# Strategic Management

creating competitive advantages *3e*

Gregory G. Dess
University of Texas at
Dallas

G. T. Lumpkin
University of Illinois at
Chicago

Alan B. Eisner
Pace University

# Strategic Management 3e

creating competitive advantages

 **McGraw-Hill Irwin**

Boston   Burr Ridge, IL   Dubuque, IA   Madison, WI   New York
San Francisco   St. Louis   Bangkok   Bogotá   Caracas   Kuala Lumpur
Lisbon   London   Madrid   Mexico City   Milan   Montreal   New Delhi
Santiago   Seoul   Singapore   Sydney   Taipei   Toronto

## McGraw-Hill
## Irwin

STRATEGIC MANAGEMENT: CREATING COMPETITIVE ADVANTAGES

Published by McGraw-Hill/Irwin, a business unit of The McGraw-Hill Companies, Inc., 1221 Avenue of the Americas, New York, NY, 10020. Copyright © 2007 by The McGraw-Hill Companies, Inc. All rights reserved. No part of this publication may be reproduced or distributed in any form or by any means, or stored in a database or retrieval system, without the prior written consent of The McGraw-Hill Companies, Inc., including, but not limited to, in any network or other electronic storage or transmission, or broadcast for distance learning.

Some ancillaries, including electronic and print components, may not be available to customers outside the United States.

This book is printed on acid-free paper.

1 2 3 4 5 6 7 8 9 0 WCK/WCK 0 9 8 7 6 5

ISBN-13: 978-0-07-312457-5
ISBN-10: 0-07-312457-5

Editorial director: *John E. Biernat*
Senior sponsoring editor: *Ryan Blankenship*
Developmental editor II: *Natalie J. Ruffatto*
Editorial coordinator: *Allison J. Clelland*
Senior marketing manager: *Lisa Nicks*
Producer, Media technology: *Damian Moshak*
Project manager: *Harvey Yep*
Production supervisor: *Gina Hangos*
Senior designer: *Adam Rooke*
Lead media project manager: *Susan Lombardi*
Cover design: *Pam Verros*
Interior design: *Pam Verros*
Typeface: *10/12 Times Roman*
Compositor: *GTS–New Delhi, India Campus*
Printer: *Quebecor World Versailles Inc.*

**Library of Congress Cataloging-in-Publication Data**

Dess, Gregory G.
    Strategic management: creating competitive advantages / Gregory G. Dess, G.T. Lumpkin,
Alan B. Eisner—3rd ed.
        p. cm.
    Includes bibliographical references and indexes.
    ISBN-13: 978-0-07-312457-5 (alk. paper)
    ISBN-10: 0-07-312457-5 (alk. paper)
    1. Strategic planning. I. Lumpkin, G. T. II. Eisner, Alan B. III. Title.
HD30.28.D4743 2007
658.4′012—dc22                                             2005056296

www.mhhe.com

# Dedication

*To my family, Margie and Taylor;*
*my parents, Bill and Mary Dess;*
*and the late Wayne D. Bodensteiner*
–Greg

*To my wife, Vicki, and my colleagues at the*
*University of Illinois at Chicago*
–Tom

*To my family, Helaine,*
*Rachel, and Jacob*
–Alan

# Brief Contents

part 1    Strategic Analysis 2

1   Strategic Management: *Creating Competitive Advantages* 4

2   Analyzing the External Environment of the Firm 40

3   Assessing the Internal Environment of the Firm 74

4   Recognizing a Firm's Intellectual Assets: *Moving beyond a Firm's Tangible Resources* 122

part 2    Strategic Formulation 158

5   Business-Level Strategy: *Creating and Sustaining Competitive Advantages* 160

6   Corporate-Level Strategy: *Creating Value through Diversification* 196

7   International Strategy: *Creating Value in Global Markets* 236

8   Digital Business Strategy: *Leveraging Capabilities in a Disruptive Environment* 274

part 3    Strategic Implementation 314

9   Strategic Control and Corporate Governance 316

10   Creating Effective Organizational Designs 352

11   Strategic Leadership: *Creating a Learning Organization and an Ethical Organization* 394

12   Managing Innovation and Fostering Corporate Entrepreneurship 432

13   Recognizing Opportunities and Creating New Ventures 468

part 4    Case Analysis 506

14   Analyzing Strategic Management Cases 508

Indexes 538

# Contents

## part 1　Strategic Analysis　2

### Chapter 1
### Strategic Management: Creating Competitive Advantages　4

**What Is Strategic Management?**　8

Defining Strategic Management　9
The Four Key Attributes of Strategic Management　10

**The Strategic Management Process**　12

Strategy Analysis　13
Strategy Formulation　16
Strategic Implementation　17

**The Role of Corporate Governance and Stakeholder Management**　18

Zero Sum or Symbiosis? Two Alternate Perspectives of Stakeholder Management　21
Social Responsibility, Social Innovation, and Environmental Sustainability: Moving Beyond the Immediate Stakeholders　22

**The Strategic Management Perspective: An Imperative Throughout the Organization**　24

Some Key Driving Forces　25
Enhancing Employee Involvement in the Strategic Management Process　27

**Ensuring Coherence in Strategic Direction**　29

Organizational Vision　29
Mission Statements　32
Strategic Objectives　33
Summary　35

### Chapter 2
### Analyzing the External Environment of the Firm　40

**Creating the Environmentally Aware Organization**　43

The Role of Scanning, Monitoring, Competitive Intelligence, and Forecasting　43
SWOT Analysis　49

**The General Environment**　49

The Demographic Segment　49
The Sociocultural Segment　52
The Political/Legal Segment　52
The Technological Segment　53
The Economic Segment　56
The Global Segment　56
Relationships among Elements of the General Environment　57

**The Competitive Environment**　57

Porter's Five-Forces Model of Industry Competition　58
Industry Analysis: A Dynamic Perspective　66
Strategic Groups within Industries　68
Summary　70

### Chapter 3
### Assessing the Internal Environment of the Firm　74

**Value-Chain Analysis**　77

Primary Activities　79
Support Activities　83
Interrelationships among Value-Chain Activities within and across Organizations　87
Applying the Value Chain to Service Organizations　88

**Resource-Based View of the Firm**　90

Types of Firm Resources　92
Firm Resources and Sustainable Competitive Advantages　94
The Generation and Distribution of a Firm's Profits: Extending the Resource-Based View of the Firm　98

**Evaluating Firm Performance: Two Approaches**　99

Financial Ratio Analysis　99
Integrating Financial Analysis and Stakeholder Perspectives: The Balanced Scorecard and the Strategy Map　102
Summary　106
Appendix to Chapter 3: Financial Ratio Analysis　111

### Chapter 4
### Recognizing a Firm's Intellectual Assets: Moving beyond a Firm's Tangible Resources　122

**The Central Role of Knowledge in Today's Economy**　124

**Human Capital: The Foundation of Intellectual Capital** 127

*Attracting Human Capital* 128
*Developing Human Capital* 131
*Retaining Human Capital* 135
*Enhancing Human Capital: The Role of Diversity in the Workforce* 138

**The Vital Role of Social Capital** 140

*How Social Capital Helps Attract and Retain Talent* 142
*The Potential Downside of Social Capital* 143

**Using Technology to Leverage Human Capital and Knowledge** 144

*Using Networks to Share Information* 144
*Electronic Teams: Using Technology to Enhance Collaboration* 145
*Codifying Knowledge for Competitive Advantage* 148
*Retaining Knowledge When Employees Leave* 148

**The Central Role of Leveraging Human Capital in Strategy Formulation** 150

*Leveraging Human Capital and Business-Level Strategy* 150
*Leveraging Human Capital and Corporate-Level Strategy* 152
*Leveraging Human Capital and International-Level Strategy* 152
*Leveraging Human Capital and Internet Strategies* 152
*Summary* 152

## part 2 Strategic Formulation 158

**Chapter 5**
**Business-Level Strategy: Creating and Sustaining Competitive Advantages** 160

**Types of Competitive Advantage and Sustainability** 163

*Overall Cost Leadership* 164
*Differentiation* 169
*Focus* 175
*Combination Strategies: Integrating Overall Low Cost and Differentiation* 177

**Industry Life Cycle Stages: Strategic Implications** 182

*Strategies in the Introduction Stage* 184
*Strategies in the Growth Stage* 184
*Strategies in the Maturity Stage* 185
*Strategies in the Decline Stage* 186
*Relating Generic Strategies to Stages of the Industry Life Cycle: The Personal Computer Industry* 187

*Turnaround Strategies* 188
*Innovation and Sustainability of Competitive Advantage* 189
*Summary* 191

**Chapter 6**
**Corporate-Level Strategy: Creating Value through Diversification** 196

**Making Diversification Work: An Overview** 199

**Related Diversification: Economies of Scope and Revenue Enhancement** 201

*Leveraging Core Competencies* 202
*Sharing Activities* 203

**Related Diversification: Market Power** 205

*Pooled Negotiating Power* 207
*Vertical Integration* 207

**Unrelated Diversification: Financial Synergies and Parenting** 211

*Corporate Parenting and Restructuring* 211
*Portfolio Management* 214
*Caveat: Is Risk Reduction a Viable Goal of Diversification?* 216

**The Means to Achieve Diversification** 217

*Mergers and Acquisitions* 217
*Strategic Alliances and Joint Ventures* 222
*Internal Development* 223

**Real Options Analysis: A Useful Tool** 224

*Applications of Real Options Analysis to Strategic Decisions* 225
*Potential Pitfalls of Real Options Analysis* 226

**How Managerial Motives Can Erode Value Creation** 228

*Growth for Growth's Sake* 228
*Egotism* 229
*Antitakeover Tactics* 230
*Summary* 231

**Chapter 7**
**International Strategy: Creating Value in Global Markets** 236

**The Global Economy: A Brief Overview** 239

**Factors Affecting a Nation's Competitiveness** 240

*Factor Conditions* 241
*Demand Conditions* 242
*Related and Supporting Industries* 242
*Firm Strategy, Structure, and Rivalry* 243
*Concluding Comment on Factors Affecting a Nation's Competitiveness* 243

**International Expansion: A Company's
Motivations and Risks**    **243**

*Motivations for International Expansion*    *243*
*Potential Risks of International Expansion*    *247*
*Global Dispersion of Value Chains:*
*Outsourcing and Offshoring*    *252*

**Achieving Competitive Advantage
in Global Markets**    **254**

*Two Opposing Pressures: Reducing Costs
and Adapting to Local Markets*    *254*
*International Strategy*    *256*
*Global Strategy*    *257*
*Multidomestic Strategy*    *258*
*Transnational Strategy*    *260*

**Entry Modes of International
Expansion**    **263**

*Exporting*    *263*
*Licensing and Franchising*    *264*
*Strategic Alliances and Joint Ventures*    *265*
*Wholly Owned Subsidiaries*    *267*
*Summary*    *269*

**Chapter 8
Digital Business Strategy:
Leveraging Capabilities in a
Disruptive Environment**    **274**

**Competitive Disruption, Strategic
Management, and the Digital Economy**    **277**

**How the Internet and Digital Technologies
Are Affecting the Five Competitive Forces**    **282**

*The Threat of New Entrants*    *282*
*The Bargaining Power of Buyers*    *284*
*The Bargaining Power of Suppliers*    *285*
*The Threat of Substitutes*    *286*
*The Intensity of Competitive Rivalry*    *288*

**How the Internet and Digital Technologies
Add Value**    **291**

*Search Activities*    *291*
*Evaluation Activities*    *291*
*Problem-Solving Activities*    *292*
*Transaction Activities*    *292*
*Other Sources of Competitive Advantage*    *293*
*Business Models*    *294*

**How the Internet and Digital Technologies
are Affecting the Competitive Strategies**    **298**

*Overall Cost Leadership*    *298*
*Differentiation*    *299*
*Focus*    *301*

**Are Digital- and Internet-Based Advantages
Sustainable?**    **304**

*Are Combination Strategies the Key to E-Business
Success?*    *305*

**Leveraging Internet Capabilities**    **307**

*Summary*    *308*

part 3    Strategic
Implementation    314

**Chapter 9
Strategic Control and Corporate
Governance**    **316**

**Ensuring Informational Control: Responding
Effectively to Environmental Change**    **318**

*A Traditional Approach to Strategic Control*    *319*
*A Contemporary Approach to Strategic Control*    *320*

**Attaining Behavioral Control: Balancing
Culture, Rewards, and Boundaries**    **322**

*Building a Strong and Effective Culture*    *323*
*Motivating with Rewards and Incentives*    *324*
*Setting Boundaries and Constraints*    *326*
*Behavioral Control in Organizations:*
*Situational Factors*    *329*
*Evolving from Boundaries to Rewards and Culture*    *329*

**The Role of Corporate Governance**    **330**

*The Modern Corporation: The Separation of Owners
(Shareholders) and Management*    *333*
*Governance Mechanisms: Aligning the
Interests of Owners and Managers*    *335*
*External Governance Control Mechanisms*    *339*
*Corporate Governance: An International Perspective*    *343*
*Summary*    *347*

**Chapter 10
Creating Effective Organizational
Designs**    **352**

**Traditional Forms of Organizational
Structure**    **355**

*Patterns of Growth of Large Corporations*    *355*
*Simple Structure*    *357*
*Functional Structure*    *357*
*Divisional Structure*    *359*
*Matrix Structure*    *362*
*International Operations: Implications for
Organizational Structure*    *363*
*Global Start-Ups: A New Phenomenon*    *365*
*How an Organization's Structure Can
Influence Strategy Formulation*    *366*

**Linking Strategic Reward and Evaluation Systems to Business-Level and Corporate-Level Strategies** 368

*Business-Level Strategy: Reward and Evaluation Systems* 368
*Corporate-Level Strategy: Strategic Reward and Evaluation Systems* 369

**Boundaryless Organizational Designs** 371

*The Barrier-Free Organization* 372
*The Modular Organization* 376
*The Virtual Organization* 377
*Boundaryless Organizations: Making Them Work* 381

**Creating Ambidextrous Organizations** 383

*The Challenge of Achieving Ambidexterity: Some Examples from Business Practice* 384
*Ambidextrous Organizations: Key Design Attributes* 385
*Summary* 388

## Chapter 11
## Strategic Leadership: Creating a Learning Organization and an Ethical Organization 394

**Leadership: Three Interdependent Activities** 397

*Setting a Direction* 398
*Designing the Organization* 399
*Nurturing a Culture Dedicated to Excellence and Ethical Behavior* 400
*Overcoming Barriers to Change and the Effective Use of Power* 402

**Emotional Intelligence: A Key Leadership Trait** 405

*Self-Awareness* 405
*Self-Regulation* 406
*Motivation* 407
*Empathy* 407
*Social Skill* 407
*Emotional Intelligence: Some Potential Drawbacks and Cautionary Notes* 408

**Developing a Learning Organization** 410

*Empowering Employees at All Levels* 411
*Accumulating and Sharing Internal Knowledge* 412
*Gathering and Integrating External Information* 414
*Challenging the Status Quo and Enabling Creativity* 416

**Creating an Ethical Organization** 417

*Individual Ethics versus Organizational Ethics* 417
*Integrity-Based versus Compliance-Based Approaches to Organizational Ethics* 421
*Role Models* 423
*Corporate Credos and Codes of Conduct* 423

*Reward and Evaluation Systems* 425
*Policies and Procedures* 425
*Summary* 426

## Chapter 12
## Managing Innovation and Fostering Corporate Entrepreneurship 432

**Managing Innovation** 435

*Types of Innovation* 436
*Challenges of Innovation* 438
*Defining the Scope of Innovation* 439
*Managing the Pace of Innovation* 441
*Collaborating with Innovation Partners* 441

**Corporate Entrepreneurship** 443

*Focused Approaches to Corporate Entrepreneurship* 446
*Dispersed Approaches to Corporate Entrepreneurship* 448
*Measuring the Success of Corporate Entrepreneurship Activities* 451

**Entrepreneurial Orientation** 454

*Autonomy* 454
*Innovativeness* 456
*Proactiveness* 458
*Competitive Aggressiveness* 459
*Risk Taking* 462
*Summary* 464

## Chapter 13
## Recognizing Opportunities and Creating New Opportunities 468

**New Ventures and Small Businesses** 471

*Categories of Entrepreneurial Ventures* 471

**Opportunity Recognition: Identifying and Developing Market Opportunities** 476

*The Opportunity Recognition Process* 476
*Characteristics of Good Opportunities* 481

**Entrepreneurial Resources** 482

*New-Venture Financing* 482
*Other Entrepreneurial Resources* 486

**Entrepreneurial Leadership** 489

*Vision* 490
*Dedication and Drive* 491
*Commitment to Excellence* 492

**Entrepreneurial Strategy** 493

*Entry Strategies* 494
*Generic Strategies* 498
*Combination Strategies* 500
*Summary* 502

## part 4   Case Analysis   506

### Chapter 14
### Analyzing Strategic
### Management Cases   508

**Why Analyze Strategic Management Cases?**   510

**How to Conduct a Case Analysis**   511

*Become Familiar with the Material*   513
*Identify Problems*   514
*Conduct Strategic Analyses*   515
*Propose Alternative Solutions*   517
*Make Recommendations*   517

**How to Get the Most from Case Analysis**   518

**Using Conflict-Inducing Decision-Making
Techniques in Case Analysis**   521

*Symptoms of Groupthink and How to Prevent It*   522
*Using Conflict to Improve Decision Making*   525

**Following the Analysis-Decision-Action
Cycle in Case Analysis**   526

*Summary*   531
*Appendix to Chapter 14: Sources of Company
and Industry Information*   531

### Indexes

*Company*   538
*Name*   543
*Subject*   551

# About the Authors

**Gregory G. Dess** is the Andrew R. Cecil Endowed Chair in Management at the University of Texas at Dallas. His primary research interests are in strategic management, organization–environment relationships, and knowledge management. He has published numerous articles on these subjects in both academic and practitioner-oriented journals. In August 2000, he was inducted into the Academy of Management Journal's Hall of Fame as one of its charter members. Professor Dess has conducted executive programs in the United States, Europe, Africa, Hong Kong, and Australia. During 1994 he was a Fulbright Scholar in Oporto, Portugal. He received his PhD in Business Administration from the University of Washington (Seattle).

**G. T. (Tom) Lumpkin** is Associate Professor of Management and Entrepreneurship at the University of Illinois at Chicago. He received his PhD in management from the University of Texas at Arlington and MBA from the University of Southern California. His research interests include entrepreneurial orientation, opportunity recognition, strategy-making processes, and innovative forms of organizing work. He has published numerous research articles and book chapters. He is a member of Editorial Review Boards of *Entrepreneurship Theory & Practice* and the *Journal of Business Venturing.* Professor Lumpkin also conducts executive programs in strategic and entrepreneurial applications of e-commerce and digital business technologies.

**Alan B. Eisner** is Associate Professor of Management and Graduate Management Program Chair at the Lubin School of Business, Pace University. He received his PhD in management from the Stern School of Business, New York University. His primary research interests are in strategic management, technology management, organizational learning, and managerial decision making. He has published research articles and cases in journals such as *Advances in Strategic Management, International Journal of Electronic Commerce, International Journal of Technology Management, American Business Review, Journal of Behavioral and Applied Management,* and *Journal of the International Academy for Case Studies.* He is the Associate Editor of the Case Association's peer reviewed journal, *The CASE Journal.*

# Preface

Welcome to the Third Edition of *Strategic Management: Creating Competitive Advantages!* We are very pleased with the positive response that our two earlier editions have received, and we are very grateful for the constructive and extensive feedback that we have obtained from the many professionals who took the time to review and critique our work. Much of this input has been invaluable and has led to what we feel are many improvements that we will summarize below. We are happy to acknowledge these important contributors later in the Preface.

We'd first like to briefly address what is, perhaps, the most obvious question: Why did we write the book? We would all agree that there are already many good strategy textbooks on the market. We felt that there was still a need for a book that students would find relevant and readable as well as rigorous. In striving for such goals, we endeavored to "cover all of the traditional bases" and to integrate some central themes throughout the book that are vital to understanding strategic management in today's global economy. These include such topics as globalization, technology, ethics, and entrepreneurship. And, to bring the concepts to life, we have included short examples from business practice to illustrate virtually every concept in the book, and we have provided over 100 Strategy Spotlights—more detailed examples—to drive home key points. We also have included four separate chapters that other strategy texts typically don't have. These chapters focus on timely topics about which all business students should have a solid understanding: the role of intellectual assets and knowledge in value creation (Chapter 4); the key role of the Internet and digital business strategies in creating competitive advantage (Chapter 8); the value of fostering entrepreneurship in established organizations (Chapter 12); and the creation of new venture start-ups (Chapter 13). We also provide an excellent set of cases to help students analyze, integrate, and apply strategic management concepts, which are available at McGraw-Hill/Irwin's custom publishing website, called Primis. Visit www.mhhe.com/primis for details.

In developing *Strategic Management* and the support materials, we did not, of course, forget the instructors. You certainly have a very challenging (and rewarding) job. And we want to do our best to help you. We provide you with a variety of supplementary materials that should help you in class preparation and delivery. We did not, like many texts, simply summarize the material in the chapters. Instead, we focused our efforts on where we felt that we could add value to your pedagogy. We worked hard to provide you with a complete package that should make your classes relevant, rigorous, and rewarding for both you and your students. We felt it was important to develop all of the supplementary materials ourselves and not farm them out to others as some other textbook authors do. We feel this has helped to ensure a consistent level of quality and consistency in all of the materials.

## What Remains the Same: Key Features from Earlier Editions

Before we discuss some of the most important changes that we have made to improve *Strategic Management* and keep it fresh and up-to-date, let's briefly address some of the exciting features that remain from the earlier editions.

- *Traditional organizing framework with four other chapters on timely topics.* Crisply written chapters cover all of the strategy bases and address contemporary topics. First, the chapters are divided logically into the traditional sequence: strategy analysis, strategy formulation, and strategy implementation. Second, we

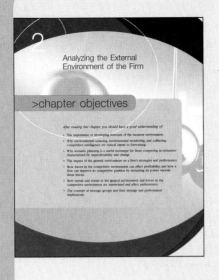

include four chapters on such timely topics as intellectual capital/knowledge management, Internet and digital strategies, innovation within the corporation, and new ventures.

- *Chapter opening cases.* What can go wrong? To enhance student interest, we begin each chapter with a case that depicts an organization that has suffered a dramatic performance drop, or outright failure, by failing to adhere to sound strategic management concepts and principles. We believe that this feature serves to underpin the value of the concepts in the course and that it is a preferred teaching approach to merely providing examples of outstanding companies that always seem to get it right! After all, isn't it better (and more challenging) to diagnose problems than admire perfection? As Dartmouth's Sydney Finkelstein, author of *Why Smart Executives Fail,* notes: "We live in a world where success is revered, and failure is quickly pushed to the side. However, some of the greatest opportunities to learn—both for individuals and organizations—come from studying what goes wrong."[1] We'll see how, for example, Coca-Cola's performance has suffered from an overbearing and intrusive board of directors and because they largely ignored the trend to non-carbonated drinks; why Jaguar has been quite a flop for its parent, Ford Motor Company; and how Charles Schwab and Company's acquisition of U.S. Trust, a financial services firm that caters to wealthy clients, has not worked out as planned.

- *Consistent chapter format and features to reinforce learning.* We have included several features in each chapter to add value and create an enhanced learning experience. First, each chapter begins with an overview and a set of bullets pointing to key learning objectives. Second, as previously noted, the opening case describes a situation in which a company's performance eroded because of a lack of proper application of strategy concepts. Third, at the end of each chapter there are four different types of questions/exercises that should help students assess their understanding and application of material:

(1) Experiential exercises.

(2) Summary review questions.

(3) Application questions and exercises.

(4) Ethics questions. Given the emergence of Internet and e-commerce, each chapter contains at least one exercise that involves the use of the Internet.

- *Clear articulation and illustration of key concepts.* Key strategy concepts are introduced in a clear and concise manner and are followed by timely and interesting examples from business practice. Such concepts include value-chain analysis, the resource-based view of the firm, Porter's five forces model, competitive advantage, boundaryless organizational designs, digital strategies, corporate governance, ethics, and entrepreneurship.

- *Extensive use of sidebars.* We include 110 sidebars (or about eight per chapter) called Strategy Spotlights. The Strategy Spotlights not only illustrate key points but also increase the readability and excitement of new strategy concepts.

[1]Personal communication, June 20, 2005.

- *Integrative themes.* The text provides a solid grounding in ethics, globalization, and technology. These topics are central themes throughout the book and form the basis for many of the Strategy Spotlights.
- *Implications of concepts for small businesses.* Many of the key concepts are applied to start-up firms and smaller businesses, which is particularly important since many students have professional plans to work in such firms.
- *Not just a textbook but an entire package. Strategic Management* features the best chapter teaching notes available today. Rather than merely summarizing the key points in each chapter, we focus on value-added material to enhance the teaching (and learning) experience. Each chapter includes dozens of questions to spur discussion, teaching tips, in-class group exercises, and about a dozen detailed examples from business practice to provide further illustrations of key concepts.
- *BusinessWeek subscription.* Students can subscribe to *BusinessWeek* for a special rate in addition to the price of the text. Students will receive a passcode card shrink-wrapped with their new text. The card directs students to a Web site where they enter the code and then gain access to *BusinessWeek*'s registration page to enter their address information and set up their print and online subscription. Please ask your McGraw-Hill/ Irwin representative for more information.

**Standard & Poor's Educational Version of Market Insight.** McGraw-Hill/Irwin is proud to partner with Standard & Poor's to offer access to the Educational Version of Standard & Poor's Market Insight©. This rich online resource provides six years of financial data, key ratio summary reports, and S&P's exclusive "Industry Surveys" that offer an in-depth look at industry trends, projections, and competitive analysis for 500 top U.S. companies in the renowned COMPUSTAT ® database. The password-protected Web site is the perfect way to bring real data into today's classroom for use in case analysis, industry analysis, and research for team and individual projects. Learn more at www.mhhe.com/edumarketinsight.

## What's New: Highlights of the Third Edition

Now, let's briefly summarize some of exciting topics and changes that we have made in the Third Edition to enhance the value of *Strategic Management* for both instructors and students.

- Ten of the 13 opening "minicases" that lead off each chapter are totally new. And the three others have been carefully updated. As we noted, we believe that it is better to analyze things that can go wrong when strategy concepts aren't followed than to observe perfection. Approximately half of the 110 Strategy Spotlights are new, and most of the others have been updated. We will address, for example, how the Sarbanes-Oxley Act has been a boon for the accounting profession, the implications of the global market for talent (especially for people in professional services industries), how VoodooPC has developed a successful differentiation focus strategy in an industry (personal computers) that is usually associated with cut-throat price competition, and how Sony develops its video games by using outsourced talent.
- **Chapter 1** expands the section on stakeholder analysis to include a more detailed discussion of social responsibility and environmental sustainability. We build on Rosabeth Kanter's advocacy that social innovation should address community needs not merely as financial donations and volunteer work but as opportunities to develop new ideas and demonstrate business technologies as well as find and serve new markets. We also reinforce the notion that organizations are becoming

more sensitive to how their operations affect the physical environment and the benefits of incorporating a "triple bottom line," which includes financial, social, and environmental performance, when assessing their firm's performance.

- **Chapter 2 (external analysis)** now includes a discussion of the dynamic nature of industries. Such a perspective has important implications for strategy, and we build on Anita McGahan's work. She suggests that an industry may follow one of four possible evolutionary trajectories that are based on two types of obsolescence: core activities and core assets. These range from radical change which occurs when both core activities and core assets face threats of obsolescence (for example, the overnight delivery industry) to progressive change when neither core assets nor core activities face imminent threats of obsolescence (e.g., commercial airline industry).

- **Chapter 3 (internal analysis)** builds on the foundation of Kaplan and Norton's balanced scorecard and introduces the strategy map concept. Strategy maps are helpful in providing a stronger link between a firm's improvements in a given area (financial, customer, internal business, learning and innovation) and the desired outcomes of an organization, helping employees see how their jobs are tied to the overall objectives of the firm, and providing insights as to how an organization can convert its assets, both tangible and intangible, into tangible outcomes. We illustrate how to develop a strategy map by using ExxonMobil as an example.

- **Chapter 4 (analysis of intellectual assets)** incorporates a discussion of electronic teams (or e-teams). More and more managers at all levels in firms are working on e-teams. We address how e-teams incorporate the three central concepts in this chapter—human capital, social capital and technology—and how their effective use can enhance a firm's performance. In addition, we address the benefits of a diverse workforce as well as the important roles of both human capital and social capital in achieving such an outcome.

- **Chapter 5 (business-level strategy)** addresses the dynamic nature of competition and how competitive advantages can be only temporary. Our presentation builds on the path-breaking work of Clayton Christensen and discusses the impact of disruptive technologies on an industry and their implications for strategy. We will discuss how resources, processes, and values help to determine whether or not a firm is able to successfully embrace an innovation.

- **Chapter 6 (corporate-level strategy)** provides a more comprehensive discussion of the trend toward consolidation in many industries, ranging from high-tech industries such as telecommunications and software to low-tech industries such as roofing supplies. In addition, we extend our prior discussion on real options analysis to address some of its potential downsides such as managerial conceit (that is, a manager's escalating commitment to a prior decision and overconfidence). This, we believe, helps to provide a more balanced discussion of this important concept.

- **Chapter 7 (international strategy)** addresses some of the potential benefits and pitfalls of offshoring (that is, when existing jobs in one country are outsourced to another country). Our discussion centers on the impacts on competitiveness, loss of jobs, and broader economic effects. Clearly, there are not many issues in business today that evoke such strong emotions!

- **Chapter 8 (Internet and digital business strategies)** discusses the role of competitive disruption in advancing economic progress and growth. Although the impact of the Internet and digital technologies has been highly disruptive, it has also created opportunities that have important strategic implications. We address the technology-driven Napster phenomenon and show that, even though its business model was unsustainable, Napster's efforts led to business development and positive change in the music industry for both new and incumbent firms.

- **Chapter 9 (strategic control and corporate governance)** extends our discussion of corporate governance to incorporate an international perspective. Here, we point out that there are many differences in corporate governance across regions and nations. For example, problems arise when there is concentrated ownership, along with extensive family ownership, business group structures, and weak protection for minority shareholders. The resulting serious conflicts tend to exist between two classes of principals—controlling shareholders and minority shareholders—giving rise to principal-principal conflicts (as opposed to principal-agent conflicts).

- **Chapter 10 (organization structure and design)** addresses how organizations can cope with the inevitable trade-offs associated with exploring new opportunities and the exploitation of existing resources and capabilities. Such dilemmas give rise to the creation of what are called "ambidextrous organizations" in which operations may become decentralized with effective means of coordination and integration at the corporate office. We also address a relatively recent phenomenon—global start-ups. They have been facilitated by an increase in the globalization of economies throughout the world and technologies associated with the Internet.

- **Chapter 11 (strategic leadership, learning organizations, and ethics)** provides a balanced perspective on one of the most popular concepts in leadership today—emotional intelligence (EI). For example, leaders can use EI to grasp what people want only to pander to such desires to gain more authority and influence. And, if leaders begin to have too much empathy for others, it may prevent them from making difficult decisions.

- **Chapter 12 (managing innovation and corporate entrepreneurship)** addresses the challenges that larger firms face when trying to foster a viable innovation strategy. We introduce a promising approach known as the "blue ocean strategy" based on the work of Chan Kim and Renee Mauborgne. Rather than outperforming competitors, the essence of a blue ocean strategy is to make them irrelevant by capturing uncontested markets. By offering innovative products and services that break down traditional industry boundaries, blue ocean strategies provide new value to both the customer and the company.

- **Chapter 13 (recognizing opportunities and creating new ventures)** addresses the important role that strategic alliances provide to young and small firms. Not only are many established firms interested in expanding their reach by partnering with entrepreneurial firms, but also young firms can use the market knowledge and resources of larger firms to overcome some of the "liability of newness" problems that often prevent new ventures from thriving.

- **Chapter 14 (case analysis)** addresses the problems that team members often face when attempting to concentrate on a problem and reach a team decision. Suggestions for managing case analysis meetings and avoiding time-wasting activities are presented.

- **Case Studies** While most textbooks that are "text only" leave instructors on their own when it comes to choosing cases, *Strategic Management: Creating Competitive Advantages* goes much further. Alan Eisner of Pace University has recommended cases that have been carefully chosen to match course concepts in a way that maximizes flexibility in using cases from *Strategic Management: Text and Cases,* the hardback version of our textbook. Instructors can use Primis's electronic publishing services to customize their own case books. In addition to the case studies selected specifically for *Strategic Management: Creating Competitive Advantages,* instructors can choose their tried-and-true favorites as well as cases from a variety of sources such as Harvard, Darden, IVEY, INSEAD, and others. Log on to Primis at www.mhhe.com/primis today!

## Acknowledgments

*Strategic Management* represents far more than just the joint efforts of the three co-authors. Rather, it is the product of the collaborative input of many people. Some of these individuals are academic colleagues, others are the outstanding team of professionals at McGraw-Hill/Irwin, and still others are those who are closest to us—our families. It is time to express our sincere gratitude.

First, we'd like to acknowledge the thorough, constructive reviews that we received from our superb team of reviewers and symposia participants. Their input was very helpful in both pointing out errors in the manuscript and suggesting areas that needed further development as additional topics. We sincerely believe that the incorporation of their ideas was critical to improving the final product. These professionals and their affiliations are:

## Reviewers for the 3rd Edition

Moses Acquaah, *University of North Carolina–Greensboro*

Joyce Beggs, *University of North Carolina–Charlotte*

Naomi A. Gardberg, *Baruch College, City University New York*

J. Michael Geringer, *Orfalea College of Business–Cal Poly*

Yezdi H. Godiwalla, *University of Wisconsin–Whitewater*

David J. Lemak, *Washington State University–Tri-Cities*

Donald L. Lester, *Arkansas State University*

John Mezias, *University of Miami*

Jeffrey R. Nystrom, *University of Colorado*

Karen L. Page, *University of Wyoming*

Matthew R. Rutherford, *Gonzaga University*

Jeremy Short, *Utah State University*

Andrew Spicer, *University of California–Riverside*

John Stanbury, *George Mason University and the Inter-University Institute of Macau, SAR China*

## Symposia Participants

Moses Acquaah, *University of North Carolina–Greensboro*

Todd Alessandri, *Syracuse University*

Kathy Anders, *Arizona State University*

William Bogner, *Georgia State University*

Jay Dial, *Ohio State University*

David Flanagan, *Western Michigan University*

Sandy Gough, *Boise State University*

Donald Hatfield, *Virginia Polytechnic Institute*

Helaine Korn, *Bernard M. Baruch College*

Jim Kroeger, *Cleveland State University*

John Logan, *University of South Carolina*

Kevin Lowe, *University of North Car-olina–Greensboro*

Catherine Maritan, *State University of New York at Buffalo*

Sarah Marsh, *Northern Illinois University*

Doug Moesel, *University of Missouri–Columbia*

Carolyn Mu, *Baylor University*

Anil Nair, *Old Dominion University*

Steve Porth, *Saint Joseph's University*

George Redmond, *Franklin University*

Ron Rivas, *Bentley College*

David Robinson, *Texas Tech University*

Simon Rodan, *San Jose State University*

Terry Sebora, *University of Nebraska–Lincoln*

John Seeger, *Bentley College*

Jamal Shamsie, *Michigan State University*

Chris Shook, *Auburn University*

Anne Smith, *University of Tennessee*

Linda Teagarden, *Virginia Tech*

Andrew Watson, *Northeastern University*

Laura Whitcomb, *California State University–Los Angeles*

Marta White, *Georgia State University*

Second, the authors would like to thank several faculty colleagues who were particularly helpful in the review, critique, and development of the book and supplementary materials. While Greg was at the University of Kentucky, faculty in the strategic management area were extremely generous with their time. They provided many excellent ideas and contributions for the book's first edition. Accordingly, he would like to thank Wally Ferrier, Gordon Holbein, Dan Lockhart, and Bruce Skaggs. His colleagues at the University of Texas at Dallas also have been helpful and supportive. These individuals include Joe Picken, Kumar Nair, Paul Gaddis, Seung-Hyun Lee, Tev Dalgic, and Jane Salk. His administrative assistant, Yung Hua, has been extremely helpful. Former MBA student Naga Damaraju, along with two doctoral students, Ted Khoury and Muthu Subbiah, have provided many useful inputs and ideas. He also appreciates the support of his dean and associate dean, Hasan Pirkul and Varghese Jacob, respectively. Tom would like to thank Gerry Hills, Abagail McWilliams, Darold Barnum, Mike Miller, Rod Shrader, James Gillespie, Lou Coco, and other colleagues at the University of Illinois at Chicago, for their support and patience throughout the process. Tom also extends a special thanks to Benyamin Lichtenstein for his support and encouragement. Both Greg and Tom wish to thank a special colleague, Abdul Rasheed at the University of Texas at Arlington, who certainly has been a valued source of friendship and ideas for us for many years. He provided many valuable contributions to the Third Edition. Alan thanks his colleagues at Pace University and the Case Association for their support in developing these fine case selections. Special thanks go to Jamal Shamsie at Michigan State University for his support in developing the case selections for this edition.

Third, we would like to thank the team at McGraw-Hill/Irwin for their outstanding support throughout the process. This begins with John Biernat, Editorial Director, who signed us to the contract. John was always available to provide support and valued input during the entire process. In editorial, Ryan Blankenship and Natalie Ruffatto kept things on track, responded quickly to our never-ending needs and requests, and offered insights and encouragement. Once the manuscript was completed and revised, project manager Harvey Yep expertly guided us through the production process. Cathy Tepper and Susan Lombardi did an outstanding job in helping us with the supplementary materials. Designer Adam Rooke and freelance designer Pam Verros provided excellent design and art work. And finally, we thank Ellen Cleary, Lisa Nicks, and Dana Woo for their energetic, competent, and thorough marketing efforts.

Finally, we would like to thank our families. For Greg this includes his parents, William and Mary Dess, who have always been there for him. His wife Margie and daughter, Taylor, have been a constant source of love and companionship. Greg would also like to acknowledge the professional collaboration and friendship that he enjoyed with the late Professor Wayne D. Bodensteiner. Wayne was a remarkable leader—a Rear Admiral in the United States Navy and a combat pilot during the Vietnam War—who also served as the Dean of the College of Business at the University of Texas at San Antonio. Greg learned a lot from him and really misses him. Tom thanks his wife Vicki for her constant love and companionship. Tom also thanks Lee Hetherington and Thelma Lumpkin for their inspiration, as well as his mom Katy, and his sister Kitty, for a lifetime of support. Alan thanks his family—his wife Helaine and his children Rachel and Jacob—for their love and support. He also thanks his parents, Gail Eisner and the late Marvin Eisner, for their support and encouragement.

# Strategic
# Management *3e*

creating competitive advantages

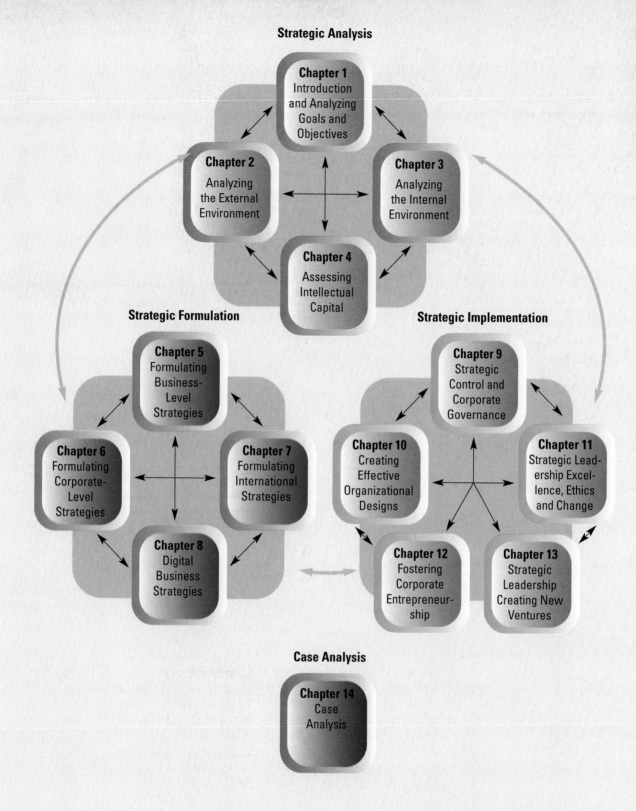

**Strategic Analysis**

**Chapter 1**
Introduction and Analyzing Goals and Objectives

**Chapter 2**
Analyzing the External Environment

**Chapter 3**
Analyzing the Internal Environment

**Chapter 4**
Assessing Intellectual Capital

**Strategic Formulation**

**Chapter 5**
Formulating Business-Level Strategies

**Chapter 6**
Formulating Corporate-Level Strategies

**Chapter 7**
Formulating International Strategies

**Chapter 8**
Digital Business Strategies

**Strategic Implementation**

**Chapter 9**
Strategic Control and Corporate Governance

**Chapter 10**
Creating Effective Organizational Designs

**Chapter 11**
Strategic Leadership Excellence, Ethics and Change

**Chapter 12**
Fostering Corporate Entrepreneurship

**Chapter 13**
Strategic Leadership Creating New Ventures

**Case Analysis**

**Chapter 14**
Case Analysis

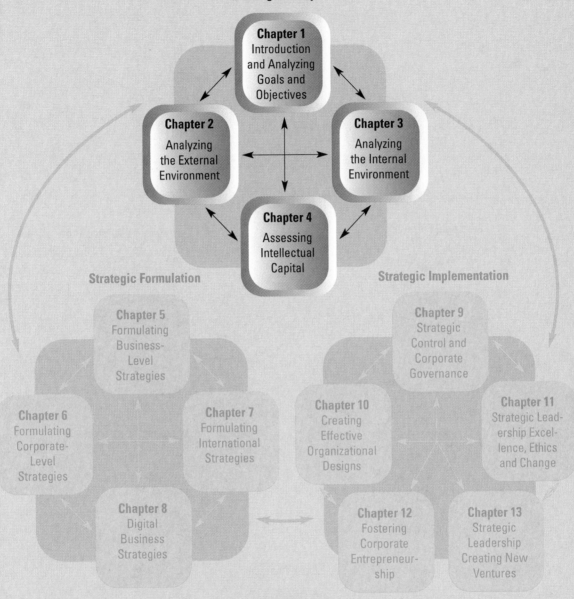

**Strategic Analysis**

**Chapter 1**
Introduction and Analyzing Goals and Objectives

**Chapter 2**
Analyzing the External Environment

**Chapter 3**
Analyzing the Internal Environment

**Chapter 4**
Assessing Intellectual Capital

**Strategic Formulation**

**Chapter 5**
Formulating Business-Level Strategies

**Chapter 6**
Formulating Corporate-Level Strategies

**Chapter 7**
Formulating International Strategies

**Chapter 8**
Digital Business Strategies

**Strategic Implementation**

**Chapter 9**
Strategic Control and Corporate Governance

**Chapter 10**
Creating Effective Organizational Designs

**Chapter 11**
Strategic Leadership Excellence, Ethics and Change

**Chapter 12**
Fostering Corporate Entrepreneurship

**Chapter 13**
Strategic Leadership Creating New Ventures

**Case Analysis**

**Chapter 14**
Case Analysis

# Strategic Analysis

1 Strategic Management: Creating Competitive Advantages

2 Analyzing the External Environment of the Firm

3 Assessing the Internal Environment of the Firm

4 Recognizing a Firm's Intellectual Assets: Moving beyond a Firm's Tangible Resources

# 1

# Strategic Management:

## *Creating Competitive Advantages*

## >chapter objectives

*After reading this chapter, you should have a good understanding of:*

- The definition of strategic management and its four key attributes.

- The strategic management process and its three interrelated and principal activities.

- The vital role of corporate governance and stakeholder management as well as how "symbiosis" can be achieved among an organization's stakeholders.

- The importance of social responsibility, including environmental sustainability, and how it can enhance a corporation's innovation strategy.

- The key environmental forces that are creating more unpredictable change and requiring greater empowerment throughout the organization.

- How an awareness of a hierarchy of strategic goals can help an organization achieve coherence in its strategic direction.

We define strategic management as *consisting of the analyses, decisions, and actions an organization undertakes in order to create and sustain competitive advantages.* At the heart of strategic management is the question: How and why do some firms outperform others? Thus, the challenge to managers is to decide on strategies that provide advantages that can be sustained over time. There are four key attributes of strategic management. It is directed at overall organizational goals, includes multiple stakeholders, incorporates short-term as well as long-term perspectives, and recognizes trade-offs between effectiveness and efficiency. We discuss the above definition and the four key attributes in the first section.

The second section addresses the strategic management process. The three major processes are strategy analysis, strategy formulation, and strategy implementation. These three components parallel the analyses, decisions, and actions in the above definition. We discuss how each of the 13 chapters addresses these three processes and provide examples from each chapter.

The third section discusses two important and interrelated concepts: corporate governance and stakeholder management. Corporate governance addresses the issue of who "governs" the corporation and determines its direction. It consists of three primary participants: stockholders (owners), management (led by the chief executive officer), and the board of directors (elected to monitor management). Stakeholder management recognizes that the interests of various stakeholders, such as owners, customers, and employees, can often conflict and create challenging decision-making dilemmas for managers. However, we discuss how some firms have been able to achieve "symbiosis" among stakeholders wherein their interests are considered interdependent and can be achieved simultaneously. We also discuss the important role of social responsibility, including the need for corporations to incorporate environmental sustainability in their strategic actions.

The fourth section addresses three interrelated factors in the business environment—globalization, technology, and intellectual capital—that have increased the level of unpredictable change for today's leaders. These factors have also created the need for a greater strategic management perspective and reinforced the role of empowerment throughout the organization.

The final section focuses on the need for organizations to ensure consistency in their vision, mission, and strategic objectives which, collectively, form a hierarchy of goals. While visions may lack specificity, they must evoke powerful and compelling mental images. Strategic objectives are much more specific and are essential for driving toward overall goals.

One of the things that makes the study of strategic management so interesting is that struggling firms can become stars, while high flyers can become earthbound very rapidly. For example, consider Coca-Cola—a firm that has experienced a hard fall from consistently being recognized as one of *Fortune* magazine's "Most Admired Firms."

As late as the 1990s, the Coca-Cola Company was one of the most respected companies in the world—a master of brand building and management in the dawning global era.[1] Under Chief Executive Officer (CEO) Roberto Goizueta's legendary leadership from March 1981 to October 1997, Coca-Cola's stock price soared an amazing 3,500 percent. He was rewarded very handsomely, becoming the first professional manager to break the $1 billion pay barrier during his 16-year tenure! However, in recent years, things have not gone well. Coke has endured many struggles, including a stale and outdated strategy that has suppressed innovation, an insular culture focused on the past, an aging and overbearing board of directors, and ineffective leadership at the top. The bottom line: Between 1990 and 1997, Coke's net income growth averaged 18 percent per year, but in recent years, it has averaged only 4 percent. And since its stock price peaked at $88 in 1998—shortly after Mr. Goizueta's death—it has dropped over 50 percent (as of mid-2005, it was selling at around $40 a share).

Part of the problem has been the erosion in Coca-Cola's marketing strategies. Goizueta's replacement, Doug Ivester, had previously served as a highly respected and talented Chief Financial Officer.[2] However, he made some serious marketing missteps. Almost immediately after becoming CEO, Ivester began shifting resources away from advertising and blanketing the world with as many vending machines, refrigerated coolers, and delivery trucks as Coke and its bottlers could muster. In his goal to strengthen market share, Ivester ignored the subtleties of brand building. Recalls one former executive: "There was no vision, no marketing. It was all growth through distribution."

Coca-Cola's core problem is that it has been stuck in a mind-set that was formed during its heyday in the 1980s, when Goizueta transformed Coke into a growth story that captivated the world. In effect, the "Goizueta Way" focused on emphasizing Coke's market share in terms of "share of stomach," as though, with the right amount of marketing, people could be persuaded to give up coffee, milk, and even water in favor of Coke. Unfortunately, an unwillingness to tamper with the structures and beliefs formed during those glory years created a culture that has left the company unable to adapt to new consumer tastes and demands. As noted by Tom Pirko, president of BevMark LLC, a consulting firm, "The whole Coke model needs to be rethought. The carbonated soft-drink model is 30 years old and out of date."

Coca-Cola has stuck to an unwavering focus on its aging group of soda-pop brands, especially Coca-Cola, Diet Coke, Sprite, and Fanta (carbonated beverages account for 82 percent of its worldwide beverage sales). Unfortunately, Coca-Cola has not been in tune with changes in consumer tastes. In recent years, demand has shifted from sodas to an array of sports drinks, vitamin-fortified waters, energy drinks, herbal teas, coffee, and other noncarbonated products. Some of these products are growing as much as *nine times* faster than cola, which has experienced a per capita decline in consumption in the United States every year since 1998.

Why has Coca-Cola been so resistant to change? A good share of the blame can be directed at the board of directors. Ten of the 14 members date back to the Goizueta era. Many of them wield enormous power. These include Warren Buffett, who is CEO of Berkshire Hathaway (Coke's largest shareholder), and Donald Keough, who was Goizueta's longtime number two executive. Consider an example of how such power was exercised. When Doug Daft (who was CEO from February 2000 to May 2004) tried to push Coke to become a "total beverage company," he met strong resistance from Coke's board. The reactions of two members were as follows:

- "That's all fine and good, but I still believe that getting the four core (soda) brands right is 85 percent of the equation."
- "[Bottled water is] something I guess we have to carry. But the fact is we're still the kings of carbonation—always have been, always will be."

Daft's credibility and confidence was severely shaken when the board of directors—urged on by Warren Buffett—vetoed his bid in November 2000 to acquire Quaker Oats Company (which included Gatorade sports drinks). Daft had, in fact, earlier assured Quaker Oats' CEO that the acquisition would be finalized! John Nash, a board consultant and former president of the National Association of Corporate Directors contends that, "The board has to challenge management's plan but should not challenge its authority." Coke's board has not only made clear its opposition to product diversification and acquisitions, but also they have been involved in many operational decisions. For example, board member Keough offended some marketing staffers in 2004 when he personally killed an edgy TV ad.

Many feel that Coke's board is responsible for the numerous rejections that it received from executives who it tried to hire to replace Doug Daft, who resigned under pressure early in 2004. Among those who passed on the opportunity to lead one of the world's most recognized brands were GE's recently retired CEO Jack Welch, James Kilts of Gillette, Robert A. Eckert of Mattel Inc., and Carlos M. Gutierrez of Kellogg. Some well-known executives were annoyed by press leaks committed by the board. One said, "It was like the search was playing out on CNN." Publicity surrounding the search was not positive. For example, A. G. Lafley, Procter and Gamble's CEO, called the search "one of the strangest processes we've ever seen," and executive recruiter Joseph D. Goodwin said, "If I were associated with that search, I would be embarrassed."

The result of the search for a new "outside" CEO resulted in the selection of Neville Isdell, a retired Coca-Cola executive with 35 years of service. Will some needed changes occur soon? It doesn't appear to be likely. As *BusinessWeek* writer Nanettte Burns puts it, "Isdell seems to have fallen into lockstep with the reigning Coke orthodoxy." Isdell says that the company's future will be directed at improving the soda operations and capitalizing on existing brands. He told Wall Street analysts in November 2004, "We are not talking about radical change in strategy. We are talking about a dramatic change in execution."

Today's leaders, such as those at Coca-Cola, face a large number of complex challenges in the global marketplace. In considering how much credit (or blame) they deserve, two perspectives of leadership come immediately to mind: the "romantic" and "external control" perspectives.[3] First, let's look at the romantic view of leadership. Here, the implicit assumption is that the leader is the key force in determining an organization's success—or lack thereof.[4] This view dominates the popular press in business magazines such as *Fortune, BusinessWeek,* and *Forbes,* wherein the CEO is either lauded for his or her firm's success or chided for the organization's demise. Consider, for example, the credit that has been bestowed on leaders such as Jack Welch, Andrew Grove, and Herb Kelleher for the tremendous accomplishments of their firms, General Electric, Intel, and Southwest Airlines, respectively.

More recently, Carlos Ghosn has been lionized in the business press for turning around Nissan's fortunes in the worldwide automobile industry. He transformed huge losses into a $7 billion profit, eliminated $23 billion of debt, and made Nissan the world's most profitable volume producer.[5] And, in the world of sports, managers and coaches, such as Bill Belichick of the New England Patriots in the National Football League, get a lot of credit for their team's outstanding success on the field.

On the other hand, when things don't go well, much of the failure of an organization can also, rightfully, be attributed to the leader. For example, when Carly Fiorina was fired as CEO of Hewlett Packard, the firm enjoyed an immediate increase in its stock price of 7 percent—hardly a strong endorsement of her leadership! And the failures of the CEOs at Coca-Cola (who followed the legendary Roberto Goizueta) to change their firm's strategies to become more consistent with dramatic changes in consumer tastes and preferences reflect shortcomings in their leadership. Coca-Cola has seen their market position and share values substantially erode.

However, this reflects only part of the picture. Consider another perspective of leadership called "external control." Here, rather than making the implicit assumption that the leader is the most important factor in determining organizational outcomes, the focus is on external factors that may positively or negatively affect a firm's success. We don't have to look far to support this perspective. For example, Coca-Cola's core business in carbonated beverages (soda) has been eroded by a shift in consumer preferences toward other beverages. The soft drink industry has been hurt by rising raw material costs, intense competition in some international markets, and price erosion. Such factors have caused *Value Line* to rate the soft drink industry 88th out of 98 industries in terms of "timeliness"—hardly an enviable industry in which to compete.[6]

The point, of course, is that, while neither the romantic nor the external control perspective is entirely correct, we must acknowledge both in the study of strategic management. Our premise is that leaders can make a difference, but they must be constantly aware of the opportunities and threats that they face in the external environment and have a thorough understanding of their firm's resources and capabilities.

In contrast to Coca-Cola, PepsiCo has leveraged its financial, marketing and distribution resources, and capabilities to aggressively diversify beyond carbonated beverages and has created many strong brands. Pepsi has been able to avoid sinking into a slow-growth pit as its core soda pop and potato chip products age.[7] As noted by Robert van Brugge of Sanford C. Bernstein & Co., "They have been early to see trends and aggressive in targeting them." For example, its Tropicana juice, Gatorade sports drinks (part of Quaker Oats which Coca-Cola failed to acquire), and Aquafina water have all become billion-dollar brands. Its CEO, Steve Reinemund, was recently named one of *BusinessWeek*'s "Best Managers."[8] His approach: "Being outside of carbonated (soft drinks) makes sure we're growing in the areas where there is growth." Not surprisingly, PepsiCo's recent performance is far stronger than Coke's. While Coke's stock price has declined slightly over the most recent five-year period, PepsiCo's is up about 60 percent.

Before we move on, we'd like to provide a rather dramatic example of the external control perspective at work: the terrorist attack on the twin towers of the World Trade Center in New York City and the Pentagon building in Arlington, Virginia, on September 11, 2001. The loss of life and injuries to innocent people were immense, and the damage to property was enormous. Wall Street suffered a loss of about $1.4 trillion in the five trading sessions after the market opened on September 17. The effect on many industries was devastating. Strategy Spotlight 1.1 looks at some high-technology industries that have recognized opportunities and benefited from the terrorist attacks and from subsequent developments such as the creation of the Department of Homeland Security, the Iraq War, and the "War on Terror."

## >>What Is Strategic Management?

Given the many challenges and opportunities in the global marketplace, today's managers must do more than set long-term strategies and hope for the best.[9] They must go beyond what some have called "incremental management," whereby they view their job as making a series of small, minor changes to improve the efficiency of their firm's operations.[10] That is fine if your firm is competing in a very stable, simple, and unchanging industry. But there aren't many of those left. As we shall discuss in this chapter and throughout the book, the pace of change is accelerating, and the pressure on managers to make both major and minor changes in a firm's strategic direction is increasing.

Rather than seeing their role as merely custodians of the status quo, today's leaders must be proactive, anticipate change, and continually refine and, when necessary, make

## Terrorism and U.S. Business

The terrorist attacks on September 11, 2001, paralyzed the U.S. economy for a few days. Their aftermath can still be felt in several industries, including airlines and tourism. Consumers, businesses, schools, and colleges have all significantly cut their technology spending. There is, however, a major purchaser of the latest technology: the federal government.

With the 2003 Iraq War and the creation of the Department of Homeland Security, government spending has become a bright spot in the technology arena. For example, according to the Morgan Keegan Investment firm, for the first half of 2004, the 13 companies related to homeland security enjoyed a 25 percent average price gain in stocks. And in the 90 days following 9/11, the same group averaged a 200 percent gain before settling down. Homeland security legislation has been passed that allocates money for homeland security to individual states, but not a lot has been spent yet, according to Michael Hoffman, a security analyst. Two firms that are likely to benefit from increased security spending are:

- Verint Systems Inc. is a maker of analytic software used in security for airports, public buildings, financial institutions, retail stores, and corporate sites. It has a large potential for growth based on future terrorist threats. Verint upgrades communication through interaction of video, voice, e-mail, and the Internet.

Sources: Kerstetter, J., Crock, S., & Hof, R. D. 2003. More bang for the bite. *BusinessWeek*, April 7: 39–40; Rae-Dupree, J. 2003. A target for tech, *U.S. News & World Report*, January 13: 30–32; Lawrence, S. 2001. Defense spending may be the mother of all invention. *Red Herring*, December 11: 17–18; www.sgi.com; and, Luckey, A. 2004. Security stocks ride fears about terrorism. *Sun-Sentinel Times*, June 20: np.

- Drexler Technology, is a maker of LaserCard optical memory cards and chip-ready Smart/Optical cards. Its cards are used in inspection procedures for immigration, border crossing visas, cargo manifests, motor vehicle registration, and identification cards.

Not all tech firms do business with the government directly. When Lockheed Martin became the prime contractor on the $200 billion Joint Strike Fighter program, it chose Silicon Graphics, Inc. (SGI) to design, evaluate, and simulate the aircraft. Similarly, when General Dynamics was asked to develop the Navy's Area Air Defense Commander Capability System—a real-time, three-dimensional view of the tactical area around the ship—high-end SGI computers were a natural fit. Apart from this, SGI now does ballistic missile defense; training systems; command, control, and surveillance systems; and weather and climate forecasting. All this has meant that for SGI, which traditionally had generated less than 28 percent of its revenues selling supercomputing defense systems, government contracts now represent 35 percent of its $1.3 billion annual revenue.

At times, high-profile success on the battlefield can provide a powerful boost for new technology that carries over to the commercial world. For example, in 1990 tiny Trimble Navigation Ltd., based in Sunnyvale, California, sold 10,000 handheld devices with global positioning systems to the military for the first Gulf War. The devices were a success in the war and a boon to Trimble and the commercial GPS market. Now Trimble is a $466 million firm, with just 3 percent of its sales from the military.

dramatic changes to their strategies. The strategic management of the organization must become both a process and a way of thinking throughout the organization.

## Defining Strategic Management

As we stated at the beginning of this chapter, strategic management consists of the analyses, decisions, and actions an organization undertakes in order to create and sustain competitive advantages. This definition captures two main elements that go to the heart of the field of strategic management.

First, the strategic management of an organization entails three ongoing processes: *analyses, decisions,* and *actions.* That is, strategic management is concerned with the *analysis* of strategic goals (vision, mission, and strategic objectives) along with the analysis of the internal and external environment of the organization. Next, leaders must make strategic decisions. These *decisions,* broadly speaking, address two basic questions: What industries should we compete in? How should we compete in those industries? These questions also often involve an organization's domestic as well as its international operations.

And last are the *actions* that must be taken. Decisions are of little use, of course, unless they are acted on. Firms must take the necessary actions to implement their strategies. This requires leaders to allocate the necessary resources and to design the organization to bring the intended strategies to reality. As we will see in the next section, this is an ongoing, evolving process that requires a great deal of interaction among these three processes.

Second, the essence of strategic management is the study of why some firms outperform others.[11] Thus, managers need to determine how a firm is to compete so that it can obtain advantages that are sustainable over a lengthy period of time. That means focusing on two fundamental questions: *How should we compete in order to create competitive advantages in the marketplace?* For example, managers need to determine if the firm should position itself as the low-cost producer, develop products and services that are unique and will enable the firm to charge premium prices, or some combination of both.

Managers must also ask how to make such advantages sustainable, instead of highly temporary, in the marketplace. That is: *How can we create competitive advantages in the marketplace that are not only unique and valuable but also difficult for competitors to copy or substitute?*[12,13]

Ideas that work are almost always copied by rivals immediately. In the 1980s, American Airlines tried to establish a competitive advantage by introducing the frequent flyer program. Within weeks, all the airlines did the same thing. Overnight, frequent flyer programs became a necessary tool for competitive parity instead of a competitive advantage. The challenge, therefore, is to create competitive advantages that are sustainable.

Michael Porter argues that sustainable competitive advantage cannot be achieved through operational effectiveness alone.[14] Most of the popular management innovations of the last two decades—total quality, just-in-time, benchmarking, business process reengineering, outsourcing—all are about operational effectiveness. Operational effectiveness means performing similar activities better than rivals. Each of these is important, but none lead to sustainable competitive advantage for the simple reason that everyone is doing them. Strategy is all about being different from everyone else. Sustainable competitive advantage is possible only through performing different activities from rivals or performing similar activities in different ways. Companies such as Wal-Mart, Southwest Airlines, and IKEA have developed unique, internally consistent, and difficult-to-imitate activity systems that have provided them with sustained competitive advantage. A company with a good strategy must make clear choices about what it wants to accomplish. Trying to do everything that your rivals do eventually leads to mutually destructive price competition, not long-term advantage.

## The Four Key Attributes of Strategic Management

Before discussing the strategic management process in more detail, let's briefly talk about four attributes of strategic management.[15] In doing so, it will become clear how this course differs from other courses that you have had in functional areas, such as accounting, marketing, operations, and finance. Exhibit 1.1 provides a definition and the four attributes of strategic management.

First, strategic management is *directed toward overall organizational goals and objectives.* That is, effort must be directed at what is best for the total organization, not just a single functional area. Some authors have referred to this perspective as "organizational versus individual rationality."[16] That is, what might look "rational" or most appropriate for one functional area, such as operations, may not be in the best interest of the overall firm. For example, operations may decide to schedule long production runs of similar products in order to lower unit costs. However, the standardized output may be counter to what the marketing department needs in order to appeal to a sophisticated

Exhibit 1.1
**Strategic
Management
Concepts**

**Definition:** Strategic management consists of the analyses, decisions, and actions an organization undertakes in order to create and sustain competitive advantages.

**Key Attributes of Strategic Management**

- Directs the organization toward overall goals and objectives.
- Includes multiple stakeholders in decision making.
- Needs to incorporate short-term and long-term perspectives.
- Recognizes trade-offs between efficiency and effectiveness.

and demanding target market. Similarly, research and development may "overengineer" the product in order to develop a far superior offering, but the design may make the product so expensive that market demand is minimal. Therefore, in this course you will look at cases and strategic issues from the perspective of the organization rather than that of the functional area(s) in which you have had the most training and experience.

Second, strategic management *includes multiple stakeholders in decision making.* Managers must incorporate the demands of many stakeholders when making decisions.[17] Stakeholders are those individuals, groups, and organizations who have a "stake" in the success of the organization, including owners (shareholders in a publicly held corporation), employees, customers, suppliers, the community at large, and so on. We'll discuss this in more detail later in this chapter. Managers will not be successful if they continually focus on a single stakeholder. For example, if the overwhelming emphasis is on generating profits for the owners, employees may become alienated, customer service may suffer, and the suppliers may become resentful of continual demands for pricing concessions. As we will see, however, many organizations have been able to satisfy multiple stakeholder needs simultaneously. For example, financial performance may actually be greater because employees who are satisfied with their jobs make a greater effort to enhance customer satisfaction, thus leading to higher profits.

Third, strategic management *requires incorporating both short-term and long-term perspectives.* Peter Senge, a leading strategic management author at the Massachusetts Institute of Technology, has referred to this need as a "creative tension."[18] That is, managers must maintain both a vision for the future of the organization as well as a focus on its present operating needs. However, as one descends the hierarchy of the organization from executive to middle-level managers to lower level managers at the level of operations, there tends to be a narrower, short-term perspective. Nonetheless, all managers throughout the organization must maintain a strategic management perspective and assess how their actions impact the overall attainment of organizational objectives. For example, laying off several valuable employees may help to cut costs and improve profits in the short term, but the long-term implications for employee morale and customer relationships may suffer, leading to subsequent performance declines.[19]

Fourth, strategic management *involves the recognition of trade-offs between effectiveness and efficiency.* Closely related to the third point above, this recognition means being aware of the need for organizations to strive to act effectively and efficiently. Some authors have referred to this as the difference between "doing the right thing" (effectiveness) and "doing things right" (efficiency).[20] While managers must allocate and use resources wisely, they must still direct their efforts toward the attainment of overall organizational objectives. Managers who are totally focused on meeting short-term budgets

## Amgen's CEO Discusses the Challenge of Managing at "Different Altitudes"

A CEO must always be switching between what I call different altitudes—tasks of different levels of abstraction and specificity. At the highest altitude you're asking the big questions: What are the company's mission and strategy? Do people understand and believe in these aims? Are decisions consistent with them? At the lowest altitude, you're looking at on-the-ground operations: Did we make that sale? What was the yield on the last lot in the factory? How many days of inventory do we have for a particular drug? And then there's everything in between: How many chemists do we need to hire this quarter? What should we pay for a small biotech company that has a promising new drug? Is our production capacity adequate to roll out a product in a new market?

You have to be working at all of these levels simultaneously, and that's not easy. . . . But most CEOs tend to gravitate toward the altitude where they are most comfortable. That's natural. Someone might choose to operate almost exclusively at the highest possible altitude: "I'm going to be responsible for the company's strategic vision." Another might choose to operate mainly at a lower altitude: "I'm going to pick the curtains in that hotel." Both altitudes are important. But most CEOs who get in trouble do so because they get stuck at a particular altitude.

Source: Reprinted by permission of *Harvard Business Review*. Excerpt from "A Time for Growth: An Interview with Amgen CEO Kevin Sharer," by Paul Hemp, July–August 2004. Copyright © 2004 by The Harvard Business School Publishing Corporation; all rights reserved.

and targets may fail to attain the broader goals of the organization. Consider the following amusing story told by Norman Augustine, former CEO of defense giant, Martin Marietta (now Lockheed Martin):

> I am reminded of an article I once read in a British newspaper which described a problem with the local bus service between the towns of Bagnall and Greenfields. It seemed that, to the great annoyance of customers, drivers had been passing long queues of would-be passengers with a smile and a wave of the hand. This practice was, however, clarified by a bus company official who explained, "It is impossible for the drivers to keep their timetables if they must stop for passengers."[21]

Clearly, the drivers who were trying to stay on schedule had ignored the overall mission. As Augustine noted, "Impeccable logic but something seems to be missing!"

Successful managers must make many trade-offs. It is central to the practice of strategic management. At times, managers must focus on the short term and efficiency; at other times the emphasis is on the long term and expanding a firm's product-market scope in order to anticipate opportunities in the competitive environment. Some authors have written on the concept of "ambidexterity"; that is, managers need to both align resources to take advantage of existing product markets and proactively exploit new opportunities.[22] We address this concept in greater detail in Chapter 10. There are other trade-offs such as how to prioritize various stakeholder needs that must be satisfied in a given situation. Strategy Spotlight 1.2 addresses an interesting top management perspective associated with managing at "different altitudes." It is provided by Kevin Sharer who is CEO of Amgen, the world's largest biotechnology company with $8.4 billion in revenues.

## >>The Strategic Management Process

We've identified three ongoing processes—analyses, decisions, and actions—that are central to strategic management. In practice, these three processes—often referred to as strategy analysis, strategy formulation, and strategy implementation—are highly interdependent. Further, these three processes do not take place one after the other in a sequential fashion in most companies.

**Exhibit 1.2   Realized Strategy and Intended Strategy: Usually Not the Same**

Source: From Mintzberg, H. & Waters, J. A., "Of Strategies: Deliberate and Emergent," *Strategic Management Joural,* Vol. 6, 1985, pp. 257–272. Copyright © John Wiley & Sons Limited. Reproduced with permission.

Henry Mintzberg, a very influential management scholar at McGill University, argues that conceptualizing the strategic management process as one in which analysis is followed by optimal decisions and their subsequent meticulous implementation neither describes the strategic management process accurately nor prescribes ideal practice.[23] In his view, the business environment is far from predictable, thus limiting our ability for analysis. Further, decisions in an organization are seldom based on optimal rationality alone, given the political processes that occur in all organizations.

Taking into consideration the limitations discussed above, Mintzberg proposed an alternative model of strategy development. As depicted in Exhibit 1.2, decisions following from analysis, in this model, constitute the *intended* strategy of the firm. For a variety of reasons, the intended strategy rarely survives in its original form. Unforeseen environmental developments, unanticipated resource constraints, or changes in managerial preferences may result in at least some parts of the intended strategy remaining *unrealized.* On the other hand, good managers will want to take advantage of a new opportunity presented by the environment, even if it was not part of the original set of intentions. For example, consider the wind energy industry.[24] In September 2004 the United States Congress renewed the wind tax credit. Legislation in 19 states now requires that electricity providers offer a certain percentage of "green" (i.e., renewable) energy. Such legislation, combined with falling clean energy costs and rising prices for coal, oil, and gas, have created a surge in demand for competitors such as GE Wind Energy, which makes large turbines and fan blades. Not surprisingly, such businesses have increased hiring and research and development, as well as revenue and profit forecasts. The final *realized* strategy of any firm is thus a combination of *deliberate* and *emergent* strategies.

In the next three subsections, we will address each of the three key strategic management processes: strategy analysis, strategy formulation, and strategy implementation. We also highlight brief examples from business practice that are based on the opening vignettes for each chapter. Throughout the book, they serve to demonstrate that effective strategic management poses complex challenges and that sometimes things can go wrong.

Exhibit 1.3 depicts the strategic management process and indicates how it ties into the chapters in the book. Consistent with our discussion above, we use two-way arrows to convey the interactive nature of the processes.

## Strategy Analysis

Strategy analysis may be looked upon as the starting point of the strategic management process. It consists of the "advance work" that must be done in order to effectively formulate and implement strategies. Many strategies fail because managers may want to

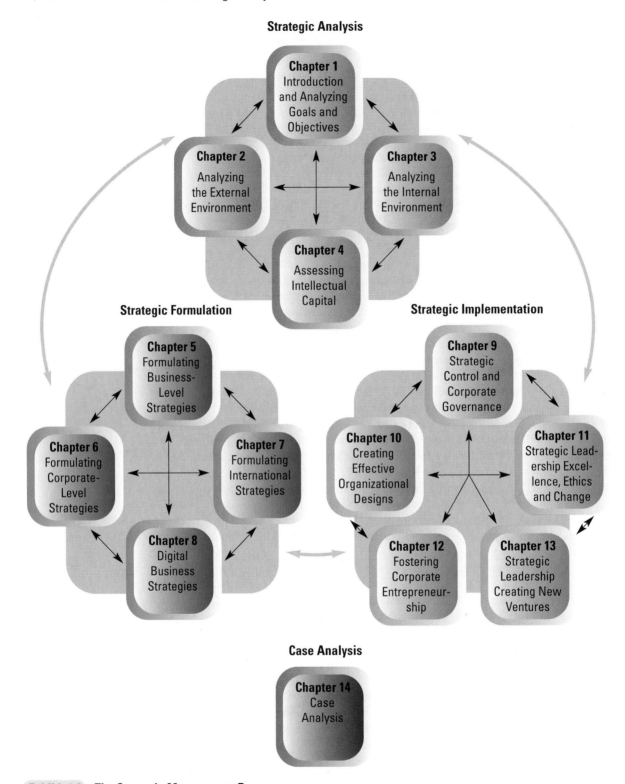

**Exhibit 1.3**    **The Strategic Management Process**

formulate and implement strategies without a careful analysis of the overarching goals of the organization and without a thorough analysis of its external and internal environment.

*Analyzing Organizational Goals and Objectives (Chapter 1)*    Later in this chapter, we will address how organizations must have clearly articulated goals and objectives in order to channel the efforts of individuals throughout the organization toward common ends. Goals and objectives also provide a means of allocating resources effectively. A firm's vision, mission, and strategic objectives form a hierarchy of goals that range from broad statements of intent and bases for competitive advantage to specific, measurable strategic objectives.

As indicated in Exhibit 1.3, this hierarchy of goals is not developed in isolation. Rather, it is developed in concert with a rigorous understanding of the opportunities and threats in the external environment (Chapter 2) as well as a thorough understanding of the firm's strengths and weaknesses (Chapters 3 and 4). The opening incident in Chapter 1 describes how Coca-Cola has failed to adapt to changes in customer tastes and demands, largely because of its outdated culture and mindset, an overbearing and entrenched board of directors, and ineffective CEO leadership.

*Analyzing the External Environment of the Firm (Chapter 2)*    Managers must monitor and scan the environment as well as analyze competitors. Such information is critical in determining the opportunity and threats in the external environment. We provide two frameworks of the external environment. First, the general environment consists of several elements, such as demographic, technological, and economic segments, from which key trends and events can have a dramatic impact on the firm. Second, the industry environment consists of competitors and other organizations that may threaten the success of a firm's products and services. We discuss how Interstate Bakeries Corporation (IBC) (makers of such American icons as Wonder Bread, Twinkies, Zingers, and Ding Dongs) was forced into bankruptcy. The problem was that IBC was unable to adjust its product mix to reflect the market's move away from high carbohydrate products and sugary snacks. Clearly, recent concerns about childhood obesity didn't help either.

*Assessing the Internal Environment of the Firm (Chapter 3)*    We provide some useful frameworks for analyzing a firm's internal environment. Such analysis helps to identify both strengths and weaknesses that can, in part, determine how well a firm will succeed in an industry. Analyzing the strengths and relationships among the activities that constitute a firm's value chain (e.g., operations, marketing and sales, and human resource management) can be a means of uncovering potential sources of competitive advantage for the firm. We discuss how Ford's Jaguar products have stumbled in the marketplace. Poor product styling, marketing, and the use of interchangeable parts with less expensive nameplates have eroded the brand. Heavy rental sales and huge rebates also have caused image problems.

*Assessing a Firm's Intellectual Assets (Chapter 4)*    The knowledge worker and a firm's other intellectual assets (e.g., patents, trademarks) are becoming increasingly important as the drivers of competitive advantages and wealth creation in today's economy. In addition to human capital, we assess how well the organization creates networks and relationships among its employees as well as its customers, suppliers, and alliance partners. We also address the need for organizations to use technology to enhance collaboration among employees as well as provide a means of accumulating and storing knowledge. We discuss how a small advertising and marketing firm, Wildflower, stumbled when it hired a "star" professional from a large, blue chip firm. The person's skills and attitude didn't fit in well at a small firm like Wildflower, and soon office morale became a serious problem. Clearly, any skills and talents the new hire could have offered were more than offset by how adversely relationships among colleagues were affected.

## Strategy Formulation

A firm's strategy formulation is developed at several levels. First, business-level strategy addresses the issue of how to compete in given business environments to attain competitive advantage. Second, corporate-level strategy focuses on two issues: (1) what businesses to compete in and (2) how businesses can be managed to achieve synergy; that is, they create more value by working together than if they operate as stand-alone businesses. Third, a firm must determine the best method to develop international strategies as it ventures beyond its national boundaries. Finally, the growing importance of the Internet has increased the necessity for firms to explore the ramifications of this new strategic platform and formulate Internet and e-business strategies.

*Formulating Business-Level Strategy (Chapter 5)*    The question of how firms compete and outperform their rivals and how they achieve and sustain competitive advantages goes to the heart of strategic management. Successful firms strive to develop bases for competitive advantage. These can be achieved through cost leadership and/or differentiation as well as by focusing on a narrow or industrywide market segment. We'll also discuss why some advantages can be more sustainable (or durable) over time and how a firm's business-level strategy changes with the industry life cycle—that is, the stages of introduction, growth, maturity, and decline. We discuss how Sharper Image erroneously based its competitive advantage on a product—an air purifier—that was easily imitated by rivals. Gains in profitability and market position became short-lived.

*Formulating Corporate-Level Strategy (Chapter 6)*    Whereas business-level strategy is concerned with how to create and sustain competitive advantage in an individual business, corporate-level strategy addresses issues concerning a firm's portfolio (or group) of businesses. That is, it asks (1) What business (or businesses) should we compete in? and (2) How can we manage this portfolio of businesses to create synergies among the businesses? In this chapter, we explore the relative advantages and disadvantages of firms pursuing strategies of related or unrelated diversification. In addition, we discuss the various means that firms can employ to diversify—internal development, mergers and acquisitions, and joint ventures and strategic alliances—as well as their relative advantages and disadvantages. We describe how a leading discount broker, Charles Schwab and Company, erred when it acquired U.S. Trust, a financial services firm that catered to wealthy clients.

*Formulating International Strategy (Chapter 7)*    When firms expand their scope of operations to include foreign markets, they encounter many opportunities and potential pitfalls. They must decide not only on the most appropriate entry strategy but also how they will go about attaining competitive advantages in international markets. Many successful international firms have been able to attain both lower costs and higher levels of differentiated products and services through the successful implementation of a "transnational strategy." We describe some of the problems experienced by Volkswagen as it tried to enter the luxury segment of the U.S. car market.

*Formulating Digital Business Strategy (Chapter 8)*    Digital technologies such as the Internet and wireless communications are changing the way business is conducted. These capabilities present both new opportunities and new threats for virtually all businesses. We believe that when firms formulate strategies, they should give explicit consideration to how digital technologies add value and impact their performance outcomes. The effective use of the Internet and digital business strategies can help an organization improve its competitive position and enhance its ability to create advantages by enhancing both cost leadership and differentiation strategies. We describe how Agillion, Inc., an application service provider founded in 1999, went bankrupt in just three years not because the Internet bubble burst, but because its product could easily be imitated. Further, it did not use digital technologies in a way that customers valued.

## Strategy Implementation

As we have noted earlier in the chapter, effective strategies are of no value if they are not properly implemented. Strategy implementation involves ensuring that a firm has proper strategic controls and organizational designs. Of particular importance is ensuring that the firm has established effective means to coordinate and integrate activities within the firm as well as with its suppliers, customers, and alliance partners. In addition, leadership plays a central role. This involves many things, including ensuring that the organization is committed to excellence and ethical behavior, promotes learning and continuous improvement, and acts entrepreneurially in creating and taking advantage of new opportunities.

*Strategic Control and Corporate Governance (Chapter 9)*   To implement strategies, firms must exercise effectively two types of strategic control. First, informational control requires that organizations continually monitor and scan the environment and respond to threats and opportunities. Second, behavioral control involves the proper balance of rewards and incentives as well as cultures and boundaries (or constraints). In addition to effective informational and behavioral controls, successful firms (those that are incorporated) practice effective corporate governance. That is, they must create mechanisms to ensure that the interests of the managers are consistent with those of the owners (shareholders) of the firm. These include an effective board of directors, actively engaged shareholders, and proper managerial reward and incentive systems. We also discuss the important role played by various external mechanisms such as the market for corporate control, auditors, banks, analysts, and the financial press in ensuring good governance. We discuss how Lantech, a $100 million manufacturing company, suffered when it implemented an ineffective reward system. The pay incentive program pitted one division against another, which resulted in intense rivalries and destructive "gamesmanship."

*Creating Effective Organizational Designs (Chapter 10)*   To succeed, firms must have organizational structures and designs that are consistent with their strategy. For example, firms that diversify into related product-market areas typically implement divisional structures. In today's rapidly changing competitive environments, firms must design their companies to ensure that their organizational boundaries—those internal to the firm and external—are more flexible and permeable. In many cases, organizations should consider creating strategic alliances in order to capitalize on the capabilities of other organizations. We discuss how the National Health Service in Great Britain experienced inefficiencies and wasted resources when its various units failed to coordinate properly.

*Creating a Learning Organization and an Ethical Organization (Chapter 11)*   Effective leaders must engage in several ongoing activities: setting a direction, designing the organization, and developing an organization that is committed to excellence and ethical behavior. In addition, given the rapid and unpredictable change in today's competitive environments, leaders need to create a "learning organization." This ensures that the entire organization can benefit from individual and collective talents. We describe how Krispy Kreme's fortunes sunk when it expanded too rapidly and its top leadership engaged in self-interested behavior in granting and managing its franchises.

***Fostering Corporate Entrepreneurship (Chapter 12)***    Today's successes do not guarantee success in the future. With rapid and unpredictable change in the global marketplace, firms must continually improve and grow as well as find new ways to renew their organizations. Corporate entrepreneurship and innovation provide firms with new opportunities, and strategies should be formulated that enhance a firm's innovative capacity. Within corporations, proactiveness and autonomous entrepreneurial behavior by product champions and other organizational members are needed to turn new ideas into corporate ventures. We present the case of Polaroid, a company that grew from a revolutionary technology—instantly developing film. However, it fell behind when it was slow to adapt to a new way of developing pictures instantly—digital photography.

***Creating New Ventures (Chapter 13)***    New ventures and small businesses represent a major engine of economic growth. Although the challenges they face are unique, especially for start-up firms entering into business for the first time, many of the concepts that we address in the text can be applied to new ventures and small businesses. Viable opportunities must be recognized, effective strategies must be implemented, and entrepreneurial leadership skills are needed to successfully launch and sustain these enterprises. We discuss the fate of Rosen Motors, a young firm with an innovative, hybrid automobile drive train that could save millions in energy costs. However, Rosen did not recognize critical market forces when implementing its start-up strategy—including the power of its most important buyers, the big automakers—and failed as a result.

We've discussed the strategic management process. In addition, Chapter 14, "Analyzing Strategic Management Cases," provides guidelines and suggestions on how to evaluate cases in this course. Thus, the concepts and techniques discussed in these 13 chapters can be applied to real-world organizations.

Let's now address two concepts—corporate governance and stakeholder management—that are critical to the strategic management process.

## >>The Role of Corporate Governance and Stakeholder Management

Most business enterprises that employ more than a few dozen people are organized as corporations. As you recall from your finance classes, the overall purpose of a corporation is to maximize the long-term return to the owners (shareholders). Thus, we may ask: Who is really responsible for fulfilling this purpose? Robert Monks and Neil Minow, in addressing this issue, provide a useful definition of corporate governance as "the relationship among various participants in determining the direction and performance of corporations. The primary participants are (1) the shareholders, (2) the management (led by the chief executive officer), and (3) the board of directors."[25] This relationship is illustrated in Exhibit 1.4.

The directors on the board of directors (BOD) are the elected representatives of the shareholders. They are charged with ensuring that the interests and motives of management are aligned with those of the owners (i.e., shareholders). In many cases, the BOD is diligent in fulfilling its purpose. For example, Intel Corporation, the giant $34 billion maker of microprocessor chips, is widely recognized as an excellent example of sound

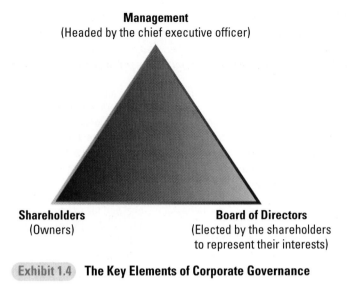

**Management**
(Headed by the chief executive officer)

**Shareholders**
(Owners)

**Board of Directors**
(Elected by the shareholders
to represent their interests)

**Exhibit 1.4    The Key Elements of Corporate Governance**

governance practices. Its BOD has established guidelines to ensure that its members are independent (i.e., not members of the executive management team and do not have close personal ties to top executives) so that they can provide proper oversight; it has explicit guidelines on the selection of director candidates (to avoid "cronyism"); and it provides detailed procedures for formal evaluations of both directors and the firm's top officers.[26] Such guidelines serve to ensure that management is acting in the best interests of shareholders.

Recently, there has been much criticism as well as cynicism by both citizens and the business press about the poor job that management and the BODs of large corporations are doing. We only have to look at the recent scandals at such firms as Arthur Andersen, WorldCom, Enron, Tyco, and ImClone Systems.[27] Such malfeasance has led to an erosion of the public's trust in the governance of corporations. For example, a recent Gallup poll found that 90 percent of Americans felt that people leading corporations could not be trusted to look after the interests of their employees, and only 18 percent thought that corporations looked after their shareholders. Forty-three percent, in fact, believed that senior executives were in it only for themselves. In Britain, that figure, according to another poll, was an astonishing 95 percent.[28] To drive home the point, consider the humorous perspective of Russell T. Lewis, CEO of the New York Times Company, in a recent speech:[29]

> Not long ago, CEOs were regarded as captains of industry—among the country's best and brightest talents—at least that's what I've been telling my parents, and they seem to have bought the line. Today, however, CEOs and their CFOs are highly reviled defendants in felony criminal proceedings. And their companies are the subjects of billion-dollar shareholder lawsuits. Things have gotten so bad that any day now I expect *Fortune* Magazine to come out with its list of "Most Wanted CEOs." No doubt this will soon be followed by a spin-off of a popular TV program. I can see the promo now: "Tonight at 8 PM—Help us catch America's Most Wanted CEOs . . . they could be hiding in our hometown."
>
> But, folks, the final indignity for this particular CEO concerns my own parents: my loving 87-year-old mother—a former public school teacher and my unfailingly supportive 94-year-old father. They no longer brag about me to the clerks at the Lake Worth, Florida, Publix supermarket. Yes, folks, it has gotten that bad.

# STRATEGY SPOTLIGHT

## 1.3

### Italy's Parmalat: Europe's Enron?

On December 15, 2003, Parmalat's founder, chairman, and CEO Calisto Tanzi resigned. And later that month on December 27, the $7.2 billion firm filed for bankruptcy. Parmalat is one of the world's largest dairy firms with headquarters in Italy and operations in 13 other countries, including the United States. Parmalat did not fail due to market and economic factors such as declining market demand, intensifying competition, or problematic foreign exchange rates. Instead, it is a textbook case of management fraud and poor corporate governance.

The defrocked Tanzi has spent 2004 and much of 2005 fighting the law. He denies prosecutors' charges of market-rigging, falsifying accounts, and obstructing Italy's stock market regulator, Consob. He is now awaiting trial on those charges, and he has confessed to siphoning off $665 million from the milk giant to a family-owned travel company. Parmalat was found to have $18 billion missing from its accounts early last year, making it one of the biggest corporate frauds in history. Italian prosecutors have discovered that managers simply invented assets to offset liabilities and falsified accounts over a 15-year period. It is uncertain whether the missing funds were used to plug operating losses, pay creditors, or illegally enrich top managers, who come from the founding family.

Several criminal and civil trials are set to get under way soon involving Tanzi and other top Parmalat executives, banks, auditing companies, and others. Tanzi, who suffers from ill health and is now under house arrest, faces up to 15 years in prison if convicted.

Prior to the outbreak of the scandal, Parmalat was already known for its poor corporate governance. Its big investors had utterly failed to use their leverage to alter the behavior of Tanzi and his executives. It is not yet clear, however, if investors made any real effort to demand better disclosure and to end "overly creative financing." Respected multinational banks such as Citigroup, J. P. Morgan, and Deutsche Bank were all too eager to construct the derivative deals by which Parmalat was able to transfer funds offshore. Although Parmalat failed to disclose a lot of information to Standard & Poor's (S&P), the agency was still content to issue investment-grade ratings on its bonds. It was only when the firm entered crisis mode that it became clear how wrong S&P had been.

Italy's government is drafting a new law on financial regulation that will overhaul both institutions and laws, forcing greater disclosure, granting regulators more investigative powers, and tightening control over accounting practices. Although leading proponents of corporate governance in Italy agree that it is still too early to see what will eventually develop, they remain confident that the once lax attitude toward self-compliance with the country's code has changed dramatically in the wake of Parmalat.

Sources: Anonymous. 2005. The worst managers. *BusinessWeek*, January 10: 74–77; Anonymous. 2005. A curious delay. *The Economist*, April 9: 52; Capell, K. et al. 2004. Europe's old ways die fast. *BusinessWeek*, May 17: 54–57; Déjà vu all over again? 2003. *The Economist*, December 20: 95–96; Turning sour. 2004. *The Economist*, January 3: 8–9; and Edmonson, G. 2004. How Parmalat went sour. *BusinessWeek*, January 12: 46–48. We would also like to thank Yi Jiang and Michael W. Peng, both of Ohio State University, for their useful input.

At times, BODs have become complacent and, in many cases, incompetent. They have often been accused of rubber stamping strategies and actions proposed by top management, and they have clearly not acted in a manner consistent with shareholder interests.

Clearly, there is a strong need for improved corporate governance, and we will address this topic in greater detail in Chapter 9. We focus on three important mechanisms to help ensure effective corporate governance: an effective and engaged board of directors, shareholder activism, and proper managerial rewards and incentives.[30] In addition to these internal controls, a key role is played by various external control mechanisms. These include the auditors, banks, analysts, an active financial press, and the threat of hostile takeovers.

Not surprisingly, the United States does not have a monopoly on executive malfeasance and poor corporate governance. For example, Strategy Spotlight 1.3 discusses the case of Italy's Parmalat. Here's a firm that has been called Europe's Enron—a label that is well deserved.

Generating long-term returns for the shareholders is the primary goal of a publicly held corporation. As noted by former Chrysler vice chairman Robert Lutz, "We are here to serve the shareholder and create shareholder value. I insist that the only person who owns the company is the person who paid good money for it."[31]

Despite the primacy of generating shareholder value, managers who focus solely on the interests of the owners of the business will often make poor decisions that lead to negative, unanticipated outcomes. For example, decisions such as mass layoffs to increase profits, ignoring issues related to conservation of the natural environment to save money, and exerting excessive pressure on suppliers to lower prices can certainly harm the firm in the long run. Such actions would likely lead to negative outcomes such as alienated employees, increased governmental oversight and fines, and disloyal suppliers.

Clearly, in addition to *shareholders,* there are other *stakeholders* that must be explicitly taken into account in the strategic management process.[32] A stakeholder can be defined as an individual or group, inside or outside the company, that has a stake in and can influence an organization's performance. Although companies can have different stakeholders, each generally has five prominent stakeholder groups:[33]

- customers
- employees and managers
- suppliers (of goods, services, and capital)
- the community at large
- owners

## Zero Sum or Symbiosis? Two Alternate Perspectives of Stakeholder Management

There are two opposing ways of looking at the role of stakeholder management in the strategic management process.[34] The first one can be termed "zero sum." In this view, the role of management is to look upon the various stakeholders as competing for the attention and resources of the organization. In essence, the gain of one individual or group is the loss of another individual or group. That is, employees want higher wages (which drive down profits), suppliers want higher prices for their inputs and slower, more flexible delivery times (which drive up costs), customers want fast deliveries and higher quality (which drive up costs), the community at large wants charitable contributions (which take money from company goals), and so on. This zero-sum thinking is rooted, in part, in the traditional conflict between workers and management, leading to the formation of unions and sometimes ending in adversarial union–management negotiations that can lead to long, bitter strikes.

Although there will always be some conflicting demands placed on the organization by its various stakeholders, there is value in exploring how the organization can achieve mutual benefit through *stakeholder symbiosis,* which recognizes that stakeholders are dependent upon each other for their success and well-being.[35] That is, managers acknowledge the interdependence among employees, suppliers, customers, shareholders, and the community at large, as we will discuss in Chapter 3 in more detail. Sears, for example, has developed a sophisticated quantitative model that demonstrates symbiosis. With this model, Sears can predict the relationship between employee satisfaction, customer satisfaction, and financial results.[36] The Sears model found that a 5 percent improvement in employee attitudes led to a 1.3 percent improvement in customer satisfaction, which, in turn, will drive a 0.5 percent improvement in revenue.

## Social Responsibility, Social Innovation, and Environmental Sustainability: Moving Beyond the Immediate Stakeholders

Organizations must acknowledge and act upon the interests and demands of stakeholders such as citizens and society in general that are beyond its immediate constituencies—customers, owners, suppliers, and employees. That is, they must consider the needs of the broader community at large and act in a socially responsible manner.[37]

Social responsibility is the expectation that businesses or individuals will strive to improve the overall welfare of society.[38] From the perspective of a business, this means that managers must take active steps to make society better by virtue of the business being in existence.[39] Similar to norms and values, actions that constitute socially responsible behavior tend to change over time. In the 1970s affirmative action was a high priority and firms responded. During the 1990s and up to the present time, the public has been concerned about the quality of the environment. Many firms have responded to this by engaging in recycling and reducing waste. And in the wake of terrorist attacks on New York City and the Pentagon as well as the continuing threat from terrorists worldwide, a new kind of priority has arisen: the need to be responsible and vigilant concerning public safety.

Today, demands for greater corporate responsibility have accelerated from a number of stakeholders.[40] These include corporate critics, social investors, activists, and, increasingly, customers who claim to assess corporate responsibility when making purchasing decisions. Such demands go well beyond product and service quality.[41] They include a focus on issues such as labor standards, environmental sustainability, financial and accounting reporting, procurement, supplier relations, environmental practices, and supply chain management.

Recent corporate scandals have intensified significant public concern about corporate responsibility, transparency, and accountability.[42] External critics reinforce the reputational damage, as Nike, Levi Strauss, Gap, Adidas, and other global brands recently found when activists directed attention to abusive labor and human rights practices in their developing-nation suppliers. Such global brands were forced to implement new systems for managing their supply chain companies in order to ensure that they were consistent with their own codes of conduct. And many large brand-name companies are adopting internal responsibility management systems to avert similar criticisms.

A key stakeholder group that appears to be particularly susceptible to corporate social responsibility (CSR) initiatives is its customers.[43] Surveys indicate a strong positive relationship between CSR behaviors and consumers' reactions to a firm's products and services. For example:

- the 2002 Corporate Citizenship poll conducted by Cone Communications found that "84 percent of Americans say they would be likely to switch brands to one associated with a good cause, if price and quality are similar."[44]
- a 2001 Hill & Knowlton/Harris Interactive poll reveals that "79 percent of Americans take corporate citizenship into account when deciding whether to buy a particular company's product and 37 percent consider corporate citizenship an important factor when making purchasing decisions."[45]

Such findings are consistent with a large body of research that confirms the positive influence of CSR on consumers' company evaluations and product purchase intentions across a broad range of product categories.

*From Social Responsibility to Social Innovation*   Rosabeth Moss Kanter, of the Harvard Business School, and her colleagues have recently found that many leading-edge companies are creating a new paradigm: moving beyond social *responsibility* to social *innovation*.[46] Such companies consider community needs not as, in effect, social ills that require "Band-Aid" solutions such as financial donations and volunteer work. Rather, they see them as valuable opportunities to develop ideas and demonstrate business technologies as well as ways to find and serve new markets.

Such innovations have both community and business payoffs. When companies approach social needs in this manner, they have a stake in the problems and they treat the effort in the same way that they would address any other project that is central to the company's operations. They deploy their best talent and their core skills. They direct their efforts to invent sophisticated solutions through a hands-on approach. Such initiatives are not viewed as charity. Rather it is R&D that strengthens their capabilities—a strategic business investment. Consider, for example, IBM's efforts in public education:

> Under the personal leadership of CEO Louis V. Gerstner, Jr., IBM began its Reinventing Education program in 1994. The program was designed to develop new tools and solutions for systemic change and now operates at 21 locations in four countries. Several product innovations, which benefit both the schools and IBM, have resulted from this initiative. For example, as part of the Wired For Learning program in four new schools in Charlotte-Mecklenburg, North Carolina, IBM created tools to connect parents to teachers digitally. This enables parents to view their children's schoolwork from home or a community center and compare it with the district's academic standards. Also, new tracking software is facilitating the introduction of flexible scheduling in Cincinnati, Ohio, including a new year-round high school. In Broward County, Florida—the fifth largest school district in the United States—IBM's data-warehousing technology provides teachers and administrators with access to extensive information on students. And, in Philadelphia, IBM created a voice recognition tool to teach reading that is based on children's high-pitched voices and speech patterns.[47]

*The Triple Bottom Line: Incorporating Financial as well as Environmental and Social Costs*   To remain viable in the long run, many companies are measuring what has been called a "triple bottom line." This technique involves assessing financial, social, and environmental performance. Shell, NEC, and Procter & Gamble, among other corporations, have recognized that failing to account for the environmental and social costs of doing business poses risks to the company and the community in which it operates.

The environmental revolution has been almost four decades in the making.[48] It has changed forever how companies do business. In the 1960s and 1970s, companies were in a state of denial regarding their firms' impact on the natural environment. However, a series of visible ecological problems created a groundswell for strict governmental regulation. In the United States, Lake Erie was dead, and in Japan, people were dying of mercury poisoning.

Stuart Hart, writing in the *Harvard Business Review*, addresses the magnitude of problems and challenges associated with the natural environment:

> The challenge is to develop a *sustainable global economy:* an economy that the planet is capable of supporting indefinitely. Although we may be approaching ecological recovery in the developed world, the planet as a whole remains on an unsustainable course. Increasingly, the scourges of the late twentieth century—depleted farmland, fisheries, and forests; choking urban pollution; poverty; infectious disease; and migration—are spilling over geopolitical

# STRATEGY SPOTLIGHT

## 1.4

### Productivity Improvement and Environmental Sustainability

Chad Holliday, CEO of DuPont, articulates his firm's innovative approach to productivity improvement:

> Many companies consider productivity to be a cost-saving operational issue. We at DuPont have elevated productivity to the strategic level because we believe that it is central to our efforts in sustainability. As a sign of our commitment in this area, we have adopted six-sigma methodology, a stringent approach that strives to reduce manufacturing defects to just several per million. At the end of last year, we had 1,100 black belts and 1,700 green belts (employees who have undergone weeks of training in the six-sigma methodology) working on 4,200 projects. . . .
>
> Altogether, our projects using six-sigma methodology are responsible for savings of more than $1 billion a year, and these efforts to improve productivity invariably result in less waste, both in energy and raw material. For example, a six-sigma team enabled a DuPont plant in Old Hickory, Tennessee, that manufactures medical gowns made of Sontara, a high-strength durable cloth, to slash its defect rate, saving the equivalent of 760,000 gowns per year. By reducing waste, our six-sigma projects connect directly to sustainable growth.

Source: Holliday, C. 2001. Sustainable growth, the DuPont way. *Harvard Business Review*, 19(9): 129–134.

borders. The simple fact is this: in meeting our needs, we are destroying the ability of future generations to meet theirs . . . corporations are the only organizations with the resources, the technology, the global reach, and, ultimately, the motivation to achieve sustainability.[49]

Environmental sustainability is now a value embraced by the most competitive and successful multinational companies.[50] The McKinsey Corporation's survey of more than 400 senior executives of companies around the world found that 92 percent agreed with former Sony President Akio Morita's contention that the environmental challenge will be one of the central issues in the 21st century.[51] Virtually all executives responding to the survey acknowledged their firm's responsibility to control pollution, and 83 percent agreed that corporations have an environmental responsibility for their products even after they are sold.

For many successful firms, environmental values are now becoming a central part of their cultures and management processes. And, as noted earlier, environmental impacts are being audited and accounted for as the "second bottom line." Such environmental impacts are not always measured in financial terms. However, they have a special value that companies are finding increasingly difficult to ignore.

> Chad Holliday, CEO of DuPont, is one executive who heads a multinational corporation that has taken a proactive approach to sustainable environmental strategies. He also chairs the World Business Council for Sustainable Development, a coalition of 150 companies from more than 30 countries that is committed to environmental protection, social equity, and economic growth. In Strategy Spotlight 1.4, Holliday shares his perspective on DuPont's strategic approach to productivity improvement that is also environment friendly.[52]

## >>The Strategic Management Perspective: An Imperative Throughout the Organization

As we have noted in this chapter, strategic management requires managers to take an integrative view of the organization and assess how all of the functional areas and activities fit together to help an organization achieve its goals and objectives. This cannot be accomplished if only the top managers in the organization take an integrative, strategic perspective of issues facing the firm and everyone else "fends for themselves" in their independent, isolated functional areas. Marketing and sales will generally favor broad, tailor-made product lines, production will demand standardized products that are relatively easy to make in order to lower manufacturing costs, research and development will design products to demonstrate technical elegance, and so on. Instead, people throughout the organization need to be striving toward overall goals.

The above argument clearly makes sense. However, the need for such a perspective is accelerating in today's increasingly complex, interconnected, ever-changing, global economy. In this section, we will address some major trends that are making the need for a strategic perspective throughout the organization even more critical. As noted by Peter Senge of MIT, the days when Henry Ford, Alfred Sloan, and Tom Watson (top executives at Ford, General Motors, and IBM, respectively) "learned for the organization are gone." He goes on to say:

> In an increasingly dynamic, interdependent, and unpredictable world, it is simply no longer possible for anyone to "figure it all out at the top." The old model, "the top thinks and the local acts," must now give way to integrating thinking and acting at all levels. While the challenge is great, so is the potential payoff. "The person who figures out how to harness the collective genius of the people in his or her organization," according to former Citibank CEO Walter Wriston, "is going to blow the competition away."[53]

In this section we will first address some of the key forces that are driving the need for a strategic perspective at all levels as well as greater participation and involvement in the strategic management process throughout the organization. Then, we will provide examples of how firms are engaging people throughout the organization to these ends.

## Some Key Driving Forces

There are many driving forces that are increasing the need for a strategic perspective and greater involvement throughout the organization.[54] Among the most important of these are globalization, technology, and intellectual capital.[55] These forces are inherently interrelated and, collectively, they are accelerating the rate of change and uncertainty with which managers at all levels must deal. The implication of such unpredictable change was probably best captured by former AOL Time Warner Chairman Stephen M. Case, in a talk to investors and analysts:

> I sometimes feel like I'm behind the wheel of a race car. . . . One of the biggest challenges is there are no road signs to help navigate. And . . . no one has yet determined which side of the road we're supposed to be on.[56]

*Globalization*   The defining feature of the global economy is not the flow of goods—international trade has existed for centuries—but the flow of capital, people, and information worldwide. With globalization, time and space are no longer a barrier to making deals anywhere in the world. Computer networks permit instantaneous transactions, and the market watchers operate around the clock on a 24/7 basis.

Along with the increasing speed of transactions and global sourcing of all forms of resources and information, managers must address the paradoxical demand to think globally and act locally. They have to move resources and information rapidly around the world to meet local needs. They also face new challenges when formulating strategies: volatile political situations, difficult trade issues, ever-fluctuating exchange rates, unfamiliar cultures, and gut-wrenching social problems.[57] Today, managers must be more literate in the ways of foreign customers, commerce, and competition than ever before.

As markets become more open—as evidenced by free trade agreements between nations—more foreign firms are likely to enter domestic markets. This increases the amount of competition. Further, since firms are operating in global markets, competitive moves in a domestic economy may negatively impact the firm in another segment of the international market. This places pressure on firms to move into international markets in order to maintain their competitiveness in areas where they already operate. Clearly, globalization requires that organizations increase their ability to learn and collaborate and to manage diversity, complexity, and ambiguity. Top-level managers can't do it all alone.

*Technology*    Technological change and diffusion of new technologies are moving at an incredible pace. Such development and diffusion accelerate the importance of innovation for firms if they are to remain competitive. David de Pury, former cochair of the board of Asea Brown Boveri, claimed that "innovate or die" is the first rule of international industrial competition. Similarly, continuous technological development and change have produced decreasing product life cycles. Andrew Grove, chairman of Intel, explained the introduction of a new product at his company. Recently, the firm introduced a sophisticated product in which it had invested considerable funds. However, later in the same year, Intel introduced a new product that would cannibalize its existing product. Thus, the firm had only 11 months to recoup that significant investment. Such time-intensive product development involves the efforts and collaboration of managers and professionals throughout the organization.

From videoconferencing to the Internet, technology has made our world smaller and faster moving. Ideas and huge amounts of information are in constant movement. The challenge for managers is to make sense of what technology offers. Not all technology adds value. In the coming years, managers in all organizations will be charged with making technology an even more viable, productive part of the work setting. They will need to stay ahead of the information curve and learn to leverage information to enhance business performance. If not, they risk being swallowed in a tidal wave of data, not ideas.

In addition to its potential benefits, technology can raise some important ethical issues that need to be addressed. Strategy Spotlight 1.5 raises the issue of "designer babies."

*Intellectual Capital*    Knowledge has become the direct source of competitive advantage(s) for companies selling ideas and relationships (e.g., professional services, software, and technology-driven companies) as well as an indirect source of competitive advantage for all companies trying to differentiate themselves from rivals by how they create value for their customers. As we will note in Chapter 4, Merck, the $52 billion pharmaceutical company, has become enormously successful because its scientists discover medicines, not because of their skills in producing pills in an efficient manner. As noted by Dr. Roy Vagelos, Merck's former CEO, "A low-value product can be made by anyone anywhere. When you have knowledge no one else has access to—that's dynamite. We guard our research even more carefully than our financial assets."[58]

Creating and applying knowledge to deliver differentiated products and services of superior value for customers requires the acquisition of superior talent, as well as the ability to develop and retain that talent.[59] However, successful firms must also create an environment with strong social and professional relationships, where people feel strong ties to their colleagues and their organization. Gary Hamel, one of today's leading strategic management writers, noted, "As the number and quality of interconnections between individuals and ideas go up, the ability to combine and recombine ideas accelerates as well."[60]

## Designer Babies

No one would dispute that it's all right to custom-design some products and services. Given individual tastes, it's only natural that people will want customization. But customization, and its associated technology, can go too far.

James D. Watson and Francis H. C. Crick's discovery of the DNA molecule in 1954 made customizing human children technologically feasible. Watson and Crick probably never foresaw this. But nearly a half century later, the potential to genetically alter babies before birth is actually here.

This raises a host of ethical questions. Imagine designer babies, children born to parents who have the financial resources to create the "perfect" child. Without a doubt, DNA experimentation has led to scientific advances, such as treatment of certain diseases, that are valuable and ethical. But when it comes to customizing a human being, the line between right and wrong can become blurry. The Honorable Michael Kirby, Justice of the High Court of Australia and a member of the International Ethics Committee of United Nations Educational, Scientific and Cultural Organization (UNESCO), raises some thought-provoking ethical questions:

> Fundamental questions are raised about the long-term effects of genetic alteration of the human species. For example, we have identified the genes that express themselves in Huntington's disease. Should the law permit, encourage, or forbid the elimination of a fetus which manifests these genes? Elimination of a fetus with likely intellectual impairment is now not uncommon, but how far do we go down that track in the quest of the "perfect" child? Should we eliminate obesity, baldness, and heart disease (if that turns out to be, at least in part, genetic)? Not to regulate these characteristics is, effectively, to permit them all.... When it becomes possible to eliminate particular genes and transplant others, what will prevent the attempted creation of a superspecies? Or an underspecies? Or an altered human species? We must be ready with our answers to these questions. It should not be assumed that sermons, political press releases, and the solemn resolutions of corporate ethics committees will have the power to prevent developments deemed undesirable by most of humanity.

Technology, with all its benefits, must also be considered in light of these and other ethical considerations.

Source: Licking, E. 2000. Ten technologies that will change our lives. *BusinessWeek*, Spring; and Kirby, M. 2000. The human genome project in the dock. *Medical Journal of Australia*, 173: 599–600.

Technologies also must be used effectively to leverage human capital to facilitate collaboration among individuals and to develop more sophisticated knowledge management systems.[61] The challenge and opportunity of management is not only to acquire and retain human capital but also to ensure that employees develop and maintain a strategic perspective as they contribute to the organization. This is essential if management is to use its talents to effectively help the organization attain its goals and objectives.

Strategy Spotlight 1.6 discusses the global market for talent. It illustrates how forces of globalization, technology, and intellectual capital can be related.

Let's now look at what some companies are doing to increase the involvement of employees throughout the organization in the strategic management process.

## Enhancing Employee Involvement in the Strategic Management Process

Today's organizations increasingly need to anticipate and respond to dramatic and unpredictable changes in the competitive environment. With the emergence of the knowledge economy, human capital (as opposed to financial and physical assets) has become the key to securing advantages in the marketplace that persist over time.

# STRATEGY SPOTLIGHT

## 1.6

### The Global Market for Talent

Globalization today involves the movement of not only goods and investments across borders, but also people and information. Many American technology-strategy consultants, who make about $150,000 annually, today are blissfully unaware of the challenge posed by the likes of Ganesh Narasimhaiya.

Ganesh is a 30-year-old Indian who enjoys cricket, R&B music, and bowling. He has a bachelor's degree in electronics and communications, and he can spin out code in a variety of languages: COBOL, Java, and UML (Unified Modeling Language), among others. Ganesh has worked on high-profile projects for Wipro, a $1 billion Indian software giant, all over the world. He has helped GE Medical Systems roll out a logistics application throughout Southeast Asia. He proposed a plan to consolidate and synchronize security solutions across a British client's e-business applications. He developed a strategy for transferring legacy system applications onto the Web for a

company in Norway. He works up to 18 or 19 hours a day at a customer site and for that he may earn as much as $7,000 a month. When he's home in Bangalore, his pay is about one-quarter of that—$21,000 a year. But by Indian standards, this is a small fortune.

Ganesh is part of Wipro's strategy of amassing a small force of high-level experts who are increasingly focused on specific industries and can compete with anyone for a given consulting project. Wipro's Trojan horse is the incredibly cheap offshore outsourcing solution that it can provide. The rise of a globally integrated knowledge economy is a blessing for developing nations. What it means for the U.S. skilled labor force is less clear. This is something strategy consultants working for Accenture or EDS in the United States need to think about. Why? Forrester Research has predicted that at least 3.3 million white-collar jobs and $136 billion in wages will shift from the U.S. to low-cost countries by 2015. With dramatically lower wage rates and the same level of service, how is the American technology professional going to compete with the likes of Ganesh and his colleagues?

Sources: Hammonds, K. H. 2003. Smart, determined, ambitious, cheap: The new face of global competition. *Fast Company,* February: 91–97; Engardio, P., Bernstein, A., & Kripalani, M. 2003. Is your job next? *BusinessWeek,* February 3: 50–60.

To develop and mobilize people and other assets in the organization, leaders are needed throughout the organization.[62] No longer can organizations be effective if the top "does the thinking" and the rest of the organization "does the work." Everyone needs to be involved in the strategic management process. Peter Senge noted the critical need for three types of leaders.

- Local line leaders who have significant profit and loss responsibility.
- Executive leaders who champion and guide ideas, create a learning infrastructure, and establish a domain for taking action.
- Internal networkers who, although they have little positional power and formal authority, generate their power through the conviction and clarity of their ideas.[63]

Sally Helgesen, author of *The Web of Inclusion: A New Architecture for Building Great Organizations,* made a similar point regarding the need for leaders throughout the organization. She asserted that many organizations "fall prey to the heroes-and-drones syndrome, exalting the value of those in powerful positions while implicitly demeaning the contributions of those who fail to achieve top rank."[64] Culture and processes in which leaders emerge at all levels, both up and down as well as across the organization, typify today's high-performing firms.[65]

Now we will provide examples of what some firms are doing to increase the involvement of employees throughout the organization. Top-level executives are key in setting the tone. Consider Richard Branson, founder of the Virgin Group, whose core businesses include retail operations, hotels, communications, and an airline. He is well known for creating a culture and an informal structure where anybody in the organization can be involved in generating and acting upon new business ideas. In an interview, he stated,

> [S]peed is something that we are better at than most companies. We don't have formal board meetings, committees, etc. If someone has an idea, they can pick up the phone and talk to me. I can vote "done, let's do it." Or, better still, they can just go ahead and do it. They know that they are not going to get a mouthful from me if they make a mistake. Rules and regulations are not our forte. Analyzing things to death is not our kind of thing. We very rarely sit back and analyze what we do.[66]

To inculcate a strategic management perspective throughout the organization, many large traditional organizations must often make a major effort to effect transformational change. This involves extensive communication, training, and development to strengthen a strategic perspective throughout the organization. Ford Motor Company is one such example.

Ford instituted a major cultural overhaul and embarked on a broad-based attempt to develop leaders throughout the organization. It wanted to build an army of "warrior-entrepreneurs"—people who have the courage and skills to reject old ideas and who believe in change passionately enough to make it happen. A few details of Ford's effort follow.

> Ford sent about 2,500 managers to its Leadership Development Center during the year for one of its four programs—Capstone, Experienced Leader Challenge, Ford Business Associates, and New Business Leader—instilling in them not just the mind-set and vocabulary of a revolutionary but also the tools necessary to achieve a revolution. At the same time, through the Business Leaders Initiative, all 100,000 salaried employees worldwide will participate in business-leadership "cascades," intense exercises that combine trickle-down communications with substantive team projects.[67]

We'd like to close with our favorite example of how inexperience can be a virtue. It further reinforces the benefits of having broad involvement throughout the organization in the strategic management process (see Strategy Spotlight 1.7)

## >>Ensuring Coherence in Strategic Direction

To be successful, employees and managers throughout the organization must strive for common goals and objectives. By specifying desired results, it becomes much easier to move forward. Otherwise, when no one knows what the firm is striving to accomplish, they have no idea of what to work toward. As the old nautical expression puts it, "No wind favors the ship that has no charted course."

Organizations express priorities best through stated goals and objectives that form a *hierarchy of goals.* The hierarchy of goals for an organization includes its vision, mission, and strategic objectives. What visions may lack in specificity, they make up for in their ability to evoke powerful and compelling mental images. On the other hand, strategic objectives tend to be more specific and provide a more direct means of determining if the organization is moving toward broader, overall goals. We will now address visions, missions, and strategic objectives in the next subsections.[68]

### Organizational Vision

The starting point for articulating a firm's hierarchy of goals is the company vision. It is often described as a goal that is "massively inspiring, overarching, and long term."[69] A vision represents a destination that is driven by and evokes passion. A vision may or may not succeed; it depends on whether everything else happens according to a firm's strategy.

# STRATEGY SPOTLIGHT

## Strategy and the Value of Inexperience

Peter Gruber, chairman of Mandalay Entertainment, explained how his firm benefited from the creative insights of an inexperienced intern.

Sometimes life is all about solving problems. In the movie business, at least, there seems to be one around every corner. One of the most effective lessons I've learned about tackling problems is to start by asking not "How to?" but rather "What if?" I learned that lesson from a young woman who was interning on a film I was producing. She actually saved the movie from being shelved by the studio.

The movie, *Gorillas in the Mist,* had turned into a logistical nightmare. We wanted to film at an altitude of 11,000 feet, in the middle of the jungle, in Rwanda—then on the verge of a revolution—and to use more than 200 animals. Warner Brothers, the studio financing the movie, worried that we would exceed our budget. But our biggest problem was that the screenplay required the gorillas to do what we wrote—in other words, to "act." If they couldn't or wouldn't, we'd have to fall back on a formula that the studio had seen fail before: using dwarfs in gorilla suits on a soundstage.

We called an emergency meeting to solve these problems. In the middle of it, a young intern asked, "What if you let the gorillas write the story?" Everyone laughed and wondered what she was doing in the meeting with experienced filmmakers. Hours later, someone casually asked her what she had meant. She said, "What if you sent a really good cinematographer into the jungle with a ton of film to shoot the gorillas. Then you could write a story around what the gorillas did on film." It was a brilliant idea. And we did exactly what she suggested: We sent Alan Root, an Academy Award–nominated cinematographer, into the jungle for three weeks. He came back with phenomenal footage that practically wrote the story for us. We shot the film for $20 million—half of the original budget!

This woman's inexperience enabled her to see opportunities where we saw only boundaries. This experience taught me three things. First, ask high-quality questions, like "what if?" Second, find people who add new perspectives and create new conversations. As experienced filmmakers, we believed that our way was the only way—and that the intern lacked the experience to have an opinion. Third, pay attention to those with new voices. If you want unlimited options for solving a problem, engage the what if before you lock onto the how to. You'll be surprised by what you discover.

Source: Gruber, P. 1998. My greatest lesson. *Fast Company* 15: 88, 90.

Developing and implementing a vision is one of a leader's central roles. In a survey of 1,500 senior leaders, 870 of them CEOs from 20 different countries, respondents were asked what they believed were the key traits that leaders must have. Ninety-eight percent responded that "a strong sense of vision" was the most important. Similarly, when asked about the critical knowledge skills, the leaders cited "strategy formulation to achieve a vision" as the most important skill. In other words, managers need to have not only a vision but also a plan to implement it. Regretfully, 90 percent reported a lack of confidence in their own skills and ability to conceive a vision for their organization. For example, T. J. Rogers, CEO of Cypress Semiconductor, an electronic chipmaker that faced some difficulties in 1992, lamented that his own shortsightedness caused the danger, "I did not have the 50,000-foot view, and got caught."[70]

One of the most famous examples of a vision is from Disneyland: "To be the happiest place on earth." Other examples are:

- "Restoring patients to full life." (Medtronic)
- "We want to satisfy all of our customers' financial needs and help them succeed financially." (Wells Fargo)
- "Our vision is to be the world's best quick service restaurant." (McDonald's)

Although such visions cannot be accurately measured by a specific indicator of how well they are being achieved, they do provide a fundamental statement of an organization's values, aspirations, and goals. Such visions go well beyond narrow financial objectives, of course, and strive to capture both the minds and hearts of employees.

The vision statement may also contain a slogan, diagram, or picture—whatever grabs attention.[71] The aim is to capture the essence of the more formal parts of the vision in a few words that are easily remembered, yet evoke the spirit of the entire vision statement. In its 20-year battle with Xerox, Canon's slogan, or battle cry, was "Beat Xerox." Motorola's slogan is "Total Customer Satisfaction." Outboard Marine Corporation's slogan is "To Take the World Boating." And Chevron strives "To Become Better than the Best."

Clearly, vision statements are not a cure-all. Sometimes they backfire and erode a company's credibility. Visions fail for many reasons, including those discussed in the following paragraphs.[72]

***The Walk Doesn't Match the Talk***   An idealistic vision can arouse employee enthusiasm. However, that same enthusiasm can be quickly dashed if employees find that senior management's behavior is not consistent with the vision. Often, vision is a sloganeering campaign of new buzzwords and empty platitudes like "devotion to the customer," "teamwork," or "total quality" that aren't consistently backed by management's action.

***Irrelevance***   A vision that is created in a vacuum—unrelated to environmental threats or opportunity or an organization's resources and capabilities—can ignore the needs of those who are expected to buy into it. When the vision is not anchored in reality, employees will reject it.

***Not the Holy Grail***   Managers often search continually for the one elusive solution that will solve their firm's problems—that is, the next holy grail of management. They may have tried other management fads only to find that they fell short of their expectations. However, they remain convinced that one exists. Visions support sound management, but they require everyone to walk the talk and be accountable for their behavior. A vision simply cannot be viewed as a magic cure for an organization's illness.

***Too Much Focus Leads to Missed Opportunities***   Clearly, one of the benefits of a sound vision statement is that it can focus efforts and excite people. However, the downside is that in directing people and resources toward a narrow perspective, exciting and innovative opportunities can be missed. Consider, for example, Komatsu:[73]

> Faced with the challenge of rival Caterpillar's entry into Komatsu's protected home market, Ryoichi Kawai, then CEO of Komatsu, focused the whole company on beating Caterpillar. "Maru-C" became the rally cry which meant "Encircle Caterpillar." And, to make the enemy visible and omnipresent, Kawai purchased the largest Caterpillar bulldozer available and placed it on the roof of Komatsu headquarters. The story is well-known of how Kawai leveraged his aggression against Caterpillar into a highly disciplined and effective process of building up Komatsu's strengths and market position. (In fact, it became the most-used Harvard case study.)
>
> However, there was a lesser-known downside. The two decades of focusing on a "life-and-death battle" with Caterpillar prevented Komatsu from identifying new opportunities in related areas of business and from pursuing genuine breakthrough innovations in its core earthmoving-equipment business. Eventually, Tetsuya Katada took over and formally abolished the "Maru-C" slogan and removed all of the symbols Kawai had built to represent the Caterpillar battle. The result was successful expansion into related areas, such as robotics, and several fundamentally different and highly innovative products, such as earthmoving equipment for undersea operations.

***An Ideal Future Irreconciled with the Present***   Although visions are not designed to mirror reality, they do need to be anchored somehow in it. People have difficulty identifying with a vision that paints a rosy picture of the future but takes no account of the often hostile environment in which the firm competes or ignores some of the firm's weaknesses. As we will see in the next section, many of these same issues can apply to mission statements.

## Mission Statements

A company's mission differs from its vision in that it encompasses both the purpose of the company as well as the basis of competition and competitive advantage.

Exhibit 1.5 contains the vision statement and mission statement of WellPoint Health Networks, a $21 billion managed health care organization. Note that while the vision statement is broad based, the mission statement is more specific and focused on the means by which the firm will compete. This includes providing branded products that will be tailor-made to customers in order to create long-term customer relationships.

Effective mission statements incorporate the concept of stakeholder management, suggesting that organizations must respond to multiple constituencies if they are to survive and prosper. Customers, employees, suppliers, and owners are the primary stakeholders, but others may also play an important role in a particular corporation. Mission statements also have the greatest impact when they reflect an organization's enduring, overarching strategic priorities and competitive positioning. Mission statements also can vary in length and specificity. The two mission statements below illustrate these issues.

- To produce superior financial returns for our shareholders as we serve our customers with the highest quality transportation, logistics, and e-commerce. (Federal Express)
- To be the very best in the business. Our game plan is status go . . . we are constantly looking ahead, building on our strengths, and reaching for new goals. In our quest of these goals, we look at the three stars of the Brinker logo and are reminded of the basic values that are the strength of this company . . . People, Quality and Profitability. Everything we do at Brinker must support these core values. We also look at the eight golden flames depicted in our logo, and are reminded of the fire that ignites our mission and makes up the heart and soul of this incredible company. These flames are: Customers, Food, Team, Concepts, Culture, Partners, Community, and Shareholders. As keeper of these flames, we will continue to build on our strengths and work together to be the best in the business. (Brinker International, whose restaurant chains include Chili's and On the Border)[74]

Few mission statements identify profit or any other financial indicator as the sole purpose of the firm. Indeed, many do not even mention profit or shareholder return.[75] Employees of organizations or departments are usually the mission's most important

---

**Exhibit 1.5**

**Comparing WellPoint Health Network's Vision and Mission**

### Vision

WellPoint *will redefine our industry:*
Through a new generation of consumer-friendly products that put individuals back in control of their future.

### Mission

The WellPoint companies provide health *security* by offering a *choice* of quality branded health and related financial services *designed* to meet the *changing* expectations of individuals, families, and their sponsors throughout a *lifelong* relationship.

Source: WellPoint Health Network company records.

## NextJet's Change of Mission

The dot-com crash was only the first blow to NextJet, Inc., a Dallas-based business launched in 1999 to ship packages overnight. The bigger blow came with the September 11 terrorist attacks, when passenger airlines were forced to add security and reduce flights. One of NextJet's strengths was its nationwide network of local courier services that got packages to and from airports, all coordinated through their proprietary software that could determine the optimal routing. However, the company's business model fell apart when it could not rely on the airlines to get packages between cities quickly enough to make the added cost for same-day delivery worthwhile.

Rather than give up, NextJet reinvented the business around the idea that its most important asset was the software itself. The company's new mission received almost immediate validation when its software was deployed successfully at United Parcel Service (UPS). NextJet's software provides Atlanta-based UPS with tools for

setting online rates and tracking packages. While a lot of same-day business did evaporate when corporations tightened the reins on spending, some things can't wait overnight to be shipped. For example, makers of hospital equipment may need to ship critical parts within a few hours. NextJet's software can help shippers make important decisions in less than a second, finding the fastest and most economical route among air, truck, and courier operations. In addition to UPS, its customers include FedEx, Greyhound, and Menlo Worldwide.

NextJet serves a very large industry segment—Service Parts & Logistics (SPL). The annual expenditures for spare parts in the United States are estimated to be $500 billion. And managers have increased their focus on the importance of effective logistics operations, given its potential impact on a firm's income. After all, whether or not a production line is running can often depend on the quick and effective installation of relatively inexpensive spare parts.

NextJet currently has 50 employees and four offices in the United States, and it seems to be on the right track with its new mission. Although executives at the privately held company will not disclose financial results, they say they are about to complete their third consecutive profitable quarter.

Sources: Goldstein, A. 2002. NextJet is hoping that its software can deliver. *Dallas Morning News,* December 4: 1–3; industry.java.sun.com/javanews/stories/story2/0,1072,34986,00.html; Nelson, M. G. 2001. NextJet network adds wireless. *Information Week,* April 30: 34; Anonymous. 2004. Who's who in e-logistics. www.americanshipper.com, September; Hudspeth, B., & Jones, J. 2004. Service parts and logistics: Should you in-source or outsource? *3pl line,* www.inboundlogistics.com, October.

audience. For them, the mission should help to build a common understanding of purpose and commitment to nurture.

Profit maximization not only fails to motivate people but also does not differentiate between organizations. Every corporation wants to maximize profits over the long term. A good mission statement, by addressing each principal theme, must communicate why an organization is special and different. Two studies that linked corporate values and mission statements with financial performance found that the most successful firms mentioned values other than profits. The less successful firms focused almost entirely on profitability.[76] In essence, profit is the metaphorical equivalent of oxygen, food, and water that the body requires. They are not the point of life, but without them, there is no life.

Although vision statements tend to be quite enduring and seldom change, a firm's mission can and should change when competitive conditions dramatically change or the firm is faced with new threats or opportunities. Strategy Spotlight 1.8 provides an example of a firm, NextJet, that changed its mission in order to realize new opportunities.

## Strategic Objectives

Thus far, we have discussed both visions and missions. Statements of vision tend to be quite broad and can be described as a goal that represents an inspiring, overarching, and emotionally driven destination. Mission statements, on the other hand, tend to be more specific and address questions concerning the organization's reason for being and the basis of its intended competitive advantage in the marketplace. Strategic objectives are used to operationalize the mission statement.[77] That is, they help to provide guidance on how the organization can fulfill or move toward the "higher goals" in the goal hierarchy—the mission and vision. As a result, they tend to be more specific and cover a more well-defined time frame.

Setting objectives demands a yardstick to measure the fulfillment of the objectives.[78] If an objective lacks specificity or measurability, it is not very useful, simply because there is no way of determining whether it is helping the organization move toward its mission and vision.

Exhibit 1.6 lists several strategic objectives of corporations, divided into financial and nonfinancial categories. While most of these strategic objectives are directed toward generating greater profits and returns for the owners of the business, others are directed at customers or society at large.

For objectives to be meaningful, they need to satisfy several criteria. They must be:

- *Measurable.* There must be at least one indicator (or yardstick) that measures progress against fulfilling the objective.
- *Specific.* This provides a clear message as to what needs to be accomplished.
- *Appropriate.* It must be consistent with the vision and mission of the organization.
- *Realistic.* It must be an achievable target given the organization's capabilities and opportunities in the environment. In essence, it must be challenging but doable.
- *Timely.* There needs to be a time frame for accomplishing the objective. After all, as the economist John Maynard Keynes once said, "In the long run, we are all dead!"

When objectives satisfy the above criteria, there are many benefits for the organization. First, they help to channel employees throughout the organization toward common goals. This helps the organization concentrate and conserve valuable resources and work collectively in a more timely manner.

Second, challenging objectives can help to motivate and inspire employees throughout the organization to higher levels of commitment and effort. A great deal of research has supported the notion that individuals work harder when they are striving toward specific goals instead of being asked simply to "do their best."

---

**Exhibit 1.6**
**Strategic Objectives**

### Strategic Objectives (Financial)

- Increase sales growth 6% to 8% and accelerate core net earnings growth to 13% to 15% per share in each of the next 5 years. (Procter & Gamble)
- Generate Internet-related revenue of $1.5 billion. (AutoNation)
- Increase the contribution of Banking Group earnings from investments, brokerage, and insurance from 16% to 25%. (Wells Fargo)
- Cut corporate overhead costs by $30 million per year. (Fortune Brands)

### Strategic Objectives (Nonfinancial)

- We want a majority of our customers, when surveyed, to say they consider Wells Fargo the best financial institution in the community. (Wells Fargo)
- We want to operate 6,000 stores by 2010—up from 3,000 in the year 2000. (Walgreen's)
- We want to be the top-ranked supplier to our customers. (PPG)
- Reduce greenhouse gases by 10 percent (from a 1990 base) by 2010. (BP Amoco)

Sources: Company documents and annual reports.

Third, as we noted earlier in the chapter, there is always the potential for different parts of an organization to pursue their own goals rather than overall company goals. Although well intentioned, these may work at cross-purposes to the organization as a whole. Meaningful objectives thus help to resolve conflicts when they arise.

Finally, proper objectives provide a yardstick for rewards and incentives. Not only will they lead to higher levels of employee motivation but they will also help to ensure a greater sense of equity or fairness when rewards are allocated.

There are, of course, still other objectives that are even more specific. These are often referred to as short-term objectives—essential components of "action plans" that are critical in implementing a firm's chosen strategy. We will discuss these issues in Chapter 9.

## Summary

We began this introductory chapter by defining strategic management and articulating some of its key attributes. Strategic management is defined as "consisting of the analyses, decisions, and actions an organization undertakes to create and sustain competitive advantages." The issue of how and why some firms outperform others in the marketplace is central to the study of strategic management. Strategic management has four key attributes: It is directed at overall organizational goals, includes multiple stakeholders, incorporates both short-term and long-term perspectives, and incorporates trade-offs between efficiency and effectiveness.

The second section discussed the strategic management process. Here, we paralleled the above definition of strategic management and focused on three core activities in the strategic management process—strategy analysis, strategy formulation, and strategy implementation. We noted how each of these activities is highly interrelated to and interdependent on the others. We also discussed how each of the 13 chapters in this text fits into the three core activities, and we provided a summary of the opening vignettes in each chapter.

Next, we introduced two important concepts—corporate governance and stakeholder management—which must be taken into account throughout the strategic management process. Governance mechanisms can be broadly divided into two groups: internal and external. Internal governance mechanisms include shareholders (owners), management (led by the chief executive officer), and the board of directors. External control is exercised by auditors, banks, analysts, and an active business press as well as the threat of takeovers. We identified five key stakeholders in all organizations: owners, customers, suppliers, employees, and society at large. Successful firms go beyond an overriding focus on satisfying solely the interests of owners. Rather, they recognize the inherent conflicts that arise among the demands of the various stakeholders as well as the need to endeavor to attain "symbiosis"—that is, interdependence and mutual benefit—among the various stakeholder groups. Managers must also recognize the need to act in a socially responsible manner which, if done effectively, can enhance a firm's innovativeness. They also should recognize and incorporate issues related to environmental sustainability in their strategic actions.

In the fourth section, we discussed three interrelated factors—globalization, technology, and intellectual capital—that have accelerated the rate of unpredictable change that managers face today. These factors, and the combination of them, have increased the need for managers and employees throughout the organization to have a strategic management perspective and to become more empowered.

The final section addressed the need for consistency among a firm's vision, mission, and strategic objectives. Collectively, they form an organization's hierarchy of goals. Visions should evoke powerful and compelling mental images. However, they are not very specific. Strategic objectives, on the other hand, are much more specific and are vital to ensuring that the organization is striving toward fulfilling its vision and mission.

## Summary Review Questions

1. How is "strategic management" defined in the text, and what are its four key attributes?
2. Briefly discuss the three key activities in the strategic management process. Why is it important for managers to recognize the interdependent nature of these activities?
3. Explain the concept of "stakeholder management." Why shouldn't managers be solely interested in stockholder management, that is, maximizing the returns for owners of the firm—its shareholders?
4. What is "corporate governance"? What are its three key elements and how can it be improved?
5. How can "symbiosis" (interdependence, mutual benefit) be achieved among a firm's stakeholders?
6. What are some of the major trends that now require firms to have a greater strategic management perspective and empowerment in the strategic management process throughout the firm?
7. What is meant by a "hierarchy of goals"? What are the main components of it, and why must consistency be achieved among them?

## Experiential Exercise

Using the Internet or library sources, select four organizations—two in the private sector and two in the public sector. Find their mission statements. Complete the following exhibit by identifying the stakeholders that are mentioned. Evaluate the differences between firms in the private sector and those in the public sector.

| | | | | |
|---|---|---|---|---|
| **Name** | | | | |
| **Mission Statement** | | | | |
| **Stakeholders (✓ = mentioned)** | | | | |
| **1.** Customers | | | | |
| **2.** Suppliers | | | | |
| **3.** Managers/employees | | | | |
| **4.** Community-at-large | | | | |
| **5.** Owners | | | | |
| **6.** Others? | | | | |
| **7.** Others? | | | | |

1. Go to the Internet and look up one of these company sites: www.walmart.com, www.ge.com, or www.fordmotor.com. What are some of the key events that would represent the "romantic" perspective of leadership? What are some of the key events that depict the "external control" perspective of leadership?

2. Select a company that competes in an industry in which you are interested. What are some of the recent demands that stakeholders have placed on this company? Can you find examples of how the company is trying to develop "symbiosis" (interdependence and mutual benefit) among its stakeholders? (Use the Internet and library resources.)

3. Provide examples of companies that are actively trying to increase the amount of empowerment in the strategic management process throughout the organization. Do these companies seem to be having positive outcomes? Why? Why not?

4. Look up the vision statements and/or mission statements for a few companies. Do you feel that they are constructive and useful as a means of motivating employees and providing a strong strategic direction? Why? Why not? (*Note:* Annual reports, along with the Internet, may be good sources of information.)

1. A company focuses solely on short-term profits to provide the greatest return to the owners of the business (i.e., the shareholders in a publicly held firm). What ethical issues could this raise?

2. A firm has spent some time—with input from managers at all levels—in developing a vision statement and a mission statement. Over time, however, the behavior of some executives is contrary to these statements. Could this raise some ethical issues?

## References

1. Byrnes, N. 2004. Gone flat. *BusinessWeek,* December 20: 76–82; Foust, D. 2004. Things aren't going better at Coke. *BusinessWeek,* August 16: 38; Trent, B. 2005. Succession screw-ups. *BusinessWeek,* January 10: 84; Morris, B. The real story. *Fortune.* May 31: 84–98; and Foust, D. 2005. Shaking up the Coke board. *BusinessWeek.* April 4: 46.

2. As CFO, Doug Ivester was responsible for the spinoff of Coke's U.S. bottling operations in 1986. This removed $2.4 billion of debt from its balance sheet. At the same time, Coca-Cola was able to maintain a 49 percent stake (and six board seats, which it packed with current and former Coke executives) in the new company, Coca-Cola Enterprises. Coke was thus able to have effective control of pricing of its concentrate as well as what the new entity charged its distributors. Interestingly, when Ivester tried to sustain profits by imposing an enormous 7.6 percent price hike on the distributors, the animosity that he created was a key factor that led to his forced resignation in 1999. Refer to Byrnes, op. cit. and Foust, 2005, op. cit. for insightful discussions of this issue.

3. For a discussion of the "romantic" versus "external control" perspective, refer to Meindl, J. R. 1987. The romance of leadership and the evaluation of organizational performance. *Academy of Management Journal* 30: 92–109; and Pfeffer, J., & Salancik, G. R. 1978. *The external control of organizations: A resource dependence perspective.* New York: Harper & Row.

4. A recent perspective on the "romantic view" of leadership is provided by: Mintzberg, H. 2004. Leadership and management development: An afterword. *Academy of Management Executive,* 18(3): 140–142.

5. Anonymous. 2005. Face value: The 10 billion dollar man. *The Economist.* February 26: 66. Interestingly, this article speculated that Mr. Ghosn could add approximately $10 billion to the market value of Ford or General Motors if he were to sign on as Chief Executive Officer. Such a perspective is clearly consistent with the "romantic view" of leadership. For an insightful perspective on the challenges faced by Mr. Ghosn as he assumes the roles of CEO for both Nissan and Renault (which owns 44 percent of Nissan), refer to: Edmondson, G. 2005. What Ghosn will do with Renault. *BusinessWeek,* April 25: 54.

6. Sanborn, S. 2005. Soft drink industry. *Value Line,* February 4: 1541.

7. Brady, D. 2004. Pepsi's thousand and one noshes. *BusinessWeek online,* June 14.

8. Anonymous. 2005. The best managers. *BusinessWeek,* January 10: 56–57; and Byrnes, op. cit.

9. For an interesting perspective on the need for strategists to maintain a global mind-set, refer to Begley, T. M., & Boyd, D. P. 2003. The need for a global mind-set. *MIT Sloan Management Review* 44(2): 25–32.

10. Porter, M. E. 1996. What is strategy? *Harvard Business Review* 74(6): 61–78.

11. See, for example, Barney, J. B., & Arikan, A. M. 2001. The resource-based view: Origins and implications. In Hitt, M. A., Freeman, R. E., & Harrison, J. S. (Eds.), *Handbook of strategic management:* 124–189. Malden, MA: Blackwell.

12. Barney, J. 1991. Firm resources and sustained competitive advantage. *Journal of Management,* 17(1): 99–120.

13. Much of Gary Hamel's work advocates the importance of not focusing on incremental change. For example, refer to Hamel, G., & Prahalad, C. K. 1994. *Competing for the future.* Boston: Harvard Business School Press; see also Christensen, C. M. 2001. The past and future of competitive advantage. *Sloan Management Review,* 42(3): 105–109.

14. Porter, M. E. 1996. What is strategy? *Harvard Business Review,* 74(6): 61–78; and Hammonds, K. H. 2001. Michael Porter's big ideas. *Fast Company,* March: 55–56.

15. This section draws upon Dess, G. G., & Miller, A. 1993. *Strategic management.* New York: McGraw-Hill.

16. See, for example, Hrebiniak, L. G., & Joyce, W. F. 1986. The strategic importance of managing myopia. *Sloan Management Review,* 28(1): 5–14.

17. For an insightful discussion on how to manage diverse stakeholder groups, refer to Rondinelli, D. A., & London, T. 2003. How corporations and environmental groups cooperate: Assessing cross-sector alliances and collaborations. *Academy of Management Executive,* 17(1): 61–76.

18. Senge, P. 1996. Leading learning organizations: The bold, the powerful, and the invisible. In Hesselbein, F., Goldsmith, M., & Beckhard, R. (Eds.), *The leader of the future:* 41–58. San Francisco: Jossey-Bass.

19. For another interesting perspective on this issue, refer to Abell, D. F. 1999. Competing today while preparing for tomorrow. *Sloan Management Review,* 40(3): 73–81.

20. Loeb, M. 1994. Where leaders come from. *Fortune,* September 19: 241 (quoting Warren Bennis).

21. Address by Norman R. Augustine at the Crummer Business School, Rollins College, Winter Park, FL, October 20, 1989.

22. For an excellent theoretical and empirical contribution on this subject, refer to Gibson, C. B., & Birkinshaw, J. 2004. The antecedents, consequences, and mediating role of organizational ambidexterity. *Academy of Management Journal,* 47(2): 209–226.

23. Mintzberg, H. 1985. Of strategies: Deliberate and emergent. *Strategic Management Journal,* 6: 257–272.

24. Carey, J. 2005. Tax credits put wind in the sails of renewables. *BusinessWeek.* January 10: 94.

25. Monks, R., & Minow, N. 2001. *Corporate governance* (2nd ed.). Malden, MA: Blackwell.

26. Intel Corp., www.intel.com/intel/finance/corp_gov.html.

27. For example, see The best (& worst) managers of the year, 2003. *BusinessWeek,* January 13: 58–92; and Lavelle, M. 2003. Rogues of the year. *Time,* January 6: 33–45.

28. Handy, C. 2002. What's a business for? *Harvard Business Review,* 80(12): 49–55.

29. From Lewis, Russel T., "The CEO's Lot is Not a Happy One . . ." *Academy of Management Executive: The Thinking Manager's Source,* 16(4): 38–39, Copyright © 2002 by Academy of Management. Reproduced by permission of Academy of Management via Copyright Clearance Center.

30. For an interesting perspective on the changing role of boards of directors, refer to Lawler, E., & Finegold, D. 2005. Rethinking governance. *MIT Sloan Management Review,* 46(2): 67–70.

31. Stakeholder symbiosis. 1998. *Fortune,* March 30: S2.

32. For a definitive, recent discussion of the stakeholder concept, refer to Freeman, R. E., & McVae, J. 2001. A stakeholder approach to strategic management. In Hitt, M. A., Freeman, R. E., & Harrison, J. S. (Eds.). *Handbook of strategic management:* 189–207. Malden, MA: Blackwell.

33. Atkinson, A. A., Waterhouse, J. H., & Wells, R. B. 1997. A stakeholder approach to strategic performance measurement. *Sloan Management Review,* 39(3): 25–38.

34. For an insightful discussion on the role of business in society, refer to Handy, op. cit.

35. Stakeholder symbiosis. op. cit., p. S3.

36. Rucci, A. J., Kirn, S. P., & Quinn, R. T. 1998. The employee-customer-profit chain at Sears. *Harvard Business Review,* 76(1): 82–97.

37. An excellent theoretical discussion on stakeholder activity is Rowley, T. J., & Moldoveanu, M. 2003. When will stakeholder groups act? An interest- and identity-based model of stakeholder group mobilization. *Academy of Management Review,* 28(2): 204–219.

38. Thomas, J. G. 2000. Macroenvironmetal forces. In Helms, M. M. (Ed.), *Encyclopedia of management.* (4th ed.): 516–520. Farmington Hills, MI: Gale Group.

39. For a strong advocacy position on the need for corporate values and social responsibility, read Hollender, J. 2004. What matters most: Corporate values and social responsibility. *California Management Review,* 46(4): 111–119.

40. Waddock, S. & Bodwell, C. 2004. Managing responsibility: What can be learned from the quality movement. *California Management Review,* 47(1): 25–37.

41. For a discussion of the role of alliances and collaboration on corporate social responsibility initiatives, refer to Pearce, J. A. II., & Doh, J. P. 2005. The high impact of collaborative social initiatives. *MIT Sloan Management Review,* 46(3): 30–40.

42. Ibid.

43. Bhattacharya, C. B., & Sen, S. 2004, Doing better at doing good: When, why, and how consumers respond to corporate social initiatives. *California Management Review,* 47(1): 9–24.

44. Cone Corporate Citizenship Study, 2002, www.coneinc.com.

45. Refer to www.bsr.org.

46. Kanter, R. M. 1999. From spare change to real change. *Harvard Business Review,* 77(3): 122–132.

47. Ibid.

48. This section draws on Hart, S. L. 1997. Beyond greening: Strategies for a sustainable world. *Harvard Business Review,* 75(1): 66–76, and Berry, M. A. & Rondinelli, D. A. 1998. Proactive corporate environmental management: A new industrial revolution. *Academy of Management Executive,* 12(2): 38–50.

49. Hart, op. cit., p. 67.

50. For a creative perspective on environmental sustainability and competitive advantage as well as ethical implications, read Ehrenfeld, J. R. 2005. The roots of sustainability. *MIT Sloan Management Review,* 46(2): 23–25.

51. McKinsey & Company. 1991. *The corporate response to the environmental challenge.* Summary Report, Amsterdam: McKinsey & Company.

52. Holliday, C. 2001. Sustainable growth, the DuPont way. *Harvard Business Review,* 79(9): 129–134.

53. Senge, P. M. 1990. The leader's new work: Building learning organizations. *Sloan Management Review,* 32(1): 7–23.

54. Barkema, G. G., Baum, A. C., & Mannix, E. A. 2002. Management challenges in a new time. *Academy of Management Journal,* 45(5): 916–930.

55. This section draws upon a variety of sources, including Tetenbaum, T. J. 1998. Shifting paradigms: From Newton to chaos. *Organizational Dynamics,* 26(4): 21–33; Ulrich, D. 1998. A new mandate for human resources. *Harvard Business Review,* 76(1): 125–135; and Hitt, M. A. 2000. The new frontier: Transformation of management for the new millennium. *Organizational Dynamics,* 28(2): 7–17.

56. Garten, J. E. 2001. *The mind of the C.E.O.* New York: Basic Books.

57. An interesting discussion on the impact of AIDS on the global economy is found in Rosen, S. 2003. AIDS *is* your business. *Harvard Business Review,* 81(2): 80–87.

58. Weber, J. 1996. Mr. nice guy with a mission. *BusinessWeek,* November 25: 137.

59. Ulrich, D. 1998. Intellectual capital: Competence × commitment. *Strategic Management Journal,* 39(2): 15–26.

60. Stewart, T. A. 2000. Today's companies won't make it, and Gary Hamel knows why. *Fortune,* September 4: 390.

61. Rivette, K. G., & Kline, D. 2000. Discovering new value in intellectual property. *Harvard Business Review,* 78(1): 54–66.

62. For an interesting perspective on the role of middle managers in the strategic management process, refer to Huy, Q. H. 2001. In praise of middle managers. *Harvard Business Review,* 79(8): 72–81.

63. Senge, 1996, op. cit., pp. 41–58.

64. Helgesen, S. 1996. Leading from the grass roots. In Hesselbein, F., Goldsmith, M., & Beckhard, R. (Eds.), *The leader of the future:* 19–24. San Francisco: Jossey-Bass.

65. Wetlaufer, S. 1999. Organizing for empowerment: An interview with AES's Roger Sant and Dennis Blake. *Harvard Business Review,* 77(1): 110–126.

66. Kets de Vries, M. F. R. 1998. Charisma in action: The transformational abilities of Virgin's Richard Branson and ABB's Percy Barnevik. *Organizational Dynamics,* 26(3): 7–21.

67. Hammonds, K. H. 2000. The next agenda. *Fast Company,* April: 140.

68. Our discussion draws on a variety of sources. These include Lipton, M. 1996. Demystifying the development of an organizational vision. *Sloan Management Review,* 37(4): 83–92; Bart, C. K. 2000. Lasting inspiration. *CA Magazine,* May: 49–50; and Quigley, J. V. 1994. Vision: How leaders develop it, share it, and sustain it. *Business Horizons,* September–October: 37–40.

69. Lipton, op. cit.

70. Quigley, op. cit.

71. Ibid.

72. Lipton, op. cit. Additional pitfalls are addressed in this article.

73. Bruch, H., & Ghoshal, S. 2004. *A bias for action.* Boston: Harvard Business School Press.

74. Company records.

75. Lipton, op. cit.

76. Sexton, D. A., & Van Aukun, P. M. 1985. A longitudinal study of small business strategic planning. *Journal of Small Business Management,* January: 8–15, cited in Lipton, op. cit.

77. For an insightful perspective on the use of strategic objectives, refer to Chatterjee, S. 2005. Core objectives: Clarity in designing strategy. *California Management Review,* 47(2): 33–49.

78. Ibid.

# Analyzing the External Environment of the Firm

>chapter objectives

*After reading this chapter, you should have a good understanding of:*

- The importance of developing forecasts of the business environment.

- Why environmental scanning, environmental monitoring, and collecting competitive intelligence are critical inputs to forecasting.

- Why scenario planning is a useful technique for firms competing in industries characterized by unpredictability and change.

- The impact of the general environment on a firm's strategies and performance.

- How forces in the competitive environment can affect profitability, and how a firm can improve its competitive position by increasing its power vis-à-vis these forces.

- How trends and events in the general environment and forces in the competitive environment are interrelated and affect performance.

- The concept of strategic groups and their strategy and performance implications.

trategies are not and should not be developed in a vacuum. They must be responsive to the external business environment. Otherwise, your firm could become, in effect, the most efficient producer of buggy whips, leisure suits, or slide rules. To avoid such strategic mistakes, firms must become knowledgeable about the business environment. One tool for analyzing trends is forecasting. In the development of forecasts, environmental scanning and environmental monitoring are important in detecting key trends and events. Managers also must aggressively collect and disseminate competitor intelligence. The information gleaned from these three activities is invaluable in developing forecasts and scenarios to minimize present and future threats as well as to exploit opportunities. We address these issues in the first part of this chapter. We also introduce a basic tool of strategy analysis—the concept of SWOT analysis (strengths, weaknesses, opportunities, and threats).

In the second part of the chapter, we present two frameworks for analyzing the external environment—the general environment and the competitive environment. The general environment consists of six segments—demographic, sociocultural, political/legal, technological, economic, and global. Trends and events in these segments can have a dramatic impact on your firm. The competitive environment is closer to home. It consists of five industry-related factors that can dramatically affect the average level of industry profitability. An awareness of these factors is critical in making decisions such as which industries to enter and how to improve your firm's current position within an industry. This is helpful in neutralizing competitive threats and increasing power over customers and suppliers. We also address industry analysis from a dynamic perspective, which reflects the rapid, unpredictable changes that are taking place in many industries. In the final part of this section, we place firms within an industry into strategic groups based on similarities in resources and strategies. As we will see, the concept of strategic groups has important implications for the intensity of rivalry and how the effects of a given environmental trend or event differ across groups.

Having well-known brands for generations will not necessarily provide a company with a permanent guarantee of success. Such firms can run into trouble if they do not effectively respond to changes in customer demands and preferences. Consider, for example, the case of the $3.5 billion Interstate Bakeries Corporation (IBC).[1] The firm has been delivering sliced bread and other bakery products since the 1930s, and many of their brands have become American icons. These include snack foods such as Twinkies, Ding Dongs, and Zingers as well as Wonder Bread. For the recent fiscal year ending May 29, 2004, IBC had a loss of $25.8 million compared to a profit of $69.8 million over the previous 2 years. Unfortunately, along with the losses, a heavy debt load of more than $1.3 billion forced the company into bankruptcy in September 2004. What went wrong with Interstate Bakeries?

> Perhaps, IBC's major shortcoming was its seeming inability to keep its brands alive. "To not innovate is a death sentence, and nostalgia won't carry you through this," says Rick Bozzelli, merchandising manager for McCaffrey's Markets, a regional supermarket in Langhorne, Pennsylvania. Enamored with its past glory, IBC never really reinvented itself. Instead, it continued to flood the baked-goods aisle with its low-priced Wonder Bread, even as consumers were turning toward fresh-baked supermarket or specialty breads. Many of its rivals' products were focused on the consumer trend toward low-carbohydrate alternatives, made popular in recent years by the Atkins diet. It is estimated that 32 million American adults follow low-carb diets such as Atkins and South Beach. It wasn't until late 2004 that IBC introduced a line of low-carb breads under the "Home Pride Carb Action" name. By then, as the old cliché goes, it was "too little too late."
>
> IBC faced similar problems with its line of snack foods. Products like Twinkies are viewed as junk foods—a sugary snack that few adults would indulge in and one lacking in appeal to a generation of children who snack on products such as Gogurt (a popular children's yogurt product). As noted by Wendell Perkins, chief investment officer at Johnson Asset Management, "I look back on Dolly Madison and Twinkies fondly and romantically from my childhood, but a lot has changed since then, and the company had a difficult time keeping up with the times." And the growing concern about child obesity in the United States certainly hasn't helped sales. Concerning IBC's bankruptcy, Kelly Brownell, director of the Yale Center for Eating and Weight Disorders contends, "I don't think there's a nutritionist in America who will shed a tear over this."
>
> IBC also failed to cut its overhead costs. Thus, it was unable to offer bargain-basement prices that would have enabled the firm to push more aggressively into mass-market channels such as Wal-Mart Stores, Inc. and Target stores. In recent years there has been a greater consolidation in the grocery industry. As some large grocery and retail chains grow in size and become more dominant, their buying power increases. This places greater pricing power on manufacturers. Thus, IBC's unfavorable cost structure put them at a significant disadvantage.

To be a successful manager, you must recognize opportunities and threats in your firm's external environment. You must be aware of what's going on outside your company. If you focus exclusively on the efficiency of internal operations, your firm may degenerate into the world's most efficient producer of buggy whips or carbon paper. But if you miscalculate the market, opportunities will be lost—hardly an enviable position for you or your firm.

In their award-winning book *Competing for the Future,* Gary Hamel and C. K. Prahalad suggest that "every manager carries around in his or her head a set of biases, assumptions, and presuppositions about the structure of the relevant 'industry,' about how one makes money in the industry, about who the competition is and isn't, about who the customers are and aren't, and so on."[2] Environmental analysis requires you to continually question these assumptions. Peter Drucker labeled these interrelated sets of assumptions the "theory of the business."[3]

A firm's strategy may be good at one point in time, but it may go astray when management's frame of reference gets out of touch with the realities of the actual business situation. This results when management's assumptions, premises, or beliefs are incorrect or when internal inconsistencies among them render the overall "theory of the business" invalid. As Warren Buffett, investor extraordinaire, colorfully notes, "Beware of past performance 'proofs.' If history books were the key to riches, the Forbes 400 would consist of librarians." And Arthur Martinez, former chairman of Sears, Roebuck & Co., states, "Today's peacock is tomorrow's feather duster."

In the business world, many peacocks have become feather dusters or at least had their plumage dulled. Consider the high-tech company Novell, which has undergone hard times.[4] Novell went head-to-head with Microsoft and bought market-share loser Word-Perfect to compete with Microsoft Word. The result was a $1.3 billion loss when Novell sold WordPerfect to Corel. And today we may wonder who will be the next Wang, Kmart, or *Encyclopaedia Britannica.*

## >>Creating the Environmentally Aware Organization

So how do managers become environmentally aware?[5] We will now address three important processes—scanning, monitoring, and gathering competitive intelligence—that managers must use to develop forecasts. Exhibit 2.1 illustrates relationships among these important activities. We also will discuss the importance of scenario planning in anticipating major future changes in the external environment and the role of SWOT analysis.[6]

### The Role of Scanning, Monitoring, Competitive Intelligence, and Forecasting

*Environmental Scanning*    Environmental scanning involves surveillance of a firm's external environment to predict environmental changes to come and to detect changes already under way.[7] Successful environmental scanning alerts the organization to critical trends and events before the changes have developed a discernible pattern and before competitors recognize them.[8] Otherwise, the firm may be forced into a reactive mode instead of being proactive.[9]

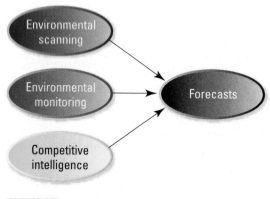

Exhibit 2.1    **Inputs to Forecasting**

Sir John Browne, chief executive officer of petroleum company BP Amoco, described in a speech the kind of environmental changes his company was experiencing.

> The next element of the change we've experienced is the growth in demand, and the changing nature of that demand. The world uses eight million more barrels of oil and 30 billion more cubic feet of natural gas every day than it did in the spring of 1990. The growth of natural gas in particular has been and continues to be spectacular, and I believe that change can legitimately be seen as part of a wider, longer-term shift to lighter, cleaner, less carbon-intensive fuels.[10]

Consider how difficult it would be for BP Amoco to develop strategies and allocate resources if it did not scan the external environment for such emerging changes in demand.

At times, your company may benefit from studies conducted by outside experts in a particular industry. A. T. Kearney, a large international consulting company, identified several key issues in the automobile industry, including:[11]

- *Globalization.* This is not a new trend but it has intensified, with enormous opportunities opening up in Asia, central and eastern Europe, and Latin America.
- *Time to Market.* Although some improvements have been made, there's still a gap between product development cycles in the United States and Europe compared to Japan. This gap may be widening as Japanese companies continue to make improvements.
- *Shifting Roles and Responsibilities.* Design responsibility, purchasing, and even project management and systems engineering are shifting from original equipment manufacturers to integrators/suppliers.

Consider how disadvantaged you would be as an executive in the global automobile industry if you were unaware of such trends.

*Environmental Monitoring*   Environmental monitoring tracks the evolution of environmental trends, sequences of events, or streams of activities. These are often uncovered during the environmental scanning process. They may be trends that the firm came across by accident or ones that were brought to its attention from outside the organization. Consider the automobile industry example. While environmental scanning may make you aware of the trends, they require close monitoring, which involves closer ongoing scrutiny. For example, you should closely monitor sales in Asia, central and eastern Europe, and Latin America. You should observe how fast Japanese companies and other competitors bring products to market compared with your firm. You should also study trends with your own suppliers/integrators in purchasing, project management, and systems engineering. Monitoring enables firms to evaluate how dramatically environmental trends are changing the competitive landscape.

One of the authors of this text recently conducted on-site interviews with executives from several industries to identify indicators that firms monitor as inputs to their strategy process. Examples of such indicators included:

- *A Motel 6 executive.* The number of rooms in the budget segment of the industry in the United States and the difference between the average daily room rate and the Consumer Price Index (CPI).
- *A Pier 1 Imports executive.* Net disposable income (NDI), consumer confidence index, and housing starts.
- *A Johnson & Johnson medical products executive.* Percentage of gross domestic product (GDP) spent on health care, number of active hospital beds, and the size and power of purchasing agents (indicates the concentration of buyers).

Such indices are critical for managers in determining a firm's strategic direction and resource allocation.

Exhibit 2.2
**What Competitive Intelligence Is and Is Not!**

**Competitive Intelligence *Is* . . .**

1. **Information** that has been analyzed to the point where you can make a decision.

2. **A tool** to alert management to early recognition of both threats and opportunities.

3. **A means to deliver reasonable assessments.** CI offers approximations of the market and competition. It is not a peek at a rival's financial books. Reasonable assessments are what modern entrepreneurs need and want on a regular basis.

4. **A way of life, a process.** If a company uses CI the way it should be used, it becomes everyone's job, not just the strategic planning or marketing staff's. It is a process by which critical information is available to those who need it.

**Competitive Intelligence *Is Not* . . .**

1. **Spying.** Spying implies illegal or unethical activities. It is a rare activity, since most corporations do not want to find themselves in court or to upset shareholders.

2. **A crystal ball.** CI gives corporations good approximations of short- and long-term reality. It does not predict the future.

3. **Database search.** Databases offer just that—data. They do not massage or analyze the data in any way. They certainly don't replace human beings who make decisions by examining the data and applying their common sense, experience, and intuition.

4. **A job for one smart person.** A CEO may appoint one person as the CI ringmaster, but one person cannot do it all. At best, the ringmaster can keep management informed and ensure that others become trained to apply this tool within their business units.

Sources: Imperato, G. 1998. Competitive intelligence—Get smart! *Fast Company,* April: 26–29; and Fuld, F. M. What competitive intelligence is and is not! www.fuld.com/whatCI.html.

***Competitive Intelligence***    Competitive intelligence (CI) helps firms define and understand their industry and identify rivals' strengths and weaknesses.[12] This includes the intelligence gathering associated with collecting data on competitors and interpreting such data for managerial decision making. Done properly, competitive intelligence helps a company avoid surprises by anticipating competitors' moves and decreasing response time.[13]

Examples of competitive analysis are evident in daily newspapers and periodicals such as *The Wall Street Journal, BusinessWeek,* and *Fortune.* For example, banks continually track home loan, auto loan, and certificate of deposit (CD) interest rates charged by peers in a given geographic region. Major airlines change hundreds of fares daily in response to competitors' tactics. Car manufacturers are keenly aware of announced cuts or increases in rivals' production volume, sales, and sales incentives (e.g., rebates and low interest rates on financing). They use this information to plan their own marketing, pricing, and production strategies. Exhibit 2.2 provides some insights on what CI is (and what it isn't).

The Internet has dramatically accelerated the speed at which firms can find competitive intelligence. Leonard Fuld, founder of the Cambridge, Massachusetts, training and consulting firm Fuld & Co., specializes in competitive intelligence.[14] His firm often

## Ethical Guidelines on Competitive Intelligence: United Technologies

United Technologies (UT) is a $28 billion global conglomerate composed of world-leading businesses with rich histories of technological pioneering, such as Otis Elevator, Carrier Air Conditioning, and Sikorsky (helicopters). It was founded in 1853 and has an impressive history of technological accomplishments. UT built the first working helicopter, developed the first commercially available hydrogen cells, and designed complete life support systems for space shuttles. UT believes strongly in a robust code of ethics. In the last decade, they have clearly articulated their principles governing business conduct. These include an antitrust guide, an ethics guide when contracting with the U.S. government and foreign governments, a policy on accepting gifts from suppliers, and guidelines for proper usage of e-mail. One such document is the Code of Ethics Guide on Competitive Intelligence. This encourages managers and workers to ask themselves these five questions whenever they have ethical concerns.

1. Have I done anything that coerced somebody to share this information? Have I, for example, threatened a supplier by indicating that future business opportunities will be influenced by the receipt of information with respect to a competitor?

2. Am I in a place where I should not be? If, for example, I am a field representative with privileges to move around in a customer's facility, have I gone outside the areas permitted? Have I misled anybody in order to gain access?

3. Is the contemplated technique for gathering information evasive, such as sifting through trash or setting up an electronic "snooping" device directed at a competitor's facility from across the street?

4. Have I misled somebody in a way that the person believed sharing information with me was required or would be protected by a confidentiality agreement? Have I, for example, called and misrepresented myself as a government official who was seeking some information for some official purpose?

5. Have I done something to evade or circumvent a system intended to secure or protect information?

Sources: Nelson, B. 2003. The thinker. *Forbes*, March 3: 62–64; and The Fuld war room—Survival kit 010. Code of Ethics (printed 2/26/01).

profiles top company and business group managers and considers these issues: What is their background? What is their style? Are they marketers? Are they cost cutters? Fuld has found that the more articles he collects and the more biographies he downloads, the better he can develop profiles.

One of Fuld & Co.'s clients needed to know if a rival was going to start competing more aggressively on costs. Fuld's analysts tracked down articles from the Internet and a local newspaper profile of the rival firm's CEO. The profile said the CEO had taken a bus to a nearby town to visit one of the firm's plants. Fuld claimed, "Those few words were a small but important sign to me that this company was going to be incredibly cost-conscious." Another client retained Fuld to determine the size, strength, and technical capabilities of a privately held company. Initially, it was difficult to get detailed information. Then one analyst used Deja News (www.dejanews.com), now part of Google, to tap into some online discussion groups. The analyst's research determined that the company had posted 14 job openings on one Usenet group. That posting was a road map to the competitor's development strategy.

At times, a firm's aggressive efforts to gather competitive intelligence may lead to unethical or illegal behaviors.[15] Strategy Spotlight 2.1 provides an example of a company, United Technologies, that has set clear guidelines to help prevent unethical behavior.

A word of caution: Executives must be careful to avoid spending so much time and effort tracking the actions of traditional competitors that they ignore new competitors. Further, broad changes and events in the larger environment may have a dramatic impact on a firm's viability. Peter Drucker, whom many consider the father of modern management, wrote:

> Increasingly, a winning strategy will require information about events and conditions outside the institution: noncustomers, technologies other than those currently used by the company and its present competitors, markets not currently served, and so on.[16]

Consider the fall of the once-mighty *Encyclopaedia Britannica*.[17] Its demise was not caused by a traditional competitor in the encyclopedia industry. It was caused by new technology. CD-ROMs came out of nowhere and devastated the printed encyclopedia industry. Why? A full set of the *Encyclopaedia Britannica* sells for about $2,000, but an encyclopedia on CD-ROM, such as Microsoft *Encarta,* sells for about $50. To make matters worse, many people receive *Encarta* free with their personal computers.

*Environmental Forecasting*    Environmental scanning, monitoring, and competitive intelligence are important inputs for analyzing the external environment. However, they are of little use unless they provide raw material that is reliable enough to help managers make accurate forecasts. Environmental forecasting involves the development of plausible projections about the direction, scope, speed, and intensity of environmental change.[18] Its purpose is to predict change. It asks: How long will it take a new technology to reach the marketplace? Will the present social concern about an issue result in new legislation? Are current lifestyle trends likely to continue?

Some forecasting issues are much more specific to a particular firm and the industry in which it competes. Consider how important it is for Motel 6 to predict future indicators, such as the number of rooms, in the budget segment of the industry. If its predictions are low, it will build too many units, creating a surplus of room capacity that would drive down room rates. Similarly, if Pier 1 Imports is overly optimistic in its forecast of future net disposable income and U.S. housing starts, it will order too much inventory and later be forced to discount merchandise drastically.

A danger of forecasting is that managers may view uncertainty as black and white and ignore important gray areas. Either they assume that the world is certain and open to precise predictions, or they assume it is uncertain and completely unpredictable.[19] The problem is that underestimating uncertainty can lead to strategies that neither defend against threats nor take advantage of opportunities. In 1977 one of the colossal underestimations in business history occurred when Kenneth H. Olsen, then president of Digital Equipment Corp., announced, "There is no reason for individuals to have a computer in their home." The explosion in the personal computer market was not easy to detect in 1977, but it was clearly within the range of possibilities that industry experts were discussing at the time. And, historically, there have been underestimates of the growth potential of new telecommunication services. The electric telegraph was derided by Ralph Waldo Emerson, and the telephone had its skeptics. More recently, an "infamous" McKinsey study in the early 1980s predicted that there would be fewer than 1 million cellular users in the United States by the year 2000. Actually, there were nearly 100 million.[20]

At the other extreme, if managers assume the world is unpredictable, they may abandon the analytical rigor of their traditional planning process and base strategic decisions on gut instinct. Such a "just do it" approach may cause executives to place misinformed bets on emerging products or markets that result in record write-offs. Entrepreneurs and venture capitalists who took the plunge and invested in questionable Internet ventures in the late 1990s provide many examples.

A more in-depth approach to forecasting involves scenario analysis. Scenario analysis draws on a range of disciplines and interests, among them economics, psychology, sociology, and demographics. It usually begins with a discussion of participants'

# STRATEGY SPOTLIGHT

## Scenario Planning at Shell Oil Company

Preparing to cope with uncertainty is one of the biggest strategic challenges faced by most businesses. There are few tools for coping with strategic uncertainty, especially over medium- to long-term horizons. One technique that has proved its usefulness is scenario planning.

Scenario planning is different from other tools for strategic planning such as trend analysis or high and low forecasts. The origins of scenario planning lie with the military, which used it to cope effectively with multiple challenges and limited resources.

In the 1960s and 1970s, Shell combined analytical tools with information to create scenarios of possible outcomes. The result of the 1973 oil embargo was a sharp increase in crude oil prices, short supplies of gasoline for consumers, and a depressed world economy. However, Shell's strategic planning, including the use of scenarios, had strongly suggested that a more unstable environment was coming, with a shift of power from oil companies to oil producers. As a result of the precautionary actions it took, Shell was in a better position than most oil companies when the 1973 embargo occurred. Shell also uses scenario planning to plan major new oil field investments because elements of risk can be identified and explored over a considerable period of time.

The Shell process of scenario planning involves the following stages:

1. Interviews with people both inside and outside the business, using an open-ended questioning technique to encourage full and frank answers.

2. Analysis of interviews by issue in order to build a "natural agenda" for further processing.

3. Synthesis of each agenda to draw out underlying areas of uncertainty/dispute and possible interrelationships among issues.

4. A small number of workshops to explore key issues to improve understanding and identify gaps for further research. These generate a wide range of strategy options.

5. A workshop to identify and build a small number of scenarios that may occur in the next 10 to 15 years or even later.

6. A testing of strategy options against the scenarios in order to assess robustness (i.e., whether or not a given strategy is effective under more than one scenario).

Other practitioners of scenario planning include Levi Strauss, which uses scenario planning to consider potential impacts of everything from cotton deregulation to the total disappearance of cotton from this planet. Also, a German insurance company anticipated the fall of the Berlin wall and made plans to expand in central Europe. And in 1990 when Nelson Mandela was released from a South African prison, he met with a panel that helped him create scenarios to chart out the country's future. Scenario planning helps by considering not just trends or forecasts but also how they could be upset by events and the outcomes that may result.

Sources: Martin, R. 2002. The oracles of oil. *Business 2.0*, January: 35–39; www.touchstonerenard.co.uk/Expertise/Strategy/Scenario_Planning/scenario_planning.htm; and Epstein, J. 1998. Scenario planning: An introduction. *The Futurist*, September: 50–52.

thoughts on ways in which societal trends, economics, politics, and technology may affect the issue under discussion.[21] For example, consider Lego. The popular Danish toy manufacturer has a strong position in the construction toys market. But what would happen if this broadly defined market should change dramatically? After all, Lego is competing not only with producers of similar products but also on a much broader canvas for a share of children's playtime. In this market, Lego has a host of competitors, many of them computer based; still others have not yet been invented. Lego may end up with an increasing share of a narrow, shrinking market (much like IBM in the declining days of the mainframe computer). To avoid such a fate, managers must consider their future in a wider context than their narrow, traditional markets. They need to lay down guidelines for at least 10 years in the future to anticipate rapid change. Strategy Spotlight 2.2 provides an example of scenario planning at Shell Oil Company.

## SWOT Analysis

To understand the business environment of a particular firm, you need to analyze both the general environment and the firm's industry and competitive environment. Generally, firms compete with other firms in the same industry. An industry is composed of a set of firms that produce similar products or services, sell to similar customers, and use similar methods of production. Gathering industry information and understanding competitive dynamics among the different companies in your industry is key to successful strategic management.

One of the most basic techniques for analyzing firm and industry conditions is SWOT analysis. SWOT stands for strengths, weaknesses, opportunities, and threats. SWOT analysis provides a framework for analyzing these four elements of a company's internal and external environment. It provides "raw material"—a basic listing of conditions both inside and surrounding your company. The strengths and weaknesses portion of SWOT refers to the internal conditions of a firm—where your firm excels (strengths) and where it may be lacking relative to competitors (weaknesses). We will address strengths and weaknesses again in Chapter 3. Opportunities and threats are environmental conditions external to the firm. These could be factors in the general environment, such as improving economic conditions, that cause lower borrowing costs or trends that benefit some companies and harm others. An example is the heightened concern with fitness, which is a threat to some companies (e.g., tobacco) and an opportunity to others (e.g., health clubs). Opportunities and threats are also present in the competitive environment among firms competing for the same customers.

## >>The General Environment

The general environment is composed of factors that can have dramatic effects on firm strategy.[22] Typically, a firm has little ability to predict trends and events in the general environment and even less ability to control them. When listening to CNBC, for example, you can hear many experts espouse totally different perspectives on what action the Federal Reserve Board may take on short-term interest rates—an action that can have huge effects on the valuation of entire economic sectors. Also, it's difficult to predict future political events such as the ongoing Middle East peace negotiations and tensions on the Korean peninsula. In addition, who would have guessed the Internet's impact on national and global economies in the past decade or two? Such dramatic innovations in information technology (e.g., the Internet) have helped keep inflation in check by lowering the cost of doing business in the United States at the beginning of the 21st century.

We divide the general environment into six segments: demographic, sociocultural, political/legal, technological, economic, and global. First, we discuss each segment and provide a summary of the segment and examples of how events and trends can impact industries. Second, we address relationships among the general environment segments. Third, we consider how trends and events can vary across industries. Exhibit 2.3 provides examples of key trends and events in each of the six segments of the general environment.

## The Demographic Segment

Demographics are the most easily understood and quantifiable elements of the general environment. They are at the root of many changes in society. Demographics include elements such as the aging population,[23] rising or declining affluence, changes in ethnic composition, geographic distribution of the population, and disparities in income level.

The impact of a demographic trend, like all segments of the general environment, varies across industries. The aging of the U.S. population has had a positive effect on the health care industry but a negative impact on the industry that produces diapers and

**Exhibit 2.3**
**General
Environment: Key
Trends and Events**

**Demographic**

- Aging population
- Rising affluence
- Changes in ethnic composition
- Geographic distribution of population
- Greater disparities in income levels

**Sociocultural**

- More women in the workforce
- Increase in temporary workers
- Greater concern for fitness
- Greater concern for environment
- Postponement of family formation

**Political/Legal**

- Tort reform
- Americans with Disabilities Act (ADA) of 1990
- Repeal of Glass-Steagall Act in 1999 (banks may now offer brokerage services)
- Deregulation of utility and other industries
- Increases in federally mandated minimum wages
- Taxation at local, state, federal levels
- Legislation on corporate governance reforms in bookkeeping, stock options, etc. (Sarbanes-Oxley Act of 2002)

**Technological**

- Genetic engineering
- Emergence of Internet technology
- Computer-aided design/computer-aided manufacturing systems (CAD/CAM)
- Research in synthetic and exotic materials
- Pollution/global warming
- Miniaturization of computing technologies
- Wireless communications
- Nanotechnology

**Economic**

- Interest rates
- Unemployment rates
- Consumer Price Index
- Trends in GDP
- Changes in stock market valuations

**Global**

- Increasing global trade
- Currency exchange rates
- Emergence of the Indian and Chinese economies
- Trade agreements among regional blocs (e.g., NAFTA, EU, ASEAN)
- Creation of WTO (leading to decreasing tariffs/free trade in services)

### Older Employees: An Increasingly Important Demographic Segment of Today's Workforce

The U.S. Bureau of Labor Statistics states that only 13 percent of American workers were 55 and older in 2000. However, by 2006 that figure will increase to 15 percent, and by 2015, 20 percent, or one in five, of all U.S. workers will be 55 or older. At the same time, the United States is expected to experience a significant drop in the percentage of younger workers ages 25 to 44, making it increasingly important for employers to find ways to recruit and retain older workers. Similarly, the National Association of Manufacturing estimates that as baby boomers continue retiring and the economy grows, the United States will have 7 million more jobs than workers by 2010. Some firms have discovered an important part of the answer to this labor shortfall: luring older workers back into their ranks.

Sources: Warner, M. 2004. Home Depot goes old school. *Business 2.0*, June: 74; and, O'Brien, S. 2005. Over 50 and looking for work? www.seniorliving. about.com.

Home Depot, the $65 billion retailer, has been partnering with the American Association of Retired Persons (AARP) to recruit more than 700 older employees—not for menial jobs, but as sales associates and managers who can help customers navigate Home Depot's towering, intimidating shelves. "We want them to have technical depth," says Cindy Milburn, Home Depot's senior hiring director. "That means plumbers, carpenters, electricians, people with millwork backgrounds, and people with design skills."

Home Depot says that there are many advantages to hiring older workers. The firm says that they stay on the job longer and don't take as many sick days as younger workers. More than two dozen companies—including Anheuser-Busch, Barnes & Noble, and Sears—are now exploring similar partnerships with the AARP.

---

baby food. Rising levels of affluence in many developed countries bode well for brokerage services as well as for upscale pets and supplies. However, these same trends may have an adverse effect on fast food restaurants because people can afford to dine at higher-priced restaurants. Fast-food restaurants depend on minimum-wage employees to operate efficiently, but the competition for labor intensifies as more attractive employment opportunities become prevalent, thus threatening the employment base for restaurants. Let's look at the details of some of these trends.

The aging population in the United States and other developed countries has important implications. With the graying of baby boomers, the demand for homes for "active elders" (as home developers refer to retirees) is bound to soar. The National Association of Home Builders estimates that people in the 55 to 74 age group will buy 281,000 homes in 2010, up from 189,000 in 1995.[24] This provides an opportunity for developers who focus on that segment of the construction industry. Another long-term projection is that by the year 2025, nearly one-fifth of the American population will be 65 or older. This may be good news for baby boomers, because there is always strength in numbers (especially in the political arena). It's also good news for drugstores, which see older patients seven times more often than younger ones.[25] Strategy Spotlight 2.3 addresses the important implications of older workers for today's workforce.

Another demographic trend is the shift in the geographic population of the United States. Although the population increased by about 13 percent (from 248 million to 281 million) during the 1990s, this growth was not evenly distributed.[26] Strong growth in the South and West—spurred in large part by an increase in the Hispanic population and relocation to economic hot spots such as Atlanta and Las Vegas—was offset by slowing growth in the North and Midwest. The resulting redistribution affects two other environmental segments: the economic well-being of those regions and the political/legal population-based representation in the U.S. House of Representatives.

## The Sociocultural Segment

Sociocultural forces influence the values, beliefs, and lifestyles of a society. Examples include a higher percentage of women in the workforce, dual-income families, increases in the number of temporary workers, greater concern for healthy diets and physical fitness, greater interest in the environment, and postponement of having children. Such forces enhance sales of products and services in many industries but depress sales in others. The increased number of women in the workforce has increased the need for business clothing merchandise but decreased the demand for baking product staples (since people would have less time to cook from scratch). A greater concern for health and fitness has had differential effects. This trend has helped industries that manufacture exercise equipment and healthful foods but harmed industries that produce unhealthful foods.

The trend toward increased educational attainment by women in the workplace has led to an increase in the number of women in upper management positions. U.S. Department of Education statistics show that women have become the dominant holders of college degrees. Based on figures of a recent graduating class, women with bachelor's degrees will outnumber their male counterparts by 27 percent. By the class of 2006–2007, the gap should surge to 38 percent. Additionally, throughout the 1990s the number of women earning MBAs increased by 29 percent compared to only 15 percent for men.[27] Given these educational attainments, it is hardly surprising that companies owned by women have been one of the driving forces of the U.S. economy; these companies (now more than 9 million in number) account for 40 percent of all U.S. businesses and have generated more than $3.6 trillion in annual revenue. In addition, women have a tremendous impact on consumer spending decisions. Not surprisingly, many companies have focused their advertising and promotion efforts on female consumers. We address this issue in Strategy Spotlight 2.4.

## The Political/Legal Segment

Political processes and legislation influence the environmental regulations with which industries must comply.[28] Some important elements of the political/legal arena include tort reform, the Americans with Disabilities Act (ADA) of 1990, the repeal of the Glass-Steagall Act in 1999 (banks may now offer brokerage services), deregulation of utilities and other industries, and increases in the federally mandated minimum wage.

As with many factors in the general environment, changes that benefit one industry may damage others. For example, tort reform (legislation designed to limit the liability of defendants in the litigation process) may be good for industries such as automobile and tire manufacturers. Witness the litigation associated with Firestone tires and Ford Explorers, for example. However, tort reform will be bad for law firms, whose fees are often linked to the size of a settlement. Many have argued that without significant tort reform, large jury awards are a constant threat to companies and lead to higher consumer prices. On the other hand, the possibility of large judgments influences companies to act in a more ethical manner. The Americans with Disabilities Act has had a profound impact on industries. Companies with more than 15 employees must provide reasonable accommodations for employees and customers, which increases their construction and maintenance costs, but companies manufacturing elevators, escalators, and ramps have benefited from such legislation.

Government legislation can also have a significant impact on the governance of corporations. The U.S. Congress passed the Sarbanes-Oxley Act in 2002, which greatly increases the accountability of auditors, executives, and corporate lawyers. This act was a response to the widespread perception that existing governance mechanisms have failed

## 2.4 STRATEGY SPOTLIGHT

# The Impact of Women on Consumer Spending Decisions

Although women may be paid less than men and may make it to the CEO suite less often, the U.S. economy is more and more female-driven. U.S. women account for about $3.3 trillion in annual consumer spending and $1.5 trillion more in business expenditures, according to Tom Peters's latest book, *Re-Imagine.* Women also comprise 47 percent of individuals with assets over $500,000 and 51.3 percent of the private wealth in the United States. According to Peters, ". . . women are not a niche. At 51 percent of the population, women are the majority. Second, in most households, the real story is that even though they're 'only' 51 percent of the population, women represent more like 80 percent of the purchasing power." Most consumer companies know that women are the key decision makers for household goods: 80 percent is the rule of thumb used by many consumer goods companies as the percentage of purchases made by women. According to Martha Barletta, CEO of Trendsight Group, women decide 92 percent of vacation plans, 62 percent of car purchases, and 52 percent of home-improvement projects.

Not surprisingly, many traditional male-oriented industries are getting in touch with their feminine sides.

Home Depot, for example, spent $1 billion in 2004 to add softer lighting and brighter signs in 300 stores. Why? It is an effort to match rival Lowe's long-standing appeal to women. And Best Buy, recognizing that women purchase 55 percent of electronics items, will add personal-shopping assistants in some stores to explain "geek speak" with which some women (and, of course, some men as well!) may not be familiar.

Companies, however, need to make sure they don't overplay the gender card. "A very important part of the home-improvement business is still more down-market, more male," says Geoff Wissman, an analyst at Retail Forward, a retail consultancy in Columbus, Ohio. After all, one-fourth of sales at home-improvement retailers come from contractors, who are predominantly male. The key is to figure out a balance between men's and women's interests.

Wilkesboro (North Carolina)-based Lowe's has found that women prefer to do larger home-improvement projects with a man—be it a boyfriend, husband, or neighbor. As a result, in addition to its "recipe card classes" (that explain various projects that take only one weekend), Lowe's offers co-ed store clinics for projects like sink installation. "Women like to feel they're given the same attention as a male customer," states Lowe's spokesperson Julie Valeant-Yenichek, who points out that most seminar attendees, whether male or female, are inexperienced.

Sources: Tsao, A. 2005. Retooling home improvement. *Businessweek.com.* February 14; Grow, B. 2004. Who wears the wallet in the family? *Business-Week,* August 16: 10.

to protect the interests of shareholders, employees, and creditors. Perhaps it is not too surprising that Sarbanes-Oxley has also created a tremendous demand for professional accounting services. We address this trend in Strategy Spotlight 2.5.

Legislation also helps companies in the high-tech sector of the economy by expanding the number of temporary visas available for highly skilled foreign professionals. For example, a bill passed in October 2000 allows 195,000 H-1B visas in each of the next three years, up from the cap of only 115,000 in 2000. The allotment for the year 2000 was used up by March, and the cap decreased to 107,500 for 2001 and a mere 65,000 each year thereafter (at least through 2005). Almost half of the visas are for professionals from India, and most of them are computer or software specialists.[29] For U.S. labor and workers' rights groups, however, the issue was a political hot potato.

## The Technological Segment

Developments in technology lead to new products and services and improve how they are produced and delivered to the end user. Innovations can create entirely new industries and alter the boundaries of existing industries.[30] Examples of technological developments and trends are genetic engineering, Internet technology, computer-aided design/computer-aided manufacturing (CAD/CAM), research in artificial and exotic

# STRATEGY SPOTLIGHT

## The Sarbanes-Oxley Act: A Boon for Accountants

Government regulation is often prompted as elected officials respond to voters' expectations. When faced with a crisis, voters often demand a solution and expect elected officials to provide one. If the politicians fail to deliver, they suffer in the next election. Consider some of the historical examples of how the U.S. government has reacted to ethical disasters with the blunt force of increased legislation.

- The creation of the Securities and Exchange Commission (SEC) and other legislation following the stock market crash of 1929.

- The Foreign Corrupt Practices Act of 1977, which followed Lockheed's bribes to government officials.

- In the wake of the Enron, WorldCom, and Andersen debacles, Congress passed the Sarbanes-Oxley Act on July 30, 2002. (The law was passed just 35 days after WorldCom announced that it had overstated its revenues by at least $3.8 billion.)

Sources: Arndt, M. 2004. A boon for bean counters. *BusinessWeek,* November 22: 13; Thomas, T., Schermerhorn, R. R., Jr., & Dienhart, J. W. 2004. Strategic leadership of ethical behavior in business. *The Academy of Management Executive,* 18(2): 56–68.

Accounting firms have really benefited from the Sarbanes-Oxley Act. They had lobbied hard to keep the act from being passed. But, fortunately for them, they lost!

Companies are working hard to comply with Section 404 of the act. The provision requires publicly traded corporations to vouch for internal financial controls and remedy problems. A recent survey by Financial Executives International (FEI) finds that, on average, companies will spend $3.1 million and 30,700 hours to comply—nearly double the estimates of an earlier poll.

Much of that expense goes to privately held accounting firms. Audit fees are expected to surge more than 50 percent, according to FEI. To deal with the increased business, the Big Four accounting firms are in a hiring frenzy and logging lots of overtime. For example, KPMG has added 850 auditors in 2004, while PricewaterhouseCoopers (PWC) has hired 400 people from English-speaking foreign countries as temporary employees. "It's a scramble," say Dennis Nally, PWC's U.S. senior partner. It seems every cloud has a silver lining.

---

materials, and, on the downside, pollution and global warming. Firms in the petroleum and primary metals industries incur significant expenses to reduce the amount of pollution they produce. Engineering and consulting firms that work with polluting industries derive financial benefits from solving such problems.

Another important technological development is the combination of information technology (IT) and the Internet. By the end of 2000, productivity in the United States was increasing at an annual rate of 5.7 percent. This represents the fastest pace in 35 years—double the historical average of 2 to 3 percent per year. According to a study conducted jointly by Harvard University and the Federal Reserve, IT is responsible for almost half of the rapid productivity gains in recent years. It also has helped offset the inflationary effects of wage increases.[31]

The Internet has reduced the cost of getting information and increased its availability, boosting company profits. How are these costs reduced? Consider two examples. The National Association of Purchasing Managers pinpoints the cost of an average in-store purchase to be $79. However, Commerce One believes the proper use of the Internet can cut it to $6. Similarly, Fidelity Investments has found that it costs $15 to handle a transaction over the phone but less than a cent to perform that same transaction on the Web.

Nanotechnology is becoming a very promising area of research with many potentially useful applications.[32] Nanotechnology takes place at industry's tiniest stage: one billionth of a meter. Remarkably, this is the size of 10 hydrogen atoms in a row.

Researchers have discovered that matter at such a tiny scale behaves very differently. While some of the science behind this phenomenon is still shrouded in mystery, the commercial potential is coming sharply into focus. Familiar materials—from gold to carbon soot—display starting and useful new properties. Some transmit light or electricity.

Exhibit 2.4
Nanotechnology:
Some Future
Applications

Groundbreaking advances in nanotechnology are expected to spread through the economy, shaking up entire industries.

| | Vision | Prognosis |
|---|---|---|
| **FIGHT CANCER** | Sensors will be able to detect a single cancer cell and will help guide nanoparticles that can burn tumors from the inside out, leaving healthy cells alone. | Diagnostics will hit the market within three years, but treatments carry far higher risk. Testing and government approvals will delay them for the next decade. |
| **TRANSFORM ENERGY** | Nano-enhanced solar panels will feed cheap electricity onto superconducting power lines made of carbon nanotubes. | Next-generation panels will emerge this decade in Japan, which leads in the technology and suffers from higher energy prices. |
| **REPLACE SILICON** | Carbon nanotubes will take over when silicon peters out, leading to far faster chips that need less power than today's. | IBM has built working nanocircuits. But in the factory, chipmakers must be able to make billions of them. The transition is unlikely before 2015. |
| **TRAVEL TO SPACE** | Podlike crawlers will carry cargo thousands of miles up a carbon-nanotube cable to a space station for billions less than rocket launches. | Today the longest nanotubes are mere millimeters. To make miles of cable, scientists must learn how to weave these into threads. A working cable is at least 20 years away. |

Source: From Baker, S., & Aston, A. 2004. "Universe in a grain of sand." *BusinessWeek*, October 11: 138–140. Reprinted with permission.

Others become harder than diamonds or turn into potent chemical catalysts. What's more, researchers have found that a tiny dose of nanoparticles can transform the chemistry and nature of far bigger things, creating everything from stronger fenders to superefficient fuel cells. Exhibit 2.4 addresses some of the promising future applications of this emerging science.

There are downsides to technology. In addition to ethical issues in biotechnology, there are threats to our environment associated with the emission of greenhouse gases. To combat such problems, some firms in the petroleum industry take a proactive approach. BP Amoco plans to decrease its greenhouse gas emissions by giving each of its 150 business units a quota of emission permits and encouraging the units to trade them. If a unit cuts emissions and has leftover permits, it can sell them to other units that are having difficulty meeting their goals. For example, Julie Hardwick, manager at the Naperville, Illinois, petrochemical division, saved up permits by fast-tracking a furnace upgrade that allowed elimination of a second furnace.[33]

## The Economic Segment

The economy has an impact on all industries, from suppliers of raw materials to manufacturers of finished goods and services, as well as all organizations in the service, wholesale, retail, government, and nonprofit sectors. Key economic indicators include interest rates, unemployment rates, the Consumer Price Index, the gross domestic product, and net disposable income. Interest-rate increases have a negative impact on the residential home construction industry but a negligible (or neutral) effect on industries that produce consumer necessities such as prescription drugs or common grocery items.

Other economic indicators are associated with equity markets. Perhaps the most watched is the Dow Jones Industrial Average (DJIA), which is composed of 30 large industrial firms. When stock market indexes increase, consumers' discretionary income rises and there is often an increased demand for luxury items such as jewelry and automobiles. But when stock valuations decrease, demand for these items shrinks.

Despite the recent mediocre stock market and overall economic performance in the United States, the housing sector continued to be one of the bright spots. This is mainly due to a series of interest rate cuts by the Federal Reserve which, by mid-2003, led to the lowest mortgage rates since World War II.

## The Global Segment

There is an increasing trend for firms to expand their operations and market reach beyond the borders of their "home" country. Globalization provides both opportunities to access larger potential markets and a broad base of factors of production such as raw materials, labor, skilled managers, and technical professionals. However, such endeavors also carry many political, social, and economic risks.

Examples of important elements in the global segment include currency exchange rates, increasing global trade, the economic emergence of China, trade agreements among regional blocs (e.g., North American Free Trade Agreement, European Union), and the General Agreement on Tariffs and Trade (GATT) (lowering of tariffs). Increases in trade across national boundaries also provide benefits to air cargo and shipping industries but have a minimal impact on service industries such as bookkeeping and routine medical services. The emergence of China as an economic power has benefited many industries, such as construction, soft drinks, and computers. However, it has had a negative impact on the defense industry in the United States as diplomatic relations between the two nations improve.

Few industries are as global as the automobile industry. Consider just a few examples of how some of the key players expanded their reach into Latin America during the 1990s. Fiat built a new plant in Argentina, Volkswagen retooled a plant in Mexico to launch the New Beetle, DaimlerChrysler built a new plant as a joint venture with BMW to produce engines in Brazil, and General Motors built a new car factory in Brazil. Why the interest? In addition to the region's low wage rates and declining trade barriers, the population of 400 million is very attractive. But the real bonus lies in the 9-to-1 ratio of people to cars in the region compared to a 2-to-1 ratio in developed countries. With this region's growth expected to be in the 3 to 4 percent range for the first part of the century, sales should increase at a healthy rate.[34]

The extent of globalization is illustrated by the Norwegian shipping industry. Despite a small population of only 4.5 million, Norway developed the world's third-largest merchant fleet. And as the world's second-largest oil exporter, it has the vessels and equipment needed to service oil fields off its storm-swept coast. When the warship *USS Cole* was severely damaged by terrorists on October 12, 2000, it was returned to the United States from Yemen aboard a giant Norwegian-owned transport ship, the *Blue Marlin.* According to Frederik Steenbuch, manager of Oslo-based Offshore Heavy Transport, which owns the *Blue Marlin,* "This has nothing to do with Norway. It is purely international. The *Blue Marlin* was built in Taiwan, flies a Panamanian flag, and has a crew from Latvia. The key machinery on board was built in Korea under a Danish license."[35]

## Relationships among Elements of the General Environment

In our discussion of the general environment, we see many relationships among the various elements.[36] For example, two demographic trends in the United States, the aging of the population and regional population shifts, have important implications for the economic segment (in terms of tax policies to provide benefits to increasing numbers of older citizens) and the political segment (because the redistribution of seats in the U.S. House of Representatives among the states increases the power of some states and reduces the power of others). Another example is the emergence of information technology as a means to increase the rate of productivity gains in the United States and other developed countries. Such use of IT results in lower inflation (an important element of the economic segment) and helps offset costs associated with higher labor rates.

Maquiladoras are manufacturing and exporting assembly plants located in Mexico that are typically owned by United States, Japanese, and European companies. Their emergence, decline, and reemergence over time illustrate how many elements of the general environment can be highly interrelated. We address this issue in Strategy Spotlight 2.6.

The effects of a trend or event in the general environment vary across industries. Governmental legislation (political/legal event) to permit the importation of prescription drugs from foreign countries is a very positive development for drugstores but a very negative event for drug manufacturers in the United States. Exhibit 2.5 on page 59 provides other examples of how the impact of trends or events in the general environment can vary across industries.

# >>The Competitive Environment

In addition to the general environment, managers must also consider the competitive environment (also sometimes referred to as the task or industry environment). The nature of competition in an industry, as well as the profitability of a firm, is often more directly influenced by developments in the competitive environment.

The competitive environment consists of many factors that are particularly relevant to a firm's strategy. These include competitors (existing or potential), customers, and suppliers. Potential competitors may include a supplier considering forward integration, such as an automobile manufacturer acquiring a rental car company, or a firm in an entirely new industry introducing a similar product that uses a more efficient technology.

In the following sections, we will discuss key concepts and analytical techniques that managers should use to assess their competitive environments. First, we examine Michael Porter's five-forces model that illustrates how these forces can be used to explain low profitability in an industry.[37] Then, we address the concept of strategic groups. This concept demonstrates that even within an industry it is often useful to group firms on the basis of similarities of their strategies. As we will see, competition tends to be more intense among firms *within* a strategic group than between strategic groups.

## Maquiladoras: Staging a Comeback

Maquiladoras originated in Mexico in the 1960s. *Maquiladora* is a Spanish word that refers to manufacturing and export assembly plants that are owned by U.S., Japanese, and European companies. Maquiladoras primarily produce electronic equipment, clothing, plastics, furniture, appliances, and auto parts, and today 80 percent of the goods produced by maquiladoras in Mexico are shipped to the United States. The plants are quite prevalent in Mexican cities such as Tijuana, Ciudad Juarez, and Matamoros that lie directly across the border from the interstate highway–connected U.S. cities of San Diego and El Paso and Brownsville, Texas.

By the late 1990s, the number of plants peaked at about 3,000 and employed over a million Mexican workers. However, from 2000 to 2003, employment declined as the competition for cheaper labor elsewhere in the world, especially China, intensified. In 2004, the sector began showing a dramatic increase. In June 2004, for example, the country's maquiladoras exported goods worth $7.72 billion—a figure that is 20 percent higher than a year earlier and an all-time monthly record. And 55,000 new maquila jobs were created in 2004.

What has caused the revitalization? There are several factors that demonstrate the interdependence between political–legal, economic, and global elements of the general environment.

First, there is the recovery in the U.S. economy. Also, the cheaper peso—down 8 percent against the dollar during a recent 1-year period—has enhanced Mexico's allure for companies looking to cut costs.

Second, there are important logistical factors that are associated with the large distance between the United States and China. Although much of the production that has been relocated to China is not expected to return, many manufacturers are favoring Mexico because they believe that the lower Chinese wages do not compensate for the logistical difficulties of supplying the U.S. market from such a great distance. According to consultant Richard N. Sinkin of Inter-American Holdings Co., "Yeah, China's great for that dollar-a-day labor, but I can't wait 30 days to get my product to a customer." And for large goods, such as cars and side-by-side refrigerators, shipping costs from China can outrun savings on labor.

Third, political issues also come into play. Heeding investor complaints, the government of Mexican president Vicente Fox has postponed until 2008 a new fiscal regime that would require maquiladora owners to pay corporate taxes in Mexico. Custom procedures also have been streamlined. Mexico recently got a boost from the U.S. Department of Commerce when it increased duties on Chinese-made TV sets to as much as 78 percent to combat "dumping" of foreign products. This measure is a boon for Japanese, Korean, and Mexican TV manufacturers based in Tijuana and Ciudad Jaurez. Another factor favoring Mexico cited by many high-tech companies is that China has weak protection of intellectual property rights.

Sources: Smith, G. 2004. Made in the maquilas—Again. *BusinessWeek*, August 16: 45; and Brezosky, L. 2004. Border factories stage a comeback in Mexico. *Dallas Morning News*, December 28: 6A.

## Porter's Five-Forces Model of Industry Competition

The "five-forces" model developed by Michael E. Porter has been the most commonly used analytical tool for examining the competitive environment. It describes the competitive environment in terms of five basic competitive forces.[38]

1. The threat of new entrants.
2. The bargaining power of buyers.
3. The bargaining power of suppliers.
4. The threat of substitute products and services.
5. The intensity of rivalry among competitors in an industry.

Each of these forces affects a firm's ability to compete in a given market. Together, they determine the profit potential for a particular industry. The model is shown in Exhibit 2.6 on page 60. As a manager, you should be familiar with the five-forces model for several reasons. It helps you decide whether your firm should remain in or exit an industry. It provides the rationale for increasing or decreasing resource commitments. The model helps you assess how to improve your firm's competitive position with regard to each of

Exhibit 2.5

The Impact of General Environmental Trends on Various Industries

| Segment/Trends and Events | Industry | Positive | Neutral | Negative |
|---|---|:---:|:---:|:---:|
| **Demographic** | | | | |
| Aging population | Health care | ✓ | | |
| | Baby products | | | ✓ |
| Rising affluence | Brokerage services | ✓ | | |
| | Fast foods | | | ✓ |
| | Upscale pets and supplies | ✓ | | |
| **Sociocultural** | | | | |
| More women in the workforce | Clothing | ✓ | | |
| | Baking products (staples) | | | ✓ |
| Greater concern for health and fitness | Home exercise equipment | ✓ | | |
| | Meat products | | | ✓ |
| **Political/legal** | | | | |
| Tort reform | Legal services | | | ✓ |
| | Auto manufacturing | ✓ | | |
| Americans with Disabilities Act (ADA) | Retail | | | ✓ |
| | Manufacturers of elevators, escalators, and ramps | ✓ | | |
| **Technological** | | | | |
| Genetic engineering | Pharmaceutical | ✓ | | |
| | Publishing | | ✓ | |
| Pollution/global warming | Engineering services | ✓ | | |
| | Petroleum | | | ✓ |
| **Economic** | | | | |
| Interest rate increases | Residential construction | | | ✓ |
| | Most common grocery products | | ✓ | |
| **Global** | | | | |
| Increasing global trade | Shipping | ✓ | | |
| | Personal service | | ✓ | |
| Emergence of China as an economic power | Soft drinks | ✓ | | |
| | Defense | | | ✓ |

the five forces. For example (and looking ahead a bit), you can use insights provided by the five-forces model to create higher entry barriers that discourage new rivals from competing with you.[39] Or you may develop strong relationships with your distribution channels. You may decide to find suppliers who satisfy the price/performance criteria needed to make your product or service a top performer.

*The Threat of New Entrants*    The threat of new entrants refers to the possibility that the profits of established firms in the industry may be eroded by new competitors.[40] The extent of the threat depends on existing barriers to entry and the combined reactions

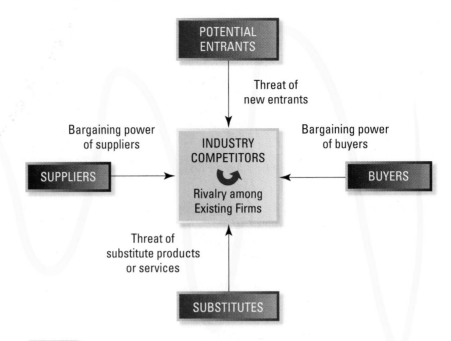

**Exhibit 2.6**    **Porter's Five-Forces Model of Industry Competition**

Source: Reprinted with permission of The Free Press, a division of Simon & Schuster Adult Publishing Group, from *Competitive Strategy: Techniques for Analyzing Industries and Competitors* by Michael E. Porter. Copyright © 1980, 1998 by The Free Press. All rights reserved.

from existing competitors. If entry barriers are high and/or the newcomer can anticipate a sharp retaliation from established competitors, the threat of entry is low. These circumstances discourage new competitors. There are six major sources of entry barriers.

***Economies of Scale*** Economies of scale refers to spreading the costs of production over the number of units produced. The cost of a product per unit declines as the absolute volume per period increases. This deters entry by forcing the entrant to come in at a large scale and risk strong reaction from existing firms or come in at a small scale and accept a cost disadvantage. Both are undesirable options.

***Product Differentiation*** When existing competitors have strong brand identification and customer loyalty, differentiation creates a barrier to entry by forcing entrants to spend heavily to overcome existing customer loyalties.

***Capital Requirements*** The need to invest large financial resources to compete creates a barrier to entry, especially if the capital is required for risky or unrecoverable up-front advertising or research and development (R&D).

***Switching Costs*** A barrier to entry is created by the existence of one-time costs that the buyer faces when switching from one supplier's product or service to another.

***Access to Distribution Channels*** The new entrant's need to secure distribution for its product can create a barrier to entry.

***Cost Disadvantages Independent of Scale*** Some existing competitors may have advantages that are independent of size or economies of scale. These derive from:

- Proprietary product
- Favorable access to raw materials

- Government subsidies
- Favorable government policies

In an environment where few, if any, of these entry barriers are present, the threat of new entry is high. For example, if a new firm can launch its business with a low capital investment and operate efficiently despite its small scale of operation, it is likely to be a threat. One company that failed because of low entry barriers in an industry is ProCD.[41] You probably never heard of this company. It didn't last very long. ProCD provides an example of a firm that failed because it entered an industry with very low entry barriers.

The story begins in 1986 when Nynex (a Baby Bell company) issued the first electronic phone book, a compact disk containing all listings for the New York City area. It charged $10,000 per copy and sold the CDs to the FBI, IRS, and other large commercial and government organizations. James Bryant, the Nynex executive in charge of the project, smelled a fantastic business opportunity. He quit Nynex and set up his own firm, ProCD, with the ambitious goal of producing an electronic directory covering the entire United States.

As expected, the telephone companies, fearing an attack on their highly profitable Yellow Pages business, refused to license digital copies of their listings to this upstart. Bryant was not deterred. He traveled to Beijing and hired Chinese workers at $3.50 a day to type every listing from every U.S. telephone book into a database. The result contained more than 70 million phone numbers and was used to create a master disk that enabled ProCD to make hundreds of thousands of copies. Each CD sold for hundreds of dollars and cost less than a dollar each to produce.

It was a profitable business indeed! However, success was fleeting. Competitors such as Digital Directory Assistance and American Business Information quickly launched competing products with the same information. Since customers couldn't tell one product from the next, the players were forced to compete on price alone. Prices for the CD soon plummeted to a few dollars each. A high-priced, high-margin product just months earlier, the CD phone book became little more than a cheap commodity.

*The Bargaining Power of Buyers*   Buyers threaten an industry by forcing down prices, bargaining for higher quality or more services, and playing competitors against each other. These actions erode industry profitability.[42] The power of each large buyer group depends on attributes of the market situation and the importance of purchases from that group compared with the industry's overall business. A buyer group is powerful under the following conditions:

- *It is concentrated or purchases large volumes relative to seller sales.* If a large percentage of a supplier's sales are purchased by a single buyer, the importance of the buyer's business to the supplier increases. Large-volume buyers also are powerful in industries with high fixed costs (e.g., steel manufacturing).
- *The products it purchases from the industry are standard or undifferentiated.* Confident they can always find alternative suppliers, buyers play one company against the other, as in commodity grain products.
- *The buyer faces few switching costs.* Switching costs lock the buyer to particular sellers. Conversely, the buyer's power is enhanced if the seller faces high switching costs.
- *It earns low profits.* Low profits create incentives to lower purchasing costs. On the other hand, highly profitable buyers are generally less price sensitive.
- *The buyers pose a credible threat of backward integration.* If buyers are either partially integrated or pose a credible threat of backward integration, they are typically able to secure bargaining concessions.

- **The industry's product is unimportant to the quality of the buyer's products or services.** When the quality of the buyer's products is not affected by the industry's product, the buyer is more price sensitive.

At times, a firm or set of firms in an industry may increase its buyer power by using the services of a third party. FreeMarkets Online is one such third party.[43] Pittsburgh-based FreeMarkets has developed software enabling large industrial buyers to organize online auctions for qualified suppliers of semistandard parts such as fabricated components, packaging materials, metal stampings, and services. By aggregating buyers, FreeMarkets increases the buyers' bargaining power. The results are impressive. In its first 48 auctions, most participating companies saved over 15 percent; some saved as much as 50 percent.

*The Bargaining Power of Suppliers*   Suppliers can exert bargaining power over participants in an industry by threatening to raise prices or reduce the quality of purchased goods and services. Powerful suppliers can squeeze the profitability of firms in an industry so far that they can't recover the costs of raw material inputs.[44] The factors that make suppliers powerful tend to mirror those that make buyers powerful. A supplier group will be powerful in the following circumstances:

- **The supplier group is dominated by a few companies and is more concentrated (few firms dominate the industry) than the industry it sells to.** Suppliers selling to fragmented industries influence prices, quality, and terms.
- **The supplier group is not obliged to contend with substitute products for sale to the industry.** The power of even large, powerful suppliers can be checked if they compete with substitutes.
- **The industry is not an important customer of the supplier group.** When suppliers sell to several industries and a particular industry does not represent a significant fraction of its sales, suppliers are more prone to exert power.
- **The supplier's product is an important input to the buyer's business.** When such inputs are important to the success of the buyer's manufacturing process or product quality, the bargaining power of suppliers is high.
- **The supplier group's products are differentiated or it has built up switching costs for the buyer.** Differentiation or switching costs facing the buyers cut off their options to play one supplier against another.
- **The supplier group poses a credible threat of forward integration.** This provides a check against the industry's ability to improve the terms by which it purchases.

When considering supplier power, we focus on companies that supply raw materials, equipment, machinery, and associated services. But the supply of labor is also an important input to businesses, and labor's power varies over time and across occupations and industries. As we enter the 21st century, the outlook is not very good for semiskilled and unskilled laborers. Annual wage gains before inflation is taken into account—typically a good measure of workers' bargaining clout in the labor market—have remained in the 3 percent range for much of the 1990s.[45] When the CPI averaged around 2 percent, that provided employees with pay increases that exceeded inflation. With higher consumer prices, however, real wage gains (wage increases above the inflation rate) have been virtually nonexistent recently.

Workers with the right skills and jobs have enjoyed the spoils of the New Economy and will likely continue to do so. However, many other employees face the same forces that kept wages flat in the early 1990s: high immigration, deunionization, and globalization. For example, steel imports surged in 2000, threatening the jobs of many U.S. steelworkers. Not surprisingly, members of the United Steel Workers (USW) have been

## Enhancing Supplier Power: The Creation of Delta Pride Catfish

The formation of Delta Pride Catfish in 1981 is an example of the power that a group of suppliers can attain if they exercise the threat of forward integration. Catfish farmers in Mississippi had historically supplied their harvest to processing plants run by large agribusiness firms such as ConAgra and Farm Fresh. When the farmers increased their production of catfish in response to growing demand in the early 1970s, they found, much to their chagrin, that processors were holding back on their plans to increase their processing capabilities in hopes of higher retail prices for catfish.

Source: Cargile, D. 2005. Personal communication. (Vice President of Sales, Delta Pride Catfish, Inc.), February 2; Anonymous. 2003. Delta Pride Catfish names Steve Osso President and CEO. www.deltabusiness.journal.com, February; and Fritz, M. 1988. Agribusiness: Catfish story. *Forbes,* December 12: 37.

What action did the farmers take? They responded by forming a cooperative, raising $4.5 million, and constructing their own processing plant, which they supplied themselves. Within two years, ConAgra's market share had dropped from 35 percent to 11 percent, and Farm Fresh's market share fell by over 20 percent.

By the late 1980s, Delta Pride controlled over 40 percent of the 280-million-pound-per-year U.S. catfish market. It has continued to grow by including value-added products such as breaded and marinated catfish products. Recently it introduced Country Crisp Catfish Strips, a bakeable, breaded product with country-style seasoning. By 2005, Delta Pride had more than 500 employees. Its approximately 100 shareholders are mostly catfish farmers who own more than 60,000 acres of catfish production ponds and produce more than 200 million pounds of live catfish each year.

---

forced to accept below-inflation pay increases. On September 1, 2000, 900 USW members at AK Steel Corp.'s Ashland, Kentucky, facility approved a pay hike of only 2.6 percent a year for the next five years. Said Roy Murray, a USW official, "We didn't want to be out there demanding more money when the industry is on its heels."

Strategy Spotlight 2.7 discusses how catfish farmers were able to enhance their bargaining power vis-à-vis their customers—large agribusiness firms—by banding together to form a cooperative.

*The Threat of Substitute Products and Services*    All firms within an industry compete with industries producing substitute products and services. Substitutes limit the potential returns of an industry by placing a ceiling on the prices that firms in that industry can profitably charge. The more attractive the price/performance ratio of substitute products, the tighter the lid on an industry's profits.

Identifying substitute products involves searching for other products or services that can perform the same function as the industry's offerings. This is a subtle task, one that leads a manager into businesses seemingly far removed from the industry. For example, the airline industry might not consider video cameras much of a threat. But as digital technology has improved and wireless and other forms of telecommunication have become more efficient, teleconferencing has become a viable substitute for business travel for many executives.

Teleconferencing can save both time and money, as IBM found out with its "Manager Jam" idea.[46] Currently, with 319,000 employees scattered around six continents, it is one of the world's largest businesses (including 32,000 managers) and can be a pretty confusing place. The shift to an increasingly mobile workplace means many managers supervise employees they rarely see face-to-face. To enhance coordination, Samuel Palmisano, IBM's new CEO, launched one of his first big initiatives: a two-year program exploring the role of the manager in the 21st century. "Manager Jam," as the project was nicknamed, was a 48-hour real-time Web event in which managers from 50 different countries swapped ideas and strategies for dealing with problems shared by all of them, regardless of geography. Some 8,100 managers logged on to the company's intranet to participate in the discussion forums.

*The Intensity of Rivalry among Competitors in an Industry*    Rivalry among existing competitors takes the form of jockeying for position. Firms use tactics like price competition, advertising battles, product introductions, and increased customer service or warranties. Rivalry occurs when competitors sense the pressure or act on an opportunity to improve their position.

Some forms of competition, such as price competition, are typically highly destabilizing and are likely to erode the average level of profitability in an industry.[47] Rivals easily match price cuts, an action that lowers profits for all firms. On the other hand, advertising battles expand overall demand or enhance the level of product differentiation for the benefit of all firms in the industry. Rivalry, of course, differs across industries. In some instances it is characterized as warlike, bitter, or cutthroat, whereas in other industries it is referred to as polite and gentlemanly. Intense rivalry is the result of several interacting factors, including the following:

- ***Numerous or equally balanced competitors.*** When there are many firms in an industry, the likelihood of mavericks is great. Some firms believe they can make moves without being noticed. Even when there are relatively few firms, and they are nearly equal in size and resources, instability results from fighting among companies having the resources for sustained and vigorous retaliation.
- ***Slow industry growth.*** Slow industry growth turns competition into a fight for market share, since firms seek to expand their sales.
- ***High fixed or storage costs.*** High fixed costs create strong pressures for all firms to increase capacity. Excess capacity often leads to escalating price cutting.
- ***Lack of differentiation or switching costs.*** Where the product or service is perceived as a commodity or near commodity, the buyer's choice is typically based on price and service, resulting in pressures for intense price and service competition. Lack of switching costs, described earlier, has the same effect.
- ***Capacity augmented in large increments.*** Where economies of scale require that capacity must be added in large increments, capacity additions can be very disruptive to the industry supply/demand balance.
- ***High exit barriers.*** Exit barriers are economic, strategic, and emotional factors that keep firms competing even though they may be earning low or negative returns on their investments. Some exit barriers are specialized assets, fixed costs of exit, strategic interrelationships (e.g., relationships between the business units and others within a company in terms of image, marketing, shared facilities, and so on), emotional barriers, and government and social pressures (e.g., governmental discouragement of exit out of concern for job loss).

Rivalry between firms is often based solely on price, but it can involve other factors. Take Pfizer's market position in the impotence treatment market. Pfizer was the first pharmaceutical firm to develop Viagra, a drug that treats impotence. International sales of Viagra were $332 million during a recent quarter. There are currently 30 million prescriptions for the drug. Pfizer would like to keep competitors from challenging this lucrative position.

In several countries, the United Kingdom among them, Pfizer faced a lawsuit by Eli Lilly & Co. and Icos Corp. challenging its patent protection. These two pharmaceutical firms recently entered into a joint venture to market Cialis, a drug to compete with Viagra. The U.K. courts agreed and lifted the patent.

This opened the door for Eli Lilly and Icos to proceed with challenging Pfizer's market position. Because Cialis has fewer side effects than Viagra, the drug has the potential to rapidly decrease Pfizer's market share in the United Kingdom if physicians switch prescriptions from Viagra to Cialis. If future patent challenges are successful, Pfizer may see its sales of Viagra erode rapidly. With projected annual sales of Cialis at $1 billion, Pfizer has reason to worry. With FDA approval, sales of Cialis could cause those of Viagra to plummet in the United States, further eroding Pfizer's market share.[48] But Pfizer is hardly standing still. It recently doubled its advertising expenditures on Viagra.

*Using Industry Analysis: A Few Caveats*   For industry analysis to be valuable, a company must collect and evaluate a wide variety of information from many sources. As the trend toward globalization accelerates, information on foreign markets as well as on a wider variety of competitors, suppliers, customers, substitutes, and potential new entrants becomes more critical. Industry analysis helps a firm not only to evaluate the profit potential of an industry, but also to consider various ways to strengthen its position vis-à-vis the five forces.

Five-forces analysis implicitly assumes a zero-sum game, determining how a firm can enhance its position relative to the forces. Yet such an approach can often be shortsighted; that is, it can overlook the many potential benefits of developing constructive win–win relationships with suppliers and customers. Establishing long-term mutually beneficial relationships with suppliers improves a firm's ability to implement just-in-time (JIT) inventory systems, which let it manage inventories better and respond quickly to market demands. A recent study found that if a company exploits its powerful position against a supplier, that action may come back to haunt the company if the position of power changes.[49] Further, by working together as partners, suppliers and manufacturers can provide the greatest value at the lowest possible cost. Later chapters address such collaborative relationships and how they can be made most effective.

The five-forces analysis also has been criticized for being essentially a static analysis. External forces as well as strategies of individual firms are continually changing the structure of all industries. The search for a dynamic theory of strategy has led to greater use of game theory in industrial organization economics research and strategy research. Based on game-theoretic considerations, Brandenburger and Nalebuff recently introduced the concept of the value net,[50] which in many ways is an extension of the five-forces analysis. It is illustrated in Exhibit 2.7. The value net represents all the players in the game and analyzes how their interactions affect a firm's ability to generate and appropriate value. The vertical dimension of the net includes suppliers and customers. The firm has direct transactions with them. On the horizontal dimension are substitutes and complements, players with whom a firm interacts but may not necessarily transact. The concept of complementors is perhaps the single most important contribution of value net analysis and is explained in more detail below.

Complements typically are products or services that have a potential impact on the value of a firm's own products or services. Those who produce complements are usually referred to as complementors. Powerful hardware is of no value to a user unless there is software that runs on it. Similarly, new and better software is possible only if the hardware on which it can be run is available. This is equally true in the video game industry, where the sales of game consoles and video games complement each other. Nintendo's success in the early 1990s was a result of their ability to manage their relationship with their complementors. They built a security chip into the hardware and then licensed the right to develop games to outside firms. These firms paid a royalty to Nintendo for each copy of the game sold. The royalty revenue enabled Nintendo to sell game consoles at

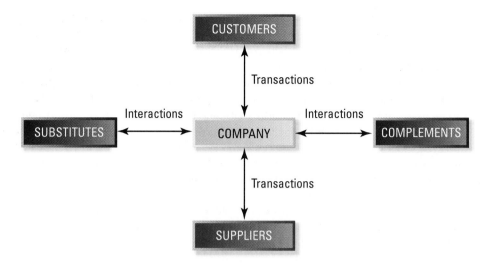

close to their cost, thereby increasing their market share, which, in turn, caused more games to be sold and more royalties to be generated.

## Industry Analysis: A Dynamic Perspective

One of the criticisms often leveled against traditional industry analysis is that it is static in nature. As we are all aware, the competitive landscape in most industries is undergoing very rapid changes due to changes in technology and customer preferences. While this does not diminish the value of the five-forces analysis at a given point in time, we need additional tools and frameworks to understand and analyze the rapid changes taking place in most industries. One very useful framework for the analysis of industry evolution has been proposed by Professor Anita McGahan of Boston University.[51] Her analysis is based on the identification of the *core activities* and the *core assets* of an industry and the threats they face. She suggests that an industry may follow one of four possible evolutionary trajectories based on two types of threats of obsolescence.

First is the threat of obsolescence faced by the *core activities* of the firm. Core activities are activities that historically have generated profits for the industry. For example, because consumers today can find all information they need to make a purchasing decision on an automobile, such as price, performance, reliability, and technical characteristics, by going online, the core selling activities of a car dealership are no longer of great value to the customer. Second is the threat of obsolescence faced by an industry's *core assets.* These refer to the resources, knowledge, and brand capital possessed by firms in an industry. For example, in the video rental industry, the core assets were traditionally locations and a wide selection. In an era of video downloads, location is of little value and typical rental outlets cannot begin to match the enormous selection offered by firms such as Netflix. The four change trajectories followed by industries based on possible combinations of threats to core activities and core assets are described in the following paragraphs.

*Radical change* occurs when both core activities and core assets face the threat of obsolescence. For example, the overnight letter delivery industry is beginning to experience this problem. The availability of cheap but instantaneous means of document delivery through fax machines and the Internet has made the core assets (delivery trucks, airplanes, and a central hub) and core activities (document tracking) of firms such as Federal Express suddenly less relevant. A similar situation was faced by typewriter manufacturers two decades ago when relatively inexpensive PCs became widely available.

*Intermediating change* occurs when core assets are not threatened but core activities are under threat. An example of an industry facing intermediating change is automobile dealerships. This occurs for a variety of reasons. First, as mentioned earlier, prospective customers can get all the information they need online. Second, as the quality and longevity of cars improve, individual purchases have become less frequent. Third, car manufacturers are now sharing the task of customer relations with the dealers. In some cases, they have even completely taken over this function. Finally, inventory management and financing are now subject to significant economies of scale that only large, integrated companies can take advantage of.

When core assets are threatened, but core activities are not, industries tend to follow the *creative change* trajectory. Examples of industries experiencing creative change include the film production industry, pharmaceuticals, oil and gas exploration, and prepackaged software. In each of these cases, there is rapid asset turnover but relatively stable relationships with suppliers and customers. For example in the pharmaceutical industry, patents for some drugs expire while new drugs get FDA approval, but the core activities of commercialization and marketing continue to be relevant.

Finally, *progressive change* occurs in industries where neither core assets nor core activities face imminent threat of obsolescence. Change does occur, but it is within the existing framework of the industry. At any given moment, changes may be incremental, but over time they cumulate to substantial changes. The commercial airline industry and the discount retailing industry are examples of two industries where progressive change has been occurring. The suppliers and the customers are, by and large, the same. The core assets and activities have changed only incrementally in any given year, but over the last decade both these industries have experienced significant changes.

Exhibit 2.8 presents the four evolutionary trajectories and the conditions under which they are likely to occur.

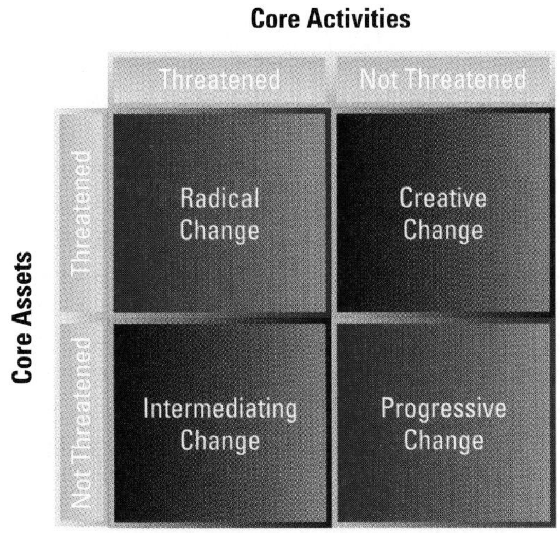

**Core Activities**

**Exhibit 2.8**   **Four Evolutionary Trajectories of Industry Change**

Each of the above four change trajectories unfolds over many years, sometimes even decades. This gives firms within an industry time to respond to the changes. Fighting change, on the other hand, seldom succeeds. When faced with *radical* or *intermediating changes,* it is wise to aggressively pursue profits in the near term while avoiding investments that could reduce strategic flexibility in the future. Another response is alliances, often with rivals, to protect common interests and defend against new competition from outsiders. For firms facing *radical change,* one option is diversification. FedEx's acquisition of Kinko's fits into this category. In order to succeed, firms facing *intermediating change* must find unconventional ways to extract profits from their core assets. For example, threatened by eBay, traditional auctioneers have responded by capitalizing on their appraisal expertise. That is, for a fee, they will certify the value of the items being sold online.

Strategies for firms facing *creative change* include spreading the risk of new-project development over a portfolio of assets as well as outsourcing project management and development tasks. Successful companies in *progressive change* industries carve out distinct positions based on geographic, technical, or marketing expertise. They also develop a system of interrelated activities that are defensible against competitors. Wal-Mart and Southwest Airlines are excellent examples of this approach. Their strategies are entirely observable and easy to understand. But they are the result of hundreds of incremental changes compounding over time and thus are difficult for rivals to match.

Industries also can change as a result of specific actions by individual firms. In Chapter 5, we will be revisiting this topic when we discuss how innovations can change the competitive landscape of an industry.

## Strategic Groups within Industries

In an industry analysis, two assumptions are unassailable: (1) No two firms are totally different, and (2) no two firms are exactly the same. The issue becomes one of identifying groups of firms that are more similar to each other than firms that are not, otherwise known as strategic groups.[52] This is important because rivalry tends to be greater among firms that are alike. Strategic groups are clusters of firms that share similar strategies. After all, is Kmart more concerned about Nordstrom or Wal-Mart? Is Mercedes more concerned about Hyundai or BMW? The answers are straightforward.[53]

These examples are not meant to trivialize the strategic groups concept. Classifying an industry into strategic groups involves judgment. If it is useful as an analytical tool, we must exercise caution in deciding what dimensions to use to map these firms. Dimensions include breadth of product and geographic scope, price/quality, degree of vertical integration, type of distribution (e.g., dealers, mass merchandisers, private label), and so on. Dimensions should also be selected to reflect the variety of strategic combinations in an industry. For example, if all firms in an industry have roughly the same level of product differentiation (or R&D intensity), this would not be a good dimension to select.

What value is the strategic groups concept as an analytical tool? First, strategic groupings help a firm identify barriers to mobility that protect a group from attacks by other groups.[54] Mobility barriers are factors that deter the movement of firms from one strategic position to another. For example, in the chainsaw industry, the major barriers protecting the high-quality/dealer-oriented group are technology, brand image, and an established network of servicing dealers.

The second value of strategic grouping is that it helps a firm identify groups whose competitive position may be marginal or tenuous. We may anticipate that these competitors may exit the industry or try to move into another group. This has been the case in recent years in the retail department store industry, where firms such as JCPenney and Sears have experienced extremely difficult times because they were stuck in the middle,

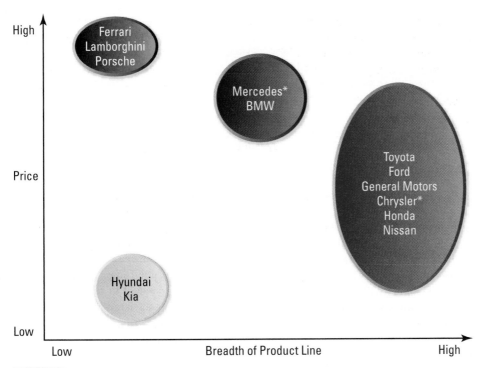

**Exhibit 2.9**  **The World Automobile Industry: Strategic Groups**

*Chrysler and Mercedes (part of DaimlerChrysler) are separated for purposes of illustration.

Note: Members of each strategic group are not inclusive, only illustrative.

neither an aggressive discount player like Wal-Mart nor a prestigious upscale player like Neiman Marcus.

Third, strategic groupings help chart the future directions of firms' strategies. Arrows emanating from each strategic group can represent the direction in which the group (or a firm within the group) seems to be moving. If all strategic groups are moving in a similar direction, this could indicate a high degree of future volatility and intensity of competition. In the automobile industry, for example, the competition in the minivan and sport utility segments has intensified in recent years as many firms have entered those product segments.

Fourth, strategic groups are helpful in thinking through the implications of each industry trend for the strategic group as a whole. Is the trend decreasing the viability of a group? If so, in what direction should the strategic group move? Is the trend increasing or decreasing entry barriers in a given group? Will the trend decrease the ability of one group to separate itself from other groups? Such analysis can help in making predictions about industry evolution. A sharp increase in interest rates, for example, would tend to have less impact on providers of higher-priced goods (e.g., Porsches) than on providers of lower-priced goods (e.g., Dodge Neons). The Dodge Neon customer base is much more price sensitive.

Exhibit 2.9 provides a strategic grouping of the worldwide automobile industry.[55] The firms in each group are representative; not all firms are included in the mapping. We have identified four strategic groups. In the top left-hand corner are high-end luxury automakers who focus on a very narrow product market. Most of the cars produced by the members of this group cost well over $100,000. Some cost many times that amount. The Ferrari F50 costs roughly $550,000 and the Lamborghini L147 $300,000[56] (in case you were wondering how to spend your employment signing bonus). Players in this market have a very exclusive clientele and face little rivalry from other strategic groups. At the other extreme, in the lower left-hand corner is a strategic group that has low-price/quality attributes and targets a narrow market. These players, Hyundai and Kia, limit competition from other strategic groups by pricing their products very low. The third group (near the middle) consists of firms high in product pricing/quality and average in their product-line breadth. The final group (at the far right) consists of firms with a broad range of products and multiple price points. These firms have entries that compete at both the lower end of the market (e.g., the Ford Focus) and the higher end (e.g., Chevrolet Corvette).

The auto market has been very dynamic and competition has intensified in recent years. Many firms in different strategic groups compete in the same product markets, such as minivans and sport utility vehicles. In the late 1990s Mercedes entered the fray with its M series, and Porsche has recent entry as well with its Cayenne, a 2004 model. Some players are also going more upscale with their product offerings. Recently, Hyundai introduced its XG300, priced at over $25,000 for a fully loaded model. This brings Hyundai into direct competition with entries from other strategic groups such as Toyota's Camry and Honda's Accord. Hyundai is offering an extensive warranty (10 years, 100,000 miles) in an effort to offset customer perceptions of their lower quality. Perhaps Ford has made the most notable efforts to go upscale. Not content to rely solely on the Lincoln nameplate to attract high-ticket buyers, Ford, like other large players, has gone on an acquisition binge. It recently acquired Volvo, Land Rover, Jaguar, and Aston Martin. Ford is aggressively accelerating its forecasted sales for each of these brands.[57] To further intensify competition, some key automakers are providing offerings in lower-priced segments. Mercedes and BMW, with their C-class and 3-series, respectively, are well-known examples. Such cars, priced in the low $30,000s, compete more directly with products from broad-line manufacturers like Ford, General Motors, and Toyota.

These new products are competing in an industry that has experienced relatively flat unit sales in the first half of this decade.[58] In addition, high-incentive–laden offerings appear to be losing some of their appeal to consumers, and there are higher levels of inventory at dealerships. Further, since manufacturers have maintained, if not increased, production schedules and plant capacity, overall competition should intensify. Don't be surprised, therefore, if rebates and discounting continue on most models.

## Summary

Managers must analyze the external environment to minimize or eliminate threats and exploit opportunities. This involves a continuous process of environmental scanning and monitoring as well as obtaining competitive intelligence on present and potential rivals. These activities provide valuable inputs for developing forecasts. In addition, many firms use scenario planning to anticipate and respond to volatile and disruptive environmental changes.

We identified two types of environment: the general environment and the competitive environment. The six segments of the general environment are demographic, sociocultural, political/legal, technological, economic, and global. Trends and events occurring in these segments, such as the aging of the population, higher percentages of women in the workplace, governmental legislation, and increasing (or decreasing) interest rates, can have a dramatic effect on a firm. A given trend or event may have a positive impact on some industries and a negative, neutral, or no impact at all on others.

The competitive environment consists of industry-related factors and has a more direct impact than the general environment. Porter's five-forces model of industry analysis includes the threat of new entrants, buyer power, supplier power, threat of substitutes, and rivalry among competitors. The intensity of these factors determines, in large part, the average expected level of profitability in an industry. A sound awareness of such factors, both individually and in combination, is beneficial not only for deciding what industries to enter but also for assessing how a firm can improve its competitive position. The limitations of five-forces analysis include its static nature and its inability to acknowledge the role of complementors. Given the rapid, unpredictable change that is occurring in many industries, we also discussed industry analysis from a dynamic perspective. Although we addressed the general environment and competitive environment in separate sections, they are quite interdependent. A given environmental trend or event, such as changes in the ethnic composition of a population or a technological innovation, typically has a much greater impact on some industries than on others.

The concept of strategic groups is also important to the external environment of a firm. No two organizations are completely different nor are they exactly the same. The question is how to group firms in an industry on the basis of similarities in their resources and strategies. The strategic groups concept is valuable for determining mobility barriers across groups, identifying groups with marginal competitive positions, charting the future directions of firm strategies, and assessing the implications of industry trends for the strategic group as a whole.

## Summary Review Questions

1. Why must managers be aware of a firm's external environment?
2. What is gathering and analyzing competitive intelligence and why is it important for firms to engage in it?
3. Discuss and describe the six elements of the external environment.
4. Select one of these elements and describe some changes relating to it in an industry that interests you.
5. Describe how the five forces can be used to determine the average expected profitability in an industry.
6. What are some of the limitations (or caveats) in using five-forces analysis?
7. Explain how the general environment and industry environment are highly related. How can such interrelationships affect the profitability of a firm or industry?
8. Explain the concept of strategic groups. What are the performance implications?

Select one of the following industries: personal computers, airlines, or automobiles. For this industry, evaluate the strength of each of Porter's five forces as well as complementors.

## Experiential Exercise

| Industry Force | High? Medium? Low? | Why? |
| --- | --- | --- |
| **1.** Threat of new entrants | | |
| **2.** Power of buyers | | |
| **3.** Power of suppliers | | |
| **4.** Power of substitutes | | |
| **5.** Rivalry among competitors | | |
| **6.** Complementors | | |

# Application Questions Exercises

1. Imagine yourself as the CEO of a large firm in an industry in which you are interested. Please (1) identify major trends in the general environment, (2) analyze their impact on the firm, and (3) identify major sources of information to monitor these trends. (Use Internet and library resources.)

2. Analyze movements across the strategic groups in the U.S. retail industry. How do these movements within this industry change the nature of competition?

3. What are the major trends in the general environment that have impacted the U.S. pharmaceutical industry?

4. Go to the Internet and look up www.kroger.com. What are some of the five forces driving industry competition that are affecting the profitability of this firm?

# Ethics Questions

1. What are some of the legal and ethical issues involved in collecting competitor intelligence in the following situations?

   a. Hotel A sends an employee posing as a potential client to Hotel B to find out who Hotel B's major corporate customers are.

   b. A firm hires an MBA student to collect information directly from a competitor while claiming the information is for a course project.

   c. A firm advertises a nonexistent position and interviews a rival's employees with the intention of obtaining competitor information.

2. What are some of the ethical implications that arise when a firm tries to exploit its power over a supplier?

# References

1. Grow, B. 2004. Can Wonder Bread rise again? *BusinessWeek,* October 18: 108, 110; Horovitz, B. 2004. Twinkie maker files for protection, gets new CEO. *USA Today,* September 22: 3B; Goglo, P. 2004. Interstate Bakeries' Twinkie defense. *BusinessWeek Online,* September 23: np; and Higgins, K. T. 2003. The world's top 100. *Food Engineering,* October: 58, 64–70.

2. Hamel, G., & Prahalad, C. K. 1994. *Competing for the future.* Boston: Harvard Business School Press.

3. Drucker, P. F. 1994. Theory of the business. *Harvard Business Review,* 72: 95–104.

4. The examples of Novell and Silicon Graphics draw on Pickering, C. I. 1998. Sorry . . . Try again next year. *Forbes ASAP,* February 23: 82–83.

5. For an insightful discussion on managers' assessment of the external environment, refer to Sutcliffe, K. M., & Weber, K. 2003. The high cost of accurate knowledge. *Harvard Business Review,* 81(5): 74–86.

6. Charitou, C. D., & Markides, C. C. 2003. Responses to disruptive strategic innovation. *MIT Sloan Management Review,* 44(2): 55–64.

7. Our discussion of scanning, monitoring, competitive intelligence, and forecasting concepts draws on several sources. These include Fahey, L., & Narayanan, V. K. 1983. *Macroenvironmental analysis for strategic management.* St. Paul, MN: West; Lorange, P., Scott, F. S., & Ghoshal, S. 1986. *Strategic control.* St. Paul, MN: West; Ansoff, H. I. 1984. *Implementing strategic management.*

Englewood Cliffs, NJ: Prentice Hall; and Schreyogg, G., & Stienmann, H. 1987. Strategic control: A new perspective. *Academy of Management Review,* 12: 91–103.

8. Elenkov, D. S. 1997. Strategic uncertainty and environmental scanning: The case for institutional influences on scanning behavior. *Strategic Management Journal,* 18: 287–302.

9. For an interesting perspective on environmental scanning in emerging economies see May, R. C., Stewart, W. H., & Sweo, R. 2000. Environmental scanning behavior in a transitional economy: Evidence from Russia. *Academy of Management Journal,* 43(3): 403–27.

10. Browne, Sir John. The new agenda. Keynote speech delivered to the World Petroleum Congress in Calgary, Canada, June 13, 2000.

11. Bowles, J. 1997. Key issues for the automotive industry CEOs. *Fortune,* August 18: S3.

12. Walters, B. A., & Priem, R. L. 1999. Business strategy and CEO intelligence acquisition. *Competitive Intelligence Review,* 10(2): 15–22.

13. Prior, V. 1999. The language of competitive intelligence, Part 4. *Competitive Intelligence Review,* 10(1): 84–87.

14. Zahra, S. A., & Charples, S. S. 1993. Blind spots in competitive analysis. *Academy of Management Executive* 7(2): 7–27.

15. Wolfenson, J. 1999. The world in 1999: A battle for corporate honesty. *The Economist* 38: 13–30.

16. Drucker, P. F. 1997. The future that has already happened. *Harvard Business Review,* 75(6): 22.

17. Evans, P. B., & Wurster, T. S. 1997. Strategy and the new economics of information. *Harvard Business Review,* 75(5): 71–82.

18. Fahey & Narayanan, op. cit., p. 41.

19. Courtney, H., Kirkland, J., & Viguerie, P. 1997. Strategy under uncertainty. *Harvard Business Review,* 75(6): 66–79.

20. Odlyzko, A. 2003. False hopes. *Red Herring,* March: 31.

21. For an interesting perspective on how Accenture practices and has developed its approach to scenario planning, refer to Ferguson, G., Mathur, S., & Shah, B. 2005. Evolving from information to insight. *MIT Sloan Management Review,* 46(2): 51–58.

22. Dean, T. J., Brown, R. L., & Bamford, C. E. 1998. Differences in large and small firm responses to environmental context: Strategic implications from a comparative analysis of business formations. *Strategic Management Journal,* 19: 709–728.

23. Colvin, G. 1997. How to beat the boomer rush. *Fortune,* August 18: 59–63.

24. Grant, P. 2000. Developing plans to serve a graying population. *Wall Street Journal,* October 18: B12.

25. Walgreens, Inc. 2000. Annual report, 20.

26. Armas, G. C. 2000. Census figures point to changes in Congress. washingtonpost.com/wpdyn/articles/A58952Dec28. html.

27. Challenger, J. 2000. Women's corporate rise has reduced relocations. *Lexington* (KY) *Herald-Leader,* October 29: D1.

28. Watkins, M. D. 2003. Government games. *MIT Sloan Management Review* 44(2): 91–95.

29. Davies, A. 2000. The welcome mat is out for nerds. *BusinessWeek,* October 16: 64.

30. Anonymous. Business ready for Internet revolution. 1999. *Financial Times,* May 21: 17.

31. The Internet example draws on Bernasek, A. 2000. How the broadband adds up. *Fortune,* October 9: 28, 30; and Kromer, E. B2B or not B2B? *UW Alumni Magazine:* 10–19.

32. Baker, S., & Aston, A. 2005. The business of nanotech. *BusinessWeek,* February 14: 64–71.

33. Ginsburg, J. 2000. Letting the free market clear the air. *BusinessWeek,* November 6: 200, 204.

34. Smith, G., Wheatley, J., & Green, J. 2000. Car power. *BusinessWeek,* October 23: 72–80.

35. Mellgren, D. 2000. Norwegian ships relied on in global disasters. *Lexington* (KY) *Herald-Leader,* November 6: A8.

36. Goll, I., & Rasheed, M. A. 1997. Rational decision-making and firm performance: The moderating role of environment. *Strategic Management Journal,* 18: 583–591.

37. This discussion draws heavily on Porter, M. E. 1980. *Competitive strategy:* Chapter 1. New York: Free Press.

38. Ibid.

39. Fryer, B. 2001. Leading through rough times: An interview with Novell's Eric Schmidt. *Harvard Business Review,* 78(5): 117–123.

40. For a discussion on the importance of barriers to entry within industries, read Greenwald, B., & Kahn, J. 2005. *Competition demystified: A radically simplified approach to business strategy.* East Rutherford, NJ: Portfolio.

41. The ProCD example draws heavily upon Shapiro, C., & Varian, H. R. 2000. Versioning: The smart way to sell information. *Harvard Business Review,* 78(1): 106–114.

42. Wise, R., & Baumgarter, P. 1999. Go downstream: The new profit imperative in manufacturing. *Harvard Business Review,* 77(5): 133–141.

43. Salman, W. A. 2000. The new economy is stronger than you think. *Harvard Business Review,* 77(6): 99–106.

44. Mudambi, R., & Helper, S. 1998. The "close but adversarial" model of supplier relations in the U.S. auto industry. *Strategic Management Journal,* 19: 775–792.

45. Bernstein, A. 2000. Workers are doing well, but will it last? *BusinessWeek,* October 9: 48.

46. Tischler, L. 2002. IBM: Manager jam. *Fast Company,* October: 48.

47. For an interesting perspective on the intensity of competition in the supermarket industry, refer to Anonymous. 2005. Warfare in the aisles. *The Economist,* April 2: 6–8.

48. Marcial, G. 2000. Giving Viagra a run for its money. *BusinessWeek,* October 23: 173.

49. Kumar, N. 1996. The power of trust in manufacturer-retailer relationship. *Harvard Business Review,* 74(6): 92–110.

50. Brandenburger, A., & Nalebuff, B. J. 1995. The right game: Use game theory to shape strategy. *Harvard Business Review,* 73(4): 57–71.

51. McGahan, A. M. 2004. How industries change. *Harvard Business Review,* 82(10): 87–94.

52. Peteraf, M., & Shanley, M. 1997. Getting to know you: A theory of strategic group identity. *Strategic Management Journal,* 18 (Special Issue): 165–186.

53. An interesting scholarly perspective on strategic groups may be found in Dranove, D., Perteraf, M., & Shanley, M. 1998. Do strategic groups exist? An economic framework for analysis. *Strategic Management Journal,* 19(11): 1029–1044.

54. This section draws on several sources, including Kerwin, K. R., & Haughton, K. 1997. Can Detroit make cars that baby boomers like? *BusinessWeek,* December 1: 134–148; and Taylor, A., III. 1994. The new golden age of autos. *Fortune.* April 4: 50–66.

55. Csere, C. 2001. Supercar supermarket. *Car and Driver,* January: 118–127.

56. Healey, J. R. 1999. Groomed so as not to marry. *USA Today,* August 6: B1.

57. Csere, op. cit.

58. Smith, J. A. 2005. Auto & Truck Industry. *Value Line,* March 4: 101.

# 3

# Assessing the Internal Environment of the Firm

## >chapter objectives

*After reading this chapter, you should have a good understanding of:*

- The benefits and limitations of SWOT analysis in conducting an internal analysis of the firm.

- The primary and support activities of a firm's value chain.

- How value-chain analysis can help managers create value by investigating relationships among activities within the firm and between the firm and its customers and suppliers.

- The resource-based view of the firm and the different types of tangible and intangible resources, as well as organizational capabilities.

- The four criteria that a firm's resources must possess to maintain a sustainable advantage and how value created can be appropriated by employees and managers.

- The usefulness of financial ratio analysis, its inherent limitations, and how to make meaningful comparisons of performance across firms.

- The value of recognizing how the interests of a variety of stakeholders can be interrelated.

*t*wo firms compete in the same industry and both have many strengths in a variety of functional areas: marketing, operations, logistics, and so on. However, one of these firms outperforms the other by a wide margin over a long period of time. How can this be so? This chapter endeavors to answer that question. We begin with two sections that include frameworks for gaining key insights into a firm's internal environment: value-chain analysis and the resource-based view of the firm. In value-chain analysis, we divide a firm's activities into a series of value-creating steps. We then explore how individual activities within the firm add value, and also how *interrelationships* among activities within the firm, and between the firm and its suppliers and customers, create value.

In the resource-based view of the firm, we analyze the firm as a collection of tangible and intangible resources as well as organizational capabilities. Advantages that tend to be sustainable over time typically arise from creating *bundles* of resources and capabilities that satisfy four criteria: they are valuable, rare, difficult to imitate, and difficult to substitute. Not all of the value created by a firm will necessarily be kept (or appropriated) by the owners. We discuss the four key factors that determine how profits will be distributed between owners as well as employees and managers.

In the closing sections, we discuss how to evaluate a firm's performance and make comparisons across firms. We emphasize both the inclusion of financial resources and the interests of multiple stakeholders. Central to our discussion are the concepts of the balanced scorecard and the strategy map, which recognize that the interests of different stakeholders can be interrelated. We also consider how a firm's performance evolves over time and how it compares with industry norms and key competitors.

Jaguar has *not* been a star in Ford Motor Company's automotive arsenal. In fact, it has been referred to in the press as CEO "Bill Ford's recurring nightmare."[1] It appears that over the 15 years that Ford has owned the British luxury marquee, each time that it seems to turn the corner, the unit begins to lose money. Jaguar's estimated losses over the past 3 years are $1.5 billion. In fact, a recent *BusinessWeek* article included a cartoon with two customers looking at a Jaguar at a dealership with the seemingly appropriate caption: "Does it come in any color other than red ink?" Let's take a look at Jaguar's recent history and the source of its problems.

In early 2002, Bill Ford vowed that Ford's Premier Automotive Group (PAG)—consisting of Land Rover, Volvo, Aston Martin, and Jaguar—would contribute nearly a third of $7 billion in pre-tax profits by 2006. Ford has recently abandoned that profit goal, in part due to Jaguar's continuing slide. For example, Jaguar's problems dragged PAG down to a $342 million loss during the first half of 2004. If Ford can't turn Jaguar around, it will be very difficult to meet the corporation's reduced profit targets.

First, the good news: Factory efficiency and quality have improved significantly in recent years. However, there is far more bad news, including some huge mistakes. A major stumble was the rollout of the Jaguar X-Type compact. Many viewed it as a poorly executed entry-level car, known as the Baby Jag, that alienated Jaguar loyalists. The share of owners who stayed with the brand when they bought new vehicles has plunged from 85 percent to 38 percent in the past few years, according to an automotive consultant. Jaguar can also be criticized for an overly ambitious expansion, a one-size-fits all marketing strategy, and stale styling. Not surprisingly, it becomes rather easy to see why Jaguar has had to discount heavily to try to meet its global sales target of 125,000 units in 2004. (With sales of 118,918 units—down one percent from 2003—it still fell short.)

Let's briefly elaborate on some of these shortcomings:

- Jaguar based the X-Type on the mass market Ford Mondeo, which cheapened the brand. Jim Sanfilippo, executive vice president of the automotive consultancy AMCI Inc. of Bloomfield Hills, Michigan, said that the X-Type "turned Jaguar into a Ford with a Jaguar badge on it."
- Sales of the revamped XJ model, Jaguar's flagship, were hurt because it looked too much like the replacement model. Perhaps, people who pay $70,000 want everyone to know they have a new Jag!
- There were major problems with Jaguar's marketing approach. It adopted a mass marketing approach and then changed it too frequently. Its current "Born to Perform" slogan emphasizes horsepower, not looks. However, style is the main reason owners cite for purchasing a Jaguar!
- Jaguar's image has been tarnished by heavy rental-car sales and large rebates. For example, in late-2004, Jaguar's U.S. sales incentives were nearly $5,000 per car. This compared to $464 and $552 for Lexus and Mercedes, respectively. This partly explains Jaguar's low resale values. In fact, the only luxury brand with lower resale values was Jag's PAG stablemate, Land Rover. Hopefully, improved products and an appealing marketing strategy will help Jaguar cut back on expensive financial sales incentives.

Under Ford, Jaguar has made great strides in operational efficiency and overall product quality. These strengths, however, do not seem to offset weaknesses in a number of areas, including marketing, engineering and styling. In addition, Jaguar has suffered from an erosion of brand image that has occurred during the past decade due to such factors as fleet sales, huge cash incentives, and the introduction of entry-level models.

Before moving ahead to value-chain analysis, let's briefly revisit SWOT analysis to discuss some of its benefits and limitations. As discussed in Chapter 2, a SWOT analysis consists of a careful listing of a firm's strengths, weaknesses, opportunities, and threats.

While we believe SWOT analysis is very helpful as a starting point, it should not form the primary basis for evaluating a firm's internal strengths and weaknesses or the opportunities and threats in the environment. Strategy Spotlight 3.1 elaborates on the limitations of the traditional SWOT approach.

We will now turn to value-chain analysis. As you will see, it provides greater insights into analyzing a firm's competitive position than SWOT analysis does by itself.

# >>Value-Chain Analysis

Value-chain analysis views the organization as a sequential process of value-creating activities. The approach is useful for understanding the building blocks of competitive advantage. Value-chain analysis was described in Michael Porter's seminal book *Competitive Advantage.*[2] In competitive terms, value is the amount that buyers are willing to pay for what a firm provides them. Value is measured by total revenue, a reflection of the price a firm's product commands and the quantity it can sell. A firm is profitable to the extent that the value it receives exceeds the total costs involved in creating its product or service. Creating value for buyers that exceeds the costs of production (i.e., margin) is a key concept used in analyzing a firm's competitive position.

Porter described two different categories of activities. First, five primary activities— inbound logistics, operations, outbound logistics, marketing and sales, and service— contribute to the physical creation of the product or service, its sale and transfer to the buyer, and its service after the sale. Second, support activities—procurement, technology development, human resource management, and general administration—either add value by themselves or add value through important relationships with both primary activities and other support activities. Exhibit 3.1 illustrates Porter's value chain.

To get the most out of value-chain analysis, you need to view the concept in its broadest context, without regard to the boundaries of your own organization. That is, place your organization within a more encompassing value chain that includes your firm's suppliers, customers, and alliance partners. Thus, in addition to thoroughly understanding how value is created within the organization, you must become aware of how value is

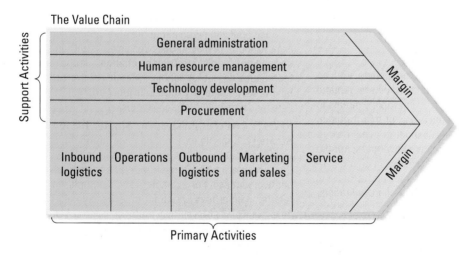

**Exhibit 3.1  The Value Chain: Primary and Support Activities**

Source: Adapted with the permission of The Free Press, a division of Simon & Schuster Adult Publishing Group, from *Competitive Advantage: Creating and Sustaining Superior Performance* by Michael E. Porter. Copyright © 1985, 1998 by Michael E. Porter. All rights reserved.

# STRATEGY SPOTLIGHT

## The Limitations of SWOT Analysis

SWOT analysis is a tried-and-true tool of strategic analysis. SWOT (strengths, weaknesses, opportunities, threats) analysis is used regularly in business to initially evaluate the opportunities and threats in the business environment as well as the strengths and weaknesses of a firm's internal environment. Top managers rely on SWOT to stimulate self-reflection and group discussions about how to improve their firm and position it for success.

But SWOT has its limitations. It is just a starting point for discussion. By listing the firm's attributes, managers have the raw material needed to perform more in-depth strategic analysis. However, SWOT cannot show them how to achieve a competitive advantage. They must not make SWOT analysis an end in itself, temporarily raising awareness about important issues but failing to lead to the kind of action steps necessary to enact strategic change.

Consider the ProCD example from Chapter 2, page 61. A brief SWOT analysis might include the following:

| Strengths | Opportunities |
|---|---|
| First-mover advantage | Demand for electronic phone books |
| Low labor cost | Sudden growth in use of digital technology |

| Weaknesses | Threats |
|---|---|
| Inexperienced new company | Easily duplicated product |
| No proprietary information | Market power of incumbent firms |

The combination of low production costs and an early-mover advantage in an environment where demand for CD-based phone books was growing rapidly seems to indicate that ProCD founder James Bryant had a golden opportunity. But the SWOT analysis did not reveal how to turn those strengths into a competitive advantage, nor did it highlight how rapidly the environment would change, allowing imitators to come into the market and erode his first-mover advantage. Let's look at some of the limitations of SWOT analysis.

**Strengths May Not Lead to an Advantage** A firm's strengths and capabilities, no matter how unique or impressive, may not enable it to achieve a competitive advantage in the marketplace. It is akin to recruiting a concert pianist to join a gang of thugs—even though such an ability is rare and valuable, it hardly helps the organization attain its goals and objectives! Similarly, the skills of a highly creative product designer would offer little competitive advantage to a firm that produces low-cost commodity products. Indeed, the additional expense of hiring such an individual could erode the firm's cost advantages. If a firm builds its strategy on a capability that cannot, by itself, create or sustain competitive advantage, it is essentially a wasted use of resources. ProCD had several key strengths, but it did not translate them into lasting advantages in the marketplace.

**SWOT's Focus on the External Environment Is Too Narrow** Strategists who rely on traditional definitions of their industry and competitive environment often focus their sights too narrowly on current customers, technologies, and competitors. Hence they fail to notice important changes on the periphery of their environment that may trigger the need to redefine industry boundaries and identify a whole new set of competitive relationships. Reconsider the example from Chapter 2 of *Encyclopaedia Britannica,* whose competitive position was severely eroded by a "nontraditional" competitor—CD-based encyclopedias (e.g., Microsoft *Encarta*) that could be used on home computers.

**SWOT Gives a One-Shot View of a Moving Target** A key weakness of SWOT is that it is primarily a static assessment. It focuses too much of a firm's attention on one moment in time. Essentially, this is like studying a single frame of a motion picture. You may be able to identify the principal actors and learn something about the setting, but it doesn't tell you much about the plot. Competition among organizations is played out over time. As circumstances, capabilities, and strategies change, static analysis techniques do not reveal the dynamics of the competitive environment. Clearly, ProCD was unaware that its competitiveness was being eroded so quickly.

**SWOT Overemphasizes a Single Dimension of Strategy** Sometimes firms become preoccupied with a single strength or a key feature of the product or service they are offering and ignore other factors needed for competitive success. For example, Food Lion, a large grocery retailer, paid a heavy price for its excessive emphasis on cost control. The resulting problems with labor and the negative publicity led to its eventual withdrawal from several markets.

SWOT analysis has much to offer, but only as a starting point. By itself, it rarely helps a firm develop competitive advantages that it can sustain over time.

Sources: Shapiro, C., & Varian, H. R. 2000. Versioning: The smart way to sell information. *Harvard Business Review,* 78(1): 99–106; and Picken, J. C., & Dess, G. G. 1997. *Mission Critical.* Burr Ridge, IL: Irwin Professional Publishing.

created for other organizations that are involved in the overall supply chain or distribution channel in which your firm participates.[3]

Next, we'll describe and provide examples of each of the primary and support activities. Then, we'll provide examples of how companies add value by means of relationships among activities within the organization as well as activities outside the organization, such as those activities associated with customers and suppliers.[4]

## Primary Activities

Five generic categories of primary activities are involved in competing in any industry, as shown in Exhibit 3.2. Each category is divisible into a number of distinct activities that depend on the particular industry and the firm's strategy.[5]

| Inbound Logistics | Operations | Outbound Logistics | Marketing and Sales | Service |
|---|---|---|---|---|
| • Location of distribution facilities to minimize shipping times.<br>• Excellent material and inventory control systems.<br>• Systems to reduce time to send "returns" to suppliers.<br>• Warehouse layout and designs to increase efficiency of operations for incoming materials. | • Efficient plant operations to minimize costs.<br>• Appropriate level of automation in manufacturing.<br>• Quality production control systems to reduce costs and enhance quality.<br>• Efficient plant layout and workflow design. | • Effective shipping processes to provide quick delivery and minimize damages.<br>• Efficient finished goods warehousing processes.<br>• Shipping of goods in large lot sizes to minimize transportation costs.<br>• Quality material handling equipment to increase order picking. | • Highly motivated and competent sales force.<br>• Innovative approaches to promotion and advertising.<br>• Selection of most appropriate distribution channels.<br>• Proper identification of customer segments and needs.<br>• Effective pricing strategies. | • Effective use of procedures to solicit customer feedback and to act on information.<br>• Quick response to customer needs and emergencies.<br>• Ability to furnish replacement parts as required.<br>• Effective management of parts and equipment inventory.<br>• Quality of service personnel and ongoing training.<br>• Appropriate warranty and guarantee policies. |

Source: Adapted with permission of The Free Press, a division of Simon & Schuster Adult Publishing Group, from *Competitive Advantage: Creating and Sustaining Superior Performance* by Michael E. Porter. Copyright © 1985, 1998 by Michael E. Porter. All rights reserved.

**Exhibit 3.2**   **The Value Chain: Some Factors to Consider in Assessing a Firm's Primary Activities**

*Inbound Logistics*   Inbound logistics is primarily associated with receiving, storing, and distributing inputs to the product. It includes material handling, warehousing, inventory control, vehicle scheduling, and returns to suppliers.

Just-in-time (JIT) inventory systems, for example, were designed to achieve efficient inbound logistics. In essence, Toyota epitomizes JIT inventory systems, in which parts deliveries arrive at the assembly plants only hours before they are needed. JIT systems will play a vital role in fulfilling Toyota's commitment to fill a buyer's new car order in just five days.[6] This standard is in sharp contrast to most competitors that require approximately 30 days' notice to build vehicles. Toyota's standard is three times faster than even Honda Motors, considered to be the industry's most efficient in order follow-through. The five days represent the time from the company's receipt of an order to the time the car leaves the assembly plant. Actual delivery may take longer, depending on where a customer lives. How can Toyota achieve such fast turnaround?

- Its 360 key suppliers are now linked to the company by way of computer on a virtual assembly line.
- Suppliers load parts onto trucks in the order in which they will be installed.
- Parts are stacked on trucks in the same place each time to help workers unload them quickly.
- Deliveries are required to meet a rigid schedule with as many as 12 trucks a day and no more than four hours between trucks.

*Operations*   Operations include all activities associated with transforming inputs into the final product form, such as machining, packaging, assembly, testing, printing, and facility operations.

Creating environmentally friendly manufacturing is one way a firm can use operations to achieve competitive advantage. Shaw Industries (now part of Berkshire Hathaway), a world-class competitor in the floor-covering industry, is well known for its strong concern for the environment.[7] It has been successful in reducing the expenses associated with the disposal of dangerous chemicals and other waste products from its manufacturing operations. Its environmental endeavors have multiple payoffs. Shaw has received numerous awards for its recycling efforts—awards that enhance its corporate reputation.

Additional examples of environmentally friendly manufacturing include: EcoSolution Q®, the industry's first nylon covering containing recycled content, which was the most successful product launch in the company's history. Shaw's residential staple polyester carpet, made from virtually 100 percent petroleum-based materials, keeps one billion plastic containers out of landfills each year through recycling. Shaw is also pioneering other innovative recycling solutions, including recycled nylon for automotive under-hood applications and ground-up carpet as an ingredient in road materials and fiber-reinforced concrete.

Strategy Spotlight 3.2 discusses how Canon was able to improve its operations by applying the principles of the Toyota Production System.

*Outbound Logistics*   The activities of outbound logistics are associated with collecting, storing, and distributing the product or service to buyers. They include finished goods, warehousing, material handling, delivery vehicle operation, order processing, and scheduling.

Campbell Soup uses an electronic network to facilitate its continuous-replenishment program with its most progressive retailers.[8] Each morning, retailers electronically inform Campbell of their product needs and of the level of inventories in their distribution

## Improving Operations at Canon

Canon, the $30 billion Japanese consumer electronics firm, dramatically improved its operational effectiveness by implementing the Toyota Production System (TPS). Could automobile manufacturing systems improve the operations of an electronics manufacturer? At the core of TPS's just-in-time manufacturing system is the elimination of waste and absolute concentration on consistent high quality by a process of continuous improvement.

In 1997, Canon hired TPS consultant Hiroshi Yamada, a one-time journalist who founded a TPS training company. Yamada advised Canon to rip the conveyor belts out of its manufacturing plants and replace them with production "cells," in which groups of employees build entire products. As might be expected, productivity declined during the first few years of the change as workers had to learn to take responsibility for the finished product instead of a single function. According to Canon CEO Fujio Mitarai, "When there were problems in the line, the production manager responsible would get an earful from our account reps."

However, believing that cell production would pay off, Mitarai stuck with it, telling subordinates he would take responsibility for problems. "As a leader, you have to remove fear," he says. Such persistence paid off. Converting 13 domestic plants and 54 overseas facilities to cells, Canon reclaimed 7.5 million square feet of space and the labor equivalent of 35,000 workers. Those workers were redeployed to increase production of key competitive components like CMOS sensors, used in digital cameras. Over the past five years, these efforts, along with research and development advances, have resulted in $2 billion in savings.

Sources: Anonymous. 2005. The car company in front. *The Economist,* January 29: 65–67; and Migliorato, P. 2004. Toyota retools Japan. *Business 2.0,* August: 39–41.

centers. Campbell uses that information to forecast future demand and to determine which products require replenishment (based on the inventory limits previously established with each retailer). Trucks leave Campbell's shipping plant that afternoon and arrive at the retailers' distribution centers the same day. The program cuts the inventories of participating retailers from about a four- to two-weeks' supply. Campbell Soup achieved this improvement because it slashed delivery time and because it knows the inventories of key retailers and can deploy supplies when they are most needed.

The Campbell Soup example also illustrates the win–win benefits of exemplary value-chain activities. Both the supplier (Campbell) and its buyers (retailers) come out ahead. Since the retailer makes more money on Campbell products delivered through continuous replenishment, it has an incentive to carry a broader line and give the company greater shelf space. Campbell found that after it introduced the program, sales of its products grew twice as fast through participating retailers as through all other retailers. Not surprisingly, supermarket chains love such programs. For example, Wegman's Food Markets in upstate New York has augmented its accounting system to measure and reward suppliers whose products cost the least to stock and sell.

*Marketing and Sales* Marketing and sales activities are associated with purchases of products and services by end users and the inducements used to get them to make purchases.[9] They include advertising, promotion, sales force, quoting, channel selection, channel relations, and pricing.[10] It is not always enough to have a great product.[11] The key is to convince your channel partners that it is in their best interests not only to carry your product but also to market it in a way that is consistent with your strategy. Consider Monsanto's efforts at educating distributors to improve the value proposition of its line of Saflex® windows.[12] The products introduced in the early 1990s had a superior attribute: The window design permitted laminators to form an exceptional type of glass by sandwiching a plastic sheet interlayer between two pieces of glass. This product is not only stronger and offers better ultraviolet protection than regular glass, but also when cracked, it adheres to the plastic sheet—an excellent safety feature for both cars and homes.

Despite these benefits, Monsanto had a hard time convincing laminators and window manufacturers to carry products made with Saflex. According to Melissa Toledo, brand manager at Monsanto, "Saflex was priced at a 30 percent premium above traditional glass, and the various stages in the value chain (distributors and retailers) didn't think there would be a demand for such an expensive glass product." What was Monsanto's solution? Subsequently, it reintroduced Saflex as KeepSafe® and worked to coordinate the product's value propositions. By analyzing the experiences of all of the players in the supply chain, it was able to create marketing programs that helped each build a business aimed at selling its products. Said Toledo, "We want to know how they go about selling those types of products, what challenges they face, and what they think they need to sell our products. This helps us a lot when we try to provide them with these needs." Thus, marketing is often a key element of competitive advantage.[13]

At times, a firm's marketing initiatives may become overly aggressive and lead to actions that are both unethical and illegal.[14] For example:

- **Burdines.** This department store chain is under investigation for allegedly adding club memberships to its customers' credit cards without prior approval.
- **Fleet Mortgage.** This company has been accused of adding insurance fees for dental coverage and home insurance to its customers' mortgage loans without the customers' knowledge.
- **HCI Direct.** Eleven states have accused this direct-mail firm with charging for panty hose samples that customers did not order.
- **Juno Online Services.** The Federal Trade Commission brought charges against this Internet service provider for failing to provide customers with a telephone number to cancel service.

**Service**    This primary activity includes all actions associated with providing service to enhance or maintain the value of the product, such as installation, repair, training, parts supply, and product adjustment.

Internet-based retailers (e-tailers) provide many examples of how superb customer service is critical for adding value. Nearly all e-tailers have faced a similar problem: They figured that the Web's self-service model would save them millions in customer service costs. But that was the last place they could afford to shave costs.[15] According to market researcher Datamonitor, 7.8 percent of abandoned online shopping carts could be salvaged through an effective customer service solution—an impressive $6.1 billion in lost annual sales. Bill Bass, senior vice president of e-commerce at catalog retailer Lands' End, Inc., claimed, "If there's a train wreck to happen, it's going to be around customer service."

Let's see what two retailers are doing to provide exemplary customer service. At Sephora.com, a customer service representative taking a phone call from a repeat customer has instant access to, for example, what shade of lipstick the customer likes best. This will help the rep cross-sell by suggesting a matching shade of lip gloss. CEO Jim Wiggett expects such personalization to build loyalty and boost sales per customer. Nordstrom, the Seattle-based department store chain, goes even a step further. It offers a cyber-assist: A service rep can take control of a customer's Web browser and literally lead her to just the silk scarf that she is looking for. CEO Dan Nordstrom believes that such a capability will close enough additional purchases to pay for the $1 million investment in software.

### Virgin Atlantic's High-Flying Service

On June 14, 2004, Virgin Atlantic's chairman and extreme sports enthusiast Richard Branson broke a 40-year-old world record for crossing the English Channel in an amphibious vehicle. He piloted a Gibbs Aquada across the 22-mile strait in an hour and 40 minutes. This might be good news for Sir Richard, but it is even better news for U.K.-based Gibbs Technologies. Orders for the sports cars have doubled since the feat. And Branson himself plans to buy a fleet of the three-seat Aquadas to ferry his Virgin Atlantic first-class passengers down the Thames River from London to Heathrow International Airport.

Source: Copeland, M. V., & Thomas, O. 2004. A new sales Channel. *Business 2.0,* August: 134; Pidcock, K. (Ed.). 2004. Virgin boss sets new record. *Orange Aero Club News,* September: 2; and Anonymous. 2003. The best of what's new. *Popular Science* (www.popsci.com).

After setting the record, Branson said "for many years our Upper Class passengers have enjoyed our complimentary limousines to and from the airport. Some people prefer our chauffeured motorbikes, but we are now planning to go one step further by introducing the chance to experience a Gibbs Aquada. This new service follows in our tradition of product innovation and fun. Using the Gibbs Aquada, we will be able to cut thirty minutes off the journey between Heathrow and The City, giving our travelers extra time for meetings or relaxation."

The Gibbs Aquada is not the only car/boat hybrid ever made, but it is by far the fastest. A 175 horsepower V-6 engine powers the three-seater at up to 100 miles per hour on land. And at sea, the same engine drives a jet that expels water out the back at high speeds to propel the boat like a jet-ski. The price is $250,000.

Strategy Spotlight 3.3 discusses a very innovative approach to customer service: Virgin Atlantic's use of amphibious vehicles to ferry their "Upper Class" passengers to London's Heathrow International Airport.

## Support Activities

Support activities in the value chain are involved with competing in any industry and can be divided into four generic categories, as shown in Exhibit 3.3. As with primary activities, each category of the support activity is divisible into a number of distinct value activities that are specific to a particular industry. For example, technology development's discrete activities may include component design, feature design, field testing, process engineering, and technology selection. Similarly, procurement may be divided into activities such as qualifying new suppliers, purchasing different groups of inputs, and monitoring supplier performance.

*Procurement*   Procurement refers to the function of purchasing inputs used in the firm's value chain, not to the purchased inputs themselves.[16] Purchased inputs include raw materials, supplies, and other consumable items as well as assets such as machinery, laboratory equipment, office equipment, and buildings.[17]

Microsoft is a company that has enhanced its procurement process (and the quality of its suppliers) by providing formal reviews of its suppliers. One of Microsoft's divisions has extended the review process used for employees to its outside suppliers.[18] The employee services group, which is responsible for everything from travel to 401(k) programs to the on-site library, outsources more than 60 percent of the services it provides. Despite all the business it was doing with suppliers, the employee services group was not providing them with enough feedback on how well Microsoft thought they were doing. This was feedback that the suppliers wanted to get and that Microsoft wanted to give. The evaluation system that Microsoft developed helped clarify its expectations to suppliers. An executive noted: "We had one supplier—this was before the new system— that would have scored a 1.2 out of 5. After we started giving this feedback, and the

**The Value Chain: Some Factors to Consider in Assessing a Firm's Support Activities**

---

**General Administration**

- Effective planning systems to attain overall goals and objectives.
- Ability of top management to anticipate and act on key environmental trends and events.
- Ability to obtain low-cost funds for capital expenditures and working capital.
- Excellent relationships with diverse stakeholder groups.
- Ability to coordinate and integrate activities across the "value system."
- High visibility to inculcate organizational culture, reputation, and values.

**Human Resource Management**

- Effective recruiting, development, and retention mechanisms for employees.
- Quality relations with trade unions.
- Quality work environment to maximize overall employee performance and minimize absenteeism.
- Reward and incentive programs to motivate all employees.

**Technology Development**

- Effective research and development activities for process and product initiatives.
- Positive collaborative relationships between R&D and other departments.
- State-of-the art facilities and equipment.
- Culture that enhances creativity and innovation.
- Excellent professional qualifications of personnel.
- Ability to meet critical deadlines.

**Procurement**

- Procurement of raw material inputs to optimize quality and speed, and to minimize the associated costs.
- Development of collaborative "win–win" relationships with suppliers.
- Effective procedures to purchase advertising and media services.
- Analysis and selection of alternate sources of inputs to minimize dependence on one supplier.
- Ability to make proper lease-versus-buy decisions.

Source: Adapted with permission of The Free Press, a division of Simon & Schuster Adult Publishing Group, from *Competitive Advantage: Creating and Sustaining Superior Performance* by Michael E. Porter. Copyright © 1985, 1998 by Michael E. Porter. All rights reserved.

---

supplier understood our expectations, its performance improved dramatically. Within six months, it scored a 4. If you'd asked me before we began the feedback system, I would have said that was impossible."

***Technology Development***    Every value activity embodies technology.[19] The array of technologies employed in most firms is very broad, ranging from technologies used to prepare documents and transport goods to those embodied in processes and equipment or the product itself. Technology development related to the product and its features

## 3.4 STRATEGY SPOTLIGHT

### An Interesting Technological Innovation: A Seaworthy Foldable Boat

When people think of foldable products, they are likely to think of lawn chairs, tables, and fans but not boats. However, last year Sandy Kaye, owner of Porta-Bote in Mountain View, California, sold nearly 10,000 dinghy-size boats for up to $1,600 each. The boat folds to 4 inches in height and it is made from a resin developed by NASA that gets stronger with each folding. With its flat design, the Porta-Bote fits on the side of a recreation vehicle, the hull of a larger boat, or even a yak! Britain's Royal Air Force Mountain Rescue Service strapped it (it only weighs about 60 pounds) on the scruffy animal for a trek up Mt. Everest and used it to cross a lake. A company spokesperson said that they have submitted an application for the Porta-Bote to appear in the *Guinness Book of World Records* as the first and only boat in to world to have "sailed" on a lake 20,000 feet above sea level.

The men from the RAF Mountain Rescue service took the folding Porta-Bote as a precaution against being stranded by melting glaciers. They expected to find the lake frozen. However, it had thawed slightly and they were able to break the ice and "set sail." Expedition leader Flight Lt. Ted Atkins said his crew used shovels as paddles to cross a glacier lake high above the Himalayas. He joked, "I've flown an RAF Nimrod at 20,000 feet before but I've never paddled a boat at that altitude."

Many might ask how a boat can be folded not just once, but many times and still have seams strong enough to never leak. Although the exact answer remains a proprietary secret of the firm, the technique is used in the aerospace industry. It involves the complex welding of the four pieces together via staple wires and some type of sealant material injected in between the panels. Whatever the exact method of welding is, it certainly does a superb job of holding the Porta-Bote together.

Sources: Anonymous. 2004. Porta-Bote. A completely collapsible watercraft that transforms from surfboard dimensions into a full-fledged boat. *TackleTour*, April 19 (www.tackletour.com); Chambers, E. Seaworthy. *BusinessWeek*, January 25: 12; and www.porta-bote.com.

---

supports the entire value chain, while other technology development is associated with particular primary or support activities.

The 2000 merger of Allied Signal and Honeywell brought together roughly 13,000 scientists and an $870 million R&D budget that promises to lead to some innovative products and services in two major areas: performance materials and control systems. Some of the possible innovations include:

- **Performance materials.** The development of uniquely shaped fibers with very high absorption capability. When employed in the company's Fram oil filters, they capture 50 percent more particles than ordinary filters. This means that cars can travel further with fewer oil changes.
- **Control systems.** Working with six leading oil companies, Honeywell developed software using "self-learning" algorithms that predict when something might go wrong in an oil refinery before it actually does. Examples include a faulty gas valve or hazardous spillage.[20]

Strategy Spotlight 3.4 addresses a unique use of technology—a foldable boat!

***Human Resource Management*** Human resource management consists of activities involved in the recruiting, hiring, training, development, and compensation of all types of personnel.[21] It supports both individual primary and support activities (e.g., hiring of engineers and scientists) and the entire value chain (e.g., negotiations with labor unions).

Like all great service companies, JetBlue Airways Corporation is obsessed with hiring superior employees.[22] But they found it difficult to attract college graduates to commit to careers as flight attendants. JetBlue developed a highly innovative recruitment program

# STRATEGY SPOTLIGHT

## SAS and Employee Turnover

Jeffrey Pfeffer, professor of organizational behavior at Stanford University, asked a managing partner at a San Francisco law firm about its employee turnover rate. Turnover had increased from 25 percent to 30 percent over the last few years. The law firm's solution was to increase recruitment of new employees. Pfeffer's response was, "What kind of doctor would you be if your patient was bleeding faster and faster, and your only response was to increase the rate of transfusion?"

It's not difficult to calculate the cost of a new hire, but what does it cost a firm when employees leave? Software developer SAS Institute puts the cost at around $50 million. David Russo, director of human resources at SAS, suggested that keeping employees is not just about caring for your employees—it also provides a strong economic advantage to the company.

Consider Russo's example: Average employee turnover in the software business is 20 percent per year. SAS's turnover rate is 4 percent. SAS has 5,000 employees earning an average of $60,000 a year. The difference between turnover in the industry and turnover at SAS is 16 percent. Multiplying 16 percent by SAS's 5,000 employees at $60,000 a year, SAS has a cost savings of nearly $50 million. SAS estimates the total cost of turnover per employee to equal the employee's annual salary.

What can a firm do with an extra $50 million? SAS spends a large portion of this sum on its employees. The SAS gym, cafeteria (with pianist), on-site medical and child care, flexible work schedules, employer retirement contributions of 15 percent of an employee's pay, and a host of other family-friendly programs help keep SAS's employee turnover level well below the industry average. Even after all these perks, SAS still has money left over.

Russo's message? "This is not tree-huggery. This is money in the bank." The bottom line is it pays to retain employees.

Sources: Levering, R., & Moskowitz, M. 2003. "The 100 Best Companies to Work For. *Fortune*, January 20: 127–152; and Webber, A. M. 1998. Danger: Toxic Company. *Fast Company*, November: 152–161.

for flight attendants—a one-year contract that gives them a chance to travel, meet lots of people, and then decide what else they might like to do. They also introduced the idea of training a friend and employee together so that they could share a job. With such employee-friendly initiatives, JetBlue has been very successful in attracting talent.

Employees often leave a firm because they reach a plateau and begin to look for new opportunities and challenges.[23] AT&T strives to retain such people with Resource Link, an in-house temporary service that enables employees with diverse management, technical, or professional skills to market their abilities to different departments for short-term assignments. This not only enables professionals to broaden their experience base but also provides a mechanism for other parts of the organization to benefit from new sources of ideas.

Strategy Spotlight 3.5 describes how SAS Institute's innovative approach to human resources provides an insightful financial justification for the broad array of benefits it provides to employees.

***General Administration*** General administration consists of a number of activities, including general management, planning, finance, accounting, legal and government affairs, quality management, and information systems. Administration (unlike the other support activities) typically supports the entire value chain and not individual activities.

Although general administration is sometimes viewed only as overhead, it can be a powerful source of competitive advantage. In a telephone operating company, for example, negotiating and maintaining ongoing relations with regulatory bodies can be among the most important activities for competitive advantage. In a similar vein, effective information systems can contribute significantly to cost position, while in some industries top management plays a vital role in dealing with important buyers.[24]

The strong and effective leadership of top executives can also make a significant contribution to an organization's success. As we discussed in Chapter 1, chief executive officers (CEOs) such as Herb Kelleher, Andrew Grove, and Jack Welch have been credited with playing critical roles in the success of Southwest Airlines, Intel, and General Electric. And Carlos Ghosn is considered one of today's top corporate leaders after his turnaround of Nissan, the Japan-based automobile manufacturer—turning losses into a $7 billion profit. He presently has been given the challenge of being CEO of *both* Nissan and its parent, Renault, the French automaker.

Information systems can also play a key role in increasing operating efficiencies and enhancing a firm's performance.[25] Consider Walgreen Co.'s introduction of Intercom Plus, a computer-based prescription management system. Linked by computer to both doctors' offices and third-party payment plans, the system automates telephone refills, store-to-store prescription transfers, and drug reordering. It also provides information on drug interactions and, coupled with revised workflows, frees up pharmacists from administrative tasks to devote more time to patient counseling.

Lawyers often receive a "bad rap," even in the corporate world! However, legal services can be a source of significant competitive advantage. One example is ensuring the protection of a firm's intellectual property through patents, trademarks, and copyrights. Although many companies are not aware of the earnings potential of their patent holdings, Texas Instruments (TI) is one notable exception.[26] In essence, TI began investing the income-generation potential of its patent portfolio in the mid-1980s, when, out of desperation, it faced bankruptcy. Since then, TI has earned an impressive $4 billion in patent royalties; its licensing revenues are estimated to be $800 million per year. Recently, TI signed yet another licensing pact for its semiconductor patents with Hyundai, an agreement that is expected to generate a total of $1 billion in additional royalties over seven years.

Strategy Spotlight 3.6 discusses how Gary Kelly, Southwest Airlines's CEO, added value to the firm when he was its chief financial officer (CFO).

## Interrelationships among Value-Chain Activities within and across Organizations

We have defined each of the value-chain activities separately for clarity of presentation, but this approach implicitly understates the importance of relationships among value-chain activities.[27] There are two levels that must be addressed: (1) interrelationships among activities within the firm and (2) relationships among activities within the firm and with other organizations (e.g., customers and suppliers) that are part of the firm's expanded value chain.[28]

With regard to the first level, recall AT&T's innovative Resource Link program wherein employees who have reached their plateau may apply for temporary positions in other parts of the organization. Clearly, this program has the potential to benefit all activities within the firm's value chain because it creates opportunities for top employees to lend their expertise to all of the organization's value-creating activities.

With regard to the second level, Campbell Soup's use of electronic networks enabled it to improve the efficiency of outbound logistics.[29] However, it also helped Campbell manage the ordering of raw materials more effectively, improve its production scheduling, and help its customers better manage their inbound logistics operations.

An example of how a firm's value-creating activity can enhance customer value is provided by Ciba Specialty Chemicals (which merged with Sandoz in 1996 to form Novartis), a Swiss manufacturer of textile dyes.[30] The firm's research and development experts have created dyes that fix more readily to the fabric and therefore require less salt. How does this innovation add value for Ciba's customers? There are three ways. First,

## How a Firm's General Administration Can Create Value

A firm's general administration can significantly impact its performance. Southwest Airlines' chief financial officer, Gary Kelly, is a key contributor to the airline's solid financial performance. He drives a red Porsche, which might lead you to believe that the 48-year-old CFO likes speed and recklessness. But he drives the car carefully and conscientiously—the very model of maturity on the road. He takes a similar approach to managing Southwest's finances.

While the rest of the airline industry was laying off workers by the thousands, Southwest did not furlough anyone. Its ability to shine in dire times is a result of its conservative financial culture that values a large cash balance and low debt. Southwest began conserving funds in 2000, when it saw a recession on the horizon. After installing a new computer system and renegotiating contracts with vendors, it managed to boost its cash on hand from $600 million to about $1 billion.

Through the years, Wall Street analysts have criticized Kelly's conservative approach and goaded him to use the extra cash to make acquisitions or buy back stock.

Goldman Sachs's airline analyst actually calls the balance sheet "too strong." Yet it is such fiscal preparedness that has kept the company's debt-to-capital ratio at around 40 percent (compared to the industry average of about 70 percent), which allows for more flexibility during tough times.

Kelly also has come up with some creative measures to get through the recent slumping economy and terrorism threats. For example, he rescheduled the delivery of 19 planes from Boeing by developing an arrangement between Boeing and a collection of banks. This arrangement, whereby the banks formed a group called the Amor Trust, allowed the trust to take delivery from Boeing as scheduled and store the planes in the Mojave Desert until Southwest needed them. The idea was to strike a balance between maintaining the good relationship with Boeing, its only supplier of planes, and holding off spending the cash on the planes it does not yet need. Darryl Jenkins, director of the Aviation Institute at George Washington University, attributes Southwest's success to two things, "Consistency, and the fact that they don't listen to other people."

*Note:* On July 15, 2004 Gary Kelly became CEO of Southwest Airlines.

Sources: Zellner, W., & Arnadt, M. 2003. Holding steady. *BusinessWeek*, February 3; and Mount, I. 2002. Southwest's Gary Kelly: A tip of the hat to the CFO at the one airline still making money. *Business 2.0*, February 12: 5–7.

it lowers the outlays for salt. Textile companies using the new dyes are able to reduce their costs for salt by up to 2 percent of revenues, a significant drop in an industry with razor-thin profit margins. Second, it reduces manufacturers' costs for water treatment. Used bathwater full of salt and unfixed dye must be treated before it is released into rivers or streams (even in low-income countries where environmental standards are typically lax). Simply put, less salt and less unfixed dye mean lower water-treatment costs. Third, the higher fixation rates of the new dyes make quality control easier, lowering the costs of rework.

We conclude this section with Strategy Spotlight 3.7. It addresses how Cardinal Health expertly integrates several value activities to create value for its suppliers and customers.

## Applying the Value Chain to Service Organizations

The value chain is often believed to apply primarily to manufacturing operations. Indeed, the concepts of inbound logistics, operations, and outbound logistics suggest managing the raw materials that might be manufactured into finished products and delivered to customers. But these three steps do not apply only to manufacturing. They correspond to any transformation process in which inputs are converted through a work process into outputs that add value. For example, accounting is a sort of transformation process that converts daily records of individual transactions into monthly financial reports. In this example, the transaction records are the inputs, accounting is the operation that adds value, and financial statements are the outputs.

# STRATEGY SPOTLIGHT

## Cardinal Health: Creating Value through the Extended Value Chain

Cardinal Health is a wholesale drug distributor that buys sprays, pills, and capsules from pharmaceutical companies and puts them on the shelves in pharmacies or into the hands of emergency-room nurses. Profitability is a problem in this business, because the company is caught between powerful manufacturers and cost-conscious customers. Cardinal, for example, buys pharmaceuticals from the likes of Pfizer (its biggest supplier) and sells them to the likes of CVS (its largest customer).

Cardinal responded to the profitability challenge by trying to add value for both customers and suppliers. It understood how urgent it was for one of its customer groups (hospitals) to control costs, so it began to offer services to hospital pharmacies. Rather than shipping medications to the hospitals' front door, it "followed the pill" into the hospital and right to the patient's room, offering pharmacy-management services and extending those services to customized surgical kits.

Sources: Slywotzky, A., & Wise, R. 2003. Double digit growth in no-growth times. *Fast Company*, April: 66–70; Stewart, T. 2002. Fueling drug growth during an economic drought. *Business 2.0*, May: 17–21; and Lashinsky, A. 2003. Big man in the "middle." *Fortune*, April 14: 161–162.

As the knowledgeable intermediary, Cardinal realized it could bring significant value to its suppliers (the pharmaceutical manufacturers) by providing services in drug formulation, testing, manufacturing, and packaging, freeing those companies to concentrate on the discovery of the next round of blockbuster medicines. Cardinal even used its position to develop new services for commercial pharmacies. Cardinal's drug-chain customers depend on third-party payments for most of the prescriptions it fills. It worked with a number of leading chains to develop a system called ScriptLINE that automates the reimbursement process for pharmacies and updates rates daily.

The result of this stream of innovations is a wave of growth and profits. Cardinal, with annual sales of $65 billion, has registered compound annual earnings growth of approximately 20 percent or better for the past 15 years.

The Cardinal Health story is a powerful example of extending the value chain and adding value to the many players involved—from the suppliers to the customers. The company found opportunities in an unpromising business landscape by identifying new customer needs related to the activities that surround the products it sells.

What are the "operations," or transformation processes, of service organizations? These could be many different things. At times, the difference between manufacturing and service is in providing a customized solution rather than the kind of mass production that is common in manufacturing. For example, a travel agent adds value by creating an itinerary that includes transportation, accommodations, and activities that are customized to your budget and your dates of travel. A law firm renders services that are specific to a client's needs and circumstances. In both cases, the work process (operation) involves the application of specialized knowledge based on the specifics of a situation (inputs) and the outcome that the client seeks to achieve (outputs). In Chapter 8, we will discuss how the Internet is adding value through unique applications of problem-solving capabilities.

The application of the value chain to service organizations suggests that the value-adding process may be configured differently depending on the type of business a firm is engaged in. As the preceding discussion on support activities suggests, activities such as procurement and legal services are critical for adding value. Indeed, the activities that may only provide support to one company may be critical to the primary value-adding activity of another firm.

Exhibit 3.4 provides two models of how the value chain might look in service industries. In the retail industry, there are no manufacturing operations. A firm, such as Circuit City, adds value by developing expertise in the procurement of finished goods and by displaying them in their stores in a way that enhances sales. Thus, the value chain makes procurement activities (i.e., partnering with vendors and purchasing goods) a primary rather than a support activity. Operations refer to the task of operating Circuit City's stores. For an engineering services firm, research and development provides inputs, the transformation

**Retail: Primary Value-Chain Activities**

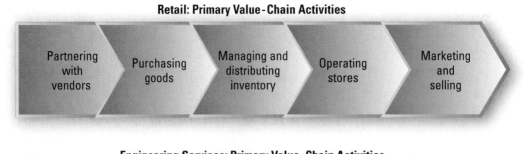

**Engineering Services: Primary Value-Chain Activities**

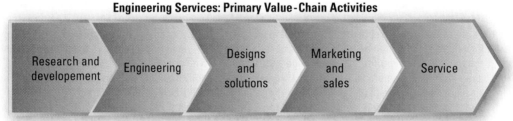

**Exhibit 3.4**   **Some Examples of Value Chains in Service Industries**

process is the engineering itself, and innovative designs and practical solutions are the outputs. Arthur D. Little, for example, is a large consulting firm with offices in 30 countries. In its technology and innovation management practice, A. D. Little strives to make the best use of the science, technology and knowledge resources available to create value for a wide range of industries and client sectors. This involves activities associated with research and development, engineering, and creating solutions as well as downstream activities such as marketing, sales, and service. These examples suggest that how the primary and support activities of a given firm are configured and deployed will often depend on industry conditions and the extent to which the company is service and/or manufacturing oriented.

## >>Resource-Based View of the Firm

The resource-based view (RBV) of the firm combines two perspectives: (1) the internal analysis of phenomena within a company and (2) an external analysis of the industry and its competitive environment.[31] It goes beyond the traditional SWOT (strengths, weaknesses, opportunities, threats) analysis by integrating internal and external perspectives. The ability of a firm's resources to confer competitive advantage(s) cannot be determined without taking into consideration the broader competitive context. That is, a firm's resources must be evaluated in terms of how valuable, rare, and hard they are for competitors to duplicate. Otherwise, at best, the firm would be able to attain only competitive parity. As noted earlier in the chapter (in Strategy Spotlight 3.1), a firm's strengths and capabilities—no matter how unique or impressive—do not necessarily lead to competitive advantages in the marketplace. The criteria for whether advantages are created and whether or not they can be sustained over time will be addressed later in this section. Thus, the RBV is a very useful framework for gaining insights as to why some competitors are more profitable than others. As we will see later in the book, the RBV is also helpful in developing strategies for individual businesses and diversified firms by revealing how core competencies embedded in a firm can help it exploit new product and market opportunities.

In the two sections that follow, we will discuss the three key types of resources that firms possess (summarized in Exhibit 3.5): tangible resources, intangible resources, and

Exhibit 3.5
**The Resource-Based
View of the Firm:
Resources and
Capabilities**

## Tangible Resources

Financial
- Firm's cash account and cash equivalents.
- Firm's capacity to raise equity.
- Firm's borrowing capacity.

Physical
- Modern plant and facilities.
- Favorable manufacturing locations.
- State-of-the-art machinery and equipment.

Technological
- Trade secrets.
- Innovative production processes.
- Patents, copyrights, trademarks.

Organizational
- Effective strategic planning processes.
- Excellent evaluation and control systems.

## Intangible Resources

Human
- Experience and capabilities of employees.
- Trust.
- Managerial skills.
- Firm-specific practices and procedures.

Innovation and creativity
- Technical and scientific skills.
- Innovation capacities.

Reputation
- Brand name.
- Reputation with customers for quality and reliability.
- Reputation with suppliers for fairness, non–zero-sum relationships.

## Organizational Capabilities

- Firm competencies or skills the firm employs to transfer inputs to outputs.
- Capacity to combine tangible and intangible resources, using organizational processes to attain desired end.

EXAMPLES:
- Outstanding customer service.
- Excellent product development capabilities.
- Innovativeness of products and services.
- Ability to hire, motivate, and retain human capital.

Source: Adapted from Barney, J. B. 1991. Firm resources and sustained competitive advantage. *Journal of Management:* 17: 101; Grant, R. M. 1991. *Contemporary Strategy Analysis:* 100–102. Cambridge England: Blackwell Business; Hitt, M. A., Ireland, R. D., & Hoskisson, R. E. 2001. *Strategic management: Competitiveness and globalization* (4th ed.). Cincinnati: South-Western College Publishing.

organizational capabilities. Then we will address the conditions under which such assets and capabilities can enable a firm to attain a sustainable competitive advantage.

It is important to note that resources by themselves typically do not yield a competitive advantage. Even if a basketball team recruited an all-star center, there would be little chance of victory if the other members of the team were continually outplayed by their opponents or if the coach's attitude was so negative that everyone, including the center, became unwilling to put forth their best efforts. And imagine how many World Series titles Joe Torre would have won as manager of the New York Yankees if none of the pitchers on his team could throw fastballs over 70 miles per hour. Although the all-star center and the baseball manager are unquestionably valuable resources, they would *not* enable the organization to attain advantages under these circumstances.

In a business context, Cardinal Health's excellent value-creating activities (e.g., logistics, drug formulation) would not be a source of competitive advantage if those activities were not integrated with other important value-creating activities such as marketing and sales. Thus, a central theme of the resource-based view of the firm is that competitive advantages are created (and sustained) through the bundling of several resources in unique combinations.

## Types of Firm Resources

We define firm resources to include all assets, capabilities, organizational processes, information, knowledge, and so forth, controlled by a firm that enable it to develop and implement value-creating strategies.

*Tangible Resources*    Assets that are relatively easy to identify are called tangible resources. They include the physical and financial assets that an organization uses to create value for its customers. Among them are financial resources (e.g., a firm's cash, accounts receivable, and its ability to borrow funds); physical resources (e.g., the company's plant, equipment, and machinery as well as its proximity to customers and suppliers); organizational resources (e.g., the company's strategic planning process and its employee development, evaluation, and reward systems); and technological resources (e.g., trade secrets, patents, and copyrights).

Many firms are finding that high-tech, computerized training has dual benefits: It develops more effective employees and reduces costs at the same time. Employees at FedEx take computer-based job competency tests every 6 to 12 months.[32] The 90-minute computer-based tests identify areas of individual weakness and provide input to a computer database of employee skills—information the firm uses in promotion decisions.

*Intangible Resources*    Much more difficult for competitors (and, for that matter, a firm's own managers) to account for or imitate are intangible resources, which are typically embedded in unique routines and practices that have evolved and accumulated over time. These include human resources (e.g., experience and capability of employees, trust, effectiveness of work teams, managerial skills), innovation resources (e.g., technical and scientific expertise, ideas), and reputation resources (e.g., brand name, reputation with suppliers for fairness and with customers for reliability and product quality). A firm's culture may also be a resource that provides competitive advantage.[33]

For example, you might not think that motorcycles, clothes, toys, and restaurants have much in common. Yet Harley-Davidson has entered all of these product and service markets by capitalizing on its strong brand image—a valuable intangible resource.[34] It has used that image to sell accessories, clothing, and toys, and it has licensed the Harley-Davidson Café in New York City to provide further exposure for its brand name and products.

*Organizational Capabilities*    Organizational capabilities are not specific tangible or intangible assets, but rather the competencies or skills that a firm employs to transform inputs into outputs.[35] In short, they refer to an organization's capacity to deploy tangible and intangible resources over time and generally in combination, and to leverage those capabilities to bring about a desired end.[36] Examples of organizational capabilities are outstanding customer service, excellent product development capabilities, superb innovation processes, and flexibility in manufacturing processes.[37]

Gillette's capability to combine several technologies has been one of the keys to its unparalleled success in the wet-shaving industry. Technologies that are central to its product development efforts include its expertise concerning the physiology of facial hair and skin, the metallurgy of blade strength and sharpness, the dynamics of a cartridge moving across skin, and the physics of a razor blade severing the hair—highly specialized areas for which Gillette has unique capabilities. Combining these technologies has helped the company to develop innovative products such as the Excel, Sensor Excel, and MACH 3 shaving systems.

Dell Inc., with annual revenues of $49 billion and net profits of $3 billion, differentiated itself by pioneering a direct sales approach with user-configurable products to address the diverse needs of the corporate and institutional customer base.[38] Exhibit 3.6 summarizes the Dell recipe for its remarkable success by integrating its tangible resources, intangible resources, and organizational capabilities.

Dell has continued to maintain this competitive advantage by further strengthening its value-chain activities and interrelationships that are critical to satisfying the largest market opportunities. They achieved this by (1) implementing e-commerce direct sales and support processes that accounted for the sophisticated buying habits

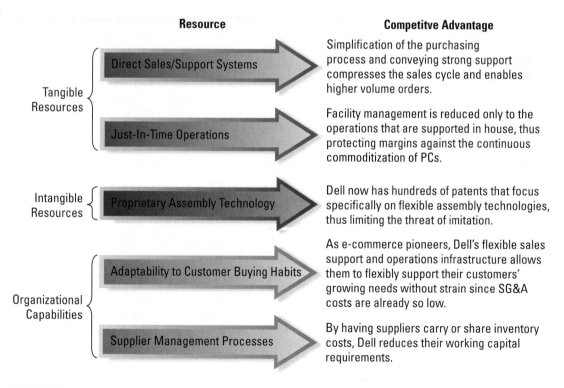

**Exhibit 3.6   Dell's Tangible Resources, Intangible Resources, and Organizational Capabilities**

of the largest markets, and (2) matching their operations to the purchase options by adopting flexible assembly processes, while leaving inventory management to its extensive supplier network. Dell has sustained these advantages by investing in intangible resources such as proprietary assembly methods and packaging configurations that help to protect against the threat of imitation. Dell recognizes that the PC is a complex product with components sourced from several different technologies and manufacturers. Thus, in working backwards from the customer's purchasing habits, Dell saw that they could build valuable solutions by organizing their resources and capabilities around the build-to-specification tastes, making both the sales and integration processes flexible, and passing on overhead expenses to their suppliers. As the PC industry has become further commoditized, Dell has been one of the few competitors which have retained solid margins. They have accomplished this by adapting their manufacturing and assembly capabilities to match the PC market's trend toward user compatibility.

## Firm Resources and Sustainable Competitive Advantages

As we have mentioned, resources alone are not a basis for competitive advantages, nor are advantages sustainable over time. In some cases, a resource or capability helps a firm to increase its revenues or to lower costs but the firm derives only a temporary advantage because competitors quickly imitate or substitute for it. Many e-commerce businesses in the early 2000s have seen their profits seriously eroded because new (or existing) competitors easily duplicated their business model. One noteworthy example is Priceline.com, which expanded its offerings from enabling customers to place bids online for airline tickets and a wide variety of other products. It was simply too easy for competitors (e.g., a consortium of major airlines) to duplicate Priceline's products and services. By the end of 2001, its market capitalization had plummeted roughly 98 percent from its 52-week high.

For a resource to provide a firm with the potential for a sustainable competitive advantage, it must have four attributes.[39] These criteria are summarized in Exhibit 3.7. First, the resource must be valuable in the sense that it exploits opportunities and/or neutralizes threats in the firm's environment. Second, it must be rare among the firm's current and potential competitors. Third, the resource must be difficult for competitors to imitate. Fourth, the resource must have no strategically equivalent substitutes. Let's examine each of these criteria.

**Exhibit 3.7**

**Four Criteria for Assessing Sustainability of Resources and Capabilities**

| Is the resource or capability . . . | Implications |
|---|---|
| Valuable | • Neutralize threats and exploit opportunities |
| Rare | • Not many firms possess |
| Difficult to imitate | • Physically unique |
| | • Path dependency (how accumulated over time) |
| | • Causal ambiguity (difficult to disentangle what it is or how it could be re-created) |
| | • Social complexity (trust, interpersonal relationships, culture, reputation) |
| Difficult to substitute | • No equivalent strategic resources or capabilities |

***Is the Resource Valuable?*** Organizational resources can be a source of competitive advantage only when they are valuable. Resources are valuable when they enable a firm to formulate and implement strategies that improve its efficiency or effectiveness. The SWOT framework suggests that firms improve their performance only when they exploit opportunities or neutralize (or minimize) threats.

The fact that firm attributes must be valuable in order to be considered resources (as well as potential sources of competitive advantage) reveals an important complementary relationship among environmental models (e.g., SWOT and five-forces analyses) and the resource-based model. Environmental models isolate those firm attributes that exploit opportunities and/or neutralize threats. Thus, they specify what firm attributes may be considered as resources. The resource-based model then suggests what additional characteristics these resources must possess if they are to develop a sustained competitive advantage.

***Is the Resource Rare?*** If competitors or potential competitors also possess the same valuable resource, it is not a source of a competitive advantage because all of these firms have the capability to exploit that resource in the same way. Common strategies based on such a resource would give no one firm an advantage. For a resource to provide competitive advantages, it must be uncommon, that is, rare relative to other competitors.

This argument can apply to bundles of valuable firm resources that are used to formulate and develop strategies. Some strategies require a mix of multiple types of resources—tangible assets, intangible assets, and organizational capabilities. If a particular bundle of firm resources is not rare, then relatively large numbers of firms will be able to conceive of and implement the strategies in question. Thus, such strategies will not be a source of competitive advantage, even if the resource in question is valuable.

***Can the Resource Be Imitated Easily?*** Inimitability (difficulty in imitating) is a key to value creation because it constrains competition.[40] If a resource is inimitable, then any profits generated are more likely to be sustainable. Having a resource that competitors can easily copy generates only temporary value. This has important implications. Since managers often fail to apply this test, they tend to base long-term strategies on resources that are imitable. IBP (Iowa Beef Processors) became the first meatpacking company in the United States to modernize by building a set of assets (automated plants located in cattle-producing states) and capabilities (low-cost "disassembly" of carcasses) that earned returns on assets of 1.3 percent in the 1970s. By the late 1980s, however, ConAgra and Cargill had imitated these resources, and IBP's profitability fell by nearly 70 percent, to 0.4 percent.

Monster.com entered the executive recruiting market by providing, in essence, a substitute for traditional bricks-and-mortar headhunting firms. Although Monster.com's resources are rare and valuable, they are subject to imitation by new rivals—other dot-com firms. Why? There are very low entry barriers for firms wanting to try their hand at recruitment. For example, many job search dot-coms have emerged in recent years, including jobsearch.com, headhunter.com, nationjob.com, and hotjobs.com. In all, there are approximately 30,000 online job boards available to job seekers. Clearly, it would be most difficult for a firm to attain a sustainable advantage in this industry.

Clearly, an advantage based on inimitability won't last forever. Competitors will eventually discover a way to copy most valuable resources. However, managers can forestall them and sustain profits for a while by developing strategies around resources that have at least one of the following four characteristics.[41]

***Physical Uniqueness*** The first source of inimitability is physical uniqueness, which by definition is inherently difficult to copy. A beautiful resort location, mineral rights, or Pfizer's pharmaceutical patents simply cannot be imitated. Many managers believe that several of their resources may fall into this category, but on close inspection, few do.

***Path Dependency*** A greater number of resources cannot be imitated because of what economists refer to as path dependency. This simply means that resources are unique and therefore scarce because of all that has happened along the path followed in their development and/or accumulation. Competitors cannot go out and buy these resources quickly and easily; they must be built up over time in ways that are difficult to accelerate.

The Gerber Products Co. brand name for baby food is an example of a resource that is potentially inimitable. Re-creating Gerber's brand loyalty would be a time-consuming process that competitors could not expedite, even with expensive marketing campaigns. Similarly, the loyalty and trust that Southwest Airlines employees feel toward their firm and its cofounder, Herb Kelleher, are resources that have been built up over a long period of time. Also, a crash R&D program generally cannot replicate a successful technology when research findings cumulate. Clearly, these path-dependent conditions build protection for the original resource. The benefits from experience and learning through trial and error cannot be duplicated overnight.

***Causal Ambiguity*** The third source of inimitability is termed causal ambiguity. This means that would-be competitors may be thwarted because it is impossible to disentangle the causes (or possible explanations) of either what the valuable resource is or how it can be re-created. What is the root of 3M's innovation process? You can study it and draw up a list of possible factors. But it is a complex, unfolding (or folding) process that is hard to understand and would be hard to imitate.

In many cases, causally ambiguous resources are organizational capabilities. They often involve a complex web of social interactions that may even depend on particular individuals. When Continental and United tried to mimic the successful low-cost strategy of Southwest Airlines, the planes, routes, and fast gate turnarounds were not the most difficult aspects for them to copy. Those were all rather easy to observe and, at least in principle, easy to duplicate. However, they could not replicate Southwest's culture of fun, family, frugality, and focus since no one can clearly specify exactly what that culture is or how it came to be.

***Social Complexity*** A final reason that a firm's resources may be imperfectly inimitable is that they may reflect a high level of social complexity. Such phenomena are typically beyond the ability of firms to systematically manage or influence. When competitive advantages are based on social complexity, it is difficult for other firms to imitate them.

A wide variety of firm resources may be considered socially complex. Examples include interpersonal relations with the managers in a firm, its culture, and its reputation with its suppliers and customers. In many of these cases, it is easy to specify how these socially complex resources add value to a firm. Hence, there is little or no causal ambiguity surrounding the link between them and competitive advantage. But an understanding that certain firm attributes, such as quality relations among managers, can improve a firm's efficiency does not necessarily lead to systematic efforts to imitate them. Such social engineering efforts are beyond the capabilities of most firms.

Although complex physical technology is not included in this category of sources of imperfect inimitability, the exploitation of physical technology in a firm typically involves the use of socially complex resources. That is, several firms may possess the same physical technology, but only one of them may have the social relations, culture, group norms, and so on to fully exploit the technology in implementing its strategies. If such complex social resources are not subject to imitation (and assuming they are valuable and rare and no substitutes exist), this firm may obtain a sustained competitive advantage from exploiting its physical technology more effectively than other firms.

Exhibit 3.8
Criteria for
Sustainable
Competitive
Advantage and
Strategic
Implications

| Is a resource or capability . . . | | | | |
|---|---|---|---|---|
| **Valuable** | **Rare** | **Difficult to Imitate** | **Without Substitutes** | **Implications for Competitiveness** |
| No | No | No | No | Competitive disadvantage |
| Yes | No | No | No | Competitive parity |
| Yes | Yes | No | No | Temporary competitive advantage |
| Yes | Yes | Yes | Yes | Sustainable competitive advantage |

Source: Adapted from Barney, J. B. 1991. Firm resources and sustained competitive advantage. *Journal of Management,* 17: 99–120.

***Are Substitutes Readily Available?*** The fourth requirement for a firm resource to be a source of sustainable competitive advantage is that there must be no strategically equivalent valuable resources that are themselves not rare or inimitable. Two valuable firm resources (or two bundles of resources) are strategically equivalent when each one can be exploited separately to implement the same strategies.

Substitutability may take at least two forms. First, though it may be impossible for a firm to imitate exactly another firm's resource, it may be able to substitute a similar resource that enables it to develop and implement the same strategy. Clearly, a firm seeking to imitate another firm's high-quality top management team would be unable to copy the team exactly. However, it might be able to develop its own unique management team. Though these two teams would have different ages, functional backgrounds, experience, and so on, they could be strategically equivalent and thus substitutes for one another.

Second, very different firm resources can become strategic substitutes. For example, Internet booksellers such as Amazon.com compete as substitutes for bricks-and-mortar booksellers such as B. Dalton. The result is that resources such as premier retail locations become less valuable. In a similar vein, several pharmaceutical firms have seen the value of patent protection erode in the face of new drugs that are based on different production processes and act in different ways, but can be used in similar treatment regimes. The coming years will likely see even more radical change in the pharmaceutical industry as the substitution of genetic therapies eliminates certain uses of chemotherapy.[42]

To recap this section, recall that resources and capabilities must be rare and valuable as well as difficult to imitate or substitute in order for a firm to attain competitive advantages that are sustainable over time.[43] Exhibit 3.8 illustrates the relationship among the four criteria of sustainability and shows the competitive implications.

In firms represented by the first row of Exhibit 3.8, managers are in a difficult situation. When their resources and capabilities do not meet any of the four criteria, it would be difficult to develop any type of competitive advantage, in the short or long term. The resources and capabilities they possess enable the firm neither to exploit environmental opportunities nor neutralize environmental threats. In the second and third rows, firms have resources and capabilities that are valuable as well as rare, respectively. However, in both cases the resources and capabilities are not difficult for competitors to imitate or substitute. Here, the firms could attain some level of competitive parity. They could perform on par with equally endowed rivals or attain a temporary competitive advantage. But their advantages would be easy for competitors to match. It is only in the fourth row, where all four criteria are satisfied, that competitive advantages can be sustained over time.

## The Generation and Distribution of a Firm's Profits: Extending the Resource-Based View of the Firm

Many scholars would agree that the resource-based view of the firm has been useful in determining when firms will create competitive advantages and enjoy high levels of profitability. However, it has not been developed to address how a firm's profits (often referred to as "rents" by economists) will be distributed to a firm's management and employees.[44] This becomes an important issue because firms may be successful in creating competitive advantages that can be sustainable for a period of time but much of the profits can be retained (or "appropriated") by its employees and managers instead of flowing to the owners of the firm (i.e., the stockholders).*

For a simple illustration, let's first consider Viewpoint DataLabs International, a Salt Lake City–based company that makes sophisticated three-dimensional models and textures for film production houses, video games, and car manufacturers. This example will help to show how employees are often able to obtain (or "appropriate") a high proportion of a firm's profits:

> Walter Noot, head of production, was having trouble keeping his highly skilled Generation X employees happy with their compensation. Each time one of them was lured away for more money, everyone would want a raise. "We were having to give out raises every six months—30 to 40 percent—then six months later they'd expect the same. It was a big struggle to keep people happy."[45]

At Viewpoint DataLabs, it is apparent that much of the profits are being generated by the highly skilled professionals working together on a variety of projects. They are able to exercise their power by successfully demanding more financial compensation. In part, management has responded favorably because they are united in their demands, and their work involves a certain amount of social complexity and causal ambiguity—given the complex, coordinated efforts that their work entails.

Four factors help explain the extent to which employees and managers will be able to obtain a proportionately high level of the profits that they generate.[46] These include:

- ***Employee Bargaining Power.*** If employees are vital to forming a firm's unique capability, they will earn disproportionately high wages. For example, marketing professionals may have access to valuable information which helps them to understand the intricacies of customer demands and expectations, or engineers may understand unique technical aspects of the products or services. Additionally, in some industries such as consulting, advertising, and tax preparation, clients tend to be very loyal to individual professionals employed by the firm, instead of to the firm itself. This enables them to "take the clients with them" if they leave. This enhances their bargaining power.
- ***Employee Replacement Cost.*** If employees' skills are idiosyncratic and rare (a source of resource-based advantage), they should have high bargaining power based on the high cost required by the firm to replace them. For example, Raymond Ozzie, the software designer who was critical in the development of Lotus Notes, was able to dictate the terms under which IBM acquired Lotus.
- ***Employee Exit Costs.*** This factor may tend to reduce an employee's bargaining power. An individual may face high personal costs when leaving the organization. Thus, that individual's threat of leaving may not be credible. In addition,

---

\* Economists define rents as profits (or prices) in excess of what is required to provide a normal return.

some of an employee's expertise may be firm-specific. Thus, it would be of limited value to other firms. A related factor is that of causal ambiguity, which would make it difficult for the employee to explain his or her specific contribution to a given project. Thus, a rival firm might be less likely to pay a high wage premium since it would be unsure of the employee's unique contribution to the firm's success.

- *Manager Bargaining Power.* Like other members of the firm, managers' power would be based on how well they create resource-based advantages. They are generally charged with creating value through the process of organizing, coordinating, and leveraging employees as well as other forms of capital such as plant, equipment, and financial capital (issues that we will address in more detail in Chapter 4). Such activities provide managers with sources of information that may not be readily available to others. Thus, although managers may not know as much about the specific nature of customers and technologies, they are in a position to have a more thorough, integrated understanding of the total operation.

We will discuss in Chapter 9 the conditions under which top-level managers (such as CEOs) of large corporations have been, at times, able to obtain levels of total compensation that would appear to be significantly disproportionate to their contributions to wealth generation as well as to top executives in peer organizations. Here, corporate governance becomes a critical control mechanism. For example, William Esrey and Ronald T. LeMay (the former two top executives at Sprint Corporation) were able to earn more than $130 million in stock options primarily because of "cozy" relationships with members of their board of directors, who tended to approve with little debate huge compensation packages.[47] Such diversion of profits from the owners of the business to top management is far less likely when the board does not consist of a high proportion of the firm's management and board members are truly independent outsiders (i.e., they do not have close ties to management). In general, given the external market for top talent, the level of compensation that executives receive is based on factors similar to the ones just discussed that determine the level of their bargaining power.[48]

# >>Evaluating Firm Performance: Two Approaches

This section addresses two approaches to use when evaluating a firm's performance. The first is financial ratio analysis, which, generally speaking, identifies how a firm is performing according to its balance sheet and income statement. As we will discuss, when performing a financial ratio analysis, you must take into account the firm's performance from a historical perspective (not just at one point in time) as well as how it compares with both industry norms and key competitors.[49]

The second perspective may be considered a broader stakeholder perspective. Firms must satisfy a broad range of stakeholders, including employees, customers, and owners, to ensure their long-term viability. Central to our discussion will be two well-known approaches—the balanced scorecard and the strategy map—that have been popularized by Robert Kaplan and David Norton.[50]

## Financial Ratio Analysis

The beginning point in analyzing the financial position of a firm is to compute and analyze five different types of financial ratios:

- Short-term solvency or liquidity
- Long-term solvency measures

- Asset management (or turnover)
- Profitability
- Market value

**The Appendix to this chapter provides detailed definitions for and discussions of each of these types of ratios as well as examples of how each is calculated.**

A meaningful ratio analysis must go beyond the calculation and interpretation of financial ratios.[51] It must include an analysis of how ratios change over time as well as how they are interrelated. For example, a firm that takes on too much long-term debt to finance operations will see an immediate impact on its indicators of long-term financial leverage. The additional debt will also have a negative impact on the firm's short-term liquidity ratio (i.e., current and quick ratios) since the firm must pay interest and principal on the additional debt each year until it is retired. Additionally, the interest expenses must be deducted from revenues, reducing the firm's profitability.

A firm's financial position should not be analyzed in isolation. Important reference points are needed. We will address some issues that must be taken into account to make financial analysis more meaningful: historical comparisons, comparisons with industry norms, and comparisons with key competitors.

*Historical Comparisons*    When you evaluate a firm's financial performance, it is very useful to compare its financial position over time. This provides a means of evaluating trends. For example, Home Depot reported revenues of $73.1 billion and net income of $5.0 billion in 2005. Almost all firms—except a few of the largest and most profitable companies in the world—would be very happy with such success. However, these figures reflect a consistent annual growth in revenue and net income of 11 percent and 18 percent, respectively, for Home Depot for the period from 2002 to 2005. Clearly, had Home Depot reported annual revenues and net income of $40.0 billion and $2.5 billion in 2005, respectively, it would still be a very large and highly profitable enterprise. However, such performance would have probably resulted in significant damage to the stock price as well as to the careers of many executives! Exhibit 3.9 illustrates a 10-year period of return on sales (ROS) for a hypothetical company. As indicated by the dotted trend lines, the rate of growth (or decline) differs substantially over time periods.

**Exhibit 3.9**
**Historical Trends: Return on Sales (ROS) for a Hypothetical Company**

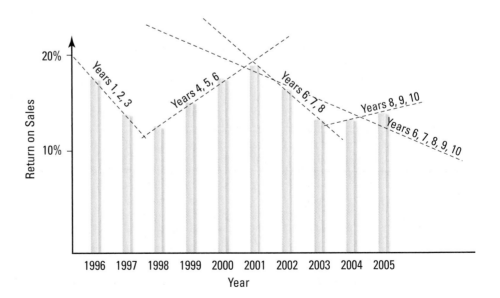

| Financial Ratio | Semiconductors | Grocery Stores | Skilled-Nursing Facilities |
|---|---|---|---|
| Quick ratio (times) | 1.9 | 0.5 | 1.1 |
| Current ratio (times) | 4.0 | 1.6 | 1.6 |
| Total liabilities to net worth (%) | 30.7 | 92.0 | 163.5 |
| Collection period (days) | 49.6 | 2.9 | 31.2 |
| Assets to sales (%) | 187.8 | 20.2 | 101.6 |
| Return on sales (%) | 5.8 | 0.8 | 1.6 |

**Exhibit 3.10**

**How Financial Ratios Differ across Industries**

Source: Dun & Bradstreet. *Industry Norms and Key Business Ratios, 2003–2004.* One Year Edition, SIC #2000-3999 (Semiconductors); SIC #5200-5499 (Grocery Stores); SIC #6100-8999 (Skilled-Nursing Facilities). New York: Dun & Bradstreet Credit Services.

*Comparison with Industry Norms*   When you are evaluating a firm's financial performance, remember also to compare it with industry norms. A firm's current ratio or profitability may appear impressive at first glance. However, it may pale when compared with industry standards or norms.

By comparing your firm with all other firms in your industry, you can calculate relative performance. Banks and other lending institutions often use such comparisons when evaluating a firm's creditworthiness. Exhibit 3.10 includes a variety of financial ratios for three industries: semiconductors, grocery stores, and skilled-nursing facilities. Why is there such variation among the financial ratios for these three industries? There are several reasons. With regard to the collection period, grocery stores operate mostly on a cash basis, so they have a very short collection period. Semiconductor manufacturers sell their output to other manufacturers (e.g., computer makers) on terms such as 2/15 net 45, which means they give a 2 percent discount on bills paid within 15 days and start charging interest after 45 days. Skilled-nursing facilities would also have a longer collection period than grocery stores because they typically rely on payments from insurance companies.

The industry norms for return on sales also highlight some differences among these industries. Grocers, with very slim margins, have a lower return on sales than either skilled-nursing facilities or semiconductor manufacturers. But how might we explain the differences between skilled-nursing facilities and semiconductor manufacturers? Health care facilities, in general, are limited in their pricing structures by Medicare/Medicaid regulations and by insurance reimbursement limits, but semiconductor producers have pricing structures determined by the market. If their products have superior performance, semiconductor manufacturers can charge premium prices.

*Comparison with Key Competitors*   Recall from Chapter 2 that firms with similar strategies are considered members of a strategic group in an industry. Furthermore, competition tends to be more intense among competitors within groups than across groups. Thus, you can gain valuable insights into a firm's financial and competitive position if you make comparisons between a firm and its most direct competitors. Consider Procter & Gamble's ill-fated efforts to enter the highly profitable pharmaceutical industry. Although P&G is a giant in consumer products, its efforts over two decades have produced nominal profits at best. In 1999 P&G spent $380 million on R&D in drugs—22 percent of its total corporate R&D budget. However, its drug unit produced only 2 percent of the company's

Exhibit 3.11

Comparison of
Procter &
Gamble's and Key
Competitors' Drug
Revenues and
R&D Expenditures

| Company (or division) | Sales* ($ billions) | R&D Budget ($ billions) |
|---|---|---|
| P&G Drug Division | $ 0.8 | $0.38 |
| Bristol-Myers Squibb | 20.2 | 1.80 |
| Pfizer | 27.4 | 4.00 |
| Merck | 32.7 | 2.10 |

Source: Berner, R. 2000. Procter & Gamble: Just say no to drugs. *BusinessWeek*, October 9: 128; data courtesy of Lehman Brothers and Procter & Gamble.

*Data: Lehman Brothers, Procter & Gamble Co.

$40 billion sales. Why? While $380 million is hardly a trivial amount of capital, its key competitors dwarf P&G. Consider the drug revenues and R&D budgets of P&G compared to its main rivals as shown in Exhibit 3.11. *BusinessWeek*'s take on P&G's chances in an article entitled "Just Say No to Drugs" was this: "Don't bet on it. P&G may be a giant in detergent and toothpaste, but the consumer-products maker is simply outclassed by the competition."[52]

### Integrating Financial Analysis and Stakeholder Perspectives: The Balanced Scorecard and the Strategy Map

In the previous section, we focused on what may be considered a good starting point in assessing a firm's performance. Clearly, it is useful to see how a firm is performing over time in terms of the several ratios. However, such traditional approaches to performance assessments can be a double-edged sword.[53] Many important transactions that managers make—investments in research and development, employee training and development, advertising and promotion of key brands, and new product development—may greatly expand a firm's market potential and create significant long-term shareholder value. But such critical investments are not reflected positively in short-term financial reports. Why? Because financial reports typically measure expenses, not the value created. Thus, managers may be penalized for spending money in the short term to improve their firm's long-term competitive viability!

Now consider the other side of the coin. A manager may be destroying the firm's future value by operating in a way that makes customers dissatisfied, depletes the firm's stock of good products coming out of R&D, or damages the morale of valued employees. Such budget cuts, however, may lead to very good short-term financials. The manager may look good in the short run and even receive credit for improving the firm's performance. In essence, such a manager has mastered denominator management, whereby decreasing investments makes the return on investment (ROI) ratio larger, even though the actual return remains constant or shrinks.

*The Balanced Scorecard*    To provide a meaningful integration of the many issues that come into evaluating a firm's performance, Kaplan and Norton developed a "balanced scorecard."[54] This is a set of measures that provide top managers with a fast but comprehensive view of the business. In a nutshell, it includes financial measures that reflect the results of actions already taken, but it complements these indicators with operational measures of customer satisfaction, internal processes, and the organization's innovation and improvement activities—operational measures that drive future financial performance.

The balanced scorecard enables managers to consider their business from four key perspectives:

- How do customers see us? (customer perspective)
- What must we excel at? (internal perspective)
- Can we continue to improve and create value? (innovation and learning perspective)
- How do we look to shareholders? (financial perspective)

***Customer Perspective*** Clearly, how a company is performing from its customers' perspective is a top priority for management. The balanced scorecard requires that managers translate their general mission statements on customer service into specific measures that reflect the factors that really matter to customers. For the balanced scorecard to work, managers must articulate goals for four key categories of customer concerns: time, quality, performance and service, and cost. For example, lead time may be measured as the time from the company's receipt of an order to the time it actually delivers the product or service to the customer. Also, quality measures may indicate the level of defective incoming products as perceived by the customer, as well as the accuracy of the company's delivery forecasts.

***Internal Business Perspective*** Although customer-based measures are important, they must be translated into indicators of what the firm must do internally to meet customers' expectations. Excellent customer performance results from processes, decisions, and actions that occur throughout organizations in a coordinated fashion, and managers must focus on those critical internal operations that enable them to satisfy customer needs. The internal measures should reflect business processes that have the greatest impact on customer satisfaction. These include factors that affect cycle time, quality, employee skills, and productivity. Firms also must identify and measure the key resources and capabilities they need to ensure continued strategic success.

***Innovation and Learning Perspective*** The customer and internal business process measures on the balanced scorecard identify the parameters that the company considers most critical to success. However, given the rapid rate of markets, technologies, and global competition, the criteria for success are constantly changing. To survive and prosper, managers must make frequent changes to existing products and services as well as introduce entirely new products with expanded capabilities. A firm's ability to improve, innovate, and learn is tied directly to its value. Simply put, only by developing new products and services, creating greater value for customers, and increasing operating efficiencies can a company penetrate new markets, increase revenues and margins, and enhance shareholder value. A firm's ability to do well from an innovation and learning perspective is more dependent on its intangible than tangible assets. Three categories of intangible assets are critically important: human capital (skills, talent, and knowledge), information capital (information systems, networks), and organization capital (culture, leadership). Chapter 4 provides a more detailed analysis of a firm's intangible assets, especially its human capital.

***Financial Perspective*** Measures of financial performance indicate whether the company's strategy, implementation, and execution are indeed contributing to bottom-line improvement. Typical financial goals include profitability, growth, and shareholder value. Periodic financial statements remind managers that improved quality, response time, productivity, and innovative products benefit the firm only when they result in improved sales, increased market share, reduced operating expenses, or higher asset turnover.[55]

Before ending our discussion of the balanced scorecard, we would like to provide an example that illustrates the causal relationships among the multiple perspectives in the model. Sears, the huge retailer, found a strong causal relationship between employee attitudes, customer attitudes, and financial outcomes.[56] Through an ongoing study, Sears developed (and continues to refine) what it calls its total performance indicators, or TPI—a set of indicators that shows how well the company is doing with customers, employees, and investors. Sears's quantitative model has shown that a 5.0 percent improvement in employee attitudes leads to a 1.3 percent improvement in customer satisfaction, which in turn will drive a 0.5 percent improvement in revenue. Thus, if a single store improved its employee attitude by 5.0 percent on a survey scale, Sears could predict with confidence that if the revenue growth in the district as a whole were 5.0 percent, the revenue growth in this particular store would be 5.5 percent. Interestingly, Sears's managers consider such numbers as rigorous as any others that they work with every year. The company's accounting firm audits management as closely as it audits the financial statements.

One final implication of the balanced scorecard is that managers do not need to look at their job as primarily balancing stakeholder demands. They need to avoid the following mind-set: "How many units in employee satisfaction do I have to give up to get some additional units of customer satisfaction or profits?" Instead, when done properly, the balanced scorecard provides a win–win approach—a means of simultaneously increasing satisfaction among a wide variety of organizational stakeholders, including employees (at all levels), customers, and stockholders. And, as we shall see in Chapter 4, indicators of employee satisfaction have become more important in a knowledge economy, where intellectual capital (as opposed to labor and financial capital) is the primary creator of wealth.

*Strategy Maps*    Building on the concepts that are the foundation of the Balanced Scorecard approach, Kaplan and Norton have recently developed a very useful tool called the strategy map.[57] Strategy maps show the cause and effect links by which specific improvements in different areas lead to a desired outcome. Strategy maps also help employees see how their jobs are related to the overall objectives of the organization. They also help us understand how an organization can convert its assets, both tangible and intangible, into tangible outcomes. We will illustrate how to develop a strategy map using ExxonMobil as an example.

A strategy map starts with the company's vision statement. ExxonMobil's vision is "to be the best integrated refiner-marketer in the United States by efficiently delivering unprecedented value to consumers." They also wanted to increase their return on capital by more than six percentage points within three years. To achieve this, they realized that they have to improve both their revenue growth and productivity (financial perspective). To improve revenue growth, the company decided to expand nongasoline sales (oil, antifreeze, wiper fluid, convenience store products) and ancillary services (car washes, oil changes). Further, within gasoline, they decided to place more emphasis on premium brands. They also decided to improve productivity by slashing operating expenses (for example, by reducing downtime at refineries). The company also decided to focus on premium customers (customers who are not price sensitive) by offering these customers fast and friendly service (customer perspective). These decisions, in turn, led to changes from an internal process perspective. They emphasized processes to create nongasoline products and services, to build best-in-class franchise teams, and to improve inventory management. Finally, from a learning and growth perspective, ExxonMobil identified that their employees needed better understanding of refining and marketing functions. These changes eventually helped the company detect and fill major gaps in its strategies and improve its profit margins.

Exhibit 3.12 presents a simplified version of ExxonMobil's strategy map.

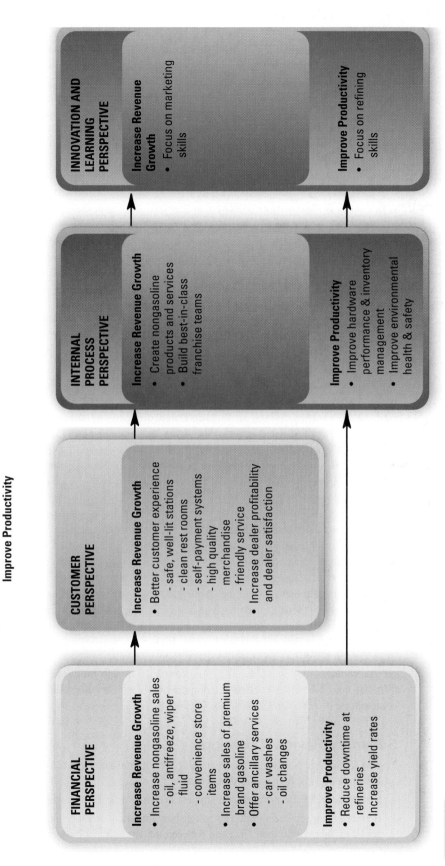

**Goal :** Increase **Return on Capital**

**Means to achieve goal:** Increase **Revenue Growth**
**Improve Productivity**

**FINANCIAL PERSPECTIVE**

**Increase Revenue Growth**
- Increase nongasoline sales
  - oil, antifreeze, wiper fluid
  - convenience store items
- Increase sales of premium brand gasoline
- Offer ancillary services
  - car washes
  - oil changes

**Improve Productivity**
- Reduce downtime at refineries
- Increase yield rates

**CUSTOMER PERSPECTIVE**

**Increase Revenue Growth**
- Better customer experience
  - safe, well-lit stations
  - clean rest rooms
  - self-payment systems
  - high quality merchandise
  - friendly service
- Increase dealer profitability and dealer satisfaction

**INTERNAL PROCESS PERSPECTIVE**

**Increase Revenue Growth**
- Create nongasoline products and services
- Build best-in-class franchise teams

**Improve Productivity**
- Improve hardware performance & inventory management
- Improve environmental health & safety

**INNOVATION AND LEARNING PERSPECTIVE**

**Increase Revenue Growth**
- Focus on marketing skills

**Improve Productivity**
- Focus on refining skills

**Exhibit 3.12** **ExxonMobil's Strategy Map**

Source: Reprinted by permission of *Harvard Business Review*. Exhibit from "Having Trouble with Your Strategy? Then Map It," by Kaplan, R. S. and Norton, D. P. 2000. Copyright © 2000 by The Harvard Business School Publishing Corporation; all rights reserved.

## Summary

In the traditional approaches to assessing a firm's internal environment, the primary goal of managers would be to determine their firm's relative strengths and weaknesses. Such is the role of SWOT analysis, wherein managers analyze their firm's strengths and weaknesses as well as the opportunities and threats in the external environment. In this chapter, we discussed why this may be a good starting point but hardly the best approach to take in performing a sound analysis. There are many limitations to SWOT analysis, including its static perspective, its potential to overemphasize a single dimension of a firm's strategy, and the likelihood that a firm's strengths do not necessarily help the firm create value or competitive advantages.

We identified two frameworks that serve to complement SWOT analysis in assessing a firm's internal environment: value-chain analysis and the resource-based view of the firm. In conducting a value-chain analysis, first divide the firm into a series of value-creating activities. These include primary activities such as inbound logistics, operations, and service as well as support activities such as procurement and human resources management. Then analyze how each activity adds value as well as how *interrelationships* among value activities in the firm and among the firm and its customers and suppliers add value. Thus, instead of merely determining a firm's strengths and weaknesses per se, you analyze them in the overall context of the firm and its relationships with customers and suppliers—the value system.

The resource-based view of the firm considers the firm as a bundle of resources: tangible resources, intangible resources, and organizational capabilities. Competitive advantages that are sustainable over time generally arise from the creation of bundles of resources and capabilities. For advantages to be sustainable, four criteria must be satisfied: value, rarity, difficulty in imitation, and difficulty in substitution. Such an evaluation requires a sound knowledge of the competitive context in which the firm exists. The owners of a business may not capture all of the value created by the firm. The appropriation of value created by a firm between the owners and employees is determined by four factors: employee bargaining power, replacement cost, employee exit costs, and manager bargaining power.

An internal analysis of the firm would not be complete unless you evaluate its performance and make the appropriate comparisons. Determining a firm's performance requires an analysis of its financial situation as well as a review of how well it is satisfying a broad range of stakeholders, including customers, employees, and stockholders. We discussed the concepts of the balanced scorecard and the strategy map, in which four perspectives must be addressed: customer, internal business, innovation and learning, and financial. Central to these concepts is the idea that the interests of various stakeholders can be interrelated. We provide examples of how indicators of employee satisfaction lead to higher levels of customer satisfaction, which in turn lead to higher levels of financial performance. Thus, improving a firm's performance does not need to involve making trade-offs among different stakeholders. Assessing the firm's performance is also more useful if it is evaluated in terms of how it changes over time, compares with industry norms, and compares with key competitors.

## Summary Review Questions

1. SWOT analysis is a technique to analyze the internal and external environment of a firm. What are its advantages and disadvantages?

2. Briefly describe the primary and support activities in a firm's value chain.

3. How can managers create value by establishing important relationships among the value-chain activities both within their firm and between the firm and its customers and suppliers?

4. Briefly explain the four criteria for sustainability of competitive advantages.

5. Under what conditions are employees and managers able to appropriate some of the value created by their firm?

6. What are the advantages and disadvantages of conducting a financial ratio analysis of a firm?

7. Summarize the concept of the balanced scorecard. What are its main advantages?

Dell Computer is a leading firm in the personal computer industry, with annual revenues of $49 billion during its 2004 fiscal year. Dell has created a very strong competitive position via its "direct model," whereby it manufactures its personal computers to detailed customer specifications.

Below we address several questions that focus on Dell's value-chain activities and inter-relationships among them as well as whether they are able to attain sustainable competitive advantage(s). (We discuss Dell in this chapter on pages 93–94.)

1. Where in Dell's value chain are they creating value for their customer?

## Experiential Exercise

| Value-Chain Activity | Yes/No | How Does Dell Create Value for the Customer? |
|---|---|---|
| **Primary:** | | |
| Inbound logistics | | |
| Operations | | |
| Outbound logistics | | |
| Marketing and sales | | |
| Service | | |
| **Support:** | | |
| Procurement | | |
| Technology development | | |
| Human resource management | | |
| General administration | | |

2. What are the important relationships among Dell's value-chain activities? What are the important interdependencies? For each activity, identify the relationships and interdependencies.

|  | Inbound logistics | Operations | Outbound logistics | Marketing and sales | Service | Procurement | Technology development | Human resource management | General administration |
|---|---|---|---|---|---|---|---|---|---|
| Inbound logistics |  |  |  |  |  |  |  |  |  |
| Operations |  |  |  |  |  |  |  |  |  |
| Outbound logistics |  |  |  |  |  |  |  |  |  |  |
| Marketing and sales |  |  |  |  |  |  |  |  |  |  |
| Service |  |  |  |  |  |  |  |  |  |  |
| Procurement |  |  |  |  |  |  |  |  |  |  |
| Technology development |  |  |  |  |  |  |  |  |  |  |
| Human resource management |  |  |  |  |  |  |  |  |  |  |
| General administration |  |  |  |  |  |  |  |  |  |  |

3. What resources, activities, and relationships enable Dell to achieve a sustainable competitive advantage?

| Resource/Activity | Is It Valuable? | Is It Rare? | Are There Few Substitutes? | Is It Difficult to Make? |
|---|---|---|---|---|
| Inbound logistics |  |  |  |  |
| Operations |  |  |  |  |
| Outbound logistics |  |  |  |  |
| Marketing and sales |  |  |  |  |
| Service |  |  |  |  |
| Procurement |  |  |  |  |
| Technology development |  |  |  |  |
| Human resource management |  |  |  |  |
| General administration |  |  |  |  |

1. Using published reports, select two CEOs who have recently made public statements regarding a major change in their firm's strategy. Discuss how the successful implementation of such strategies requires changes in the firm's primary and support activities.

2. Select a firm that competes in an industry in which you are interested. Drawing upon published financial reports, complete a financial ratio analysis. Based on changes over time and a comparison with industry norms, evaluate the firm's strengths and weaknesses in terms of its financial position.

3. How might exemplary human resource practices enhance and strengthen a firm's value-chain activities?

4. Using the Internet, look up your university or college. What are some of its key value-creating activities that provide competitive advantages? Why?

Application
Questions
Exercises

1. What are some of the ethical issues that arise when a firm becomes overly zealous in advertising its products?

2. What are some of the ethical issues that may arise from a firm's procurement activities? Are you aware of any of these issues from your personal experience or businesses you are familiar with?

Ethics
Questions

## References

1. Halliday, J., & Sanders, L. 2004. Troubled Jaguar searches for marketing panacea. *Automotive News,* November 22: 28; Kerwin, K. 2004. The care and feeding of Jaguar. *BusinessWeek,* October 4: 38; Anonymous. 2005. Jaguar's problems hold back PAG profits. *Birmingham Post,* January 12: np; and, Smith, C. 2004. Don't run down the messenger. *Marketing,* November 10: 28.

2. Our discussion of the value chain will draw on Porter, M. E. 1985. *Competitive advantage:* chap. 2. New York: Free Press.

3. Dyer, J. H. 1996. Specialized supplier networks as a source of competitive advantage: Evidence from the auto industry. *Strategic Management Journal,* 17: 271–291.

4. For an insightful perspective on value-chain analysis, refer to Stabell, C. B., & Fjeldstad, O. D. 1998. Configuring value for competitive advantage: On chains, shops, and networks. *Strategic Management Journal,* 19: 413–437. The authors develop concepts of value chains, value shops, and value networks to extend the value-creation logic across a broad range of industries. Their work builds on the seminal contributions of Porter, 1985, op. cit., and others who have addressed how firms create value through key interrelationships among value-creating activities.

5. Ibid.

6. Maynard, M. 1999. Toyota promises custom order in 5 days. *USA Today,* August 6: B1.

7. Shaw Industries. 1999. Annual report: 14–15.

8. Fisher, M. L. 1997. What is the right supply chain for your product? *Harvard Business Review,* 75(2): 105–116.

9. Jackson. M. 2001. Bringing a dying brand back to life. *Harvard Business Review,* 79(5): 53–61.

10. Anderson, J. C., & Nmarus, J. A. 2003. Selectively pursuing more of your customer's business. *MIT Sloan Management Review,* 44(3): 42–50.

11. An insightful discussion of the role of identity marketing—that is, the myriad labels that people use to express who they are—in successful marketing activities is found in Reed, A., II, & Bolton, L. E. 2005. The complexity of identify. *MIT Sloan Management Review,* 46(3): 18–22.

12. Berggren, E., & Nacher, T. 2000. Why good ideas go bust. *Management Review,* February: 32–36.

13. For an insightful perspective on creating effective brand portfolios, refer to Hill, S., Ettenson, R., & Tyson, D. 2005. Achieving the ideal brand portfolio. *MIT Sloan Management Review,* 46(2): 85–90.

14. Haddad, C., & Grow, B. 2001. Wait a second—I didn't order that! *BusinessWeek,* July 16: 45.

15. Brown, J. 2000. Service, please. *BusinessWeek* E. Biz, October 23: EB 48–50.

16. For a scholarly discussion on the procurement of technology components, read Hoetker, G. 2005. How much you know versus how well I know you: Selecting a supplier for a technically innovative component. *Strategic Management Journal,* 26(1): 75–96.

17. For a discussion on criteria to use when screening suppliers for back-office functions, read Feeny, D., Lacity, M., & Willcocks, L. P. 2005. Taking the measure of outsourcing providers. *MIT Sloan Management Review,* 46(3): 41–48.

18. Imperato, G. 1998. How to give good feedback. *Fast Company,* September: 144–156.

19. Bensaou, B. M., & Earl, M. 1998. The right mindset for managing information technology. *Harvard Business Review,* 96(5): 118–128.

20. Donlon, J. P. 2000. Bonsignore's bid for the big time. *Chief Executive,* March: 28–37.

21. Ulrich, D. 1998. A new mandate for human resources. *Harvard Business Review,* 96(1): 124–134.

22. Wood, J. 2003. Sharing jobs and working from home: The new face of the airline industry. *AviationCareer.net,* February 21.

23. Follow AT&T's lead in this tactic to retain "plateaued" employees. n.d. *Recruitment & Retention:* 1.

24. For a cautionary note on the use of IT, refer to McAfee, A. 2003. When too much IT knowledge is a dangerous thing. *MIT Sloan Management Review,* 44(2): 83–90.

25. Walgreen Co. 1996. *Information technology and Walgreen's: Opportunities for employment,* January; and Dess, G. G., & Picken, J. C. 1997. *Beyond productivity.* New York: AMACOM.

26. Rivette, K. G., & Kline, D. 2000. Discovering new value in intellectual property. *Harvard Business Review,* 78(1): 54–66.

27. For an interesting perspective on some of the potential downsides of close customer and supplier relationships, refer to Anderson, E., & Jap, S. D. 2005. The dark side of close relationships. *MIT Sloan Management Review,* 46(3): 75–82.

28. Day, G. S. 2003. Creating a superior customer-relating capability. *MIT Sloan Management Review,* 44(3): 77–82.

29. To gain insights on the role of electronic technologies in enhancing a firm's connections to outside suppliers and customers, refer to Lawrence, T. B., Morse, E. A., & Fowler, S. W. 2005. Managing your portfolio of connections. *MIT Sloan Management Review,* 46(2): 59–66.

30. Reinhardt, F. L. 1999. Bringing the environment down to earth. *Harvard Business Review,* 77(4): 149–157.

31. Collis, D. J., & Montgomery, C. A. 1995. Competing on resources: Strategy in the 1990's. *Harvard Business Review,* 73(4): 119–128; and Barney, J. 1991. Firm resources and sustained competitive advantage. *Journal of Management,* 17(1): 99–120.

32. Henkoff, R. 1993. Companies that train the best. *Fortune,* March 22: 83; and Dess & Picken, *Beyond productivity,* p. 98.

33. Barney, J. B. 1986. Types of competition and the theory of strategy: Towards an integrative framework. *Academy of Management Review,* 11(4): 791–800.

34. Harley-Davidson. 1993. Annual report.

35. For a rigorous, academic treatment of the origin of capabilities, refer to Ethiraj, S. K., Kale, P., Krishnan, M. S., & Singh, J. V. 2005. Where do capabilities come from and how do they matter? A study of the software services industry. *Strategic Management Journal,* 26(1): 25–46.

36. For an academic discussion on methods associated with organizational capabilities, refer to Dutta, S., Narasimhan, O., & Rajiv, S. 2005. Conceptualizing and measuring capabilities: Methodology and empirical application. *Strategic Management Journal,* 26(3): 277–286.

37. Lorenzoni, G., & Lipparini, A. 1999. The leveraging of interfirm relationships as a distinctive organizational capability: A longitudinal study. *Strategic Management Journal,* 20: 317–338.

38. The following discussion of Dell and Exhibit 3.6 draw on the following sources: Serwer, A. 2005. America's most admired companies. *Fortune,* March 7: 72–82; Weiss, J., & Hughes, J. 2005. Execution without excuses. *Harvard Business Review,* 83(3): 102–111; Brown, E., & Costa, Len A. 1999. America's most admired companies. *Fortune,* March 1: 68–74; Hamel, G., & Sampler, J. 1998. The E-Corporation. *Fortune,* December 7: 80–88; and Rivkin, J. W., & Porter, M. Matching Dell. *Harvard Business School Case* 9-799-158. We would like to thank Ted Khoury, a Ph.D. student at the University of Texas at Dallas, for his assistance in preparing this example.

39. Barney, J. 1991. Firm resources and sustained competitive advantage. *Journal of Management,* 17(1): 99–120.

40. Barney, 1986, op. cit. Our discussion of inimitability and substitution draws upon this source.

41. Deephouse, D. L. 1999. To be different, or to be the same? It's a question (and theory) of strategic balance. *Strategic Management Journal,* 20: 147–166.

42. Yeoh, P. L., & Roth, K. 1999. An empirical analysis of sustained advantage in the U.S. pharmaceutical industry: Impact of firm resources and capabilities. *Strategic Management Journal,* 20: 637–653.

43. Robins, J. A., & Wiersema, M. F. 2000. Strategies for unstructured competitive environments: Using scarce resources to create new markets. In Bresser, R. F., et al., (Eds.), *Winning strategies in a deconstructing world:* 201–220. New York: John Wiley.

44. Amit, R., & Schoemaker, J. H. 1993. Strategic assets and organizational rent. *Strategic Management Journal,* 14(1): 33–46; Collis, D. J., & Montgomery, C. A. 1995. Competing on resources: Strategy in the 1990's. *Harvard Business Review,* 73(4): 118–128; Coff, R. W. 1999. When competitive advantage doesn't lead to performance: The resource-based view and stakeholder bargaining power. *Organization Science,* 10(2): 119–133; and Blyler, M., & Coff, R. W. 2003. Dynamic capabilities, social capital, and rent appropriation: Ties that split pies. *Strategic Management Journal,* 24: 677–686.

45. Munk, N. 1998. The new organization man. *Fortune,* March 16: 62–74.

46. Coff, op. cit.

47. Lavelle, L. 2003. Sprint's board needs a good sweeping, too. *BusinessWeek,* February 24: 40; Anonymous. 2003. Another nail in the coffin. *The Economist,* February 15: 69–70; and Byrnes, N., Dwyer, P., & McNamee, M. 2003. Hacking away at tax shelters, *BusinessWeek,* February 24: 41.

48. We have focused our discussion on how internal stake-holders (e.g., employees, managers, and top executives) may appropriate a firm's profits (or rents). For an interesting discussion of how a firm's innovations may be appropriated by external stakeholders (e.g., customers, suppliers) as well as competitors, refer to Grant, R. M. 2002. *Contemporary strategy analysis* (4th ed.): 335–340. Malden, MA: Blackwell.

49. Luehrman, T. A. 1997. What's it worth? A general manager's guide to valuation. *Harvard Business Review,* 45(3): 132–142.

50. See, for example, Kaplan, R. S., & Norton, D. P. 1992. The balanced scorecard: Measures that drive performance. *Harvard Business Review,* 69(1): 71–79.

51. Hitt, M. A., Ireland, R. D., & Stadter, G. 1982. Functional importance of company performance: Moderating effects of grand strategy and industry type. *Strategic Management Journal,* 3: 315–330.

52. Berner, R. 2000. Procter & Gamble: Just say no to drugs. *BusinessWeek,* October 9: 128.

53. Kaplan & Norton, op. cit.

54. Ibid.

55. For a discussion of the relative value of growth versus increasing margins, read Mass, N. J. 2005. The relative value of growth. *Harvard Business Review,* 83(4): 102–112.

56. Rucci, A. J., Kirn, S. P., & Quinn, R. T. 1998. The employee-customer-profit chain at Sears. *Harvard Business Review,* 76(1): 82–97.

57. Kaplan, R. S., & Norton, D. P. 2000. Having trouble with your strategy? Then map it. *Harvard Business Review,* 78(10): 167–176.

# APPENDIX TO CHAPTER 3

# Financial Ratio Analysis
## Standard Financial Statements

One obvious thing we might want to do with a company's financial statements is to compare them to those of other, similar companies. We would immediately have a problem, however. It's almost impossible to directly compare the financial statements for two companies because of differences in size.

For example, Oracle and IBM are obviously serious rivals in the computer software market, but IBM is much larger (in terms of assets), so it is difficult to compare them directly. For that matter, it's difficult to even compare financial statements from different points in time for the same company if the company's size has changed. The size problem is compounded if we try to compare IBM and, say, SAP (of Germany). If SAP's financial statements are denominated in German marks, then we have a size *and* a currency difference.

To start making comparisons, one obvious thing we might try to do is to somehow standardize the financial statements. One very common and useful way of doing this is to work with percentages instead of total dollars. The resulting financial statements are called *common-size statements.* We consider these next.

## Common-Size Balance Sheets

For easy reference, Prufrock Corporation's 2004 and 2005 balance sheets are provided in Exhibit 3A.1. Using these, we construct common-size balance sheets by expressing each item as a percentage of total assets. Prufrock's 2004 and 2005 common-size balance sheets are shown in Exhibit 3A.2.

Notice that some of the totals don't check exactly because of rounding errors. Also notice that the total change has to be zero since the beginning and ending numbers must add up to 100 percent.

In this form, financial statements are relatively easy to read and compare. For example, just looking at the two balance sheets for Prufrock, we see that current assets were 19.7 percent of total assets in 2004, up from 19.1 percent in 2005. Current liabilities declined from 16.0 percent to 15.1 percent of total liabilities and equity over that same time. Similarly, total equity rose from 68.1 percent of total liabilities and equity to 72.2 percent.

Source: Adapted from Rows, S. A., Westerfield, R. W., & Jordan, B. D. 1999. *Essentials of Corporate Finance* (2nd ed.). chap. 3. NewYork: McGraw-Hill. 1999.

**Exhibit 3A.1**

**Prufrock
Corporation**
Balance Sheets as of
December 31, 2004
and 2005
($ in millions)

|  | 2004 | 2005 |
|---|---|---|
| **Assets** | | |
| Current assets | | |
| Cash | $ 84 | $ 98 |
| Accounts receivable | 165 | 188 |
| Inventory | 393 | 422 |
| Total | $ 642 | $ 708 |
| Fixed assets | | |
| Net plant and equipment | $2,731 | $2,880 |
| Total assets | $3,373 | $3,588 |
| **Liabilities and Owners' Equity** | | |
| Current liabilities | | |
| Accounts payable | $ 312 | $ 344 |
| Notes payable | 231 | 196 |
| Total | $ 543 | $ 540 |
| Long-term debt | $ 531 | $ 457 |
| Owners' equity | | |
| Common stock and paid-in surplus | $ 500 | $ 550 |
| Retained earnings | 1,799 | 2,041 |
| Total | $2,299 | $2,591 |
| Total liabilities and owners' equity | $3,373 | $3,588 |

Overall, Prufrock's liquidity, as measured by current assets compared to current liabilities, increased over the year. Simultaneously, Prufrock's indebtedness diminished as a percentage of total assets. We might be tempted to conclude that the balance sheet has grown "stronger."

## Common-Size Income Statements

A useful way of standardizing the income statement, shown in Exhibit 3A.3, is to express each item as a percentage of total sales, as illustrated for Prufrock in Exhibit 3A.4.

This income statement tells us what happens to each dollar in sales. For Prufrock, interest expense eats up $.061 out of every sales dollar and taxes take another $.081. When all is said and done, $.157 of each dollar flows through to the bottom line (net income), and that amount is split into $.105 retained in the business and $.052 paid out in dividends.

These percentages are very useful in comparisons. For example, a relevant figure is the cost percentage. For Prufrock, $.582 of each $1.00 in sales goes to pay for goods sold. It would be interesting to compute the same percentage for Prufrock's main competitors to see how Prufrock stacks up in terms of cost control.

## Ratio Analysis

Another way of avoiding the problems involved in comparing companies of different sizes is to calculate and compare *financial ratios*. Such ratios are ways of comparing and investigating the

| | 2004 | 2005 | Change |
|---|---|---|---|
| **Assets** | | | |
| Current assets | | | |
|   Cash | 2.5% | 2.7% | + .2% |
|   Accounts receivable | 4.9 | 5.2 | + .3 |
|   Inventory | 11.7 | 11.8 | + .1 |
|     Total | 19.1 | 19.7 | + .6 |
| Fixed assets | | | |
|   Net plant and equipment | 80.9 | 80.3 | − .6 |
| Total assets | 100.0% | 100.0% | .0% |
| **Liabilities and Owners' Equity** | | | |
| Current liabilities | | | |
|   Accounts payable | 9.2% | 9.6% | + .4% |
|   Notes payable | 6.8 | 5.5 | − 1.3 |
|     Total | 16.0 | 15.1 | − .9 |
| Long-term debt | 15.7 | 12.7 | − 3.0 |
| Owners' equity | | | |
|   Common stock and paid-in surplus | 14.8 | 15.3 | + .5 |
|   Retained earnings | 53.3 | 56.9 | +3.6 |
|     Total | 68.1 | 72.2 | +4.1 |
| Total liabilities and owners' equities | 100.0% | 100.0% | .0% |

**Exhibit 3A.2**
**Prufrock Corporation**
Common-Size Balance Sheets as of December 31, 2004 and 2005 (%)

Note: Numbers may not add up to 100.0% due to rounding.

| | | |
|---|---|---|
| Sales | | $2,311 |
| Cost of goods sold | | 1,344 |
| Depreciation | | 276 |
| Earnings before interest and taxes | | $ 691 |
| Interest paid | | 141 |
| Taxable income | | $ 550 |
| Taxes (34%) | | 187 |
| Net income | | $ 363 |
|   Dividends | $121 | |
|   Addition to retained earnings | 242 | |

**Exhibit 3A.3**
**Prufrock Corporation**
2005 Income Statement ($ in millions)

| Sales | | 100.0% |
|---|---|---|
| Cost of goods sold | | 58.2 |
| Depreciation | | 11.9 |
| Earnings before interest and taxes | | 29.9 |
| Interest paid | | 6.1 |
| Taxable income | | 23.8 |
| Taxes (34%) | | 8.1 |
| Net income | | 15.7% |
| Dividends | 5.2% | |
| Addition to retained earnings | 10.5 | |

relationships between different pieces of financial information. We cover some of the more common ratios next, but there are many others that we don't touch on.

One problem with ratios is that different people and different sources frequently don't compute them in exactly the same way, and this leads to much confusion. The specific definitions we use here may or may not be the same as others you have seen or will see elsewhere. If you ever use ratios as a tool for analysis, you should be careful to document how you calculate each one, and, if you are comparing your numbers to those of another source, be sure you know how its numbers are computed.

For each of the ratios we discuss, several questions come to mind:

1. How is it computed?
2. What is it intended to measure, and why might we be interested?
3. What is the unit of measurement?
4. What might a high or low value be telling us? How might such values be misleading?
5. How could this measure be improved?

Financial ratios are traditionally grouped into the following categories:

1. Short-term solvency, or liquidity, ratios.
2. Long-term solvency, or financial leverage, ratios.
3. Asset management, or turnover, ratios.
4. Profitability ratios.
5. Market value ratios.

We will consider each of these in turn. In calculating these numbers for Prufrock, we will use the ending balance sheet (2005) figures unless we explicitly say otherwise. The numbers for the various ratios come from the income statement and the balance sheet.

## Short-Term Solvency, or Liquidity, Measures

As the name suggests, short-term solvency ratios as a group are intended to provide information about a firm's liquidity, and these ratios are sometimes called *liquidity measures*. The primary concern is the firm's ability to pay its bills over the short run without undue stress. Consequently, these ratios focus on current assets and current liabilities.

For obvious reasons, liquidity ratios are particularly interesting to short-term creditors. Since financial managers are constantly working with banks and other short-term lenders, an understanding of these ratios is essential.

One advantage of looking at current assets and liabilities is that their book values and market values are likely to be similar. Often (though not always), these assets and liabilities just don't live long enough for the two to get seriously out of step. On the other hand, like any type of near cash, current assets and liabilities can and do change fairly rapidly, so today's amounts may not be a reliable guide to the future.

**Current Ratio**   One of the best-known and most widely used ratios is the *current ratio*. As you might guess, the current ratio is defined as:

$$\text{Current ratio} = \frac{\text{Current assets}}{\text{Current liabilities}}$$

For Prufrock, the 2005 current ratio is:

$$\text{Current ratio} = \frac{\$708}{\$540} = 1.31 \text{ times}$$

Because current assets and liabilities are, in principle, converted to cash over the following 12 months, the current ratio is a measure of short-term liquidity. The unit of measurement is either dollars or times. So, we could say Prufrock has $1.31 in current assets for every $1 in current liabilities, or we could say Prufrock has its current liabilities covered 1.31 times over.

To a creditor, particularly a short-term creditor such as a supplier, the higher the current ratio, the better. To the firm, a high current ratio indicates liquidity, but it also may indicate an inefficient use of cash and other short-term assets. Absent some extraordinary circumstances, we would expect to see a current ratio of at least 1, because a current ratio of less than 1 would mean that net working capital (current assets less current liabilities) is negative. This would be unusual in a healthy firm, at least for most types of businesses.

The current ratio, like any ratio, is affected by various types of transactions. For example, suppose the firm borrows over the long term to raise money. The short-run effect would be an increase in cash from the issue proceeds and an increase in long-term debt. Current liabilities would not be affected, so the current ratio would rise.

Finally, note that an apparently low current ratio may not be a bad sign for a company with a large reserve of untapped borrowing power.

**Quick (or Acid-Test) Ratio**   Inventory is often the least liquid current asset. It's also the one for which the book values are least reliable as measures of market value, since the quality of the inventory isn't considered. Some of the inventory may later turn out to be damaged, obsolete, or lost.

More to the point, relatively large inventories are often a sign of short-term trouble. The firm may have overestimated sales and overbought or overproduced as a result. In this case, the firm may have a substantial portion of its liquidity tied up in slow-moving inventory.

To further evaluate liquidity, the *quick,* or *acid-test, ratio* is computed just like the current ratio, except inventory is omitted:

$$\text{Quick ratio} = \frac{\text{Current assets} - \text{Inventory}}{\text{Current liabilities}}$$

Notice that using cash to buy inventory does not affect the current ratio, but it reduces the quick ratio. Again, the idea is that inventory is relatively illiquid compared to cash.

For Prufrock, this ratio in 2005 was:

$$\text{Quick ratio} = \frac{\$708 - 422}{\$540} = .53 \text{ times}$$

The quick ratio here tells a somewhat different story than the current ratio, because inventory accounts for more than half of Prufrock's current assets. To exaggerate the point, if this inventory consisted of, say, unsold nuclear power plants, then this would be a cause for concern.

**Cash Ratio**   A very short-term creditor might be interested in the *cash ratio:*

$$\text{Cash ratio} = \frac{\text{Cash}}{\text{Current liabilities}}$$

You can verify that this works out to be .18 times for Prufrock.

## Long-Term Solvency Measures

Long-term solvency ratios are intended to address the firm's long-run ability to meet its obligations, or, more generally, its financial leverage. These ratios are sometimes called *financial leverage ratios* or just *leverage ratios*. We consider three commonly used measures and some variations.

*Total Debt Ratio*   The *total debt ratio* takes into account all debts of all maturities to all creditors. It can be defined in several ways, the easiest of which is:

$$\text{Total debt ratio} = \frac{\text{Total assets} - \text{Total equity}}{\text{Total assets}}$$

$$= \frac{\$3,588 - 2,591}{\$3,588} = .28 \text{ times}$$

In this case, an analyst might say that Prufrock uses 28 percent debt.[1] Whether this is high or low or whether it even makes any difference depends on whether or not capital structure matters.

Prufrock has $.28 in debt for every $1 in assets. Therefore, there is $.72 in equity ($1 − .28) for every $.28 in debt. With this in mind, we can define two useful variations on the total debt ratio, the *debt-equity ratio* and the *equity multiplier:*

$$\text{Debt-equity ratio} = \text{Total debt/Total equity}$$

$$= \$.28/\$.72 = .39 \text{ times}$$

$$\text{Equity multiplier} = \text{Total assets/Total equity}$$

$$= \$1/\$.72 = 1.39 \text{ times}$$

The fact that the equity multiplier is 1 plus the debt-equity ratio is not a coincidence:

$$\text{Equity multiplier} = \text{Total assets/Total equity} = \$1/\$.72 = 1.39$$

$$= (\text{Total equity} + \text{Total debt})/\text{Total equity}$$

$$= 1 + \text{Debt-equity ratio} = 1.39 \text{ times}$$

The thing to notice here is that given any one of these three ratios, you can immediately calculate the other two, so they all say exactly the same thing.

*Times Interest Earned*   Another common measure of long-term solvency is the *times interest earned* (TIE) *ratio*. Once again, there are several possible (and common) definitions, but we'll stick with the most traditional:

$$\text{Times interest earned ratio} = \frac{\text{EBIT}}{\text{Interest}}$$

$$= \frac{\$691}{\$141} = 4.9 \text{ times}$$

As the name suggests, this ratio measures how well a company has its interest obligations covered, and it is often called the interest coverage ratio. For Prufrock, the interest bill is covered 4.9 times over.

*Cash Coverage*   A problem with the TIE ratio is that it is based on earnings before interest and taxes (EBIT), which is not really a measure of cash available to pay interest. The reason

---

[1] Total equity here includes preferred stock, if there is any. An equivalent numerator in this ratio would be (Current liabilities + Long-term debt).

is that depreciation, a noncash expense, has been deducted. Since interest is most definitely a cash outflow (to creditors), one way to define the *cash coverage ratio* is:

$$\text{Cash coverage ratio} = \frac{\text{EBIT} + \text{Depreciation}}{\text{Interest}}$$

$$= \frac{\$691 + 276}{\$141} = \frac{\$967}{\$141} = 6.9 \text{ times}$$

The numerator here, EBIT plus depreciation, is often abbreviated EBDIT (earnings before depreciation, interest, and taxes). It is a basic measure of the firm's ability to generate cash from operations, and it is frequently used as a measure of cash flow available to meet financial obligations.

## Asset Management, or Turnover, Measures

We next turn our attention to the efficiency with which Prufrock uses its assets. The measures in this section are sometimes called *asset utilization ratios.* The specific ratios we discuss can all be interpreted as measures of turnover. What they are intended to describe is how efficiently, or intensively, a firm uses its assets to generate sales. We first look at two important current assets: inventory and receivables.

*Inventory Turnover and Days' Sales in Inventory* During the year, Prufrock had a cost of goods sold of $1,344. Inventory at the end of the year was $422. With these numbers, *inventory turnover* can be calculated as:

$$\text{Inventory turnover} = \frac{\text{Cost of goods sold}}{\text{Inventory}}$$

$$= \frac{\$1,344}{\$422} = 3.2 \text{ times}$$

In a sense, we sold off, or turned over, the entire inventory 3.2 times. As long as we are not running out of stock and thereby forgoing sales, the higher this ratio is, the more efficiently we are managing inventory.

If we know that we turned our inventory over 3.2 times during the year, then we can immediately figure out how long it took us to turn it over on average. The result is the average *days' sales in inventory:*

$$\text{Days' sales in inventory} = \frac{365 \text{ days}}{\text{Inventory turnover}}$$

$$= \frac{365}{3.2} = 114 \text{ days}$$

This tells us that, on average, inventory sits 114 days before it is sold. Alternatively, assuming we used the most recent inventory and cost figures, it will take about 114 days to work off our current inventory.

For example, we frequently hear things like "Majestic Motors has a 60 days' supply of cars." This means that, at current daily sales, it would take 60 days to deplete the available inventory. We could also say that Majestic has 60 days of sales in inventory.

*Receivables Turnover and Days' Sales in Receivables* Our inventory measures give some indication of how fast we can sell products. We now look at how fast we collect on those sales. The *receivables turnover* is defined in the same way as inventory turnover:

$$\text{Receivables turnover} = \frac{\text{Sales}}{\text{Accounts receivable}}$$

$$= \frac{\$2,311}{\$188} = 12.3 \text{ times}$$

Loosely speaking, we collected our outstanding credit accounts and reloaned the money 12.3 times during the year.[2]

This ratio makes more sense if we convert it to days, so the *days' sales in receivables* is:

$$\text{Days' sales in receivables} = \frac{365 \text{ days}}{\text{Receivables turnover}}$$

$$= \frac{365}{12.3} = 30 \text{ days}$$

Therefore, on average, we collect on our credit sales in 30 days. For obvious reasons, this ratio is very frequently called the *average collection period* (ACP).

Also note that if we are using the most recent figures, we can also say that we have 30 days' worth of sales currently uncollected.

*Total Asset Turnover*   Moving away from specific accounts like inventory or receivables, we can consider an important "big picture" ratio, the *total asset turnover ratio*. As the name suggests, total asset turnover is:

$$\text{Total asset turnover} = \frac{\text{Sales}}{\text{Total assets}}$$

$$= \frac{\$2,311}{\$3,588} = .64 \text{ times}$$

In other words, for every dollar in assets, we generated $.64 in sales.

A closely related ratio, the *capital intensity ratio,* is simply the reciprocal of (i.e., 1 divided by) total asset turnover. It can be interpreted as the dollar investment in assets needed to generate $1 in sales. High values correspond to capital intensive industries (e.g., public utilities). For Prufrock, total asset turnover is .64, so, if we flip this over, we get that capital intensity is $1/.64 = $1.56. That is, it takes Prufrock $1.56 in assets to create $1 in sales.

## Profitability Measures

The three measures we discuss in this section are probably the best known and most widely used of all financial ratios. In one form or another, they are intended to measure how efficiently the firm uses its assets and how efficiently the firm manages its operations. The focus in this group is on the bottom line, net income.

*Profit Margin*   Companies pay a great deal of attention to their *profit margin:*

$$\text{Profit margin} = \frac{\text{Net income}}{\text{Sales}}$$

$$= \frac{\$363}{\$2,311} = 15.7\%$$

This tells us that Prufrock, in an accounting sense, generates a little less than 16 cents in profit for every dollar in sales.

All other things being equal, a relatively high profit margin is obviously desirable. This situation corresponds to low expense ratios relative to sales. However, we hasten to add that other things are often not equal.

For example, lowering our sales price will usually increase unit volume, but will normally cause profit margins to shrink. Total profit (or, more importantly, operating cash flow) may go up or down; so the fact that margins are smaller isn't necessarily bad. After all, isn't it possible that,

---

[2]Here we have implicitly assumed that all sales are credit sales. If they were not, then we would simply use total credit sales in these calculations, not total sales.

as the saying goes, "Our prices are so low that we lose money on everything we sell, but we make it up in volume!"[3]

***Return on Assets***    *Return on assets* (ROA) is a measure of profit per dollar of assets. It can be defined several ways, but the most common is:

$$\text{Return on assets} = \frac{\text{Net income}}{\text{Total equity}}$$

$$= \frac{\$363}{\$3,588} = 10.12\%$$

***Return on Equity***    *Return on equity* (ROE) is a measure of how the stockholders fared during the year. Since benefiting shareholders is our goal, ROE is, in an accounting sense, the true bottom-line measure of performance. ROE is usually measured as:

$$\text{Return on equity} = \frac{\text{Net income}}{\text{Total assets}}$$

$$= \frac{\$363}{\$2,591} = 14\%$$

For every dollar in equity, therefore, Prufrock generated 14 cents in profit, but, again, this is only correct in accounting terms.

Because ROA and ROE are such commonly cited numbers, we stress that it is important to remember they are accounting rates of return. For this reason, these measures should properly be called *return on book assets* and *return on book equity*. In addition, ROE is sometimes called *return on net worth*. Whatever it's called, it would be inappropriate to compare the results to, for example, an interest rate observed in the financial markets.

The fact that ROE exceeds ROA reflects Prufrock's use of financial leverage. We will examine the relationship between these two measures in more detail below.

## Market Value Measures

Our final group of measures is based, in part, on information not necessarily contained in financial statements—the market price per share of the stock. Obviously, these measures can only be calculated directly for publicly traded companies.

We assume that Prufrock has 33 million shares outstanding and the stock sold for $88 per share at the end of the year. If we recall that Prufrock's net income was $363 million, then we can calculate that its earnings per share were:

$$\text{EPS} = \frac{\text{Net income}}{\text{Shares outstanding}} = \frac{\$363}{33} = \$11$$

***Price-Earnings Ratio***    The first of our market value measures, the *price-earnings*, or PE, *ratio* (or multiple), is defined as:

$$\text{PE ratio} = \frac{\text{Price per share}}{\text{Earnings per share}}$$

$$= \frac{\$85}{\$11} = 8 \text{ times}$$

In the vernacular, we would say that Prufrock shares sell for eight times earnings, or we might say that Prufrock shares have, or "carry," a PE multiple of 8.

Since the PE ratio measures how much investors are willing to pay per dollar of current earnings, higher PEs are often taken to mean that the firm has significant prospects for future growth.

---

[3]No, it's not; margins can be small, but they do need to be positive!

Of course, if a firm had no or almost no earnings, its PE would probably be quite large; so, as always, be careful when interpreting this ratio.

*Market-to-Book Ratio*   A second commonly quoted measure is the *market-to-book ratio:*

$$\text{Market-to-book ratio} = \frac{\text{Market value per share}}{\text{Book value per share}}$$

$$= \frac{\$88}{(\$2,591/33)} = \frac{\$88}{\$78.5} = 1.12 \text{ times}$$

Notice that book value per share is total equity (not just common stock) divided by the number of shares outstanding.

Since book value per share is an accounting number, it reflects historical costs. In a loose sense, the market-to-book ratio therefore compares the market value of the firm's investments to their cost. A value less than 1 could mean that the firm has not been successful overall in creating value for its stockholders.

## Conclusion

This completes our definition of some common ratios. Exhibit 3A.5 summarizes the ratios we've discussed.

**I.  Short-term solvency, or liquidity, ratios**

$$\text{Current ratio} = \frac{\text{Current assets}}{\text{Current liabilities}}$$

$$\text{Quick ratio} = \frac{\text{Current assets} - \text{Inventory}}{\text{Current liabilities}}$$

$$\text{Cash ratio} = \frac{\text{Cash}}{\text{Current liabilities}}$$

**II.  Long-term solvency, or financial leverage, ratios**

$$\text{Total debt ratio} = \frac{\text{Total assets} - \text{Total equity}}{\text{Total assets}}$$

$$\text{Debt-equity ratio} = \text{Total debt/Total equity}$$

$$\text{Equity multiplier} = \text{Total assets/Total equity}$$

$$\text{Times interest earned ratio} = \frac{\text{EBIT}}{\text{Interest}}$$

$$\text{Cash coverage ratio} = \frac{\text{EBIT} + \text{Depreciation}}{\text{Interest}}$$

**III.  Asset utilization, or turnover, ratios**

$$\text{Inventory turnover} = \frac{\text{Cost of goods sold}}{\text{Inventory}}$$

$$\text{Days' sales in inventory} = \frac{365 \text{ days}}{\text{Inventory turnover}}$$

$$\text{Receivables turnover} = \frac{\text{Sales}}{\text{Accounts receivable}}$$

$$\text{Days' sales in receivables} = \frac{365 \text{ days}}{\text{Receivables turnover}}$$

$$\text{Total asset turnover} = \frac{\text{Sales}}{\text{Total assets}}$$

$$\text{Capital intensity} = \frac{\text{Total assets}}{\text{Sales}}$$

**IV.  Profitability ratios**

$$\text{Profit margin} = \frac{\text{Net income}}{\text{Sales}}$$

$$\text{Return on assets (ROA)} = \frac{\text{Net income}}{\text{Total assets}}$$

$$\text{Return on equity (ROE)} = \frac{\text{Net income}}{\text{Total equity}}$$

$$\text{ROE} = \frac{\text{Net income}}{\text{Sales}} \times \frac{\text{Sales}}{\text{Assets}} \times \frac{\text{Assets}}{\text{Equity}}$$

**V.  Market value ratios**

$$\text{Price-earnings ratio} = \frac{\text{Price per share}}{\text{Earnings per share}}$$

$$\text{Market-to-book ratio} = \frac{\text{Market value per share}}{\text{Book value per share}}$$

**Exhibit 3A.5**

# 4

# Recognizing a Firm's Intellectual Assets:

*Moving beyond a Firm's Tangible Resources*

## >chapter objectives

*After reading this chapter, you should have a good understanding of:*

- Why the management of knowledge professionals and knowledge itself are so critical in today's organizations.

- The importance of recognizing the interdependence of attracting, developing, and retaining human capital.

- The key role of social capital in leveraging human capital within and across the firm.

- Why teams are critical in combining and leveraging knowledge in organizations and how they can be made more effective.

- The vital role of technology in leveraging knowledge and human capital.

- How technology can help to retain knowledge even when employees cannot be retained by the organization.

- How leveraging human capital is critical to strategy formulation at the business, corporate, international, and Internet levels.

One of the most important trends that managers must consider is the significance of the knowledge worker in today's economy. Managers must both recognize the importance of top talent and provide mechanisms to enhance the leveraging of human capital to innovate and, in the end, develop products and services that create value.

The first section addresses the increasing role of knowledge as the primary means of wealth generation in today's economy. A company's value is not derived solely from its physical assets, such as plant, equipment, and machinery. Rather, it is based on knowledge, know-how, and intellectual assets—all embedded in people.

The second section discusses the key resource itself, human capital, which is the foundation of intellectual capital. We explore ways in which the organization can attract, develop, and retain top talent—three important, interdependent activities. With regard to attracting human capital, we address issues such as "hiring for attitude, training for skill." One of the issues regarding developing human capital is encouraging widespread involvement throughout the organization. Our discussion on retaining human capital addresses issues such as the importance of having employees identify with an organization's mission and values. We also address the value of a diverse workforce.

The attraction, development, and retention of human capital are necessary but not sufficient conditions for organizational success. In the third section we address social capital—networks of relationships among a firm's members. This is especially important where collaboration and sharing information are critical. In this section we address why social capital can be particularly important in attracting human capital and making teams effective.

The fourth section addresses the role of technology in leveraging human capital. Examples range from e-mail and the use of networks to facilitate collaboration among individuals to more complex forms of technologies, such as sophisticated knowledge management systems. We discuss how electronic teams can be effectively managed. We also address how technology can help to retain knowledge.

The fifth and final section discusses how leveraging human capital is vital to each of the four levels of strategy formulation—business, corporate, international, and Internet.

Some companies excel in attracting top talent and leveraging such talent. This often leads to positive relationships among individuals within the firm, promoting a social infrastructure that is critical for gaining consensus on major decisions, sharing information, and promoting cooperation. However, at times, hiring top talent or "stars" can have a big downside. Consider the experience of The Wildflower Group, a New York–based licensing and marketing group that represents the trademark owners of such products as home furnishings, giftware, and popular characters, including ALF and Newton's Law (a small bear extremely popular in Great Britain).

> To Michael Carlisle, one of Wildflower's partners, it seemed like the coup of a lifetime.[1] Although his firm was just three years old and had only 10 employees, it was able to recruit a highly regarded salesperson from one of the industry's largest and most prestigious companies. She was a bona fide superstar, with a blue-chip resume, a Rolodex brimming with contacts, and a track record for landing top-dollar clients. The excited Carlisle remembers thinking, "She could do a lot for us."
>
> But that was then . . . and things didn't work out as planned. The new employee was accustomed to the comforts and amenities of a large corporation. She became testy and unpleasant when asked to, for example, troubleshoot her own computer problems or alter her travel plans to take advantage of cheaper airfares. And she hardly created warm, positive feelings among her coworkers by trying to fob off administrative chores such as sending faxes. To make matters worse, she was not bringing in new business for Wildflower. Finally, and not too surprisingly, she did not take direction very well. Carlisle would lay out Wildflower's sales plan, and she'd argue about it.
>
> Carlisle and his partner, Fred Paprin, spent many unproductive hours discussing how to best salvage the situation. However, as the complaints mounted, Carlisle began to worry about losing other employees. The final straw came when Carlisle noticed that several younger employees were beginning to emulate the star's poor behavior. The partners agreed it was time for the company to cut its losses. Wildflower's big hiring coup lasted less than 10 months.

Managers are always hunting for stellar employees who can raise the organization to the next level. Unfortunately, as Carlisle discovered, bulletproof credentials are far from a "happily ever after" guarantee. Just the opposite may come true instead.

In this chapter, we will discuss how attracting, developing, and retaining talent is a necessary but not sufficient condition for success. Many firms have experienced problems leveraging talent and technologies into successful products and services. In today's knowledge economy, it doesn't matter too much how big your stock of resources is— whether it be top-level talent, physical resources such as buildings and machinery, or financial capital. Rather, the question becomes: How good is the organization at attracting top talent and leveraging that talent to produce a stream of products and services valued by the marketplace?

## >>The Central Role of Knowledge in Today's Economy

Central to our discussion is an enormous change that has accelerated over the past few decades and its implications for the strategic management of organizations.[2] That is, for most of the 20th century, managers were primarily concerned with tangible resources such as land, equipment, and money as well as intangibles such as brands, image, and customer loyalty. Most efforts were directed more toward the efficient allocation of labor and capital—the two traditional factors of production.

How times have changed. Today, more than 50 percent of the gross domestic product (GDP) in developed economies is knowledge-based; that is, it is based on intellectual assets and intangible people skills.[3] In the United States, intellectual and information processes create most of the value for firms in large service industries (e.g., software, medical care, communications, and education), which make up 76 percent of the U.S. GDP. In the manufacturing sector, intellectual activities like R&D, process design, product design, logistics, marketing, or technological innovation produce the preponderance of value added.[4] To drive home the point, consider the perspective of Gary Hamel and C. K. Prahalad, two leading writers in strategic management:

> The machine age was a physical world. It consisted of things. Companies made and distributed things (physical products). Management allocated things (capital budgets); management invested in things (plant and equipment).
>
> In the machine age, people were ancillary, and things were central. In the information age, things are ancillary, knowledge is central. A company's value derives not from things, but from knowledge, know-how, intellectual assets, competencies—all embedded in people.[5]

In a similar vein, Robert Reich, former U. S. Secretary of Labor, provides an example of everyday products:[6]

> The real value of my shirt-and-trouser order lies in the system that translates it into digital instructions along the way, monitors every step to make sure it's done quickly and correctly, and then speeds it back to me. The apparel industry that departed New England in the first half of the twentieth century in pursuit of cheaper labor in the South, and then promptly moved on to Southeast Asia, where labor was even cheaper, is being transformed largely into design, marketing, and software systems located wherever the designers, marketers, and software engineers reside. Only a small fraction of the price of that final garment has anything to do with routine sewing and cutting. I'm mostly buying intangible services.

In the knowledge economy, wealth is increasingly created through the effective management of knowledge workers instead of by the efficient control of physical and financial assets. The growing importance of knowledge, coupled with the move by labor markets to reward knowledge work, tells us that someone who invests in a company is, in essence, buying a set of talents, capabilities, skills, and ideas—intellectual capital— not physical and financial resources.[7]

Let's provide a few examples. People don't buy Microsoft's stock because of its software factories; it doesn't own any. Rather, the value of Microsoft is bid up because of its ability to set standards for personal-computing software, exploit the value of its name, and forge alliances with other companies. Similarly, Merck didn't become the "Most Admired" company, for seven consecutive years in *Fortune*'s annual survey, because it can manufacture pills, but because its scientists can discover medicines. P. Roy Vagelos, who was CEO of Merck, the $23 billion pharmaceutical giant, during its long run atop the "Most Admired" survey, said, "A low-value product can be made by anyone anywhere. When you have knowledge no one else has access to—that's dynamite. We guard our research even more carefully than our financial assets."[8]

To apply some numbers to our arguments, let's ask, What's a company worth?[9] Start with the "big three" financial statements: income statement, balance sheet, and statement of cash flow. If these statements tell a story that investors find useful, then a company's market value* should roughly (but not precisely, because the market looks forward and the books look backward) be the same as the value that accountants ascribe to it—the book value of the firm. However, this is not the case. A study compared the market value with the book value of 3,500 U.S. companies over a period of two decades. In 1978 the

---

* The market value of a firm is equal to the value of a share of its common stock times the number of shares outstanding. The book value of a firm is primarily a measure of the value of its tangible assets. It can be calculated by the formula: total assets − total liabilities.

Exhibit 4.1
Ratio of Market Value
to Book Value for
Selected Companies

| Company | Annual Sales ($ billions) | Market Value ($ billions) | Book Value ($ billions) | Ratio of Market to Book Value |
|---|---|---|---|---|
| Google | 3.2 | 60.4 | 2.9 | 20.8 |
| Genentech | 3.9 | 75.0 | 6.8 | 11.0 |
| Yahoo! | 3.6 | 47.9 | 7.1 | 6.7 |
| eBay | 3.2 | 42.8 | 6.7 | 6.4 |
| Southwest Airlines | 6.5 | 11.7 | 5.5 | 2.1 |
| Union Pacific (Railroad) | 12.2 | 16.7 | 12.7 | 1.3 |
| Ford Motor Company | 171.6 | 16.7 | 16.0 | 1.0 |

Note: The data on market valuations are as of May 1, 2005. All other financial data is based on the most recently available balance sheets and income statements.

two were pretty well matched: Book value was 95 percent of market value. However, the gap between market values and book values has widened significantly. Twenty years later, book value was just 28 percent of market value. A colorful commentary comes from Robert A. Howell, an expert on the changing role of finance and accounting, "The big three financial statements . . . are about as useful as an 80-year-old Los Angeles road map."

As we might expect based on the above discussion, the gap between a firm's market value and book value is far greater for knowledge-intensive corporations than for firms with strategies based primarily on tangible assets. Exhibit 4.1 shows the ratio of market-to-book value for a selected set of companies. In firms where knowledge and the management of knowledge workers are relatively important contributors to developing products and services—and physical resources are less critical—the ratio of market-to-book value tends to be much higher. Many writers have defined intellectual capital as the difference between a firm's market value and book value—that is, a measure of the value of a firm's intangible assets.[10] This admittedly broad definition includes assets such as reputation, employee loyalty and commitment, customer relationships, company values, brand names, and the experience and skills of employees.[11] Thus, simplifying, we have:

Intellectual capital = Market value of the firm − Book value of the firm

The issue becomes: How do companies create value in the knowledge-intensive economy? As we stated above, the general answer is to attract and leverage human capital effectively through mechanisms that create products and services of value over time. Let's articulate a few of the basic concepts that we will be talking about in this chapter.

First, consider human capital. Human capital is the "*individual* capabilities, knowledge, skills, and experience of the company's employees and managers."[12] This is knowledge that is relevant to the task at hand, as well as the capacity to add to this reservoir of knowledge, skills, and experience through learning.[13]

Second, social capital can be defined as "the network of relationships that individuals have throughout the organization." Such relationships are critical in sharing and leveraging knowledge and in acquiring resources.[14] Social capital also can extend beyond the organizational boundaries to include relationships between the firm and its suppliers, customers, and alliance partners.[15]

Third is the concept of "knowledge," which comes in two different forms. On the one hand, there is explicit knowledge that is codified, documented, easily reproduced, and widely distributed. Examples include engineering drawings, software code, sales collateral, and patents. The other type of knowledge is tacit knowledge.[16] This is knowledge that is, in essence, in the minds of employees and is based on their experiences and backgrounds. Tacit knowledge is shared only with the consent and participation of the individual.

New knowledge is constantly being created in organizations. It involves the continual interaction of explicit and tacit knowledge. Consider, for example, two software engineers working together on a computer code. The computer code itself is the explicit knowledge. However, through their sharing of ideas based on each individual's experience—that is, their tacit knowledge—new knowledge is created when they make modifications to the existing code. Another important issue is the role of "socially complex processes," which include leadership, culture, and trust.[17] These processes play a central role in the creation of knowledge.[18] They represent the "glue" that holds the organization together and helps to create a working environment where individuals are more willing to share their ideas, work in teams, and, in the end, create products and services of value. In a later section, we will address the importance of social capital in the value creation process.

Numerous books have been written on the subject of knowledge management and the central role that it has played in creating wealth in organizations and countries throughout the developed world.[19] Here, we focus on some of the key issues that organizations must address to compete through knowledge.

We will now turn our discussion to the central resource itself—human capital—and some guidelines on how it can be attracted/selected, developed, and retained. Tom Stewart, editor of the *Harvard Business Review,* noted that organizations must also undergo significant efforts to protect their human capital. A firm may "diversify the ownership of vital knowledge by emphasizing teamwork, guard against obsolescence by developing learning programs, and shackle key people with golden handcuffs."[20] In addition, people are less likely to leave an organization if there are effective structures to promote teamwork and information sharing, strong leadership that encourages innovation, and cultures that demand excellence and ethical behavior. Such issues are also central to the topic of this chapter. Although we touch on these issues throughout this chapter, we provide more detail in later chapters. We discuss organizational controls (culture, rewards, and boundaries) in Chapter 9, organization structure and design in Chapter 10, and a variety of leadership and entrepreneurship topics in Chapters 11, 12, and 13.

## >>Human Capital: The Foundation of Intellectual Capital

To be successful, organizations must recruit talented people—employees at all levels with the proper sets of skills and capabilities coupled with the right values and attitudes. Such skills and attitudes must be continually developed, strengthened, and reinforced, and each employee must be motivated and his or her efforts focused on the organization's goals and objectives.

The rise to prominence of the knowledge worker as a vital source of competitive advantage is changing the balance of power in today's organization. Knowledge workers place professional development and personal enrichment (financial and otherwise) above company loyalty. Attracting, recruiting, and hiring the "best and the brightest," is a critical first step in the process of building intellectual capital. At a symposium for CEOs, Bill Gates said, "The thing that is holding Microsoft back . . . is simply how [hard] we find it to go out and recruit the kind of people we want to grow our research team."[21]

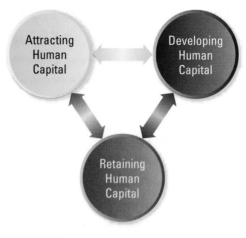

**Exhibit 4.2    Human Capital: Three Interdependent Activities**

But hiring is only the first of three vital processes in which all successful organizations must engage to build and leverage their human capital. Firms must also *develop* employees at all levels and specialties to fulfill their full potential in order to maximize their joint contributions. Finally, the first two processes are for naught if firms can't provide the working environment and intrinsic and extrinsic rewards to *retain* their best and brightest.

These three activities are highly interrelated. We would like to suggest the imagery of a three-legged stool (see Exhibit 4.2).[22] If one leg is weak or broken, the stool collapses.

To illustrate such interdependence, poor hiring impedes the effectiveness of development and retention processes. In a similar vein, ineffective retention efforts place additional burdens on hiring and development. Consider the following anecdote, provided by Jeffrey Pfeffer of the Stanford University Business School:

> Not long ago, I went to a large, fancy San Francisco law firm—where they treat their associates like dog doo and where the turnover is very high. I asked the managing partner about the turnover rate. He said, "A few years ago, it was 25 percent, and now we're up to 30 percent." I asked him how the firm had responded to that trend. He said, "We increased our recruiting." So I asked him, "What kind of doctor would you be if your patient was bleeding faster and faster, and your only response was to increase the speed of the transfusion?"[23]

Clearly, stepped-up recruiting is a poor substitute for weak retention. Although there are no simple, easy-to-apply answers, we can learn from what leading-edge firms are doing to attract, develop, and retain human capital in today's highly competitive and rapidly changing marketplace. Let's begin by discussing hiring and selection practices.

## Attracting Human Capital

All we can do is bet on the people we pick. So my whole job is picking the right people.

**Jack Welch,** former chairman, General Electric Company[24]

As we have noted, the first step in the process of building superior human capital is input control: attracting and selecting the right person. Many human resource professionals still approach employee selection from a "lock and key" mentality—that is, fit a key (a job candidate) into a lock (the job). Such an approach involves a thorough analysis of both the person and the job. Only then can the right decision be made as to how well the two will fit together. How can you fail, the theory goes, if you get a precise match of knowledge, ability, and skill profiles? Frequently, however, the precise matching approach places its primary emphasis on task-specific skills (e.g., motor skills, specific information gathering and processing capabilities, and communication skills) and puts less emphasis on the broad general knowledge and experience, social skills, values, beliefs, and attitudes of employees.

Many have questioned the precise matching approach. Instead, they argue that firms can identify top performers by focusing on key employee mind-sets, attitudes, social skills, and general orientations that lead to success in nearly all jobs. These firms reason that if they get these elements right, the task-specific skills can be learned in relatively short order. (This does not imply, however, that task-specific skills are unimportant; rather, it suggests that the requisite skill sets must be viewed as a necessary but not sufficient condition.) This leads us to a phrase that is popular with many organizations today and serves as the title of the next section.

*"Hire for Attitude, Train for Skill"*   Organizations are increasingly placing their emphasis on the general knowledge and experience, social skills, values, beliefs, and attitudes of employees. Consider Southwest Airlines's hiring practices, with their strong focus on employee values and attitudes. Given its strong team orientation, Southwest uses an "indirect" approach. For example, the interviewing team asks a group of employees to prepare a five-minute presentation about themselves. During the presentations, the interviewers observe which candidates are enthusiastically supporting their peers and which candidates are focused on polishing their own presentations while the others are presenting.[25] The former are, of course, favored.

Social skills are also important. You need to be both pleasant and collegial to be hired by Rosenbluth International, a travel-management company based in Philadelphia, with annual revenues over $5 billion. Here, job applicants are asked to play a trial game of softball with the company team. Potential executives are frequently flown to the firm's North Dakota ranch to help repair fences or drive cattle. Do athletic ability or ranching skills matter? Not at all. According to Keami Lewis, Rosenbluth's diversity manager, "You can teach a person almost anything. But you can't teach him or her how to be nice."[26] Or, as Tom Stewart has suggested, "You can make a leopard a better leopard, but you can't change its spots."[27]

Alan Cooper, president of Cooper Software, Inc., in Palo Alto, California, goes a few steps further. He cleverly *uses technology* to hone in on the problem-solving ability of his applicants and their attitudes before an interview even takes place. He has devised a "Bozo Filter," a test administered online (see Strategy Spotlight 4.1) that can be applied to any industry. Before you spend time figuring out whether job candidates will work out satisfactorily, find out how their minds work. Cooper advised, "Hiring was a black hole. I don't talk to bozos anymore because 90 percent of them turn away when they see our test. It's a self-administering bozo filter."[28]

The central point is what some have called the Popeye Principle, "I y'am what I y'am," borrowing from the famous cartoon sailor. Many have argued that the most common, and fatal, hiring mistake is to select individuals with the right skills but the wrong mind-set on the theory that "we can change them." According to Alan Davidson, an industrial psychologist in San Diego whose clients include Chevron, Merrill Lynch, and the Internal Revenue Service, "The single best predictor of future behavior is past behavior. Your personality (largely reflecting values, beliefs, attitudes, and social skills) is going to be essentially the same throughout your life."[29]

# STRATEGY SPOTLIGHT

## Cooper Software's "Bozo Filter"

Hiring is often easier than firing. Even when unemployment rates are low and labor is scarce, it's still easier to find employees than it is to get them out the door if they don't work out. Not only do poor employees affect the morale of better talent, but they also cost the company money in lost productivity.

Cooper Software has found an innovative way to prevent the problem of hiring bad employees. CEO Alan Cooper asks job applicants to visit the company's Web site, where the applicants will find a test that takes between two and five hours to complete. The test asks questions designed to see how prospective employees approach problem-solving tasks. For example, one key question asks software engineer applicants to design a new table-creation software program for Microsoft Word. Candidates provide pencil sketches and a description of

Sources: Cardin, R. 1997. Make your own bozo filter. *Fast Company*, October–November: 56; Coop, A. 1997. Getting design across. Unpublished manuscript, November 23: 1–8; and www.cooper.com.

the new user interface. Another question is used for design communicators. They are asked to develop a marketing strategy for a new touch-tone phone—directed at consumers in the year 1850. Candidates e-mail their answers back to the company, and the answers are circulated around the firm to solicit feedback. Only candidates with the highest marks get interviews.

Jonathan Korman, a design communicator, suggested that the test "told me more about real job duties than any description could." Josh Seiden, a software designer, is even more positive: "It was a fun puzzle—much more engaging than most of what I was doing at my previous job."

That's exactly the kind of attitude Cooper wants. "We get e-mail from some people saying, 'Before I take this test, is the position still open?' I say no, because I don't want anybody who sees it as an effort," claims Cooper. "People who really care take the test and love it. Other people say it's hard. We don't want those people."

***Sound Recruiting Approaches and Networking*** Companies that take hiring seriously must also take recruiting seriously. The number of jobs that successful knowledge-intensive companies must fill is astonishing. Ironically, many companies still have no shortage of applicants. Southwest Airlines typically gets 150,000 résumés a year, yet hires only about 5,000 new employees. And Netscape (now part of Time Warner) reviews 60 résumés for every hire.[30] The challenge becomes having the right job candidates, not the greatest number of them.

Few firms are as thorough as Microsoft when it comes to recruiting. Each year the firm scans the entire pool of 25,000 U.S. computer-science graduates and identifies the 8,000 in which they are interested. After further screening, 2,600 are invited for on-campus interviews at their universities. Out of these, only 800 are invited to the company's Redmond, Washington, headquarters. Of these, 500 receive offers, and usually 400 accept. These massive efforts, however, provide less than 20 percent of the company's hiring needs. To find the other talent, Microsoft maintains a team of 300 recruiting experts whose full-time job is to locate the best and brightest in the industry.[31]

GE Medical Systems, which builds CT scanners and magnetic resonance imaging (MRI) systems, relies extensively on networking. They have found that current employees are the best source for new ones. Recently, Steven Patscot, head of staffing and leadership development, made a few simple changes to double the number of referrals. First, he simplified the process—no complex forms, no bureaucracy, and so on. Second, he increased incentives. Everyone referring a qualified candidate received a gift certificate from Sears. For referrals who were hired, the "bounty" was increased to $2,000 (or $3,000 if the referral was a software engineer). Although this may sound like a lot of money, it is "peanuts" compared to the $15,000 to $20,000 fees that GE typically pays

## The "War for Talent": Possible Downsides

Various organizational processes and dynamics arise when organizations adopt a "war for talent" mind-set that can lead to many adverse outcomes. Dr. Jeffrey Pfeffer, a professor at Stanford University's Business School, cautions that not only should a firm *not* try to "win" the war for talent but also that even adopting this imagery to guide recruiting initiatives can be hazardous to an organization's health.

When a firm engages in a war for talent, there is:

- An inevitable emphasis on individual performance (rewarding "stars"). This tends to erode teamwork, increase internal competition, and reduce learning and the spread of best practices within the firm.

- A tendency to become enamored with the talents of those outside the firm and discount the talents and abilities of insiders. This generally leads to decreased motivation in the firm's existing employees and greater turnover, and often causes more

difficulties in future recruiting as the company tries to replace those who left.

- A self-fulfilling prophecy. Those labeled as less capable become less able because they are often asked to do less and are given fewer resources, training, and mentoring. In the process, the organization has far too many people who are in the process of dropping out of the competitive fray.

- A reduced emphasis on repairing the systemic, cultural, and business process issues that are typically much more important for enhanced performance. Why? The company seeks success solely by getting the right people into the company.

- The creation of an elitist, arrogant attitude. After all, once a firm has successfully completed the war for talent, it develops an attitude that makes building a wise organization extremely difficult. In wise organizations, people know what they know and what they don't know. However, companies that believe they have won the war for talent think they are so full of smart people that they know everything!

Source: Pfeffer, J. 2001. Fighting the war for talent is hazardous to your organization's health. *Organizational Dynamics*, 29(4): 248–259.

to headhunters for each person hired.[32] Also, when someone refers a former colleague or friend for a job, his or her credibility is on the line. Thus, employees will tend to be careful in recommending people for employment unless they are reasonably confident that these people are good candidates. This provides a good "screen" for the firm in deciding whom to hire. After all, hiring the right people makes things a lot easier: fewer rules and regulations, less need for monitoring and hierarchy, and greater internalization of organizational norms and objectives.

Before moving on, it is useful to point out an important caveat. While it is important to strive to attract "top talent," managers must avoid a mind-set where they engage in "war for talent." We address this issue in Strategy Spotlight 4.2.

## Developing Human Capital

It is not enough to hire top-level talent and expect that the skills and capabilities of those employees remain current throughout the duration of their employment. Rather, training and development must take place at all levels of the organization.[33] For example, Solectron assembles printed circuit boards and other components for its Silicon Valley clients.[34] Its employees receive an average of 95 hours of company-provided training each year. Chairman Winston Chen observed, "Technology changes so fast that we estimate 20 percent of an engineer's knowledge becomes obsolete each year. Training is an obligation we owe to our employees. If you want high growth and high quality, then training is a big part of the equation." Although the financial returns on training may be hard to calculate, most experts believe it is not only real, but also essential. One company that has calculated the benefit from training is Motorola. This high-technology firm has calculated that every dollar spent on training returns $30 in productivity gains over the following three years.

Cinergy, the $12 billion Cincinnati-based gas, electric, and energy services company, is another firm that recognizes that all employees must be the prime investors and beneficiaries of learning.[35] Gone is the focus on executive leadership. In its place is "talent development" which is available to everyone. Elizabeth Lanier, the legal chief of staff, stated, "The premise is that we want to have the smartest people in every layer of the job. If it's the janitor in a power plant, I want him smarter than any other janitor." Lanier is convinced that if you only recruit and train your best talent, you run the risk of having that talent take your investment to the competition.

In addition to the importance of training and developing human capital throughout the organization, let's now discuss three other related topics: encouraging widespread involvement, monitoring and tracking employee development, and evaluating human capital.[36]

*Encouraging Widespread Involvement*   The development of human capital requires the active involvement of leaders at all levels throughout the organization. It won't be successful if it is viewed only as the responsibility of the human resources department. Each year at General Electric, 200 facilitators, 30 officers, 30 human resource executives, and many young managers actively participate in GE's orientation program at the firm's impressive Crotonville training center outside New York City. Topics include global competition, winning on the global playing field, and personal examination of the new employee's core values vis-à-vis GE's values. As a senior manager once commented, "There is nothing like teaching Sunday school to force you to confront your own values."

The "cascade approach" is another way that managers at multiple levels in an organization become actively involved in developing human capital. For example, Robert Galvin, former chairman of Motorola, requested a workshop for more than 1,000 Motorola senior executives to help them understand the market potential of selected Asian countries. However, rather than bringing in outside experts, participants were asked to analyze the existing competition and to determine how Motorola could compete in these markets. After researching their topics, the executives traveled around the world to directly observe local market developments. Then they taught the concepts of globalization to the next level of 3,000 Motorola managers. By doing so, they not only verified their impressions with firsthand observations, but they also reinforced their learning and shared it by teaching others.

*Transferring Knowledge*   Often in our lives, we need to either transfer our knowledge to someone else (a child, a junior colleague, a peer) or access accumulated bits of wisdom—someone else's tacit knowledge.[37] A vital aspect of developing human capital is transferring unique and specialized knowledge. However, before we can even begin to plan such a transfer, we need to understand how our brains process incoming information. According to Dorothy Leonard Barton of Harvard University:

> Our existing tacit knowledge determines how we assimilate new experiences. Without receptors—hooks on which to hang new information—we may not be able to perceive and process the information. It is like being sent boxes of documents but having no idea how they could or should be organized.

This cognitive limitation also applies to the organizational level as well. For example, when GE Healthcare sets up or transfers operations from one location to another, it appoints an experienced manager to be the "pitcher" and a team in the receiving plant to be the "catcher." These two teams work together, often over a period of years—first at the pitcher's location and then at the catcher's. In order to ensure a smooth transition, the pitching team needs to be sensitive to the catching team's level of experience and familiarity with GE Healthcare procedures.

How does this work in practice? Here's one example: When a veteran operations manager arrived at a growing GE Healthcare plant in China, the local team was getting ready to move raw materials from the manufacturing facility into a warehouse. Although the operations manager could see numerous potential problems with the chosen site, he knew that simply vetoing it would have transferred little knowledge. Thus, he helped the team to develop a list of critical-to-quality (CTQ) sites. (Although this technique is standard operating procedure at GE, the Chinese plant was not familiar with it.) The list included such factors as proximity to the manufacturing plant, easy access for large trucks, road conditions between facilities, and basic amenities for employees. With the list in hand, the catchers visited the selected site and they could see that it met few of their criteria. Thus, they understood the reasons for using the CTQ model for even apparently simple choices. They now had a framework and some basic experience on which to build future decisions.

***Monitoring Progress and Tracking Development***   Whether a firm uses on-site formal training, off-site training (e.g., universities), or on-the-job training, tracking individual progress—and sharing this knowledge with both the employee and key managers—becomes essential. At Citibank (part of Citigroup, the large financial services organization), a talent inventory program keeps track of roughly 10,000 employees worldwide—how they're doing, what skills they need to work on, and where else in the company they might thrive. Larry Phillips, head of human resources, considers the program critical to the company's global growth.[38]

Like many leading-edge organizations, GlaxoSmithKline places increasingly greater emphasis on broader experiences over longer periods of time. Dan Phelan, senior vice president and director of human resources, explained, "We ideally follow a two-plus-two-plus-two formula in developing people for top management positions." The formula reflects the belief that SmithKline's best people should gain experience in two business units, two functional units (such as finance and marketing), in two countries. Interestingly, when vacancies occur among the firm's top 300 positions, the company will consider looking outside for talent. According to CEO Jan Leschly, "A little new blood doesn't hurt. If you're not the best person for the job, we'll show no hesitancy to go outside."

***Evaluating Human Capital***   In today's competitive environment, collaboration and interdependence have become vital to organizational success. Individuals must share their knowledge and work together constructively to achieve collective, not just individual, goals. However, traditional evaluation systems evaluate performance from a single perspective (i.e., "top down") and generally don't address the "softer" dimensions of communications and social skills, values, beliefs, and attitudes.[39]

To address the limitations of the traditional approach, many organizations have begun to use 360-degree evaluation and feedback systems.[40] In these systems, superiors, direct reports, colleagues, and even internal and external customers rate a person's skills. Managers also rate themselves in order to have a personal benchmark. The 360-degree feedback system complements teamwork, employee involvement, and organizational flattening. As organizations continue to push responsibility downward,

**Exhibit 4.3**

**An Excerpt from General Electric's 360-Degree Leadership Assessment Chart**

| | |
|---|---|
| Vision | • Has developed and communicated a clear, simple, customer-focused vision/direction for the organization.<br>• Forward-thinking, stretches horizons, challenges imaginations.<br>• Inspires and energizes others to commit to Vision. Captures minds. Leads by example.<br>• As appropriate, updates Vision to reflect constant and accelerating change affecting the business. |

Customer/Quality Focus

Integrity

Accountability/Commitment

Communication/Influence

Shared Ownership/Boundaryless

Team Builder/Empowerment

Knowledge/Expertise/Intellect

Initiative/Speed

Global Mind-Set

Source: Adapted from Slater, R. 1994. *Get better or get beaten:* 152–155. Burr Ridge, IL: Irwin Professional Publishing.

Note: This evaluation system consists of 10 "characteristics"—Vision, Customer/Quality Focus, Integrity, and so on. Each of these characteristics has four "performance criteria." For illustrative purposes, the four performance criteria of "Vision" are included.

traditional top-down appraisal systems become insufficient. For example, a manager who previously managed the performance of 3 supervisors might now be responsible for 10 and might be less likely to have the in-depth knowledge needed to appraise and develop each sufficiently and fairly. Exhibit 4.3 provides a portion of GE's 360-degree evaluation system.

In addition to being more accurate, companies are also adopting multirater feedback systems to shorten the process for developing human capital. "What might have taken four or five years for people to realize about themselves before can happen in much less time," claimed Stella Estevez of Warner-Lambert (now merged into Pfizer), a pharmaceutical firm that uses 360-degree feedback. Similarly, Jerry Wallace of Saturn (a division of General Motors) learned that, although he considered himself flexible, his subordinates did not. Instead they felt that he used excessive control. Wallace claimed, "I got a strong message that I need to delegate more. I thought I'd been doing it. But I need to do it more and sooner."

Finally, evaluation systems must ensure that a manager's success does not come at the cost of compromising the organization's core values. Clearly, such behavior generally leads to only short-term wins for both the manager and the organization. The organization typically suffers long-term losses in terms of morale, turnover, productivity, and so on. Accordingly, Merck's chairman, Ray Gilmartin, told his employees, "If someone is achieving results but not demonstrating the core values of the company, at the expense of our people, that manager does not have much of a career here."

Strategy Spotlight 4.3 summarizes General Electric's "Session C"—an integral part of its leadership evaluation and development process.

## General Electric's "Session C" Leadership Evaluation

General Electric, long regarded as one of the top talent producers in the corporate world, has relied on what it calls "Session C" leadership evaluation as an important means of ensuring that its leadership resources are consistent with its business direction. Session C is GE's annual, dialogue-intensive review and one of its most valuable tools for evaluating CEO candidates and for helping its rising stars evaluate themselves.

Every year, GE chooses a different set of 20 to 25 leaders who might eventually become CEOs or top leaders in functional areas. It conducts a three- to four-hour session with each of them along with two human resource executives from outside of the person's own business unit. The HR executives trace these high potential leaders' progression from early childhood (where they grew up, how their parents influenced their style of thinking, what their early values were) through their recent accomplishments. The

HR executives then conduct an extensive fact-finding mission both inside and outside the organization, including 360-degree reviews; thorough reference checks; and interviews with their bosses, direct reports, customers, and peers. Rather than relying on psychology, the assessment focuses on observed, measurable performance within the business.

The outcome of this effort is a 15- to 20-page document that summarizes the promising leader's work and development over decades. The report is full of accolades but also includes details on how the leaders can improve their effectiveness. The report is also distributed to the individual's manager, the senior human-resource executive of his or her unit, and to corporate headquarters. There, it is closely reviewed by GE's chairman, the three vice chairmen, and Bill Conaty, senior vice president for corporate human resources. Claims Conaty, "I usually wait until the end of the workday to read one of these because it takes an hour or so. You find out incredibly interesting things about people in the process."

Source: Charan, R. 2005. Ending the CEO succession crisis. *Harvard Business Review,* 83(2): 72–81.

## Retaining Human Capital

It has been said that talented employees are like "frogs in a wheelbarrow."[41] They can jump out at any time. By analogy, the organization can either try to force employees to stay in the firm or try to keep them from wanting to jump out by creating incentives. In other words, today's leaders can either provide the work environment and incentives to keep productive employees and management from wanting to bail out, or they can rely on legal means such as employment contracts and noncompete clauses.[42] Clearly, firms must provide mechanisms that prevent the transfer of valuable and sensitive information outside the organization. Failure to do so would be, among other things, the neglect of a leader's fiduciary responsibility to shareholders. However, greater efforts should be directed at the former (e.g., good work environment and incentives), but, as we all know, the latter (e.g., employment contracts and noncompete clauses) have their place.[43]

Let's now discuss the importance of an individual's identification with the organization's mission and values, challenging work and stimulating environment, and financial and nonfinancial rewards and incentives in retaining a firm's human capital.

*Identifying with an Organization's Mission and Values*  People who identify with and are more committed to the core mission and values of the organization are less likely to stray or bolt to the competition. Consider Medtronic, Inc., a $9 billion medical products firm based in Minneapolis.[44] Former CEO Bill George stated, "Shareholder value is a hollow notion as the sole source of employee motivation. If you do business that way, you'll end up like ITT." What motivates its workers to go well beyond Medtronic's 34 percent total return to shareholders? Simply put, it's helping sick people get well. The company's motto is "Restoring patients to full life," and its symbol is an image of a supine human rising toward upright wellness. That sounds good, but how does the "resurrection" imagery come to life?

> Each December, at the company's holiday party, patients, their families, and their doctors are flown in to tell their survival stories. It's for employees—who are moved to tears year after year—and journalists are generally not invited. President Art Collins, a strapping guy with a firm handshake who is not prone to crying fits, said, "I remember my first holiday party and someone asked me if I had brought my Kleenex. I assumed I'd be fine, but these parents got up with their daughter who was alive because of our product. Even surgeons who see this stuff all the time were crying."

So much for the all-consuming emphasis on profits.

Employees can also form strong alliances to organizations that create simple and straightforward missions—"strategic intents"—that channel efforts and generate intense loyalties.[45] Examples include Canon's passion to "beat Xerox" and Honda's early quest to become a second Ford. Likewise, leaders can arouse passions and loyalty by reinforcing the firm's quest to "topple Goliath" or by constantly communicating a history of overcoming adversity and life-threatening challenges.[46] For example, CEO Richard Branson of the Virgin Group constantly uses the "David and Goliath" imagery, pitting his company against such powerful adversaries as British Airways and Coca-Cola. A key part of Southwest Airlines's folklore is its struggle for survival in the Texas courts against such entrenched (and now bankrupt) rivals as Braniff and Texas Air. Southwest does not exist because of regulated or protected markets, but despite them; during its first three years of existence, no planes left the ground!

In addition to identifying with the organization, "tribal loyalty" is another key factor that links people to the organization.[47] A tribe is not the organization as a whole (unless it is very small). Rather, it is teams, communities of practice, and other groups within an organization or occupation.

Brian Hall, CEO of Values Technology in Santa Cruz, California, documented a shift in people's emotional expectations from work. From the 1950s on, a "task first" relationship to the company—"tell me what the job is, and let's get on with it"—dominated employee attitudes. Emotions and personal life were checked at the door. In the past few years, a "relationship-first" set of values has challenged the task orientation. Hall believes that it will become dominant. Employees want to share attitudes and beliefs as well as workspace. They want to establish the relationship (with one another and with the company) before buckling down to the task.

***Challenging Work and a Stimulating Environment***    Arthur Schawlow, winner of the 1981 Nobel Prize in physics, was once asked what he believed made the difference between highly creative and less creative scientists. His reply: "The labor of love aspect is very important. The most successful scientists often are not the most talented. But they are the ones impelled by curiosity. They've got to know what the answer is."[48]

Such insights highlight the importance of intrinsic motivation: the motivation to work on something because it is interesting, exciting, satisfying, or personally challenging. Consider the perspective of Jorgen Wedel, executive vice president of Gillette's international division, on the relative importance of pay compared with the meaningfulness of work: "I get calls from headhunters who offer bigger salaries, signing bonuses, and such. But the excitement of what I am doing here is equal to a 30 percent pay raise."

To keep competitors from poaching talent, organizations must keep employees excited about the challenges and opportunities available. Scott Cook, chairman of Intuit, understands this reality, "I wake up every morning knowing that if my people don't sense a compelling vision and a big upside, they'll simply leave."[49]

One way successful firms keep highly mobile employees motivated and challenged is through an internal market for opportunities that lower the barriers to an employee's mobility within a company. For example, Shell Oil Company has created an "open sourcing" model for talent. Jobs are listed on Shell's intranet, and, with a two-month notice, employees can go to work on anything that interests them. Monsanto[50] has developed a similar approach. According to one executive:

> Because we don't have a lot of structure, people will flow toward where success and innovation are taking place. We have a free-market system where people can move, so you have an outflow of people in areas where not much progress is being made. Before, the HR function ran processes like management development and performance evaluation. Now it also facilitates this movement of people.

*Financial and Nonfinancial Rewards and Incentives*    Without a doubt, financial rewards are a vital organizational control mechanism (as we will discuss in Chapter 9). Money—whether in the form of salary, bonus, stock options, and so forth—can mean many different things to people. For some it might mean security, to others recognition, and to still others, a sense of freedom and independence.

An article in *Organizational Dynamics* raised the point that there is little evidence that simply paying people more is the most important factor in attracting and retaining human capital.[51] Most surveys show that money is not the most important reason why people take or leave jobs, and that money, in some surveys, is not even in the top 10. Consistent with these findings, Tandem Computers (now part of Hewlett-Packard) never used to tell people being recruited what their salaries would be. People who asked were told that their salaries were competitive. If they persisted along this line of questioning, they would not be offered a position. Why? Tandem realized a rather simple idea: People who come for money will leave for money. Clearly, money can't be ignored, but it shouldn't be the primary mechanism to attract and retain talent.

Without the proper retention mechanisms (and as we all know, there are no easy answers), organizations can commit time and resources to inadvertently helping the competition develop their human capital.[52] And, given the importance of networking and teams, losses tend to multiply and intensify. The exodus of talent can erode a firm's competitive advantages in the marketplace. Let's now consider what some firms are doing to improve flexibility and amenities.[53]

When discussing firms with an impressive array of amenities to retain (and attract) employees, few compare with USAA, the San Antonio–based insurance and financial services company.

> If you're not keen on driving to work, the company sponsors a van pool. A run in your hose? Pick up a pair at the on-site store. There's also a dry cleaning service, a bank, and several ATMs. Even the cafeteria food is so tasty that several years ago employees began demanding dinner to go. The athletic facilities are striking. The three gyms rival those of many upscale health clubs and one is open 24 hours a day. Outside, employees compete in intramural leagues in basketball and tennis as well as on the softball and tennis courts. Into golf? There's also a driving range.
>
> Many return to campus on weekends with their families. Donna Castillo, a sales manager in consumer finance and auto service, said, "There are playgrounds where they can run around, and it's nice to take pictures when the bluebonnets come out in the spring." USAA also scores high on the emerging trend for on-site child care. The facility can handle 300 children. Raul Navarez, a security officer, said, "My wife and I visited 10 or 12 day care facilities . . . there was no competition."[54]

# STRATEGY SPOTLIGHT

## How Dow Chemical Evaluates Its Success in Retaining Top Talent

Dow Chemical is a $40 billion company that develops and sells chemicals, plastic materials, and agricultural and other specialized products and services. In the March 7, 2005, issue of *Fortune* magazine, Dow was ranked second out of 10 companies in the chemical industry, up from ninth place last year. Fortune noted that "Dow Chemical sharply boosted its image among industry peers, jumping a whopping seven places this year. Management finesse and strong ratings for 'community work' lifted its score."

Perhaps an important attribute of Dow Chemical's management system is its ability to fill important positions with internal candidates. Here, the firm has developed explicit benchmarks to evaluate its success in this endeavor.

At Dow Chemical, an internal hire rate of 75 to 80 percent is considered a sign of success. In fact, an outside hire for a role that is considered critical to the firm is viewed as a failure in the internal development process. (The company assumes that some external hires are important in maintaining a fresh perspective and for filling unanticipated roles.)

Dow also measures the attrition rate of its "future leaders," compared to the attrition rate of its entire employee population. "Future leaders" are those individuals who are advanced in their rate of development, perform at a competency level well above that of their colleagues, and are believed to have the potential to fill jobs at senior levels. In 2000, for example, the future leaders' rate of attrition was only 1.5 percent, compared to an overall attrition rate of 5 percent. Dow considers this to be a positive signal that its future leaders are receiving the developmental opportunities that they want and need. It is also useful to note that Dow's top 14 executives have all had cross-functional development opportunities that helped to prepare them for the demands of senior management.

Sources: Useem, J. 2005. America's most admired companies. *Fortune*, March 7: 66–70, 85–97; Cogner, J. A., & Fulmer, R. M. 2003. Developing your leadership pipeline. *Harvard Business Review*, 81(12): 78–85; and, Dychtwald, K., Erickson, T., & Morison, B. 2004. It's time to retire retirement. *Harvard Business Review*, 82(3): 48–56.

Another nonfinancial reward involves accommodating working families with children. Coping with the conflicting demands of family and work is a problem at some point for virtually all employees. After all, women represent 44 percent of today's U.S. workforce, and mothers of children under age six represent the fastest-growing segment. Mothers are often the primary caregivers in a family. It is estimated that 60 percent of working-age women are employed outside the home. And, according to a recent study, 13 percent of women with preschoolers indicated that they would work more hours if additional or better child care were provided.[55]

Strategy Spotlight 4.4 discusses Dow Chemical evaluates how well it retains top talent.

## Enhancing Human Capital: The Role of Diversity in the Workforce

Today, a combination of demographic trends and accelerating globalization of business has made the management of cultural differences a critical issue for corporate leaders.[56] Workforces, which reflect demographic changes in the overall population, will be increasingly heterogeneous along dimensions such as gender, race, ethnicity, and nationality. For example, demographic trends in the United States indicate a growth in Hispanic Americans from 6.9 million in 1960 to over 35 million in 2000. This figure also is expected to increase to over 55 million by 2020. Similarly, the Asian-American population should grow to 20 million in 2020 from 12 million in 2000 and only 1.5 million in 1970. And the African-American population is becoming more ethnically heterogeneous. Census estimates project that by 2010 as many as 10 percent of Americans of African descent will be immigrants from Africa or the Caribbean.[57]

Such demographic changes have implications not only for the labor pool but also for customer bases which are also becoming more diverse. This creates important organizational challenges and opportunities. For example:

- Minorities are the majority in six out of the eight largest metropolitan areas in the United States.
- The combined African-American, Hispanic-American and Asian-American buying power is more than $750 billion a year.
- Women are the primary investors in more than half of U. S. households.[58]

Clearly, the effective management of diversity can enhance the social responsibility goals of an organization.[59] However, there are many other benefits as well. Six other areas where sound management of diverse workforces can improve an organization's effectiveness and competitive advantages are: (1) cost, (2) resource acquisition, (3) marketing, (4) creativity, (5) problem-solving, and (6) organizational flexibility. The first two items—cost and resource acquisition—may be considered "inevitability-of-diversity" issues. After all, competitiveness is affected by the need (because of national and cross-national workforce demographic trends) to hire more minorities, women, and foreign nationals. However, the marketing, creativity, problem-solving, and system flexibility arguments are derived from what can be called the "value-in-diversity hypothesis," which states that diversity brings net-added value to organization processes. Here is a summary of the six ways diversity benefits an organization:

- **Cost Argument.** As organizations become more diverse, firms effective in managing diversity will have a cost advantage over those that are not.
- **Resource Acquisition Argument.** Firms with excellent reputations as prospective employers for women and ethnic minorities will have an advantage in the competition for top talent. As labor pools shrink and change in composition, such advantages will become even more important.
- **Marketing Argument.** For multinational organizations, the insight and cultural sensitivity that members with roots in other countries bring to marketing efforts will be very useful. A similar rationale applies to subpopulations within domestic operations.
- **Creativity Argument.** Less emphasis on conformity to norms of the past and a diversity of perspectives will improve the level of creativity.
- **Problem-solving Argument.** Heterogeniety in decision-making and problem-solving groups potentially produces better decisions because of a wider range of perspectives as well as more thorough and critical analysis of issues. To illustrate, Jim Schiro, CEO of PriceWaterhouseCoopers, explains, "When you make a genuine commitment to diversity, you bring a greater diversity of ideas, approaches, and experiences and abilities that can be applied to client problems. After all, six people with different perspectives have a better shot at solving complex problems than sixty people who all think alike."[60]
- **System Flexibility Argument.** With effective programs to enhance workplace diversity, systems become less determinant, less standardized, and therefore more fluid. Such fluidity should lead to greater flexibility to react to environmental changes. Reactions should be faster and less costly.

Many successful companies have been included in *Fortune's* list of the Best Companies for Minorities for their exemplary diversity programs.[61] One of these firms is Enterprise Rent-a-Car, which is discussed in Strategy Spotlight 4.5.

## The Effective Diversity Program at Enterprise Rent-a-Car

Enterprise Rent-a-Car, with locations in 200 countries and territories, is an exemplar of effective diversity programs. It recently sponsored a diversity study with the National Urban League, which surveyed 5,500 American workers, including managers and CEOs. Only 32 percent of U. S. employees think their companies do a good job of hiring and promoting people other than white males. Fewer than half (47 percent) of the executives think that their own diversity efforts are successful, and 59 percent say it's partly their fault for not being more involved. (The complete study "Diversity Practices That Work: The American Worker Speaks," is available at www.nul.org.)

The study singled out eight companies in which diversity is more than a buzzword and described in detail what they are doing. One of these companies was Enterprise Rent-a-Car.

Given the multicultural nature of its customer base, Enterprise Rent-a-Car gets a broad mix in the 6,500 management-track employees that it hires each year. It dispatches diverse teams of recruiters—men, women, African Americans, whites, Asians, and people of widely differing ages. It takes a similar approach in its TV advertisements. The firm also rewards managers for hiring and developing people who reflect local markets. Since its branches are mostly in neighborhoods (only 150 of 5,700 are at airports), staffing in San Francisco, for example, is quite different from that in San Antonio or St. Louis. "We want people who speak the same language, literally and figuratively, as our customers," claims Ed Adams, VP of human resources. "We don't set quotas. We say, 'Reflect your local market.'"

Enterprise has several diversity initiatives. First, from the St. Louis headquarters and working with the company's executive leaders, the Corporate Diversity Manager is responsible for implementing the firm's overall diversity strategy. Second, the National Diversity Team aids the regions in recruiting, developing, and retaining the workforce. Local diversity teams complement the work of the national team by helping individual groups, regions, or business units attain local diversity goals. Third, Enterprise conducts diversity leadership training companywide for its employees. The emphasis is on diversity training that helps create better leaders and managers. Fourth, Enterprise wants its supplier base to bear a reasonable relationship to the communities in which Enterprise does business. Their supplier diversity program identifies and encourages equal opportunities for minority-owned, women-owned and disadvantaged businesses. Enterprise's "deeds" clearly reflect the "words" of its Chairman and CEO, Andrew Taylor: "Enterprise is fully committed to providing every employee with an inclusive workplace that offers respect, training and opportunities to succeed. That's simply who we are as a company, who we are as individuals and how we will continue to build our success in the 21st century."

Such a strategy contributed to Enterprise's recent success—its revenues increased fourfold to $7.4 billion in the past decade, reflecting a compounded growth rate of 15 percent. It is now the industry leader.

Source: Fisher, A. 2004. How you can do better on diversity. *Fortune*, November 15: 60, www.erac.com/recruit/diversity.asp?navID=diversity; and www.nul.org.

## >>The Vital Role of Social Capital

Successful firms are well aware that the attraction, development, and retention of talent *is a necessary but not sufficient condition* for creating competitive advantages.[62] In the knowledge economy, it is not the stock of human capital that is important, but the extent to which it is combined and leveraged. In a sense, developing and retaining human capital becomes less important as key players (talented professionals, in particular) take the role of "free agents" and bring with them the requisite skill in many cases. Rather, the development of social capital (that is, the friendships and working relationships among talented individuals) gains importance, because it helps tie knowledge workers to a given firm.[63] Knowledge workers often exhibit greater loyalties to their colleagues and their profession than their employing organization, which may be "an amorphous, distant, and sometimes threatening entity."[64] Thus, a firm must find ways to create "ties" among its knowledge workers.

To illustrate, let's look at a hypothetical example. Two pharmaceutical firms are fortunate enough to hire Nobel Prize–winning scientists to work in their laboratories.[65] In one

## How Nucor Shares Knowledge within and between Its Manufacturing Plants

Nucor, with 2003 revenues of $6.3 billion, is the most efficient steel producer in the world. A key aspect of its strategy is to develop strong social relationships and a team-based culture throughout the firm. It is effectively supported by a combination of work-group, plant-level, and corporatewide financial incentives and rewards, wherein knowledge and best practices are eagerly shared by everyone in the organization. How does Nucor do it?

**Within Plant Knowledge Transfers.** Nucor strives to develop a social community within each plant that promotes trust and open communication. People know each other very well throughout each plant, and they are encouraged to interact. To accomplish this, the firm's policy is to keep the number of employees at each plant between 250 and 300. Such a relatively small number, combined with employees' long tenure, fosters a high degree of interpersonal familiarity. Additionally, each plant's general manager regu-

larly holds dinner meetings for groups of 25 to 30, inviting every employee once a year. The format is free and open and includes a few ground rules: All comments are to remain business-related and are not to be directed to specific individuals. In turn, managers guarantee that they will carefully consider and respond to all suggestions and criticisms.

**Between Plant Knowledge Transfers.** Nucor uses several mechanisms to transfer knowledge among its plants. First, detailed performance data on each mill are regularly distributed to all of the plant managers. Second, all plant general managers meet as a group three times a year to review each facility's performance and develop formal plans on how to transfer best practices. Third, plant managers, supervisors, and machine operators regularly visit each other's mills. These visits enable operations personnel to go beyond performance data in order to understand firsthand the factors that make particular practices superior or inferior. After all, they possess the true process knowledge. Fourth, given the inherent difficulties in transferring complex knowledge, Nucor selectively assigns people from one plant to another on the basis of their expertise.

Source: Gupta, A. K., & Govindarajan, V. 2000. Knowledge management's social dimension: Lessons from Nucor steel. *Organizational Dynamics*, Fall 2000: 71–80.

case, the scientist is offered a very attractive salary, outstanding facilities and equipment, and told to "go to it!" In the second case, the scientist is offered approximately the same salary, facilities, and equipment plus one additional ingredient. He or she will be working in a laboratory with 10 highly skilled and enthusiastic scientists. Part of the job is to collaborate with these peers and jointly develop promising drug compounds. There is little doubt as to which scenario will lead to a higher probability of retaining the scientist. Clearly, the interaction, sharing, and collaboration will create a situation in which the scientist will develop firm-specific ties and be less likely to "bolt" for a higher salary offer. Such ties are critical because knowledge-based resources tend to be more tacit in nature, as we mentioned early in this chapter. Therefore, they are much more difficult to protect against loss (i.e., the individual quitting the organization) than other types of capital, such as equipment, machinery, and land.

Another way to view this situation is in terms of the resource-based view of the firm that we discussed in Chapter 3. That is, competitive advantages tend to be harder for competitors to copy if they are based on "unique bundles" of resources.[66] So, if employees are working effectively in teams and sharing their knowledge and learning from each other, not only will they be more likely to add value to the firm, but they also will be less likely to leave the organization, because of the loyalties and social ties that they develop over time. Strategy Spotlight 4.6 discusses how Nucor, a highly successful steel manufacturer, develops social capital among its employees and managers. This promotes the sharing of ideas within and across its manufacturing plants.

Next, we'll address a key concept in the New Economy—the Pied Piper Effect. Here, groups of professionals join (or leave) organizations en masse, not one at a time.

## How Social Capital Helps Attract and Retain Talent

The importance of social ties among talented professionals is creating a significant challenge (and opportunity) for organizations today. In the *Wall Street Journal,* Bernard Wysocki described the increasing prevalence of a type of "Pied Piper Effect," in which teams or networks of people are leaving one company for another.[67] The trend is to recruit job candidates at the crux of social networks in organizations, particularly if they are seen as having the potential to bring with them a raft of valuable colleagues. This is a process that is referred to as "hiring via personal networks." Let's look at one instance of this practice.

> Gerald Eickhoff, founder of an electronic commerce company called Third Millennium Communications, tried for 15 years to hire Michael Reene. Why? Mr. Eickhoff says that he has "these Pied Piper skills." Mr. Reene was a star at Andersen Consulting in the 1980s and at IBM in the 1990s. He built his businesses and kept turning down overtures from Mr. Eickhoff.
>
> However, in early 2000, he joined Third Millennium as chief executive officer, with a salary of just $120,000 but with a 20 percent stake in the firm. Since then, he has brought in a raft of former IBM colleagues and Andersen subordinates. One protégé from his time at Andersen, Mary Goode, was brought on board as executive vice president. She promptly tapped her own network and brought along a half-dozen friends and former colleagues.
>
> Wysocki considers the Pied Piper effect one of the underappreciated factors in the war for talent today. This is because one of the myths of the New Economy is rampant individualism, wherein individuals find jobs on the Internet career sites and go to work for complete strangers. Perhaps, instead of Me Inc., the truth is closer to We Inc.[68]

Another example of social networks causing human capital mobility is the emigration of talent from an organization to form start-up ventures. Microsoft is perhaps the best-known example of this phenomenon.[69] Professionals have frequently left Microsoft en masse to form venture capital and technology start-ups built around teams of software developers. One example is Ignition Corporation, of Bellevue, Washington, which was formed by Brad Silverberg, a former Microsoft senior vice president. Eight former Microsoft executives, among others, founded the company. Exhibit 4.4 provides a partial listing of other companies that have been formed by groups of former Microsoft employees.

**Exhibit 4.4**

**Microsoft Employees Who Have Left the Company for Other Businesses**

| Company | What It Does | Defectors from Microsoft |
|---|---|---|
| Crossgain | Builds software around XML computer language | 23 of 60 employees |
| ViAir | Makes software for wireless providers | Company declines to specify |
| CheckSpace | Builds online payment service for small businesses | Company says "a good chunk" of its 30 employees |
| digiMine | Sells data mining service | About 15% of 62 employees in addition to the 3 founders |
| Avogadro | Builds wireless notification software | 8 of 25 employees |
| Tellme Networks | Offers information like stock quotes and scores over the phone | About 40 of 250 employees; another 40 from the former Netscape |

Source: From Rebecca Buckman, "Tech Defectors from Microsoft Resettle Together," *Wall Street Journal,* Eastern Edition, 2000. Copyright © 2000 by Dow Jones & Company, Inc. Reproduced with permission of Dow Jones & Company, Inc. via Copyright Clearance Center.

## Alumni Programs: A Great Way to Stay in Touch

Michael Jacobson had worked in securities practices at Cooley Godward, a Palo Alto, California law firm, for a dozen years. Nobody was happy when he gave notice in 1998. Everyone felt that it would be difficult to get along without him.

However, a few months later, Cooley Godward's managers couldn't have been happier. Why? Jacobson's new job was as general counsel at a little-known online auction site called eBay! When the site needed outside counsel, Jacobsen tapped his former employer. A few months later, Cooley Godward was lead counsel for eBay's record-breaking $1.3 billion initial public offering. "It's a great relationship," says Mark Pitchford, partner and chief operating officer of the firm.

With such a "lucky break," Cooley Godward no longer leaves such matters to chance. In January 2004, it launched an alumni program to help the firm stay in touch with its former attorneys. Such programs are not particu-larly new to corporate America. Firms such as McKinsey & Company, Ernst & Young, and Procter & Gamble have had them in place for years. However, as partners at Cooley Godward have found, smaller firms can also benefit from alumni initiatives. "Former employees are a resource," says John Izzo, president of Izzo Consulting, a firm based in Vancouver, Washington. The firm advises small businesses on employee training and retention issues.

Despite the potential benefits of maintaining active contact with former employees, many employers treat them as just another name in the Rolodex—or even worse, as a competitive threat. Izzo warns that this can be a big mistake. Often, he claims, former staffers can act as good-will ambassadors for their former employers, helping to refer new talent and clients. They may even return at a later point and will requiring little training. And with the job market now showing signs of improvement and many employees more likely to move on, alumni programs could become very important, especially at firms that have a hard time recruiting and retaining qualified professionals.

Source: Rich, L. 2005. Don't be a stranger. *Inc.*, January: 32–33.

---

The importance of the Pied Piper Effect for today's firms is rather self-evident. Leaders must be aware of social relationships among professionals as important recruiting and retention mechanisms. Some good advice for professionals would be to not invest all their time and effort in enhancing their human capital (skills and competences). Rather, they should be sure to also develop their social networks.[70]

Social networks can provide an important mechanism for obtaining both resources and information from individuals and organizations outside the boundary of a firm.[71] Strategy Spotlight 4.7 touts the benefits of firms' alumni programs. It describes how eBay's general counsel became an excellent source of business for his prior employer.

## The Potential Downside of Social Capital

Some companies have been damaged by high social capital that breeds "groupthink"—a tendency not to question shared beliefs.[72] When people identify strongly with a group, they sometimes support ideas that are suboptimal or simply wrong. Too many warm and fuzzy feelings among group members prevent people from challenging one another with tough questions and discourage them from engaging in the "creative abrasion" that Dorothy Leonard of Harvard University described as a key source of innovation.[73] Two firms well known for their collegiality, strong sense of employee membership, and humane treatment—Digital Equipment (now part of Hewlett-Packard Co.) and Polaroid—suffered greatly from market misjudgments and strategic errors. The aforementioned aspects of their culture contributed to their problems.

A recent study of 60 teams in 11 companies representing a variety of industries also provides insight into the drawbacks of too much social capital:[74]

> In the most effective teams, about half of the relationships among members were close enough
> to be considered friendships. However, in teams where that number approached 100 percent,

performance dropped dramatically. Such groups suffer lower performance because they are insular, impermeable to outside influences, and unhealthily self-reliant. Sometimes those problems can be avoided by brainstorming or by assigning someone in the group to be a devil's advocate. But where friendships are especially close, even those techniques are unlikely to produce widely different perspectives.

The friendships that benefit teams most were formed outside the group. Business-centered relationships with people in other parts of the company are more important for transmitting simple work flow information. However, even more important are relationships that extended into the social sphere—to lunches and dinners and after-work drinks—because they are especially fertile sources of social capital. Team members who socialize in this way, particularly with top managers and leaders of other teams, bring back to their groups strategic information, task-related advice, and political and social support.

Additionally, some have argued that socialization processes whereby individuals are "socialized in the norms, values, and ways of working inherent to the workgroup and the organization" can be potentially expensive in terms of financial resources and managerial commitment.[75] Such expenses may represent a significant opportunity cost that should be evaluated in terms of the potential costs and benefits. Clearly, if such expenses become excessive, profitability may be eroded.

In general, however, the effects of high social capital are strongly positive. Engagement, collaboration, loyalty, persistence, and dedication are important benefits.[76] Firms such as United Parcel Service, Hewlett-Packard, and SAS Institute have made significant investments in social capital that enable them to attract and retain talent and help them to do their best work. Few of these companies seem to face any imminent danger from an overdose of a good thing.

## >>Using Technology to Leverage Human Capital and Knowledge

Sharing knowledge and information throughout the organization can be a means of conserving resources, developing products and services, and creating new opportunities. In this section we will discuss how technology can be used to leverage human capital and knowledge within organizations as well as with customers and suppliers beyond their boundaries. We will start with simple applications, such as the use of e-mail and networks for product development, and then we will discuss how technology can help to enhance the competitive position of knowledge-intensive firms in industries such as consulting, health care, and personal computers. We will close by discussing how technology can help firms to retain employees' knowledge even when they leave, because, even in the most desirable workplaces, people will leave. Technology can help us to make sure they don't take all of the valuable knowledge with them.

### Using Networks to Share Information

As we all know, e-mail is an effective means of communicating a wide variety of information. It is quick, easy, and almost costless. Of course, it can become a problem when employees use it extensively for personal reasons and it detracts from productivity. Consider how fast jokes or rumors can spread within and across organizations! For example, at Computer Associates, the $3 billion software giant, e-mail is banned from 10 a.m. to noon and again from 2 p.m. to 4 p.m. because the firm's former chairman, Charles Wang, believes that it detracts from productivity.[77]

Managers and employees must be very careful when using e-mail. Once e-mails are sent, the sender has no control over where they are forwarded or where they are stored. Consider, for example, what can happen when an executive sends out a very negative and threatening mass e-mail.[78]

Neal Patterson, CEO of Cerner Corporation, sent out a rather scathing e-mail to about 400 company managers. He felt that his managers had created "a very unhealthy work environment" and he was troubled by the nearly empty parking lot outside his Kansas City offices at 7:30 a.m. and 6:00 p.m.—a testament, he felt, to a lax work ethic. In his e-mail, he listed punishments that he planned to implement, including having some employees punch a clock as well as possibly laying off some people. In addition, he said that he wanted to see the parking lot "substantially full at 7:30 a.m. and 6:00 p.m. and on Saturday morning." After giving his managers two weeks to turn the situation around, he ended his e-mail with an ominous "Tick, tock."

Unfortunately, after clicking "send," the e-mail took on a life of its own and ended up being posted on Yahoo!, where anybody could read it. This included analysts and investors who took the harsh message as an indication that something was clearly wrong at Cerner. After the leak, the trading volume for Cerner surged, and its stock price dropped 22 percent!

E-mail can, however, be a means for top executives to communicate information efficiently. For example, Martin Sorrell, chairman of WPP Group PLC, a $2.4 billion advertising and public relations firm, is a strong believer in the use of e-mail.[79] He e-mails all of his employees once a month. He discusses how the company is doing, addresses specific issues, and offers his perspectives on hot issues, such as new business models for the Internet. He believes that it is a great way to keep people abreast of what he is working on.

Technology can also enable much more sophisticated forms of communication in addition to knowledge sharing. Consider, for example, Buckman Laboratories, a $300 million specialty chemicals company based in Memphis, Tennessee, with approximately 1,300 employees in over 100 countries. Buckman has successfully used its global knowledge sharing network—known as K'Netix—to enhance its competitive advantages in the marketplace:[80]

Buckman produces more than 1,000 different specialty chemicals in eight factories throughout the world. It competes in a wide variety of industries, including pulp and paper processing and water treatment to leather, agriculture, and personal care. Unlike a typical multinational corporation, it is relatively small, and its competitive advantage is largely due to its ability to apply the power of all of its employees to every customer engagement. Central to this valuable capability is its global knowledge sharing network called K'Netix, which is integral to Buckman's information infrastructure.

Here's an example of how the network can be applied. One of Buckman's paper customers in Michigan realized that the peroxide it was adding to remove ink from old magazines was no longer working. A Buckman sales manager presented this problem to the knowledge network. Within two days, salespeople from Belgium and Finland identified a likely cause: Bacteria in the paper slurry was producing an enzyme that broke down the peroxide. The sales manager recommended a chemical to control the bacteria, and the problem was solved. You can imagine how positive the customer must feel about doing business with Buckman. And with the company and the customer co-creating knowledge, a new level of trust and value can emerge.

As you might expect, the idea of top executives sharing ideas with many or all individuals in their company is hardly new.[81] In the 1800s at British American Tobacco (BAT), the chief executive would write a monthly report to all of BAT's country managers. The executive used a fountain pen, and it generally took about three months for the report to reach India. With e-mail the message gets out in seconds—an enormous difference. Clearly, e-mail can be an effective tool, but it must be used judiciously.

## Electronic Teams: Using Technology to Enhance Collaboration

The use of technology has also enabled professionals to work as part of electronic, or virtual, teams to enhance the speed and effectiveness with which products are developed.

For example, Microsoft has concentrated much of its development on electronic teams that are networked together throughout the company.[82] This helps to accelerate design and testing of new software modules that use the Windows-based framework as their central architecture. Microsoft is able to foster specialized technical expertise while sharing knowledge rapidly throughout the organization. This helps the firm learn how its new technologies can be applied rapidly to new business ventures such as cable television, broadcasting, travel services, and financial services.

What are electronic teams (or e-teams)? There are two key differences between e-teams and more traditional teams.[83] First, e-team members either work in geographically separated work places or they may work in the same space but at different times. E-teams may have members working in different spaces and time zones, as is the case with many multinational teams. Second, most of the interactions among members of e-teams occur through electronic communication channels such as fax machines and groupware tools such as e-mail, bulletin boards, chat, and videoconferencing.

The use of e-teams has expanded exponentially in recent years.[84] Organizations face increasingly high levels of complex, dynamic change and environmental uncertainty. E-teams are also effective in helping businesses cope with global challenges. Most e-teams perform very complex tasks and most knowledge-based teams are charged with developing new products, improving organizational processes, and satisfying challenging customer problems. For example, Eastman Kodak's e-teams design new products, Hewlett Packard's e-teams solve clients' computing problems, and Sun Microsystems' e-teams generate new business models.

There are multiple advantages of e-teams.[85] In addition to the rather obvious use of technology to facilitate communications, the potential benefits parallel the other two major sections in this chapter—human capital and social capital. First, e-teams are less restricted by the geographic constraints that are placed on face-to-face teams. Thus, e-teams have the potential to acquire a broader range of "human capital" or the skills and capacities that are necessary to complete complex assignments. So, e-team leaders can draw upon a greater pool of talent to address a wider range of problems since they are not constrained by geographic space. Once formed, e-teams can be more flexible in responding to unanticipated work challenges and opportunities because team members can be rotated out of projects when demands and contingencies alter the team's objectives.

Second, e-teams can be very effective in generating "social capital"—the quality of relationships and networks that leaders and team members form. Such capital is a key lubricant in work transactions and operations. Given the broader boundaries associated with e-teams, members and leaders generally have access to a wider range of social contacts than would be typically available in more traditional face-to-face teams. Such contacts are often connected to a broader scope of clients, customers, constituents, and other key stakeholders.

However, there are challenges associated with making e-teams effective. Successful action by both traditional teams and e-teams requires that:

- Members *identify* who among them can provide the most appropriate knowledge and resources, and,
- E-team leaders and key members know how to *combine* individual contributions in the most effective manner for a coordinated and appropriate response.

Group psychologists have termed such activities "identification and combination" activities and teams that fail to perform them face a "process loss."[86] Process losses prevent teams from reaching high levels of performance because of inefficient interaction dynamics among team members. Such poor dynamics require that some collective energy, time, and effort be devoted to dealing with team inefficiencies, thus diverting the team away from its objectives. For example, if a team member fails to communicate important information at critical phases of a project, other members may waste time and energy. This can lead to conflict and resentment as well as to decreased motivation to work hard to complete tasks. Clearly, team leaders and other members must expend collective energy to repair the breach, resulting in a process loss.

The potential for process losses tends to be more prevalent in e-teams than in traditional teams because the geographical dispersion of members increases the complexity of establishing effective interaction and exchanges. Generally, teams suffer process loss because of low cohesion, low trust among members, a lack of appropriate norms or standard operating procedures, or a lack of shared understanding among team members about their tasks. With e-teams, members are more geographically or temporally dispersed, and the team becomes more susceptible to the risk factors that can create process loss. Such problems can be exacerbated when team members have less than ideal competencies and social skills. This can erode problem-solving capabilities as well as the effective functioning of the group as a social unit.

A recent study explored what made e-teams at Texas-based Sabre computerized reservation system (used by most major airlines) more or less successful in achieving their objectives. Sabre has over 6,000 employees in 45 countries and processes approximately 400 million travel bookings a year. The 65 e-teams in the study were cross-functional, based in the United States and Canada, and averaged about eight members. Sabre's e-teams are highly interdependent and conduct activities such as selling reservation systems, scheduling installation and training appointments, and handling billing and collections. Members communicate via e-mail, telephone, videoconferencing, and Web-based conferencing.

What were the study's key findings? Below, we summarize some of the key challenges that the e-teams faced and how the most successful teams overcame them:

- ***Develop Trust Based on Performance Consistency Rather than Social Bonds.*** Rapid responses by team members fostered trust, and team leaders played a key role in reinforcing timeliness and interaction. Levels of trust based on performance helped to compensate for a lack of social interaction.
- ***Overcome Group Process Losses Associated with Virtual Teams.*** Extensive training in virtual team leadership, conflict management, and meetings management as well as adaptation of decision-making software were used to facilitate problem solving and decision making.
- ***Create an Environment of Inclusiveness and Involvement.*** Individual preferences were taken into account when selecting e-team members. Team members were given a realistic preview of the potential for feeling detached and were provided opportunities for face-to-face contact with clients and other team members.
- ***Identify Team Members with a Proper Balance of Technical and Interpersonal Skills.*** Behavioral interviewing techniques and simulation were used as part of the selection process, and other team members were asked to help recruit and select new team members to ensure a good balance of technical and social skills. Such activities also help to socialize newly appointed team members.
- ***Create Proper Mechanisms for Evaluating Team Members and Providing Coaching and Support.*** A comprehensive evaluation approach that includes both quantitative and qualitative measures was employed to assess idea generation, leadership, and problem-solving skills. Team-member peer reviews were used to assess individual contributions to team effectiveness and online training and development resources were created to enhance members' knowledge, skills, and abilities.

## Codifying Knowledge for Competitive Advantage

As we discussed early in this chapter, there are two different kinds of knowledge. Tacit knowledge is embedded in personal experience and shared only with the consent and participation of the individual. Explicit (or codified) knowledge, on the other hand, is knowledge that can be documented, widely distributed, and easily replicated. One of the challenges of knowledge-intensive organizations is to capture and codify the knowledge and experience that, in effect, resides in the heads of its employees. Otherwise, they will have to constantly "reinvent the wheel," which is both expensive and inefficient. Also, the "new wheel" may not necessarily be superior to the "old wheel."[87]

Once a knowledge asset (e.g., a software code or processes, routines for a consulting firm) is developed and paid for, it can be reused many times at very low cost, assuming that it doesn't have to be substantially modified each time. Let's take the case of a consulting company, such as Accenture (formerly Andersen Consulting).[88] Since the knowledge of its consultants has been codified and stored in electronic repositories, it can be employed in many jobs by a huge number of consultants. Additionally, since the work has a high level of standardization (i.e., there are strong similarities across the numerous client engagements), there generally tends to be a rather high ratio of consultants to partners. For example, the ratio of consultants to partners is roughly 30, which is quite high. As one might expect, there must be extensive training of the newly hired consultants for such an approach to work. The recruits are trained at Accenture's Center for Professional Education, a 150-acre campus in St. Charles, Illinois. Using the center's knowledge-management respository, the consultants work through many scenarios designed to improve business processes. In effect, the information technologies enable the consultants to be "implementers, not inventors."

Access Health, a call-in medical center, also uses technology to capture and share knowledge. When someone calls the center, a registered nurse uses the company's "clinical decision architecture" to assess the caller's symptoms, rule out possible conditions, and recommend a home remedy, doctor's visit, or trip to the emergency room. The company's knowledge repository contains algorithms of the symptoms of more than 500 illnesses. According to CEO Joseph Tallman, "We are not inventing a new way to cure disease. We are taking available knowledge and inventing processes to put it to better use." At Access Health, the codified knowledge is in the form of software algorithms. They were very expensive to develop, but the investment has been repaid many times over. The first 300 algorithms that Access Health developed have each been used an average of 8,000 times a year. Further, the company's paying customers—insurance companies and provider groups—save money because many callers would have made expensive trips to the emergency room or the doctor's office had they not been diagnosed over the phone.

The use of information technology in codifying knowledge can also help a firm integrate activities among its internal value-chain activities, customers, and suppliers. Strategy Spotlight 4.8 shows how Dell Computer's sophisticated knowledge-management system is an integral part of its widely admired business model.

## Retaining Knowledge When Employees Leave

All organizations—with a few exceptions, such as prisons and the military during periods of conscription—suffer the adverse consequences of voluntary turnover. As we noted in Chapter 3, even SAS Institute, consistently one of *Fortune* magazine's "Most Desirable Places to Work," has a 4 percent turnover (far below the software industry's average of 20 percent). So, turnover—to a high, moderate, or low degree—is simply an organizational

# STRATEGY SPOTLIGHT

## Dell's Knowledge Management System

A company that can successfully assemble and sell 11 million personal computers (PCs) a year, using 40,000 possible configurations (compared with about 100 for competitors), is clearly one that has learned something about knowledge management. Dell Computer Corporation has recruited talented engineers to design these processes, but the company's real strength is found in the way it has codified these processes.

By investing heavily in the ability to determine the necessary configurations up front. Dell is able to reuse this knowledge to its advantage. Although each configuration is used on average only about 275 times each year, Dell has captured the knowledge of its talented engineers in the processes used to custom assemble PCs en masse.

Sources: Hansen, M. T., Nohria, N., & Tierney, T. 1999. What's your strategy for managing knowledge? *Harvard Business Review,* 77 (2): 106–117; Magretta, J. 1998. The power of virtual integration: An interview with Dell Computer's Michael Dell. *Harvard Business Review,* 76(2): 73–84.

Key to Dell's knowledge-management system is a repository that contains a list of available components. Dell uses this system to its competitive advantage through cost containment that is passed on, in part, to consumers. This low-cost advantage provides Dell with a 25 percent share of the U.S. personal computer market.

Dell effectively uses its knowledge-management system to integrate assembly activities from the initial customer order to product delivery. The company's external supply chain is linked to the assembly process by an elaborate inventory-control system that enables the firm to know what parts are currently available, matching these to possible configurations. This enhances Dell's link with customers by giving customers the flexibility to order PCs to their desired specifications. By integrating the entire value chain with its knowledge-management system, Dell has given itself an edge in the intensely competitive PC market.

---

fact of life. However, many leading firms are devising ways to minimize the loss of knowledge when employees leave.

Information technology can often help employers cope with turnover by saving some tacit knowledge that the firm would otherwise lose.[89] Customer relationship software, for example, automates sales and provides salespeople with access to client histories, including prior orders and complaints. This enables salespeople to quickly become familiar with client accounts (about which they might otherwise know nothing). Similarly, groupware applications such as Lotus Notes can standardize interactions and keep records of decisions and crucial contextual information, providing something like an electronic record of employee knowledge. Other programs, such as Open Text's Livelink, enable all employees to track and share documents on their firm's intranet. New simulation software for team-based project management, such as Thinking Tools's Project Challenge, enables new teams to learn how to work together much more rapidly than on-the-job experience alone would permit.

Even a simple technology such as e-mail can help when key employees leave an organization. For example, Pamela Hirshman, a project manager at Young & Rubicam, a large international advertising firm, was asked to take over a project after the entire original project team bolted.[90] Noted Hirshman, "The project file had a record of all the e-mails between the team and the client, and after reviewing about 50 of these, I was up to speed on the problems of the client and where the project was headed."

Motivation is a key issue in such knowledge-management systems. That is, what are the incentives for people to contribute their knowledge? Some organizations have found that such systems work best when they are incorporated into the firm's evaluation and reward system. For example, Bruce Strong, founder and CEO of Context Integration, a Web consulting firm, decided to develop a knowledge-management system to help employees unlock their thoughts and, collectively, help them to be more productive.[91] Six months and a half-million dollars later, he unveiled IAN (Intellectual Assets Network). The objective was to provide a medium for his consultants to share ideas, ask questions, and trace earlier journeys on similar projects. The theory was fine, but Strong was disappointed with the lack of involvement by his employees. This is not surprising. Carla O'Dell, president of the American Productivity and Quality Center, said that of the companies trying knowledge management, fewer than 10 percent succeeded in making it part of their culture.

Why didn't the consultants embrace IAN? There were many reasons:

- Consultants saw depositing notes or project records into the database as one more task in a busy day.
- The task didn't appear to have any urgency.
- Consultants generally did not like to admit they couldn't solve a problem.
- They resented management trying to impose what consultants perceived as a rigid structure on their work.

What was Strong to do? He began to reinforce the many benefits of the system, such as providing better and more consistent service. He also publicly recognized people who stood out as strong IAN contributors, and he made this part of everyone's job description. Perhaps most important, he began paying people to use it. He assigned points when people used the system—for example, one point for posting a résumé on the system, five points for creating a project record, and so on. The results were tallied every three months and the score accounted for 10 percent of a consultant's quarterly bonus. Over a two-month period, overall IAN usage almost doubled. However, more important, many consultants became enthusiastic converts once they had a positive experience with IAN. Not only does IAN continue to help many of them provide excellent service to their clients, but also some of their knowledge remains in the firm when they leave.

We close this section with a series of questions managers should consider in determining (1) how effective their organization is in attracting, developing, and retaining human capital and (2) how effective they are in leveraging human capital through social capital and technology. These questions, included in Exhibit 4.5, summarize some of the key issues addressed in this chapter.

## >>The Central Role of Leveraging Human Capital in Strategy Formulation

In this chapter we have emphasized the importance of human capital and how such intangible assets can create the greatest value in today's successful organizations. As we have noted throughout the chapter, attracting top talent is a necessary, but not a sufficient, condition for competitive advantage. It must be not only developed and retained, but also leveraged through effective use of social capital and technology. In this section we will discuss how leveraging human capital is vital to each of the levels of strategy that we will address in the next four chapters (5, 6, 7, and 8) of the book.

### Leveraging Human Capital and Business-Level Strategy

At the business level (Chapter 5), firms strive to create advantages that are sustainable over time. To do this, managers must integrate the primary and support activities in their firm's value chain (discussed in Chapter 3). We will discuss how much of Siebel Systems' success can be attributed to its excellent customer relationships, fostered by the firm's insistence on having customer input before the software is written. And FedEx has provided its drivers with handheld computers—a valuable technology—to help them effectively track customer packages. The Siebel Systems and FedEx examples point out how social capital and technology can help a firm enhance business-level strategies by leveraging its human capital.

## Human Capital

### Recruiting "Top-Notch" Human Capital

- Does the organization assess attitude and "general makeup" instead of focusing primarily on skills and background in selecting employees at all levels?
- How important are creativity and problem solving ability? Are they properly considered in hiring decisions?
- Do people throughout the organization engage in effective networking activities to obtain a broad pool of worthy potential employees? Is the organization creative in such endeavors?

### Enhancing Human Capital through Employee Development

- Does the development and training process inculcate an "organizationwide" perspective?
- Is there widespread involvement, including top executives, in the preparation and delivery of training and development programs?
- Is the development of human capital effectively tracked and monitored?
- Are there effective programs for succession at all levels of the organization, especially at the top-most levels?
- Does the firm effectively evaluate its human capital? Is a 360-degree evaluation used? Why? Why not?
- Are mechanisms in place to assure that a manager's success does not come at the cost of compromising the organization's core values?

### Retaining the Best Employees

- Are there appropriate financial rewards to motivate employees at all levels?
- Do people throughout the organization strongly identify with the organization's mission?
- Are employees provided with a stimulating and challenging work environment that fosters professional growth?
- Are valued amenities provided (e.g., flex time, child-care facilities, telecommuting) that are appropriate given the organization's mission, strategy, and how work is accomplished?
- Is the organization continually devising strategies and mechanisms to retain top performers?

## Social Capital

- Are there positive personal and professional relationships among employees?
- Is the organization benefiting (or being penalized) by hiring (or by voluntary turnover) en masse?
- Does an environment of caring and encouragement rather than competition enhance team performance?
- Does the organization minimize the adverse effects of excessive social capital, such as excessive costs and "groupthink"?

## Technology

- Has the organization used technologies such as e-mail and networks to develop products and services?
- Does the organization effectively use technology to transfer best practices across the organization?
- Does the organization use technology to leverage human capital and knowledge both within the boundaries of the organization and among its suppliers and customers?
- Has the organization effectively used technology to codify knowledge for competitive advantage?
- Does the organization try to retain some of the knowledge of employees when they decide to leave the firm?

Source: Adapted from Dess, G. G., & Picken, J. C. 1999. *Beyond Productivity:* 63–64. New York: AMACON.

**Exhibit 4.5**

**Issues to Consider in Creating Value through Human Capital, Social Capital, and Technology**

## Leveraging Human Capital and Corporate-Level Strategy

In Chapter 6 on corporate-level strategy, we will discuss how firms can create value by managing their business to create synergy; that is, how more value can be created by working together across business units than if they were freestanding units. Managers must determine what important relationships (products, markets, technologies) exist across businesses and how they can be leveraged. We will discuss how Procter & Gamble is able to reapply its customer knowledge and understanding of technologies across many different product markets. For example, P&G's knowledge of oral hygiene and bleaching agents enabled it to develop a special film technology that whitened teeth within 14 days. For such knowledge transfer to occur, managers must be aware of not only their human capital (tacit knowledge), but also their organization's codified knowledge and relationships among key professionals and across business units.

## Leveraging Human Capital and International-Level Strategy

In Chapter 7 we will address how companies create value by leveraging resources and knowledge across national boundaries. Here firms are faced with two opposing forces: how to achieve economies of scale and how to adapt to local market needs. We will discuss how some leading-edge firms are able to successfully attain a "transnational strategy" wherein not only do the firms achieve lower costs through economies of scale, but also they are able to adapt successfully to local markets. To do so, firms must facilitate the flow of information and knowledge between business units in different countries. This requires not only attracting, developing, and retaining superior talent, but also leveraging their knowledge and skills through effective working relationships (i.e., social capital) and use of technology.

## Leveraging Human Capital and Internet Strategies

Chapter 8 addresses the role of digital and Internet-based technologies in creating competitive advantages. These technologies have enormous strategic implications for managers who use them to lower costs, enhance customer service, and improve performance. We provide the example of BP Amoco, a company that has pursued an aggressive policy of implementing Internet-based capabilities. Managers are able to tap into the company's reservoir of knowledge by using the personalized Web pages that all BP Amoco employees use to report on their areas of expertise. In one example, engineers drilling for oil in the Caribbean saved $600,000 by using a process that had been developed in Norway just a few days earlier. To make such technologies effective, of course, requires both talented professionals to develop and apply knowledge as well as strong, positive working relationships between managers and technology experts.

## Summary

Firms throughout the industrial world are recognizing that the knowledge worker is the key to success in the marketplace. However, we also recognize that human capital, although vital, is still only a necessary, but not a sufficient, condition for creating value. We began the first section of the chapter by addressing the importance of human capital and how it can be attracted, developed, and retained. Then we discussed the role of social capital and technology in leveraging human capital for competitive success. We pointed out that intellectual capital—the difference between a firm's market value and its book value—has increased significantly over the past few decades. This is particularly true for firms in knowledge-intensive industries, especially where there are relatively few tangible assets, such as software development.

The second section of the chapter addressed the attraction, development, and retention of human capital. We viewed these three activities as a "three-legged stool"—that is, it is difficult for firms to be successful if they ignore or are unsuccessful in any one of these activities. Among the issues we discussed in *attracting* human capital were "hiring for attitude, training for skill" and the value of using social networks to attract human capital. In particular, it is important to attract employees who can collaborate with others, given the importance of collective efforts such as teams and task forces. With regard to *developing* human capital, we discussed the need to encourage widespread involvement throughout the organization, monitor progress and track the development of human capital, and evaluate human capital. Among the issues that are widely practiced in evaluating human capital is the 360-degree evaluation system. Employees are evaluated by their superiors, peers, direct reports, and even internal and external customers. We also addressed the value of maintaining a diverse workforce. Finally, some mechanisms for retaining human capital are employees' identification with the organization's mission and values, providing challenging work and a stimulating environment, the importance of financial and nonfinancial rewards and incentives, and providing flexibility and amenities. A key issue here is that a firm should not overemphasize financial rewards. After all, if individuals join an organization for money, they also are likely to leave for money. With money as the primary motivator, there is little chance that employees will develop firm-specific ties to keep them with the organization.

The third section of the chapter discussed the importance of social capital in leveraging human capital. Social capital refers to the network of relationships that individuals have throughout the organization as well as with customers and suppliers. Such ties can be critical in obtaining both information and resources. With regard to recruiting, for example, we saw how some firms are able to hire en masse groups of individuals who are part of social networks. Social relationships can also be very important in the effective functioning of groups. Finally, we discussed some of the potential downsides of social capital. These include the expenses that firms may bear when promoting social and working relationships among individuals as well as the potential for "groupthink," wherein individuals are reluctant to express divergent (or opposing) views on an issue because of social pressures to conform.

The fourth section addressed the role of technology in leveraging human capital. We discussed relatively simple means of using technology, such as e-mail and networks where individuals can collaborate by way of personal computers. We provided suggestions and guidelines on how electronic teams can be effectively managed. We also addressed more sophisticated uses of technology, such as sophisticated management systems. Here knowledge can be codified and reused at very low cost, as we saw in the examples of firms in the consulting, health care, and high-technology industries. Also, given that there will still be some turnover—voluntary or involuntary—even in the most desirable places to work, technology can be a valuable means of retaining knowledge when individuals terminate their employment with a firm.

The final section addressed how the leveraging of human capital is critical in strategy formulation at all levels. This includes the business, corporate, international, and Internet levels.

## Summary Review Questions

1. Explain the role of knowledge in today's competitive environment.

2. Why is it important for managers to recognize the interdependence in the attraction, development, and retention of talented professionals?

3. What are some of the potential downsides for firms that engage in a "war for talent"?

4. Discuss the need for managers to use social capital in leveraging their human capital both within and across their firm.

5. Discuss the key role of technology in leveraging knowledge and human capital.

## Experiential Exercise

Johnson & Johnson, a leading health care firm with $47 billion in 2004 revenues, is often rated as one of *Fortune*'s "Most Admired Firms." It is also considered an excellent place to work and has generated high return to shareholders. Clearly, they value their human capital. Using the Internet and/or library resources, identify some of the actions/strategies Johnson & Johnson has taken to attract, develop, and retain human capital. What are their implications?

| Activity | Actions/Strategies | Implications |
|---|---|---|
| Attracting human capital | | |
| Developing human capital | | |
| Retaining human capital | | |

## Application Questions Exercises

1. Look up successful firms in a high-technology industry as well as two successful firms in more traditional industries such as automobile manufacturing and retailing. Compare their market values and book values. What are some implications of these differences?

2. Select a firm for which you believe its social capital—both within the firm and among its suppliers and customers—is vital to its competitive advantage. Support your arguments.

3. Choose a company with which you are familiar. What are some of the ways in which it uses technology to leverage its human capital?

4. Using the Internet, look up a company with which you are familiar. What are some of the policies and procedures that it uses to enhance the firm's human and social capital?

## Ethics Questions

1. Recall an example of a firm that recently faced an ethical crisis. How do you feel the crisis and management's handling of it affected the firm's human capital and social capital?

2. Based on your experiences or what you have learned in your previous classes, are you familiar with any companies that used unethical practices to attract talented professionals? What do you feel were the short-term and long-term consequences of such practices?

## References

1. Wellner, A. S. 2004. The perils of hiring stars. *Inc.,* August: 32–33; Molaro, R. 2005. Bear season. *The Art of Licensing,* Winter: S-11–S13; and personal communication with Michael Carlisle and the authors, February 10, 2005.

2. Parts of this chapter draw upon some of the ideas and examples from Dess, G. G., & Picken, J. C. 1999. *Beyond Productivity.* New York: AMACOM.

3. An acknowledged trend: The world economic survey. 1996. *The Economist,* September 28: 25–28.

4. Quinn, J. B., Anderson, P., & Finkelstein, S. 1996. Leveraging intellect. *Academy of Management Executive,* 10(3): 7–27.

5. Hamel, G., & Prahalad, C. K. 1996. Competing in the new economy: Managing out of bounds. *Strategic Management Journal,* 17: 238.

6. Reich, R. B. 2000. *The future of success:* 21. New York: Random House.

7. Stewart, T. A. 1997. *Intellectual capital: The new wealth of organizations.* New York: Doubleday/Currency.

8. Leif Edvisson and Michael S. Malone have a similar, more detailed definition of *intellectual capital:* "the combined knowledge, skill, innovativeness, and ability to meet the task at hand." They consider intellectual capital to equal human capital plus structural capital. *Structural capital* is defined as "the hardware, software, databases, organization structure, patents, trademarks, and everything else of organizational capability that supports those employees' productivity—in a word, everything left at the office when the employees go home." Edvisson, L., & Malone, M. S. 1997. *Intellectual capital: Realizing your company's true value by finding its hidden brainpower:* 10–14. New York: HarperBusiness.

9. Stewart, T. A. 2001. Accounting gets radical. *Fortune,* April 16: 184–194.

10. Thomas Stewart has suggested this formula in his book *Intellectual Capital.* He provides an insightful discussion on pages 224–225, including some of the limitations of this approach to measuring intellectual capital. We recognize, of course, that during the late 1990s and in early 2000, there were some excessive market valuations of high-technology and Internet firms. For an interesting discussion of the extraordinary market valuation of Yahoo!, an Internet company, refer to Perkins, A. B. 2001. The Internet bubble encapsulated: Yahoo! *Red Herring,* April 15: 17–18.

11. Roberts, P. W., & Dowling, G. R. 2002. Corporate reputation and sustained superior financial performance. *Strategic Management Journal,* 23(12): 1077–1095.

12. For a recent study on the relationships between human capital, learning, and sustainable competitive advantage, read Hatch, N. W., & Dyer, J. H. 2005. Human capital and learning as a source of sustainable competitive advantage. *Strategic Management Journal,* 25: 1155–1178.

13. One of the seminal contributions on knowledge management is Becker, G. S. 1993. *Human capital: A theoretical and empirical analysis with special reference to education* (3rd ed.). Chicago: University of Chicago Press.

14. For an excellent overview of the topic of social capital, read Baron, R. A. 2005. Social capital. In Hitt, M. A., & Ireland, R. D. (Eds.), *The Blackwell encyclopedia of management* (2nd ed.): 224–226. Malden, MA: Blackwell.

15. For an excellent discussion of social capital and its impact on organizational performance, refer to Nahapiet, J., & Ghoshal, S. 1998. Social capital, intellectual capital, and the organizational advantage. *Academy of Management Review,* 23: 242–266.

16. Polanyi, M. 1967. *The tacit dimension.* Garden City, NY: Anchor Publishing.

17. Barney, J. B. 1991. Firm resources and sustained competitive advantage. *Journal of Management,* 17: 99–120.

18. For an interesting perspective of empirical research on how knowledge can adversely affect performance, read Haas, M. R., & Hansen, M. T. 2005. When using knowledge can hurt performance: The value of organizational capabilities in a management consulting company. *Strategic Management Journal,* 26(1): 1–24.

19. Some of the notable books on this topic include Edvisson & Malone, op. cit.; Stewart, op. cit.; and Nonaka, I., & Takeuchi, I. 1995. *The knowledge creating company.* New York: Oxford University Press.

20. Stewart, T. A. 2000. Taking risk to the marketplace. *Fortune,* March 6: 424.

21. Dutton, G. 1997. Are you technologically competent? *Management Review,* November: 54–58.

22. Dess & Picken, op. cit.: 34.

23. Webber, A. M. 1998. Danger: Toxic company. *Fast Company,* November: 152–161.

24. Morris, B. 1997. Key to success: People, people, people. *Fortune,* October 27: 232.

25. Martin, J. 1998. So, you want to work for the best . . . . *Fortune,* January 12: 77.

26. Carbonara, P. 1997. Hire for attitude, train for skill. *Fast Company,* August–September: 66–67.

27. Stewart, T. A. 1996. Why value statements don't work. *Fortune,* June 10: 138.

28. Cardin, R. 1997. Make your own Bozo Filter. *Fast Company,* October–November: 56.

29. Carbonara, op. cit.

30. Martin, op. cit.; Henkoff, R. 1993. Companies that train best. *Fortune,* March 22: 53–60.

31. Bartlett, C. A., & Ghoshal, S. 2002. Building competitive advantage through people. *MIT Sloan Management Review,* 43(2): 34–41.

32. Ibid.

33. An interesting perspective on developing new talent rapidly when they join an organization can be found in Rollag, K., Parise, S., & Cross, R. 2005. Getting new hires up to speed quickly. *MIT Sloan Management Review,* 46(2): 35–41.

34. Stewart, T. A. 1998. Gray flannel suit? moi? *Fortune,* March 18: 80–82.

35. Ibid.

36. An interesting perspective on how Cisco Systems develops its talent can be found in Chatman, J., O'Reilly, C., & Chang, V. 2005. Cisco Systems: Developing a human capital strategy. *California Management Review,* 47(2): 137–166.

37. This section is based on Leonard, D., & Swap, W. 2004. Deep smarts. *Harvard Business Review,* 82(9): 88–97.

38. Morris, B. op. cit.

39. For an innovative perspective on the appropriateness of alternate approaches to evaluation and rewards, refer to Seijts, G. H., & Lathan, G. P. 2005. Learning versus performance goals: When should each be used? *Academy of Management Executive,* 19(1): 124–132.

40. The discussion of the 360-degree feedback system draws on UPS. 1997. 360-degree feedback: Coming from all

sides. *Vision* (a UPS Corporation internal company publication), March: 3; Slater, R. 1994. *Get better or get beaten: Thirty-one leadership secrets from Jack Welch.* Burr Ridge, IL: Irwin; Nexon, M. 1997. General Electric: The secrets of the finest company in the world. *L'Expansion,* July 23: 18–30; and Smith, D. 1996. Bold new directions for human resources. *Merck World* (internal company publication), October: 8.

41. Kets de Vries, M. F. R. 1998. Charisma in action: The transformational abilities of Virgin's Richard Branson and ABB's Percy Barnevik. *Organizational Dynamics,* Winter: 20.

42. We have only to consider the most celebrated case of industrial espionage in recent years, wherein José Ignacio Lopez was indicted in a German court for stealing sensitive product planning documents from his former employer, General Motors, and sharing them with his executive colleagues at Volkswagen. The lawsuit was dismissed by the German courts, but Lopez and his colleagues were investigated by the U.S. Justice Department. Also consider the recent litigation involving noncompete employment contracts and confidentiality clauses of *International Paper v. Louisiana-Pacific, Campbell Soup v. H. J. Heinz Co.,* and *PepsiCo v. Quaker Oats's Gatorade.* In addition to retaining valuable human resources and often their valuable network of customers, firms must also protect proprietary information and knowledge. For interesting insights, refer to Carley, W. M. 1998. CEO gets hard lesson in how not to keep his lieutenants. *Wall Street Journal,* February 11: A1, A10; and Lenzner, R., & Shook, C. 1998. Whose Rolodex is it, anyway? *Forbes,* February 23: 100–103.

43. For an insightful discussion of retention of knowledge workers in today's economy, read Davenport, T. H. 2005. *The care and feeding of the knowledge worker.* Boston, MA: Harvard Business School Press.

44. Lieber, R. B. 1998, Why employees love these companies. *Fortune,* January 12: 72–74.

45. The examples in this section draw upon a variety of sources, including Lubove, S. 1998. New age capitalist. *Forbes,* April 6: 42–43; Kets de Vries, op. cit.; Pfeffer, J. 1995. Producing sustainable competitive advantage through the effective management of people. *Academy of Management Executive,* 9(1): 55–69. The concept of strategic intent is generally credited to Hamel, G., & Prahalad, C. K. 1989. Strategic intent. *Harvard Business Review,* 67: 63–76.

46. Kets de Vries, op. cit.: 73–92.

47. Stewart, T. A. 2001. *The wealth of knowledge.* New York: Currency.

48. Amabile, T. M. 1997. Motivating creativity in organizations: On doing what you love and loving what you do. *California Management Review,* Fall: 39–58.

49. The discussion of internal markets for human capital draws on Hamel, G. 1999. Bringing Silicon Valley inside. *Harvard Business Review,* 77(5): 71–84.

50. Monsanto has been part of Pharmacia since 2002. *Hoover's Handbook of Am. Bus. 2004:* 562.

51. Pfeffer, J. 2001. Fighting the war for talent is hazardous to your organization's health. *Organizational Dynamics,* 29(4): 248–259.

52. For an insightful discussion on strategies for retaining and developing human capital, refer to Coff, R. W. 1997. Human assets and management dilemmas: Coping with hazards on the road to resource-based theory. *Academy of Management Review,* 22(2): 374–402.

53. For an insightful study on the effects of tuition reimbursement on voluntary employee turnover, see Benson, G. S., Finegold, D., & Mohrman, S. A. 2004. You paid for the skills, now keep them: Tuition reimbursement and voluntary turnover. *Academy of Management Journal,* 47(3): 315–331.

54. The examples in this section draw upon the following sources: Stewart, *Intellectual capital;* and Fisher, A. 1998. The 100 best companies to work for in America. *Fortune,* January 12: 69–70.

55. The statistics on child care trends are drawn from Bubbar, S. E., & Aspelin, D. J. 1998. The overtime rebellion: Symptom of a bigger problem? *Academy of Management Executive,* 12: 68–76. The other examples in this section are drawn from various sources, including Munk, N. 1998. The new organization man. *Fortune,* March 16: 68–72; and Hammonds, K. H., Furchgott, R., Hamm, S., & Judge, P. C. 1997. Work and family. *BusinessWeek,* September 15: 96–104.

56. Cox, T. L. 1991. The multinational organization. *Academy of Management Executive,* 5(2): 34–47. Without doubt, a great deal has been written on the topic of creating and maintaining an effective diverse workforce. Some excellent, recent books include: Harvey, C. P., & Allard, M. J. 2005. *Understanding and managing diversity: Readings, cases, and exercises.* (3rd ed.). Upper Saddle River, NJ: Pearson Prentice-Hall; Miller, F. A., & Katz, J. H. 2002. *The inclusion breakthrough: Unleashing the real power of diversity.* San Francisco: Berrett Koehler; and Williams, M. A. 2001. *The 10 lenses: Your guide to living and working in a multicultural world.* Sterling, VA: Capital Books.

57. www.rand.org/publications/RB/RB/5050.

58. www.shrm.org/diversity/businesscase.asp.

59. This section, including the six potential benefits of a diverse workforce, draws on Cox, T. H., & Blake, S. 1991. Managing cultural diversity: Implications for organizational competitiveness. *Academy of Management Executive,* 5(3): 45–56.

60. www.pwcglobal.com/us/eng/careers/diversity/index.html.

61. Refer to www.fortune.com/diversity.

62. This discussion draws on Dess, G. G., & Lumpkin, G. T. 2001. Emerging issues in strategy process research. In Hitt, M. A., Freeman, R. E., & Harrison, J. S. (Eds.). *Handbook of strategic management:* 3–34. Malden, MA: Blackwell.

63. Adler, P. S., & Kwon, S. W. 2002. Social capital: Prospects for a new concept. *Academy of Management Review,* 27(1): 17–40.

64. Capelli, P. 2000. A market-driven approach to retaining talent. *Harvard Business Review,* 78(1): 103–113.

65. This hypothetical example draws on Peteraf, M. 1993. The cornerstones of competitive advantage. *Strategic Management Journal,* 14: 179–191.

66. Wernerfelt, B. 1984. A resource-based view of the firm. *Strategic Management Journal,* 5: 171–180.

67. Wysocki, B., Jr. 2000. Yet another hazard of the new economy: The Pied Piper Effect. *Wall Street Journal,* March 20: A1–A16.

68. Ibid.

69. Buckman, R. C. 2000. Tech defectors from Microsoft resettle together. *Wall Street Journal,* October: B1–B6.

70. For an insightful discussion on the creation of social capital, see Bolino, M. C., Turnley, W. H., & Bloodgood, J. M. 2002. Citizenship behavior and the creation of social capital in organizations. *Academy of Management Review,* 27(4): 505–522.

71. An insightful discussion of the interorganizational aspects of social capital can be found in Dyer, J. H., & Singh, H. 1998. The relational view: Cooperative strategy and sources of interorganizational competitive advantage. *Academy of Management Review,* 23: 66–79.

72. Prusak, L., & Cohen, D. 2001. How to invest in social capital. *Harvard Business Review,* 79(6): 86–93.

73. Leonard, D., & Straus, S. 1997. Putting your company's whole brain to work. *Harvard Business Review,* 75(4): 110–122.

74. Oh, H., Chung, M., & Labianca, G. 2004. Group social capital and group effectiveness: The role of informal socializing ties. *Academy of Management Journal,* 47(6): 860–875; and Labianca, J. 2004. The ties that bind. *Harvard Business Review,* 82(10): 19.

75. Leana, C. R., & Van Buren, H. J., III. 1999. Organizational social capital and employment practices. *Academy of Management Review,* 24: 538–555.

76. Prusak & Cohen, op. cit.: 86–93.

77. Teitelbaum, R. 1997. Tough guys finish first. *Fortune,* July 21: 82–84.

78. Collins, D. 2003. *Communication in a virtual organization.* Mason, OH: Thompson South-Western; and Winston, S. 2004. *Organized for success: Top executives and CEOs reveal the organizing principles that helped them reach the top.* New York: Crown Business.

79. Taylor, W. C. 1999. Whatever happened to globalization? *Fast Company,* December: 228–236.

80. Prahalad, C. K., & Ramaswamy, V. 2004. *The future of competition: Co-creating value with customers.* Boston: Harvard Business School Press.

81. Ibid.

82. Lei, D., Slocum, J., & Pitts, R. A. 1999. Designing organizations for competitive advantage: The power of unlearning and learning. *Organizational Dynamics,* Winter: 24–38.

83. This section draws upon Zaccaro, S. J., & Bader, P. 2002. E-Leadership and the challenges of leading e-teams: Minimizing the bad and maximizing the good. *Organizational Dynamics,* 31(4): 377–387.

84. Kirkman, B. L., Rosen, B., Tesluk, P. E., & Gibson, C. B. 2004. The impact of team empowerment on virtual team performance: The moderating role of face-to-face interaction. *Academy of Management Journal,* 47(2): 175–192.

85. The discussion of the advantages and challenges associated with e-teams draws on Zacarro & Bader, op. cit.

86. For a recent study exploring the relationship between team empowerment, face-to-face interaction, and performance in virtual teams, read Kirkman, Rosen, Tesluk, & Gibson, op. cit.

87. For an innovative study on how firms share knowledge with competitors and the performance implications, read Spencer, J. W. 2003. Firms' knowledge sharing strategies in the global innovation system: Empirical evidence from the flat panel display industry. *Strategic Management Journal,* 24(3): 217–235.

88. The examples of Andersen Consulting and Access Health draw upon Hansen, M. T., Nohria, N., & Tierney, T. 1999. What's your strategy for managing knowledge? *Harvard Business Review,* 77(2): 106–118.

89. Capelli, op. cit.

90. Ibid.

91. Koudsi, S. 2000. Actually, it is brain surgery. *Fortune,* March 20: 233.

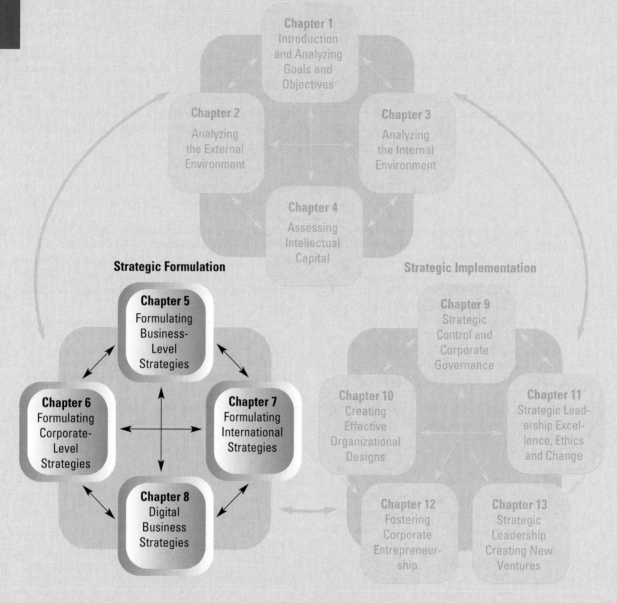

**Strategic Analysis**

**Chapter 1**
Introduction
and Analyzing
Goals and
Objectives

**Chapter 2**
Analyzing
the External
Environment

**Chapter 3**
Analyzing
the Internal
Environment

**Chapter 4**
Assessing
Intellectual
Capital

**Strategic Formulation**

**Chapter 5**
Formulating
Business-
Level
Strategies

**Chapter 6**
Formulating
Corporate-
Level
Strategies

**Chapter 7**
Formulating
International
Strategies

**Chapter 8**
Digital
Business
Strategies

**Strategic Implementation**

**Chapter 9**
Strategic
Control and
Corporate
Governance

**Chapter 10**
Creating
Effective
Organizational
Designs

**Chapter 11**
Strategic Lead-
ership Excel-
lence, Ethics
and Change

**Chapter 12**
Fostering
Corporate
Entrepreneur-
ship

**Chapter 13**
Strategic
Leadership
Creating New
Ventures

**Case Analysis**

**Chapter 14**
Case
Analysis

# part two

# Strategic Formulation

5

Business-Level Strategy: Creating and Sustaining
Competitive Advantages

6

Corporate-Level Strategy: Creating Value through Diversification

7

International Strategy: Creating Value in Global Markets

8

Digital Business Strategies: Leveraging Internet and E-Business
Capabilities

# 5

# Business-Level Strategy:
## Creating and Sustaining Competitive Advantages

## >chapter objectives

*After reading this chapter, you should have a good understanding of:*

- The central role of competitive advantage in the study of strategic management.

- The three generic strategies: overall cost leadership, differentiation, and focus.

- How the successful attainment of generic strategies can improve a firm's relative power vis-à-vis the five forces that determine an industry's average profitability.

- The pitfalls managers must avoid in striving to attain generic strategies.

- How firms can effectively combine the generic strategies of overall cost leadership and differentiation.

- The importance of considering the industry life cycle to determine a firm's business-level strategy and its relative emphasis on functional area strategies and value-creating activities.

- The need for turnaround strategies and a dynamic perspective on industry change and evolution that enable a firm to reposition its competitive position in an industry.

*h*ow firms compete with each other and how they attain and sustain competitive advantages go to the heart of strategic management. In short, the key issue becomes: Why do some firms outperform others and enjoy such advantages over time? This subject, business-level strategy, is the focus of Chapter 5.

The first part of the chapter draws on Michael Porter's framework of generic strategies. He identifies three strategies—overall cost leadership, differentiation, and focus—that firms may apply to outperform their rivals in an industry. We begin by describing each of these strategies and provide examples of firms that have successfully attained them as a means of outperforming competitors in their industry. Next, we address how these strategies help a firm develop a favorable position vis-à-vis the "five forces" (Chapter 2). We then suggest some of the pitfalls that managers must avoid if they are to successfully pursue these generic strategies. We close this section with a discussion of the conditions under which firms may effectively combine generic strategies to outperform rivals. Firms that fail to consider carefully the potential downsides associated with the generic strategies—separately and in combination—will have the most difficulty either creating or sustaining competitive advantages over time.

The second part of Chapter 5 discusses a vital consideration in the effective use of business-level strategies: industry life cycles. The four stages of the industry life cycle—introduction, growth, maturity, and decline—are indicative of an evolving management process that affects factors such as the market growth rate and the intensity of competition. Accordingly, the stages of an industry's life cycle are an important contingency that managers should take into account when making decisions concerning the optimal overall business-level strategies and the relative emphasis to place on functional capabilities and value-creating activities. At times, firms are faced with performance declines and must find ways to revitalize their competitive positions. The actions followed to do so are referred to as turnaround strategies, which may be needed at any stage of the industry life cycle. However, they occur more frequently during the maturity and decline stages. Finally, managers must recognize the dynamic nature of industry change and evolution. Advantages can be short lived. Managers need to be able to embrace innovations and strive to sustain competitive advantages.

Sharper Image, with revenues of $736 million, was founded in 1987 and established itself with such gadgets as fogless mirrors and water-proof shower radios.[1] In the late 1990s it cashed in on the Razor scooter fad. When that faded, Sharper Image introduced the Ionic Breeze Quadra, which helped it to double annual sales between 1999 and 2003. However, as the firm found out, relying on a single product that rivals can easily imitate can be a very risky strategy.

> For several years, the $350 Ionic Breeze Quadra air purifier was Sharper Image's primary money machine, accounting for about 16 percent of its total revenues in a recent year. However, rivals have begun to enter the market and Sharper Image's purifier is facing intense competition. Its most direct rival, Brookstone, is selling its new Pure-Ion UV air purifier for $300. Home Depot and RadioShack are selling their own versions for $200. Sharper Image tried to prop up sales by coming up with an easier-to-clean model. However, the price was too expensive at $400, and it failed to generate significant new sales.
>
> If Sharper Image's product was far superior to its competition, customers might be willing to spend the extra money. However, the firm's product was panned in research conducted by that venerable consumer watchdog *Consumer Reports* (CR). In February 2002, CR published a lengthy article reviewing 16 air purifiers. It placed the Ionic Breeze Quadra dead last in its ranking, saying that the device produced "no measurable reduction in airborne particles." Sharper Image complained because it felt that the tests were unfair since their model needed to run longer in order to be effective. So, according to Steve Williams, an attorney for Consumers Union (the publisher of *Consumer Reports*), they "went back and tested again, this time seeing how much cigarette smoke could be removed over 19 hours. It couldn't even clean the smoke from one-eighth of a cigarette." In addition, CR had its test procedures reviewed by an independent expert who confirmed the validity of their procedure. CR then ran a second article. The result was that the Ionic Breeze Quadra ended up near the bottom of the magazine's rankings.
>
> Sharper Image sued the research group in 2003, alleging product disparagement. Unfortunately, in November 2004, the San Francisco district court ruled that there was "no reasonable probability" that Sharper Image could prove its case. The judge then dismissed the suit under California's so-called anti-SLAPP law, which is designed to deter "strategic litigation against public participation," that is, frivolous suits filed by big companies to silence critics. Sharper Image was also required to reimburse Consumers Union $525,000 for its costs and attorneys' fees. And, to add insult to injury, in the May 2005 issue of *Consumer Reports*, the magazine reported that not only does the Ionic Breeze Quadra fail to significantly clean the air, but it also releases potentially unhealthy levels of ozone.
>
> How much of the product's sales decline is due to CR's negative evaluation and how much is due to intensified competition is, of course, open to question. However, few would argue that the large drop in demand for Sharper Image's major product is a primary reason for the firm's overall recent poor performance. For 2004, the firm's same store sales were down one percent, and its overall profit was down nearly 50 percent from the previous year. And not surprisingly, its stock price has been hit very hard. In early 2005, shares were trading at about $17 a share—down from its all-time high of $40 a year earlier.

Sharper Image's problem was three-fold. First, the Ionic Breeze Quadra did not enjoy any clear differentiation advantage along any product attributes such as quality, styling, or performance. Second, at $350, it did not enjoy a cost advantage either. Third, the Ionic Breeze Quadra was easily imitated by rivals. In addition, when negative product reviews came in, Sharper Image went on a legal offensive instead of addressing the real problem.

Since all firms endeavor to enjoy above-average returns (or profits), the question of how management should go about this is a core issue in strategic management. Organizations that have created sustainable competitive advantages don't rely on a single strength, as Sharper Image has done, but strive for well-rounded strategies. This increases the chances that advantages will be more lasting, or sustainable, instead of temporary.

These avenues of competitive advantage take several forms, known as generic strategies. There are three major types: overall low cost, differentiation, and focus. In the next section, we will discuss how Michael Porter's three generic strategies contribute to a firm's competitive advantage and how firms can successfully combine multiple strategies.

## >>Types of Competitive Advantage and Sustainability

Michael Porter presented three generic strategies that a firm can use to overcome the five forces and achieve competitive advantage.[2] Each of Porter's generic strategies has the potential to allow a firm to outperform rivals within the same industry. The first, *overall cost leadership,* is based on creating a low-cost-position relative to a firm's peers. With this strategy, a firm must manage the relationships throughout the entire value chain and be devoted to lowering costs throughout the entire chain. On the other hand, *differentiation* requires a firm (or business unit) to create products and/or services that are unique and valued. Here, the primary emphasis is on "nonprice" attributes for which customers will gladly pay a premium. Finally, a firm following a *focus* strategy must direct its attention (or "focus") toward narrow product lines, buyer segments, or targeted geographic markets. A firm emphasizing a focus strategy must attain advantages either through differentiation or a cost leadership approach. Whereas the overall cost leadership and differentiation strategies strive to attain advantages industrywide, focusers build their strategy with a narrow target market in mind. Exhibit 5.1 illustrates these three strategies on two dimensions: competitive advantage and strategic target.

Before moving on to each generic strategy, it is important to note that both casual observation and research support the notion that firms that identify with one or more of the forms of competitive advantage that Porter identified outperform those that do not.[3] There has been a rich history of strategic management research addressing this topic. One study analyzed 1,789 strategic business units and found that businesses combining multiple forms of competitive advantage (differentiation and overall cost leadership)

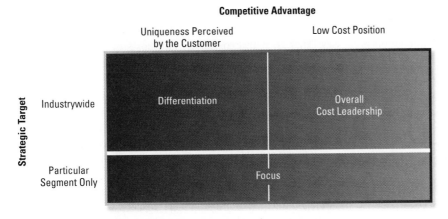

**Exhibit 5.1   Three Generic Strategies**

| Competitive Advantage | | | | | | |
| Performance | Differentiation and Cost | Differentiation | Cost | Differentiation and Focus | Cost and Focus | Stuck in the Middle |
| --- | --- | --- | --- | --- | --- | --- |
| Return on investment (%) | 35.5 | 32.9 | 30.2 | 17.0 | 23.7 | 17.8 |
| Sales growth (%) | 15.1 | 13.5 | 13.5 | 16.4 | 17.5 | 12.2 |
| Gain in market share (%) | 5.3 | 5.3 | 5.5 | 6.1 | 6.3 | 4.4 |
| Sample size | 123 | 160 | 100 | 141 | 86 | 105 |

**Exhibit 5.2**   **Competitive Advantage and Business Performance**

outperformed businesses that used only a single form. The lowest performers were those that did not identify with even a single type of advantage. They were classified as "stuck in the middle." Results of this study are presented in Exhibit 5.2.[4]

## Overall Cost Leadership

The first generic strategy is overall cost leadership. Cost leadership requires a tight set of interrelated tactics that include:

- Aggressive construction of efficient-scale facilities.
- Vigorous pursuit of cost reductions from experience.
- Tight cost and overhead control.
- Avoidance of marginal customer accounts.
- Cost minimization in all activities in the firm's value chain, such as R&D, service, sales force, and advertising.

Exhibit 5.3 draws on the value-chain concept (see Chapter 3) to provide examples of how a firm can attain an overall cost leadership strategy in its primary and support activities.

An important concept related to an overall cost leadership strategy is the experience curve, which refers to how business "learns" how to lower costs as it gains experience with production processes. That is, with experience, unit costs of production decline as output increases in most industries. The experience curve concept is discussed in Strategy Spotlight 5.1 and Exhibit 5.4 (page 167).

To generate above-average performance, a firm following an overall cost leadership position must attain parity on the basis of differentiation relative to competitors. In other words, a firm achieving parity is similar to its competitors, or "on par," with respect to differentiated products.[5] Parity on the basis of differentiation permits a cost leader to translate cost advantages directly into higher profits than competitors. Thus, the cost leader earns above-average returns.[6]

The failure to attain parity on the basis of differentiation can be illustrated with an example from the automobile industry—the ill-fated Yugo. Below is an excerpt from a speech by J. W. Marriott, Jr., Chairman of the Marriott Corporation:[7]

> . . . money is a big thing. But it's not the only thing. In the 1980s, a new automobile reached North America from behind the Iron Curtain. It was called the Yugo, and its main attraction was price. About $3,000 each. But the only way they caught on was as the butt of jokes. Remember the guy who told his mechanic, "I want a gas cap for my Yugo." "OK," the mechanic replied, "that sounds like a fair trade."

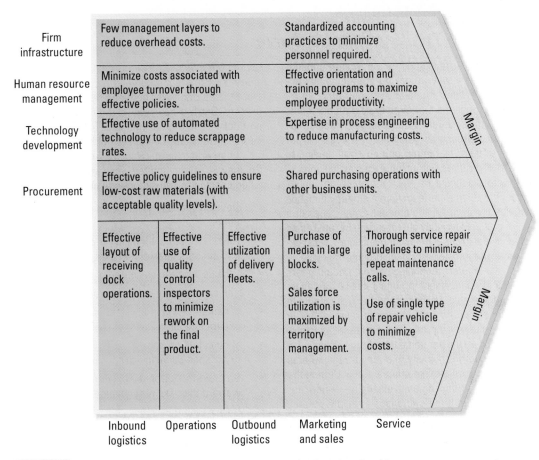

| Firm infrastructure | Few management layers to reduce overhead costs. | Standardized accounting practices to minimize personnel required. | | | |
| Human resource management | Minimize costs associated with employee turnover through effective policies. | Effective orientation and training programs to maximize employee productivity. | | | |
| Technology development | Effective use of automated technology to reduce scrappage rates. | Expertise in process engineering to reduce manufacturing costs. | | | |
| Procurement | Effective policy guidelines to ensure low-cost raw materials (with acceptable quality levels). | Shared purchasing operations with other business units. | | | |
| | Effective layout of receiving dock operations. | Effective use of quality control inspectors to minimize rework on the final product. | Effective utilization of delivery fleets. | Purchase of media in large blocks. Sales force utilization is maximized by territory management. | Thorough service repair guidelines to minimize repeat maintenance calls. Use of single type of repair vehicle to minimize costs. |
| | Inbound logistics | Operations | Outbound logistics | Marketing and sales | Service |

**Exhibit 5.3  Value-Chain Activities: Examples of Overall Cost Leadership**

Source: Adapted with the permission of The Free Press, a division of Simon & Schuster Adult Publishing Group, from *Competitive Advantage: Creating and Sustaining Superior Performance* by Michael E. Porter. Copyright © 1985, 1998 by Michael E. Porter. All rights reserved.

Yugo was offering a lousy value proposition. The cars literally fell apart before your eyes. And the lesson was simple. Price is just one component of value. No matter how good the price, the most cost-sensitive consumer won't buy a bad product.

Below, we discuss some examples of how firms enhance cost leadership position in their industries.

While other managed care providers were having a string of weak years, WellPoint, based in Thousand Oaks, California, has had a number of banner years and recently enjoyed a profit growth of 75 percent to approximately $960 million over the past two years.[8] Chairman Leonard Schaeffer credits the company's focus on innovation for both expanding revenues and cutting costs. Recently, for example, WellPoint asked the Food and Drug Administration (FDA) to make the allergy drug Claritin available over the counter. Surprisingly, this may be the first time that an insurer has approached the FDA with this type of request. Schaeffer claimed, "They were kind of stunned," but the FDA agreed to consider it. It was a smart move for WellPoint. If approved as an over-the-counter drug, Claritin would reduce patient visits to the doctor and eliminate the need for prescriptions—two reimbursable expenses for which WellPoint would otherwise be responsible.

Stephen Sanger, CEO of General Mills, recently came up with an idea that helped his firm cut costs.[9] To improve productivity, he sent technicians to watch pit crews during a

# STRATEGY SPOTLIGHT

## 5.1

### The Experience Curve

The experience curve, developed by the Boston Consulting Group in 1968, is a way of looking at efficiencies developed through a firm's cumulative experience. In its basic form, the experience curve relates production costs to production output. As output doubles, costs decline by 10 percent to 30 percent. For example, if it costs $1 per unit to produce 100 units, the per unit cost will decline to between 70 to 90 cents as output increases to 200 units.

What factors account for this increased efficiency? First, the success of an experience curve strategy depends on the industry life cycle for the product. Early stages of a product's life cycle are typically characterized by rapid gains in technological advances in production efficiency. Most experience curve gains come early in the product life cycle.

Second, the inherent technology of the product offers opportunities for enhancement through gained experience. High-tech products give the best opportunity for gains in production efficiencies. As technology is developed, "value engineering" of innovative production processes is implemented, driving down the per unit costs of production.

Third, a product's sensitivity to price strongly affects a firm's ability to exploit the experience curve. Cutting the price of a product with high demand elasticity—where demand increases when price decreases—rapidly creates consumer purchases of the new product. By cutting prices, a firm can increase demand for its product. The increased demand in turn increases product manufacture, thus increasing the firm's experience in the manufacturing process. So by decreasing price and increasing demand, a firm gains manufacturing experience in that particular product, which drives down per unit production costs.

Fourth, the competitive landscape factors into whether or not a firm might benefit from an experience curve strategy. If other competitors are well positioned in the market, have strong capital resources, and are known to promote their product lines aggressively to gain market share, an experience curve strategy may lead to nothing more than a price war between two or more strong competitors. But if a company is the first to market with the product and has good financial backing, an experience curve strategy may be successful.

In an article in the *Harvard Business Review,* Pankaj Ghemawat recommended answering several questions when considering an experience curve strategy.

- Does my industry exhibit a significant experience curve?
- Have I defined the industry broadly enough to take into account interrelated experience?
- What is the precise source of cost reduction?
- Can my company keep cost reductions proprietary?
- Is demand sufficiently stable to justify using the experience curve?
- Is cumulated output doubling fast enough for the experience curve to provide much strategic leverage?
- Do the returns from an experience curve strategy warrant the risks of technological obsolescence?
- Is demand price-sensitive?
- Are there well-financed competitors who are already following an experience curve strategy or are likely to adopt one if my company does?

Michael Porter suggested, however, that the experience curve is not useful in all situations. Whether or not to base strategy on the experience curve depends on what specifically causes the decline in costs. For example, if costs drop from efficient production facilities and not necessarily from experience, the experience curve is not helpful. But as Sharon Oster pointed out in her book on competitive analysis, the experience curve can help managers analyze costs when efficient learning, rather than efficient machinery, is the source of cost savings.

Sources: Ghemawat, P. 1985. Building strategy on the experience curve. *Harvard Business Review,* March–April: 143–149; Porter, M. E. 1996. *On competition.* Boston: Harvard Business Review Press; Oster, S. M. 1994. *Modern competitive analysis* (2nd ed.). New York: Oxford University Press.

NASCAR race. That experience inspired the techies to figure out how to reduce the time it takes to switch a plant line from five hours to 20 minutes. This provided an important lesson: Many interesting benchmarking examples can take place far outside of an industry. Often, process improvements involve identifying the best practices in other industries and adapting them for implementation in your own firm. After all, when firms benchmark competitors in their own industry, the end result is often copying and playing catch-up.[10]

A business that strives for a low-cost advantage must attain an absolute cost advantage relative to its rivals. This is typically accomplished by offering a no-frills product

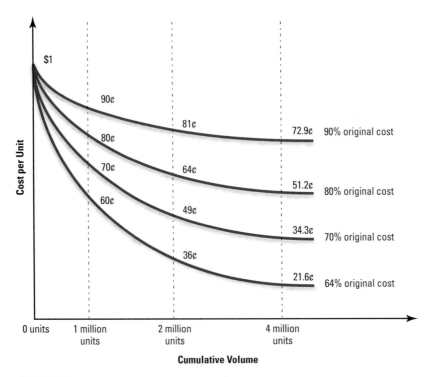

**Exhibit 5.4**   **Comparing Experience Curve Effects**

or service to a broad target market using standardization to derive the greatest benefits from economies of scale and experience. However, such a strategy may fail if a firm is unable to attain parity on important dimensions of differentiation such as quick responses to customer requests for services or design changes. Strategy Spotlight 5.2 discusses ING Direct, a financial services company that provides a "no frills" service but very generous rates on savings accounts and other services. In part, it succeeds by providing parity on differentiation through very good account security, ease and speed for customers in open-ing accounts, and very thorough online and paper account statements."[11]

*Overall Cost Leadership: Improving Competitive Position vis-à-vis the Five Forces*   An overall low-cost position enables a firm to achieve above-average returns despite strong competition. It protects a firm against rivalry from com-petitors, because lower costs allow a firm to earn returns even if its competitors eroded their profits through intense rivalry. A low-cost position also protects firms against pow-erful buyers. Buyers can exert power to drive down prices only to the level of the next most efficient producer. Also, a low-cost position provides more flexibility to cope with demands from powerful suppliers for input cost increases. The factors that lead to a low-cost position also provide substantial entry barriers from economies of scale and cost advantages. Finally, a low-cost position puts the firm in a favorable position with respect to substitute products introduced by new and existing competitors.

A few examples will illustrate these points. ING Direct's close attention to costs helps to protect them from buyer power and intense rivalry from competitors. Thus, they are able to drive down costs and enjoy relatively high power over their customers. By increasing its productivity and lowering unit costs, General Mills (and its competitors in that industry) enjoy greater scale economies and erect higher entry barriers for others

## ING Direct: A Highly Successful Low-Cost Strategy

ING Direct, considered the fast-food chain of the financial services industry, may be an extreme example of a low-cost strategy. However, it has been highly successful. For the year 2004, its pretax profit of $250 million was more than twice its profit of $110 million in 2003.

ING Direct has a limited offering of financial services, including savings accounts, CDs, and home equity loans. It is a unit of the Dutch giant ING, which offers banking, insurance, and asset management to over 60 million private, corporate and institutional clients in more than 50 countries. ING employs over 112,000 people in 65 countries, including more than 11,000 in the United States.

ING Direct attracts people who need very little hand-holding—that is, low maintenance customers—with very high interest rates. In fact, its Orange savings account pays 2.6 percent, which is over four times the .56 percent average for a money-market account at a bank. It is able to offer such enticing rates because it does 75 percent of its transactions online and it avoids amenities such as checking.

However, a unique aspect of ING Direct's approach to driving down costs is that it typically "fires" about 3,600 of its 2 million customers each year! It saves about $1 million annually by getting rid of customers who are too time-consuming. ING has driven its cost per account to about one-third of the industry average, even as its total assets have climbed to $30 billion since it entered the U. S. market in 2000.

CEO Arkadi Kuhlmann provides an interesting perspective on how ING Direct gets rid of its overly demanding customers:

> The difference between ING Direct and the rest of the financial industry is like the difference between take-out food and a sit-down restaurant. The business isn't based on relationships; it's based on a commodity product that's high-volume and low-margin. We need to keep expenses down, which doesn't work well when customers want a lot of empathetic contact.
>
> If the average customer phone call costs us $5.25 and the average account revenue is $12 per month, all it takes is 100,000 misbehaving customers for costs to go through the roof. So when a customer calls too many times or wants too many exceptions to the rule, our sales associate can basically say: "Look, this doesn't fit you. You need to go back to your community bank and get the kind of contact you're comfortable with." Of course, we have to use judgment. In some cases, people have legitimate questions. But often it's customers with large balances who are used to special treatment. They like premiums, platinum cards, and special rates. But you don't get that kind of stuff at the take-out window.

Source: Stone, A. 2005. Bare bones, plump profits. *BusinessWeek*, March 14: 88; Esfahani, E. 2004. How to get tough with bad customers. *Business 2.0*, October: 52; and www.home.ingdirect.com.

who want to enter the industry. Finally, as competitors such as WellPoint lower costs through means such as petitioning the FDA to make certain drugs available over the counter, they become less vulnerable to substitutes such as Internet-based competitors.

*Potential Pitfalls of Overall Cost Leadership Strategies*    There are many benefits from following a strategy of overall cost leadership. However, there are some pitfalls to avoid:

- *Too much focus on one or a few value-chain activities.* Would you consider a person to be astute if he cancelled his newspaper subscription and quit eating out to save money, but then "maxed out" several credit cards, requiring him to pay hundreds of dollars a month in interest charges? Of course not. Similarly, firms need to pay attention to all activities in the value chain to manage their overall costs. Too often managers make big cuts in operating expenses, but don't question year-to-year spending on capital projects. Or managers may decide to cut selling and marketing expenses but leave manufacturing expenses untouched. Managers should explore *all* value-chain activities, including relationships among them, as candidates for cost reductions.

- *All rivals share a common input or raw material.* Firms that compete on overall low-cost strategies are vulnerable to price increases in the factors of production.

Since they're competing on costs, they are less able to pass on price increases, because customers can easily take their business to competitors who have lower prices. Consider the hardship experienced by fertilizer producers in early 2001 when energy prices spiked.[12] The dramatic increase—a quadrupling of prices to $10 per thousand cubic feet of natural gas—forced firms to shut down nearly half of their production capacity. Why? Natural gas accounts for over 70 percent of the fertilizer's cost. According to Betty-Ann Hegge, senior vice president of Potash Corporation of Saskatchewan, Inc., North America's second largest producer, "Many companies are not even covering their cash costs at these prices."

- *The strategy is imitated too easily.* One of the common pitfalls of a cost-leadership strategy is that a firm's strategy may consist of value-creating activities that are easy to imitate.[13] Such was the case with online brokers in recent years.[14] As of early 2001, there were about 140 online brokers, hardly symbolic of an industry where imitation is extremely difficult. But according to Henry McVey, financial services analyst at Morgan Stanley, "We think you need five to ten" online brokers.

  What are some of the dynamics? First, although online brokers were geared up to handle 1.2 million trades a day by early 2001, volume had shrunk to about 834,000—a 30 percent drop. Thus, competition for a smaller pool of business is increasingly intense. Second, when the stock market is down, many investors trust their instincts less and seek professional guidance from brokerages that offer differentiated services. Eric Rajendra of A. T. Kearney, an international consulting company, claimed, "The current (online broker) model is inadequate for the pressures the industry is facing now."

- *A lack of parity on differentiation.* As noted earlier, firms endeavoring to attain cost leadership advantages need to obtain a level of parity on differentiation. An example is organizations providing online degree programs to adults working full-time. Although such firms may offer low prices, they may not be successful unless they can offer instruction that is perceived as comparable to traditional providers. For them, parity can be achieved on differentiation dimensions such as reputation and quality and through signaling mechanisms such as national and regional accreditation agencies.

- *Erosion of cost advantages when the pricing information available to customers increases.* This is becoming a more significant challenge as the Internet dramatically increases both the quantity and volume of information available to consumers about pricing and cost structures. Life insurance firms offering whole life insurance provide an interesting example.[15] One study found that for each 10 percent increase in consumer use of the Internet, there is a corresponding reduction in insurance prices to consumers of 3 to 5 percent. Recently, the nationwide savings (or, alternatively, reduced revenues to providers) was between $115 and $125 million annually.

## Differentiation

As the name implies, the strategy of differentiation consists of creating differences in the firm's product or service offering by creating something that is perceived *industrywide* as unique and valued by customers. Differentiation can take many forms:

- Prestige or brand image (Adam's Mark hotels, BMW automobiles).[16]
- Technology (Martin guitars, Marantz stereo components, North Face camping equipment).
- Innovation (Medtronic medical equipment, Nokia cellular phones).

| Firm infrastructure | Superior MIS—To integrate value-creating activities to improve quality. | | Facilities that promote firm image. | | Widely respected CEO enhances firm reputation. | |
| Human resource management | Programs to attract talented engineers and scientists. | | | Provide training and incentives to ensure a strong customer service orientation. | | Margin |
| Technology development | Superior material handling and sorting technology. | | | Excellent applications engineering support. | | |
| Procurement | Purchase of high-quality components to enhance product image. | | Use of most prestigious outlets. | | | |
| | Superior material handling operations to minimize damage.  Quick transfer of inputs to manufacturing process. | Flexibility and speed in responding to changes in manufacturing specifications.  Low defect rates to improve quality. | Accurate and responsive order processing.  Effective product replenishment to reduce customer inventory. | Creative and innovative advertising programs.  Fostering of personal relationship with key customers. | Rapid response to customer service requests.  Complete inventory of replacement parts and supplies. | Margin |
| | Inbound logistics | Operations | Outbound logistics | Marketing and sales | Service | |

**Exhibit 5.5**    **Value-Chain Activities: Examples of Differentiation**

Source: Adapted with the permission of The Free Press, a division of Simon & Schuster Adult Publishing Group, from *Competitive Advantage: Creating and Sustaining Superior Performance* by Michael E. Porter. Copyright © 1985, 1998 by Michael E. Porter. All rights reserved.

- Features (Cannondale mountain bikes, Honda Goldwing motorcycles).
- Customer service (Nordstrom department stores, Sears lawn equipment retailing).
- Dealer network (Lexus automobiles, Caterpillar earth-moving equipment).

Exhibit 5.5 draws on the concept of the value chain as an example of how firms may differentiate themselves in primary and support activities.

Firms may differentiate themselves along several different dimensions at once. For example, BMW is known for its high prestige, superior engineering, and high-quality automobiles. Another example is Harley-Davidson, which differentiates on image and dealer services.[17]

Firms achieve and sustain differentiation advantages and attain above-average performance when their price premiums exceed the extra costs incurred in being unique.[18] For example, both BMW and Harley-Davidson must increase consumer costs to offset added marketing expenses. Thus, a differentiator will always seek out ways of distinguishing itself from similar competitors to justify price premiums greater than the costs incurred by differentiating. Clearly, a differentiator cannot ignore costs. After all, its premium prices would be eroded by a markedly inferior cost position. Therefore, it must attain a level of cost *parity* relative to competitors. Differentiators can do this by reducing costs in all areas that do not affect differentiation. Porsche, for example, invests heavily in engine design—an area in which its customers demand excellence—but it is less concerned and spends fewer resources in the design of the instrument panel or the arrangement of switches on the radio.[19]

Many companies successfully follow a differentiation strategy.[20] For example, some firms have been able to appeal to a very upscale and discriminating segment of the market by offering products with an excellent image and strong brand identification. If you are interested in one of Ferrari's lower-priced models, the 360 Modena, be prepared to pay about $160,000. But it might take more than money; you'll need patience. Recently, there was a 50-person, 18-month waiting list for the all-aluminum, 400-horsepower V8-powered model.[21] And if you want the top-of-the-line Destiny yacht, a 135 footer, be prepared to spend around $13 million. If that is a little steep, a 94-foot model is only $6 million.[22]

Siebel Systems, a leader in software that manages customer relations, is well known for its customer service.[23] No software is written until the customer has significant input. Outside consultants routinely poll clients on satisfaction, and the compensation of managers and technical professionals is heavily based on such reports. How successful is Siebel? In the seven years since its founding, its sales have exceeded $1 billion faster than any other software maker, including Microsoft. CEO Tom Siebel is confident the firm will sustain its growth rate as long as the company, as he expressed it, "shows respect for the customer."

FedEx's CEO and founder, Fred Smith, claims that the key to his firm's success is innovation.[24] He contends his management team didn't understand their real goal when they started the firm in 1971: "We thought that we were selling the transportation of goods; in fact, we were selling peace of mind." To that end, they now provide each driver with a handheld computer and a transmitting device that makes it possible for customers to track their packages right from their desktop PCs.

Lexus, a division of Toyota, provides an example of how a firm can strengthen its differentiation strategy by *achieving integration at multiple points along the value chain.*[25] Although the luxury car line was not introduced until the late 1980s, by the early 1990s the cars had already soared to the top of J. D. Power & Associates's customer satisfaction ratings.

In the spirit of benchmarking, one of Lexus's competitors hired Custom Research Inc. (CRI), a marketing research firm, to find out why Lexus owners were so satisfied. CRI conducted a series of focus groups in which Lexus drivers eagerly offered anecdotes about the special care they experienced from their dealers. It became clear that, although Lexus was manufacturing cars with few mechanical defects, it was the extra care shown by the sales and service staff that resulted in satisfied customers. Such pampering is reflected in the feedback from one customer who claimed she never had a problem with her Lexus. However, upon further probing, she said, "Well, I suppose you could call the four times they had to replace the windshield a 'problem.' But frankly, they took care of it so well and always gave me a loaner car, so I never really considered it a problem until you mentioned it now." An insight gained in CRI's research is that perceptions of product quality (design, engineering, and manufacturing) can be strongly influenced by downstream activities in the value chain (marketing and sales, service).

Let's take a closer look at the Lexus example to reiterate some of the key points of a successful differentiation strategy.[26] The example illustrates how strong relationships among value activities reinforce and strengthen the customer's total perception of value. Value activity integration creates value for the end user. Clearly, Lexus must establish and maintain close ties with its dealers by providing resources such as advertising

## VoodooPC: A Successful Differentiation Strategy

When we think of personal computers, commodity products driven by low costs and competitive pricing usually comes to mind. Such is clearly not the case with VoodooPC, a highly successful Canadian company that competes at the high end of the market. As one of its accountants, Jennifer Fraser, notes, "We have an unconventional position in a market saturated by big boring giants."

VoodooPC Ltd. is a world leader in the design and manufacturing of high-performance and stylish personal computer entertainment systems. VoodooPC has won the prestigious Ultimate Gaming Machine Award for the past three years in a row.

Each VoodooPC is unique and custom made for each customer. To buy a Voodoo computer, you order what you think you need through the Voodoo Web site. Then, a Voodoo engineer contacts you to ensure that your Voodoo PC will exactly match your unique requirements. Ninety-five percent of all orders are further refined after customers talked to Voodoo engineers.

In a sense, VoodooPCs are not just PCs. Rather, they are works of art. The cases for VoodooPCs have 11 coats of European automobile paint for maximum gloss and color choice. Their desktops have art cut into the side of the computer tower and they are illuminated from the inside, casting a mysterious glow. Also, the inside of the

computer looks different, starting with beautifully folded wires, which they call "origami cabling." Similar to designers of Mercedes Benz cars, the creators of each VoodooPC sign their names on the inside of the case.

Obviously, VoodooPC does not compete on price. While there are some lower-end models, the typical prices are between $4,000 and $5,000. Some of their clientele are willing to pay $19,000 for dual processors, two video chips, and a liquid cooling system. The company even sold a 22-karat-gold-plated desktop for $52,000.

VoodooPC was founded by brothers Rahul and Ravi Sood who branded Voodoo as the PC company for the hard-core game geek. The strategy has worked. During the past four years, Voodoo's sales have soared past $20 million. And while the profit margin on the typical PC is 10 percent, the Soods' gaming machines generally get about 30 percent.

Voodoo prides itself on its custom design capabilities and customer service. It makes sure that the machine fits the buyer like an expensive, custom-made suit. Rahul Sood says, "We sometimes try to undersell you." That approach builds trust and positive buzz in the tight-knit gaming community. Voodoo also claims that it will (literally) go to the ends of the earth to service its machines. In fact, in 2002, it sent a tech support employee all the way to Sydney, Australia, to fix a PC. Rahul claims that the company won enough word-of-mouth sales from that one visit to more than justify the $828 plane ticket.

Sources: Malik, O. 2004. The 22-Karat PC. *Business 2.0*, May: 78; and, Anonymous. 2005. VoodooPC. *Cool Companies*, Calgary and Edmonton Edition: 120–121.

materials, training, parts, supplies, and automobile inventories. Yet you could easily imagine the futility of Lexus's superb marketing, sales, and service efforts if the company could not maintain high production quality, or if procurement were unable to acquire high-quality components. Superb marketing and service alone would be inadequate to support Lexus's strategy. Thus, successful differentiation requires attention to and integration with all parts of a firm's value chain.

Strategy Spotlight 5.3 discusses how VoodooPC has been highly successful with its differentiation strategy in what is generally considered to be a commodity industry—personal computers. Like Lexus, its success can be partially explained by its excellence in downstream activities such as customer service, as well as by its reputation for product excellence.

***Differentiation: Improving Competitive Position vis-à-vis the Five Forces*** Achieving differentiation is a viable strategy for earning above-average returns by creating a defensible position for overcoming Porter's five competitive forces. Differentiation provides protection against rivalry since brand loyalty lowers customer sensitivity to price and raises customer switching costs. By increasing a firm's margins, differentiation also avoids the need for a low-cost position. Higher entry barriers result because of customer loyalty and the firm's ability to provide uniqueness in its products or services. Differentiation also provides higher margins that enable a firm to deal with supplier power. And it reduces buyer power, because buyers lack comparable alternatives and are therefore less price sensitive. Supplier power is also decreased because there is a certain amount of prestige associated with being the supplier to a producer of highly differentiated products and services. Last, a firm that uses differentiation will enjoy high customer loyalty, thus experiencing less threat from substitutes than its competitors.

The examples in this section will be used to illustrate the above points. Lexus has enjoyed enhanced power over buyers because its top J. D. Power ranking makes buyers more willing to pay a premium price. This lessens rivalry, since buyers become less price-sensitive. The prestige associated with these upper-crust brand names such as Destiny yachts and Ferrari automobiles also lowers supplier power since margins are high. Suppliers would probably desire to be associated with prestige brands, thus lessening their incentives to drive up prices. Finally, the loyalty and "peace of mind" associated with a service provider such as FedEx or Siebel Systems make these firms less vulnerable to rivalry or substitute products and services.

*Potential Pitfalls of Differentiation Strategies*    Along with the benefits of differentiation, there are also pitfalls.

*   *Uniqueness that is not valuable.* A differentiation strategy must provide unique bundles of products and/or services that customers value highly. It's not enough just to be "different." An example is Gibson's Dobro bass guitar. Gibson came up with a unique idea: Design and build an acoustic bass guitar with sufficient sound volume so that amplification wasn't necessary. The problem with other acoustic bass guitars was that they did not project enough volume because of the low-frequency bass notes. By adding a resonator plate on the body of the traditional acoustic bass, Gibson increased the sound volume. Gibson believed this product would serve a particular niche market—bluegrass and folk artists who played in small group "jams" with other acoustic musicians. Unfortunately, Gibson soon discovered that its targeted market was content with their existing options: an upright bass amplified with a microphone or an acoustic electric guitar. Thus, Gibson developed a unique product, but it was not perceived as valuable by its potential customers.[27]

*   *Too much differentiation.* Firms may strive for quality or service that is higher than customers desire. Thus, they are vulnerable to competitors who provide an appropriate level of quality at a lower price. For example, consider the expensive Mercedes-Benz S-Class, which ranges in price between $75,000 and $125,000.[28] *Consumer Reports* recently described it as "sumptuous," "quiet and luxurious," and a "delight to drive." The magazine also considered it to be the least reliable sedan available in the United States. According to David Champion, who runs their testing program, the problems are electronic. "The engineers have gone a little wild," he says. "They've put every bell and whistle that they think of, and sometimes they don't have the attention to detail to make these systems work." Consider some features of these models: a computer-driven suspension that reduces body roll as the vehicle whips around a corner; cruise control that automatically slows the car down if it gets too close to another car; and seats that are adjustable 14 ways and that are ventilated by a system that uses eight fans to whisk away perspiration. Perhaps it is not too surprising that an executive at Mercedes, Sephan Wolfsried, told a symposium in Germany that he eliminated 600 functions from the Mercedes vehicles, "functions nobody needed and nobody

knew how to use." And drivers who responded to the *Consumer Reports'* surveys cited "serious" problems with the vehicle's electrical systems, power equipment and accessories. Through the end of October 2004, sales of the S-Class were down 12 percent from the previous year.

- ***Too high a price premium.*** This pitfall is quite similar to too much differentiation. Customers may desire the product, but they are repelled by the price premium compared to that of competitors. For example, Duracell (a division of Gillette) recently charged too high a price for batteries.[29] The firm tried to sell consumers on its superior quality products, but the mass market wasn't convinced. Why? The price differential was simply too high. At a CVS drugstore just one block from Gillette's headquarters, a four-pack of Energizer AA batteries was on sale at $2.99 compared with a Duracell four-pack at $4.59. Not only did Duracell's market share drop 2 percent in a recent two-year period, but its profits declined over 30 percent. Clearly, the price/performance proposition Duracell offered customers was not being accepted.

- ***Differentiation that is easily imitated.*** As we noted in Chapter 3, resources that are easily imitated cannot lead to sustainable advantages. Similarly, firms may strive for, and even attain, a differentiation strategy that is successful for a time. However, the advantages are eroded through imitation. L.A. Gear, a maker of high-end fashion sneakers and shoes, shows what can happen when a firm creates a product that is easy to imitate.[30] At one time, L.A. Gear enjoyed rapid success. Its revenues increased from $36 million in 1986 to $902 million in 1990. But by the early 1990s, intense competition eroded L.A. Gear's competitive position. Sales dropped to $416 million by 1994, but L.A. Gear failed to cut back its investments.

  Several problems plagued L.A. Gear. First, there was increasing price competition. Given low switching costs, rivals were able to attract L.A. Gear's customers with lower prices. Second, L.A. Gear had specialized assets and inventories that locked the company into its position. Thus, as competition intensified, the firm could not exit the industry without walking away from valuable assets.

- ***Dilution of brand identification through product-line extensions.*** Firms may erode their quality brand image by adding products or services with lower prices and less quality. Although this can increase short-term revenues, it may be detrimental in the long run. Profits don't necessarily follow revenues. Consider the case of Gucci.[31] In the 1980s Gucci was determined to capitalize on its prestigious brand name by launching an aggressive strategy of revenue growth. It added a set of lower-priced canvas goods to its product line. It also pushed goods heavily into department stores and duty-free channels and allowed its name to appear on a host of licensed items such as watches, eyeglasses, and perfumes. In the short term, this strategy worked. Sales soared. However, the strategy carried a high price. Gucci's indiscriminate approach to expanding its products and channels tarnished its sterling brand. Sales of its high-end goods (with higher profit margins) fell, causing profits to decline.

- ***Perceptions of differentiation may vary between buyers and sellers.*** The issue here is that "beauty is in the eye of the beholder." Companies must realize that although they may perceive their products and services as differentiated, their customers may view them as commodities. Indeed, in today's marketplace, many products and services have been reduced to commodities.[32] Thus, a firm could overprice its offerings and lose margins altogether if it has to lower prices to reflect market realities.

## Focus

The third generic strategy, focus, is based on the choice of a narrow competitive scope within an industry. A firm following this strategy selects a segment or group of segments and tailors its strategy to serve them. The focuser achieves competitive advantages by dedicating itself to these segments exclusively. The essence of focus is the exploitation of a particular market niche that is different from the rest of the industry. As you might expect, narrow focus itself (like merely "being different" as a differentiator) is simply not sufficient for above-average performance. The focus strategy, as indicated in Exhibit 5.1, has two variants. In a cost focus, a firm strives to create a cost advantage in its target segment. In a differentiation focus, a firm seeks to differentiate in its target market. Both variants of the focus strategy rely on providing better service than broad-based competitors who are trying to serve the focuser's target segment. Cost focus exploits differences in cost behavior in some segments, while differentiation focus exploits the special needs of buyers in other segments.

Let's look at examples of two firms that have successfully implemented focus strategies. Network Appliance (NA) has developed a more cost-effective way to store and distribute computer files.[33] Its larger rival, EMC, makes mainframe-style products priced over $1 million that store files and accommodate Internet traffic. NA makes devices that cost under $200,000 for particular storage jobs such as caching (temporary storage) of Internet content. Focusing on such narrow segments has certainly paid off for NA; it has posted a remarkable 20 straight quarters of revenue growth.

The above example was drawn from the high-technology industry. Our next example, Bessemer Trust, competes in the private banking industry.[34] A differentiation focuser, Bessemer targets families with a minimum of $5 million in assets, who desire both capital preservation and wealth accumulation. In other words, these are not people who want to put all their "eggs in a dot-com basket." Bessemer configures its activities for highly personalized service by assigning one account officer for every 14 families. Meetings are more likely to be held at a client's ranch or yacht than in Bessemer's office. Bessemer offers a wide range of customized services, such as investment management, estate administration, oversight of oil and gas investments, and accounting for race horses and aircraft. Despite the industry's most generous compensation of account officers and the highest personnel cost as a percentage of operating expenses, Bessemer's focused differentiation strategy is estimated to yield the highest return on equity in the industry.

Strategy Spotlight 5.4 provides an example of a well-known company that has a successful differentiation focus strategy—Porsche. Here's a firm that thrives by making products nobody needs but everyone seems to want!

*Focus: Improving Competitive Position vis-à-vis the Five Forces*    As we have seen, firms pursuing a focus strategy can earn above-average returns. Focus requires that a firm either have a low-cost position with its strategic target, high differentiation, or both. As we discussed with regard to cost and differentiation strategies, these positions provide defenses against each competitive force. Focus is also used to select niches that are least vulnerable to substitutes or where competitors are weakest.

Let's look at our examples to illustrate some of these points. First, Bessemer Trust and Porsche experienced less rivalry and lower buyer bargaining power by providing products and services to a targeted market segment that was less price-sensitive. New rivals would have difficulty attracting customers away from these firms based only on lower prices. Similarly, the brand image and quality that these brands evoked heightened the entry barriers for rivals trying to gain market share. Additionally, we could reasonably speculate that these two firms enjoyed some protection against substitute products and services because of their

# STRATEGY SPOTLIGHT

**5.4**

## Porsche: Winning through Differentiation Focus

After nearly filing for bankruptcy in the 1990s, Porsche has emerged as a company in a class by itself. It embodies the essence of a differentiation focus strategy. Porsche has one manufacturing plant in Stuttgart, Germany, and the entire company employs only 8,200 employees—fewer than just two or three Detroit automobile factories. And the worst thing (or best?) is that no one *needs* a Porsche.

What's their secret? The answer lies in Porsche's very specific market niche. In fact, their Cayenne, a new sport utility vehicle that was introduced in late 2002, is a "very expensive toy that caters to the person who wants everything," according to Ron Pinelli, an analyst with Autodata Corporation in Woodcliff Lake, New Jersey. Target marketing to a focal segment is Porsche's key to success. Current sales of 40,000 cars a year pales in comparison to the Big Three automakers. To illustrate, General Motors

stopped making the Pontiac Fiero when sales fell below 40,000. By contrast, Porsche's sales of 40,000 units give it enough room to profitably restructure its operations and pull itself out of potential bankruptcy without merging or being acquired by a larger firm. With a break-even point of only 12,000 to 14,000 unit sales, Porsche certainly has a comfortable cushion. Further, with growth in its traditional products and the success of its Cayenne, it will increase annual sales to about 80,000 units.

Their differentiation focus strategy has successfully positioned the company as a producer of highly sought-after luxury sports cars. As noted by CEO Wendelin Wiedekig, "Porsche wants to grow and we want to have exclusive products. That means we will keep following the niche strategy." A recent research report from Deutsche Bank states, "It is the design, the technology, and the brand that make a Porsche stand out." If you can't afford to buy a Porsche, but still want to enjoy the experience, take heart: You can rent a Porsche 996 for a day for *only* $749 at the Driven Image agency in Las Vegas, Nevada.

Sources: Taylor, III, A. "Porsche's Risky Recipe," *Fortune,* February 17, 2003, pp. 90–94; Curry, A. "Dude, Where's My Porsche," *U.S. News & World Report,* November 25, 2002, p. D8; Suhr, J. 2001, "Porsche Has High Hopes for SUV in '02," *Lexington* (KY) *Herald-Leader,* February 2001, p. B10; and Healey, J. "Groomed so as Not to Marry," *USA Today,* August 6, 1999, pp. B1–B2.

relatively high reputation, brand image, and customer loyalty. With regard to the strategy of cost focus, Network Appliances, the successful rival to EMC in the computer storage industry, was better able to absorb pricing increases from suppliers as a result of its lower cost structure. Thus, the effects of supplier power were lessened.

***Potential Pitfalls of Focus Strategies*** Along with the benefits, managers must be aware of the pitfalls of a focus strategy.

- ***Erosion of cost advantages within the narrow segment.*** The advantages of a cost focus strategy may be fleeting if the cost advantages are eroded over time. For example, Dell's pioneering direct selling model in the personal computer industry, while still the industry standard, is constantly being challenged by competitors as other computer makers gain experience with Dell's distribution method. Similarly, other firms have seen their profit margins drop as competitors enter their product segment.

- ***Even product and service offerings that are highly focused are subject to competition from new entrants and from imitation.*** Some firms adopting a focus strategy may enjoy temporary advantages because they select a small niche with few rivals. However, their advantages may be short-lived as rivals invade their market niche. A notable example is the multitude of dot-com firms that specialize in very narrow segments such as pet supplies, ethnic foods, and vintage automobile accessories. The entry barriers tend to be low, there is little buyer loyalty, and competition becomes intense. And since the marketing strategies and technologies employed by most rivals are largely nonproprietary, imitation is easy. Over time, revenues fall, profits margins are squeezed, and only the strongest players survive the shakeout.

176

- *Focusers can become too focused to satisfy buyer needs.* Some firms attempting to attain competitive advantages through a focus strategy may have too narrow a product or service. Examples include many retail firms. Hardware chains such as Ace and True Value are losing market share to rivals such as Lowe's and Home Depot who offer a full line of home and garden equipment and accessories. Similarly, many specialty ethnic and gourmet food stores may see their sales and profits shrink as large, national grocers such as Kroger's expand their already broad product lines to include such items. And given the enormous purchasing power of the national chains, it would be difficult for such specialty retailers to attain parity on costs.

## Combination Strategies: Integrating Overall Low Cost and Differentiation

There has been ample evidence—in the popular press and in research studies—about the strategic benefits of combining generic strategies. In the beginning of this section, we provided some evidence from nearly 1,800 strategic business units (see Exhibit 5.2) to support this contention. As you will recall, the highest performers were businesses that attained both cost and differentiation advantages, followed by those that had either one or the other. Those strategic business units that had the lowest performance identified with neither generic strategy; that is, they were "stuck in the middle." Results from other studies are consistent with these findings across a wide variety of industries including low-profit industries, the paints and allied products industry, the Korean electronics industry, the apparel industry, and the screw machine products industry.[35]

Perhaps the primary benefit to be enjoyed by firms that successfully integrate low-cost and differentiation strategies is that it is generally harder for competitors to duplicate or imitate. An integrated strategy enables a firm to provide two types of value to customers: differentiated attributes (e.g., high quality, brand identification, reputation) and lower prices (because of the firm's lower costs in value-creating activities). The goal becomes one of providing unique value to customers in an efficient manner.[36] Some firms are able to attain both types of advantages simultaneously. For example, superior quality can lead to lower costs because of less need for rework in manufacturing, fewer warranty claims, a reduced need for customer service personnel to resolve customer complaints, and so forth. Thus, the benefits of combining advantages can be additive, instead of merely involving trade-offs. Next, we consider three approaches to combining overall low-cost and differentiation competitive strategies.

*Automated and Flexible Manufacturing Systems*   Given the advances in manufacturing technologies such as CAD/CAM (computer aided design and computer aided manufacturing) as well as information technologies, many firms have been able to manufacture unique products in relatively small quantities at lower costs—a concept known as "mass customization."[37]

Let's consider the case of Andersen Windows of Bayport, Minnesota—a $1 billion manufacturer of windows for the building industry.[38] Until about 15 years ago, Andersen was a mass producer, in small batches, of a variety of standard windows. However, to meet changing customer needs, Andersen kept adding to its product line. The result was catalogs of ever-increasing size and a bewildering set of choices for both homeowners and contractors. Over a 6-year period, the number of products tripled, price quotes took several hours, and the error rate increased. This not only damaged the company's reputation, but also added to its manufacturing expenses.

To bring about a major change, Andersen developed an interactive computer version of its paper catalogs that it sold to distributors and retailers. Salespersons can now customize each window to meet the customer's needs, check the design for structural soundness, and provide a price quote. The system is virtually error free, customers get exactly what they want, and the time to develop the design and furnish a quotation has been cut by 75 percent. Each showroom computer is connected to the factory, and customers are assigned a code number that permits them to track the order. The manufacturing system has been developed to use some common finished parts (e.g., mullions, the vertical or horizontal strips separating window panes and sashes), but it also allows considerable variation in the final products. Despite its huge investment in time and money, Andersen has found that the new system has lowered costs, enhanced quality and variety, and improved its response time to customers.

*Exploiting the Profit Pool Concept for Competitive Advantage*   A profit pool can be defined as the total profits in an industry at all points along the industry's value chain.[39] Although the concept is relatively straightforward, the structure of the profit pool can be complex. The potential pool of profits will be deeper in some segments of the value chain than in others, and the depths will vary within an individual segment. Segment profitability may vary widely by customer group, product category, geographic market, or distribution channel. Additionally, the pattern of profit concentration in an industry is very often different from the pattern of revenue generation.

Consider the automobile industry profit pool in Exhibit 5.6. Here we see little relationship between the generation of revenues and capturing of profits. While manufacturing generates most of the revenue, this value activity is far smaller profitwise than other

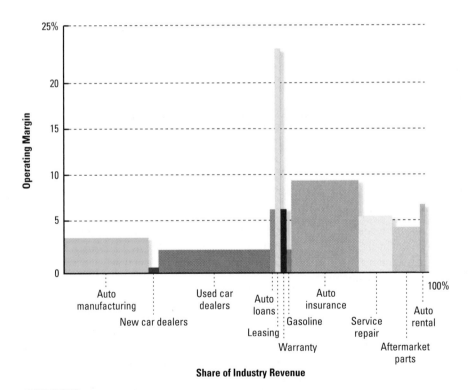

**Exhibit 5.6   The U.S. Automobile Industry's Profit Pool**

Source: Adapted and reprinted by permission of Harvard Business Review, Exhibit from "Profit Pools: A Fresh Look at Strategy," by O. Gadiesh and J. L. Gilbert, May–June 1998. Copyright © 1998 by the Harvard Business School Publishing Corporation; all rights reserved.

value activities such as financing and extended warranty operations. So while a car manufacturer may be under tremendous pressure to produce cars efficiently, much of the profit (at least proportionately) can be captured in the aforementioned downstream operations. Thus, a carmaker would be ill-advised to focus solely on manufacturing and leave downstream operations to others through outsourcing.

The profit pool concept helps explain U-Haul's success in the truck rental business. Its 10 percent operating margin is far superior to the industry average of less than 3 percent. U-Haul's largest competitor, Ryder, even abandoned the consumer rental business and sold off its fleet in 1996.

What is the key to U-Haul's outstanding performance? Unlike its competitors, U-Haul looked past its core truck rental business and found an untapped source of profit. That source was the accessories business—the sale of boxes and insurance, rentals of trailers and storage space—all the ancillary products and services customers need to complete the moving job that begins when they rent the truck. Profit margins for moving-truck rentals are small; customers shop for the lowest daily rate. But accessories are a different story. With virtually no competition in this part of the value chain, the accessories business enjoys attractive margins. And once a customer signs a rental agreement for a truck, his or her comparison shopping ends. Although the accessory business requires a greater variety of offerings, customers are largely "a captive market" and are, therefore, less price-sensitive. Thus, U-Haul's strategy became one of tightly managing its costs and prices to consumers in the low-profit truck rental part of the business. This enabled them to attract more customers to whom they sold high-margin accessories.

*Coordinating the "Extended" Value Chain by Way of Information Technology*    Many firms have achieved success by integrating activities throughout the "extended value chain" by using information technology to link their own value chain with the value chains of their customers and suppliers. As noted in Chapter 3, this approach enables a firm to add value not only through its own value-creating activities, but also for its customers and suppliers.

Such a strategy often necessitates redefining the industry's value chain. A number of years ago, Wal-Mart took a close look at its industry's value chain and decided to reframe the competitive challenge.[40] Although its competitors were primarily focused on retailing—merchandising and promotion—Wal-Mart determined that it was not so much in the retailing industry as in the transportation logistics and communications industries. Here, linkages in the extended value chain became central. That became Wal-Mart's chosen battleground. By redefining the rules of competition that played to its strengths, Wal-Mart has attained competitive advantages and dominates its industry.

Strategy Spotlight 5.5 provides some details of how Wal-Mart was able to combine differentiation and overall cost leadership to become the dominant retailer in the world. We also discuss why the company's strategy is highly sustainable; competitors would have a very difficult time imitating it or finding substitutes.

*Integrated Overall Low-Cost and Differentiation Strategies: Improving Competitive Position vis-à-vis the Five Forces*    Firms that successfully integrate both differentiation and cost advantages create an enviable position relative to industry forces. For example, Wal-Mart's integration of information systems, logistics, and transportation helps it to drive down costs and provide outstanding product selection. This dominant competitive position, along with its excellent reputation, serves to erect high entry barriers to potential competitors that have neither the financial nor physical resources to compete head-to-head. Wal-Mart's size—$288 billion in 2004 sales—provides the chain with enormous bargaining power over suppliers. Its low pricing and

## How Wal-Mart Combines Advantages

One of the most successful retailers of all time, Wal-Mart has trounced its competitors by combining competitive advantages. With net income of $10 billion from total revenues of $288 billion in 2004, Wal-Mart continued to post very impressive performance numbers. During the three-year period from 2001 to 2004, it experienced annual growth rates in revenues and net income of 10 percent and 16 percent, respectively. Wal-Mart has broadened its product offerings in recent years and now offers a diverse product line, including groceries, deli items, pharmaceuticals, and fast food. It has expanded internationally by exporting its data systems and models of efficiency to international markets, including Canada, Mexico, China, Indonesia, the United Kingdom, and Brazil.

Much of Wal-Mart's success can be attributed to its strategic focus, emphasis on key value-chain activities, and combination of competitive advantages. The value chains of merchandise retailers such as Kmart and Target have been much like that of grocery retailers. These value chains focused on cost control, efficiency in distribution and purchasing, and low-overhead facilities. Rivalry in this sector has centered on store location, pricing, and promotion.

Over the past decade, Wal-Mart has left its competitors behind by differentiating itself. In addition to the diverse product lines previously mentioned, Wal-Mart has distinguished itself from competitors by offering optical shops and photofinishing. By moving into such nontraditional areas, Wal-Mart challenges competitors in industries other than traditional discount retailers. Grocery chains, optical shops, fast-food restaurants, photofinishing stores, and pharmacies must now be concerned with the impact on market share each time Wal-Mart opens a new store in their town.

What is Wal-Mart's secret? We'll look at how Wal-Mart competes successfully on multiple forms of competitive advantage. A central feature of Wal-Mart's strategy is the logistics technique of cross-docking. Goods are continuously delivered to the company's warehouses, where they are selected, repacked, and then distributed to stores, often without being placed in inventory. Instead of wasting valuable time in warehouses, merchandise moves across one loading dock to another in 48 hours or less. This lets Wal-Mart achieve economies associated with full-truckload purchasing while avoiding the usual inventory and handling costs. Impressively, this reduces Wal-Mart's cost of sales by 2 to 3 percent compared to its competitors.

The benefits to Wal-Mart and its customers multiply. Lower costs help make possible the retailer's everyday low prices. This, in turn, saves money with less frequent promotions. Stable prices lead to more predictable sales, thus reducing stockouts and excess inventory. Fewer stockouts increase customer loyalty, while inventory control allows quick response to changing customer preferences. Everyday low prices bring in more customer traffic, which translates into more sales.

These economies allow Wal-Mart to staff stores with greeters and additional checkout clerks and to reward employees with stock ownership through a profit-sharing plan. Loyal, dedicated employees and enhanced customer service are elements of differentiation that translate into more customer loyalty and increased sales.

Despite the value of cross-docking, it's not easily copied by competitors. If it were, Wal-Mart's advantage would have long since vanished. The key is that cross-docking is complicated to manage. Wal-Mart made strategic investments in a variety of interlocking support systems that are difficult to imitate. The systems involve:

- Continuous contact between Wal-Mart's distribution centers, suppliers, and every point of sale in each store, so that orders can be executed within hours.

- Fast, responsive transportation, including 19 distribution centers serviced by nearly 2,000 company-owned trucks.

- Fundamental changes in managerial control that allow the stores to pull products when and where they need them rather than having suppliers push products into the system. With less centralized control, a premium is placed on frequent, informed cooperation between stores, distribution centers, and suppliers.

- Information systems that provide store managers with detailed information about customer behavior and a fleet of airplanes that regularly ferry store managers to Wal-Mart's Bentonville, Arkansas, headquarters for training on market trends and merchandising.

- A video link connecting each store.

- Profit sharing for employees, to encourage high customer responsiveness.

The cross-docking logistics strategy and sophisticated information systems reduce costs in a number of ways. By reducing inventories and shortening procurement cycle times, Wal-Mart can increase its flexibility and responsiveness to changing customer preferences. Wal-Mart has understood the business as a process and expanded its boundaries to include customers and *(continued)* wide selection reduce the power of buyers (its customers), because there are relatively few competitors that can provide a comparable cost/value proposition. This reduces the possibility of intense head-to-head rivalry, such as protracted price wars. Finally, Wal-Mart's overall value proposition makes potential substitute products (e.g., Internet competitors) a less viable threat.

*Pitfalls of Integrated Overall Cost Leadership and Differentiation Strategies*    Firms that attain both types of competitive advantage enjoy high returns. However, as with each generic strategy taken individually, there are some pitfalls to avoid.

- *Firms that fail to attain both strategies may end up with neither and become "stuck in the middle."* A key issue in strategic management is the creation of competitive advantages that enable a firm to enjoy above-average returns. Some firms may become "stuck in the middle" if they try to attain both cost and differentiation advantages. J. C. Penney Co., for example, has become, in the words of a *BusinessWeek* writer, "trapped in no-man's land . . . its fashions are tired, its prices unreasonable . . . and [it has] lost . . . cachet with customers."[41] Why? Penney's tried to achieve differentiation and cost control at the same time, but succeeded in neither. It struggled to fend off discounters such as Wal-Mart and Target on one front, and upscale department stores such as Macy's on the other. Not surprisingly, Penney's stock dropped about 80 percent between 1998 and 2000. As you might expect, the key elements of J. C. Penney's CEO Allen Questrom's turnaround plan include elements of both differentiation and cost control:
  - Improve store presentations.
  - Radically rethink merchandise.
  - Market the company brand more effectively.
  - Slash costs, including closing 44 stores and cutting 5,000 jobs.
  - Overhaul management ranks, including more outside recruitment.

- *Underestimating the challenges and expenses associated with coordinating value-creating activities in the extended value chain.* Successfully integrating activities across a firm's value chain with the value chain of suppliers and customers involves a significant investment in financial and human resources. Managers must not underestimate the expenses linked to technology investment, managerial time and commitment, and the involvement and investment required by the firm's customers and suppliers. The firm must be confident that it can generate a sufficient scale of operations and revenues to justify all associated expenses.

- *Miscalculating sources of revenue and profit pools in the firm's industry.* Firms may fail to accurately assess sources of revenue and profits in their value chain. This can occur for several reasons. For example, a manager may be biased due to his or her functional area background, work experiences, and educational background. If the manager's background is in engineering, he or she might perceive that proportionately greater revenue and margins were being created in manufacturing, product, and process design than a person whose background is in a "downstream" value-chain activity such as marketing and sales. Or politics could make managers "fudge" the numbers to put their area of operations in a more favorable light. This would make them responsible for a greater proportion of the firm's profits, thus improving their bargaining position for their share of the firm's internal resources.

A related problem is directing an overwhelming amount of managerial time, attention, and resources to value-creating activities that produce the greatest margins—to the detriment of other important, albeit less profitable, activities. For example, an automobile manufacturer may focus too much on downstream activities, such as warranty fulfillment and financing operations, to the detriment of differentiation and cost of the automobiles themselves. Or, as described earlier in the case of the truck rental industry, management might let the quality of rental trucks deteriorate while directing attention to the more profitable accessory side of the business.

## >>Industry Life Cycle Stages: Strategic Implications

The life cycle of an industry refers to the stages of introduction, growth, maturity, and decline that occur over the life of an industry. In considering the industry life cycle, it is useful to think in terms of broad product lines such as personal computers, photocopiers, or long-distance telephone service. Yet the industry life cycle concept can be explored from several levels, from the life cycle of an entire industry to the life cycle of a single variation or model of a specific product or service.

Why is it important to consider industry life cycles?[42] The emphasis on various generic strategies, functional areas, value-creating activities, and overall objectives varies over the course of an industry life cycle. Managers must become even more aware of their firm's strengths and weaknesses in many areas to attain competitive advantages. For example, firms depend on their research and development (R&D) activities in the introductory stage of the life cycle. R&D is the source of new products and features that everyone hopes will appeal to customers. Firms develop products and services to stimulate consumer demand. Later, during the maturity phase, the functions of the product have been defined, more competitors have entered the market, and competition is intense. Managers then place greater emphasis on production efficiencies and process (as opposed to the product) engineering in order to lower manufacturing costs. This helps to protect the firm's market position and to extend the product life cycle because the firm's lower costs can be passed on to consumers in the form of lower prices, and price-sensitive customers will find the product more appealing.

Exhibit 5.7 illustrates the four stages of the industry life cycle and how factors such as generic strategies, market growth rate, intensity of competition, and overall objectives change over time. As we noted earlier, managers must strive to emphasize the key functional areas during each of the four stages and to attain a level of parity in all functional areas and value-creating activities. For example, even though controlling production costs may be a primary concern during the maturity stage, managers should not totally ignore other functions such as marketing and R&D. If they do, they can become so focused on lowering costs that they miss market trends or fail to incorporate important product or process designs. In such cases, the firm may attain low-cost products that have limited market appeal.

It is important to point out a caveat. While the life cycle idea is analogous to a living organism (i.e., birth, growth, maturity, and death), the comparison does have limitations.[43]

| Stage<br>Factor | Introduction | Growth | Maturity | Decline |
|---|---|---|---|---|
| Generic strategies | Differentiation | Differentiation | Differentiation<br>Overall cost leadership | Overall cost leadership<br>Focus |
| Market growth rate | Low | Very large | Low to moderate | Negative |
| Number of segments | Very few | Some | Many | Few |
| Intensity of competition | Low | Increasing | Very intense | Changing |
| Emphasis on product design | Very high | High | Low to moderate | Low |
| Emphasis on process design | Low | Low to moderate | High | Low |
| Major functional area(s) of concern | Research and development | Sales and marketing | Production | General management and finance |
| Overall objective | Increase market awareness | Create consumer demand | Defend market share and extend product life cycles | Consolidate, maintain, harvest, or exit |

**Exhibit 5.7**  **Stages of the Industry Life Cycle**

Products and services go through many cycles of innovation and renewal. For the most part, only fad products have a single life cycle. Maturity stages of an industry can be "transformed" or followed by a stage of rapid growth if consumer tastes change, technological innovations take place, or new developments occur in the general environment. The cereal industry is a good example. When medical research indicated that oat consumption reduced a person's cholesterol, sales of Quaker Oats increased dramatically.[44]

Next we will discuss each stage of the industry life cycle. Then we will summarize how each stage poses important implications for a firm's generic strategies. To do this, we will briefly discuss the evolution of the personal computer industry. Finally, we will discuss turnaround strategies—that is, strategies that are necessary in order to reverse performance erosion and regain competitive position.

## Strategies in the Introduction Stage

In the introduction stage, products are unfamiliar to consumers.[45] Market segments are not well defined, and product features are not clearly specified. The early development of an industry typically involves low sales growth, rapid technological change, operating losses, and the need for strong sources of cash to finance operations. Since there are few players and not much growth, competition tends to be limited.

Success in the introduction stage requires an emphasis on research and development and marketing activities to enhance awareness of the product or service. The challenge becomes one of (1) developing the product and finding a way to get users to try it, and (2) generating enough exposure so the product emerges as the "standard" by which all other competitors' products are evaluated.

There's an advantage to being the "first mover" in a market.[46] Consider Coca-Cola's success in becoming the first soft-drink company to build a recognizable global brand. Moving first enabled Caterpillar to get a lock on overseas sales channels and service capabilities. Being a first mover allowed Matsushita to establish Video Home Source (VHS) as the global standard for videocassette recorders.

However, there can also be a benefit to being a "late mover." Target carefully thought out the decision to delay its Internet strategy. Compared to its competitors Wal-Mart and Kmart, Target was definitely the industry laggard. Strategy Spotlight 5.6 explains why its strategy paid off.

Examples of products currently in the introductory stages of the industry life cycle include electric vehicles, digital cameras, and high-definition television (HDTV).

## Strategies in the Growth Stage

The second stage of the industry life cycle—growth—is characterized by strong increases in sales. The potential for strong sales (and profits) attracts other competitors who also want to benefit. As products enter the growth stage, the primary key to success is to build consumer preferences for specific brands. This requires strong brand recognition, differentiated products, and the financial resources to support a variety of value-chain activities such as marketing and sales, customer service, and research and development. Whereas marketing and sales initiatives were mainly directed at spurring *aggregate* demand—that is, demand for all such products in the introduction stage—efforts in the growth stage are directed toward stimulating *selective* demand, in which a firm's product offerings are chosen instead of those of its rivals.

Revenues in the growth stage increase at an accelerating rate because (1) new consumers are trying the product and (2) a growing proportion of satisfied consumers are making repeat purchases.[47] In general, as a product moves through its life cycle, the proportion of repeat buyers to new purchasers increases. Conversely, new products and services often fail if there are relatively few repeat purchases. This is especially true with many consumer products that are characterized by relatively low price and frequent purchase. For example, Alberto-Culver introduced Mr. Culver's Sparklers, which were solid air fresheners that looked like stained glass. Although the product quickly went from the introductory to the growth stage, sales then plummeted. Why? Unfortunately, there were few repeat purchasers because buyers treated them as inexpensive window decorations, left them there, and felt little need to purchase new ones. Examples of products currently in the growth stage of the industry life cycle include Internet servers and personal digital assistants (e.g., Palm Pilots).

# STRATEGY SPOTLIGHT

## Target: An Example of "Late Mover" Advantage

All cutting-edge retailers have Web sites. The first retailer with a Web site gains the largest market share. Only technologically inept stores don't rush to reach customers though the Internet. At least that's the conventional wisdom. Looking back on the success (or lack thereof) gained from these strategies shows that conventional wisdom is sometimes conventional thoughtlessness.

Two of the first movers in Web-based retailing were Kmart and Wal-Mart. While Kmart faltered with Blue-Light.com and Wal-Mart struggled with Walmart.com, Target patiently waited. Electronic retailing, or "e-tailing," was a new area for low-cost retailers. Target's strategy was to learn from the mistakes of the first movers. Target waited until it understood *how* to attract customers with a Web site before it actually tried to attract customers with one. It seems like the conventional wisdom of Kmart and Wal-Mart was just a little too unconventional for Target.

By waiting, Target gained a "late mover" advantage. The store was able to use competitors' mistakes as its own learning curve. This saved money, and customers didn't seem to mind the wait: When Target finally opened its Web site, it quickly captured market share from both Kmart and Wal-Mart Internet shoppers. Forrester Research Internet analyst Stephen Zrike commented, "There's no question, in our mind, that Target has a far better understanding of how consumers buy online."

"I think the first mover advantage was grossly overrated on the Web," according to Jerry Storch, president of financial services and new business for Target. The conventional wisdom says that the first to market will capture the largest market share. This is often true, but only if the company that is first to market has the ability to do things right. Otherwise, customers become disgruntled; this affects not only the firm's Web store, but also the reputation of its bricks-and-mortar facilities. By waiting until it could do things right, Target now has more Web market share than either of its early mover rivals.

Sources: Stoughton, S. 2000. Target aimed carefully at Web sales, then stepped up and hit the bull's-eye. *Lexington* (KY) *Herald-Leader*, November 20 (Business Monday): 2; Neuborne, E. 2000. E-tailers hit the relaunch key. *Business Week*, October 17: 62.

## Strategies in the Maturity Stage

In the third stage—maturity—aggregate industry demand begins to slow. Since markets are becoming saturated, there are few opportunities to attract new adopters. It's no longer possible to "grow around" the competition, so direct competition becomes predominant.[48] With few attractive prospects, marginal competitors begin to exit the market. At the same time, rivalry among existing competitors intensifies because there is often fierce price competition at the same time that expenses associated with attracting new buyers are rising. Advantages based on efficient manufacturing operations and process engineering become more important for keeping costs low as customers become more price sensitive. It also becomes more difficult for firms to differentiate their offerings, because users have a greater understanding of products and services.

An article in *Fortune* magazine that addressed the intensity of rivalry in mature markets was aptly titled "A Game of Inches." It stated, "Battling for market share in a slowing industry can be a mighty dirty business. Just ask laundry soap archrivals Unilever and Procter & Gamble."[49] These two firms have been locked in a battle for market share since 1965. Why is the competition so intense? There is not much territory to gain. In 2000, total sales for the industry were flat at $6 billion a year. A Lehman Brothers analyst noted, "People aren't getting any dirtier." Thus, the only way to win is to take market share from the competition. To increase its share, Procter & Gamble (P&G) spends $100 million a year promoting its Tide brand on television, billboards, subways, buses, magazines, and the Internet. But Unilever isn't standing still. Armed with a new $80 million budget, it recently launched a soap tablet product named Wisk Dual Action Tablets. On January 7, 2001, it delivered samples of this product to 24 million U.S. homes in Sunday newspapers, followed by a series of TV ads. P&G launched a counteroffensive with Tide Rapid Action Tablets ads showed in side-by-side comparisons of the two products dropped into beakers of water. In the promotion, P&G claimed that its product is superior because it dissolves faster than Unilever's product. A minor point, but Unilever is challenging P&G in court. And the beat goes on . . . .

Although this is only one example, many product classes and industries, including consumer products such as beer, automobiles, and televisions, are in the maturity stage.

## Strategies in the Decline Stage

Although all decisions in the phases of an industry life cycle are important, they become particularly difficult in the decline stage. Hard choices must be made, and firms must face up to the fundamental strategic choices of either exiting or staying and attempting to consolidate their position in the industry.[50]

The decline stage occurs when industry sales and profits begin to fall. Typically, changes in the business environment are at the root of an industry or product group entering this stage.[51] Changes in consumer tastes or a technological innovation can push a product into decline. Typewriters have entered into the decline stage because of the word processing capabilities of personal computers. Compact disks have forced cassette tapes into decline in the prerecorded music industry, and digital video disks (DVDs) may soon replace compact disks. About 20 years earlier, of course, cassette tapes had led to the demise of long-playing records (LPs).

When a product enters the decline stage, it often consumes a large share of management time and financial resources relative to its potential worth. Not only are sales and profits declining, but also competitors may start drastically cutting their prices to raise cash and remain solvent in the short term. The situation is further aggravated by the wholesale liquidation of assets, including inventory, of some of the competitors that have failed. This further intensifies price competition.

In the decline stage, a firm's strategic options become dependent on the actions of rivals. If many competitors decide to leave the market, sales and profit opportunities increase. On the other hand, prospects are limited if all competitors remain.[52] If some competitors merge, their increased market power may erode the opportunities for the remaining players. Managers must carefully monitor the actions and intentions of competitors before deciding on a course of action.

Four basic strategies are available in the decline phase: *maintaining, harvesting, exiting,* or *consolidating.*[53]

- *Maintaining* refers to keeping a product going without significantly reducing marketing support, technological development, or other investments, in the hope that competitors will eventually exit the market. Many offices, for example, still use typewriters for filling out forms and other purposes that cannot be completed on a personal computer. In some rural areas, rotary (or dial) telephones persist because of the older technology used in central switching offices. Thus, if a firm remains in the business and others exit, there may still be the potential for revenues and profits.

- *Harvesting* involves obtaining as much profit as possible and requires that costs in the decline stage be reduced quickly. Managers should consider the firm's value-creating activities and cut associated budgets. Value-chain activities to consider are primary (e.g., operations, sales and marketing) and support (e.g., procurement, information systems, technology development). The objective is to wring out as much profit as possible.

- *Exiting the market* involves dropping the product from a firm's portfolio. Since a residual core of consumers may still use the product, eliminating it should be considered carefully. If the firm's exit involves product markets that affect important relationships with other product markets in the corporation's overall portfolio, an exit could have repercussions for the whole corporation. For example, it may involve the loss of valuable brand names or human capital with a broad variety of expertise in many value-creating activities such as marketing, technology, and operations.

- *Consolidation* involves one firm acquiring at a reasonable price the best of the surviving firms in an industry. This enables firms to enhance market power and acquire valuable assets. One example of a consolidation strategy took place in the defense industry in the early 1990s. As the cliché suggests, "peace broke out" at the end of the Cold War and overall U.S. defense spending levels plummeted.[54] Many companies that make up the defense industry saw more than 50 percent of their market disappear. Only one-quarter of the 120,000 companies that once supplied the Department of Defense still serve in that capacity; the others have shut down their defense business or dissolved altogether. But one key player, Lockheed Martin, became a dominant rival by pursuing an aggressive strategy of consolidation. During the 1990s, it purchased 17 independent entities, including General Dynamics's tactical aircraft and space systems divisions, GE Aerospace, Goodyear Aerospace, and Honeywell ElectroOptics. These combinations enabled Lockheed Martin to emerge as the top provider to three governmental customers: the Department of Defense, the Department of Energy, and NASA. Despite several downsizing initiatives, the firm was ranked for the first time in the Fortune 25 (the largest 25 industrial concerns in the United States). Clearly, the prospects for industry prosperity have increased in the aftermath of the September 11, 2001, terrorist attacks, the wars in Iraq and Afghanistan, and the "War on Terror."

Examples of products currently in the decline stage of the industry life cycle include automotive spark plugs (replaced by electronic fuel ignition), videocassette recorders (replaced by digital video disk recorders), and personal computer zip drives (replaced by compact disk read-write drives). As we mentioned previously, compact disks may soon be replaced by digital video disks (DVDs).

## Relating Generic Strategies to Stages of the Industry Life Cycle: The Personal Computer Industry

The personal computer (PC) industry provides an example of how a firm's generic strategies can vary over stages of the industry life cycle. In the introduction and growth stages, there were many players, such as IBM, Compaq, and others, who endeavored to create brand recognition and build loyal followings for their entries. To do so required well-developed and executed differentiation strategies. Apple was further differentiated because it was the only player to have a graphical user interface (GUI). However, well within a decade, the market matured, particularly when the "Wintel" standard (Microsoft's Windows operating system and Intel's microprocessor units) was widely adopted. This, in effect, eroded Apple's unique feature. Price competition then quickly intensified. Why? Consumer awareness and sophistication with personal computers quickly accelerated and the market became saturated with similar products. Here, overall low-cost strategies became the dominant form of competition. However, some firms, such as Dell Computer, were still able to make differentiation a key part of their business-level strategy by offering superior service and rapid fulfillment of customer orders. It now appears that many Web appliances, such as Oracle TalkBack and Intel's Dot.Station (each priced at approximately $200), may become viable substitute products. These products provide many features similar to those of personal computers—Internet access, e-mail delivery, and personal calendars. Thus, demand for these products may drive the personal computer industry into the decline stage by significantly lowering aggregate consumer demand. If, faced with the decline stage, the personal computer companies have to intensify their cost-reduction initiatives and develop focus strategies to seek out niches in the market, that may prove more viable than exiting the industry altogether.

## Turnaround Strategies

One problem with the life cycle analogy is that we tend to think that decline is inevitably followed by death. In the case of businesses, however, decline can be reversed by strategies that lead to turnaround and rejuvenation. Such a need for turnaround may occur at any stage in the life cycle. However, it is more likely to occur during the maturity or decline stage.

Most turnarounds require a firm to carefully analyze the external and internal environments. The external analysis leads to identification of market segments or customer groups that may still find the product attractive. Internal analysis results in actions aimed at reduced costs and higher efficiency. Typically, a firm needs to undertake a mix of both internally and externally oriented actions to effect a turnaround.[55]

A study of 260 mature businesses in need of a turnaround identified three strategies used by successful companies.[56]

- *Asset and cost surgery.* Very often, mature firms tend to have assets that do not produce any returns. These include real estate, buildings, etc. Outright sales or sale and leaseback free up considerable cash and improve returns. Investment in new plants and equipment can be deferred. Firms in turnaround situations try to aggressively cut administrative expenses and inventories and speed up collection of receivables. Costs also can be reduced by outsourcing production of various inputs for which market prices may be cheaper than in-house production costs.

- *Selective product and market pruning.* Most mature or declining firms have many product lines that are losing money or are only marginally profitable. One strategy is to discontinue these product lines and focus all resources on a few core profitable areas. For example, in the early 1980s, faced with possible bankruptcy, Chrysler Corporation sold off all their nonautomotive businesses as well as all their production facilities abroad. Focus on the North American market and identification of a profitable niche—namely, minivans—were keys to their eventual successful turnaround.

- *Piecemeal productivity improvements.* There are hundreds of ways in which a firm can eliminate costs and improve productivity. Although individually these are small gains, they cumulate over a period of time to substantial gains. Improving business processes by reengineering them, benchmarking specific activities against industry leaders, encouraging employee input to identify excess costs, reducing R&D and marketing expenses, increasing capacity utilization, and improving employee productivity lead to a significant overall gain.

The turnaround of software maker Intuit is an interesting case of a quick but well-implemented turnaround strategy. After stagnating and stumbling during the dot-com boom, Intuit, which is known for its Quickbook and Turbotax software, hired Stephen M. Bennett, a 22-year GE veteran, in 1999. He immediately discontinued Intuit's online finance, insurance, and bill-paying operations that were losing money. Instead, he focused on software for small businesses that employ less than 250 people. He also instituted a performance-based reward system that greatly improved employee productivity. Within a few years, Intuit was once again making substantial profits and its stock was up 42 percent.[57]

Even when an industry is in overall decline, pockets of profitability remain. These are segments with customers who are relatively price insensitive. For example, the replacement demand for vacuum tubes affords its manufacturers an opportunity to earn above normal returns although the product itself is technologically obsolete. Surprisingly, within

## Mitchell Caplan's Successful Turnaround at E*Trade

Mitchell Caplan is an optimist. He was confident that E*Trade Financial Corporation would survive and prosper. However, such optimism seemed to be misplaced given the fact that the shares of the online broker and bank had plunged from $60 at the peak of the Internet frenzy to a low of $3 in 2002. In 2001 and 2002, the firm lost a total of $428 million.

Fortunately for E*Trade (and their shareholders), Mr. Caplan was elevated to the CEO position in 2003, and he initiated what became a very successful turnaround. Let's take a look at how he did it.

First, Caplan had to change the firm's general approach to business. E*Trade had traditionally ignored the red ink as long as the stock price climbed. However, Caplan realized that he had to cut costs and sell off unrelated businesses. This included sharply reducing marketing and advertising expenses. E*Trade no longer splurges on $2 million Super Bowl commercials. In fact, one year, the company spent $500 million on marketing—more than the entire U. S. liquor industry! Now it only spends about $140 million a year. There are also fewer employees—down to about 4,000 now from a peak of 5,000. He also sold off businesses and assets that were unrelated to E*Trade's core. This included a national ATM network, kiosks in Target stores, a palatial New York retail branch that sold E*Trade souvenirs, and a TV business-news service. In addition, new ventures, such as a string of small storefront offices in major cities, are now rigorously analyzed for profitability. Notes Caplan, "I am adamant—and as a team we are adamant—about financial returns."

Mitch Caplan also felt that he needed to change the organization's culture and instill more discipline. He moved the headquarters from Menlo Park, California, to New York City. In effect, he left behind the propeller beanies, rubber chickens, and geeky props that made the firm's atmosphere rather loose. In its place are jackets and ties.

In addition to cutting costs and changing the culture, Caplan also focused E*Trade on leveraging its core banking operations. Here, it had a clear edge over rivals Charles Schwab Corp. and Ameritrade Inc. By offering banking products such as checking accounts and loans at reduced rates to customers who had brokerage accounts, E*Trade has built the nation's eighth-largest thrift. It also has become a big profit center, accounting for 40 percent of all revenues and 48 percent of profits. Now the company has about 632,000 bank accounts and 2.9 million active brokerage accounts—up from 170,00 bank accounts and 2.4 million brokerage accounts in early 2000.

By focusing on its core business, E*Trade's revenues were only $1.6 billion for the year 2004, which is less than the roughly $2 billion for the years 2003, 2002, 2001. However, profits have soared to $389 million in 2004 compared to an average *loss* of about $75 million for the three previous years. And E*Trade was recently recognized by *InformationWeek* as one of the 40 top firms in the financial services industry for delivering IT solutions to solve business problems.

Source: Weber, J. 2005. E*Trade rises from the ashes. *BusinessWeek*, January 17: 58–59; and Schmerken, I. 2004. Innovation in motion. *Wall Street & Technology*, October: 22–26.

declining industries, there may still be segments that are either stable or growing. Cigars and chewing tobacco are examples of profitable segments within the tobacco industry. Although fountain pens ceased to be the writing instrument of choice a long time ago, the fountain pen industry has successfully reconceptualized the product as a high margin luxury item that signals accomplishment, success, and appreciation of the finer things in life. In the final analysis, every business has the potential for rejuvenation. But it takes creativity, persistence, and most of all a clear strategy to translate that potential into reality.

Strategy Spotlight 5.7 summarizes how Mitchell Caplan conducted a successful turnaround at E*Trade. He was able to effectively cut costs and sell off unrelated businesses, change the firm's general approach to business and its culture, and leverage its core banking operations.

## Innovation and the Sustainability of Competitive Advantage

Our discussion of competitive advantages and industry life cycle so far has two major limitations. First, it may appear as if once a firm establishes a competitive advantage, all it has to do is to keep investing more resources to sustain that advantage. Second, the industry life cycle seems to suggest that every industry goes through a sequence of gradual and predictable stages. In recent years, at least in some industries, evidence shows that both these assumptions may be far from valid. Rapid technological changes and resulting innovations in products and services have unleashed a "gale of creative destruction"—a concept introduced by famed economist Joseph Schumpeter that has made competitive advantages fleeting and the life cycle of industries far from the predictable sequence of gradual changes that the life cycle analogy suggests.

As we mentioned already, innovation lies at the root of short-lived competitive advantages and abrupt ends to industry life cycles before they have progressed through all the stages. Innovations generally can be divided into two categories: *sustaining innovations* and *disruptive innovations*.[58] Innovations that help incumbents in an industry earn higher margins by selling better products to their best customers are called *sustaining innovations*. Even when incumbents are not the first to innovate, in most cases they end up winning because of their resource advantages and their ties to the existing customers. *Disruptive innovations,* on the other hand, appeal to customers whom the current incumbents are not seeking because they are not considered attractive enough to the existing players in the industry. Unfortunately for incumbents, these customer segments that were once considered unattractive have a way of becoming attractive growth markets subsequently.

Compaq's adoption of Intel's 32-bit 386 microprocessor, Merrill Lynch's introduction of the Cash Management Account (which allowed customers to write checks against their equity holdings), and the recent adoption of online banking by most major banks are examples of sustaining innovations. Each of these innovations enabled the firm to serve an existing customer segment better than before, often realizing better margins in the process as well. On the other hand, Apple's introduction of PCs, Charles Schwab's early entry into discount brokerage services, and the entry of airlines such as EasyJet and RyanAir into the European aviation industry represent disruptive innovations. In each of these cases, the innovation didn't address next-generation needs of leading customers in current markets. Instead, they appealed to a class of customers who were previously out of the market. And better still, the disruptive innovations improved at such a rapid pace that they began to pull in the customers of the mainstream markets by addressing their needs as well.

What determines a company's ability to embrace innovations and sustain their competitive advantages? Three organizational factors play a critical role. First, a firm's *resources,* both tangible and intangible, play a big part in determining what a firm can and cannot do. Access to abundant resources may increase a firm's odds of coping with change, but resources by themselves are seldom enough. Second, the internal *processes* within an organization play an even more important role. Internal processes include patterns of interaction, coordination, communication, and decision making. It is these processes that enable managers to transform resources into products and services and add value to them. Processes developed for a specific task and perfected through countless repetitions over several years can seldom meet the demands of a completely different task. Spotlight 5.8 explains how Digital Equipment Corporation failed to embrace the disruptive innovation of PCs because their internal processes were created to produce minicomputers. Finally, a firm's *values* also determine how successfully it can cope with innovations. Values refer to the standards by which managers set priorities. Values help them prioritize factors such as how to allocate scarce organizational resources, which products to develop, and which customers to sell. Again, in the case of Digital, an organizational value was that products with gross margins of less than 40 percent were not worth making or selling. Similarly, one of Toyota's organizational values has been developing cars with higher and higher margins. Together, resources, processes, and values determine whether a firm is able to successfully embrace an innovation.

## Failure to Cope with Disruptive Innovation: Digital Equipment Corporation

Digital Equipment Corporation was a phenomenally successful maker of minicomputers during the 1960s, 1970s, and 1980s. It would seem that Digital's success should have continued into the age of personal computers. After all, a maker of minicomputers is closer to the PC market than makers of large mainframes. It looked as if Digital had all the resources to succeed in the PC business. They had a trusted brand, great technology, and plenty of cash. Their engineers routinely built minicomputers which were more sophisticated than PCs. Why did Digital fail to take the obvious road to success in the growing PC industry?

First, Digital designed and built most of the key components of minicomputers internally and then integrated those components into proprietary configurations. This process was time consuming, often taking as many as three years to design a new product platform. PC makers, on the other hand, outsourced most components based on cost, quality, and technological currency, thereby keeping the capital investments low while assembling technologically up-to-date products. This also enabled them to bring

new computer designs into the market in 6 to 12 months. Second, Digital assembled minicomputers in batch mode and sold directly to corporate engineering departments. PCs, in contrast, were manufactured in high volume assembly lines and sold to end users through retail channels. Thus, despite having the technological and financial ability to make and market PCs, Digital was handicapped by processes that were designed and perfected for an industry with an altogether different set of performance characteristics.

Digital was also prevented from entering the PC business by their own resource allocation rules. Digital's financial criteria for new product development were based on gross margins. If a product could generate gross margins of 50 percent or more, it was considered a good business. If gross margins were lower than 40 percent, the product would be abandoned. This was a rule that served them well in the high overhead minicomputer business. PCs are high volume, low margin products and thus did not appeal to Digital! They walked away from a high growth business with few established competitors (at that time) just because it did not meet a decision criterion that was set up for a very different business!

Source: Christensen, C. M., & Overdorf, M. 2000. Meeting the challenge of disruptive change. *Harvard Business Review*, March–April: 66–76.

How and why firms outperform each other goes to the heart of strategic management. In this chapter, we identified three generic strategies and discussed how firms are able not only to attain advantages over competitors, but also to sustain such advantages over time. Why do some advantages become long-lasting while others are quickly imitated by competitors?

The three generic strategies—overall cost leadership, differentiation, and focus—form the core of this chapter. We began by providing a brief description of each generic strategy (or competitive advantage) and furnished examples of firms that have successfully implemented these strategies. Successful generic strategies invariably enhance a firm's position vis-à-vis the five forces of that industry—a point that we stressed and illustrated with examples. However, as we pointed out, there are pitfalls to each of the generic strategies. Thus, the sustainability of a firm's advantage is always challenged because of imitation or substitution by new or existing rivals. Such competitor moves erode a firm's advantage over time.

We also discussed the viability of combining (or integrating) overall cost leadership and generic differentiation strategies. If successful, such integration can enable a firm to enjoy superior performance and improve its competitive position. However, this is challenging, and managers must be aware of the potential downside risks associated with such an initiative.

The concept of the industry life cycle is a critical contingency that managers must take into account in striving to create and sustain competitive advantages. We identified the four stages of the industry life cycle—introduction, growth, maturity, and decline—and suggested

## Summary

how these stages can play a role in decisions that managers must make at the business level. These include overall strategies as well as the relative emphasis on functional areas and value-creating activities.

When a firm's performance severely erodes, turnaround strategies are needed to reverse its situation and enhance its competitive position. We have discussed three approaches—asset cost surgery, selective product and market pruning, and piecemeal productivity improvements. In addition, managers must be aware of disruptive change that can revolutionize an industry. They need to be able to embrace innovations and strive to sustain competitive advantages.

## Summary Review Questions

1. Explain why the concept of competitive advantage is central to the study of strategic management.

2. Briefly describe the three generic strategies—overall cost leadership, differentiation, and focus.

3. Explain the relationship between the three generic strategies and the five forces that determine the average profitability within an industry.

4. What are some of the ways in which a firm can attain a successful turnaround strategy?

5. Describe some of the pitfalls associated with each of the three generic strategies.

6. Can firms combine the generic strategies of overall cost leadership and differentiation? Why or why not?

7. Explain why the industry life cycle concept is an important factor in determining a firm's business-level strategy.

## Experiential Exercise

What are some examples of primary and support activities that enable Nucor, an $11 billion steel manufacturer, to achieve a low-cost strategy?

| Value Chain Activity | Yes/No | How Does Nucor Create Value for the Customer? |
|---|---|---|
| **Primary:** | | |
| Inbound logistics | | |
| Operations | | |
| Outbound logistics | | |
| Marketing and sales | | |
| Service | | |
| **Support:** | | |
| Procurement | | |
| Technology development | | |
| Human resource management | | |
| General administration | | |

1. Go to the Internet and look up www.walmart.com. How has this firm been able to combine overall cost leadership and differentiation strategies?

2. Choose a firm with which you are familiar in your local business community. Is the firm successful in following one (or more) generic strategies? Why or why not? What do you think are some of the challenges it faces in implementing these strategies in an effective manner?

3. Think of a firm that has attained a differentiation focus or cost focus strategy. Are their advantages sustainable? Why? Why not? (*Hint:* Consider its position vis-à-vis Porter's five forces.)

4. Think of a firm that successfully achieved a combination overall cost leadership and differentiation strategy. What can be learned from this example? Are these advantages sustainable? Why? Why not? (*Hint:* Consider its competitive position vis-à-vis Porter's five forces.)

## Application Questions Exercises

1. Can you think of a company (other than the opening case of Sharper Image) that suffered ethical consequences as a result of an overemphasis on a cost leadership strategy? What do you think were the financial and nonfinancial implications?

2. In the introductory stage of the product life cycle, what are some of the unethical practices that managers could engage in to enhance their firm's market position? What could be some of the long-term implications of such actions?

## Ethics Questions

## References

1. Armstrong, D. 2004. A mighty wind. *Forbes,* July 5: 62; Lomax, A. 2004. Sharper Image's dull holidays. *Yahoo finance.com,* December 27; Parloff, R. 2004. The Ionic Breeze is no match for Consumer Reports. *Fortune,* December 13: 57–58; Lee, L. 2004. Sharper Image needs . . . a sharper image. *BusinessWeek,* September 20: 45–46; and, Anonymous. 2005. Magazine taking aim at Sharper Image's air purifier. *Dallas Morning News,* April 5: 5D.

2. For a recent perspective by Porter on competitive strategy, refer to Porter, M. E. 1996. What is strategy? *Harvard Business Review,* 74(6): 61–78.

3. Some useful ideas on maintaining competitive advantages can be found in Ma, H., & Karri, R. 2005. Leaders beward: Some sure ways to lose your competitive advantage. *Organizational Dynamics,* 343(1): 63–76.

4. Miller, A., & Dess, G. G. 1993. Assessing Porter's model in terms of its generalizability, accuracy, and simplicity. *Journal of Management Studies,* 30(4): 553–585.

5. For a scholarly discussion and analysis of the concept of competitive parity, refer to Powell, T. C. 2003. Varieties of competitive parity. *Strategic Management Journal,* 24(1): 61–86.

6. Rao, A. R., Bergen, M. E., & Davis, S. 2000. How to fight a price war. *Harvard Business Review,* 78(2): 107–120.

7. Marriot, J. W. Jr. Our competitive strength: Human capital. A speech given to the Detroit Economic Club on October 2, 2000.

8. Whalen, C. J., Pascual, A. M., Lowery, T., & Muller, J. 2001. The top 25 managers. *BusinessWeek,* January 8: 63.

9. Ibid.

10. For an interesting perspective on the need for creative strategies, refer to Hamel, G., & Prahalad, C. K. 1994. *Competing for the Future.* Boston: Harvard Business School Press.

11. www.epinions.com/content_674557508.

12. Symonds, W. C., Arndt, M., Palmer, A. T., Weintraub, A., & Holmes, S. 2001. Trying to break the choke hold. *BusinessWeek,* January 22: 38–39.

13. For a perspective on the sustainability of competitive advantages, refer to Barney, J. 1995. Looking inside for competitive advantage. *Academy of Management Executive,* 9(4): 49–61.

14. Thornton, E., 2001, Why e-brokers are broker and broker. *BusinessWeek,* January 22: 94.

15. Koretz, G. 2001. E-commerce: The buyer wins. *BusinessWeek,* January 8: 30.

16. For an interesting perspective on the value of corporate brands and how they may be leveraged, refer to Aaker, D. A. 2004, *California Management Review,* 46(3): 6–18.

17. MacMillan, I., & McGrath, R. 1997. Discovering new points of differentiation. *Harvard Business Review,* 75(4): 133–145; Wise, R., & Baumgarter, P. 1999. Beating the clock: Corporate responses to rapid change in the PC industry. *California Management Review,* 42(1): 8–36.

18. For a discussion on quality in terms of a company's software and information systems, refer to Prahalad, C. K., & Krishnan, M. S. 1999. The new meaning of quality in the information age. *Harvard Business Review,* 77(5): 109–118.

19. Taylor, A., III. 2001. Can you believe Porsche is putting its badge on this car? *Fortune,* February 19: 168–172.

20. Ward, S., Light, L., & Goldstine, J. 1999. What high-tech managers need to know about brands. *Harvard Business Review,* 77(4): 85–95.

21. Zesiger, S. 1999. Silicon speed. *Fortune,* September 13: 120.

22. Blank, D. 2001. Down to the sea in mega-yachts. *BusinessWeek,* October 30: 18.

23. Whalen et al., op. cit.

24. Rosenfeld, J. 2000. Unit of one. *Fast Company,* April: 98.

25. Markides, C. 1997. Strategic innovation. *Sloan Management Review,* 38(3): 9–23.

26. Dess, G. G., & Picken, J. C. 1997. *Mission Critical:* 84. Burr Ridge, IL: Irwin.

27. The authors would like to thank Scott Droege, a faculty member at Western Kentucky University, for providing this example.

28. Flint, J. 2004. Stop the nerds. *Forbes,* July 5: 80; and, Fahey, E. 2004. Over-engineering 101. *Forbes,* December 13: 62.

29. Symonds, W. C. 2000. Can Gillette regain its voltage? *BusinessWeek,* October 16: 102–104.

30. McGahan, A. M. 1999. Competition, strategy, and business performance. *California Management Review,* 41(3): 74–102.

31. Gadiesh, O., & Gilbert, J. L. 1998. Profit pools: A fresh look at strategy. *Harvard Business Review,* 76(3): 139–158.

32. Colvin, G. 2000. Beware: You could soon be selling soybeans. *Fortune,* November 13: 80.

33. Whalen et al., op. cit.: 63.

34. Porter, M. E. 1996. What is strategy? *Harvard Business Review,* 74(6): 61–78.

35. Hall, W. K. 1980. Survival strategies in a hostile environment, *Harvard Business Review,* 58: 75–87; on the paint and allied products industry, see Dess, G. G., & Davis, P. S. 1984. Porter's (1980) generic strategies as determinants of strategic group membership and organizational performance. *Academy of Management Journal,* 27: 467–488; for the Korean electronics industry, see Kim, L., & Lim, Y. 1988. Environment, generic strategies, and performance in a rapidly developing country: A taxonomic approach. *Academy of Management Journal,* 31: 802–827; Wright, P., Hotard, D., Kroll, M., Chan, P., & Tanner, J. 1990. Performance and multiple strategies in a firm: Evidence from the apparel industry. In Dean, B. V., & Cassidy, J. C. (Eds.). *Strategic management: Methods and studies:* 93–110. Amsterdam: Elsevier-North Holland; and Wright, P., Kroll, M., Tu, H.,

& Helms, M. 1991. Generic strategies and business performance: An empirical study of the screw machine products industry. *British Journal of Management,* 2: 1–9.

36. Gilmore, J. H., & Pine, B. J., II. 1997. The four faces of customization. *Harvard Business Review,* 75(1): 91–101.

37. Ibid. For interesting insights on mass customization, refer to Cattani, K., Dahan, E., & Schmidt, G. 2005. Offshoring versus "spackling." *MIT Sloan Management Review,* 46(3): 6–7.

38. Goodstein, L. D., & Butz, H. E. 1998. Customer value: The linchpin of organizational change. *Organizational Dynamics,* Summer: 21–34.

39. Gadiesh & Gilbert, op. cit.: 139–158.

40. This example draws on Dess & Picken. 1997. op. cit.

41. Forest, S. A. 2001. Can an outsider fix J. C. Penney? *BusinessWeek,* February 12: 56, 58.

42. For an interesting perspective on the influence of the product life cycle and rate of technological change on competitive strategy, refer to Lei, D., & Slocum, J. W. Jr. 2005. Strategic and organizational requirements for competitive advantage. *Academy of Management Executive,* 19(1): 31–45.

43. Dickson, P. R. 1994. *Marketing Management:* 293. Fort Worth, TX: Dryden Press; Day, G. S. 1981. The product life cycle: Analysis and application. *Journal of Marketing Research,* 45: 60–67.

44. Bearden, W. O., Ingram, T. N., & LaForge, R. W. 1995. *Marketing principles and practices.* Burr Ridge, IL: Irwin.

45. MacMillan, I. C. 1985. Preemptive strategies. In Guth, W. D. (Ed.). *Handbook of Business Strategy:* 9-1–9-22. Boston: Warren, Gorham & Lamont; Pearce, J. A., & Robinson, R. B. 2000. *Strategic management* (7th ed.). New York: McGraw-Hill; Dickson, op. cit.: 295–296.

46. Bartlett, C. A., & Ghoshal, S. 2000. Going global: Lessons for late movers. *Harvard Business Review,* 78(2): 132–142.

47. Berkowitz, E. N., Kerin, R. A., & Hartley, S. W. 2000. *Marketing* (6th ed.). New York: McGraw-Hill.

48. MacMillan, op. cit.

49. Brooker, K. 2001. A game of inches. *Fortune,* February 5: 98–100.

50. MacMillan, op. cit.

51. Berkowitz et al., op. cit.

52. Bearden et al., op. cit.

53. The discussion of these four strategies draws on MacMillan, op. cit.; Berkowitz et al., op. cit.; and Bearden et al., op. cit.

54. Augustine, N. R. 1997. Reshaping an industry: Lockheed Martin's survival story. *Harvard Business Review,* 75(3): 83–94.

55. For some useful ideas on effective turnarounds and handling downsizings, refer to Marks, M. S., & De Meuse, K. P. 2005. Resizing the organization: Maximizing the gain

while minimizing the pain of layoffs, divestitures and closings. *Organizational Dynamics,* 34(1): 19–36.

56. Hambrick, D. C., & Schecter, S. M. 1983. Turnaround strategies for mature industrial product business units. *Academy of Management Journal,* 26(2): 231–248.

57. Mullaney, T. J. 2002. The wizard of Intuit. *BusinessWeek,* October 28: 60–63.

58. This section draws on Christensen, C. M., & Overdorf, M. 2000. Meeting the challenge of disruptive change. *Harvard Business Review,* March-April: 66–76; and Christensen, C. M., Johnson, M. W., & Rigby, D. K. 2002. Foundations for growth: How to identify and build disruptive new businesses. *Sloan Management Review,* Spring: 22–31.

6

# Corporate-Level Strategy:

## Creating Value through Diversification

## >chapter objectives

*After reading this chapter, you should have a good understanding of:*

- How managers can create value through diversification initiatives.

- The reasons for the failure of many diversification efforts.

- How corporations can use related diversification to achieve synergistic benefits through economies of scope and market power.

- How corporations can use unrelated diversification to attain synergistic benefits through corporate restructuring, parenting, and portfolio analysis.

- The various means of engaging in diversification—mergers and acquisitions, joint ventures/strategic alliances, and internal development.

- The benefits and potential drawbacks of real options analysis (ROA) in making resource allocation decisions under conditions of high uncertainty.

- Managerial behaviors that can erode the creation of value.

*C* orporate-level strategy addresses two related issues: (1) what businesses should a corporation compete in, and (2) how can these businesses be managed so they create "synergy"—that is, more value by working together than if they were freestanding units? As we will see, these questions present a key challenge for today's managers. Many diversification efforts fail or, in many cases, provide only marginal returns to shareholders. Thus, determining how to create value through entering new markets, introducing new products, or developing new technologies is a vital issue in strategic management.

We begin by discussing why diversification initiatives, in general, have not yielded the anticipated benefits. Then, in the next three sections of the chapter, we explore the two key alternative approaches: related and unrelated diversification. With related diversification, corporations strive to enter product-markets that share some resources and capabilities with their existing business units or increase their market power. Here we suggest four means of creating value: leveraging core competencies, sharing activities, pooled negotiating power, and vertical integration. With unrelated diversification, there are few similarities in the resources and capabilities among the firm's business units, but value can be created in multiple ways. These include restructuring, corporate parenting, and portfolio analysis approaches. Whereas the synergies to be realized with related diversification come from *horizontal relationships* among the business units, the synergies from unrelated diversification are derived from *hierarchical relationships* between the corporate office and the business units.

The last three sections address (1) the various means that corporations can use to achieve diversification, (2) real options analysis, and (3) managerial behaviors (e.g., self-interest) that serve to erode shareholder value. We address merger and acquisitions (M&A), joint ventures/strategic alliances, and internal development. Each of these involves the evaluation of important trade-offs. We also discuss the benefits and potential drawbacks of real options analysis (ROA)—an increasingly popular technique for making resource allocation decisions. Detrimental managerial behaviors, often guided by a manager's self-interest, are "growth for growth's sake," egotism, and antitakeover tactics. Some of these behaviors raise ethical issues because managers, in some cases, are not acting in the best interests of a firm's shareholders.

The pioneering discount broker Charles Schwab and Company became the industry leader through its focus on the customer and the innovative use of information technology. Faced with intense competition from deep-discount Internet brokerages in the late 1990s, Schwab tried to greatly expand its services to wealthy clientele by acquiring U.S. Trust. Below, we discuss why things didn't work out as planned.

"Clicks and mortar" broker Charles Schwab Corp. bought U.S. Trust Corp. in mid-2000 for $3.2 billion, joining a 147-year-old private-client wealth management firm with a leading provider of discount investor services.[1] Schwab paid a premium of 63.5 percent to U.S. Trust shareholders. The steep premium for U.S. Trust reflects the broker's deep pockets as well as its interest in becoming a full-service investment firm. At the time of the acquisition, Schwab was the nation's number one Internet and discount broker and number four financial services company overall.

Several synergies were expected from this acquisition. According to Schwab, the move expanded on its already developed offerings for wealthy clientele, including Schwab's Advisor Source and Signature Services. Schwab saw great potential for growth in the market represented by high-net-worth individuals and hoped its combination of Internet savvy and U.S. Trust's high-touch business lines would be tailor-made for that segment. In all, Schwab expected to leverage on its core competency in investor services to build greater market power.

But the news out of Charles Schwab and Co. has not been good. The bear market took a big bite out of Schwab's trading volume, revenues, and profits. With investment returns eroding, customers were much more sensitive to brokerage and commission fees. The management shake-up at U.S. Trust Corp. in October 2002 also raised serious questions. In its eagerness to tap upscale markets and become more than the people's broker, did the normally savvy Schwab miss serious warning signs at U.S. Trust? What went wrong?

The apparent synergies have not worked out, and deeper incompatibilities surfaced. Former U.S. Trust employees claimed that Schwab was overly enamored by the glossy brand and pedigreed clients of U.S. Trust. The company was too optimistic about Schwab's ability to direct their high-end clients to U.S. Trust, but very few Schwab customers have $2 million in assets, the minimum for U.S. Trust's pricey hand holding. Even those referred were often turned down by the subsidiary. Therefore, the main hope for the acquisition—stopping Schwab's richest customers from defecting to full-service brokerages such as Merrill Lynch—has not panned out. Also, many key managers left when their retention agreements expired in May 2002, taking their clients with them.

By mid-2004, more than 300 wealth advisers had departed. Wealth advisers are the core of U.S. Trust's businesses because they have the direct relationships with the wealthy families that make up its core clientele. When advisers leave, clients often follow them. U.S. Trust has been forced to offer hefty pay packages and bonuses to retain some of its top talent.

Perhaps, the core problem has been a clash between the two cultures. The low-cost discount-broker culture of Schwab discouraged big pay packages and provided only limited services to clients. U.S. Trust, with its plush dining rooms and lavish pay packages, prides itself on its highly personal service to wealthy families. Schwab executives complained about U.S. Trust's arrogance and refusal to adapt to fast-changing financial markets and customer demands. U.S. Trust executives, in contrast, frowned on Schwab's lack of sophistication and obsessive focus on cutting costs. According to one U.S. Trust executive, "It's like the battle between old wealth versus new wealth. U.S. Trust represented the established wealth and complicated needs of wealthy families. Schwab was the upstart that saw the market in more simple terms."

Another major problem has been technology. Despite reports of federal regulators' hinting at system-related problems, Schwab thought it was manageable and was content with its inspection of U.S. Trust's system. However, it eventually discovered the magnitude of the problem when the computer systems failed to detect suspicious patterns of cash transactions. The bank had to pay $10 million in July 2001 to settle charges by the New York State Banking Department and Federal Reserve that it was not complying with anti–money laundering rules. (The bank did not admit or deny fault.) The severity of the technology problem is illustrated by the fact that U.S. Trust did not even use the standard Windows operating system until the late 1990s. Furthermore, its 30 branches are not on a single computer system, hindering back-office operations such as order processing.

Compounding the problems after the compliance fiasco, U.S. Trust started screening clients so closely that it alienated them. This consumed time and money that could otherwise have been spent generating new business. Cost cutting has been another area of concern. U.S. Trust's executives dragged their feet on consolidating their numerous bank charters and cutting costs at offices outside New York, adding to the disappointing performance. Several weak branches will likely be closed.

With problems mounting, Schwab replaced U.S. Trust CEO Jeffrey S. Maurer and the president, Amribeth S. Rahe. They named Alan J. Weber, former head of Citibank's international operations, to be CEO and president. Weber faces the Herculean task of making things work. "The wild card is whether Schwab can transform a high-net-worth business from (one of) steady earnings growth to more dynamic earnings growth," says a Wall Street analyst. It seems that marrying up has not been the ticket to wealth it was supposed to be.

Schwab is not alone in having a disappointing experience with an acquisition. Many large multinational firms and recent big acquirers have failed to effectively integrate their acquisitions, paid too high a premium for the target's common stock, or were unable to understand how the acquired firm's assets would fit with their own lines of business. And, at times, top executives may not have acted in the best interests of shareholders. That is, the motive for the acquisition may have been to enhance the executives' power and prestige rather than improve shareholder returns. At times, the only other people who may have benefited were the shareholders of the *acquired* firms.

Exhibit 6.1 summarizes some of the bottom line results of several studies that were conducted over a variety of time periods. Here are a few examples of the enormous amount of shareholder wealth that has been lost within a few years after some of the more recent well-chronicled acquisitions and mergers.[2]

* Glaxo/SmithKline (2000)   $40 billion lost
* Chase/J. P. Morgan (2000)   $26 billion lost
* SBC/Ameritech (1999)   $68 billion lost
* WorldCom/MCI (1998)   $94 billion lost
* Daimler/Chrysler (1998)   $36 billion lost

Many acquisitions ultimately result in divestiture—an admission that things didn't work out as planned. In fact, some years ago, a writer for *Fortune* magazine lamented, "Studies show that 33 percent to 50 percent of acquisitions are later divested, giving corporate marriages a divorce rate roughly comparable to that of men and women."[3]

Admittedly, we have been rather pessimistic so far. Clearly, many diversification efforts have worked out very well—whether through mergers and acquisitions, strategic alliances and joint ventures, or internal development. We will discuss many success stories throughout this chapter. Next, we will discuss the primary rationales for diversification.

## >>Making Diversification Work: An Overview

Not all diversification moves, including those involving mergers and acquisitions, erode performance. For example, acquisitions in the oil industry, such as British Petroleum PLC's purchases of Amoco and Arco, are performing well, as is the merger of Exxon and Mobil. Similarly, many leading high-tech firms, such as Microsoft and Intel, have

The summaries of the studies below consistently support the notion that attaining the intended payoffs from diversification efforts is very elusive.

- Michael Porter of Harvard University studied the diversification records of 33 large, prestigious U.S. companies from 1950 to 1986 and found that most of them had divested many more acquisitions than they had kept. The corporate strategies of most companies had dissipated rather than enhanced shareholder value. By taking over companies and breaking them up, corporate raiders had thrived on failed strategies.

- Another study evaluated the stock market reaction to 600 acquisitions over the period between 1975 and 1991. The results indicated that the acquiring firms suffered an average 4 percent drop in market value (after adjusting for market movements) in the three months following the acquisitions announcement.

- A study conducted jointly by *BusinessWeek* and Mercer Management Consulting, Inc., analyzed 150 acquisitions worth more than $500 million that took place between July 1990 and July 1995. Based on total stock returns from three months before the announcement and up to three years after the announcement:
  - 30 percent substantially eroded shareholder returns.
  - 20 percent eroded some returns.
  - 33 percent created only marginal returns.
  - 17 percent created substantial returns.

- In a study by Salomon Smith Barney of U.S. companies acquired since 1997 in deals for $15 billion or more, the stocks of the acquiring firms have, on average, underperformed the S&P stock index by 14 percentage points and underperformed their peer group by 4 percentage points after the deals were announced.

- A study of 12,023 acquisitions from 1980 to 2001 found that acquiring-firm shareholders lost 12 cents per dollar spent on acquisition, for a total loss of $240 billion from 1998 through 2001, whereas they lost only $7 billion in all of the 1980s, or 1.6 cents per dollar spent. The 1998 to 2001 aggregate dollar loss of acquiring-firm shareholders is so large because of a small number of acquisitions with negative synergy gains by firms with extremely high valuations. Without these acquisitions, the wealth of acquiring-firm shareholders would have increased.

Sources: Moeller, S. B., Schlingemann, F. P., & Stulz, R. M. 2005. Wealth destruction on a massive scale? A study of acquiring-firm returns in the recent merger wave. *Journal of Finance* (forthcoming); Lipin, S., & Deogun, N. 2000. Big mergers of the 90s prove disappointing to shareholders. *The Wall Street Journal*, October 30: C1; Dr. G. William Schwert, University of Rochester study cited in Pare, T. P. 1994. The new merger boom. *Fortune*, November 28: 96; and, Porter, M. E. 1987. From competitive advantage to corporate strategy. *Harvard Business Review*, 65(3): 43.

dramatically increased their revenues, profits, and market values through a wide variety of diversification moves, including mergers and acquisitions, strategic alliances and joint ventures, and internal development.

So the question becomes: Why do some diversification efforts pay off and others produce disappointing results? In this chapter we will address this question. Whereas Chapter 5 focused on business-level strategy—that is, how to achieve sustainable advantages in a given business or product market—this chapter addresses two related issues: (1) What businesses should a corporation compete in? and (2) How should these businesses be managed to jointly create more value than if they were freestanding units?

Diversification initiatives—whether through mergers and acquisitions, strategic alliances and joint ventures, or internal development—must be justified by the creation of value for shareholders. But this is not always the case. For example, as noted earlier, acquiring firms typically pay high premiums when they acquire a target firm. However, you and I, as private investors, can diversify our portfolio of stocks very cheaply. With the advent of the intensely competitive online brokerage industry, we can acquire hundreds (or thousands) of shares for a transaction fee of as little as $10.00 or less—a far cry from the 30 to 40 percent (or higher) premiums that corporations typically must pay to acquire companies.

Given the seemingly high inherent downside risks and uncertainties, it might be reasonable to ask why companies should even bother with diversification initiatives. The answer, in a word, is *synergy,* derived from the Greek word *synergos,* which means "working together." This can have two different, but not mutually exclusive, meanings. First, a firm may diversify into *related* businesses. Here, the primary potential benefits to be derived come from *horizontal relationships;* that is, businesses sharing intangible resources (e.g., core competences) and tangible resources (e.g., production facilities, distribution channels). Additionally, firms can enhance their market power through pooled negotiating power and vertical integration. As we will see in this chapter, Procter & Gamble enjoys many synergies from having businesses that share distribution resources.

Second, a corporation may diversify into *unrelated* businesses. In these instances, the primary potential benefits are derived largely from *hierarchical relationships;* that is, value creation derived from the corporate office. Examples of the latter would include leveraging some of the support activities in the value chain that we discussed in Chapter 3, such as information systems or human resource practices. Cooper Industries, another firm we will discuss, has followed a successful strategy of unrelated diversification. There are few similarities in the products it makes or the industries in which it competes. However, the corporate office adds value through such activities as superb human resource practices as well as planning and budgeting systems.

It is important to note that the aforementioned horizontal (derived from related diversification) and hierarchical (derived from related and unrelated diversification) relationships are not mutually exclusive. Many firms that diversify into related areas benefit from information technology expertise in the corporate office, and firms diversifying into unrelated areas often benefit from the "best practices" of sister businesses even though their products, markets, and technologies may differ dramatically.

Exhibit 6.2 provides an overview of how we will address the various means by which firms create value through both related and unrelated diversification and also include a summary of some examples that we will address in this chapter.[4]

## >>Related Diversification: Economies of Scope and Revenue Enhancement

As discussed earlier, related diversification enables a firm to benefit from horizontal relationships across different businesses in the diversified corporation by leveraging core competencies and sharing activities (e.g., production facilities and distribution facilities). This enables a corporation to benefit from economies of scope. *Economies of scope* refers to cost savings from leveraging core competencies or sharing related activities among businesses in the corporation. A firm can also enjoy greater revenues if two businesses attain higher levels of sales growth combined than either company could attain independently.

For example, a sporting goods store with one or several locations may acquire other stores. This enables it to leverage, or reuse, many of its key resources—favorable reputation, expert staff and management skills, efficient purchasing operations—the basis

Exhibit 6.2

**Creating Value through Related and Unrelated Diversification**

**Related Diversification: Economies of Scope**

Leveraging core competences
- 3M leverages its competencies in adhesives technologies to many industries, including automotive, construction, and telecommunications.

Sharing activities
- McKesson, a large distribution company, sells many product lines, such as pharmaceuticals and liquor, through its superwarehouses.

**Related Diversification: Market Power**

Pooled negotiating power
- The Times Mirror Company increases its power over customers by providing "one-stop shopping" for advertisers to reach customers through multiple media—television and newspapers—in several huge markets such as New York and Chicago.

Vertical integration
- Shaw Industries, a giant carpet manufacturer, increases its control over raw materials by producing much of its own polypropylene fiber, a key input to its manufacturing process.

**Unrelated Diversification: Parenting, Restructuring, and Financial Synergies**

Corporate restructuring and parenting
- The corporate office of Cooper Industries adds value to its acquired businesses by performing such activities as auditing their manufacturing operations, improving their accounting activities, and centralizing union negotiations.

Portfolio management
- Novartis, formerly Ciba-Geigy, uses portfolio management to improve many key activities, including resource allocation and reward and evaluation systems.

of its competitive advantage(s), over a larger number of stores.[5] Let's next address how to create value by leveraging core competencies.

## Leveraging Core Competencies

The concept of core competencies can be illustrated by the imagery of the diversified corporation as a tree.[6] The trunk and major limbs represent core products; the smaller branches are business units; and the leaves, flowers, and fruit are end products. The core competencies are represented by the root system, which provides nourishment, sustenance, and stability. Managers often misread the strength of competitors by looking only at their end products, just as we can fail to appreciate the strength of a tree by looking only at its leaves. Core competencies may also be viewed as the "glue" that binds existing businesses together or as the engine that fuels new business growth.

Core competencies reflect the collective learning in organizations—how to coordinate diverse production skills, integrate multiple streams of technologies, and market and merchandise diverse products and services. The theoretical knowledge necessary to put a radio on a chip does not in itself assure a company of the skill needed to produce a miniature radio approximately the size of a business card. To accomplish this, Casio, a giant electronic products producer, must synthesize know-how in miniaturization, microprocessor design, material science, and ultrathin precision castings. These are the same skills that it applies in its miniature card calculators, pocket TVs, and digital watches.

For a core competence to create value and provide a viable basis for synergy among the businesses in a corporation, it must meet three criteria.[7]

- ***The core competence must enhance competitive advantage(s) by creating superior customer value.*** It must enable the business to develop strengths relative to the competition. Every value-chain activity has the potential to provide a viable basis for building on a core competence.[8] At Gillette, for example, scientists developed the Mach 3 and Sensor Excel after the introduction of the tremendously successful Sensor System because of a thorough understanding of several phenomena that underlie shaving. These include the physiology of facial hair and skin, the metallurgy of blade strength and sharpness, the dynamics of a cartridge moving across skin, and the physics of a razor blade severing hair. Such innovations are possible only with an understanding of such phenomena and the ability to combine such technologies into innovative products. Customers have consistently been willing to pay more for such technologically differentiated products.

- ***Different businesses in the corporation must be similar in at least one important way related to the core competence.*** It is not essential that the products or services themselves be similar. Rather, at least one element in the value chain must require similar skills in creating competitive advantage if the corporation is to capitalize on its core competence. At first glance you might think that motorcycles, clothes, and restaurants have little in common. But at Harley-Davidson, they do.[9] Harley-Davidson has capitalized on its exceptionally strong brand image as well as merchandising and licensing skills to sell accessories, clothing, and toys and has licensed the Harley-Davidson Café in New York City—further evidence of the strength of its brand name and products.

- ***The core competencies must be difficult for competitors to imitate or find substitutes for.*** As we discussed in Chapter 5, competitive advantages will not be sustainable if the competition can easily imitate or substitute them. Similarly, if the skills associated with a firm's core competencies are easily imitated or replicated, they are not a sound basis for sustainable advantages. Consider Sharp Corporation, a $17 billion consumer electronics giant.[10] It has a set of specialized core competencies in optoelectronics technologies that are difficult to replicate and contribute to its competitive advantages in its core businesses. Its most successful technology has been liquid crystal displays (LCDs) that are critical components in nearly all of Sharp's products. Its expertise in this technology enabled Sharp to succeed in videocassette recorders (VCRs) with its innovative LCD viewfinder and led to the creation of its Wizard, a personal electronic organizer.

Strategy Spotlight 6.1 discusses how UPS leverages its core competence in logistics. It ships broken Toshiba laptops to its facility in Louisville, Kentucky, to diagnose and repair them.

## Sharing Activities

As we saw above, leveraging core competencies involves transferring accumulated skills and expertise across business units in a corporation. When carried out effectively, this leads to advantages that can become quite sustainable over time. Corporations also can achieve synergy by sharing tangible activities across their business units. These include

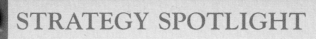

# STRATEGY SPOTLIGHT 6.1

## UPS: Leveraging Its Core Competence in Logistics

Toshiba has recently handed over its entire laptop repair operation to United Parcel Service (UPS) Supply Chain Solutions, the shipper's $2.4 billion logistics outsourcing division. UPS will ship broken Toshiba laptops to its facility in Louisville, Kentucky, where UPS will diagnose and repair defects. The facility consists of a campus that occupies 2 million square feet devoted to more than 70 companies. Consumers will enjoy an immediate benefit. In the past, repairs could take weeks, depending on whether Toshiba needed components from Japan. However, since the UPS repair site is adjacent to its air hub, customers should get their machines back, as good as new, in a matter of days.

Why would Toshiba let a shipping company repair its laptops? Simply put, the challenge of computer repair is more logistical than technical. "Moving a unit around and getting replacement parts consumes most of the time," says Mark Simons, general manager of Toshiba's digital products division. "The actual service only takes about an hour." Plus, UPS already has experience in this area. The company has repaired Lexmark and Hewlett-Packard

printers since 1996 and has performed initial inspections on laptops being returned by Toshiba since 1999.

The expanded relationship with Toshiba is another step in UPS's strategy to broaden its business beyond package delivery into commerce services. Its new marketing mission in 2004 was to market a set of capabilities that go along with its new slogan, "Synchronizing the world of commerce." According to Larry Bloomenkranz, Vice President, Global Brand Management and Advertising, "It's not just the same old UPS. We are a one-brand supplier up and down the supply chain." UPS currently works with clients to manage inventory, ordering, and customs processes, and it has just introduced a service to dispose of unwanted electronics.

If Toshiba's customers are satisfied with the new UPS repair services, other electronics manufacturers will likely also consider UPS as an outsourcing partner. As pointed out by Roger Kay, Vice President for Client Computing at research firm IDC, "A logistics partner who can also do repair is a rare and wonderful thing." Clearly, UPS is able to leverage its core competencies in logistics (e.g., shipping, spare parts supply management) into the seemingly unrelated area of laptop repair to enhance its revenues and profitability.

Sources: James, G. 2004. The next delivery? Computer repairs by UPS. *Business 2.0*, July: 30; Blanchard, D. 2004. It takes a supply chain village. *www.logisticstoday.com*, November: 9; and, Podmolik, M. 2004. UPS promotes commerce, supply-chain capabilities. *B to B*, 89(12): 18.

value-creating activities such as common manufacturing facilities, distribution channels, and sales forces. As we will see, sharing activities can potentially provide two primary payoffs: cost savings and revenue enhancements.

***Deriving Cost Savings through Sharing Activities*** Typically, this is the most common type of synergy and the easiest to estimate. Peter Shaw, head of mergers and acquisitions at the British chemical and pharmaceutical company ICI refers to cost savings as "hard synergies" and contends that the level of certainty of their achievement is quite high. Cost savings come from many sources, including elimination of jobs, facilities, and related expenses that are no longer needed when functions are consolidated, or from economies of scale in purchasing. Cost savings are generally highest when one company acquires another from the same industry in the same country. Shaw Industries, recently acquired by Berkshire Hathaway, is the nation's largest carpet producer. Over the years, it has dominated the competition through a strategy of acquisition which has enabled Shaw, among other things, to consolidate its manufacturing operations in a few, highly efficient plants and to lower costs through higher capacity utilization.

It is important to note that sharing activities inevitably involve costs that the benefits must outweigh. One often overlooked cost is the greater coordination required to manage a shared activity. Even more important is the need to compromise the design or performance of an activity so that it can be shared. For example, a salesperson handling the products of two business units must operate in a way that is usually not what either unit would choose if it were independent. If the compromise erodes the unit's effectiveness, then sharing may reduce rather than enhance competitive advantage.

### *Enhancing Revenue and Differentiation through Sharing Activities*

Often an acquiring firm and its target may achieve a higher level of sales growth together than either company could on its own. Shortly after Gillette acquired Duracell, it confirmed its expectation that selling Duracell batteries through Gillette's existing channels for personal care products would increase sales, particularly internationally. Gillette sold Duracell products in 25 new markets in the first year after the acquisition and substantially increased sales in established international markets. In a similar vein, a target company's distribution channel can be used to escalate the sales of the acquiring company's product. Such was the case when Gillette acquired Parker Pen. Gillette estimated that it could gain an additional $25 million in sales of its own Waterman pens by taking advantage of Parker's distribution channels.

Firms also can enhance the effectiveness of their differentiation strategies by means of sharing activities among business units. A shared order-processing system, for example, may permit new features and services that a buyer will value. Also, sharing can reduce the cost of differentiation. For instance, a shared service network may make more advanced, remote service technology economically feasible. To illustrate the potential for enhanced differentiation though sharing, consider $5.1 billion VF Corporation—producer of such well-known brands as Lee, Wrangler, Vanity Fair, and Jantzen.

> VF's acquisition of Nutmeg Industries and H. H. Cutler provided it with several large customers that it didn't have before, increasing its plant utilization and productivity. But more importantly, Nutmeg designs and makes licensed apparel for sports teams and organizations, while Cutler manufactures licensed brand-name children's apparel, including Walt Disney kids' wear. Such brand labeling enhances the differentiation of VF's apparel products. According to VF President Mackey McDonald, "What we're doing is looking at value-added knitwear, taking our basic fleece from Basset-Walker [one of its divisions], embellishing it through Cutler and Nutmeg, and selling it as a value-added product." Additionally, Cutler's advanced high-speed printing technologies will enable VF to be more proactive in anticipating trends in the fashion-driven fleece market. Claims McDonald, "Rather than printing first and then trying to guess what the customer wants, we can see what's happening in the marketplace and then print it up."[11]

As a cautionary note, managers must keep in mind that sharing activities among businesses in a corporation can have a negative effect on a given business's differentiation. For example, with the merger of Chrysler and Daimler-Benz, many consumers may lower their perceptions of Mercedes's quality and prestige if they feel that common production components and processes are being used across the two divisions. And the Jaguar division of Ford Motor Company may be adversely affected as consumers come to understand that it shares many components with its sister divisions at Ford, including Lincoln.

Strategy Spotlight 6.2 discusses how Freemantle Media leverages its hit television show *American Idol* through its core competences and shared activities to create multiple revenue streams.

## >>Related Diversification: Market Power

In the previous section, we explained how leveraging core competencies and sharing activities help firms create economies of scale and scope through related diversification. In this section, we discuss how companies achieve related diversification through market power. We also address the two principal means by which firms achieve synergy through market power: *pooled negotiating power* and *vertical integration*. It is important to recognize that managers have limits on their ability to use market power for diversification,

# STRATEGY SPOTLIGHT

## *American Idol:* Far More than Just a Television Show

*American Idol* is one of several of FremantleMedia's (FM) hit television shows. FM is a division of German media giant Bertlesmann, which has approximately $20 billion in revenues. Some of FM's other well-known television shows are *The Apprentice, The Swan*, and at a ripe old age of 48—*The Price Is Right*.

First shown in the United States in June 2002, *American Idol* became a tremendous overnight success. Although the show may be crass and occasionally cruel, it is undeniably brilliant. It's become the ultimate testament to a singular business achievement: FM has become extremely successful at creating truly global programming. In part, that is due to the creative minds at Fremantle; it has some of the best professionals in the business who have a talent for developing shows that appeal to huge populations with different backgrounds and circumstances.

Amazingly, FM, which created *Pop Idol* in Britain in 2001, is now rolling out the show in its 30th country. There's *Belgium Idool, Portugal Idolos, Deutschland Sucht den SuperStar* (Germany), *SuperStar KZ* (Kazakhstan), and of course, the largest and best-known show, *American Idol*, in the United States. *American Idol* is the primary reason that Fremantle's revenue is up 9 percent to more than $1 billion since the show was launched. According to Fremantle's CEO Tony Cohen, "*Idol* has become a national institution in lots of countries." To illustrate, fans cast more than 65 million votes for the *American Idol* finale in May, 2004—that is two-thirds as many people as voted in the 2004 U.S. presidential election.

The real key to Fremantle's success is not just adapting its television hits to other countries, but systematically leveraging its core product—television shows—to create multiple revenue streams. In essence, the "Fremantle Way" holds lessons not just for show business but for all business. It enables a company to use its core competence of making products of mass appeal and then to customize them for places with widely varying languages, cultures, and mores. It then milks the hits for every penny through tie-ins, spinoffs, innovative uses of technology, and marketing masterstrokes.

The *Idol* franchise has created a wide variety of new revenue streams for Fremantle's German parent, Bertelsmann. Here's how much *American Idol* has generated in its first two years since its June 2002 launch:

- *Products ($50 million).* Brand extensions range from videogames and fragrances to a planned microphone-shaped soap-on-a-rope. Fremantle receives a licensing fee from manufacturers.

- *TV Licensing ($75 million).* For its rights fee, Fox gets to broadcast the show and, in turn, sell ads and lucrative sponsorships.

- *Compact Discs (CDs) ($130 million).* The most successful performers on the *Idols* shows have sold millions of CDs; more than one-third of the revenue goes to BMG, which, like Fremantle, is an affiliate of Bertelsmann.

- *Concerts ($35 million).* Although artists and their management get the bulk of the take, concerts sell records and merchandise and promote the next *Idol* show.

In addition, Fremantle Licensing Worldwide signed Warner Brothers Publications to produce and distribute *Idol* audition books with CDs for the United States, Canada, United Kingdom, and Australia. The new books/CDs—*Pop Idol* (UK), *Australian Idol,* and *Canadian Idol*—join the *American Idol* book/CD.

Sources: Sloan, P. 2004. The reality factory. *Business 2.0,* August: 74–82; Cooney, J. 2004. In the news. *License!,* March: 48; and, Anonymous. 2005. Fox on top in Feb; NBC languishing at the bottom. www.indiantelevision.com, March 2.

because government regulations can sometimes restrict the ability of a business to gain very large shares of a particular market.

When General Electric (GE) announced a $41 billion bid for Honeywell, the European Union stepped in. GE's market clout would have expanded significantly as a result of the deal, with GE supplying over one-half the parts needed to build several aircraft engines. The commission's concern, causing them to reject the acquisition, was that GE could use its increased market power to dominate the aircraft engine parts market and crowd out competitors.[12] Thus, while managers need to be aware of the strategic advantages of market power, they must at the same time be aware of regulations and legislation.

## Pooled Negotiating Power

Similar businesses working together or the affiliation of a business with a strong parent can strengthen an organization's bargaining position in relation to suppliers and customers and enhance its position vis-à-vis competitors. Compare, for example, the position of an independent food manufacturer with the same business within Nestlé. Being part of Nestlé Corporation provides the business with significant clout—greater bargaining power with suppliers and customers—since it is part of a firm that makes large purchases from suppliers and provides a wide variety of products to its customers. Access to the parent's deep pockets increases the business's strength relative to rivals. Further, the Nestlé unit enjoys greater protection from substitutes and new entrants. Not only would rivals perceive the unit as a more formidable opponent, but the unit's association with Nestlé would also provide greater visibility and improved image.

Consolidating an industry can also increase a firm's market power. This is clearly an emerging trend in the multimedia industry.[13] All of these mergers and acquisitions have a common goal: to control and leverage as many news and entertainment channels as possible. In total, more than $261 billion in mergers and acquisitions in the media industry were announced in 2000—up 12 percent from 1999. For example, consider the Tribune Company's $8 billion purchase of the Times Mirror Company.

> The merger doubled the size of the Tribune and secured its position among the top tier of major media companies. The enhanced scale and scope helped it to compete more effectively and grow more rapidly in two consolidating industries—newspaper and television broadcasting. The combined company would increase its power over customers by providing a "one-stop shop" for advertisers desiring to reach consumers through multiple media in enormous markets such as Chicago, Los Angeles, and New York. The company has estimated its incremental revenue from national and cross-media advertising will grow from $40 to $50 million in 2001 to $200 million by 2005. The combined company should also increase its power relative to its suppliers. The company's enhanced size is expected to lead to increased efficiencies when purchasing newsprint and other commodities.[14]

When acquiring related businesses, a firm's potential for pooled negotiating power vis-à-vis its customers and suppliers can be very enticing. However, managers must carefully evaluate how the combined businesses may affect relationships with actual and potential customers, suppliers, and competitors. For example, when PepsiCo diversified into the fast-food industry with its acquisitions of Kentucky Fried Chicken, Taco Bell, and Pizza Hut (since spun off as Tricon, Inc.), it clearly benefited from its position over these units that served as a captive market for its soft-drink products. However, many competitors such as McDonald's have refused to consider PepsiCo as a supplier of its own soft-drink needs because of competition with Pepsi's divisions in the fast-food industry. Simply put, McDonald's did not want to subsidize the enemy! Thus, although acquiring related businesses can enhance a corporation's bargaining power, it must be aware of the potential for retaliation.

## Vertical Integration

Vertical integration represents an expansion or extension of the firm by integrating preceding or successive productive processes.[15] That is, the firm incorporates more processes toward the original source of raw materials (backward integration) or toward the ultimate consumer (forward integration). For example, an automobile manufacturer might supply its own parts or make its own engines to secure sources of supply. Or it might control its own system of dealerships to ensure retail outlets for its products. Similarly, an oil refinery might secure land leases and develop its own drilling capacity to

# STRATEGY SPOTLIGHT

**6.3**

## Vertical Integration at Shaw Industries

Shaw Industries (now part of Berkshire Hathaway) is an example of a firm that has followed a very successful strategy of vertical integration. By relentlessly pursuing both backward and forward integration, Shaw has become the dominant manufacturer of carpeting products in the United States. According to CEO Robert Shaw, "We want to be involved with as much of the process of making and selling carpets as practical. That way, we're

in charge of costs." For example, Shaw acquired Amoco's polypropylene fiber manufacturing facilities in Alabama and Georgia. These new plants provide carpet fibers for internal use and for sale to other manufacturers. With this backward integration, fully one-quarter of Shaw's carpet fiber needs are now met in-house. In early 1996 Shaw began to integrate forward, acquiring seven floor-covering retailers in a move that suggested a strategy to consolidate the fragmented industry and increase its influence over retail pricing. Exhibit 6.3 provides a simplified depiction of the stages of vertical integration for Shaw Industries.

Sources: White, J. 2003. Shaw to home in on more with Georgia Tufters deal. *HFN: The Weekly Newspaper for the Home Furnishing Network*, May 5: 32; Shaw Industries. 1993, 2000. Annual reports; and Server, A. 1994. How to escape a price war. *Fortune*, June 13: 88.

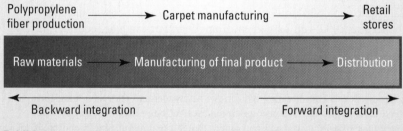

**Exhibit 6.3** *Simplified Stages of Vertical Integration: Shaw Industries*

ensure a constant supply of crude oil. Or it could expand into retail operations by owning or licensing gasoline stations to guarantee customers for its petroleum products.

Clearly, vertical integration can be a viable strategy for many firms. Strategy Spotlight 6.3 discusses Shaw Industries, a carpet manufacturer that has attained a dominant position in the industry via a strategy of vertical integration. Shaw has successfully implemented strategies of both forward and backward integration.

*Benefits and Risks of Vertical Integration*    Although vertical integration is a means for an organization to reduce its dependence on suppliers or its channels of distribution to end users, it represents a major decision that an organization must carefully consider. The benefits associated with vertical integration—backward or forward—must be carefully weighed against the risks.[16]

The *benefits* of vertical integration include (1) a secure supply of raw materials or distribution channels that cannot be "held hostage" to external markets where costs can fluctuate over time, (2) protection and control over assets and services required to produce and deliver valuable products and services, (3) access to new business opportunities and new forms of technologies, and (4) simplified procurement and administrative procedures since key activities are brought inside the firm, eliminating the need to deal with a wide variety of suppliers and distributors.

Winnebago, the leader in the market for drivable recreational vehicles with a 19.3 percent market share, illustrates some of vertical integration's benefits.[17] The word Winnebago means "big RV" to most Americans. And the firm has a sterling reputation for great quality. The firm's huge northern Iowa factories do everything from extruding aluminum for body parts to molding plastics for water and holding tanks and dashboards. Such vertical integration at the factory may appear to be outdated and expensive, but it guarantees excellent quality. The Recreational Vehicle Dealer Association started giving a quality award in 1996, and Winnebago has won it every year.

The *risks* of vertical integration include (1) the costs and expenses associated with increased overhead and capital expenditures to provide facilities, raw material inputs, and distribution channels inside the organization; (2) a loss of flexibility resulting from the inability to respond quickly to changes in the external environment because of the huge investments in vertical integration activities that generally cannot be easily deployed elsewhere; (3) problems associated with unbalanced capacities or unfilled demand along the value chain; and (4) additional administrative costs associated with managing a more complex set of activities. Exhibit 6.4 summarizes the benefits and risks of vertical integration.

In making decisions associated with vertical integration, four issues should be considered.[18]

1. *Is the company satisfied with the quality of the value that its present suppliers and distributors are providing?* If the performance of organizations in the vertical chain—both suppliers and distributors—is satisfactory, it may not, in general, be appropriate for a company to perform these activities themselves. Firms in the athletic footwear industry such as Nike and Reebok have traditionally outsourced the manufacture of their shoes to countries such as China and Indonesia where labor costs are low. Since the strengths of these companies are typically in design and marketing, it would be advisable to continue to outsource production operations and continue to focus on where they can add the most value.

2. *Are there activities in the industry value chain presently being outsourced or performed independently by others that are a viable source of future profits?* Even if a firm is outsourcing value-chain activities to companies that are doing a credible job, it may be missing out on substantial profit opportunities. To illustrate, consider the automobile industry's profit pool. As you may recall from Chapter 5, there is much more potential profit in many downstream activities (e.g., leasing, warranty, insurance, and service) than in the manufacture of automobiles. Not surprising, carmakers such as Ford and General Motors are undertaking forward integration strategies to become bigger players in these high-profit activities.

---

**Exhibit 6.4**
**Benefits and Risks of Vertical Integration**

**Benefits**

- A secure source of raw materials or distribution channels.
- Protection of and control over valuable assets.
- Access to new business opportunities.
- Simplified procurement and administrative procedures.

**Risks**

- Costs and expenses associated with increased overhead and capital expenditures.
- Loss of flexibility resulting from large investments.
- Problems associated with unbalanced capacities along the value chain.
- Additional administrative costs associated with managing a more complex set of activities.

3. *Is there a high level of stability in the demand for the organization's products?*
High demand or sales volatility would not be conducive to a vertical integration
strategy. With the high level of fixed costs in plant and equipment as well as
operating costs that accompany endeavors toward vertical integration, widely
fluctuating sales demand can either strain resources (in times of high demand)
or result in unused capacity (in times of low demand). The cycles of "boom and
bust" in the automobile industry are a key reason why the manufacturers have
increased the amount of outsourced inputs in recent years.

4. *How high is the proportion of additional production capacity actually absorbed by
existing products or by the prospects of new and similar products?* The smaller
the proportion of production capacity to be absorbed by existing or future products, the lower is the potential for achieving scale economies associated with the
increased capacity—either in terms of backward integration (toward the supply of
raw materials) or forward integration (toward the end user). Alternatively, if there
is excess capacity in the near term, the strategy of vertical integration may be
viable if there is the anticipation of future expansion of products.

### *Analyzing Vertical Integration: The Transaction Cost Perspective*

Another approach that has proved very useful in understanding vertical integration is the
*transaction cost perspective.*[19] According to this perspective, every market transaction
involves some *transaction costs.* First, a decision to purchase an input from an outside
source leads to *search* costs (i.e., the cost to find where it is available, the level of quality, etc.). Second, there are costs associated with *negotiating.* Third, a *contract* needs to
be written spelling out future possible contingencies. Fourth, parties in a contract have
to *monitor* each other. Finally, if a party does not comply with the terms of the contract,
there are *enforcement* costs. Transaction costs are thus the sum of search costs, negotiation costs, contracting costs, monitoring costs, and enforcement costs. These transaction
costs can be avoided by internalizing the activity, in other words, by producing the input
in-house.

A related problem with purchasing a specialized input from outside is the issue of
*transaction-specific investments.* For example, when an automobile company needs an input
specifically designed for a particular car model, the supplier may be unwilling to make the
investments in plant and machinery necessary to produce that component for two reasons.
First, the investment may take many years to recover but there is no guarantee the automobile company will continue to buy from them after the contract expires, typically in one
year. Second, once the investment is made, the supplier has no bargaining power. That is,
the buyer knows that the supplier has no option but to supply at ever-lower prices because
the investments were so specific that they cannot be used to produce alternative products.
In such circumstances, again, vertical integration may be the only option.

Vertical integration, however, gives rise to a different set of costs. These costs are
referred to as *administrative costs.* Coordinating different stages of the value chain now
internalized within the firm causes administrative costs to go up. Decisions about vertical integration are, therefore, based on a comparison of transaction costs and administrative costs. If transaction costs are lower than administrative costs, it is best to resort to
market transactions and avoid vertical integration. For example, McDonald's may be the
world's biggest buyer of beef, but they do not raise cattle. The market for beef has low
transaction costs and requires no transaction-specific investments. On the other hand, if
transaction costs are higher than administrative costs, vertical integration becomes an
attractive strategy. Most automobile manufacturers produce their own engines because the
market for engines involves high transaction costs and transaction-specific investments.

*Vertical Integration: Further Considerations*   As many companies would attest, successfully executing strategies of vertical integration can be very difficult. For example, Unocal, a major petroleum refiner, which once owned retail gas stations, was slow to capture the potential grocery and merchandise side business that might have resulted from customer traffic to its service stations. Unocal lacked the competencies to develop a separate retail organization and culture. The company eventually sold the assets and brand to Tosco (now part of Phillips Petroleum Co.). Eli Lilly, the pharmaceutical firm, tried to achieve forward integration by acquiring a pharmaceutical mail-order business in 1994, but it was unsuccessful in increasing market share because it failed to integrate its operations. Two years later, Lilly wrote off the venture.

Last, as with our earlier discussion of pooled negotiating power, managers must carefully consider the impact that vertical integration may have on existing and future customers, suppliers, and competitors. After Lockheed Martin, a dominant defense contractor, acquired Loral Corporation, an electronics supplier, for $9.1 billion, it had an unpleasant and unanticipated surprise. Loral, as a captive supplier of Lockheed, is now perceived and treated as a competitor by many of its previous customers. McDonnell Douglas (MD), for example, announced that it would switch its business from Loral to other suppliers of electronic systems such as Litton Industries or Raytheon. Thus, before Lockheed Martin can realize any net synergies from this acquisition, it must make up for the substantial lost business resulting from MD's (now part of Boeing) decision to switch suppliers.

In these two sections we have addressed four means by which firms can achieve synergies through related diversification: leveraging core competences, sharing activities, pooled negotiating power, and vertical integration. In Strategy Spotlight 6.4, we address how Procter & Gamble strengthened its competitive position by combining all four means. We next turn our attention to unrelated diversification.

# >>Unrelated Diversification: Financial Synergies and Parenting

With unrelated diversification, unlike related diversification, few benefits are derived from *horizontal relationships*—that is, the leveraging of core competencies or the sharing of activities across business units within a corporation. Instead, potential benefits can be gained from *vertical (or hierarchical) relationships*—the creation of synergies from the interaction of the corporate office with the individual business units. There are two main sources of such synergies. First, the corporate office can contribute to "parenting" and restructuring of (often acquired) businesses. Second, the corporate office can add value by viewing the entire corporation as a family or "portfolio" of businesses and allocating resources to optimize corporate goals of profitability, cash flow, and growth. Additionally, the corporate office enhances value by establishing appropriate human resource practices and financial controls for each of its business units.

## Corporate Parenting and Restructuring

So far, we have discussed how corporations can add value through related diversification by exploring sources of synergy *across* business units. In this section, we will discuss how value can be created *within* business units as a result of the expertise and support provided by the corporate office. Thus, we look at these as *hierarchical* sources of synergy.

The positive contributions of the corporate office have been referred to as the "parenting advantage."[20] Many firms have successfully diversified their holdings without

## Procter & Gamble: Using Multiple Means to Achieve Synergies

To accomplish successful related diversification, a company must combine multiple facets of its business to create synergies across the organization. Procter & Gamble (P&G) is a prime example of such a firm. Using related diversification, it creates synergies by leveraging core competencies, sharing activities, pooling negotiating power, and vertically integrating certain product lines as part of its corporate-level strategy. The following excerpt from a speech by Clayt Daley, Procter & Gamble's chief financial officer, illustrates how the company has done this.

### Remarks to Financial Analysts

Today, we already sell 10 brands with sales of one billion dollars or more. Seven of these 10 brands surpassed the billion-dollar sales mark during the '90s. And, in total, these 10 brands accounted for more than half of our sales growth during the decade. Beyond these 10, there are several brands with the potential to achieve a billion dollars in sales by 2005. Olay could surpass a billion dollars in sales in 2001, Iams by 2002.

P&G's unmatched lineup of billion-dollar leadership brands generates consistently strong returns. In virtually every case, P&G's leading brands achieve higher margins and deliver consistently strong shareholder returns. Having a stable of such strong global brands creates significant advantages for P&G—and our total company scale multiplies those advantages.

We can obviously take advantage of our purchasing power for things as varied as raw materials and advertising media. We can leverage the scale of our manufacturing and logistics operations. But we can do far more.

We have the scale of our intellectual property—the knowledge and deep insight that exists throughout our organization. We have scale in our technologies—the enormous breadth of expertise we have across our product categories. There is scale in our go-to-market capabilities and our global customer relationships.

Let me give you three quick examples. First, scale of consumer knowledge. We are able to learn, reapply, and multiply knowledge across many brands with a similar target audience. For example, teens. The teen market is global. Teens in New York, Tokyo, and Caracas wear the same clothes, listen to the same music, and have many of the same attitudes. We have categories they buy and use: cosmetics, hair care, skin care, personal cleansing and body products, feminine protection, snacks and beverages, oral care, and others. Our scale enables us to develop unique insights on teens—like how to identify teen chat leaders—and then reapply that across all our teen-focused businesses.

Another way we can leverage scale is through the transfer of product technologies across categories. We can connect seemingly unrelated technologies to create surprising new products. Our new Crest White Strips are a great example of the innovation that can result. This new product provides a major new tooth-whitening benefit that can be achieved in the home. We have combined our knowledge in oral hygiene, and our knowledge of bleaching agents, with a special film technology to provide a safe and effective product that can whiten teeth within 14 days.

Another important source of scale is our go-to-market capability. No other consumer products company works with retailers the way we do. Our Customer Business Development approach is a fundamentally different way of working with our trade partners. We seek to build businesses across common goals.

We bring a philosophy that encourages a simple, transparent shopping experience—with simple, transparent pricing, efficient assortment, efficient in-store promotion, and efficient replenishment. This approach has helped us build extremely strong relationships with our customers. For example, in the annual Cannondale "Power-Ranking Survey," U.S. retailers consistently ranked P&G at the top on brands, consumer information, supply-chain management, category management, and more.

Source: Daley, C. 2000. Remarks to Financial Analysts. Speech excerpt. Procter & Gamble Company, September 28.

strong evidence of the more traditional sources of synergy (i.e., horizontally across business units). Diversified public corporations such as BTR, Emerson Electric, and Hanson and leveraged buyout firms such as Kohlberg, Kravis, Roberts & Company, and Clayton, Dublilier & Rice are a few examples.[21] These parent companies create value through management expertise. How? They improve plans and budgets and provide especially competent central functions such as legal, financial, human resource management, procurement, and the like. Additionally, they help subsidiaries make wise choices in their own acquisitions, divestitures, and new internal development decisions. Such contributions often help business units to substantially increase their revenues and profits. Consider Texas-based Cooper Industries' acquisition of Champion International, the spark plug company, as an example of corporate parenting.[22]

Cooper applies a distinctive parenting approach designed to help its businesses improve their manufacturing performance. New acquisitions are "Cooperized"—Cooper audits their manufacturing operations; improves their cost accounting systems; makes their planning, budgeting, and human resource systems conform with its systems; and centralizes union negotiations. Excess cash is squeezed out through tighter controls and reinvested in productivity enhancements, which improve overall operating efficiency. As one manager observed, "When you get acquired by Cooper, one of the first things that happens is a truckload of policy manuals arrives at your door." Such active parenting has been effective in enhancing the competitive advantages of many kinds of manufacturing businesses.

*Restructuring* is another means by which the corporate office can add substantial value to a business.[23] The central idea can be captured in the real estate phrase "buy low and sell high." Here, the corporate office tries to find either poorly performing firms with unrealized potential or firms in industries on the threshold of significant, positive change. The parent intervenes, often selling off parts of the business; changing the management; reducing payroll and unnecessary sources of expenses; changing strategies; and infusing the company with new technologies, processes, reward systems, and so forth. When the restructuring is complete, the firm can either "sell high" and capture the added value or keep the business in the corporate family and enjoy the financial and competitive benefits of the enhanced performance.[24]

For the restructuring strategy to work, the corporate management must have both the insight to detect undervalued companies (otherwise the cost of acquisition would be too high) or businesses competing in industries with a high potential for transformation.[25] Additionally, of course, they must have the requisite skills and resources to turn the businesses around, even if they may be in new and unfamiliar industries.

Restructuring can involve changes in assets, capital structure, or management. *Asset restructuring* involves the sale of unproductive assets, or even whole lines of businesses, that are peripheral. In some cases, it may even involve acquisitions that strengthen the core business. *Capital restructuring* involves changing the debt-equity mix, or the mix between different classes of debt or equity. Although the substitution of equity with debt is more common in buyout situations, occasionally the parent may provide additional equity capital. *Management restructuring* typically involves changes in the composition of the top management team, organizational structure, and reporting relationships. Tight financial control, rewards based strictly on meeting short- to medium-term performance goals, and reduction in the number of middle-level managers are common steps in management restructuring. In some cases, parental intervention may even result in changes in strategy as well as infusion of new technologies and processes.

Hanson, plc, a British conglomerate, made numerous such acquisitions in the United States in the 1980s, often selling these firms at significant profits after a few years of successful restructuring efforts. Hanson's acquisition and subsequent restructuring of the SCM group is a classic example of the restructuring strategy. Hanson acquired SCM, a diversified manufacturer of industrial and consumer products (including Smith-Corona typewriters, Glidden paints, and Durkee Famous Foods), for $930 million in 1986 after a bitter takeover battle. In the next few months, Hanson sold SCM's paper and pulp operations for $160 million, the chemical division for $30 million, Glidden paints for $580 million, and Durkee Famous Foods for $120 million, virtually recovering the entire original investment. In addition, Hanson also sold the SCM headquarters in New York for $36 million and reduced the headquarters staff by 250. They still retained several profitable divisions, including the titanium dioxide operations and managed them with tight financial controls that led to increased returns.[26]

## Portfolio Management

During the 1970s and early 1980s, several leading consulting firms developed the concept of portfolio matrices to achieve a better understanding of the competitive position of an overall portfolio (or family) of businesses, to suggest strategic alternatives for each of the businesses, and to identify priorities for the allocation of resources. Several studies have reported widespread use of these techniques among American firms.[27]

The key purpose of portfolio models was to assist a firm in achieving a balanced portfolio of businesses.[28] This consisted of businesses whose profitability, growth, and cash flow characteristics would complement each other and add up to a satisfactory overall corporate performance. Imbalance, for example, could be caused either by excessive cash generation with too few growth opportunities or by insufficient cash generation to fund the growth requirements in the portfolio. Monsanto, for example, used portfolio planning to restructure its portfolio, divesting low-growth commodity chemicals businesses and acquiring businesses in higher-growth industries such as biotechnology.

The Boston Consulting Group's (BCG) growth/share matrix is among the best known of these approaches.[29] In the BCG approach, each of the firm's strategic business units (SBUs) is plotted on a two-dimensional grid in which the axes are relative market share and industry growth rate. The grid is broken into four quadrants. Exhibit 6.5 depicts the BCG matrix. Following are a few clarifications:

1.  Each circle represents one of the corporation's business units. The size of the circle represents the relative size of the business unit in terms of revenues.
2.  Relative market share, measured by the ratio of the business unit's size to that of its largest competitor, is plotted along the horizontal axis.
3.  Market share is central to the BCG matrix. This is because high relative market share leads to unit cost reduction due to experience and learning curve effects and, consequently, superior competitive position.

Each of the four quadrants of the grid has different implications for the SBUs that fall into the category:

*   *Stars* are SBUs competing in high-growth industries with relatively high market shares. These firms have long-term growth potential and should continue to receive substantial investment funding.

*   *Question marks* are SBUs competing in high-growth industries but having relatively weak market shares. Resources should be invested in them to enhance their competitive positions.

*   *Cash cows* are SBUs with high market shares in low-growth industries. These units have limited long-run potential but represent a source of current cash flows to fund investments in "stars" and "question marks."

*   *Dogs* are SBUs with weak market shares in low-growth industries. Because they have weak positions and limited potential, most analysts recommend that they be divested.

In using portfolio strategy approaches, a corporation tries to create synergies and shareholder value in a number of ways.[30] Since the businesses are unrelated, synergies

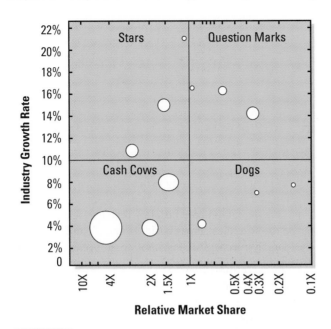

**Exhibit 6.5**   **The Boston Consulting Group (BCG) Portfolio Matrix**

that develop are those that result from the actions of the corporate office with the individual units (i.e., hierarchical relationships) instead of among business units (i.e., horizontal relationships). First, portfolio analysis provides a snapshot of the businesses in a corporation's portfolio; therefore, the corporation is in a better position to allocate resources among the business units according to prescribed criteria (e.g., use cash flows from the "cash cows" to fund promising "stars"). Second, the expertise and analytical resources in the corporate office provide guidance in determining what firms may be attractive (or unattractive) acquisitions. Third, the corporate office is able to provide financial resources to the business units on favorable terms that reflect the corporation's overall ability to raise funds. Fourth, the corporate office can provide high-quality review and coaching for the individual businesses. Fifth, portfolio analysis provides a basis for developing strategic goals and reward/evaluation systems for business managers. For example, managers of cash cows would have lower targets for revenue growth than managers of stars, but the former would have higher threshold levels of profit targets on proposed projects than the managers of star businesses. Compensation systems would also reflect such realities. Cash cows understandably would be rewarded more on the basis of cash that their businesses generate than would managers of star businesses. Similarly, managers of star businesses would be held to higher standards for revenue growth than managers of cash cow businesses.

To see how companies can benefit from portfolio approaches, consider Ciba-Geigy.

In 1994 Ciba-Geigy adopted portfolio planning approaches to help it manage its business units, which competed in a wide variety of industries, including chemicals, dyes, pharmaceuticals, crop protection, and animal health.[31] It placed each business unit in a category corresponding to the BCG matrix. The business unit's goals, compensation programs, personnel selection, and resource allocation were strongly associated with the category within which the business was placed. For example, business units classified as "cash cows" had much higher hurdles for obtaining financial resources (from the corporate office) for expansion than "question marks" since the latter were businesses for which Ciba-Geigy had high hopes for accelerated future growth and profitability. Additionally, the compensation of a business unit manager in a cash cow would be strongly associated with its success in generating cash to fund other businesses, whereas a manager of a question mark business would be rewarded on his or her ability to increase revenue growth and market share. The portfolio planning approaches appear to be working. In 2004, Ciba-Geigy's (now Novartis) revenues and net income stood at $22 billion and $5.0 billion, respectively. This represents a rather modest 40 percent increase in revenues but a most impressive 150 percent growth in net income over a seven-year period.

Despite the potential benefits of portfolio models, there are also some notable downsides. First, they compare SBUs on only two dimensions, making the implicit but erroneous assumption that (1) those are the only factors that really matter and (2) every unit can be accurately compared on that basis. Second, the approach views each SBU as a stand-alone entity, ignoring common core business practices and value-creating activities that may hold promise for synergies across business units. Third, unless care is exercised, the process becomes largely mechanical, substituting an oversimplified graphical model for the important contributions of the CEO's (and other corporate managers's) experience and judgment. Fourth, the reliance on "strict rules" regarding resource allocation across SBUs can be detrimental to a firm's long-term viability. For example, according to one study, over one-half of all the businesses that should have been cash users (based on the BCG matrix) were instead cash providers.[32] Finally, while colorful and easy to comprehend, the imagery of the BCG matrix can lead to some troublesome and overly simplistic prescriptions. According to one author:

> The dairying analogy is appropriate (for some cash cows), so long as we resist the urge to oversimplify it. On the farm, even the best-producing cows eventually begin to dry up. The farmer's solution to this is euphemistically called "freshening" the cow: The farmer arranges a date for the cow with a bull, she has a calf, the milk begins flowing again. Cloistering the cow—isolating her from everything but the feed trough and the milking machines—assures that she will go dry.[33]

To see what can go wrong, consider Cabot Corporation.

> Cabot Corporation supplies carbon black for the rubber, electronics, and plastics industries. Following the BCG matrix, Cabot moved away from its cash cow, carbon black, and diversified into stars such as ceramics and semiconductors in a seemingly overaggressive effort to create more revenue growth for the corporation. Predictably, Cabot's return on assets declined as the firm shifted away from its core competence to unrelated areas. The portfolio model failed by pointing the company in the wrong direction in an effort to spur growth—away from their core business. Recognizing its mistake, Cabot Corporation returned to its mainstay carbon black manufacturing and divested unrelated businesses. Today the company is a leader in its field with $1.8 billion in 2003 revenues.[34]

## Caveat: Is Risk Reduction a Viable Goal of Diversification?

Analysts and academics have suggested that one of the purposes of diversification is to reduce the risk that is inherent in a firm's variability in revenues and profits over time. In essence, the argument is that if a firm enters new products or markets that are affected differently by seasonal or economic cycles, its performance over time will be more stable. For example, a firm manufacturing lawn mowers may diversify into snow blowers to even out its annual sales. Or a firm manufacturing a luxury line of household furniture may introduce a lower-priced line since affluent and lower-income customers are affected differently by economic cycles.

At first glance the above reasoning may make sense, but there are some problems with it. First, a firm's stockholders can diversify their portfolios at a much lower cost than a corporation. As we have noted in this chapter, individuals can purchase their shares with almost no premium (e.g., only a small commission is paid to a discount broker), and they don't have to worry about integrating the acquisition into their portfolio. Second, economic cycles as well as their impact on a given industry (or firm) are difficult to predict with any degree of accuracy.

Notwithstanding the above, some firms have benefited from diversification by lowering the variability (or risk) in their performance over time. Consider Emerson Electronic.

> Emerson Electronic is a $16 billion manufacturer that has enjoyed an incredible run—43 consecutive years of earnings growth![35] It produces a wide variety of products, including measurement devices for heavy industry, temperature controls for heating and ventilation systems, and power tools sold at Home Depot. Recently, many analysts questioned Emerson's purchase of companies that sell power systems to the volatile telecommunications industry. Why? This industry is expected to experience, at best, minimal growth. However, CEO David Farr maintained that such assets could be acquired inexpensively because of the aggregate decline in demand in this industry. Additionally, he argued that the other business units, such as the sales of valves and regulators to the now-booming oil and natural gas companies, were able to pick up the slack. Therefore, while net profits in the electrical equipment sector (Emerson's core business) sharply decreased, Emerson's overall corporate profits increased 1.7 percent.

In summary, risk reduction in and of itself is rarely viable as a means to create shareholder value. It must be undertaken with a view of a firm's overall diversification strategy.

# >>The Means to Achieve Diversification

In the prior three sections, we have addressed the types of diversification (e.g., related and unrelated) that a firm may undertake to achieve synergies and create value for its shareholders. In this section, we address the means by which a firm can go about achieving these desired benefits.

We will address three basic means. First, through acquisitions or mergers, corporations can directly acquire the assets and competencies of other firms. Second, corporations may agree to pool the resources of other companies with their resource base. This approach is commonly known as a joint venture or strategic alliance. Although these two forms of partnerships are similar in many ways, there is an important difference. Joint ventures involve the formation of a third-party legal entity where the two (or more) firms each contribute equity, whereas strategic alliances do not. Third, corporations may diversify into new products, markets, and technologies through internal development. This approach, sometimes called corporate entrepreneurship, involves the leveraging and combining of a firm's own resources and competencies to create synergies and enhance shareholder value.

## Mergers and Acquisitions

The rate of mergers and acquisitions (M&A) had dropped off beginning in 2001. This trend was largely a result of a recession, corporate scandals, and a declining stock market. However, the situation has changed dramatically. Recently, several large mergers and acquisitions were announced. These include:[36]

- Sprint's merger with Nextel for $39 billion.
- Johnson & Johnson's $25 billion acquisition of medical device maker Guidant.
- Exelon's acquisition of Public Service Enterprise Group for $12 billion.
- SBC's purchase of AT&T for $16 billion.
- Procter & Gamble's purchase of Gillette for $54 billion.
- Kmart Holding Corp.'s acquisition of Sears, Roebuck & Co. for $11 billion.

**Let's make some deals**
The value of U.S. mergers and acquisitions has been steadily increasing since 2002.

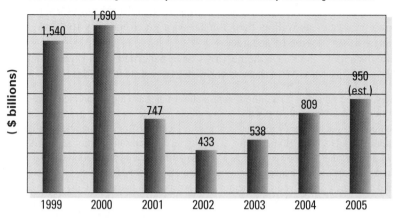

Exhibit 6.6   **U.S. Mergers and Acquisitions**

Sources: Thomson Financial; and, Coy, P., Thornton, E., Arndt, M. Grow, B. 2005. Shake rattle, and merge. *BusinessWeek,* January 10:34.

Exhibit 6.6 illustrates the dramatic increase in merger and acquisition activity in the United States in the past few years. While the volume is not expected soon to reach the peak level of 1999 and 2000, when the dollar amount totaled over $3 trillion, several factors help to explain the recent rise. First, there is the robust economy and the increasing corporate profits that have boosted stock prices and cash. For example, the Standard & Poor's 500 stock index companies, including financial companies, have a record $2 trillion in cash and other short-term assets, according to S&P Compustat.

Second, the weak U.S. dollar makes U.S. assets more attractive to other countries. That is, from the perspective of a foreign acquirer, compared to any other period in recent memory, U.S. companies are "cheap" today. For example, a Euro which was worth only 80 cents in 1999 was worth $1.25 by early 2005. This makes U.S. companies a relative bargain for a European acquirer. And third, stricter governance standards are requiring poorly performing CEOs and boards of directors to consider unsolicited offers. In essence, top executives and board members are less likely to be protected by anti-takeover mechanisms such as greenmail, poison pills and golden parachutes (which we will discuss at the end of the chapter).

Next, we will address some of the motives and potential benefits of mergers and acquisitions as well as their potential limitations.

*Motives and Benefits*   Growth through mergers and acquisitions has played a critical role in the success of many corporations in a wide variety of high-technology and knowledge-intensive industries. Here, market and technology changes can occur very quickly and unpredictably.[37] Speed—speed to market, speed to positioning, and speed to becoming a viable company—is critical in such industries. For example, Alex Mandl, then AT&T's president, was responsible for the acquisition of McCaw Cellular. Although many industry experts felt the price was too steep, he believed that cellular technology was a critical asset for the telecommunications business and that it would have been extremely difficult to build that business from the ground up. Mandl claimed, "The plain fact is that acquiring is much faster than building."[38]

As we discussed earlier in the chapter, mergers and acquisitions also can be a means of *obtaining valuable resources that can help an organization expand its product offerings and services.* For example, Cisco Systems, a dominant player in networking equipment, acquired more than 70 companies from 1993 to early 2000.[39] This provides Cisco with access to the latest in networking equipment. Then it uses its excellent sales force to market the new technology to its corporate customers and telephone companies. Cisco also provides strong incentives to the staff of acquired companies to stay on. In order to realize the greatest value from its acquisitions, Cisco also has learned to integrate acquired companies efficiently and effectively.[40]

Mergers and acquisitions also can *provide the opportunity for firms to attain the three bases of synergy that were addressed earlier in the chapter—leveraging core competencies, sharing activities, and building market power.* Consider Procter & Gamble's $54 billion proposed acquisition of Gillette.[41] First, it should help Procter & Gamble to leverage its core competencies in marketing and product positioning in the area of grooming and personal care brands. For example, P&G has experience in repositioning brands such as Old Spice in this market (which recently passed Gillette's Right Guard brand to become No. 1 in the deodorant market). Gillette has very strong brands in razors and blades. Thus, P&G's marketing expertise should help it to enhance its market position. Second, there are opportunities to share value-creating activities. Gillette will benefit from P&G's stronger distribution network in developing countries where the potential growth rate for the industry's products remains higher than in the United States, Europe, or Japan. Consider the insight of A. F. Lafley, P&G's CEO:

> When I was in Asia in the 90s, we had already gone beyond the top 500 cities in China. Today, we're way down into the rural areas. So we add three, four, five Gillette brands, and we don't even have to add a salesperson.

Finally, the addition of Gillette will enhance P&G's market power. In recent years, the growth of powerful global retailers such as Wal-Mart, Carrefour, and Costco has eroded much of the consumer goods industry's pricing power. A central part of P&G's recent strategy has been to focus its resources on enhancing its core brands. Today, 16 of its brands (each with revenues of over $1 billion) account for $30 billion of the firm's $51.4 billion in total revenues. Gillette, with $10.5 billion in total revenues, adds five brands which also have revenues of over $1 billion. P&G anticipates that its growing stable of "superbrands" will help it to weather the industry's tough pricing environment and enhance its power relative to large, powerful retailers.

Merger and acquisition activity also can *lead to consolidation within an industry and can force other players to merge.*[42] In the pharmaceutical industry, the patents for many top-selling drugs are expiring and M&A activity is expected to heat up.[43] For example, SG Cowen Securities predicts that between 2000 and 2005, U.S. patents will expire on pharmaceutical products with annual domestic sales of approximately $34.6 billion. Clearly, this is an example of how the political-legal segment of the general environment (discussed in Chapter 2) can affect a corporation's strategy and performance. Although health care providers and patients are happy about the lower-cost generics that will arrive, drug firms are being pressed to make up for lost revenues. Combining top firms such as Pfizer Inc. and Warner-Lambert Co. as well as Glaxo Wellcome and SmithKline Beecham has many potential long-term benefits. They not only promise significant post-merger cost savings, but also the increased size of the combined companies brings greater research and development possibilities.

Two other industries where consolidation is the primary rationale are telecommunications and software.[44] In 2004, Cingular Wireless became number one in the industry by acquiring AT&T Wireless Communications. Subsequently, Sprint agreed to buy Nextel to form a stronger number three. SBC Communications Inc. desires to have full ownership of Cingular, but BellSouth does not want to sell its 40 percent ownership. Will SBC simply buy all of BellSouth? Says SBC chief operating officer (COO) Randall Stephenson, "I don't want to speculate, but who knows? This industry is going to continue to consolidate." In software, the primary motive for merger is to offer customers a fuller portfolio of products. Many niche players are selling out to serial buyers like Oracle Corp., which recently acquired PeopleSoft Inc. after a long and heated struggle. Symantec Corp. agreed to acquire Veritas Software Corporation for $13.5 billion. Such consolidation raises questions about whether smaller players such as McAfee, BEA Systems, and Siebel Systems are big enough to remain independent. According to Joseph M. Tucci, president and CEO of data-storage giant EMC, "This is going to be a big boys' game. They're going to move very aggressively and quickly."

Strategy Spotlight 6.5 discusses how Ken Hendricks was able to successfully consolidate the highly fragmented, and low-margin industry of roofing supplies. The example shows that industry consolidation can take place in lesser known, and more mundane, industries.

Corporations can also *enter new market segments by way of acquisitions.* Although Charles Schwab & Co. is best known for providing discount trading services for middle America, it clearly is interested in other target markets.[45] In late 2000 Schwab surprised its rivals by paying $2.7 billion to acquire U.S. Trust Corporation, a 147-year-old-financial services institution that is a top estate planner for the wealthy, as noted in the chapter's opening case. However, Schwab is in no way ignoring its core market. The firm also purchased Cybercorp Inc., a Texas brokerage company, for $488 million. That firm offers active online traders sophisticated quotes and stock-screening tools.

*Potential Limitations*    As noted in the previous section, mergers and acquisitions provide a firm with many potential benefits. However, at the same time, there are many potential drawbacks or limitations to such corporate activity.[46]

First, *the takeover premium that is paid for an acquisition is very high.* Two times out of three, the stock price of the acquiring company falls once the deal is made public. Since the acquiring firm often pays a 30 percent to 40 percent premium for the target company, the acquirer must create synergies and scale economies that result in sales and market gains exceeding the premium price. Firms paying higher premiums set the performance hurdle even higher. For example, Household International paid an 82 percent premium to buy Beneficial, and Conseco paid an 83 percent premium to acquire Green Tree Financial. Historically, paying a high premium over the stock price has been a largely unprofitable strategy.

Second, *competing firms often can imitate any advantages realized or copy synergies that result from the M&A.* Thus, a firm can often see its advantages quickly evaporate if it plans to achieve competitive advantage through M&A activity. Unless the advantages are sustainable and difficult to copy, investors will not be willing to pay a high premium for the stock. Similarly, the time value of money must be factored into the stock price. M&A costs are paid up front. Conversely, firms pay for research and development, ongoing marketing, and capacity expansion over time. This stretches out the payments needed to gain new competencies. The M&A argument is that a large initial investment is worthwhile because it creates long-term advantages. However, stock analysts want to see immediate results from such a large cash outlay. If the acquired firm does not produce results quickly, investors often sell the stock, driving the price down.

Third, *managers' credibility and ego can sometimes get in the way of sound business decisions.* If the M&A does not perform as planned, managers who pushed for the deal find that their reputation may be at stake. Sometimes, this can lead these managers

## How Ken Hendricks Consolidated the Roofing Industry

As a child growing up in Janesville, Wisconsin, Ken Hendricks sensed the contempt "the country club set" had for his blue-collar family because of his father's humble job as a roofer. "They looked down their noses at him," Hendricks says. "He went to work every single day of his life. That wasn't good enough? Some kid got to go to a fancy school and that made him different than me? That just sets in your gut."

Whatever has driven Mr. Hendricks, he has become a remarkable success. Last year, his Beloit, Wisconsin–based American Builders & Contractors Supply (ABC) was the largest wholesaler of roofing supplies in the United States and among the largest supplies of vinyl sidings and windows. In 2004, the firm netted $67 million in profits on revenues of $1.8 billion. And as the sole owner of the privately held company, Hendricks joined the Forbes 400 with an estimated net worth of $850 million.

In his early years, Ken worked as an independent roofer, picking up jobs where he could, and subcontracting out some of the work. He had his big break when a major hailstorm hit a small town near where he lived. He met with the insurance company's claims adjuster and he offered to charge his normal pricing in exchange for a contract that combined all of the damaged roofs. (Most of his rivals typically inflated their prices in order to exploit the situation.) Eventually word spread, and before he was 30 years old, he had about 500 roofers working for him around the country.

Several years later—after selling off his business and settling into a leisurely life pursuing a sideline of renovating real estate—he began thinking about the need for a national distribution chain. He recalled that as a contractor he was constantly frustrated by dealing with dozens of suppliers, none of which could sell everything he needed.

And he sensed that there was a tremendous amount of complacency, waste, and room for improvement.

In 1982, Hendricks bought his first three distributors and intensified his acquisition activities over the next 15 years. By 1997, Hendricks had 157 outlets, $789 million in revenues, and a profit of $10 million. In total, he has made over 60 acquisitions, and ABC now has 280 locations in the United States.

He made it work by negotiating volume discounts with manufacturers and exercising very tight cost control. He used to deliver shingles to job sites with used trucks instead of buying new ones. He recycles pallets and sells them back to the manufacturer. ABC's point-of-sales system was built with a $20,000 software package, and it is still the heart of the company's computer system today.

Although Hendricks does not have the latest customer-relationship software, he does have an understanding of customer needs. "I've been up on the roof. I know what those guys are going through. My whole life has been about making that profession respectable."

But how will the competition from the big hardware and home-improvement chains affect ABC? Replies Hendricks, "We've got 256 different shingles by brand, weight, and color. Home Depot's not going to waste the shelf space. It's a low-margin business."

A testimony from a satisfied customer exemplifies ABC's commitment to excellent customer service. Robert Shannon, a contractor in Mineola, New York, has 50 roofers working for him. That makes him a very desirable customer for ABC as well as Home Depot. Some bad customer-service experiences soured him on Home Depot, and he is now loyal to ABC. Says Shannon, "They've delivered shingles overnight from Boston, stuff I needed the next day. No other supplier does that. They understand if you have nine crew members standing around with nothing to do, that costs money."

Sources: Armstrong, D. 2004. Up on the roof. *Forbes*, November 29: 184–188; and Welles, E. O. 2001. Roll your own. *Inc.*, February: 68–72.

to protect their credibility by funneling more money, or escalating their commitment, into an inevitably doomed operation. Further, when a merger fails and a firm tries to unload the acquisition, managers often find that they must sell at a huge discount. These problems further compound the costs and weaken the stock price.

Fourth, *there can be many cultural issues that may doom the intended benefits from M&A endeavors.* Consider, for example, the insights of Joanne Lawrence, who played an important role as vice president and director of communications and investor relations at SmithKline Beecham, in the merger between SmithKline and the Beecham Group, a diversified consumer-oriented group headquartered in the United Kingdom.[47]

The key to a strategic merger is to create a new culture. This was a mammoth challenge during the SmithKline Beecham merger. We were working at so many different cultural levels, it was dizzying. We had two national cultures to blend—American and British—that compounded the challenge of selling the merger in two different markets with two different shareholder bases. There were also two different business cultures: One was very strong, scientific, and academic; the other was much more commercially oriented. And then we had to consider within both companies the individual businesses, each of which has its own little culture.[48]

## Strategic Alliances and Joint Ventures

Strategic alliances and joint ventures are assuming an increasingly prominent role in the strategy of leading firms, both large and small.[49] Such cooperative relationships have many potential advantages. Among these are entering new markets, reducing manufacturing (or other) costs in the value chain, and developing and diffusing new technologies.[50]

*Entering New Markets*    Often a company that has a successful product or service wants to introduce it into a new market. However, it may not have the requisite marketing expertise because it does not understand customer needs, know how to promote the product, or have access to the proper distribution channels.

The partnerships formed between Time-Warner, Inc., and three African American–owned cable companies in New York City are examples of joint ventures created to serve a domestic market. Time-Warner built a 185,000-home cable system in the city and asked the three cable companies to operate it. Time-Warner supplied the product, and the cable companies supplied the knowledge of the community and the know-how to market the cable system. Joining with the local companies enabled Time-Warner to win the acceptance of the cable customers and to benefit from an improved image in the black community.

*Reducing Manufacturing (or Other) Costs in the Value Chain*    Strategic alliances (or joint ventures) often enable firms to pool capital, value-creating activities, or facilities in order to reduce costs. For example, Molson Companies and Carling O'Keefe Breweries in Canada formed a joint venture to merge their brewing operations. Although Molson had a modern and efficient brewery in Montreal, Carling's was outdated. However, Carling had the better facilities in Toronto. In addition, Molson's Toronto brewery was located on the waterfront and had substantial real estate value. Overall, the synergies gained by using their combined facilities more efficiently added $150 million of pretax earnings during the initial year of the venture. Economies of scale were realized and facilities were better utilized.

*Developing and Diffusing New Technologies*    Strategic alliances also may be used to build jointly on the technological expertise of two or more companies in order to develop products technologically beyond the capability of the companies acting independently. STMicroelectronics (ST) is a high-tech company based in Geneva, Switzerland, that has thrived—largely due to the success of its strategic alliances.[51] The firm develops and manufactures computer chips for a variety of applications such as mobile phones, set-top boxes, smart cards, and flash memories. In 1995 it teamed up with Hewlett-Packard to develop powerful new processors for various digital applications that are now nearing completion. Another example was its strategic alliance with Nokia to develop a chip that would give Nokia's phones a longer battery life. Here, ST produced a chip that tripled standby time to 60 hours—a breakthough that gave Nokia a huge advantage in the marketplace.

The firm's CEO, Pasquale Pistorio, was among the first in the industry to form R&D alliances with other companies. Now ST's top 12 customers, including HP, Nokia, and Nortel, account for 45 percent of revenues. According to Pistorio, "Alliances are in our DNA." Such relationships help ST keep better-than-average growth rates, even in difficult times. That's because close partners are less likely to defect to other suppliers. ST's financial results are most impressive. During 2000 its revenues grew 55 percent—nearly double the industry average.

Despite their promise, many alliances and joint ventures fail to meet expectations for a variety of reasons. First, without the proper partner, a firm should never consider undertaking an alliance, even for the best of reasons. Each partner should bring the desired complementary strengths to the partnership. Ideally, the strengths contributed by the partners are unique; thus synergies created can be more easily sustained and defended over the longer term. The goal must be to develop synergies between the contributions of the partners, resulting in a win–win situation for both. Moreover, the partners must be compatible and willing to trust each other. Unfortunately, often little attention is given to nurturing the close working relationships and interpersonal connections that bring together the partnering organizations. The human or people factors are not carefully considered or, at worst, they are dismissed as an unimportant consideration.

## Internal Development

Firms can also diversify by means of corporate entrepreneurship and new venture development. In today's economy, internal development is such an important means by which companies expand their businesses that we have devoted a whole chapter to it (see Chapter 12). Sony and the Minnesota Mining & Manufacturing Co. (3M), for example, are known for their dedication to innovation, R&D, and cutting-edge technologies. For example, 3M has developed its entire corporate culture to support its ongoing policy of generating at least 25 percent of total sales from products created within the most recent four-year period. During the 1990s, 3M exceeded this goal by achieving about 30 percent of sales per year from new internally developed products.

Many companies use some form of internal development to extend their product lines or add to their service offerings. This approach to internal development is used by many large publicly held corporations as well as small firms. An example of the latter is Rosa Verde, a small but growing business serving the health care needs of San Antonio, Texas.

> This small company began with one person who moved from Mexico to San Antonio, Texas, to serve the health care needs of inner-city residents.[52] Beginning as a sole proprietor, Dr. Lourdes Pizana started Rosa Verde Family Health Care Group in 1995 with only $10,000 obtained from credit card debt. She has used a strategy of internal development to propel the company to where it is today—six clinics, 30 doctors, and a team of other health care professionals.
>
> How was Dr. Pizana able to accomplish this in such a short time? She emphasizes the company's role in the community, forging links with community leaders. In addition, she hires nearly all her professional staff as independent contractors to control costs. These professionals are paid based on the volume of work they do rather than a set salary; Pizana splits her revenue with them, thus motivating them to work efficiently. Her strategy is to grow the company from the inside out through high levels of service, commitment to the community she serves, and savvy leadership. By committing to a solid plan, Pizana has proven that internal growth and development can be a successful strategy.

The luxury hotel chain Ritz-Carlton has long been recognized for its exemplary service. In fact, it is the only service company ever to win two Malcolm Baldrige National Quality Awards. It has built on this capability by developing a highly successful internal venture to offer leadership development programs—both to its employees as well as to outside companies. We address this internal venture in Strategy Spotlight 6.6.

Compared to mergers and acquisitions, firms that engage in internal development are able to capture the value created by their own innovative activities without having to "share the wealth" with alliance partners or face the difficulties associated with combining activities across the value chains of several companies or merging corporate cultures. Another advantage is that firms can often develop new products or services at a relatively lower

## The Ritz-Carlton Leadership Center: A Successful Internal Venture

Companies worldwide often strive to be the "Ritz-Carlton" of their industries. Ritz-Carlton, the large luxury hotel chain, is the only service company to have won the prestigious Malcolm Baldrige National Quality Award twice—in 1992 and 1999 (one year after being acquired by Marriott). It also has placed first in guest satisfaction among luxury hotels in the most recent J.D. Power & Associates hotel survey.

Until a few years ago, being "Ritz-Carlton-like" was just a motivational simile. However, in 2000, the company launched the Ritz-Carlton Leadership Center, where it offers 12 leadership development programs for its employees and seven benchmarking seminars and workshops to outside companies. It also conducts 35 off-site presentations on such topics as "Creating a Dynamic Employee Orientation," and "The Key to Retaining and Selecting Talented Employees." (Incidentally, Ritz-Carlton's annual turnover rate among nonmanagement employees is 25 percent— roughly half the average rate for U.S. luxury hotels.)

Within its first four years of operation, 800 different companies from such industries as health care, banking and finance, hospitality, and the automotive industries have participated in the Leadership Center's programs. And to date it has generated over $2 million in revenues. Ken Yancey, CEO of the nonprofit small-business consultancy, Score, says the concepts he learned, like "the three steps of service," apply directly to his business. "Hotels are about service to a client," he says. "And we are too."

To give a few specifics on one of the Leadership Center's programs, consider its "Legendary Service I" course. The topics that are covered include empowerment, using customer recognition to boost loyalty, and Ritz-Carlton's approach to quality. The course lasts two days and costs $2,000 per attendee. Well-known companies that have participated include Microsoft, Morgan Stanley, and Starbucks.

Sources: McDonald, D. 2004. Roll out the blue carpet. *Business 2.0*, May: 53; and Johnson, G. 2003. Nine tactics to take your corporate university from good to GREAT. *Training*, July/August: 38–41.

cost and thus rely on their own resources rather than turning to external funding. There are also potential disadvantages. Internal development may be time consuming; thus, firms may forfeit the benefits of speed that growth through mergers or acquisitions can provide. This may be especially important among high-tech or knowledge-based organizations in fast-paced environments where being an early mover is critical. Thus, firms that choose to diversify through internal development must develop capabilities that allow them to move quickly from initial opportunity recognition to market introduction.

## >>Real Options Analysis: A Useful Tool

*Real options analysis* (ROA) is an investment analysis tool from the field of finance. It has been slowly, but increasingly, adopted by consultants and executives to support strategic decision making in firms. What does real options analysis consist of and how can it be appropriately applied to the investments required to initiate strategic decisions? To understand *real* options it is first necessary to have a basic understanding of what *options* are.

Options exist when the owner of the option has the right but not the obligation to engage in certain types of transactions. The most common are stock options. A stock option grants the holder the right to buy (call option) or sell (put option) shares of the stock at a fixed price (strike price) at some time in the future.[53] Another aspect of stock options important to note is that the investment to be made immediately is small, whereas the investment to be made in the future is generally larger. For example, an option to buy a rapidly rising stock currently priced at $50 might cost as little as $.50.[54] An important point to note is that owners of such a stock option have limited their losses to $.50 per share, while the upside potential is unlimited. This aspect of options is attractive because options offer the prospect of high gains with relatively small up-front investments that represent limited losses.

The phrase "real options" applies to situations where options theory and valuation techniques are applied to real assets or physical things as opposed to financial assets. Some of the most common applications of real options are with property and insurance. A real estate option grants the holder the right to buy or sell a piece of property at an established price some time in the future. The actual market price of the property may rise above the established (or strike) price—or the market value may sink below the strike price. If the price of the property goes up, the owner of the option is likely to buy it. If the market value of the property drops below the strike price, the option holder is unlikely to execute the purchase. In the latter circumstance, the option holder has limited his or her loss to the cost of the option, but during the life of the option retains the right to participate in whatever the upside potential might be. Casualty insurance is another variation of real options. With casualty insurance, the owner of the property has limited the loss to the cost of the insurance, while the upside potential is the actual loss, ranging, of course, up to the limit of the insurance.[55]

## Applications of Real Options Analysis to Strategic Decisions

The concept of options can also be applied to strategic decisions where management has flexibility; that is, the situation will permit management to decide whether to invest additional funds to grow or accelerate the activity, perhaps delay in order to learn more, shrink the scale of the activity, or even abandon it. Decisions to invest in business activities such as R&D, motion pictures, exploration and production of oil wells, and the opening and closing of copper mines often have this flexibility.[56] Important issues to note are the following:

- Real options analysis is appropriate to use when investments can be staged; in other words, a smaller investment up front can be followed by subsequent investments. In short, real options can be applied to an investment decision that gives the company the right, but not the obligation, to make follow-on investments.

- The strategic decision makers have "tollgates" or key points at which they can decide whether to continue, delay, or abandon the project. In short, the executives have the flexibility. There are opportunities to make other go or no–go decisions associated with each phase.

- It is expected that there will be increased knowledge about outcomes at the time of the next investment and that additional knowledge will help inform the decision makers about whether to make additional investments (i.e., whether the option is in the money or out of the money).

Many strategic decisions have the characteristic of containing a series of options. The phenomenon is called "embedded options," a series of investments in which at each stage of the investment there is a go/no–go decision. For example, pharmaceutical companies have successfully used real options analysis in evaluating decisions about investments in pharmaceutical R&D projects since the early 1990s.[57] Pharmaceuticals have at least four stages of investments: basic research yielding compounds and the three FDA-mandated phases of clinical trials. Generally, each phase is more expensive to undertake than the previous phase. However, as each phase unfolds, management knows more about the underlying drug and the many sources of uncertainty, including the technical difficulties with the drugs themselves as well as external market conditions, such as the results of competitors' research.[58] Management can make the decision to invest more with the intent of speeding up the process, delay the start of the next phase, reduce investment, or even abandon the R&D.[59]

As noted above, the use of real options analysis can provide the firm with many opportunities for learning. In many cases, such learning can extend beyond the specific investment or project at hand. For example, consider Eli Lilly's 1984 investment in a start-up biotechnology firm, Hybritech:[60]

> Within two years of making its investment in Hybritech, Eli Lilly acquired the firm outright, acquiring full access to drugs that Hybritech was pursuing. The first and primary benefit for Eli Lilly was access to a drug before it had been approved by the FDA, allowing them to acquire it at a much lower cost than if they had waited for FDA approval. They also acquired access to Hybritech's management and existing knowledge—another benefit. The benefit easiest to overlook, however, was learning how to partner with a biotechnology start-up with different expertise (i.e., Eli Lilly was engaged in chemical-based science; Hybritech was genetically based). This enabled them to learn how to better work with their biotechnology partners and how to transmit that information inside Eli Lilly more efficiently. They wrote an option to acquire Hybritech and also wrote an option to learn how to partner with other biotechnology firms. Long term, the latter appears to have been the more valuable real option. Lilly has brought more drugs to market from its collaboration with its partners than has nearly anyone else. Lilly's recent FDA-approved drug, Cialis, resulted from a partnership with another biotechnology firm, Icos.

Strategy Spotlight 6.7 provides two examples of companies using ROA to guide their decision-making process.

## Potential Pitfalls of Real Options Analysis

Despite the many benefits that can be gained from using real options analysis, managers must be aware of its potential limitations or pitfalls. Below we will address three major issues.[61]

*Agency Theory and the Back-Solver Dilemma*    Let's assume that companies adopting a real-options perspective invest heavily in training and that their people understand how to effectively estimate variance—that is, the amount of dispersion or range that is estimated for potential outcomes. Such training can help them use ROA. However, it does not solve another inherent problem: managers may have an incentive and the know-how to "game the system." Most electronic spreadsheets permit users to simply back-solve any formula; that is, you can type in the answer you want and ask what values are needed in a formula to get that answer. If managers know that a certain option value must be met in order for the proposal to get approved, they can back-solve the model to find a variance estimate needed to arrive at the answer that upper management desires. What would be the manager's motive to do this?

Agency problems are typically inherent in investment decisions. They may occur when the managers of a firm are separated from its owners—that is, when managers act as "agents" rather than "principals" (owners). Such problems could occur because a manager may have something to gain by not acting in the owner's best interests, or the interests of managers and owners are not co-aligned. Agency theory suggests that as managerial and owner interests diverge, managers will follow the path of their own self-interests. Sometimes this is to secure better compensation. At other times, those interests involve exerting less effort. In terms of securing better compensation, agency problems arise because managers who propose projects may believe that if their projects are approved, they stand a much better chance of getting promoted. So while managers have an incentive to propose projects that *should* be successful, they also have an incentive to propose projects that *might* be successful. And because of the subjectivity involved in formally modeling a real option, managers may have an incentive to choose variance values that increase the likelihood of approval.

*Managerial Conceit: Overconfidence and the Illusion of Control*
Often, poor decisions are the result of such traps as biases, blind spots, and other human frailties. Much of this literature falls under the concept of *managerial conceit*.[62]

# Applications of Real Options Analysis

The following two examples illustrate how real options analysis (ROA) is enjoying increasing popularity among strategists facing the task of allocating resources in an era of great uncertainty. In the first example, a privately held biotechnology firm is using ROA to analyze an internal development decision. In the second example pharmaceutical giant Merck uses this tool to decide whether to enter into a strategic alliance. In each of these cases, ROA led to a different decision outcome than that of more traditional net present value (NPV) analysis. NPV is the sum of costs and revenues for the life of the project, discounted typically by current interest rates to reflect the time value of money.

- A privately held biotechnology firm had developed a unique technology for introducing the coat protein of a particular virus into animal feedstock. Ingesting the coat protein generated an immune response, thus protecting the animal from the virus. The firm was at the beginning of the preclinical trials stage, the first of a series of tests required by FDA regulation and conducted through the FDA subagency called the Center for Veterinary Medicine. The company expected the stage to take 18 months and cost $2 million. Long-standing experience indicated that 95 percent of new drug investigations are abandoned during this phase. Subsequent stages would decrease somewhat in terms of the possibility of rejection, but costs would rise, with a total outflow from 2002 through anticipated launch in 2007 of at least $18.5 million. The company's best estimate of the market from 2007 through 2017 was about $85 million per year, with the possibility of taking as much as a 50 percent market share. In short, there was huge potential, but in the interim there was tremendous chance of

failure (i.e., high risk), significant early outflows, and delayed inflows. Analysis using a traditional NPV analysis yielded a negative $2 million with an 11 percent risk-adjusted discount rate. Viewing the investment as a multistage option, however, and incorporating management's flexibility to change its decision at a minimum of four points between 2002 and 2007, changes the valuation markedly. A real options analysis approach to the analysis demonstrated a present value of about $22 million. The question was not whether to risk $18.5 million, but whether to invest $2 million today for the opportunity to earn $22 million.

- Merck has applied real options analysis to a number of its strategic decisions. One was the agreement it signed with Biogen, which in the late 1990s had developed an asthma drug. Instead of purchasing Biogen outright, Merck created a real options arrangement. Merck paid Biogen $15 million up front and retained the right to invest up to an additional $130 million at various points as the biotechnology company reached specified milestones. In essence, Merck purchased a stream of options: the right to scale up and scale down, or even abandon, the option. Merck's potential in the deal was unlimited, while its downside risk was limited to the extent of the milestone payments. Analysis suggested that the present value of the deal was about $275 million, considerably more than the present value of the up-front and milestone payments. Using traditional NPV methods would have killed this deal. However, real options analysis encouraged Merck to undertake the arrangement, in part, because Merck was in the process of learning about the underlying technology. Biogen, on the other hand, gained the advantage of committed cash flow to continue development—provided that developments from the various phases continued to be favorable.

Sources: Stockley, R. L., Jr., Curtis, S., Jafari, J., and Tibbs, K. 2003. The option value of an early-stage biotechnology investment. *Journal of Applied Finance,* 15(2): 44–55; and Mauboussin, M. H. 1999. Get real: Using real options in security analysis. *Equity Research Series by Credit Suite/First Boston,* 10, June 23: 18.

Understanding how these traps affect decision makers can help to improve decision making.

First, managerial conceit occurs when managers who have made successful choices in the past may come to believe that they possess superior expertise for managing uncertainty. They believe that their abilities can, therefore, reduce the risks inherent in decision making to a much greater extent than they actually can. Such managers are more likely to shift away from analysis to trusting their own judgment. In the case of real options, they can simply declare that any given decision is a real option and proceed as before. If asked to formally model their decision, they are more likely to employ variance estimates that support their viewpoint.

Second, employing the real-options perspective can encourage decision makers toward a bias for action. Such a bias may lead to carelessness. Managerial conceit is as much a problem (if not more so) for small decisions as for big ones. Why? The cost to write the first stage of an option is much smaller than the cost of full commitment, and managers pay less attention to small decisions than to large ones. Because real options are designed to minimize potential losses while preserving potential gains, any problems that arise are likely to be smaller at first, causing less concern for the manager. Managerial conceit could suggest that managers will assume that those problems are the easiest to solve and control—a concern referred to as the illusion of control. Managers may fail to respond appropriately because they overlook the problem or believe that since it is small, they can easily resolve it. Thus, managers may approach each real-option decision with less care and diligence than if they had made a full commitment to a larger investment.

*Managerial Conceit: Irrational Escalation of Commitment*    A strength of a real options perspective is also one of its Achilles heels. Both real options and decisions involving escalation of commitment require specific environments with sequential decisions.[63] As the escalation-of-commitment literature indicates, simply separating a decision into multiple parts does not guarantee that decisions made will turn out well. This condition is potentially present whenever the exercise decision retains some uncertainty, which most still do. The decision to abandon also has strong psychological factors associated with it that affect the ability of managers to make correct exercise decisions.[64]

An option to exit requires reversing an initial decision made by someone in the organization. Organizations typically encourage managers to "own their decisions" in order to motivate them. One result is that as managers invest themselves in their decision, it proves harder for them to lose face by reversing course. In effect, for managers making the decision, it feels as if they made the wrong decision in the first place, even if it was initially a good decision. The more specific the manager's human capital becomes, the harder it is to transfer it to other organizations. Hence, there is a greater likelihood that managers will stick around and try to make an existing decision work. They are more likely to continue an existing project even if it should perhaps be ended.[65]

## >>How Managerial Motives Can Erode Value Creation

Thus far in the chapter we have implicitly assumed that CEOs and top executives are "rational beings"; that is, they act in the best interests of shareholders to maximize long-term shareholder value. In the real world, however, this is not the case. Frequently, they may act in their own self-interest. Next we address some managerial motives that can serve to erode, rather than enhance, value creation. These include "growth for growth's sake," excessive egotism, and the creation of a wide variety of antitakeover tactics.

### Growth for Growth's Sake

There are huge incentives for executives to increase the size of their firm, and many of these are hardly consistent with increasing shareholder wealth. Top managers, including the CEO, of larger firms typically enjoy more prestige, higher rankings for their companies on the Fortune 500 list (which is based on revenues, not profits), greater incomes, more job security, and so on. There is also the excitement and associated recognition of making a major acquisition. As noted by Harvard's Michael Porter, "There's a tremendous allure to mergers and acquisitions. It's the big play, the dramatic gesture. With one stroke of the pen you can add billions to size, get a front-page story, and create excitement in markets."[66]

In recent years many high-tech firms have suffered from the negative impact of their uncontrolled growth. Consider, for example, Priceline.com's ill-fated venture into an online service to offer groceries and gasoline.[67] A myriad of problems—perhaps most importantly, a lack of participation by manufacturers—caused the firm to lose more than $5 million a *week* prior to abandoning these ventures. Similarly, many have questioned the profit potential of Amazon.com's recent ventures into a variety of products such as tools and hardware, cell phones, and service. Such initiatives are often little more than desperate moves by top managers to satisfy investor demands for accelerating revenues. Unfortunately, the increased revenues often fail to materialize into a corresponding hike in earnings.

At times, executives' overemphasis on growth can result in a plethora of ethical lapses, which can have disastrous outcomes for their companies. A good example (of bad practice) is Joseph Bernardino's leadership at Andersen Worldwide. Bernardino had a chance early on to take a hard line on ethics and quality in the wake of earlier scandals at clients such as Waste Management and Sunbeam. Instead, according to former executives, he put too much emphasis on revenue growth. Consequently, the firm's reputation quickly eroded when it audited and signed off on the highly flawed financial statements of such infamous firms as Enron, Global Crossing, and WorldCom. WorldCom, in fact, is recognized as the biggest financial fraud of all time. Bernardino ultimately resigned in disgrace in March 2002, and his firm was dissolved later that year.[68]

## Egotism

Most would agree that there is nothing wrong with ego, per se. After all, a healthy ego helps make a leader confident, clearheaded, and able to cope with change. CEOs, by their very nature, are typically fiercely competitive people in the office as well as on the tennis court or golf course. However, sometimes when pride is at stake, individuals will go to great lengths to win—or at least not to back down. Consider the following anecdote:

> When Warner Bros. CEO Robert Daly walked into the first postmerger gathering of senior Time Warner management in the Bahamas, he felt a hand on his shoulder. It was a Time Inc. executive whom he had never met. The magazine man asked the studio executive if he ever considered that General Motors purchased $30 million worth of advertising in Time Inc. publications before Daly acquired *Roger and Me,* a scathing cinematic indictment of the carmaker.
>
> Daly replied, "No. Did you consider that Warner Bros. spent over $50 million on *Batman* before *Time* ran its lousy review of the movie?" The Time executive smiled, patted his new colleague's shoulder and suggested that they continue their jobs in their own way!

Egos can get in the way of a "synergistic" corporate marriage. Few executives (or lower-level managers) are exempt from the potential downside of excessive egos. Consider, for example, the reflections of General Electric's former CEO Jack Welch, considered by many to be the world's most admired executive. He admitted to his regrettable decision for GE to acquire Kidder Peabody.[69] According to Welch, "My hubris got in the way in the Kidder Peabody deal. [He was referring to GE's buyout of the soon-to-be-troubled Wall Street firm.] I got wise advice from Walter Wriston and other directors who said, 'Jack, don't do this.' But I was bully enough and on a run to do it. And I got whacked right in the head." In addition to poor financial results, Kidder Peabody was wracked by a widely publicized trading scandal that tarnished the reputations of both GE and Kidder Peabody. Welch ended up selling Kidder in 1994.

The business press has included many stories of how egotism and greed have infiltrated organizations. Some incidents are considered rather astonishing, such as Tyco's former (and now convicted) CEO Dennis Kozlowski's well-chronicled purchase of a $6,000 shower curtain and vodka-spewing, full-size replica of Michaelangelo's David.[70] Other well-known examples of power grabs and extraordinary consumption of compensation and perks include

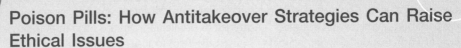

# STRATEGY SPOTLIGHT

## 6.8

### Poison Pills: How Antitakeover Strategies Can Raise Ethical Issues

Poison pills are almost always good for managers but not always so good for shareholders. They present managers with an ethical dilemma: How can they balance their own interests with their fiduciary responsibility to shareholders?

Here's how poison pills work. In the event of a takeover bid, existing shareholders have the option to buy additional shares of stock at a discount to the current market price. This action is typically triggered when a new shareholder rapidly accumulates more than a set percentage of ownership (usually 20 percent) through stock purchases. When this happens, managers fear that the voting rights and increased proportional ownership of the new shareholder might be a ploy to make a takeover play.

To protect existing shareholders, stock is offered at a discount, but only to existing shareholders. As the existing owners buy the discounted stock, the stock is diluted (i.e., there are now more shares, each with a lower value). If there has been a takeover offer at a set price per share, the overall price for the company immediately goes up

since there are now more shares. This assures stockholders of receiving a fair price for the company.

Sounds good, but here's the problem. Executives on the company's board of directors retain the right to allow the stock discount. The discounted stock price for existing shareholders may or may not be activated when a takeover is imminent. This brings in the issue of motive: Why did the board enact the poison pill provision in the first place? At times, it may have been simply to protect the existing shareholders. At other times, it may have been to protect the interests of those on the board of directors. In other words, the board may have enacted the rule not to protect shareholders, but to protect their own jobs.

When the board receives a takeover offer, the offering company will be aware of the poison pill provision. This gives negotiating power to board members of the takeover target. They may include as part of the negotiation that the new company keep them as members of the board. In exchange, the board members would not enact the discounted share price; existing stockholders would lose, but the jobs of the board members would be protected.

When a company offers poison pill provisions to shareholders, the shareholders should keep in mind that things are not always as they seem. The motives may reflect concern for shareholders. But on the other hand . . .

Sources: Vicente, J. P. 2001. Toxic treatment: Poison pills proliferate as Internet firms worry they've become easy marks. *Red Herring*, May 1 and 15: 195; Chakraborty, A., & Baum, C. F. 1998. Poison pills, optimal contracting and the market for corporate control: Evidence from Fortune 500 firms. *International Journal of Finance*, 10(3): 1120–1138; Sundaramurthy, C. 1996. Corporate governance within the context of antitakeover provisions. *Strategic Management Journal*, 17: 377–394.

executives at Enron, the Rigas family who were convicted of defrauding Adelphia of roughly $1 billion, former CEO Bernie Ebbers's $408 million loan from WorldCom, and so on. However, executives in the United States clearly don't have a monopoly on such deeds. Consider, for example, Jean-Marie Messier, former CEO of Vivendi Universal.[71]

> In striving to convert a French utility into a global media conglomerate, Messier seldom passed up a chance for self-promotion. Although most French executives have a preference for discreet personal lives, Messier hung out with rock stars and moved his family into a $17.5 million Park Avenue spread paid for by Vivendi. He pushed the company to the brink of collapse by running up $19 billion in debt from an acquisition spree and confusing investors with inconsistent financial transactions which are now under investigation by authorities in both the United States and France. Not one to accept full responsibility, less than five months after his forced resignation, he published a book, *My True Diary*, that blames a group of French business leaders for plotting against him. And his ego is clearly intact: At a recent Paris press conference, he described his firing as a setback for French capitalism.

### Antitakeover Tactics

Unfriendly or hostile takeovers can occur when a company's stock becomes undervalued. A competing organization can buy the outstanding stock of a takeover candidate in sufficient quantity to become a large shareholder. Then it makes a tender offer to gain full control of the company. If the shareholders accept the offer, the hostile firm buys the target company and either fires the target firm's management team or strips them of their power. For this reason, antitakeover tactics are common. Three of these are greenmail, golden parachutes, and poison pills.[72]

The first, *greenmail,* is an effort by the target firm to prevent an impending takeover. When a hostile firm buys a large block of outstanding target company stock and the target firm's management feels that a tender offer is impending, they offer to buy the stock back from the hostile company at a higher price than the unfriendly company paid for it. The positive side is that this often prevents a hostile takeover. On the downside, the same price is not offered to preexisting shareholders. However, it protects the jobs of the target firm's management.

The second strategy is a *golden parachute.* A golden parachute is a prearranged contract with managers specifying that, in the event of a hostile takeover, the target firm's managers will be paid a significant severance package. Although top managers lose their jobs, the golden parachute provisions protect their income.

Strategy Spotlight 6.8 illustrates how poison pills are used to prevent takeovers. *Poison pills* are means by which a company can give shareholders certain rights in the event of a takeover by another firm. In addition to "poison pills," they are also known as shareholder rights plans.

As you can see, antitakeover tactics can often raise some interesting ethical issues.

## Summary

A key challenge for today's managers is to create "synergy" when engaging in diversification activities. As we discussed in this chapter, corporate managers do not, in general, have a very good track record in creating value in such endeavors when it comes to mergers and acquisitions. Among the factors that serve to erode shareholder values are paying an excessive premium for the target firm, failing to integrate the activities of the newly acquired businesses into the corporate family, and undertaking diversification initiatives that are too easily imitated by the competition.

We addressed two major types of corporate-level strategy: related and unrelated diversification. With *related diversification* the corporation strives to enter into areas in which key resources and capabilities of the corporation can be shared or leveraged. Synergies come from horizontal relationships between business units. Cost savings and enhanced revenues can be derived from two major sources. First, economies of scope can be achieved from the leveraging of core competencies and the sharing of activities. Second, market power can be attained from greater, or pooled, negotiating power and from vertical integration.

When firms undergo *unrelated diversification* they enter product markets that are dissimilar to their present businesses. Thus, there is generally little opportunity to either leverage core competencies or share activities across business units. Here, synergies are created from vertical relationships between the corporate office and the individual business units. With unrelated diversification, the primary ways to create value are corporate restructuring and parenting, as well as the use of portfolio analysis techniques.

Corporations have three primary means of diversifying their product markets—mergers and acquisitions, joint ventures/strategic alliances, and internal development. There are key trade-offs associated with each of these. For example, mergers and acquisitions are typically the quickest means to enter new markets and provide the corporation with a high level of control over the acquired business. However, with the expensive premiums that often need to be paid to the shareholders of the target firm and the challenges associated with integrating acquisitions, they can also be quite expensive. Strategic alliances between two or more firms, on the other hand, may be a means of reducing risk since they involve the sharing and combining of resources. But such joint initiatives also provide a firm with less control (than it would have with an acquisition) since governance is shared between two independent entities. Also, there is a limit to the potential upside for each partner because returns must be shared as well. Finally, with internal development, a firm is able to capture all of the value from its initiatives (as opposed to sharing it with a merger or alliance partner). However, diversification by means of internal development can be very time-consuming—a disadvantage that becomes even more important in fast-paced competitive environments.

Traditional tools such as net present value (NPV) analysis are not always very helpful in making resource allocation decisions under uncertainty. Real options analysis (ROA) is increasingly used to make better quality decisions in such situations. We also addressed the potential limitations of ROA.

Finally, some managerial behaviors may serve to erode shareholder returns. Among these are "growth for growth's sake," egotism, and antitakeover tactics. As we discussed, some of these issues—particularly antitakeover tactics—raise ethical considerations because the managers of the firm are not acting in the best interests of the shareholders.

## Summary Review Questions

1. Discuss how managers can create value for their firm through diversification efforts.
2. What are some of the reasons that many diversification efforts fail to achieve desired outcomes?
3. How can companies benefit from related diversification? Unrelated diversification? What are some of the key concepts that can explain such success?
4. What are some of the important ways in which a firm can restructure a business?
5. Discuss some of the various means that firms can use to diversify. What are the pros and cons associated with each of these?
6. Discuss some of the actions that managers may engage in to erode shareholder value.

## Experiential Exercise

Time Warner (formerly AOL Time Warner) is a firm that follows a strategy of related diversification. Evaluate its success (or lack thereof) with regard to how well it has: (1) built on core competencies, (2) shared infrastructures, and (3) increased market power.

| Rationale for Related Diversification | Successful/Unsuccessful? | Why? |
|---|---|---|
| **1.** Build on core competencies | | |
| **2.** Share infrastructures | | |
| **3.** Increase market power | | |

1. What were some of the largest mergers and acquisitions over the last two years? What was the rationale for these actions? Do you think they will be successful? Explain.

2. Discuss some examples from business practice in which an executive's actions appear to be in his or her self-interest rather than the corporation's well-being.

3. Discuss some of the challenges that managers must overcome in making strategic alliances successful. What are some strategic alliances with which you are familiar? Were they successful or not? Explain.

4. Use the Internet and select a company that has recently undertaken diversification into new product markets. What do you feel were some of the reasons for this diversification (e.g., leveraging core competencies, sharing infrastructures)?

**Application Questions Exercises**

1. In recent years there has been a rash of corporate downsizing and layoffs. Do you feel that such actions raise ethical considerations? Why or why not?

2. What are some of the ethical issues that arise when managers act in a manner that is counter to their firm's best interests? What are the long-term implications for both the firms and the managers themselves?

**Ethics Questions**

## References

1. Craig, S., & Brown, K. 2004. Schwab ousts Pottruck as CEO; Founder returns to take the helm. *Wall Street Journal,* July 21: A1; Tabb, L. 2004. Wealth management: Can a leopard change its spots? www.wallstreetand_tech.com, November; Frank, R. 2004. U.S. Trust feels effects of switch; Schwab unit was perceived as ousted CEO's deal; shake-up is likely in offing. *Wall Street Journal,* July 21: A8; Lee, L. 2002, Closed eyes, open wallet. *BusinessWeek,* November 4: 116–117; Shilling, A. G. 2003. Wall Street's fat. *Forbes,* April 14: 242; and Schwab acquires U.S. Trust. 2000. *CNN Money* (online), January 13.

2. Hammonds, K. H. 2002. The numbers don't lie. *Fast Company,* September: 80.

3. Pare, T. P. 1994. The new merger boom. *Fortune,* November 28: 96.

4. Our framework draws upon a variety of sources, including Goold, M., & Campbell, A. 1998. Desperately seeking synergy. *Harvard Business Review,* 76(5): 131–143; Porter, M. E. 1987. From advantage to corporate strategy. *Harvard Business Review,* 65(3): 43–59; and Hitt, M. A., Ireland, R. D., & Hoskisson, R. E. 2001. *Strategic management: competitiveness and globalization* (4th ed.). Cincinnati, OH: South-Western.

5. Collis, D. J., & Montgomery, C. A. 1987. *Corporate strategy: Resources and the scope of the firm.* New York: McGraw-Hill.

6. This imagery of the corporation as a tree and related discussion draws on Prahalad, C. K., & Hamel, G. 1990. The core competence of the corporation. *Harvard Business Review,* 68(3): 79–91. Parts of this section also draw on Picken, J. C., & Dess, G. G. 1997. *Mission critical:* chap. 5. Burr Ridge, IL: Irwin Professional Publishing.

7. This section draws on Prahalad & Hamel, op. cit.; and Porter, op. cit.

8. A recent study that investigates the relationship between a firm's technology resources, diversification, and performance can be found in Miller, D. J. 2004. Firms' technological resources and the performance effects of diversification. A longitudinal study. *Strategic Management Journal,* 25: 1097–1119.

9. Harley-Davidson. 1993. Annual report.

10. Collis & Montgomery, op. cit.

11. Henricks, M. 1994. VF seeks global brand dominance. *Apparel Industry Magazine,* August: 21–40; VF Corporation. 1993. First quarter corporate summary report. *1993 VF Annual Report.*

12. Hill, A., & Hargreaves, D. 2001. Turbulent times for GE-Honeywell deal. *Financial Times,* February 28: 26.

13. Lowry, T. 2001. Media. *BusinessWeek,* January 8: 100–101.

14. The Tribune Company. 1999. *Annual report.*

15. This section draws on Hrebiniak, L. G., & Joyce, W. F. 1984. *Implementing strategy.* New York: MacMillan; and Oster, S. M. 1994. *Modern competitive analysis.* New York: Oxford University Press.

16. The discussion of the benefits and costs of vertical integration draws on Hax, A. C., & Majluf, N. S. 1991. *The strategy concept and process: A pragmatic approach:* 139. Englewood Cliffs, NJ: Prentice Hall.

17. Fahey, J. 2005. Gray winds. *Forbes.* January 10: 143.

18. This discussion draws on Oster, op. cit.; and Harrigan, K. 1986. Matching vertical integration strategies to competitive conditions. *Strategic Management Journal,* 7(6): 535–556.

19. For a scholarly explanation on how transaction costs determine the boundaries of a firm, see Oliver E. Williamson's pioneering books *Markets and Hierarchies: Analysis and Antitrust Implications* (New York: Free Press, 1975) and

*The Economic Institutions of Capitalism* (New York: Free Press, 1985).

20. Campbell, A., Goold, M., & Alexander, M. 1995. Corporate strategy: The quest for parenting advantage. *Harvard Business Review,* 73(2): 120–132; and Picken & Dess, op. cit.

21. Anslinger, P. A., & Copeland, T. E. 1996. Growth through acquisition: A fresh look. *Harvard Business Review,* 74(1): 126–135.

22. Campbell et al., op. cit.

23. This section draws on Porter, op. cit.; and Hambrick, D. C. 1985. Turnaround strategies. In Guth, W. D. (Ed.). *Handbook of business strategy:* 10-1–10-32. Boston: Warren, Gorham & Lamont.

24. There is an important delineation between companies that are operated for a long-term profit and those that are bought and sold for short-term gains. The latter are sometimes referred to as "holding companies" and are generally more concerned about financial issues than strategic issues.

25. Casico. W. F. 2002. Strategies for responsible restructuring. *Academy of Management Executive,* 16(3): 80–91; and Singh, H. 1993. Challenges in researching corporate restructuring. *Journal of Management Studies,* 30(1): 147–172.

26. Cusack, M. 1987. *Hanson Trust: A review of the company and its prospects.* London: Hoare Govett.

27. Hax & Majluf, op. cit. By 1979, 45 percent of Fortune 500 companies employed some form of portfolio analysis, according to Haspelagh, P. 1982. Portfolio planning: Uses and limits. *Harvard Busines Review,* 60: 58–73. A later study conducted in 1993 found that over 40 percent of the respondents used portfolio analysis techniques, but the level of usage was expected to increase to more than 60 percent in the near future: Rigby, D. K. 1994. Managing the management tools. *Planning Review,* September–October: 20–24.

28. Goold, M., & Luchs, K. 1993. Why diversify? Four decades of management thinking. *Academy of Management Executive,* 7(3): 7–25.

29. Other approaches include the industry attractiveness–business strength matrix developed jointly by General Electric and McKinsey and Company, the life-cycle matrix developed by Arthur D. Little, and the profitability matrix proposed by Marakon. For an extensive review, refer to Hax & Majluf, op. cit.: 182–194.

30. Porter, op. cit.: 49–52.

31. Collis, D. J. 1995. Portfolio planning at Ciba-Geigy and the Newport investment proposal. Harvard Business School Case No. 9-795-040. Novartis AG was created in 1996 by the merger of Ciba-Geigy and Sandoz.

32. Buzzell, R. D., & Gale, B. T. 1987. *The PIMS Principles: Linking Strategy to Performance.* New York: Free Press; and Miller, A., & Dess, G. G. 1996. *Strategic Management,* (2nd ed.). New York: McGraw-Hill.

33. Seeger, J. 1984. Reversing the images of BCG's growth share matrix. *Strategic Management Journal,* 5(1): 93–97.

34. Picken & Dess, op. cit.; Cabot Corporation. 2001. 10-Q filing, Securities and Exchange Commission, May 14.

35. Koudsi, S. 2001. Remedies for an economic hangover. *Fortune,* June 25: 130–139.

36. Coy, P., Thornton, E., Arndt, M., & Grow, B. 2005. Shake, rattle, and merge. *BusinessWeek,* January 10: 32–35; and Anonymous. 2005. Love is in the air. *Economist,* February 5: 9.

37. For an interesting study of the relationship between mergers and a firm's product-market strategies, refer to Krisnan, R. A., Joshi, S., & Krishnan, H. 2004. The influence of mergers on firms' product-mix strategies. *Strategic Management Journal,* 25: 587–611.

38. Carey, D., moderator. 2000. A CEO roundtable on making mergers succeed. *Harvard Business Review,* 78(3): 146.

39. Shinal, J. 2001. Can Mike Volpi make Cisco sizzle again? *BusinessWeek,* February 26: 102–104; Kambil, A. Eselius, E. D., & Monteiro, K. A. 2000. Fast venturing: The quick way to start Web businesses. *Sloan Management Review,* 41(4): 55–67; and Elstrom, P. 2001. Sorry, Cisco: The old answers won't work. *BusinessWeek,* April 30: 39.

40. Like many high-tech firms during the economic slump that began in mid-2000, Cisco Systems has experienced declining performance. On April 16, 2001, it announced that its revenues for the quarter closing April 30 would drop 5 percent from a year earlier—and a stunning 30 percent from the previous three months—to about $4.7 billion. Furthermore, Cisco announced that it would lay off 8,500 employees and take an enormous $2.5 billion charge to write down inventory. By late October 2002, its stock was trading at around $10, down significantly from its 52-week high of $70. Elstrom, op. cit.: 39.

41. Coy, P., Thornton, E., Arndt, M. & Grow, B. 2005, Shake, rattle, and merge. *BusinessWeek,* January 10: 32–35; and, Anonymous. 2005. The rise of the superbrands. *Economist.* February 5: 63–65; and, Sellers, P. 2005. It was a no-brainer. *Fortune,* February 21: 96–102.

42. For a discussion of the trend toward consolidation of the steel industry and how Lakshmi Mittal is becoming a dominant player, read Reed, S., & Arndt, M. 2004. The Raja of steel. *BusinessWeek,* December 20: 50–52.

43. Barrett, A. 2001. Drugs. *BusinessWeek,* January 8: 112–113.

44. Coy, P., et al. 2005, op. cit.

45. Whalen, C. J., Pascual, A. M., Lowery, T., & Muller, J. 2001. The top 25 managers. *BusinessWeek,* January 8: 63.

46. This discussion draws upon Rappaport, A., & Sirower, M. L. 1999. Stock or cash? The trade-offs for buyers and sellers in mergers and acquisitions. *Harvard Business Review,* 77(6): 147–158; and Lipin, S., & Deogun, N. 2000. Big mergers of 90s prove disappointing to shareholders. *Wall Street Journal,* October 30: C1.

47. Mouio, A. (Ed.). 1998. Unit of one. *Fast Company,* September: 82.

48. Ibid.

49. For scholarly perspectives on the role of learning in creating value in strategic alliances, refer to Anard, B. N., & Khanna, T. 2000. Do firms learn to create value? *Strategic*

*Management Journal,* 12(3): 295–317; and Vermeulen, F., & Barkema, H. P. 2001. Learning through acquisitions. *Academy of Management Journal,* 44(3): 457–476.

50. This section draws on Hutt, M. D., Stafford, E. R., Walker, B. A., & Reingen, P. H. 2000. Case study: Defining the strategic alliance. *Sloan Management Review,* 41(2): 51–62; and Walters, B. A., Peters, S., & Dess, G. G. 1994. Strategic alliances and joint ventures: Making them work. *Business Horizons,* 4: 5–10.

51. Edmondson, G., & Reinhardt, A. 2001. From niche player to Goliath. *BusinessWeek,* March 12: 94–96.

52. Clayton, V. 2000. Lourdes Pizana's passions: Confessions and lessons of an accidental business owner. *E-Merging Business,* Fall–Winter: 73–75.

53. Hoskin, R. E. 1994. *Financial Accounting.* New York: Wiley.

54. We know stock options as derivative assets—that is, "an asset whose value depends on or is derived from the value of another, the underlying asset": Amram, M., & Kulatilaka, N. 1999. *Real options: Managing strategic investment in an uncertain world:* 34. Boston: Harvard Business School Press.

55. Neufville, R. de. 2001. Real options: Dealing with uncertainty in systems planning and design, paper presented to the Fifth International Conference on Technology Policy and Innovation at the Technical University of Delft, Delft, Netherlands, June 29.

56. For an interesting discussion on why it is difficult to "kill options," refer to Royer, I. 2003. Why bad projects are so hard to kill. *Harvard Business Review,* 81(2): 48–57.

57. Triantis, A., et al. 2003. University of Maryland roundtable on real options and corporate practice. *Journal of Applied Corporate Finance,* 15(2): 8–23.

58. Interesting insights on how CEOs use their financial preferences in making decisions is found in Prince, E. T. 2005. The fiscal behavior of CEOs. *MIT Sloan Management Review,* 46(3): 23–26.

59. For a more in-depth discussion of ROA, refer to Copeland, T. E., & Keenan, P. T. 1998. Making real options real. *McKinsey Quarterly,* 3; and Luehrman, T. A. 1998. Strategy as a portfolio of real options. *Harvard Business Review,* September–October.

60. Janney, J. J., & Dess, G. G. 2004. Can real-options analysis improve decision making? Promises and pitfalls. *Academy of Management Executive,* 18(4): 60–75.

61. This section draws on Janney, J. J., & Dess, G. G. 2004. Can real options analysis improve decision-making?

Promises and pitfalls. *Academy of Management Executive,* 18(4): 60–75. For additional insights on pitfalls of real options, consider McGrath, R. G. 1997. A real options logic for initiating technology positioning investment. *Academy of Management Review,* 22(4): 974–994; Coff, R. W., & Laverty, K. J. 2001. Real options on knowledge assets: Panacea or Pandora's box. *Business Horizons,* 73: 79, McGrath, R. G. 1999. Falling forward: Real options reasoning and entrepreneurial failure. *Academy of Management Review,* 24(1): 13–30; and, Zardkoohi, A. 2004.

62. For an understanding of the differences between how managers say they approach decisions and how they actually do, March and Shapira's discussion is perhaps the best. March, J. G., & Shapira, Z. 1987. Managerial perspectives on risk and risk-taking. *Management Science,* 33(11): 1404–1418.

63. A discussion of some factors that may lead to escalation in decision making is included in Choo, C. W. 2005. Information failures and organizational disasters. *MIT Sloan Management Review,* 46(3): 8–10.

64. For an interesting discussion of the use of real options analysis in the application of wireless communications, which helped to lower the potential for escalation, refer to McGrath, R. G., Ferrier, W. J., & Mendelow, A. L. 2004. Real options as engines of choice and heterogeneity. *Academy of Management Review,* 29(1): 86–101.

65. One very useful solution for reducing the effects of managerial conceit is to incorporate an "exit champion" into the decision process. Exit champions provide arguments for killing off the firm's commitment to a decision. For a very insightful discussion on exit champions, refer to Royer, I. 2003. Why bad projects are so hard to kill. *Harvard Business Review,* 81(2): 49–56.

66. Porter, op. cit.: 43–59.

67. Angwin, J. S., & Wingfield, N. 2000. How Jay Walker built WebHouse on a theory that he couldn't prove. *Wall Street Journal,* October 16: A1, A8.

68. *BusinessWeek.* 2003. The fallen. January 13: 80–82.

69. The Jack Welch example draws upon Sellers, P. 2001. Get over yourself. *Fortune,* April 30: 76–88.

70. Polek, D. 2002. The rise and fall of Dennis Kozlowski. *BusinessWeek,* December 23: 64–77.

71. *BusinessWeek.* 2003. op. cit.: 80.

72. This section draws on Weston, J. F., Besley, S., & Brigham, E. F. 1996. *Essentials of Managerial Finance* (11th ed.): 18–20. Fort Worth, TX: Dryden Press, Harcourt Brace.

# 7

# International Strategy:
## Creating Value in Global Markets

## >chapter objectives

*After reading this chapter, you should have a good understanding of:*

- The importance of international expansion as a viable diversification strategy.

- The sources of national advantage; that is, why an industry in a given country is more (or less) successful than the same industry in another country.

- The motivations (or benefits) and the risks associated with international expansion, including the emerging trend for greater offshoring and outsourcing activity.

- The two opposing forces—cost reduction and adaptation to local markets— that firms face when entering international markets.

- The advantages and disadvantages associated with each of the four basic strategies: international, global, multidomestic, and transnational.

- The four basic types of entry strategies and the relative benefits and risks associated with each of them.

*t*he global marketplace provides many opportunities for firms to increase their revenue base and their profitability. Furthermore, in today's knowledge-intensive economy, there is the potential to create advantages by leveraging firm knowledge when crossing national boundaries to do business. At the same time, however, there are pitfalls and risks that firms must avoid in order to be successful. In this chapter we will provide insights on how to be successful and create value when diversifying into global markets.

After some introductory comments on the global economy, we address the question: What explains the level of success of a given industry in a given country? To provide a framework for analysis, we draw on Michael Porter's "diamond of national advantage," in which he identified four factors that help to explain performance differences.

In the second section of the chapter, we shift our focus to the level of the firm and discuss some of the major motivations and risks associated with international expansion. Recognizing such potential benefits and risks enables managers to better assess the growth and profit potential in a given country. We also address important issues associated with a topic of growing interest in the international marketplace—offshoring and outsourcing.

Next, in the third section—the largest in this chapter—we address how firms can attain competitive advantages in the global marketplace. We discuss two opposing forces firms face when entering foreign markets: cost reduction and local adaptation. Depending on the intensity of each of these forces, they should select among four basic strategies: international, global, multidomestic, and transnational. We discuss both the strengths and limitations of each of these strategies.

The final section addresses the four categories of entry strategies that firms may choose in entering foreign markets. These strategies vary along a continuum from low investment, low control (exporting) to high investment, high control (wholly owned subsidiaries and greenfield ventures). We discuss the pros and cons associated with each.

Volkswagen has experienced problems with some of the new, high-priced models that it has introduced into the U.S. automobile market. This illustrates that, regardless of a firm's size or resource base, all companies face new opportunities and threats when they venture beyond the boundaries of their home nation.

A number of carmakers worldwide want to get into the luxury vehicle segment. But competition is very tough in this segment, and a high price no longer guarantees a high profit.[1] Volkswagen (VW), the European car manufacturer, also has recently jumped onto this bandwagon, and is currently in the process of transforming itself into a luxury-vehicle company. Ferdinand Piesch, VW's previous chief executive, spent hundreds of millions of dollars to acquire luxury brand names such as Lamborghini, Rolls-Royce/Bentley, and Bugatti. He also started work on VW's own line of luxury models. New production facilities had to be created for manufacturing the luxury models. VW is one of the most successful European car manufacturers in the United States, and it decided to introduce its luxury models in the United States too.

One of these models, the Touareg, launched in January 2003, is a sport utility vehicle (SUV) and costs around $35,000 to $40,000. The Phaeton, launched during the summer in 2003, costs even more—well over $60,000.

However, the results so far have not been encouraging. The Passat W-8 did not generate the excitement that was expected, and VW sold only 2,000 vehicles of this model in the United States by December 2002—much below the expected 5,000. The Phaeton is a question mark because Americans may hesitate to pay such a high price for a Volkswagen, even if the model is a credible competitor to the Mercedes S class. The Touareg's future is also not clear.

Then, there is the problem with the brand name. "The name may sound strange, but we wanted to differentiate the vehicle from everything else," says Jens Neumann, VW's board member responsible for U.S. operations. The name "Touareg" refers to a nomadic tribe in the Sahara who are known for their blue-dyed bodies and their talent for torture. This foreign name is odd and is something that Americans cannot spell or pronounce easily. It is unclear how well this name would be received by U.S. customers. But company officials seem confident. According to Volkswagen spokesman Tony Fouladpour, "Touareg is the name of a resilient, athletic African tribe known for surviving in very hostile environments, including the Sahara desert. So it's a good name for a tough, resilient sport-utility that's athletic on roads and can compete with the best off road." He adds, "Don't forget that Volkswagen is a German company, and the Touareg tribe is well known in Germany, where it's highly regarded. We will sell the Touareg sport-ute internationally and see no reason to give it a different name for America. We knew many Americans wouldn't accept that name at first, but find that many have become accustomed to it now. After all, Volkswagen has used other seemingly obscure names for our cars, such as Passat (the name of a prevailing Atlantic ocean wind), which now are widely accepted."

How have things turned out? Far fewer than the targeted 35,000 units were sold in the United States in 2004. The Touareg was outsold by many comparably equipped competitors, including the Volvo XC90, Nissan's Infiniti FX 35/45, and the Cadillac SRX. In fact, Toyota Motor's $35,000 Lexus RX 330 sold more than three times as many units as Volkswagen's model.

It seems the name "Touareg" itself was the least of Volkswagen's concerns. The major problem was really quite straightforward: price versus perceived value. Despite VW's effort to increase its stature as a luxury brand, it is fighting for the same piece of the market as other already established models by Lexus, BMW, and Mercedes-Benz. Even though the Mercedes ML model is quite dated and does not have the interior feel of the Touareg, it sells almost as well because of that big star (Mercedes' logo) on the hood. And the BMW X5, though fading because it has not been updated, still outsells the VW by several thousand units. Again, it is the "badge thing"—that is, consumers' preoccupation with a car's brand. Overall, VW sales were down 16 percent in 2004.

According to *Forbes* magazine, this is because not only has it failed to find firm footing as a luxury marquee, but also the rest of its lineup is old and uncompetitive with what is really hot in North America—mid-priced near-luxury sedans and crossovers and lower-priced crossovers.

Will Volkswagen eventually succeed in the U.S. luxury car segment? We'll have to wait and see. Some are pessimistic. Stephen Cheetham, an analyst at Sanford C. Bernstein and Co. in London, believes that Volkswagen "is facing the mother of all marketing problems."

# >>The Global Economy: A Brief Overview

In this chapter we will discuss how firms can create value and achieve competitive advantage—as well as how to avoid pitfalls—in the global marketplace. We will discuss not only the factors that can influence a nation's success in a particular industry but also how firms can become successful when they diversify by expanding the scope of their business to include international operations. But first, let's talk about some of the broader issues in the global economy.

Today's managers face many opportunities and risks when they diversify abroad.[2] As we know, the trade among nations has increased dramatically in recent years. It is estimated that by 2015, the trade *across* nations will exceed the trade within nations. And in a variety of industries such as semiconductors, automobiles, commercial aircraft, telecommunications, computers, and consumer electronics, it is virtually impossible to survive unless firms scan the world for competitors, customers, human resources, suppliers, and technology.[3]

Fred Hasan, Chairman and CEO of the $8 billion pharmaceutical giant, Schering-Plough, emphasizes the importance of such a perspective:[4]

> We have long lead times—it can take 5 to 15 years for a new product to be born. Individual product bets are into hundreds of millions, if not billions, of dollars. Once you've got an idea that's been turned into a product, you need to pay back the high cost of R&D, so you need to sell it around the world. Good ideas can come from anywhere, and good products can be sold anywhere. The more places you are, the more ideas you will get. And the more ideas you get, the more places you can sell them and the more competitive you will be. Managing in many places requires a willingness to accept good ideas no matter where they come from— which means having a global attitude.

The rise of globalization—meaning the rise of market capitalism around the world— has undeniably contributed to the economic boom in America's New Economy, where knowledge is the key source of competitive advantage and value creation. It is estimated that it has brought phone service to about 300 million households in developing nations and a transfer of nearly $2 trillion from rich countries to poor countries through equity, bond investments, and commercial loans.[5]

Without doubt, there have been extremes in the effect of global capitalism on national economies and poverty levels around the world.[6] Clearly, the economies of East Asia have attained rapid growth, but there has been comparatively little progress in the rest of the world. For example, income in Latin America grew by only 6 percent in the past two decades when the continent was opening up to global capitalism. Average incomes in sub-Saharan Africa and the old Eastern European bloc have actually declined. Indeed, the World Bank estimates that the number of people living on $1 per day has *increased* to 1.3 billion over the past decade.

Such disparities in wealth among nations raise an important question: Why do some countries and their citizens enjoy the fruits of global capitalism while others are mired in poverty? Stated differently, why do some governments make the best use of inflows of foreign investment and know-how and others do not? There are many explanations. Among these are the need of governments to have track records of business-friendly policies to attract multinationals and local entrepreneurs to train workers, invest in modern technology, and nurture local suppliers and managers. Also, it means carefully managing the broader economic factors in an economy, such as interest rates, inflation, and unemployment, as well as a good legal system that protects property rights, strong educational systems, and a society where prosperity is widely shared.

The above policies are the type that East Asia—in locations such as Hong Kong, Taiwan, South Korea, and Singapore—has employed to evolve from the sweatshop economies of the 1960s and 1970s to industrial powers today. On the other hand, many countries have moved in the other direction. For example, in Guatemala, among other unfavorable indicators, only 52.0 percent of males complete fifth grade and an astonishing 39.8 percent of the population subsists on less than $1 per day.[7] (By comparison, the corresponding numbers for South Korea are 98 percent and less than 2 percent, respectively.)

Strategy Spotlight 7.1 provides an interesting perspective on global trade—marketing to the "bottom of the pyramid." This refers to the practice of a multinational firm targeting its goods and services to the nearly 5 billion poor people in the world who inhabit developing countries. Collectively, this represents a very large market with $14 trillion in purchasing power.

In the next section, we will address in more detail the question of why some nations and their industries are more competitive. This discussion establishes an important context or setting for the remainder of the chapter. After we discuss why some *nations and their industries* outperform others, we will be better able to address the various strategies that *firms* can take to create competitive advantage when they expand internationally.

## >>Factors Affecting a Nation's Competitiveness

Michael Porter of Harvard University conducted a four-year study in which he and a team of 30 researchers looked at the patterns of competitive success in 10 leading trading nations. He concluded that there are four broad attributes of nations that individually, and as a system, constitute what is termed "the diamond of national advantage." In effect, these attributes jointly determine the playing field that each nation establishes and operates for its industries. These factors are:

- *Factor conditions.* The nation's position in factors of production, such as skilled labor or infrastructure, necessary to compete in a given industry.
- *Demand conditions.* The nature of home-market demand for the industry's product or service.
- *Related and supporting industries.* The presence or absence in the nation of supplier industries and other related industries that are internationally competitive.
- *Firm strategy, structure, and rivalry.* The conditions in the nation governing how companies are created, organized, and managed, as well as the nature of domestic rivalry.

We will now briefly discuss each of these factors.[8] Then we will provide an integrative example—the Indian software industry—to demonstrate how these attributes interact to explain India's high level of competitiveness in this industry.

# STRATEGY SPOTLIGHT

## Marketing to the "Bottom of the Pyramid"

Many executives wrongly believe that profitable opportunities to sell consumer goods exist only in countries where income levels are high. Even when they expand internationally, they often tend to limit their marketing to only the affluent segments within the developing countries. Such narrow conceptualizations of the market cause them to ignore the vast opportunities that exist at "the bottom of the pyramid," according to University of Michigan professor C. K. Prahalad. The *bottom of the pyramid* refers to the nearly 5 billion poor people who inhabit the developing countries. Surprisingly, they represent $14 trillion in purchasing power! And they are looking for products and services that can improve the quality of their lives such as clean energy, personal-care products, lighting, and medicines. Multinationals are missing out on growth opportunities if they ignore this vast segment of the market.

How can the poor buy if they do not have the money? The key is to bring the cost structures of the companies and their product offerings within the reach of the low-income customers. Unilever started marketing single serve sachets of shampoo to the poor in India several years ago. Selling for about a penny, single serve sales account for 60 percent of the total value of shampoo sold in India today! A 20-ounce shampoo bottle may cost more than a farm worker's daily income and thus may be out of her reach. However, the need for shampoo is almost universal. The challenge is to sell it in a way in which the poor can satisfy their need for shampoo.

Other innovative firms have found creative ways to serve the poor and still make a profit. Grameen Bank in Bangladesh is very different from the money center banks of London or New York. Pioneers of the concept of micro-credit, Grameen Bank extends small loans—sometimes as small as $20—to thousands of struggling micro-entrepreneurs who have no collateral to offer. Not only are their loan recovery rates comparable to big banks, but they are also changing the lives of thousands of people while making a profit as well. Casas Bahias, the Brazilian retailer, has built a $2.5 billion-a-year chain selling to the poor who live in the *favelas*, the illegal shanty towns. Another amazing example is Aravind Eye Care, an Indian hospital that specializes in cataract surgeries. Today they are the largest eye care facility in the world, performing more than 200,000 surgeries per year. The secret of their volume: The surgeries cost only about $25! A comparable surgery in the West costs $3,000. And best of all, Aravind has a return on equity of more than 75 percent!

As the above examples demonstrate, in order to sell to the bottom of the pyramid, managers must rethink their costs, quality, scale of operations, and even their use of capital. What prevents managers from selling to this vast market? Often they are victims of their own false assumptions. First, they think that the poor have no purchasing power. But $14 trillion can buy a lot. Second, they assume that poor people have no need for new technologies. We only have to see the demand for cell phones from entrepreneurs who run microbusinesses in villages in India to dispel this myth. Third, they assume that the poor have no use for their products and services. Shampoo, detergents, and banking satisfy universal needs, not just the needs of the rich. Fourth, they assume that managers may not be excited about working in these markets. Recent experience shows that this may be a more exciting environment than dogs fighting for fractions of market shares in the mature markets of the developed countries.

No one is helped by viewing the poor as the wretched of the earth. Instead, they are the latest frontier of opportunity for those who can meet their needs. A vast market that is barely tapped, the bottom of the pyramid offers enormous opportunities.

Sources: Prahalad, C. K. 2004. Why selling to the poor makes for good business. *Fortune,* 150(9): 32–33; Overholt, A. 2005. A new path to profit. *Fast Company,* January: 25–26; and Prahalad, C. K. 2005. *The fortune at the bottom of the pyramid: Eradicating poverty through profits.* Philadelphia: Wharton School Publishing.

## Factor Conditions[9]

Classical economics suggests that factors of production such as land, labor, and capital are the building blocks that create usable consumer goods and services.[10] But this tells only part of the story when we consider the global aspects of economic growth. Companies in advanced nations seeking competitive advantage over firms in other nations *create* many of the factors of production. For example, a country or industry dependent on scientific innovation must have a skilled human resource pool to draw upon. This resource pool is not inherited; it is created through investment in industry-specific knowledge and talent. The supporting infrastructure of a country—that is, its transportation and communication systems as well as its banking system—are also critical.

To achieve competitive advantage, factors of production must be developed that are industry and firm specific. In addition, the pool of resources a firm or a country has at its disposal is less important than the speed and efficiency with which these resources are deployed. Thus, firm-specific knowledge and skills created within a country that are rare, valuable, difficult to imitate, and rapidly and efficiently deployed are the factors of production that ultimately lead to a nation's competitive advantage.

For example, the island nation of Japan has little land mass, making the warehouse space needed to store inventory prohibitively expensive. But by pioneering just-in-time inventory management, Japanese companies managed to create a resource from which they gained advantage over companies in other nations that spent large sums to warehouse inventory.

## Demand Conditions

Demand conditions refer to the demands that consumers place on an industry for goods and services. Consumers who demand highly specific, sophisticated products and services force firms to create innovative, advanced products and services to meet the demand. This consumer pressure presents challenges to a country's industries. But in response to these challenges, improvements to existing goods and services often result, creating conditions necessary for competitive advantage over firms in other countries.

Demanding consumers push firms to move ahead of companies in other countries where consumers are less demanding and more complacent. Countries with demanding consumers drive firms in that country to meet high standards, upgrade existing products and services, and create innovative products and services. Thus, the conditions of consumer demand influence how firms view a market, with more demanding consumers stimulating advances in products and services. This in turn helps a nation's industries to better anticipate future global demand conditions and proactively respond to product and service requirements before competing nations are even aware of the need for such products and services.

Denmark, for instance, is known for its environmental awareness. Demand from consumers for environmentally safe products has spurred Danish manufacturers to become leaders in water pollution control equipment—products it successfully exports to other nations.

## Related and Supporting Industries

Related and supporting industries enable firms to manage inputs more effectively. For example, countries with a strong supplier base benefit by adding efficiency to downstream activities. A competitive supplier base helps a firm obtain inputs using cost-effective, timely methods, thus reducing manufacturing costs. Also, close working relationships with suppliers provide the potential to develop competitive advantages through joint research and development and the ongoing exchange of knowledge, helping both suppliers and manufacturers.

Related industries offer similar opportunities through joint efforts among firms. In addition, related industries create the probability that new entrants will enter the market, increasing competition and forcing existing firms to become more competitive through efforts such as cost control, product innovation, and novel approaches to distribution. Combined, these give the home country's industries a source of competitive advantage over less competitive nations.

In the Italian footwear industry the supporting industries show how they can lead to national competitive advantage. In Italy, shoe manufacturers are geographically located near their suppliers. The manufacturers have ongoing interactions with leather suppliers and learn about new textures, colors, and manufacturing techniques while a shoe is still in the prototype stage. The manufacturers are able to project future demand and gear their factories for new products long before companies in other nations become aware of the new styles. Similarly, geographic proximity of industries related to the pharmaceutical industry (e.g., the dye industry) in Switzerland has given that nation a leadership position in this market, with firms such as Ciba-Geigy, Hoffman LaRoche, and Sandoz using dyes from local manufacturers in many pharmaceutical products.

## Firm Strategy, Structure, and Rivalry

Rivalry is particularly intense in nations with conditions of strong consumer demand, strong supplier bases, and high new entrant potential from related industries. This competitive rivalry in turn increases the efficiency with which firms develop, market, and distribute products and services within the home country. Domestic rivalry thus provides a strong impetus for firms to innovate and find new sources of competitive advantage.

Interestingly, this intense rivalry forces firms to look outside their national boundaries for new markets, setting up the conditions necessary for global competitiveness. Among all the points on Porter's diamond of national advantage, domestic rivalry is perhaps the strongest indicator of global competitive success. Firms that have experienced intense domestic competition are more likely to have designed strategies and structures that allow them to successfully compete in world markets.

In the United States, for example, intense rivalry has spurred companies such as Dell Computer to find innovative ways to produce and distribute its products. This is largely a result of competition from IBM and Hewlett-Packard.

Strategy Spotlight 7.2 discusses India's software industry. It provides an integrative example of how Porter's "diamond" can help to explain the relative degree of success of an industry in a given country.

## Concluding Comment on Factors Affecting a Nation's Competitiveness

Porter drew his conclusions based on case histories of firms in more than 100 industries. Despite the differences in strategies employed by successful global competitors, a common theme did emerge: Firms that succeeded in global markets had first succeeded in intense competition in their home markets. We can conclude that competitive advantage for global firms typically grows out of relentless, continuing improvement, innovation, and change.

Now that we have talked about the important role that nations play in international strategy, let's turn to the level of the individual firm.[11] In the next section, we will discuss a company's motivations and the risks associated with international expansion.

# >>International Expansion: A Company's Motivations and Risks

## Motivations for International Expansion

As you would expect, there are many motivations for a company to pursue international expansion. The most obvious one is to *increase the size of potential markets* for a firm's products and services.[12] By the middle of 2005, the world's population approached

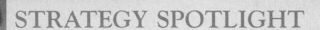

# STRATEGY SPOTLIGHT

## India and the Diamond of National Advantage

Consider the following facts:

- SAP, the German software company, has developed new applications for notebook PCs at its 500-engineer Bangladore facility.

- General Electric plans to invest $100 million and hire 2,600 scientists to create the world's largest research and development lab in Bangalore, India.

- Microsoft plans to invest $400 million in new research partnerships in India.

- Over one-fifth of Fortune 1000 companies outsource their software requirements to firms in India.

- McKinsey & Co. projects that the Indian software and services industry will be an $87 billion business by 2008; $50 billion of this will be exported.

- For the past decade, the Indian software industry has grown at a 50 percent annual rate.

- More than 800 firms in India are involved in software services as their primary activity.

- Software and information technology firms in India are projected to employ 2.2 million people by 2008.

What is causing such global interest in India's software services industry? Porter's diamond of national advantage helps clarify this question. See Exhibit 7.1.

First, *factor conditions* are conducive to the rise of India's software industry. Through investment in human resource development with a focus on industry-specific knowledge, India's universities and software firms have literally created this essential factor of production. *(continued)*

Sources: Kripalani, M. 2002. Calling Bangalore: Multinationals are making it a hub for high-tech research *BusinessWeek,* November 25: 52–54; Kapur, D., & Ramamurti, R. 2001. India's emerging competitive advantage in services. 2001. *Academy of Management Executive,* 15(2): 20–33; World Bank. *World development report:* 6. New York: Oxford University Press. Reuters. 2001. Oracle in India push, taps software talent. *Washington Post Online,* July 3.

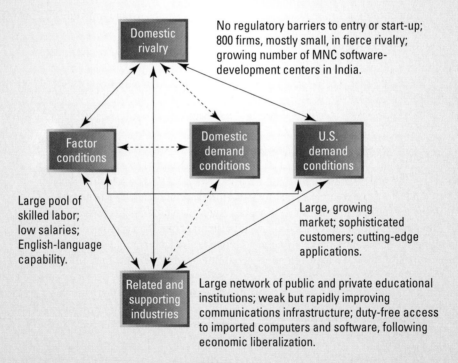

No regulatory barriers to entry or start-up; 800 firms, mostly small, in fierce rivalry; growing number of MNC software-development centers in India.

Large pool of skilled labor; low salaries; English-language capability.

Large, growing market; sophisticated customers; cutting-edge applications.

Large network of public and private educational institutions; weak but rapidly improving communications infrastructure; duty-free access to imported computers and software, following economic liberalization.

Note: Dashed lines represent weaker interactions.

**Exhibit 7.1** *India's Diamond in Software*

Source: From Kampur D. and Ramamurti R., "India's Emerging Competition Advantage in Services," *Academy of Management Executive: The Thinking Manager's Source* Copyright © 2001 by Academy of Management. Reproduced with permission of Academy of Management via Copyright Clearance Center.

*(continued)* For example, India produces the second largest annual output of scientists and engineers in the world, behind only the United States. In a knowledge-intensive industry such as software, development of human resources is fundamental to both domestic and global success.

Second, *demand conditions* require that software firms stay on the cutting edge of technological innovation. India has already moved toward globalization of its software industry; consumer demand conditions in developed nations such as Germany, Denmark, parts of Southeast Asia, and the United States created the consumer demand necessary to propel India's software makers toward sophisticated software solutions.*

Third, India has the *supplier base as well as the related industries* needed to drive competitive rivalry and

* Although India's success cannot be explained in terms of its home market demand (according to Porter's model), the nature of the industry enables software to be transferred among different locations simultaneously by way of communications links. Thus, competitiveness of markets outside India can be enhanced without a physical presence in those markets.

enhance competitiveness. In particular, information technology (IT) hardware prices declined rapidly in the 1990s. Furthermore, rapid technological change in IT hardware meant that latecomers like India were not locked into older-generation technologies. Thus, both the IT hardware and software industries could "leapfrog" older technologies. In addition, relationships among knowledge workers in these IT hardware and software industries offer the social structure for ongoing knowledge exchange, promoting further enhancement of existing products. Further infrastructure improvements are occurring rapidly.

Fourth, with over 800 firms in the software services industry in India, *intense rivalry forces firms to develop competitive strategies and structures.* Although firms like TCS, Infosys, and Wipro have become large, they were quite small only five years ago. And dozens of small and midsized companies are aspiring to catch up. This intense rivalry is one of the primary factors driving Indian software firms to develop overseas distribution channels, as predicted by Porter's diamond of national advantage.

6.5 billion, with the United States representing less than 5 percent. Exhibit 7.2 lists the population of the United States compared to other major markets abroad.

Many multinational firms are intensifying their efforts to market their products and services to countries such as India and China as the ranks of their middle class have increased over the past decade. These include Procter & Gamble's success in achieving a 50 percent share in China's shampoo market as well as PepsiCo's impressive inroads in the Indian soft-drink market.[13] Strategy Spotlight 7.3 discusses the opportunities that are presented by China's emerging middle class.

Expanding a firm's global presence also automatically increases its scale of operations, providing it with a larger revenue and asset base. As we noted in Chapter 5 in discussing overall cost leadership strategies, such an increase in revenues and asset base potentially enables a firm to *attain economies of scale*. This provides multiple benefits. One advantage is the spreading of fixed costs such as research and development over a larger volume of production. Examples would include the sale of Boeing's commercial aircraft and Microsoft's operating systems in many foreign countries.

| Country | May 2005 (estimated) |
|---|---|
| China | 1,305,034,000 |
| India | 1,077,886,000 |
| United States | 295,280,000 |
| Japan | 127,418,000 |
| Germany | 82,438,000 |
| World Total | 6,379,157,000 |
| Source: www.geohive.com/global/pop_data2.php. | |

**Exhibit 7.2**
**Populations of Selected Nations and the World**

# STRATEGY SPOTLIGHT

## 7.3

### The Opportunities Presented by China's Emerging Middle Class

For many years, Western companies have dreamed of selling to China's 1.3 billion people, only to find out that not enough Chinese can afford their foreign goods. However, China's middle class has finally attained a critical mass—between 35 million and 200 million people, depending on whose definition you prefer. The larger number is preferred by Fan Gong, director of China's National Economic Research Institute, who fixes the lower boundary of "middle" as a family income of $10,000.

Sociologist Bao Degong of China's Northeast University puts the number at about 80 million. He says that the middle class people are primarily found in the coastal areas where the economy rapidly develops. In particular, they tend to be owners of small and medium private enterprises as well as the new and high-tech specialists. The central government's emphasis on science and technologies has boosted the rapid development of higher education, which is the incubator of the middle class, claims Bao.

John Chen, chief executive of American software maker Sybase, whose Chinese revenue has doubled in three years to $40 million, sells to businesses that sell to the new consumers. Chen asserts that "The middle class is really taking off. It is now worth selling one widget to every Chinese who can afford it."

What is happening in China may be viewed as a new example of economies of scale. Many American companies already have factories in China exporting goods. Now that there is a domestic market to go along with the export market, those factories can increase their output with little additional cost. That is one reason why many foreign companies' profits in China have been so strong in recent years.

Consider Kodak. It invested $1.2 billion in China in 1998, planning on a 10- or 12-year payback period. However, Kodak initially overestimated the Chinese market. In the early years domestic demand for cameras and film was well below company forecasts and China operations were in the red, says Ying Yeh, a Chinese-born American and chairman of Kodak's Greater China region. Things have turned around. In recent years, Kodak's sales in China have climbed from very little to a first-place position in the market. In fact, revenues grew 40 percent in the first half of 2004 and the company says it is now ahead of its plan to recoup its investment, with China's profit margins on par with those worldwide. Not surprisingly, China has really helped on the cost side—95 percent of Kodak cameras are made there, some by contract manufacturers but most in its Shanghai factory, which runs three shifts a day.

Sources: Meredith, R. 2004. Middle kingdom, middle class. *Forbes*, November 15: 188–192; and Anonymous. 2004. Middle class becomes rising power in China. www.Chinadaily.com, November 6.

A second advantage would be *reducing the costs of research and development as well as operating costs.* Recall, for example, the establishment of software development operations by Microsoft and other firms in talent-rich India (see Strategy Spotlight 7.2). A final advantage would be the attainment of greater purchasing power by pooling purchases. For example, as McDonald's increases the number of outlets it has all over the world, it is able to place larger orders for equipment and supplies, thus increasing its bargaining power with suppliers.

International expansion can also *extend the life cycle of a product* that is in its maturity stage in a firm's home country but that has greater demand potential elsewhere. As we noted in Chapter 5, products (and industries) generally go through a four-stage life cycle of introduction, growth, maturity, and decline. In recent decades, U.S. soft-drink producers such as Coca-Cola and PepsiCo have aggressively pursued international markets to attain levels of growth that simply would not be available in the United States. Similarly, personal computer manufacturers such as Dell and Hewlett-Packard have sought out foreign markets to offset the growing saturation in the U.S. market. The worldwide automobile industry is also intensely competitive. Firms such as General Motors and Ford have invested billions of dollars in Latin America in an effort to capture market share in that growing market.

Finally, international expansion can enable a firm to *optimize the physical location for every activity in its value chain.* Recall from our discussions in Chapters 3 and 5 that the value chain represents the various activities in which all firms must engage to produce products and services. They include primary activities, such as inbound logistics, operations, and marketing, as well as support activities, such as procurement, research and development, and human resource management. All firms have to make critical decisions as to where each activity will take place.[14] Optimizing the location for every activity in the value chain can yield one or more of three strategic advantages: performance enhancement, cost reduction, and risk reduction. We will now discuss each of these.

*Performance Enhancement*    Microsoft's decision to establish a corporate research laboratory in Cambridge, England, is an example of a location decision that was guided mainly by the goal of building and sustaining world-class excellence in selected value-creating activities.[15] This strategic decision provided Microsoft with access to outstanding technical and professional talent. Location decisions can affect the quality with which any activity is performed in terms of the availability of needed talent, speed of learning, and the quality of external and internal coordination.

*Cost Reduction*    Two location decisions founded largely on cost-reduction considerations are (1) Nike's decision to source the manufacture of athletic shoes from Asian countries such as China, Vietnam, and Indonesia, and (2) the decision of many multinational companies to set up production operations just south of the United States–Mexico border to access lower-cost labor. These operations are called *maquiladoras*. Such location decisions can affect the cost structure in terms of local manpower and other resources, transportation and logistics, and government incentives and the local tax structure.

Performance enhancement and cost-reduction benefits parallel the business-level strategies (discussed in Chapter 5) of differentiation and overall cost leadership. They can at times be attained simultaneously. Consider our example in the previous section on the Indian software industry. When Oracle set up a development operation in that country, the company benefited both from lower labor costs and operational expenses as well as from performance enhancements realized through the hiring of superbly talented professionals.

Managing across borders can lead to challenging ethical dilemmas. One issue that has received a good deal of attention in the recent business press is the issue of child labor. Strategy Spotlight 7.4 discusses how two multinational companies have taken different approaches to address this issue.

*Risk Reduction*    Given the erratic swings in the exchange ratios between the U.S. dollar and the Japanese yen (in relation to each other as well as other major currencies), an important basis for cost competition between Ford and Toyota has been their relative ingenuity at managing currency risks. One of the ways for such competitors to manage currency risks has been to spread the high-cost elements of their manufacturing operations across a few select and carefully chosen locations around the world. Location decisions such as these can affect the overall risk profile of the firm with respect to currency, economic, and political risks.[16]

## Potential Risks of International Expansion

When a company expands its international operations, it does so to increase its profits or revenues. As with any other investment, however, there are potential risks to accompany the anticipated returns.[17] To help companies assess the risk of entering foreign markets, rating systems have been developed to evaluate political, economic, and financial and credit risks.[18] *Euromoney* magazine publishes a semiannual "Country Risk Rating" that evaluates political, economic, and other risks that entrants potentially face. Exhibit 7.3 depicts a sample of country risk ratings, published by the World Bank, from the 178

# STRATEGY SPOTLIGHT

## Child Labor: How Two Companies Have Addressed This Issue

It is interesting to consider how multinational companies have taken different approaches to address the issue of child labor in their overseas operations. Nike, for example, has revised its code of conduct a few times since 1992, including increasing the minimum age from 14 to 18 years for footwear factory workers and from 14 to 16 for equipment and apparel, which is quite a bit higher than other company codes and the International Labor Organization's (ILO) convention. The company also has started an internal compliance program, supplemented with external monitoring. However, this does not seem to have silenced the staunchest critics. Nike's Web site reflects the way in which the company tries to openly address this critique, providing ample information about the monitoring of facilities and the dilemmas the company faces after the introduction of its latest code.

Chiquita Banana almost completely follows the SA 8000 standard, including all references to international conventions, but with a few modifications, primarily to take account of workplace issues specific to agriculture. (The SA 8000 standard is developed by the Council on Economic Priorities Accreditation Agency and is widely recognized and accepted. It is based on ILO and United Nations conventions.) The company's strict child labor provisions do not apply to family farms or to small-scale holdings in the seasonal, nonbanana business, which do not regularly employ hired workers. This is also meant to allow for employment of a farmer's own children in seasonal activities. In line with its standard, Chiquita Banana tries to address the problem associated with children found to be working in supplying factories by giving "adequate support to enable such children to attend and remain in school until no longer a child."

Source: Kolk, A., & Tulder, R. V. 2004. Ethics in international business: Multinational approaches to child labor. *Journal of World Business,* 39: 49–60.

countries that *Euromoney* evaluates. In the exhibit, note that the lower the score, the higher the country's expected level of risk.

Next we will discuss the four main types of risk: political risk, economic risk, currency risk, and management risk.

*Political and Economic Risk*   Generally speaking, the business climate in the United States is very favorable. However, some countries around the globe may be

**Exhibit 7.3**

**A Sample of International Country Risk Rankings**

| Rank | Country | Total Risk Assessment | Economic Performance | Political Risk | Total of Debt Indicators | Total of Credit and Access to Finance Indicators |
|------|---------|-----------------------|----------------------|----------------|--------------------------|--------------------------------------------------|
| 1 | Luxembourg | 99.51 | 25.00 | 24.51 | 20.00 | 30.00 |
| 2 | Switzerland | 98.84 | 23.84 | 25.00 | 20.00 | 30.00 |
| 3 | United States | 98.37 | 23.96 | 24.41 | 20.00 | 30.00 |
| 40 | China | 71.27 | 18.93 | 16.87 | 19.73 | 15.74 |
| 55 | Poland | 57.12 | 18.56 | 13.97 | 9.36 | 15.23 |
| 63 | Vietnam | 52.04 | 14.80 | 11.91 | 18.51 | 6.82 |
| 86 | Russia | 42.62 | 11.47 | 8.33 | 17.99 | 4.83 |
| 114 | Albania | 34.23 | 8.48 | 5.04 | 19.62 | 1.09 |
| 161 | Mozambique | 21.71 | 3.28 | 2.75 | 13.85 | 1.83 |
| 178 | Afghanistan | 3.92 | 0.00 | 3.04 | 0.00 | 0.88 |

Source: Adapted from worldbank.org/html/prddr/trans/so96/art7.htm.

hazardous to the health of corporate initiatives because of political risk.[19] Forces such as social unrest, military turmoil, demonstrations, and even violent conflict and terrorism can pose serious threats.[20] Consider, for example, the ongoing tension and violence in the Middle East between Israelis and Palestinians, and the social and political unrest in Indonesia and Iraq.[21] Because such conditions increase the likelihood of destruction of property and disruption of operations as well as nonpayment for goods and services, countries that are viewed as high risk are less attractive for most types of business. Typical exceptions include providers of munitions and counterintelligence services.

The laws, as well as the enforcement of laws, associated with the protection of intellectual property rights can be a significant potential risk in entering new countries. Microsoft, for example, has lost billions of dollars in potential revenue through piracy of its software products in many countries, including China. Other areas of the globe, such as the former Soviet Union and some eastern European nations, have piracy problems as well. Firms rich in intellectual property have encountered financial losses as imitations of their products have grown due to a lack of law enforcement of intellectual property rights.[22]

Strategy Spotlight 7.5 discusses a problem that presents a severe threat to global trade— piracy. As we will see, estimates are that counterfeiting accounts for between 5 percent and 7 percent of global merchandise trade—the equivalent of as much as $512 billion a year. And the potential corrosive effects include health and safety, not just economic, damage.

*Currency Risks*   Currency fluctuations can pose substantial risks. A company with operations in several countries must constantly monitor the exchange rate between its own currency and that of the host country. Even a small change in the exchange rate can result in a significant difference in the cost of production or net profit when doing business overseas. When the U.S. dollar appreciates against other currencies, for example, U.S. goods can be more expensive to consumers in foreign countries. At the same time, however, appreciation of the U.S. dollar can have negative implications for American companies that have branch operations overseas. The reason for this is that profits from abroad must be exchanged for dollars at a more expensive rate of exchange, reducing the amount of profit when measured in dollars. For example, consider an American firm doing business in Italy. If this firm had a 20 percent profit in euros at its Italian center of operations, this profit would be totally wiped out when converted into U.S. dollars if the euro had depreciated 20 percent against the U.S. dollar. (U.S. multinationals typically engage in sophisticated "hedging strategies" to minimize currency risk. The discussion of this is beyond the scope of this section.)

It is important to note that even when government intervention is well intended, the macroeconomic effects of such action can be very negative for multinational corporations. Such was the case in 1997 when Thailand suddenly chose to devalue its currency, the baht, after months of trying to support it at an artificially high level. This, in effect, made the baht worthless compared to other currencies. And in 1998 Russia not only devalued its ruble but also elected not to honor its foreign debt obligations.

*Management Risks*   Management risks may be considered the challenges and risks that managers face when they must respond to the inevitable differences that they encounter in foreign markets (as was the case in our opening example of Volkswagen). These take a variety of forms: culture, customs, language, income levels, customer preferences, distribution systems, and so on.[23] As we will note later in the chapter, even in the case of apparently standard products, some degree of local adaptation will become necessary.

Differences in cultures across countries can also pose unique challenges for managers.[24] Cultural symbols can evoke deep feelings.[25] For example, in a series of advertisements aimed at Italian vacationers, Coca-Cola executives turned the Eiffel Tower, Empire State

## Piracy: A Key Threat to World Trade

From the Barbary pirates to the rumrunners of Prohibition to today's e-mail spammers, every period has its unique form of economic criminal: People who flout or break the rules of commerce for their own economic gain. Such problems cannot be eliminated, but a successful society keeps them under control.

By that measure, the era of globalization may be facing one of its greatest challenges. The rapid expansion of manufacturing capability in developed countries, notably China, has raised incomes and boosted trade around the world. But the same production and distribution also have created a threatening phenomenon—an ever-rising flood of counterfeits and fakes coming onto world markets.

What products are involved? Kiwi Shoe Polish, Callaway Golf clubs, Intel computer chips, Bosch power drills, BP oil. We could pick any product from any well-known brand, and the chances are pretty good that there is a counterfeit version of it. Of course, this is not a new phenomenon. Fakes have been around for decades. And only the most naïve person would think that the $20 Rolex watch on Silom Road in Bangkok or the $30 Louis Vuitton bag on New York's Canal Street are genuine.

However, counterfeiting has grown up and has become a major threat to multinational corporations. "We've seen a massive increase in the last five years, and there is a risk that it will spiral out of control," claims Anthony Simon, marketing chief of Unilever Bestfoods. "It is no longer a cottage industry."

The figures are astounding. The World Customs Organization estimates that counterfeiting accounts for about 5 percent to 7 percent of global merchandise trade—equivalent to as much as $512 billion. Seizures of fakes by United States customs jumped 46 percent last year as counterfeiters boosted exports to Western markets. Unilever Groups says that knockoffs of its shampoos, soaps, and teas are growing at a rate of 30 percent annually.

Such counterfeiting can also have health and safety implications as well. The World Health Organization says up to 10 percent of medicines worldwide are counterfeit—a deadly hazard that could be costing the pharmaceutical industry $46 billion a year. "You won't die from purchasing a pair of counterfeit blue jeans or a counterfeit golf club. You can die from taking counterfeit pharmaceutical products. And there's no doubt that people have died in China from bad medicine," says John Theirault, head of global security for American pharmaceutical giant, Pfizer. And,

sadly, cases like the one in China, where fake baby formula recently killed 60 infants, have investigators stepping up enforcement at U.S. ports. Injuries from overheating counterfeit cell phone batteries purchased right on Verizon store shelves sparked a recall. According to Hal Stratton, of the Consumer Product Safety Commission, "We know of at least one apartment fire that's occurred. We know of at least one burn situation of someone's face that's occurred." And bogus car parts are a $12 billion market worldwide. "Counterfeiting has gone from a local nuisance to a global threat," says Hanns Glatz, DaimlerChrysler's point man on intellectual property.

China is the key to any solution. Given the country's economic power, its counterfeiting is turning into quite the problem itself, accounting for nearly two-thirds of all fake and pirated goods worldwide. Dan Chow, a law professor at Ohio State University who specializes in Chinese counterfeiting provides some perspective: "We have never seen a problem of this size and magnitude in world history. There's more counterfeiting going on in China now than we've ever seen anywhere. We know that 15 to 20 percent of all goods in China are counterfeit."

As more Chinese interests have seen profits suffer because of counterfeiting, there may be a tougher response from Beijing. For example, Li-Ning Co., China's number one homegrown athletic footwear and apparel company, has gotten the ultimate compliment from counterfeiters: They're faking its shoes. So today, Li-Ning has three full-time employees who track counterfeiters. The state tobacco monopoly is conducting joint raids with big international tobacco companies, since counterfeiters have started cranking out Double Happiness, Chunghwa, and other Chinese brands. And the government is finally realizing that piracy, which accounts for 92 percent of all software used in the mainland, isn't just setting back the likes of Microsoft Corp. "Piracy is a big problem for the development of the local software industry," says Victor Zhang, senior representative for China of the Business Software Alliance, an industry group. Some fear that Western companies may cut research spending in China if the mainland doesn't crack down.

China, of course, is not alone. Counterfeiting continues to spread. According to *BusinessWeek,* Pakistan and Russia are huge producers of fake pharmaceuticals; while in Italy an estimated 10 percent of all designer clothing is fake, much of it produced locally. Gangs in Paraguay funnel phony cosmetics, designer jeans, and toys from China to the rest of South America. And Bulgarians are masters at bootlegging U.S. liquor brands. This is one fight that will take years to win.

Source: Balfour, F. 2005. Fake! *BusinessWeek,* February 7: 54–64; Anonymous. 2005. Editorial. *BusinessWeek.* February 7: 96; and Simon, B. 2004. The world's greatest fakes. www.cbsnews.com, August 8.

Exhibit 7.4
**How Culture Varies
across Nations:
Implications for
Business**

### Ecuador:

- Dinners at Ecuadorian homes last for many hours. Expect drinks and appetizers around 8:00 p.m., with dinner not served until 11:00 p.m. or midnight. You will dismay your hosts if you leave as early as 1:00 a.m. A party at an Ecuadorian home will begin late and end around 4:00 a.m. or 5:00 a.m. Late guests may sometimes be served breakfast before they leave.

### France:

- Most English-speaking French have studied British-style English, which can lead to communication breakdowns with speakers of American-style English. For example, in the United States a presentation that "bombs" has failed, but in England it has succeeded.
- Words in French and English may have the same roots but different meanings or connotations. For example, a French person might "demand" something because *demander* in French means "to ask."

### Hong Kong:

- Negotiations occur over cups of tea. Always accept an offer of tea whether you want it or not. When you are served, wait for the host to drink first.
- Chinese negotiators commonly use teacups as visual aids. One cup may be used to represent your company, another cup to represent the Hong Kong company, and the position of the cups will be changed to indicate how far apart the companies are on the terms of an agreement.

### Singapore:

- Singaporeans associate all of the following with funerals—do not give them as gifts:
  - (a) Straw sandals
  - (b) Clocks
  - (c) A stork or crane
  - (d) Handkerchiefs (they symbolize sadness or weeping)
  - (e) Gifts or wrapping paper where the predominant color is white, black, or blue.
- Also avoid any gifts of knives, scissors, or cutting tools; to the Chinese they suggest the severing of a friendship. If you're giving flowers, give an even number of flowers—an odd number would be very unlucky.

Source: Morrison, T., Conaway, W., & Borden, G. 1994. *Kiss, bow, or shake hands.* Avon, MA: Adams Media; and www.executiveplanet.com/business-culture/112565157281.html.

Building, and the Tower of Pisa into the familiar Coke bottle. So far, so good. However, when the white marble columns of the Parthenon that crowns the Acropolis in Athens were turned into Coke bottles, the Greeks became outraged. Why? Greeks refer to the Acropolis as the "holy rock," and a government official said the Parthenon is an "international symbol of excellence" and that "whoever insults the Parthenon insults international culture." Coca-Cola apologized for the ad. Exhibit 7.4 demonstrates how cultures

At times, a lack of understanding and awareness of local customs can provide some frustrating and embarrassing situations. Such customs can raise issues that must be taken into account in order to make good decisions.

For example, consider the unique problem that Larry Henderson, plant manager, and John Lichthental, manager of human resources, were faced with when they

Source: Harvey, M., & Buckley, M. R. 2002. Assessing the "conventional wisdoms" of management for the 21st century organization. *Organizational Dynamics*, 30(4): 368–378.

were assigned by Celanese Chemical Corp. to build a new plant in Singapore. The $125 million plant was completed in July, but according to local custom, a plant should only be christened on "lucky" days. Unfortunately, the next "lucky" day was not until September 3.

Henderson and Lichthental had to convince executives at Celanese's Dallas headquarters to delay the plant opening. It wasn't easy. But after many heated telephone conversations and flaming e-mails, the president agreed to open the new plant on the "lucky" day—September 3.

vary across countries and some of the implications for the conduct of business across national boundaries.

Strategy Spotlight 7.6 addresses a rather humorous example of how a local custom can affect operations at a manufacturing plant.

Thus far, we have addressed several of the motivations and risks associated with international expansion. A major trend in recent years has been the dispersion of the value chains of multinational corporations across different countries; that is, the various activities that constitute the value chain of a firm are now spread across several countries and continents. Such dispersion of value occurs mainly through increasing offshoring and outsourcing. Next we address some of the primary benefits and costs associated with this new trend.

### Global Dispersion of Value Chains: Outsourcing and Offshoring

A report issued by the World Trade Organization describes the production of a particular U.S. car as follows: "30 percent of the car's value goes to Korea for assembly, 17.5 percent to Japan for components and advanced technology, 7.5 percent to Germany for design, 4 percent to Taiwan and Singapore for minor parts, 2.5 percent to U.K. for advertising and marketing services, and 1.5% to Ireland and Barbados for data processing. This means that only 37 percent of the production value is generated in the U.S."[26] Similarly, in the production of a Barbie doll, Mattel purchases plastic and hair from Taiwan and Japan, the molds from the United States, the doll clothing from China, and paint from the U.S. and assembles the product in Indonesia and Malaysia for sales worldwide. In today's economy these are not isolated examples. Instead, we are increasingly witnessing two interrelated trends: *outsourcing and offshoring. Outsourcing* occurs when a firm decides to utilize other firms to perform value-creating activities that were previously performed in-house.[27] In some cases, it may be a new activity that the firm is perfectly capable of doing, but it still chooses to have someone else perform the function for cost or quality reasons. Outsourcing can be to either a domestic company or a foreign firm.

*Offshoring* takes place when a firm decides to shift an activity that they were previously performing in a domestic location to a foreign location. For example, both Microsoft and Intel now have R&D facilities in India, employing a large number of

Indian scientists and engineers. In many cases, offshoring and outsourcing go together; that is, a firm may outsource an activity to a foreign supplier, thereby causing the work to be offshored as well.

The recent explosion in the volume of outsourcing and offshoring is due to a variety of factors. Up until the 1960s, for most companies, the entire value chain was in one location. Further, the production took place close to where the customers were in order to keep transportation costs under control. In the case of service industries, it was generally believed that offshoring was not possible because the producer and consumer had to be present at the same place at the same time. After all, a haircut could not be performed if the barber and the client were separated!

In the case of manufacturing industries, the rapid decline in transportation and coordination costs has enabled firms to disperse their value chains over different locations. For example, Nike's R&D takes place in the United States, raw materials are procured from a multitude of countries, actual manufacturing takes place in China or Indonesia, advertising is produced in the United States, and sales and service take place in practically all the countries. Each value-creating activity is performed in the location where the cost is the lowest or the quality is the best. Without finding optimal locations for each activity and the resultant dispersion of the value chain, Nike could not have attained its position as the world's largest shoe company.

The experience of the manufacturing sector was repeated in the service sector as well by the mid-1990s. A trend that began with the outsourcing of low-level programming and data entry work to countries such as India and Ireland suddenly grew manyfold, encompassing a variety of white collar and professional activities ranging from call-centers to R&D. Today, the technical support lines of a large number of U.S. companies are answered from call centers in faraway locations. The cost of a long distance call from the United States to India has come down from about $3 to $0.03 in the last 20 years, thereby making it possible to have call centers located in countries like India where a combination of low labor costs and English proficiency presents an ideal mix of factor conditions. Bangalore, India, in recent years, has emerged as a location where more and more U.S. tax returns are prepared. Sitting in India, U.S.-trained and licensed radiologists interpret chest X-rays and CT scans from U.S. hospitals for half the cost. The advantages from offshoring go beyond mere cost savings today. In many specialized occupations in science and engineering, there is a shortage of qualified professionals in developed countries whereas countries like India, China, and Singapore have what seems like an inexhaustible supply.[28]

For most of the 20th century, domestic companies catered to the needs of local populations. However, with the increasing homogenization of customer needs around the world and the institutionalization of free trade and investment as a global ideology (especially after the creation of the WTO), competition has become truly global. Each company has to keep its costs low in order to survive global competition. They also must find the best suppliers and the most skilled workers. Further, they have to locate each stage of the value chain in places where factor conditions are most conducive. Thus, outsourcing and offshoring are no longer mere options to consider, but an imperative for competitive survival for today's multinationals.

While there is a compelling logic for companies to engage in offshoring, there are many pitfalls associated with it. Strategy Spotlight 7.7 discusses the experience of Misiu Systems, a U.S. alarm systems manufacturer that found out the hard way that offshoring is not for everyone.

Let's now look at how firms can attain competitive advantages when they move beyond the boundaries of their home nation.

## Misiu Systems: Outsourcing Is Not for Everyone

When Todd Hodgen, CEO of Misiu Systems, a Bothell, Washington–based manufacturer of alarm systems, learned that he could save 65 percent of his design costs by outsourcing it to a Taiwanese firm, he was really excited. In addition to cost savings, an added bonus was that the Taiwanese engineers would be working after Misiu's engineers had gone home because of the time differences. This meant that the product development cycle could be greatly accelerated. For a start-up financed mostly with loans from friends and family, the twin advantages of cost savings and reduced cycle time were too much to resist.

After several months of discussions with the contractor and a visit to Taiwan, Hodgen signed the outsourcing agreement. However, things did not quite work out as he had expected. His feedback to the design team in Taiwan often went unheeded. The design was eventually delivered eight months late and the quality fell well short of expectations. Why? The Taiwanese engineers who were supposed to be working solely for him were also working for other clients. Business from a small firm like Misiu was not given the same priority that was given to bigger clients. Eventually Hodgen ended up terminating the agreement with the Taiwanese firm and hiring a U.S. firm to finish the project!

Source: Wahlgren, E. 2004. The outsourcing dilemma. *Inc.*, April: 41–43.

## >>Achieving Competitive Advantage in Global Markets

We will begin this section by discussing the two opposing forces that firms face when they expand into global markets: cost reduction and adaptation to local markets. Then we will address the four basic types of international strategies that they may pursue: international, global, multidomestic, and transnational. The selection of one of these four types of strategies is largely dependent on a firm's relative pressure to address each of the two forces.

### Two Opposing Pressures: Reducing Costs and Adapting to Local Markets

Many years ago, the famed marketing strategist Theodore Levitt advocated strategies that favored global products and brands. That is, he suggested that firms should standardize all of their products and services for all of their worldwide markets. Such an approach would help a firm lower its overall costs by spreading its investments over as large a market as possible. Levitt's approach rested on three key assumptions:

1.  Customer needs and interests are becoming increasingly homogeneous worldwide.
2.  People around the world are willing to sacrifice preferences in product features, functions, design, and the like for lower prices at high quality.
3.  Substantial economies of scale in production and marketing can be achieved through supplying global markets.[29]

However, we can find ample evidence to refute each of these assumptions.[30] With regard to the first assumption—the increasing worldwide homogeneity of customer needs and interests—consider the number of product markets, ranging from watches and handbags to soft drinks and fast foods. Here companies have successfully identified global customer segments and developed global products and brands targeted to those segments. In addition, many other companies adapt lines to idiosyncratic country preferences and develop local brands targeted to local market segments. For example, Nestlé's line of pizzas marketed in the United Kingdom includes cheese with ham and pineapple topping on a French bread crust. Similarly, Coca-Cola in Japan markets Georgia (a tonic drink) as well as Classic Coke and Hi-C.

Consider the second assumption—the sacrifice of product attributes for lower prices. While there is invariably a price-sensitive segment in many product markets, there is no indication that this is on the increase. On the contrary, in many product and service markets—ranging from watches, personal computers, and household appliances, to banking and insurance—there appears to be a growing interest in multiple product features, product quality, and service.

Finally, the third assumption is that significant economies of scale in production and marketing could be achieved for global products and services. Although standardization may lower manufacturing costs, such a perspective does not consider three critical and interrelated points. First, as we discussed in Chapter 5, technological developments in flexible factory automation enable economies of scale to be attained at lower levels of output and do not require production of a single standardized product. Second, the cost of production is only one component, and often not the critical one, in determining the total cost of a product. Third, a firm's strategy should not be product-driven. It should also consider other activities in the firm's value chain, such as marketing, sales, and distribution.

Based on the above, we would have a hard time arguing that it is wise to develop the same product or service for all markets throughout the world. While there are some exceptions, such as Harley-Davidson motorcycles and some of Coca-Cola's soft-drink products, managers must also strive to tailor their products to the culture of the country in which they are attempting to do business. Few would argue that "one size fits all" generally applies. But let's look at what happened when Ford took this approach with the launch of its Escort automobile in Europe in the 1980s. According to the company's then CEO, Jacques Nasser:

> The Escort, which was intended to be our first global product, was engineered on two continents—North America and Europe. Obviously, that made it impossible for us to capitalize on global sourcing for components. And it was launched individually in every country. Not only did every country come up with its own positioning for the car, but each devised its own advertising message and hired its own advertising agency to get that message across. So you had one car and a substantial number of value propositions. One market was saying, "Yeah, this car's a limousine." And another market was saying it was a sports vehicle. That made it impossible for us to get customers' input into the product after it was out there.[31]

What we have briefly discussed so far are two opposing pressures that managers face when they compete in markets beyond their national boundaries. These forces place conflicting demands on firms as they strive to be competitive.[32] On the one hand, competitive pressures require that firms do what they can to lower unit costs so that consumers will not perceive their product and service offerings as too expensive. This may lead them to consider locating manufacturing facilities where labor costs are low and developing products that are highly standardized across multiple countries.

In addition to responding to pressures to lower costs, managers also must strive to be responsive to local pressures in order to tailor their products to the demand of the local market in which they do business. This requires differentiating their offerings and strategies from country to country to reflect consumer tastes and preferences and making changes to reflect differences in distribution channels, human resource practices, and governmental regulations. However, since the strategies and tactics to differentiate products and services to local markets can involve additional expenses, a firm's costs will tend to rise.

The two opposing pressures result in four different basic strategies that companies can use to compete in the global marketplace: international, global, multidomestic, and

**Exhibit 7.5**

**Opposing Pressures and Four Strategies**

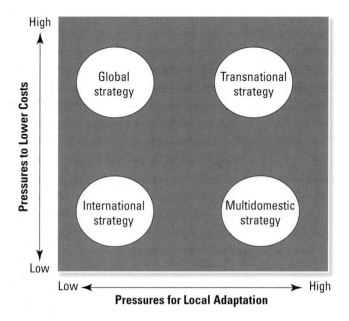

transnational. The strategy that a firm selects depends on the degree of pressure that it is facing for cost reductions and the importance of adapting to local markets. Exhibit 7.5 shows the conditions under which each of these strategies would be most appropriate. As we would expect, there are advantages and disadvantages associated with each of these strategies. In the following sections we will summarize each strategy, discuss where each is most appropriate, and identify relative advantages and disadvantages.

It is important to note that we consider these strategies to be "basic" or "pure"; that is, in practice, all firms will tend to have some elements of international, global, multidomestic, and transnational strategies.

## International Strategy

There are a small number of industries in which pressures for both local adaptation and lowering costs are rather low. An extreme example of such an industry is the "orphan" drug industry. These are medicines for diseases that are severe but affect only a small number of people. Diseases such as the Gaucher disease and Fabry disease fit into this category. Companies such as Genzyme and Oxford GlycoSciences are active in this segment of the drug industry. There is virtually no need to adapt their products to the local markets. And the pressures to reduce costs are low; even though only a few thousand patients are affected, the revenues and margins are significant because patients are charged up to $100,000 per year.

An international strategy is based on diffusion and adaptation of the parent company's knowledge and expertise to foreign markets. Country units are allowed to make some minor adaptations to products and ideas coming from the head office, but they have far less independence and autonomy compared to multidomestic companies. The primary goal of the strategy is worldwide exploitation of the parent firm's knowledge and capabilities. All sources of core competencies are centralized.

For most of its history, Ericsson, a Swedish telecommunications firm, has followed this strategy. Because its home market (Sweden) was too small to support the R&D effort necessary in the industry, Ericsson built its strategy on its ability to transfer and adapt its innovative products and process technologies to international markets. This strategy of sequential diffusion of innovation developed at home helped it compete successfully against NEC, which followed a global strategy, and ITT, which followed a multidomestic strategy.[33]

The majority of large U.S. multinationals pursued the international strategy in the decades following World War II. These companies centralized R&D and product development but established manufacturing facilities as well as marketing organizations abroad. Companies such as McDonald's and Kellogg are examples of firms following such a strategy. Although these companies do make some local adaptations, they are of a very limited nature. With increasing pressures to reduce costs due to global competition, especially from low-cost countries, opportunities to successfully employ international strategy are becoming more limited. This strategy is most suitable in situations where a firm has distinctive competencies that local companies in foreign markets lack.

Below, we address some of the risks and challenges associated with an international strategy.

- Different activities in the value chain typically have different optimal locations. That is, R&D may be optimally located in a country with an abundant supply of scientists and engineers, whereas assembly may be better conducted in a low-cost location. Nike, for example, designs its shoes in the United States, but all the manufacturing is done in countries like China or Thailand. The international strategy, with its tendency to concentrate most of its activities in one location, fails to take advantage of the benefits of an optimally distributed value chain.

- The lack of local responsiveness may result in the alienation of local customers. Worse still, the firm's inability to be receptive to new ideas and innovation from its foreign subsidiaries may lead to missed opportunities.

## Global Strategy

As indicated in Exhibit 7.5, a firm whose emphasis is on lowering costs tends to follow a global strategy. Competitive strategy is centralized and controlled to a large extent by the corporate office. Since the primary emphasis is on controlling costs, the corporate office strives to achieve a strong level of coordination and integration across the various businesses.[34] Firms following a global strategy strive to offer standardized products and services as well as to locate manufacturing, R&D, and marketing activities in only a few locations.[35]

A global strategy emphasizes economies of scale due to the standardization of products and services, and the centralization of operations in a few locations. As such, one advantage may be that innovations that come about through efforts of either a business unit or the corporate office can be transferred more easily to other locations. Although costs may be lower, the firm following a global strategy may, in general, have to forgo opportunities for revenue growth since it does not invest extensive resources in adapting product offerings from one market to another.

Consistent with Exhibit 7.5, a global strategy is most appropriate when there are strong pressures for reducing costs and comparatively weak pressures for adaptation to local markets. Identifying potential economies of scale becomes an important consideration.[36] Advantages to increased volume may come not only from larger production plants or runs but also from more efficient logistics and distribution networks. Worldwide volume is also especially important in supporting high levels of investment in research and development. As we would expect, many industries requiring high levels of R&D, such as pharmaceuticals, semiconductors, and jet aircraft, follow global strategies.

Another advantage of a global strategy is that it can enable a firm to create a standard level of quality throughout the world. Let's look at what Tom Siebel, chairman of

Siebel Systems, the $2 billion developer of e-business application software, has to say about global standardization.

> Our customers—global companies like IBM, Zurich Financial Services, and Citicorp—expect the same high level of service and quality, and the same licensing policies, no matter where we do business with them around the world. Our human resources and legal departments help us create policies that respect local cultures and requirements worldwide, while at the same time maintaining the highest standards. We have one brand, one image, one set of corporate colors, and one set of messages, across every place on the planet. An organization needs central quality control to avoid surprises.[37]

There are, of course, some risks associated with a global strategy.[38]

- A firm can enjoy scale economies only by concentrating scale-sensitive resources and activities in one or few locations. Such concentration, however, becomes a "double-edged sword." For example, if a firm has only one manufacturing facility, it must export its output (e.g., components, subsystems, or finished products) to other markets, some of which may be a great distance from the operation. Thus, decisions about locating facilities must weigh the potential benefits from concentrating operations in a single location against the higher transportation and tariff costs that result from such concentration.

- The geographic concentration of any activity may also tend to isolate that activity from the targeted markets. Such isolation may be risky since it may hamper the facility's ability to quickly respond to changes in market conditions and needs.

- Concentrating an activity in a single location also makes the rest of the firm dependent on that location. Such dependency on a sole source implies that, unless the location has world-class competencies, the firm's competitive position can be eroded if problems arise. A European executive of Ford Motor Co., reflecting on the firm's concentration of activities during a global integration program in the mid-1990s, lamented, "Now if you misjudge the market, you are wrong in 15 countries rather than only one."

## Multidomestic Strategy

According to Exhibit 7.5, a firm whose emphasis is on differentiating its product and service offerings to adapt to local markets follows a multidomestic strategy. In contrast to a global strategy in which decision-making authority tends to be highly centralized in the corporate office, decisions evolving from a multidomestic strategy tend to be more decentralized to permit the firm to tailor its products and respond rapidly to changes in demand. This enables a firm to expand its market and to charge different prices in different markets. For firms following this strategy, differences in language, culture, income levels, customer preferences, and distribution systems are only a few of the many factors that must be considered. Even in the case of relatively standardized products, at least some level of local adaptation is often necessary. Consider, for example, Honda motorcycles.

> Although we could argue that a good product knows no national boundaries, there are subtle differences in ways that a product is used and what customers expect of it. Thus, while Honda uses a common basic technology, it must develop different types of motorcycles for different regions of the world. For example, North Americans primarily use motorcycles for leisure and sports; thus aggressive looks and high horsepower are key. Southeast Asians provide a counterpoint. Here, motorcycles are a basic means of transportation. Thus, they require low cost and ease of maintenance. And, in Australia and New Zealand, shepherds use motorcycles to herd sheep. Therefore, they demand low-speed torque, rather than high speed and maintenance.[39]

# STRATEGY SPOTLIGHT

## Dealing with Bribery Abroad

Most multinational firms experience difficult dilemmas when it comes to the question of adapting rules and guidelines, both formal and informal, while operating in foreign countries. A case in point is the Foreign Corrupt Practices Act of 1977, which makes it illegal for U.S. companies to bribe foreign officials to gain business or facilitate approvals and permissions. Unfortunately, in many parts of the world, bribery is a way of life, with large payoffs to government officials and politicians the norm to win government contracts. At a lower level, goods won't clear customs unless routine illegal, but well-accepted, payments, are made to officials. What is an American company to do in such situations?

Intel follows a strict rule-based definition of bribery as "a thing of value given to someone with the intent of obtaining favorable treatment from the recipient." The company strictly prohibits payments to expedite a shipment through customs if the payment did not "follow applicable rules and regulations, and if the agent gives money or payment in kind to a government official for personal benefit." Texas Instruments, on the other hand, follows a middle approach. They require employees to "exercise good judgment" in questionable circumstances "by avoiding activities that could create even the appearance that our decisions could be compromised." And Analog Devices has set up a policy manager as a consultant to overseas operations. The policy manager does not make decisions for country managers. Instead, the policy manager helps country managers think through the issues and provides information on how the corporate office has handled similar situations in the past.

Source: Begley, T. M., & Boyd, D. P. 2003. The need for a corporate global mind-set. *MIT Sloan Management Review*, Winter: 25–32.

In addition to the products themselves, how they are packaged must sometimes be adapted to local market conditions. Some consumers in developing countries are likely to have packaging preferences very different from consumers in the West. For example, single-serve packets, or sachets, are very popular in India.[40] They permit consumers to purchase only what they need, experiment with new products, and conserve cash at the same time. Products as varied as detergents, shampoos, pickles, and cough syrup are sold in sachets in India. It is estimated that they make up 20 percent to 30 percent of the total sold in their categories. In China, sachets are also spreading as a marketing device for such items as shampoos. This reminds us of the importance of considering all activities in a firm's value chain (discussed in Chapters 3 and 5) in determining where local adaptations may be advisable.

Cultural differences may also require a firm to adapt its personnel practices when it expands internationally.[41] For example, some facets of Wal-Mart stores have been easily "exported" to foreign operations, while others have required some modifications.[42] When the retailer entered the German market in 1997, it took along the company "cheer"— Give me a W! Give me an A! Give me an L! Who's Number One? The Customer!— which suited German employees as much as their U.S. counterparts. However, Wal-Mart's 10-Foot Rule, which requires employees to greet any customer within a 10-foot radius, was not so well received in Germany, where employees and shoppers alike weren't comfortable with the custom.

Strategy Spotlight 7.8 describes how U.S. multinationals have adapted to the problem of bribery in various countries while adhering to strict federal laws on corrupt practices abroad.

As you might expect, there are some risks associated with a multidomestic strategy. Among these are the following:

- Typically, local adaptation of products and services will increase a company's cost structure. In many industries, competition is so intense that most firms can ill afford any competitive disadvantages on the dimension of cost. A key challenge of managers is to determine the trade-off between local adaptation and its cost structure. For example, cost considerations led Procter & Gamble to standardize its diaper design across all European markets. This was done despite research data indicating that Italian mothers, unlike those in other countries, preferred diapers that covered the baby's navel. Later, however, P&G recognized that this feature was critical to these mothers, so the company decided to incorporate this feature for the Italian market despite its adverse cost implications.

- At times local adaptations, even when well intentioned, may backfire. When the American restaurant chain TGI Fridays entered the South Korean market, it purposely incorporated many local dishes, such as kimchi (hot, spicy cabbage), in its menu. This responsiveness, however, was not well received. Company analysis of the weak market acceptance indicated that Korean customers anticipated a visit to TGI Fridays as a visit to America. Thus, finding Korean dishes was inconsistent with their expectations.

- Consistent with other aspects of global marketing, the optimal degree of local adaptation evolves over time. In many industry segments, a variety of factors, such as the influence of global media, greater international travel, and declining income disparities across countries, may lead to increasing global standardization. On the other hand, in other industry segments, especially where the product or service can be delivered over the Internet (such as music), the need for even greater customization and local adaptation may increase over time. Firms must recalibrate the need for local adaptation on an ongoing basis; excessive adaptation extracts a price as surely as underadaptation.

## Transnational Strategy

Let's briefly review global and multidomestic strategies before we discuss how a transnational strategy can be a vehicle for overcoming the limitations of each of these strategies and, in effect, "getting the best of both worlds."[43]

With a *global strategy,* resources and capabilities are concentrated at the center of the organization. Authority is highly centralized. Thus, a global company achieves efficiency primarily by exploiting potential scale economies in all of its value-chain activities. Since innovation is highly centralized in the corporate office, there is often a lack of understanding of the changing market needs and production requirements outside the local market, and there are few incentives to adapt.

The *multidomestic strategy* can be considered the exact opposite of the global strategy. Resources are dispersed throughout many countries in which a firm does business, and a subsidiary of the multinational company can more effectively respond to local needs. However, such fragmentation inevitably carries efficiency penalties. Learning also suffers because knowledge is not consolidated in a centralized location and does not flow among the various parts of the company.

A multinational firm following a *transnational strategy* strives to optimize the trade-offs associated with efficiency, local adaptation, and learning.[44] It seeks efficiency not for its own sake, but as a means to achieve global competitiveness. It recognizes the importance of local responsiveness but as a tool for flexibility in international operations.[45] Innovations are regarded as an outcome of a larger process of organizational learning that includes the contributions of everyone in the firm.[46] Additionally, a core tenet of the transnational model is that a firm's assets and capabilities are dispersed according to the most beneficial location for a specific activity. Thus, managers avoid the tendency to either concentrate activities in a central location (as with a global strategy) or disperse them across many locations to enhance adaptation (as with a multidomestic strategy). Peter Brabeck, CEO of Nestlé, the giant food company, provides such a perspective.

> We believe strongly that there isn't a so-called global consumer, at least not when it comes to food and beverages. People have local tastes based on their unique cultures and traditions—a good candy bar in Brazil is not the same as a good candy bar in China. Therefore, decision making needs to be pushed down as low as possible in the organization, out close to the markets. Otherwise, how can you make good brand decisions? That said, decentralization has its limits. If you are too decentralized, you can become too complicated—you get too much complexity in your production system. The closer we come to the consumer, in branding, pricing, communication, and product adaptation, the more we decentralize. The more we are dealing with production, logistics, and supply-chain management, the more centralized decision making becomes. After all, we want to leverage Nestlé's size, not be hampered by it.[47]

The Nestlé example illustrates a common approach in determining whether or not to centralize or decentralize a value-chain activity. Typically, primary activities that are "downstream" (e.g., marketing, sales, and service), or closer to the customer, tend to require more decentralization in order to adapt to local market conditions. On the other hand, primary activities that are "upstream" (e.g., logistics and operations), or further away from the customer, tend to be centralized. This is because there is less need for adapting these activities to local markets and the firm can benefit from economies of scale. Additionally, many support activities, such as information systems and procurement, tend to be centralized in order to increase the potential for economies of scale.

A central philosophy of the transnational organization is enhanced adaptation to all competitive situations as well as flexibility by capitalizing on communication and knowledge flows throughout the organization.[48] A principal characteristic is the integration of unique contributions of all units into worldwide operations. Thus, a joint innovation by headquarters and by one of the overseas units can lead potentially to the development of relatively standardized and yet flexible products and services that are suitable for multiple markets.

Asea Brown Boveri (ABB) is a firm that successfully follows a transnational strategy. ABB, with its home bases in Sweden and Switzerland, illustrates the trend toward cross-national mergers that lead firms to consider multiple headquarters in the future. It is managed as a flexible network of units, and one of management's main functions is the facilitation of information and knowledge flows between units. ABB's subsidiaries have complete responsibility for product categories on a worldwide basis. Such a transnational strategy enables ABB to benefit from access to new markets and the opportunity to utilize and develop resources wherever they may be located.

As with the other strategies, there are some unique risks and challenges associated with a transnational strategy.

- The choice of a seemingly optimal location cannot guarantee that the quality and cost of factor inputs (i.e., labor, materials) will be optimal. Managers must ensure that the relative advantage of a location is actually realized, not squandered because of weaknesses in productivity and the quality of internal operations. Ford Motor Co., for example, has benefited from having some of its manufacturing operations in Mexico. While some have argued that the benefits of lower wage rates will be partly offset by lower productivity, this does not always have to be the case. Since unemployment in Mexico is higher than in the United States, Ford can be more selective in its hiring practices for its Mexican operations. And, given the lower turnover among its Mexican employees, Ford can justify a high level of investment in training and development. Thus, the net result can be not only lower wage rates but also higher productivity than in the United States.

Exhibit 7.6

Strengths and
Limitations of Various
Strategies

| Strategy | Strengths | Limitations |
| --- | --- | --- |
| International | • Leverage and diffusion of parent's knowledge and core competencies.<br>• Lower costs because of less need to tailor products and services.<br>• Greater level of worldwide coordination. | • Limited ability to adapt to local markets.<br>• Inability to take advantage of new ideas and innovations occurring in local markets. |
| Global | • Strong integration across various businesses.<br>• Standardization leads to higher economies of scale, which lowers costs.<br>• Helps to create uniform standards of quality throughout the world. | • Limited ability to adapt to local markets.<br>• Concentration of activities may increase dependence on a single facility.<br>• Single locations may lead to higher tariffs and transportation costs. |
| Multidomestic | • Ability to adapt products and services to local market conditions.<br>• Ability to detect potential opportunities for attractive niches in a given market, enhancing revenue. | • Less ability to realize cost savings through scale economies.<br>• Greater difficulty in transferring knowledge across countries.<br>• May lead to "overadaptation" as conditions change. |
| Transnational | • Ability to attain economies of scale.<br>• Ability to adapt to local markets.<br>• Ability to locate activities in optimal locations.<br>• Ability to increase knowledge flows and learning. | • Unique challenges in determining optimal locations of activities to ensure cost and quality.<br>• Unique managerial challenges in fostering knowledge transfer. |

• Although knowledge transfer can be a key source of competitive advantage, it does not take place "automatically." For knowledge transfer to take place from one subsidiary to another, it is important for the source of the knowledge, the target units, and the corporate headquarters to recognize the potential value of such unique know-how. Given that there can be significant geographic, linguistic, and cultural distances that typically separate subsidiaries, the potential for knowledge transfer can become very difficult to realize. Firms must create mechanisms to systematically and routinely uncover the opportunities for knowledge transfer.

Exhibit 7.6 summarizes the relative advantages and disadvantages of international, global, multidomestic, and transnational strategies.

We've discussed the types of strategies that firms pursue in international markets and their relative advantages and disadvantages. Let's now turn to the types of entry modes that companies may use to enter international markets.

## >>Entry Modes of International Expansion

A firm has many options available to it when it decides to expand into international markets. Given the challenges associated with such entry, many firms first start on a small scale and then increase their level of investment and risk as they gain greater experience with the overseas market in question.[49]

Exhibit 7.7 illustrates a wide variety of modes of foreign entry, including exporting, licensing, franchising, joint ventures, strategic alliances, and wholly owned subsidiaries.[50] As the exhibit indicates, the various types of entry form a continuum that ranges from exporting (low investment and risk, low control) to a wholly owned subsidiary (high investment and risk, high control).[51]

Admittedly, there can at times be frustrations and setbacks as a firm evolves its international entry strategy from exporting to more expensive types, including wholly owned subsidiaries. For example, according to the CEO of a large U.S. specialty chemical company:

> In the end, we always do a better job with our own subsidiaries; sales improve, and we have greater control over the business. But we still need local distributors for entry, and we are still searching for strategies to get us through the transitions without battles over control and performance.[52]

Let's discuss each of these international entry modes.[53]

### Exporting

Exporting consists of producing goods in one country to sell in another. This entry strategy enables a firm to invest the least amount of resources in terms of its product, its organization, and its overall corporate strategy. Not surprisingly, many host countries dislike this entry strategy because it provides less local employment than other modes of entry.[54]

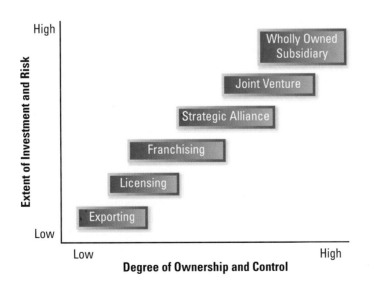

**Exhibit 7.7**
**Entry Modes for International Expansion**

Multinationals often stumble onto a stepwise strategy for penetrating markets, beginning with the exporting of products. This often results in a series of unplanned actions to increase sales revenues. As the pattern recurs with entries into subsequent markets, this approach, named a "beachhead strategy," becomes official policy in many organizations.

Such an approach definitely has its advantages. After all, firms start from scratch in sales and distribution when they enter new markets. Because many foreign markets are nationally regulated and dominated by networks of local intermediaries, firms need to partner with local distributors to benefit from their valuable expertise and knowledge of their own markets. Multinationals, after all, recognize that they cannot master local business practices, meet regulatory requirements, hire and manage local personnel, or gain access to potential customers without some form of local partnership.

In addition to the need to partner with local firms, multinationals also want to minimize their own risk. They do this by hiring local distributors and investing very little in the undertaking. In essence, the firm gives up control of strategic marketing decisions to the local partners—much more control than they would be willing to give up in their home market.

As we might expect, exporting is a relatively inexpensive way to enter foreign markets. However, it can still have significant downsides. In a study of 250 instances in which multinational firms used local distributors to implement their exporting entry strategy, the results were dismal. In the vast majority of the cases, the distributors were bought (to increase control) by the multinational firm or fired. In contrast, successful distributors shared two common characteristics:

- They carried product lines that complemented, rather than competed with, the multinational's products.

- They behaved as if they were business partners with the multinationals. They shared market information with the corporations, they initiated projects with distributors in neighboring countries, and they suggested initiatives in their own or nearby markets. Additionally, these distributors took on risk themselves by investing in areas such as training, information systems, and advertising and promotion in order to increase the business of their multinational partners.

The key point is the importance of developing collaborative, win–win relationships.

To ensure more control over operations without incurring significant risks, many firms have used licensing and franchising as a mode of entry. Let's now discuss these and their relative advantages and disadvantages.

## Licensing and Franchising

Licensing as an entry mode enables a company to receive a royalty or fee in exchange for the right to use its trademark, patent, trade secret, or other valuable item of intellectual property.[55] In international markets, the advantage is that the firm granting the license incurs little risk, since it does not have to invest any significant resources into the country itself. In turn, the licensee (the firm receiving the license) gains access to the trademark, patent, and so on, and is able to potentially create competitive advantages. In many cases, the country also benefits from the product being manufactured locally. For example, Yoplait yogurt is licensed by General Mills from Sodima, a French cooperative, for sale in the United States. The logos of college and professional athletic teams in the United States are another source of trademarks that generate significant royalty income domestically and internationally.

There are, of course, some important disadvantages with this type of entry. For example, the licensor gives up control of its product and forgoes potential revenues and profits. Furthermore, the licensee may eventually become so familiar with the patent and trade secrets that it may become a competitor; that is, the licensee may make some modifications to the product and manufacture and sell it independently of the licensor without having to pay a royalty fee. This potential situation is aggravated in countries that have relatively weak laws to protect intellectual property. Additionally, if the licensee selected by the multinational firm turns out to be a poor choice, the brand name and reputation of the product may be tarnished.[56]

Although licensing and franchising are both forms of contractual arrangements, franchise contracts generally include a broader range of factors in an operation and have a longer time period during which the agreement is in effect. Franchising has the advantage of limiting the risk exposure that a firm has in overseas markets while expanding the revenue base of the parent company. The other side of the coin is that the multinational firm receives only a portion of the revenues, in the form of franchise fees, instead of the entire revenue, as would be the case if the firm set up the operation itself (e.g., a restaurant) through direct investment.

Franchising remains an overwhelmingly American form of business. According to a recent survey, more than 400 U.S. franchisers have international exposure.[57] This is greater than the combined totals of the next four largest franchiser home countries—France, the United Kingdom, Mexico, and Austria.

Companies often desire a closer collaboration with other firms in order to increase revenue, reduce costs, and enhance their learning—often through the diffusion of technology. To achieve such objectives, they enter into strategic alliances or joint ventures, two entry modes we will discuss next.

## Strategic Alliances and Joint Ventures

Joint ventures and strategic alliances have become in recent years an increasingly popular way for firms to enter and succeed in foreign markets. These two forms of partnership differ in that joint ventures entail the creation of a third-party legal entity, whereas strategic alliances do not. In addition, strategic alliances generally focus on initiatives that are smaller in scope than joint ventures.

As we discussed in Chapter 6, these strategies have been effective in helping firms increase revenues and reduce costs as well as enhance learning and diffuse technologies. These partnerships enable firms to share the risks as well as the potential revenues and profits. Also, by gaining exposure to new sources of knowledge and technologies, such partnerships can help firms develop core competencies that can lead to competitive advantages in the marketplace.[58] Finally, entering into partnerships with host country firms can provide very useful information on local market tastes, competitive conditions, legal matters, and cultural nuances.[59] Strategy Spotlight 7.9 discusses how Microsoft has used a variety of partnerships to strengthen its position in East Asia.

Despite the potential benefits, managers must be aware of the risks associated with strategic alliances and joint ventures and how they can be minimized.[60] First, there needs to be a clearly defined strategy that is strongly supported by the organizations that are party to the partnership. Otherwise, the firms may work at cross-purposes and not achieve any of their goals. Second, and closely allied to the first issue, there must be a clear understanding of capabilities and resources that will be central to the partnership. Without such clarification, there will be fewer opportunities

# STRATEGY SPOTLIGHT

## Microsoft's Partnerships in East Asia

Microsoft is forming strategic alliances and joint ventures with companies in East Asia. Rather than competing with existing firms, Microsoft has entered several countries by cooperating with these firms. It has entered the Japanese and Taiwanese markets by joining efforts with mobile phone operator NTT DoCoMo, which has already established itself as a successful provider of cellular phone service through its Mobimagic service. By teaming with Microsoft, both companies stand to profit by integrating Microsoft's software applications, such as e-mail, into the existing service of cell-phone subscribers. Akio Fujii, head of new product development for Microsoft Japan, envisions adding a Web browser to these cell-phone services.

GigaMedia has 100,000 broadband subscribers offering sports, music, news, video-on-demand, as well as online karaoke. By hooking up with Microsoft, GigaMedia is now able to move its services from personal computers (PCs) to televisions, with the television serving as the monitor and a set-top box similar to a cable television box functioning as the PC. In exchange for its contribution, Microsoft gleans 2 percent of GigaMedia's broadband subscriber fees and significant revenue from GigaMedia's e-commerce sales. In a similar move, the Koos Group, owner of KG Telecom, the second largest cell-phone operator in Taiwan, has joined ranks with Microsoft to integrate Internet capabilities on the televisions and cell phones of subscribers.

Microsoft has taken strategic moves to blunt competition from Palm by joining forces in an alliance with Psion in London, one of Palm's chief rivals. Microsoft has also reduced Palm's competitive threat in the cell-phone market by partnering with Stockholm's Ericsson, a leading manufacturer of mobile phones.

Microsoft has utilized forward-thinking vision to achieve win–win relationships through several joint ventures and strategic alliances throughout the globe. By doing so, it is successfully exporting its influence from an entrenched position in the United States to a global presence. This is good not only for Microsoft and its shareholders; stockholders of other firms around the world stand to prosper from the cooperative agreements Microsoft has forged with their firms. In addition, the added competition from a powerhouse like Microsoft forces other international firms to compete for efficiencies, thus benefiting overall economic prosperity.

Source: Chowdhury, N. 2000. Gates & Co. attack Asia. *Fortune.com*, April 17; Mariano, G. 2001. Palm to groove with liquid audio music. *New York Times Online*, April 11.

for learning and developing competences that could lead to competitive advantages. Third, trust is a vital element. Phasing in the relationship between alliance partners permits them to get to know each other better and develop trust. According to Philip Benton, Jr., former president of Ford Motor Co. (which has been involved in multiple international partnerships over the years), "The first time two companies work together, the chances of succeeding are very slight. But once you find ways to work together, all sorts of opportunities arise." Without trust, one party may take advantage of the other by, for example, withholding its fair share of resources and gaining access to privileged information through unethical (or illegal) means. Fourth, cultural issues that can potentially lead to conflict and dysfunctional behaviors need to be addressed. An organization's culture is the set of values, beliefs, and attitudes that influence the behavior and goals of its employees. Thus, recognizing cultural differences as well as striving to develop elements of a "common culture" for the partnership is vital. Without a unifying culture, it will become difficult to combine and leverage resources that are increasingly important in knowledge-intensive organizations (discussed in Chapter 4).[61]

As we know, not all partnerships are successful, for a variety of reasons. One of the most famous in recent business history was the joint venture formed by General Motors and Daewoo Motor Co.

In the mid-1980s General Motors sought cheap labor in Korea while Daewoo (of Korea) wanted to export automobiles. Thus, the two companies joined forces in 1986 to manufacture the ill-fated Pontiac LeMans. Things did not work out as planned. The LeMans experienced a sales decline of 39 percent from 1988 to 1990 and further declines in 1990 until the partnership was dissolved shortly thereafter.

What went wrong? The first cars had quality problems: GM sent engineers to Korea to correct them. Korea's cheap labor didn't materialize because of economic improvement, devaluation of the dollar, and increasingly strong demands from the newly formed labor unions for higher wages. However, the biggest problem was the differing goals of the two firms. While Daewoo wanted to upgrade the models to gain a larger share of the domestic market, GM wanted to keep costs down.

In effect, the alliance failed from the start, due to minimal understanding of each other's objectives and a lack of effort to reevaluate plans when problems appeared.[62]

Finally, the success of a firm's alliance should not be left to chance.[63] To improve their odds of success, many companies have carefully documented alliance-management knowledge by creating guidelines and manuals to help them manage specific aspects of the entire alliance life cycle (e.g., partner selection and alliance negotiation and contracting). For example, Lotus Corp. (part of IBM) created what it calls its "35 rules of thumb" to manage each phase of an alliance from formation to termination. Hewlett-Packard developed 60 different tools and templates, which it placed in a 300-page manual for guiding decision making in specific alliance situations. The manual included such tools as a template for making the business case for an alliance, a partner evaluation form, a negotiation template outlining the roles and responsibilities of different departments, a list of the ways to measure alliance performance, and an alliance termination checklist.

When a firm desires the highest level of control over its international operations, it develops wholly owned subsidiaries. Although wholly owned subsidiaries can generate the greatest returns, they also come with the highest levels of investment and risk. We will now discuss them.

## Wholly Owned Subsidiaries

A wholly owned subsidiary is a business in which a multinational company owns 100 percent of the stock. There are two means by which a firm can establish a wholly owned subsidiary. It can either acquire an existing company in the home country or it can develop a totally new operation. The latter is often referred to as a "greenfield venture." Establishing a wholly owned subsidiary is the most expensive and risky of the various entry modes. However, as expected, it can also yield the highest returns. In addition, it provides the multinational company with the greatest degree of control of all activities, including manufacturing, marketing, distribution, and technology development.[64]

Wholly owned subsidiaries as well as direct investment in greenfield ventures are most appropriate where a firm already has the appropriate knowledge and capabilities that it can leverage rather easily through multiple locations in many countries. Examples range from restaurants to semiconductor manufacturers. To lower costs, for example, Intel Corporation builds semiconductor plants throughout the world—all of which use virtually the same blueprint. In establishing wholly owned subsidiaries, knowledge can be further leveraged by the hiring of managers and professionals from the firm's home country, often through hiring talent from competitors.

As noted, wholly owned subsidiaries are typically the most expensive and risky of the various modes for entering international markets. With franchising, joint ventures, or

# STRATEGY SPOTLIGHT

**7.10**

## Häagen-Dazs's Unique Entry Strategy

The ice-cream and frozen yogurt company Häagen-Dazs has taken a unique route for cross-border entry. Rather than follow traditional entry modes, the Bronx, New York–based company has an unconventional way of moving beyond the boundaries of the United States.

The company uses a three-step process. First, it uses high-end retailers to introduce the brand. Next, it finds high-traffic areas to build company-owned stores. The last step is to sell Häagen-Dazs products in convenience stores and supermarkets.

Häagen-Dazs is quick to adapt to local needs. For instance, freezers in some European stores are notorious for their unreliability. Clearly, a freezer malfunction would ruin a store's stock of Häagen-Dazs products. So Häagen-Dazs buys high-quality freezers for stores willing to carry its brand. Small sacrifices such as this have grown the company from a small ice-cream manufacturer in the Bronx to a worldwide franchiser with 650 stores in 55 countries, including Belgium, France, Japan, and the United Kingdom.

Sources: Meremenot, M. 1991. Screaming for Häagen-Dazs. *BusinessWeek*, October 14: 121; Häagen-Dazs. 2001. Information for franchisees. Häagen-Dazs company document: 1–24.

strategic alliances, the risk is shared with the firm's partners. With wholly owned subsidiaries, the entire risk is assumed by the parent company. The risks associated with doing business in a new country (e.g., political, cultural, and legal) can be lessened by hiring local talent.

Wal-Mart's expansion into South Korea points out some of the challenges and risks of creating greenfield ventures.

> Prior to Wal-Mart entering South Korea, local competitors were fearful that the giant retailer would "devour the local fish" with its extensive financial resources and global buying power. However, after its initial foray, many are now talking about what went wrong with Wal-Mart's initial efforts. For one thing, Wal-Mart used a membership approach similar to the one used by its Sam's warehouse stores. According to Song Kye-Hyon, a financial analyst, "It turned out to be a strategic flaw of Wal-Mart when it first adopted the Western policy of the membership where customers were required to pay a membership fee for shopping privileges and no food (only merchandise)." In South Korea, fresh, quality food is a key ingredient of success. It generates half of a store's revenues. To make matters worse, one of Wal-Mart's competitors, E-Mart, has several thousand local food suppliers with which it has nurtured long-term relationships. E-Mart even owns its own farm that supplies its stores.
>
> The local competitors have also developed mechanisms to create greater customer loyalty. They employ green-capped young men who help bring the shopping carts to the customers' cars in the parking lot. And they operate shuttle buses to go through neighborhoods to pick up customers and drop them off at their homes after they have completed their shopping.
>
> Wal-Mart remains undaunted. It has changed course to adopt the supercenter Wal-Mart concept in which it scrapped the memberships and introduced food. Wal-Mart and its competitors have vowed to further expand their operations in an effort to grab a larger piece of the discount retail market which is expected to reach $25 billion by 2004.[65]

In this closing section, we have addressed entry strategies as a progression from exporting through the creation of wholly owned subsidiaries. However, we must point out that many firms do not follow such an evolutionary approach. Instead, such firms follow rather unique entry strategies; see the discussion of Häagen-Dazs in Strategy Spotlight 7.10.

We live in a highly interconnected global community where many of the best opportunities for growth and profitability lie beyond the boundaries of a company's home country. Along with the opportunities, of course, there are many risks associated with diversification into global markets.

The first section of the chapter addressed the factors that determine a nation's competitiveness in a particular industry. The framework was developed by Professor Michael Porter of Harvard University and was based on a four-year study that explored the competitive success of 10 leading trading nations. The four factors, collectively termed the "diamond of national advantage," were factor conditions, demand characteristics, related and supporting industries, and firm strategy, structure, and rivalry.

The discussion of Porter's "diamond" helped, in essence, to set the broader context for exploring competitive advantage at the firm level. In the second section, we discussed the primary motivations and the potential risks associated with international expansion. The primary motivations included increasing the size of the potential market for the firm's products and services, achieving economies of scale, extending the life cycle of the firm's products, and optimizing the location for every activity in the value chain. On the other hand, the key risks included political and economic risks, currency risks, and management risks. Management risks are the challenges associated with responding to the inevitable differences that exist across countries such as customs, culture, language, customer preferences, and distribution systems. We also addressed some of the managerial challenges and opportunities associated with offshoring and outsourcing.

Next, we addressed how firms can go about attaining competitive advantage in global markets. We began by discussing the two opposing forces—cost reduction and adaptation to local markets—that managers must contend with when entering global markets. The relative importance of these two factors plays a major part in determining which of the four basic types of strategies to select: international, global, multidomestic, or transnational. The chapter covered the benefits and risks associated with each type of strategy.

The final section discussed the four types of entry strategies that managers may undertake when entering international markets. The key trade-off in each of these strategies is the level of investment or risk versus the level of control. In order of their progressively greater investment/risk and control, the strategies range from exporting to licensing and franchising, to strategic alliances and joint ventures, to wholly owned subsidiaries. The relative benefits and risks associated with each of these strategies were addressed.

## Summary Review Questions

1. What are some of the advantages and disadvantages associated with a firm's expansion into international markets?

2. What are the four factors described in Porter's diamond of national advantage? How do the four factors explain why some industries in a given country are more successful than others?

3. Explain the two opposing forces—cost reduction and adaptation to local markets—that firms must deal with when they go global.

4. There are four basic strategies—international, global, multidomestic, and transnational. What are the advantages and disadvantages associated with each?

5. Describe the basic entry strategies that firms have available when they enter international markets. What are the relative advantages and disadvantages of each?

**Summary**

## Experiential Exercise

The United States is considered a world leader in the motion picture industry. Using Porter's diamond framework for national competitiveness, explain the success of this industry.

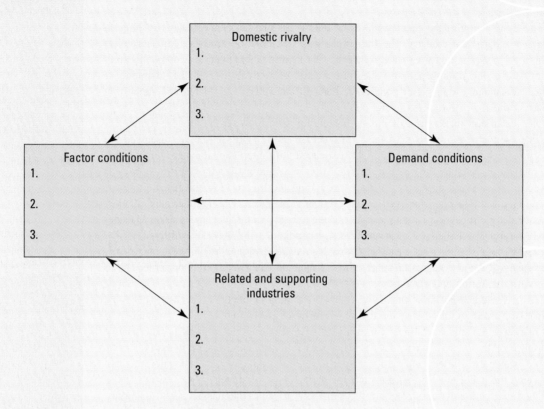

## Application Questions Exercises

1. Data on the "competitiveness of nations" can be found at www.imd.ch/wcy/ranking/. This Web site provides a ranking on a variety of criteria for 49 countries. How might Porter's diamond of national advantage help to explain the rankings for some of these countries for certain industries that interest you?

2. The Internet has lowered the entry barriers for smaller firms that wish to diversify into international markets. Why is this so? Provide an example.

3. Many firms fail when they enter into strategic alliances with firms that link up with companies based in other countries. What are some reasons for this failure? Provide an example.

4. Many large U.S.-based management consulting companies such as McKinsey and Company and the BCG Group have been very successful in the international marketplace. How can Porter's diamond explain their success?

## Ethics Questions

1. Over the past few decades, many American firms have relocated most or all of their operations from the United States to countries such as Mexico and China that pay lower wages. What are some of the ethical issues that such actions may raise?

2. Business practices and customs vary throughout the world. What are some of the ethical issues concerning payments that must be made in a foreign country to obtain business opportunities?

# References

1. Edmondson, G. 2003. Volkswagen needs a jump. *Business-Week,* May 12: 48–49; Flint, J. 2002. Luxury: The cure du jour. *Forbes,* December 9: 88; Snarkhunting.com. 2003. www.snarkhunting.com/2003_01_01_archive.html, January; The name game Touareg? Murano? Where do they get those new car names? 2003. *Chicago Sun-Times,* January 30, www.automobilemag.com/news/news_30_5/; www.vw.com/autoshow/pdf/touareg.pdf; and Frank, M. 2004. Test drives: 2005 Volkswagen Touareg V-10. *Forbes.com,* November 18.

2. For a recent discussion on globalization by one of international business's most respected authors, read Ohmae, K. 2005. *The next global stage: Challenges and opportunities in our borderless world.* Philadelphia: Wharton School Publishing.

3. Our discussion of globalization draws upon Engardio, P., & Belton, C. 2000. Global capitalism: Can it be made to work better? *BusinessWeek,* November 6: 72–98.

4. Green, S., Hasan, F., Immelt, J., Marks, M., & Meiland, D. 2003. In search of global leaders. *Harvard Business Review,* 81(8): 41.

5. Engardio & Belton, op. cit.

6. For insightful perspectives on strategy in emerging economies, refer to the article entitled: Strategy research in emerging economies: Challenging the conventional wisdom in the January 2005 issue of *Journal of Management Studies,* 42(1).

7. The above discussion draws on Clifford, M. L., Engardio, P., Malkin, E., Roberts, D., & Echikson, W. 2000. Up the ladder. *BusinessWeek,* November 6: 78–84.

8. For another interesting discussion on a country perspective, refer to Makino, S. 1999. MITI Minister Kaora Yosano on reviving Japan's competitive advantages. *Academy of Management Executive,* 13(4): 8–28.

9. The following discussion draws heavily upon Porter, M. E. 1990. The competitive advantage of nations. *Harvard Business Review,* March–April: 73–93.

10. Landes, D. S. 1998. *The wealth and poverty of nations.* New York: W. W. Norton.

11. A recent study that investigates the relationship between international diversification and firm performance is Lu, J. W., & Beamish, P. W. 2004. International diversification and firm performance: The s-curve hypothesis. *Academy of Management Journal,* 47(4): 598–609.

12. Part of our discussion of the motivations and risks of international expansion draws upon Gregg, F. M. 1999. International strategy. In Helms, M. M. (Ed.). *Encyclopedia of management:* 434–438. Detroit: Gale Group.

13. These two examples are discussed, respectively, in Dawar, N., & Frost, T. 1999. Competing with giants: Survival strategies for local companies in emerging markets. *Harvard Business Review,* 77(2): 119–129; and Prahalad, C. K., & Lieberthal, K. 1998. The end of corporate imperialism. *Harvard Business Review,* 76(4): 68–79.

14. This discussion draws upon Gupta, A. K., & Govindarajan, V. 2001. Converting global presence into global competitive advantage. *Academy of Management Executive,* 15(2): 45–56.

15. Stross, R. E. 1997. Mr. Gates builds his brain trust. *Fortune,* December 8: 84–98.

16. For a good summary of the benefits and risks of international expansion, refer to Bartlett, C. A., & Ghoshal, S. 1987. Managing across borders: New strategic responses. *Sloan Management Review,* 28(5): 45–53; and Brown, R. H. 1994. *Competing to win in a global economy.* Washington, DC: U.S. Department of Commerce.

17. For an interesting insight into rivalry in global markets, refer to MacMillan, I. C., van Putten, A. B., & McGrath, R. G. 2003. Global gamesmanship. *Harvard Business Review,* 81(5): 62–73.

18. It is important for firms to spread their foreign operations and outsourcing relationships with a broad, well-balanced mix of regions and countries to reduce risk and increase potential reward. For example, refer to Vestring, T., Rouse, T., & Reinert, U. 2005. Hedge your offshoring bets. *MIT Sloan Management Review,* 46(3): 27–29.

19. For a discussion of some of the challenges associated with government corruption regarding entry strategies in foreign markets, read Rodriguez, P., Uhlenbruck, K., & Eden, L. 2005. Government corruption and entry strategies of multinationals. *Academy of Management Review,* 30(2): 383–396.

20. For a discussion of the political risks in China for United States companies, refer to Garten, J. E. 1998. Opening the doors for business in China. *Harvard Business Review,* 76(3): 167–175.

21. Shari, M. 2001. Is a holy war brewing in Indonesia? *BusinessWeek,* October 15: 62.

22. Gikkas, N. S. 1996. International licensing of intellectual property: The promise and the peril. *Journal of Technology Law & Policy,* 1(1): 1–26.

23. For an excellent theoretical discussion of how cultural factors can affect knowledge transfer across national boundaries, refer to Bhagat, R. S., Kedia, B. L., Harveston, P. D., & Triandis, H. C. 2002. Cultural variations in the cross-border transfer of organizational knowledge: An integrative framework. *Academy of Management Review,* 27(2): 204–221.

24. To gain insights on the role of national and regional cultures on knowledge management models and frameworks, read Pauleen, D. J., & Murphy, P. 2005. In praise of cultural bias. *MIT Sloan Management Review,* 46(2): 21–22.

25. Berkowitz, E. N. 2000. *Marketing* (6th ed.). New York: McGraw-Hill.

26. World Trade Organization. *Annual Report 1998.* Geneva: World Trade Organization.

27. Lei, D. 2005. Outsourcing. In Hitt, M. A., & Ireland, R. D. (Eds.). *The Blackwell encyclopedia of management*. Entrepreneurship: 196–199. Malden, MA: Blackwell.

28. The discussion above draws from Colvin, J. 2004. Think your job can't be sent to India? Just watch. *Fortune,* December 13: 80; Schwartz, N. D. 2004. Down and out in white collar America. *Fortune,* June 23: 321–325; Hagel, J. 2004. Outsourcing is not just about cost cutting. *Wall Street Journal,* March 18: A3.

29. Levitt, T. 1983. The globalization of markets. *Harvard Business Review,* 61(3): 92–102.

30. Our discussion of these assumptions draws upon Douglas, S. P., & Wind, Y. 1987. The myth of globalization. *Columbia Journal of World Business,* Winter: 19–29.

31. Wetlaufer, S. 1999. Driving change: An interview with Ford Motor Company's Jacques Nasser. *Harvard Business Review,* 77(2): 76–81.

32. Ghoshal, S. 1987. Global strategy: An organizing framework. *Strategic Management Journal,* 8: 425–440.

33. Bartlett, C. A., & Ghoshal, S. 1989. *Managing across borders: The transnational solution.* Boston: Harvard Business School Press.

34. For insights on global branding, refer to Aaker, D. A., & Joachimsthaler, E. 1999. The lure of global branding. *Harvard Business Review,* 77(6): 137–146.

35. For an interesting perspective on how small firms can compete in their home markets, refer to Dawar & Frost, op. cit.: 119–129.

36. Hout, T., Porter, M. E., & Rudden, E. 1982. How global companies win out. *Harvard Business Review,* 60(5): 98–107.

37. Fryer, B. 2001. Tom Siebel of Siebel Systems: High tech the old-fashioned way. *Harvard Business Review,* 79(3): 118–130.

38. The risks that are discussed for the global, multidomestic, and transnational strategies draw upon Gupta & Govindarajan, op. cit.

39. Sigiura, H. 1990. How Honda localizes its global strategy. *Sloan Management Review,* 31: 77–82.

40. Prahalad & Lieberthal, op. cit.: 68–79. Their article also discusses how firms may have to reconsider their brand management, costs of market building, product design, and approaches to capital efficiency when entering foreign markets.

41. Hofstede, G. 1980. *Culture's consequences: International differences in work-related values.* Beverly Hills, CA: Sage; Hofstede, G. 1993. Cultural constraints in management theories. *Academy of Management Executive,* 7(1): 81–94; Kogut, B., & Singh, H. 1988. The effect of national culture on the choice of entry mode. *Journal of International Business Studies,* 19: 411–432; and Usinier, J. C. 1996. *Marketing across cultures.* London: Prentice Hall.

42. McCune, J. C. 1999. Exporting corporate culture. *Management Review,* December: 53–56.

43. This discussion draws upon Bartlett and Ghoshal, op. cit.; and Raisinghani, M. 2000. Transnational organization. In Helms, M. M. (Ed.). *Encyclopedia of management* (4th ed.): 968–969. Detroit: Gale Group.

44. Prahalad, C. K., & Doz, Y. L. 1987. *The multinational mission: Balancing local demands and global vision.* New York: Free Press.

45. Kidd, J. B., & Teramoto, Y. 1995. The learning organization: The case of Japanese RHQs in Europe. *Management international review,* 35 (Special Issue): 39–56.

46. Gupta, A. K., & Govindarajan, V. 2000. Knowledge flows within multinational corporations. *Strategic Management Journal,* 21(4): 473–496.

47. Wetlaufer, S. 2001. The business case against revolution: An interview with Nestlé's Peter Brabeck. *Harvard Business Review,* 79(2): 112–121.

48. Nobel, R., & Birkinshaw, J. 1998. Innovation in multinational corporations: Control and communication patterns in international R&D operations. *Strategic Management Journal,* 19(5): 461–478.

49. For a rigorous analysis of performance implications of entry strategies, refer to Zahra, S. A., Ireland, R. D., & Hitt, M. A. 2000. International expansion by new venture firms: International diversity, modes of entry, technological learning, and performance. *Academy of Management Journal,* 43(6): 925–950.

50. Li, J. T. 1995. Foreign entry and survival: The effects of strategic choices on performance in international markets. *Strategic Management Journal,* 16: 333–351.

51. For a discussion of how home-country environments can affect diversification strategies, refer to Wan, W. P., & Hoskisson, R. E. 2003. Home country environments, corporate diversification strategies, and firm performance. *Academy of Management Journal,* 46(1): 27–45.

52. Arnold, D. 2000. Seven rules of international distribution. *Harvard Business Review,* 78(6): 131–137.

53. Sharma, A. 1998. Mode of entry and ex-post performance. *Strategic Management Journal,* 19(9): 879–900.

54. This section draws upon Arnold, op. cit.: 131–137; and Berkowitz, op. cit.

55. Kline, D. 2003. Strategic licensing. *MIT Sloan Management Review,* 44(3): 89–93.

56. Arnold, op. cit.; and Berkowitz, op. cit.

57. Martin, J. 1999. Franchising in the Middle East. *Management Review,* June: 38–42.

58. Manufacturer-supplier relationships can be very effective in global industries such as automobile manufacturing. Refer to Kotabe, M., Martin, X., & Domoto, H. 2003. Gaining from vertical partnerships: Knowledge transfer, relationship duration, and supplier performance improvement in the U.S. and Japanese automotive industries. *Strategic Management Journal,* 24(4): 293–316.

59. For a good discussion, refer to Merchant, H., & Schendel, D. 2000. How do international joint ventures create shareholder value? *Strategic Management Journal,* 21(7): 723–738.

60. This discussion draws upon Walters, B. A., Peters, S., & Dess, G. G. 1994. Strategic alliances and joint ventures: Making them work. *Business Horizons,* 37(4): 5–11.

61. For a rigorous discussion of the importance of information access in international joint ventures, refer to Reuer, J. J., & Koza, M. P. 2000. Asymmetric information and joint venture performance: Theory and evidence for domestic and international joint ventures. *Strategic Management Journal,* 21(1): 81–88.

62. Treece, J. 1991. Why Daewoo wound up on the road to nowhere. *BusinessWeek,* September 23: 55.

63. Dyer, J. H., Kale, P., & Singh, H. 2001. How to make strategic alliances work. *MIT Sloan Management Review,* 42(4): 37–43.

64. For a discussion of some of the challenges in managing subsidiaries, refer to O'Donnell, S. W. 2000. Managing foreign subsidiaries: Agents of headquarters, or an independent network? *Strategic Management Journal,* 21(5): 525–548.

65. Mi-Young, A. 2000. Wal-Mart has to adapt to the South Korean consumer. *Deutsche-Presse-agentur,* November 8: 1–3.

# Digital Business Strategy:

## Leveraging Capabilities in a Disruptive Environment

## >chapter objectives

*After reading this chapter, you should have a good understanding of:*

- How new technologies contribute to competitive disruption and foster economic progress.

- Why use of Internet and digital technologies is more important to achieving competitive advantage than the technologies themselves.

- How the Internet and digitally based capabilities are affecting the five competitive forces and industry profitability.

- How firms are using Internet technologies to add value and achieve unique advantages.

- How Internet-enabled business models are being used to improve strategic positioning.

- How firms can improve their competitive position by effectively deploying digital strategies and avoiding the pitfalls associated with using the Internet and digital technologies.

*t*he technological advances that have swept in the new digital economy and created many Internet- and Web-based business opportunities have enormous strategic implications. Some of the changes require that business be conducted in entirely new ways. Others make it important to pursue traditional business strategies more effectively. This chapter helps sort out the ramifications of the Internet and digitally based capabilities for strategic management practices.

We begin by revisiting Porter's five-forces approach to industry analysis. We outline how industry and competitive practices are being affected by the capabilities provided by Internet technologies. On the one hand, some of the five forces are stronger in a digital economy, thus potentially suppressing profitability in a given industry. On the other hand, new opportunities created by digital technologies are providing firms with new ways to adapt to and overcome the five forces to achieve a competitive advantage. For each of the five forces, we provide examples that illustrate how these technological changes are shifting the nature of competition in several critical ways.

The second section explores how Internet-based businesses and incumbent firms are using digital technologies to add value. We consider four activities—search, evaluation, problem solving, and transaction—as well as three types of content—customer feedback, expertise, and entertainment programming. These technology-enhanced capabilities are providing new means with which firms can achieve competitive advantages.

The third section addresses how competitive strategies should be revised and redeployed in light of the shifts in industry and competitive forces caused by the Internet and digital technologies. Examples show new ways firms are providing low-cost leadership, differentiating, and focusing. For many firms, combination strategies provide the best avenue for building a solid strategy by integrating the new capabilities with sound strategic principles.

Sometimes new technologies are introduced and adopted so rapidly that current practices and business norms are seriously disrupted. Disruptive technologies (see Chapter 5) typically affect whole industries as well as relationships across industries. The innovations that flow from disruptive technologies may have legal ramifications and often pit technically sophisticated entrepreneurial firms against powerful incumbent firms in a struggle for who will control or suppress the use of the new technologies. Such struggles nearly always have enormous strategic implications. Consider the case of Napster.[1]

Created by 19-year-old reformed hacker Shawn Fanning, Napster provided software that enabled digital music files to be shared over the Internet. It was a combination of new technologies that made Napster possible—capabilities that were hardly possible at all just a few years earlier. First, there was MP3 technology, which allows for the kind of digital music typically found on CDs to be compressed into files 10 times smaller without loss of quality. Second, there was a new form of network architecture known as peer-to-peer (P2P) that allowed files to be distributed directly between computers in the network (in contrast to a client/server architecture). Finally, there was the Internet itself, which provided the network through which MP3 files could be shared. The result was that nearly 70 million registered users exchanged billions of high-quality music files simply by going to Napster, finding someone online who had a copy, and downloading it—for free. The technology made Napster the fastest-growing company in history.

To the millions of tech-savvy listeners who were accustomed to paying $10 to $20 to acquire a CD, it was unbelievably good news. But to the music industry giants such as Sony and EMI, who were accustomed to receiving payment every time a CD was sold or even played on the radio, it was nothing less than stealing. In June 2000, the Record Industry Association of America (RIAA), backed by the five major music publishers, filed suit to prohibit Napster from giving away its music. It was David versus Goliath all over again.

Napster claimed that it was not stealing but simply facilitating an exchange. In fact, the company claimed that the Audio Home Recording Act provided for this type of sharing. But RIAA argued that such laws were written when songs were recorded one-at-a-time and could not be applied in an era when new technologies made simultaneous and superfast Internet downloads possible. More importantly, the music industry believed it was losing huge sums of money. And apparently it was. On the weekend before a judge threatened to suddenly close Napster, Massachusetts-based Webnoize Research estimated that 250 million songs were downloaded. This translates into a loss for the music industry of approximately $270 million in a 48-hour period.

On July 1, 2001, after months of court battles, the Napster Web site was shut down and it seemed that Goliath had won. But by then, billions of music files had already been downloaded and competing online music Web sites were waiting to pick up where Napster left off. The online file sharing genie was out of the bottle. And Napster was a household word.

But Napster, the company, would never be the same. It had never been financially strong because it did not charge for its service (which is one reason it could claim in court that it was not profiting from the file-sharing activity). Nor did it make money in other ways, such as by selling online advertising or branded products. When it attempted to save itself by making content licensing agreements with the music publishers, internal squabbling among the founders and conflict with its venture capital firm stymied its efforts to become legitimate. The court action forced Napster to face its strategic and financial shortcomings. During this period, Jupiter Media Metrix senior analyst Aram Sinnreich said of Napster, "It has no clout, no leverage, pending lawsuits, a brand that's fading in the minds of consumers, and nothing that's really proprietary to the company."

This assessment, however, did not stop Bertelsmann AG, the German conglomerate that owned the BMG music label, from pouring $85 million into Napster to keep it from failing during the time it was shut down by the courts. Bertelsmann wanted to buy Napster in bankruptcy. In spite of the support Bertelsmann provided, however, a judge eventually prohibited the sale. Why? Again, it was the other big music labels that objected, claiming the acquisition would give BMG an unfair advantage in the online music business.

Eventually Roxio, a company that made CD-burning software, bought Napster's assets, including its name, for $5 million. Once the sale was complete, Roxio changed its name to Napster, sold its software division and entered the online music market as a legitimate company hoping to capitalize on the Napster name. But the new Napster set sail in a sea of competitors, including market leader Apple iTunes and major players such as Sony, Yahoo, RealNetworks, and even Wal-Mart. By the end of 2004, while Apple was boasting 100 million downloads per quarter at 99 cents per song, Napster was still operating at a loss and could claim just 270,000 subscribers to its Napster To Go subscription service, which allows unlimited downloads for $14.95 per month. And, in the file-sharing universe, unlicensed downloads continued to outpace paid transactions. According to BigChampagne LLC, a company that tracks file sharing activity, 1 billion songs were downloaded in January 2005 alone using P2P networks such as Kazaa, Grokster, and eDonkey. In such an environment, it is unlikely that Napster will ever achieve anything close to its former glory.

*What Went Wrong at Napster?*   Napster's failure was due, in part, to its extraordinary success. Such failures are rather common among firms that grow faster than their financial resources or ability to manage operations would enable them. From the beginning, Napster was cash-strapped and poorly organized, had a weak management team, and never had a concrete business plan.[2] But it was its greatest asset—the technological innovation that makes Internet-based file sharing possible—that made Napster a threat to the music industry giants. Legal action by these companies may have spurred the company's rapid growth and made Napster a household word, but it also led to the court injunction that shut down the fledgling company and caused it to declare bankruptcy.

Another critical reason for Napster's failure was that it never developed a viable revenue model. In this respect, Napster was like so many firms that grew up too fast during the great Internet expansion of the late 1990s. During that period, Napster was just one of the companies that was caught up in a kind of technological euphoria that was based more on what was technologically possible than on how much money could be earned. However the venture capitalists who sank billions of dollars into Internet businesses did not know that. All they knew was that something big was happening technologically. They, and the millions who invested, knew only that eventually there were great profits to be made and they did not want to be left out when that happened.

For these reasons, Napster in particular, and the Internet bubble in general, are somewhat extreme examples of technological disruption. Both happened so fast and with such profound impact that millions of lives were affected and literally trillions of dollars were involved. Between March 2000 and March 2001, more than $3 trillion of investment wealth was wiped out of the U.S. stock markets, due in large part to the collapse of the dot-com surge.[3] Yet both the Internet and a rather humbled version of Napster are still around. In essence, both have "gone mainstream."

In this chapter we will address the impact of the technological disruptions brought on by the digital revolution and the Internet on business practices and the strategic forces that guide business decisions and actions. The next section describes several dimensions of the digital economy and illustrates the importance of technological innovation to strategic decision making and economic growth. We will also highlight both potential benefits and drawbacks of digitally based capabilities on the future of strategic management.

## >>Competitive Disruption, Strategic Management, and the Digital Economy

The Napster case illustrates the important role that technological innovation can have in shaping the strategic forces and competitive pressures affecting business. Schumpeter referred to such impact as one of "creative destruction." This occurs when the creative efforts of a few pioneers who introduce new innovative solutions unravel existing industry relationships and clear the way for a new technological regime with different economic players.[4] The Napster that Shawn Fanning created is no longer viable, but the revolution it brought about has irrevocably changed how the music industry sells music, relates to its customers, and manages its intellectual property.

Another such revolution was brought about in the early 1980s when Apple introduced the first personal computer. Traditional ways of computing, characterized by mainframes and mini-computers were suddenly challenged in unexpected ways. As the desktop PC became the dominant design, not one of the companies that made the previously dominant types of computers became a major player in the personal computer industry.[5] Apple itself has struggled mightily to survive in the face of stiff competition. It made a key strategic error in its early days by refusing to license use of its operating system.[6] As a result MS-DOS, an operating system that is arguably less efficient than Apple's, became dominant and firms such as Microsoft and Dell surged ahead. But Apple's superior technology and its continuous innovation helped it to remain viable. It's ironic that the new Napster's biggest rival today is the once iconoclastic Apple. With its hugely successful iPod MP3 player and its iTunes file-sharing business, Apple has become a dominant incumbent player.

These examples illustrate the importance of technological innovation and competitive disruptions in advancing economic development. In his book *The Free-Market Innovation Machine* economist William J. Baumol argues that the drive to innovate has been more important than price-based competition in explaining the success of free-market economies.[7] Baumol describes a cycle in which breakthrough innovations by entrepreneurial new entrants bring new technologies into mainstream use. Some of these new firms can leverage their early success to become dominant players. Most, however, are acquired by existing large firms that are hungry for fresh ideas to propel them forward. Once disruptive technologies are absorbed, innovation becomes more routine. As more and more firms adopt the technologies, competition intensifies and factors that drive industry competition and sustainable competitive advantage, such as the five forces, the value chain, and cost and differentiation strategies, become increasingly important.

Yet, according to Baumol, for both incumbents and the new firms, it is innovation-driven competition that determines who will succeed or fail. Thus a company like Apple, even though it has faced fierce price competition, has continued to be a viable contender because of its technological leadership and willingness to seize opportunities that are based on disruptive technologies.

Few technologically driven phenomena have been as disruptive, or as brimming with opportunity, as the Internet. Napster, iTunes, and thousands of new technology-driven enterprises would not be possible if it were not for the Internet. According to Jack Welch, former chairman of General Electric, the Internet is "the single most important event in the U.S. economy since the Industrial revolution."[8] Indeed, the Internet has dramatically changed the way business is conducted in every corner of the globe.

The impact of the information technology revolution, however, goes beyond the Internet. At a more basic level, it is the shift from analog to digital technologies that is responsible for so many new IT capabilities. Analog was once the primary technology for conveying information such as music recordings, voice communications, and television signals. It represents a type of physical information that requires large amounts of storage and often works only with hard-wired equipment. By contrast, digital technologies use information in the form of bits, that is, electronic signals expressed as either on or off, one or zero. These bits can be stored in tiny chips, easily reproduced and transferred rapidly and wirelessly.[9] Many technologies have made the switch from analog to digital—phones, photographs, television signals, and even books—and the trend suggests digitization is here to stay. As a result, digital technology capabilities, which, in essence, make the Internet possible, are a major driver in today's economy. Strategy Spotlight 8.1 addresses types of business activity, including the Internet, that have been enabled by digital technology.

These technology-driven initiatives—the Internet, wireless communications, and other digital technologies—are having a significant impact on the economy. They have done so by changing the ways businesses interact with each other and with consumers. These changes, though initially disruptive, create opportunities for firms to address needs more effectively and compete more efficiently.

According to C. K. Prahalad and Venkat Ramaswamy, authors of *The Future of Competition,* the "ubiquitous connectivity" and feedback systems provided the by Internet and digital technologies are contributing to major changes in competitive practices.[10] Because today's consumers are more networked than ever, they can interact with the companies they do business with and thus influence decisions and choices companies make about product design, services features, and so forth.[11] Manufacturing systems are more flexible, databases can be updated instantaneously, and alternative choices can be evaluated in real time. As a result, customers can be involved from the beginning in developing end products.[12] Thus, they are able to personally experience the value creation process.

The authors describe several examples of companies engaged in such co-creation processes:

- Intuit, the maker of Quicken® and other financial software, which has grown by continuously expanding customer's access to financial management capabilities and Internet-based information resources.

- Deere & Company, the farm machinery manufacturer, which is equipping its tractors and combines with global positioning systems (GPS) and biosensor systems that monitor soil conditions, analyze crops, and diagnose equipment problems in advance.

- Sumerset Houseboats, the world's largest houseboat builder, which actively involves customers throughout the houseboat design process.

To excel, these companies are drawing on four building blocks: dialogue, access, risk assessment, and transparency (DART). Exhibit 8.1 illustrates how the Internet is being used to enable the co-creation process.

The Internet has created a new climate for business in which sound principles of strategic management are *more,* not less important.[13] Indeed, the changes caused by the Internet and digital economy have made strategizing more challenging. Rapid improvements in technology, globalization, shifting patterns of demand, and uncertainty about costs and revenues are highlighting the importance of strategy formulation. Successful implementation may be even more difficult in this climate because of the uncertainty surrounding the new technology. Even so, the digital business phenomenon is steadily expanding.

Clearly, the Internet phenomenon has heightened the need for effective strategic management. Digital business success requires a new strategic perspective that builds on the possibilities provided by information technologies and permits Internet connectivity to transform the way business is conducted. Despite the rapid change and competitive disruption, an important lesson about the strategic implications of the Internet and digital technologies remains: It is the actual use of the technologies for profitable transactions,

| Building Blocks | Definitions | Role in Co-Creation Process | Internet-based Examples |
|---|---|---|---|
| Dialogue | Sharing and exchanging knowledge to increase levels of understanding among companies, consumers, and communities of interest.<br>• It requires forums in which dialogue can occur. | Generates new knowledge | Using online Internet forums such as newsgroups, weblogs ("blogs") and chat rooms to exchange information.<br>• Used by the "Open Source" software movement (in developing Linux and other programs) to establish guidelines and create standards of quality. |
| Access | Creating opportunities for experiences at multiple points of interaction.<br>• If users can access capabilities, they don't have to own them to experience them. | Provides experiences | Using computers networked via the Internet to provide resources for on-demand computing.<br>• Companies such as Gateway and IBM are investing in online networks and grid computing systems that make using on-demand computing power just like using electricity. |
| Risk Assessment | Assessing not just the benefits but the risks associated with using goods and services.<br>• If consumers understand potential dangers, they can make more informed decisions and take action to reduce potential harm. | Promotes shared responsibility | Using the Internet to disclose and disseminate medical information.<br>• Companies such as Iceland's deCODE Genetics are exchanging genetic information and disclosing the latest research findings. |
| Transparency | Promoting openness, sharing discoveries, and eliminating information asymmetries.<br>• It requires that companies disclose information about prices, costs, and profit margins. | Creates trust | Using the Internet to share scientific knowledge, cumulate findings, and make manufacturing processes and other operations more visible.<br>• Used in the Human Genome Project to promote information sharing and collaboration among scientists. |

Sources: Dennis, C. 2003. Draft guidelines ease restrictions on use of genome sequence data. *Nature*, 421: 877–878; Kambil, A., Friesen, G. B., & Sundaram, A. 1999. Co-creation: A new source of value. *Outlook Magazine*, 3(2): 23–29; Nerney, C. 2002. IBM, Grid computing groups to unveil grid services protocols. *Internet News*, www.internetnews.com, February 1; Prahalad, C. K., & Ramaswamy, V. 2004. *The future of competition*. Boston, MA: Harvard Business School Press; and www.decode.com.

**Exhibit 8.1**

**The DART Framework: How the Internet Contributes to the Co-Creation Process**

## Beyond the Internet: The Wireless, Digital Economy

The Internet is a leading and highly visible component of a broader technological phenomenon—the emergence of digital technology. The Internet is like a staging area, a platform through which numerous applications of digital technology can be routed. Even technologies that don't require the Internet to function, such as wireless phones and GPS, rely on the Internet for data transfer and communications.

One of the key factors behind the growth of Internet-based applications of digital technologies is the implementation of broadband Internet connections (primarily cable and DSL). At-home broadband use grew 36 percent in 2004; at that rate, over 70 percent of all U.S. homes will have broadband connections by 2006. Worldwide broadband adoptions grew even faster—a one-year increase of about 50 percent in 2004. Since broadband connections are always on, users can get online much faster, and usually do. Broadband users spend 34 percent more time online than users with slower connections. Once there, they also spend more. In a recent period, 69 percent of online purchases were conducted over broadband connections, and broadband users spent 34 percent more than shoppers without broadband. Exhibit 8.2 illustrates worldwide growth trends in Internet use.

Business applications of the Internet are continuing to grow in many sectors of the economy. For example, the banking industry, which was slow to adopt Internet technologies, has experienced such rapid growth that it now has more services available online. Forty-four percent of all Internet users—53 million Americans—were using some form of online banking service by 2005. Small-and medium-sized enterprises (SMEs) are also relying on the Internet more than ever. A recent study found that 87 percent of SMEs are receiving monthly revenue from their Web site, and 42 percent derive more than a quarter of their monthly revenue from their Internet presence. According to Joel Kocher, CEO of Interland, "We are getting to the point in most small-business categories where it will soon be safe to say that if you're not online, you're not really serious about being in business."

This growth is not limited to Internet use. Wireless technologies are increasingly being used by businesses for everything from mission critical communications to

attracting singles to a nightclub with text messages that offer free drinks. Mobile devices that connect to the Internet through wireless networks make it possible to conduct business anywhere, anytime. These "always on" technologies, in effect, make the customer the point of sale.

Wireless technologies are being improved in ways that will increase their reach and reliability and threaten existing communication systems. For example, several companies are developing "smart antennas" that concentrate radio signals in a narrow band rather than broadcasting in all directions at once. Using a cluster of 128 pencil size antennas, San Francisco start-up Vivato, Inc has developed a system than can project signals as far as 2.5 miles. This is well beyond the current range of just 300 feet for most Wi-Fi systems.

Wireless and digital technologies still face numerous challenges, however. For example, international standards for wireless communication are still in flux. As a result, cell phones and other devices that work in the U.S. are often useless in many parts of Europe and Asia. And, unlike analog systems, electronic bits of data that are zooming through space can be more easily lost, stolen, or manipulated. However, even with these problems, wireless and digital technologies are undoubtedly the (air) wave of the future. As Alan Greenspan, chairman of the U.S. Federal Reserve System, stated, "the revolution in information technology has altered the structure of the way the American economy works."

Sources: Anonymous. 2005. SMBs believe in the Web. *eMarketer*, www.emarketer.com, May 16. Greenspan, A. U.S. Congressional hearing. Quoted in Lewis, M. 2000. *The new, new thing*. New York: W.W. Norton; McGann, R. 2005. Broadband: High speed, high spend. *ClickZ Network*, www.clickz.com, January 24; McGann, R. 2005. Online banking increased 47 percent since 2002. *ClickZ Network*, www.clickz.com, February 9; Ward, L. 2003. Is M-Commerce dead and buried? *E-Commerce Times*, www.ecommercetimes.com, May 9; Yang, C. 2003. Beyond Wi-Fi: A new wireless age. *BusinessWeek*, December 15: 84–88.

| Internet Use Worldwide | | |
|---|---|---|
| | **Internet Users (in millions)** | |
| **Geographic Region** | **2004** | **2009 (estimated)** |
| North America | 206,000 | 274,560 |
| Western Europe | 195,865 | 303,072 |
| Eastern Europe/Russia | 61,292 | 124,510 |
| Asia-Pacific | 362,388 | 689,616 |
| South/Central America | 65,483 | 131,821 |
| Middle East/Africa | 43,452 | 110,109 |
| Total Internet Users | 934,480 | 1,633,688 |

**Exhibit 8.2** *Growth in Internet Activity*
Sources: *Computer Industry Almanac.*

not the technology itself, that matters to a company's bottom line. Yet it is the technology that is making it possible to conduct new types of transactions and enhance interactions with nearly every important stakeholder—customers, suppliers, employees, stockholders, competitors, government regulators, and others. Thus, the Internet presents a new strategic challenge: how to make the best use of the new technology without losing sight of important business fundamentals.

As we have seen, strategy can play a key role in the success of Internet-based and digital economy enterprises. Next, we will evaluate Michael Porter's five-forces model in terms of the actual use of the Internet and the new technological capabilities that it makes possible.

## >>How the Internet and Digital Technologies Are Affecting the Five Competitive Forces

### The Threat of New Entrants

In most industries, the threat of new entrants has increased because digital and Internet-based technologies lower barriers to entry. For example, it is relatively inexpensive for a new firm to create a Web presence that is even more impressive than the Web site of a larger or more established competitor. Unlike the traditional "Main Street" business, where customers could assess the firm's size and quality by walking in the door, businesses that exist in cyberspace can create an appearance that makes them seem like strong competitors, regardless of their actual size or the quality of their operations. Thus, scale economies may be less important in this context and new entrants can go to market with lower capital costs.

Beyond mere appearances, businesses that reach customers primarily through the Internet may enjoy savings on other traditional expenses such as office rent, sales force salaries, printing, and postage. This may encourage more entrants who, because of the lower start-up expenses, see an opportunity to capture market share by offering a product or performing a service more efficiently than existing competitors. Thus, a new cyberentrant can use the savings provided by the Internet to charge lower prices and compete on price despite the incumbent's scale advantages. Alternatively, because digital technologies often make it possible for young firms to provide services that are equivalent or superior to an incumbent, a new entrant may be able to serve a market more effectively, with more personalized services and greater attention to product details. A new firm may be able to build a reputation in its niche and charge premium prices. By so doing, it can capture small pieces of an incumbent's business and erode profitability.

Advances in technology also have created a flood of new entrants in several industries, including software, electronic equipment manufacturing, and online retailing. Strategy Spotlight 8.2 addresses the Internet telephony phenomenon known as VOIP, a digitally based technology that is causing major disruptions in the telecom industry. Not only does this technology change the way phone communications actually take place, but it also is changing how much customers pay for phone service, or if they pay for it at all.

Another potential benefit of Web-based business is access to distribution channels. Manufacturers or distributors that can reach potential outlets for their products more efficiently by means of the Internet may be encouraged to enter markets that were previously closed to them. Such access is not guaranteed, however, because of the strong barriers to entry that may exist in certain industries.[14]

# VOIP: The Telecom Industry's New Threat

"Every week, I see at least one new company pop up and try to sell Internet-based phone service to consumers," writes Om Malik, senior writer for *Business 2.0* magazine. Few digital technologies have inspired a rush of new entrants as intense as Voice over Internet Protocol (VOIP), also known as Internet Voice. Although the technology has been around since the mid-1990s, it is only now being perfected. More importantly, it is finally becoming commercially viable.

Early VOIP users typically sat in front of a computer with a microphone exchanging wavy and halting chunks of conversations over the Internet. But because it was free, it was worth it. Today the technology allows voice information to flow more smoothly and reliably. With some low-cost equipment and a little software, dialers with a broadband connection can make phone calls over the Internet.

The implications are enormous. Federal Communications Commission Chairman Michael Powell claims that VOIP represents the "most significant paradigm shift in the entire history of modern communications since the invention of the telephone." *Fortune* magazine reports:

> VOIP's impact will be more profound than that of either cell phones or the Internet, largely because it encompasses both. Like the wireless and Internet phenomena, VOIP has the potential to buoy a raft of new household brands. Fortunes will rise and fall as traditional phone companies, cable operators, and upstarts fight to sell you more convenient, cheaper and way cooler phone services. And it will increasingly marginalize the century-old traditional phone network, replacing it with a sleek new system of interconnecting data pipelines that will deliver calls, movies, messages, games and whatever else can be digitized.

Such heady predictions have created a frenzy of new entrants. Yet Internet voice systems are far from perfect. Service can be interrupted if Internet connections go down and emergency calls into 911 systems using VOIP are currently unable to inform the dispatcher of the physical location. But using Internet Voice is so much cheaper that many business users are willing to take these risks. For example, Smyth Solutions, a 100-person staffing and recruiting company in New Jersey, has cut its local and long distance phone bill from $100,000 to $80,000 by using

VOIP. Savings on phone bills of 20 to 30 percent are common. "The low cost of Internet voice makes it as disruptive as e-mail," says Frost & Sullivan market analyst Jon Arnold. And, as in the early days of e-mail, there are several online companies offering VOIP for free including Skype, a service started by the group that created the free music-sharing service Kazaa.

Clearly VOIP is a major threat to traditional phone service providers. Analysts predict that by 2008, 16 percent of U.S. homes, or about 17.5 million users, will be "VOIPing," while the revenue of Verizon, SBC, and other regional carriers will slip by 12 percent, or $8 billion. Even so, these large phone companies should be in a strong position to capitalize on VOIP with their market power and brand names. Most users prefer to work with the reliable big phone providers. This raises an interesting question: Who are the new entrants and what are they selling?

Perhaps the biggest threat to traditional phone companies comes from cable operators such as Cox Communications and Comcast, which can use their cable connections to offer Internet voice. By packaging VOIP with its video, voice, and data service, New York-based Cablevision became the second largest VOIP provider in just six months. Upstart Vonage, the largest provider, has a strong following and an aggressive marketing campaign that includes selling do-it-yourself installation kits at Radio Shack and Best Buy.

Hundreds of other new entrants have developed equipment, software, and services that build on VOIP technology. New York–based M5 Networks is using a combination of digital and traditional phone lines to improve sound quality. 8×8, a Santa Clara, California start-up, is offering free videoconferencing and developing a *Hollywood Squares*–style approach that puts multiple people on the video screen at the same time. Because it is digital, VOIP phone systems can be integrated with other digital information such as customer databases. This would allow, for example, law firms to log phone calls into the firm's accounting system automatically, making it easier to account for billable hours.

Eventually there will be a shakeout as weak firms fail and the large incumbents acquire the small companies with good ideas. Industry incumbents will pay handsomely to acquire successful new entrants, and some of those young firms will survive to become major players themselves. Meanwhile, the entire phenomenon is driving prices down, and that will be a threat to the telecom industry for years to come.

Sources: Ferguson, K. 2005. Talk gets cheaper. *BusinessWeek Online,* www.businessweek.com, March 14; Fitzgerald, M. 2004. Can you hear me now? *Inc. Magazine,* November: 63–64; Malik, O. 2005. VOIP madness looks familiar. *Business 2.0,* www.business2.com, January 14; Malik, O. 2004. The technology of the year: Internet Voice. *Business 2.0,* 5(9): 109–110; and, Mehta, S. N. 2004. The future is on the line. *Fortune,* www.fortune.com, July 12.

## The Bargaining Power of Buyers

The Internet and wireless technologies may increase buyer power by providing consumers with more information to make buying decisions and by lowering switching costs. But these technologies may also suppress the power of traditional buyer channels that have concentrated buying power in the hands of a few, giving buyers new ways to access sellers. In industries such as book publishing and grocery retailing, where the flow of products to market has traditionally been determined by strong intermediaries such as wholesalers and distributors, buyer power is shifting because of the Internet. To sort out these differences, let's first distinguish between two types of buyers: end users and buyer channel intermediaries.

*End users,* as the name implies, are the final customers in a distribution channel. They are the consumers who actually buy a product and put it to use. Internet sales activity that is labeled "B2C"—that is, business-to-consumer—is concerned with end users. The Internet is likely to increase the power of these buyers for several reasons. First, a large amount of consumer information is available on the Internet. This gives end users the information they need to shop for quality merchandise and bargain for price concessions. The automobile industry provides an excellent example of this phenomenon. For a small fee, agencies such as Consumers Union (publishers of *Consumer Reports*) will provide customers with detailed information about actual automobile manufacturer costs.[15] This information, available online, can be used to bid down dealers' profits.

Second, an end user's switching costs are also potentially much lower because of the Internet. Setting aside the psychological cost of switching due to an unwillingness by consumers to switch brands, the physical cost of switching may involve only a few clicks of the mouse to find and view a competing product or service online. As a result, according to Web strategist David Siegel, businesses that are serious about selling online will need to become increasingly customer-led. That is, they must be willing to listen to customers more often and respond to them more quickly. "E-customers aren't loyal to a brand," says Siegel. "They may be attracted to a specific business proposition, but their memories are very short. Solve one problem for them, and they have another. Companies must earn their networked customers' loyalty with *every* new deal."[16] In this environment, buyers are likely to have much more bargaining power.[17]

The bargaining power of distribution channel buyers may decrease because of the Internet. *Buyer channel intermediaries* are the wholesalers, distributors, and retailers who serve as intermediaries between manufacturers and end users. In some industries, they are dominated by powerful players that control who gains access to the latest goods or the best merchandise. The Internet and wireless communications, however, make it much easier and less expensive for businesses to reach customers directly. This is especially valuable for specialized companies that can focus their promotional efforts on marketplace segments that are more easily identified via the Internet. Thus, the Internet may increase the power of incumbent firms relative to that of traditional buyer channels.

The book publishing industry illustrates some of the changes brought on by the Internet that have affected the two types of buyers. Prior to the Internet, book publishers worked primarily through large distributors. These intermediaries such as Tennessee-based Ingram, one of the largest and most powerful distributors, exercised strong control over the movement of books from publishers to bookstores. This power was especially strong relative to small, independent publishers who often found it difficult to get their books into bookstores and in front of potential customers. The Internet has changed these relationships. Publishers can now negotiate distribution agreements directly with online retailers such as Amazon and Books-A-Million. And small publishers can use the Internet to sell directly to end users and publicize new titles, without depending on buyer channel intermediaries to handle their books.

Business customers are not the only buyers turning to the Internet to find better deals. State and local governments in the U.S. also have significantly increased their use of online procurement systems to obtain supplies and equipment more efficiently. In a recent period, Minnesota saved 10.6 percent using online procurement to buy commodities such as vehicles, electronic devices, and uniforms; Florida saved $18.3 million (30.4 percent) on purchases of office supplies and paper. To achieve these savings, both states used forms of Internet-based reverse auctions (where multiple sellers bid to do business with one buyer). INPUT, a government marketing intelligence organization, estimates that between 2004 and 2007, government use of reverse auctions for procurement will increase 300 percent.[18]

## The Bargaining Power of Suppliers

Use of the Internet and digital technologies to speed up and streamline the process of acquiring supplies is already benefiting many sectors of the economy. But the net effect of the Internet on supplier power will depend on the nature of competition in a given industry. As with buyer power, the extent to which the Internet is a benefit or a detriment may also hinge on the supplier's position along the supply chain.

The role of suppliers typically involves providing products or services to other businesses. Thus, the term "B2B"—that is, business-to-business—is often used to refer to businesses that supply or sell to other businesses. The effect of the Internet on the bargaining power of suppliers is a double-edged sword. On the one hand, Internet technologies make it possible for suppliers to access more of their business customers at a relatively lower cost per customer. On the other hand, suppliers may not be able to hold onto these customers, because buyers can do comparative shopping and price negotiations so much faster on the Internet and can turn to other suppliers with a few clicks of the mouse. This is especially damaging to supply-chain intermediaries, such as product distributors, who may not be able to stop suppliers from directly accessing other potential business customers.

In general, one of the greatest threats to supplier power is that the Internet inhibits the ability of suppliers to offer highly differentiated products or unique services. Most procurement technologies can be imitated by competing suppliers, and the technologies that make it possible to design and customize new products rapidly are being used by all competitors. For example, Moen, the faucet manufacturer, sends digital designs of new faucets by way of e-mail to its suppliers worldwide to review. Suggestions for improvement are consolidated and final adjustments are made simultaneously. In a recent period, these practices cut design time from 24 to 16 months and boosted sales by 17 percent.[19] However, Delta and other competitors have implemented similar techniques to improve their own cycle time and boost sales.

Other factors may also contribute to stronger supplier power. First, the growth of new Web-based business in general may create more downstream outlets for suppliers to sell to. Second, suppliers may be able to create Web-based purchasing arrangements that make purchasing easier and discourage their customers from switching. Online procurement systems, for example, create a direct link between suppliers and customers that reduces transaction costs and paperwork.[20] Third, the use of proprietary software that links buyers to a supplier's Web site may create a rapid, low-cost ordering capability that discourages the buyer from seeking other sources of supply. Amazon.com, for example, created and patented One-Click purchasing technology that speeds up the ordering process for customers who enroll in the service.[21]

Finally, suppliers will have greater power to the extent that they can reach end users directly without intermediaries. Previously, suppliers often had to work through intermediaries who brought their products or services to market for a fee. But a process known as *disintermediation* is removing the organizations or business process layers responsible for intermediary steps in the value chain of many industries.[22] This is a major new business reality that the Internet has made possible, and it has significant strategic implications. As Larry Downes and Chunka Mui state in their book, *Unleashing the Killer App:*

> If buyers and sellers can find each other cheaply over the Internet, who needs agents (for instance, insurance) and distributors (for instance, home computers)? Complex transactions are becoming disaggregated, and middlemen who are not adding sufficient value relative to the open market are being disintermediated.[23]

Just as the Internet is eliminating some business functions, it is creating an opening for new functions. These new activities are entering the value chain by a process known as *reintermediation*—the introduction of new types of intermediaries. Many of these new functions are affecting traditional supply chains. In consumer markets, for example, delivery services are enjoying a boom because of the Internet. Many more consumers are choosing to have products delivered to their door rather than going out to pick them up. Electronic delivery is also becoming common. In business markets, e-commerce has created the need for new types of financial intermediaries that can perform clearing functions for purchases made online. New products (e.g., online credit cards) and new services (e.g., online escrow services) have been introduced as use of the Internet has grown. Consider the following examples of reintermediation:

- **Extremetix, Inc.**—Developed ClicknPrint Tickets®, an online ticketing system that allows tickets to be printed at home using any standard ink-jet or laser printer. The tickets, which contain a two-dimensional bar-code, can be e-mailed to others for printing. If lost or damaged, a new one with a new number can be printed, canceling the previous ticket. In 2004, Extremetix became the largest provider of eTicketing to independent amusement parks, waterparks, and attractions.[24]

- **Pitney Bowes**—Used its knowledge of electronic billing, encryption, and document management to turn around its 84-year-old postal meter business. By acquiring several market-leading digital communication companies and leveraging its relationship with the U.S. Postal Service, its profit growth jumped to 13 percent a year. Recently, eBay chose it to be its online postage provider.[25]

- **E-Trade**—Developed Club eTrade, an online service designed to provide personal attention to high net worth customers. The system has improved customer service and significantly boosted performance. In the first four months of operation, it generated $460 million in new assets by directing 2,200 existing customers to new financial products.[26]

Exhibit 8.3 demonstrates how the processes of disintermediation and reintermediation are altering the traditional channels by which manufacturers reach consumers.

## The Threat of Substitutes

Along with traditional marketplaces, the Internet has created a new marketplace; along with traditional channels, it has become a new channel. In general, therefore, the threat of substitutes is heightened because the Internet introduces new ways to accomplish the same tasks.

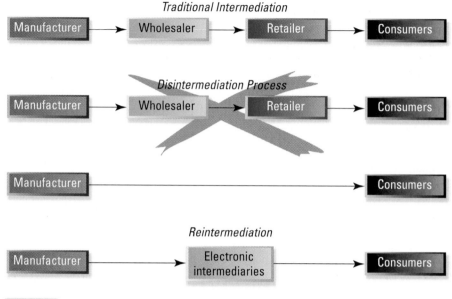

**Exhibit 8.3   Disintermediation and Reintermediation**

The primary factor that leads to substitution is economic. Consumers will generally choose to use a product or service until a substitute that meets the same need becomes available at a lower cost. The economies created by Internet technologies have led to the development of numerous substitutes for traditional ways of doing business. For example, a company called Conferenza is offering an alternative way to participate in conferences for people who don't want to spend the time and money to attend. The Web site provides summaries of many conference events, quality ratings using an "event intelligence" score, and schedules of upcoming events.[27]

Another example of substitution is in the realm of electronic storage. With expanded use of desktop computing capabilities during the last 20 years, the need to store information electronically has increased dramatically. Until recently, the trend has been to create increasingly larger desktop storage capabilities and techniques for compressing information that create storage efficiencies. But a viable substitute has recently emerged: storing information on the Internet. Companies such as My Docs Online Inc. are providing Web-based storage that firms can access simply by going online. Rather than purchasing more megabytes of storage space, firms can now lease cyberspace. Since these storage places are virtual, they can be accessed anywhere the Web can be accessed. This makes it possible for a traveler to access important documents and files without transporting them physically from place to place. Cyberstorage is not free, but it is still cheaper and more convenient than purchasing and carrying additional disk storage.[28]

Another substitute is in market research, which was traditionally conducted through mailed questionnaires and test marketing. These can be expensive to plan and administer. Questionnaires must be designed, printed, and mailed—all activities that have a hard cost. New products were often rolled out one city at a time to test the responses of a typical group of a few shoppers before a major launch. But Web technologies have reduced the time and cost of marketing. Insight Express is an online market research firm that can survey 300 people for around $1,000. Initially launched to conduct test marketing for mom-and-pop operations, the company is now test-marketing new names,

# STRATEGY SPOTLIGHT

## Adware and Spyware: Bad News *and* Good News?

Internet technologies have created new and far-reaching ways to invade consumer privacy. The way Internet service is provided creates many of these problems. For example, whenever you visit a Web site, a record of that visit is stored as a data packet on your own hard drive. These data packets are known as cookies and are used to speed up processing by remembering information such as products left in a shopping cart. But they can also be used to gather name and address information as well as a Web user's browsing habits.

Another example relates to the increased use of broadband for Internet access. Everyone knows the advantage of broadband is speed. But to provide speed, the Internet connection is typically always on (unless you turn off your computer or manually terminate the connection). This always-on feature increases the chance that unwelcome visitors are peering in on your Internet activity or leaving a "bug" that enables them to spy on you in the future.

Such bugs, appropriately labeled "spyware," are actually software applications that secretly track your behavior by monitoring system activity. Some spyware can even capture login data, including passwords, and transmit them to a remote computer. Spyware applications may be bundled with other legitimate software that an individual or business willingly downloads. Most users have no idea how spyware ever got on their computers.

Adware uses spyware technology but with a twist: They have your permission. Have you ever downloaded a free program, such as the file-sharing software Kazaa,

without actually reading the user agreement? If so, at least in the case of Kazaa, you would have also downloaded and agreed to the terms of Claria's GAIN, the leading source of adware. Claria then tracks your online activity and uses that information to plaster your screen with targeted ads. Such advertising antics are not just part of some Internet underground; Claria's customers include American Express and Sprint.

A Dell executive who recently testified to the FTC about invasive software reported that adware and spyware had become the number one reason that customers call Dell's tech support. But even though it may be a nuisance, is it unethical? Would you feel invaded if your personal buying habits were linked to your Internet surfing history, and this information was sold to businesses that wanted to send you targeted advertising? Or is this simply a case of "let the buyer beware"? That is, is using such software just a form of clever marketing, and is it ultimately the responsibility of consumers to know it and protect themselves?

Whatever the ethics of the situation may be, it can be said that this phenomenon has been good for business in two ways. First, adware seems to improve advertising effectiveness. Surfers click on adware-informed pop-ups 20 percent of the time according to WhenU, Claria's biggest adware rival. This is far better than the click rate for traditional, untargeted pop-ups. Second, the market for products that combat spyware—such as Spy Sweeper and PestPatrol, which was recently acquired by Computer Associates—will exceed $100 million in 2005. It seems certain that spyware fighters will profit from the battle to protect your privacy.

Source: Desmond, M. 2004. Threat assessment. *PCWorld*, www.pcworld.com, August 26; Deutschman, A. 2004. The ad agency on your hard drive. *Fast Company*, 88: 46; and Myser, M. 2005. Invasion of the corporate spyware. *Business 2.0*, 6(2): 30.

---

logos, product ideas, and even business concepts for major online players such as E-Trade and Yahoo![29]

Products can be tested more quickly in cyberspace. This is driven in part by the Internet's ability to capture detailed information about a person's Web-surfing habits, including information such as how long a visitor views a Web page, whether he or she clicks through a banner ad, and whether a purchase is made.[30] Such detailed information is invaluable to marketers trying to determine how to target their advertising. However, it can also be used maliciously to steal personal information or invade consumer privacy. Strategy Spotlight 8.3 describes some of the ethical issues surrounding this powerful new Internet capability.

## The Intensity of Competitive Rivalry

Because the Internet creates more tools and means for competing, rivalry among competitors is likely to be more intense. Only those competitors that can use digital technologies and the Web to give themselves a distinct image, create unique product offerings, or provide "faster, smarter, cheaper" services are likely to capture greater profitability with the new technology. Such gains are hard to sustain, however, because in most cases the new technology can be imitated quickly. Thus, the Internet tends to increase rivalry by making it difficult for firms to differentiate themselves and by shifting customer attention to issues of price.

As we saw in Chapter 2, rivalry is more intense when switching costs are low and product or service differentiation is minimized. Because the Internet makes it possible to shop around with a few clicks of the mouse, it has "commoditized" products that might previously have been regarded as rare or unique. Since the Internet eliminates the importance of location, products that previously had to be sought out in geographically distant outlets are now readily available online. This makes competitors in cyberspace seem more equally balanced, thus intensifying rivalry.

The problem is made worse for marketers by the presence of shopping robots ("bots") and infomediaries that search the Web for the best possible prices. Consumer Web sites like mySimon and PriceSCAN seek out all the Web locations that sell similar products and provide price comparisons.[31] Obviously, this hinders a firm's ability to establish unique characteristics and focuses the consumer exclusively on price. Some shopping infomediaries, such as BizRate and CNET, not only search for the lowest prices on many different products but also rank the customer service quality of different sites that sell similarly priced items.[32] This is important because research indicates that customer service is three times more important than price to repeat online sales.[33] Such infomediary services are good for consumers because they give them the chance to compare services as well as price. For businesses, however, they increase rivalry by consolidating the marketing message that consumers use to make a purchase decision to a few key pieces of information over which the selling company has little control.

Recognizing that this phenomenon is part of the new Internet reality, many companies willingly participate in such services.[34] For example, BestBookBuys.com is a site that searches for the best prices among the Web sites of 24 different booksellers, including major ones such as Amazon and Barnes & Noble.[35] The booksellers featured on the site are member participants. They have agreed to have their prices included because it provides another kind of access to consumers. If they refused to be included, book buyers might never consider doing business with them. At least this way, there is a possibility that a new buyer will be attracted to a bookseller's site and make a return visit.

The online music business, discussed earlier in the chapter, provides a good example of how Internet and digital technologies have increased competitive rivalry. In addition to Napster and Apple iTunes, dozens of online music providers are vying for business. The competition is heating up around issues of price and capacity, i.e., the number of available titles. Competitors such as RealNetworks have offered songs for as little as $0.49 each (compared to about $0.99 on Apple iTunes).[36] The Internet amplifies this price-based rivalry in several ways. Switching costs are very low for Internet-based businesses. Compared to physically visiting another store to purchase music, alternative Web sites can be visited quickly and easily. The end products themselves are almost completely undifferentiated—one digital version of a song is virtually the same as another. The fact that the deliverable is digital also makes distribution very simple. All a consumer needs is access to a computer and the software (which is generally provided free) with which to download. These Internet-enabled factors make rivalry in the music selling industry more competitive than ever.

Exhibit 8.4 summarizes many of the ways the Internet is affecting industry structure. These influences will also change how companies develop and deploy strategies to generate above-average profits and sustainable competitive advantage. We turn to these topics next.

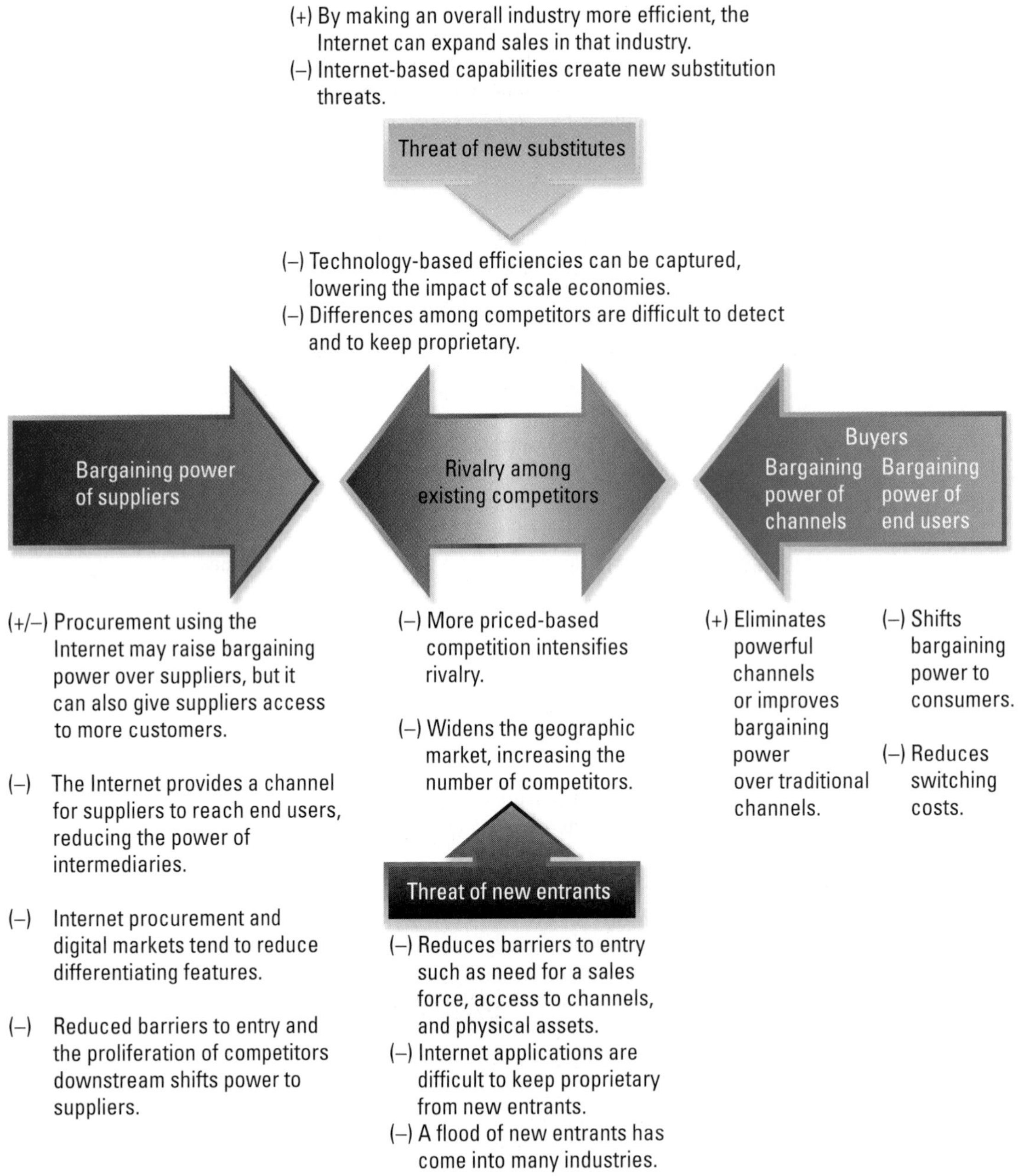

(+) By making an overall industry more efficient, the Internet can expand sales in that industry.
(–) Internet-based capabilities create new substitution threats.

**Threat of new substitutes**

(–) Technology-based efficiencies can be captured, lowering the impact of scale economies.
(–) Differences among competitors are difficult to detect and to keep proprietary.

**Bargaining power of suppliers**

**Rivalry among existing competitors**

**Buyers**
**Bargaining power of channels    Bargaining power of end users**

(+/–) Procurement using the Internet may raise bargaining power over suppliers, but it can also give suppliers access to more customers.

(–) The Internet provides a channel for suppliers to reach end users, reducing the power of intermediaries.

(–) Internet procurement and digital markets tend to reduce differentiating features.

(–) Reduced barriers to entry and the proliferation of competitors downstream shifts power to suppliers.

(–) More priced-based competition intensifies rivalry.

(–) Widens the geographic market, increasing the number of competitors.

**Threat of new entrants**

(–) Reduces barriers to entry such as need for a sales force, access to channels, and physical assets.
(–) Internet applications are difficult to keep proprietary from new entrants.
(–) A flood of new entrants has come into many industries.

(+) Eliminates powerful channels or improves bargaining power over traditional channels.

(–) Shifts bargaining power to consumers.

(–) Reduces switching costs.

**Exhibit 8.4    How the Internet Influences Industry Structure**

Source: Adapted and reprinted by permission of *Harvard Business Review.* Exhibit from "Strategy and the Internet," by M. E. Porter, March 2001. Copyright © 2001 by the Harvard Business School Publishing Corporation; all rights reserved.

# >>How the Internet and Digital Technologies Add Value

Using a five-forces framework, we have identified how the Internet and other digital technologies are influencing the competitive landscape. Next we turn to how companies can use these technologies to add value and create competitive advantages. As we noted earlier, the technology itself, whether it is digital or Internet, becomes strategically significant only when its practical application creates new value.

Clearly, the Internet has changed the way business is conducted. By conducting business online and using digital technologies to streamline operations, the Internet is helping companies create new value propositions. Let's take a look at several ways these changes have added new value. Exhibit 8.5 illustrates four related activities that are being revolutionized by the Internet—search, evaluation, problem solving, and transaction.[37]

## Search Activities

*Search* refers to the process of gathering information and identifying purchase options. The Internet has enhanced both the speed of information gathering and the breadth of information that can be accessed. This enhanced search capability is one of the key reasons the Internet has lowered switching costs—by decreasing the cost of search. These efficiency gains have greatly benefited buyers. Suppliers also have benefited. Small suppliers that had difficulty getting noticed can more easily be found, and large suppliers can publish thousands of pages of information for a fraction of the cost that hard-copy catalogs once required. Additionally, online search engines have accelerated the search process to incredible speeds. Consider the example of Google:

> Google, a search engine developed as a project by two graduate students, became the number one search service in just four years. Why? Because it is capable of incredible things: Using 10,000 networked computers, it searches 3 billion Web pages in an average of 500 milliseconds. To do the same search manually, by thumbing through 3 billion pages at the rate of one minute per page, would take 5,707 years. This ability has made Google an essential tool for many businesses. As a result, Google has built a powerful advertising business. Mark Kini, who runs a small limousine service in Boston, spends 80 percent of his advertising budget on Google and other search engines. "It's how we survive," says Kini.[38]

## Evaluation Activities

*Evaluation* refers to the process of considering alternatives and comparing the costs and benefits of various options. Online services that facilitate comparative shopping, provide

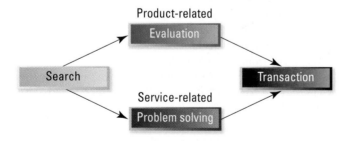

**Exhibit 8.5**    **Internet Activities That Add Value**

Sources: Adapted from Zeng, M., & Reinartz, W. 2003. Beyond online search: The road to profitability. *California Management Review,* Winter: 107–130; and Stabell, C. B., & Fjeldstad, O. D. 1998. Configuring value for competitive advantage: On chains, shops, and networks. *Strategic Management Journal,* 19: 413–437.

product reviews, and catalog customer evaluations of performance have made the Internet a valuable resource.[39] For example, BizRate.com offers extensive product ratings that can help evaluate products. Sites such as CNET that provide comparative pricing have helped lower prices even for quality products that have traditionally maintained premium prices. Opinion-based sites such as ePinions.com and PlanetFeedback.com provide reports of consumer experiences with various vendors.

Many Internet businesses, according to digital business experts Ming Zeng and Werner Reinartz, could improve their performance by making a stronger effort to help buyers evaluate purchases.[40] Even so, only certain types of products can be evaluated online. Products such as CDs that appeal primarily to the sense of sound sell well on the Internet. But products that appeal to multiple senses are harder to evaluate online. This explains why products such as furniture and fashion have never been strong online sellers. It's one thing to look at a leather sofa, but to be able to sit in it, touch, and smell the leather online are impossible.

## Problem-Solving Activities

*Problem solving* refers to the process of identifying problems or needs and generating ideas and action plans to address those needs. Whereas evaluation is primarily product-related, problem solving is typically used in the context of services. Customers usually have unique problems and therefore are handled one at a time. For example, online travel services such as Travelocity help customers select from many options to form a unique travel package. Furthermore, problem solving often involves providing answers immediately (compared to the creation of a new product). Firms in industries such as medicine, law, and engineering are using the Internet and digital technologies to deliver many new solutions.

Many products involve both a service and a product component; therefore, both problem solving and evaluation may be needed. Dell Computer's Web site is an example of a site that has combined the benefits of both. By creating a Web site that allows for customization of individual computers, they address the unique concerns of customers "one computer at a time." But the site also features a strong evaluative component because it allows users to compare the costs and features of various options. Shoppers can even compare their customized selection to refurbished Dell computers that are available at a substantially lower cost.

## Transaction Activities

*Transaction* refers to the process of completing the sale, including negotiating and agreeing contractually, making payments, and taking delivery. Numerous types of Internet-enabled activities have contributed to lowering this aspect of overall transaction costs. Auctions of various sorts, from raw materials used in manufacturing to collectibles sold on eBay, facilitate the process of arriving at mutually agreed-on prices. Services such as PayPal provide a third-party intermediary that facilitates transactions between parties who never have (and probably never will!) meet. Amazon.com's One-Click technology allows for very rapid purchases, and Amazon's overall superiority in managing order fulfillment has made its transactions process rapid and reliable. Amazon's success today can be attributed to a large extent to its having sold this transaction capability to other companies such as Target, Toys "R" Us and even Borders (another bookstore!).[41]

These four factors are primary ways that organizations go about adding value. Strategy Spotlight 8.4 describes several examples of how the automobile industry and car buyers have used each of these activities to benefit their own value-adding efforts.

## Adding Value in the Auto Industry

The auto industry jumped on the Internet bandwagon in a big way. One of the early successes was Autobytel, and many online auto sales Web sites quickly followed. Today, the automakers—and the auto-buying public—have found ways to use the Internet profitably. Here are a few examples:

**Search** EBay, the online auction giant that makes searching for products of all sorts fast and simple, has become a serious player in the used car business. Beginning with a few private individuals, the auto auction business took off unexpectedly, so the company formed eBay Motors, which contributed about $100 million to eBay's total revenue of $1.2 billion in a recent year. EBay's technology speeds the process of online search, and buyers who may have been reluctant to shop for cars online are comforted by eBay's reputation. EBay and other online auto sales sites make searching for insurance and auto financing easier as well.

**Problem Solving** To help its dealers manage inventories more effectively, General Motors developed SmartAuction. For vehicles that are coming off lease, SmartAuction notifies customers to bring in cars for an inspection before the lease expires. The condition of the car is logged into the system and sent to GM dealers, who use it to purchase cars electronically for their used car lots. The system helps dealers find cars that fit their target audience, manages the auto titling process, and shortens the time cars are carried in inventory.

**Evaluation** In the early days of the Internet, most thought that cars would never sell online, because customers like to kick the tires and take a test drive. This is often still true. But customers who go for a test drive and also have already researched the car online usually save money when they buy. Economists researching this phenomenon have labeled it the "information effect"—auto shoppers who first gather information online are better able to evaluate their purchase.

**Transaction** Auto referral services such as CarsDirect have streamlined the transaction process by brokering purchases between dealers and consumers. Through these companies, both new and used cars can be purchased online, sight unseen. One shopper, who bought a used car online, flew to Fort Worth, Texas, to pick it up, and drove it 18 hours back home to Ohio, said, "In retrospect, I had more information about this vehicle than if I had gone onto a dealer's lot and started haggling over price." Online auto shoppers typically save money due to the "contract effect," which occurs because third-party auto referral services monitor the information provided by dealers and facilitate the transaction.

Sources: Postrell, V. 2003. How much is that Civic online? *New York Times*, April 24, www.nytimes.com; Stepanek, M. 2003. New routes in the Internet car business. *CIO Insight*, January 23, www.cioinsight.com; and, Wingfield, N., & Lundegaard, K. 2003. EBay is emerging as unlikely giant in used-car sales. *Wall Street Journal*, February 7.

## Other Sources of Competitive Advantage

There are other factors that can be important sources of competitive advantage. One of the most important of these is content. The Internet makes it possible to capture vast amounts of content at a very low cost. REI.com, for example, a provider of recreational equipment and apparel, has over 78,000 items described on its 45,000-page Web site.[42] But firms have not always managed content in ways that add value. Garden.com, a site that started strongly in 1999 and raised enormous venture capital, spent millions on creating detailed and attractive content. But the expense did not generate sales. Content adds value only if it contributes to the overall value proposition. As a result, Garden.com failed in early 2001 (but the name is still being used by the Burpee Company, a 125-year-old supplier of garden products, who bought rights to the name).[43]

Three types of content can improve the value proposition of a Web site—customer feedback, expertise, and entertainment programming.

- **Customer feedback.** Buyers often trust what other buyers say more than a company's promises. One type of content that can enhance a Web site is customer testimonials. Remember the leather sofa in the example above? Even though individuals can't feel and smell a sofa online, the testimonials of other buyers can build confidence and add to the chances that the purchaser will buy online sight unseen. This is one way that content can be a source of competitive advantage. Being able to interact with like-minded customers by reading their experiences or hearing how they have responded to a new product offering builds a sense of belonging that is otherwise hard to create.

- *Expertise.* The Internet has emerged as a tremendously important learning tool. Fifty-one percent of users compare the Internet to a library.[44] The prime reason many users go to the Web is to gain expertise. Web sites that provide new knowledge or unbiased information are highly valuable. Additionally the problem-solving function often involves educating consumers regarding options and implications of various choices. For example, LendingTree.com, the online loan company, provides a help center that includes extensive information and resources about obtaining loans, maintaining good credit, and so forth. Further, the expertise function is not limited to consumer sites. In the case of B2B businesses, Web sites that facilitate sharing expert knowledge help build a sense of community in industry or professional groups.

- *Entertainment programming.* The Internet is being used by more and more people as an entertainment medium. With technologies such as streaming media, which allows the Internet to send televisionlike images and sound, computers can provide everything from breaking news to video games to online movies. A study by the Pew Internet and American Life Project indicates that among people using high-speed broadband service, TV viewing is down and online activity has increased. One reason is that the technology is interactive, which means that viewers don't just passively watch, but they use the Web to create art or play online games. Businesses have noticed this trend, of course, and are creating Web content that is not just informative but entertaining. Strategy Spotlight 8.5 tells how online game developer Skyworks Technologies is using games to increase product sales.

These three types of content—customer feedback, expertise, and entertainment programming—are potential sources of competitive advantage. That is, they create advantages by making the value creation process even stronger. Or, if they are handled poorly, they diminish performance.

Next we turn to the topic of Internet business models. How the Internet creates value depends to a great extent on how a value proposition is enacted. Business models provide a guide to the effectiveness of the value-adding process.

## Business Models

The Internet provides a unique platform or staging area for business activity, which has become, in some ways, like a new marketplace. How do firms conduct business in this new arena? One way of addressing this question is by describing various Internet business models. A business model is a method and a set of assumptions that explain how a business creates value and earns profits in a competitive environment. Some of these models are quite simple and traditional even when applied in an Internet context. Others have features that are unique to the digitally networked, online environment. In this section, we discuss seven Internet business models that account for the vast majority of business conducted online.[45]

- *Commission-based* models are used by businesses that provide services for a fee. The business is usually a third-party intermediary, and the commission charged is

## "Advergaming": Making Advertisements Interactive and Fun

Video games were popular well before the Web came along. But new digital technologies have made it possible to feature some of the best games online. Combine this with advertisers' need to use the Net's interactivity to make online ads more interesting and what do you get? Advergaming—online games that weave advertisements into the experience. Here are some examples:

- A game designed for Pepsi involves an auto race in which the goal is to recover a stolen shipment of Mountain Dew Code Red. The top 100 gamers received a free case of the soft drink.

- Some games make you buy something to play. To play the Pebbles Big Barney Chase game, players must answer a question; to learn the answer, you have to purchase a box of Post Cereal.

- Candystand.com, a Web site developed by Skyworks Technologies to promote Life Savers for Kraft Foods, features dozens of card, racing, and arcade games and ranks as the sixth most popular gaming destination on the Web.

Sources: Athitakis, M. 2003. The entertainer. *Business 2.0*, May: 88; Suciu, P. 2003. Mobility takes the forum. *GameSpy*, May 2, www.gamespy.com; www.candystand.com; www.skyworkstech.com; Keighley, G. 2004. Quick-change ads for the joystick generation. *Business 2.0*, 5(8): 31–32; and www.ssx3.com.

- SSX 3, an extreme sports games that pits gamers against the thrills and perils of a massive mountain, lets players snowboard through the open door of a Honda Element SUV.

Spending on advergaming is expected to more than double from $21 million in 2004 to $44 million in 2007. This kind of growth was enough to prompt Nielsen Interactive Entertainment (compiler of the all-important Nielsen Ratings) to develop a "people meter" to gauge how long people play games, which ads they see while playing, and how long they see them. "Measured media is going to lend credibility to the videogame space," says Sam Bloom of Camelot Communications, a media marketing firm whose clients include Blockbuster and Southwest Airlines.

According to Skyworks founder Garry Kitchen, advergaming can leave a deeper and more positive impression than television commercials. The idea is catching on. In a recent year, Skyworks made $4.3 million in revenues, and industry analyst Kent Allen of the Aberdeen Group expects the trend to continue, especially among consumer packaged-goods marketers. "The consumer guys are starting to understand advergaming," says Allen. "They're realizing it's a great way to connect with people."

---

often based on the size of the transaction. The most common type is a brokerage service, such as a stockbroker (e.g., Schwab.com), real estate broker (e.g., Remax. com), or transaction broker (e.g., Paypal.com). This category also includes auction companies such as eBay. In exchange for putting buyers and sellers together, eBay earns a commission.

- ***Advertising-based*** models are used by companies that provide content and/or services to visitors and sell advertising to businesses that want to reach those visitors. It is similar to the broadcast television model, in which viewers watch shows produced with advertising dollars. A key difference is that online visitors can interact with both the ads and the content. Large portals such as Yahoo.com are in this category as well as specialty portals such as iNest.com, which provides services for buyers of newly constructed homes. EPinions.com, a recommender system, is just one example of the many types of content that are often available.

- ***Markup-based*** models are used by businesses that add value in marketing and sales (rather than production) by acquiring products, marking up the price, and reselling them at a profit. Also known as the merchant model, it applies to both wholesalers and retailers. Amazon.com is the best-known example in this category.

It also includes bricks-and-mortar companies such as Wal-Mart, which has a very successful online operation, and vendors whose products are purely digital such as Fonts.com, which sells downloadable fonts and photographs.

- *Production-based* models are used by companies that add value in the production process by converting raw materials into value-added products. Thus, it is also referred to as the manufacturing model. The Internet adds value to this model in two key ways. First, it lowers marketing costs by enabling direct contact with end users. Second, such direct contact facilitates customization and problem solving. Dell's online ordering system is supported by a state-of-the-art customized manufacturing process. Travelocity uses its rich database of travel options and customer profiles to identify, produce, and deliver unique solutions.

- *Referral-based* models are used by firms that steer customers to another company for a fee. One type is the affiliate model, in which a vendor pays an affiliate a fee each time a visitor clicks through the affiliate's Web site and makes a purchase from the vendor. Many name-brand companies use affiliate programs. For example, WeddingChannel.com, which provides a bridal registry where wedding guests can buy gifts from companies such as Tiffany's, Macy's, or Crate & Barrel, receives a fee each time a sale is made through its Web site. Another referral-based example is Yesmail.com, which generates leads using e-mail marketing.

- *Subscription-based* models are used by businesses that charge a flat fee for providing either a service or proprietary content. Internet service providers are one example of this model. Companies such as America Online and Earthlink supply Internet connections for fees that are charged whether buyers use the service or not. Subscription-based models are also used by content creators such as the *Economist* or the *New York Times.* Although these recognizable brands often provide free content, only a small portion is available free. The *Economist,* for example, advertises that 70 percent of its content is available only to subscribers.

- *Fee-for-service-based* models are used by companies that provide ongoing services similar to a utility company. Unlike the commission-based model, the fee-for-service model involves a pay-as-you-go system. That is, activities are metered and companies pay only for the amount of service used. Application service providers fall in this category. For example, eProject.com provides virtual work space where people in different physical locations can collaborate online. Users essentially rent Internet space, and a host of tools that make it easy to interact, for a fee based on their usage.

Exhibit 8.6 summarizes the key feature of each Internet business model, suggests what role content may play in the model, and addresses how the four value-adding activities—search, evaluation, problem solving, and transaction—can be sources of competitive advantage.

It's important to keep in mind that many companies combine these models to achieve competitive advantages. For example, a company such as LendingTree not only sells advertising but also earns a commission as a third-party intermediary and earns fees by referring viewers to other sites through its affiliate programs.

Next, we turn to the topic of how the Internet and digital technologies are influencing the three competitive strategies—overall low cost, differentiation, and focus—and

Exhibit 8.6

**Internet Business Models**

| Type | Features and Content | Sources of Competitive Advantage |
|---|---|---|
| **Commission-based** | Charges commissions for brokerage or intermediary services. Adds value by providing expertise and/or access to a wide network of alternatives. | Search<br>Evaluation<br>Problem solving<br>Transaction |
| **Advertising-based** | Web content paid for by advertisers. Adds value by providing free or low-cost content—including customer feedback, expertise, and entertainment programming—to audiences that range from very broad (general content) to highly targeted (specialized content). | Search<br>Evaluation |
| **Markup-based** | Resells marked-up merchandise. Adds value through selection, through distribution efficiencies, and by leveraging brand image and reputation. May use entertainment programming to enhance sales. | Search<br>Transaction |
| **Production-based** | Sells manufactured goods and custom services. Adds value by increasing production efficiencies, capturing customer preferences, and improving customer service. | Search<br>Problem solving |
| **Referral-based** | Charges fees for referring customers. Adds value by enhancing a company's product or service offering, tracking referrals electronically, and generating demographic data. Expertise and customer feedback often included with referral information. | Search<br>Problem solving<br>Transaction |
| **Subscription-based** | Charges fees for unlimited use of service or content. Adds value by leveraging strong brand name, providing high-quality information to specialized markets, or providing access to essential services. May consist entirely of entertainment programming. | Evaluation<br>Problem solving |
| **Fee-for-service-based** | Charges fees for metered services. Adds value by providing service efficiencies, expertise, and practical outsourcing solutions. | Problem solving<br>Transaction |

Sources: Afuah, A., & Tucci, C. L. 2003. *Internet business models and strategies* (2nd ed.). New York: McGraw-Hill; Rappa, M. 2005. Business models on the Web, digitalenterprise.org/models/models.html; and Timmers, P. 1999. *Electronic commerce.* New York: Wiley.

discuss further the role of combination strategies in creating competitive advantages for Internet companies.

## >>How the Internet and Digital Technologies Are Affecting the Competitive Strategies

As we have seen, the Internet and digital technologies are sweeping across the economy and affecting in many ways how business is conducted. The Internet is a resource that companies around the world can access. Thus, to stay competitive, firms must update their strategies to reflect the new possibilities and constraints that these phenomena represent. In this section we will revisit the three competitive strategies introduced in Chapter 5—overall cost leadership, differentiation, and focus—and address how the Internet and digital technologies can be used to enhance firm performance. We will also consider two major impacts that the Internet is having on business: lowering transaction costs and enabling mass customization. Finally, we will briefly discuss the pitfalls associated with using the new technologies and will address the role of combination strategies in achieving competitive advantages.

### Overall Cost Leadership

An overall low-cost leadership strategy involves managing costs in every activity of a firm's value chain and offering no-frills products that are an exceptional value at the best possible price. We have seen how companies such as Wal-Mart and Southwest Airlines achieved this position through vigilant attention to cost control. Internet and digital technologies now provide even more opportunities to manage costs and achieve greater efficiencies. But these capabilities are available to many competing firms, and even specialized capabilities (i.e., those that firms might realize by using proprietary software) often provide only a short-lived advantage.

Nevertheless, managing costs, and even changing the cost structures of certain industries, is a key feature of the new digital economy. Most analysts agree that the Internet's ability to lower transaction costs will transform business. Broadly speaking, *transaction costs* refer to all the various expenses associated with conducting business. It applies not just to buy/sell transactions but to the costs of interacting with every part of a firm's value chain, within and outside the firm. Think about it. Hiring new employees, meeting with customers, ordering supplies, addressing government regulations—all of these exchanges have some costs associated with them. Because business can be conducted differently on the Internet, new ways of saving money are changing the competitive landscape.

Consider how one company, British Petroleum (BP), has used the Internet and digital technologies to lower procurement costs and create efficient methods to communicate:[46]

> British Petroleum has achieved a number of strategic advantages with its Internet initiatives, including a $300 million savings in a recent year. Led by John Leggate, BP's group vice president for digital business, the company has pursued an aggressive policy of implementing Internet-based cost savings. For example:
>
> - Instead of sending teams to far-off exploration targets, BP scientists now gather in any of 15 data centers around the globe to view digital 3-D images of drilling sites sent over the Internet. *Payoff:* Up to $250 million in annual savings.
> - All BP employees have personalized Web pages listing their areas of expertise. This helps managers tap into BP's reservoir of knowledge. *Payoff:* In one case, engineers in the Caribbean saved $600,000 by adopting a drilling process developed in Norway just a few days earlier.

Such practices are strengthening the role of the Internet and digital technologies in cutting expenses and managing transaction costs throughout the value chain.

Other factors also help to lower transaction costs. The process of disintermediation, described earlier in this chapter, has a similar effect. Each time intermediaries are used in a transaction, additional costs are added. Removing those intermediaries lowers transaction costs. The Internet reduces the costs of traveling to a location to search for a product or service, whether it is a retail outlet (as in the case of consumers) or a trade show (as in the case of business-to-business shoppers). Not only is the need for travel eliminated, but so is the need to maintain a physical address, whether it's a permanent retail location or a temporary presence at a trade show.

In terms of strategizing, therefore, the Internet and digital technologies are creating new opportunities for firms to achieve low-cost advantages.[47] Of course, the same potential benefits are available to all companies relatively equally, but some companies have adopted these capabilities more rapidly or implemented them more efficiently. These cost savings are available throughout a firm's value chain, in both primary and support activities:

- Direct access to progress reports and the ability for customers to periodically check work in progress is minimizing rework.
- Online bidding and order processing are eliminating the need for sales calls and are minimizing sales force expenses.
- Online purchase orders are making many transactions paperless, thus reducing the costs of procurement and paper.
- Collaborative design efforts using Internet technologies that link designers, materials suppliers, and manufacturers are reducing the costs and speeding the process of new-product development.
- Human resources departments are using online testing and evaluation techniques in the hiring process and in online training after they hire.

*Potential Internet-Related Pitfalls for Low-Cost Leaders*   As Internet and digital technologies become more widespread, the cost advantages that early users of these technologies enjoyed may be available to many firms. One of the biggest threats to low-cost leaders is imitation. This problem is intensified for business done on the Internet. Most of the advantages associated with contacting customers directly, and even capabilities that are software driven (e.g., customized ordering systems or real-time access to the status of work in progress that lowers the cost of rework), can be duplicated quickly and without threat of infringement on proprietary information.

Another major pitfall for low-cost providers is the availability of information online that allows consumers to comparison shop much more easily. Also, companies that become overly enamored with the Internet and its ability to cut costs may suffer if they place too much attention on one business activity and ignore others. They may jeopardize customer relations or neglect other cost centers, such as providing services or controlling turnover and recruiting expenses, which then dig into their cost advantages.

## Differentiation

A differentiation strategy involves providing unique, high-quality products and services that promote a favorable reputation and strong brand identity and usually command a premium price. Throughout this text we have seen examples of strong differentiators—Disney, Nokia, BMW, and others. The Internet and digital technologies have created new ways for firms to achieve a competitive advantage. Some of these capabilities are being used to threaten the position of companies that have traditionally maintained the best reputations or strong leadership positions. Other technologies are being employed by industry leaders to make their position even stronger.

Consider the example of emachineShop.com, which provides computer-aided design (CAD) software for free to companies seeking to custom-design machine-made parts.[48] The downloadable software not only allows users to create three-dimensional designs, but also analyzes the shape, materials, and finished appearance and automatically informs the user of any limitations of the design. Once the design is finalized, the software prices the finished product and orders the parts over the Internet. Then, eMachineShop.com actually manufactures the part. The process is far faster than previous methods and the easy-to-use software allows for direct customer involvement in the end product.

Among the most striking trends that the new technologies foster are new ways to interact with consumers. In particular, the Internet is creating new ways of differentiating by enabling *mass customization,* which improves the response of companies to customer wishes. Mass customization is not a new phenomenon; it has been growing for years as flexible manufacturing systems have made manufacturing more adaptable and electronic data interchange has made communications more direct. But the Internet has generated a giant leap forward in the amount of control customers can have in influencing the process. Such capabilities are changing the way companies develop unique product and service offerings, make their reputation, and preserve their brand image. The new technology may affect the structure of entire industries. In the old days, manufacturers built products and waited for customers to respond. Now they are taking directions from customers before manufacturing any products. Consider the following examples.

- Dell Computer has strengthened its leadership position by creating an online ordering system that allows customers to configure their own computers before they are built.[49]

- 7 Eleven, a convenience store operator, has created a finely tuned feedback system that monitors subtle shifts in customer demand and recommends revisions to its product offerings on a daily basis.[50]

- Footwear giant Nike lets customers choose the color of their shoes and add a personal name or nickname through its NIKEiD program. Customers can view their selection at the Nike.com Web site before finalizing the order.[51]

Methods like mass customization, which are changing the way companies go to market, are challenging some of the tried-and-true techniques of differentiation. Traditionally, companies reached customers in various ways—the high-end catalog, the showroom floor, the personal sales call—and used numerous means to make products more inviting—prestige packaging, celebrity endorsements, charity sponsorships. All of these avenues are still available and may still be effective, depending on a firm's competitive environment. But many consumers now judge the quality and uniqueness of a product or service by their ability to be involved in planning and design, combined with speed of delivery and reliability of results. Internet and digitally based capabilities are thus changing the way differentiators make exceptional products and achieve superior service. And these improvements are being made at a reasonable cost, allowing firms to achieve parity on the basis of overall cost leadership relative to competitors (see Chapter 5).

Here again, opportunities to differentiate using Internet and digital technologies are available in all parts of a company's value chain. Some of the techniques firms are using to achieve competitive advantage are fast becoming industry norms; successful differentiators will need to remain attentive to the evolving capabilities of the new technologies. These capabilities are evident in both primary and support activities.

- Internet-based knowledge management systems that link all parts of the organization are shortening response times and accelerating organization learning.

- Personalized online access provides customers with their own "site within a site" in which their prior orders, status of current orders, and requests for future orders are processed directly on the supplier's Web site.

- Quick online responses to service requests and rapid feedback to customer surveys and product promotions are enhancing marketing efforts.

- Online access to real-time sales and service information is being used to empower the sales force and continually update R&D and technology development efforts.

- Automated procurement and payment systems provide both suppliers and customers with access to detailed status reports and purchasing histories.

*Potential Internet-Related Pitfalls for Differentiators*   As applications of these technologies become part of the mainstream, it will become harder to use the Web to differentiate. The sustainability of Internet-based gains from differentiation will deteriorate if companies offer differentiating features that customers don't want or create a sense of uniqueness that customers don't value. This has been the case with some of the personalization and customization software that early dot-com companies added to their sites at great expense. Users did not care about these features and that led to a failed value proposition—the value companies thought they were offering did not translate into sales. Other problems can result from overpricing products and services or developing brand extensions that dilute a company's image or reputation.

Now consider the efforts of one firm that has drawn on the Internet's technological capabilities to attempt a new approach to strategizing. Strategy Spotlight 8.6 profiles Buy.com, an Internet company with an unusual approach. Is it a differentiator or an overall cost leader? Whether the answer is "neither" or "both," Buy.com appears so far to have defied traditional strategic thinking.

## Focus

A focus strategy involves targeting a narrow market segment with customized products and/or specialized services. For companies that pursue focus strategies, the Internet offers new avenues in which to compete because they can access markets less expensively (low cost) and provide more services and features (differentiation). Some claim that the Internet has opened up a new world of opportunities for niche players who seek to access small markets in a highly specialized fashion.[52] Niche businesses are among the most active users of digital technologies and e-business solutions. According to the ClickZ.com division of Jupitermedia Corporation, 77 percent of small businesses agree that a Web site is essential for small business success. Small businesses also report that the Internet has helped them grow (58 percent), made them more profitable (51 percent), and helped reduce business costs (49 percent).[53] Clearly, niche players and small businesses are using the Internet and digital technologies to create more viable focus strategies.

Nevertheless, even though the Internet and digital technologies present some exciting new possibilities, the same problems that low-cost leaders and differentiators face in

# STRATEGY SPOTLIGHT

## Buy.Com's Risky Strategy

In terms of Michael Porter's competitive strategies, Buy.com tried something very risky. It tried to build brand with an overall cost leadership strategy. Developing a brand image that customers will turn to and rely on is traditionally associated with a differentiation strategy. Heavy investments in advertising to create brand recognition are generally considered ineffective for low-cost providers because customers seeking the lowest price tend to be less loyal. They follow the low price, not the brand.

This didn't stop Buy.com, an online retailer of electronics, books, video games, and more. From the beginning it sought to build a reputation as the lowest-cost provider with the advertising slogan "lowest prices on earth." It purchased hundreds of domain names that started with the term "buy": BuyNokia.com, BuySony.com, and so forth. Then it offered incredibly low prices, well below market value. In the case of hot, new high-demand products, it sold loss leaders at negative gross margins to attract buyers. It hoped to make up the difference in advertising revenues. As a self-proclaimed "superstore" offering 30,000 different products, Buy.com sought to build a reputation as the best place to shop for low prices and thus an ideal venue for the ads of other vendors.

Has this strategy worked? It's still too early to tell. Buy.com did achieve $100 million in sales faster than any other company in history, but it also chalked up significant losses. In addition to negative profitability, Buy.com has had numerous problems with order fulfillment and has developed a reputation for advertising products that were back-ordered for weeks. Its hopes for advertising revenue were not fulfilled either, as the luster of banner ads faded and the dot-com downturn caused everyone to have second thoughts about online advertising.

In late 2001, Buy.com founder Scott Blum reacquired the company for $23.6 million and took it private. This purchase price was equivalent to 17 cents per share even though at one time the company's stock sold for $35 per share. Blum, who earlier in 2001 had provided Buy.com with $9 million in interim financing, said he would return the company to its "Internet Superstore" roots and relaunch its "Lowest Prices on Earth" marketing campaign. More recently, Buy.com has launched a glossy magazine and boasted it will outperform Amazon.com by offering free shipping on everything.

Such features are costly and make Buy.com appear to be differentiating. However, it continues to position itself as an overall low-cost leader in terms of pricing. "I do not believe that Buy.com's pricing assault on Amazon.com is sustainable," said Ken Cassar, senior analyst at Jupiter Media Metrix. "It is very likely . . . that Buy.com will steal market share from Amazon in the short term. Whether that is sustainable will depend upon whether customers will come back to Buy.com when there is no promotion."

Clearly the firm's long-term prospects are still uncertain. But that hasn't kept Blum, who owns 98 percent of the stock, from pursuing another unorthodox strategy. In 2005, he filed papers with the SEC to take Buy.com public—again. Will investors bite? "Buy.com has lot of a baggage," according to Tom Taulli, co-founder of CurrentOfferings.com. "Seven years ago Buy.com had sizzle. But this doesn't have a lot of sizzle to it." Indeed, in its eight years of existence, the company has never had a profitable year. And at the end of 2004, it had about $22 million in debt. Repaying that debt will be a top priority with the proceeds from the initial public offering (IPO).

Others see it more positively. Pattie Freeman Evans, a retail analyst for Jupiter Research says, "They've expanded in ways that make sense—like moving into books through books about computers." Buy.com's 2004 sales were $290.8 million. Still, that's way down from the $787.6 million in revenues for 2000. During the same period Overtock.com, one of its closest competitors, grew revenues from $25.5 million in 2000 to $494.6 million in 2004.

Buy.com continues to invest in its potentially risky strategy. Now it is asking investors to buy in as well.

Sources: *Economist.* 1999. Playing i-ball. November 6: 65; Porter, M. E. 2001. Strategy and the Internet. *Harvard Business Review,* March: 63–78; Cox, B. 2002. E-commerce price war escalates, Amazon expands. *InternetNews,* June 25, www.internetnews.com; Cox, B. 2002. And now, Buy.com the magazine. *InternetNews,* February 27; Singer, M. 2001. Scott Blum re-acquires. Buy.com. *InternetNews,* November 28; B. Cox. 2001. Buy.com returns to its roots. *InternetNews,* September 25. Lacy, S. 2005. Back to the future at Buy.com. *BusinessWeek Online,* www.businessweek.com, January 26; Hellweg, E. 2005. BuyersBeware.com. *Business 2.0,* www.business2.com, January 31; and www.hoovers.com.

a digital economy will affect focusers as well. Achieving competitive advantage will depend on how effectively firms use Internet technologies and deploy focus strategies. Let's look at SalvageSale, Inc., an online broker of salvage goods.

SalvageSale, Inc., has become the top choice of insurance and transportation companies that need to quickly liquidate commercial salvage goods. The Houston-based company has been successful by carefully watching costs, relying on word-of-mouth advertising, and staying focused on the narrow salvage goods market. Traditionally, when salvage goods become available, insurance adjusters and transportation agents seek bids from local brokers using faxes and telephone calls. But SalvageSale posts such information online, where many brokers can bid using an eBay-style auction. Because of the time saved by this method and the larger number of bidders reached, companies are getting higher prices for the salvaged goods. This, in turn, raises the total earnings of SalvageSale even though it charges considerably lower commissions than traditional brokers. The result: SalvageSale has become a leader in the $50 billion salvage goods industry.[54]

To create focus strategies that work, firms must consider how best to deploy their resources throughout every value-creating activity. Both primary and support activities can be enhanced using the kind of singlemindedness that is characteristic of a focus strategy. Companies that have adapted their strategies to serve specialized markets, however, may enjoy only a temporary advantage unless they seize the capabilities that the Internet provides for focusers:

- Permission marketing techniques are focusing sales efforts on specific customers who opt to receive advertising notices.

- Chat rooms, discussion boards, and member functions that create community for customers with common interests are increasing Web site usage.

- Niche portals that target specific groups are providing advertisers with access to viewers with specialized interests.

- Virtual organizing and online "officing" are being used to minimize firm infrastructure requirements.

- Procurement technologies that use Internet software to match buyers and sellers are highlighting specialized buyers and drawing attention to smaller suppliers.

*Potential Internet-Related Pitfalls for Focusers*    Many aspects of the Internet economy seem to favor focus strategies because niche players and small firms can often implement Internet capabilities as effectively as their larger competitors. However, the same technologies—and the same cost savings—that are creating new opportunities for focusers are also available to major players. Thus, focusers must use the new technology to provide the kinds of advantages that have been the hallmark of a focus strategy in the past: specialized knowledge, rapid response, and strong customer service.

These advantages may be challenged if focusers misread the scope and interests of their target markets. This can cause them to focus on segments that are too narrow to be profitable or to lose their uniqueness by going after overly broad niches, making them vulnerable to imitators or new entrants. What happens when an e-business focuser tries to overextend its niche? Efforts to appeal to a broader audience—by carrying additional inventory, developing additional content, or offering additional services—can cause it to lose the cost advantages associated with a limited product or service offering. Conversely, when focus strategies become too narrow, the e-business may have trouble generating enough activity to justify the expense of operating the Web site.

The wireless technology firm Bluetooth provides an example of a venture that has effectively managed the scope of its product/service offering. In the late 1990s, Bluetooth was considered the leading provider of personal area networks which are used to wirelessly connect equipment such as laptops and personal digital assistants (PDAs). Because Bluetooth had limited function and range, however, it was written off as overly

# STRATEGY SPOTLIGHT

## Bluetooth's Comeback

The technology known as Bluetooth refers to a wireless method of communicating over short distances. It's a sort of personal area network that enables devices such as cell phones and laptops to communicate with each other. When it was introduced in the late 1990s, it promised to get rid of all the cables that make using multiple gadgets so messy. However, after the initial hype, analysts said it was too costly and complex. Early versions had poor battery life and couldn't reliably perform key functions. Disagreements over a unified technology standard also delayed product introduction and many technology pundits wrote off Bluetooth as overly geeky and too narrowly focused.

Today, Bluetooth is back. Over 1,400 products incorporated Bluetooth technology in 2004, from cell phones and laptops to cars and medical equipment. Here are a few examples of how it is being used:

- Wireless headsets that communicate with cell phones are commonplace in Europe and are catching on fast in the United States. The Plantronics

Sources: Jacques, R. 2005. Wireless lans point to Bluetooth decay. *Forbes*, www.forbes.com, March 22; Maier, M. 2004. The comeback of the year: Bluetooth. *Business 2.0*, 5(9): 112; Miller, M. J. 2001. A tangled, wireless web. *PC Magazine*, www.pcmagazine.com, February 2; and Wildstrom, S. 2005. The new Bluetooth: More on the beam. *BusinessWeek Online*, www.businessweek.com, April 7.

version offers multiple methods of recharging the battery.

- Automobiles such as the Toyota Prius and Acura TL use Bluetooth to facilitate hands-free phones. In the TL, the handset is integrated with the car so the stereo system works as a speaker phone and caller information is displayed on the instrument panel.

- Apple Computers was among the first to release a new, faster version of Bluetooth. It comes standard in the Macintosh, which will automatically sync with a Bluetooth keyboard or mouse that it recognizes during set-up. Apple's new line of PowerBook laptops are also using it to sync and swap files with gadgets such as Bluetooth-enabled Treo Palm phones and Tungsten PDAs.

"Bluetooth is now in everything from consumer goods to medical devices," says Joyce Putscher of market research firm In-Stat. "It's no longer niche." Apparently not: 69 million Bluetooth semiconductors were shipped in 2003. Despite looming competition from VOIP wireless technologies (see Strategy Spotlight 8.2), the number is expected to reach 700 million by 2008, with a projected market value of $1.7 billion. For a product that many declared dead on arrival, that's an impressive comeback.

specialized. But Bluetooth persisted and its technology improved. Strategy Spotlight 8.7 describes the comeback of a strategic focuser that is effectively leveraging its unique digital technology.

## >>Are Digital- and Internet-Based Advantages Sustainable?

The Internet provides many ways to achieve above-average returns, but it may create even more possibilities for eroding unique advantages. So what's the bottom line? Strategy is about achieving competitive advantage and sustaining it. Do digital technologies and the Internet contribute to or detract from a firm's efforts to attain sustainable competitive advantages?

On the one hand, it appears that the Internet and the achievements in digital technology that it makes possible are creating new opportunities for strategic success. A few business models—those that offer capabilities that are unique to the Internet, such as eBay's auction system—seem to be providing strong, *lasting* opportunities for above-average profitability. Such new applications also have created opportunities for companies that supply equipment to run the Internet, such as Cisco Systems and Sun Microsystems, and companies that provide software applications management and online fulfillment services, such as Juniper Networks and SAP. As applications of these technologies mature, many more firms are finding ways to alter the competitive landscape and pursue new business opportunities. Traditional companies are also using the Internet and digital capabilities to create new strategic ventures. Consider InnoCentive, the Internet-based initiative launched by pharmaceutical giant Eli Lilly:

> InnoCentive, as the name implies, provides incentives for innovation. It does so by providing a platform for scientists from around the world to work in virtual communities to solve complex problems. The effort not only benefits Lilly but provides a virtual, open source R&D organization that any member company can use. Here's how it works: Drug companies, called "Seekers," put up "Wanted" posters describing problems that need addressing. Bounty-hunting scientists, labeled "Solvers," sign confidentiality agreements that gain them admission to a secure project room where they can access data and product specifications related to the problem. If they solve the problem, they get a reward—around $25,000 to $30,000 depending on the problem. According to InnoCentive president and CEO Darren J. Carroll, what Lilly has done is revolutionary. By creating a global community of scientists, "We're punching a hole in the side of the laboratory and exposing mission-critical problems to the outside world," says Carroll. "It's using the Net to communicate, collaborate, and innovate."[55]

On the other hand, the cycle of dot-com failures that burst the Internet bubble suggests that applications of Internet and digital technologies may be only temporary if they are built on an unsustainable base. Most observers agree that the downturn resulted, to a great extent, from overestimating the importance of the technology itself, ignoring business fundamentals, or overlooking basic economic requirements. Another major reason why so many start-ups failed was that the service or capability that they offered could be imitated easily. This was especially damaging for the young start-ups and "pure plays" (i.e., firms that exist only in cyberspace and have no other physical outlets). The reason? Larger firms with greater resources could observe what was working over time and bring more resources and talent to bear on an effective imitation strategy.

Thus, Internet technologies can benefit firms that use them effectively in ways that genuinely set them apart from rivals. But the extent to which the Internet can create advantages that are rare and difficult to imitate is highly questionable. Perhaps combination strategies (see Chapter 5) hold the key to successful digital business.

## Are Combination Strategies the Key to E-Business Success?

Because of the changing dynamics presented by digital- and Internet-based technologies, new strategic combinations that make the best use of the competitive strategies just described may hold the greatest promise for future success.[56] Several things are clear in this regard. First, the Internet in general is eroding opportunities for sustainable advantage. Many experts agree that the net effect of the digital economy is fewer rather than more opportunities for sustainable advantages.[57] This means strategic thinking is even more important in the Internet age.

More specifically, the Internet has provided all companies with greater tools for managing costs. So it may be that cost management and control will increase in importance as a management tool. In general, this may be good if it leads to an economy that makes more efficient use of its scarce resources. However, for individual companies, it may shave critical percentage points off profit margins and create a climate that makes it impossible to survive, much less achieve sustainable above-average profits.

Many differentiation advantages are also diminished by the Internet. The ability to comparison shop—to check product reviews and inspect different choices with a few clicks of the mouse—is depriving some companies, such as auto dealers, of the unique

## Liberty Mutual's Electronic Invoice System: Combining Low Cost and Differentiation Advantages

Boston-based Liberty Mutual Group is a leading global insurer and the sixth largest property and casualty insurer in the United States. Its largest line of business is personal automobile insurance. Liberty Mutual has $64.4 billion in assets and $16.6 billion in annual revenues—ranking the firm 116th on the Fortune 500 list of the largest corporations.

In 2000, Liberty Mutual became one of the first companies to experiment with electronic invoices. It set up a pilot program with a few law firms to submit its bills through a secured Web site. These firms, for the most part, handle claims litigation for Liberty, defending its policyholders in lawsuits. Its success with this program convinced Liberty that it could achieve significant cost savings and also pass along differentiating features to its customers and strategic partners. Liberty now processes nearly 400,000 electronic legal-services invoices a year—70 percent of the total invoices that the firm receives.

As expected, the initial transition was quite expensive. The company invested nearly $1 million in the first four years. However, Liberty estimates that the electronic invoice program saves the company $750,000 a year in direct costs by streamlining the distribution, payment, storage, and retrieval of invoices. E-invoices enable Liberty to move from intake to payment with half the staff that it had taken to process paper invoices. The firm has also created new efficiencies by cutting costs resulting from data entry errors, late payments, and overpayments. As a relatively minor issue, Liberty saves more than $20,000 per year on postage, photocopying, archiving, and retrieval costs.

The legal invoices are organized by litigation phase or task—for example, taking a deposition or reporting a witness statement. Work is diced into tiny increments of six minutes or less. A single invoice that covers a month of complex litigation, for example, can include well over 1,000 lines. However, by building and mining a database of law firm billing practices, Liberty is able to generate a highly granular report card about law firm activities and performance. The new knowledge generated by this system not only increases internal effectiveness but also allows Liberty to provide detailed feedback to clients and other external stakeholders.

Online invoicing has also helped speed up both processing and response time. Liberty can instantaneously see how firms deploy and bill for partners, paralegals, and other staff; how they compare with each other on rates, hours, and case outcomes; and whether, how, and how often they send duplicate invoices or charge for inappropriate services. The system also allows Liberty to instantly review all of the time billed for a particular attorney across many cases, enabling the firm to reconstruct the total time billed to Liberty during a single day. More than once they have found that attorneys have billed more than 24 hours in a day. Liberty is also able to easily expose prohibited formula billing patterns (wherein, for example, they are billed a set amount for a service instead of actual time spent). In two cases in which formula billing was used, Liberty found that there were more than $28,000 in suspected overcharges.

Liberty Mutual is in the process of developing a large database of law firms' billing practices on different types of cases. The database should eventually enable Liberty to evaluate a law firm's billing activities and compare them to the norms of all of its partner firms. With such intelligence, it will be a rather straightforward matter to rate each firm's cost effectiveness in handling certain types of cases and match firms with cases accordingly.

Liberty's decision to use electronic invoices was initially based on the potential for cost savings. But the differentiating advantages it has achieved—in terms of rapid feedback, decreased response time, and a knowledge trove in databases that can be electronically mined—has provided the company with a fruitful combination of Internet-based strategic advantages.

Sources: Coyle, M., & Cusolito, J. 2005. Liberty Mutual Group (LMG) to release 2004 financial results on March 2, 2005. www.libertymutual.com; and Smunt, T. L., & Sutcliffe, C. L. 2004. There's gold in them bills. *Harvard Business Review*, 82(9): 24–25.

advantages that were the hallmark of their success in a previous time. Differentiating is still an important strategy, of course. But how firms achieve it may change, and the best approach may be to combine a differentiation strategy with other competitive strategies. Strategy Spotlight 8.8 describes the efforts of Liberty Mutual, a traditional firm that has used digital technology to achieve both differentiation and cost advantages.

Perhaps the greatest beneficiaries are the focusers, who can use the Internet to capture a niche that previously may have been inaccessible. Even this is not assured, however, because the same factors that make it possible for a small niche player to be a contender may make that same niche attractive to a big company. That is, an incumbent firm that previously thought a niche market was not worth the effort may use Internet technologies to enter that segment for a lower cost than in the past. The larger firm can then bring its market power and resources to bear in a way that a smaller competitor cannot match.

Firms using combination strategies may also fall short if they underestimate the demands of combining strategic approaches and get "stuck in the middle." This can lead to inaccurately assessing the costs and benefits of a strategy that combines differentiating and low-cost features. Firms may believe they can keep prices and costs low but still offer high-end services that are expensive to provide.

Another potential pitfall for companies using combination strategies relates to the difficulty of managing complex strategies. Managers tend to develop a bias in favor of the functional areas with which they are most familiar. Furthermore, companies in general tend to fall into the trap of believing that there is "one best way" to accomplish organizational goals. A combination strategy, by definition, challenges a company to carefully blend alternative strategic approaches and remain mindful of the impact of different decisions on the firm's value-creating processes and its extended value-chain activities. Strong leadership is needed to maintain a bird's-eye perspective on a company's overall approach and to coordinate the multiple dimensions of a combination strategy.

Indeed, the key to effectively implementing any digital- or Internet-based strategy is for the leaders of today's firms to recognize that the digital economy has forever changed the way business is conducted and to adopt practices that use the advantages that new technologies have to offer without ignoring business fundamentals. Companies will increasingly need to adapt to the Internet and implement the capabilities that make digitally based business possible because, as Intel's former Chairman Andy Grove expressed it, "The world now runs on Internet time."[58]

# >>Leveraging Internet Capabilities

In this chapter we have emphasized the importance of the Internet and digital technologies in creating new business capabilities and new strategic initiatives. We have addressed how the Internet is affecting the five competitive forces and how it contributes to a firm's efforts to add value and create competitive advantages. We conclude by discussing how digital technologies and Internet-based capabilities can affect business-level strategy (Chapter 5), corporate-level strategy (Chapter 6), and international-level strategy (Chapter 7).

*Leveraging Internet Capabilities and Business-Level Strategy*    Chapter 5 addressed attributes and potential pitfalls of business-level strategies. Earlier in this chapter, we presented a rather detailed section on how the Internet and digital technologies are affecting overall low-cost, differentiation, and focus strategies and how combination strategies may be effective in the context of e-business. By providing new ways to add value and shifting the power of the five competitive forces, the Internet and digital technologies have altered the competitive climate in numerous industries. These changes often require modifications in generic strategies, sometimes leading to new strategic combinations. While many strategic imperatives remain the same, in some cases, such as Buy.com, this has led to a complete rethinking of how firms use resources and position themselves in a competitive environment.

### *Leveraging Internet Capabilities and Corporate-Level Strategy*

Chapter 6 addressed how firms strategically diversify and manage portfolios of businesses at the corporate level. In the case of related diversification, the Internet has created new means of generating synergies and enhancing revenue among elements of a diverse firm. For example, by linking sources of supply more efficiently and streamlining distribution, digital technologies can enhance profitability. In the case of unrelated diversification, corporate offices that manage portfolios of businesses can use the Internet to deal with suppliers more efficiently and can increase negotiating power. In both cases, when the Internet becomes integrated into a corporation's infrastructure and procurement system, it supports activities that contribute to the bottom line. In terms of internal development and acquisition as avenues of corporate growth, e-business models that have proven successful can be a welcome addition to a firm's portfolio. Internet-related business initiatives, such as the online postage capability developed by Pitney-Bowes, are creating new strategic advantages for many corporations.

### *Leveraging Internet Capabilities and International-Level Strategies*

Chapter 7 addressed how and why businesses grow beyond their national boundaries. Expanding into international markets involves special challenges that may be mitigated by using Internet and digital technologies. In terms of controlling costs, the Internet has enhanced the ability to conduct business without the time and expense of physically traveling to various locations. In terms of adapting to local markets, the ability to conduct research and communicate online has increased the level of access to local cultures and market conditions. This combination of capabilities has, in some cases, enhanced the ability of firms to pursue a transnational strategy by addressing both cost reduction and local adaptation issues. The Internet also has allowed firms to leapfrog the usual path of international development with technologies that reach customers and facilitate transactions around the globe. Whereas prior to the Internet, local distributors or licensees were essential international partners for firms expanding into new regions, now an online presence can accomplish the same thing. Additionally, new types of international commerce are possible, as suggested by Eli Lilly's InnoCentive venture, which enables scientists from around the world to address difficult problems. Collaboration at such a scale was virtually impossible prior to the Internet.

## Summary

New technologies often unleash forces in the economy that are highly disruptive. The innovations that flow from such technologies often radically change the competitive landscape. Under such conditions innovation-driven competition creates new strategic capabilities that alter the rules of competition. Few technologically driven phenomena have been as disruptive— or as rich with opportunity—as the Internet, wireless communications, and other digital technologies. As Internet-based capabilities and related information technologies become more widespread in all parts of the globe, strategic managers need to increasingly integrate the Internet and digital capabilities into their strategic plans.

In terms of the competitive environment, most of the changes brought about by the digital economy can be understood in the context of Porter's five-forces model of industry analysis. The threat of new entrants is expected to increase as digital and Internet technologies reduce many barriers to entry. The process of disintermediation has enhanced the power of some suppliers by simplifying supply chains, but it may also shift bargaining power to customers. Buyer power has increased for many end users due to lower switching costs. The threat of substitutes will generally be higher, because Internet and digital technologies are providing new methods for achieving old tasks. Finally, intensity of rivalry among similar competitors is heightened in the digital economy as competition tends to be more price-oriented and technology-based advantages are easily imitated.

The Internet and digital technologies have created new opportunities for firms to add value. Four value-adding activities that have been enhanced by Internet capabilities are search, evaluation, problem solving, and transaction. Search activities include processes for gathering information and identifying purchase options. Evaluation activities refers to the process of considering alternatives and comparing the costs and benefits of various options. Problem-solving activities include identifying problems or needs and generating ideas and action plans to address those needs. Transaction activities involve the process of completing a sale, including negotiating and agreeing contractually, making payments, and taking delivery. These four activities are supported by three different types of content that Internet businesses often use—customer feedback, expertise, and entertainment programming. Strategic use of these attributes can help build competitive advantages and contribute to profitability. Seven business models have been identified that are proving successful for use by Internet firms. These include commission, advertising, markup, production, referral, subscription, and fee-for-service based models. Firms also have found that combinations of these business models can contribute to greater success.

The way companies formulate and deploy strategies is also changing because of the impact of the Internet and digital technologies on many industries. Overall low-cost strategies may be more important as some firms use Internet technologies to lower transaction costs and increase the efficiency of their operations. Differentiation strategies may be harder to achieve for many firms, because the Internet is eroding some of their most unique features. Further, Internet technologies are enabling the mass customization capabilities of greater numbers of competitors. Focus strategies are likely to increase in importance because the Internet provides highly targeted and lower-cost access to narrow or specialized markets. These strategies are not without their pitfalls, however, and firms need to understand the dangers as well as the potential benefits of Internet-based approaches.

Thus, the digital economy, while promising to provide new opportunities for creating value and fostering growth, may make the competitive landscape more challenging for many firms. In this chapter we have addressed both the potential and the pitfalls of the Internet and digital technology in today's economy.

## Summary Review Questions

1. How do Porter's five competitive forces affect companies that compete primarily on the Internet? Provide an example.

2. What effects do digital capabilities and the Internet have on the three competitive strategies—overall low-cost, differentiation, and focus? How does this relate to a firm's competitive advantage?

3. What effect do digital technologies and the Internet have on the profitability an industry is able to achieve? How can companies use these technologies to enhance their own profitability?

4. Explain the difference between the effective use of technology and the technology *itself* in terms of achieving and sustaining competitive advantages.

5. Describe how the three competitive strategies can be combined to create competitive advantages among firms that compete primarily by leveraging digital capabilities.

# Experiential Exercise

Using the Internet, identify two firms—one an Internet "pure play" and the second a traditional bricks-and-mortar company—that have a strong Internet presence. Consider how each of these firms is adding value by using the Internet and digital technologies.

1. Bricks-and-mortar firm: _____

Which of the following Internet-based activities is the company using to add value?

| Value-Adding Activity | Examples of How the Company Uses the Activity | Is It Creating Value? (Yes/No) |
|---|---|---|
| **Type:** | | |
| Search | | |
| Evaluation | | |
| Problem solving | | |
| Transaction | | |
| **Content:** | | |
| Customer feedback | | |
| Expertise | | |
| Entertainment programming | | |

2. Internet pure-play firm: _____

Which of the following Internet-based activities is the company using to add value?

| Value-Adding Activity | Examples of How the Company Uses the Activity | Is It Creating Value? (Yes/No) |
|---|---|---|
| **Type:** | | |
| Search | | |
| Evaluation | | |
| Problem solving | | |
| Transaction | | |
| **Content:** | | |
| Customer feedback | | |
| Expertise | | |
| Entertainment programming | | |

3. How do the two firms compare? Is one adding more value than the other? What is the pure play doing that might help the bricks-and-mortar firm? What is the bricks-and-mortar firm doing that could benefit the pure play?

1. Select a company that has used digital technologies to change or enhance its competitive strategy. Look up the company on the Internet and discuss how it has increased (or decreased) its competitive advantage vis-à-vis Porter's five forces.

2. Choose an Internet pure play that is competing with a bricks-and-mortar company. What are the relative advantages and disadvantages of the Internet pure play? Do you think it will be successful in the long term?

3. Select a small firm that has used the Internet to its advantage in entering international markets. Do you believe such advantages will be sustainable over time? Explain.

4. How can a firm use the Internet and/or digital technologies to enhance its overall cost leadership or differentiation competitive advantages? Provide examples.

1. Discuss the ethical implications of the use of adware or spyware by companies to track customer Internet surfing and shopping activities.

2. Discuss the ethical implications of online music file sharing. Can Internet companies that provide free access to other users' computers to download copyrighted material (e.g., Kazaa) guard against infringing on the rights of the artists who develop the material?

## References

1. Banerjee, S., & Garrity, B. 2004. Roxio bets future on Napster brand. *Billboard,* 116(34): 8, 62; Garrity, B. 2002. Embattled Napster rumored for sale. *Billboard,* 114(17): 10; McGuire, D. 2005. Downloading: The next generation. *BizReport,* www.bizreport.com, February 28; Menn, J. 2003. *All the rave: The rise and fall of Shawn Fanning's Napster.* New York: Crown Business; Taylor, K. 2005. Napster: Can iTunes do this? *The Motley Fool,* www.fool.com, March 11; and Wood, C. 2001. The heirs of Napster. *Maclean's,* 114(9): 52–53.

2. Menn, op. cit.

3. Coy, P., & Vickers, M. 2001. How bad will it get? *BusinessWeek,* March 12: 36–42.

4. Schumpeter, J. A. 1934. *The theory of economic development.* Cambridge, MA: Harvard University Press.

5. Christensen, C. M. 1997. *The innovator's dilemma.* Boston: Harvard University Press.

6. Linzmayer, O. W. 2004. *Apple Confidential 2.0: The definitive history of the world's most colorful company* (2nd ed.). San Francisco, CA: No Starch Press.

7. Baumol, W. J. 2002. *The free-market innovation machine.* Princeton, NJ: Princeton University Press.

8. Quoted in Mandel, M. J., & Hof, R. D. 2001. Rethinking the Internet. *BusinessWeek,* March 26: 117–122.

9. Evans, P., & Wurster, T. S. 2000. *Blown to bits.* Cambridge, MA: Harvard Business School Press; Negroponte, N. 1995. *Being digital.* New York: Alfred A. Knopf.

10. Prahalad, C. K., & Ramaswamy, V. 2004. *The future of competition.* Boston: Harvard Business School Press.

11. For an interesting discussion of the role of interactivity on the performance of Internet-based businesses, see Auger, P. 2005. The impact of interactivity and design sophistication on the performance of commercial websites for small businesses. *Journal of Small Business Management,* 43(2): 119–137.

12. For interesting insights on the role of customers in co-creating value see Groth, M. 2005. Customers as good soldiers: Examining citizenship behaviors in Internet service deliveries. *Journal of Management,* 31(1): 7–27; Sawhney, M., Prandelli, E., & Verona, G. 2003. The power of innomediation. *Sloan Management Review,* 44(2): 77–82; and Xue, M., & Harker, P. T. 2002 Customer efficiency: Concepts and its impact on e-business management. *Journal of Service Research,* 4: 253–267.

13. Porter, M. E. 2001. Strategy and the Internet. *Harvard Business Review,* 79: 63–78.

14. For an interesting perspective on changing features of firm boundaries, refer to Afuah, A. 2003. Redefining firm boundaries in the face of Internet: Are firms really shrinking? *Academy of Management Review,* 28(1): 34–53.

15. www.consumerreports.org.

16. Siegel, D. 1999. *Futurize your enterprises:* New York: Wiley.

17. For an alternative perspective on the role of customers in an Internet environment, refer to Nambisan, S. 2002. Designing virtual customer environments for new product development: Toward a theory. *Academy of Management Review,* 27(3): 392–413.

18. Brynda, T. 2004. Reverse auction use by states to increase 300 percent, but low impact on IT. *INPUT/Output,* December: 1–7.

19. Keenan, F. 2001. Opening the spigot. *BusinessWeek e.biz,* June 4: EB17–EB20.

20. Time to rebuild. 2001. *Economist,* May 19: 55–56.

21. www.amazon.com.

22. For more on the role of the Internet as an electronic intermediary, refer to Carr, N. G. 2000. Hypermediation: Commerce as clickstream. *Harvard Business Review,* 78(1): 46–48.

23. Downes, L., & Mui, C. 1998. *Unleashing the killer app:* 45–46. Boston: Harvard Business School Press.

24. Dawson, J. D. 2002. Company turns computers into box offices with click of a ticket. *Houston Business Journal,* www.bizjournals.com/houston, September 27; and www.tickettrends.com.

25. McDonald, D. 2004. Meet eBay's new postman. *Business 2.0,* 5(8): 52–54.

26. Collins, A. 2001. Personal touch pays off. *Business 2.0,* www.business2.com, March.

27. Olofson, C. 2001. The next best thing to being there. *Fast Company,* April: 175; and www.conferenza.com.

28. Lelii, S. R. 2001. Free online storage a thing of the past? *eWEEK,* April 22.

29. McKay, N. 2000. Ballpark figures. *Red Herring,* May: 360; www.insightexpress.com.

30. www.privacy.net; and www.epic.org.

31. www.mysimon.com; and www.pricescan.com.

32. www.cnet.com; and www.bizrate.com.

33. Hanrahan, T. 1999. Price isn't everything. *Wall Street Journal,* July 12: R20.

34. For a discussion of strategic implications of partnering and competing, refer to Gulati, R., Nohria, N., and Zaheer, A.

2000. Strategic networks. *Strategic Management Journal,* 21: 203–215.

35. www.bestbookbuys.com.

36. McGuire, op. cit.

37. The ideas in this section draw on several sources, including Zeng, M., & Reinartz, W. 2003. Beyond online search: The road to profitability. *California Management Review,* Winter: 107–130; and Stabell, C. B., & Fjeldstad, O. D. 1998. Configuring value for competitive advantage: On chains, shops, and networks. *Strategic Management Journal,* 19: 413–437.

38. Hardy, Q. 2003. All eyes on Google. *Forbes,* May 26, www.forbes.com.

39. For an interesting discussion of how successful Internet-based companies are using evaluation to add value see Weiss, L. M., Capozzi, M. M., & Prusak, L. 2004. Learning from the Internet giants. *Sloan Management Review,* 45(4): 79–84.

40. Zeng & Reinartz, op. cit.

41. Bayers, C. 2002. The last laugh. *Business 2.0,* September: 86–93.

42. Yamada, K. 2001. Web trails. *Forbes,* December 3; and www.rei.com.

43. Weintraub, A. 2001. E-assets for sale—dirt cheap. *BusinessWeek e.biz,* May 14: EB20–EB22.

44. Greenspan, R. 2003. Internet not for everyone. *CyberAtlas,* April 16, www.cyberatlas.com.

45. Afuah, A., & Tucci, C. L. 2003. *Internet business models and strategies* (2nd ed.). New York: McGraw-Hill; Timmers, P. 1999. *Electronic commerce.* New York: Wiley.

46. Echikson, W. 2001. When oil gets connected. *BusinessWeek,* www.businessweek.com, December 3: EB28–EB30.

47. For an interesting discussion of the cost and pricing implications of Internet technology, refer to Sinha, I. 2000. Cost transparency: The net's real threat to prices and brands. *Harvard Business Review,* 78(2): 43–51.

48. Wailgum, T. 2004. Machine shop dreams. *CIO Magazine,* www.cio.com, November 15; www.emachineshop.com.

49. Evans, P., & Wurster, T. S. 2000. *Blown to bits:* 82–83. Boston: Harvard Business School Press.

50. Over the counter e-commerce. 2001. *Economist,* May 26: 77–78.

51. Collett, S. 1999. Nike offers mass customization online. *ComputerWorld,* November 23.

52. Seybold, P. 2000. Niches bring riches. *Business 2.0,* June 13: 135.

53. Greenspan, R. 2004. Net drives profits to small biz. *ClickZ.com,* March 25, www.clickz.com; Greenspan, R. 2002. Small biz benefits from Internet tools. *ClickZ.com,* March 28, www.clickz.com.

54. Lii, J. 2001. Salvagesale.com gets the goods where they're needed. *Lexington* (KY) *Herald-Leader,* February 25: H2.

55. Breen, B. 2002. Lilly's R&D prescription. *Fast Company,* 57: 44. Sawhney, M. 2002. What lies ahead: Rethinking the global corporation, *Digital Frontier Conference 2002,* www. mohansawhney.com; and www. innocentive.com.

56. Empirical support for the use of combination strategies in an e-business context can be found in Kim, E., Nam, D., & Stimpert, J. L. 2004. The applicability of Porter's generic strategies in the Digital Age: Assumptions, conjectures, and suggestions. *Journal of Management,* 30(5): 569–589.

57. Porter, op. cit.: 63–78.

58. Downes & Mui, op. cit.: 13.

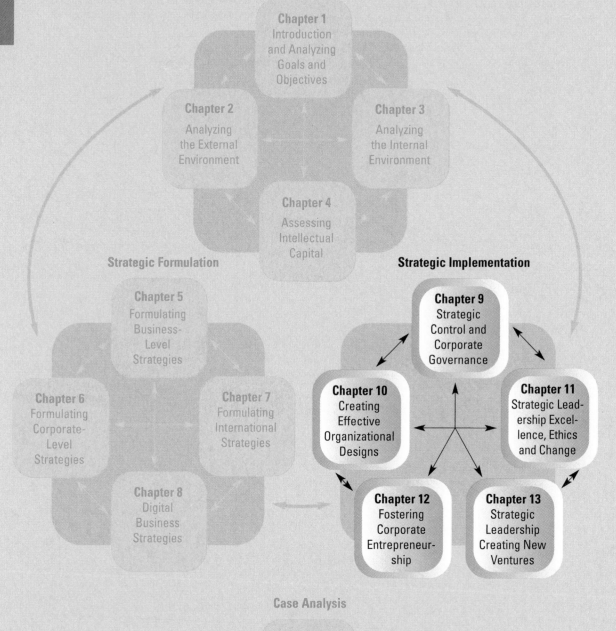

**Strategic Analysis**

**Chapter 1**
Introduction and Analyzing Goals and Objectives

**Chapter 2**
Analyzing the External Environment

**Chapter 3**
Analyzing the Internal Environment

**Chapter 4**
Assessing Intellectual Capital

**Strategic Formulation**

**Chapter 5**
Formulating Business-Level Strategies

**Chapter 6**
Formulating Corporate-Level Strategies

**Chapter 7**
Formulating International Strategies

**Chapter 8**
Digital Business Strategies

**Strategic Implementation**

**Chapter 9**
Strategic Control and Corporate Governance

**Chapter 10**
Creating Effective Organizational Designs

**Chapter 11**
Strategic Leadership Excellence, Ethics and Change

**Chapter 12**
Fostering Corporate Entrepreneurship

**Chapter 13**
Strategic Leadership Creating New Ventures

**Case Analysis**

**Chapter 14**
Case Analysis

# part three

# Strategic Implementation

**9** Strategic Control and Corporate Governance

**10** Creating Effective Organizational Designs

**11** Strategic Leadership: Creating a Learning Organization and an Ethical Organization

**12** Managing Innovation and Fostering Corporate Entrepreneurship

**13** Recognizing Opportunities and Creating New Ventures

# Strategic Control
# and Corporate Governance

## >chapter objectives

*After reading this chapter, you should have a good understanding of:*

- The value of effective strategic control systems in strategy implementation.

- The key difference between "traditional" and "contemporary" control systems.

- The imperative for "contemporary" control systems in today's complex and rapidly changing competitive and general environments.

- The benefits of having the proper balance among the three levers of behavioral control: culture, rewards and incentives, and boundaries.

- The three key participants in corporate governance: shareholders, management (led by the CEO), and the board of directors.

- The role of corporate governance mechanisms in ensuring that the interests of managers are aligned with those of shareholders from both the United States and international perspectives.

*O*rganizations must have effective strategic controls if they are to successfully implement their strategies. This includes systems that exercise both informational control and behavioral control. In addition, a firm must promote sound corporate governance as well as have controls that are consistent with the strategy that the firm is following.

In the first section, we address the need to have effective informational control, contrasting two approaches to informational control. The first approach, which we call "traditional," is highly sequential. Goals and objectives are set, then implemented, and after a set period of time, performance is compared to the desired standards. In contrast, the second approach, termed "contemporary," is much more interactive. Here, the internal and external environments are continually monitored, and managers determine whether the strategy itself needs to be modified. Today the contemporary approach is required, given the rapidly changing conditions in virtually all industries.

Next, we discuss behavioral control. Here the firm must strive to maintain a proper balance between culture, rewards, and boundaries. We also argue that organizations that have strong, positive cultures and reward systems can rely less on boundaries, such as rules, regulations, and procedures. When individuals in the firm internalize goals and strategies, there is less need for monitoring behavior, and efforts are focused more on important organizational goals and objectives.

The third section addresses the role of corporate governance in ensuring that managerial and shareholder interests are aligned. We provide examples of both effective and ineffective corporate governance practices. We discuss three governance mechanisms for aligning managerial and shareholder interests: a committed and involved board of directors, shareholder activism, and effective managerial rewards and incentives. Public companies are also subject to external control. We discuss several external control mechanisms, such as the market for corporate control, auditors, banks and analysts, the media, and public activists. We close with a discussion of corporate governance from an international perspective.

Incentives are designed to boost productivity and help a company achieve its goals.[1] This works as long as the incentives are designed with organizational goals in mind. Problems can arise quickly when incentives are not designed in a way that aligns the goals of employees with those of the firm.

Consider the case of Lantech, a $100 million company headquartered in Louisville, Kentucky, that had to face this problem. The firm has a dominant position in a market that it pioneered—stretch wrapping equipment that encases pallet loads of products (such as Kellogg's Corn Flakes) in clear plastic film for shipment to customers.

> Lantech wanted to increase the productivity of its workers, and the obvious way seemed to be to reward high-performing divisions with productivity incentives. Each of the firm's manufacturing divisions was offered a productivity bonus that could increase the pay of each employee in the division by 10 percent.
>
> Unfortunately, the results weren't exactly what Lantech's managers had in mind. The bonus was based on each division's productivity, and because one measure of productivity is the ratio of costs to revenues, employees began to devise ways to decrease costs in their division. But rather than *cutting* costs, employees focused their efforts on *shifting* costs.
>
> Production at Lantech required mutual cooperation between divisions; each division relied on the others for parts and engineering expertise. However, the incentive plan inadvertently encouraged workers to assign costs to other divisions while claiming revenue for themselves. Workers argued over who was responsible for shared costs, with no division wanting to accept its fair share. But, needless to say, they were all willing to claim responsibility for revenues. It got to the point that one division wanted to assign a greater percentage of toilet paper costs to another division with a higher number of employees of a certain gender, arguing that one gender used more toilet paper than the other!
>
> Chairman Pat Lancaster claimed that he spent 95 percent of his time resolving arguments after he had initiated this new incentive plan. He claimed that, "The bonuses moved managers in the direction of favoring short-term profit over long-term customer satisfaction. They were so busy fighting over who was going to pay for what that they couldn't make decisions that were good for the customers as a whole." And CEO Jim Lancaster, his son, said that the new system caused "so much secrecy, politicking, and sucking noise that you wouldn't believe it."

It should come as no surprise that the plan was eliminated after just a short period. In its place, Lantech offered a profit-sharing plan where employees benefited only if the entire firm performed well. The bottom line is that incentive plans must align the employees' desire for extra income with the firm's need for profits.

In this chapter, we will focus on how organizations can develop and use effective strategic control.[2] We first explore two central aspects of strategic control: (1) *informational control,* which is the ability to respond effectively to environmental change, and (2) *behavioral control,* which is the appropriate balance and alignment among a firm's culture, rewards, and boundaries. In the final section of this chapter, we focus on strategic control from a much broader perspective—what is referred to as *corporate governance.* Here, we direct our attention to the need for a firm's shareholders (the owners) and their elected representatives (the board of directors) to ensure that the firm's executives (the management team) strive to fulfill their fiduciary duty of maximizing long-term shareholder value.

## >>Ensuring Informational Control: Responding Effectively to Environmental Change

In this section we will discuss two broad types of control systems. The first one, which we label "traditional," is based largely on a feedback approach; that is, there is little or no action taken to revise strategies, goals, and objectives until the end of the time period in question, usually a quarter or a month. The second one, which we call "contemporary,"

**Exhibit 9.1**   **Traditional Approach to Strategic Control**

emphasizes the importance of continually monitoring the environment (both internal and external) for trends and events that signal the need to make modifications to a firm's strategies, goals, and objectives. As both general and competitive environments become more unpredictable and complex, the need for contemporary systems increases.

## A Traditional Approach to Strategic Control

The traditional approach to strategic control is sequential: (1) strategies are formulated and top management sets goals, (2) strategies are implemented, and (3) performance is measured against the predetermined goal set, as illustrated in Exhibit 9.1.

Control is based on a feedback loop from performance measurement to strategy formulation. This process typically involves lengthy time lags, often tied to a firm's annual planning cycle. Such traditional control systems, termed "single-loop" learning by Chris Argyris of Harvard University, simply compare actual performance to a predetermined goal.[3] They are most appropriate when the environment is stable and relatively simple, goals and objectives can be measured with a high level of certainty, and there is little need for complex measures of performance. Sales quotas, operating budgets, production schedules, and similar quantitative control mechanisms are typical. The appropriateness of the business strategy or standards of performance is seldom questioned.[4]

The idea that well-managed companies should move forward in accordance with detailed and precise plans has come under attack from several directions.[5] James Brian Quinn of Dartmouth College has argued that grand designs with precise and carefully integrated plans seldom work. Rather, most strategic change proceeds incrementally— one step at a time. Leaders can best serve their organizations by introducing some sense of direction, some logic in incremental steps.[6]

Similarly, McGill University's Henry Mintzberg has written about leaders "crafting" a strategy.[7] Drawing on the parallel between the potter at her wheel and the strategist, Mintzberg pointed out that the potter begins work with some general idea of the artifact she wishes to create, but the details of design—even possibilities for a different design— emerge as the work progresses. For businesses facing complex and turbulent business environments, the craftsperson's method seems more appropriate than that provided by the traditional, more rational, planner. The former helps us deal with the uncertainty about how a design will work out in practice and allows for a creative element.

Mintzberg's argument, like Quinn's, casts doubt on the value of rigid planning and goal-setting processes. Fixed strategic goals also become dysfunctional for firms competing in highly unpredictable competitive environments where strategies need to change frequently and opportunistically. An inflexible commitment to predetermined goals and milestones can prevent the very adaptability that is often required of a good strategy.

Even organizations that have been extremely successful in the past can become complacent or fail to adapt their goals and strategies to the new conditions. An example of such a firm is Cisco Systems, whose market value at one time approached an astonishing $600 billion, but as of late 2005 was about $110 billion. Cisco has minimized the potential for such problems in the future by improving its informational control systems. Other firms

## When the Tech Bubble Burst

We can learn some lessons from fallen stars. Cisco Systems, Inc., once the invincible momentum stock adored by Wall Street, came crashing down just as we were beginning the 21st century. What went wrong?

Problems started when Cisco announced a $2.2 billion inventory write-off; Wall Street severely punished the stock as a result. With all of its experience, why didn't Cisco see the problems coming? Cisco made a common mistake: It projected the past into the future.

Past demand had been vigorous, but customers were requiring less and less of the firm's products. And financing was cheap—it was no problem for a company like Cisco to find capital to finance ongoing operations even when things didn't look so bright on the horizon. Overtaken by its own success, Cisco failed to see the slowdown in

Sources: Weber, J. 2001. Management lessons from the bust. *BusinessWeek*, August 27: 104–112; Morrison, S. 2001. Positive sales news takes the sting out of Cisco revamp. *Financial Times Online*, August 26; Reuters. 2001. Siebel sees economic rebound late 2002: August 20.

customer demand. John Sterman at MIT sums up the situation: "If you were in the pasta business, you want to know how much pasta people are cooking and eating, not how much they're buying, and certainly not how much supermarkets and distributors are ordering from the factory." Consumers ultimately determine demand; Cisco missed this important point and inaccurately forecast new sales orders. When the orders didn't materialize, a stockpile of inventory sat on the shelves while Wall Street annulled the short-lived marriage between investors and their beloved Cisco.

In contrast, Siebel Systems, Inc., kept its eye on the future. The company rewarded its sales force for providing accurate information concerning future demand. Salespeople receive commissions not only for sales, but also for forecast information. Haim Mendelson at Stanford University remarked that this provides the company "with a deep understanding of what customers are going to do."

such as Siebel Systems have been more successful in anticipating change and have made proper corrections to their strategies. We discuss these firms in Strategy Spotlight 9.1.

Without doubt, the traditional "feedback" approach to strategic control has some important limitations. Is there another, better, way?

## A Contemporary Approach to Strategic Control

Adapting to and anticipating both internal and external environmental change is an integral part of strategic control. The relationships between strategy formulation, implementation, and control are highly interactive, as suggested by Exhibit 9.2. It also illustrates two different types of strategic control: informational control and behavioral control. Informational control is primarily concerned with whether or not the organization is "doing the right things." Behavioral control, on the other hand, asks if the organization is "doing things right" in the implementation of its strategy. Both the informational and behavioral components of strategic control are necessary, but not sufficient, conditions for success. That is, what good is a well-conceived strategy that cannot be implemented? Or, alternatively, what use is an energetic and committed workforce if it is focused on the wrong strategic target?

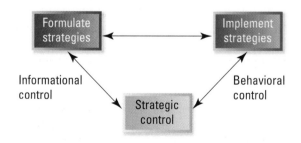

**Exhibit 9.2** Contemporary Approach to Strategic Control

John Weston is the former CEO of ADP Corporation, the largest payroll and tax-filing processor in the world. He captures the essence of contemporary control systems.

> At ADP, 39 plus 1 adds up to more than 40 plus 0. The 40-plus-0 employee is the harried worker who at 40 hours a week just tries to keep up with what's in the "in" basket. He tries to do whatever he thinks he's supposed to do. Because he works with his head down, he takes zero hours to think about what he's doing, why he's doing it, and how he's doing it. Does he need to do it in the first place? On the other hand, the 39-plus-1 employee takes at least 1 of those 40 hours to think about what he's doing and why he's doing it. That's why the other 39 hours are far more productive.[8]

Informational control deals with the internal environment as well as the external strategic context. It addresses the assumptions and premises that provide the foundation for an organization's strategy. The key question addressed by information control is: Do the organization's goals and strategies still "fit" within the context of the current strategic environment?

This involves two key issues. First, managers must scan and monitor the external environment, as we discussed in Chapter 2. Recall, for example, the failure of Interstate Bakeries Corporation (IBC) to change their strategies to reflect changes in consumer tastes, such as the trend toward healthier foods and low-carb diets. Also, conditions can change in the internal environment of the firm, as we discussed in Chapter 3, requiring changes in the strategic direction of the firm. These may include, for example, the resignation of key executives or delays in the completion of major production facilities.

In the contemporary approach, information control is part of an ongoing process of organizational learning that continuously updates and challenges the assumptions that underlie the organization's strategy. In such "double-loop" learning, the organization's assumptions, premises, goals, and strategies are continuously monitored, tested, and reviewed. The benefits of continuous monitoring are evident—time lags are dramatically shortened, changes in the competitive environment are detected earlier, and the organization's ability to respond with speed and flexibility is enhanced.

A key question becomes: OK, but how is this done? Contemporary control systems must have four characteristics to be effective.[9]

1. They must focus on constantly changing information that top managers identify as having potential strategic importance.
2. The information is important enough to demand frequent and regular attention from operating managers at all levels of the organization.
3. The data and information generated by the control system are best interpreted and discussed in face-to-face meetings of superiors, subordinates, and peers.
4. The contemporary control system is a key catalyst for an ongoing debate about underlying data, assumptions, and action plans.

Contemporary control systems track the strategic uncertainties that may keep senior managers awake at night. Depending on the type of business, such uncertainties may relate to changes in technology, customer tastes, government regulation, and industry competition. Since control systems must be designed to gather information that might challenge the strategic visions of the future, they are, by definition, hot buttons for senior managers.

An executive's decision to use the control system interactively—in other words, to invest the time and attention to review and evaluate new information—sends a clear signal to the organization about what is important. The dialogue and debate that emerge from such an interactive process can often lead to new strategies and innovations.

## USA Today's Interactive Control System

Top managers at Gannett-owned *USA Today* meet each Friday to discuss ongoing strategy. Every week, they review information ranging from day-to-day operations to year-to-date data. This information enables top management to check the pulse of the industry on a frequent basis and minimizes the surprises that frequently beset other companies that don't keep close tabs on available information. Senior managers frequently meet with operations-level managers for intensive discussion to analyze the weekly information. The results of these high-level meetings on information control allow managers from the operating core of the newspaper to respond to industry trends and events on nearly a real-time basis.

By controlling information, *USA Today* managers:

- Compare projected advertising volume with actual volume.

- Assess new advertising revenues by client type to better target client markets.

- Quickly discover revenue shortfalls before major problems arise.

- Become aware of unexpected successes that have often led to innovations.

These weekly meetings have returned significant rewards for *USA Today.* Innovations that have been implemented as a result of high information control include:

- A new market survey service targeted at the automobile industry (a potential source of high-volume advertising).

- The addition of fractional page color advertising (increasing the number of advertisers that use color, thereby increasing advertising revenue).

- Expanding the job function of circulation employees to include regional sales of advertising space.

- Developing a program of advertising inserts targeted toward specific customers and products.

Sources: Simons, R. 1995. Control in an age of empowerment. *Harvard Business Review,* 73(2): 80–88; Caney, D. 2001. Gannett, Knight Ridder walloped by ad slump. Reuters, July 17.

Strategy Spotlight 9.2 discusses how executives at *USA Today,* Gannett Co.'s daily newspaper, review information delivered each Friday.

Let's now turn our attention to behavioral control.

## >>Attaining Behavioral Control: Balancing Culture, Rewards, and Boundaries

Behavioral control is focused on implementation—doing things right. Effectively implementing strategy requires manipulating three key control "levers": culture, rewards, and boundaries. These three levers are illustrated in Exhibit 9.3. Furthermore, there are two compelling reasons for an increased emphasis on culture and rewards in implementing a system of behavioral controls.

First, the competitive environment is increasingly complex and unpredictable, demanding both flexibility and quick response to its challenges. As firms simultaneously downsize and face the need for increased coordination across organizational boundaries, a control system based primarily on rigid strategies and rules and regulations is dysfunctional. Thus, the use of rewards and culture to align individual and organizational goals becomes increasingly important.

Second, the implicit long-term contract between the organization and its key employees has been eroded.[10] Today's younger managers have been conditioned to see themselves as "free agents" and view a career as a series of opportunistic challenges. As managers are advised to "specialize, market yourself, and have work, if not a job," the importance of culture and rewards in building organizational loyalty claims greater importance. (We addressed this issue at length in Chapter 4.)

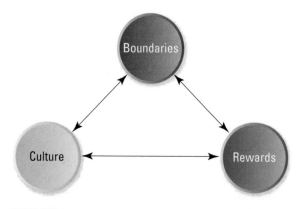

**Exhibit 9.3**  **Essential Elements of Behavioral Control**

Each of the three levers—culture, rewards, and boundaries—must work in a balanced and consistent manner. Let's consider the role of each.

## Building a Strong and Effective Culture

What is culture? Consistent with our discussion in Chapter 4, organizational culture is a system of shared values (what is important) and beliefs (how things work) that shape a company's people, organizational structures, and control systems to produce behavioral norms (the way we do things around here). How important is culture? Very. Over the years, numerous best sellers, such as *Theory Z, Corporate Cultures, In Search of Excellence,* and *Good to Great,*[11] have emphasized the powerful influence of culture on what goes on within organizations and how they perform.

Collins and Porras argued in *Built to Last* that the key factor in sustained exceptional performance is a cultlike culture.[12] You can't touch it, you can't write it down, but it's there, in every organization, and its influence is pervasive. It can work for you or against you.[13] Effective leaders understand its importance and strive to shape and use it as one of their important levers of strategic control.[14]

*The Role of Culture*  Culture wears many different hats, each woven from the fabric of those values that sustain the organization's primary source of competitive advantage. Some examples are:

- Federal Express and Southwest Airlines focus on customer service.
- Lexus (a division of Toyota) and Hewlett-Packard emphasize product quality.
- Newell Rubbermaid and 3M place a high value on innovation.
- Nucor (steel) and Emerson Electric are concerned, above all, with operational efficiency.

Culture sets implicit boundaries—that is, unwritten standards of acceptable behavior—in dress, ethical matters, and the way an organization conducts its business.[15] By creating a framework of shared values, culture encourages individual identification with the organization and its objectives. Thus, culture acts as a means of reducing monitoring costs.[16]

*Sustaining an Effective Culture*  Powerful organizational cultures just don't happen overnight, and they don't remain in place without a strong commitment—both in terms of words and deeds—by leaders throughout the organization. A viable and productive organizational culture can be strengthened and sustained. However, it cannot be "built" or "assembled"; instead, it must be cultivated, encouraged, and "fertilized."

Storytelling is one way effective cultures are maintained. Many are familiar with the story of how Art Fry's failure to develop a strong adhesive led to 3M's enormously successful Post-it Notes. Perhaps less familiar is the story of Francis G. Okie.[17] In 1922 Okie came up with the idea of selling sandpaper to men as a replacement for razor blades. The idea obviously didn't pan out, but Okie was allowed to remain at 3M. Interestingly, the technology developed by Okie led 3M to develop its first blockbuster product: a waterproof sandpaper that became a staple of the automobile industry. Such stories foster the importance of risk taking, experimentation, freedom to fail, and of course innovation—all vital elements of 3M's culture.

Rallies or "pep talks" by top executives also serve to reinforce a firm's culture. The late Sam Walton was well known for his pep rallies at local Wal-Mart stores. Four times a year, the founders of Home Depot—CEO Bernard Marcus and Arthur Blank—used to don orange aprons and stage Breakfast with Bernie and Arthur, a 6:30 a.m. pep rally, broadcast live over the firm's closed-circuit TV network to most of its 45,000 employees.[18]

Southwest Airlines' "Culture Committee" is a unique vehicle designed to perpetuate the company's highly successful culture. The following excerpt from an internal company publication describes its objectives:

> The goal of the Committee is simple—to ensure that our unique Corporate Culture stays alive. . . . Culture Committee members represent all regions and departments across our system and they are selected based upon their exemplary display of the "Positively Outrageous Service" that won us the first-ever Triple Crown; their continual exhibition of the "Southwest Spirit" to our Customers and to their fellow workers; and their high energy level, boundless enthusiasm, unique creativity, and constant demonstration of teamwork and love for their fellow workers.[19]

## Motivating with Rewards and Incentives

Reward and incentive systems represent a powerful means of influencing an organization's culture, focusing efforts on high-priority tasks, and motivating individual and collective task performance.[20] Just as culture deals with influencing beliefs, behaviors, and attitudes of people within an organization, the reward system—by specifying who gets rewarded and why—is an effective motivator and control mechanism.[21] Strategy Spotlight 9.3 discusses how the China-based Legend Group varies its incentives based upon the different hierarchical levels in its organization.

*The Potential Downside*    Generally speaking, people in organizations act rationally, each motivated by his or her personal best interest.[22] However, the collective sum of individual behaviors of an organization's employees does not always necessarily result in what is best for the organization; that is, individual rationality does not always guarantee organizational rationality.

As corporations grow and evolve, they often develop different business units with multiple reward systems. They may differ based on industry contexts, business situations, stage of product life cycles, and so on. Thus, subcultures within organizations may reflect differences among an organization's functional areas, products, services, and divisions. To the extent that reward systems reinforce such behavioral norms, attitudes, and belief systems, organizational cohesiveness is reduced; important information is hoarded rather than shared, individuals begin working at cross-purposes, and they lose sight of overarching goals and objectives.

Such conflicts are commonplace in many organizations. For example, sales and marketing personnel promise unrealistically quick delivery times to bring in business, much to the dismay of operations and logistics; overengineering by R&D creates headaches for manufacturing; and so on. Conflicts also arise across divisions when divisional profits

# STRATEGY SPOTLIGHT

## Legend Group: Providing Incentives at All Levels

One of the key tasks of management is to keep the employees motivated. Designing the right kind of incentives that meet the expectations of employee groups at different levels in the hierarchy is a big challenge. Here is how Liu Chuanzhi, chairman of Legend Group, dealt with this issue. Legend is a global personal computer manufacturer based in Beijing, China.

> Our executive team needs a sense of ownership in the company. Many state-owned enterprises in China face a special challenge: They cannot give their senior executives stock. But we took an untraditional approach; we reformed our ownership structure to make Legend a joint stock company, enabling us to give all our executive team members stock. In addition, senior executives need recognition, so we provide them with opportunities

to speak to the media. To date, we've lost no senior executives to other companies.

> Midlevel managers want to become senior managers, so they respond best to challenges—to opportunities to display and hone their talents. We set very high performance standards for our middle managers, and we let them participate in strategic processes, in designing their own work, and in making and executing their own decisions. If they get good results, they are handsomely rewarded.

> Line employees need a sense of stability. If they take responsibility and are conscientious, they earn a predictable bonus. We also tie team performance to company or unit performance, and individual performance to team performance. For example, we might let the team decide how to allocate a percentage of their team bonus to individuals, with some general guidelines from the corporate level.

Source: Chuanzhi, L. 2003. Set different incentive levels. *Harvard Business Review*, 81(1): 47.

become a key compensation criterion. As ill will and anger escalate, personal relationships and performance may suffer.

***Creating Effective Reward and Incentive Programs***    To be effective, incentive and reward systems need to reinforce basic core values and enhance cohesion and commitment to goals and objectives. They also must not be at odds with the organization's overall mission and purpose.[23]

Consider how incentives are used at General Mills. To ensure a manager's interest in the overall performance of his or her unit, half of a manager's annual bonus is linked to business-unit results and half to individual performance.[24] For example, if a manager simply matches a rival manufacturer's performance, his or her salary is roughly 5 percent lower. However, if a manager's product ranks in the industry's top 10 percent in earnings growth and return on capital, the manager's total compensation can rise to nearly 30 percent beyond the industry norm.

Effective reward and incentive systems share a number of common characteristics.

* Objectives are clear, well understood, and broadly accepted.
* Rewards are clearly linked to performance and desired behaviors.
* Performance measures are clear and highly visible.
* Feedback is prompt, clear, and unambiguous.
* The compensation "system" is perceived as fair and equitable.
* The structure is flexible; it can adapt to changing circumstances.[25]

The perception that a plan is "fair and equitable" is critically important. Similarly, the firm must have the flexibility to respond to changing requirements as its direction and objectives change. In recent years many companies have begun to place more emphasis on growth. Emerson Electric is one company that has shifted its emphasis from cost cutting to growth. To ensure that changes take hold, the management compensation formula has been changed from a largely bottom-line focus to one that emphasizes growth, new products, acquisitions, and international expansion. Discussions about profits are handled separately, and a culture of risk taking is encouraged.[26]

## Setting Boundaries and Constraints

In an ideal world, a strong culture and effective rewards should be sufficient to ensure that all individuals and subunits work toward the common goals and objectives of the whole organization.[27] In the real world, however, this is not usually the case. Counterproductive behavior can arise because of motivated self-interest, lack of a clear understanding of goals and objectives, or outright malfeasance. Boundaries and constraints, when used properly, can serve many useful purposes for organizations, including:

- Focusing individual efforts on strategic priorities.
- Providing short-term objectives and action plans to channel efforts.
- Improving efficiency and effectiveness.
- Minimizing improper and unethical conduct.

*Focusing Efforts on Strategic Priorities*    Boundaries and constraints play a valuable role in focusing a company's strategic priorities. A well-known strategic boundary in U.S. industry is Jack Welch's (former CEO of General Electric) demand that any business in the corporate portfolio be ranked first or second in its industry. In a similar vein, Eli Lilly has reduced its research efforts to five broad areas of disease, down from eight or nine a decade ago.[28] This concentration of effort and resources provides the firm with greater strategic focus and the potential for stronger competitive advantages in the remaining areas.

Norman Augustine, Lockheed Martin's former chairman, provided four criteria for selecting candidates for diversification into "closely related" businesses.[29] They must (1) be high tech, (2) be systems-oriented, (3) deal with large customers (either corporations or government) as opposed to consumers, and (4) be in growth businesses. Augustine said, "We have found that if we can meet most of those standards, then we can move into adjacent markets and grow."

Boundaries also have a place in the nonprofit sector. For example, a British relief organization uses a system to monitor strategic boundaries by maintaining a list of companies whose contributions it will neither solicit nor accept. Such boundaries clearly go beyond simply taking the moral high road. Rather, they are essential for maintaining legitimacy with existing and potential benefactors.

*Providing Short-Term Objectives and Action Plans*    In Chapter 1 we discussed the importance of a firm having a vision, mission, and strategic objectives that are internally consistent and that provide strategic direction. In addition, short-term objectives and action plans provide similar benefits. That is, they represent boundaries that help to allocate resources in an optimal manner and to channel the efforts of employees at all levels throughout the organization.[30] To be effective, short-term objectives must have several attributes. They should:

- Be specific and measurable.
- Include a specific time horizon for their attainment.
- Be achievable, yet challenging enough to motivate managers who must strive to accomplish them.

Research has found that performance is enhanced when individuals are encouraged to attain specific, difficult, yet achievable, goals (as opposed to vague "do your best" goals).[31]

Short-term objectives must provide proper direction and at the same time provide enough flexibility for the firm to keep pace with and anticipate changes in the external environment. Such changes might include new government regulations, a competitor introducing a substitute product, or changes in consumer taste. Additionally, unexpected events within a firm may require a firm to make important adjustments in both strategic and short-term objectives. For example, the emergence of new industries can have a drastic effect on the demand for products and services in more traditional industries.

Along with short-term objectives, action plans are critical to the implementation of chosen strategies. Unless action plans are specific, there may be little assurance that managers have thought through all of the resource requirements for implementing their strategies. In addition, unless plans are specific, managers may not understand what needs to be implemented or have a clear time frame for completion. This is essential for the scheduling of key activities that must be implemented. Finally, individual managers must be held accountable for the implementation of action plans. This helps to provide the necessary motivation and "sense of ownership" to implement action plans on a timely basis. Strategy Spotlight 9.4 illustrates how action plans fit into the mission statement and objectives of a small manufacturer of aircraft interior components.

***Improving Operational Efficiency and Effectiveness***   Rule-based controls are most appropriate in organizations with the following characteristics:

- Environments are stable and predictable.
- Employees are largely unskilled and interchangeable.
- Consistency in product and service is critical.
- The risk of malfeasance is extremely high (e.g., in banking or casino operations), and controls must be implemented to guard against improper conduct.[32]

For example, McDonald's Corp. has extensive rules and regulations that regulate the operation of its franchises.[33] Its policy manual states, "Cooks must turn, never flip, hamburgers. If they haven't been purchased, Big Macs must be discarded in 10 minutes after being cooked and French fries in 7 minutes. Cashiers must make eye contact with and smile at every customer."

Guidelines can also be effective in setting spending limits and the range of discretion for employees and managers, such as the $2,500 limit that hotelier Ritz-Carlton uses to empower employees to placate dissatisfied customers. Regulations also can be initiated to improve the use of an employee's time at work.[34] Computer Associates restricts the use of e-mail during the hours of 10 a.m. to noon and 2 p.m. to 4 p.m. each day.[35]

***Minimizing Improper and Unethical Conduct***   Guidelines can be useful in specifying proper relationships with a company's customers and suppliers.[36] For example, many companies have explicit rules regarding commercial practices, including the prohibition of any form of payment, bribe, or kickback. Cadbury Schweppes has followed a rather simple but effective step in controlling the use of bribes by specifying that all payments, no matter how unusual, are recorded on the company's books. Its chairman, Sir Adrian Cadbury, contended that such a practice causes managers to pause and consider whether a payment is simply a bribe or a necessary and standard cost of doing business.[37] Consulting companies, too, typically have strong rules and regulations directed at protecting client confidentiality and conflicts of interest.

Regulations backed up with strong sanctions can also help an organization avoid conducting business in an unethical manner. In the wake of the corporate scandals of the early 21st century and the passing of the Sarbanes-Oxley Act (which, among other things, provides for stiffer penalties for financial reporting misdeeds), many chief financial officers (CFOs) have taken steps to ensure ethical behavior in the preparation of financial statements. For example, Home Depot's CFO, Carol B. Tome, strengthened the firm's code of ethics and developed stricter guidelines. Now all 25 of her subordinates must sign

# STRATEGY SPOTLIGHT

## Developing Meaningful Action Plans: Aircraft Interior Products, Inc.

MSA Aircraft Interior Products, Inc., is a manufacturing firm based in San Antonio, Texas, that was founded in 1983 by Mike Spraggins and Robert Plenge. The firm fulfills a small but highly profitable niche in the aviation industry with two key products. The Accordia line consists of patented, lightweight, self-contained window-shade assemblies. MSA's interior cabin shells are state-of-the-art assemblies that include window panels, side panels, headliners, and suspension system structures. MSA's products have been installed on a variety of aircraft, such as the Gulfstream series; the Cessna Citation; and Boeing's 727, 737, 757, and 707.

Much of MSA's success can be attributed to carefully articulated action plans consistent with the firm's mission and objectives. During the past five years, MSA has increased its sales at an annual rate of 15 to 18 percent. It has also succeeded in adding many prestigious companies to its customer base. Below are excerpts from MSA's mission statement and objectives as well as the action plans to achieve a 20 percent annual increase in sales.

### Mission Statement

- Be recognized as an innovative and reliable supplier of quality interior products for the high-end, personalized transportation segments of the aviation, marine, and automotive industries.

- Design, develop, and manufacture interior fixtures and components that provide exceptional value to the customer through the development of innovative designs in a manner that permits decorative design flexibility while retaining the superior functionality, reliability, and maintainability of well-engineered, factory-produced products.

- Grow, be profitable, and provide a fair return, commensurate with the degree of risk, for owners and stockholders.

### Objectives

1. Achieve sustained and profitable growth over the next three years:

    - 20 percent annual growth in revenues
    - 12 percent pretax profit margins
    - 18 percent return on shareholder's equity

2. Expand the company's revenues through the development and introduction of two or more new products capable of generating revenues in excess of $8 million a year by 2008.

3. Continue to aggressively expand market opportunities and applications for the Accordia line of window-shade assemblies, with the objective of sustaining or exceeding a 20 percent annual growth rate for at least the next three years.

Exhibit 9.4 details an "Action Plan" for Objective 3.

| Description | Primary Responsibility | Target Date |
|---|---|---|
| 1. Develop and implement 2006 marketing plan, including specific plans for addressing Falcon 20 retrofit programs and expanded sales of cabin shells. | R. H. Plenge (V.P. Marketing) | December 15, 2005 |
| 2. Negotiate new supplier agreement with Gulfstream Aerospace. | M. Spraggins (President) | March 1, 2006 |
| 3. Continue and complete the development of the UltraSlim window and have a fully tested and documented design ready for production at a manufacturing cost of less than $900 per unit. | D. R. Pearson (V.P. Operations) | June 15, 2006 |
| 4. Develop a window design suitable for L-1011 and similar wide-body aircraft and have a fully tested and documented design ready for production at a manufacturing cost comparable to the current Boeing window. | D. R. Pearson (V.P. Operations) | September 15, 2006 |

**Exhibit 9.4** *Action Plan for Objective 3*

*(continued)*

**(continued)**

MSA's action plans are supported by detailed month-by-month budgets and strong financial incentives for its

Source: For purposes of confidentiality, some of the information presented in this spotlight has been disguised. We would like to thank company management and Joseph Picken, consultant, for providing us with the information used in this application.

executives. Budgets are prepared by each individual department and include all revenue and cost items. Managers are motivated by their participation in a profit-sharing program, and the firm's two founders each receive a bonus equal to 3 percent of total sales.

personal statements that all of their financial statements are correct—just as she and her boss, CEO Robert Nardelli, have to do now according to the congressional legislation.[38]

## Behavioral Control in Organizations: Situational Factors

We have discussed the behavioral dimension of control. Here, the focus is on ensuring that the behavior of individuals at all levels of an organization is directed toward achieving organizational goals and objectives. The three fundamental types of control are culture, rewards and incentives, and boundaries and constraints. An organization may pursue one or a combination of them on the basis of a variety of internal and external factors.

Not all organizations place the same emphasis on each type of control.[39] For example, in professional organizations, such as high-technology firms engaged in basic research, members may work under high levels of autonomy. Here, an individual's performance is generally quite difficult to measure accurately because of the long lead times involved in research and development activities. Thus, internalized norms and values become very important.

In organizations where the measurement of an individual's output or performance is quite straightforward, control depends primarily on granting or withholding rewards. Frequently, a sales manager's compensation is in the form of a commission and bonus tied directly to his or her sales volume, which is relatively easy to determine. Here, behavior is influenced more strongly by the attractiveness of the compensation than by the norms and values implicit in the organization's culture. Furthermore, the measurability of output precludes the need for an elaborate system of rules to control behavior.

Control in bureaucratic organizations has long been recognized as dependent on members following a highly formalized set of rules and regulations. In such situations, most activities are routine and the desired behavior can be specified in a detailed manner because there is generally little need for innovative or creative activity. In business organizations, for example, managing an assembly plant requires strict adherence to many rules as well as exacting sequences of assembly operations. In the public sector, the Department of Motor Vehicles in most states must follow clearly prescribed procedures when issuing or renewing driver licenses.

Exhibit 9.5 provides alternate approaches to behavioral control and some of the situational factors associated with them.

## Evolving from Boundaries to Rewards and Culture

In most environments, organizations should strive to provide a system of rewards and incentives, coupled with a culture strong enough that boundaries become internalized. This reduces the need for external controls such as rules and regulations. We suggest several ways to move in this direction.

Exhibit 9.5
Organizational Control:
Alternative
Approaches

| Approach | Some Situational Factors |
|---|---|
| *Culture:* A system of unwritten rules that forms an internalized influence over behavior. | • Often found in professional organizations.<br>• Associated with high autonomy.<br>• Norms are the basis for behavior. |
| *Rules:* Written and explicit guidelines that provide external constraints on behavior. | • Associated with standardized output.<br>• Tasks are generally repetitive and routine.<br>• Little need for innovation or creative activity.<br>• Measurement of output and performance is rather straightforward. |
| *Rewards:* The use of performance-based incentive systems to motivate. | • Most appropriate in organizations pursuing unrelated diversification strategies.<br>• Rewards may be used to reinforce other means of control. |

First, hire the right people—individuals who already identify with the organization's dominant values and have attributes consistent with them. We addressed this issue in detail in Chapter 4; recall the "Bozo Filter" that was developed by Cooper Software of Palo Alto, California. Microsoft's David Pritchard is well aware of the consequences of failing to hire properly.

> If I hire a bunch of bozos, it will hurt us, because it takes time to get rid of them. They start infiltrating the organization and then they themselves start hiring people of lower quality. At Microsoft, we are always looking for people who are better than we are.

Second, training plays a key role. For example, in elite military units such as the Green Berets and Navy SEALs, the training regimen so thoroughly internalizes the culture that individuals, in effect, lose their identity. The group becomes the overriding concern and focal point of their energies. At firms such as FedEx, training not only builds skills, but also plays a significant role in building a strong culture on the foundation of each organization's dominant values.

Third, managerial role models are vital. Andy Grove at Intel doesn't need (or want) a large number of bureaucratic rules to determine who is responsible for what, who is supposed to talk to whom, and who gets to fly first class (no one does). He encourages openness by not having many of the trappings of success—he works in a cubicle like all the other professionals. Can you imagine any new manager asking whether or not he can fly first class? Grove's personal example eliminates such a need.

Fourth, reward systems must be clearly aligned with the organizational goals and objectives. Where do you think rules and regulations are more important in controlling behavior—Home Depot, with its generous bonus and stock option plan, or Kmart, which does not provide the same level of rewards and incentives?

## >>The Role of Corporate Governance

In the first two sections of this chapter we addressed how management can exercise strategic control over the firm's overall operations through the use of informational and behavioral controls. Now we address the issue of strategic control in a broader perspective, typically referred to as "corporate governance." Here we focus on the need for both shareholders (the owners of the corporation) and their elected representatives, the board of directors, to actively ensure that management fulfills its overriding purpose of increasing long-term shareholder value.

Robert Monks and Nell Minow, two leading scholars in corporate governance, define it as "the relationship among various participants in determining the direction and performance of corporations. The primary participants are (1) the shareholders, (2) the management (led by the chief executive officer), and (3) the board of directors."\* Consistent with Monks and Minow's definition, our discussion will center on how corporations can succeed (or fail) in aligning managerial motives with the interests of the shareholders and their elected representatives, the board of directors. As you will recall from Chapter 1, we discussed the important role of boards of directors and provided some examples of effective and ineffective boards.[40]

There is little doubt that effective corporate governance can affect a firm's bottom line. Good corporate governance plays an important role in the investment decisions of major institutions, and a premium is often reflected in the price of securities of companies that practice it. The corporate governance premium is larger for firms in countries with sound corporate governance practices compared to countries with weaker corporate governance standards.[41] In addition, there is a strong correlation between strong corporate governance and superior financial performance. Strategy Spotlight 9.5 briefly summarizes three studies that provide support for this contention.

As indicated in our discussion above and in Strategy Spotlight 9.5, there is solid evidence linking good corporate governance with higher performance. At the same time, few topics in the business press are generating as much interest (and disdain!) as corporate governance.

Some recent notable examples of flawed corporate governance include:[42]

- Board members of Nortel Networks meet with governance-minded investors to discuss possible changes to the board. This is after 10 executives and accounting officials are fired for artificially boosting the company's 2003 financial results. (September 30, 2004)
- The Chairman of Boeing Company, Philip M. Condit, presides over a series of manipulations in accounting, acquisitions, and strategy. He conceals a $2.6 billion cost overrun from shareholders for months while his merger with McDonnell Douglas Corporation is completed, and as a result, he is forced to resign by the board. (December 15, 2003)
- Royal Ahoud NV (owner of Stop and Shop), the world's third largest supermarket operator, fires its CEO and CFO for inappropriate accounting for discounts from suppliers. The company also reduces earnings for the prior two years by $500 million. (February 25, 2003)
- AOL buys Time Warner in a deal worth $183 billion—which later results in a $54 billion write-off, the largest ever. (April 25, 2002)
- The New York State Attorney General charges that Merrill Lynch analysts were privately referring to certain stocks as "crap" and "junk" while publicly recommending them to investors. (April 8, 2002)

---

\* Management, of course, cannot ignore the demands of other important firm stakeholders such as creditors, suppliers, customers, employees, and government regulators. At times of financial duress, powerful creditors can exert strong and legitimate pressures on managerial decisions. In general, however, the attention to stakeholders other than the owners of the corporation must be addressed in a manner that is still consistent with maximizing long-term shareholder returns. For a seminal discussion on stakeholder management, refer to Freeman, R. E. 1984. *Strategic management: A stakeholder approach.* Boston: Pitman.

# STRATEGY SPOTLIGHT

## Good Corporate Governance and Performance: Research Evidence

Three studies found a positive relationship between the extent to which a firm practices good corporate governance and its performance outcomes. The results of these studies are summarized below.

1. *A strong correlation between corporate governance and price performance of large companies.* Over a recent three-year period, the average return of large capitalized firms with the best governance practices was more than five times higher than the performance of firms in the bottom corporate governance quartile.

2. *Across emerging markets.* In 10 of the 11 Asian and Latin American markets, companies in the top corporate governance quartile for their respective regions had a significantly higher (averaging 10 percentage points) return on capital employed (ROCE) than their market sample. In 12 of the emerging markets analyzed, companies in the lowest corporate governance quartile had a lower ROCE than the market average.

Sources: McKinsey & Company. 2000. *Investor opinion survey on corporate governance,* June; Gill, Amar, Credit Lyonnais Securities (Asia). 2001. *Corporate governance in emerging markets: Saints and sinners,* April; and Low, C. K. 2002. *Corporate governance: An Asia-Pacific critique.* Hong Kong: Sweet & Maxwell Asia.

3. *Attitudes toward investing.* McKinsey & Company conducted three surveys from September 1999 to April 2000 that studied attitudes toward investing in Asia, Europe, the United States, and Latin America. Over three-quarters of the more than 200 investors surveyed agreed that "board practices were at least as important as financial performance." Over 80 percent of investors agreed that they "would pay a premium for the shares of a better-governed company than for those of a poorly governed company with comparable financial performance." Interestingly, the study demonstrated that the value of good corporate governance—that is, the premium that investors are willing to pay—varied across regions. Good corporate governance in the United States and the United Kingdom brought the lowest premium at 18 percent. However, for investments in Asian and Latin American countries, the premium rose to between 20 and 28 percent. The difference in the premium reflected the lack of good corporate governance standards in Asia and Latin America compared to the standards of companies in the United States and the United Kingdom.

- Tyco International discloses that it paid a director $10 million in cash and gave an additional $10 million to his favorite charity in exchange for his help in closing an acquisition deal. (January 29, 2002)
- Global Crossing, once a high-flying telecom service provider, files for Chapter 11. In the preceding three years, the company's insiders had cashed in $1.3 billion in stock. (January 28, 2002)
- Former company CEO Al Dunlap agrees to pay $15 million to settle a lawsuit from Sunbeam shareholders and bondholders alleging that he cooked the books of the small appliances maker. (January 11, 2002)
- Arthur Andersen, the accounting firm, agrees to pay $110 million to settle a shareholders suit for alleged fraud in its audit of Sunbeam. (May, 2001)
- Oracle CEO Larry Ellison exercises 23 million stock options for a record gain of more than $706 million—weeks before lowering earnings forecasts. (January, 2001)

Clearly, because of the many lapses in corporate governance, we can see the benefits associated with effective practices. However, corporate managers may behave in their own self-interest, often to the detriment of shareholders. Next we address the implications of the separation of ownership and management in the modern corporation, and some mechanisms that can be used to ensure consistency (or alignment) between the interests of shareholders and those of the managers to minimize potential conflicts.

## The Modern Corporation: The Separation of Owners (Shareholders) and Management

Some of the proposed definitions for a *corporation* include:

- "The business corporation is an instrument through which capital is assembled for the activities of producing and distributing goods and services and making investments. Accordingly, a basic premise of corporation law is that a business corporation should have as its objective the conduct of such activities with a view to enhancing the corporation's profit and the gains of the corporation's owners, that is, the shareholders." (Melvin Aron Eisenberg, *The Structure of Corporation Law*)
- "A body of persons granted a charter legally recognizing them as a separate entity having its own rights, privileges, and liabilities distinct from those of its members." (*American Heritage Dictionary*)
- An ingenious device for obtaining individual profit without individual responsibility." (Ambrose Bierce, *The Devil's Dictionary*)[43]

All of these definitions have some validity and each one (including that from *The Devil's Dictionary!*) reflects a key feature of the corporate form of business organization—its ability to draw resources from a variety of groups and establish and maintain its own persona that is separate from all of them. As Henry Ford once said, "A great business is really too big to be human."

Simply put, a corporation is a mechanism created to allow different parties to contribute capital, expertise, and labor for the maximum benefit of each party. The shareholders (investors) are able to participate in the profits of the enterprise without taking direct responsibility for the operations. The management can run the company without the responsibility of personally providing the funds. And, in order to make both of these possible, the shareholders have limited liability as well as rather limited involvement in the company's affairs. However, they reserve the right to elect directors who have the fiduciary obligation to protect their interests.

Over 70 years ago, Columbia University professors Adolf Berle and Gardiner C. Means addressed the divergence of the interests of the owners of the corporation from the professional managers who are hired to run it. They warned that widely dispersed ownership "released management from the overriding requirement that it serve stockholders." The separation of ownership from management has given rise to a set of ideas called "agency theory." Central to agency theory is the relationship between two primary players—the *principals* who are the owners of the firm (stockholders) and the *agents,* who are the people paid by principals to perform a job on their behalf (management). The stockholders elect and are represented by a board of directors that has a fiduciary responsibility to ensure that management acts in the best interests of stockholders to ensure long-term financial returns for the firm.

Agency theory is concerned with resolving two problems that can occur in agency relationships.[44] The first is the agency problem that arises (1) when the goals of the principals and agents conflict, and (2) when it is difficult or expensive for the principal to verify what the agent is actually doing. In a corporation, this means that the board of directors would be unable to confirm that the managers were actually acting in the shareholders' interests because, in most cases, managers are "insiders" with regard to the businesses they operate and thus are better informed than the principals. Thus, managers may act "opportunistically" in pursuing their own interests—to the detriment of the corporation.[45] Managers may, for example, spend corporate funds on expensive perquisites (e.g., company jets and expensive art), devote time and resources to pet projects (initiatives in which they have a personal interest but that have limited market potential), engage in power struggles (where they may fight

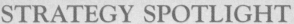
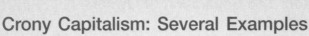

# STRATEGY SPOTLIGHT

### 9.6

## Crony Capitalism: Several Examples

When President George W. Bush signed the Sarbanes-Oxley Act into law on July 30, 2002, one of its goals was to prevent the kind of self-dealing and other conflicts of interest that had brought down Enron, WorldCom, Adelphia, and other corporate giants. Among other things, the Sarbanes-Oxley Act bans company loans to executives and prohibits extending the terms of existing loans.

Many companies, however, acted quickly *before* the bill was signed. For example, *one day* before the bill was signed, Crescent Real Estate Equities of Fort Worth, Texas, extended the payback deadline by 10 years on a loan of $26 million to its chief executive, John Goff. And Electronic Arts gave a $4 million loan to Warren Johnson, its chief financial officer, admitting in a filing that it was doing so a month prior to the "prohibition on loans to executive officers."

Despite legislation such as Sarbanes-Oxley and pressures from shareholders, related-party deals are quite common. According to the Corporate Library, a research group in Portland, Maine, 75 percent of 2,000 companies that were studied still engage in them. In essence, that means that companies must make embarrassing disclosures in their proxy statements about nepotism, property leased from top managers, corporate-owned apartments, and other forms of "insiderism."

Consider some examples:

- Two hundred companies have leased or bought airplanes from insiders. For example, Pilgrim's Pride of

Pittsburgh, Texas, a chicken processor with $2.6 billion in annual sales has leased an airplane from its chief executive and founder Lonnie Pilgrim since 1985. Mr. Pilgrim made $656,000 in fiscal 2003 from this deal to go along with his $1.7 million in compensation. The company defends the pact as cost-efficient since its headquarters is located in a small town. Pilgrim also provides some bookkeeping services for his personal businesses, but he won't provide details.

- Micky M. Arison is chief executive of Carnival, the big cruise line. He is also chief executive and owner of the Miami Heat of the National Basketball Association. Carnival paid the Heat $675,000 in fiscal 2002 and 2003 for sponsorship and advertising as well as season tickets. Although that may be a rather small sum, given Carnival's $2.2 billion in net income for the period, we could still ask if the money would have been spent on something else if Arison didn't own the team.

- Alliance Semiconductor CEO N. Damodar Reddy has committed $20 million to Solar Ventures, a venture capital company run by his brother C. N. Reddy. Other unnamed insiders purchased undisclosed stakes in Solar. However, Alliance won't disclose whether its CEO is one of them. To date it has invested $12.5 million in Solar. Beth Young, senior research associate of the Corporate Library poses an interesting question: "Is Reddy using shareholder capital just to keep afloat his brother's fund and the insiders' investment?"

Source: MacDonald, E. 2004. Crony capitalism. *Forbes*, June 21: 140–146.

---

over resources for their own betterment and to the detriment of the firm), and negate (or sabotage) attractive merger offers because they may result in increased employment risk.[46]

The second issue is the problem of risk sharing. This arises when the principal and the agent have different attitudes and preferences toward risk. For example, the executives in a firm may favor additional diversification initiatives because, by their very nature, they increase the size of the firm and thus the level of executive compensation. At the same time, such diversification initiatives may erode shareholder value because they fail to achieve some of the synergies that we discussed in Chapter 6 (e.g., building on core competencies, sharing activities, or enhancing market power). In effect, agents (executives) may have a stronger preference toward diversification than shareholders because it reduces their personal level of risk from potential loss of employment. In contrast, research has shown that executives who have large holdings of stock in their firms were more likely to have diversification strategies that were more consistent with shareholder interests—that is, increasing long-term returns.[47]

At times, top-level managers engage in actions that reflect their self-interest rather than the interests of shareholders. Some examples of such conflicts of interest are addressed in Strategy Spotlight 9.6.

# Governance Mechanisms: Aligning the Interests of Owners and Managers

As noted above, a key characteristic of the modern corporation is the separation of ownership from control. To minimize the potential for managers to act in their own self-interest, or "opportunistically," the owners can implement some governance mechanisms.[48] We address three of these in the next sections. First, there are two primary means of monitoring the behavior of managers. These include (1) a committed and involved *board of directors* that acts in the best interests of the shareholders to create long-term value for shareholders and (2) *shareholder activism,* wherein the owners of the corporation view themselves as share*owners* instead of share*holders* and become actively engaged in the governance of the corporation. As we will see later in this section, shareholder activism has increased dramatically in recent years. Finally, there are managerial incentives, sometimes called "contract-based outcomes," which consist of *reward and compensation agreements.* Here the goal is to carefully craft managerial incentive packages to align the interests of management with those of the stockholders.

*A Committed and Involved Board of Directors*    The board of directors acts as a fulcrum between the owners and controllers of a corporation. In effect, they are the intermediaries who provide a balance between a small group of key managers in the firm based at the corporate headquarters and a sometimes vast group of shareholders typically spread out over the world. In the United States, the law imposes on the board a strict and absolute fiduciary duty to ensure that a company is run consistent with the long-term interests of the owners—the shareholders. The reality, as we have seen, is somewhat more ambiguous.[49]

The Business Roundtable, representing the largest U.S. corporations, describes the duties of the board as follows:

1. Select, regularly evaluate, and, if necessary, replace the chief executive officer. Determine management compensation. Review succession planning.
2. Review and, where appropriate, approve the financial objectives, major strategies, and plans of the corporation.
3. Provide advice and counsel to top management.
4. Select and recommend to shareholders for election an appropriate slate of candidates for the board of directors; evaluate board processes and performance.
5. Review the adequacy of the systems to comply with all applicable laws/regulations.[50]

Given these principles, what makes for a good board of directors? According to the Business Roundtable, the most important quality is a board of directors who are active, critical participants in determining a company's strategies.[51] That does not mean board members should micromanage or circumvent the CEO. Rather, they should provide strong oversight that goes beyond simply approving the chief executive's plans. Today, a board's primary responsibilities are to ensure that strategic plans undergo rigorous scrutiny, evaluate managers against high performance standards, and take control of the succession process.

Although boards in the past were often dismissed as CEO's rubber stamps, increasingly they are playing a more active role by forcing out CEOs who cannot deliver on performance. According to a recent study by the consulting firm Booz Allen Hamilton, the rate of CEO departures for performance reasons has more than tripled, from 1.3 percent to 4.2 percent, between 1995 and 2002.[52] Well-known CEOs like Gerald M. Levin of AOL Time Warner and Jack M. Greenberg of McDonald's paid the price for poor financial performance by being forced to leave. Others, such as Bernard Ebbers of WorldCom, Inc., and Dennis Kozlowski of Tyco International, lost their jobs due to scandals. "Deliver or depart" is clearly the new message from the boards.

Another key component of top-ranked boards is director independence. Governance experts believe that a majority of directors should be free of all ties to either the CEO or the company. That means a minimum of "insiders" (past or present members of the management team) should serve on the board, and that directors and their firms should be barred from doing consulting, legal, or other work for the company.[53] Interlocking directorships—in which CEOs and other top managers serve on each other's boards—are not desirable. But perhaps the best guarantee that directors act in the best interests of shareholders is the simplest: Most good companies now insist that directors own significant stock in the company they oversee.[54]

Such guidelines are not always followed. At times, it would appear that the practices of the boards of directors of some companies are the antithesis of such guidelines. Consider the Walt Disney Co. Over a recent five-year period, Michael Eisner pocketed an astonishing $531 million. Although, over a 10-year period, Eisner had led Disney to provide shareholder returns of over 20 percent, he likely had very little resistance from his board of directors.

> Many investors view the Disney board as an anachronism. Among Disney's 16 directors is Eisner's personal attorney—who for several years was chairman of the company's compensation committee! There was also the architect who designed Eisner's Aspen home and his parents' apartment. Joining them are the principal of an elementary school once attended by his children and the president of a university to which Eisner donated $1 million. The board also includes the actor Sidney Poitier, seven current and former Disney executives, and an attorney who does business with Disney. Moreover, most of the outside directors own little or no Disney stock. "It is an egregiously bad board—a train wreck waiting to happen," warns Michael L. Useem, a management professor at the University of Pennsylvania's Wharton School.[55]

This example also demonstrates that "outside directors" are only beneficial to strong corporate governance if they are engaged and vigilant in carrying out their responsibilities.[56] As humorously suggested by Warren Buffett, founder and chairman of Berkshire Hathaway: "The ratcheting up of compensation has been obscene. . . . There is a tendency to put cocker spaniels on compensation committees, not Doberman pinschers."[57]

Many firms do have exemplary board practices. Below, for example, we list some of the excellent practices at Intel Corp., the world's largest semiconductor chip manufacturer, with $34 billion in revenues:[58]

- *Mix of inside and outside directors.* The board believes that there should be a majority of independent directors on the board. However, the board is willing to have members of management, in addition to the chief executive officer, as directors.

- *Board presentations and access to employees.* The board encourages management to schedule managers to be present at meetings who: (a) can provide additional insight into the items being discussed because of personal involvement in these areas, or (b) have future potential that management believes should be given exposure to the board.

## 9.7 | STRATEGY SPOTLIGHT

### Continental Airlines: Selecting Competent Directors for its Board

Continental Airlines took explicit action to select directors who could face the challenges of its industry. The board thoroughly analyzed Continental's business issues in order to assess what skills and experience it needed and zeroed in on the knowledge of the airline and travel industries, an understanding of marketing and consumer behavior, access to key business and political contacts, and experience with industry reconfiguration.

The board then defined the capabilities and qualities that were required of all directors, such as independence,

business credibility, confidence, and teamwork. To be as representative as possible, it determined the directors' knowledge of geographic markets, especially their knowledge of key Continental hubs, CEO experience, leadership in business sectors, and gender and ethnic diversity.

After this analysis, the board evaluated all of its directors and mapped their skills, experience, and backgrounds against the new criteria. The gaps became critical information for targeting new directors. Ultimately, several board members voluntarily resigned to make way for new directors who had the capabilities and background that Continental needed to compete more successfully.

Source: Nadler, D. A. 2004. Building better boards. *Harvard Business Review,* 82(5): 102–111.

---

- *Formal evaluation of officers.* The Compensation Committee conducts, and reviews with the outside directors, an annual evaluation to help determine the salary and executive bonus of all officers, including the chief executive officer.

To be effective, boards of directors also have to be composed of members who have the requisite competencies and backgrounds. Strategy Spotlight 9.7 discusses the intricate process that Continental Airlines has undertaken to improve the quality of the members of its board of directors.

*Shareholder Activism*   As a practical matter, there are so many owners of the largest American corporations that it makes little sense to refer to them as "owners" in the sense of individuals becoming informed and involved in corporate affairs. However, even an individual shareholder has several rights, including (1) the right to sell the stock, (2) the right to vote the proxy (which includes the election of board members), (3) the right to bring suit for damages if the corporation's directors or managers fail to meet their obligations, (4) the right to certain information from the company, and (5) certain residual rights following the company's liquidation (or its filing for reorganization under bankruptcy laws), once creditors and other claimants are paid off.[59]

Collectively, shareholders have the power to direct the course of corporations.[60] This may involve acts such as being party to shareholder action suits and demanding that key issues be brought up for proxy votes at annual board meetings. In addition, the power of shareholders has intensified in recent years because of the increasing influence of large institutional investors such as mutual funds (e.g., T. Rowe Price and Fidelity Investments) and retirement systems such as TIAA-CREF (for university faculty members and school administrative staff).[61] Institutional investors hold approximately 50 percent of all listed corporate stock in the United States.

Many institutional investors are aggressive in protecting and enhancing their investments. In effect, they are shifting from traders to owners. They are assuming the role of permanent shareholders and rigorously analyzing issues of corporate governance. In the process they are reinventing systems of corporate monitoring and accountability.[62]

Consider the proactive behavior of CalPERS, the California Public Employees' Retirement System, which manages approximately $150 billion in assets and is the third largest pension fund in the world. Every year CalPERS reviews the performance of U.S. companies in its stock portfolio and identifies those that are among the lowest long-term relative performers and have governance structures that do not ensure full accountability to company owners. This generates a long list of companies, each of which may potentially be publicly identified as a CalPERS "Focus Company"—corporations to which CalPERS directs specific suggested governance reforms. CalPERS meets with the directors of each of these companies to discuss performance and governance issues. The CalPERS Focus List contains those companies that continue to merit public and market attention at the end of the process.

Emerson Electric, based in St. Louis, Missouri, has $5 billion in revenues and is one of the four firms on the CalPERS 2004 Focus List. CalPERS holds 2.19 million shares (0.52 percent of the total outstanding shares). Following is list of the governance changes that CalPERS wants Emerson to make:[63]

- Formalize director evaluations.
- Commit to independent board members and reduce the employee representation on the board.
- Provide an analysis of retaining former CEO Charles Knight as Chairman of the Board member and commit to renegotiating the excessive terms of Mr. Knight's contract and perquisites.
- Seek shareholder approval of the company's poison pill.
- Seek shareholder approval to eliminate the supermajority requirements and declassify the board by the 2005 annual meeting.
- Tie a significant portion of the company's long-term compensation to performance-based measures.
- Improve communication and transparency of good governance initiatives.

While appearing punitive to company management, such aggressive activism has paid significant returns for CalPERS (and other stockholders of the "Focused" companies). For example, a Wilshire Associates study of the "CalPERS Effect" of corporate governance examined the performance of 62 targets over a five-year period. The results indicated that, while the stock of these companies trailed the Standard & Poors Index by 89 percent in the five-year period before CalPERS acted, the same stocks outperformed the index by 23 percent in the following five years, adding approximately $150 million annually in additional returns to the fund.

*Managerial Rewards and Incentives*    As we discussed earlier in the chapter, incentive systems must be designed to help a company achieve its goals. Similarly, from the perspective of governance, one of the most critical roles of the board of directors is to create incentives that align the interests of the CEO and top executives with the interests of owners of the corporation—long-term shareholder returns.[64] After all, shareholders rely on CEOs to adopt policies and strategies that maximize the value of their shares.[65] A combination of three basic policies may create the right monetary incentives for CEOs to maximize the value of their companies:

1. Boards can require that the CEOs become substantial owners of company stock.
2. Salaries, bonuses, and stock options can be structured so as to provide rewards for superior performance and penalties for poor performance.
3. Threat of dismissal for poor performance can be a realistic outcome.

In recent years the granting of stock options has enabled top executives of publicly held corporations to earn enormous levels of compensation. In 2001 the CEOs of large corporations in the United States averaged $11 million, or 411 times as much as the average factory worker. Over the past decade, the wages of rank-and-file workers increased only 36 percent while the pay of CEOs climbed 340 percent. Many boards have awarded huge option grants despite poor executive performance, and others have made performance goals easier to reach. In 2002 nearly 200 companies swapped or repriced options—all to enrich wealthy executives who are already among the country's richest people. However, stock options can be a valuable governance mechanism to align the CEO's interests with those of the shareholders. The extraordinarily high level of compensation can often be grounded in sound governance principles.[66] For example, Howard Solomon, CEO of Forest Laboratories, received a total compensation of $148.5 million in 2001.[67] This represented $823,000 in salary, $400,000 in bonus, and $147.3 million in stock options that were exercised. However, shareholders also did well, receiving gains of 40 percent. The firm has enjoyed spectacular growth over the past five years and Solomon has been CEO since 1977. Thus, huge income is attributed largely to gains that have built up over many years. As stated by compensation committee member Dan Goldwasser, "If a CEO is delivering substantial increases in shareholder value . . . it's only appropriate that he be rewarded for it."

However, the "pay for performance" principle doesn't always hold. Consider Oracle, for example.

> By 2001, with the tech bubble bursting, Oracle stock was in a free fall. Rather than sit tight in a show of confidence, CEO Laurence Ellison sold 29 million shares in a single week in January, flooding the market when investors already were jittery. He exercised 23 million options the same week for a gain of more than $706 million. Within a month, Oracle stock had lost a third of its value and the company was announcing that it would miss third-quarter forecasts. That triggered further price declines and a rash of shareholder lawsuits alleging that Ellison engaged in "what appears to be the largest insider trading in the history of the U.S. financial market," according to one suit. Ellison's stock sales were a factor in the sell-off that followed, says Henry Asher, president of Northstar Group, Inc., which owns 48,000 Oracle shares. "Was that a ringing endorsement for the company's short-term prospects?" asks Asher. "I don't think so."[68]

In addition to the granting of stock options, boards of directors are often failing to fulfill their fiduciary responsibilities to shareholders when they lower the performance targets that executives need to meet in order to receive millions of dollars. At General Motors, for example, CEO G. Richard Wagoner, Jr., and other top executives were entitled to a special performance bonus if the company's net profit margin reached 5 percent by the end of 2003. However, the 5 percent target was later lowered.

TIAA-CREF has provided several principles of corporate governance with regard to executive compensation.[69] These include the importance of aligning the rewards of all employees—rank and file as well as executives—to the long-term performance of the corporation; general guidelines on the role of cash compensation, stock, and "fringe benefits"; and the mission of a corporation's compensation committee. Exhibit 9.6 addresses TIAA-CREF's principles on the role of stock in managerial compensation.

## External Governance Control Mechanisms

Our discussion so far has been on internal governance mechanisms. Internal controls, however, are not always enough to ensure good governance. The separation of ownership and control that we discussed earlier requires multiple control mechanisms, some internal and some external, to ensure that managerial actions lead to shareholder value maximization. Further, society-at-large wants some assurance that this goal is met without harming other stakeholder groups. In this section, we discuss several external control mechanisms that have developed in most modern economies. These include the market for corporate control, auditors, governmental regulatory bodies, banks and analysts, media, and public activists.

Stock-based compensation plans are a critical element of most compensation programs and can provide opportunities for managers whose efforts contribute to the creation of shareholder wealth. In evaluating the suitability of these plans, considerations of reasonableness, scale, linkage to performance, and fairness to shareholders and all employees also apply. TIAA-CREF, the largest pension system in the world, has set forth the following guidelines for stock-based compensation. Proper stock-based plans should:

- Allow for creation of executive wealth that is reasonable in view of the creation of shareholder wealth. Management should not prosper through stock while shareholders suffer.
- Have measurable and predictable outcomes that are directly linked to the company's performance.
- Be market oriented, within levels of comparability for similar positions in companies of similar size and business focus.
- Be straightforward and clearly described so that investors and employees can understand them.
- Be fully disclosed to the investing public and be approved by shareholders.

Source: www.tiaa-cref.org/pubs.

*The Market for Corporate Control*    Let us assume for a moment that internal control mechanisms in a company are failing. This means that the board is ineffective in monitoring managers and is not exercising the oversight required of them and that shareholders are passive and are not taking any actions to monitor or discipline managers. Theoretically, under these circumstances managers may behave opportunistically.[70] Opportunistic behavior can take many forms. First, they can *shirk* their responsibilities. Shirking means that managers fail to exert themselves fully, as is required of them. Second, they can engage in *on the job consumption.* Examples of on the job consumption include private jets, club memberships, expensive artwork in the offices, and so on. Each of these represents consumption by managers that does not in any way increase shareholder value. Instead, they actually diminish shareholder value. Third, managers may engage in *excessive product-market diversification.*[71] As we discussed in Chapter 6, such diversification serves to reduce only the employment risk of the managers rather than the financial risk of the shareholders, who can more cheaply diversify their risk by owning a portfolio of investments. Is there any external mechanism to stop managers from shirking, consumption on the job, and excessive diversification?

The market for corporate control is one such external mechanism that provides at least some partial solution to the problems described. If internal control mechanisms fail and the management is behaving opportunistically, the likely response of most shareholders will be to sell their stock rather than engage in activism.[72] As more and more stockholders vote with their feet, the value of the stock begins to decline. As the decline continues, at some point the market value of the firm becomes less than the book value. That is, a corporate raider can take over the company for a price less than the book value of the assets of the company. The first thing that the raider may do on assuming control over the company will be to fire the underperforming management. The risk of being acquired by a hostile raider is often referred to as the *takeover constraint.* The takeover constraint deters management from engaging in opportunistic behavior.[73]

Although in theory the takeover constraint is supposed to limit managerial opportunism, in recent years its effectiveness has become diluted as a result of a number of defense tactics adopted by incumbent management (see Chapter 6). Foremost among them are poison pills, greenmail, and golden parachutes. Poison pills are provisions adopted by the company to reduce its worth to the acquirer. An example would be payment of a huge one-time dividend, typically financed by debt. Greenmail involves buying back the stock from the acquirer, usually at an attractive premium. Golden parachutes are employment contracts that cause the company to pay lucrative severance packages to top managers fired as a result of a takeover, often running to several million dollars.

*Auditors*    Even when there are stringent disclosure requirements, there is no guarantee that the information disclosed will be accurate. Managers may deliberately disclose false information or withhold negative financial information. It is also possible that they may use accounting methods that distort results based on highly subjective interpretations. Therefore, all accounting statements are required to be audited and certified to be accurate by external auditors. These auditing firms are independent organizations staffed by certified professionals who verify the books of accounts of the company. Audits can unearth financial irregularities and ensure that financial reporting by the firm conforms to standard accounting practices.

Recent developments leading to the bankruptcy of firms such as Enron and WorldCom and a spate of earnings restatements raise questions about the failure of the auditing firms to act as effective external control mechanisms. Why did an auditing firm like Arthur Andersen, with decades of reputation in the auditing profession at stake, fail to raise red flags about accounting irregularities? First, auditors are appointed by the firm being audited. The desire to continue that business relationship sometimes makes them overlook financial irregularities. Second, most auditing firms also do consulting work and often have lucrative consulting contracts with the firms that they audit. Understandably, some of them tend not to ask too many difficult questions, because they fear jeopardizing the consulting business, which is often more profitable than the auditing work.

The recent restatement of earnings by Xerox is an example of the lack of independence of auditing firms. The Securities and Exchange Commission filed a lawsuit against KPMG, the world's third largest accounting firm, in January 2003 for allowing Xerox to inflate its revenues by $3 billion between 1997 and 2000. Of the $82 million that Xerox paid KPMG during these four years, only $26 million was for auditing. The rest was for consulting services. When one of the auditors objected to Xerox's practice of booking revenues for equipment leases earlier than it should have, Xerox asked KPMG to replace him, which it did.[74]

*Banks and Analysts*    Two external groups that monitor publicly held firms are financial institutions and stock analysts. Commercial and investment banks do so because they have lent money to corporations and therefore have to ensure that the borrowing firm's finances are in order and that the loan covenants are being followed. Stock analysts conduct ongoing in-depth studies of the firms that they follow and make recommendations to their clients to buy, hold, or sell. Their rewards and reputation depend on the quality of these recommendations. Their access to information, knowledge of the industry and the firm, and the insights they gain from interactions with the management of the company enable them to alert the investing community of both positive and negative developments relating to a company.

In reality, it is generally observed that analyst recommendations are often more optimistic than warranted by facts. "Sell" recommendations tend to be exceptions rather than the norm. Many analysts seem to have failed to grasp the gravity of the problems surrounding failed companies such as Enron and Global Crossing till the very end. Part of the explanation may lie in the fact that most analysts work for firms that also have investment banking relationships with the companies they follow. Negative recommendations by analysts can displease the management, who may decide to take their investment banking business to a rival firm. Thus, otherwise independent and competent analysts may be pressured to overlook negative information or tone down their criticism. A recent settlement between the Securities and Exchange Commission and the New York State Attorney General with 10 banks requires them to pay $1.4 billion in penalties and to fund independent research for investors.[75]

*Regulatory Bodies*    All corporations are subject to some regulation by the government. The extent of regulation is often a function of the type of industry. Banks, utilities, and pharmaceuticals, for example, are subject to more regulatory oversight because of their importance to society. Public corporations are subject to more regulatory requirements than private corporations. All public corporations are required to disclose a substantial amount of financial information by bodies such as the Securities and Exchange Commission. These include quarterly and annual filings of financial performance, stock trading by insiders, and details of executive compensation packages. There are two primary reasons behind such requirements. First, markets can operate efficiently only when the investing public has faith in the market system. In the absence of disclosure requirements, the average investor suffers from a lack of reliable information and therefore may completely stay away from the capital market. This will negatively impact an economy's ability to grow. Second, disclosure of information such as insider trading protects the small investor to some extent from the negative consequences of information asymmetry. That is, the insiders and large investors typically have more information than the small investor and can therefore use that information to buy or sell before the information becomes public knowledge.

The failure of a variety of external control mechanisms led the U.S. Congress to pass the Sarbanes-Oxley Act in 2002. This act calls for many stringent measures that would ensure better governance of U.S. corporations. Some of these measures include:[76]

- *Auditors* are barred from certain types of nonaudit work. They are not allowed to destroy records for five years. Lead partners auditing a client should be changed at least every five years.
- *CEOs* and *CFOs* must fully reveal off-balance-sheet finances and vouch for the accuracy of the information revealed.
- *Executives* must promptly reveal the sale of shares in firms they manage and are not allowed to sell when other employees cannot.
- *Corporate lawyers* must report to senior managers any violations of securities law lower down.

Strategy Spotlight 9.8 discusses some of the expenses that companies have incurred in complying with the Sarbanes-Oxley Act. You may wonder whether the costs outweigh some of the benefits.

*Media and Public Activists*    The press is not usually recognized as an external control mechanism in the literature on corporate governance. There is, however, no denying that in all developed capitalist economies, the financial press and media play an important indirect role in monitoring the management of public corporations. In the United States, business magazines such as *BusinessWeek* and *Fortune,* financial newspapers such as *The Wall Street Journal* and *Investors Business Daily,* as well as television networks like Financial News Network and CNBC are constantly reporting on companies. Public perceptions about

## Governance Reform: The Costs Add Up

In the aftermath of Enron and Worldcom and a spate of corporate scandals early in the decade, the U.S. Congress passed the Sarbanes-Oxley Act in 2002. It was an effort to restore investor confidence in the governance of corporations in general and financial reporting in particular. Three years later, a backlash seems to be developing among executives about the high compliance costs and some of the more draconian requirements.

The major source of resentment is the issue of cost. It is estimated that large corporations with revenues over $4 billion have to spend an average of $35 million a year to implement Sarbanes-Oxley. Medium-sized companies spend $3.1 million a year on average. Smaller companies find the cost of compliance particularly burdensome because they have a smaller revenue base. Some critics go to the extent of arguing that this amounts to a form of regressive taxation against small businesses. Many are even considering delisting to avoid compliance costs.

Costs are not the only problem that companies face. Meeting the requirements of Sarbanes-Oxley is very time consuming as well. For example, the law requires that financial numbers such as value of inventory and receivables are cross-checked. But it requires an army of additional people and significant additional costs to ensure this. Yellow Roadway Corporation, the nation's largest trucking firm, had to use 200 employees and $9 million to accomplish this in 2004. This was 3% of their total profits. And just think of the lost productivity!

How much has Sarbanes-Oxley succeeded in improving governance and ensuring the accuracy and reliability of financial reporting? While it is too early to assess the impact, there is at least some anecdotal evidence that it is having some impact. Visteon Corp., an auto-parts supplier, reported that they uncovered problems with their accounts receivable while complying with the requirements of the act. Similarly, SunTrust Banks Inc. fired three officers after discovering errors in the calculation of loan allowances in their portfolios. Tough but fair regulations can improve governance, but the costs of compliance cannot be ignored.

Source: Henry, D. 2005. Death, taxes & Sarbanes-Oxley? *BusinessWeek*, January 17: 28–31.

---

a company's financial prospects and the quality of its management are greatly influenced by the media. For example, Food Lion's reputation was sullied when ABC's *Prime Time Live* in 1992 charged the company with employee exploitation, false package dating, and unsanitary meat handling practices. Bethany McLean of *Fortune* magazine is often credited as the first to raise questions about Enron's long-term financial viability.[77]

Similarly, consumer groups and activist individuals often take a crusading role in exposing corporate malfeasance. Well-known examples include Ralph Nader and Erin Brockovich, who played important roles in bringing to light the safety issues related to GM's Corvair and environmental pollution issues concerning Pacific Gas and Electric Company, respectively. Exhibit 9.7 summarizes the many watchdog groups founded by Ralph Nader to monitor and change the behavior and strategies of major corporations.

## Corporate Governance: An International Perspective

As we have noted in this chapter (and in Chapter 1), the topic of corporate governance has long been dominated by agency theory and based on the explicit assumption of the separation of ownership and control.[78] The central conflicts are principal–agent conflicts between shareholders and management. However, such an underlying assumption seldom applies outside of the United States and the United Kingdom. This is particularly true in emerging economies and continental Europe. Here, there is often concentrated ownership, along with extensive family ownership and control, business group structures, and weak legal protection for minority shareholders. Thus, serious conflicts tend to exist between two classes of principals: controlling shareholders and minority shareholders. Such conflicts can be called

Ralph Nader, an activist politician in the United States, established more than 30 public interest groups to act as "watchdogs" for corporate America. Together, the loose federation of independent groups constitutes, in effect, an anticorporate conglomerate. Here are a few examples.

- **Aviation Consumer Action Project:** Works to propose new rules to prevent flight delays, impose penalties for deceiving passengers about problems, and push for higher compensation for lost luggage.

- **Center for Auto Safety:** Helps consumers find plaintiff lawyers and agitates for vehicle recalls, increased highway safety standards, and lemon laws.

- **Center for Study of Responsive Law:** This is Nader's headquarters. Home of a consumer project on technology, this group sponsored seminars on Microsoft remedies and pushed for tougher Internet privacy rules. It also took on the drug industry over costs.

- **Commercial Alert:** This group fights excessive commercialism. Its targets include Primedia for delivering ads in educational programming and Coke and Pepsi for aggressive sales tactics in schools.

- **Pension Rights Center:** This center helped employees of IBM, General Electric, and other companies to organize themselves against cash-balance pension plans.

- **Public Citizen:** This is the umbrella organization that sponsors Global Trade Watch, Congress Watch, the Critical Mass Energy & Environment program, Health Research Group, and Public Citizen Litigation Group. Issues taken up include tort reform, oil mergers, and reform of campaign finance.

Source: From Bernstein, A., "Too Much Corporate Power?" *BusinessWeek*, Sept. 2000. Reprinted with permission.

**Exhibit 9.7**

**Watchdogs for Corporate America**

*principal–principal* (PP) conflicts as opposed to *principal–agent* conflicts. Exhibits 9.8 and 9.9 address how principal–principal conflicts and principal–agent conflicts differ.

Strong family control is one of the leading indicators of concentrated ownership. For example, in East Asia (excluding China), approximately 57 percent of the corporations have board chairmen and CEOs from the controlling families. In continental Europe, this number is 68 percent. A very common practice is the appointment of family members as board chairman, CEOs, and other top executives. This happens because the families are controlling (not necessarily majority) shareholders. For example, in 2003, 30-year-old James Murdoch was appointed CEO of British Sky Broadcasting (BSkyB), Europe's largest satellite broadcaster. There was very vocal resistance by minority shareholders. Why was he appointed in the first place? James's father just happened to be Rupert Murdoch, who controlled 35 percent of BSkyB and chaired the board. Clearly, this is a case of a principal–principal conflict.

In general, three conditions must be met for PP conflicts to occur. First, there must be a dominant owner or group of owners who have interests that are distinct from minority shareholders. Second, there must be motivation for the controlling shareholders to exercise their dominant positions to their advantage. And third, there must be few formal (such as legislation or regulatory bodies) or informal constraints that would discourage or prevent the controlling shareholders from exploiting their advantageous positions.

The result is often that family managers, who represent (or actually are) the controlling shareholders, engage in *expropriation* of minority shareholders, which is defined as activities that enrich the controlling shareholders at the expense of minority shareholders. What is their motive? After all, controlling shareholders have incentives to maintain firm value. But controlling shareholders may take actions that decrease aggregate firm

| | **Principal–Agent Conflicts** | **Principal–Principal Conflicts** |
|---|---|---|
| Goal Incongruence | Between shareholders and professional managers who own a relatively small portion of the firm's equity. | Between controlling shareholders and minority shareholders. |
| Ownership Pattern | Dispersed—5%–20% is considered "concentrated ownership." | Concentrated—Often greater than 50% of equity is controlled by controlling shareholders. |
| Manifestations | Strategies that benefit entrenched managers at the expense of shareholders in general (e.g., shirking, pet projects, excessive compensation, and empire building). | Strategies that benefit controlling shareholders at the expense of minority shareholders (e.g., minority shareholder expropriation, nepotism, and cronyism). |
| Institutional Protection of Minority Shareholders | Formal constraints (e.g., judicial reviews and courts) set an upper boundary on potential expropriation by majority shareholders. Informal norms generally adhere to shareholder wealth maximization. | Formal institutional protection is often lacking, corrupted, or un-enforced. Informal norms are typically in favor of the interests of controlling shareholders ahead of those of minority investors. |

Source: Adapted from Young, M., Peng, M. W., Ahlstrom, D., & Bruton, G. 2002. Governing the corporation in emerging economies: A principal–principal perspective. *Academy of Management Best Papers Proceedings,* Denver.

**Exhibit 9.8**

**Traditional Principal–Agent Conflicts versus Principal–Principal Conflicts: How they Differ Along Dimensions**

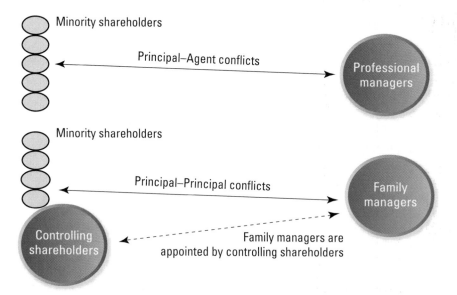

**Exhibit 9.9**    **Principal–Agent Conflicts and Principal–Principal Conflicts: A Diagram**

Source: Young, M. N., Peng, M. W., Ahlstrom, D., Bruton, G. D., Jiang, Y. 2005. Principal–principal conflicts in corporate governance (unpublished manuscript); and Peng, M. V. 2006. *Global strategy.* Cincinnati: Thomson South-Western. We are very appreciative of the helpful comments of Mike Young of the Chinese University of Hong Kong and Mike Peng of the Ohio State University.

# STRATEGY SPOTLIGHT

## Effective and Ineffective Corporate Governance in Hong Kong

Finding examples of exemplary corporate governance in Hong Kong isn't easy due to the high incidence of family-controlled corporations and the lack of laws to protect minority shareholders. An exception is CLP, one of the largest electric utilities in Asia, which is 35 percent controlled by Chairman Michael Kadoorie and his family. Admirers say it is an example of how even a family-controlled company can move toward more transparency. The company's board has several independent directors, and its Web site gives comprehensive information on its corporate governance policy. Kadoorie says family shareholders are treated the same as others.

At the other end of the continuum is Henderson Land Development. The company is controlled by Lee Shau Kee, one of Hong Kong's wealthiest tycoons. In its latest corporate-governance snafu, Henderson attempted to buy 73 percent of its publicly listed subsidiary, Henderson Investment, for 30 percent below its reported net asset value. However, the related transaction was thwarted by minority shareholders, including the powerful Templeton Asset Management. At the time, Henderson Land Vice-Chairman Colin Lam insisted the dissenting investors had placed "a very, very high valuation on Henderson Investment," implying that this placed too high a value on its shares. Needless to say, the minority shareholders would hardly agree. However, it was perfectly legal in Hong Kong, and had it gone through, the minority shareholders would have been left holding the bag.

Had the Henderson Investment deal occurred in the United States, a shareholder lawsuit would have been launched. In Hong Kong, however, class-action lawsuits are not allowed. Consider the sentiment of Andrew Sheng, head of the Hong Kong Securities & Futures Commission, in the face of an action by another company taking advantage of minority shareholders: if the investors didn't like what was happening, they could simply sell their shares. Such a "buyer beware" attitude, even by regulatory bodies in one of the most developed emerging economies, causes firms to trade at a discount compared to firms in more mature economies.

Sources: Balfour, F., & Tashiro, H. 2004. A change in attitude. *BusinessWeek*, May 17: 48–50; Clifford, M. 2002. China Journal: Hong Kong's cautionary Christmas carol. *BusinessWeek* Online, August; and Young, M. N., Peng, M. W., Ahlstrom, D., Bruton, G. D., & Jiang, Y. 2005. Principal–principal conflicts in corporate governance Unpublished manuscript.

performance if their personal gains from expropriation exceed their personal losses from their firm's lowered performance.

Another ubiquitous feature of corporate life outside of the United States and Great Britain are *business groups* such as the keiretsus of Japan and the chaebols of South Korea. This is particularly dominant in emerging economies. A business group is "a set of firms which, though legally independent, are bound together by a constellation of formal and informal ties and are accustomed to taking coordinated action."[79] Business groups are especially common in emerging economies, and they are different from other organizational forms in that the groups are communities of firms without clear boundaries. Business groups have many advantages that can enhance the value of a firm. For example, they often facilitate technology transfer or intergroup capital allocation that otherwise might be impossible because of inadequate institutional infrastructure such as excellent financial services firms. On the other hand, informal ties—such as cross-holdings, board interlocks, and coordinated actions—can often result in intragroup activities and transactions, often at very favorable terms to member firms. For example, expropriation can be legally done through *related transactions,* which can occur when controlling owners sell firm assets to another firm they own at below market prices or spin off the most profitable part of a public firm and merge it with another of their private firms. Strategy Spotlight 9.9 provides examples from Hong Kong of effective corporate governance as well as how a firm attempted a related transaction that would have benefited controlling shareholders at the expense of minority shareholders.

For firms to be successful, they must practice effective strategic control and corporate governance. Without such controls, the firm will not be able to achieve competitive advantages and outperform rivals in the marketplace.

**Summary**

We began the chapter with the key role of informational control. We contrasted two types of control systems: what we termed "traditional" and "contemporary" information control systems. Whereas traditional control systems may have their place in placid, simple competitive environments, there are fewer of those in today's economy. Instead, we advocated the contemporary approach wherein the internal and external environment are constantly monitored so that when surprises emerge, the firm can modify its strategies, goals, and objectives.

Behavioral controls are also a vital part of effective control systems. We argued that firms must develop the proper balance between culture, rewards and incentives, and boundaries and constraints. Where there are strong and positive cultures and rewards, employees tend to internalize the organization's strategies and objectives. This permits a firm to spend fewer resources on monitoring behavior, and assures the firm that the efforts and initiatives of employees are more consistent with the overall objectives of the organization.

In the final section of this chapter, we addressed corporate governance, which can be defined as the relationship between various participants in determining the direction and performance of the corporation. The primary participants include shareholders, management (led by the chief executive officer), and the board of directors. We reviewed studies that indicated a consistent relationship between effective corporate governance and financial performance. There are also several internal and external control mechanisms that can serve to align managerial interests and shareholder interests. The internal mechanisms include a committed and involved board of directors, shareholder activism, and effective managerial incentives and rewards. The external mechanisms include the market for corporate control, banks and analysts, regulators, the media, and public activists. We also addressed corporate governance from both a United States and an international perspective.

## Summary Review Questions

1. Why are effective strategic control systems so important in today's economy?

2. What are the main advantages of "contemporary" control systems over "traditional" control systems? What are the main differences between these two systems?

3. Why is it important to have a balance between the three elements of behavioral control—culture, rewards and incentives, and boundaries?

4. Discuss the relationship between types of organizations and their primary means of behavioral control.

5. Boundaries become less important as a firm develops a strong culture and reward system. Explain.

6. Why is it important to avoid a "one best way" mentality concerning control systems? What are the consequences of applying the same type of control system to all types of environments?

7. What is the role of effective corporate governance in improving a firm's performance? What are some of the key governance mechanisms that are used to ensure that managerial and shareholder interests are aligned?

8. Define principal–principal (PP) conflicts. What are the implications for corporate governance?

## Experiential Exercise

McDonald's Corporation, the world's largest fast-food restaurant chain, with revenues of $19 billion, has encountered declining shareholder value in the early 2000s. Using the Internet or library sources, evaluate the quality of the corporation in terms of management, the board of directors, and shareholder activism. Are the issues you list favorable or unfavorable for sound corporate governance?

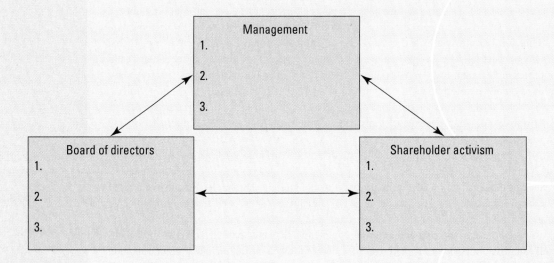

## Application Questions Exercises

1. The problems of many firms may be attributed to a "traditional" control system that failed to continuously monitor the environment and make necessary changes in their strategy and objectives. What companies are you familiar with that responded appropriately (or inappropriately) to environmental change?

2. How can a strong, positive culture enhance a firm's competitive advantage? How can a weak, negative culture erode competitive advantages? Explain and provide examples.

3. Use the Internet to research a firm that has an excellent culture and/or reward and incentive system. What are this firm's main financial and nonfinancial benefits?

4. Using the Internet, go to the Web site of a large, publicly held corporation in which you are interested. What evidence do you see of effective (or ineffective) corporate governance?

## Ethics Questions

1. Strong cultures can have powerful effects on employee behavior. How does this create inadvertent control mechanisms? That is, are strong cultures an ethical way to control behavior?

2. Rules and regulations can help reduce unethical behavior in organizations. To be effective, however, what other systems, mechanisms, and processes are necessary?

# References

1. Limperis, J. 2004. Frame of mind. *The Manufacturer.com,* October 31; Cavanaugh, M. 2001. When the wheels start turning. *Business First,* March 9: B3; Nulty, P. 1995. Incentive plans can be crippling. *Fortune,* November 13: 235; and Lancaster, P. R. 1994. Incentive pay isn't good for your company. *Inc.,* September: 23–24.

2. This chapter draws upon Picken, J. C., & Dess, G. G. 1997. *Mission critical.* Burr Ridge, IL: Irwin Professional Publishing.

3. Argyris, C. 1977. Double-loop learning in organizations. *Harvard Business Review,* 55: 115–125.

4. Simons, R. 1995. Control in an age of empowerment. *Harvard Business Review,* 73: 80–88. This chapter draws on this source in the discussion of informational control.

5. Goold, M., & Quinn, J. B. 1990. The paradox of strategic controls. *Strategic Management Journal,* 11: 43–57.

6. Quinn, J. B. 1980. *Strategies for change.* Homewood, IL: Richard D. Irwin.

7. Mintzberg, H. 1987. Crafting strategy. *Harvard Business Review,* 65: 66–75.

8. Weston, J. S. 1992. Soft stuff matters. *Financial Executive,* July–August: 52–53.

9. This discussion of control systems draws upon Simons, op. cit.

10. For an interesting perspective on this issue and how a downturn in the economy can reduce the tendency toward "free agency" by managers and professionals, refer to Morris, B. 2001. White collar blues. *Fortune,* July 23: 98–110.

11. Ouchi, W. 1981. *Theory Z.* Reading, MA: Addison-Wesley; Deal, T. E., & Kennedy, A. A. 1982. *Corporate cultures.* Reading, MA: Addison-Wesley; Peters, T. J., & Waterman, R. H. 1982. *In search of excellence.* New York: Random House; Collins, J. 2001. *Good to great.* New York: HarperCollins.

12. Collins, J. C., & Porras, J. I. 1994. *Built to last: Successful habits of visionary companies.* New York: HarperBusiness.

13. Lee, J., & Miller, D. 1999. People matter: Commitment to employees, strategy, and performance in Korean firms. *Strategic Management Journal,* 6: 579–594.

14. For an insightful discussion of IKEA's unique culture, see Kling, K., & Goteman, I. 2003. IKEA CEO Anders Dahlvig on international growth and IKEA's unique corporate culture and brand identity. *Academy of Management Executive,* 17(1): 31–37.

15. For a discussion of how professionals inculcate values, refer to Uhl-Bien, M., & Graen, G. B. 1998. Individual self-management: Analysis of professionals' self-managing activities in functional and cross-functional work teams. *Academy of Management Journal,* 41(3): 340–350.

16. A perspective on how antisocial behavior can erode a firm's culture can be found in Robinson, S. L., & O'Leary-Kelly, A. M. 1998. Monkey see, monkey do: The influence of work groups on the antisocial behavior of employees. *Academy of Management Journal,* 41(6): 658–672.

17. Mitchell, R. 1989. Masters of innovation. *BusinessWeek,* April 10: 58–63.

18. Sellers, P. 1993. Companies that serve you best. *Fortune,* May 31: 88.

19. Southwest Airlines Culture Committee. 1993. *Luv Lines* (company publication), March–April: 17–18; for an interesting perspective on the "downside" of strong "cultlike" organizational cultures, refer to Arnott, D. A. 2000. *Corporate cults.* New York: AMACOM.

20. Kerr, J., & Slocum, J. W., Jr. 1987. Managing corporate culture through reward systems. *Academy of Management Executive,* 1(2): 99–107.

21. For a unique perspective on leader challenges in managing wealthy professionals, refer to Wetlaufer, S. 2000. Who wants to manage a millionaire? *Harvard Business Review,* 78(4): 53–60.

22. These next two subsections draw upon Dess, G. G., & Picken, J. C. 1997. *Beyond Productivity.* New York: AMACOM.

23. For a discussion of the benefits of stock options as executive compensation, refer to Hall, B. J. 2000. What you need to know about stock options. *Harvard Business Review,* 78(2): 121–129.

24. Tully, S. 1993. Your paycheck gets exciting. *Fortune,* November 13: 89.

25. For a recent discussion linking pay to performance, refer to Rappaport, A. 1999. New thinking on how to link pay to performance. *Harvard Business Review,* 77(2): 91–105.

26. Zellner, W., Hof, R. D., Brandt, R., Baker, S., & Greising, D. 1995. Go-go goliaths. *BusinessWeek,* February 13: 64–70.

27. This section draws on Dess & Picken, op. cit.: chap. 5.

28. Simons, op. cit.

29. Davis, E. 1997. Interview: Norman Augustine. *Management Review,* November: 11.

30. This section draws upon Dess, G. G., & Miller, A. 1993. *Strategic management.* New York: McGraw-Hill.

31. For a good review of the goal-setting literature, refer to Locke, E. A., & Latham, G. P. 1990. *A theory of goal setting and task performance.* Englewood Cliffs, NJ: Prentice Hall.

32. For an interesting perspective on the use of rules and regulations that is counter to this industry's (software) norms, refer to Fryer, B. 2001. Tom Siebel of Siebel Systems: High tech the old fashioned way. *Harvard Business Review,* 79(3): 118–130.

33. Thompson, A. A., Jr., & Strickland, A. J., III. 1998. *Strategic management: Concepts and cases* (10th ed.): 313. New York: McGraw-Hill.

34. Ibid.

35. Teitelbaum, R. 1997. Tough guys finish first. *Fortune,* July 21: 82–84.

36. Weaver, G. R., Trevino, L. K., & Cochran, P. L. 1999. Corporate ethics programs as control systems: Influences of executive commitment and environmental factors. *Academy of Management Journal,* 42(1): 41–57.

37. Cadbury, S. A. 1987. Ethical managers make their own rules. *Harvard Business Review,* 65: 3, 69–73.

38. Weber, J. 2003. CFOs on the hot seat. *BusinessWeek,* March 17: 66–70.

39. William Ouchi has written extensively about the use of clan control (which is viewed as an alternate to bureaucratic or market control). Here, a powerful culture results in people aligning their individual interests with those of the firm. Refer to Ouchi, op. cit. This section also draws on Hall, R. H. 2002. *Organizations: Structures, processes, and outcomes* (8th ed.). Upper Saddle River, NJ: Prentice Hall.

40. Monks, R., & Minow, N. 2001. *Corporate governance* (2nd ed.). Malden, MA: Blackwell.

41. Pound, J. 1995. The promise of the governed corporation. *Harvard Business Review,* 73(2): 89–98.

42. Heinzl, M. 2004. Nortel's directors and investors discuss changes to the board. *Wall Street Journal,* September 30: B4; Editorial. 2003. Pulling Boeing out of a tailspin. *BusinessWeek,* December 15: 136; and Zimmerman, A., Ball, D., & Veen, M. 2003. A global journal report: Supermarket giant Ahoud ousts CEO in big accounting scandal. *Wall Street Journal,* February 25: A1; Ibid.

43. This discussion draws upon Monks & Minow, op. cit.

44. Eisenhardt, K. M. 1989. Agency theory: An assessment and review. *Academy of Management Review,* 14(1): 57–74. Some of the seminal contributions to agency theory include Jensen, M., & Meckling, W. 1976. Theory of the firm: Managerial behavior, agency costs, and ownership structure. *Journal of Financial Economics,* 3: 305–360; Fama, E., & Jensen, M. 1983. Separation of ownership and control. *Journal of Law and Economics,* 26: 301, 325; and Fama, E. 1980. Agency problems and the theory of the firm. *Journal of Political Economy,* 88: 288–307.

45. Managers may also engage in "shirking"—that is, reducing or withholding their efforts. See, for example, Kidwell, R. E., Jr., & Bennett, N. 1993. Employee propensity to withhold effort: A conceptual model to intersect three avenues of research. *Academy of Management Review,* 18(3): 429–456.

46. For an interesting perspective on agency and clarification of many related concepts and terms, visit the following Web site: www.encycogov.com.

47. Argawal, A., & Mandelker, G. 1987. Managerial incentives and corporate investment and financing decisions. *Journal of Finance,* 42: 823–837.

48. For an insightful, recent discussion of the academic research on corporate governance, and in particular the role of boards of directors, refer to Chatterjee, S., & Harrison, J. S. 2001. Corporate governance. In Hitt, M. A., Freeman, R. E., & Harrison, J. S. (Eds.). *Handbook of strategic management:* 543–563. Malden, MA: Blackwell.

49. This opening discussion draws on Monks & Minow, op. cit. 164, 169; see also Pound, op. cit.

50. Business Roundtable. 1990. *Corporate governance and American competitiveness,* March: 7.

51. Byrne, J. A., Grover, R., & Melcher, R. A. 1997. The best and worst boards. *BusinessWeek,* November 26: 35–47. The three key roles of boards of directors are monitoring the actions of executives, providing advice, and providing links to the external environment to provide resources. See Johnson, J. L., Daily, C. M., & Ellstrand, A. E. 1996. Boards of directors: A review and research agenda. *Academy of Management Review,* 37: 409–438.

52. McGeehan, P. 2003. More chief executives shown the door, study says. *New York Times,* May 12: C2.

53. There are benefits, of course, to having some insiders on the board of directors. Inside directors would be more aware of the firm's strategies. Additionally, outsiders may rely too often on financial performance indicators because of information asymmetries. For an interesting discussion, see Baysinger, B. D., & Hoskisson, R. E. 1990. The composition of boards of directors and strategic control: Effects on corporate strategy. *Academy of Management Review,* 15: 72–87.

54. Hambrick, D. C., & Jackson, E. M. 2000. Outside directors with a stake: The linchpin in improving governance. *California Management Review,* 42(4): 108–127.

55. Ibid.

56. Disney has begun to make many changes to improve its corporate governance, such as assigning only independent directors to important board committees, restricting directors from serving on more than three boards, and appointing a lead director who can convene the board without approval by the CEO. In recent years, the Disney Co. has shown up on some "best" board lists. In addition Eisner has recently relinquished the chairman position.

57. Talk show. 2002. *BusinessWeek,* September 30: 14.

58. Ward, R. D. 2000. *Improving corporate boards.* New York: Wiley.

59. Monks and Minow, op. cit.: 93.

60. A discussion of the factors that lead to shareholder activism is found in Ryan, L. V., & Schneider, M. 2002. The antecedents of institutional investor activism. *Academy of Management Review,* 27(4): 554–573.

61. There is strong research support for the idea that the presence of large block shareholders is associated with value-maximizing decisions. For example, refer to Johnson, R. A., Hoskisson, R. E., & Hitt, M. A. 1993. Board of director involvement in restructuring: The effects of board versus managerial controls and characteristics. *Strategic Management Journal,* 14:33–50.

62. For an interesting perspective on the impact of institutional ownership on a firm's innovation strategies, see Hoskisson, R. E., Hitt, M. A., Johnson, R. A., & Grossman, W. 2002. *Academy of Management Journal,* 45(4): 697–716.

63. www.calpers.ca/gov/index.

64. Jensen, M. C., & Murphy, K. J. 1990. CEO incentives—It's not how much you pay, but how. *Harvard Business Review,* 68(3): 138–149.

65. For a perspective on the relative advantages and disadvantages of "duality"—that is, one individual serving as both Chief Executive Office and Chairman of the Board, see Lorsch, J. W., & Zelleke, A. 2005. Should the CEO be the chairman. *MIT Sloan Management Review,* 46(2): 71–74.

66. Research has found that executive compensation is more closely aligned with firm performance in companies with compensation committees and boards dominated by outside directors. See, for example, Conyon, M. J., & Peck, S. I. 1998. Board control, remuneration committees, and top management compensation. *Academy of Management Journal,* 41: 146–157.

67. Lavelle, L., Jespersen, F. F., & Arndt, M. 2002. Executive pay. *BusinessWeek,* April 15: 66–72.

68. Ibid.

69. www.tiaa-cref.org/pubs.

70. Such opportunistic behavior is common in all principal-agent relationships. For a description of agency problems, especially in the context of the relationship between shareholders and managers, see Jensen, M. C., & Meckling, W. H. 1976. Theory of the firm: Managerial behavior, agency costs, and ownership structure. *Journal of Financial Economics,* 3: 305–360.

71. Hoskisson, R. E., & Turk, T. A. 1990. Corporate restructuring: Governance and control limits of the internal market. *Academy of Management Review,* 15: 459–477.

72. For an insightful perspective on the market for corporate control and how it is influenced by knowledge intensity, see Coff, R. 2003. Bidding wars over R&D-intensive firms: Knowledge, opportunism, and the market for corporate control. *Academy of Management Journal,* 46(1): 74–85.

73. Walsh, J. P., & Kosnik, R. D. 1993. Corporate raiders and their disciplinary role in the market for corporate control. *Academy of Management Journal,* 36: 671–700.

74. Gunning for KPMG. 2003. *Economist,* February 1: 63.

75. Timmons, H. 2003. Investment banks: Who will foot their bill? *BusinessWeek,* March 3: 116.

76. Wishy-washy: The SEC pulls its punches on corporate-governance rules. 2003. *Economist,* February 1: 60.

77. McLean, B. 2001. Is Enron overpriced? *Fortune,* March 5: 122–125.

78. This section draws upon Young, M. N., Peng, M. W., Ahlstrom, D., Bruton, G. D., Jiang, Y. 2005. Principal-principal conflicts in corporate governance (unpublished manuscript); and, Peng, M. W. 2006. *Global strategy.* Cincinnati: Thomson South-Western. We are very appreciative of the helpful comments of Mike Young of the Chinese University of Hong Kong and Mike Peng of the Ohio State University.

79. Khanna, T., & Rivkin, J. 2001. Estimating the performance effects of business groups in emerging markets. *Strategic Management Journal,* 22: 45–74.

# 10

# Creating Effective Organizational Designs

## >chapter objectives

*After reading this chapter, you should have a good understanding of:*

- The importance of organizational structure and the concept of the "boundaryless" organization in implementing strategies.

- The growth patterns of major corporations and the relationship between a firm's strategy and its structure.

- Each of the traditional types of organizational structure: simple, functional, divisional, and matrix.

- The relative advantages and disadvantages of traditional organizational structures.

- The implications of a firm's international operations for organizational structure.

- Why there is no "one best way" to design strategic reward and evaluation systems, and the important contingent roles of business- and corporate-level strategies.

- The different types of boundaryless organizations—barrier-free, modular, and virtual—and their relative advantages and disadvantages.

- The need for creating ambidextrous organizational designs that enable firms to explore new opportunities and effectively integrate existing operations.

*t*o implement strategies successfully, firms must have appropriate organizational structures. These include the processes and integrating mechanisms necessary to ensure that boundaries among internal activities and external parties, such as suppliers, customers, and alliance partners, are flexible and permeable. A firm's performance will suffer if its managers don't carefully consider both of these organizational design attributes.

In the first section, we begin by discussing the growth patterns of large corporations to address the important relationships between the strategy that a firm follows and its corresponding structure. For example, as firms diversify into related product-market areas, they change their structure from functional to divisional. We then address the different types of traditional structures—simple, functional, divisional, and matrix—and their relative advantages and disadvantages. We close with a discussion of the implications of a firm's international operations for the structure of its organization. The primary factors that are taken into account are (1) the type of international strategy (e.g., global or multidomestic), (2) the level of product diversity, and (3) the extent to which a firm depends on foreign sales.

The second section takes the perspective that there is no "one best way" to design an organization's strategic reward and evaluation system. Here we address two important contingencies: business- and corporate-level strategy. For example, when strategies require a great deal of collaboration, as well as resource and information sharing, there must be incentives and cultures that encourage and reward such initiatives.

The third section discusses the concept of the "boundaryless" organization. We do *not* argue that organizations should have no internal and external boundaries. Instead, we suggest that in rapidly changing and unpredictable environments, organizations must strive to make their internal and external boundaries both flexible and permeable. We suggest three different types of boundaryless organizations: barrier-free, modular, and virtual. Whereas the barrier-free type focuses on creating flexible and permeable internal and external boundaries, the modular type addresses the strategic role of outsourcing, and the virtual type centers on the viability of strategic alliances and network organizations in today's global economy.

The fourth section focuses on the need for managers to recognize that they typically face two opposing challenges: (1) being proactive in taking advantage of new opportunities and (2) ensuring the effective coordination and integration of existing operations. This suggests the need for ambidextrous organizations, that is, firms that can both be efficient in how they manage existing assets and competencies and take advantage of opportunities in rapidly changing and unpredictable environments—conditions that are becoming more pronounced in today's global markets.

The National Health Service (NHS) was created in July 1948 to provide health care for all British citizens, based on need, not on the ability to pay.[1] The NHS, whose 2005 budget was 63 billion British pounds (about $110 billion), was originally split into three parts:

- Hospital services
- Family doctors, dentists, opticians, and pharmacists
- Local authority health services, including community nursing

As you would imagine, since 1948, there have been huge increases in the overall budget as well as major changes to both the organizational structure and the way that patient services are provided. And, in 2001, the NHS Modernization Agency was established to bring together individuals and teams from the NHS with reputations for modernizing services and developing leadership within the NHS. A few of the eight teams that make up the agency are the Leadership Center, the Redesign, and the New Ways of Working Team. However, as we note below, even with the Modernization Agency, the NHS does not seem to be a paragon of efficiency.

> One of the examples of waste was played out in a hospital where catering staff provided dozens of meals a day for nonexistent patients in wards that had been closed to save money. Management confirmed that this occurred and that it went on for days. The explanation was that there had been a breakdown in communications between staff. One of the NHS hospitals explained that the extra meals were cooked because of a failure to notify the catering staff of the unit closures. "We advise our wards to give as much notice to the catering departments as possible," a spokeswoman said. "As is often the case, it's a matter of improving communication and reminding staff of procedures and letting other people know what's happening." However, the hospital was also wasting money by routinely sending patient referral letters for surgeries to doctors by first-class mail, even though an internal delivery system had been set up specifically to deal with such correspondence.
>
> The details of such waste had been disclosed by David James, a doctor who is leading the Conservative Party's investigation of public sector waste. He contends that it may be typical of "a whole culture of management which is deficient" and which, across the entire NHS, will see millions of pounds of taxpayers' money, in effect, thrown away.
>
> In 2001, an investigation revealed that the NHS was wasting more than 18 million British pounds (about $30 million) every year in its catering operations. The study attributed the waste to bad practice and poor standards. The whistle-blower who contacted Dr. James felt that little had been done to correct things since that inquiry was conducted.
>
> The meals were repeatedly delivered when it was clear they were not being eaten. Perhaps, this is evidence of staff having learned to follow procedures rather than to think for themselves. Or could it be an indication of a culture of sticking to the job description and not worrying about costs that may be incurred in the process?

One of the central concepts in this chapter is the importance of boundaryless organizations. That is, successful organizations create permeable boundaries among the internal activities as well as between the organization and its external customers, suppliers, and alliance partners. We introduced this idea in Chapter 3 in our discussion of the value-chain concept, which consisted of several primary (e.g., inbound logistics, marketing and sales) and support activities (e.g., procurement, human resource management). Clearly, the underlying cause of NHS's problem was its inability to establish close and effective working relationships between its internal departments.

The most important implication of this chapter is that today's managers are faced with two ongoing and vital activities in structuring and designing their organizations. First, they must decide on the most appropriate type of organizational structure. Second, they need to assess what mechanisms, processes, and techniques are most helpful in enhancing the permeability of the internal and external boundaries of their organization.

# >>Traditional Forms of Organizational Structure

Organizational structure refers to the formalized patterns of interactions that link the tasks, technologies, and people of a firm.[2] Structures are designed to ensure that resources are used most effectively toward accomplishing an organization's mission. Structure provides managers with a means of balancing two conflicting forces: a need for the division of tasks into meaningful groupings and the need to integrate such groupings in order to ensure organizational efficiency and effectiveness. Structure identifies the executive, managerial, and administrative organization of a firm and indicates responsibilities and hierarchical relationships. It also influences the flow of information as well as the context and nature of human interactions.

Most organizations begin very small and either die or remain small. Those few that survive and prosper embark on strategies designed to increase the overall scope of operations and enable them to enter new product-market domains. Such growth places additional pressure on executives to control and coordinate the firm's increasing size and diversity. The most appropriate type of structure depends on the nature and magnitude of growth in a firm. In this section, we address various types of structural forms, their advantages and disadvantages, and their relationships to the strategies that organizations undertake.

## Patterns of Growth of Large Corporations

A firm's strategy and structure change as it increases in size, diversifies into new product markets, and expands its geographic scope.[3] Exhibit 10.1 illustrates some of the common growth patterns that firms may follow.

A new firm with a *simple structure* typically increases its sales revenue and volume of outputs over time. It may also engage in some vertical integration to secure sources of supply (backward integration) as well as channels of distribution (forward integration). After a time, the simple-structure firm implements a *functional structure* to concentrate efforts on both increasing efficiency and enhancing its operations and products. This structure enables the firm to group its operations into either functions, departments, or geographic areas. As its initial markets mature, a firm looks beyond its present products and markets for possible expansion. Such a strategy of related diversification requires a need to reorganize around product lines or geographic markets. This leads to a *divisional structure.* As the business expands in terms of sales revenues, and domestic growth opportunities become somewhat limited, a firm may seek opportunities in international markets. At this time, a firm has a wide variety of structures to choose from. These include *international division, geographic area, worldwide product division, worldwide functional,* and *worldwide matrix.* As we will see later in this section, deciding upon the most appropriate structure when a firm has international operations depends on three primary factors: the extent of international expansion, type of strategy (global, multidomestic, or transnational), and the degree of product diversity.[4]

There are some other common growth patterns. For example, some firms may find it advantageous to diversify into several product lines rather than focus their efforts on strengthening distributor and supplier relationships through vertical integration. Thus, they would organize themselves according to product lines by implementing a divisional structure. Also, some firms may choose to move into unrelated product areas, typically by acquiring existing businesses. Frequently, their rationale is that acquiring assets and competencies is more economical or expedient than developing them internally. Such an unrelated, or conglomerate, strategy requires relatively little integration across businesses

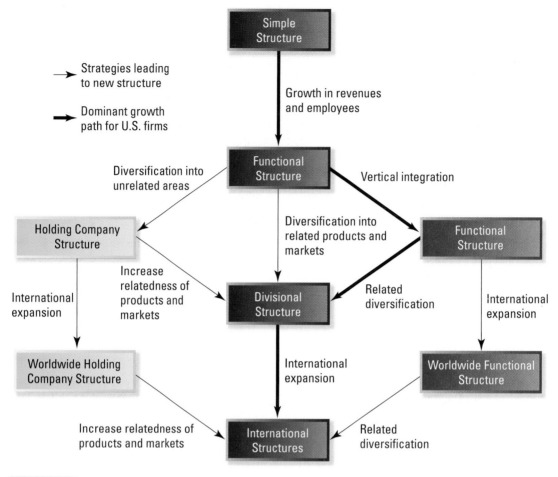

**Exhibit 10.1    Dominant Growth Patterns of Large Corporations**

Source: From *Strategy Implementation: The Role of Structure and Process,* 2nd edition by J. R. Galbraith and R. K. Kazanjian. Copyright © 1986. Reprinted with permission of South-Western, a division of Thomson Learning: www.thomsonrights.com. Fax: 800-730-2215.

and sharing of resources. Thus, a *holding company structure* becomes appropriate. As we would expect, there are many other growth patterns, but these are the most common.*

Now we will discuss some of the most common types of organizational structures—simple, functional, divisional (including two variants: *strategic business unit* and *holding company*), and matrix and their advantages and disadvantages. We will close the section with a discussion of the structural implications when a firm expands its operations into international markets.

---

* The lowering of transaction costs and globalization have led to some changes in the common historical patterns that we have discussed. Some firms are, in effect, bypassing the vertical integration stage. Instead, they focus on core competencies and outsource other value-creation activities. Also, even relatively young firms are going global early in their history because of lower communication and transportation costs. For an interesting perspective on global start-ups, see McDougall, P. P., & Oviatt, B. M. 1996. New venture internationalization, strategic change and performance: A follow-up study. *Journal of Business Venturing,* 11: 23–40; and McDougall, P. P., & Oviatt, B. M. (Eds.). 2000. The special research forum on international entrepreneurship. *Academy of Management Journal,* October: 902–1003.

## Simple Structure

As we might expect, the simple structure is the oldest, and most common, organizational form. After all, most organizations are very small and have a single or very narrow product line in which the owner-manager (or top executive) makes almost all of the decisions. In effect, the owner-manager controls all activities, and the staff serves as an extension of the top executive's personality.

The simple structure is highly informal and the coordination of tasks is accomplished by direct supervision. Decision making is highly centralized, there is little specialization of tasks, few rules and regulations, and an informal evaluation and reward system. Although the owner-manager is intimately involved in almost all phases of the business, a manager is often employed to oversee day-to-day operations.

A small firm with a simple structure may often foster creativity and individualism since there are generally few rules and regulations. However, such "informality" may lead to problems. Employees may not clearly understand their responsibilities, which can lead to conflict and confusion. Employees also may take advantage of the lack of regulations and act in their own self-interest. Such actions can erode motivation and satisfaction as well as lead to the possible misuse of organizational resources. Further, small organizations have flat structures (i.e., few vertical, hierarchical levels) that limit opportunities for upward mobility. Without the potential for future advancement, recruiting and retaining talent may become very difficult.

## Functional Structure

When an organization is small (15 employees or less), it is not necessary to have a variety of formal arrangements and groupings of activities. However, as firms grow, excessive demands may be placed on the owner-manager in order to obtain and process all of the information necessary to run the business. Chances are the owner will not be skilled in all specialties (e.g., accounting, engineering, production, marketing) at a level necessary to run a growing business. Thus, he or she will need to hire specialists in the various functional areas. Such growth in the overall scope and complexity of the business necessitates a functional structure wherein the major functions of the firm are grouped internally and led by a specialist. The coordination and integration of the functional areas becomes one of the most important responsibilities of the chief executive of the firm. Exhibit 10.2 presents a diagram of a functional structure.

Functional structures are generally found in organizations in which there is a single or closely related product or service, high production volume, and some vertical integration. Initially, firms tend to expand the overall scope of their operations by penetrating existing markets, introducing similar products in additional markets, or increasing

**Exhibit 10.2**   **Functional Organizational Structure**

# STRATEGY SPOTLIGHT

## 10.1

### Two Examples of Successful Functional Organization Structures

Sharp Corporation is a top performer in the consumer electronics industry, with $21 billion in annual sales. The firm is organized into functional units, allowing coordination of tasks involving research and development, production, marketing, and management. Key components such as LCDs (liquid crystal displays) are developed and produced in single functional units using the talents of these specialties. By using a centralized, functional structure, Sharp is able to achieve economies of scale with its applied research and manufacturing skills. It would be much more expensive if such skills and resources were distributed over many different, relatively autonomous business units. To make sure that these units are not completely sealed off from the other business units in the firm, product managers have the responsibility of coordinating similar products in multiple functional areas throughout the organization.

Sources: Stewart, C. 2003. The perfect yarn. *The Manufacturer.com,* July 31; www.parkdalemills.com; Berman, P. 1987. The fast track isn't always the best track. *Forbes,* November 2: 60–64; personal communication with Duke Kimbrell, March 11, 2005; and Collins, D. J., & Montgomery, C. A. 1998. Creating corporate advantage. *Harvard Business Review,* 76(3): 70–83.

For more than 80 years, Parkdale Mills, with approximately $1 billion in revenues, has been the industry leader in the production of cotton and cotton blend yarns. Their expertise comes by concentrating on a single product line, perfecting processes, and welcoming innovation. According to CEO Andy Warlick, "I think we've probably spent more than any two competitors combined on new equipment and robotics. We do this because we have to compete in a global market where a lot of the competition has a lower wage structure and gets subsidies that we don't receive, so we really have to focus on consistency and cost control." Yarn making is generally considered to be a commodity business, and Parkdale is the industry's low-cost producer.

Tasks are highly standardized and authority is centralized with Duke Kimbrell, founder and chairman, and CEO Andy Warlick. The firm operates a bare-bones staff with a small staff of top executives. Kimbrell and Warlick are considered shrewd about the cotton market, technology, customer loyalty, and incentive pay.

the level of vertical integration. Such expansion activities clearly increase the scope and complexity of the operations. Fortunately, the functional structure provides for a high level of centralization that helps to ensure integration and control over the related product-market activities or multiple primary activities (from inbound logistics to operations to marketing, sales, and service) in the value chain (addressed in Chapters 3 and 4).

Strategy Spotlight 10.1 provides two examples of effective functional organization structures—Sharp Corporation and Parkdale Mills.

As with any type of organizational structure, there are some relative advantages and disadvantages associated with the functional structure. By bringing together specialists into functional departments, a firm is able to enhance its coordination and control within each of the functional areas. The structure also ensures that decision making in the firm will be centralized at the top of the organization. This enhances the organizational-level (as opposed to functional area) perspective across the various functions in the organization. In addition, the functional structure provides for a more efficient use of managerial and technical talent since functional area expertise is pooled in a single department (e.g., marketing) instead of being spread across a variety of product-market areas. Finally, career paths and professional development in specialized areas are facilitated.

There also are some significant disadvantages associated with the functional structure. First, the differences in values and orientations among functional areas may impede communication and coordination. Edgar Schein of MIT has argued that shared assumptions, often based on similar backgrounds and experiences of members, form around functional units in an organization. This leads to what are often called "stove pipes" or "silos," in which departments view themselves as isolated, self-contained units with little need for interaction and coordination with other departments. This erodes communication because functional groups may have not only different goals but also differing meanings of words and concepts. According to Schein:

> The word "marketing" will mean product development to the engineer, studying customers through market research to the product manager, merchandising to the salesperson, and constant change in design to the manufacturing manager. When they try to work together, they will often attribute disagreements to personalities and fail to notice the deeper, shared assumptions that color how each function thinks.[5]

Such narrow functional orientations also may lead to short-term thinking based largely upon what is best for the functional area, not the organization as a whole. For example, in a manufacturing firm, sales may want to offer a wide range of customized products to appeal to the firm's customers; research and development may overdesign products and components to achieve technical elegance; and manufacturing may favor no-frills products that can be produced at low cost by means of long production runs. In addition, functional structures may overburden the top executives in the firm because conflicts have a tendency to be "pushed up" to the top of the organization since there are no managers who are responsible for the specific product lines. Finally, functional structures make it difficult to establish uniform performance standards across the whole organization. Whereas it may be relatively easy to evaluate production managers on the basis of production volume and cost control, establishing performance measures for engineering, research and development, and accounting become more problematic.

## Divisional Structure

The divisional structure (sometimes called the multidivisional structure or M-Form) is organized around products, projects, or markets. Each of the divisions, in turn, includes its own functional specialists who are typically organized into departments. A divisional structure encompasses a set of relatively autonomous units governed by a central corporate office. The operating divisions are relatively independent and consist of products and services that are different from those of the other divisions. Operational decision making in a large business places excessive demands on the firm's top management. In order to attend to broader, longer-term organizational issues, top-level managers must delegate decision making to lower-level managers. Thus, divisional executives play a key role. In conjunction with corporate-level executives, they help to determine the product-market and financial objectives for the division as well as their division's contribution to overall corporate performance.[6] The rewards are based largely on measures of financial performance such as net income and revenue. Exhibit 10.3 illustrates a divisional structure.

General Motors was among the earliest firms to adopt the divisional organizational structure.[7] In the 1920s the company formed five major product divisions (Cadillac, Buick, Oldsmobile, Pontiac, and Chevrolet) as well as several industrial divisions. Since then, many firms have discovered that as they diversified into new product-market activities, functional structures—with their emphasis on single functional departments—were unable to manage the increased complexity of the entire business.

There are many advantages associated with the divisional structure. By creating separate divisions to manage individual product markets, there is a separation of strategic and operating control. That is, divisional managers can focus their efforts on improving operations in the product markets for which they are responsible, and corporate officers can devote their time to overall strategic issues for the entire corporation. The focus on a division's products and markets—by the divisional executives—provides the corporation with an enhanced ability to respond quickly to important changes in the external

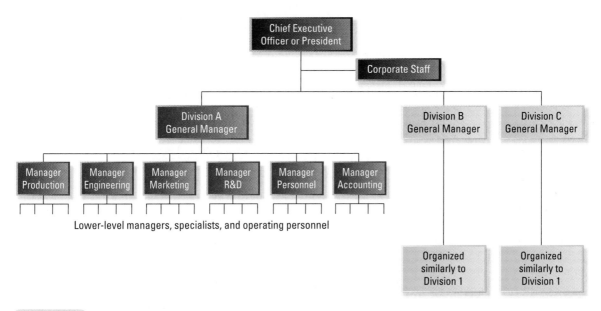

**Lower-level managers, specialists, and operating personnel**

**Exhibit 10.3    Divisional Organizational Structure**

environment. Since there are functional departments within each division of the corporation, the problems associated with sharing resources across functional departments are minimized. Finally, because there are multiple levels of general managers (that is, executives responsible for integrating and coordinating all functional areas), the development of general management talent is enhanced. Strategy Spotlight 10.2 discusses the rationale behind Brinker Corporation's change in structure from functional to divisional.

As you would expect, a divisional structure also has potential disadvantages. First, it can be very expensive; that is, there can be increased costs due to the duplication of personnel, operations, and investment since each division must staff multiple functional departments. There also can be dysfunctional competition among divisions since each division tends to become concerned solely about its own operations. Furthermore, divisional managers are often evaluated on common measures such as return on assets and sales growth. Thus, if goals are conflicting, there can be a sense of a "zero-sum" game that would discourage sharing ideas and resources among the divisions for the common good of the corporation. As noted by Ghoshal and Bartlett, two leading scholars in strategic management:

> As their label clearly warns, divisions divide. The divisional model fragmented companies' resources; it created vertical communication channels that insulated business units and prevented them from sharing their strengths with one another. Consequently, the whole of the corporation was often less than the sum of its parts.[8]

Another potential disadvantage is that with many divisions providing different products and services, there is the chance that differences in image and quality may occur across divisions. For example, one division may offer no-frills products of lower quality that may erode the brand reputation of another division that has top quality, highly differentiated offerings. Finally, since each division is evaluated in terms of financial measures such as return on investment and revenue growth, there is often an urge to focus on short-term performance. For example, if corporate management uses quarterly profits as

## Brinker International's Change in Organizational Structure

Although Brinker International had a traditional functional structure, changes in its competitive outlook forced management to take a closer look at the organizational design of the firm. The firm controls a variety of restaurant chains and bakeries, including Wildfire, Big Bowl, and Chili's.

With all these interests under one corporate roof, management of these disparate entities became difficult. The fragmented $330 billion restaurant and bakery industry caters to highly focused market niches. The original functional design of the Brinker chain had some disadvan-

tages as the company grew. With areas separated by function, it became hard to focus efforts on a single restaurant chain. The diverse markets served by the bakeries and restaurants began to lose their focus.

As a result, Brinker International changed to a divisional structure. This allowed the company to consolidate individuals who worked with a single restaurant or bakery chain into a separate division. Brinker referred to these as concept teams, with each concept team responsible for the operation of a single line of business. This focused effort streamlined the company's ability to concentrate on the market niche served by each of its restaurants and bakeries.

Source: CEO interview: Ronald A. McDougall, Brinker International. 1999. *Wall Street Transcript*, January 20: 1–4.

the key performance indicator, divisional management may tend to put significant emphasis on "making the numbers" and minimizing activities, such as advertising, maintenance, and capital investments, which would detract from short-term performance measures.

Before moving on, we'll discuss two variations of the divisional form of organizational structure: the strategic business unit (SBU) and holding company structures.

***Strategic Business Unit (SBU) Structure***    Corporations that are highly diversified such as ConAgra, a $15 billion food producer, may consist of dozens of different divisions.[9] If ConAgra were to use a purely divisional structure, it would be nearly impossible for the corporate office to plan and coordinate activities because the span of control would be too large. Instead, to attain synergies, ConAgra has put its diverse businesses into three primary SBUs: food service (restaurants), retail (grocery stores), and agricultural products.

With an SBU structure, divisions with similar products, markets, and/or technologies are grouped into homogenous groups in order to achieve some synergies. These include those discussed in Chapter 6 for related diversification, such as leveraging core competencies, sharing infrastructures, and market power. Generally speaking, the more related businesses are within a corporation, the fewer SBUs will be required. Each of the SBUs in the corporation operates as a profit center.

The major advantage of the SBU structure is that it makes the task of planning and control by the corporate office more manageable. Also, since the structure provides greater decentralization of authority, individual businesses can react more quickly to important changes in the environment than if all divisions had to report directly to the corporate office.

There are also some disadvantages to the SBU structure. Since the divisions are grouped into SBUs, it may become difficult to achieve synergies across SBUs. That is, if divisions that are included in different SBUs have potential sources of synergy, it may become difficult for them to be realized. The additional level of management increases the number of personnel and overhead expenses, while the additional hierarchical level removes the corporate office further from the individual divisions. Thus, the corporate office may become unaware of key developments that could have a major impact on the corporation.

*Holding Company Structure*    The holding company structure (sometimes referred to as a *conglomerate*) is also a variation of the divisional structure. Whereas the SBU structure is often used when similarities exist between the individual businesses (or divisions), the holding company structure is appropriate when the businesses in a corporation's portfolio do not have much in common. Thus, the potential for synergies is limited.

Holding company structures are most appropriate for firms that follow a strategy of unrelated diversification. Companies such as Hanson Trust, ITT, and the CP group of Thailand have relied on the holding company structure to implement their unrelated diversification strategies. Since there are few similarities across the businesses, the corporate offices in these companies provide a great deal of autonomy to operating divisions and rely on financial controls and incentive programs to obtain high levels of performance from the individual businesses. As you would expect, corporate staffs at these firms tend to be small because their involvement in the overall operation of their various businesses is limited.[10]

An important advantage of the holding company structure is the cost savings associated with fewer personnel and the lower overhead resulting from a small corporate office and fewer levels in the corporate hierarchy. In addition, the autonomy of the holding company structure increases the motivational level of divisional executives and enables them to respond quickly to market opportunities and threats.

The primary disadvantage of the holding company structure is the inherent lack of control and dependence that corporate-level executives have on divisional executives. Major problems could arise if key divisional executives leave the firm, because the corporate office has very little "bench strength"—that is, additional managerial talent ready to fill key positions on short notice. And, if problems arise in a division, it may become very difficult to turn around individual businesses because of limited staff support in the corporate office.

## Matrix Structure

At times, managers may find that none of the structures that we have described above fully meet their needs. One approach that tries to overcome the inadequacies inherent in the other structures is the matrix structure. It is, in effect, a combination of the functional and divisional structures. Most commonly, functional departments are combined with product groups on a project basis. For example, a product group may want to develop a new addition to its line; for this project, it obtains personnel from functional departments such as marketing, production, and engineering. These personnel work under the manager of the product group for the duration of the project, which can vary from a few weeks to an open-ended period of time. The individuals who work in a matrix organization become responsible to two managers: the project manager and the manager of their functional area. Exhibit 10.4 illustrates a matrix structure.

In addition to the product-function matrix, other bases may be related in a matrix. Some large multinational corporations rely on a matrix structure to combine product groups and geographical units. Product managers have global responsibility for the development, manufacturing, and distribution of their own line, while managers of geographical regions have responsibility for the profitability of the businesses in their regions. In the mid-1990s, Caterpillar, Inc., implemented this type of structure.

Michael Eisner, CEO of Disney, relies on the matrix concept—with its dual-reporting responsibility—to enhance synergy. Consider the perspective that he shared in an interview.[11]

> We're also trying to increase the amount of synergy in our global operations country by country. We've just reorganized our international organization into a hybrid type of structure, so the person running movies in Italy, for instance, not only reports to an executive in the movie

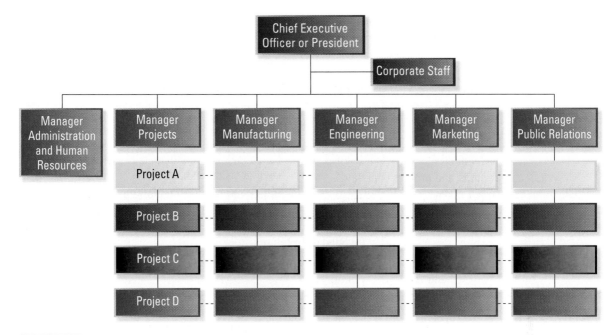

**Exhibit 10.4**  **Matrix Organizational Structure**

division, as he or she did before, but also reports to a country head. That country head is responsible for synergy. Hopefully, this will duplicate what we do in Burbank [Disney's head-quarters] every week.

A primary advantage of the matrix structure is that it facilitates the use of special-ized personnel, equipment, and facilities. Rather than duplicating functions, as would be the case in a divisional structure based on products, the resources are shared as needed. Individuals with high expertise can divide their time among multiple projects at one time. Such resource sharing and collaboration enable a firm to use resources more efficiently and to respond more quickly and effectively to changes in the competitive environment. In addition, the flexibility inherent in a matrix structure provides professionals with a broader range of responsibility. Such experience enables them to develop their skills and competencies.

There are also many potential disadvantages associated with matrix structures. The dual-reporting structures can result in uncertainty and lead to intense power struggles and conflict over the allocation of professional personnel and other resources. Addition-ally, working relationships become more complicated. This may result in excessive reliance on group processes and teamwork, along with a diffusion of responsibility, which in turn may erode timely decision making. Exhibit 10.5 briefly summarizes the advantages and disadvantages of the functional, divisional, and matrix organizational structures.

## International Operations: Implications for Organizational Structure

Today's managers must maintain an international outlook on their firm's businesses and competitive strategies. To be successful in the global marketplace, managers must ensure consistency between their strategies (at the business, corporate, and international levels)

## Functional Structure

| Advantages | Disadvantages |
|---|---|
| • Pooling of specialists enhances coordination and control. | • Differences in functional area orientation impede communication and coordination. |
| • Centralized decision making enhances an organizational perspective across functions. | • Tendency for specialists to develop short-term perspective and narrow functional orientation. |
| • Efficient use of managerial and technical talent. | • Functional area conflicts may overburden top-level decision makers. |
| • Facilitates career paths and professional development in specialized areas. | • Difficult to establish uniform performance standards. |

## Divisional Structure

| Advantages | Disadvantages |
|---|---|
| • Increases strategic and operational control, permitting corporate-level executives to address strategic issues. | • Increased costs incurred through duplication of personnel, operations, and investment. |
| • Quick response to environmental changes. | • Dysfunctional competition among divisions may detract from overall corporate performance. |
| • Increases focus on products and markets. | • Difficult to maintain uniform corporate image. |
| • Minimizes problems associated with sharing resources across functional areas. | • Overemphasis on short-term performance. |
| • Facilitates development of general managers. | |

## Matrix Structure

| Advantages | Disadvantages |
|---|---|
| • Increases market responsiveness through collaboration and synergies among professional colleagues. | • Dual-reporting relationships can result in uncertainty regarding accountability. |
| • Allows more efficient utilization of resources. | • Intense power struggles may lead to increased levels of conflict. |
| • Improves flexibility, coordination, and communication. | • Working relationships may be more complicated and human resources duplicated. |
| • Increases professional development through a broader range of responsibility. | • Excessive reliance on group processes and teamwork may impede timely decision making. |

**Exhibit 10.5**

**Functional, Divisional, and Matrix Organizational Structures: Advantages and Disadvantages**

and the structure of their organization. As firms expand into foreign markets, they generally follow a pattern of change in structure that parallels the changes in their strategies. Three major contingencies that seem to influence the structure adopted by firms with international operations are (1) the type of strategy that is driving a firm's foreign operations, (2) product diversity, and (3) the extent to which a firm is dependent on foreign sales.[12]

As international operations become an important part of a firm's overall operations, managers must make changes that are consistent with their firm's structure. The primary types of structures used to manage a firm's international operations are:[13]

- International division
- Geographic-area division
- Worldwide functional
- Worldwide product division
- Worldwide matrix

As we discussed in Chapter 7, multidomestic strategies are driven by political and cultural imperatives that require managers within each country to respond to local conditions. The structures that would be consistent with such a strategic orientation are the *international division* and *geographic-area division* structures. Here local managers are provided with a high level of autonomy to manage their operations within the constraints and demands of their geographic market. As a firm's foreign sales increase as a percentage of its total sales, it will likely change from an international division structure to a geographic-area division structure. And, as a firm's product and/or market diversity becomes large, it is more likely to benefit from a *worldwide matrix structure.*

Global strategies, on the other hand, are driven by economic pressures that require managers to view operations in different geographic areas as only a component of an overall operation that must be managed for overall efficiency. The structures consistent with the efficiency perspective are the *worldwide functional* and *worldwide product division* structures. Here, division managers view the marketplace as homogeneous and devote relatively little attention to local market, political, and economic factors. The choice between these two types of structures is guided largely by the extent of product diversity. Firms with relatively low levels of product diversity may opt for a worldwide product division structure. However, when a firm has significant product-market diversity resulting from a series of highly unrelated international acquisitions, a worldwide holding company structure is likely to be implemented. Such firms are characterized by very little commonality among products, markets, or technologies, and have little need for integration.

## Global Start-Ups: A New Phenomenon

Our discussion of dominant patterns of growth earlier in the section suggested that international expansion occurs rather late in the history of most corporations, typically after possibilities of domestic growth are exhausted. Increasingly, we are seeing two interrelated phenomena. First, many firms now decide to expand internationally relatively early in their history. Second, some firms are "born global"—that is, from the very beginning, many start-ups are global in their activities. For example, Logitech Inc., the leading producer of the "mouse" that helps you use the personal computer, was global in its operations from day one. Founded in 1982 by a Swiss national and two Italians, the company was headquartered both in California and Switzerland. R&D and manufacturing were also conducted in both locations and, subsequently, in Taiwan and Ireland as well.[14]

The success of companies such as Logitech challenges the conventional wisdom that a company must first build up assets, internal processes, and experience before venturing into faraway lands. It also raises a number of questions: What exactly is a global start-up? Under what conditions should a company start out as a global start-up? What does it take to succeed as a global start-up?

A global start-up has been defined as a business organization that, from inception, seeks to derive significant competitive advantage from the use of resources and the sale of outputs in multiple countries. That is, right from the beginning, it uses inputs from around the world and sells its products and services to customers around the world. Geographical boundaries of nation-states are, by and large, irrelevant for a global start-up.

There is no reason for every start-up to be global. Being global necessarily involves higher communication, coordination, and transportation costs. Therefore, it is important to identify the circumstances under which going global from the beginning is advantageous.[15] First, if the required human resources are globally dispersed, going global may be the best way to access those resources. For example, Italians are masters in fine leather and Europeans in ergonomics. Second, in many cases foreign financing may be easier to obtain and more suitable for the project. Traditionally, U.S. venture capitalists have shown greater willingness to bear risk, but have shorter time horizons in their expectations for return. If a U.S. start-up is looking for patient capital, it may be better off looking overseas. Third, the target customers in many specialized industries are located in other parts of the world. Fourth, in many industries a gradual move from domestic markets to foreign markets is no longer possible because, if a product is successful, foreign competitors may immediately imitate it. Therefore, preemptive entry into foreign markets may be the only option. Finally, because of high up-front development costs, a global market is necessary to recover the costs in many industries. This is particularly true for start-ups from smaller nations that do not have access to large domestic markets.

Successful management of a global start-up presents many challenges. As already mentioned, communication and coordination across time zones and cultures are always problematic. Given that most global start-ups have far less resources than well-established corporations, one key for success is to internalize a minimal proportion of activities and outsource the rest. It is absolutely important that managers of such firms have considerable prior international experience so that they can successfully handle the communication problems and cultural conflicts that are inevitable. Another key for success is to keep the communication and coordination costs low. The only way to achieve this is by creating less costly administrative mechanisms. The boundaryless organizational designs that we discuss in the next section are particularly suitable for global start-ups because of their flexibility and low cost.

Strategy Spotlight 10.3 discusses two global start-ups that are based in Israel.

## How an Organization's Structure Can Influence Strategy Formulation

Generally speaking, discussions of the relationship between strategy and structure strongly imply that structure follows strategy. That is, the strategy that a firm chooses (e.g., related diversification) dictates such structural elements as the division of tasks, the appropriate patterns of information flow, the need for integration of activities, and authority relationships within the organization. However, we must also recognize the role that an existing structure can play in strategy formulation. For example, once a firm's structure is in place, it is very difficult and expensive to change.[16] Executives may not be able to modify their duties and responsibilities greatly, or may not welcome the disruption associated with a transfer to a new location. Further, there may be costs associated with hiring, training, and replacing executive, managerial, and operating personnel. Thus, strategy cannot be formulated without considering structural elements.

The type of organizational structure can also strongly influence a firm's strategy, day-to-day operations and performance.[17] For example, as we discussed earlier, the functional structure of Sharp Corp., the consumer electronics giant, enables the company to achieve economies of scale with its applied research and manufacturing skills. Also,

## Israel: Home of Global Start-Ups

Israel may be a minor player in the world of international commerce, but surprisingly, the country has been the home base for a disproportionately large number of global start-ups. Blue chip venture capital firms and private equity firms from the United States funded as many as 111 start-ups in Israel in the fourth quarter of 2003. Here are some examples:

- Cash-U, founded by Gal Nachum and Amir Peleg, initially thought of developing games for cell phones but soon realized that it was difficult to come up with games that have universal appeal. Instead, they now supply a software platform that helps others develop games for cell phones. Once they created the product in their labs outside Tel Aviv, they opened sales offices in London and Singapore. Today, their customers include firms such as Vodafone and Telefonica and their revenue growth is around 75 percent annually.

- Baradok Pridor, 38, and Yonatan Aumann, 42, founders of ClearForest, developed an innovative software product—a program that can analyze unstructured electronic data, such as a Web page or a video clip, as if it were already in a spreadsheet or database. Instead of waiting for customers to show up, right from the beginning, they started sending their engineers to make presentations to potential

clients around the world. Today the company's customers include Dow Chemical, Thomson Financial, and the FBI itself! They have raised $33 million so far in three rounds of venture financing. Interestingly, the headquarters of the 83-person company is in Boston!

- HyperRoll, a company that makes software for analyzing massive databases, has raised $28 million in venture funding. Referring to their hiring practices, Yossi Matias, founder of HyperRoll, says, "We build the strongest team possible, unconstrained by locality, affinity, or culture. It requires every employee to accept and support a multicultural environment." Although essentially an Israeli start-up, he even banned the use of Hebrew in the office to facilitate greater integration between the American and Israeli employees!

Why is Israel home to so many global start-ups? First, being a small country of 6 million people, the home market is too small to support the growth of domestic companies. Second, the political uncertainties of the region encourage entrepreneurs to diversify their risk by establishing an international presence. Third, many younger generation Israelis have international networks of contacts either due to education or travel. More importantly, the country has an educated workforce with a work ethic second to none. No wonder, many international start-ups are blooming in this desert country!

Sources: Copeland, M. V. 2004. The start-up oasis. *Business 2.0*, August 46–48; and Brown, E. 2004. Global start-up. *Forbes*, November 29: 150–161.

managers have the responsibility to coordinate similar products in multiple functional areas throughout the organization. Such structural arrangements should help increase operating performance because of lower costs and should enable Sharp to enter new product markets through its applied research. These opportunities would likely not be realized if Sharp had extensive redundant manufacturing resources throughout its divisions and did not effectively coordinate functional area operations across its divisions. Sharp's successful history of functional structure also suggests that the company is unlikely to consider diversification—a strategy that would require them to move away from the functional structure. Similarly, we discussed Brinker International's move to a divisional structure in order to organize its restaurant groups into different units to focus on market niches. This new structure should enable the firm to adapt to change more rapidly and innovate more effectively with the various restaurant brands. Brinker's management did not feel that they were as effective with their previous functional organizational structure.

Today, most organizations compete in environments that may be characterized as rapidly changing and unpredictable. To succeed, they must make their boundaries more flexible and permeable. Later in the chapter, we will discuss three types of what we term "boundaryless" organizations: barrier-free, modular, and virtual.

## >>Linking Strategic Reward and Evaluation Systems to Business-Level and Corporate-Level Strategies

The effective use of reward and evaluation systems can play a critical role in motivating managers to conform to organizational strategies, achieve performance targets, and reduce the gap between organizational and individual goals. In contrast, reward systems, if improperly designed, can lead to behaviors that either are detrimental to organizational performance or can lower morale and cause employee dissatisfaction.

As we will see in this section, there is no "one best way" to design reward and evaluation systems for an organization. Instead, it is contingent on many factors. Two of the most important factors are a firm's business-level strategy (see Chapter 5) and its corporate-level strategy (see Chapter 6).

### Business-Level Strategy: Reward and Evaluation Systems

In Chapter 5 we discussed two different approaches that firms may take to secure competitive advantages in the marketplace: overall cost leadership and differentiation.[18] As we might expect, implementing these strategies requires fundamentally different organizational arrangements, approaches to control, and reward and incentive systems.

*Overall Cost Leadership*    This strategy requires that product lines remain rather stable and that innovations deal mostly with production processes. Given the emphasis on efficiency, costly changes even in production processes tend to be rare. Since products are quite standardized and change rather infrequently, procedures can be developed to divide work into its basic components—those that are routine, standardized, and ideal for semiskilled and unskilled employees. As such, firms competing on the basis of cost must implement tight cost controls, frequent and comprehensive reports to monitor the costs associated with outputs, and highly structured tasks and responsibilities. As we might expect, incentives tend to be based on explicit financial targets since innovation and creativity are expensive and might tend to erode competitive advantages. Let's look at Nucor, a highly successful steel producer with $11 billion in revenues.

Nucor competes primarily on the basis of cost and, has a reward and incentive system that is largely based on financial outputs and financial measures.[19] Nucor uses four incentive compensation systems that correspond to the levels of management.

1.  *Production incentive program.* Groups of 20 to 40 people are paid a weekly bonus based on either anticipated product time or tonnage produced. Each shift and production line is in a separate bonus group.
2.  *Department managers.* Bonuses are based on divisional performance, primarily measured by return on assets.
3.  *Employees not directly involved in production.* These include engineers, accountants, secretaries, receptionists, and others. Bonuses are based on two factors: divisional and corporate return on assets.
4.  *Senior incentive programs.* Salaries are lower than comparable companies, but a significant portion of total compensation is based on return on stockholder equity. A portion of pretax earnings is placed in a pool and divided among officers as bonuses that are part cash and part stock.

As we might expect, the culture at Nucor reflects its reward and incentive system. Since incentive compensation can account for more than half of their paychecks, employees become nearly obsessed with productivity and apply a lot of pressure on each other. Ken Iverson, a former CEO, recalled an instance in which one employee arrived at work in sunglasses instead of safety glasses, preventing the team from doing any work. Furious, the other workers chased him around the plant with a piece of angle iron!

*Differentiation*    This strategy typically involves the development of innovative products and services that require using experts who can identify the crucial elements of intricate, creative designs and marketing decisions. Highly trained professionals such as scientists and engineers are essential for devising, assessing, implementing and continually changing complex product designs. New product design also requires extensive collaboration and cooperation among specialists and functional managers from different areas within a firm. Such individuals must, for example, evaluate and implement a new design, constantly bearing in mind marketing, financial, production, and engineering considerations.

Given the need for cooperation and coordination among professionals in many functional areas, it becomes quite difficult to evaluate individuals using set quantitative criteria. It also is difficult to measure specific outcomes of such efforts and attribute outcomes to specific individuals. Thus, more behavioral measures (such as how effectively employees collaborate and share information) and intangible incentives and rewards become necessary to support a strong culture and to motivate employees. Consider 3M, a highly innovative company whose core value is innovation.

> At 3M, rewards are tied closely to risk-taking and innovation-oriented behavior. Managers are not penalized for product failures; instead, those same people are encouraged to work on another project that borrows from their shared experience and insight. A culture of creativity and "thinking out of the box" is reinforced by their well-known "15 percent rule," which permits employees to set aside 15 percent of their work time to pursue personal research interests. And a familiar 3M homily, "Thou shall not kill new ideas for products," is known as the 11th commandment. It is the source of countless stories, including one that tells how L. D. DeSimone (3M's former CEO) tried five times (and failed) to kill the project that yielded the 3M blockbuster product, Thinsulate.[20]

## Corporate-Level Strategy: Strategic Reward and Evaluation Systems

In Chapter 6 we discussed two broad types of diversification strategies: related and unrelated. The type of diversification strategy that a firm follows has important implications for the type of reward and evaluation systems that it should use.

Sharp Corporation, a $21 billion Japanese consumer electronics giant, that we discussed earlier in this chapter, follows a strategy of *related* diversification.[21] Its most successful technology has been liquid crystal displays (LCDs) that are critical components in nearly all of the firm's products. With their expertise in this area, they are moving into high-end displays for cellular telephones, hand-held computers, and digital computers.[22]

Given the need to leverage such technologies across multiple product lines, Sharp must have reward and evaluation systems that foster coordination and sharing. It must focus more on individuals' behavior rather than on short-term financial outcomes. For example, promotion is the most powerful incentive, and it is generally based on seniority and subtle skills exhibited over time, such as teamwork and communication. It is critical to ensure that the company's reward system will not reward short-term self-interested orientations.

Like many Japanese companies, Sharp's culture reinforces the view that the firm is a family or community whose members should cooperate for the greater good. In accordance with the policy of lifetime employment, turnover is low. This encourages employees to pursue what is best for the entire company. Such an outlook lessens the inevitable conflict over sharing important resources such as R&D knowledge.

In contrast to Sharp, firms such as Hanson PLC (a British conglomerate) followed a strategy of unrelated diversification for most of its history. At one time it owned as many as 150 operating companies in areas such as tobacco, footwear, building products, brewing, and food. There were limited product similarities across businesses and therefore little need for sharing of resources and knowledge across divisional boundaries. James Hanson and Gordon White, founders of the company, actually did not permit any sharing of resources between operating companies even if it was feasible!

Their reward and evaluation system placed such heavy emphasis on individual accountability that they viewed resource sharing, with its potential for mutual blaming, unacceptable. The operating managers had more than 60 percent of their compensation tied to annual financial performance of their subsidiaries. All decision making was decentralized so that subsidiary managers could be held responsible for the return on capital they employed. However, there was one area in which they had to obtain approval from the corporate office. No subsidiary manager was allowed to incur a capital expenditure greater than $3,000 without permission from the corporate office. Hanson managed to be successful with a very small corporate office because of its decentralized structure, tight financial controls, and an incentive system that motivated managers to meet financial goals. Gordon White was proud of claiming that he had never visited any of the operating companies that were part of the Hanson empire.[23]

To summarize our discussion of the contingent relationship between levels of strategy and evaluation and reward systems, the key issue becomes the need for *inde*pendence versus *inter*dependence. In the cases of cost leadership strategies and unrelated diversification, there tends to be less need for interdependence. Thus, the reward and evaluation systems focus more on the use of financial indicators because unit costs, profits, and revenues can be rather easily attributed to a given business unit or division.

In contrast, firms that follow differentiation or related diversification strategies have intense needs for tight interdependencies among the functional areas and business units within the corporation. In these firms, sharing of resources, including raw materials, R&D knowledge, marketing information, and so on, is critical to organizational success. That is, it is more important to achieve synergies with value-creating activities and business units than with cost leadership or unrelated strategies. To facilitate sharing and collaboration, reward and evaluation systems tend to incorporate more behavioral indicators. Exhibit 10.6 summarizes our discussion of the relationship between strategies and control systems.

**Exhibit 10.6**

**Summary of Relationships between Reward and Evaluation Systems and Business-Level and Corporate-Level Strategies**

| Level of Strategy | Types of Strategy | Need for Interdependence | Primary Type of Reward and Evaluation System |
|---|---|---|---|
| Business-level | Overall cost leadership | Low | Financial |
| Business-level | Differentiation | High | Behavioral |
| Corporate-level | Related diversification | High | Behavioral |
| Corporate-level | Unrelated diversification | Low | Financial |

## 10.4 STRATEGY SPOTLIGHT

### Boundary Types

There are primarily four types of boundaries that place limits on organizations. In today's dynamic business environment, different types of boundaries are needed to foster high degrees of interaction with outside influences and varying levels of permeability.

1. *Vertical boundaries between levels in the organization's hierarchy.* SmithKline Beecham asks employees at different hierarchical levels to brainstorm ideas for managing clinical trial data. The ideas are incorporated into action plans that significantly cut the new product approval time of its breakthrough pharmaceuticals. This would not have been possible if the barriers between levels of individuals in the organization had been too high.

2. *Horizontal boundaries between functional areas.* Fidelity Investments makes the functional barriers more porous and flexible among divisions, such as marketing, operations, and customer service, in order to offer customers a more integrated experience when conducting business with the company. Customers can take their questions to one person, reducing the chance that customers will "get the runaround" from employees who feel customer service is not their responsibility. At Fidelity, customer service is everyone's business, regardless of functional area.

3. *External boundaries between the firm and its customers, suppliers, and regulators.* GE Lighting, by working closely with retailers, functions throughout the value chain as a single operation. This allows GE to track point-of-sale purchases, giving it better control over inventory management.

4. *Geographic boundaries between locations, cultures, and markets.* The global nature of today's business environment spurred PricewaterhouseCoopers to use a global groupware system. This allows the company to instantly connect to its 26 worldwide offices.

Source: Ashkenas, R. 1997. The organization's new clothes. In Hesselbein, F., Goldsmith, M., and Beckhard, R. (Eds.). *The organization of the future:* 104–106. San Francisco: Jossey Bass.

---

Finally, we must apply an important caveat. Exhibit 10.6 suggests guidelines on how an organization should match its strategies to its evaluation and reward systems. In actual practice, there is clearly a need for all organizations to have combinations of both financial and behavioral rewards. Both overall cost leadership and unrelated diversification strategies require a need for collaboration and the sharing of best practices across both value-creating activities and business units. General Electric, for example, has developed many integrating mechanisms to enhance sharing "best practices" across what would appear to be rather unrelated businesses such as jet engines, appliances, and network television. And for both differentiation and related diversification strategies, financial indicators such as revenue growth and profitability should not be overlooked at both the business-unit and corporate levels.

## >>Boundaryless Organizational Designs

The term *boundaryless* may bring to mind a chaotic organizational reality in which "anything goes." This is not the case. As Jack Welch, GE's former CEO, has suggested, boundaryless does not imply that all internal and external boundaries vanish completely. Although boundaries may continue to exist in some form, they become more open and permeable.[24] Strategy Spotlight 10.4 discusses four types of boundaries and provides examples of how organizations have made them more permeable.

We are not suggesting that boundaryless structures replace the traditional forms of organizational structure, but rather that they should complement them. For example, Sharp Corp. has implemented a functional structure to attain economies of scale with its applied research and manufacturing skills. However, to bring about this key objective,

371

Sharp has relied on several integrating mechanisms and processes that are key attributes of the boundaryless concept.

> To prevent functional groups from becoming vertical chimneys that obstruct product development, Sharp's product managers have responsibility—but not authority—for coordinating the entire set of value-chain activities. And the company convenes enormous numbers of cross-unit and corporate committees to ensure that shared activities, including the corporate R&D unit and sales forces, are optimally configured and allocated among the different product lines. Sharp invests in such time-intensive coordination to minimize the inevitable conflicts that arise when units share important activities.[25]

We will discuss three approaches to making boundaries more permeable. In the process, these approaches help to facilitate the widespread sharing of knowledge and information across both the internal and external boundaries of the organization. We'll begin with the *barrier-free* type, which involves making all organizational boundaries—internal and external—more permeable. We'll place particular emphasis on team concepts, because we view teams as a central building block for implementing the boundaryless organization. In the next two sections, we will address the *modular* and *virtual* types of organizations. These forms focus on the need to create seamless relationships with external organizations such as customers or suppliers. While the modular type emphasizes the outsourcing of noncore activities, the virtual (or network) organization focuses on alliances among independent entities formed to exploit specific market opportunities.

## The Barrier-Free Organization

The "boundary" mind-set is ingrained deeply into bureaucracies. It is evidenced by such clichés as "That's not my job," "I'm here from corporate to help," or endless battles over transfer pricing. In the traditional company, boundaries are clearly delineated in the design of an organization's structure. These boundaries are rigid. Their basic advantage is that the roles of managers and employees are simple, clear, well-defined, and long-lived. A major shortcoming was pointed out to the authors during an interview with a high-tech executive: "Structure tends to be divisive; it leads to territorial fights."

Today such structures are being replaced by fluid, ambiguous, and deliberately ill-defined tasks and roles. Just because work roles are no longer defined by traditional structures, however, does not mean that differences in skills, authority, and talent disappear.

A barrier-free organization enables a firm to bridge real differences in culture, function, and goals to find common ground that facilitates information sharing and other forms of cooperative behavior. Eliminating the multiple boundaries that stifle productivity and innovation can enhance the potential of the entire organization.

Strategy Spotlight 10.5 describes how GE has used the boundaryless concept to develop its wind energy business. This business unit draws on GE's expertise in transportation and jet engines.

***Creating Permeable Internal Boundaries***    For barrier-free organizations to work effectively, the level of trust and shared interests among all parts of the organization must be raised. Similarly, the organization needs to develop among its employees the skill level needed to work in a more democratic organization. Barrier-free organizations also require a shift in the organization's philosophy from executive development to organizational development, and from investments in high-potential individuals to investments in leveraging the talents of all individuals.

## Boundarylessness: A Key to GE's Success in Wind Energy

Among GE's most promising businesses is a business unit that sells wind-power turbines. GE Wind Energy's revenues are more than $1 billion annually, and the company has become the world's number 2 maker of wind-power systems.

GE Wind Energy primarily designs and builds turbines at plants in California, Florida, Germany, Spain, and the Netherlands. Sometimes the company provides services to wind farms. Other times, it plans major projects, installs the turbines, and operates the plants, as seen in the Clear Sky project in Texas. Thanks to heavy government support in some U.S. states and overseas, GE has won many major projects recently from Colorado to California and from Britain to Belgium.

The key to GE's success comes from a combination of buying into the business and bringing to bear technologies and expertise from all across the giant company. GE acquired Enron's wind assets in 2002 for $285 million and immediately faced a big problem: The erratic nature of the power source—wind gusts—is taxing on turbine components, especially the gearbox, which is vital for transforming the spinning of the blades into electricity. GE has extensive expertise in gearboxes. Its transportation division makes huge, highly efficient ones, including those used in 300-ton mining trucks. Such expertise helped GE develop more reliable wind-turbine gearboxes.

GE jet-engine scientists began working on fiber composites to lighten the giant blades—each about the size of a Boeing 747's wingspan. They plan to cut the blades' weight by 25 percent. GE also has teams of PhDs in India and China working on computer simulations to test components for new wind turbine models (there are 23 now, each designed for specific wind conditions). "We really understand the physics of the machine," says Steve Zwolinski, GE Wind's CEO.

Such efforts are paying off. The wind turbines are much more durable and efficient than when GE acquired the business. Manufacturing costs have also come down 30 percent. Wind power is expected to become an increasingly important part of the global energy picture.

Industry experts predict wind energy—the world's fastest-growing energy source—to expand at least 20 percent annually between 2003 and 2008. Although pragmatic about the chances of wind dominating the world's energy portfolio, John Rice, GE Power Systems CEO and president, asserts that return on sales could be 10 percent in five years. "Is it a $2 billion to $3 billion business or a $5 to $6 billion business over the next five or ten years?" Rice asks. "Either way, I think it's going to be substantial."

Sources: Carey, J. 2005. Tax credits put wind in the sails of renewables. *BusinessWeek*, January 10: 94; Schonfeld, E. 2004. GE sees the light. *Business 2.0*, July: 80–86; and, Rubner, J. 2003. GE Power rides wind energy. *Atlanta Business Chronicle*, November 7: 10–12.

Teams can be an important aspect of barrier-free structures.[26] Jeffrey Pfeffer, author of several insightful books, including *The Human Equation,* suggests that teams have three primary advantages.[27] First, teams substitute peer-based control for hierarchical control of work activities. In essence, employees control themselves, reducing the time and energy management needs to devote to control.

Second, teams frequently develop more creative solutions to problems because they encourage the sharing of the tacit knowledge held by individual team members.[28] Brainstorming, or group problem solving, involves the pooling of ideas and expertise to enhance the chances that at least one group member will think of a way to solve the problems at hand.

Third, by substituting peer control for hierarchical control, teams permit the removal of layers of hierarchy and absorption of administrative tasks previously performed by specialists. This avoids the cumbersome costs of having people whose sole job is to watch the people who watch other people do the work. To carry the argument one step further, Norman Augustine humorously pointed out in *Augustine's Laws* that "If a sufficient number of management layers are superimposed on top of each other, it can be assured that disaster is not left to chance!"[29]

Effective barrier-free organizations must go beyond achieving close integration and coordination within divisions in a corporation. Past research on the multidivisional type of organization has pointed to the importance of interdivisional coordination and resource sharing.[30] Means to this end include interdivisional task forces and committees, reward and incentive systems that emphasize interdivisional cooperation, and common training programs.

A study of professional service firms provides some additional insights.[31] The most important assets of these firms were not the individual technical expertise of their members. That was merely a precondition at these firms. Rather, the collective wisdom of multidisciplinary teams was what set them apart. Further, the researchers found that the average performers excel at using the combined knowledge of boundary-crossing teams to solve especially complex problems with the speed and efficiency that competitors could not match. The competitor of a top-performing investment bank lamented:

> They are the team to beat. Why? They don't slow themselves down with the clutter of bureaucracy. They overwhelm the problem. That *could* yield inefficiency, but it doesn't. They are smart and quick and work seamlessly together.

Given the importance of collaboration and collective efforts, what makes a good team becomes of critical importance. Frank Carruba (former head of Hewlett-Packard's labs) provides some interesting insights.[32] He discovered over time that the difference between mediocre teams and good teams was generally varying levels of motivation and talent. But what explained the difference between good teams and truly superior teams? Carruba found that the key difference—and this explained a 40 percent overall difference in performance—was the way members treated each other; that is, the degree to which they believed in one another and created an atmosphere of encouragement rather than competition. In other words, vision, talent, and motivation could carry a team only so far. What clearly stood out in the "super" teams were higher levels of authenticity and caring, which allowed the full synergy of their individual talents, motivation, and vision to be expressed without barriers.

### Developing Effective Relationships with External Constituencies

In barrier-free organizations, managers must also create flexible, porous organizational boundaries and establish communication flows and mutually beneficial relationships with internal (e.g., employees) and external (e.g., customers) constituencies. Michael Dell, founder and CEO of Dell Computer, is a strong believer in fostering close relationships with his customers. In an interview, he explained:

> We're not going to be just your PC vendor anymore. We're going to be your IT department for PCs. Boeing, for example, has 100,000 Dell PCs, and we have 30 people that live at Boeing, and if you look at the things we're doing for them or for other customers, we don't look like a supplier, we look more like Boeing's PC department. We become intimately involved in planning their PC needs and the configuration of their network.
>
> It's not that we make these decisions by ourselves. They're certainly using their own people to get the best answer for the company. But the people working on PCs together, from both Dell and Boeing, understand the needs in a very intimate way. They're right there living it and breathing it, as opposed to the typical vendor who says, "Here are your computers. See you later."[33]

Thus far, we have argued that barrier-free organizations create successful relationships between both internal and external constituencies. However, there is one additional constituency—competitors—with whom some organizations have benefited as they developed cooperative relationships.

For example, after years of seeing its empty trucks return from warehouses back to production facilities after deliveries, General Mills teamed up with 16 of its competitors to form an e-commerce business that allows the companies to find carriers with empty cargo trailers to piggyback freight loads to distributors near the production facilities.[34] This increases revenue for all network members and reduces wasted carrier miles.

***Risks, Challenges, and Potential Downsides***   In spite of its potential benefits, many firms are discovering that creating and managing a barrier-free organization can be frustrating.[35] For example, Puritan-Bennett Corporation, a Lenexa, Kansas, manufacturer of respiratory equipment, found that its product development time more than doubled after it adopted team management. Roger J. Dolida, director of R&D, attributed this failure to a lack of top management commitment, high turnover among team members, and infrequent meetings. Very often, managers trained in rigid hierarchies find it difficult to make the transition to the more democratic, participative style that teamwork requires.

Christopher Barnes, now a consultant with PricewaterhouseCoopers in Atlanta, previously worked as an industrial engineer for Challenger Electrical Distribution (a subsidiary of Westinghouse, now part of CBS) at a plant in Jackson, Mississippi, which produced circuit-breaker boxes. His assignment was to lead a team of workers from the plant's troubled final-assembly operation with the mission: "Make things better." Not surprisingly, that vague notion set the team up for failure.

After a year of futility, the team was disbanded. In retrospect, and after several successes with teams, Barnes identified several reasons for the debacle in Jackson: (1) limited personal credibility—he was viewed as an "outsider"; (2) a lack of commitment to the team—everyone involved was forced to be on the team; (3) poor communications—nobody was told why the team was important; (4) limited autonomy—line managers refused to give up control over team members; and (5) misaligned incentives—the culture rewarded individual performance over team performance. Barnes's experience has important implications for all types of teams, whether they are composed of managerial, professional, clerical, or production personnel.[36] The pros and cons of barrier-free structures are summarized in Exhibit 10.7.

| Pros | Cons |
| --- | --- |
| • Leverages the talents of all employees. | • Difficult to overcome political and authority boundaries inside and outside the organization. |
| • Enhances cooperation, coordination, and information sharing among functions, divisions, SBUs, and external constituencies. | • Lacks strong leadership and common vision, which can lead to coordination problems. |
| • Enables a quicker response to market changes through a single-goal focus. | • Time-consuming and difficult-to-manage democratic processes. |
| • Can lead to coordinated win–win initiatives with key suppliers, customers, and alliance partners. | • Lacks high levels of trust, which can impede performance. |

**Exhibit 10.7**
**Pros and Cons of Barrier-Free Structures**

## The Modular Organization

As Charles Handy, author of *The Age of Unreason,* has noted:

> Organizations have realized that, while it may be convenient to have everyone around all the time, having all of your workforce's time at your command is an extravagant way of marshaling the necessary resources. It is cheaper to keep them outside the organization, employed by themselves or by specialist contractors, and to buy their services when you need them.[37]

To capture Handy's vision, the modular organization type outsources nonvital functions, tapping into the knowledge and expertise of "best in class" suppliers of goods and services, but retains strategic control. Outsiders may be used to manufacture parts, handle logistics, or perform accounting activities. As we discussed in Chapters 3 and 5, the value chain can be used as a framework to identify the key primary and support activities performed by a firm to create value. The key question becomes: Which activities do we keep "in-house" and which activities do we outsource to suppliers?[38] In effect, the organization becomes a central hub surrounded by networks of outside suppliers and specialists and, much like Lego blocks, parts can be added or taken away. Both manufacturing and service units may be modular.[39]

In the personal computer industry, the shift to the modular structure has been pioneered by relative newcomers like Dell and Gateway, as well as by workstation innovators like Sun Microsystems. These companies either buy their products ready-made or purchase all the parts from suppliers and perform only the final assembly. Their larger, more established competitors—IBM and Hewlett-Packard—produce most of their parts in-house. As a result, the smaller modular companies are often ahead of their older rivals in profitability.[40]

Apparel is another industry in which the modular type has been widely adopted. Nike and Reebok, for example, have succeeded by concentrating on their strengths: designing and marketing high-tech, fashionable footwear. Nike has very limited production facilities and Reebok owns no plants. These two companies contract virtually all their footwear production to suppliers in Taiwan, South Korea, and other countries with low-cost labor. Avoiding large investments in fixed assets helps them derive large profits on minor sales increases. By being modular, Nike and Reebok can keep pace with changing tastes in the marketplace because their suppliers have become expert at rapidly retooling for the manufacture of new products.

In a modular company, outsourcing the noncore functions offers three advantages.

1. A firm can decrease overall costs, stimulate new product development by hiring suppliers whose talent may be superior to that of in-house personnel, avoid idle capacity, realize inventory savings, and avoid becoming locked into a particular technology.

2. Outsourcing enables a company to focus scarce resources on the areas where it holds a competitive advantage. These benefits can translate into more funding for research and development, hiring the best engineers, and providing continuous training for sales and service staff.

3. By enabling an organization to tap into the knowledge and expertise of its specialized supply-chain partners, it adds critical skills and accelerates organizational learning.[41]

The modular type enables a company to leverage relatively small amounts of capital and a small management team to achieve seemingly unattainable strategic objectives.[42] Freed from the need to make big investments in fixed assets, the modular company can achieve rapid growth. Certain preconditions must exist or be created, however, before the modular approach can be successful. First, the company must work closely with suppliers to ensure that the interests of each party are being fulfilled. Companies need to find loyal, reliable vendors who can be trusted with trade secrets. They also need assurances that suppliers will dedicate their financial, physical, and human resources to satisfy strategic objectives such as lowering costs or being first to market. Second, the modular company must make sure that it selects the proper competencies to keep in-house. For Nike and Reebok, the core competencies are design and marketing, not shoe manufacturing; for Honda, the core competence is engine technology. These firms are unlikely to outsource any activity that involves their core competence. An organization must be wary of outsourcing components of its business that may compromise long-term competitive advantages.

*Strategic Risks of Outsourcing*   While adopting the modular form clearly has some advantages, managers must also weigh associated risks. The main strategic concerns are (1) loss of critical skills or developing the wrong skills, (2) loss of cross-functional skills, and (3) loss of control over a supplier.[43]

Too much outsourcing can result in a firm "giving away" too much skill and control. Outsourcing relieves companies of the requirement to maintain skill levels needed to manufacture essential components. Over time, these skills that were once part of the knowledge base of the company disappear. At one time, semiconductor chips seemed like a simple technology to outsource. But now, they have become a critical component of a wide variety of products. Companies that have outsourced the manufacture of these chips run the risk of losing the ability to manufacture them as the technology has rapidly escalated. Thus, they may become increasingly dependent upon their suppliers.

Cross-functional skills refer to the skills acquired through the interaction of individuals in various departments within a company. Often, such interaction assists a department in solving problems as employees interface with others across functional units. However, if a firm outsources key functional responsibilities, such as manufacturing, communication across departments can become more difficult. This is because a firm and its employees must now integrate their activities with a new, outside supplier. This typically brings about new challenges in the coordination of joint efforts.

Another serious drawback can occur when the outsourced products give suppliers too much power over the manufacturer. This can happen when the manufacturer is dependent on a single supplier, or just a few suppliers, for critical components. Suppliers that are key to a manufacturer's success can, in essence, hold the manufacturer "hostage." Nike manages this potential problem by sending full-time "product expatriates" to work at the plants of its suppliers. Also, the company often brings top members of supplier management and technical teams to Nike headquarters. This way, Nike keeps close tabs on the pulse of new developments, builds rapport and trust with suppliers, and develops long-term relationships with suppliers to prevent hostage situations.

Strategy Spotlight 10.6 discusses how Sony outsources for talent to develop games for its highly successful video game business. Exhibit 10.8 summarizes the pros and cons of modular structures.[44]

## The Virtual Organization

In contrast to the "self-reliant" thinking that guided traditional organizational designs, the strategic challenge today has become doing more with less and looking outside the firm for opportunities and solutions to problems. The virtual type of organization provides a new means of leveraging resources and exploiting opportunities.[45]

# STRATEGY SPOTLIGHT

## Outsourcing for Talent: How Sony Develops Video Games

The convergence of Hollywood and Silicon Valley has led to the explosive growth of the worldwide video game industry, with revenues of $24.5 billion in 2004. Recently, it has overtaken the movie industry's box office receipts. The industry's sales are expected to soar to $55 billion by 2008, according to PricewaterhouseCoopers.

While broadcast TV audiences dwindle and moviegoing stagnates, gaming is emerging as the newest and perhaps strongest pillar in the media world. So it's no surprise that film studios, media giants, gamemakers, and Japanese electronics companies are all battling to win the "Games Wars." "This is a huge shift we're seeing, and nobody wants to be left behind," says Sony Entertainment Chairman, Michael Lynton.

In this sprawling market where controlling a broad portfolio of businesses is crucial, nobody is better positioned than Sony. Unlike other rivals, it has already assembled all of the pieces of a true video game empire. It sells hardware with its PlayStation consoles, and it has developed its handheld PlayStation Portable product. It also develops games such as the popular *Gran Turismo* racing and *EverQuest* online. And it owns Sony Pictures and MGM movie studios, whose Spider-Man and James Bond franchises have been mega hit games for Activision and EA. This combination has enabled

Sony to sell 80 million Play Station 2 (PS2) consoles worldwide.

The real payoff for Sony comes in game software sales. While Sony and other console makers sell their hardware for a loss, they typically make $5 to $10 in royalties for every game sold on their platform. PS2 has more than 2,000 software titles, with more than 775 million total game copies sold.

Central to Sony's strategy is how it has used outside developers to produce most of its games. It has even reached out to gamers themselves. "We didn't want outside developers to be peripheral to our business model," says Andrew House, an early PlayStation team member and executive vice president of Sony Computer Entertainment America. "We knew that the widest variety of content possible was the best way to build the largest consumer base possible."

Sony has searched high and low for talent. In 1997, it launched a developer kit aimed at hobbyists. "We sent it to budding college developers who wanted to try their hands," House says. Ideas from those amateurs made their way into commercial games in Japan. Meanwhile, externally developed titles like *Final Fantasy* and *Madden NFL Football* helped put Sony's second generation console, the PS2, at the top of the heap in 2001. Sony also launched a Linux developer kit for just $199 in 2002. "It's our way of feeding the market for the future. Some of the first great games were developed by people at home in their garages," say House. "If we're not getting people involved and looking for opportunities very early on, we really are missing out."

Sources: House, A. 2004. Sony. *Fast Company*, April: 65; and Grover, R. Edwards, C., Rowley, I., & Moon, I. 2005. Game wars. *BusinessWeek*, February 28: 35–40.

---

**Exhibit 10.8**

**Pros and Cons of Modular Structures**

| Pros | Cons |
|---|---|
| • Directs a firm's managerial and technical talent to the most critical activities. | • Inhibits common vision through reliance on outsiders. |
| • Maintains full strategic control over most critical activities—core competencies. | • Diminishes future competitive advantages if critical technologies or other competences are outsourced. |
| • Achieves "best in class" performance at each link in the value chain. | • Increases the difficulty of bringing back into the firm activities that now add value due to market shifts. |
| • Leverages core competencies by outsourcing with smaller capital commitment. | • Leads to an erosion of cross-functional skills. |
| • Encourages information sharing and accelerates organizational learning. | • Decreases operational control and potential loss of control over a supplier. |

The virtual type can be viewed as a continually evolving network of independent companies—suppliers, customers, even competitors—linked together to share skills, costs, and access to one another's markets.[46] The members of a virtual organization, by pooling and sharing the knowledge and expertise of each of the component organizations, simultaneously "know" more and can "do" more than any one member of the group could do alone. By working closely together in a cooperative effort, each gains in the long run from the resulting individual and organizational learning that takes place.[47] The term *virtual,* meaning "being in effect but not actually so," is commonly used in the computer industry. A computer's ability to appear to have more storage capacity than it really possesses is called virtual memory. Similarly, by assembling resources from a variety of entities, a virtual organization may seem to have more capabilities than it really possesses.[48]

The virtual organization consists of a grouping of units of different organizations that have joined in an alliance to exploit complementary skills in pursuing common strategic objectives. A case in point is Lockheed Martin's use of specialized coalitions between and among three entities—the company, academia, and government—to enhance competitiveness. According to former CEO Norman Augustine:

> The underlying beauty of this approach is that it forces us to reach outward. No matter what your size, you have to look broadly for new ideas, new approaches, new products. Lockheed Martin used this approach in a surprising manner when it set out during the height of the Cold War to make stealth aircraft and missiles. The technical idea came from research done at the Institute of Radio Engineering in Moscow in the 1960s that was published, and publicized, quite openly in the academic media.
>
> Despite the great contrasts among government, academia and private business, we have found ways to work together that have produced very positive results, not the least of which is our ability to compete on a global scale.[49]

Virtual organizations need not be permanent. Participating firms may be involved in multiple alliances at any one time. Virtual organizations may involve different firms performing complementary value activities, or different firms involved jointly in the same value activities, such as production, R&D, advertising, and distribution. The percentage of activities that are jointly performed with alliance partners may vary significantly from alliance to alliance.[50]

How does the virtual type of structure differ from the modular type? Unlike the modular type, in which the focal firm maintains full strategic control, the virtual organization is characterized by participating firms that give up part of their control and accept interdependent destinies. Participating firms pursue a collective strategy that enables them to cope with uncertainty in the environment through cooperative efforts. The benefit is that, just as virtual memory increases storage capacity, the virtual organizations enhance the capacity or competitive advantage of participating firms. Strategy Spotlight 10.7 addresses the variety of collaborative relationships in the biotechnology industry.

Each company (as Strategy Spotlight 10.7 illustrates) that links up with others to create a virtual organization contributes only what it considers its core competencies. It will mix and match what it does best with the best of other firms by identifying its critical capabilities and the necessary links to other capabilities.[51]

*Challenges and Risks*   Despite their many advantages, such alliances often fail to meet expectations. For example, the alliance between IBM and Microsoft soured in early 1991 when Microsoft began shipping Windows in direct competition to OS/2, which was jointly developed by the two firms. The runaway success of Windows frustrated IBM's

## Collaborative Relationships in Biotechnology

Collaboration in biotechnology has benefited a variety of firms. Amgen collaborates with a number of smaller firms including ARRIS, Environgen, Glycomex, and Interneuron, among others. The companies work on joint marketing projects and bring R&D scientists together to explore opportunities for new pharmaceutical product development. In exchange for the expertise of the scientists and marketers at the smaller companies, Amgen provides financial clout and technical assistance when new-product opportunities are identified.

Another biotech company that utilizes collaborative relationships with competitors is Biogen. This large pharmaceutical firm once outsourced clinical testing of its new drugs. But now, the company brings experts from other firms to Biogen laboratories to work with their scientists.

Chiron, one of the largest pharmaceutical firms, with over 7,500 employees, makes extensive use of collaborative efforts with its competitors. The company currently collaborates with over 1,400 companies, tapping into the knowledge base of R&D experts with a wide variety of skill and expertise in the field. Chiron considers this network one of its core competencies.

Source: Powell, W. W. 1998. Learning from collaboration: Knowledge and networks in the biotechnology and pharmaceutical industries. *California Management Review,* 40 (3): 228–240; Williams, E., & Langreth, R. 2001. "A biotech wonder grows up. *Forbes,* September 3: 118.

ability to set an industry standard. In retaliation, IBM entered into an alliance with Microsoft's archrival, Novell, to develop network software to compete with Microsoft's LAN Manager.

The virtual organization demands a unique set of managerial skills. Managers must build relationships with other companies, negotiate win–win deals for all parties involved, find the right partners with compatible goals and values, and provide the temporary organization with the right balance of freedom and control. In addition, information systems must be designed and integrated to facilitate communication with current and potential partners.

An ever-changing pattern of alliances that is constantly being formed and dissolved does not necessarily imply mutually exploitative arrangements or lack of long-term relationships. The key is for managers to be clear about the strategic objectives while forming alliances. Some objectives are time bound, and those alliances need to be dissolved once the objective is fulfilled. Some alliances may have relatively long-term objectives and will need to be clearly monitored and nurtured to produce mutual commitment and avoid bitter fights for control. The highly dynamic personal computer industry, for example, is characterized by multiple temporary alliances among hardware, operating systems, and software producers.[52] But alliances in the more stable automobile industry, such as those involving Nissan and Volkswagen as well as Mazda and Ford, have long-term objectives and tend to be relatively stable.

The virtual organization is a logical culmination of joint-venture strategies of the past. Shared risks, shared costs, and shared rewards are the facts of life in a virtual organization.[53] When virtual organizations are formed, they involve tremendous challenges for strategic planning. As with the modular corporation, it is essential to identify core competencies. However, for virtual structures to be successful, a strategic plan is also needed to determine the effectiveness of combining core competencies.

The strategic plan must address the diminished operational control and overwhelming need for trust and common vision between the partners. This new structure may be appropriate for firms whose strategies require merging technologies (e.g., computing and communication) or for firms exploiting shrinking product life cycles that require simultaneous entry into multiple geographical markets. Further, it may be effective for firms

| Pros | Cons |
|---|---|
| • Enables the sharing of costs and skills. | • Harder to determine where one company ends and another begins, due to close interdependencies among players. |
| • Enhances access to global markets. | |
| • Increases market responsiveness. | |
| • Creates a "best of everything" organization since each partner brings core competencies to the alliance. | • Leads to potential loss of operational control among partners. |
| • Encourages both individual and organizational knowledge sharing and accelerates organizational learning. | • Results in loss of strategic control over emerging technology. |
| | • Requires new and difficult-to-acquire managerial skills. |

Source: Miles, R. E., & Snow, C. C. 1986. Organizations: New concepts for new forms. *California Management Review,* Spring: 62–73; Miles & Snow. 1999. Causes of failure in network organizations. *California Management Review,* Summer: 53–72; and Bahrami, H. 1991. The emerging flexible organization: Perspectives from Silicon Valley. *California Management Review,* Summer: 33–52.

**Exhibit 10.9**
**Pros and Cons of Virtual Structures**

that desire to be quick to the market with a new product or service; an example is the recent profusion of alliances among airlines, primarily motivated by the need to provide seamless travel demanded by the full-fare paying business traveler. Exhibit 10.9 summarizes the advantages and disadvantages of the virtual form.

## Boundaryless Organizations: Making Them Work

Designing an organization that simultaneously supports the requirements of an organization's strategy, is consistent with the demands of the environment, and can be effectively implemented by the people around the manager is a tall order for any manager.[54] Many times, the most effective solution is a combination of organizational types. That is, a firm may outsource many parts of its value chain to reduce costs and increase quality, engage simultaneously in multiple alliances to take advantage of technological developments or penetrate new markets, and break down barriers within the organization to enhance flexibility. In Strategy Spotlight 10.8, we look at how an innovative firm, Technical Computer Graphics, effectively combines both barrier-free and virtual forms of an organization.

When an organization faces external pressures, resource scarcity, and declining performance, it tends to become more internally focused, rather than directing its efforts toward managing and enhancing relationships with existing and potential external stakeholders. We believe that this may be the most opportune time for managers to carefully analyze their value-chain activities and evaluate the potential for adopting elements of modular, virtual, and barrier-free organizational types.

Regardless of the form of organization ultimately chosen, achieving the coordination and integration necessary to maximize the potential of an organization's human capital involves much more than just creating a new structure. Techniques and processes designed and implemented to ensure the necessary coordination and integration of an organization's key value-chain activities are critical. Teams are key building blocks of the new organizational forms, and teamwork requires new and flexible approaches to coordination and integration.

# STRATEGY SPOTLIGHT

**10.8**

## Technical Computer Graphics' Boundaryless Organization

The Technical Computer Graphics (TCG) group manufactures items such as handheld bar code readers and scanning software. The company uses 13 "alliances," or small project teams, employing a total of 200 employees. Each team is responsible for either specific customers or specific products. Alliance teams share a common infrastructure, but they can develop new business opportunities without approval from upper management. Projects often emerge from listening to what customers need.

TCG uses a "triangulation approach"—alliances that include customers, suppliers, and other alliances. Suppliers and customers who provide funding are involved at the outset of the project. The alliances recognize that attaining the initial customer funding is crucial; it stimulates them to focus on what customers have to say. With an emphasis on speed, new products come to market quickly, providing the firm and its partners with tangible benefits.

Source: Snow, C. 1997. Twenty-first century organizations: Implications for a new marketing paradigm. *Journal of the Academy of Marketing Science*, Winter: 72–74; Allred, B. Snow, C. & Miles, R. 1996. Characteristics of managerial careers of the 21st century. *Academy of Management Executive*, November: 17–27; Herzog, V. L. 2001. Trust building on corporate collaborative teams. *Project Management Journal*, March: 28–41.

Sometimes another alliance acts as either the customer or the supplier and provides funding.

While each alliance is independent, it shares financial concern for other alliance teams. When a new business opportunity is discovered, an alliance draws on technical expertise from the other alliances. The purpose is not only to acquire additional knowledge, but also to share accumulated learning. There's no benefit to hoarding information: Learning gained from one software project might prove especially valuable to one under way in another alliance. This technological diffusion of information produces products that quickly reach the market.

TCG's formal structure is designed to ensure that such knowledge diffusion occurs. The company's culture is structured to encourage this as well. The TCG culture attracts both the entrepreneur and the team-oriented person at the same time. Working with multiple stakeholders through TCG's triangulation model forces employees to listen to the customers and respond quickly. Because the customer matters more than the functional title, teams lend expertise to each other in return for sharing the gains realized from supplying value to the customer.

Often managers trained in rigid hierarchies find it difficult to make the transition to the more democratic, participative style that teamwork requires. As Douglas K. Smith, coauthor of *The Wisdom of Teams*, pointed out, "A completely diverse group must agree on a goal, put the notion of individual accountability aside and figure out how to work with each other. Most of all, they must learn that if the team fails, it's everyone's fault."[55] Within the framework of an appropriate organizational design, managers must select a mix and balance of tools and techniques to facilitate the effective coordination and integration of key activities. Some of the factors that must be considered include:

- Common culture and shared values.
- Horizontal organizational structures.
- Horizontal systems and processes.
- Communications and information technologies.
- Human resource practices.

***Common Culture and Shared Values*** Shared goals, mutual objectives, and a high degree of trust are essential to the success of boundaryless organizations. It is neither feasible nor desirable to attempt to "control" suppliers, customers, or alliance partners in the traditional sense. In the fluid and flexible environments of the new organizational architectures, common cultures, shared values, and carefully aligned incentives are often less expensive to implement and are often a more effective means of strategic control than rules, boundaries, and formal procedures.

382

*Horizontal Organizational Structures*   Horizontal organizational structures, which group similar or related business units under common management control, facilitate sharing resources and infrastructures to exploit synergies among operating units and help to create a sense of common purpose. Consistency in training and the development of similar structures across business units facilitates job rotation and cross training and enhances understanding of common problems and opportunities. Cross-functional teams and interdivisional committees and task groups represent important opportunities to improve understanding and foster cooperation among operating units.

*Horizontal Systems and Processes*   Organizational systems, policies, and procedures are the traditional mechanisms for achieving integration among functional units. Too often, however, existing policies and procedures do little more than institutionalize the barriers that exist from years of managing within the framework of the traditional model. The concept of business reengineering focuses primarily on these internal processes and procedures. Beginning with an understanding of basic business processes in the context of "a collection of activities that takes one or more kinds of input and creates an output that is of value to the customer," Michael Hammer and James Champy's 1993 best-selling *Reengineering the Corporation* outlined a methodology for redesigning internal systems and procedures that has been embraced, in its various forms, by many organizations.[56] Proponents claim that successful reengineering lowers costs, reduces inventories and cycle times, improves quality, speeds response times, and enhances organizational flexibility. Others advocate similar benefits through the reduction of cycle times, total quality management, and the like.

*Communications and Information Technologies*   Improved communications through the effective use of information technologies can play an important role in bridging gaps and breaking down barriers between organizations. Electronic mail and videoconferencing can improve lateral communications across long distances and multiple time zones and, by short-circuiting vertical structures, tend to circumvent many of the barriers of the traditional model. Information technology can be a powerful ally in the redesign and streamlining of internal business processes and in improving coordination and integration between suppliers and customers. Internet technologies have eliminated the paperwork of purchase order and invoice documentation in many buyer–supplier relationships, enabling cooperating organizations to reduce inventories, shorten delivery cycles, and reduce operating costs. Today information technology must be viewed more as a prime component of an organization's overall strategy than simply in terms of its more traditional role as administrative support. The close relationships that must exist between technology and other value-creating activities were addressed in Chapters 3, 4, and 8.

*Human Resource Practices*   Change, whether in structure, process, or procedure, always involves and impacts the human dimension of organizations. As we noted in Chapter 4, the attraction, development, and retention of human capital are vital to value creation. As boundaryless structures are implemented, processes are reengineered, and organizations become increasingly dependent on sophisticated information technologies, the skills of workers and managers alike must be upgraded to realize the full benefits.

# >>Creating Ambidextrous Organizations

In rapidly changing and complex competitive environments, organizations face two opposing challenges.[57] First, firms must explore new opportunities and adjust to volatile markets in order to avoid complacency. They must ensure that they maintain *adaptability* and remain proactive in expanding and/or modifying their product-market scope to anticipate and satisfy market conditions. Such competences are especially challenging when change is rapid and unpredictable—conditions that are becoming more pronounced in global markets.

Second, organizations must also effectively exploit the value of their existing assets and competencies. They need to have *alignment,* which is a clear sense of how value is being created in the short term and how activities are integrated and properly coordinated. Firms that achieve both adaptability and alignment are considered *ambidextrous organizations*—aligned and efficient in how they manage today's business but flexible enough to changes in the environment so that they will prosper tomorrow.

As we would expect, handling such opposing demands is difficult because there will always be some degree of conflict. Such trade-offs can never really be entirely eliminated, and firms often suffer when they place too strong a priority on either adaptability or alignment. If it places too much focus on adaptability, the firm will suffer low profitability in the short term. On the other hand, if managers direct their efforts primarily at alignment, they will likely miss out on promising business opportunities.

## The Challenge of Achieving Ambidexterity: Some Examples from Business Practice

Clearly, it is hard to become an ambidextrous organization and get the balance of adaptability and alignment just right. Let's look at a couple of brief cases in which firms went too far in one direction.

- Lloyds TSB Bank Plc, based in the United Kingdom, became highly successful in providing stellar shareholder returns throughout the 1980s and 1990s by focusing on a single performance indicator—return on equity. Under the direction of CEO Brian Pittman, little attention was paid to monitoring and understanding either the changing needs of their customer base or the morale of the workforce—two factors that ultimately eroded the bank's performance. Too much emphasis was placed on maintaining efficient operations. The result was that between 1998 and 2003, Lloyds TSB lost 60 percent of its market value. Clearly, this was a situation of too much alignment and a lack of adaptability.

- Sweden's Ericsson made the opposite mistake—too much adaptability at the expense of short-term performance. The firm led in the development of the telephony industry and developed one of the first analog mobile systems. In addition, it was a leader in designing the global system of mobile communication and pioneered third-generation mobile technology standards. Unfortunately, the impressive growth in sales came at a very high cost and a bloated organization structure. There was a great deal of duplication of effort, largely because of an R&D organization that had grown to 30,000 people in approximately 100 technology centers. When the crash in the telecom industry hit in 2000, Ericsson suffered much more than its rivals. The firm eventually cut 60,000 employees and closed most of its technology centers in its effort to become profitable again.

Fortunately, some firms do seem to make the right trade-offs and, in essence, get the "best of both worlds." For example, Finland's Nokia Corp. is experimenting with a wide array of mobile technologies. At the same time, it continues to invest in its dominant handset franchise. And GlaxoSmithKline PLC is experimenting with alternative organization models, alliance partners, and technologies in its search for new blockbuster drugs. At the same time, the pharmaceutical firm is striving to maximize the return from the existing drug portfolio.

## Ambidextrous Organizations: Key Design Attributes

A recent study by Charles O'Reilly and Michael Tushman[58] provides some insights into how some firms were able to create successful ambidextrous organizations. These researchers and their colleagues investigated companies that attempted to simultaneously pursue modest, incremental innovations as well as more dramatic, breakthrough innovations. In all, the team investigated 35 attempts to launch breakthrough innovations undertaken by 15 business units in nine different industries. They studied the organizational designs and the processes, systems, and cultures associated with the breakthrough projects as well as their impact on the operations and performance of the traditional businesses.

Companies tended to structure their breakthrough projects in one of four primary ways:

- Seven were carried out within existing *functional organizational structures*. The projects were completely integrated into the regular organizational and management structure.

- Nine were organized as *cross-functional teams*. The groups operated within the established organization but outside of the existing management structure.

- Four were organized as *unsupported teams*. Here, they became independent units set up outside the established organization and management hierarchy.

- Fifteen were conducted within *ambidextrous organizations*. Here, the breakthrough efforts were organized within structurally independent units, each having its own processes, structures, and cultures. However, they were integrated into the existing senior management structure.

Exhibit 10.10 depicts each of these four organization structures. The performance results of the 35 initiatives were tracked along two dimensions:

- Their success in creating desired innovations was measured by either the actual commercial results of the new product or the application of practical market or technical learning.

- The performance of the existing business was evaluated.

The study found that the organizational structure and management practices employed had a direct and significant impact on the performance of both the breakthrough initiative and the traditional business. The ambidextrous organizational designs were more effective than the other three designs on both dimensions: launching breakthrough products or services (i.e., adaptation) and improving the performance of the existing business (i.e., alignment).

Why was the ambidextrous organization the most effective structure? The study found that there were many factors. A clear and compelling vision, consistently communicated by the company's senior management team was critical in building the ambidextrous designs. The structure enabled cross-fertilization among business units while avoiding cross-contamination. The tight coordination and integration at the managerial levels enabled the newer units to share important resources from the traditional units such as cash, talent, expertise, and so on. Such sharing was encouraged and facilitated by effective reward systems that emphasized overall company goals. At the same time, the organizational separation ensured that the new units' distinctive processes, structures, and cultures were not overwhelmed by the forces of "business as usual." Furthermore, the established units were shielded from the distractions of launching new businesses, and they continued to focus

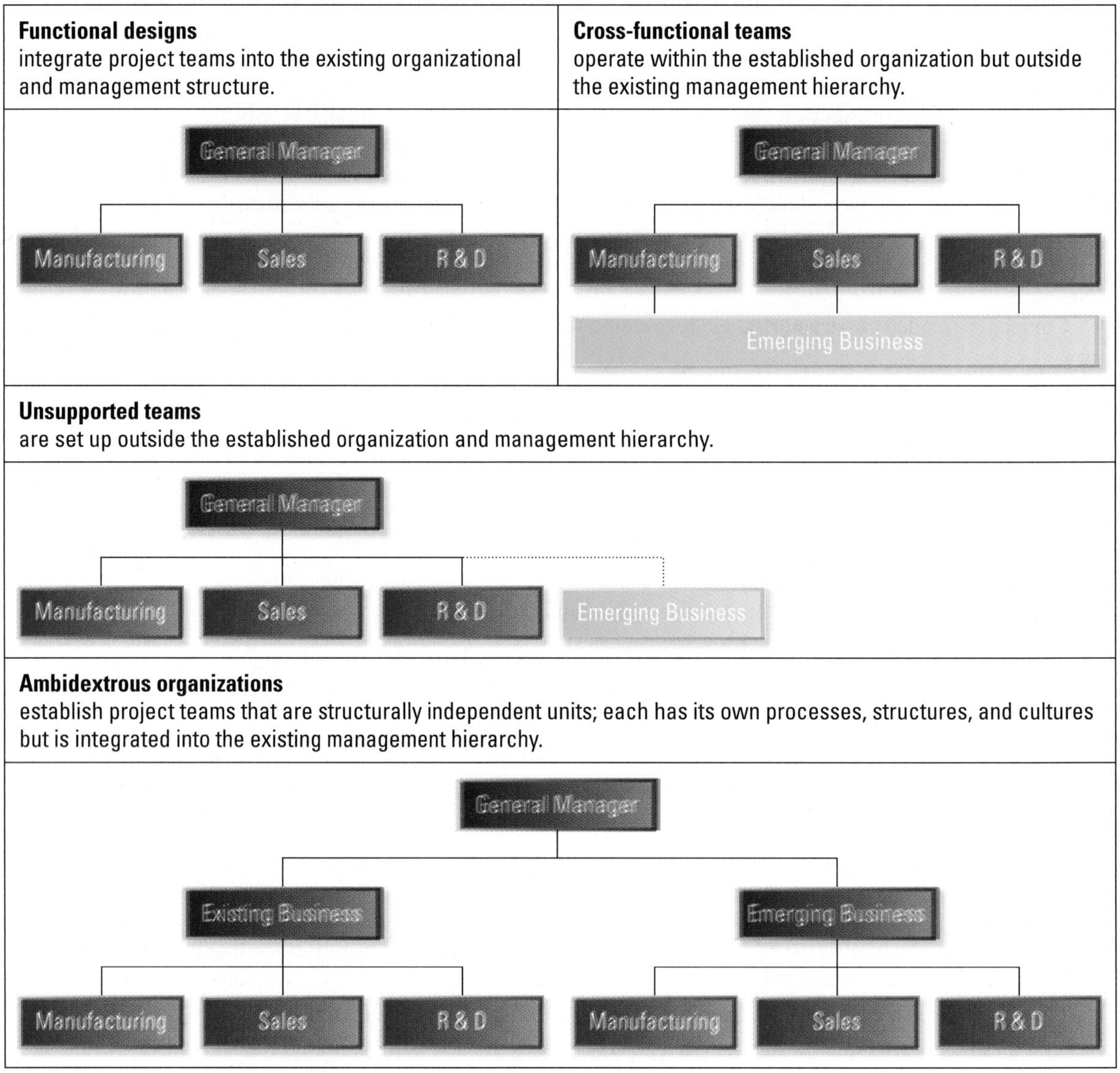

**Functional designs**
integrate project teams into the existing organizational and management structure.

**Cross-functional teams**
operate within the established organization but outside the existing management hierarchy.

**Unsupported teams**
are set up outside the established organization and management hierarchy.

**Ambidextrous organizations**
establish project teams that are structurally independent units; each has its own processes, structures, and cultures but is integrated into the existing management hierarchy.

**Exhibit 10.10**   **Organizational Designs for Adaptation and Alignment**

In an examination of 35 different attempts at breakthrough innovation, businesses tended to apply one of four organizational designs to develop and deliver their innovations. More than 90 percent of businesses using the ambidextrous structure succeeded in their attempts, while none of the cross-functional or unsupported teams and only 25 percent of those using functional designs reached their goals.

Source: Reprinted by permission of *Harvard Business Review.* Exhibit from "The Ambidextrous organization," by O' Reilly, C. A. and Tushman, M. L. 2004. Copyright © 2004 by the Harvard Business School Publishing Corporation; all rights reserved.

all of their attention and energy on refining their operations, enhancing their products, and serving their customers.

Let's look at one of these organizations in more detail. Strategy Spotlight 10.9 discusses *USA Today*'s success and helps us identify some of the key managerial and organizational characteristics that underpin the ambidextrous organization and how it attains both adaptability and alignment.

## USA Today: Success through an Ambidextrous Organization

USA Today was not an overnight success. Launched in 1982 as a division of the Gannett Corporation, its colorful brand of journalism was widely ridiculed by critics. However, during the 1990s it turned around an initial decade of losses and posted some impressive profits. It became the most widely read daily newspaper in the United States. Well-heeled business travelers made up a good chunk of its subscriber base and, not surprisingly, USA Today became an attractive platform for national advertisers.

By the end of the 1990s, however, some unfavorable external trends were emerging. Newspaper readership was steadily decreasing, especially among young people. Competition was intensifying, as more customers were looking toward television and Internet media outlets for their news. Furthermore, newsprint costs were escalating.

Tom Curley, USA Today's president and publisher, knew that he could not keep operating "business as usual." He recognized that he would have to move the company beyond its traditional print media in order to maintain strong growth and profits. Such expansion, he realized, would require dramatic innovations and the company would need to discover ways to apply the existing news-gathering and editing capabilities to entirely new media.

In 1999, Curley decided that USA Today should adopt a "network strategy," in which it would share news content across three platforms: the newspaper, USATODAY.com (an online news service), and Gannett's 21 local television stations. Curley explained his vision: "We're no longer in the newspaper business—we're in the news information space, and we'd better learn to deliver content regardless of forms."

Sounds like a great vision, but how did Curley make it work? To execute the strategy, Curley knew he needed to create an ambidextrous organization by sustaining the print business and also pursuing innovations in broadcasting and online news. To launch the bold initiative, Curley appeared at a company meeting dressed as a cyberpunk, complete with blue hair. The message, he recalled, was "It's a new world, and we need to be ready to move into it." In addition to the theatrics, he appointed a new leader in 2000 for USATODAY.com who was a strong supporter of the network strategy, and he brought in an outsider to create a television operation, USAToday Direct. Both the online and television organizations remained separate and distinct from the newspaper, maintaining unique processes, structures and cultures. However, Curley demanded that the senior leadership of all three businesses be tightly integrated and coordinated.

Karen Jurgenson, the editor of USA Today, and the leaders of the online and television units instituted daily editorial meetings to review stories and assignments, share ideas, and identify other potential synergies. They quickly saw, for example, that eliciting the cooperation of USA Today's reporters would be vital to the success of the strategy (print journalists are notorious for hoarding stories), and they jointly decided to train the print reporters in television and Web broadcasting and equip them with video cameras so that they could file stories simultaneously in the different media. These moves quickly paid off; reporters soon realized that they would have the chance to appear on TV. And a new position of "network editor" was also created in the newsroom to help reporters sharpen their stories for the broadcast media.

All along, Curley knew that he had to make some broader changes to the organization in terms of its culture, processes, structures, and personnel. He fired several senior executives who clearly did not "buy in" to his network strategy. Such firm action was required to ensure that his team would present a united front and deliver consistent messages to all employees. He also changed the incentive program for executives by replacing an emphasis on unit-specific goals with a common bonus program tied to growth targets across all three media. Human resource policies were changed to encourage transfers of talent across the three units, and promotion and compensation decisions began to include people's willingness to share stories and other content. As part of the overall effort, a "Friends of the Network" recognition was established to explicitly reward cross-unit accomplishments.

Yet while all of the sharing and synergy was being emphasized, the organizational integrity of the three units was carefully maintained. The three units were physically separate, and they each followed different staffing models. For example, the employees at USATODAY.com were, on average, much younger than the newspaper's reporters, and they remained far more collaborative and fast paced. Reporters continued to be fiercely independent and focused more on in-depth coverage of stories than the television staff.

USA Today, with its ambidextrous organization, has been able to compete aggressively in the mature business of daily print news, develop a strong Internet franchise, and provide Gannett television stations with coverage of breaking news. And, during the Internet collapse several years ago, USA Today made $60 million. This success was largely due to the company's ability to continue to attract national advertisers and revenues from its profitable USAToday.com operation.

Source: O'Reilly, C. A. III., & Tushman, M. L. 2004. The ambidextrous organization. *Harvard Business Review*, 82(4): 74–81.

# Summary

Successful organizations must ensure that they have the proper type of organizational structure. Furthermore, they must ensure that their firms incorporate the necessary integration and processes so that the internal and external boundaries of their firms are flexible and permeable. Such a need is increasingly important as the environments of firms become more complex, rapidly changing, and unpredictable.

In the first section of the chapter, we discussed the growth patterns of large corporations. Although most organizations remain small or die, some firms continue to grow in terms of revenues, vertical integration, and diversity of products and services. In addition, their geographical scope may increase to include international operations. We traced the dominant pattern of growth, which evolves from a simple structure to a functional structure as a firm grows in terms of size and increases its level of vertical integration. After a firm expands into related products and services, its structure changes from a functional to a divisional form of organization. Finally, when the firm enters international markets, its structure again changes to accommodate the change in strategy.

We also addressed the different types of organizational structure—simple, functional, divisional (including two variations—strategic business unit and holding company), and matrix as well as their relative advantages and disadvantages. We closed the section with a discussion of the implications for structure when a firm enters international markets. The three primary factors to take into account when determining the appropriate structure are type of international strategy, product diversity, and the extent to which a firm is dependent on foreign sales.

In the second section, we took a contingency approach to the design of reward and evaluation systems. That is, we argued that there is no one best way to design such systems; rather, it is dependent on a variety of factors. The two that we discussed are business- and corporate-level strategies. With an overall cost leadership strategy and unrelated diversification, it is appropriate to rely primarily on cultures and reward systems that emphasize the production outcomes of the organization, because it is rather easy to quantify such indicators. In contrast, differentiation strategies and related diversification require cultures and incentive systems that encourage and reward creativity initiatives as well as the cooperation among professionals in many different functional areas. Here it becomes more difficult to measure accurately each individual's contribution, and more subjective indicators become essential.

The third section of the chapter introduced the concept of the boundaryless organization. We did not suggest that the concept of the boundaryless organization replaces the traditional forms of organizational structure. Rather, it should complement them. This is necessary to cope with the increasing complexity and change in the competitive environment. We addressed three types of boundaryless organizations. The barrier-free type focuses on the need for the internal and external boundaries of a firm to be more flexible and permeable. The modular type emphasizes the strategic outsourcing of noncore activities. The virtual type centers on the strategic benefits of alliances and the forming of network organizations. We discussed both the advantages and disadvantages of each type of boundaryless organization as well as suggested some techniques and processes that are necessary to successfully implement them. These are common culture and values, horizontal organizational structures, horizontal systems and processes, communications and information technologies, and human resource practices.

The final section addresses the need for managers to develop ambidextrous organizations. In today's rapidly changing global environment, managers must be responsive and proactive in order to take advantage of new opportunities. At the same time, they must effectively integrate and coordinate existing operations. Such requirements call for organizational designs that establish project teams that are structurally independent units, with each having its own processes, structures, and cultures. But, at the same time, each unit needs to be effectively integrated into the existing management hierarchy.

## Summary Review Questions

1. Why is it important for managers to carefully consider the type of organizational structure that they use to implement their strategies?

2. Briefly trace the dominant growth pattern of major corporations from simple structure to functional structure to divisional structure. Discuss the relationship between a firm's strategy and its structure.

3. What are the relative advantages and disadvantages of the types of organizational structure—simple, functional, divisional, matrix—discussed in the chapter?

4. When a firm expands its operations into foreign markets, what are the three most important factors to take into account in deciding what type of structure is most appropriate? What are the types of international structures discussed in the text and what are the relationships between strategy and structure?

5. Briefly describe the three different types of boundaryless organizations: barrier-free, modular, and virtual.

6. What are some of the key attributes of effective groups? Ineffective groups?

7. What are the advantages and disadvantages of the three types of boundaryless organizations: barrier-free, modular, and virtual?

8. When are ambidextrous organizational designs necessary? What are some of their key attributes?

## Experiential Exercise

Many firms have recently moved toward a modular structure. For example, they have increasingly outsourced many of their information technology (IT) activities. Identify three such organizations. Using secondary sources, evaluate (1) the firm's rationale for IT outsourcing and (2) the implications for performance.

| Firm | Rationale | Implication(s) for Performance |
|---|---|---|
| 1. | | |
| 2. | | |
| 3. | | |

## Application Questions Exercises

1. Select an organization that competes in an industry in which you are particularly interested. Go on the Internet and determine what type of organizational structure this organization has. In your view, is it consistent with the strategy that it has chosen to implement? Why? Why not?

2. Choose an article from *BusinessWeek, Fortune, Forbes, Fast Company,* or any other well-known publication that deals with a corporation that has undergone a significant change in its strategic direction. What are the implications for the structure of this organization?

3. Go on the Internet and look up some of the public statements or speeches of an executive in a major corporation about a significant initiative such as entering into a joint venture or launching a new product line. What do you feel are the implications for making the internal and external barriers of the firm more flexible and permeable? Does the executive discuss processes, procedures, integrating mechanisms, or cultural issues that should serve this purpose? Or are other issues discussed that enable a firm to become more boundaryless?

4. Look up a recent article in the publications listed in question 2 above that addresses a firm's involvement in outsourcing (modular organization) or in strategic alliance or network organizations (virtual organization). Was the firm successful or unsuccessful in this endeavor? Why? Why not?

## Ethics Questions

1. If a firm has a divisional structure and places extreme pressures on its divisional executives to meet short-term profitability goals (e.g., quarterly income), could this raise some ethical considerations? Why? Why not?

2. If a firm enters into a strategic alliance but does not exercise appropriate behavioral control of its employees (in terms of culture, rewards and incentives, and boundaries—as discussed in Chapter 9) that are involved in the alliance, what ethical issues could arise? What could be the potential long-term and short-term downside for the firm?

## References

1. Wheatcroft, P. 2004. An expensive farce has been played out in NHS. *The Times,* April 24: 58; and www.nhs.uk.

2. This introductory discussion draws upon Hall, R. H. 2002. *Organizations: Structures, processes, and outcomes* (8th ed.). Upper Saddle River, NJ: Prentice Hall; and Duncan, R. E. 1979. What is the right organization structure? Decision-tree analysis provides the right answer. *Organizational Dynamics,* 7(3): 59–80. For an insightful discussion of strategy-structure relationships in the organization theory and strategic management literatures, refer to Keats, B., & O'Neill, H. M. 2001. Organization structure: Looking through a strategy lens. In Hitt, M. A., Freeman, R. E., & Harrison, J. S. 2001. *The Blackwell handbook of strategic management:* 520–542. Malden, MA: Blackwell.

3. This discussion draws upon Chandler, A. D. 1962. *Strategy and structure.* Cambridge, MA: MIT Press; Galbraith J. R., & Kazanjian, R. K. 1986. *Strategy implementation: The role of structure and process.* St. Paul, MN: West Publishing;

and Scott, B. R. 1971. Stages of corporate development. Intercollegiate Case Clearing house, 9-371-294, BP 998. Harvard Business School.

4. Our discussion of the different types of organizational structures draws on a variety of sources, including Galbraith & Kazanjian, op. cit.; Hrebiniak, L. G., & Joyce, W. F. 1984. *Implementing strategy.* New York: Macmillan; Distelzweig, H. 2000. Organizational structure. In Helms, M. M. (Ed.). *Encyclopedia of management:* 692–699. Farmington Hills, MI: Gale; and Dess, G. G., & Miller, A. 1993. *Strategic management.* New York: McGraw-Hill.

5. Schein, E. H. 1996. Three cultures of management: The key to organizational learning. *Sloan Management Review,* 38(1): 9–20.

6. For a discussion of performance implications, refer to Hoskisson, R. E. 1987. Multidivisional structure and performance: The contingency of diversification strategy. *Academy of Management Journal,* 29: 625–644.

7. For a thorough and seminal discussion of the evolution toward the divisional form of organizational structure in the United States, refer to Chandler, op. cit. A rigorous empirical study of the strategy and structure relationship is found in Rumelt, R. P. 1974. *Strategy, structure, and economic performance.* Cambridge, MA: Harvard Business School Press.

8. Ghoshal, S., & Bartlett, C. A. 1995. Changing the role of management: Beyond structure to processes. *Harvard Business Review,* 73(1): 88.

9. Koppel, B. 2000. Synergy in ketchup? *Forbes,* February 7: 68–69; and Hitt, M. A., Ireland, R. D., & Hoskisson, R. E. 2001. *Strategic management: Competitiveness and globalization* (4th ed.). Cincinnati, OH: Southwestern Publishing.

10. Pitts, R. A. 1977. Strategies and structures for diversification. *Academy of Management Journal,* 20(2): 197–208.

11. Wetlaufer, S. 2000. Common sense and conflict: An interview with Disney's Michael Eisner. *Harvard Business Review,* 78(1): 121.

12. Daniels, J. D., Pitts, R. A., & Tretter, M. J. 1984. Strategy and structure of U.S. multinationals: An exploratory study. *Academy of Management Journal,* 27(2): 292–307.

13. Habib, M. M., & Victor, B. 1991. Strategy, structure, and performance of U.S. manufacturing and service MNCs: A comparative analysis. *Strategic Management Journal,* 12(8): 589–606.

14. Our discussion of global start-ups draws from Oviatt, B. M., & McDougall, P. P. 2005. The internationalization of entrepreneurship. *Journal of International Business Studies,* 36(1): 2–8; Oviatt, B. M., & McDougall, P. P. 1994. Toward a theory of international new ventures. *Journal of International Business Studies,* 25(1): 45–64; and Oviatt, B. M., & McDougall, P. P. 1995. Global start-ups: Entrepreneurs on a worldwide stage. *Academy of Management Executive,* 9(2): 30–43.

15. Some useful guidelines for global start-ups are provided in Kuemmerle, W. 2005. The entrepreneur's path for global expansion. *MIT Sloan Management Review,* 46(2): 42–50.

16. See, for example, Miller, D., & Friesen, P. H. 1980. Momentum and revolution in organizational structure. *Administrative Science Quarterly,* 13: 65–91.

17. Many authors have argued that a firm's structure can influence a firm's strategy and performance. These include Amburgey, T. L., & Dacin, T. 1995. As the left foot follows the right? The dynamics of strategic and structural change. *Academy of Management Journal,* 37: 1427–1452; Dawn, K., & Amburgey, T. L. 1991. Organizational inertia and momentum: A dynamic model of strategic change. *Academy of Management Journal,* 34: 591–612; Fredrickson, J. W. 1986. The strategic decision process and organization structure. *Academy of Management Review,* 11: 280–297; Hall, D. J., & Saias, M. A.

1980. Strategy follows structure! *Strategic Management Journal,* 1: 149–164; and Burgelman, R. A. 1983. A model of the interaction of strategic behavior, corporate context, and the concept of strategy. *Academy of Management Review,* 8: 61–70.

18. This discussion of generic strategies and their relationship to organizational control draws upon Porter, M. E. 1980. *Competitive strategy.* New York: Free Press; and Miller, D. 1988. Relating Porter's business strategies to environment and structure: Analysis and performance implications. *Academy of Management Journal,* 31(2): 280–308.

19. Rodengen, J. L. 1997. *The legend of Nucor Corporation.* Fort Lauderdale, FL: Write Stuff Enterprises.

20. The 3M example draws upon *Blueprints for service quality.* 1994. New York: American Management Association; personal communication with Katerine Hagmeier, program manager, external communications, 3M Corporation, March 26, 1998; Lei, D., Slocum, J. W., & Pitts, R. A. 1999. Designing organizations for competitive advantage: The power of unlearning and learning. *Organizational Dynamics,* 27(3): 24–38; and Graham, A. B., & Pizzo, V. G. 1996. A question of balance: Case studies in strategic knowledge management. *European Management Journal,* 14(4): 338–346.

21. The Sharp Corporation and Hanson plc examples are based on Collis, D. J., & Montgomery, C. A. 1998. Creating corporate advantage. *Harvard Business Review,* 76(3): 70–83.

22. Kunii, I. 2002. Japanese companies' survival skills. *BusinessWeek,* November 18: 18.

23. White, G. 1988. How I turned $3,000 into $10 billion. *Fortune,* November 7: 80–89. After the death of the founders, the Hanson plc conglomerate was found to be too unwieldy and was broken up into several separate, publicly traded corporations. For more on its more limited current scope of operations, see www.hansonplc.com.

24. An interesting discussion on how the Internet has affected the boundaries of firms can be found in Afuah, A. 2003. Redefining firm boundaries in the face of the Internet: Are firms really shrinking? *Academy of Management Review,* 28(1): 34–53.

25. Collis & Montgomery, op. cit.

26. For a discussion of the role of coaching on developing high performance teams, refer to Kets de Vries, M. F. R. 2005. Leadership group coaching in action: The zen of creating high performance teams. *Academy of Management Executive,* 19(1): 77–89.

27. Pfeffer, J. 1998. *The human equation: Building profits by putting people first.* Cambridge, MA: Harvard Business School Press.

28. For a discussion on how functional area diversity affects performance, see Bunderson, J. S., & Sutcliffe, K. M. 2002. *Academy of Management Journal,* 45(5): 875–893.

29. Augustine, N. R. 1983. *Augustine's laws.* New York: Viking Press.

30. See, for example, Hoskisson, R. E., Hill, C. W. L., & Kim, H. 1993. The multidivisional structure: Organizational fossil or source of value? *Journal of Management,* 19(2): 269–298.

31. Kuedtjam, H., Haskins, M. E., Rosenblum, J. W., & Weber, J. 1997. The generative cycle: Linking knowledge and relationships. *Sloan Management Review,* 39(1): 47–58.

32. Pottruck, D. A. 1997. Speech delivered by the co-CEO of Charles Schwab Co., Inc., to the Retail Leadership Meeting, San Francisco, CA, January 30; and Miller, W. 1999. Building the ultimate resource. *Management Review,* January: 42–45.

33. Magretta, J. 1998. The power of virtual integration: An interview with Dell Computer's Michael Dell. *Harvard Business Review,* 76(2): 75.

34. Forster, J. 2001. Networking for cash. *BusinessWeek,* January 8: 129.

35. Dess, G. G., Rasheed, A. M. A., McLaughlin, K. J., & Priem, R. 1995. The new corporate architecture. *Academy of Management Executive,* 9(3): 7–20.

36. Barnes, C. 1998. A fatal case. *Fast Company,* February–March: 173.

37. Handy, C. 1989. *The age of unreason.* Boston: Harvard Business School Press; Ramstead, E. 1997. APC maker's low-tech formula: Start with the box. *Wall Street Journal,* December 29: B1; Mussberg, W. 1997. Thin screen PCs are looking good but still fall flat. *Wall Street Journal,* January 2: 9; Brown, E. 1997. Monorail: Low cost PCs. *Fortune,* July 7: 106–108; and Young, M. 1996. Ex-Compaq executives start new company. *Computer Reseller News,* November 11: 181.

38. For a discussion of some of the downsides of outsourcing, refer to Rossetti, C., & Choi, T. Y. 2005. On the dark side of strategic sourcing: Experiences from the aerospace industry. *Academy of Management Executive,* 19(1): 46–60.

39. Tully, S. 1993. The modular corporation. *Fortune,* February 8: 196.

40. For a recent review of the relationship between outsourcing and firm performance, see Gilley, K. M., & Rasheed, A. 2000. Making more by doing less: An analysis of outsourcing and its effects on firm performance. *Journal of Management,* 26(4): 763–790.

41. Quinn, J. B. 1992. *Intelligent enterprise: A knowledge and service based paradigm for industry.* New York: Free Press.

42. For an insightful perspective on outsourcing and its role in developing capabilities, read Gottfredson, M., Puryear, R., & Phillips, C. 2005. Strategic sourcing: From periphery to the core. *Harvard Business Review,* 83(4): 132–139.

43. This discussion draws upon Quinn, J. B., & Hilmer, F. C. 1994. Strategic outsourcing. *Sloan Management Review,* 35(4): 43–55.

44. See also Stuckey, J., & White, D. 1993. When and when not to vertically integrate. *Sloan Management Review,* Spring: 71–81; Harrar, G. 1993. Outsource tales. *Forbes ASAP,* June 7: 37–39, 42; and Davis, E. W. 1992. Global outsourcing: Have U.S. managers thrown the baby out with the bath water? *Business Horizons,* July–August: 58–64.

45. For a discussion of knowledge creation through alliances, refer to Inkpen, A. C. 1996. Creating knowledge through collaboration. *California Management Review,* 39(1): 123–140; and Mowery, D. C., Oxley, J. E., & Silverman, B. S. 1996. Strategic alliances and interfirm knowledge transfer. *Strategic Management Journal,* 17 (Special Issue, Winter): 77–92.

46. Doz, Y., & Hamel, G. 1998. *Alliance advantage: The art of creating value through partnering.* Boston: Harvard Business School Press.

47. DeSanctis, G., Glass, J. T., & Ensing, I. M. 2002. Organizational designs for R&D. *Academy of Management Executive,* 16(3): 55–66.

48. Barringer, B. R., & Harrison, J. S. 2000. Walking a tightrope: Creating value through interorganizational alliances. *Journal of Management,* 26: 367–403.

49. Davis, E. 1997. Interview: Norman Augustine. *Management Review,* November: 14.

50. One contemporary example of virtual organizations is R&D consortia. For an insightful discussion, refer to Sakaibara, M. 2002. Formation of R&D consortia: Industry and company effects. *Strategic Management Journal,* 23(11): 1033–1050.

51. Bartness, A., & Cerny, K. 1993. Building competitive advantage through a global network of capabilities. *California Management Review,* Winter: 78–103. For an insightful historical discussion of the usefulness of alliances in the computer industry, see Moore, J. F. 1993. Predators and prey: A new ecology of competition. *Harvard Business Review,* 71(3): 75–86.

52. See Lorange, P., & Roos, J. 1991. Why some strategic alliances succeed and others fail. *Journal of Business Strategy,* January–February: 25–30; and Slowinski, G. 1992. The human touch in strategic alliances. *Mergers and Acquisitions,* July–August: 44–47. A compelling argument for strategic alliances is provided by Ohmae, K. 1989. The global logic of strategic alliances. *Harvard Business Review,* 67(2): 143–154.

53. Some of the downsides of alliances are discussed in Das, T. K., & Teng, B. S. 2000. Instabilities of strategic alliances: An internal tensions perspective. *Organization Science,* 11: 77–106.

54. This section draws upon Dess, G. G., & Picken, J. C. 1997. *Mission critical.* Burr Ridge, IL: Irwin Professional Publishing.

55. Katzenbach, J. R., & Smith, D. K. 1994. *The wisdom of teams: Creating the high performance organization.* New York: HarperBusiness.

56. Hammer, M., & Champy, J. 1993. *Reengineering the corporation: A manifesto for business revolution.* New York: HarperCollins.

57. This section draws on Birkinshaw, J., & Gibson, C. 2004. Building ambidexterity into an organization. *MIT Sloan Management Review,* 45(4): 47–55; and Gibson, C. B., & Birkinshaw, J. 2004. The antecedents, consequences, and mediating role of organizational ambidexterity. *Academy of Management Journal,* 47(2): 209–226. Robert Duncan is generally credited with being the first to coin the term "ambidextrous organizations" in his article entitled: Designing dual structures for innovation. In Kilmann, R. H., Pondy, L. R., & Slevin, D. (Eds.). 1976. *The management of organizations,* vol. 1: 167–188. For a seminal academic discussion of the concept of exploration and exploitation, which parallels adaptation and alignment, refer to: March, J. G. 1991. Exploration and exploitation in organizational learning. *Organization Science,* 2: 71–86.

58. This section is based on O'Reilly, C. A., & Tushman, M. L. 2004. The ambidextrous organization. *Harvard Business Review,* 82(4): 74–81.

# Strategic Leadership:

## Creating a Learning Organization and an Ethical Organization

*After reading this chapter, you should have a good understanding of:*

- The three key activities in which all successful leaders must be continually engaged.

- The importance of recognizing the interdependence of the three key leadership activities and the salience of power in overcoming resistance to change.

- The crucial role of emotional intelligence (EI) in successful leadership as well as its potential drawbacks.

- The value of creating and maintaining a "learning organization" in today's global marketplace.

- The five central elements of a "learning organization."

- The leader's role in establishing an ethical organization.

- The benefits of developing an ethical organization.

- The high financial and nonfinancial costs associated with ethical crises.

*t*o compete in the global marketplace, organizations need to have strong and effective leadership. This involves the active process of both creating and implementing proper strategies. In this chapter we address key activities in which leaders throughout the organization must be involved to be successful in creating competitive advantages.

In the first section we provide a brief overview of the three key leadership activities. These are (1) setting a direction, (2) designing the organization, and (3) nurturing a culture committed to excellence and ethical behavior. Each of these activities is "necessary but not sufficient"; that is, to be effective, leaders must give proper attention to each of them. We also address the importance of a leader's effective use of power to overcome resistance to change.

The second section discusses the vital role of emotional intelligence (EI) in effective strategic leadership. EI refers to an individual's capacity for recognizing his or her emotions and those of others. It consists of five components: self-awareness, self-regulation, motivation, empathy, and social skills. We also address potential downsides or drawbacks that may result from the ineffective use of EI.

Next we address the important role of a leader in creating a "learning organization." Here leaders must strive to harness the individual and collective talents of individuals throughout the entire organization. Creating a learning organization becomes particularly important in today's competitive environment, which is increasingly unpredictable, dynamic, and interdependent. Clearly, everyone must be involved in learning. It can't be only a few people at the top of the organization. The key elements of a learning organization are inspiring and motivating people with a mission or purpose, empowering employees at all levels, accumulating and sharing internal and external information, and challenging the status quo to enable creativity.

The final section discusses a leader's challenge in creating and maintaining an ethical organization. There are many benefits of having an ethical organization. In addition to financial benefits, it can enhance human capital and help to ensure positive relationships with suppliers, customers, society at large, and governmental agencies. On the other hand, the costs of ethical crises can be very expensive for many reasons. We address four key elements of an ethical organization: role models, corporate credos and codes of conduct, reward and evaluation systems, and policies and procedures.

Scott A. Livengood was fired as Chief Executive Officer (CEO) of Krispy Kreme on January 19, 2005.[1] He hasn't received very much good news lately. The firm's stock went up 10 percent the day of that announcement. And he received the rather dubious honor of being recognized as one of *BusinessWeek*'s seven "Worst Managers" of 2004.

What brought about the demise of Livengood, a 28-year veteran of the doughnut maker who had been CEO since 1998? Let's look at two of the central issues.

First, under his direction Krispy Kreme expanded far too rapidly. After its initial public offering in 2001, it continued to open stores at breakneck speed. Hoping to cash in on the nation's sweet tooth, the chain created media events in places like New York, San Francisco, and Boston. At times, cars would line up for blocks just to bring a box of the tasty confections to work. Unfortunately, while the craze faded, the costs of operating the franchises did not. By 2003, same-store sales had declined 16 percent, while the company's overhead continued to rise. In short, the brand quickly lost its novelty. Soon Krispy Kreme realized that many of its franchises would fail.

Recent financial results reflect the poor strategy. The once high-flying company posted a $3 million third-quarter loss in November 2004—its second losing quarter of the year. And in February 2005, the firm stated that it would restate earnings for the previous year, lowering previously reported income by as much as 8.6 percent.

Second, there are what *Fortune* has called "shady deals" surrounding how the firm conducted buybacks of some franchises owned by corporate insiders. For example, Krispy Kreme didn't disclose that a California franchise it repurchased in 2004 was partly owned by Livengood's ex-wife, whose stake was valued at $1.5 million. While executives aren't required to disclose transactions with former spouses, Livengood could be in trouble if the deal was made as part of a settlement or in lieu of alimony.

An even more troubling transaction is the 2003 deal in which the chain repurchased six stores in Dallas and Shreveport, Louisiana, that were partly owned by Krispy Kreme's former chairman and current director, Joseph McAleer. McAleer got a pretty good deal—$67 million (or $11 million per store). This comes to more than three times what the firm paid for many other shops! According to David Gourevitch, a former Securities and Exchange Commission (SEC) enforcement attorney, "At some point a transaction is not remotely reasonable, and it approximates a gift or payoff." Worst case scenario: The SEC could impose fines and require some officials to step down.

The SEC continues to investigate the firm and it upgraded its informal inquiry to a formal probe. Although customers may continue to enjoy Krispy Kreme's products, the investors have hardly had a pleasant experience. Krispy Kreme's stock price has continued to sink. By late 2005 it was at $7—less than one-sixth of the $45 peak that it reached in July 2003. This fall reflects a loss of market capitalization of over $2 billion.

Clearly, many of the decisions and actions of Scott A. Livengood were not in the best interests of the firm and its shareholders. In contrast, effective leaders play an important and often pivotal role in the development and implementation of strategies.

This chapter provides insights into how organizations can more effectively manage, change, and cope with increased environmental complexity and uncertainty. Below we will define leadership and introduce what are considered to be the three most important leadership activities as well as the important role of power. The second section focuses on a key trait—emotional intelligence—that has become increasingly recognized as critical to successful leadership. Then, the third major section, "Developing a Learning Organization," provides a useful framework for how leaders can help their firms learn and proactively adapt in the face of accelerating change. Central to this contemporary idea is the concept of empowerment, wherein employees and managers throughout the organization truly come to have a sense of self-determination, meaning, competence, and impact. The fourth section addresses the leader's role in building an ethical organization. Here, we address both the value of an ethical culture for a firm as well as the key elements that it encompasses.

# >>Leadership: Three Interdependent Activities

In today's chaotic world, few would argue against the need for leadership, but how do we go about encouraging it? Let's focus on business organizations. Is it enough to merely keep the organization afloat, or is it essential to make steady progress toward some well-defined objective? We believe custodial management is not leadership. Rather, leadership is proactive, goal-oriented, and focused on the creation and implementation of a creative vision. *Leadership is the process of transforming organizations from what they are to what the leader would have them become.* This definition implies a lot: *dissatisfaction* with the status quo, a *vision* of what should be, and a *process* for bringing about change. An insurance company executive recently shared the following insight on leadership, "I lead by the Noah Principle: It's all right to know when it's going to rain, but, by God, you had better build the ark."

Doing the right thing is becoming increasingly important in today's competitive environment. After all, many industries are declining; the global village is becoming increasingly complex, interconnected, and unpredictable; and product and market life cycles are becoming increasingly compressed. Recently, when asked to describe the life cycle of his company's products, the CEO of a supplier of computer components replied, "Seven months from cradle to grave—and that includes three months to design the product and get it into production!" Richard D'Aveni, author of *Hypercompetition,* went even further. He argued that in a world where all dimensions of competition appear to be compressed in time and heightened in complexity, *sustainable* competitive advantages are no longer possible.

Despite the importance of doing the "right thing," leaders must also be concerned about doing "things right." Charan and Colvin argued strongly that implementation (or execution) is also essential to success.

> Any way that you look at it, mastering execution turns out to be the odds-on best way for a CEO to keep his job. So what's the right way to think about that sexier obsession, strategy? It's vitally important—obviously. The problem is that our age's fascination feeds the mistaken belief that developing exactly the right strategy will enable a company to rocket past competitors. In reality, that's less than half the battle.[2]

Thus, leaders are change agents whose success is measured by how effectively they implement a strategic vision and mission.

Accordingly, many authors contend that successful leaders must recognize three interdependent activities that must be continually reassessed for organizations to succeed. As shown in Exhibit 11.1, these are: (1) determining a direction, (2) designing the organization, and (3) nurturing a culture dedicated to excellence and ethical behavior.[3]

The interdependent nature of these three activities is self-evident. Consider an organization with a great mission and a superb organizational structure and design, but a culture that implicitly encourages shirking and unethical behavior. Or a strong culture and organizational design but little direction and vision—in caricature, a highly ethical and efficient buggy whip manufacturer. Or one with a sound direction and strong culture, but counterproductive teams and a "zero-sum" reward system that leads to the dysfunctional situation in which one party's gain is viewed as another party's loss, and collaboration and sharing are severely hampered. Obviously, the examples could go on and on. We contend that much of the failure of today's organizations can be attributed to a lack of equal consideration of these three activities. The imagery of a three-legged stool is instructive: It will collapse if one leg is missing or broken. Let's briefly look at each of these activities. We'll also address the important role of a leader's power in overcoming resistance to change.

**Exhibit 11.1**    **Three Interdependent Activities of Leadership**

## Setting a Direction

Leaders need a holistic understanding of an organization's stakeholders. This requires an ability to scan the environment to develop a knowledge of all of the company's stakeholders (e.g., customers, suppliers, shareholders) and other salient environmental trends and events and integrate this knowledge into a vision of what the organization could become. It necessitates the capacity to solve increasingly complex problems, become proactive in approach, and develop viable strategic options. Developing a strategic vision provides many benefits: a clear future direction; a framework for the organization's mission and goals; and enhanced employee communication, participation, and commitment. Strategy Spotlight 11.1 discusses how Chairman Howard Schultz's vision of Starbucks as a "third place" has spurred the firm's remarkable growth.

At times the creative process involves what the CEO of Yokogawa, GE's Japanese partner in the Medical Systems business, called "bullet train" thinking.[4] That is, if you want to increase the speed by 10 miles per hour, you look for incremental advances. However, if you want to double the speed, you've got to think "out of the box" (e.g., widen the track, change the overall suspension system). In today's challenging times, leaders typically need more than just keeping the same train with a few minor tweaks. Instead, they must come up with more revolutionary visions.

Consider how Robert Tillman, CEO of Lowe's, dramatically revitalized his firm by setting a clear and compelling direction. He made it into a formidable competitor to Home Depot, Inc., the Goliath of the home-improvement and hardware retailing industry.[5] In his six years as CEO, Tillman has transformed the $36.5 billion chain, based in Wilkesboro, North Carolina. Its shares have more than doubled over the past four years, while Home Depot's have fallen about 20 percent.

Tillman has redirected Lowe's strategy by responding effectively to research showing that women initiate 80 percent of home projects. While Home Depot has focused on the professionals and male customers, Tillman has redesigned Lowe's stores to give them a brighter appearance, stocked them with more appliances, and focused on higher-margin goods (including everything from Laura Ashley paints to high-end bathroom fixtures). And, like Wal-Mart, Lowe's has one of the best inventory systems in retailing. As a result, Lowe's profits are expected to continue to rise faster than Home Depot's.

### Howard Schultz's Vision of Starbucks as a "Third Place"

Most people think of Starbucks as an expensive place to get a cup of coffee. However, Chairman Howard Schultz sees the 8,000-store chain as a "third place" for people to hang out besides home and work. That is why the seemingly unrelated service of offering wireless Net access in its stores that started in 2002 turned out to be so successful. Although Starbucks Corp. will not quantify the revenue impact, people using the service typically stay nine times longer than the usual five minutes—almost certainly enough time to consume more lattes. Further, 90 percent of customers who log on are doing so after peak morning hours, which helps to fill the stores during previously slow periods. According to Anne Saunders, Starbucks' senior vice-president of marketing, "If we'd only thought of ourselves as a coffee company, we wouldn't have done this."

The wireless network also inspired a new initiative that could again remake the Seattle-based company. Its recently introduced Hear Music Coffeehouses features dozens of listening stations where people can make custom CDs, at about a dollar a tune, from hundreds of thousands of songs. Eventually, Starbucks plans to have a Hear Music media bar in about half of its stores. In addition to offering this new service, Schultz has said he thinks Starbucks could transform the music business. Although that might be debatable, he's transforming Starbucks once again. And who would have ever thought that Apple and Starbucks might become competitors?

Source: Burrows, P., Hamm, S., Brady, D. & Rowley, I. 2004. Managing for innovation. *BusinessWeek*, October 11: 192–200; and Gray, S. 2005. Starbucks brews broader menu; coffee chain's cup runneth over with breakfast, lunch, music. *Wall Street Journal*, February 9: B9.

Let's now turn to another key leadership activity: the design of the organization's structure, processes, and evaluation and control systems.

## Designing the Organization

At times, almost all leaders have difficulty implementing their vision and strategies. Such problems—many of which we discussed in Chapter 10—may stem from a variety of sources, including:

- Lack of understanding of responsibility and accountability among managers.
- Reward systems that do not motivate individuals (or collectives such as groups and divisions) toward desired organizational goals.
- Inadequate or inappropriate budgeting and control systems.
- Insufficient mechanisms to coordinate and integrate activities across the organization.

Successful leaders are actively involved in building structures, teams, systems, and organizational processes that facilitate the implementation of their vision and strategies. For example, we discussed the necessity for consistency between business-level and corporate-level strategies and organizational control in Chapter 9. Clearly, a firm would generally be unable to attain an overall low-cost advantage without closely monitoring its costs through detailed and formalized cost and financial control procedures. In a similar vein, achieving a differentiation advantage would necessitate encouraging innovation, creativity, and sensitivity to market conditions. Such efforts would be typically impeded by the use of a huge set of cumbersome rules and regulations, as well as highly centralized decision making. With regard to corporate-level strategy, in Chapter 9 we addressed how a related diversification strategy would necessitate reward systems that emphasize behavioral measures to promote sharing across divisions within a firm, whereas an unrelated strategy should rely more on financial (or objective) indicators of

## Marshall Industries: Problems with Incentives

Marshall Industries is a large Los Angeles distributor of 170,000 different electronic components. The company has 30,000 customers and receives supplies from more than 150 suppliers. CEO Rod Rodin became concerned about some irregularities in the company. He saw that an average of 20 percent of monthly sales were being shipped in the last three days of the month. He discovered that divisions within the company were hiding customer returns and opening bad credit accounts to beef up monthly numbers. Employees in divisions with scarce supplies were hiding the supplies from other divisions. Sales representatives, working on commission, were constantly fighting with one another over how commissions should be split on joint sales efforts.

Rodin came to the conclusion that his employees were doing exactly what they were being paid to do. The commission structure encouraged employees to hide returns, put in nonexistent orders the last few days of a month to make their monthly sales goals, and hide resources from one another. The key objective, of course, was sales, but the compensation structure failed to motivate employees in that direction. "Creative accounting" could easily make sure representatives made their sales goals each month whether or not the sales actually occurred. Until Rodin noticed the irregularities, there were few control mechanisms in place to integrate sales activities between divisions.

Rodin's solution? Scrap the commission system. From now on, all salespeople would receive a salary plus a bonus based on company profitability. *Electronic Buyers News* published an editorial criticizing the decision. Most people thought it was a crazy idea. But sometimes crazy ideas work pretty well. Four years after the change, sales had grown from $582 million to $1.2 billion, and the stock price of Marshall Industries had nearly quadrupled. Aligning the goals of employees with the objectives of the company seemed to be just the thing needed to bring control, integration, and coordination out of chaos.

Sources: Dess, G. G., & Picken, J. C. 1999. *Beyond productivity.* New York: AMACOM; Muoio, A. 1998. The truth is, the truth hurts. *Fast Company,* April–May: 93–102; Wilson, T. 1998. Marshall Industries: Wholesale shift to the Web. *InternetWeek,* July 20: 14–15.

performance, such as revenue gains and profitability, since there is less need for collaboration across business units because they would have little in common.

Strategy Spotlight 11.2 focuses on how the reward and evaluation system at Marshall Industries had unintended consequences, making budgeting and control very difficult. However, Rod Rodin, Marshall's CEO, recognized the problem and took decisive and bold action. This example shows how leaders must, at times, make decisions that appear to be counter to "conventional wisdom."

### Nurturing a Culture Dedicated to Excellence and Ethical Behavior

In Chapter 9 we discussed how organizational culture can be an effective and positive means of organizational control. Leaders play a key role in developing and sustaining—as well as changing, when necessary—an organization's culture. Strategy Spotlight 11.3 discusses how the leadership at the Container Store has created such an exemplary culture.

Leaders actions can, of course, also have a very detrimental effect on a firm's culture and ethics. Consider Kenneth Lay, the infamous former CEO of Enron. He, along with other top executives, led Enron into a megascandal that resulted in bankruptcy and an investor loss of $67 billion. He will stand trial in Houston, Texas, in early 2006 on criminal conspiracy charges.[6] Sherron Watkins, a former vice president at Enron, provides an interesting example of and perspective on how Lay's actions served to erode Enron's culture and ethical standards:[7]

> Ken Lay, although well known for his charitable giving and his verbal commitment to Enron's four core values (Respect, Integrity, Communication, and Excellence), was not quite walking

## The Container Store: The Best Place to Work in America

The Container Store, a Dallas-based chain of 20 specialty retail stores that sell everything you need to organize your home, office, car, or even your life, has been consistently ranked as one of the "Best Companies to Work For" by *Fortune* magazine. In the five years from 2000 to 2004, they were always ranked in the top three, and they were number one in 2000 and 2001. This is truly surprising considering that the retail industry typically has a very high employee turnover, poorly trained workers on minimum wages, and low skill levels. The Container Store is also one of the 14 companies that Dr. Leonard Berry identified as providing exemplary service through values-driven marketing. What makes the Container Store so special?

First of all, they pay very well. The average salary for salespersons is $36,000—one of the highest salaries in the industry. The benefits are substantial too. But the financial benefits are only a small part of the story. The employees consider the Container Store a happy place to work. It is a community that they belong to. Nearly 40 percent of the company's new hires are referrals from existing employees. The company invests heavily in employee training. Stores welcome new employees with Foundation Week, a week-long orientation to the company, its products, and philosophy along with a welcome box that contains $150 worth of company products as gifts. During the first year, an employee receives 235 hours of training! At the headquarters, the Fun Committee builds a sense of community among employees through lunch-time activities such as silent auctions. At birthday celebrations, teams gather for lunch and cake. It is the birthday person's responsibility to bring cake for the next birthday honoree. The company offers employees yoga classes, chair massages, and an online exercise and nutrition diary personalized to every employee! More importantly, the company's books are open to every employee every day. This helps them make better business decisions.

The company has no thick policy manuals. Instead, they are guided by six Foundational Principles that are easy to remember:

1. "Fill the other guy's basket to the brim." Each employee is trained to work with the customer in creative and imaginative ways to help them choose the best products for organizing.

2. "Man-in-the-desert." A thirsty man reaching an oasis needs more than just water. Similarly, each employee is expected to "astonish" the customer by exceeding his expectations.

3. "1 average person = 3 lousy people. 1 good person = 3 average people. 1 great person = 3 good people." The Container Store seeks only great people. Others may be happy with 9 lousy people!

4. "Intuition does not come to the unprepared mind." The heavy emphasis on training helps to prepare the employees to create unique solutions for customers.

5. "The best selection of products anywhere + the best service anywhere + the best pricing in our markets."

6. "Air of excitement." Three steps into the door and customers realize that they are in a different place.

Kip Tindal, CEO of the Container Store, explains:

> TCS's Foundational Principles empower employees to serve the customer in the true sense of the word. Employees are trusted to make whatever decision necessary to help a customer. TCS is said to provide exemplary service through values-driven marketing practices. Its employees delight in helping customers solve problems—and they possess the freedom and confidence to do so. The quest for excellence pays off in human terms, as well as financial terms.

Sources: Gavin, J. H., & Mason, R. O. 2004. The virtuous organization: The value of happiness in the workplace. *Organizational Dynamics*, 33(4): 379–392; and Berry, L. 1999. *Discovering the soul of service: Nine drivers of sustainable business success*. New York: Free Press.

the walk. For example, he always had Enron employees use his sister's travel agency. And not just us; the local Andersen office and Enron's outside attorneys, Vinson and Elkins, were pressured into using her agency as well. Trouble was that it provided neither low cost nor good service. Domestically, you could manage, but when it came to international travel—that agency sucked. I was stuck in Third World countries, where I didn't speak the language, without a hotel room or with an insufficient airline ticket home, despite paperwork that indicated otherwise. The incompetence was hard to understand. I would try using a different agency, but after one or two expense reports, I'd get a finger-wagging voice mail or e-mail reminding me that I needed to use Enron's preferred agency, Travel Agency in the Park. We called it Travel Agency in the Dark.

   In some perverse way, Andy Fastow (Enron's Chief Financial Officer) might have justified his behavior by saying to himself, "Well, my LJM partnership is helping Enron meet its financial statement goals. Why can't I just take a little for myself, just like Lay has been taking a little Enron money and transferring it to his sister for all these years?"[8]

Clearly, a leader's ethical behavior can make a strong impact on an organization—for good or for bad. Given the importance of this topic, we address it in detail in the last major section of this chapter.

Managers and top executives must also accept personal responsibility for developing and strengthening ethical behavior throughout the organization. They must consistently demonstrate that such behavior is central to the vision and mission of the organization. Several elements must be present and reinforced for a firm to become a highly ethical organization: role models, corporate credos and codes of conduct, reward and evaluation systems, and policies and procedures.

## Overcoming Barriers to Change and the Effective Use of Power

Now that we have discussed the three interdependent activities that leaders perform, we must address a key question: What are the barriers to change that leaders often encounter, and how can they use power to bring about meaningful change in their organizations? After all, people generally have some level of choice about how strongly they support or resist a leader's change initiatives. Why is there often so much resistance? There are many reasons why organizations and managers at all levels are prone to inertia and are slow to learn, adapt, and change.

1.  Many people have *vested interests in the status quo.* There is a broad stream of organizational literature on the subject of "escalation," wherein certain individuals (in both controlled laboratory settings and actual management practice) continue to throw "good money at bad decisions" despite negative performance feedback.[9]
2.  There are *systemic barriers.* Here, the design of the organization's structure, information processing, reporting relationships, and so forth impede the proper flow and evaluation of information. A bureaucratic structure with multiple layers, onerous requirements for documentation, and rigid rules and procedures will often "inoculate" the organization against change.
3.  *Behavioral barriers* are associated with the tendency of managers to look at issues from a biased or limited perspective. This can be attributed to their education, training, work experiences, and so forth. For example, consider an incident shared by David Lieberman, marketing director at GVO, an innovation consulting firm based in Palo Alto, California.

     A company's creative type had come up with a great idea for a new product. Nearly everybody loved it. However, it was shot down by a high-ranking manufacturing representative who exploded: "A new color? Do you have any idea of the spare-parts problem that it will create?" This was not a dimwit exasperated at having to build a few storage racks at the warehouse. He'd been hearing for years about cost cutting, lean inventories, and "focus." Lieberman's comment: "Good concepts, but not always good for innovation."

4.  *Political barriers* refer to conflicts arising from power relationships. This can be the outcome of a myriad of symptoms such as vested interests (e.g., the aforementioned escalation problems), refusal to share information, conflicts over resources, conflicts between departments and divisions, and petty interpersonal differences.

5. *Personal time constraints* bring to mind the old saying about "not having enough time to drain the swamp when you are up to your neck in alligators." In effect, Gresham's law of planning states that operational decisions will drive out the time necessary for strategic thinking and reflection. This tendency is accentuated in organizations experiencing severe price competition or retrenchment wherein managers and employees are spread rather thin.

Successful leadership requires effective use of power in overcoming barriers to change.[10] Power refers to a leader's ability to get things done in a way he or she wants them to be done. It is the ability to influence other people's behavior, to persuade them to do things that they otherwise would not do, and to overcome resistance and opposition to changing direction. Effective exercise of power is essential for successful leadership.[11]

A leader derives his or her power from several sources or bases. Numerous classifications of such sources or bases abound in the literature on power. However, the simplest way to understand the bases of power is by classifying them as organizational and personal, as shown in Exhibit 11.2.

Organizational bases of power refer to the power that a person wields because of holding a formal management position. These include legitimate power, reward power, coercive power, and information power. *Legitimate power* is derived from organizationally conferred decision-making authority and is exercised by virtue of a manager's position in the organization. *Reward power* depends on the ability of the leader or manager to confer rewards for positive behaviors or outcomes. *Coercive power* is the power a manager exercises over employees using fear of punishment for errors of omission or commission. *Information power* arises from a manager's access, control, and distribution of information that is not freely available to everyone in an organization.

Apart from the organizationally derived power, a leader might be able to influence subordinates because of his or her personality characteristics and behavior. These would be considered the "personal" bases of power. The personal bases of power are referent power and expert power. The source of *referent power* is a subordinate's identification with the leader. A leader's personal attributes or charisma might influence subordinates and make them devoted to that leader. On the other hand, the source of *expert power* is the leader's

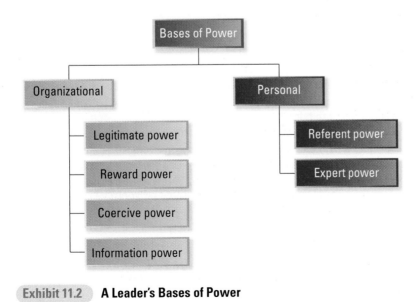

**Exhibit 11.2    A Leader's Bases of Power**

## William Bratton: Using Multiple Bases of Power

William Bratton, Chief of the Los Angeles Police Department has an enviable track record in turning around police departments in crime-ridden cities. First, while running the police division of Massachusetts Bay Transit Authority (MBTA) in Boston, then as police commissioner of New York in the mid-1990s, and now in Los Angeles since 2002, Chief Bratton is credited with reducing crime and improving police morale in record time. An analysis of his success at each of these organizations reveals very similar patterns both in terms of the problems he faced and the many ways in which he used the different bases of power to engineer a rapid turnaround.

In Boston, New York, and Los Angeles, Chief Bratton faced similar hurdles: organizations wedded to the status quo, limited resources, demotivated staffs, and opposition from powerful vested interests. But he does not give up in the face of these seemingly insurmountable problems. He is persuasive in calls for change, capable of mobilizing the commitment of key players, silencing vocal naysayers, and building rapport with superiors and subordinates while building bridges with external constituencies.

Chief Bratton's persuasion tactics are unconventional, yet effective. When he was running the MBTA police, the Transit Authority decided to buy small squad cars, which are cheaper to buy and to run, but very inadequate for the police officer's task. Instead of arguing, Bratton invited the general manager for a tour of the city. He rode with the general manager in exactly the same type of car that was ordered for ordinary officers, and drove over every pothole on the road. He

moved the seats forward so that the general manager could feel how little leg room was there. And he put on his belt, cuffs, and gun so that the general manager could understand how limited the space was. After two hours in the cramped car, the general manager was ready to change the order and get more suitable cars for the officers!

Another tactic Bratton used effectively was insisting on community meetings between police officers and citizens. This went against the long-standing practice of detachment between police and community to decrease the chances of corruption. The result was that his department had a better understanding of public concerns and rearranged their priorities, which in turn led to better community relations. For internal communications, he relied mainly on professionally produced videos instead of long, boring memos.

Chief Bratton also shows a remarkable talent for building political bridges and silencing naysayers. As he was introducing his zero-tolerance policing approach that aggressively targets "quality of life" crimes such as panhandling, drunkenness, and prostitution, opposition came from the city's courts which feared being inundated by a large number of small-crimes cases. Bratton enlisted the support of Rudolph Giuliani, the mayor of New York, who had considerable influence over the district attorneys, the courts, and the city jail. He also took the case to the *New York Times,* and managed to get the issue of zero-tolerance on the front pages of the newspaper. The courts were left with no alternative but to cooperate.

To a great extent, Bratton's success can be attributed to his understanding of the subtleties of power, including persuasion, motivation, coalition building, empathy for subordinates, and a focus on goals.

Sources: Chan Kim, W., & Renee Mauborgne, R. 2003. Tipping point leadership. *Harvard Business Review,* 81(4): 60–69; and McCarthy, T. 2004. The gang buster. *Time,* January 19: 56–58.

expertise and knowledge in a particular field. The leader is the expert on whom subordinates depend for information that they need to do their jobs successfully.

Successful leaders use the different bases of power, and often a combination of them, as appropriate to meet the demands of a situation, such as the nature of the task, the personality characteristics of the subordinates, the urgency of the issue, and other factors. Leaders must recognize that persuasion and developing consensus are often essential, but so is pressing for action. Clearly, at some point stragglers must be prodded into line.[12] Peter Georgescu, who recently retired as CEO of Young & Rubicam (an advertising and media giant acquired by the UK-based WPP Group in 2000), summarized a leader's dilemma brilliantly (and humorously), "I have knee pads and a .45. I get down and beg a lot, but I shoot people too."[13]

Strategy Spotlight 11.4 addresses some of the subtleties of power. It focuses on William Bratton, Chief of the Los Angeles Police Department, who has enjoyed a very successful career in law enforcement.

## >>Emotional Intelligence: A Key Leadership Trait

In the previous section, we discussed three of the salient activities of strategic leadership. In a sense, the focus was on "what leaders *do*." In this section, the issue becomes "who leaders *are*," that is, what are the most important traits (or capabilities) of leaders. Clearly, these two issues are related, because successful leaders possess the valuable traits that enable them to perform effectively in order to create value for their organization.

There has been, as we would expect, a vast amount of literature on the successful traits of leaders, including business leaders at the highest level.[14] These traits include integrity, maturity, energy, judgment, motivation, intelligence, expertise, and so on. However, for simplicity, these traits may be grouped into three broad sets of capabilities:

- Purely technical skills (like accounting or operations research).
- Cognitive abilities (like analytical reasoning or quantitative analysis).
- Emotional intelligence (such as the ability to work with others and a passion for work).

One attribute of successful leaders that has become popular in both the literature and management practice in recent years is "emotional intelligence."[15] Some evidence of this popularity is that *Harvard Business Review* articles published in 1998 and 2000 by psychologist/journalist Daniel Goleman, who is most closely associated with the concept, have become this widely read management journal's most highly requested reprint articles. And two of Goleman's recent books, *Emotional Intelligence* and *Working with Emotional Intelligence,* were both on the *New York Times*'s best-seller lists. Goleman defines emotional intelligence (EI) as the capacity for recognizing one's own emotions and those of others.[16]

Recent studies of successful managers have found that effective leaders consistently have a high level of emotional intelligence.[17] Findings indicate, for example, that EI is a better predictor of life success (economic well-being, satisfaction with life, friendship, family life), including occupational attainments, than IQ. Such evidence has been extrapolated to the catchy phrase: "IQ gets you hired, but EQ (Emotional Quotient) gets you promoted." And surveys show that human resource managers believe this statement to be true, and perhaps even for highly technical jobs such as those of scientists and engineers.

This is not to say that IQ and technical skills are irrelevant. Obviously, they do matter, but they should be viewed as "threshold capabilities." That is, they are the necessary requirements for attaining higher-level managerial positions. EI, on the other hand, is essential for leadership success. Without it, Goleman has argued, a manager can have excellent training, an incisive analytical mind, and many smart ideas but will still not be a great leader.

There are five components of EI: self-awareness, self-regulation, motivation, empathy, and social skill. They are included in Exhibit 11.3. Next, we will briefly discuss each of them.

### Self-Awareness

Self-awareness is the first component of EI and brings to mind that Delphic oracle who gave the advice "know thyself" thousands of years ago. Self-awareness involves a person having a deep understanding of his or her emotions, strengths, weaknesses, and drives. People with strong self-awareness are neither overly critical nor unrealistically optimistic. Instead, they are honest with themselves and others.

| | Definition | Hallmarks |
|---|---|---|
| **Self-management skills:** | | |
| Self-awareness | • The ability to recognize and understand your moods, emotions, and drives, as well as their effect on others. | • Self-confidence<br>• Realistic self-assessment<br>• Self-deprecating sense of humor |
| Self-regulation | • The ability to control or redirect disruptive impulses and moods.<br>• The propensity to suspend judgment—to think before acting. | • Trustworthiness and integrity<br>• Comfort with ambiguity<br>• Openness to change |
| Motivation | • A passion to work for reasons that go beyond money or status.<br>• A propensity to pursue goals with energy and persistence. | • Strong drive to achieve<br>• Optimism, even in the face of failure<br>• Organizational commitment |
| **Managing relationships:** | | |
| Empathy | • The ability to understand the emotional makeup of other people.<br>• Skill in treating people according to their emotional reactions. | • Expertise in building and retaining talent<br>• Cross-cultural sensitivity<br>• Service to clients and customers |
| Social skill | • Proficiency in managing relationships and building networks.<br>• An ability to find common ground and build rapport. | • Effectiveness in leading change<br>• Persuasiveness<br>• Expertise in building and leading teams |

Source: Adapted and reprinted by permission of *Harvard Business Review*. Exhibit from "What Makes a Leader," by D. Goleman, January 2004. Copyright © 2004 by the Harvard Business School Publishing Corporation; all rights reserved.

**Exhibit 11.3**

**The Five Components of Emotional Intelligence at Work**

People generally admire and respect candor. Further, leaders are constantly required to make judgment calls that require a candid assessment of capabilities—their own and those of others. People who assess themselves honestly (i.e., self-aware people) are well suited to do the same for the organizations they run.

### Self-Regulation

Biological impulses drive our emotions. Although we cannot do away with them, we can strive to manage them. Self-regulation, which is akin to an ongoing inner conversation, frees us from being prisoners of our feelings. People engaged in such conversation feel bad moods and emotional impulses just as everyone else does. However, they find ways to control them and even channel them in useful ways.

People who are in control of their feelings and impulses are able to create an environment of trust and fairness. In such an environment, political behavior and infighting are sharply reduced and productivity tends to be high. Further, people who have mastered their emotions are better able to bring about and implement change in an organization. When a new initiative is announced, they are less likely to panic; rather, they are able to suspend judgment, seek out information, and listen to executives explain the new program.

## Motivation

Successful executives are driven to achieve beyond expectations—their own and everyone else's. They are driven to achieve. Although many people are driven by external factors, such as money and prestige, those with leadership potential are driven by a deeply embedded desire to achieve for the sake of achievement.

How can a person tell if he or she is motivated by a drive for achievement instead of external rewards? Look for a sign of passion for the work itself, such as seeking out creative challenges, a love of learning, and taking pride in a job well done. Also, motivated people have a high level of energy to do things better as well as a restlessness with the status quo. They are eager to explore new approaches to their work.

## Empathy

Empathy is probably the most easily recognized component of EI. In a business setting, empathy means thoughtfully considering an employee's feelings, along with other factors, in the process of making intelligent decisions. Empathy is particularly important in today's business environment for at least three reasons: the increasing use of teams, the rapid pace of globalization, and the growing need to retain talent.[18]

When leading a team, a manager is often charged with arriving at a consensus—often in the face of a high level of emotions. Empathy enables a manager to sense and understand the viewpoints of everyone around the table.

Globalization typically involves cross-cultural dialogue that can easily lead to miscues. Empathetic people are attuned to the subtleties of body language; they can hear the message beneath the words being spoken. In a more general sense, they have a deep understanding of the existence and importance of cultural and ethnic differences.

Empathy also plays a key role in retaining talent. As we discussed in Chapter 4, human capital is particularly important to a firm in the knowledge economy when it comes to creating advantages that are sustainable. Leaders need empathy to develop and keep top talent. Today, that's even more important, because when high performers leave, they take their tacit knowledge with them.

## Social Skill

While the first three components of emotional intelligence are all self-management skills, the last two—empathy and social skill—concern a person's ability to manage relationships with others. Social skill may be viewed as friendliness with a purpose: moving people in the direction you desire, whether that's agreement on a new marketing strategy or enthusiasm about a new product.

Socially skilled people tend to have a wide circle of acquaintances as well as a knack for finding common ground and building rapport. They recognize that nothing gets done alone, and they have a network in place when the time for action comes.

Social skill can be viewed as the culmination of the other dimensions of EI. People will be effective at managing relationships when they can understand and control their own emotions and can empathize with the feelings of others. Motivation also contributes to social skill. People who are driven to achieve tend to be optimistic, even when confronted with setbacks or failure. And when people are upbeat, their "glow" is cast upon conversations and other social encounters. They are popular, and for good reason.

# STRATEGY SPOTLIGHT

## Emotional Intelligence: Pat Croce

Every businessperson knows the story of a highly qualified, well-trained executive who was promoted to a leadership position, only to fail at the job. This is not because the executive didn't have a high IQ or sound technical fundamentals. It is about the presence or lack of *emotional intelligence*. When Pat Croce took over as the new president of the Philadelphia 76ers in May 1996, people were skeptical of his cornball style and unabashed attitude. At his national debut as the president of the 76ers, he erupted with glee as the team wound up with the number one pick at the nationally televised broadcast of the NBA's draft lottery. He leaped to his feet, pumped his fists and slapped the palms of the other team representatives. But that was not all. He then hugged David Stern, the gray-haired, tight-laced NBA commissioner, kissing him on the cheek and patting him on the sleeve of his suit jacket.

People who meet Croce on the street or at work salute him with either a high-five or a "Hey dude." Those who know him say his high energy and red-bloodedness are infectious and his vivacious style is how he exhibits the virtues of a can-do attitude and never-say-die perseverance. A self-made man, Croce founded a fitness center called the Sports Physical Therapists (SPT), successfully turned it into an 11-state chain, and eventually sold it off for $40 million in 1993.

His record as the basketball baron is no less impressive. His team was the Cinderella story of the NBA. Before he took over, the team's dismal business management and apathetic player attitudes had led to a very unimpressive record. Croce is widely credited with reinvigorating the business with his hurricane-force personality and leading the born-again team to its first chance to compete in the NBA finals in more than a decade. And for all this, Croce has but his emotional intelligence to thank. His self-awareness, motivation, and social skills make him detail-oriented and competitive—the stereotypical qualities of a successful entrepreneur.

Sources: Rosenbloom, J. 2002. Why it's Pat Croce's world. *Inc.*, April: 77–83; www.patcroce.com/NonMember/pages/index.html; and Brokaw, L. 2002. Pat Croce's bottom line. *Fast Company*, January 1: 45–47.

Strategy Spotlight 11.5 discusses Pat Croce's approach to leadership and illustrates some of the components of emotional intelligence. Croce is president of the National Basketball Association's Philadelphia 76ers.

Consider some comments from Dan Goleman, who has made many important contributions to our understanding of EI.

> It would be foolish to assert that good old-fashioned IQ and technical ability are not important ingredients to strong leadership. But the recipe would not be complete without emotional intelligence. It was once thought that the components of emotional intelligence were "nice to have" in business leaders. But now we know that, for the sake of performance, these are ingredients that leaders "need to have."
>
> It is fortunate, then, that emotional intelligence can be learned. The process is not easy. It takes time and, most of all, commitment. But the benefits that come from having a well-developed emotional intelligence, both for the individual and for the organization, make it worth the effort.[19]

### Emotional Intelligence: Some Potential Drawbacks and Cautionary Notes

Many great leaders have been found to have great reserves of empathy, interpersonal astuteness, awareness of their own feelings, and an awareness of their impact on others.[20] And, more importantly, they apply these capabilities judiciously as best benefits the situation. In essence, the key to this is self-regulation; having some minimum level of these emotional intelligences will help a person be effective as a leader as long as they are channeled appropriately. However, if a person has a high level of these capabilities it may become "too much of a good thing" if they are allowed to drive inappropriate behaviors. Let's consider two insights from experts that appeared in a 2004 *Harvard Business Review* article:[21]

> . . . there is always a danger in being preoccupied with, or overusing, one aspect of EI. For example, if you overemphasize the emotional intelligence competencies of initiative or achievement, you'll always be changing things at your company. Nobody would know what you are going to do next, which would be quite destabilizing for the organization. If you overuse empathy, you might never fire anybody. If you overuse teamwork, you might never build diversity or listen to a lone voice. Balance is essential.

> If you're extremely self-aware but short on empathy, you might come off as self-obsessed. If you're excessively empathetic, you risk being too hard to read. If you're great at self-management but not very transparent, you might seem inauthentic. Finally, at times, leaders have to deliberately avoid getting too close to the troops in order to ensure that they're seeing the bigger picture. Emotionally intelligent leaders know when to rein it in.

Some additional potential drawbacks of EI can be gleaned from the flip side of the benefits from some of its essential components.

***Effective Leaders Have Empathy for Others***   However, they also must be able to make the "tough decisions." Leaders must be able to appeal to logic and reason and acknowledge others' feelings so that people feel the decisions are correct. However, it is easy to overidentify with others or confuse empathy with sympathy. This will make it more difficult to make the tough decisions.

***Effective Leaders Are Astute Judges of People***   A danger is that leaders may become judgmental and overly critical about the shortcomings they perceive in others. They are likely to dismiss other people's insights, making them feel disrespected and undervalued.

***Effective Leaders Are Passionate about What They Do, and They Show It***   This doesn't necessarily mean that they are always cheerleaders. Rather, they may express their passion as persistence in pursuing an objective or a relentless focus on a valued principle. However, there is a fine line between being excited about something and letting your passion close your mind to other possibilities or cause you to ignore realities that others see.

***Effective Leaders Create Personal Connections with Their People***   Most effective leaders take time to engage employees individually and in groups, listening to their ideas, suggestions and concerns, and responding in ways that make people feel that their ideas are respected and appreciated. However, the downside of such visibility is that if the leader makes too many unannounced visits, it may create a culture of fear and micromanagement. Clearly, striking a correct balance is essential.

Finally, from a moral standpoint, emotional leadership is neither good nor bad. Emotional leaders can be altruistic, focused on the general welfare of the company and its employees, and highly principled. On the other hand, they can be manipulative, selfish, and dishonest. For example, if a person is using leadership solely to gain formal or informal power, that is not leadership at all.[22] Rather, they are using their EI to grasp what people want and pander to those desires in order to gain authority and influence. After all, easy answers sell.

Many people with high emotional intelligence and charisma aren't interested in asking the deeper questions, because they get so much emotional gain from the adoring crowd.[23] For them, that is the end in itself. They are satisfying their own hungers and vulnerabilities—their need to be liked, their need for power and control, or their need to be needed and to feel important—which renders them vulnerable to grandiosity. But that's not leadership. It's hunger for authority.[24]

In the next section, we will discuss some guidelines for developing a "learning organization." In today's competitive environment, the old saying about "a chain is only as strong as the weakest link" applies more than ever before. People throughout organizations must become involved in leadership processes and play greater roles in the formulation and implementation of an organization's strategies and tactics. Put another way, to learn and adapt proactively, firms need "eyes, ears, and brains" throughout all parts of the organization. One person, or a small group of individuals, can no longer think and learn for the entire entity.

## >>Developing a Learning Organization

Charles Handy, author of *The Age of Unreason* and *The Age of Paradox* and one of today's most respected business visionaries, shared an amusing story:

> The other day, a courier could not find my family's remote cottage. He called his base on his radio, and the base called us to ask directions. He was just around the corner, but his base managed to omit a vital part of the directions. So he called them again, and they called us again. Then the courier repeated the cycle a third time to ask whether we had a dangerous dog. When he eventually arrived, we asked whether it would not have been simpler and less aggravating to everyone if he had called us directly from the roadside telephone booth where he had been parked. "I can't do that," he said, "because they won't refund any money I spend." "But it's only pennies!" I exclaimed. "I know," he said, "but that only shows how little they trust us!"[25]

At first glance, it would appear that the story simply epitomizes the lack of empowerment and trust granted to the hapless courier: Don't ask questions, Do as you're told![26] However, implicit in this scenario is also the message that learning, information sharing, adaptation, decision making, and so on are *not* shared throughout the organization. In contrast to this admittedly rather extreme case, leading-edge organizations recognize the importance of having everyone involved in the process of actively learning and adapting. As noted by today's leading expert on learning organizations, MIT's Peter Senge, the days when Henry Ford, Alfred Sloan, and Tom Watson *"learned **for** the organization"* are gone.

> In an increasingly dynamic, interdependent, and unpredictable world, it is simply no longer possible for anyone to "figure it all out at the top." The old model, "the top thinks and the local acts," must now give way to integrating thinking and acting at all levels. While the challenge is great, so is the potential payoff. "The person who figures out how to harness the collective genius of the people in his or her organization," according to former Citibank CEO Walter Wriston, "is going to blow the competition away."[27]

Learning and change typically involve the ongoing questioning of an organization's status quo or method of procedure. This means that all individuals throughout the organization—not just those at the top—must reflect. Although this seems simple enough, it is easy to ignore. After all, organizations, especially successful ones, are so caught up in carrying out their day-to-day work that they rarely, if ever, stop to think objectively about themselves and their businesses. They often fail to ask the probing questions that might lead them to call into question their basic assumptions, to refresh their strategies, or to reengineer their work processes. According to Michael

Hammer and Steven Stanton, the pioneer consultants who touched off the reengineering movement:

> Reflection entails awareness of self, of competitors, of customers. It means thinking without preconception. It means questioning cherished assumptions and replacing them with new approaches. It is the only way in which a winning company can maintain its leadership position, by which a company with great assets can ensure that they continue to be well deployed.[28]

Successful learning organizations create a proactive, creative approach to the unknown, actively solicit the involvement of employees at all levels, and enable all employees to use their intelligence and apply their imagination. Higher-level skills are required of everyone, not just those at the top. A learning environment involves organizationwide commitment to change, an action orientation, and applicable tools and methods.[29] It must be viewed by everyone as a guiding philosophy and not simply as another change program that is often derisively labeled the new "flavor of the month."

A critical requirement of all learning organizations is that everyone feels and supports a compelling purpose. In the words of William O'Brien, CEO of Hanover Insurance, "Before there can be meaningful participation, people must share certain values and pictures about where we are trying to go. We discovered that people have a real need to feel that they're part of an enabling mission."[30]

Inspiring and motivating people with a mission or purpose is a necessary but not sufficient condition for developing an organization that can learn and adapt to a rapidly changing, complex, and interconnected environment. In the next four sections, we'll address four other critical ongoing processes of learning organizations:

- Empowering employees at all levels.
- Accumulating and sharing internal knowledge.
- Gathering and integrating external information.
- Challenging the status quo and enabling creativity.

## Empowering Employees at All Levels

"The great leader is a great servant," asserted Ken Melrose, CEO of Toro Company and author of *Making the Grass Greener on Your Side.*[31] A manager's role becomes one of creating an environment where employees can achieve their potential as they help move the organization toward its goals. Instead of viewing themselves as resource controllers and power brokers, leaders must truly envision themselves as flexible resources willing to assume numerous (and perhaps unaccustomed) roles as coaches, information providers, teachers, decision makers, facilitators, supporters, or listeners, depending on the needs of their employees.

The central key to empowerment is effective leadership. Empowerment can't occur in a leadership vacuum. According to Melrose, "I came to understand that you best lead by serving the needs of your people. You don't do their jobs for them; you enable them to learn and progress on the job." In their article in *Organizational Dynamics,* Robert Quinn and Gretchen Spreitzer made an interesting point regarding what may be viewed as two diametrically opposite perspectives on empowerment.[32] In the top-down perspective, empowerment is about delegation and accountability—senior management has developed a clear vision and has communicated specific plans to the rest of the organization. This strategy for empowerment encompasses the following:

- Start at the top.
- Clarify the organization's mission, vision, and values.

- Clearly specify the tasks, roles, and rewards for employees.
- Delegate responsibility.
- Hold people accountable for results.

By contrast, the bottom-up view looks at empowerment as concerned with risk taking, growth, and change. It involves trusting people to "do the right thing" and having a tolerance for failure. It encourages employees to act with a sense of ownership and typically "ask for forgiveness rather than permission." Here the salient elements of empowerment are:

- Start at the bottom by understanding the needs of employees.
- Teach employees self-management skills and model desired behavior.
- Build teams to encourage cooperative behavior.
- Encourage intelligent risk taking.
- Trust people to perform.

Clearly, these two perspectives draw a sharp contrast in assumptions that people make about trust and control. Interestingly, Quinn and Spreitzer recently shared these contrasting views of empowerment with a senior management team. After an initial heavy silence, someone from the first group voiced a concern about the second group's perspective, "We can't afford loose cannons around here." A person in the second group retorted, "When was the last time you saw a cannon of any kind around here?"

Many leading-edge organizations are moving in the direction of the second perspective—recognizing the need for trust, cultural control, and expertise (at all levels) instead of the extensive and cumbersome rules and regulations inherent in hierarchical control.[33] Some have argued that too often organizations fall prey to the "heroes-and-drones syndrome," wherein the value of those in powerful positions is exalted and the value of those who fail to achieve top rank is diminished. Such an attitude is implicit in phrases such as "Lead, follow, or get out of the way" or, even less appealing, "Unless you're the lead horse, the view never changes." Of course, few will ever reach the top hierarchical positions in organizations, but in the information economy, the strongest organizations are those that effectively use the talents of all the players on the team. Strategy Spotlight 11.6 illustrates how one company, Chaparral Steel, empowers its employees.

## Accumulating and Sharing Internal Knowledge

Effective organizations must also *redistribute information, knowledge* (i.e., skills to act on the information), and *rewards*.[34] For example, a company might give frontline employees the power to act as "customer advocates," doing whatever is necessary to please the customers. Employees, however, also need to have the appropriate training to act as businesspeople. The company needs to disseminate information by sharing customer expectations and feedback as well as financial information. The employees need to know about the goals and objectives of the business as well as how key value-creating activities in the organization are related to each other. Finally, organizations should allocate rewards on the basis of how effectively employees use information, knowledge, and power to improve customer service quality and the company's financial performance.

Jack Stack is the president and CEO of Springfield ReManufacturing Corporation (SRC) in Springfield, Missouri, and author of *The Great Game of Business*. He is generally considered the pioneer of "open book" management—an innovative way to gather and disseminate internal information. Implementing this system involves three core activities.[35] First, numbers are generated daily for each of the company's employees, reflecting his or her work performance and production costs. Second, this information is aggregated once

# STRATEGY SPOTLIGHT

## Employee Empowerment at Chaparral Steel

Managers at Chaparral Steel, a steel minimill in Midlothian, Texas, are convinced that employee ownership empowers workers to act in the best interests of the company. They believe that ownership is not composed solely of the firm's equity but also of its knowledge. By sharing financial and knowledge resources with employees, Chaparral Steel is a model of employee empowerment—90 percent of its employees own company stock and everyone is salaried, wears the same white hard hats, drinks the same free coffee, and has access to the knowledge that goes into the innovative processes at the firm's manufacturing plants.

Rather than using managers as buffers between customers and line workers, Chaparral directly involves employees with customers. Customer concerns are routed directly to the line workers responsible for manufacturing a customer's specific products. "Everyone here is part of the sales department," president and CEO Gordon Forward said. "They carry their own business cards. If they visit a customer, we want them to come back and look at their own process differently. This helps employees from all levels to view operations from the customer's perspective." Forward believes that "if a melt shop crew understands why a customer needs a particular grade of steel, it will make sure the customer gets that exact grade."

This encourages employees to think beyond traditional functional boundaries and find ways to improve the organization's processes. By integrating the customer's perspective into their efforts, employees at Chaparral Steel become more than just salaried workers; they feel responsible to the firm as if each production process was their own creation and responsibility.

Sources: Johnson, D. 1998. Catching the third wave: How to succeed in business when it's changing at the speed of light. *Futurist*, March: 32–38; Petry, C. 1997. Chaparral poised on the brink of breakthrough: Chaparral Steel developing integrated automobile shredder-separation facility. *American Metal Market*, September 10: 18; Leonard-Barton, D. 1992. The factory as a learning laboratory. *Sloan Management Review*, 34: 23–38; and TXI Chaparral Steel Midlothian registered to ISO 2002. Chaparral Steel press release, July 8, 2001.

a week and shared with all of the company's people from secretaries to top management. Third, employees receive extensive training in how to use and interpret the numbers—how to understand balance sheets as well as cash flows and income statements.

In explaining why SRC embraces open book management, Stack provided an insightful counterperspective to the old adage "Information is power."

> We are building a company in which everyone tells the truth every day—not because everyone is honest but because everyone has access to the same information: operating metrics, financial data, valuation estimates. The more people understand what's really going on in their company, the more eager they are to help solve its problems. Information isn't power. It's a burden. Share information, and you share the burdens of leadership as well.

These perspectives help to point out both the motivational and utilitarian uses of sharing company information. It can apply to organizations of all sizes. Let's look at a very small company—Leonhardt Plating Company, a $1.5 million company that makes steel plating.

> Its CEO, Daniel Leonhardt, became an accidental progressive, so to speak. Recently, instead of trying to replace his polishing foreman, he resorted to a desperate, if cutting-edge, strategy. He decided to let the polishing department rule itself by committee.
>
> The results? Revenues have risen 25 percent in the past year. After employees had access to company information such as material prices, their decisions began paying off for the whole firm. Says Leonhardt: "The workers are showing more interest in the company as a whole." Not surprisingly, he plans to introduce committee rule to other departments.[36]

Additional benefits of management sharing company information can be gleaned from a look at Whole Foods Market, Inc., the largest natural foods grocer in the United States.[37] An important benefit of the sharing of internal information at Whole Foods becomes the active process of *internal benchmarking*. Competition is intense at Whole Foods. Teams compete against their own goals for sales, growth, and productivity; they compete against different teams in their stores; and they compete against similar teams at different stores and regions. Similarly, there is an elaborate system of peer reviews through which teams benchmark each other. The "Store Tour" is the most intense. On a periodic schedule, each Whole Foods store is toured by a group of as many as 40 visitors from another region. The tour is a mix of social interaction, reviews, performance audits, and structured feedback sessions. Lateral learning—discovering what your colleagues are doing right and carrying those practices into your organization—has become a driving force at Whole Foods.

In addition to enhancing the sharing of company information both up and down as well as across the organization, leaders also have to develop means to tap into some of the more informal sources of internal information. In a recent survey of presidents, CEOs, board members, and top executives in a variety of nonprofit organizations, respondents were asked what differentiated the successful candidates for promotion. The consensus: The executive was seen as a person who listens. According to Peter Meyer, the author of the study, "The value of listening is clear: You cannot succeed in running a company if you do not hear what your people, customers, and suppliers are telling you. Poor listeners do not survive. Listening and understanding well are key to making good decisions."[38]

John Chambers, president and CEO of Cisco Systems, the networking giant, also uses an effective vehicle for getting candid feedback from employees and for discovering potential problems.[39] Every year during their birthday month, employees at Cisco's corporate headquarters in San Jose, California, receive an e-mail invitation to a "birthday breakfast" with Chambers. Each month, several dozen of the employees fire some pretty tough questions, including bruising queries about partnering strategy and stark assessments of perceived management failings. Any question is fair game, and directors and vice presidents are strongly discouraged from attending.

Although not always pleasant, Chambers believes it is an indispensable hour of unmediated interaction. At times, he finds there is inconsistency between what his executives say they are doing and what is actually happening. For example, at one quarterly meeting with 500 managers, Chambers asked how many managers required potential hires to have five interviews. When all raised their hands, he retorted, "I have a problem, because at the past three birthday breakfasts, I asked the new hires how many had interviewed that way, and only half raised their hands. You've got to fix it." His take on the birthday breakfasts: "I'm not there for the cake."

Strategy Spotlight 11.7 discusses how Intel Corporation effectively shares information through a unique mentoring program.

## Gathering and Integrating External Information

Recognizing opportunities, as well as threats, in the external environment is vital to a firm's success. Focusing exclusively on the efficiency of internal operations may result in a firm becoming, in effect, the world's most efficient producer of manual typewriters or leisure suits—hardly an enviable position! As organizations *and* environments become more complex and evolve rapidly, it is far more critical for employees and managers to become more aware of environmental trends and events—both general and industry-specific—and more knowledgeable about their firm's competitors and customers. Next, we will discuss some ideas on how to do it.

First, the Internet has dramatically accelerated the speed with which anyone can track down useful information or locate people who might have useful information. Prior to the Net, locating someone who used to work at a company—always a good source of

## Information Sharing through Mentoring Relationships at Intel

Intel veteran Ann Otero seems to be an unlikely mentor. She is neither a star engineer nor a fast-track sales executive. She has, however, been with the company for the past 12 years and is currently a senior administrative assistant. Ann is part of Intel's new wedge—an innovative new mentoring movement that matches people not by job title or years of service but by specific skills that are in demand. The program uses an intranet-based questionnaire to match partners with the right mentor, creating relationships that stretch across state lines and national boundaries. The system works by having potential mentors list their top skills at Circuit, Intel's internal employee site. Partners click on topics they want to master, then an algorithm computes all of the variables and the database

hashes out a list of possible matches. Once a match is made, an automatic e-mail goes to the mentor asking her to set up a time to meet and talk. The mentor and partner learn and follow some simple guidelines:

1. The partner controls the relationship.

2. A mentoring contract is drawn up about what needs to be accomplished by the end of the mentoring.

3. Both the partner and the mentor decide what to talk about.

Unlike many corporations, Intel does not use its mentoring for career advancement. Its style is all about learning and sharing the knowledge pool of someone whom you have probably never met.

Sources: www.intel.com/jobs/news/news.htm; Warner, F. 2002. Inside Intel's mentoring movement. *Fast Company*, April: 67–69.

---

information—was quite a challenge. However, today people post their résumés on the Web; they participate in discussion groups and talk openly about where they work. It is pretty straightforward.

An example of the effective use of the Internet is provided by Marc Friedman, manager of market research at Andrew Corporation, a fast-growing manufacturer of wireless communications products with annual revenues of nearly $1 billion.[40] One of Friedman's preferred sites to visit is Corptech's Web site, which provides information on 45,000 high-tech companies and more than 170,000 executives. One of his firm's product lines consisted of antennae for air-traffic control systems. He got a request to provide a country-by-country breakdown of upgrade plans for various airports. Although he knew nothing about air-traffic control at the time, he found a site on the Internet for the International Civil Aviation Organization. Fortunately, it had a great deal of useful data, including several research companies working in his area of interest.

Second, in addition to the Internet, company employees at all levels can use "garden variety" traditional sources to acquire external information. Much can be gleaned by reading trade and professional journals, books, and popular business magazines such as *BusinessWeek, Forbes, Fortune,* and *Fast Company.* (Some professional journals might have an extremely narrow focus and, while they could prove to be very useful, they are not fireside reading for the general public.) Other venues for gathering external information include membership in professional or trade organizations and attendance at meetings and conventions. Networking among colleagues inside and outside of your industry is also very useful. Intel's Andy Grove, for example, gathers information from people like DreamWorks SKG's Steven Spielberg and Tele-Communications Inc.'s John Malone.[41] He believes that such interaction provides insights into how to make personal computers more entertaining and better at communicating. Internally, Grove spends time with the young "propeller-heads" who run Intel Architecture labs, an Oregon-based facility that Grove hopes will become the de facto R&D lab for the entire PC industry.

Third, benchmarking can be a useful means of employing external information. Here managers seek out the best examples of a particular practice as part of an ongoing effort to improve the corresponding practice in their own organization.[42] There are two primary types of benchmarking. *Competitive benchmarking* restricts the search for best practices to competitors, while *functional benchmarking* endeavors to determine best practices regardless of industry. Industry-specific standards (e.g., response times required to repair power outages in the electric utility industry) are typically best handled through competitive benchmarking, whereas more generic processes (e.g., answering 1-800 calls) lend themselves to functional benchmarking because the function is essentially the same in any industry.

Ford Motor Company benefited from benchmarking by studying Mazda's accounts payable operations.[43] Its initial goal of a 20 percent cut in its 500-employee accounts payable staff was ratcheted up to 75 percent—and met. Ford's benchmarkers found that staff spent most of their time trying to match often conflicting data in a mass of paper, including purchase orders, invoices, and receipts. Following Mazda's example, Ford created an "invoiceless system" in which invoices no longer trigger payments to suppliers. The receipt does the job.

Fourth, focus directly on customers for information. For example, William McKnight, head of 3M's Chicago sales office, required that salesmen of abrasives products talk directly to the workers in the shop to find out what they needed, instead of calling on only front-office executives.[44] This was very innovative at the time—1909! But it illustrates the need to get to the end user of a product or service. (McKnight went on to become 3M's president from 1929 to 1949 and chairman from 1949 to 1969.) More recently, James Taylor, senior vice president for global marketing at Gateway 2000, discussed the value of customer input in reducing response time, a critical success factor in the PC industry.

> We talk to 100,000 people a day—people calling to order a computer, shopping around, looking for tech support. Our Web site gets 1.1 million hits per day. The time it takes for an idea to enter this organization, get processed, and then go to customers for feedback is down to minutes. We've designed the company around speed and feedback.[45]

## Challenging the Status Quo and Enabling Creativity

Earlier in this chapter we discussed some of the barriers that leaders face when trying to bring about change in an organization. These included vested interests in the status quo, systemic barriers, behavioral barriers, political barriers, and personal time constraints. For a firm to become a "learning organization," it must overcome such barriers in order to foster creativity and enable it to permeate the firm. This becomes quite a challenge, of course, if the firm is entrenched in a status quo mentality.

Perhaps the primary means to directly challenge the status quo is for the leader to forcefully create a sense of urgency. For example, Tom Kasten, vice president of Levi Strauss, has a direct approach to initiating change. He is charged with leading the campaign to transform the company for the 21st century.

> You create a compelling picture of the risks of *not* changing. We let our people hear directly from customers. We videotaped interviews with customers and played excerpts. One big customer said, "We trust many of your competitors implicitly. We sample their deliveries. We open *all* Levi's deliveries." Another said, "Your lead times are the worst. If you weren't Levi's, you'd be gone." It was powerful. I wish we had done more of it.[46]

Such initiative—if sincere and credible—establishes a shared mission and the need for major transformations. If effective, it can channel energies to bring about both change and creative endeavors.

Establishing a "culture of dissent" can be another effective means of questioning the status quo and serving as a spur toward creativity. Here norms are established whereby dissenters can openly question a superior's perspective without fear of retaliation or retribution. Consider the perspective of Steven Balmer, Microsoft's CEO.

> Bill [Gates] brings to the company the idea that conflict can be a good thing. . . . Bill knows it's important to avoid that gentle civility that keeps you from getting to the heart of an issue quickly. He likes it when anyone, even a junior employee, challenges him, and you know he respects you when he starts shouting back.[47]

Motorola has, in effect, gone a step further and institutionalized its culture of dissent.[48] By filing a "minority report," an employee can go above his or her immediate supervisor's head and officially lodge a different point of view on a business decision. According to former CEO George Fisher, "I'd call it a healthy spirit of discontent and a freedom by and large to express your discontent around here or to disagree with whoever it is in the company, me or anybody else."

Closely related to the culture of dissent is the fostering of a culture that encourages risk taking. "If you're not making mistakes, you're not taking risks, and that means you're not going anywhere," claimed John Holt, coauthor of *Celebrate Your Mistakes.*[49] "The key is to make errors faster than the competition, so you have more chances to learn and win."

Companies that cultivate cultures of experimentation and curiosity make sure that *failure* is not, in essence, an obscene word. People who stretch the envelope and ruffle feathers are protected. More importantly, they encourage mistakes as a key part of their competitive advantage. Wood Dickinson, CEO of the Kansas City–based Dickinson movie theater chain, told his property managers that he wanted to see them committing "intelligent failures in the pursuit of service excellence."[50] This philosophy was shared by Stan Shih, CEO of Acer, a Taiwan-based computer company. If a manager at Acer took an intelligent risk and made a mistake—even a costly one—Shih wrote off the loss as tuition payment for the manager's education. Such a culture must permeate the entire organization. As a high-tech executive told us during an interview: "Every person has a freedom to fail."

Strategy Spotlight 11.8 provides examples of how failures led to highly successful innovations.

## >>Creating an Ethical Organization

What is ethics?[51] Ethics may be defined as a system of right and wrong. Ethics assists individuals in deciding when an act is moral or immoral, socially desirable or not. There are many sources for an individual's ethics. These include religious beliefs, national and ethnic heritage, family practices, community standards and expectations, educational experiences, and friends and neighbors. Business ethics is the application of ethical standards to commercial enterprise.

### Individual Ethics versus Organizational Ethics

Many leaders may think of ethics as a question of personal scruples, a confidential matter between employees and their consciences. Such leaders are quick to describe any wrongdoing as an isolated incident, the work of a rogue employee. They assume the company should not bear any responsibility for an individual's misdeeds—it may not ever even enter their minds. After all, in their view, ethics has nothing to do with leadership.

In fact, ethics has everything to do with leadership. Seldom does the character flaw of a lone actor completely explain corporate misconduct. Instead, unethical business practices typically involve the tacit, if not explicit, cooperation of others and reflect the values,

Experimentation can often fail. At times, such failures can be the seeds that lead to very successful products. As the famous writer James Joyce once said, "Mistakes are the portals for discovery." Below, we summarize three failures that evolved into remarkable innovations.

W. L. Gore & Associates is the well-known company that produces such innovative products as Gore-Tex, the material that is used in many outdoor clothing products to help keep out moisture, and Glide, a dental floss. It also has become the second-leading manufacturer in the $100 million stringed-instrument business—largely as the result of a failed product.

In 1997, a team at Gore was testing a material for the cables that control puppets at Disney's theme parks. The prototype failed. But it was the beginning of a successful product. "We gave it to guitar players to try out, and they were amazed that it didn't go dead," explains Steve Young, who now heads Gore's Elixir business.

It turned out that Gore's strings lasted up to five times longer than most others then available. However, they cost twice as much. How did they market the new product? Gore went straight to the musicians. It bought magazine subscriber lists and showed up at festivals, giving out

samples and building some buzz. It hired musically trained sales reps to develop relationships with retailers and got Taylor Guitars, a leading acoustical manufacturer, to install Elixir on all of its guitars. Today, Elixir Strings are sold by more than half the music stores in the United States.

Rubber shortages during World War II prompted the U.S. government to try to develop a synthetic rubber. It seemed to make sense to make this substitute out of something that was very plentiful. Silicone seemed to be the logical solution. An inventor at General Electric added a little boric acid to silicone oil and developed a gooey, bouncy substance.

Although the substance failed as a substitute for rubber, after the war it became a very popular toy—Silly Putty. Apollo 8 astronauts later used it to stabilize their tools in zero gravity. (The astronauts carried their Silly Putty in sterling silver eggs.) Today Binney & Smith produces about 20,000 eggs' worth of Silly Putty a day.

Wilson Greatbatch, a medical researcher, was working on a device to record irregular heartbeats. He accidentally inserted a resistor of the wrong size and he noticed that the circuit pulsed, stopped, and pulsed again—just like a human heart. After two years of tinkering, Greatbatch developed the first implantable pacemaker. He later invented a corrosion-free lithium battery to power it. Millions have benefited from his efforts.

Sources: Sacks, D. 2003. The Gore-Tex of guitar strings. *Fast Company,* December: 46; Jones, C. 1994. *Mistakes that worked.* New York: Random House; and Brokenbrough, M. 2005. *The greatest mistakes of all time.* encarta. msn.com, January 8: np.

attitudes, and behavior patterns that define an organization's operating culture. Clearly, ethics is as much an organizational as a personal issue. Leaders who fail to provide proper leadership to institute proper systems and controls that facilitate ethical conduct share responsibility with those who conceive, execute, and knowingly benefit from corporate misdeeds.

The ethical orientation of a leader is generally considered to be a key factor in promoting ethical behavior among employees. Ethical leaders must take personal, ethical responsibility for their actions and decision making. Leaders who exhibit high ethical standards become role models for others in the organization and raise its overall level of ethical behavior. In essence, ethical behavior must start with the leader before the employees can be expected to perform accordingly.

Over the last few decades, there has been a growing interest in corporate ethical performance. Perhaps some reasons for this trend may be the increasing lack of confidence regarding corporate activities, the growing emphasis on quality of life issues, and a spate of recent corporate scandals at such firms as Enron and Tyco. Clearly, concerns about protecting the environment, fair employment practices, and the distribution of unsafe products have served to create powerful regulatory agencies such as the Environmental Protection Agency, the Equal Opportunity Commission, and the Federal Drug Administration. Recently, however, other concerns are becoming salient, such as problems associated with fetal tissue for research, disproportionate executive pay levels, corporate crises such as the Firestone/Ford Explorer tire fiasco, race debacles at Texaco and at Denny's Restaurants, the *Exxon Valdez* oil spill, and the practices of major financial services institutions in the wake of the dot-com crash. Merely adhering to the minimum regulatory standards may not be enough to remain competitive in a world that is becoming more socially conscious.

Without a strong ethical culture, the chance of ethical crises occurring is enhanced. Ethical crises can be very expensive—both in terms of financial costs and in the erosion of human capital and overall firm reputation. Consider, for example, Texaco's class-action discrimination lawsuit.

> In 1994 a senior financial analyst, Bari-Ellen Roberts, and one of her co-workers, Sil Chambers, filed a class-action discrimination suit against Texaco after enduring racial slurs and being passed over for promotion on several occasions. The discrimination suit charged Texaco with using an "old boys network" to systematically discriminate against African Americans.
>
> Roberts remembers, "The hardest part of the suit was deciding to do it. I'd worked so hard to get where I was, and I had to risk all of that. Then I had to deal with loneliness and isolation. Even some of the other African Americans viewed me as a troublemaker. When you're standing up and calling for change, it makes people fear for their own security."
>
> Two years later, in 1996, Texaco settled the suit, paying $141 million to its African-American workers. This was followed with an additional $35 million to remove discriminatory practices.[52]

Please note that the financial cost alone of $176 million was certainly not the proverbial "drop in the bucket." This amount represented nearly 10 percent of Texaco Inc.'s entire net income for 1996.

As we are all aware, the past several years have been characterized by numerous examples of unethical and illegal behavior by many top-level corporate executives. These include executives of firms such as Enron, Tyco, Worldcom, Inc., Adelphia, and Healthsouth Corp., who were all forced to resign and are facing (or have been convicted of) criminal charges. Exhibit 11.4 briefly summarizes the unethical and/or illegal activities of other well-known corporate leaders.

The ethical organization is characterized by a conception of ethical values and integrity as a driving force of the enterprise.[53] Ethical values shape the search for opportunities, the design of organizational systems, and the decision-making process used by individuals and groups. They provide a common frame of reference that serves as a unifying force across different functions, lines of business, and employee groups. Organizational ethics helps to define what a company is and what it stands for.

There are many potential benefits of an ethical organization, but they are often indirect. The research literature in organizational behavior has found somewhat inconsistent results concerning the overall relationship between ethical performance and measures of financial performance.[54] However, positive relationships have generally been found between ethical performance and strong organizational culture, increased employee efforts, lower turnover, higher organizational commitment, and enhanced social responsibility.

Clearly, the advantages of a strong ethical orientation can have a positive effect on employee commitment and motivation to excel. This is particularly important in today's knowledge-intensive organizations, where human capital is critical in creating value and competitive advantages. As we discussed in Chapter 4, positive, constructive relationships among individuals (i.e., social capital) are vital in leveraging human capital and other resources in an organization. However, there are many other potential benefits as well. Drawing on the concept of stakeholder management that we discussed in Chapter 1, an ethically sound organization can also strengthen its bonds among its suppliers,

**Exhibit 11.4**

**Unethical and Illegal Behavior by Top-Level Corporate Executives**

| | |
|---|---|
| Martha Stewart, CEO Martha Stewart Living Omnimedia | In December 2001, Stewart sold over one-quarter million dollars' worth of ImClone Systems stock prior to the stock's subsequent plunge. Her defense claimed that she had discussed selling the large sum of stock since the stock had dropped below $60 per share. However, it was later revealed that she and her broker were guilty of insider trading based on inside information from ImClone Systems' CEO Sam Waksal (who also was found guilty of the same felony and is now serving six years in a Pennsylvania prison camp). On July 16, 2004, Stewart was sentenced to five months in federal prison and five months house arrest and was fined $30,000. |
| Harry C. Stonecipher, CEO Boeing Co. | There are ethical dilemmas, of course, that fall outside the more recent focus on corrupt financial behavior. Boeing's Stonecipher engaged in an extramarital affair with fellow executive, Deborah Peabody. This raised a particularly difficult decision for Boeing's board of directors. In only 15 months on the job, Stonecipher had helped the company recover from ethical credibility problems created by a Pentagon scandal that landed two of its executives in prison. During Stonecipher's brief time at the top, the company's market valuation had climbed 50 percent. On February 28, 2005, Boeing's board requested that he cease his relationship with Peabody. The 68-year-old Stonecipher, ignoring the shareholder consequences of his questionable image, declined this request. The board responded with a demand for his resignation. |
| Maurice Greenberg, CEO American Insurance Group (AIG) | The Greenberg family may show that unethical behavior can be hereditary. In September 2004, New York Attorney General Eliot Spitzer insisted that the son of AIG's CEO Maurice "Hank" Greenberg, Jeffrey Greenberg, CEO of the world's largest insurance broker, Marsh & McLennan, resign due to account fixing and bid rigging charges. In Marsh's case, the defense attempted to plead that Jeffrey Greenberg "did not understand how the insurance business operated." In November 2004, AIG paid an $80 million fine to the U.S. Department of Justice to settle complaints concerning the crooked sale of insurance products. In April 2005, AIG's board requested that Maurice Greenberg, 79, step down from his position in the face of similar scandals associated with rigging bids of nontraditional insurance products that were pitched to the heads of other companies. |

Sources: Kahn, J. 2004. Why CEOs should hope Martha walks. *Fortune,* February 9: 24–25; Sellers, P. 2004. Why Martha may choose jail now. *Fortune,* August 9: 36; Revell, J. 2004. Martha gets 5 to 20; Investors get life. *Fortune,* March 22: 40; Holmes, S. 2005. Why Boeing's culture breeds turmoil. *BusinessWeek,* March 21: 34–36; Henry, D., France, M., & Lavelle, Louis. 2005. The boss on the sidelines. April 25: 86–96; Elkind, P., & Devin, L. 2005. More bad news for AIG's Greenberg? *Fortune,* March 7: 28; Condon, B., & Coolidge, C. 2005. When gray becomes black-and-white. *Forbes,* May 9: 90–92; and http://www.insurancejournal.com/news/national/2004/10/15/46937.htm.

# STRATEGY SPOTLIGHT

## Procter & Gamble: Using Ethics to "Build the Spirit of the Place"

John Pepper, former CEO and chairman of Procter & Gamble Company, shares his perspective on ethics.

Let me start by saying that while ethics may seem like a soft concept—not as hard, say, as strategy or budgeting or operations—it is, in fact, a very hard concept. It is tangible. It is crucial . . . it is good for business.

There are several reasons for this. First, a company's values have a tremendous impact on who is attracted to your company and who will stay with it. We only have one life to live. All of us want to live it as part of an institution committed to high goals and high-sighted means of reaching these goals. This is true everywhere I've been. In our most mature countries and our newest.

Strong corporate values greatly simplify decision making. It is important to know the things you won't even think about doing. Diluting a product. Paying a bribe. Not being fair to a customer or an employee.

Strong values earn the respect of customers and suppliers and governments and other companies, too. This is absolutely crucial over the long term.

A company which pays bribes in a foreign market becomes an open target for more bribes when the word gets out. It never stops.

A company which is seen to be offering different trade terms to different customers based on how big they are or how hard they push will forever be beset by requests for special terms.

A company which is seen by a government as having weak or varying standards will not be respected by that government.

And more positively, governments and other companies really do want to deal with companies they feel are pursuing sound values because in many, if not most, cases, they believe it will be good for them.

One final but very fundamental reason for operating ethically is that strong values create trust and pride among employees. Simply put, they build the spirit of the place.

Source: Pepper, J. E. 1997. The boa principle: Operating ethically in today's business environment. Speech presented at Florida A&M University, Tallahassee, January 30.

---

customers, and governmental agencies. John E. Pepper, former chairman of Procter & Gamble, addresses such a perspective in Strategy Spotlight 11.9.

## Integrity-Based versus Compliance-Based Approaches to Organizational Ethics

Before discussing the key elements for building an ethical organization, it is important to understand the essential links between organizational integrity and the personal integrity of an organization's members.[55] There cannot be high-integrity organizations without high-integrity individuals. At the same time, individual integrity is rarely self-sustaining. Even good people can lose their bearings when faced with pressures, temptations, and heightened performance expectations in the absence of organizational support systems and ethical boundaries. Organizational integrity, on the other hand, is beyond personal integrity. It rests on a concept of purpose, responsibility, and ideals for an organization as a whole. An important responsibility of leadership in building organizational integrity is to create this ethical framework and develop the organizational capabilities to make it operational.

It is also important to know the approaches or strategies organizations take in dealing with ethics. Lynn Paine, a researcher at Harvard, identifies two such approaches: the compliance-based approach and the integrity-based approach. (See Exhibit 11.5 for a comparison of compliance-based and integrity-based strategies.) Faced with the prospect of litigation, several organizations reactively implement compliance-based ethics programs. Such programs are typically designed by a corporate counsel with the goal of preventing, detecting, and punishing legal violations. But being ethical is much more

| Characteristics | Compliance-Based Approach | Integrity-Based Approach |
|---|---|---|
| Ethos | Conformity with externally imposed standards | Self-governance according to chosen standards |
| Objective | Prevent criminal misconduct | Enable responsible conduct |
| Leadership | Lawyer-driven | Management-driven with aid of lawyers, HR, and others |
| Methods | Education, reduced discretion, auditing and controls, penalties | Education, leadership, accountability, organizational systems and decision processes, auditing and controls, penalties |
| Behavioral Assumptions | Autonomous beings guided by material self-interest | Social beings guided by material self-interest, values, ideals, peers |

Source: Paine, L. S. 1994. Managing for organizational integrity. *Harvard Business Review,* 72(2): 113 (with permission).

**Exhibit 11.5**
**Approaches to Ethics Management**

than being legal, and an integrity-based approach addresses the issue of ethics in a more comprehensive manner.

An integrity-based approach to ethics management combines a concern for law with an emphasis on managerial responsibility for ethical behavior. This approach is broader, deeper, and more demanding than a legal compliance initiative. It is broader in that it seeks to enable responsible conduct. It is deeper in that it cuts to the ethos and operating systems of an organization and its members, their core guiding values, thoughts, and actions. And it is more demanding because it requires an active effort to define the responsibilities and aspirations that constitute an organization's ethical compass. Most importantly, in this approach, organizational ethics is seen as the work of management. A corporate counsel may play a role in designing and implementing integrity strategies, but it is managers at all levels and across all functions that are involved in the process. Once integrated into the day-to-day operations of an organization, such strategies can help prevent damaging ethical lapses, while tapping into powerful human impulses for moral thought and action. Ethics then become the governing ethos of an organization and not burdensome constraints to be adhered to. Here is an example of an organization that goes beyond mere compliance to laws in building an ethical organization:

> In teaching ethics to its employees, Texas Instruments, the $8 billion chip and electronics manufacturer, asks them to run an issue through the following steps: Is it legal? Is it consistent with the company's stated values? Will the employee feel bad doing it? What will the public think if the action is reported in the press? Does the employee think it is wrong? Further, if the employees are not sure of the ethicality of the issue, they are encouraged to ask someone until they are clear about it. In the process, employees can approach high-level personnel and even the company's lawyers. As can be clearly noted, at Texas Instruments, the question of ethics goes much beyond merely being legal. It is no surprise, therefore, that this company is a benchmark for corporate ethics and has been a recipient of three ethics awards: the David C. Lincoln Award for Ethics and Excellence in Business, American Business Ethics Award, and Bentley College Center for Business Ethics Award.[56]

To sum up, compliance-based approaches are externally motivated—that is, based on the fear of punishment for doing something unlawful. On the other hand, integrity-based approaches are driven by a personal and organizational commitment to ethical behavior.

A firm must have several key elements before it can become a highly ethical organization. These elements must be both present and constantly reinforced in order for the firm to be successful:

- Role models.
- Corporate credos and codes of conduct.
- Reward and evaluation systems.
- Policies and procedures.

These elements are highly interrelated. For example, reward structures and policies will be useless if leaders throughout the organization are not sound role models. That is, leaders who implicitly say, "Do as I say, not as I do," will quickly have their credibility eroded and such actions will, in effect, sabotage other elements that are essential to building an ethical organization.

## Role Models

For good or for bad, leaders are role models in their organizations. As we noted in Chapter 9, leaders must "walk the talk"; that is, they must be consistent in their words and deeds. The values as well as the character of leaders become transparent to an organization's employees through their behaviors. In addition, when leaders do not believe in the ethical standards that they are trying to inspire, they will not be effective as good role models. Being an effective leader often includes taking responsibility for ethical lapses within the organization—even though the executives themselves are not directly involved. Consider, for example, the perspective of Dennis Bakke, CEO of AES, the $8 billion global electricity company based in Arlington, Virginia.

> There was a major breach (in 1992) of the AES values. Nine members of the water treatment team in Oklahoma lied to the EPA about water quality at the plant. There was no environmental damage, but they lied about the test results. A new, young chemist at the plant discovered it, and she told a team leader, and, of course, we then were notified. Now, you could argue that the people who lied were responsible and were accountable, but the senior management team also took responsibility by taking pay cuts. My reduction was about 30 percent.[57]

Such action enhances the loyalty and commitment of employees throughout the organization. Many would believe that it would have been much easier (and personally less expensive!) for Bakke and his management team to merely take strong punitive action against the nine individuals who were acting contrary to the behavior expected in AES's ethical culture. However, by taking responsibility for the misdeeds, the top executives—through their highly visible action—made it very clear that responsibility and penalties for ethical lapses go well beyond the "guilty" parties. Such courageous behavior by leaders helps to strengthen an organization's ethical environment.

## Corporate Credos and Codes of Conduct

Corporate credos or codes of conduct are another important element of an ethical organization. Such mechanisms provide a statement and guidelines for norms and beliefs as well as guidelines for decision making. They provide employees with a clear understanding of the organization's position regarding employee behavior. Such guidelines also provide the basis for employees to refuse to commit unethical acts and help to make them aware of issues before they are faced with the situation. For such codes to be truly effective, organization members must be aware of them and what behavioral guidelines they contain.[58]

Large corporations are not the only ones to develop and use codes of conduct. Consider the example of Wetherill Associates (WAI), a small, privately held supplier of electrical parts to the automotive market.

> Rather than a conventional code of conduct, WAI has a Quality Assurance Manual—a combination of philosophy text, conduct guide, technical manual, and company profile—that describes the company's commitment to honesty, ethical action, and integrity.
>
> Interestingly, WAI doesn't have a corporate ethics officer, because the company's corporate ethics officer is top management. Marie Bothe, WAI's chief executive officer, sees her main function as keeping the 350-employee company on the path of ethical behavior and looking for opportunities to help the community. She delegates the "technical" aspects of the business—marketing, finance, personnel, and operations—to other members of the organization.[59]

Perhaps the best-known credo, a statement describing a firm's commitment to certain standards, is that of Johnson & Johnson (J&J). It is reprinted in Exhibit 11.6. The credo stresses honesty, integrity, superior products, and putting people before profits. What

**Exhibit 11.6**

**Johnson & Johnson's Credo**

We believe our first responsibility is to the doctors, nurses and patients, to mothers and fathers and all others who use our products and services. In meeting their needs everything we do must be of high quality. We must constantly strive to reduce our costs in order to maintain reasonable prices. Customers' orders must be serviced promptly and accurately. Our suppliers and distributors must have an opportunity to make a fair profit.

We are responsible to our employees, the men and women who work with us throughout the world. Everyone must be considered as an individual. We must respect their dignity and recognize their merit. They must have a sense of security in their jobs. Compensation must be fair and adequate, and working conditions clean, orderly, and safe. We must be mindful of ways to help our employees fulfill their family responsibilities. Employees must feel free to make suggestions and complaints. There must be equal opportunity for employment, development, and advancement for those qualified. We must provide competent management, and their actions must be just and ethical.

We are responsible to the communities in which we live and work and to the world community as well. We must be good citizens—support good works and charities and bear our fair share of taxes. We must encourage civic improvements and better health and education. We must maintain in good order the property we are privileged to use, protecting the environment and natural resources.

Our final responsibility is to our stockholders. Business must make a sound profit. We must experiment with new ideas. Research must be carried on, innovative programs developed, and mistakes paid for. New equipment must be purchased, new facilities provided, and new products launched. Reserves must be created to provide for adverse times. When we operate according to these principles, the stockholders should realize a fair return.

Source: Reprinted with permission of Johnson & Johnson Co.

distinguishes the J&J credo from those of other firms is the amount of energy the company's top managers devote to ensuring that employees live by its precepts.

Over a three-year period, Johnson & Johnson undertook a massive effort to assure that its original credo, already decades old, was still valid. More than 1,200 managers attended two-day seminars in groups of 25, with explicit instructions to challenge the credo. The president or CEO of the firm personally presided over each session. In the end, the company came out of the process believing that its original document was still valid. However, the questioning process continues. Such "challenge meetings" are still replicated every other year for all new managers. These efforts force J&J to question, internalize, and then implement its credo. Such investments have paid off handsomely many times—most notably in 1982, when eight people died from swallowing capsules of Tylenol, one of its flagship products, that someone had laced with cyanide. Leaders such as James Burke, who without hesitation made an across-the-board recall of the product even though it affected only a limited number of untraceable units, send a strong message throughout their organization.

## Reward and Evaluation Systems

It is entirely possible for a highly ethical leader to preside over an organization that commits several unethical acts. How? It may reflect a flaw in the organization's reward structure. A reward and evaluation system may inadvertently cause individuals to act in an inappropriate manner if rewards are seen as being distributed on the basis of outcomes instead of the means by which goals and objectives are achieved.[60]

Consider the example of Sears, Roebuck & Co.'s automotive operations. Here, unethical behavior, rooted in a faulty reward system, took place primarily at the operations level: its automobile repair facilities.[61]

> In 1992 Sears was flooded with complaints about its automotive service business. Consumers and attorneys general in more than 40 states accused the firm of misleading customers and selling them unnecessary parts and services, from brake jobs to front-end alignments. What were the causes?
>
> In the face of declining revenues and eroding market share, Sears's management attempted to spur the performance of its auto centers by introducing new goals and incentives for mechanics. Automotive service advisers were given product-specific quotas for a variety of parts and repairs. Failure to meet the quotas could lead to transfers and reduced hours. Many employees spoke of "pressure, pressure, pressure" to bring in sales.
>
> Not too surprisingly, the judgment of many employees suffered. In essence, employees were left to chart their own course, given the lack of management guidance and customer ignorance. The bottom line: In settling the spate of lawsuits, Sears offered coupons to customers who had purchased certain auto services over the most recent two-year period. The total cost of the settlement, including potential customer refunds, was estimated to be $60 million. The cost in terms of damaged reputation? Difficult to assess, but certainly not trivial.

The Sears automotive example makes two important points. First, inappropriate reward systems may cause individuals at all levels throughout an organization to commit unethical acts that they might not otherwise commit. Second, the penalties in terms of damage to reputations, human capital erosion, and financial loss—in the short run and long run—are typically much higher than any gains that could be obtained through such unethical behavior.

## Policies and Procedures

Many situations that a firm faces have regular, identifiable patterns. Typically, leaders tend to handle such routine by establishing a policy or procedure to be followed that can

# STRATEGY SPOTLIGHT 11.10

## No More Whistleblowing Woes!

The landmark Sarbanes-Oxley Act of 2002 gives those who expose corporate misconduct strong legal protection. Henceforth, an executive who retaliates against the corporate whistleblower can be held criminally liable and imprisoned for up to 10 years. That's the same sentence a mafia don gets for threatening a witness. The Labor Department can order a company to rehire an employee without going to court. If the fired workers feel their case is moving too slowly, they can request a federal jury after six months.

Companies need to revisit their current policies, including nondisclosure pacts. They may no longer be able to enforce rules requiring employees to get permission to speak to the media or lawyers. Even layoffs should be planned in advance, lest they seem retaliatory.

Sources: www.sarbanes-oxley.com/pcaob.php/level=2&pub_id=Sarbanes-Oxley&chap_id=PCAOB11; Dwyer, P., Carney, D., Borrus, A., Woellert, L., & Palmeri, C. 2002. Year of the WhistleBlower. *BusinessWeek*, December 16: 107–109; and www.buchalter.com/FSL5CS/articles/articles204.asp.

Employees of publicly traded companies are now the most protected whistleblowers. Provisions coauthored by Senator Grassley in the Sarbanes-Oxley corporate-reform law:

- Make it unlawful to "discharge, demote, suspend or threaten, harass, or in any manner discriminate against" a whistleblower.

- Establish criminal penalties of up to 10 years in jail for executives who retaliate against whistleblowers.

- Require board audit committees to establish procedures for hearing whistleblower complaints.

- Allow the secretary of labor to order a company to rehire a terminated whistleblower with no court hearings whatsoever.

- Give a whistleblower a right to jury trial, bypassing months or years of cumbersome administrative hearings.

be applied rather uniformly to each occurrence. As we noted in Chapter 9, such guidelines can be useful in specifying the proper relationships with a firm's customers and suppliers. For example, Levi Strauss has developed stringent global sourcing guidelines and Chemical Bank (now part of J. P. Morgan Chase Bank) has a policy of forbidding any review that would determine whether or not suppliers are Chemical customers when the bank awards contracts.

Clearly, it is important to carefully develop policies and procedures to guide behavior so that all employees will be encouraged to behave in an ethical manner. However, it is not enough merely to have policies and procedures "on the books." Rather, they must be reinforced with effective communication, enforcement, and monitoring, as well as sound corporate governance practices. Strategy Spotlight 11.10 describes how the recently enacted Sarbanes-Oxley Act provides considerable legal protection to employees of publicly traded companies who report unethical or illegal practices.

## Summary

Strategic leadership is vital in ensuring that strategies are formulated and implemented in an effective manner. Leaders must play a central role in performing three critical and interdependent activities: setting the direction, designing the organization, and nurturing a culture committed to excellence and ethical behavior. In the chapter we provided the imagery of these three activities as a "three-legged stool." If leaders ignore or are ineffective at performing any one of the three, the organization will not be very successful. Leaders must also use power effectively to overcome barriers to change.

For leaders to effectively fulfill their activities, emotional intelligence (EI) is very important. Five elements that contribute to EI are self-awareness, self-regulation, motivation, empathy, and social skill. The first three elements pertain to self-management skills, whereas the last two are associated with a person's ability to manage relationships with others. We also addressed some of the potential drawbacks from the ineffective use of EI. These include the dysfunctional use of power as well as a tendency to become overly empathetic, which may result in unreasonably lowered performance expectations.

Leaders must also play a central role in creating a learning organization. Gone are the days when the top-level managers "think" and everyone else in the organization "does." With the rapidly changing, unpredictable, and complex competitive environments that characterize most industries, leaders must engage everyone in the ideas and energies of people throughout the organization. Great ideas can come from anywhere in the organization—from the executive suite to the factory floor. The five elements that we discussed as central to a learning organization are inspiring and motivating people with a mission or purpose, empowering people at all levels throughout the organization, accumulating and sharing internal knowledge, gathering external information, and challenging the status quo to stimulate creativity.

In the final section of the chapter, we addressed a leader's central role in instilling ethical behavior in the organization. We discussed the enormous costs that firms face when ethical crises arise—costs in terms of financial and reputational loss as well as the erosion of human capital and relationships with suppliers, customers, society at large, and governmental agencies. And, as we would expect, the benefits of having a strong ethical organization are also numerous. We contrasted compliance-based and integrity-based approaches to organizational ethics. Compliance-based approaches are largely externally motivated; that is, they are motivated by the fear of punishment for doing something that is unlawful. Integrity-based approaches, on the other hand, are driven by a personal and organizational commitment to ethical behavior. We also addressed the four key elements of an ethical organization: role models, corporate credos and codes of conduct, reward and evaluation systems, and policies and procedures.

## Summary Review Questions

1. Three key activities—setting a direction, designing the organization, and nurturing a culture and ethics—are all part of what effective leaders do on a regular basis. Explain how these three activities are interrelated.

2. Define emotional intelligence (EI). What are the key elements of EI? Why is EI so important to successful strategic leadership?

3. The knowledge a firm possesses can be a source of competitive advantage. Describe ways that a firm can continuously learn to maintain its competitive position.

4. How can the five central elements of "learning organizations" be incorporated into global companies?

5. What are the benefits to firms and their shareholders of conducting business in an ethical manner?

6. Firms that fail to behave in an ethical manner can incur high costs. What are these costs and what is their source?

7. What are the most important differences between an "integrity organization" and a "compliance organization" in a firm's approach to organizational ethics?

8. What are some of the important mechanisms for promoting ethics in a firm?

## Experiential Exercise

Select two well-known business leaders—one you admire and one you do not. Evaluate each of them on the five characteristics of emotional intelligence.

| Emotional Intelligence Characteristics | Admired Leader | Leader Not Admired |
|---|---|---|
| Self-awareness | | |
| Self-regulation | | |
| Motivation | | |
| Empathy | | |
| Social skills | | |

## Application Questions Exercises

1. Identify two CEOs whose leadership you admire. What is it about their skills, attributes, and effective use of power that causes you to admire them?
2. Founders have an important role in developing their organization's culture and values. At times, their influence persists for many years. Identify and describe two organizations in which the cultures and values established by the founder(s) continue to flourish. You may find research on the Internet helpful in answering these questions.
3. Some leaders place a great emphasis on developing superior human capital. In what ways does this help a firm to develop and sustain competitive advantages?
4. In this chapter we discussed the five elements of a "learning organization." Select a firm with which you are familiar and discuss whether or not it epitomizes some (or all) of these elements.

## Ethics Questions

1. Sometimes organizations must go outside the firm to hire talent, thus bypassing employees already working for the firm. Are there conditions under which this might raise ethical considerations?
2. Ethical crises can occur in virtually any organization. Describe some of the systems, procedures, and processes that can help to prevent such crises.

# References

1. Gagnier, M. 2005. Kremed again. *BusinessWeek,* January 17:40; Anonymous. 2005. Worst managers. *BusinessWeek,* January 10: 74–77; Stires, D. 2004. Krispy Kreme is in the hole—again. *Fortune,* November 11: 42–43; and, McGowan, W. P. 2005. Krispy Kreme: A recipe for business failure. *Canyon News,* 19: 23.

2. Charan, R., & Colvin, G. 1999. Why CEOs fail. *Fortune,* June 21: 68–78.

3. These three activities and our discussion draw from Kotter, J. P. 1990. What leaders really do. *Harvard Business Review,* 68(3): 103–111; Pearson, A. E. 1990. Six basics for general managers. *Harvard Business Review,* 67(4): 94–101; and Covey, S. R. 1996. Three roles of the leader in the new paradigm. In *The leader of the future:* 149–160. Hesselbein, F., Goldsmith, M., & Beckhard, R. (Eds.). San Francisco: Jossey-Bass. Some of the discussion of each of the three leadership activity concepts draws on Dess, G. G., & Miller, A. 1993. *Strategic management:* 320–325. New York: McGraw-Hill.

4. Day, C., Jr., & LaBarre, P. 1994. GE: Just your average everyday $60 billion family grocery store. *Industry Week,* May 2: 13–18.

5. The best (& worst) managers of the year. 2003. *Business-Week,* January 13: 63.

6. Johnson, C. 2005. Lay, Skilling go on trial in January. *Washington Post,* February 25: E3.

7. Watkins, S. 2003. Former Enron vice president Sherron Watkins on the Enron collapse. *Academy of Management Executive,* 17(4): 119–125. Ms. Watkins has been widely recognized as a "whistleblower" and for her courage in bringing the Enron scandal to light. For example, she was one of three individuals to be recognized as *Time* magazine's Persons of the Year in 2002. She also received the Scales of Justice Award, Everyday Hero's Award, Women Mean Business Award, and the Academy of Management's 2003 Distinguished Executive Speaker.

8. In January 2004, Fastow agreed to serve a 10-year sentence, pay a $23 million fine, and cooperate with the U.S. government's continuing investigation. He had been charged with 78 counts of fraud, money laundering, and conspiracy.

9. For insightful perspectives on escalation, refer to Brockner, J. 1992. The escalation of commitment to a failing course of action. *Academy of Management Review,* 17(1): 39–61; and Staw, B. M. 1976. Knee-deep in the big muddy: A study of commitment to a chosen course of action. *Organizational Behavior and Human Decision Processes,* 16: 27–44. The discussion of systemic, behavioral, and political barriers draws on Lorange, P., & Murphy, D. 1984. Considerations in implementing strategic control. *Journal of Business Strategy,* 5: 27–35. In a similar vein, Noel M. Tichy has addressed three types of resistance to change in the context of General Electric: technical resistance, political resistance, and cultural resistance. See Tichy, N. M. 1993. Revolutionalize your company. *Fortune,* December 13: 114–118. Examples draw from O'Reilly, B. 1997. The secrets of America's most admired corporations: New ideas and new products. *Fortune,* March 3: 60–64.

10. This section draws on Champoux, J. E. 2000. *Organizational behavior: Essential tenets for a new millennium.* London: South-Western; and The mature use of power in organizations. 2003. *RHR International-Executive Insights,* May 29, 12.19.168.197/execinsights/8-3.htm.

11. An insightful perspective on the role of power and politics in organizations is provided in Ciampa, K. 2005. Almost ready: How leaders move up. *Harvard Business Review,* 83(1): 46–53.

12. A discussion of the importance of persuasion in bringing about change can be found in Garvin, D. A., & Roberto, M. A. 2005. Change through persuasion. *Harvard Business Review,* 83(4): 104–113.

13. Lorsch, J. W., & Tierney, T. J. 2002. *Aligning the stars: How to succeed when professionals drive results.* Boston: Harvard Business School Press.

14. For a review of this literature, see Daft, R. 1999. *Leadership: Theory and practice.* Fort Worth, TX: Dryden Press.

15. This section draws on Luthans, F. 2002. Positive organizational behavior: Developing and managing psychological strengths. *Academy of Management Executive,* 16(1): 57–72; and Goleman, D. 1998. What makes a leader? *Harvard Business Review,* 76(6): 92–105.

16. EI has its roots in the concept of "social intelligence" that was first identified by E. L. Thorndike in 1920 (Intelligence and its uses. *Harper's Magazine,* 140: 227–235). Psychologists have been uncovering other intelligences for some time now and have grouped them into such clusters as abstract intelligence (the ability to understand and manipulate verbal and mathematical symbols), concrete intelligence (the ability to understand and manipulate objects), and social intelligence (the ability to understand and relate to people). See Ruisel, I. 1992. Social intelligence: Conception and methodological problems. *Studia Psychologica,* 34(4–5): 281–296. Refer to trochim.human. cornell.edu/gallery.

17. See, for example, Luthans, op. cit.; Mayer, J. D., Salvoney, P., & Caruso, D. 2000. Models of emotional intelligence. In Sternberg, R. J. (Ed.). *Handbook of intelligence.* Cambridge, UK: Cambridge University Press; and Cameron, K. 1999. Developing emotional intelligence at the Weatherhead School of Management. *Strategy: The Magazine of the Weatherhead School of Management,* Winter: 2–3.

18. An insightful perspective on leadership, which involves discovering, developing and celebrating what is unique about each individual, is found in Buckingham, M. 2005. *What great managers do. Harvard Business Review,* 83(3): 70–79.

19. Goleman, op. cit.: 102.

20. This section draws upon Klemp. G. 2005. *Emotional intelligence and leadership: What really matters.* Cambria Consulting, Inc., www.cambriaconsulting.com.

21. Mayer, J. D. et al. 2004. Leading by feel. *Harvard Business Review,* 82(1): 27–37.

22. Heifetz, R. 2004. Question authority. *Harvard Business Review,* 82(1): 37.

23. Ibid.

24. For another insightful perspective, refer to Goleman, D., Boyztzis, R., & McKee, A. 2002. *Primal leadership: Realizing the power of emotional Intelligence.* Boston: Harvard Business School. In particular, this book addresses the advantages and drawbacks of six leadership styles that draw upon the EI concept.

25. Handy, C. 1995. Trust and the virtual organization. *Harvard Business Review,* 73(3): 40–50.

26. This section draws upon Dess, G. G., & Picken, J. C. 1999. *Beyond productivity.* New York: AMACOM. The elements of the learning organization in this section are consistent with the work of Dorothy Leonard-Barton. See, for example, Leonard-Barton, D. 1992. The factory as a learning laboratory. *Sloan Management Review,* 11: 23–38.

27. Senge, P. M. 1990. The leader's new work: Building learning organizations. *Sloan Management Review,* 32(1): 7–23.

28. Hammer, M., & Stanton, S. A. 1997. The power of reflection. *Fortune,* November 24: 291–296.

29. For some guidance on how to effectively bring about change in organizations, refer to Wall, S. J. 2005. The protean organization: Learning to love change. *Organizational Dynamics,* 34(1): 37–46.

30. Covey, S. R. 1989. *The seven habits of highly effective people: Powerful lessons in personal change.* New York: Simon & Schuster.

31. Melrose, K. 1995. *Making the grass greener on your side: A CEO's journey to leading by servicing.* San Francisco: Barrett-Koehler.

32. Quinn, R. C., & Spreitzer, G. M. 1997. The road to empowerment: Seven questions every leader should consider. *Organizational Dynamics,* 25: 37–49.

33. Helgesen, S. 1996. Leading from the grass roots. In *Leader of the future:* 19–24 Hesselbein et al.

34. Bowen, D. E., & Lawler, E. E., III. 1995. Empowering service employees. *Sloan Management Review,* 37: 73–84.

35. Stack, J. 1992. *The great game of business.* New York: Doubleday/Currency.

36. Lubove, S. 1998. New age capitalist. *Forbes,* April 6: 42–43.

37. Schafer, S. 1997. Battling a labor shortage? It's all in your imagination. *Inc.,* August: 24.

38. Meyer, P. 1998. So you want the president's job . . . . *Business Horizons,* January–February: 2–8.

39. Goldberg, M. 1998. Cisco's most important meal of the day. *Fast Company,* February–March: 56.

40. Imperato, G. 1998. Competitive intelligence: Get smart! *Fast Company,* May: 268–279.

41. Novicki, C. 1998. The best brains in business. *Fast Company,* April: 125.

42. The introductory discussion of benchmarking draws on Miller, A. 1998. *Strategic management:* 142–143. New York: McGraw-Hill.

43. Port, O., & Smith, G. 1992. Beg, borrow—and benchmark. *BusinessWeek,* November 30: 74–75.

44. Main, J. 1992. How to steal the best ideas around. *Fortune,* October 19: 102–106.

45. Taylor, J. T. 1997. What happens after what comes next? *Fast Company,* December–January: 84–85.

46. Sheff, D. 1996. Levi's changes everything. *Fast Company,* June–July: 65–74.

47. Isaacson, W. 1997. In search of the real Bill Gates. *Time,* January 13: 44–57.

48. Baatz, E. B. 1993. Motorola's secret weapon. *Electronic Business,* April: 51–53.

49. Holt, J. W. 1996. *Celebrate your mistakes.* New York: McGraw-Hill.

50. Harari, O. 1997. Flood your organization with knowledge. *Management Review,* November: 33–37.

51. This opening discussion draws upon Conley, J. H. 2000. Ethics in business. In Helms, M. M. (Ed.). *Encyclopedia of management* (4th ed.): 281–285; Farmington Hills, MI: Gale Group; Paine, L. S. 1994. Managing for organizational integrity. *Harvard Business Review,* 72(2): 106–117; and Carlson, D. S., & Perrewe, P. L. 1995. Institutionalization of organizational ethics through transformational leadership. *Journal of Business Ethics,* 14: 829–838.

52. Kiger, P. J. 2001. Truth and consequences. *Working Woman,* May: 57–61.

53. Soule, E. 2002. Managerial moral strategies—in search of a few good principles. *Academy of Management Review,* 27(1): 114–124.

54. Carlson & Perrewe, op. cit.

55. This discussion is based upon Paine. Managing for organizational integrity; Paine, L. S. 1997. *Cases in leadership, ethics, and organizational integrity: A Strategic approach.* Burr Ridge, IL: Irwin; and Fontrodona, J. 2002. Business ethics across the Atlantic. Business Ethics Direct, www.ethicsa.org/BED_art_fontrodone.html.

56. www.ti.com/corp/docs/company/citizen/ethics/benchmark. shtml; and www.ti.com/corp/docs/company/citizen/ethics/ quicktest.shtml.

57. Wetlaufer, S. 1999. Organizing for empowerment: An interview with AES's Roger Sant and Dennis Bakke. *Harvard Business Review,* 77(1): 110–126.

58. For an insightful, academic perspective on the impact of ethics codes on executive decision making, refer to Stevens, J. M., Steensma, H. K., Harrison, D. A., & Cochran, P. S.

2005. Symbolic or substantive document? The influence of ethics code on financial executives' decisions. *Strategic Management Journal,* 26(2): 181–195.

59. Paine. Managing for organizational integrity.

60. For a recent study on the effects of goal setting on unethical behavior, read Schweitzer, M. E., Ordonez, L., & Douma, B. 2004. Goal setting as a motivator of unethical behavior. *Academy of Management Journal,* 47(3): 422–432.

61. Paine. Managing for organizational integrity.

# Managing Innovation and Fostering Corporate Entrepreneurship

## >chapter objectives

*After reading this chapter, you should have a good understanding of:*

- The importance of implementing strategies and practices that foster innovation.
- The challenges and pitfalls of managing corporate innovation processes.
- The role of product champions and exit champions in internal corporate venturing.
- How independent venture teams and business incubators are used to develop corporate ventures.
- How corporations create an internal environment and culture that promote entrepreneurial development.
- How an entrepreneurial orientation can enhance a firm's efforts to develop promising corporate venture initiatives.

*t*o remain competitive, established firms must continually seek out opportunities for growth and new methods for strategically renewing their performance. Changes in customer needs, new technologies, and shifts in the competitive landscape require that companies continually innovate and initiate corporate ventures in order to compete effectively. This chapter addresses how entrepreneurial activities can be an avenue for achieving competitive advantages.

In the first section, we address the importance of innovation in identifying venture opportunities and strategic renewal. Innovations can take many forms, including radical breakthrough innovations as well as incremental innovative improvements, and be used either to update products or renew organizational processes. We discuss how firms can successfully manage the innovation process. Impediments and challenges to effective innovation are discussed and examples of good innovation practices are presented.

We discuss the unique role of corporate entrepreneurship in the strategic management process in the second section. Here we highlight two types of activities corporations use to remain competitive—focused and dispersed. New venture groups and business incubators are often used to focus a firm's entrepreneurial activities. In other corporations, the entrepreneurial spirit is dispersed throughout the organization and gives rise to product champions and other autonomous strategic behaviors that organizational members engage in to foster internal corporate venturing.

In the final section we describe how a firm's entrepreneurial orientation can contribute to its growth and renewal as well as enhance the methods and processes strategic managers use to recognize opportunities and develop initiatives for internal growth and development. The chapter also evaluates the pitfalls that firms may encounter when implementing entrepreneurial strategies.

Companies often grow by commercializing new technologies. This is one of the most important paths to corporate entrepreneurship. But technologies change and yesterday's exciting innovation eventually becomes today's old news. Consider the case of Polaroid, a company that captivated the marketplace with its instant photography technology and grew to become a multibillion dollar enterprise on the strength of that innovation.[1]

Polaroid Corporation's founder, Edward Land, was a Harvard dropout. He was also a genius in optics, chemistry, and engineering who started his Cambridge, Massachusetts, company in 1937 to focus on sunglasses and other technologies that polarize light. During World War II, the company built infrared filters for gunsights and dark-adaptation goggles. It was after the war, however, that one of Land's innovations struck gold. In 1947 he introduced a single-step photographic process that would develop film in 60 seconds and launched the Land Camera. Over the next 30 years, the camera and its film evolved into the Polaroid One-Step, and sales surged to $1.4 billion by 1978.

In the process, Polaroid became one of the most admired companies and a best bet among stock pickers. It was a member of the "Nifty Fifty," a group of companies known for their innovative ideas whose stocks regularly traded at 40 or more times earnings. In 1991 it won a huge patent infringement lawsuit against rival Eastman Kodak, which had to pay Polaroid $925 million. The company also continued to launch new products using its instant film technology in a variety of different cameras with updated features.

On the surface, Polaroid seemed to be the picture of success. Land had been hailed as a new breed of corporate leader—both technically savvy and entrepreneurial. But by 1991, the year Land died, the company he built was unraveling. Instead of using the cash from the Kodak lawsuit to pay down its heavy debt, Polaroid spent the money to develop a new camera—the Captiva—which flopped in the marketplace. A few years later the I-Zone Pocket Camera, a product targeted at adolescents, had weak sales because the image quality was inconsistent and replacement film was considered too expensive for teens. Meanwhile, internally, Polaroid was spending 37 percent of its sales on administrative costs, compared to Kodak's 21 percent. Even though the company continued to sell millions of cameras each year—a record 13.1 million in 2000—its strength was deteriorating.

Polaroid's most serious problems began when it failed to get on the digital photography bandwagon. Rather than make the move into digital, Polaroid decided to stick with its proprietary technology. Once Polaroid realized the extent of the digital photography trend, it was too late. It eventually introduced digital cameras but they were often ranked low in consumer ratings. Polaroid even developed digital printing technologies, called Opal and Onyx, designed to deliver high resolution digital images. But because of its weakened financial state, it could not get the funding from investors to advertise and develop them. By 2001, it was in real trouble. Its debt was $950 million, it laid off 2,950 employees—35 percent of its workforce—and began missing interest payments to bondholders. In October 2001, it filed for Chapter 11 bankruptcy protection. Sale of its stock, which had traded as high as $60 in July 1997, was halted at 28 cents per share on the New York Stock Exchange.

The final blow to its reputation came in 2005 when it was announced, as part of a deal to sell Polaroid to a Minnesota-based conglomerate, that thousands of former Polaroid employees would have their pensions wiped out. Retirees and ex-employees, who also lost their health coverage and life insurance, received a total of just $47 for their years of service, while four former Polaroid executives split a $30 million dollar settlement among them![2]

***What Went Wrong at Polaroid?*** Considered by many to be one of the first great research-based companies, Polaroid failed largely because it lost its ability to effectively innovate and launch new products. Many factors contributed to its downfall. Clearly, its failure to respond quickly to the digital photography phenomenon caused a serious setback. But the roots of the problem were deeper. As one writer put it, "They overestimated the value of their core business." That is, Polaroid's overconfidence in its early success prevented it from envisioning a purpose beyond its instant imaging capability. This phenomenon is sometimes referred to as "the innovator's dilemma"—firms become so preoccupied with meeting current needs that they fail to take steps to meet future needs.[3] This dilemma inhibited Polaroid's ability to change and affected every aspect of its business:

- Even though sales of its core products were strong, it lost touch with its customers. As a result, several of its innovations failed in the marketplace.

- It did not have a long-term strategy for financing growth. Because it relied heavily on investors to finance new product initiatives, when one failed, it created cash flow problems. To regain profitability, Polaroid would offer more shares and bonds to investors, which, in turn, devalued the stock and created even more indebtedness. Eventually, investors turned away.

- Buoyed by revenues that grew annually for over 30 years, it failed to control personnel costs and was weighed down by too many employees. Eventually these expenses overtook its sales.

In short, Polaroid stopped thinking and acting like an entrepreneurial firm. The Polaroid brand is still loved by many, and its products can still be found in the marketplace. (In 2002, Polaroid's assets were purchased by OEP Imaging Operating Corporation and, as part of the agreement, OEPI changed its name to Polaroid Corporation.) But the company that had once changed the world of photography was itself unable to make the changes necessary to remain viable. As a result of its lack of vision and failure to change, what had once been a leading innovator and top financial performer slowly fizzled out.[4]

Managing change, as we suggested in Chapter 11, is one of the most important functions performed by strategic leaders. The transformative activity of bringing organizations "from what they are to what the leader would have them become" requires fresh ideas and a vision of the future. Most organizations want to grow. To do so, they must expand their product offering, reach into new markets, and obtain new customers. Sometimes profitability can be increased by streamlining processes and operating more efficiently. These activities inevitably involve change, and a firm's leaders must be effective change agents.

What options are available to organizations that want to change and grow? This chapter addresses two major avenues through which companies can expand or improve their business—innovation and corporate entrepreneurship. These two activities go hand-in-hand because they both have similar aims. The first is strategic renewal. Innovations help an organization stay fresh and reinvent itself as conditions in the business environment change. This is why managing innovation is such an important strategic implementation issue. The second is the pursuit of venture opportunities. Innovative breakthroughs, as well as new product concepts, evolving technologies, and shifting demand, create opportunities for corporate venturing. In this chapter we will explore these topics—how change and innovation can stimulate strategic renewal and foster corporate entrepreneurship. First we turn to the challenge of managing innovation.

# >>Managing Innovation

One of the most important sources of growth opportunities is innovation. Innovation involves using new knowledge to transform organizational processes or create commercially viable products and services. The sources of new knowledge may include the latest technology, the results of experiments, creative insights, or competitive information. However it comes about, innovation occurs when new combinations of ideas and information bring about positive change.

# STRATEGY SPOTLIGHT

## Rubbermaid: Building Advantages through Marketing Innovations

Rubbermaid is a consistent winner of innovation kudos, including the *Chicago Sun-Times* Innovation Awards and *Retail Merchandiser*'s 2002 Marketing Innovation award winner in two categories. Yet Rubbermaid's innovations would rarely be considered "high-tech." Although the company (which consolidated in 1999 to form Newell Rubbermaid, Inc.) is known for its synthetic rubber materials, it is the application of those materials to develop innovative products that is responsible for its winning strategies. Here are some examples:

**Tool Tower**—Consumers have been crying out for help in organizing their garages, according to Adrian Fernandez, director of product management for Rubbermaid's Home Products unit. In fact, storing tools efficiently is the number one complaint by homeowners about garages. The Tool Tower, a simple and efficient plastic rack designed to hold long- and short-handle tools in one place, was a welcome solution. It is easily assembled, takes up little space, and is much safer than hanging tools on nails or racks.

**High-Heat Scraper**—While on site at one of its restaurant customers, a Rubbermaid business team noticed that chefs preferred synthetic rubber scrapers instead of metal spatulas when using nonstick cookware. But the scrapers quickly warped from the heat and lost their shape. Based on this experience, a new scraper of pliable synthetic rubber was developed with chefs in mind. It still did not scratch but could sustain temperatures as high as 500 degrees Fahrenheit.

**Hardware Blue**—Many products are tested in the company's "Everything Rubbermaid" experimental lab stores. Rubbermaid noticed that more and more women were buying tool boxes and workshop organizers. They wondered how women shoppers liked their traditional colors—yellow, black, and gray. Through focus groups, they identified a new color, "Hardware Blue," that outsold all other colors and appealed to both men and women.

Clearly, the high-heat scraper required technological know-how to develop. But the impetus for it came from proactive customer contact, and the product itself was simple. As can be seen from these examples, Rubbermaid is concerned not only with technologically based innovations but also with marketing innovations.

Sources: Kuczmarski, T. D. 2005. Award winners find innovation is profitable. *Chicago Sun-Times,* June 16; www.suntimes.com; Schmitt, W. 1997. Rubbermaid Inc. In Kanter, R. M., Kao, J., & Wiersma, F. (Eds.), *Innovation: Breakthrough thinking at 3M, DuPont, GE, Pfizer, and Rubbermaid:* 168–170. New York: HarperCollins; www.retail-merchandiser.com; and www.rubbermaid .com.

The emphasis on newness is a key point. For example, for a patent application to have any chance of success, one of the most important attributes it must possess is novelty. You can't patent an idea that has been copied. This is a central idea. In fact, the root of the word *innovation* is the Latin *novus,* which means new. Innovation involves introducing or changing to something new.[5]

Among the most important sources of new ideas is new technology. Technology creates new possibilities. Technology provides the raw material that firms use to make innovative new products and services. But technology is the only source of innovations. There can be innovations in human resources, firm infrastructure, marketing, service, or in many other value-adding areas that have little to do with anything "high-tech." Strategy Spotlight 12.1 highlights three innovations by the Rubbermaid Corporation that met customer needs and generated sales but were relatively low-tech.

As the Rubbermaid example suggests, innovation can take many forms. Next we will consider two frameworks that are often used to distinguish types of innovation.

### Types of Innovation

Although innovations are not always high-tech, changes in technology can be an important source of change and growth. When an innovation is based on a sweeping new technology, it often has a more far-reaching impact. However, sometimes even a small innovation can add value and create competitive advantages. Innovation can and should occur throughout an organization—in every department and all aspects of the value chain.

One way to view the impact of an innovation is in terms of its degree of innovativeness, which falls somewhere on a continuum that extends from incremental to radical.[6]

- *Radical innovations* produce fundamental changes by evoking major departures from existing practices. These breakthrough innovations usually occur because of technological change. They tend to be highly disruptive and can transform a company or even revolutionize a whole industry. They may lead to products or processes that can be patented, giving a firm a strong competitive advantage. Examples include electricity, the telephone, the transistor, desktop computers, fiber optics, artificial intelligence, and genetically engineered drugs.

- *Incremental innovations* enhance existing practices or make small improvements in products and processes. They may represent evolutionary applications within existing paradigms of earlier, more radical innovations. Because they often sustain a company by extending or expanding its product line or manufacturing skills, incremental innovations can be a source of competitive advantage. They increase revenues by creating a new marketplace offering or reduce costs by providing new capabilities that minimize expenses or speed productivity. Examples include frozen food, sports drinks, steel-belted radial tires, electronic bookkeeping, shatterproof glass, and digital telephones.

Some innovations are highly radical; others are only slightly incremental. But most innovations fall somewhere between these two extremes. Exhibit 12.1 shows where several innovations fall along the radical–incremental continuum.

Another distinction that is often used when discussing innovation is between process innovation and product innovation.[7] *Product innovation* refers to efforts to create product designs and applications of technology to develop new products for end users. Recall from Chapter 5 how generic strategies were typically different depending on the stage of the industry life cycle. Product innovations tend to be more radical and are more common during the earlier stages of an industry's life cycle. As an industry matures, there

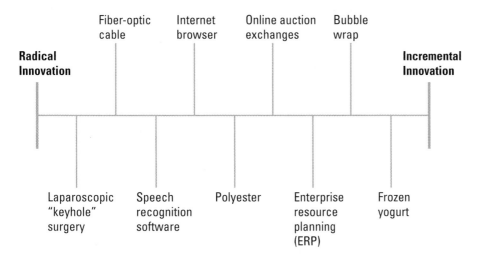

**Exhibit 12.1**   **Continuum of Radical and Incremental Innovations**

are fewer opportunities for newness, so the innovations tend to be more incremental. Product innovations are also commonly associated with a differentiation strategy. Firms that differentiate by providing customers with new products or services that offer unique features or quality enhancements often engage in product innovation.

*Process innovation,* by contrast, is typically associated with improving the efficiency of an organizational process, especially manufacturing systems and operations. By drawing on new technologies and an organization's accumulated experience (Chapter 5), firms can often improve materials utilization, shorten cycle time, and increase quality. Process innovations are more likely to occur in the later stages of an industry's life cycle as companies seek ways to remain viable in markets where demand has flattened out and competition is more intense. As a result, process innovations are often associated with overall cost leader strategies, because the aim of many process improvements is to lower the costs of operations.

As you can see from this discussion of different types of innovation, the innovation process itself has numerous strategic implications. Innovation is a force in both the external environment (technology, competition) and also a factor affecting a firm's internal choices (generic strategy, value-adding activities). Nevertheless, innovation can be quite difficult for some firms to manage, especially those that have become comfortable with the status quo. Next, we turn to the challenges associated with successful innovation.

## Challenges of Innovation

Innovation is essential to sustaining competitive advantages. Recall from Chapter 3 that one of the four elements of the Balanced Scorecard is the innovation and learning perspective. The extent and success of a company's innovation efforts are indicators of its overall performance. As management guru Peter Drucker warned, "An established company which, in an age demanding innovation, is not capable of innovation is doomed to decline and extinction."[8] To put it simply, in today's competitive environment, most firms have only one choice: "Innovate or die."

As with change, however, firms are often resistant to innovation. Only those companies that actively pursue innovation, even though it is often difficult and uncertain, will get a payoff from their innovation efforts. But managing innovation is challenging. As former Pfizer chairman and CEO William Steere puts it: "In some ways, managing innovation is analogous to breaking in a spirited horse. You are never sure of success until you achieve your goal. In the meantime, everyone takes a few lumps."[9]

What is it that makes innovation so difficult? Clearly the uncertainty about outcomes is one factor. Companies that keep an eye on their bottom line (and most of them do!) are often reluctant to invest time and resources into activities with an unknown future. Another factor is that the innovation process involves so many choices. These choices present five dilemmas that companies must wrestle with when pursuing innovation.[10]

- *Seeds versus Weeds.* Most companies have an abundance of innovative ideas. They must decide which of these is most likely to bear fruit—the "Seeds"—and which should be cast aside—the "Weeds." This is an ongoing dilemma that is often complicated by the fact that some innovation projects require a considerable level of investment before a firm can fully evaluate whether they are worth pursuing. As a result, firms need a mechanism with which they can choose among various innovation projects.

- *Experience versus Initiative.* Companies must decide who will lead an innovation project. Senior managers may have experience and credibility but tend to be more risk averse. Midlevel employees, who may be the innovators themselves, may have more enthusiasm because they can see firsthand how an innovation would address specific problems. As a result, firms need to support and reward organizational members who bring new ideas to light.

- **Internal versus External Staffing.** Innovation projects need competent staffs to succeed. People drawn from inside the company may have greater social capital and know the organization's culture and routines. But this knowledge may actually inhibit them from thinking outside the box. Staffing innovation projects with external personnel requires that project managers justify the hiring and spend time recruiting, training, and relationship building. As a result, firms need to streamline and support the process of staffing innovation efforts.

- **Building Capabilities versus Collaborating.** Innovation projects often require new sets of skills. Firms can seek help from other departments and/or partner with other companies that bring resources and experience as well as share costs of development. However, such arrangements can create dependencies and inhibit internal skills development. Further, struggles over who contributed the most or how the benefits of the project are to be allocated may arise. As a result, firms need a mechanism for forging links with outside parties to the innovation process.

- **Incremental versus Preemptive Launch.** Companies must manage the timing and scale of new innovation projects. An incremental launch is less risky because it requires fewer resources and serves as a market test. But a launch that is too tentative can undermine the project's credibility. It also opens the door for a competitive response. A large-scale launch requires more resources, but it can effectively preempt a competitive response. As a result, firms need to make funding and management arrangements that allow for projects to hit the ground running and be responsive to market feedback.

These dilemmas highlight why the innovation process can be daunting even for highly successful firms. Strategy Spotlight 12.2 addresses the challenges and pitfalls that Microsoft faces in its efforts to be a strong innovator. How can companies successfully address these innovation challenges? Next, we consider three steps that firms can take to manage the innovation process.[11]

## Defining the Scope of Innovation

Firms must have a means to focus their innovation efforts. By defining the "strategic envelope"—that is, the scope of a firm's innovation efforts—firms ensure that their innovation efforts are not wasted on projects that are highly uncertain or outside the firm's domain of interest. Strategic enveloping defines the range of acceptable projects. As Alistair Corbett, an innovation expert who directs the Toronto office of the global consulting firm Bain & Company, recently said, "One man's radical innovation is another man's incremental innovation."[12] Thus, a strategic envelope creates a firm-specific view of innovation that defines how a firm can create new knowledge and learn from an innovation initiative even if the project fails. Although such limitations might seem overly constraining, they also give direction to a firm's innovation efforts, which helps separate seeds from weeds and build internal capabilities.

One way to determine which projects to work on is to focus on a common technology. Then, innovation efforts across the firm can aim at developing skills and expertise in a given technical area. Another potential focus is on a market theme.

### Microsoft's Innovation Challenges

You would think that Microsoft, the dominant software seller in the world with a $6.8 billion annual research and development budget, would be a major innovator. Instead, innovation seems to be Microsoft's Achilles' heel. From its earliest days, Microsoft has had far more success as an imitator than an innovator. Despite having well-funded research labs at its Redmond, Washington, headquarters, Microsoft has little to show for years of efforts to come up with the next big breakthrough innovation. Why is Microsoft is so innovation-challenged?

- **Innovation is hard.** There is no doubt that Microsoft is working hard at it. From 2000 to 2005, Microsoft acquired 2,188 patents to protect its researchers' work. But creating a commercially viable breakthrough innovation such as the Web browser (created by Netscape), the streaming media player (by RealNetworks) or interactive television (TiVo) is not easy. In many cases, it is more about luck and timing than money, dedication, and brilliance.

- **Bigger isn't better.** Large companies simply find it more difficult than smaller ones to sustain rapid growth through innovation. Good ideas are scarce everywhere and most new innovations take a few

years to get off the ground. Because of Microsoft's sheer size, the contribution that a new product can make is relatively small. For example, if Microsoft had matched Google's recent growth record, that business activity would have added only 4 percent to Microsoft's top line.

- **Defense is easier.** Most of Microsoft's research efforts go to helping it sustain its strong leadership in software products such as MS Office. Of every dollar it spends on research and development (R&D), "probably something on the order of 90 percent is directly in line, or in service of, the existing business groups," according to Craig Mundie, Microsoft's co-chief technology officer. In this respect, Microsoft is a victim of "the innovator's dilemma"—spending so much more time protecting its established lines of business and satisfying existing customers that it misses opportunities to make breakthroughs.

Microsoft continues to support innovation and its breakthrough product may come any day. But even its new project, the second generation videogame console known as XBox 360, lags far behind Sony's PlayStation2 in sales and market penetration. Microsoft may not be producing the next big thing, but as a fast follower of technology breakthroughs, it has been highly successful.

Sources: Grossman, L. 2005. Out of the Xbox. *Time*, May 23: 44–53; and Hawn, C. 2004. What money can't buy. *Fast Company*, 89: 68–73.

Consider how DuPont responded to a growing concern for environmentally sensitive products:

> In the early 1990s, DuPont sought to use its knowledge of plastics to identify products to meet a growing market demand for biodegradable products. Over the next decade, it conducted numerous experiments with a biodegradable polyester resin it named Biomax. By trying different applications and formulations demanded by potential customers, the company was finally able to create a product that could be produced economically and had market appeal. Recently, Biomax was certified biodegradable and compostable by the Biodegradable Products Institute, an endorsement that should further boost sales.[13]

In defining a strategic envelope, companies must be clear not only about the kinds of innovation they are looking for but also the expected results. Therefore, each company needs to develop a set of questions to ask itself about its innovation efforts:

- How much will the innovation initiative cost?
- How likely is it to actually become commercially viable?
- How much value will it add; that is, what will it be worth if it works?
- What will be learned if it does not pan out?

In other words, however a firm envisions its innovation goals, it needs to develop a systematic approach to evaluating its results and learning from its innovation initiatives. Viewing innovation from this perspective helps firms manage the process.[14]

## Managing the Pace of Innovation

Along with clarifying the scope of an innovation by defining a strategic envelope, firms also need to regulate the pace of innovation. An advantage of assessing the extent to which an innovation is radical or incremental is that it helps determine how long it will take for an innovation initiative to realistically come to fruition. The project time line of an incremental innovation may be six months to 2 years, whereas a more radical innovation is typically long term—10 years or more.[15] Thus, radical innovations often begin with a long period of exploration in which experimentation makes strict timelines unrealistic. In contrast, firms that are innovating incrementally in order to exploit a window of opportunity may use a milestone approach that is more stringently driven by goals and deadlines. As suggested in Chapter 9, this kind of sensitivity to realistic time frames helps companies separate dilemmas temporally so they are easier to manage.

The idea of time pacing can also be a source of competitive advantage, because it helps a company manage transitions and develop an internal rhythm.[16] In their book *Competing on the Edge*, Shona Brown and Kathleen Eisenhardt contrasted time pacing with event pacing. They argue that, by controlling the pace of the innovation process (time pacing), a company can more effectively learn from it and grow internally. In contrast, when outside events, such as shifts in technology or the actions of competitors, determine the pace of innovation (event pacing), then firms lose their ability to manage the change process. Time pacing does not mean the company ignores the demands of market timing. Instead, it means that companies have a sense of their own internal clock in a way that allows them to thwart competitors by controlling the innovation process.

Not all innovation lends itself to speedy development, however. Radical innovation often involves open-ended experimentation and time-consuming mistakes. Further, the creative aspects of innovation are often difficult to time. When software maker Intuit's new CEO, Steve Bennett, began to turn around that troubled business, he required every department to implement Six Sigma, a quality control management technique that focuses on being responsive to customer needs. Everybody, that is, but the techies.

> "We're not GE, we're not a company where Jack says 'Do it,' and everyone salutes," says Bill Hensler, Intuit's vice president for process excellence. That's because software development, according to many, is more of an art than a science. At the Six Sigma Academy, president of operations Phil Samuel says even companies that have embraced Six Sigma across every other aspect of their organization usually maintain a hands-off policy when it comes to software developers. Techies, it turns out, like to go at their own pace.[17]

The example of software developers makes an important point about strategic pacing: some projects can't be rushed. Companies that hurry up their research efforts or go to market before they are ready can damage their ability to innovate—and their reputation. Thus, managing the pace of innovation can be an important factor in long-term success.

## Collaborating with Innovation Partners

Innovation involves gathering new knowledge and learning from your mistakes. It is rare for any one work group or department to have all the information it needs to carry an innovation from concept to commercialization. Even a company that is highly competent with its current operations usually needs new capabilities to achieve new results. Innovation partners can provide the skills and insights that are often needed to make innovation projects succeed.

Partners can come from several sources:

- Other personnel within the department.
- Personnel within the firm but from another department.
- Partners outside the firm.

Innovation partners may also come from nonbusiness sources, including research universities and the federal government. Each year the federal government issues requests for proposals (RFPs) asking private companies for assistance in improving services or finding solutions to public problems. Universities are another type of innovation partner. Chip-maker Intel, for example, has benefited from underwriting substantial amounts of university research. Rather than hand universities a blank check, Intel bargains for rights to patents that emerge from Intel-sponsored research. The university retains ownership of the patent, but Intel gets royalty-free use of it.[18]

Strategic partnering has other benefits as well. It requires firms to identify their strengths and weaknesses and make choices about which capabilities to leverage, which need further development, and which are outside the firm's current or projected scope of operations. Such knowledge can bring a level of realism to the process. It also helps managers get clear about what they need partners to do.

Consider the example of Nextel in its decision to partner with RadioFrame Networks, a Seattle-based start-up.

> RadioFrame had developed an innovative radio transmitter that could be used inside buildings to make cell-phone signals clearer. Nextel, which did not have as much network capacity as some of its larger competitors, saw this as a way to increase bandwidth and add value to its existing set of services. Not only did the two firms form a partnership, but Nextel also became involved in the development process by providing senior engineers and funding to help build the system. "We really worked hand-in-hand with Nextel," says RadioFrame CEO Jeff Brown, "from user requirements to how to physically get the finished product into their distribution systems."[19]

Firms need a mechanism to help decide whom to partner with. Several factors will enter into the decision, including the issues mentioned above regarding the pace and scope of innovation initiatives. To choose partners, firms need to ask what competencies they are looking for and what the innovation partner will contribute. These contributions might include knowledge of markets, technology expertise, or contacts with key players in an industry. Innovation partnerships also typically need to specify how the rewards of the innovation will be shared and who will own the intellectual property that is developed.[20]

Innovation efforts that involve multiple partners and the speed and ease with which partners can network and collaborate are changing the way innovation is conducted. These changes have prompted one Harvard University professor to claim that the innovation process itself has experienced a paradigm shift. Strategy Spotlight 12.3 emphasizes the role of collaboration and partnerships in a new approach to innovation labeled "open innovation."

As this section indicates, managing innovation is an important and challenging organizational activity. For it to be successful, the innovation process has to stay focused on its ultimate purpose—to introduce new products and/or deploy new processes that build competitive advantages and make the company profitable. Innovation involves a companywide commitment because the results of innovation affect every part of the organization. Innovation also requires an entrepreneurial spirit and skill set to be effective. One of the most important ways that companies improve and grow is when innovation is put to the task of creating new corporate ventures. We will look at that topic next.

# STRATEGY SPOTLIGHT

## Open Innovation: A Better Way to Build Value?

Recall from Chapter 8 the example of InnoCentive, the Internet-based collaboration platform launched by Eli Lilly to provide an open source, virtual R&D community to solve complex scientific problems. Not only is InnoCentive a savvy application of digital technology, it is also an example of what Harvard business professor Henry Chesbrough calls "open innovation." The concept of open innovation builds on two other concepts seen in previous chapters—the importance of intellectual assets in today's economy (Chapter 4) and the use of boundaryless organizational arrangements to achieve strategic ends (Chapter 10).

Chesbrough claims that the open innovation model will become increasingly important in the future. His argument is as follows: Innovation teams and R&D departments have acted with a fairly traditional mind-set for years about how to profit from innovation initiatives. The old mind-set, however, has created a paradox—in an era when ideas and knowledge abound, innovation and industrial research seem less effective. The old way of innovating no longer seems to be bearing fruit, because new technologies and the speed of innovation are creating new demands on companies to look beyond their traditional boundaries and share their intellectual property (IP). The innovation process itself, according to Chesbrough, needs innovating.

The old approach to innovation, labeled "closed innovation," operates on several key assumptions:

1. The smart people in our field work for us.

2. We should control the IP developed by our smart people so that competitors don't profit from our ideas.

3. To profit from R&D and innovation, we have to discover it, develop it, and ship it ourselves.

Source: Chesbrough, H. 2003. The era of open innovation. *MIT Sloan Management Review*, 44(3): 35–41; Chesbrough, H. 2003. *Open innovation: The new imperative for creating and profiting from technology*. Boston: Harvard Business School Press.

4. If we discover it first, we will get it to market first.

5. If we get it to market first, we win.

In contrast, Chesbrough argues, the open way to successfully innovate involves collaborating and drawing on the knowledge and resources of competitors and other strategic partners. In other words, disclose your intellectual property, cross organizational boundaries to achieve innovation goals, and let others share in the wealth. Here are the contrasting assumptions that are central to open innovation:

1. Not all the smart people work for us. Some of the smart people that we need to work with work somewhere else.

2. We should profit when others use our IP and be willing to buy their IP if it advances our innovation business model.

3. Internal R&D is not the only way to add value; external R&D can also benefit us.

4. We don't have to originate the research to profit from it.

5. Building a smarter innovation business model is better than getting to market first.

In his book, Chesbrough describes how innovation leader IBM, once an exemplar of the closed innovation approach, has transformed itself by being willing to cross boundaries and share its IP with others. He also describes how companies such as Cisco and Intel have succeeded by using an open approach while their rivals Lucent and Xerox have struggled. It remains to be seen whether other companies will adopt open innovation, but Chesbrough is convinced that the ones that are willing to seize this new approach will be the long-term winners.

## >>Corporate Entrepreneurship

Corporate entrepreneurship (CE) has two primary aims: the pursuit of new venture opportunities and strategic renewal.[21] The innovation process keeps firms alert by exposing them to new technologies, making them aware of marketplace trends, and helping them evaluate new possibilities. Corporate entrepreneurship uses the fruits of the innovation process to help firms build new sources of competitive advantage and renew their value propositions. Just as the innovation process helps firms to make positive improvements, corporate entrepreneurship helps firms identify opportunities and launch new ventures. In Chapter 6 we addressed corporate growth through mergers and acquisitions as well as through joint ventures and strategic alliances. Here the focus is on internal venture development and growth.

Corporate new venture creation was labeled "intrapreneuring" by Gifford Pinchot because it refers to building entrepreneurial businesses within existing corporations.[22] However, to engage in corporate entrepreneurship that yields above-average returns and contributes to sustainable advantages, it must be done effectively. In this section we will examine the sources of entrepreneurial activity within established firms and the methods large corporations use to stimulate entrepreneurial behavior.

In a typical corporation, what determines how entrepreneurial projects will be pursued? That depends on many factors, including:

- Corporate culture.
- Leadership.
- Structural features that guide and constrain action.
- Organizational systems that foster learning and manage rewards.

In other words, all of the factors that influence the strategy implementation process will also shape how corporations engage in internal venturing.

Other factors will also affect how entrepreneurial ventures will be pursued.

- The use of teams in strategic decision making.
- Whether the company is product or service oriented.
- Whether its innovation efforts are aimed at product or process improvements.
- The extent to which it is high-tech or low-tech.

Because these factors are different in every organization, some companies may be more involved than others in identifying and developing new venture opportunities. These factors will also influence the nature of the CE process. In this section, we will address several avenues by which companies pursue growth and profit opportunities through entrepreneurial activities.

Successful corporate entrepreneurship typically requires firms to reach beyond their current operations and markets in the pursuit of new opportunities. In fact, it is often the breakthrough opportunities that provide the greatest returns. A recent study found that 86 percent of firms expand by making incremental improvements such as extending an existing product line. Only 14 percent ventured into arenas that were new to the world or new to the firm. Although line extensions provided 62 percent of the total revenues, they accounted for only 39 percent of total profits. By contrast, the companies that entered new markets and industries enjoyed total profits of 61 percent from 38 percent of total revenues.[23]

These findings led W. Chan Kim and Renee Mauborgne in their new book *Blue Ocean Strategy* to conclude that companies that are willing to venture into market spaces where there is little or no competition—labeled "blue oceans"—will outperform those firms that limit growth to incremental improvements in competitively crowded industries—labeled "red oceans." Companies that identify and pursue blue ocean strategies follow somewhat different rules than those that are "bloodied" by the competitive practices in red oceans. Consider the following elements of a blue ocean strategy:

- ***Create uncontested market space.*** By seeking opportunities where they are not threatened by existing competitors, blue ocean firms can focus on customers rather than on competition.

- ***Make the competition irrelevant.*** Rather than using the competition as a benchmark, blue ocean firms cross industry boundaries to offer new and different products and services.

## Cirque du Soleil's Blue Ocean Strategy

The blue ocean strategy of Cirque du Soleil is a prime example of creating new market space within a declining industry. The promotional tagline that the Canadian-based circus company sometimes uses explains how they did it: "We reinvent the circus." By altering the industry boundaries that had traditionally defined the circus concept, Cirque has created a new type of circus experience that audiences have enthusiastically embraced. Since 1984, when it was founded by a group of street performers, Cirque du Soleil has staged a variety of different productions that have been seen by over 40 million people in some 90 cities around the world.

How did they do it? One of the keys to redefining the circus business was to challenge conventional thinking and create a new vision of circus entertainment. Since the days of Ringling Bros. and Barnum & Bailey, the circus had consisted of animal acts, star performers, and Bozo-like clowns. Cirque questioned this formula and sought to understand what its audiences really wanted. It found that interest in animal acts was declining in part because of public concerns over the treatment of circus animals. Since managing animals—and the celebrity trainers who performed with them—created a heavy economic burden, Cirque eliminated them.

Instead Cirque has focused on three elements of the classic circus tent event that still captivated audiences: acrobatic acts, clowns, and the tent itself. Elegant acrobatics

Sources: Kim, W. C., & Mauborgne, R. 2004. Blue ocean strategy. *Harvard Business Review*, 82(10): 76–84; and Tischler, L. 2005. Join the circus. *Fast Company*, 96: 52–58.

became a central feature of its performances, and clown humor became more sophisticated and less slapstick. Cirque also preserved the image of the tent by creating exotic facades that captured the symbolic elements of the traditional tent.

For Cirque to sail into a blue ocean, however, it had to make even bigger changes. It did so by introducing theatrical elements into its circus acts. Each production provides a range of features more commonly found in theatres than in circus tents—from using theatrical story lines to replacing hard benches with comfortable seating. Rather than displaying three different acts simultaneously, as in the classic three-ring circus, Cirque offers multiple productions giving audiences a reason to go to the circus more often. Each production has a different theme and its own original musical score.

As it has rolled out all of these changes, Cirque has kept its eye on the bottom line. In fact, a key motivator for many of its changes was to find ways to lower costs and increase revenues in the declining circus industry. Cutting the cost of animal acts and star performers as well as boosting revenues by offering a variety of productions has allowed it to achieve both low cost and differentiation advantages. Such a strategy creates value for both the company and its customers. The essence of its success, however, lies not in the extent to which it has outperformed competitors, but in how it has surpassed them by redefining the circus concept and becoming a prime mover in the market space it created.

- *Create and capture new demand.* Rather than fighting over existing demand, blue ocean companies seek opportunities in uncharted territory.

- *Break the value/cost trade-off.* Blues ocean firms reject the idea that a trade-off between value and cost is inevitable and instead seek opportunities in areas that benefit both their cost structure and their value proposition to customers.

- *Pursue differentiation and low cost simultaneously.* By integrating the range of a firm's utility, price, and cost activities, blue ocean companies align their whole system to create sustainable strategies.

As the above imperatives suggest, the essence of blue ocean strategy is not just to find an uncontested market, but to create one. Some blue oceans arise because new technologies create new possibilities, such as eBay's online auction business. Yet technological innovation is not a defining feature of a blue ocean strategy. Most blue oceans are created from within red oceans by companies that push beyond the existing industry boundaries. Strategy Spotlight 12.4 describes how Cirque du Soleil created a new market for circus entertainment by making traditional circus acts more like theatrical productions.

Once created, a blue ocean strategy is difficult to imitate. If customers flock to blue ocean creators, firms rapidly achieve economies of scale, learning advantages, and synergies across their organizational systems. Wal-Mart, for example, was able to integrate its operations and functions so efficiently that would-be imitators were effectively discouraged. Another example is Body Shop, which chartered new territory by refusing to focus solely on beauty products. Traditional competitors such as Estee Lauder and L'Oreal, whose brands are based on promises of eternal youth and beauty, found it difficult to imitate this approach without repudiating their current images.

These factors suggest that blue ocean strategies provide an avenue by which firms can pursue corporate entrepreneurship. Such strategies are not without risks, however. In the sections that follow, we will address some of the strategic choice and implementation issues that influence the success or failure of CE activities. How various companies approach corporate venturing is a key factor. Two distinct approaches to corporate venturing are found among firms that pursue entrepreneurial aims. The first is *focused* corporate venturing, in which CE activities are isolated from a firm's existing operations and worked on by independent work units. The second approach to CE is *dispersed,* in which all parts of the organization and every organization member are engaged in intrapreneurial activities. In the next two sections, we will address these approaches and provide examples of each.

## Focused Approaches to Corporate Entrepreneurship

Firms using a focused approach typically separate the corporate venturing activity from the other ongoing operations of the firm. That is, corporate entrepreneurship is usually the domain of autonomous work groups that pursue entrepreneurial aims independent of the rest of the firm. The advantage of this approach is that it frees entrepreneurial team members to think and act without the constraints imposed by existing organizational norms and routines. This independence is often necessary for the kind of open-minded creativity that leads to strategic breakthroughs. The disadvantage is that, because of their isolation from the corporate mainstream, the work groups that concentrate on internal ventures may fail to obtain the resources or support needed to carry an entrepreneurial project through to completion. Two forms—new venture groups (NVGs) and business incubators—are among the most common types of focused approaches.

*New Venture Groups (NVGs)*   Corporations often form new venture groups whose goal is to identify, evaluate, and cultivate venture opportunities. These groups typically function as semi-autonomous units with little formal structure. The new venture group may simply be a committee that reports to the president on potential new ventures. Or it may be organized as a corporate division with its own staff and budget. The aims of the new venture group may be open-ended in terms of what ventures it may consider. Alternatively, some corporations use them to promote concentrated effort on a specific problem. In both cases, they usually have a substantial amount of freedom to take risks and a supply of resources to do it with.[24]

New venture groups usually have a larger mandate than a typical R&D department. That is, their involvement extends beyond innovation and experimentation to coordinating with other corporate divisions, identifying potential venture partners, gathering resources, and, in some cases, actually launching the venture.

Nortel Networks, a global producer of telecom equipment, provides an example of how the NVG of a major corporation successfully launches new ventures.[25] Responsibility for its venturing activities lies with a senior vice president who oversees corporate strategy, alliances, and venturing, including the company's NVG. Company employees

# STRATEGY SPOTLIGHT

## Corporate Venture Capital

What does a company do when it wants to enjoy the benefits of an entrepreneurial start-up but does not want to acquire a venture or take time to develop one internally? It finances one by providing venture capital.

Since the 1970s, major U.S. corporations such as Exxon Mobil have invested in externally generated business ideas in order to strengthen their innovation profile. Some firms invest in technologies that are similar to their core business or provide potential future synergies. Intel, for example, has invested in several e-business start-ups that are in a position to increase demand for Intel processors. With the high growth potential of industries such as information technology and biotechnology, the level of corporate venture capital is increasing. During the booming dot-com era, corporate venture unit investments jumped by a factor of five, from $1.4 billion to $7.8 billion. In 2000 alone, corporations worldwide invested nearly $17 billion in venture capital.

Several major corporations have launched venture financing efforts. In Germany alone there are over 20 corporate venture funds, including global players Siemens, Bertelsmann, and Deutsche Telekom. Even utilities are investing in emerging companies. AEP, a major U.S. electric power company, recently invested in PHPK, a cryogenics firm based in Columbus, Ohio. PHPK is poised to provide support of superconductivity applications, a rapidly growing energy niche that is seeking innovations. AEP prefers expansion-stage firms that need capital and guidance rather than earlier-stage firms. And AEP invests only in energy-related companies. PHPK has nearly doubled its business since AEP made its investment, which served as an immediate endorsement of PHPK's technology and capabilities.

The result? Intel, for one, has enjoyed tremendous returns. It has a portfolio of businesses worth $8 billion. But Intel's goal is not just to make money—it is looking for ways to cement ties early with promising start-ups. "Companies have discovered that it's a good way to do market development," according to Les Vadasz, head of Intel's venture program. "I do see it as a competitive weapon."

Louis Rajczi, managing partner at Siemens Venture Capital, agrees. Unlike traditional VCs which invest in businesses strictly for the financial returns, corporations invest in new ventures to advance their strategic vision and beat the competition. "If we get in on more good deals at an earlier stage than our competitors, we'll end up getting ahead," says Rajczi. "That will increase the value of the company and increase our returns."

Even so, corporate funding for external ventures dried up rapidly after the technology bubble burst in the early 2000s. In the first half of 2002, only $1.1 billion was invested, compared to $17 billion in 2000. Not only have new investments by corporations dropped dramatically, but also corporations such as Hewlett-Packard and Accenture have sold off large portions of their portfolios. Nevertheless, as a long-term strategy, corporate venture funding can benefit both new ventures and corporations and remains a viable alternative to internal corporate venturing.

Sources: Stein, T. 2002. Rip cord. *Red Herring*, November 28, www.redherring.com; Franzke, E. 2001. Four keys to corporate venturing success. *European Venture Capital Journal*, June 1: 36–37; Letzelter, J. 2000. The new venture capitalists: Utilities go shopping for deals. *Public Utilities Fortnightly*, December: 34–38; Rabinovitz, J. 2000. Venture capital, Inc. *Industry Standard*, April 17: 88–90; and, Worrell, D. 2003. The big guns. *Entrepreneur*, November, www.entrepreneur.com.

submit ideas through a company intranet. Once the NVG decides to pursue an opportunity, two teams are set up—an opportunity team, which investigates the marketability of the venture concept, and a commercialization team, which manages venture investments and value development. Nortel's NVG is only interested in ventures that are likely to become stand-alone businesses, not extensions of current product lines. As a result, governance of new ventures usually includes outside board members and external investors who can be involved in managing the venture once it is spun off. Recently, Nortel used this process to create a spin-off called NetActive, which offers digital rights management (DRM) technology used to protect Internet-based content.

Firms that want to expand by way of new venture start-ups usually acquire existing ventures, as discussed in Chapter 6, or develop ventures internally. Strategy Spotlight 12.5 describes a third alternative for firms that want to be entrepreneurial but still maintain their autonomy: corporate venture funding.

*Business Incubators*   The term *incubator* was originally used to describe a device in which eggs are hatched. Business incubators are designed to "hatch" new businesses. They are a type of corporate new venture group with a somewhat more specialized purpose—to support and nurture fledgling entrepreneurial ventures until they can thrive on their own as stand-alone businesses. Corporations often use incubators as a way to grow businesses identified by the new venture group. Although they often receive support from many parts of the corporation, they still operate independently until they are strong enough to go it alone. Then, depending on the type of business, they are either integrated into an existing corporate division or continue to operate as a subsidiary of the parent firm. Additionally, the type of corporate venturing support reported in Strategy Spotlight 12.5 that external new ventures receive may also include allowing a young venture into the corporation's incubator.

Incubators are sometimes found outside the domain of corporate entrepreneurship (see Chapter 13). However, a company-sponsored incubator often has advantages because of the experience and resources that the parent corporation can provide. Incubators typically provide some or all of the following five functions.[26]

- *Funding.* Usually includes capital investments but may also include in-kind investments and loans.

- *Physical space.* A common problem for new ventures; incubators in which several start-ups share space often provide fertile ground for new ideas and collaboration.

- *Business services.* Along with office space, young ventures need basic services and infrastructure; may include anything from phone systems and computer networks to public relations and personnel management.

- *Mentoring.* Senior executives and skilled technical personnel often provide coaching and experience-based advice.

- *Networking.* Contact with other parts of the firm and external resources such as suppliers, industry experts, and potential customers facilitates problem solving and knowledge sharing.

As the above list suggests, business incubators provide a safe and supportive environment for corporate ventures. Nevertheless, the risk associated with launching ventures should not be overlooked. Companies have at times spent millions incubating new ideas with very little to show for it. Major corporations such as Lucent, British Airways, and Hewlett-Packard inactivated their incubators and scaled back new venture portfolios after experiencing major declines in value since the early 2000s.[27]

Thus, to encourage entrepreneurship, corporations sometimes need to do more than create independent work groups or venture incubators to generate new enterprises. In some firms, the entrepreneurial spirit is spread throughout the organization. It is this dispersed approach to corporate entrepreneurship that we turn to next.

## Dispersed Approaches to Corporate Entrepreneurship

The second type of corporate entrepreneurship is dispersed. For some companies, a dedication to the principles and practices of entrepreneurship is spread throughout the organization. One advantage of this approach is that organizational members don't have to be reminded to think entrepreneurially or be willing to change. The ability to change is considered to be a core capability. Such corporations often have a reputation for being entrepreneurial. This leads to a second advantage: Because of this entrepreneurial reputation, stakeholders such as vendors, customers, or alliance partners can bring new ideas or venture opportunities to anyone in the organization and expect them to be well-received. Such opportunities make it possible for the firm to stay ahead of the competition.

However, there are disadvantages as well. Firms that are overzealous about corporate entrepreneurship sometimes feel they must change for the sake of change, causing them to lose vital competencies or spend heavily on R&D and innovation to the detriment of the bottom line. Two related aspects of dispersed entrepreneurship include entrepreneurial cultures that have an overarching commitment to CE activities and the use of product champions in promoting entrepreneurial behaviors.

*Entrepreneurial Culture*   In some large corporations, the corporate culture embodies the spirit of entrepreneurship. A culture of entrepreneurship is one in which the search for venture opportunities permeates every part of the organization. Recall from Chapter 3 that the key to creating value successfully is viewing every value-chain activity as a source of competitive advantage. In a similar way, the effect of corporate entrepreneurship on a firm's strategic success is strongest when it animates all parts of an organization. It is found in companies where the strategic leaders and the culture together generate a strong impetus to innovate, take risks, and seek out new venture opportunities.

In companies with an entrepreneurial culture, everyone in the organization is attuned to opportunities to leverage the assets and capabilities of the corporation to help create new businesses. Many such firms use a top-down approach to stimulate entrepreneurial activity. That is, the top leaders of the organization support programs and incentives that foster a climate of entrepreneurship. Many of the best ideas for new corporate ventures, however, come from the bottom up. Here's what Martin Sorrell, CEO of the WPP Group, a London-based global communication services group, says about drawing on the talents of lower-level employees:

> The people at the so-called bottom of an organization know more about what's going on than the people at the top. The people in the trenches are the ones in the best position to make critical decisions. It's up to the leaders to give those people the freedom and the resources they need.[28]

Thus, an entrepreneurial culture is one in which change and renewal are on everybody's mind. Sony, 3M, Intel, and Cisco are among the corporations best known for their corporate venturing activities. Many fast-growing young corporations also attribute much of their success to an entrepreneurial culture. Virgin Group, the British conglomerate that began as Virgin Airlines under the leadership of Richard Branson, has spawned nearly 200 new businesses in its short history. Strategy Spotlight 12.6 describes a few of Virgin's start-up successes as well as some ambitious future plans.

*Product Champions*   CE does not always involve making large investments in start-ups or establishing incubators to spawn new divisions. Often, innovative ideas emerge in the normal course of business and are brought forth and become part of the way of doing business. In many firms, especially small, informally run ones, this may happen organically through the energetic efforts of individuals with good ideas. Larger firms often have more formal efforts to encourage innovation among their employees. In both cases, it is often product champions who are needed to take charge of internally generated ventures. Product (or project) champions are those individuals working within a corporation who bring entrepreneurial ideas forward, identify what kind of market exists for the product or service, find resources to support the venture, and promote the venture concept to upper management.[29]

When lower-level employees identify a product idea or novel solution, they will take it to their supervisor or someone in authority. Similarly, a new idea that is generated in a technology lab may be introduced to others by its inventor. If the idea has merit, it gains support and builds momentum across the organization.[30] Thus, even though the corporation may not be looking for new ideas or have a program for cultivating internal ventures, the independent behaviors of a few organizational members can have important strategic consequences.

# STRATEGY SPOTLIGHT

## Growing New Ventures at Virgin Group

While most large companies have to work hard to stoke the fires of entrepreneurship, they burn with ferocious intensity at the Virgin Group. As a $4.25 billion U.S. company that has created nearly 200 businesses, it stands as clear evidence that ideas, capital, and talent can flow as freely in big, far-flung organizations as they can among the start-ups of Silicon Valley.

The mix of businesses that Virgin has spawned is indicative of the fun-loving, eclectic culture that its chairman, Richard Branson, has developed. Branson and his deputies have worked hard to create a culture where employees speak up and share their ideas. There are no gleaming corporate headquarters or executive privileges, just a large house in London where meetings are held in a small room. "Rules and regulations are not our forte," Branson said. "Analyzing things to death is not our kind of thing."

There aren't even any job descriptions at Virgin, because they are thought to place too many limits on what people can do. Instead, senior executives work shoulder to shoulder with first-line employees. Branson believes that employees should be given top priority, and he has created a friendly, nonhierarchical, familylike environment in which people have fun and enjoy themselves. His advice to his employees reflects his personal philosophy: "Do things that you like. If your work and your hobby are the same, you will work long hours because you are motivated."

The result is that Virgin's businesses include entertainment megastores, cinemas, a fun-to-fly airline, an all-in-one consumer banking system, a hip radio station, and a passenger train service. Smaller ventures have also been launched by persistent employees with good ideas. "We've got people all over the world who are coming up with great new ideas, and trying them doesn't actually cost us a lot relative to the overall size of the group," says Branson.

Some of those good ideas are now integral parts of the Virgin legend:

- A woman who believed the company's airline should offer passengers onboard massages camped on Branson's doorstep until she was allowed to give him a neck and shoulder rub. Now an in-flight massage is a valued perk in Virgin Atlantic's Upper Class.

- A soon-to-be-married flight attendant came up with the idea of offering an integrated bridal planning service, everything from wedding apparel and catering to limousines and honeymoon reservations. She became the first CEO of Virgin Bride.

Virgin's latest ambitions are out of this world—literally. Branson recently teamed-up with Burt Rutan, winner of the X-Prize competition which awarded $10 million to the first nongovernment-funded flight to reach an altitude of 62 miles twice with the same vehicle. With Rutan's help, Virgin wasted no time in forming a new spin-off: Virgin Galactic. The enterprise will use a "stretch" version of SpaceShipOne, the name of the winning vehicle, to ferry ordinary citizens to outer space. Tickets on these flights are already selling for about $210,000 each, and the flights are expected to begin in 2008. According to Rutan, "Space tourism will be a multibillion-dollar industry." It's just that kind of vision—and risk taking—that has made the 54-year-old Branson's Virgin Group one of the most exciting and profitable examples of corporate entrepreneurship.

Sources: Hamel, G. 1999. Bringing Silicon Valley inside. *Harvard Business Review*, 77(5): 71–84; Kets de Vries, M. F. R. 1998. The transformational abilities of Virgin's Richard Branson and ABB's Percy Barnevik. *Organizational Dynamics*, 26(3): 7–21; Freedman, D. H. 2005. Burt Rutan, entrepreneur of the year. *Inc. Magazine*, January: 58–66; Hopkins, M. J. 2005. Richard Branson. *Inc. Magazine*, April: 100–102; and Port, O. 2004. SpaceShipOne's heady flight path. *BusinessWeek Online*, October 1, www.businessweek.com.

No matter how an entrepreneurial idea comes to light, however, a new venture concept must pass through two critical stages or it may never get off the ground: project definition and project impetus:

1. **Project definition.** A promising opportunity has to be justified in terms of its attractiveness in the marketplace and how well it fits with the corporation's other strategic objectives.

2. **Project impetus.** For a project to gain impetus, its strategic and economic impact must be supported by senior managers who have experience with similar projects. The project then becomes an embryonic business with its own organization and budget.

For a project to advance through these stages of definition and impetus, a product champion is often needed to generate support and encouragement. Champions are especially important during the time after a new project has been defined but before it gains momentum. They form a link between the definition and impetus stages of internal development, which they do by procuring resources and stimulating interest for the product among potential customers.[31] Often, they must work quietly and alone. Consider the example of Ken Kutaragi, the Sony engineer who championed the PlayStation.

> Even though Sony had made the processor that powered the first Nintendo video games, no one at Sony in the mid-1980s saw any future in such products. "It was a kind of snobbery," Kutaragi recalled. "For Sony people, the Nintendo product would have been very embarrassing to make because it was only a toy." But Kutaragi was convinced he could make a better product. He began working secretly on a video game. Kutaragi said, "I realized that if it was visible, it would be killed." He quietly began enlisting the support of senior executives, such as the head of R&D. He made a case that Sony could use his project to develop capabilities in digital technologies that would be important in the future. It was not until 1994, after years of "underground" development and quiet building of support, that Sony introduced the PlayStation. By the year 2000, Sony had sold 55 million of them, and Kutaragi became CEO of Sony Computer Entertainment. By 2005, Kutagari was Sony's Chief Operating Officer, and plans to launch the third generation version of the market-leading PlayStation (PS3) were well under way.[32]

Thus, product champions play an important entrepreneurial role in a corporate setting by encouraging others to take a chance on promising new ideas.[33]

## Measuring the Success of Corporate Entrepreneurship Activities

At this point in the discussion, it is reasonable to ask whether corporate entrepreneurship is successful. Corporate venturing, like the innovation process, usually requires a tremendous effort. Is it worth it? In this section we consider factors that corporations need to take into consideration when evaluating the success of CE programs. We also examine techniques that companies can use to limit the expense of venturing or to cut their losses when CE initiatives appear doomed.

*Comparing Strategic and Financial CE Goals*   Not all corporate venturing efforts are financially rewarding. Recall the example of NetActive, the Nortel Networks venture. The company was greeted with great enthusiasm once Nortel spun it off, and it attracted over $20 million in capital investment from the venture community. It also provided a technology that was highly demanded. But NetActive became . . . inactive. The company's Web site went dark, and it was put up for sale, a victim of the dot-com crash.[34] By most accounts, Nortel Networks did all the right things in developing NetActive in terms of establishing it as a stand-alone business and endowing it with assets and funding. But the business was a flop financially.

In terms of financial performance, slightly more than 50 percent of corporate venturing efforts reach profitability (measured by ROI) within six years of their launch.[35] If this were the only criterion for measuring success, it would seem to be a rather poor return. On the one hand, these results should be expected, because CE is riskier than other investments such as expanding ongoing operations. On the other hand, corporations expect a higher return from corporate venturing projects than from normal operations. Thus, in terms of the risk-return trade-off, it seems that CE often falls short of expectations.[36]

There are several other important criteria, however, for judging the success of a corporate venture initiative. In addition to financial goals, most CE programs have strategic goals. The strategic reasons for undertaking a corporate venture include strengthening competitive position, entering into new markets, expanding capabilities by learning and acquiring new knowledge, and building the corporation's base of resources and experience. Different corporations may emphasize some of these goals more than others, but in general three questions should be used to assess the effectiveness of a corporation's venturing initiatives:[37]

1. *Are the products or services offered by the venture accepted in the marketplace?* That is, is the venture considered to be a market success? If so, the financial returns are likely to be satisfactory. In addition, the venture may open doors into other markets and suggest avenues for other venture projects.
2. *Are the contributions of the venture to the corporation's internal competencies and experience valuable?* That is, does the venture add to the worth of the firm internally? If so, strategic goals such as leveraging existing assets, building new knowledge, and enhancing firm capabilities are likely to be met.
3. *Is the venture able to sustain its basis of competitive advantage?* That is, does the value proposition offered by the venture insulate it from competitive attack? If so, it is likely to place the corporation in a stronger position relative to competitors and provide a base from which to build other advantages.

As you can see, these criteria include both strategic and financial goals of CE. Another way to evaluate a corporate venture is in terms of the four criteria from the Balanced Scorecard (Chapter 3). In a successful venture, not only are financial and market acceptance (customer) goals met but so are the internal business and innovation and learning goals. Thus, when assessing the success of corporate venturing, it is important to look beyond simple financial returns and consider a well-rounded set of criteria.[38]

Next, we revisit the concept of real options as a way to evaluate the progress of a venture development program and consider the role of "exit champions" in helping corporations limit their exposure to venture projects that are unlikely to succeed.

*Exit Champions*   Although a culture of championing venture projects is advantageous for stimulating an ongoing stream of entrepreneurial initiatives, many—in fact, most—of the ideas will not work out. At some point in the process, a majority of initiatives will be abandoned. Sometimes, however, companies wait too long to terminate a new venture and do so only after large sums of resources are used up or, worse, result in a marketplace failure. Motorola's costly global satellite telecom project known as Iridium provides a useful illustration. Even though problems with the project existed during the lengthy development process, Motorola refused to pull the plug. Only after investing $5 billion and years of effort was the project abandoned.[39]

How can companies avoid these costly and discouraging defeats? One way is to support a key role in the CE process: "exit champions." In contrast to product champions and other entrepreneurial enthusiasts within the corporation, exit champions are willing to question the viability of a venture project.[40] By demanding hard evidence and challenging the belief system that is carrying an idea forward, exit champions hold the line on ventures that appear shaky.

Both product champions and exit champions must be willing to energetically stand up for what they believe. Both put their reputations on the line. But they also differ in important ways. Product champions deal in uncertainty and ambiguity. Exit champions reduce ambiguity by gathering hard data and developing a strong case for why a project should be killed. Product champions are often thought to be willing to violate procedures and operate outside normal channels. Exit champions, by contrast, often have to reinstate procedures and reassert the decision-making criteria that are supposed to guide venture decisions. Whereas product champions often emerge as heroes, exit champions run the risk of losing status by opposing popular projects.

Thus, the role of exit champion may seem unappealing. But it is one that could save a corporation both financially and in terms of its reputation in the marketplace. It is especially important because one measure of the success of a firm's CE efforts is the extent to which it knows when to cut its losses and move on.

*Real Options*   Another way firms can minimize failure and avoid losses from pursuing faulty ideas is to apply the logic of real options (Chapter 6). Applied to entrepreneurship, real options suggest a path that corporations can use to manage the uncertainty associated with launching new ventures.

Options are created whenever a company begins to explore a new venture concept. That is, initial investments, such as conducting market tests, building prototypes, and forming venture teams, bestow an option to invest further. Retail giant Wal-Mart provides an interesting example of this limited approach. It's safe to say Wal-Mart could enter just about any market it wanted to in a big way. But its recent decision to enter the used-car business began with an experiment. Four dealerships were set up in the Houston, Texas, area under a brand called Price 1 Auto Stores. According to Ira Kalish, chief economist for Retail Forward, Inc., a consulting group that specializes in retailing, "Wal-Mart will seek to test the outer boundaries of what consumers are willing to let Wal-Mart be."[41]

With its four-store experiment, Wal-Mart is obtaining an option to invest more at a later date. The results of Wal-Mart's market test will be factored into the next round of decisions. This is consistent with the logic of real options—based on feedback at each stage of development, firms decide whether to exercise their options by making further investments. Alternatively, they may decide that the idea is not worth further consideration. In so doing—that is, by making smaller and more incremental investments—firms keep their total investment low and minimize downside risk. Often it's the job of an exit champion or some other practically minded organization member to decide that a project does not warrant further investment.

Consider the real options logic that Johnson Controls, a maker of car seats, instrument panels, and interior control systems uses to advance or eliminate entrepreneurial ideas.[42] Johnson options each new innovative idea by making a small investment in it. To decide whether to exercise an option, the idea must continue to prove itself at each stage of development. Here's how Jim Geschke, vice president and general manager of electronics integration at Johnson, describes the process:

> Think of Johnson as an innovation machine. The front end has a robust series of gates that each idea must pass through. Early on, we'll have many ideas and spend a little money on each of them. As they get more fleshed out, the ideas go through a gate where a go or no-go decision is made. A lot if ideas get filtered out, so there are far fewer items, and the spending on each goes up. . . . Several months later each idea will face another gate. If it passes, that means it's a serious idea that we are going to develop. Then the spending goes way up, and the number of ideas goes way down. By the time you reach the final gate, you need to have a credible business case in order to be accepted. At a certain point in the development process, we take our idea to customers and ask them what they think. Sometimes they say, "That's a terrible idea. Forget it." Other times they say, "That's fabulous. I want a million of them."

This process of evaluating ideas by separating winning ideas from losing ones in a way that keeps investments low has helped Johnson Controls grow its revenues at a double-digit rate to over $28 billion a year. Thus, using real options logic to advance the development process is a key way that firms reduce uncertainty and minimize innovation-related failures.[43]

The types of venture projects and entrepreneurial initiatives that corporations pursue are more likely to succeed if their organizational members behave entrepreneurially. In the next section, we look at the practices and characteristics that are associated with an entrepreneurial orientation.

## >>Entrepreneurial Orientation

Firms that want to engage in successful corporate entrepreneurship need to have an entrepreneurial orientation (EO). EO refers to the strategy-making practices that businesses use in identifying and launching corporate ventures. It represents a frame of mind and a perspective toward entrepreneurship that is reflected in a firm's ongoing processes and corporate culture.[44]

An entrepreneurial orientation has five dimensions that permeate the decision-making styles and practices of the firm's members. These are autonomy, innovativeness, proactiveness, competitive aggressiveness, and risk taking. These factors can work together to enhance a firm's entrepreneurial performance. But even those firms that are strong in only a few aspects of EO can be very successful.[45] Exhibit 12.2 summarizes the dimensions of an entrepreneurial orientation. Below we discuss the five dimensions of entrepreneurial orientation and how they have been used to enhance internal venture development.

### Autonomy

*Autonomy* refers to a willingness to act independently in order to carry forward an entrepreneurial vision or opportunity. It applies to both individuals and teams that operate outside an organization's existing norms and strategies. In the context of corporate entrepreneurship, autonomous work units are often used to leverage existing strengths in new arenas, identify opportunities that are beyond the organization's current capabilities, and encourage development of new ventures or improved business practices.[46]

**Exhibit 12.2**

**Dimensions of Entrepreneurial Orientation**

| Dimension | Definition |
|---|---|
| Autonomy | Independent action by an individual or team aimed at bringing forth a business concept or vision and carrying it through to completion. |
| Innovativeness | A willingness to introduce novelty through experimentation and creative processes aimed at developing new products and services as well as new processes. |
| Proactiveness | A forward-looking perspective characteristic of a marketplace leader that has the foresight to seize opportunities in anticipation of future demand. |
| Competitive aggressiveness | An intense effort to outperform industry rivals characterized by a combative posture or an aggressive response aimed at improving position or overcoming a threat in a competitive marketplace. |
| Risk taking | Making decisions and taking action without certain knowledge of probable outcomes; some undertakings may also involve making substantial resource commitments in the process of venturing forward. |

Source: Dess, G. G., & Lumpkin, G. T. 2005. The role of entrepreneurial orientation in stimulating effective corporate entrepreneurship. *Academy of Management Executive,* 19(1): 147–156; Covin, J. G., & Slevin, D. P. 1991. A conceptual model of entrepreneurship as firm behavior. *Entrepreneurship Theory & Practice,* Fall: 7–25; Lumpkin, G. T., and Dess, G. G. 1996. Clarifying the entrepreneurial orientation construct and linking it to performance. *Academy of Management Review,* 21: 135–172; Miller, D. 1983. The correlates of entrepreneurship in three types of firms. *Management Science,* 29: 770–791.

The need for autonomy may apply to either dispersed or focused entrepreneurial efforts. Clearly, because of the emphasis on venture projects that are being developed outside of the normal flow of business, a focused approach suggests a working environment that is relatively autonomous. But autonomy may also be important in an organization where entrepreneurship is part of the corporate culture. Everything from the methods of group interaction to the firm's reward system must make organizational members feel as if they can think freely about venture opportunities, take time to investigate them, and act without fear of condemnation. This implies a respect for the autonomy of each individual and an openness to the independent thinking that goes into championing a corporate venture idea. Thus, autonomy represents a type of empowerment (see Chapter 11) that is directed at identifying and leveraging entrepreneurial opportunities.

Two techniques that organizations often use to promote autonomy include:

1. *Using skunkworks to foster entrepreneurial thinking.* To help managers and other employees set aside their usual routines and practices, companies often develop independent work units called "skunkworks" to encourage creative thinking and brainstorming about new venture ideas. The term is used to represent a work environment that is often physically separate from corporate headquarters and free of the normal job requirements and pressures. Nearly every major corporation that grows by means of entrepreneurship uses some form of skunkworks.[47] That's what Overstock.com, the successful online retailer, did when it decided to explore creating an auction service that would compete with eBay. Led by 29-year-old Holly MacDonald-Korth, a group of Overstock staffers set up shop in a corner of one of its company warehouses. The group started by reselling merchandise that had been returned to Overstock on eBay. "We started this business on eBay just like someone would probably start it in their garage," says MacDonald-Korth. "I really wanted to understand all the problems a small business would face." Within four months, their e-selling experiment was bringing in about $30,000 per week. Soon after, they used their newly gained knowledge of selling online to create a new division called Overstock Auctions. The Overstock approach aims to improve on eBay's service in a few key ways, including offering listing fees that are 30 percent lower and extending auctions to prevent last minute bidders from scooping up items during the last few seconds of an auction.[48]

2. *Designing organization structures that support independent action.* Sometimes corporations need to do more than create independent think tanks to help stimulate new ideas. Changes in organizational structure may also be necessary. Established firms with traditional structures often have to break out of such molds in order to remain competitive. This was the conclusion of Deloitte Consulting, a division of Deloitte Touche Tohmatsu, one of the world's largest accounting consultancies. After losing millions in consulting jobs to young Internet-based consultancies, Deloitte decided to reorganize. The first step was to break the firm into small, autonomous groups called "chip-aways" that could operate with the speed and flexibility of a start-up. "This allows them to react more like a Navy SEAL team rather than an Army division," according to Tom Rodenhauser, author of *Inside Consulting*. One of Deloitte's first chip-aways was Roundarch, a Web technology and marketing venture that projected first-year revenues of $40 million and beat its own projections by 10 percent.[49] Other organization structures may also help promote autonomy, such as virtual organizations that allow people to work independently and communicate via the Web.

Creating autonomous work units and encouraging independent action may have pitfalls that can jeopardize their effectiveness. Autonomous teams, for example, often lack coordination. Excessive decentralization has a strong potential to create inefficiencies, such as duplication of effort and wasting resources on projects with questionable feasibility. For example, Chris Galvin, former CEO of Motorola, scrapped the skunkworks approach the company had been using to develop new wireless phones. Fifteen teams had created 128 different phones, which led to spiraling costs and overly complex operations.[50]

Thus, for autonomous work units and independent projects to be effective, such efforts have to be measured and monitored. This requires a delicate balance for corporations. They must have the patience and budget to tolerate the explorations of autonomous groups and have the strength to cut back efforts that are not bearing fruit. It must be undertaken with a clear sense of purpose—namely, to generate new sources of competitive advantage.

## Innovativeness

*Innovativeness* refers to a firm's efforts to find new opportunities and novel solutions. In the beginning of this chapter we discussed innovation; here the focus is on innovativeness—that is, a firm's attitude toward innovation and willingness to innovate. It involves creativity and experimentation that result in new products, new services, or improved technological processes. Innovativeness is one of the major components of an entrepreneurial strategy. As indicated at the beginning of the chapter, however, the job of managing innovativeness can be very challenging.

Innovativeness requires that firms depart from existing technologies and practices and venture beyond the current state of the art. Inventions and new ideas need to be nurtured even when their benefits are unclear. However, in today's climate of rapid change, effectively producing, assimilating, and exploiting innovations can be an important avenue for achieving competitive advantages.

As our earlier discussion of CE indicated, many corporations owe their success to an active program of innovation-based corporate venturing.[51] Few, however, have a more exemplary reputation for effective entrepreneurship than W. L. Gore. Exhibit 12.3 describes the policies that create a climate of innovativeness at W. L. Gore.

Two of the methods companies can use to enhance their competitive position through innovativeness are:

1. *Fostering creativity and experimentation.* To innovate successfully, firms must break out of the molds that have shaped their thinking. They also must create avenues for employees to express themselves. Tim Warren, director of research and technical services at the oil giant Royal Dutch/Shell, was sure that Shell's employees had vast reserves of innovative talent that had not been tapped. He also felt that more radical innovations were needed for Shell to achieve its performance goals. So Warren allocated $20 million to be used for breakthrough ideas that would change the playing field. He also asked his people to devote up to 10 percent of their time to nonlinear thinking. The initiative became known as the "GameChanger." With the help of Strategos Consulting, the GameChanger review panel developed an Innovation Lab to help employees develop game-changing ideas. The first lab attracted 72 would-be entrepreneurs who learned how to uncover new opportunities and challenge industry conventions. By the end of the three-day lab, a portfolio of 240 ideas had been generated. The GameChanger process, which now provides funding of $100,000 to $600,000 within 10 days after approval, has now found a permanent home within Shell and has become a critical part of its internal entrepreneurial process.[52]

2. *Investing in new technology, R&D, and continuous improvement.* For successful innovation, companies must seek advantages from the latest technologies. This

Exhibit 12.3
W. L. Gore's New
Rules for Fostering
Innovativeness

| Rule | Implications |
|---|---|
| **The power of small teams** | Gore believes that small teams promote familiarity and autonomy. Even its manufacturing plants are capped at just 200 people. That way everyone can get to know one another on a first-name basis and work together with minimal rules. This also helps to cultivate "an environment where creativity can flourish," according to CEO Chuck Carroll. |
| **No ranks, no titles, no bosses** | Because Gore believes in maximizing individual potential, employees, dubbed "associates," decide for themselves what new commitments to take on. Associates have "sponsors," rather than bosses, and there are no standardized job descriptions or categories. Everyone is supposed to take on a unique role. Committees of co-workers evaluate each team member's contribution and decide on compensation. |
| **Take the long view** | Although impatient about the status quo, Gore exhibits great patience with the time—often years, sometimes decades—it takes to nurture and develop breakthrough products and bring them to market. |
| **Make time for face time** | Gore avoids the traditional hierarchical chain of command, opting instead for a team-based environment that fosters personal initiative. Gore also discourages memos and e-mail and promotes direct, person-to-person communication among all associates— anyone in the company can talk to anyone else. |
| **Lead by leading** | Associates are encouraged to spend about 10 percent of their time pursuing speculative new ideas. Anyone is free to champion products, as long as they have the passion and ideas to attract followers. Many of Gore's breakthroughs started with one person acting on his or her own initiative and developed as colleagues helped in their spare time. |
| **Celebrate failure** | When a project doesn't work out and the team decides to kill it, they celebrate just as they would if it had been a success—with some beer and maybe a glass of champagne. Rather than condemning failure, Gore figures that celebrating it encourages experimentation and risk taking. |

Source: Deutschman, A. 2004. The fabric of creativity. *Fast Company*, 89: 54–62; Levering, R., & Moskowitz, M. 2005. The 100 best companies to work for. *Fortune*, 151(2): 61–72; and www.gore.com.

often requires a substantial investment. Consider, for example, Dell Computer Corp.'s new production capability. With its new OptiPlex manufacturing system, Dell is attempting to revolutionize the way computers are made. Of course, it is still necessary to connect part A to part B—that is, to conduct the basic assembly process. But how those parts are received, handled, and turned into finished product is changing radically because of Dell's state-of-the-art automation techniques. The OptiPlex factory is managed by a network of computers that takes in orders, communicates with suppliers, draws in components, organizes the assembly process, and arranges shipping. The result: Hundreds of computers can be custom-built in an eight-hour shift, productivity per person increased 160 percent, and most parts are kept on hand for a mere two hours. Dell was already leading other major PC manufacturers by maintaining product inventories for only 5 or 6 days compared with the industry average of 50 to 90 days. With its latest innovation, Dell now expects to cut inventory turnover down to $2\frac{1}{2}$ days.[53]

Innovativeness can be a source of great progress and strong corporate growth, but there are also major pitfalls for firms that invest in innovation. Expenditures on R&D aimed at identifying new products or processes can be a waste of resources if the effort does not yield results. Another danger is related to the competitive climate. Even if a company innovates a new capability or successfully applies a technological breakthrough, another company may develop a similar innovation or find a use for it that is more profitable. Finally, in many firms, R&D and other innovation efforts are among the first to be cut back during an economic downturn.

Therefore, even though innovativeness is an important means of internal corporate venturing, it also involves major risks because investments in innovations may not pay off. For strategic managers of entrepreneurial firms, however, successfully developing and adopting innovations can generate competitive advantages and provide a major source of growth for the firm.

## Proactiveness

*Proactiveness* refers to a firm's efforts to seize new opportunities. Proactive organizations monitor trends, identify the future needs of existing customers, and anticipate changes in demand or emerging problems that can lead to new venture opportunities. Proactiveness involves not only recognizing changes but also being willing to act on those insights ahead of the competition. Strategic managers who practice proactiveness have their eye on the future in a search for new possibilities for growth and development.

Such a forward-looking perspective is important for companies that seek to be industry leaders. Many proactive firms seek out ways not only to be future oriented but also to change the very nature of competition in their industry. From its beginning, Dell sold personal computers directly to consumers, diminishing the role of retail stores as a way to reach customers. Its success changed the way PCs were sold.[54]

Proactiveness is especially effective at creating competitive advantages, because it puts competitors in the position of having to respond to successful initiatives. The benefit gained by firms that are the first to enter new markets, establish brand identity, implement administrative techniques, or adopt new operating technologies in an industry is called first mover advantage.[55]

First movers usually have several advantages. First, industry pioneers, especially in new industries, often capture unusually high profits because there are no competitors to drive prices down. Second, first movers that establish brand recognition are usually able to retain their image and hold on to the market share gains they earned by being first. Sometimes these benefits also accrue to other early movers in an industry, but, generally speaking, first movers have an advantage that can be sustained until firms enter the maturity phase of an industry's life cycle.[56]

First movers are not always successful. For one thing, the customers of companies that introduce novel products or embrace breakthrough technologies may be reluctant to commit to a new way of doing things. In his book *Crossing the Chasm,* Geoffrey A. Moore noted that most firms seek evolution, not revolution, in their operations. This makes it difficult for a first mover to sell promising new technologies.[57] Second, some companies try to be a first mover before they are ready. Consider Apple Computer's Newton.

Newton, the first personal digital assistant (PDA), was released in 1993. Because it was revolutionary, it generated a great deal of media attention and initial sales success. But the Newton was troubled from the beginning because it was launched before it was ready. For too many customers, it could not do what it claimed: recognize handwriting. But Apple was desperate to launch ahead of Microsoft. "We cut corners and ignored problems . . . to gain an edge in a reckless public relations battle," said Larry Tesler, who headed the Newton group until a few months before its release. In 1998, after five years of trying to recover from its initial failure, the Newton project was killed.[58]

Even with these caveats, however, companies that are first movers can enhance their competitive position. Firms can use two other methods to act proactively.

1. ***Introducing new products or technological capabilities ahead of the competition.*** Maintaining a high level of proactiveness is central to the corporate culture of some major corporations. Sony's mission statement asserts, for example, "We should always be the pioneers with our products—out front leading the market. We believe in leading the public with new products rather than asking them what kind of products they want."[59] Sony has launched numerous new products that not only have succeeded financially but have changed the competitive landscape. Walkman, PlayStation, Betacam, and Vaio laptop computers are just a few of the many leading products that Sony has introduced.

2. ***Continuously seeking out new product or service offerings.*** Firms that provide new resources or sources of supply can benefit from a proactive stance. Aerie Networks is a Denver company that aspires to expand the U.S. fiber-optic network extensively. Two factors make its efforts especially proactive. First, it is laying cable that contains 432 fibers (compared with the 96 strands that established companies like AT&T typically install). This approach fits Aerie's goal of being the low-cost wholesaler of bandwidth to long-distance carriers and other fiber users. Second, it worked for over a year to form an alliance with gas pipeline rivals that made it possible to use up to 25,000 miles of pipeline rights-of-way across 26 states. The partnering was more difficult than the technology—Aerie had to give a 30 percent stake to the gas pipeline companies—but the potential payoff is enormous.[60]

Being an industry leader does not always lead to competitive advantages. Some firms that have launched pioneering new products or staked their reputation on new brands have failed to get the hoped-for payoff. Two major beverage companies—Coca-Cola and PepsiCo—invested $75 million to launch sodas that would capitalize on the low-carb diet trend. But with half the carbohydrates taken out, neither *C2,* Coke's entry, nor *Pepsi Edge* tasted very good. The two new brands combined never achieved more than one percent market share. PepsiCo announced in would halt production in 2006 and Coca-Cola was expected to follow suit.[61] Such missteps are indicative of the dangers of trying to proactively anticipate demand. Strategy Spotlight 12.7, in contrast, describes another type of proactiveness—how some organizations are using entrepreneurial thinking and practices to effectively promote corporate social responsibility.

Thus, careful monitoring and scanning of the environment, as well as extensive feasibility research, are needed for a proactive strategy to lead to competitive advantages. Firms that do it well usually have substantial growth and internal development to show for it. Many of them have been able to sustain the advantages of proactiveness for years.

## Competitive Aggressiveness

*Competitive aggressiveness* refers to a firm's efforts to outperform its industry rivals. Companies with an aggressive orientation are willing to "do battle" with competitors.

## Socially Responsible Corporate Entrepreneurship

One of the most important trends in U.S. business today is corporate social responsibility (CSR). Proactively oriented firms are seizing opportunities to take a leading role in issues such as the environment, product safety, and fair trade. Among the most interesting examples of this, as suggested in the Chapter 1 section on social innovation, are those firms that are taking an entrepreneurial approach to CSR. That is, they are using new technologies, environmentally friendly ventures, and entrepreneurial practices to advance their social responsibility goals. Following is a sample of three corporations that are taking a very entrepreneurial approach to corporate social responsibility.

### Whirlpool Corporation—From efficiency to advocacy

Whirlpool is perhaps best known for its "white boxes"—the refrigerators, freezers, and laundry appliances that account for over 60 percent of its $13 billion in annual sales. To explore what creates customer loyalty, Whirlpool conducted a global survey of its customers. "We discovered there is a strong correlation between a company's performance in appliance markets and their social response to issues such as energy efficiency and pollution," said Steve Willis, director of Whirlpool's global environment, health, and safety programs. One result has been its innovative Duet Series of washers and dryers that significantly reduces energy consumption. Recently, Whirlpool decided to take its environmental efforts a step farther: It joined The Natural Step, an entrepreneurial organization that is advancing the movement toward environmental sustainability by advocating the development of innovative products that meet high standards of ecological sustainability.

### Interface, Inc.—Doing more with less

In Chapter 1, we saw how some companies have changed their corporate missions to include socially responsible goals like protecting the environment. Carpet maker Interface Inc. has found a way not only to become more environmentally friendly but also to achieve a universal entrepreneurial objective: Do more with less. By leasing rather than selling carpets, Georgia-based Interface is able to take back worn carpets and "remanufacture" them. As a

result, it has cut its raw materials input costs by nearly 100 percent and its business customers get to deduct the cost of leasing. "Our costs are down, not up," according to CEO Ray Anderson. "Sustainability doesn't cost more, it saves." Recently, Interface instituted a program known as EcoSense to educate its employees about sustainability and reward them for making environmental improvements. These savings helped Interface survive the 40 percent decline in sales of office furnishings that followed the dot-com collapse and the September 11th terrorist attack. "We might not have made it if it were not for our EcoSense programs," says Anderson.

### Green Mountain Coffee Roasters—Empowering local entrepreneurs

As the name suggests, this NASDAQ-listed corporation (GMCR) is located in the Green Mountains of Vermont. But its reach is global. As a roaster and distributor of specialty coffees, GMCR has become a leading advocate for fair trade practices and providing financial support for local coffee growers. "Our president and CEO Robert Stiller visited places where coffee is grown and was struck by the levels of poverty. He wanted to do something about it," said Rick Peyser, director of public relations. As a result, GMCR now purchases coffee beans from small farm cooperatives in Peru, Mexico, and Sumatra. It also provides micro-loans to underwrite family businesses that are trying to create more diverse agricultural economies. Back home in its Waterbury, Vermont, roasting facility, GMCR uses a 95-kilowatt cogeneration system that captures waste heat from its propane-fired generator and recycles it for both coffee roasting and space heating.

Each of these companies has recently been named one of the 100 Best Corporate Citizens by *Business Ethics* magazine. However, major corporations still have their critics. In fact, companies that claim to be making progress in advancing CSR are often the most loudly criticized. For example, British Petroleum, which has endeavored to be an oil industry leader in supporting environmentally sensitive energy development, is often attacked by environmental groups despite initiatives such as investing $48 million to develop the world's largest solar energy project. Despite such criticism, it is encouraging to note that entrepreneurial activities can help companies achieve their social responsibility goals as well as their innovation and growth goals.

Sources: Asmus, P. 2005. 100 best corporate citizens for 2005. *Business Ethics*, www.business-ethics.com; Asmus, P. 2003. 100 best corporate citizens for 2003. *Business Ethics*, www.business-ethics.com; Baker, M. 2001. BP anounces world's largest solar project. *Business Respect*, 1: April 6; Hawken, P., Lovins, A., & Lovins, H. 2000. *Natural capitalism*. Boston: Back Bay Books; see also www.bp.com; www.domini.com; www.hoovers.com; and www.ifsia.com.

They might slash prices and sacrifice profitability to gain market share or spend aggressively to obtain manufacturing capacity. As an avenue of firm development and growth, competitive aggressiveness may involve being very assertive in leveraging the results of other entrepreneurial activities such as innovativeness or proactiveness.

Unlike innovativeness and proactiveness, however, which tend to focus on market opportunities, competitive aggressiveness is directed toward competitors. The SWOT (strengths, weaknesses, opportunities, threats) analysis discussed in Chapters 2 and 3 provides a useful way to distinguish between these different approaches to corporate entrepreneurship. Proactiveness, as we saw in the last section, is a response to opportunities—the O in SWOT. Competitive aggressiveness, by contrast, is a response to threats—the T in SWOT. A competitively aggressive posture is important for firms that seek to enter new markets in the face of intense rivalry.

Strategic managers can use competitive aggressiveness to combat industry trends that threaten their survival or market position. Sometimes firms need to be forceful in defending the competitive position that has made them an industry leader. Firms often need to be aggressive to ensure their advantage by capitalizing on new technologies or serving new market needs.

Two of the ways competitively aggressive firms enhance their entrepreneurial position are:

1. ***Entering markets with drastically lower prices.*** Smaller firms often fear the entry of resource-rich large firms into their marketplace. Because the larger firms usually have deep pockets, they can afford to cut prices without being seriously damaged by an extended period of narrow margins. In the mid-1990s, the retail record store business was nearly wiped out when larger new entrants launched a price war. It started when Best Buy, a "big box" electronics retailer with hundreds of stores, was looking for a way to increase traffic in its large suburban stores. It decided to sell compact disks (CDs). Most record stores were paying about $10 at wholesale for CDs and selling them for $14 or more. Best Buy priced new releases at $9.98. Soon, archrival Circuit City also started retailing CDs and a major price war followed. Within two years, seven record stores declared bankruptcy. The Best Buy executive who championed the CD policy said, "The whole goal of getting into business is taking market share and building your business. That's what it's about."[62]

2. ***Copying the business practices or techniques of successful competitors.*** We've all heard that imitation is the highest form of flattery. But imitation may also be used to take business from competitors; as long as the idea or practice is not protected by intellectual property laws, it's not illegal. This was the conclusion of Chris Bogan, CEO of Best Practices, LLC, a North Carolina consulting group with $8 million in revenues. Best Practices seeks out best practices in order to repackage and resell them or use them internally. Its mission is to find superstar performers in the business world and then sell their secrets to others. Best Practices's revenues come from one-time consulting projects and products like databases and benchmarking reports on subjects such as managing call centers and launching new products. Bogan's philosophy is that companies don't have to invent solutions to their problems; they can "steal" them from successful companies.[63]

Another practice companies use to overcome the competition is to make preannouncements of new products or technologies. This type of signaling is aimed not only at potential customers but also at competitors to see how they will react or to discourage them from launching similar initiatives. Sometimes the preannouncements are made just to scare off competitors, an action that has potential ethical implications.

Competitive aggressiveness may not always lead to competitive advantages. Some companies (or their CEOs) have severely damaged their reputations by being overly aggressive. Microsoft is a good example. Although it continues to be a dominant player, its highly aggressive profile makes it the subject of scorn by some businesses and individuals. Microsoft's image also contributed to the huge antitrust suit brought against it by the U.S. government and several states. Efforts to find viable replacements for the Microsoft products upon which users have become overly dependent may eventually erode Microsoft's leading role as a software provider.

Therefore, competitive aggressiveness is a strategy that is best used in moderation. Companies that aggressively establish their competitive position and vigorously exploit opportunities to achieve profitability may, over the long run, be better able to sustain their competitive advantages if their goal is to defeat, rather than decimate, their competitors.

## Risk Taking

*Risk taking* refers to a firm's willingness to seize a venture opportunity even though it does not know whether the venture will be successful—to act boldly without knowing the consequences. To be successful through corporate entrepreneurship, firms usually have to take on riskier alternatives, even if it means forgoing the methods or products that have worked in the past. To obtain high financial returns, firms take such risks as assuming high levels of debt, committing large amounts of firm resources, introducing new products into new markets, and investing in unexplored technologies.

In some ways, all of the approaches to internal development that we have discussed are potentially risky. Whether they are being aggressive, proactive, or innovative, firms on the path of corporate entrepreneurship must act without knowing how their actions will turn out. Before launching their strategies, corporate entrepreneurs must know their firm's appetite for risk. How far is it willing to go without knowing what the outcome will be?

Three types of risk that organizations and their executives face are business risk, financial risk, and personal risk:

- *Business risk taking* involves venturing into the unknown without knowing the probability of success. This is the risk associated with entering untested markets or committing to unproven technologies.

- *Financial risk taking* requires that a company borrow heavily or commit a large portion of its resources in order to grow. In this context, risk is used to refer to the risk/return trade-off that is familiar in financial analysis.

- *Personal risk taking* refers to the risks that an executive assumes in taking a stand in favor of a strategic course of action. Executives who take such risks stand to influence the course of their whole company, and their decisions also can have significant implications for their careers.

In many business situations, all three types of risk taking are present. Taking bold new actions rarely affects just one part of the organization. Consider the example of David D'Alessandro of John Hancock Financial Services, Inc.

David D'Alessandro joined insurance giant John Hancock in 1984 as its vice president of corporate communications. At the time, Hancock's image was weak due in part to a series of forgettable TV ads that failed to distinguish it from other insurance carriers. D'Alessandro championed a new advertising campaign that featured "real life" images, such as a husband and wife arguing, and a lesbian couple adopting a Vietnamese baby. Although it was costly to produce and risky for the image of the traditional insurance carrier, sales surged 17 percent in the first year of the ad campaign. The risk also paid off for D'Alessandro personally: In

May 2000 he was named the youngest chairman and CEO in John Hancock's history. (In 2004, John Hancock was acquired by Toronto-based Manulife Financial Corporation.)[64]

Even though risk taking involves taking chances, it is not gambling. The best-run companies investigate the consequences of various opportunities and create scenarios of likely outcomes. Their goal is to reduce the riskiness of business decision making. As we saw in the section on product champions, a key to managing entrepreneurial risks is to evaluate new venture opportunities thoroughly enough to reduce the uncertainty surrounding them.

Companies can use the following two methods to strengthen their competitive position through risk taking.

1. ***Researching and assessing risk factors to minimize uncertainty.*** Although all new business endeavors are inherently risky, firms that do their homework can usually reduce their risk. For example, Graybar Electric Co., a privately held 136-year-old provider of data and telecom equipment, had to revamp its warehouse and distribution system. The Internet was creating booming demand. But with 231 local distribution centers, each run independently, Graybar could not get its products to customers fast enough. After careful analysis, the company hatched a plan that consolidated 16 supply warehouses without displacing any local managers, thus preserving the quality of service for both customers and employees. The changeover was expensive—$144 million over four years. But the plan called for a payback after five years, and even with telecom sector sales slipping, Graybar's prudent risk taking led to a 21 percent surge in sales in 2000. By 2004, its annual revenues exceeded $4 billion.[65]

2. ***Using techniques that have worked in other domains.*** Risky methods that other companies have applied successfully may be used to advance corporate ventures. Consider the actions of Autobytel.com, one of the first companies to sell cars online. Although it had enjoyed early success by being a first mover, it wanted to jump-start its sales. It decided to make a risky move. In a year when Autobytel.com earned only $6 million in revenues, it committed $1.2 million to a 30-second TV advertisement. But that ad was run during the Super Bowl and Autobytel was the first dot-com ever to use that venue. The free publicity and favorable business press it received extended far beyond the 30 seconds that Autobytel's $1.2 million had bought it.[66]

Risk taking, by its nature, involves potential dangers and pitfalls. Only carefully managed risk is likely to lead to competitive advantages. Actions that are taken without sufficient forethought, research, and planning may prove to be very costly. The era of dot-com start-ups and subsequent failures proved that businesses are often launched—at great expense—without a clear sense of the long-term or even, in some cases, short-term consequences. When the Internet bubble burst, more than $3 trillion of investment wealth was wiped out of the U.S. stock markets, due in large part to the collapse of the dot-com surge.[67] Along with the financial losses, the business and personal losses were enormous.

Strategic managers must always remain mindful of potential risks. In his book *Innovation and Entrepreneurship,* Peter Drucker argued that successful entrepreneurs are typically not risk takers. Instead, they take steps to minimize risks by carefully understanding them. That is how they avoid focusing on risk and remain focused on opportunity.[68] Thus, risk taking is a good place to close this chapter on corporate entrepreneurship. Companies that choose to grow through internal corporate venturing must remember that entrepreneurship always involves embracing what is new and uncertain.

# Summary

To remain competitive in today's economy, established firms must find new avenues for development and growth. This chapter has addressed how innovation and corporate entrepreneurship can be a means of internal venture creation and strategic renewal, and how an entrepreneurial orientation can help corporations enhance their competitive position.

Innovation is one of the primary means by which corporations grow and strengthen their strategic position. Innovations can take several forms, ranging from radical breakthrough innovations to incremental improvement innovations. Innovations are often used to update products and services or for improving organizational processes. Managing the innovation process is often challenging, because it involves a great deal of uncertainty and there are many choices to be made about the extent and type of innovations to pursue. By defining the scope of innovation, managing the pace of innovation, and collaborating with innovation partners, firms can more effectively manage the innovation process.

We also discussed the role of corporate entrepreneurship in venture development and strategic renewal. Entrepreneurial firms that pursue a blue ocean strategy find success by breaking down traditional industry barriers and creating new arenas in which to achieve market dominance. Other corporations usually take either a focused or dispersed approach to corporate venturing. Firms with a focused approach usually separate the corporate venturing activity from the ongoing operations of the firm in order to foster independent thinking and encourage entrepreneurial team members to think and act without the constraints imposed by the corporation. In corporations where venturing activities are dispersed, a culture of entrepreneurship permeates all parts of the company in order to induce strategic behaviors by all organizational members. In measuring the success of corporate venturing activities, both financial and strategic objectives should be considered.

Most entrepreneurial firms need to have an entrepreneurial orientation: the methods, practices, and decision-making styles that strategic managers use to act entrepreneurially. Five dimensions of entrepreneurial orientation are found in firms that pursue corporate venture strategies. Autonomy, innovativeness, proactiveness, competitive aggressiveness, and risk taking each make a unique contribution to the pursuit of new opportunities. When deployed effectively, the methods and practices of an entrepreneurial orientation can be used to engage successfully in corporate entrepreneurship and new venture creation. However, strategic managers must remain mindful of the pitfalls associated with each of these approaches.

## Summary Review Questions

1. What is meant by the concept of a continuum of radical and incremental innovations?
2. What are the dilemmas that organizations face when deciding what innovation projects to pursue? What steps can organizations take to effectively manage the innovation process?
3. What is the difference between focused and dispersed approaches to corporate entrepreneurship?
4. How are business incubators used to foster internal corporate venturing?
5. What is the role of the product champion in bringing a new product or service into existence in a corporation? How can companies use product champions to enhance their venture development efforts?
6. Explain the difference between proactiveness and competitive aggressiveness in terms of achieving and sustaining competitive advantage.
7. Describe how the entrepreneurial orientation (EO) dimensions of innovativeness, proactiveness, and risk taking can be combined to create competitive advantages for entrepreneurial firms.

Select two different major corporations from two different industries (you might use Fortune 500 companies to make your selection). Compare and contrast these organizations in terms of their entrepreneurial orientation.

| Entrepreneurial Orientation | Company A | Company B |
|---|---|---|
| Autonomy | | |
| Innovativeness | | |
| Proactiveness | | |
| Competitive Aggressiveness | | |
| Risk Taking | | |

## Based on Your Comparison:

1. How is the corporation's entrepreneurial orientation reflected in its strategy?
2. Which corporation would you say has the stronger entrepreneurial orientation?
3. Is the corporation with the stronger entrepreneurial orientation also stronger in terms of financial performance?

1. Select a firm known for its corporate entrepreneurship activities. Research the company and discuss how it has positioned itself relative to its close competitors. Does it have a unique strategic advantage? Disadvantage? Explain.
2. Explain the difference between product innovations and process innovations. Provide examples of firms that have recently introduced each type of innovation. What are the types of innovations related to the strategies of each firm?
3. Using the Internet, select a company that is listed on the NASDAQ or New York Stock Exchange. Research the extent to which the company has an entrepreneurial culture. Does the company use product champions? Does it have a corporate venture capital fund? Do you believe its entrepreneurial efforts are sufficient to generate sustainable advantages?
4. How can an established firm use an entrepreneurial orientation to enhance its overall strategic position? Provide examples.

1. Innovation activities are often aimed at making a discovery or commercializing a technology ahead of the competition. What are some of the unethical practices that companies could engage in during the innovation process? What are the potential long-term consequences of such actions?
2. Discuss the ethical implications of using entrepreneurial policies and practices to pursue corporate social responsibility goals. Are these efforts authentic and genuine or just an attempt to attract more customers?

# References

1. Sources for the Polaroid example include Charan, R., & Useem, J. 2002. Why companies fail. *Fortune,* May 15; Knox, N. 2001. Rivals push Polaroid toward Chapter 11. *USA Today,* October 11; McLaughlin, T. 2001. Harvard dropout made Polaroid an icon. *Toronto Star,* October 15; Pope, J. 2001. Polaroid's fortunes rose with Land, but fell under the burden of debt. *Daily Kent Stater* (OH), October 15; and www.polaroid.com.

2. Eagan, M. 2005. How did Polaroid's faithful ever land in this predicament? *Boston Herald,* April 28: 20; and St. Anthony, N. 2005. Petters wraps up Polaroid. *Star Tribune,* April 28: 1D.

3. Christensen, C. M. 1997. *The innovator's dilemma: When new technologies cause great firms to fail.* Cambridge, MA: Harvard Business School Press.

4. For a discussion about Polaroid, see Gavetti, G., & Levinthal, D. 2000. Looking forward and looking backward: Cognitive and experiential search. *Administrative Science Quarterly,* 45: 113–137.

5. For an interesting discussion, see Johannessen, J. A., Olsen, B., & Lumpkin, G. T. 2001. Innovation as newness: What is new, how new, and new to whom? *European Journal of Innovation Management,* 4(1): 20–31.

6. The discussion of radical and incremental innovations draws from Leifer, R., McDermott, C. M., Colarelli, G., O'Connor, G. C., Peters, L. S., Rice, M. P., & Veryzer, R. W. 2000. *Radical innovation: How mature companies can outsmart upstarts.* Boston: Harvard Business School Press; Damanpour, F. 1996. Organizational complexity and innovation: Developing and testing multiple contingency models. *Management Science,* 42(5): 693–716; and Hage, J. 1980. *Theories of organizations.* New York: Wiley.

7. The discussion of product and process innovation is based on Roberts, E. B. (Ed.). 2002. *Innovation: Driving product, process, and market change.* San Francisco: Jossey-Bass; Hayes, R., & Wheelwright, S. 1985. Competing through manufacturing. *Harvard Business Review,* 63(1): 99–109; and Hayes, R., & Wheelwright, S. 1979. Dynamics of product-process life cycles. *Harvard Business Review,* 57(2): 127–136.

8. Drucker, P. F. 1985. *Innovation and entrepreneurship:* 2000 New York: Harper & Row.

9. Steere, W. C., Jr., & Niblack, J. 1997. Pfizer, Inc. In Kanter, R. M., Kao, J., & Wiersema, F. (Eds.), *Innovation: Breakthrough thinking at 3M, DuPont, GE, Pfizer, and Rubbermaid:* 123–145. New York: HarperCollins.

10. Morrissey, C. A. 2000. Managing innovation through corporate venturing. *Graziadio Business Report,* Spring, gbr.pepperdine.edu; and Sharma, A. 1999. Central dilemmas of managing innovation in large firms. *California Management Review,* 41(3): 147–164.

11. Sharma, op. cit.

12. Canabou, C. 2003. Fast ideas for slow times. *Fast Company,* May: 52.

13. Biodegradable Products Institute. 2003. "Compostable Logo" of the Biodegradable Products Institute gains momentum with approval of DuPont™ Biomax® resin, www.bpiworld.org, June 12; Leifer et al., op. cit.

14. For more on defining the scope of innovation, see Valikangas, L., & Gibbert, M. 2005. Boundary-setting strategies for escaping innovation traps. *MIT Sloan Management Review,* 46(3): 58–65.

15. Leifer et al., op. cit.

16. Bhide, A. V. 2000. *The origin and evolution of new businesses.* New York: Oxford University Press; Brown, S. L., & Eisenhardt, K. M. 1998. *Competing on the edge: Strategy as structured chaos.* Cambridge, MA: Harvard Business School Press.

17. Caulfield, B. 2003. Why techies don't get Six Sigma. *Business 2.0,* June: 90.

18. Chesbrough, H. 2003. *Open innovation: The new imperative for creating and profiting from technology.* Boston: Harvard Business School Press.

19. Bick, J. 2003. Gold bond. *Entrepreneur,* March: 54–57.

20. For an interesting perspective on the role of collaboration among multinational corporations see Hansen, M. T., & Nohria, N. 2004. How to build collaborative advantage. *MIT Sloan Management Review,* 46(1): 22–30.

21. Guth, W. D., & Ginsberg, A. 1990. Guest editor's introduction: Corporate entrepreneurship. *Strategic Management Journal,* 11: 5–15.

22. Pinchot, G. 1985. *Intrapreneuring.* New York: Harper & Row.

23. Kim, W. C., & Mauborgne, R. 2005. *Blue ocean strategy.* Boston, MA: Harvard Business School Press; and Kim, W. C., & Mauborgne, R. 2005. Blue ocean strategy: From theory to practice. *California Management Review,* 47(3): 105–121.

24. Birkinshaw, J. 1997. Entrepreneurship in multinational corporations: The characteristics of subsidiary initiatives. *Strategic Management Journal,* 18(3): 207–229; and Kanter, R. M. 1985. *The change masters.* New York: Simon & Schuster.

25. The information in this example is from Leifer et al., op. cit.; Vance, A. 2000. NetActive looks to role as download police. *IDG News Service,* November 14, www.idg.net; and www.hoovers.com.

26. Hansen, M. T., Chesbrough, H. W., Nohria, N., & Sull, D. 2000. Networked incubators: Hothouses of the new economy. *Harvard Business Review,* 78(5): 74–84.

27. Stein, T. 2002. Corporate venture investors are bailing out. *Red Herring,* December: 74–75.

28. Is your company up to speed? 2003. *Fast Company,* June: 86.

29. For an interesting discussion, see Davenport, T. H., Prusak, L., & Wilson, H. J. 2003. Who's bringing you hot ideas and how are you responding? *Harvard Business Review,* 80(1): 58–64.

30. Howell, J. M. 2005. The right stuff. Identifying and developing effective champions of innovation. *Academy of Management Executive,* 19(2): 108–119. See also Greene, P., Brush, C., & Hart, M. 1999. The corporate venture champion: A resource-based approach to role and process. *Entrepreneurship theory & practice,* 23(3): 103–122; and Markham, S. K., & Aiman-Smith, L. 2001. Product champions: Truths, myths and management. *Research Technology Management,* May–June: 44–50.

31. Burgelman, R. A. 1983. A process model of internal corporate venturing in the diversified major firm. *Administrative Science Quarterly,* 28: 223–244.

32. Hamel, G. 2000. *Leading the revolution.* Boston: Harvard Business School Press.

33. Greene, Brush, & Hart, op. cit.; and Shane, S. 1994. Are champions different from non-champions? *Journal of Business Venturing,* 9(5): 397–421.

34. Vance, op. cit.; and www.info-mech.com/netactive.html.

35. Block, Z., & MacMillan, I. C. 1993. *Corporate venturing—Creating new businesses with the firm.* Cambridge, MA: Harvard Business School Press.

36. For an interesting discussion of these trade-offs, see Stringer, R. 2000. How to manage radical innovation. *California Management Review,* 42(4): 70–88; and Gompers, P. A., & Lerner, J. 1999. *The venture capital cycle.* Cambridge, MA: MIT Press.

37. Albrinck, J., Hornery, J., Kletter, D., & Neilson, G. 2001. Adventures in corporate venturing. *Strategy + Business,* 22: 119–129; and McGrath, R. G., & MacMillan, I. C. 2000. *The entrepreneurial mind set.* Cambridge, MA: Harvard Business School Press.

38. For an interesting discussion of how different outcome goals affect organizational learning and employee motivation, see Seijts, G. H., & Latham, G. P. 2005. Learning versus performance goals: When should each be used? *Academy of Management Executive,* 19(1): 124–131.

39. Crockett, R. O. 2001. Motorola. *BusinessWeek,* July 15: 72–78.

40. The ideas in this section are drawn from Royer, I. 2003. Why bad projects are so hard to kill. *Harvard Business Review,* 80(1): 48–56.

41. Breen, B. 2003. How does a 900-pound gorilla get to be an 1,800-pound gorilla? *Fast Company,* January: 87–89.

42. Slywotzky, A., & Wise, R. 2003. Double-digit growth in no-growth times. *Fast Company,* April: 66–72; www.hoovers .com; and www.johnsoncontrols.com.

43. For more on the role of real options in entrepreneurial decision making, see Folta, T. B., & O'Brien, J. P. 2004. Entry in the presence of dueling options. *Strategic Management Journal,* 25: 121–138.

44. Covin, J. G., & Slevin, D. P. 1991. A conceptual model of entrepreneurship as firm behavior. *Entrepreneurship Theory and Practice,* 16(1): 7–24; Lumpkin, G. T., & Dess, G. G. 1996. Clarifying the entrepreneurial orientation construct and linking it to performance. *Academy of Management Review,* 21(1): 135–172; and McGrath, R. G., & MacMillan, I. C. 2000. *The entrepreneurial mind set.* Cambridge, MA: Harvard Business School Press.

45. Lumpkin, G. T., & Dess, G. G. 2001. Linking two dimensions of entrepreneurial orientation to firm performance: The moderating role of environment and life cycle. *Journal of Business Venturing,* 16: 429–451.

46. For an interesting discussion, see Day, J. D., Mang, P. Y., Richter, A., & Roberts, J. 2001. The innovative organization: Why new ventures need more than a room of their own, *McKinsey Quarterly,* 2: 21–31.

47. Quinn, J. B. 1992. *Intelligent enterprise.* New York: Free Press.

48. Wagner, M. 2005. Out of the skunkworks. *Internet Retailer,* January, www.internetretailer.com.

49. Cross, K. 2001. Bang the drum quickly. *Business 2.0,* May 1: 28–30.

50. Crockett, R. O. 2001. Chris Galvin shakes things up—again. *BusinessWeek,* May 28: 38–39.

51. For an interesting discussion of the impact of innovativeness on organizational outcomes see Cho, H. J., & Pucik, V. 2005. Relationship between innovativeness, quality, growth, profitability, and market value. *Strategic Management Journal,* 26(6): 555–575.

52. Hamel, G. 1999. Bringing Silicon Valley inside. *Harvard Business Review,* 77(5): 71–84.

53. Perman, S. 2001. Automate or die. www.business2.com, July; and Dell, M. 1999. *Direct from Dell.* New York: HarperBusiness.

54. Evans, P., & Wurster, T. S. 2000. *Blown to bits.* Boston: Harvard Business School Press.

55. Lieberman, M. B., & Montgomery, D. B. 1988. First mover advantages. *Strategic Management Journal,* 9 (Special Issue): 41–58.

56. The discussion of first mover advantages is based on several articles, including Lambkin, M. 1988. Order of entry and performance in new markets. *Strategic Management Journal,* 9: 127–140; Lieberman & Montgomery, op. cit.: 41–58; and Miller, A., & Camp, B. 1985. Exploring determinants of success in corporate ventures. *Journal of Business Venturing,* 1(2): 87–105.

57. Moore, G. A. 1999. *Crossing the chasm* (2nd ed.). New York: HarperBusiness.

58. Tesler, L. 2001. Why the Apple Newton failed, www.techtv .com/print/story/0,23102,3013675,00.html; Veitch, M. 1998. Apple kills off Newton PDA, news.zdnet.co.uk/story/ printer/0,,s2067739,00.html.

59. Collins, J. C. & Porras, J. I. 1997. *Built to last.* New York: HarperBusiness; see also www.sony.com.

60. Hardy, Q., & Godwin, J. 2000. Other people's money. *Forbes,* August 7: 116–118.

61. Mallas, S. 2005. PepsiCo loses its Edge. *The Motley Fool,* June 1, www.fool.com.

62. Carvell, T., 1997, The crazy record business: These prices are really insane. *Fortune,* August 4: 109–16.

63. Bogan, C. E., & English, M. J. 1994. *Benchmarking for best practices.* New York: McGraw-Hill; Mochari, I. 2001. Steal this strategy. *Inc.,* July: 62–67.

64. Helman, C. 2001. Stand-up brand. *Forbes,* July 9: 27; and www.hoovers.com.

65. Keenan, F., & Mullaney, T. J. 2001. Clicking at Graybar. *BusinessWeek,* June 18: 132–134; and www.graybar.com.

66. Weintraub, A. 2001. Make or break for Autobytel. *BusinessWeek e.biz,* July 9: EB30–EB32; see also www.autobytel.com.

67. Coy, P., & Vickers, M. 2001. How bad will it get? *BusinessWeek,* March 12: 36–42.

68. Drucker, op. cit., pp. 109–110.

# Recognizing Opportunities and Creating New Ventures

## >chapter objectives

*After reading this chapter, you should have a good understanding of:*

- The role of new ventures and small businesses in the U.S. economy.

- The importance of opportunity recognition, as well as the role of opportunities, resources, and entrepreneurs, in successfully pursuing new ventures.

- The role of vision, dedication, and commitment to excellence in determining the quality of entrepreneurial leadership.

- The different types of financing that are available to new ventures depending on their stage of development.

- The importance of human capital and social capital as well as government resources in supporting new ventures and small businesses.

- The three types of entry strategies—pioneering, imitative, and adaptive—that are commonly used to launch a new venture.

- How the generic strategies of overall cost leadership, differentiation, and focus are used by new ventures and small businesses.

*n*ew technologies, shifting social and demographic trends, and sudden changes in the business environment create opportunities for entrepreneurship. New ventures, which often emerge under such conditions, face unique strategic challenges if they are going to survive and grow. Small businesses, which are a major engine of growth in the U.S. economy because of their role in job creation and innovation, must rely on sound strategic principles to be successful.

This chapter addresses how new ventures and small businesses can achieve competitive advantages. In the first section we review various perspectives of entrepreneurship and how the size, age, and growth goals of a firm affect small businesses and entrepreneurial firms. We also examine the contribution of small businesses to the U.S economy.

In the second section we address the role of opportunity recognition in the process of new venture creation. We highlight the importance of three factors in determining whether a potential venture opportunity should be pursued—the nature of the opportunity itself, the resources available to undertake it, and the characteristics of the entrepreneur(s) pursuing it.

In section three we expand on the topic of entrepreneurial resources. We discuss various types of financing that may be available during early and later stages of the new venture creation process. We also address how other factors, including human capital, social capital, and government programs aimed at supporting entrepreneurial firms, provide important resources for the small business owner.

In the fourth section we focus on the qualities of entrepreneurial leadership. Business founders need vision in order to conceive realities that do not yet exist. Dedication and drive are essential to maintain the level of motivation and persistence needed to succeed. A commitment to excellence as seen in the quality of products and services, the talent and skill level of employees, and superior customer service are other elements of effective entrepreneurial leadership.

In section five we show how many of the strategic concepts discussed in this text apply to new ventures and small businesses. Three different types of new entry strategies are discussed—pioneering, imitative, and adaptive. Then, the generic strategies (discussed in Chapter 5) as well as combination strategies are addressed in terms of how they apply to new ventures and entrepreneurial firms. Additionally, some of the pitfalls associated with each of these strategic approaches are presented.

The success of an entrepreneurial venture—whether it is undertaken by a major corporation or a small start-up—depends on many factors. The right combination of resources, know-how, and strategic action can lead to above-average profitability and new advantages. However, many things can go wrong. To see how a firm's entrepreneurial efforts can turn to failure, consider the example of Great Plains Airlines.

The airlines industry is both competitive and volatile. For many years it was regulated in an effort to make sure all markets were served and to prevent any one airline from becoming overly dominant. After the industry was deregulated, however, some of the major airlines abandoned unprofitable markets and consolidated their efforts around hub cities such as Dallas, Atlanta, Los Angeles, and New York. A notable exception was Southwest Airlines, which became highly successful by avoiding expensive hub operations in favor of point-to-point flights into smaller airports. Start-up airlines, which began to flourish after deregulation, tended to imitate the Southwest model. One such start-up was Great Plains Airlines, Inc., a regional airline launched in Tulsa, Oklahoma.[1]

> The goal of founders James Swartz and John Knight was to fly 50-seater airplanes nonstop between Tulsa and the U.S. coasts. Not only did the entrepreneurs aim to focus on unserved markets, but they also sought a competitive advantage by avoiding big hubs and flying into underutilized airports. From the start, the entrepreneurs pledged not to compete head-on with the major airlines and pinned their hopes on the belief that the big airlines would return the favor.
>
> The early going for Great Plains seemed very promising. Key members of the Tulsa Chamber of Commerce along with support from the Tulsa City Council and local airport and industrial officials helped Great Plains amass $30 million in start-up capital. *The Wall Street Journal* named Great Plains one of four start-ups to watch in 2001 in their series labeled "The Challengers," which highlighted young new entrant firms that were challenging existing big players.
>
> From the start, however, it seemed that Great Plains was in for a rocky ride. Even with $30 million under its belt, the company was plagued by insufficient resources. "The one big problem is, they are undercapitalized," said Darryl Jenkins, an airline consultant and director of the aviation-studies program at George Washington University. The lack of resources dogged the founders as they shopped for airplanes. Although they were able to obtain two 32-seaters by purchasing nearly defunct Ozark Air, the planes did not hold enough fuel to make trips to the coast. With the two planes, service was started to Nashville and Albuquerque instead.
>
> Another problem came from the incumbent airlines, which took steps to squash the fledgling airlines. Soon after Great Plains announced it would offer service to the west coast, American Airlines announced it would inaugurate nonstop service between Tulsa and Los Angeles. "We tried for years to get them to fly that route," said Brent Kitchen, director of the Tulsa airport authority. "I think American figured, 'We're going to try it before Great Plains gets there.'"
>
> Finally, the funding Great Plains received was apparently obtained illegally through a convoluted loan agreement that violated a federal ban against local airports subsidizing airlines. By March 2004, when the loan came due, Great Plains defaulted. The airline had already filed for Chapter 11 bankruptcy protection and suspended service. After an investigation by the FBI and U.S. Department of Transportation, Great Plains filed a Chapter 7 bankruptcy in January 2005 and closed down for good.

***What Went Wrong with Great Plains Airlines?***     Great Plains failed because it could not get off the ground fast enough to prevent major airlines from entering the same markets and preempting its planned services. It also made a classic entrepreneurial mistake by starting with insufficient resources. Great Plains' problems were compounded by their lack of strategic planning. Its business plan called for leasing planes since, at $20 million each, purchasing a fleet would be very costly. But airplane leasing is highly complicated and time consuming. The founders, who had successfully launched Jet Arizona, an air ambulance service, seemed unprepared for the delays a leasing agreement would create. The 50-seat planes were also in short supply, something that better research would likely have revealed. Finally, even though it recognized the need to form strong alliances and a network of support, Great Plains got mixed up in a shady and very public financing debacle.

The Great Plains case illustrates the importance of thinking and acting strategically in the entrepreneurial process. Even though Great Plains aimed to fill a market need and obtained $30 million of financial support, it was not able to convert its investment into a profitable business. Even when market conditions are creating new opportunities, poor planning and industry and competitive forces may prevent a new entrant from reaching the marketplace. Thus, to be successful, new ventures need to apply the lessons of strategic management to evaluate business conditions, assess their internal capabilities, formulate effective strategies, and implement sound business practices. New ventures and small businesses are often vulnerable because they lack experience and/or resources, and because established firms may be relatively more powerful. In this chapter we address how new ventures and small businesses, by applying the principles and practices of strategic management, can improve their chances of success. To begin our discussion, we address some of the differences and similarities found among the many types of entrepreneurial firms and address the importance of entrepreneurship to the economy.

## >>New Ventures and Small Businesses

The majority of new business creation is the result of entrepreneurial efforts by new ventures and small businesses. The strategic concepts introduced in this text can be applied to the effective management of entrepreneurial firms. Because there are several types of entrepreneurial firms, the application of these principles may differ somewhat depending on factors such as the size, age, or growth goals of the firm. Generally speaking, however, entrepreneurial activities will be more successful if strategic thinking guides decision making.

In this section we will investigate several types of entrepreneurial ventures and how the unique circumstances surrounding each type affect the strategies they pursue. First, let's consider the important role that small business and entrepreneurship play in the U.S. economy. Strategy Spotlight 13.1 addresses some of the reasons why small business and entrepreneurship are viewed favorably in the United States.

### Categories of Entrepreneurial Ventures

There are many ways to categorize entrepreneurial ventures. The term *entrepreneurship* itself has come to represent a wide array of meanings.[2] For example:

- Working for oneself rather than for someone else for a salary.
- Entering into a new or established market with new or existing products or services.
- Operating a firm in which there is no separation between ownership and management.
- Discovering, evaluating, and exploiting opportunities.
- Creating new organizations.

All of these definitions have been used to characterize entrepreneurial firms and/or small businesses. For purposes of strategic analysis, it is useful to note three differences among entrepreneurial firms, because these distinctions have strategic implications. The first of these is size. Small businesses, of course, are small. However, some ventures are small because they are new. This leads to the second criterion—age. Start-ups and new ventures are often considered to be entrepreneurial simply because they are young. That is, size is often correlated with age. New ventures usually begin small and grow over time as their business activity increases. Thus, as the age of a firm increases, so does its size. There is a third factor, however, that may limit an entrepreneurial firm's size—its growth goals.

Firms that do not aspire to grow large usually don't. Therefore, a young firm's growth goals often determine whether it will remain small as it ages or grow large. In

# STRATEGY SPOTLIGHT

## The Contribution of Small Business and Entrepreneurship to the U.S. Economy

In the late 1970s, MIT professor David Birch launched a study to explore the sources of business growth. "I wasn't really looking for anything in particular," says Birch. But the findings surprised him: Small businesses create the most jobs. Since then, Birch and others have shown that it's not just big companies that power the economy. The actual number of businesses, as measured by tax returns, has been growing faster than the civilian labor force for the past three decades. There is no sign of a reversal in that trend. Small business and entrepreneurship have become a major component of the economy.

Here are the facts:

- In the United States, there are approximately 5.7 million companies with fewer than 100 employees.

Another 100,000 companies have 100 to 500 employees. In addition, 17.0 million individuals are nonemployer sole proprietors.

- Small businesses create the majority of new jobs. According to recent data, small business created three-quarters of U.S. net new jobs in a recent period (2.5 million of the 3.4 million total). A small percentage of the fastest growing entrepreneurial firms (5 to 15 percent) account for a majority of the new jobs created.

- Small businesses (fewer than 500 employees) employ more than half of the private sector workforce (54 million in 2001) and account for more *(continued)*

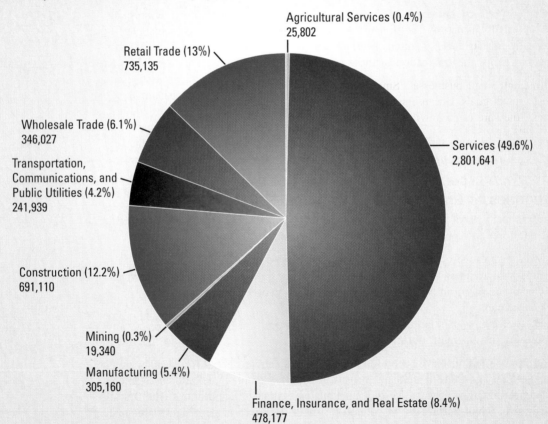

**Exhibit 13.1** *All U.S. Small Companies by Industry**

* *Businesses with 500 or fewer employees in 2001.*

Source: Small Business Administration's Office of Advocacy, based on data provided by the U.S. Census Bureau, statistics of U.S. businesses. (Percentages don't add to 100% because of rounding.)

*(continued)* than 50 percent of nonfarm private gross domestic product (GDP).

- Small firms produce 13 to 14 times more patents per employee than large patenting firms and employ 39 percent of high-tech workers (such as scientists, engineers, and computer workers). In addition, smaller entrepreneurial firms account for 55 percent of all innovations.

- Small businesses make up 97 percent of all U.S. exporters and accounted for 29 percent of known U.S. export value in 2001.

Sources: Small Business Administration. 2004. *The small business economy.* Washington, DC: U.S. Government Printing Office; Small Business Administration. 2005. Small business by the numbers. *SBA Office of Advocacy,* June, www.sba.gov/advo/; *Inc.* 2001. Small business 2001: Where we are now. May 29: 18–19; Dennis, Jr., W. J. 1999. *Business starts and stops.* Washington, DC: National Federation of Independent Business; Mioniti, M., & Bygrave, W. D. 2004. *Global entrepreneurship monitor—National entrepreneurship assessment: United States of America 2004, executive report.* Kansas City, MO: Kauffman Center for Entrepreneurial Leadership; and *Fortune.* 2001. The heroes: A portfolio. October 4: 74.

Exhibit 13.1 shows the number of small businesses in the United States and how they are distributed through different sectors of the economy.

Even though thousands of small businesses are formed each year, thousands also close. In a recent year, between 600,000 and 800,000 businesses with employees were formed. This translates into an annual birth rate of 14 to 16 percent. But in the same year, 12 to 14 percent of existing businesses were terminated, resulting in a net annual increase of about 2 percent. Among those that close each year, about one-fourth are sold or transferred (e.g., through inheritance). Another half simply "fade away," (i.e., the owners allow them to become inactive). Some of the deactivated firms are terminated not because they were unprofitable, but because the owner found a better business opportunity elsewhere. Thus, even though some businesses fail or turn out to be less lucrative than expected, the overall trend is positive. Small business and entrepreneurship will continue to be a major force in the economy for years to come.

fact, growth goals are one of the key factors used to distinguish between entrepreneurial firms and small businesses. Small businesses are generally thought to have low or modest growth goals. Because small business owners prefer to maintain control of their business, they are often unwilling to take steps that are necessary to grow, even though they may have growth potential. These steps include, most notably, borrowing heavily or going public to obtain the funding needed to finance growth. As a result, they remain small businesses.

By contrast, entrepreneurial firms generally favor growth. Because growth is a priority, founders with high growth goals will often sell a share of the business (thus giving up some control) in order to finance growth. As a result, successful businesses founded by high-growth entrepreneurs develop a life of their own. In contrast, small businesses are often associated so closely with their founders that when the founder is gone, the business ceases to operate. Of course, there may be intervening factors that affect growth outcomes unexpectedly. For example, some entrepreneurs may want to grow large businesses but cannot, and others may become bigger than they ever expected because market forces propel them onto a growth curve they did not anticipate. But in general, the difference between entrepreneurial firms and small businesses is related to their path of growth.

These three factors—size, age, and growth goals—are captured in a model of entrepreneurial firms that was developed by David Birch, the famed small-business researcher whose findings are presented in Spotlight 13.1 Birch identified three categories of firms—elephants, mice, and gazelles. Let's look briefly at each of these.

*Elephants*   As the name suggests, these are large firms. They also tend to be older and are the types of firms that appear in the Fortune 500. They have some disadvantages relative to entrepreneurial firms. For one thing, they cannot change direction quickly, and it is sometimes difficult to get them to move forward at all. As a group, these large firms have laid off more people than they have hired in the last 25 years.[3] On the other hand, they have obvious advantages. They can be hard chargers and move quite rapidly because of their overall power in the marketplace. Like elephants, these large firms usually command respect and can influence marketplace conditions (competition, technology) as well as business conditions (political/legal) in their industry.

As you might imagine from the image of the lumbering elephant, it is often difficult for such firms to be entrepreneurial. That's why some of the large firms introduced in Chapter 12 that have been strong innovators and generated an entrepreneurial spirit—3M, Sony, W. L. Gore, Virgin Group—have been so highly successful.

*Mice*    This term refers to the many small firms that power the U.S. economy. Over 80 percent of all firms in the United States have fewer than 20 employees.[4] The mice represent the many types of locally run businesses, including small retailers, small manufacturers, and all kinds of local service firms from auto repair shops and heating and air conditioning contractors to restaurants and banks. Mice typically do not have as much market power as large firms, but they can change direction more quickly in response to changes in business conditions.

As suggested earlier, many of these firms do not aspire to grow large as long as they remain profitable and competitive. Even so, since 1980, small businesses have added more jobs than large firms.[5] Even small firms that are committed to remaining small often add jobs or become the target of corporate takeovers. Consider the example of Timbuk2, a small manufacturer that decided to remain small rather than pursue rapid growth when a major buyer came calling:

> When CompUSA agreed to carry its urban shoulder bag products, California-based Timbuk2 thought it had it made. But after just four months, CEO Mark Dwight cancelled the deal. CompUSA's high-volume, low-margin requirements were eating too far into Timbuk2's profits. Going mainstream also threatened Timbuk2's quirky messenger bag image. "We're a specialty brand," says Dwight. By refocusing on specialty retailers such as REI and the Apple Stores, Timbuk2 has increased its margins, strengthened its specialty image, and helped double sales to over $10 million in just two years.[6]

Small businesses represent a bedrock of economic strength in the U.S. economy. Although many have chosen to remain small, many others aspire to grow into major corporations. It is these growth-oriented firms that we turn to next.

*Gazelles*    An important third category identified by Birch is known as gazelles. These are the firms that seek rapid growth and above average profitability. They are likely to be listed in the *Inc.* 500 or the *Entrepreneur* Hot 100, both of which highlight the fastest-growing small companies. To be a gazelle, a firm must grow at least 20 percent a year for four years, from a base of at least $100,000 in revenues.[7] A firm that meets these criteria doubles in size during the four-year period.

Gazelles are important to the economy for several reasons. For one thing, their value proposition often includes a radical innovation or the implementation of a new technology. Thus, they are an important engine for innovation in the U.S. economy. For example, Sur-Modics, Inc. is a Minnesota-based manufacturer of coatings for medical devices such as stents—metal coils that help hold blood vessels open after heart surgery. SurModics's coatings help make stents more slippery, which reduces the risk of stroke and makes them less likely to carry infections, thus improving their effectiveness. By partnering with companies such as Johnson & Johnson, which pays SurModics to conduct innovative research and then pays again to license the technology, SurModics has created a winning business model that recently earned it a place on the Fortune FSB 100 list of fast-growing small businesses. In a recent year, with fewer than 200 employees, it had revenues of $43.2 million and posted sales growth of 31 percent and net income growth of 47 percent.[8]

## Ariat International: Riding High on the Heels of Success

For the twenty million horseback riders around the world, Ariat International is the Reebok of riding boots. Founded by Beth Cross, who, as a Bain & Company consultant, once helped Reebok market innovative materials such as gel padding and air pockets, Ariat has become a leading manufacturer of performance footwear for equestrians. Ariat's ergonomically designed boots have caught the attention of both cowboys and city slickers. Between 2000 and 2004, the company grew more than 25 percent per year and now owns about 17 percent of the U.S. market for western wear. Not bad, considering that Ariat's two leading competitors—Justin Boots and Tony Lama—have been around since the days of Wyatt Earp and are now owned by Warren Buffet.

Cross founded the company in her Union City, California home in 1991. At first it was slow going. With $250,000 from family and friends, initially she was able to produce only a few styles. But with some patents under her belt and an infusion of venture funding in 1996, the company began to take off. Recent growth has been propelled by a string of awards including the prestigious Innovation Award from the British Equestrian Trade Association (BETA) and Manufacturer of the Year Award from The National Foundation Quarter Horse Association (NFQHA). According to Sam Summers, NFQHA's Editor in Chief, "While attending horse shows, we sometimes gather around the horse trailer camps after the day's events and inevitably the subject of boots comes up. Ariat is always leading the discussion for its comfort and craftsmanship."

Here are some of the factors that helped Ariat succeed:

- **Find the Market's Blind Spot**—Having grown up on a horse farm, Cross knew about boots. While working on the Reebok account, Cross recognized that leather-soled riding boots was a niche that could probably benefit from an upgrade. Market research helped convince her there was room for another brand.

- **Make Friends in High Places**—In the early days of Ariat, Cross was able to attract a key supporter—Angel Martinez, Reebok's head of business development, whose daughter rode horses. With Martinez on board, Cross was able to recruit other high-profile board members with expertise in footwear, retailing, and finance. These industry bigwigs, in turn, helped Ariat secure an estimated $9 million in venture funding.

- **Pay Less, Charge More**—Ariat has only 100 employees; most of them are in sales and customer service. China-based manufacturers who were already making boots for Timberland and Wolverine produce the boots using leather sourced from Europe and various components patented by Ariat. Compared to Justin, which manufactures its boots in Texas and Missouri, Ariat is able to charge more but has significantly lower costs.

- **Create Your Own Demand**—In the early days, Ariat had a very small marketing budget, but it did have boots. So Cross traveled to rodeos and horse shows and actually gave the boots away to young hotshots and promising amateurs. Once others saw these rising stars wearing Ariats, they began asking western stores and tack shops to carry them. "There's no better way to get a retailer to stock your product than to have people start calling for it," says Cross.

Ariat's rapid growth has created new opportunities. It now offers several new product lines including riding pants, shirts, and clogs. And the boots have become a fashion item. In 2004, Ariat was featured in *Vogue* magazine and was chosen to participate in New York City's famed "Fashion Week" event. With its 25 percent growth rate and sales over $80 million in a recent year, the privately held company is leaving other boot makers in the dust.

Sources: Copeland, M. V. 2004. These boots really were made for walking. *Business 2.0*, 5(9): 72–74; Grant, K. 2004. Ariat International featured on runway of New York's famed "Fashion Week." *Ariat International*, www.ariat.com, February 12; Grant, K. 2004. NFQHA names Ariat International "Manufacturer of the Year." *Ariat International*, www.ariat.com, May 4; and www.elle.com.

Although technology is often a hot growth area, the majority of gazelles are not in high-tech fields. Some are using existing technologies in new arenas. Strategy Spotlight 13.2 describes Ariat International, a fast growing boot maker that has adapted athletic footwear technology to the making of riding and cowboy boots. Approximately 30 percent are in retail and wholesale trades (primarily low-tech) and another 30 percent are in services (including both high- and low-tech). Gazelles are not necessarily young either. Although some young firms take off rapidly from birth, many firms have growth spurts only after a long period of gradual development. Around one-fifth of gazelles have been in operation 30 years or more.[9]

Perhaps the most important contribution gazelles make is in job growth. Because gazelles are highly entrepreneurial, they seek growth rather than control. As they grow, their need for additional employees also increases rapidly.[10] As a result, the Small Business Administration (SBA) has estimated that gazelles, of which there were approximately 386,000 in 2002, have created as many jobs during the last 25 years as have the mice, which numbered around 17 million in 2002.[11] Thus, it is no surprise that local and state governments often seek out gazelles because of their role in boosting economic development in a region.

There are many other ways to categorize new ventures and small businesses. For example, according to the IRS, over 20 million self employment tax returns (Schedule C) were filed in a recent year, indicating that a large proportion of the adult population is engaged in money-making enterprises. Exhibit 13.2 identifies three other major business categories that are generally considered to be entrepreneurial in nature—franchises, family businesses, and home-based businesses.

All entrepreneurial firms that wish to launch a new venture must first identify a strong business opportunity. Thus, next we address the strategic issues and techniques that firms use to recognize and develop new venture opportunities.

## >>Opportunity Recognition: Identifying and Developing Market Opportunities

The starting point for any new venture is the presence of an entrepreneurial opportunity. Where do opportunities come from? For new business start-ups, opportunities come from many sources—current or past work experiences, hobbies that grow into businesses or lead to inventions, suggestions by friends or family, or a chance event that makes an entrepreneur aware of an unmet need. For established firms, new business opportunities come from the needs of existing customers, suggestions by suppliers, or technological developments that lead to new advances.[12] For all types of firms, there is a major, overarching factor that is behind all viable opportunities that emerge in the business landscape: change. Change creates opportunities. Entrepreneurial firms make the most of changes brought about by new technology, sociocultural trends, and shifts in consumer demand. Even tragedy stimulates business development. Since September 11, 2001, initiatives related to strengthening homeland security and building military capabilities have stimulated billions of dollars of demand for new products and services such as night vision systems and unmanned aerial vehicles.[13]

### The Opportunity Recognition Process

How do changes in the external environment lead to new business creation? They spark creative new ideas and innovation. Businesspeople often have ideas for entrepreneurial ventures. However, not all such ideas are good ideas—that is, viable business opportunities. To determine which ideas are strong enough to become new ventures, entrepreneurs must go through a process of identifying, selecting, and developing potential opportunities. This is the process of opportunity recognition.

Opportunity recognition refers to more than just the "Eureka!" feeling that people sometimes experience at the moment they identify a new idea. Although such insights

Exhibit 13.2
**Types of
Entrepreneurial
Ventures**

| Type | Characteristics |
|---|---|
| **Family businesses** | • *Definition:* A family business, broadly defined, is a privately held firm in which family members have some degree of effective control over the strategic direction of the firm and intend for the business to remain within the family. |
| | • *Scope:* According to the Family Firm Institute (FFI), family-owned businesses that meet the broad definition above comprise 80 to 90 percent of all business enterprises in North America, 30 to 35 percent of the Fortune 500 companies, and the majority of enterprises internationally. Further, 50 percent of the U.S. Gross Domestic Product (GDP), over $3.3 trillion, is generated by family-owned businesses. |
| **Franchises** | • *Definition:* A franchise exists when a firm that already has a successful product or service (franchisor) contracts with another business to be a dealer (franchisee) by using the franchisor's name, trademark, and business system in exchange for a fee. There are several types, but the most common is the business format franchise, in which the franchisor provides a complete plan, or format, for managing the business. |
| | • *Scope:* According to the International Franchise Association (IFA), franchising accounted for $1 trillion in annual retail sales in the United States since 2000. There are about 320,000 franchise businesses employing more than 8 million people in 75 different industries. |
| **Home-based businesses** | • *Definition:* A home-based business, also commonly referred to as SOHO (small office/home office), consists of a company with 20 or fewer employees, including the self-employed, free agents, e-lancers, telecommuters, or other independent professionals working from a home-based setting. |
| | • *Scope:* According to the National Association of Home-Based Businesses (NAHBB), approximately 20 million businesses are home-based. The U.S. Commerce Department estimates that more than half of all small businesses are home-based. |

are often very important, the opportunity recognition process involves two phases of activity—discovery and formation—that lead to viable new venture opportunities.[14]

The discovery phase refers to the process of becoming aware of a new business concept.[15] Many entrepreneurs report that their idea for a new venture occurred to them in an instant, as a sort of "Aha!" experience—that is, they had some insight or epiphany, often based on their prior knowledge, that gave them an idea for a new business. This may occur unintentionally, because the discovery of new opportunities is often spontaneous and unexpected. For example, Howard Schultz, CEO of Starbucks, was in Milan, Italy, when he suddenly realized that the coffee-and-conversation café model that was common in Europe would work in the United States as well. According

# STRATEGY SPOTLIGHT

## 13.3

### Opportunity Recognition: Great Businesses that Started with a Simple Idea

In the founding of a business, there is always a moment when the opportunity is first recognized. The recognition may unfold in tiny steps over time or appear suddenly as an Aha! experience. When founding entrepreneurs act on such realizations, the rest, as they say, is history. And speaking of history, here are a few examples of the initial sparks that eventually resulted in some very big businesses.

#### Carl Westcott, founder of 1-800-Flowers

While visiting Los Angeles in 1979, Carl Westcott decided to send flowers back home to his wife. It was late but he finally found a florist that was open. The only problem was, it wouldn't take his credit card over the phone. "Bottom line," recalls Westcott, "I didn't send the flowers." While trying to get the florist to take his order, however, he noticed that the word "flowers" had seven digits. The next day he dialed 1-800-356-9377. The backhaul trucker that answered wasn't too surprised—he had already heard from FTD. But Westcott persisted and offered the man $15,000 and 3 percent of the 1-800-FLOWERS business. Both the trucker and Westcott made out pretty well when he sold the business for $4 million just 18 months later.

#### David Cook, founder of TollTags

When David Cook heard that the Los Alamos National Laboratories in New Mexico was going to implant miniaturized radio frequency chips under the skin of cattle to track their location, he laughed and thought, "That's just insane—and tough to market." Soon after, while driving on a toll road, he realized the same technology could be used to enable drivers to pay tolls automatically. To prove that TollTags would work, he raised $6 million from investors to build an electronic payment system on a toll road in Dallas, Texas, with the agreement that the tollway authority could scrap the system with just 24 hours notice. "It was by far the riskiest thing I've ever done in my life," recalls Cook. But it paid off. Today the North Texas Tollway Authority sells nearly 1 million TollTags annually. As for opportunity recognition, Cook says, "You have to believe in your idea and your ability to take your accumulated knowledge and intuition and apply that as you build your business."

#### Ross Perot, founder of Electronic Data Systems (EDS)

Ross Perot was a salesman at IBM when he had his epiphany: Computer customers don't especially care about computer hardware. What they really need is computing *power*. "It was obvious to me . . . that people wanted a system that worked, which included the computer, the software, the whole package," recalls Perot. He took the idea to his bosses who weren't interested. At the time, 80 cents of every dollar spent on computing was for hardware and IBM dominated the market. But Perot knew he was onto something. "I was sitting in a barbershop reading an old *Reader's Digest* that had a quote from Thoreau that said, 'The mass of men lead lives of quiet desperation.' That's when I made the decision that I had to try it." With $1,000 of his wife's money, he launched EDS in 1962. Today, this provider of information technology and business process outsourcing services enjoys annual revenues of about $20 billion.

Sources: Hall, C. 2004. The big ideas that started here. *Dallas Morning News*, December 26: 1D–6D. www.eds.com; www.hoovers.com; and, www.ntta.org.

---

to Schultz, he didn't need to do research to find out if Americans would pay $3 for a cup of coffee—he just *knew*. Starbucks was just a small business at the time but Schultz began literally shaking with excitement about growing it into a bigger business.[16] Strategy Spotlight 13.3 tells how three other highly successful entrepreneurs identified their business opportunities.

Opportunity discovery also may occur as the result of a deliberate search for new venture opportunities or creative solutions to business problems. New venture ideas often emerge only after a concerted effort to identify good opportunities or realistic solutions. It is very similar to a creative process, which may be unstructured and "chaotic" at first but eventually leads to a practical solution or business innovation. To stimulate the discovery of new opportunities, companies often encourage creativity, out-of-the-box thinking, and brainstorming. Consider the example of Oakshire Mushroom Farm, Inc.

While trying to figure out how to recover from its 40 percent decline in market share for shii-take mushrooms, Oakshire came up with an idea that at first seemed ridiculous—selling a product to competitors. "We kicked around a lot of ideas—franchising, expanding geograph-ically to be more local" to supermarkets and restaurants, explained Gary Schroeder, CEO of the Kennett Square, Pennsylvania, grower. "But these other competitors were already there." Finally, they decided to sell rival farms their most unique innovation: a sawdust log for grow-ing shiitakes that reduces the harvest time from four years to four months. The solution worked, and sales increased 45 percent to $5 million in the first year and nearly doubled the next. Now the logs account for about 10 percent of its revenues, and Oakshire has become a vendor within other segments of its industry.[17]

New ventures are often launched because founding entrepreneurs find innovative ways to apply new technologies. This is supported by the statistics in Strategy Spotlight 13.1, which indicates that a majority of patents and innovations come from small firms. Why is this so? Research indicates that entrepreneurial firms are often more successful at discovering radically different technology-based venture opportunities than large firms. Strategy Spotlight 13.4 explains why young firms often have a competitive edge when it comes to technological innovation.

Opportunity formation, which occurs after an opportunity has been identified, involves evaluating an opportunity to determine whether it is viable and strong enough to be developed into a full-fledged new venture. Ideas that have been developed by new-product groups or in brainstorming sessions are tested by various methods, includ-ing talking to potential target customers and discussing operational requirements with production or logistics managers. A technique known as feasibility analysis is used to evaluate these and other critical success factors. This type of analysis often leads to the decision that a new venture project should be discontinued. If the venture concept continues to seem viable, a more formal business plan may be developed.

Among the most important factors to evaluate is the market potential for the prod-uct or service. Established firms tend to operate in established markets. They have to adjust to market trends and to shifts in consumer demand, of course, but they usually have a customer base for which they are already filling a marketplace need. New ventures, in contrast, must first determine whether a market exists for the product or service they are contemplating. Thus, a critical element of opportunity recognition is assessing to what extent the opportunity is viable *in the marketplace.* Most definitions of entrepreneurial opportunity suggest that, for it to be an opportunity, it must be viable in terms of its potential to earn a profit.

Several of the techniques suggested in Chapters 2 and 3 can be used to assess the market potential of a business concept. Questions that might emerge in a test of the mar-ket for a new product or service include:

- Do market forces support the product's introduction? For example, is market demand growing because of shifting demographics or sociocultural trends?
- How is the need that it addresses currently being met?
- What firms would be the closest competitors?
- How are competitive products priced?
- What is its value proposition—that is, in what ways does it add value relative to products or services already being sold?
- Can its value be enhanced by combining it with other value-adding activities?

For a more complete assessment of how well a new business concept would be received, marketing techniques such as product concept testing, focus groups, and/or extended trial runs with end users are often necessary. In some respects, assessing

# STRATEGY SPOTLIGHT

## Technological Innovation: Why Entrepreneurial Firms Have a Competitive Advantage

Young firms have a knack for seeing things differently. As a result, they tend to be net winners in the game of technological innovation. This was also the finding of Harvard Professor Clayton M. Christensen, author of *The Innovator's Dilemma.* In his study of disruptive technologies (technologies that change the rules of an industry, similar to radical innovations) in the computer disk drive industry, Christensen found that new entrants outperformed incumbent firms—"from the simplest to the most radical, the firms that led the industry in every instance of developing and adopting disruptive technologies were entrants to the industry, not its incumbent leaders."

What makes entrepreneurial firms better innovators? For one thing, they are able to recognize possibilities and approach problems with a fresh perspective. They are not burdened by old ways of thinking or beliefs about how things have always been. Here are three examples of what entrepreneurial firms do to excel at innovation:

1. ***Painting pictures, not assembling puzzles.*** Innovative thinking requires a broad perspective, just as a painter needs to draw on a full palette of colors when creating an image that is wholly new. Entrepreneurial firms often have the freedom to see the big picture as well as its component parts. Large companies, because of the constraints under which they operate, are often required to approach innovation as they would assembling a puzzle—piecing together a set number of predetermined shapes (in the form of personnel, budgets, existing technologies, and so forth) that someone else has devised.

   > Consider the example of Carol Latham, a staff chemist at British Petroleum (BP), who discovered how plastic parts could be used to keep computers cool. When she approached the top brass with her idea at BP's Ohio research lab where she worked, they weren't interested. It turns out that BP, generally considered to be entrepreneurially minded, was having a bad year—oil stock values were down—and the company did not want to fund any initiatives that detracted from its core business. Perhaps more importantly, most of Latham's colleagues were researching ceramics, and her plastics idea seemed threatening to their efforts. BP just couldn't see what she could see. But Latham was sure she was on to something. She quit her job, labored for months in her basement with mixing bowls and a blender, and formed Thermagon, Inc.

   > Once she had an actual product—superthin polymer sheets cut to fit between computer components, they sold themselves. After being named to the *Inc.* 500 list of fastest growing companies three years in a row and reaching annual revenues of $19 million, Thermagon was acquired by Laird Technologies of St. Louis, Missouri, in April 2004.

2. ***Solving the big guy's little problems.*** Small firms often succeed by forming alliances with larger firms. And quite often, the big firms need the help. As an incumbent firm grows, the task of management becomes more complicated. Some large firms find it difficult to manage internal processes because their problem-solving capability does not match the complexity of their problems. The innovation process is loaded with choices and uncertainties, making it one of the areas where large firms often lose their edge. One of the ways large firms deal with such problems is by turning to small firms for help.

   > Foster-Miller is an engineering and technology development firm that specializes in innovative solutions. With its staff of 200 engineers and scientists, Foster-Miller tackles problems the big firms can't seem to solve. For example, Nabisco, the largest cookie maker in the world, was having trouble making a low-fat version of its Fig Newton because the fat-free batter kept sticking to the cutting equipment. Unable to solve the problem, Nabisco called in Foster-Miller, which designed a noncontact cookie cutter that solved the problem.

3. ***Setting up a big tent.*** Recall from Strategy Spotlight 12.3 the closed model of innovation. According to that perspective, many large firms believe they should "go it alone and do it ourselves" when it comes to innovation. The problem with that approach, according to *Open Innovation* author Henry Chesbrough, is that firms miss out on talent and resources that could make the innovation process more efficient and cost effective. Additionally, other firms that might benefit from an innovation are left out or left to discover it on their own.

   > MicroUnity, Inc., a designer of microprocessor software for communications, approaches innovation differently. For one thing, it accepts the fact that it is small. As a result, the private ***(continued)***

marketability is as much an art as it is a science. Nevertheless, it is essential to create a model of how the product or service will perform in the marketplace in order to develop a plan for launching it. Thus, the aim of the opportunity recognition process is to explore and test a new venture concept in order to determine whether it is a viable opportunity.

## Characteristics of Good Opportunities

The opportunity recognition process involves discovering and forming business concepts into realistic business opportunities. For an opportunity to be viable, it needs to have four qualities.[18]

- *Attractive.* The opportunity must be attractive in the marketplace; that is, there must be market demand for the new product or service.

- *Achievable.* The opportunity must be practical and physically possible.

- *Durable.* The opportunity must be attractive long enough for the development and deployment to be successful; that is, the window of opportunity must be open long enough for it to be worthwhile.

- *Value creating.* The opportunity must be potentially profitable; that is, the benefits must surpass the cost of development by a significant margin.

If a new business concept meets these criteria, two other factors must be considered before the opportunity is launched as a business. First, the readiness and skills of the entrepreneurial founder or team must be evaluated. Do the founders have the necessary knowledge and experience to make the venture successful? Second, the availability and access to resources needed for the launch must be considered. Given an analysis of the start-up costs and operational expenses, can the venture obtain the necessary funding? These three factors—the nature of the opportunity itself, the resources available to undertake it, and the characteristics of the entrepreneur(s) pursuing it—are essential for the successful launch of a new venture.[19] Exhibit 13.3 identifies the three factors that are needed to successfully proceed—opportunity, resources, and entrepreneur(s). In the next section, we address the issue of entrepreneurial resources; following that, we address the importance of entrepreneurial leadership.

**Exhibit 13.3    Opportunity Analysis Framework**

Sources: Based on Timmons, J. A., & Spinelli, S. 2004. *New venture creation* (6th ed.). New York: McGraw-Hill/Irwin; and Bygrave, W. D. 1997. The entrepreneurial process. In W. D. Bygrave (Ed.), *The portable MBA in entrepreneurship* (2nd ed.). New York: Wiley.

## >>Entrepreneurial Resources

As Exhibit 13.3 indicates, resources are an essential component of a successful entrepreneurial launch. One of the major challenges that entrepreneurial firms face is a lack of resources. For start-ups, the most important resource is usually money. A new firm typically has to expend substantial sums just to start up the business. However, financial resources are not the only kind of resource a young firm needs. Human capital and social capital are also important during the early days of a new venture and throughout the life of a small business. Some small firms also rely on government resources to help them thrive.

Young and small firms have many of the same needs as larger firms—financial resources, skilled and experienced workers, and the ability to operate in a network of beneficial relationships. But they also have unique needs that stem from being young or small. Nearly all young firms face the liability of newness.[20] This phrase refers to the vulnerability that most new firms feel because they lack experience, are unknown in their industry, and are unfamiliar to customers. Until they have proven themselves, young firms lack credibility: Banks often will not lend them money, and suppliers may not extend them credit.

To overcome the liability of newness and build credibility, therefore, founders must find practical ways to obtain resources. These include financial as well as other resources. In this section we will address some of the resource requirements of entrepreneurial firms and how they can meet their needs.

### New-Venture Financing

Hand-in-hand with the importance of markets (and marketing) to new-venture creation, start-up firms must also have financing. In fact, the level of available financing is often a strong determinant of how the business is launched and its eventual success. Cash finances are, of course, highly important. But access to capital, such as a line of credit or favorable payment terms with a supplier, can also help a start-up to succeed.

A new firm's financing requirements and sources of funds typically change as it grows. In the next two sections, we address sources of financing in the earlier and later stages of launching a new venture.

*Early-Stage Financing*   The vast majority of new firms are low-budget start-ups launched with personal savings and the contributions of family and friends.[21] Even among firms included in the *Entrepreneur* list of the 100 fastest-growing new businesses in a recent year, 61 percent reported that their start-up funds came from personal savings.[22] Although bank financing, public financing, and venture capital are important sources of small business finance, these types of financial support are typically available only after a company has started to conduct business and generate sales. Therefore, the founders usually carry the initial burden of financing most new firms.

The burdens are many: renting space, buying inventory, installing phones and equipment, obtaining insurance, and paying salaries. How does a cash-strapped entrepreneur make ends meet? One way is by *bootstrapping*. The term is used to describe persons who rely on their personal resources and resourcefulness to succeed. Applied to entrepreneurs, it refers to techniques used to minimize borrowing and avoid selling parts of a business to investors or venture capitalists. For the young start-up, this involves getting the most out of every dollar and doing without anything but the bare necessities. It may mean buying used equipment, operating out of a basement, or forgoing a new car purchase in order to reinvest in the business.

The typical new business owner has just $4,000 invested the day the business opens.[23] Therefore, bootstrapping to make ends meet is a common practice among start-up entrepreneurs. For example, Brad and Gia Boyle of Moab, Utah, got their start running Walkabout Travel Gear out of a 37-foot recreational vehicle. Using a motor home as an office not only helped them save money on rent, it also kept them in touch with their industry—travel. Their bootstrapping philosophy is expressed by a quote on their Web site: "A tight budget is the mother of adventure." In a recent year, the business brought in about $250,000.[23]

Bootstrapping may shift a start-up's priorities. To successfully bootstrap, a new firm may have to get cash-generating products or services to market quickly in order to jump-start cash flow. As a result, the new firm may postpone development activities or investments in technology. Consider the example of Stacy's Pita Chip Co.:

> In 1996 founders Mark and Stacy Andrus were operating a successful pita-wrap sandwich business that was ready to grow. But customers kept asking for the baked chips they made every night from leftover pita bread and handed out free to customers waiting in line. "We thought we could get bigger faster with the chips," said Stacy. The couple, who were still paying off six-figure student loans, decided to take their chips nationwide. The business they created is a model of bootstrapping efficiency. The paper sign on the door, folding tables, and used dining room chairs are the first signs of their spartan approach to business. They also saved over $250,000 buying used equipment. "Everything goes into the business," said Stacy, who takes home a scavenger-level salary. But it has paid off. Their baked pita chips' annual revenues recently hit $1.3 million, with sales in 37 states.[24]

If personal savings and bootstrapping efforts are insufficient to finance the business, entrepreneurs must turn to other sources of funds. One of the most common mistakes business founders make, as suggested by the Great Plains Airline opening incident, is trying to launch a business with insufficient capital. Thus, seeking external sources of financing is often essential for start-up success.

Funding that comes from others, unless it is a gift, will take one of two forms—debt or equity. There are important differences between the two types of financing:

- **Debt.** This refers to borrowed funds, such as an interest-bearing loan, that must be repaid regardless of firm performance. To obtain it usually requires that some business or personal assets be used as collateral.

- **Equity.** This refers to invested funds, such as in shares of stock, that increase or decrease in value depending on the performance of the business. To obtain it usually requires that business founders give up some ownership and control of the business.

There are many possible sources of external funding. One of the most important sources is family and friends. This can be an especially helpful resource during the very early stages of a new venture. Among the *Entrepreneur* 100 fastest-growing firms, 18 percent received start-up financing from family and friends.[25] This type of financing may be in the form of either debt or equity.

To preserve cash, another technique start-up businesses use involves relying on unconventional or creative financing sources. For example, credit card financing is one of the fastest growing techniques for financing a start-up. About half of all small businesses finance their launch or expansion with credit cards.[26] Another example is supplier financing in which suppliers give buyers as long as 60 or 90 days to pay for purchases. This arrangement, which may also help suppliers increase sales, is an alternative that can help a cash-strapped start-up.[27]

*Later-Stage Financing*   Once an entrepreneur has a going concern, certain types of financing become more readily available. Young firms that have contracted with a first customer or can demonstrate several months of sales are considered a better risk by investors and creditors. Even "angel" investors—private individuals who provide seed capital during the early stages of a new venture—favor companies that already have a winning business model and dominance in a market niche.[28] According to Cal Simmons, coauthor of *Every Business Needs an Angel,* "I would much rather talk to an entrepreneur who has already put his money and his effort into proving the concept. And I think most angels I know feel the same way right now."[29]

Angel investors are an important source of equity investment for many entrepreneurial firms. They often invest modest amounts—under $1 million—and help firms that are trying to grow beyond their initial start-up success. Angels also provide mentoring and contacts for young firms that are trying to become established.

Start-ups that involve large capital investments or extensive development costs—such as manufacturing or engineering firms that are trying to commercialize an innovative product—may have high cash requirements soon after they are founded. Others need financing only when they are on the brink of rapid growth. To obtain such funding, entrepreneurial firms often seek venture capital. Venture capital is a form of private equity financing through which entrepreneurs raise money by selling shares in the new venture. In contrast to angel investors, who are actively engaged in investing their own money, venture capital companies are organized to place the funds of private investors into lucrative business opportunities. Equity financing, however, often comes with strings attached. On the one hand, venture capitalists often have high performance expectations and demand a regular accounting. On the other hand, sometimes these "strings" can enhance a firm's chances for success. Venture capital groups often provide important managerial advice, links to key contacts in an industry, and the peace of mind of knowing that financial backers support your project. But founders who use venture capital forfeit part of the payoff if the venture succeeds. Further, they must agree to let the venture capitalists influence management decisions.

Venture capital is an important source of funding for certain types of entrepreneurial firms.[30] Entrepreneurs who seek large infusions of capital usually turn to some form of private capital financing. Venture capital was a primary driver of the rapid growth in Internet start-ups. Although loans by venture capitalists have declined sharply since their rapid expansion during the Internet boom of 1999 to 2000, annual venture capital investing remains over $21 billion.[31] Despite the importance of venture capital to many fast-growing firms, the vast majority of funding for young and small firms comes from informal sources such as family and friends. Exhibit 13.4, based on the *Global Entrepreneurship Monitor* survey of entrepreneurial firms, demonstrates this dramatic difference. A closer look, however, reveals an interesting fact: Firms that obtain venture capital receive funding of about $2.6 million each. In contrast, companies that obtain funding from informal sources typically receive only about $10,000 each. Although relatively few companies receive venture funding, they are attractive to venture capitalists because their profit potential and impact on innovation, job growth, and wealth creation tends to be much greater.

Venture capital groups also help start-ups by sponsoring independent business incubators. Recall from Chapter 12 the use of in-house incubators by large corporations to

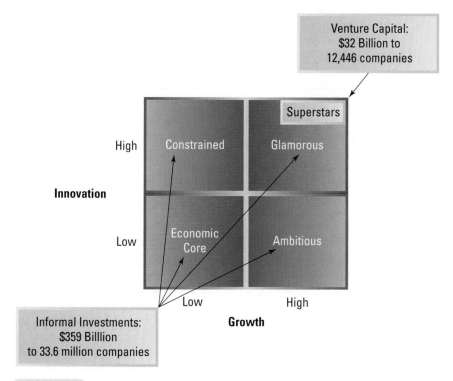

**Exhibit 13.4** **How Different Types of Young Firms Are Financed: Informal Investment versus Venture Capital**

Source: Reynolds, P. D., Bygrave, W. D., & Autio, E. 2004. *Global Entrepreneurship Monitor: 2003 executive report.* Babson College, London Business School, and the Kauffman Foundation. The classification of companies system used by GEM is based on Kirchhoff, B. 1994. *Entrepreneurship and dynamic capitalism.* London: Praeger.

launch new ventures. Incubators are also used by or in conjunction with venture capital groups to help facilitate the growth of both start-up and later-stage companies. The venture capital groups provide management assistance; the incubators provide office space, technology infrastructure, and business support services. An example is TechSpace, an international network of incubators with offices in New York, California, and several other global locations. Besides providing the usual incubator services, TechSpace and its venture capital partners often invest in the young firms that reside in its office communities.[32]

Angels and venture capitalists provide equity investments for entrepreneurial firms. Another important source of funding is from debt. The primary provider of debt financing for new ventures is commercial banks. Although credit cards often provide an important source of funding for very young firms (see Exhibit 13.4), banks provide an important source of ongoing funding. Because banks make their money by receiving interest on the loans as well as a return of principal, they are keenly interested in the firm's ability to repay the loan. That is why businesses with a track record of generating revenues are more likely to get bank loans. Besides cash flow, banks are also interested in collateral—assets that an entrepreneurial firm could sell to repay its loan in the event of a default. As a result, one of the ways that young firms often get start-up capital is through a home equity loan. Why? Because the house provides collateral which, in the event that the entrepreneur fails to make payments, the bank could force the homeowner to sell to satisfy its debt.

Clearly, financial resources are essential for new ventures and small businesses.[33] But other types of resources are also vitally important. In the next section, we will address the role of human capital, social capital, and government resources in the entrepreneurial start-up process.

## Other Entrepreneurial Resources

Whether an entrepreneur starts by bootstrapping or brings a large sum of assets to a new venture, founders often turn to three other types of resources that were discussed in Chapter 4: human capital, social capital, and government resources. Young and small firms have many of the same needs as larger firms—skilled and experienced workers and the ability to operate in a network of beneficial relationships. But they also have unique needs that stem from being young or small. By relying on the talents of other people, their network of contacts, and support services provided by government programs, entrepreneurial firms can often strengthen their ability to survive and succeed.

*Human Capital*   The most important human capital may be in the founding team. Bankers, venture capitalists, and angel investors who invest in start-up firms and small businesses agree that the most important asset an entrepreneurial firm can have is strong and skilled management. According to Stephen Gaal, founding member of Walnut Venture Associates, venture investors do not invest in businesses; instead "We invest in people . . . very smart people with very high integrity." Managers need to have a strong base of experience and extensive domain knowledge, as well as an ability to make rapid decisions and change direction as shifting circumstances may require. Additionally, among start-ups, more is better. New ventures that are started by teams of three, four, or five entrepreneurs are more likely to succeed in the long run than are ventures launched by "lone wolf" entrepreneurs.[34]

*Social Capital*   New ventures founded by entrepreneurs who have extensive social contacts are more likely to succeed than are ventures started without the support of a social network.[35] This is one of the major avenues for overcoming the liability problem of newness. Even though a firm may be new, if the founders have contacts who will vouch for them, they gain exposure and build legitimacy faster.[36] This support can come from several sources: prior jobs, industry organizations, and local business groups such as the chamber of commerce. These contacts can all contribute to a growing network that provides support for the young or small firm. Janina Pawlowski, cofounder of the online lending company E-Loan, attributes part of her success to the strong advisors she persuaded to serve on her board of directors, including Tim Koogle, CEO of Yahoo![37]

Strategic alliances represent a type of social capital that can be especially important to young and small firms. Strategy Spotlight 13.5 presents a few examples of alliances and some potential pitfalls of using alliances.

*Government Resources*   In the United States, the federal government is an important resource for many young and small businesses. It provides support for entrepreneurial firms in two key arenas—financing and government contracting. The Small Business Administration (SBA) has several loan guarantee programs designed to support the growth and development of entrepreneurial firms. The government itself does not lend money but underwrites loans made by banks to small businesses, thus reducing the risk associated with lending to firms that have unproven records. The SBA also offers training, counseling, and support services through its local offices and Small Business Development Centers.[38]

Another key area of support is in government contracting. Programs sponsored by the SBA and other government agencies ensure that small businesses have the opportunity to bid on contracts to provide goods and services to the government. Strategy Spotlight 13.6 on page 490 describes how several small firms have benefited from government contracts.

State and local governments also have hundreds of programs to provide funding, contracts, and other support for new ventures and small businesses. Local economic development initiatives such as the Southwest Minnesota Initiative Fund (SWMIF) are often designed specifically to stimulate small business activity. State-sponsored microenterprise funds such as the Utah Microenterprise Loan Fund (UMLF) provide funding as well as training for companies with fewer than five employees that are seeking less than $25,000.[39] Consider the example of Lissa D'Aquanni, who launched a gourmet chocolate business in her basement in 1998. As the business grew, she needed more space. To get it, she combined creative financing with government support.

> D'Aquanni had her eye on an abandoned building close to her home, but it cost $95,000 and needed $260,000 of renovation—more than her business could afford. So she turned to the local community. First, she asked for the support of local residents who were attracted to her plans to revitalize an empty building in the neighborhood and helped raised $25,000. Then the Albany Local Development Corporation, an economic development group, loaned her $95,000 to buy the building. A local credit union provided her with a government guaranteed loan to begin the renovations. A community development group helped her apply to a state program that funds energy-efficient upgrades such as windows, siding, and light fixtures. A matching grant program to encourage commercial development provided funds to upgrade the buildings facade. Eventually, she got the whole job done. "There are pockets of money out there, whether it be municipalities, counties, chambers of commerce," says Bill Brigham, director of the Albany Small Business Development Center. "Those are the loan programs that no one seems to have information about. A lot of these programs will not require the collateral and cash that is typical of traditional [loans]."[40]

As you can see from the example above, the government provides numerous funding opportunities for small business and new ventures. Although working with the government sometimes has its drawbacks in terms of issues of regulation and time-consuming decision

# STRATEGY SPOTLIGHT

## Strategic Alliances: A Key Entrepreneurial Resource

Strategic alliances provide a key avenue for growth by entrepreneurial firms. By partnering with other companies, young or small firms can expand or give the appearance of entering numerous markets and/or handling a range of operations. Here are several examples of alliances that have been used to extend or strengthen entrepreneurial firms:

### Technology Alliances

Often large firms seek out tech-savvy entrepreneurial firms that have mastered a new technology. The alliance allows the large firm to enhance its capabilities and expands the revenue and reach of the smaller firm. Such was the case when Intel announced in 2005 that it was forming an alliance with ArrayComm, LLC, a start-up formed to develop "smart" antenna technology. These antennas can be used to provide wireless Internet access for whole cities using a technology known as WiMax, an extended version of WiFi technology. Intel is a strong proponent of WiMax and sought the alliance to help it develop new chips that meet the standards needed for communicating with ArrayComm's smart antenna technology.

### Manufacturing Alliances

Outsourcing with foreign manufacturers was once considered something that only big firms could manage. But enhanced global communications and a worldwide spirit of entrepreneurship is changing all that. Not only are some firms "born global" as discussed in Chapter 7, but also there are new ventures that can profitably launch only because their products are manufactured overseas. This is how Philip McCaleb was able to introduce the Stella scooter, a Vespa knock-off manufactured in India. McCaleb had run a scooter parts business for nine years when he learned that Vespa was going to end its production alliance with scooter maker LML. McCaleb and a staff of three partnered with LML and in just three years rolled out 2,500 Stellas. McCaleb expects to double that number by 2006. The scooters sell for just $2,699—37 percent less than a comparable Vespa.

Sources: Clark, D. 2005. Intel deal could link start-up to nascent WiMax technology. *The Wall Street Journal,* June 22: B5; Copeland, M. V., & Tilin, A. 2005. Get someone to build it. *Business 2.0,* 6(5): 88–90; Monahan, J. 2005. All systems grow. *Entrepreneur,* March: 78–82; Prince, C. J. 2005. Foreign affairs. *Entrepreneur,* March: 56; Torres, N. L. 2005. Love thine enemy. *Entrepreneur,* March: 102; and Weaver, K. M., & Dickson, P. 2004. Strategic alliances. In W. J. Dennis, Jr. (Ed.), *NFIB national small business poll.* Washington, DC: National Federation of Independent Business.

### Retail Alliances

One of the best ways for small businesses to extend their sales is through licensing. Although the company gives up some profits with a license agreement, it also shifts some of the financial burden and expands its market. This helped Taggies, Inc., a maker of blankets and toys with satiny tags, expand its sales from $2 million to $3 million in one year when children's book publisher Scholastica, Inc., licensed its products for use in book promotions.

Licensing can also be used to go global. Specialty products—the types sometimes made by entrepreneurial firms—often seem more exotic when sold in another country. This was the view of a Japanese vendor that approached Meliorra, an Idaho-based beauty supply manufacturer, about selling its products in Japan. The young company was skeptical at first because it required a shift in priorities. But once it crunched the numbers, Meliorra realized it was an opportunity not to be missed. The deal is estimated to account for 30 percent of its 2005 sales—about $4.5 million.

### Alliances with Competitors

Lee Labrada, founder of a line of low-carb food products name CarbWatchers, was surprised one day when he was surfing the Internet and found a company using the very same name for a low-carb weight loss center in New York City. Because he trademarked the name, Labrada figured he could solve the problem by sending a cease and desist letter. But then he had a better idea. When the owner of the New York company called to resolve the problem, he suggested she carry his products in her store. Both would profit from the partnership as well as build their brand awareness. "We came to a meeting of the minds," says Labrada, one that helped his company grow to $20 million in yearly sales.

According to the National Federation of Independent Business (NFIB), nearly two-thirds of small businesses currently hold or have held some type of alliance. Strategic alliances among entrepreneurial firms can take many different forms. Exhibit 13.5 shows the different types of partnering that small businesses and small manufacturers in the NFIB study often use.

Although such alliances often sound good, there are also potential pitfalls. Lack of oversight and control is one danger of partnering with foreign firms. Problems with product quality, timely delivery, and receiving payments can also sour an alliance relationship *(continued)*

*(continued)* if it is not carefully managed. With technology alliances, there is a risk that big firms may take advantage of the technological know-how of their entrepreneurial partners. However, even with these potential problems, strategic alliances provide a good means for young and small firms to develop and grow.

| Type of Alliance and/or Long-Term Agreement* | Small Manufacturers | Small Businesses |
|---|---|---|
| Licensing | 20.0% | 32.5% |
| Export/Import | 14.4% | 7.3% |
| Franchise | 5.0% | 5.3% |
| Marketing | 18.0% | 25.2% |
| Distribution | 20.1% | 20.5% |
| Production | 26.5% | 11.3% |
| Product/Services R&D | 12.2% | 12.6% |
| Process R&D | 6.7% | 5.3% |
| Purchaser/Supplier | 23.5% | 13.9% |
| Outside Contracting | 23.2% | 28.5% |

*Columns add to over 100 percent because firms may use multiple alliances.

**Exhibit 13.5** *Use of Strategic Alliances by Small Businesses and Small Manufacturers*

Source: From Weaver, K. M., & Dickson, P. 2004. Strategic Alliances. In W. J. Dennis, Jr. (Ed.), *NFIB National Small Business Poll.* Washington, DC: National Federation of Independent Business. Reprinted with permission.

making, programs to support young and small firms constitute an important resource for firms to use during the start-up and growth process.

Clearly, the resource needs of new ventures are enormous. Unlike established firms, which often have a stockpile of resources—both human and physical—to draw upon, entrepreneurial firms are usually starting from scratch. Meeting the resource requirements of a new venture can be critically important to its success in the short run and over the long term. In the next section we will consider another type of capability that is especially important for the success of small or young firms: entrepreneurial leadership.

## >>Entrepreneurial Leadership

Whether a venture is launched by an individual entrepreneur or an entrepreneurial team, effective leadership is needed. Launching a new venture requires a special kind of leadership. It involves courage, belief in your convictions, and the energy to work hard even in difficult circumstances. Entrepreneurs and small business owners work for themselves. They don't have bosses to inspire them or tell them what to do. Their next paycheck will arrive only as a result of their own efforts. They must oversee all aspects of a company's operations as well as monitor quality and performance. Yet these are the very challenges that motivate most business owners. Entrepreneurs put themselves to the test and get their satisfaction from acting independently, overcoming obstacles, and thriving financially. To

## Government Work: It's Good Enough for Many Small Businesses

Homeland security, the war in Afghanistan, the rebuilding of Iraq—these projects and more have been keeping the U.S. government busy since the September 11 tragedies. To meet the needs created by these initiatives, more and more private companies are being called on to serve as contractors. Federal spending on information technology (IT) alone increased 18 percent from 2002 to 2003 to $59 billion, and it is expected to grow. This has allowed companies such as Cyveillance, a northern Virginia start-up that specializes in Internet espionage software, to grow its business by providing online monitoring services for the government.

To encourage businesses to bid on contracts, government agencies are proactively seeking bidders. This has created numerous opportunities for small businesses, because federal law requires that prime contracts use subcontractors on any job that is larger than $500,000. Although the big contracts go to major contractors like Boeing, Unisys, and Lockheed Martin, there are many subcontracting opportunities. This is how Gryphon Technologies, an IT logistics company, got its start. Its first contract was a small job for Northrop Grumman. Although at the time it seemed to founder Pam Braden like a low-level opportunity, she did not hesitate to take it. This led to bigger contracts, and now Gryphon is a prime contractor for the Department of Defense. "If you want to be a large business, which I want to be," says Braden, "you need to network the big companies and the government itself."

Not all of the government work is IT related. Thousands of projects, ranging from high-end engineering to maintenance and supply projects, are available to small business subcontractors. There are many peacetime opportunities available as well. The Small Business Administration (SBA) in cooperation with the National Science Foundation (NSF) runs a program known as Small Business Innovation Research (SBIR). The program recently funded nearly $2 billion in research, including $1 billion for the Department of Defense in 2005. Here is a description of SBIR's goals from its Web site:

> SBIR targets the entrepreneurial sector because that is where most innovation and innovators thrive. However, the risk and expense of conducting serious R&D efforts are often beyond the means of many small businesses. By reserving a specific percentage of federal R&D funds for small business, SBIR protects the small business and enables it to compete on the same level as larger businesses. SBIR funds the critical start-up and development stages, and it encourages the commercialization of the technology, product, or service, which, in turn, stimulates the U.S. economy.

As these various programs suggest, the federal government is potentially a rich resource for small firms, which supports innovation and the successful commercialization of new venture opportunities. Dealing with the government, however, can be time consuming and involve lots of "red tape"—that is, reporting requirements and regulations that are quite demanding. Even so, many small companies owe their success to the support they have gotten from government-sponsored programs.

Sources: Chen, C. Y. 2003. Getting a piece of the D.C. pie. *Fortune*, May 12:34; Kurtz, R. 2003. What your country can do for you. *Inc.*, July: 33–34; www.cyveillance.com; and www.sba.gov/sbir/.

do so, they must embody three characteristics of leadership—vision, dedication and drive, and commitment to excellence—and pass these on to all those who work with them.

### Vision

Vision may be an entrepreneur's most important asset. The entrepreneur has to envision realities that do not yet exist. This may consist of a new product or a unique service. It may include a competitive goal, such as besting a close competitor. For many entrepreneurs, the vision may be personal—building something from scratch, being your own boss, making a difference, achieving financial security. In every case, entrepreneurs must exercise a kind of transformational leadership that aims to create something new and, in some way, change their world. Not all founders of new ventures succeed. Indeed, the majority fail. But without a vision, most entrepreneurs would never even get a new business off the ground.

The idea of creating something new is captured in the vision of Paul Robbins, founder of Caribbean Shipping & Cold Storage.

> In a run-down part of Jacksonville, Florida, Paul Robbins envisioned opportunity. Where others saw a stretch of ramshackle houses, a lot strewn with rubble, and an abandoned warehouse, Robbins saw promise and profits. Caribbean Shipping & Cold Storage handles food products that need cold storage on their way to Puerto Rico and other Caribbean islands. In the past, shipments from far-flung U.S. locations might be transferred from truck to train to ship as many as six times. Instead of making arrangements with all those carriers, customers such as Outback Steakhouse and the Ritz-Carlton have Robbins handle the entire shipment. So why the run-down lot in Jacksonville? Because it's one block from Interstate 95 and only half a mile from Interstate 10. CSX train lines are so close that train whistles interrupt meetings. And the lot is adjacent to Jacksonville's shipping port. In other words, it's a crossroads—one that has paid off. Caribbean Shipping's revenues rose from $3.5 million to $20 million in just four years.[41]

By itself, however, just having a vision is not enough. The new venture idea must be effectively articulated as well. To develop support, get financial backing, and attract employees, entrepreneurial leaders must share their vision with others. The following leadership skills are needed to enact an entrepreneurial vision:[42]

- ***Be able to communicate with a wide audience.*** Entrepreneurial founders must reach a diverse collection of stakeholders. Understanding how these constituencies differ and fitting the vision message to their concerns is an important element of good leadership.
- ***Be willing to make unpopular decisions.*** As the new venture concept is developed, tough decisions will have to be made that define and shape the boundaries of the vision. Good leaders realize their decisions will not please everyone, but they still have to make them and move on.
- ***Be determined to make sure your message gets through.*** Employees of a venture start-up must have a clear sense of the leader's vision. But it's not enough to just make a vision statement. Good leaders must demonstrate how it is defining the direction of the company so the employees internalize it.
- ***Create and implement quality systems and methods that will survive.*** For a vision to be meaningful on a daily basis, leaders need to think of it as a tool. As such, it can be used to identify benchmarks that are needed to maintain quality, control outcomes, and measure success.

Creating and articulating a vision provide an essential starting point for an entrepreneurial venture. Without enthusiasm and perseverance, however, many ventures never get off the ground. Next, we turn to the important qualities of dedication and drive.

## Dedication and Drive

Dedication and drive are key success factors for the start-up entrepreneur. Dedication and drive are reflected in hard work. They require patience, stamina, and a willingness to work long hours. One of the key reasons that start-up businesses fail is that the founders lack commitment and neglect the business. Thus, drive involves internal motivation, while dedication calls for an intellectual commitment to the enterprise that keeps the entrepreneur going even in the face of bad news or poor luck. Entrepreneurs typically have a strong enthusiasm, not just for their venture but for life in general. As a result, their dedication and drive are like a magnet that draws people to the business and builds confidence in what the entrepreneurs are doing. Consider the example of Bill Nguyen.

Bill Nguyen is the founder and CEO of Seven Networks, a wireless software development start-up. Nguyen, who is only 30 years old and sleeps just three hours a night, has already been a part of six high-tech start-ups. One month after selling his previous start-up, Onebox.com, to Openwave Systems for $850 million, Nguyen launched Seven Networks and started raising venture capital. Initially, the venture capital firm Ignition and Greylock told him, "Bill, we love you, but it's not going to work." This didn't stop Nguyen. He went home and worked on the technical problems for three days straight with no sleep. When he showed up at Ignition's offices with a revised plan, he had solved the problem. Soon thereafter, the venture capitalists pledged $34 million to Nguyen's Seven Networks venture. According to Brad Silverberg, CEO at Ignition, "He's a rocket; you just strap in and try to hold on."[43]

Clearly, Nguyen is an example of a driven entrepreneur who has used his personal experience and sheer stamina to make his businesses succeed. Such dedication may be more important for some entrepreneurial firms. However, a business built on the heroic efforts of one person may suffer in the long run, especially if something happens to that person. Dedication and drive are important to success. But even hard-charging entrepreneurs can fail if they don't make an effort to do quality work or lack the competencies to achieve their aims. It is this commitment to excellence that we turn to next.

## Commitment to Excellence

Successfully managing the many elements of an entrepreneurial start-up requires a commitment to excellence. As we learned previously, new firms are often vulnerable because they lack credibility and experience. To improve the chances of survival, entrepreneurial founders must devote themselves to surpassing the performance of other competitors. To do so, they need to develop a sensitivity to how the elements of their value chain fit together and contribute to overall success. To achieve excellence, therefore, venture founders and small business owners must:

- Understand the customer.
- Provide quality products and services.
- Manage the business knowledgeably and expertly.
- Pay attention to details.
- Learn continuously.

Having this type of "whole organization" perspective can help a venture founder manage the synergies that might exist between different value-adding functions in a firm's value chain. For the firm to survive and become successful, the entrepreneurial leader must manage a firm's value proposition and set high standards for quality and customer service. Consider the example of Sue Bhatia and Rose International:

Rose International is a fast-growing information technology firm located in St. Louis, Missouri. Its CEO is Sue Bhatia, whose commitment to excellence helped her firm grow to 250 employees in just seven years despite its being a minority, female-owned firm in a male-dominated industry. Bhatia said, "I think it's important to remember that the customer is looking for good service. They don't care what your gender or race is. They want to see you deliver your service better than anyone, every time. If you can do that, you have a chance." According to Joe Hartmann, president of Digital Dimensions, Inc., who hired Bhatia's company to provide database architecture and network management solutions, Rose is a model of excellence. "Rose International has delivered more than promised since day one," Hartmann said. "They listen, and have an ability to draw upon their nationwide resources to provide the best solution possible."[44]

Another indicator of an entrepreneur's commitment to excellence is what kind of people they surround themselves with. Founders who think they can "do it all" and fail to recognize the importance of drawing on the talents and experience of others often fail.

Successful entrepreneurs often report that they owe their success to hiring people smarter than themselves to make things happen.

In his book *Good to Great,* Jim Collins makes an important point: Great companies are typically not led by lone-wolf leaders. Building a start-up on the vision or charisma of a single person can hinder a young firm, because when that person leaves, it creates a vacuum that may be hard to fill. In fact, the reason some companies never go from good to great is because they never fill the void left by the founder. Instead, business leaders with a commitment to excellence recognize that skilled and experienced people are needed to make the business successful. Such people are themselves leaders who attract other top-quality people to the organization.[45]

Another important practice is to let people go who don't fit with the company's culture. Even skilled persons can create problems for a firm if they do not embrace the company's goals and work ethic. Success requires focused and disciplined action. In the case of employees, that means leaders must have a willingness to get rid of people who are not working out. In an excellent company, says Collins, "Those people who do not share the company's core values find themselves surrounded by corporate antibodies and ejected like a virus."[46]

Although entrepreneurs must also exhibit other qualities of strong leadership, as we have suggested in earlier chapters, the combined elements of vision, dedication, drive, and commitment to excellence are especially important to the start-up entrepreneur. Next, we will turn to the elements of entrepreneurial strategy that are commonly associated with successful new venture creation.

## >>Entrepreneurial Strategy

Successfully creating new ventures requires several ingredients. As indicated in Exhibit 13.3, three factors are necessary—a viable opportunity, sufficient resources, and a skilled and dedicated entrepreneur or entrepreneurial team. The previous three sections have addressed these requirements. Once these elements are in place, the new venture needs a strategy. For any given venture, the best strategy for the enterprise will be determined to some extent by the unique features of the opportunity, resources, and entrepreneur(s) in combination with other conditions in the business environment. But there are still numerous strategic choices to be made. The tools and techniques introduced in this text, such as five-forces and value-chain analyses, can also be used to guide decision making among new ventures and small businesses. In this section, we consider several different strategic factors that are unique to new ventures and also how the generic strategies introduced in Chapter 5 can be applied to entrepreneurial firms. We also indicate how combination strategies might benefit young and small firms and address the potential pitfalls associated with launching new venture strategies.

To be successful, small and new ventures must evaluate industry conditions, the competitive environment, and market opportunities in order to position themselves strategically. However, a traditional strategic analysis may have to be altered somewhat to fit the entrepreneurial situation. For example, five-forces analysis (as discussed in Chapter 2) is typically used by established firms. It can also be applied to the analysis of new ventures to assess the impact of industry and competitive forces. But you may ask, How does a new entrant evaluate the threat of new entrants?

First, the new entrant needs to examine barriers to entry. If the barriers are too high, the potential entrant may decide not to enter or to gather more resources before attempting to do so. Compared to an older firm with an established reputation and available resources, the barriers to entry may be insurmountable for an entrepreneurial start-up. Therefore, understanding the force of these barriers is critical in making a decision to launch.

A second factor that may be especially important to a young or small firm is the threat of retaliation by incumbents. In many cases, entrepreneurial ventures *are* the new entrants that pose a threat to incumbent firms. Therefore, in applying the five-forces model to young firms, the threat of retaliation by established firms needs to be considered. This threat can be deadly for a young start-up.

New ventures often face challenges that threaten their survival. They tend to have less power than large firms, which can put them at a disadvantage. To overcome this problem, small firms and start-ups must look for a strategic opportunity to offer a unique value proposition to potential customers. Part of any decision about what opportunity to pursue is a consideration of how a new entrant will actually enter a new market. The concept of entry strategies provides a useful means of addressing the types of choices that new ventures have, and that is the subject we turn to next.

## Entry Strategies

As suggested earlier, one of the most challenging aspects of launching a new venture is finding a way to begin doing business that generates cash flow, builds credibility, attracts good employees, and overcomes the liability of newness. One aspect of that effort is the initial decision about how to get a foothold in the market. The idea of an entry strategy or "entry wedge" describes several approaches that firms may take.[47] Several factors discussed earlier will affect this decision.

- Does the entrepreneur prefer control or growth?
- Is the product/service high-tech or low-tech?
- What resources are available for the initial launch?
- What are the industry and competitive conditions?
- What is the overall market potential?

In some respects, any type of entry into a market for the first time may be considered entrepreneurial. But the entry strategy will vary depending on how risky and innovative the new business concept is. New-entry strategies typically fall into one of three categories—pioneering new entry, imitative new entry, or adaptive new entry.

*Pioneering New Entry*    A young firm with a radical new product or highly innovative service may change the way business is conducted in an industry. This kind of pioneering—creating new ways to solve old problems or meeting customer's needs in a unique new way—is referred to as a pioneering new entry. If the product or service is unique enough, a pioneering new entrant may actually have little direct competition. The first personal computer was a pioneering product; there had never been anything quite like it and it revolutionized computing. The first Internet browser provided a type of pioneering service. These breakthroughs created whole new industries and changed the competitive landscape. But breakthrough innovations continue to inspire pioneering entrepreneurial efforts. Consider the example of SkyTower Telecommunications, a year 2000 start-up that is hoping to take wireless communications to new heights:

> Wireless communications systems have only three ways to get to your cell phone or computer—radio towers that are often not tall enough, satellites that cost $50 million to $400 million to launch, and short-range Wi-Fi transmitters (see Chapter 8). SkyTower proposes a fourth alternative: unmanned, solar-powered airplanes that look like flying wings and send out Internet, mobile phone, and high-definition TV signals. The planes have already been successfully tested over Hawaii. They are able to fly at an altitude of 12 miles in a tight 2,000-foot-wide circle for six months at a time without landing. Designed as private communication systems for both businesses and consumers, they are able to deliver Internet service for about a third of the cost

of DSL or cable. SkyTower has already received the backing of NASA and $80 million in investment capital. Its target customers are major Internet Service Providers (ISPs). The plan is not without problems, however. For one thing, the Federal Aviation Administration (FAA) currently prohibits the launch of unpiloted planes. Even so, SkyTower's flying wing satellite is a breakthrough technology that addresses the increasing demand for cost-effective wireless communications.[48]

The pitfalls associated with a pioneering new entry are numerous. For one thing, there is a strong risk that the product or service will not be accepted by consumers. The history of entrepreneurship is littered with new ideas that never got off the launching pad. Take, for example, Smell-O-Vision, an invention designed to pump odors into movie theatres from the projection room at preestablished moments in a film. It was tried only once (for the film *Scent of a Mystery*) before it was declared a major flop. Innovative? Sure. But hardly a good idea at the time.[49]

A pioneering new entry is disruptive to the status quo of an industry. It is likely based on a technological breakthrough such as the one proposed by SkyTower. If it is successful, other competitors will rush in to copy it. This can create issues of sustainability for an entrepreneurial firm, especially if a larger company with greater resources introduces a similar product. For a new entrant to sustain its pioneering advantage, therefore, it may be necessary to protect its intellectual property, advertise heavily to build brand recognition, form alliances with businesses that will adopt its products or services, and offer exceptional customer service.

*Imitative New Entry*   In many respects, an imitative new-entry strategy is the opposite of entering by way of pioneering. Whereas pioneers are often inventors or tinkerers with new technology, imitators usually have a strong marketing orientation. They look for opportunities to capitalize on proven market successes. An imitation strategy is used by entrepreneurs who see products or business concepts that have been successful in one market niche or physical locale and introduce the same basic product or service in another segment of the market.

Sometimes the key to success with an imitative strategy is to fill a market space where the need had previously been filled inadequately. This was the approach used by Fixx Services, Inc., a restaurant and retail store maintenance service.

> Maintenance and repairs is hardly a new business concept. But Mark Bucher found that restaurants and retail stores were poorly served. He provides a facility management service designed to alleviate the headaches associated with keeping everything running. "Customers want one number to call if their oven breaks or if someone throws a brick through their front window," says Bucher. Founded in 1999, home-based and self-funded for the first three years, Fixx Services now has 12 employees and annual sales of nearly $10 million.[50]

Entrepreneurs are also prompted to be imitators when they realize that they have the resources or skills to do a job better than an existing competitor. This can actually be a serious problem for entrepreneurial start-ups if the imitator is an established company. Consider the example of Hugger Mugger Yoga Products, a Salt Lake City producer of yoga apparel and equipment such as yoga mats for practitioners of the ancient exercise art, with sales of $7.5 million annually.

> When founder Sara Chambers started the business in the mid-1980s, there was little competition. But once yoga went mainstream and became the subject of celebrity cover stories, other competitors saw an opportunity to imitate. Then Nike and Reebok jumped into the business with their own mats, clothes, and props. Hugger Mugger was a leading provider and had enjoyed 50 percent annual growth. But even after introducing a mass market line for stores such as Linens 'n' Things and hiring 50 independent sales reps, its growth rate has leveled off.[51]

## Franchising: A Tried-and-True Imitative Strategy

Franchising, by any measure, is a success story. One of every 12 retail businesses is a franchise—just over 8 percent of all retailers. Yet these businesses account for 40 percent of all retail sales in the United States. Franchising as an opportunity to own a business and work independently continues to expand. Industry experts estimate that a new franchise outlet opens somewhere in the United States every eight minutes, and franchising is rapidly becoming a global phenomenon.

Many people are familiar with major franchises. The first names that come to mind when most people think of franchises are the fast-food chains—McDonald's, Wendy's, Subway. But there are hundreds of other franchise businesses in industries such as accounting, printing and copying, advertising services, home repair and remodeling, environmental services, education services, and automotive repairs, to name a few. These businesses provide entrepreneurial opportunities for business owners and employment for hundreds of thousands of workers.

The most common type of franchise is known as the business format franchise, in which the franchisor provides the franchisee with a step-by-step guide for managing all major aspects of the business. With this approach, everything from the operational systems to the name, logo, and color scheme are prescribed by the franchisor. Regulations have been introduced during the last 10 years to provide franchisees with the essential information they need to choose a franchisor. This has taken away some of the mystery in the deals being offered by franchisors and made franchisees more confident about buying in. At the same time, the procedures for operating the business

systems have also improved. "It's easier for a new franchisee to enter the system now," says Paul Sweeney, a McDonald's franchisee in Cranberry Township, Pennsylvania. "They give you handbooks that tell you how to run your business so you don't have to come up with the context for construction and development on your own."

Clearly, franchising is built on the idea of imitating what another business has already done. If a business format is so easy to imitate, can it possibly have any competitive advantages? In the minds of many consumers of franchise products and services, the advantage is *because of* imitation. That is, consumers have confidence in franchises because they are familiar with them. "As time has gone by, the public has come to embrace franchising because they're familiar with the successful franchises and brand," claims Tony DeSio, founder of Mail Boxes Etc. "They know that, from one location to another, they can rely on product consistency." Thus, imitation is one of the central reasons why franchises are successful.

Even though consistency and sameness are highly valued in a franchise system, most franchisors are also open to suggestions for how to improve. Franchisees who think of a better way to market a service or showcase products are usually welcome to do so. For example, Navin Bhatia, owner of nine Valvoline Instant Oil Changes in San Antonio, Texas, masterminded the "good, better, best" marketing strategy for differentiating between the type of oil and level of service that is recommended to customers. Thus, through the efforts of independent franchisees, many franchises are able to continually improve their systems and hone their product and service offerings. Of course, when that happens, what do most of the other franchisees in the system do? They imitate it.

Sources: Williams, G. 2002. Keep thinking. *Entrepreneur*, September: 100–103; Smith, D. 2002. Want franchises with that? *Entrepreneur*, May: 102–106; and www.franchise.org.

Recall from Chapter 3 that the quality "difficult to imitate" was viewed as one of the keys to building sustainable advantages. A strategy that can be imitated, therefore, seems like a poor way to build a business. In essence, this is true. But then consider the example of a franchise. Strategy Spotlight 13.7 addresses the question of how and why the franchise approach to imitation has worked well for many entrepreneurs.

**Adaptive New Entry**   Most new entrants use a strategy somewhere between "pure" imitation and "pure" pioneering. That is, they offer a product or service that is somewhat new and sufficiently different to create new value for customers and capture market share. Such firms are adaptive in the sense that they are aware of marketplace conditions and conceive entry strategies to capitalize on current trends.

According to business creativity coach Tom Monahan, "Every new idea is merely a spin of an old idea. [Knowing that] takes the pressure off from thinking [you] have to

## AltiTunes: Success through Adaptation

"Darwin said it is not the strongest or fastest that survive but those that can adapt quickly," says Thomas Barry, chief investment officer at Bjurman, Barry & Associates. That's what Amy Nye Wolf learned when she launched her AltiTunes Partners LP business. She had been listening to the same music over and over during a six-week backpacking trip through Europe. At the end of the trip, she was elated to find a store selling music at London's Heathrow Airport. "I was so sick of the music I had, and I was just happy to see it."

About five years later, after finishing college and working as an investment banker, Wolf remembered her experience in the airport. She realized that selling CDs

was not an original idea but she thought there might be a need anyway. "I stole the idea," says Wolf, "and then did some serious adapting." Airports, she figured, constituted a unique market niche. She estimated that if she could sell just 30 CDs per day, she could keep the business afloat. Naming her business AltiTunes, Wolf took the plunge.

Today, AltiTunes sells 3,000 to 4,000 CDs per day at 27 stores in 20 airports and one train station. Sales of CDs and products such as portable stereos and computer games now exceed $15 million annually. And Wolf is still adapting. Her latest innovation is a gadget that lets shoppers roam around the store and sample any CD on the racks. It's a PDA-sized device developed by a company name MusiKube, LLC, that shoppers use by scanning a CD bar code to hear selections of music. It's just the latest improvement in Wolf's plan to stay cutting edge by continually adapting what she calls her "small format, extraordinary-location," music retailing business.

Sources: Barrett, A., & Foust, D. 2003. Hot growth companies. *BusinessWeek*, June 9: 74–77; Goldsmith, G. 2003. Retailers try new devices to make CD purchasing more enjoyable. *Wall Street Journal*, June 12, www.wsj.com; Williams, G. 2002. Looks like rain. *Entrepreneur*, September: 104–111; and www.altitunes.com.

be totally creative. You don't. Sometimes it's one slight twist to an old idea that makes all the difference."[52] Thus, an adaptive approach does not involve "reinventing the wheel," nor is it merely imitative either. It involves taking an existing idea and adapting it to a particular situation. Let's look at the example of Citipost:

> Richard Trayford was working temporarily while he waited for his new job in music promotion to begin. But he noticed that the bicycle-messenger company he was working for charged just one dollar for overnight delivery as a gimmick to get customers to use its more expensive same-day delivery service. Trayford realized that some customers would pay much more as long as it was less expensive than UPS and FedEx. So he borrowed $19,500 and launched Citipost. His strategy was to adapt an overnight delivery service to high-volume customers in New York's central business district. Citipost's first customer was Random House, a publisher that sends hundreds of overnight packages to agents, reviewers, and others within Manhattan every day. The service saved Random House 50 percent on delivery costs, and within four months Citipost was handling all of its deliveries. Twice named to the *Inc.* 500 list of the fastest-growing companies, Citipost now operates low-cost central city overnight delivery services in a dozen cities around the globe and earns revenues of $30 million annually.[53]

There are several pitfalls that might limit the success of an adaptive new entrant. First, the value proposition set forth by the new entrant firm must be perceived as unique. Unless potential customers believe a new product or service does a superior job of meeting their needs, they will have little motivation to try them out. Second, there is nothing to prevent a close competitor from mimicking the new firm's adaptation as a way to hold on to its customers. Third, once an adaptive entrant achieves initial success, the challenge is to keep the idea fresh. If the attractive features of the new business wear off or are copied, the entrepreneurial firm must find ways to adapt and improve the product or service offering. Strategy Spotlight 13.8 describes how adaptive new entrant Amy Nye Wolf has continually improved her entrepreneurial venture in order to hold her customers' interest and grow her business.

A new entrant must decide not only the best way to enter into business for the first time, but also what type of strategic positioning will work best as the business goes forward. Those strategic choices can be informed by the guidelines suggested for the generic strategies. We turn to that subject next.

## Generic Strategies

Typically, an entrepreneurial firm begins with a single business model that is equivalent in scope to a business-level strategy (Chapter 5). Thus, most small businesses and new ventures can benefit from applying the generic strategies. There is rarely any reason for a new venture to consider a corporate-level strategy (Chapter 6) except in a case when an entrepreneur decides to diversify into related or unrelated businesses or to purchase an existing business. Then, some of the guidelines that make the acquisition process more successful may be helpful to new entrants. In general, however, new ventures are single-business firms using business-level strategies. In this section we address how overall low cost, differentiation, and focus strategies can be used by new ventures to achieve competitive advantages.

*Overall Cost Leadership*    One of the ways entrepreneurial firms achieve success is by doing more with less. That is, by holding down costs or making more efficient use of resources than larger competitors, new ventures are often able to offer lower prices and still be profitable. Thus, under the right circumstances, a low-cost leader strategy is a viable alternative for some new ventures. The way new ventures achieve low-cost leadership, however, is typically different for young or small firms. Let's look first at why a cost-leadership strategy might be difficult for a new venture.

Recall from Chapter 5 that three of the features of a low-cost approach included operating at a large enough scale to spread costs over many units of production (i.e., economies of scale), making substantial capital investments in order to increase scale economies, and using knowledge gained from experience to make cost-saving improvements. These elements of a cost-leadership strategy may be unavailable to new ventures. Because new ventures are typically small, they usually don't have high economies of scale relative to competitors. Because they are usually cash strapped, they can't make large capital investments to increase their scale advantages. And because they are young, they often don't have a wealth of accumulated experience to draw on to achieve cost reductions.

Given these constraints, how can new ventures successfully deploy cost-leader strategies? Compared to large firms, new ventures often have simple organizational structures that make decision making both easier and faster. The smaller size also helps young firms change more quickly when upgrades in technology or feedback from the marketplace indicate that improvements are needed. New ventures are also able to make decisions at the time they are founded that help them deal with the issue of controlling costs. For example, they may source materials from a supplier that provides them more cheaply or set up manufacturing facilities in another country where labor costs are especially low. Thus, new firms have several avenues for achieving low cost leadership.

Consider the example of UTStarcom, a fast-growing wireless phone service being marketed in mainland China:

> Taiwan-born founder Hong Liang Lu was an executive at Japan's Kyocera Corp. when he made his first visit to China in 1990. He found a population that badly needed decent phone service. "Before that trip, I hadn't really thought about doing business in China. Afterward, I felt it made no sense to do business anywhere else." Using Personal Access System (PAS), a technology that had never caught on in Japan, he created a low-cost service that uses existing copper networks as its backbone. The service costs only $100 per subscriber to deploy, about half the price of cellular-based systems. Customers pay nothing for incoming calls and outgoing ones are 25 percent of the cellular rate. Competing against the big telecom providers was difficult at first, but once they marketed the "Little Smart" as a low cost alternative to cellular, sales took off. Average

annual revenues have grown 73 percent since 1999, and 2003 sales reached $1.96 billion. Says CEO Lu, "Our biggest problem is keeping up with demand."[54]

Whatever methods young firms use to achieve a low-cost advantage, this has always been a way that entrepreneurial firms take business away from incumbents—by offering a comparable product or service at a lower price.

*Differentiation*   Both pioneering and adaptive entry strategies involve some degree of differentiation. That is, the new entry is based on being able to offer a differentiated value proposition. Clearly, in the case of pioneers, the new venture is attempting to do something strikingly different, either by using a new technology or deploying resources in a way that radically alters the way business is conducted. Often, entrepreneurs do both.

Jeff Bezos set out to use Internet technology to revolutionize the way books are sold. He garnered the ire of other booksellers and the attention of the public by making bold claims about being the world's largest bookseller. As a bookseller, Bezos was not doing anything that had not been done before. But two key differentiating features—doing it on the Internet and offering extraordinary customer service—have made Amazon a differentiated success.

Even though the Internet and new technologies have provided many opportunities for entrepreneurs, differentiators don't have to be highly sophisticated to succeed. Consider the example of Spry Learning Co., a Portland, Oregon, start-up begun in 2000.

> Founders Sarah Chapman and Devin Williams believed that older people would benefit from using computers and surfing the Internet—if they only knew how. Working with gerontologists and instructional designers, they designed a computer-skills curriculum aimed at seniors. After piloting the program at two retirement communities, they successfully launched the differentiated service and, after just a few years, projected annual revenues over $4 million.[55]

There are several factors that make it more difficult for young firms to be successful as differentiators. For one thing, the strategy is generally thought to be expensive to enact. For example, differentiation is often associated with strong brand identity, and establishing a brand is usually considered to be expensive because of the cost of advertising and promotion, paid endorsements, exceptional customer service, aggressive warranties and return guarantees, as well as other expenses typically associated with building brand. Differentiation successes are sometimes built on superior innovation or use of technology. These are also factors where it may be challenging for young firms to excel relative to established competitors.

On the other hand, all of these areas—innovation, technology, customer service, distinctive branding—are also arenas where new ventures have sometimes made a name for themselves even though they must operate with limited resources and experience. To be successful, according to Garry Ridge, CEO of the WD-40 Company, "You need to have a great product, make the end user aware of it, and make it easy to buy."[56] It sounds simple, but it is a difficult challenge for entrepreneurs with differentiation strategies.

*Focus*   Because of the competitive environment facing most ventures, focus or "niche" strategies provide one of the most effective strategies for any new firm. A niche represents a small segment within a market. A young or small firm can play an important role in such a market space if there is an opportunity to thrive in that environment. Typically, a focus strategy is used to pursue a niche. Focus strategies are associated with small businesses because there is a natural fit between the narrow scope of the strategy and the small size of the firm. As we learned earlier, a focus strategy may include elements of differentiation and overall cost leadership, as well as combinations of these approaches. But to be successful within a market niche, the key strategic requirement is to stay focused. Here's why:

Despite all the attention given to fast-growing new industries, most start-ups enter industries that are mature.[57] In mature industries, growth in demand tends to be slow and there are often many competitors. Therefore, if a start-up wants to get a piece of the action, it often has to take business away from an existing competitor. If a start-up enters a market with a broad or aggressive strategy, it is likely to evoke retaliation from a more powerful competitor. Therefore, young firms can often succeed best by finding a market niche where they can get a foothold and make small advances that erode the position of existing competitors.[58] From this position, they can build a name for themselves and grow. Consider the example of Corporate Interns, Inc.:

> When Jason Engen was an undergraduate student at the University of St. Thomas in St. Paul, Minnesota, he learned the value of internships in which students worked for local companies. He wrote a business plan for one of his classes about forming an internship placement service in which he would screen students and match them with local companies. It's a "win–win situation," said Engen. "The student gets the experience, and the company gets eager talent." The interest in his idea was high, and a week after graduation he started Corporate Interns, Inc. It was difficult at first, however, because companies handle internships differently than other placement activities. But as Engen learned more, he realized this difference was an advantage: By positioning himself only in the college intern market, he avoided competing directly with large staffing companies. "Specialization is important," says Engen. "You have to stay focused on that niche." For Engen, that niche now generates $2 million in annual revenues.[59]

As the Corporate Interns example indicates, many small businesses are very successful even though their share of the market is quite small. Giant companies such as Procter & Gamble, Johnson & Johnson, and Ford are often described in terms of their market share—that is, their share of sales in a whole market. But many of the industries that small firms participate in have thousands of participants that are not direct competitors. For example, small restaurants and auto repair shops in California don't compete with those in Michigan or Georgia. These industries are considered "fragmented" because no single company is strong enough to have power over other competitors. Therefore, small firms need to focus on the market share only in their trade area. This may be defined as a geographical area or a small segment of a larger product group.

Consider, for example, the "Miniature Editions" line of books launched by Running Press, a small Philadelphia publisher. The books are palm-sized minibooks positioned at bookstore cash registers as point-of-sale impulse items costing about $4.95. Beginning with just 10 titles in 1993, Running Press grew rapidly and within 10 years had sold over 20 million copies. Even though these books represent just a tiny fraction of total sales in the $23 billion publishing industry, they have been a mainstay for Running Press, which eventually had to sue other publishers to protect its two-and-a-half by three-inch "trade dress" format.[60]

Although each of the three strategies holds promise, and pitfalls, for new ventures and small businesses, firms that can make unique combinations of the generic approaches may have the greatest chances of success. It is that subject we turn to next.

## Combination Strategies

Strategic positioning has different implications for small firms and entrepreneurial start-ups. For small firms, the issues they face in terms of their marketplace are often confined to a geographical locale or a small class of products. For start-ups, a key issue is the scope of their strategic efforts relative to those of their competitors. In determining a strategic position, both types of firms must address fundamental issues of how to achieve a distinct competitive advantage that will earn above-average profits as well as how to create value for their customers in the marketplace.

## Combining Strategies at AllDorm.com

"There are two ways to be successful in e-commerce," according to Jim Crawford, vice president at the research firm Retail Forward. "Operate on a large scale, or find an audience that isn't served by brick-and-mortar stores." It was the second of those two ways that motivated All-Dorm.com co-founder Ryan Garman. Standing in line at 5:00 a.m. with 2,400 other students after a grueling 13-hour drive pulling a U-Haul packed with his stuff, the entering freshman figured there had to be a better way. With that bleary-eyed epiphany, he found his unserved niche: college students moving into dorm rooms. A year and a half later, Garman and three college sophomore buddies founded AllDorm.com . . . in a dorm room.

Alldorm.com is an online retailer that specializes in the furnishings and accessories that students need to live in the shared and usually cramped space of a dorm room. According to the National Retail Federation, students and parents spend $2.6 billion annually furnishing dorm rooms and student apartments.

Beyond focusing on a lucrative niche, AllDorm has other strategic advantages as well. Its product selection—over 6,000 items—gives AllDorm differentiation advantages. For one thing, the products it offers are not just

the usual bean bag chair and mini-fridge. AllDorm goes for the latest in dorm design trends. "Students know what they want," says Gina LaGuardia of *The College Bound Network,* a magazine that targets the precollege market. "Practical items that have that funky element to them will really sell." Beside furnishings, it also sells hard-to-find products, such as extra long bedsheets, and products useful for group living, such as shower kits with sandals for trips to the communal bathroom. The company also coordinates deliveries with universities to make sure that shipments do not arrive too early.

Alldorm also concentrates on controlling costs. To help select products and keep in touch with trends in the student market, current college students are hired as interns to test new items. It also carefully controls back-end costs; rather than maintaining large inventories, AllDorm uses proprietary e-commerce software to coordinate direct shipments from suppliers.

Garman and his partners reflected recently on their success: "When you're in college, you have time to do things well. You can study, you can party, or you can start a company. We chose to start a company." Theirs was a good decision, apparently. Just four years after it was founded, AllDorm's revenues jumped to over $25 million per year and it's still growing.

Source: Torres, N. L. 2005. Inside job. *Entrepreneur,* March: 132; Myser, M. 2004. Giving college kids a smoother move. *Business 2.0,* June: 82; and www.alldorm.com.

One of the best ways for new ventures and small businesses to achieve success is by pursuing combination strategies. By combining the best features of low-cost, differentiation, and focus strategies, young and small firms can often achieve something that is truly distinctive.

Entrepreneurial firms are often in a strong position to offer a combination strategy, because they have the flexibility to approach situations uniquely. For example, holding down expenses can be difficult for big firms because each layer of bureaucracy adds to the cost of communicating and doing business. To get a part made, for example, or to outsource it, may be complicated and expensive for many large firms. By contrast, the Nartron Corporation, a small engineering firm whose innovations include the first keyless automobile entry system, solves that problem by building everything itself. By engineering its own products from its own designs, it not only saves money but also creates better parts. "Our parts look different from other people's because we keep adding functionality," says Nartron CEO Norman Rautiola. According to Rautiola, this capability allows the company to "run rings" around its competitors, which include Texas Instruments and Motorola.[61]

A similar argument could be made about entrepreneurial firms that differentiate. Large firms often find it difficult to offer highly specialized products or superior customer services. Entrepreneurial firms, by contrast, can often create high-value products and services through their unique differentiating efforts. Strategy Spotlight 13.9 examines AllDorm, a start-up founded by college students who made good use of a combination strategy.

For nearly all small firms, one of the major dangers is that a large firm with more resources will copy what they are doing. That is, well-established larger competitors that observe the success of a new entrant's product or service will copy it and use their market power to overwhelm the smaller firm. Although this happens often, the threat may be lessened for firms that use combination strategies. Because of the flexibility and quick decision-making ability of entrepreneurial firms, they can often enact their combination strategies in ways that the large firms cannot copy. This makes the strategies much more sustainable.

Perhaps more threatening than large competitors for many entrepreneurial firms are other small firms that are close competitors. Because they have similar structural features that help them adjust quickly and be flexible in decision making, close competitors are often a danger to young and small firms. Here again, a carefully crafted and executed combination strategy may be the best way for an entrepreneurial firm to thrive in a competitive environment.

## Summary

New ventures and small businesses that capitalize on marketplace opportunities make an important contribution to the U.S. economy. They are leaders in terms of implementing new technologies and introducing innovative products and services. Entrepreneurial firms face unique challenges if they are going to survive and grow. The size, age, and growth goals of small firms affect how they achieve competitive advantages.

To successfully launch new ventures or implement new technologies, firms must develop a strong ability to recognize viable opportunities. Opportunity recognition is a process of determining which venture ideas are, in fact, promising business opportunities. It consists of two phases. First is the discovery phase, in which new ideas are identified by alert individuals or generated by means of deliberate search processes. Second is the formation phase, in which the feasibility of opportunities is evaluated and plans are made to support and fund the new venture. In addition to strong opportunities, entrepreneurial firms need sufficient resources and entrepreneurial leadership to thrive.

The resources that start-ups need include financial resources as well as human capital and social capital. Strategic alliances are another resource that often benefits young and small firms. Many small firms also benefit from government programs that support their development and growth. Various avenues for obtaining resources are available to start-ups, depending on whether the new venture is in early or later stages of development. In early stages, personal savings and financial support from family and friends are the most common types of initial funding. Most start-ups can also benefit from bootstrapping, that is, operating economically and relying on as few outside resources as possible. Bank financing and venture capital are often used by entrepreneurial firms in later stages of development.

Young and small firms thrive best when they are led by founders or owners who have vision, drive and dedication, and a commitment to excellence. Vision provides entrepreneurial leaders with an ability to conceive of realities that do not yet exist. Dedication and drive are needed in order to persist in the face of difficulties and keep up the level of motivation necessary to succeed. Commitment to excellence is reflected in an entrepreneurial leader's focus on quality and customer service as well as a desire to be surrounded by talented and skilled employees.

New ventures and small businesses face numerous strategic challenges. However, many of the tools of strategic management can be applied to these firms. Decisions about the strategic positioning of young and small firms can benefit from applying five-forces analysis and evaluating the requirements of niche markets. Entry strategies used by new ventures take several forms, including pioneering new entry, imitative new entry, and adaptive new entry. Entrepreneurial firms can benefit from using overall low-cost, differentiation, and focus strategies, although each of these approaches has pitfalls that are unique to young and small firms. Entrepreneurial firms are also in a strong position to benefit from combination strategies.

## Summary Review Questions

1. Explain how an entrepreneurial firm's size, age, and growth goals help determine its character and strategic direction.

2. What is the difference between discovery and formation in the process of opportunity recognition? Give an example of each.

3. What types of financing are typically available to entrepreneurs in early stages and later stages of a new venture start-up?

4. How can bootstrapping help a young start-up or small business minimize its resource requirements? How might bootstrapping efforts affect decisions about strategic positioning?

5. Describe the three characteristics of entrepreneurial leadership: vision, dedication and drive, and commitment to excellence.

6. Briefly describe the three types of entrepreneurial entry strategies: pioneering, imitative, and adaptive.

7. Explain why entrepreneurial firms are often in a strong position to use combination strategies.

E-Loan is a young firm that offers lending services over the Internet. Evaluate the qualities of the opportunity E-Loan identified in terms of the four characteristics of an opportunity. In each category:

1. Evaluate the extent to which they met the criteria (using high, medium, or low).

2. Explain your rationale. That is, what features of the opportunity account for the score you gave them?

## Experiential Exercise

| Characteristics | High/Medium/Low | Rationale |
|---|---|---|
| 1. Attractive | | |
| 2. Achievable | | |
| 3. Durable | | |
| 4. Value Creating | | |

## Application Questions Exercises

1. Using the Internet, research the Web site of the Small Business Administration (www.sba.gov). What different types of financing are available to small firms? Besides financing, what other programs are available to support the growth and development of small businesses?

2. Think of an entrepreneurial firm that has been successfully launched in the last 10 years. What are the characteristics of the entrepreneur(s) who launched the firm?

3. Select a small business that you are familiar with in your local community. Research the company and discuss how it has positioned itself relative to its close competitors. Does it have a unique strategic advantage? Disadvantage? Explain.

4. Using the Internet, find an example of a young entrepreneurial firm (founded within the last five years). What kind of entry strategy did it use—pioneering, imitative, or adaptive? Since the firm's initial entry, how has it used or combined overall low-cost, differentiation, and/or focus strategies?

## Ethics Questions

1. Imitation strategies are based on the idea of copying another firm's idea and using it for your own purposes. Is this unethical or simply a smart business practice? Discuss the ethical implications of this practice (if any).

2. The prices of some foreign products that enter the United States are regulated to keep prices high, and "dumping" laws have been established to prevent some foreign companies from selling below wholesale prices. Should price wars that drive small businesses or new entrants out of business be illegal? What ethical considerations are raised (if any)?

## References

1. Lassek, P. J. 2004. No criminal activity found in city probe. *Tulsa World,* November 11, www.tulsaworld.com; Wysocki, B. 2001. Airline faces turbulence enroute to takeoff. *WSJ.com Startup Journal,* April 16, www.startupjournal.com; Wysocki, B. 2001. Airline's plan flies away as big carriers take root. *WSJ.com Startup Journal,* August 21, www.startupjournal.com; and www.tulsatoday.com.

2. Shane, S., & Venkataraman, S. 2000. The promise of entrepreneurship as a field of research. *Academy of Management Review,* 25(1): 217–226; Lumpkin, G. T., & Dess, G. G. 1996. Clarifying the entrepreneurial orientation construct and linking it to performance. *Academy of Management Review,* 21(1): 135–172; and Gartner, W. B. 1988. Who is an entrepreneur? is the wrong question. *American Journal of Small Business,* 12(4): 11–32.

3. Martin, J., & Birch, D. 2002. Slump? What slump? *Fortune,* December 1, www.fortune.com.

4. Dennis, W. J., Jr. 2000. *NFIB small business policy guide.* Washington, DC: National Federation of Independent Business; and www.nfib.com.

5. Small Business Administration. 2002. A report from Advocacy's 25th anniversary symposium. *SBA Office of Advocacy,* February 22, www.sba.gov/advo/.

6. Tilin, A. 2005. Bagging the right customers. *Business 2.0,* 6(4): 56–57.

7. Case, J. 2001. The gazelle theory. *Inc.,* May 15, www.inc.com; and Birch, D. 1979. *The job generation process.* MIT Program on Neighborhood and Regional Change. Cambridge, MA: MIT Press.

8. Sloane, J. 2003. Hearts and minds. *Fortune,* July 11, www.fortune.com; www.surmodics.com; and www.hoovers.com.

9. Case, J., op. cit.

10. Maintaining high levels of both wealth creation and employment growth is very challenging for most small firms. For an interesting perspective on how small ad medium-sized enterprises can manage fluctuations in growth, see Nicholls-Nixon, C. L. 2005. Rapid growth and high performance: The entrepreneur's "impossible dream"? *Academy of Management Executive,* 19(1): 77–89.

11. Small Business Administration, op. cit.

12. Fromartz, S. 1998. How to get your first great idea. *Inc.,* April 1: 91–94; and Vesper, K. H. 1990. *New venture strategies* (2nd ed.). Englewood Cliffs, NJ: Prentice Hall.

13. Carey, J., & Yang, C. 2001. From smart to brilliant weapons. *BusinessWeek,* October 8: 62–63.

14. Gaglio, C. M. 1997. Opportunity identification: Review, critique and suggested research directions. In J. A. Katz (Ed.), *Advances in entrepreneurship, firm emergence and growth,* vol. 3: 139–202. Greenwich, CT: JAI Press; Hills, G. E., Shrader, R. C., & Lumpkin, G. T. 1999. Opportunity recognition as a creative process. In *Frontiers of entrepreneurship research:* 216–227. Wellesley, MA: Babson College; and Long, W., & McMullan, W. E. 1984. Mapping the new venture opportunity identification process. In *Frontiers of entrepreneurship research:* 567–590. Wellesley, MA: Babson College.

15. For an interesting discussion of different aspects of opportunity discovery, see Shepherd, D. A., & DeTienne, D. R. 2005. Prior knowledge, potential financial reward, and opportunity identification. *Entrepreneurship Theory & Practice,* 29(1): 91–112; and Gaglio, C. M. 2004. The role of mental simulations and counterfactual thinking in the

opportunity identification process. *Entrepreneurship Theory & Practice,* 28(6): 533–552.

16. Stewart, T. A. 2002. How to think with your gut. *Business 2.0,* November: 99–104.

17. Bennet, E. 2000. Fungus fanatic. *Philadelphia Business Journal,* February 18, www.bizjournals.com/philadelphia/; and Greco, S. 1998. Where great ideas come from. *Inc.,* April: 76–86.

18. Timmons, J. A. 1997. Opportunity recognition. In Bygrave, W. D. (Ed.). *The portable MBA in entrepreneurship* (2nd ed.): 26–54. New York: Wiley.

19. Timmons, J. A., & Spinelli, S. 2004. *New venture creation* (6th ed.). New York: McGraw-Hill/Irwin; and Bygrave, W. D. 1997. The entrepreneurial process. In W. D. Bygrave (Ed.), *The portable MBA:* 1–26.

20. Stinchcombe, A. L. 1965. Social structure in organizations. In March, J. G. (Ed.), *Handbook of organizations:* 142–193. Chicago: Rand McNally.

21. *Inc.* 2001. Small business 2001: Where are we now? May 29: 18–19; and Zacharakis, A. L., Bygrave, W. D., & Shepherd, D. A. 2000. *Global entrepreneurship monitor—National entrepreneurship assessment: United States of America 2000 executive report.* Kansas City, MO: Kauffman Center for Entrepreneurial Leadership.

22. Cooper, S. 2003. Cash cows. *Entrepreneur,* June: 36.

23. Small business 2001: Where are we now? op. cit.; and Dennis, W. J., Jr. 1997. *Business starts and stops.* Washington, DC: National Federation of Independent Business.

23. www.keepwalking.com; and www.walkabouttravelgear.com.

24. Stuart, A. 2001. The pita principle. *Inc.,* August: 58–64.

25. Cooper, op. cit.

26. Gossage, B. 2004. Charging ahead. *Inc.,* January: 42–44.

27. Fraser, J. A. 2001. Plans for growth. *Inc.,* March: 56–57; and Fraser, J. A. 1998. A hitchhiker's guide to capital resources. *Inc.,* February: 74–82.

28. Seglin, J. L. 1998. What angels want. *Inc.,* May: 43–44.

29. Torres, N. L. 2002. Playing an angel. *Entrepreneur,* May: 130–138.

30. Fraser, J. A. 2001. The money hunt. *Inc.,* March: 49–63.

31. Lefteroff, T. T. 2003. The thrill of the chase. *Entrepreneur,* July: 56.

32. *Economist.* 2000. Hatching a new plan, August 12: 53–54; www.techspace.com; and www.nbia.org.

33. For more on how different forms of organizing entrepreneurial firms as well as different stages of new firm growth and development affect financing, see Cassar, G. 2004. The financing of business start-ups. *Journal of Business Venturing,* 19(2): 261–283.

34. Eisenhardt, K. M., & Schoonhoven, C. B. 1990. Organizational growth: Linking founding team, strategy, environment, and growth among U.S. semiconductor ventures, 1978–1988. *Administrative Science Quarterly* 35: 504–529.

35. Dubini, P., & Aldrich, H. 1991. Personal and extended networks are central to the entrepreneurship process. *Journal of Business Venturing,* 6(5): 305–333.

36. For more on the role of social contacts in helping young firms build legitimacy, see Chrisman, J. J., & McMullan, W. E. 2004. Outside assistance as a knowledge resource for new venture survival. *Journal of Small Business Management,* 42(3): 229–244.

37. Vogel, C. 2000. Janina Pawlowski. *Working Woman,* June: 70.

38. For more information, go to the Small Business Administration Web site at www.sba.gov.

39. Torres, N. L. 2002. Under the microscope. *Entrepreneur,* August: 106–109.

40. Detamore-Rodman, C. 2003. Out on a limb. *Entrepreneur,* March: 78–83.

41. Tanner, J. 2000. Meals on wheels (and rails and water). *Inc.,* May: 124–126.

42. Based on Kurlantzick, J. 2003. Got what it takes? *Entrepreneur,* March: 52.

43. Briody, D. 2001. Top ten entrepreneurs: Bill Nguyen. *Red Herring,* August 1: 58–60.

44. Himanshu "Sue" Bhatia. 2000. *Working Woman,* June: 91; see also roseint.com.

45. Collins, J. 2001. *Good to great.* New York: HarperBusiness.

46. Ibid.; and Collins, J. 2003. Bigger, better, faster. *Fast Company,* June: 74–78.

47. The idea of entry wedges was discussed by Vesper, K. 1990. *New venture strategies* (2nd ed.). Englewood Cliffs, NJ: Prentice Hall; and Drucker, P. F. 1985. *Innovation and entrepreneurship.* New York: HarperBusiness.

48. Frauenfelder, M. 2002. Look! Up in the sky! It's a flying cell phone tower! *Business 2.0,* November: 108–112.

49. Maiello, M. 2002. They almost changed the world. *Forbes,* December 22: 217–220.

50. Pedroza, G. M. 2003. Blanket statement. *Entrepreneur,* March: 92.

51. Gull, N. 2003. Just say om. *Inc.,* July: 42–44.

52. Williams, G. 2002. Looks like rain. *Entrepreneur,* September: 104–111.

53. Fromartz, op. cit.; and Grossman, J. 1999. Courier's foreign niche. *Inc.,* October 15: 57.

54. Burrows, P. 2003. Ringing off the hook in China. *BusinessWeek,* June 9: 80–82; www.hoovers.com.

55. Pedroza, G. M. 2002. Tech tutors. *Entrepreneur,* September: 120.

56. Barrett, A. 2003. Hot growth companies. *BusinessWeek,* June 9: 74–77.

57. Dennis, W. J., Jr. 1992. *The state of small business: A report of the president, 1992:* 65–90. Washington, DC: U.S. Government Printing Office.

58. Romanelli, E. 1989. Environments and strategies of organization start-up: Effects on early survival. *Administrative Science Quarterly,* 34(3): 369–387.

59. Torres, N. L. 2003. A perfect match. *Entrepreneur,* July: 112–114.

60. Wallace, B. 2000. Brothers. *Philadelphia Magazine,* April: 66–75.

61. Buchanan, L. 2003. The innovation factor: A field guide to innovation. *Forbes,* April 21, www.forbes.com.

**Strategic Analysis**

**Chapter 1**
Introduction
and Analyzing
Goals and
Objectives

**Chapter 2**
Analyzing
the External
Environment

**Chapter 3**
Analyzing
the Internal
Environment

**Chapter 4**
Assessing
Intellectual
Capital

**Strategic Formulation**

**Chapter 5**
Formulating
Business-
Level
Strategies

**Chapter 6**
Formulating
Corporate-
Level
Strategies

**Chapter 7**
Formulating
International
Strategies

**Chapter 8**
Digital
Business
Strategies

**Strategic Implementation**

**Chapter 9**
Strategic
Control and
Corporate
Governance

**Chapter 10**
Creating
Effective
Organizational
Designs

**Chapter 11**
Strategic Lead-
ership Excel-
lence, Ethics
and Change

**Chapter 12**
Fostering
Corporate
Entrepreneur-
ship

**Chapter 13**
Strategic
Leadership
Creating New
Ventures

**Case Analysis**

**Chapter 14**
Case
Analysis

# Case Analysis

## 14
Analyzing Strategic Management Cases

Cases

# Analyzing Strategic Management Cases

## >chapter objectives

*After reading this chapter, you should have a good understanding of:*

- How strategic case analysis is used to simulate real-world experiences.

- How analyzing strategic management cases can help develop the ability to differentiate, speculate, and integrate when evaluating complex business problems.

- The steps involved in conducting a strategic management case analysis.

- How conflict-inducing discussion techniques can lead to better decisions.

- How to get the most out of case analysis.

- How to use the strategic insights and material from each of the 13 previous chapters in the text to analyze issues posed by strategic management cases.

*C*ase analysis is one of the most effective ways to learn strategic management. It provides a complement to other methods of instruction by asking you to use the tools and techniques of strategic management to deal with an actual business situation. Strategy cases include detailed descriptions of management challenges faced by executives and business owners. By studying the background and analyzing the strategic predicaments posed by a case, you first see that the circumstances businesses confront are often difficult and complex. Then you are asked what decisions you would make to address the situation in the case and how the actions you recommend will affect the company. Thus, the processes of analysis, formulation, and implementation that have been addressed by this textbook can be applied in a real-life situation.

In this chapter we will discuss the role of case analysis as a learning tool in both the classroom and the real world. One of the benefits of strategic case analysis is to develop the ability to differentiate, speculate, and integrate. We will also describe how to conduct a case analysis and address techniques for deriving the greatest benefit from the process, including the effective use of conflict-inducing decision techniques. Finally, we will discuss how case analysis in a classroom setting can enhance the process of analyzing, making decisions, and taking action in real-world strategic situations.

# >>Why Analyze Strategic Management Cases?

It is often said that the key to finding good answers is to ask good questions. Strategic managers and business leaders are required to evaluate options, make choices, and find solutions to the challenges they face every day. To do so, they must learn to ask the right questions. The study of strategic management poses the same challenge. The process of analyzing, decision making, and implementing strategic actions raises many good questions.

- Why do some firms succeed and others fail?
- Why are some companies higher performers than others?
- What information is needed in the strategic planning process?
- How do competing values and beliefs affect strategic decision making?
- What skills and capabilities are needed to implement a strategy effectively?

How does a student of strategic management answer these questions? By strategic case analysis. Case analysis simulates the real-world experience that strategic managers and company leaders face as they try to determine how best to run their companies. It places students in the middle of an actual situation and challenges them to figure out what to do.[1]

Asking the right questions is just the beginning of case analysis. In the previous chapters we have discussed issues and challenges that managers face and provided analytical frameworks for understanding the situation. But once the analysis is complete, decisions have to be made. Case analysis forces you to choose among different options and set forth a plan of action based on your choices. But even then the job is not done. Strategic case analysis also requires that you address how you will implement the plan and the implications of choosing one course of action over another.

A strategic management case is a detailed description of a challenging situation faced by an organization.[2] It usually includes a chronology of events and extensive support materials, such as financial statements, product lists, and transcripts of interviews with employees. Although names or locations are sometimes changed to provide anonymity, cases usually report the facts of a situation as authentically as possible.

One of the main reasons to analyze strategic management cases is to develop an ability to evaluate business situations critically. In case analysis, memorizing key terms and conceptual frameworks is not enough. To analyze a case, it is important that you go beyond textbook prescriptions and quick answers. It requires you to look deeply into the information that is provided and root out the essential issues and causes of a company's problems.

The types of skills that are required to prepare an effective strategic case analysis can benefit you in actual business situations. Case analysis adds to the overall learning experience by helping you acquire or improve skills that may not be taught in a typical lecture course. Three capabilities that can be learned by conducting case analysis are especially useful to strategic managers—the ability to differentiate, speculate, and integrate.[3] Here's how case analysis can enhance those skills.

1. ***Differentiate.*** Effective strategic management requires that many different elements of a situation be evaluated at once. This is also true in case analysis. When analyzing cases, it is important to isolate critical facts, evaluate whether assumptions are useful or faulty, and distinguish between good and bad information. Differentiating between the factors that are influencing the situation presented by a case is necessary for making a good analysis. Strategic management also involves understanding that problems are often complex and multilayered. This applies to case analysis as well. Ask whether the case deals with operational, business-level, or corporate issues. Do the problems stem from weaknesses in the internal value chain or threats

in the external environment? Dig deep. Being too quick to accept the easiest or least controversial answer will usually fail to get to the heart of the problem.

2. **Speculate.** Strategic managers need to be able to use their imagination to envision an explanation or solution that might not readily be apparent. The same is true with case analysis. Being able to imagine different scenarios or contemplate the outcome of a decision can aid the analysis. Managers also have to deal with uncertainty since most decisions are made without complete knowledge of the circumstances. This is also true in case analysis. Case materials often seem to be missing data or the information provided is contradictory. The ability to speculate about details that are unknown or the consequences of an action can be helpful.

3. **Integrate.** Strategy involves looking at the big picture and having an organization-wide perspective. Strategic case analysis is no different. Even though the chapters in this textbook divide the material into various topics that may apply to different parts of an organization, all of this information must be integrated into one set of recommendations that will affect the whole company. A strategic manager needs to comprehend how all the factors that influence the organization will interact. This also applies to case analysis. Changes made in one part of the organization affect other parts. Thus, a holistic perspective that integrates the impact of various decisions and environmental influences on all parts of the organization is needed.

In business, these three activities sometimes "compete" with each other for your attention. For example, some decision makers may have a natural ability to differentiate among elements of a problem but are not able to integrate them very well. Others have enough innate creativity to imagine solutions or fill in the blanks when information is missing. But they may have a difficult time when faced with hard numbers or cold facts. Even so, each of these skills is important. The mark of a good strategic manager is the ability to simultaneously make distinctions and envision the whole, and to imagine a future scenario while staying focused on the present. Thus, another reason to conduct case analysis is to help you develop and exercise your ability to differentiate, speculate, and integrate.

Case analysis takes the student through the whole cycle of activity that a manager would face. Beyond the textbook descriptions of concepts and examples, case analysis asks you to "walk a mile in the shoes" of the strategic decision maker and learn to evaluate situations critically. Executives and owners must make decisions every day with limited information and a swirl of business activity going on around them. Consider the example of Sapient Health Networks, an Internet start-up that had to undergo some analysis and problem solving just to survive. Strategy Spotlight 14.1 describes how this company transformed itself after a serious self-examination during a time of crisis.

As you can see from the experience of Sapient Health Networks, businesses are often faced with immediate challenges that threaten their lives. The Sapient case illustrates how the strategic management process helped it survive. First, the company realistically assessed the environment, evaluated the marketplace, and analyzed its resources. Then it made tough decisions, which included shifting its market focus, hiring and firing, and redeploying its assets. Finally, it took action. The result was not only firm survival, but also a quick turnaround leading to rapid success.

## >>How to Conduct a Case Analysis

The process of analyzing strategic management cases involves several steps. In this section we will review the mechanics of preparing a case analysis. Before beginning, there are two things to keep in mind that will clarify your understanding of the process and make the results of the process more meaningful.

# STRATEGY SPOTLIGHT

## Analysis, Decision Making, and Change at Sapient Health Network

Sapient Health Network (SHN) had gotten off to a good start. CEO Jim Kean and his two cofounders had raised $5 million in investor capital to launch their vision: an Internet-based health care information subscription service. The idea was to create an Internet community for people suffering from chronic diseases. It would provide members with expert information, resources, a message board, and chat rooms so that people suffering from the same ailments could provide each other with information and support. "Who would be more voracious consumers of information than people who are faced with life-changing, life-threatening illnesses?" thought Bill Kelly, one of SHN's cofounders. Initial market research and beta tests had supported that view.

During the beta tests, however, the service had been offered for free. The troubles began when SHN tried to convert its trial subscribers into paying ones. Fewer than 5 percent signed on, far less than the 15 percent the company had projected. Sapient hired a vice president of marketing who launched an aggressive promotion, but after three months of campaigning SHN still had only 500 members. SHN was now burning through $400,000 per month, with little revenue to show for it.

At that point, according to SHN board member Susan Clymer, "there was a lot of scrambling around trying to figure out how we could wring value out of what we'd already accomplished." One thing SHN had created was an expert software system which had two components: an "intelligent profile engine" (IPE) and an "intelligent query

Sources: Brenneman, K. 2000. Healtheon/WebMD's local office is thriving. *Business Journal of Portland*, June 2; Raths, D. 1998. Reversal of fortune. *Inc. Technology*, 2: 52–62.

engine" (IQE). SHN used this system to collect detailed information from its subscribers.

SHN was sure that the expert system was its biggest selling point. But how could they use it? Then the founders remembered that the original business plan had suggested there might be a market for aggregate data about patient populations gathered from the Web site. Could they turn the business around by selling patient data? To analyze the possibility, Kean tried out the idea on the market research arm of a huge East Coast health care conglomerate. The officials were intrigued. SHN realized that its expert system could become a market research tool.

Once the analysis was completed, the founders made the decision: They would still create Internet communities for chronically ill patients, but the service would be free. And they would transform SHN from a company that processed subscriptions to one that sold market research.

Finally, they enacted the changes. Some of it was painful, including laying off 18 employees. Instead, SHN needed more health care industry expertise. It even hired an interim CEO, Craig Davenport, a 25-year veteran of the industry, to steer the company in its new direction. Finally, SHN had to communicate a new message to its members. It began by reimbursing the $10,000 of subscription fees they had paid.

All of this paid off dramatically in a matter of just two years. Revenues jumped to $1.9 million in 1998. Early in 1999 SHN was purchased by WebMD and less than a year later, WebMD merged with Healtheon. The combined company still operates a thriving office out of SHN's original location in Portland, Oregon.

First, unless you prepare for a case discussion, there is little you can gain from the discussion and even less that you can offer. Effective strategic managers don't enter into problem-solving situations without doing some homework—investigating the situation, analyzing and researching possible solutions, and sometimes gathering the advice of others. Good problem solving often requires that decision makers be immersed in the facts, options, and implications surrounding the problem. In case analysis, this means reading and thoroughly comprehending the case materials before trying to make an analysis.

The second point is related to the first. To get the most out of a case analysis you must place yourself "inside" the case—that is, think like an actual participant in the case situation. However, there are several positions you can take. These are discussed in the following paragraphs:

- **Strategic decision maker.** This is the position of the senior executive responsible for resolving the situation described in the case. It may be the CEO, the business owner, or a strategic manager in a key executive position.

- **Board of directors.** Since the board of directors represents the owners of a corporation, it has a responsibility to step in when a management crisis threatens the company. As a board member, you may be in a unique position to solve problems.

- **Outside consultant.** Either the board or top management may decide to bring in outsiders. Consultants often have an advantage because they can look at a situation objectively. But they also may be at a disadvantage since they have no power to enforce changes.

Before beginning the analysis, it may be helpful to envision yourself assuming one of these roles. Then, as you study and analyze the case materials, you can make a diagnosis and recommend solutions in a way that is consistent with your position. Try different perspectives. You may find that your view of the situation changes depending on the role you play. As an outside consultant, for example, it may be easy for you to conclude that certain individuals should be replaced in order to solve a problem presented in the case. However, if you take the role of the CEO who knows the individuals and the challenges they have been facing, you may be reluctant to fire them and will seek another solution instead.

The idea of assuming a particular role is similar to the real world in various ways. In your career, you may work in an organization where outside accountants, bankers, lawyers, or other professionals are advising you about how to resolve business situations or improve your practices. Their perspective will be different from yours but it is useful to understand things from their point of view. Conversely, you may work as a member of the audit team of an accounting firm or the loan committee of a bank. In those situations, it would be helpful if you understood the situation from the perspective of the business leader who must weigh your views against all the other advice that he or she receives. Case analysis can help develop an ability to appreciate such multiple perspectives.

One of the most challenging roles to play in business is as a business founder or owner. For small businesses or entrepreneurial start-ups, the founder may wear all hats at once—key decision maker, primary stockholder, and CEO. Hiring an outside consultant may not be an option. However, the issues faced by young firms and established firms are often not that different, especially when it comes to formulating a plan of action. Business plans that entrepreneurial firms use to raise money or propose a business expansion typically revolve around a few key issues that must be addressed no matter what the size or age of the business. Strategy Spotlight 14.2 reviews business planning issues that are most important to consider when evaluating any case, especially from the perspective of the business founder or owner.

Next we will review five steps to follow when conducting a strategic management case analysis: becoming familiar with the material, identifying the problems, analyzing the strategic issues using the tools and insights of strategic management, proposing alternative solutions, and making recommendations.[4]

## Become Familiar with the Material

Written cases often include a lot of material. They may be complex and include detailed financials or long passages. Even so, to understand a case and its implications, you must become familiar with its content. Sometimes key information is not immediately apparent. It may be contained in the footnotes to an exhibit or an interview with a lower-level employee. In other cases the important points may be difficult to grasp because the subject matter is so unfamiliar. When you approach a strategic case try the following technique to enhance comprehension:

- Read quickly through the case one time to get an overall sense of the material.
- Use the initial read-through to assess possible links to strategic concepts.
- Read through the case again, in depth. Make written notes as you read.

Established businesses often have to change what they are doing in order to improve their competitive position or sometimes simply to survive. To make the changes effectively, businesses usually need a plan. Business plans are no longer just for entrepreneurs. The kind of market analysis, decision making, and action planning that is considered standard practice among new ventures can also benefit going concerns that want to make changes, seize an opportunity, or head in a new direction.

The best business plans, however, are not those loaded with decades of month-by-month financial projections or that depend on rigid adherence to a schedule of events that is impossible to predict. The good ones are focused on four factors that are critical to new-venture success. These same factors are important in case analysis as well because they get to the heart of many of the problems found in strategic cases.

1.  *The People.* "When I receive a business plan, I always read the résumé section first," says Harvard Professor William Sahlman. The people questions that are critically important to investors include: What are their skills? How much experience do they have? What is their reputation? Have they worked together as a team? These same questions also may be used in case analysis to evaluate the role of individuals in the strategic case.

2.  *The Opportunity.* Business opportunities come in many forms. They are not limited to new ventures. The chance to enter new markets, introduce new

products, or merge with a competitor provide many of the challenges that are found in strategic management cases. What are the consequences of such actions? Will the proposed changes affect the firm's business concept? What factors might stand in the way of success? The same issues are also present in most strategic cases.

3.  *The Context.* Things happen in contexts that cannot be controlled by a firm's managers. This is particularly true of the general environment where social trends, economic changes, or events such as the September 11, 2001, terrorist attacks can change business overnight. When evaluating strategic cases, ask: Is the company aware of the impact of context on the business? What will it do if the context changes? Can it influence the context in a way that favors the company?

4.  *Risk and Reward.* With a new venture, the entrepreneurs and investors take the risks and get the rewards. In strategic cases, the risks and rewards often extend to many other stakeholders, such as employees, customers, and suppliers. When analyzing a case, ask: Are the managers making choices that will pay off in the future? Are the rewards evenly distributed? Will some stakeholders be put at risk if the situation in the case changes? What if the situation remains the same? Could that be even riskier?

Whether a business is growing or shrinking, large or small, industrial or service oriented, the issues of people, opportunities, context, and risks and rewards will have a large impact on its performance. Therefore, you should always consider these four factors when evaluating strategic management cases.

Sources: Wasserman, E. 2003. A simple plan. *MBA Jungle*, February: 50–55; DeKluyver, C. A. 2000. *Strategic thinking: An executive perspective.* Upper Saddle River, NJ: Prentice Hall; Sahlman, W. A. 1997. How to write a great business plan. *Harvard Business Review*, 75(4): 98–108.

- Evaluate how strategic concepts might inform key decisions or suggest alternative solutions.
- After formulating an initial recommendation, thumb through the case again quickly to help assess the consequences of the actions you propose.

## Identify Problems

When conducting case analysis, one of your most important tasks is to identify the problem. Earlier we noted that one of the main reasons to conduct case analysis was to find solutions. But you cannot find a solution unless you know the problem. Another saying you may have heard is, "A good diagnosis is half the cure." In other words, once you have determined what the problem is, you are well on your way to identifying a reasonable solution.

Some cases have more than one problem. But the problems are usually related. For a hypothetical example, consider the following: Company A was losing customers to a new competitor. Upon analysis, it was determined that the competitor had a 50 percent faster delivery time even though its product was of lower quality. The managers of company A could not understand why customers would settle for an inferior product. It turns out that no one was marketing to company A's customers that its product was superior. A second problem was that falling sales resulted in cuts in company A's sales force. Thus, there were two related problems: inferior delivery technology and insufficient sales effort.

When trying to determine the problem, avoid getting hung up on symptoms. Zero in on the problem. For example, in the company A example above, the symptom was losing customers. But the problems were an underfunded, understaffed sales force combined with an outdated delivery technology. Try to see beyond the immediate symptoms to the more fundamental problems.

Another tip when preparing a case analysis is to articulate the problem.[5] Writing down a problem statement gives you a reference point to turn to as you proceed through the case analysis. This is important because the process of formulating strategies or evaluating implementation methods may lead you away from the initial problem. Make sure your recommendation actually addresses the problems you have identified.

One more thing about identifying problems: Sometimes problems are not apparent until *after* you do the analysis. In some cases the problem will be presented plainly, perhaps in the opening paragraph or on the last page of the case. But in other cases the problem does not emerge until after the issues in the case have been analyzed. We turn next to the subject of strategic case analysis.

## Conduct Strategic Analyses

This textbook has presented numerous analytical tools (e.g., five-forces analysis and value-chain analysis), contingency frameworks (e.g., when to use related rather than unrelated diversification strategies), and other techniques that can be used to evaluate strategic situations. The previous 13 chapters have addressed practices that are common in strategic management, but only so much can be learned by studying the practices and concepts. The best way to understand these methods is to apply them by conducting analyses of specific cases.

The first step is to determine which strategic issues are involved. Is there a problem in the company's competitive environment? Or is it an internal problem? If it is internal, does it have to do with organizational structure? Strategic controls? Uses of technology? Or perhaps the company has overworked its employees or underutilized its intellectual capital. Has the company mishandled a merger? Chosen the wrong diversification strategy? Botched a new product introduction? Each of these issues is linked to one or more of the concepts discussed earlier in the text. Determine what strategic issues are associated with the problems you have identified. Remember also that most real-life case situations involve issues that are highly interrelated. Even in cases where there is only one major problem, the strategic processes required to solve it may involve several parts of the organization.

Once you have identified the issues that apply to the case, conduct the analysis. For example, you may need to conduct a five-forces analysis or dissect the company's competitive strategy. Perhaps you need to evaluate whether its resources are rare, valuable, difficult to imitate, or difficult to substitute. Financial analysis may be needed to assess the company's economic prospects. Perhaps the international entry mode needs to be reevaluated because of changing conditions in the host country. Employee empowerment techniques may need to be improved to enhance organizational learning. Whatever the case, all the strategic concepts introduced in the text include insights for assessing their effectiveness. Determining how well a company is doing these things is central to the case analysis process.

| Ratio | What It Measures |
|---|---|
| **Short-term solvency, or liquidity, ratios:** | |
| Current ratio | Ability to use assets to pay off liabilities. |
| Quick ratio | Ability to use liquid assets to pay off liabilities quickly. |
| Cash ratio | Ability to pay off liabilities with cash on hand. |
| **Long-term solvency, or financial leverage, ratios:** | |
| Total debt ratio | How much of a company's total assets are financed by debt. |
| Debt-equity ratio | Compares how much a company is financed by debt with how much it is financed by equity. |
| Equity multiplier | How much debt is being used to finance assets. |
| Times interest earned ratio | How well a company has its interest obligations covered. |
| Cash coverage ratio | A company's ability to generate cash from operations. |
| **Asset utilization, or turnover, ratios:** | |
| Inventory turnover | How many times each year a company sells its entire inventory. |
| Days' sales in inventory | How many days on average inventory is on hand before it is sold. |
| Receivables turnover | How frequently each year a company collects on its credit sales. |
| Days' sales in receivables | How many days on average it takes to collect on credit sales (average collection period). |
| Total asset turnover | How much of sales is generated for every dollar in assets. |
| Capital intensity | The dollar investment in assets needed to generate $1 in sales. |
| **Profitability ratios:** | |
| Profit margin | How much profit is generated by every dollar of sales. |
| Return on assets (ROA) | How effectively assets are being used to generate a return. |
| Return on equity (ROE) | How effectively amounts invested in the business by its owners are being used to generate a return. |
| **Market value ratios:** | |
| Price-earnings ratio | How much investors are willing to pay per dollar of current earnings. |
| Market-to-book ratio | Compares market value of the company's investments to the cost of those investments. |

**Exhibit 14.1**

**Summary of Financial Ratio Analysis Techniques**

Financial analysis is one of the primary tools used to conduct case analysis. The Appendix to Chapter 3 includes a discussion and examples of the financial ratios that are often used to evaluate a company's performance and financial well-being. Exhibit 14.1 provides a summary of the financial ratios presented in the Appendix to Chapter 3.

In this part of the overall strategic analysis process, it is also important to test your own assumptions about the case.[6] First, what assumptions are you making about the case materials? It may be that you have interpreted the case content differently than your team members or classmates. Being clear about these assumptions will be important in determining how to analyze the case. Second, what assumptions have you made about the best way to resolve the problems? Ask yourself why you have chosen one type of analysis over another. This process of assumption checking can also help determine if you have gotten to the heart of the problem or are still just dealing with symptoms.

As mentioned earlier, sometimes the critical diagnosis in a case can only be made after the analysis is conducted. However, by the end of this stage in the process, you should know the problems and have completed a thorough analysis of them. You can now move to the next step: finding solutions.

## Propose Alternative Solutions

It is important to remember that in strategic management case analysis, there is rarely one right answer or one best way. Even when members of a class or a team agree on what the problem is, they may not agree upon how to solve the problem. Therefore, it is helpful to consider several different solutions.

After conducting strategic analysis and identifying the problem, develop a list of options. What are the possible solutions? What are the alternatives? First, generate a list of all the options you can think of without prejudging any one of them. Remember that not all cases call for dramatic decisions or sweeping changes. Some companies just need to make small adjustments. In fact, "Do nothing" may be a reasonable alternative in some cases. Although that is rare, it might be useful to consider what will happen if the company does nothing. This point illustrates the purpose of developing alternatives: to evaluate what will happen if a company chooses one solution over another.

Thus, during this step of a case analysis, you will evaluate choices and the implications of those choices. One aspect of any business that is likely to be highlighted in this part of the analysis is strategy implementation. Ask how the choices made will be implemented. It may be that what seems like an obvious choice for solving a problem creates an even bigger problem when implemented. But remember also that no strategy or strategic "fix" is going to work if it cannot be implemented. Once a list of alternatives is generated, ask:

- Can the company afford it? How will it affect the bottom line?
- Is the solution likely to evoke a competitive response?
- Will employees throughout the company accept the changes? What impact will the solution have on morale?
- How will the decision affect other stakeholders? Will customers, suppliers, and others buy into it?
- How does this solution fit with the company's vison, mission, and objectives?
- Will the culture or values of the company be changed by the solution? Is it a positive change?

The point of this step in the case analysis process is to find a solution that both solves the problem and is realistic. A consideration of the implications of various alternative solutions will generally lead you to a final recommendation that is more thoughtful and complete.

## Make Recommendations

The basic aim of case analysis is to find solutions. Your analysis is not complete until you have recommended a course of action. In this step the task is to make a set of recommendations that your analysis supports. Describe exactly what needs to be done. Explain why this course of action will solve the problem. The recommendation should also include suggestions for how best to implement the proposed solution because the recommended actions and their implications for the performance and future of the firm are interrelated.

Recall that the solution you propose must solve the problem you identified. This point cannot be overemphasized; too often students make recommendations that treat only symptoms or fail to tackle the central problems in the case. Make a logical argument that shows how the problem led to the analysis and the analysis led to the recommendations you are proposing. Remember, an analysis is not an end in itself; it is useful only if it leads to a solution.

The actions you propose should describe the very next steps that the company needs to take. Don't say, for example, "If the company does more market research, then I would recommend the following course of action. . . ." Instead, make conducting the research part of your recommendation. Taking the example a step further, if you also want to suggest subsequent actions that may be different *depending* on the outcome of the market research, that's OK. But don't make your initial recommendation conditional on actions the company may or may not take.

In summary, case analysis can be a very rewarding process but, as you might imagine, it can also be frustrating and challenging. If you will follow the steps described above, you will address the different elements of a thorough analysis. This approach can give your analysis a solid footing. Then, even if there are differences of opinion about how to interpret the facts, analyze the situation, or solve the problems, you can feel confident that you have not missed any important steps in finding the best course of action.

Students are often asked to prepare oral presentations of the information in a case and their analysis of the best remedies. This is frequently assigned as a group project. Or you may be called upon in class to present your ideas about the circumstances or solutions for a case the class is discussing. Exhibit 14.2 provides some tips for preparing an oral case presentation.

## >>How to Get the Most from Case Analysis

One of the reasons case analysis is so enriching as a learning tool is that it draws on many resources and skills besides just what is in the textbook. This is especially true in the study of strategy. Why? Because strategic management itself is a highly integrative task that draws on many areas of specialization at several levels, from the individual to the whole of society. Therefore, to get the most out of case analysis, expand your horizons beyond the concepts in this text and seek insights from your own reservoir of knowledge. Here are some tips for how to do that.[7]

- *Keep an open mind.* Like any good discussion, a case analysis discussion often evokes strong opinions and high emotions. But it's the variety of perspectives that makes case analysis so valuable: Many viewpoints usually lead to a more complete analysis. Therefore, avoid letting an emotional response to another person's style or opinion keep you from hearing what he or she has to say. Once you evaluate what is said, you may disagree with it or dismiss it as faulty. But unless you keep an open mind in the first place, you may miss the importance of the other person's contribution. Also, people often place a higher value on the opinions of those they consider to be good listeners.

- *Take a stand for what you believe.* Although it is vital to keep an open mind, it is also important to state your views proactively. Don't try to figure out what your friends or the instructor wants to hear. Analyze the case from the perspective of your own background and belief system. For example, perhaps you feel that a

| Rule | Description |
|------|-------------|
| **Organize your thoughts.** | Begin by becoming familiar with the material. If you are working with a team, compare notes about the key points of the case and share insights that other team members may have gleaned from tables and exhibits. Then make an outline. This is one of the best ways to organize the flow and content of the presentation. |
| **Emphasize strategic analysis.** | The purpose of case analysis is to diagnose problems and find solutions. In the process, you may need to unravel the case material as presented and reconfigure it in a fashion that can be more effectively analyzed. Present the material in a way that lends itself to analysis—don't simply restate what is in the case. This involves three major categories with the following emphasis:<br><br>      Background/Problem Statement    10–20%<br>      Strategic Analysis/Options        60–75%<br>      Recommendations/Action Plan    10–20%<br><br>As you can see, the emphasis of your presentation should be on analysis. This will probably require you to reorganize the material so that the tools of strategic analysis can be applied. |
| **Be logical and consistent.** | A presentation that is rambling and hard to follow may confuse the listener and fail to evoke a good discussion. Present your arguments and explanations in a logical sequence. Support your claims with facts. Include financial analysis where appropriate. Be sure that the solutions you recommend address the problems you have identified. |
| **Defend your position.** | Usually an oral presentation is followed by a class discussion. Anticipate what others might disagree with and be prepared to defend your views. This means being aware of the choices you made and the implications of your recommendations. Be clear about your assumptions. Be able to expand on your analysis. |
| **Share presentation responsibilities.** | Strategic management case analyses are often conducted by teams. Each member of the team should have a clear role in the oral presentation, preferably a speaking role. It's also important to coordinate the different parts of the presentation into a logical, smooth-flowing whole. How well a team works together is usually very apparent during an oral presentation. |

**Exhibit 14.2**

**Preparing an Oral Case Presentation**

decision is unethical or that the managers in a case have misinterpreted the facts. Don't be afraid to assert that in the discussion. For one thing, when a person takes a strong stand, it often encourages others to evaluate the issues more closely. This can lead to a more thorough investigation and a more meaningful class discussion.

- **Draw on your personal experience.** You may have experiences from work or as a customer that shed light on some of the issues in a case. Even though one of the purposes of case analysis is to apply the analytical tools from this text, you may be able to add to the discussion by drawing on your outside experiences and background. Of course, you need to guard against carrying that to extremes. In other words, don't think that your perspective is the only viewpoint that matters! Simply recognize that firsthand experience usually represents a welcome contribution to the overall quality of case discussions.

- *Participate and persuade.* Have you heard the phrase, "Vote early . . . and often"? Among loyal members of certain political parties, it has become rather a joke. Why? Because a democratic system is built on the concept of one person, one vote. Even though some voters may want to vote often enough to get their candidate elected, it is against the law. Not so in a case discussion. People who are persuasive and speak their mind can often influence the views of others. But to do so, you have to be prepared and convincing. Being persuasive is more than being loud or long-winded. It involves understanding all sides of an argument and being able to overcome objections to your own point of view. These efforts can make a case discussion more lively. And they parallel what happens in the real world; in business, people frequently share their opinions and attempt to persuade others to see things their way.

- *Be concise and to the point.* In the previous point, we encouraged you to speak up and "sell" your ideas to others in a case discussion. But you must be clear about what you are selling. Make your arguments in a way that is explicit and direct. Zero in on the most important points. Be brief. Don't try to make a lot of points at once by jumping around between topics. Avoid trying to explain the whole case situation at once. Remember, other students usually resent classmates who go on and on, take up a lot of "airtime," or repeat themselves unnecessarily. The best way to avoid this is to stay focused and be specific.

- *Think out of the box.* It's OK to be a little provocative; sometimes that is the consequence of taking a stand on issues. But it may be equally important to be imaginative and creative when making a recommendation or determining how to implement a solution. Albert Einstein once stated, "Imagination is more important than knowledge." The reason is that managing strategically requires more than memorizing concepts. Strategic management insights must be applied to each case differently—just knowing the principles is not enough. Imagination and out-of-the-box thinking help to apply strategic knowledge in novel and unique ways.

- *Learn from the insights of others.* Before you make up your mind about a case, hear what other students have to say. Get a second opinion, and a third, and so forth. Of course, in a situation where you have to put your analysis in writing, you may not be able to learn from others ahead of time. But in a case discussion, observe how various students attack the issues and engage in problem solving. Such observation skills also may be a key to finding answers within the case. For example, people tend to believe authority figures, so they would place a higher value on what a company president says. In some cases, however, the statements of middle managers may represent a point of view that is even more helpful for finding a solution to the problems presented by the case.

- *Apply insights from other case analyses.* Throughout the text, we have used examples of actual businesses to illustrate strategy concepts. The aim has been to show you how firms think about and deal with business problems. During the course, you may be asked to conduct several case analyses as part of the learning experience. Once you have performed a few case analyses, you will see how the concepts from the text apply in real-life business situations. Incorporate the insights learned from the text examples and your own previous case discussions into each new case that you analyze.

- *Critically analyze your own performance.* Performance appraisals are a standard part of many workplace situations. They are used to determine promotions, raises, and work assignments. In some organizations, everyone from the top executive down is subject to such reviews. Even in situations where the owner or CEO is not evaluated by others, they often find it useful to ask themselves regularly, Am I being effective? The same can be applied to your performance in a case analysis situation. Ask yourself, Were my comments insightful? Did I make a good contribution? How might I improve next time? Use the same criteria on yourself that you use to evaluate others. What grade would you give yourself? This technique will not only make you more fair in your assessment of others but also will indicate how your own performance can improve.

- *Conduct outside research.* Many times, you can enhance your understanding of a case situation by investigating sources outside the case materials. For example, you may want to study an industry more closely or research a company's close competitors. Recent moves such as mergers and acquisitions or product introductions may be reported in the business press. The company itself may provide useful information on its Web site or in its annual reports. Such information can usually spur additional discussion and enrich the case analysis. (*Caution:* It is best to check with your instructor in advance to be sure this kind of additional research is encouraged. Bringing in outside research may conflict with the instructor's learning objectives.)

Several of the points suggested above for how to get the most out of case analysis apply only to an open discussion of a case, like that in a classroom setting. Exhibit 14.3 provides some additional guidelines for preparing a written case analysis.

# >>Using Conflict-Inducing Decision-Making Techniques in Case Analysis

Next we address some techniques often used to improve case analyses that involve the constructive use of conflict. In the classroom—as well as in the business world—you will frequently be analyzing cases or solving problems in groups. While the word *conflict* often has a negative connotation (e.g., rude behavior, personal affronts), it can be very helpful in arriving at better solutions to cases. It can provide an effective means for new insights as well as for rigorously questioning and analyzing assumptions and strategic alternatives. In fact, if you don't have constructive conflict, you may only get consensus. When this happens, decisions tend to be based on compromise rather than collaboration.

In your organizational behavior classes, you probably learned the concept of "groupthink."[8] Groupthink, a term coined by Irving Janis after he conducted numerous studies on executive decision making, is a condition in which group members strive to reach agreement or consensus without realistically considering other viable alternatives. In effect, group norms bolster morale at the expense of critical thinking and decision making is impaired.[9]

Many of us have probably been "victims" of groupthink at one time or another in our life. We may be confronted with situations when social pressure, politics, or "not wanting to stand out" may prevent us from voicing our concerns about a chosen course of action. Nevertheless, decision making in groups is a common practice in the management of many businesses. Most companies, especially large ones, rely on input from various top managers to provide valuable information and experience from their specialty area as well as their unique perspectives. Chapter 11 emphasized the importance of empowering individuals at all levels to participate in decision-making processes. In terms of this course, case analysis

| Rule | Description |
|---|---|
| **Be thorough.** | Many of the ideas presented in Exhibit 14.2 about oral presentations also apply to written case analysis. However, a written analysis typically has to be more complete. This means writing out the problem statement and articulating assumptions. It is also important to provide support for your arguments and reference case materials or other facts more specifically. |
| **Coordinate team efforts.** | Written cases are often prepared by small groups. Within a group, just as in a class discussion, you may disagree about the diagnosis or the recommended plan of action. This can be healthy if it leads to a richer understanding of the case material. But before committing your ideas to writing, make sure you have coordinated your responses. Don't prepare a written analysis that appears contradictory or looks like a patchwork of disconnected thoughts. |
| **Avoid restating the obvious.** | There is no reason to restate material that everyone is familiar with already, namely, the case content. It is too easy for students to use up space in a written analysis with a recapitulation of the details of the case—this accomplishes very little. Stay focused on the key points. Only restate the information that is most central to your analysis. |
| **Present information graphically.** | Tables, graphs, and other exhibits are usually one of the best ways to present factual material that supports your arguments. For example, financial calculations such as break-even analysis, sensitivity analysis, or return on investment are best presented graphically. Even qualitative information such as product lists or rosters of employees can be summarized effectively and viewed quickly by using a table or graph. |
| **Exercise quality control.** | When presenting a case analysis in writing, it is especially important to use good grammar, avoid misspelling words, and eliminate typos and other visual distractions. Mistakes that can be glossed over in an oral presentation or class discussion are often highlighted when they appear in writing. Make your written presentation appear as professional as possible. Don't let the appearance of your written case keep the reader from recognizing the importance and quality of your analysis. |

**Exhibit 14.3**

**Preparing a Written Case Analysis**

involves a type of decision making that is often conducted in groups. Strategy Spotlight 14.3 provides guidelines for making team-based approaches to case analysis more effective.

Clearly, understanding how to work in groups and the potential problems associated with group decision processes can benefit the case analysis process. Therefore, let's first look at some of the symptoms of groupthink and suggest ways of preventing it. Then, we will suggest some conflict-inducing decision-making techniques—devil's advocacy and dialectical inquiry—that can help to prevent groupthink and lead to better decisions.

## Symptoms of Groupthink and How to Prevent It

Irving Janis identified several symptoms of groupthink, including:

- *An illusion of invulnerability.* This reassures people about possible dangers and leads to overoptimism and failure to heed warnings of danger.

- *A belief in the inherent morality of the group.* Because individuals think that what they are doing is right, they tend to ignore ethical or moral consequences of their decisions.

# STRATEGY SPOTLIGHT

## Making Case Analysis Teams More Effective

Working in teams can be very challenging. Not all team members have the same skills, interests, or motivations. Some team members just want to get the work done. Others see teams as an opportunity to socialize. Occasionally, there are team members who think they should be in charge and make all the decisions; other teams have free-loaders—team members who don't want to do anything except get credit for the team's work.

One consequence of these various styles is that team meetings can become time wasters. Disagreements about how to proceed, how to share the work, or what to do at the next meeting tend to slow down teams and impede progress toward the goal. While the dynamics of case analysis teams are likely to always be challenging depending on the personalities involved, one thing nearly all members realize is that, ultimately, the team's work must be completed. Most team members also aim to do the highest quality work possible. The following guidelines provide some useful insights about how to get the work of a team done more effectively.

### Spend More Time Together

One of the factors that prevents teams from doing a good job with case analysis is their failure to put in the necessary time. Unless teams really tackle the issues surrounding case analysis—both the issues in the case itself and organizing how the work is to be conducted—the end result will probably be lacking because decisions that are made too quickly are unlikely to get to the heart of the problem(s) in the case. "Meetings should be a precious resource, but they're treated like a necessary evil," says Kenneth Sole, a consultant who specializes in organizational behavior. As a result, teams that care more about finishing the analysis than getting the analysis right often make poor decisions.

Therefore, expect to have a few meetings that run long, especially at the beginning of the project when the work is being organized and the issues in the case are being sorted out, and again at the end when the team must coordinate the components of the case analysis that will be presented. Without spending this kind of time together, it is doubtful that the analysis will be comprehensive and the presentation is likely to be choppy and incomplete.

### Make a Focused and Disciplined Agenda

To complete tasks and avoid wasting time, meetings need to have a clear purpose. To accomplish this at Roche, the Swiss drug and diagnostic product maker, CEO Franz Humer implemented a "decision agenda." The agenda focuses only on Roche's highest value issues and discussions are limited to these major topics. In terms of case analysis, the

major topics include sorting out the issues of the case, linking elements of the case to the strategic issues presented in class or the text, and assigning roles to various team members. Such objectives help keep team members on track.

Agendas also can be used to address issues such as the time line for accomplishing work. Otherwise the purpose of meetings may only be to manage the "crisis" of getting the case analysis finished on time. One solution is to assign a team member to manage the agenda. That person could make sure the team stays focused on the tasks at hand and remains mindful of time constraints. Another role could be to link the team's efforts to the steps presented in Exhibits 14.2 and 14.3 on how to prepare a case analysis.

### Pay More Attention to Strategy

Teams often waste time by focusing on unimportant aspects of a case. These may include details that are interesting but irrelevant or operational issues rather than strategic issues. It is true that useful clues to the issues in the case are sometimes embedded in the conversations of key managers or the trends evident in a financial statement. But once such insights are discovered, teams need to focus on the underlying strategic problems in the case. To solve such problems, major corporations such as Cadbury Schweppes and Boeing hold meetings just to generate strategic alternatives for solving their problems. This gives managers time to consider the implications of various courses of action. Separate meetings are held to evaluate alternatives, make strategic decisions, and approve an action plan.

Once the strategic solutions or "course corrections" are identified—as is common in most cases assigned—the operational implications and details of implementation will flow from the strategic decisions that companies make. Therefore, focusing primarily on strategic issues will provide teams with insights for making recommendations that are based on a deeper understanding of the issues in the case.

### Produce Real Decisions

Too often, meetings are about discussing rather than deciding. Teams often spend a lot of time talking without reaching any conclusions. As Raymond Sanchez, CEO of Florida-based Security Mortgage Group, says, meetings are often used to "rehash the hash that's already been hashed." To be efficient and productive, team meetings need to be about more than just information sharing and group input. For example, an initial meeting may result in the team realizing that it needs to study the case in greater depth and examine links to strategic issues more carefully. Once more analysis is conducted, the team needs to reach a *(continued)*

- *Stereotyped views of members of opposing groups.* Members of other groups are viewed as weak or not intelligent.

- *The application of pressure to members who express doubts about the group's shared illusions or question the validity of arguments proposed.*

- *The practice of self-censorship.* Members keep silent about their opposing views and downplay to themselves the value of their perspectives.

- *An illusion of unanimity.* People assume that judgments expressed by members are shared by all.

- *The appointment of mindguards.* People sometimes appoint themselves as mind-guards to protect the group from adverse information that might break the climate of consensus (or agreement).

Clearly, groupthink is an undesirable and negative phenomenon that can lead to poor decisions. Irving Janis considers it to be a key contributor to such faulty decisions as the failure to prepare for the attack on Pearl Harbor, the escalation of the Vietnam conflict, and the failure to prepare for the consequences of the Iraqi invasion. Many of the same sorts of flawed decision making occur in business organizations—as we discussed above with the EDS example. Janis has provided several suggestions for preventing groupthink that can be used as valuable guides in decision making and problem solving:

- Leaders must encourage group members to address their concerns and objectives.
- When higher-level managers assign a problem for a group to solve, they should adopt an impartial stance and not mention their preferences.
- Before a group reaches its final decision, the leader should encourage members to discuss their deliberations with trusted associates and then report the perspectives back to the group.
- The group should invite outside experts and encourage them to challenge the group's viewpoints and positions.
- The group should divide into subgroups, meet at various times under different chairpersons, and then get together to resolve differences.
- After reaching a preliminary agreement, the group should hold a "second chance" meeting which provides members a forum to express any remaining concerns and rethink the issue prior to making a final decision.

# Using Conflict to Improve Decision Making

In addition to the above suggestions, the effective use of conflict can be a means of improving decision making. Although conflict can have negative outcomes, such as ill will, anger, tension, and lowered motivation, both leaders and group members must strive to assure that it is managed properly and used in a constructive manner.

Two conflict-inducing decision-making approaches that have become quite popular are *devil's advocacy* and *dialectical inquiry.* Both approaches incorporate conflict into the decision-making process through formalized debate. A group charged with making a decision or solving a problem is divided into two subgroups and each will be involved in the analysis and solution.

*Devil's Advocacy*    With the devil's advocate approach, one of the groups (or individuals) acts as a critic to the plan. The devil's advocate tries to come up with problems with the proposed alternative and suggest reasons why it should not be adopted. The role of the devil's advocate is to create dissonance. This ensures that the group will take a hard look at its original proposal or alternative. By having a group (or individual) assigned the role of devil's advocate, it becomes clear that such an adversarial stance is legitimized. It brings out criticisms that might otherwise not be made.

Some authors have suggested that the use of a devil's advocate can be very helpful in helping boards of directors to ensure that decisions are addressed comprehensively and to avoid groupthink.[10] And Charles Elson, a director of Sunbeam Corporation, has argued that:

> Devil's advocates are terrific in any situation because they help you to figure a decision's numerous implications. . . . The better you think out the implications prior to making the decision, the better the decision ultimately turns out to be. That's why a devil's advocate is always a great person, irritating sometimes, but a great person.

As one might expect, there can be some potential problems with using the devil's advocate approach. If one's views are constantly criticized, one may become demoralized. Thus, that person may come up with "safe solutions" in order to minimize embarrassment or personal risk and become less subject to criticism. Additionally, even if the devil's advocate is successful with finding problems with the proposed course of action, there may be no new ideas or counterproposals to take its place. Thus, the approach sometimes may simply focus on what is wrong without suggesting other ideas.

*Dialectical Inquiry*    Dialectical inquiry attempts to accomplish the goals of the devil's advocate in a more constructive manner. It is a technique whereby a problem is approached from two alternative points of view. The idea is that out of a critique of the opposing perspectives—a thesis and an antithesis—a creative synthesis will occur. Dialectical inquiry involves the following steps:

1. Identify a proposal and the information that was used to derive it.
2. State the underlying assumptions of the proposal.
3. Identify a counterplan (antithesis) that is believed to be feasible, politically viable, and generally credible. However, it rests on assumptions that are opposite to the original proposal.
4. Engage in a debate in which individuals favoring each plan provide their arguments and support.
5. Identify a synthesis which, hopefully, includes the best components of each alternative.

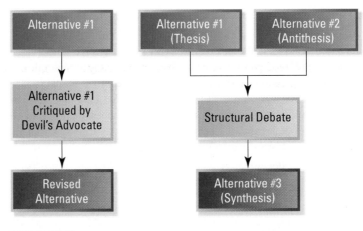

Exhibit 14.4    **Two Conflict-Inducing Decision-Making Processes**

There are some potential downsides associated with dialectical inquiry. It can be quite time consuming and involve a good deal of training. Further, it may result in a series of compromises between the initial proposal and the counterplan. In cases where the original proposal was the best approach, this would be unfortunate.

Despite some possible limitations associated with these conflict-inducing decision-making techniques, they have many benefits. Both techniques force debate about underlying assumptions, data, and recommendations between subgroups. Such debate tends to prevent the uncritical acceptance of a plan that may seem to be satisfactory after a cursory analysis. The approach serves to tap the knowledge and perspectives of group members and continues until group members agree on both assumptions and recommended actions. Given that both approaches serve to use, rather than minimize or suppress, conflict, higher quality decisions should result. Exhibit 14.4 briefly summarizes these techniques.

## >>Following the Analysis-Decision-Action Cycle in Case Analysis

In Chapter 1 we defined strategic management as the analysis, decisions, and actions that organizations undertake to create and sustain competitive advantages. It is no accident that we chose that sequence of words because it corresponds to the sequence of events that typically occurs in the strategic management process. In case analysis, as in the real world, this cycle of events can provide a useful framework. First, an analysis of the case in terms of the business environment and current events is needed. To make such an analysis, the case background must be considered. Next, based on that analysis, decisions must be made. This may involve formulating a strategy, choosing between difficult options, moving forward aggressively, or retreating from a bad situation. There are many possible decisions, depending on the case situation. Finally, action is required. Once decisions are made and plans are set, the action begins. The recommended action steps and the consequences of implementing these actions are the final stage.

Each of the previous 13 chapters of this book includes techniques and information that may be useful in a case analysis. However, not all of the issues presented will be important in every case. As noted earlier, one of the challenges of case analysis is to identify the most critical points and sort through material that may be ambiguous or unimportant.

In this section we draw on the material presented in each of the 13 chapters to show how it informs the case analysis process. The ideas are linked sequentially and in terms of an overarching strategic perspective. One of your jobs when conducting case analysis is to see how the parts of a case fit together and how the insights from the study of strategy can help you understand the case situation.

1. **Analyzing organizational goals and objectives.** A company's vision, mission, and objectives keep organization members focused on a common purpose. They also influence how an organization deploys its resources, relates to its stakeholders, and matches its short-term objectives with its long-term goals. The goals may even impact how a company formulates and implements strategies. When exploring issues of goals and objectives, you might ask:

   - Has the company developed short-term objectives that are inconsistent with its long-term mission? If so, how can management realign its vision, mission, and objectives?
   - Has the company considered all of its stakeholders equally in making critical decisions? If not, should the views of all stakeholders be treated the same or are some stakeholders more important than others?
   - Is the company being faced with an issue that conflicts with one of its long-standing policies? If so, how should it compare its existing policies to the potential new situation?

2. **Analyzing the external environment.** The business environment has two components. The general environment consists of demographic, sociocultural, political/legal, technological, economic, and global conditions. The competitive environment includes rivals, suppliers, customers, and other factors that may directly affect a company's success. Strategic managers must monitor the environment to identify opportunities and threats that may have an impact on performance. When investigating a firm's external environment, you might ask:

   - Does the company follow trends and events in the general environment? If not, how can these influences be made part of the company's strategic analysis process?
   - Is the company effectively scanning and monitoring the competitive environment? If so, how is it using the competitive intelligence it is gathering to enhance its competitive advantage?
   - Has the company correctly analyzed the impact of the competitive forces in its industry on profitability? If so, how can it improve its competitive position relative to these forces?

3. **Analyzing the internal environment.** A firm's internal environment consists of its resources and other value-adding capabilities. Value-chain analysis and a resource-based approach to analysis can be used to identify a company's strengths and weaknesses and determine how they are contributing to its competitive advantages. Evaluating firm performance can also help make meaningful comparisons with competitors. When researching a company's internal analysis, you might ask:

   - Does the company know how the various components of its value chain are adding value to the firm? If not, what internal analysis is needed to determine its strengths and weakness?
   - Has the company accurately analyzed the source and vitality of its resources? If so, is it deploying its resources in a way that contributes to competitive advantages?
   - Is the company's financial performance as good as or better than that of its close competitors? If so, has it balanced its financial success with the performance criteria of other stakeholders such as customers and employees?

4. ***Assessing a firm's intellectual assets.*** Human capital is a major resource in today's knowledge economy. As a result, attracting, developing, and retaining talented workers is a key strategic challenge. Other assets such as patents and trademarks are also critical. How companies leverage their intellectual assets through social networks and strategic alliances, and how technology is used to manage knowledge may be a major influence on a firm's competitive advantage. When analyzing a firm's intellectual assets, you might ask:

- Does the company have underutilized human capital? If so, what steps are needed to develop and leverage its intellectual assets?
- Is the company missing opportunities to forge strategic alliances? If so, how can it use its social capital to network more effectively?
- Has the company developed knowledge-management systems that capture what it learns? If not, what technologies can it employ to retain new knowledge?

5. ***Formulating business-level strategies.*** Firms use the competitive strategies of differentiation, focus, and overall cost leadership as a basis for overcoming the five competitive forces and developing sustainable competitive advantages. Combinations of these strategies may work best in some competitive environments. Additionally, an industry's life cycle is an important contingency that may affect a company's choice of business-level strategies. When assessing business-level strategies, you might ask:

- Has the company chosen the correct competitive strategy given its industry environment and competitive situation? If not, how should it use its strengths and resources to improve its performance?
- Does the company use combination strategies effectively? If so, what capabilities can it cultivate to further enhance profitability?
- Is the company using a strategy that is appropriate for the industry life cycle in which it is competing? If not, how can it realign itself to match its efforts to the current stage of industry growth?

6. ***Formulating corporate-level strategies.*** Large firms often own and manage portfolios of businesses. Corporate strategies address methods for achieving synergies among these businesses. Related and unrelated diversification techniques are alternative approaches to deciding which business should be added to or removed from a portfolio. Companies can diversify by means of mergers, acquisitions, joint ventures, strategic alliances, and internal development. When analyzing corporate-level strategies, you might ask:

- Is the company competing in the right businesses given the opportunities and threats that are present in the environment? If not, how can it realign its diversification strategy to achieve competitive advantages?
- Is the corporation managing its portfolio of businesses in a way that creates synergies among the businesses? If so, what additional business should it consider adding to its portfolio?
- Are the motives of the top corporate executives who are pushing diversification strategies appropriate? If not, what action can be taken to curb their activities or align them with the best interests of all stakeholders?

7. ***Formulating international-level strategies.*** Foreign markets provide both opportunities and potential dangers for companies that want to expand globally. To decide which entry strategy is most appropriate, companies have to evaluate the trade-offs between two factors that firms face when entering foreign markets: cost reduction and local adaptation. To achieve competitive advantages, firms will typically

choose one of three strategies: global, multidomestic, or transnational. When evaluating international-level strategies, you might ask:

- Is the company's entry into an international marketplace threatened by the actions of local competitors? If so, how can cultural differences be minimized to give the firm a better chance of succeeding?
- Has the company made the appropriate choices between cost reduction and local adaptation to foreign markets? If not, how can it adjust its strategy to achieve competitive advantages?
- Can the company improve its effectiveness by embracing one international strategy over another? If so, how should it choose between a global, multidomestic, or transnational strategy?

8. *Formulating Internet strategies.* The Internet and digital technologies have created a new arena for strategic analysis, decisions, and action. The technologies and applications that the Internet makes possible are having an impact on competitive forces in many industries. Internet business models and value-adding strategies that combine elements of low cost, differentiation, and focus are creating new wealth in this new economy. When conducting an analysis that involves Internet strategies, you might ask:

- Has the company correctly assessed shifts in the five competitive forces that have been brought about by the Internet? If so, what new strategies should it formulate to take advantage of—or defend itself—in the new Internet economy?
- Does the company have an opportunity to lower its transaction costs by using digital technologies or doing business over the Internet? If so, what supply-chain or distribution channel relationships might be disrupted?
- Is the company using the right mix of competitive strategies to make the most of Internet-based technologies? If not, how might it deploy its resources and capabilities differently?

9. *Achieving effective strategic control.* Strategic controls enable a firm to implement strategies effectively. Informational controls involve comparing performance to stated goals and scanning, monitoring, and being responsive to the environment. Behavioral controls emerge from a company's culture, reward systems, and organizational boundaries. When assessing the impact of strategic controls on implementation, you might ask:

- Is the company employing the appropriate informational control systems? If not, how can it implement a more interactive approach to enhance learning and minimize response times?
- Does the company have a strong and effective culture? If not, what steps can it take to align its values and rewards system with its goals and objectives?
- Has the company implemented control systems that match its strategies? If so, what additional steps can be taken to improve performance?

10. *Creating effective organizational designs.* Organizational designs that align with competitive strategies can enhance performance. As companies grow and change, their structures must also evolve to meet new demands. In today's economy, firm boundaries must be flexible and permeable to facilitate smoother interactions with external parties such as customers, suppliers, and alliance partners. New forms of organizing are becoming more common. When evaluating the role of organizational structure on strategy implementation, you might ask:

- Has the company implemented organizational structures that are suited to the type of business it is in? If not, how can it alter the design in ways that enhance its competitiveness?

- Is the company employing boundaryless organizational designs where appropriate? If so, how are senior managers maintaining control of lower-level employees?
- Does the company use outsourcing to achieve the best possible results? If not, what criteria should it use to decide which functions can be outsourced?

11. ***Creating a learning organization and an ethical organization.*** Strong leadership is essential for achieving competitive advantages. Two leadership roles are especially important. The first is creating a learning organization by harnessing talent and encouraging the development of new knowledge. Second, leaders play a vital role in motivating employees to excellence and inspiring ethical behavior. When exploring the impact of effective strategic leadership, you might ask:

- Do company leaders promote excellence as part of the overall culture? If so, how has this influenced the performance of the firm and the individuals in it?
- Is the company committed to being a learning organization? If not, what can it do to capitalize on the individual and collective talents of organizational members?
- Have company leaders exhibited an ethical attitude in their own behavior? If not, how has their behavior influenced the actions of other employees?

12. ***Fostering corporate entrepreneurship.*** Many firms continually seek new growth opportunities and avenues for strategic renewal. In some corporations, autonomous work units such as business incubators and new-venture groups are used to focus corporate venturing activities. In other corporate settings, product champions and other firm members provide companies with the impetus to expand into new areas. When investigating the impact of entrepreneurship on strategic effectiveness, you might ask:

- Has the company resolved the dilemmas associated with managing innovation? If so, is it effectively defining and pacing its innovation efforts?
- Has the company developed autonomous work units that have the freedom to bring forth new product ideas? If so, has it used product champions to implement new venture initiatives?
- Does the company have an entrepreneurial orientation? If not, what can it do to encourage entrepreneurial attitudes in the strategic behavior of its organizational members?

13. ***Creating new ventures.*** Young and small firms launch ventures that add jobs and create new wealth. In order to do so, they must identify opportunities that will be viable in the marketplace. The strategic management concepts introduced in this text can guide new ventures and small businesses in their efforts to identify markets, obtain resources, and create effective strategies. When examining the role of strategic thinking on the success of small business management and new venture creation, you might ask:

- Is the company engaged in an ongoing process of opportunity recognition? If not, how can it enhance its ability to recognize opportunities?
- Do the entrepreneurs who are launching new ventures have vision, dedication and drive, and a commitment to excellence? If so, how have these affected the performance and dedication of other employees involved in the venture?
- Have strategic principles been used in the process of obtaining valuable resources and crafting effective entrepreneurial strategies? If not, how can the venture apply the tools of five-forces and value-chain analyses to improve its strategy making and performance?

# Summary

Strategic management case analysis provides an effective method of learning how companies analyze problems, make decisions, and resolve challenges. Strategic cases include detailed accounts of actual business situations. The purpose of analyzing such cases is to gain exposure to a wide variety of organizational and managerial situations. By putting yourself in the place of a strategic decision maker, you can gain an appreciation of the difficulty and complexity of many strategic situations. In the process you can learn how to ask good strategic questions and enhance your analytical skills. Presenting case analyses can also help develop oral and written communication skills.

In this chapter we have discussed the importance of strategic case analysis and described the five steps involved in conducting a case analysis: becoming familiar with the material, identifying problems, analyzing strategic issues, proposing alternative solutions, and making recommendations. We have also discussed how to get the most from case analysis. Finally, we have described how the case analysis process follows the analysis-decision-action cycle of strategic management and outlined issues and questions that are associated with each of the previous 13 chapters of the text.

# References

1. The material in this chapter is based on several sources, including Barnes, L. A., Nelson, A. J., & Christensen, C. R. 1994. *Teaching and the case method: Text, cases and readings.* Boston: Harvard Business School Press: Guth, W. D. 1985. Central concepts of business unit and corporate strategy. In W. D. Guth (Ed.). *Handbook of business strategy:* 1–9. Boston: Warren, Gorham & Lamont; Lundberg, C. C., & Enz, C. 1993. A framework for student case preparation. *Case Research Journal,* 13 (Summer): 129–140; and Ronstadt, R. 1980. *The art of case analysis: A guide to the diagnosis of business situations.* Dover, MA: Lord Publishing.

2. Edge, A. G., & Coleman, D. R. 1986. *The guide to case analysis and reporting* (3rd ed.). Honolulu, HI: System Logistics.

3. Morris, E. 1987. Vision and strategy: A focus for the future. *Journal of Business Strategy* 8: 51–58.

4. This section is based on Lundberg & Enz, op. cit., and Ronstadt, op. cit.

5. The importance of problem definition was emphasized in Mintzberg, H., Raisinghani, D., & Theoret, A. 1976. The structure of "unstructured" decision processes. *Administrative Science Quarterly,* 21(2): 246–275.

6. Drucker, P. F. 1994. The theory of the business. *Harvard Business Review,* 72(5): 95–104.

7. This section draws on Edge & Coleman, op. cit.

8. Irving Janis is credited with coining the term *groupthink,* and he applied it primarily to fiascos in government (such as the Bay of Pigs incident in 1961). Refer to Janis, I. L. 1982. *Victims of groupthink* (2nd ed.). Boston: Houghton Mifflin.

9. Much of our discussion is based upon Finkelstein, S., & Mooney, A. C. 2003. Not the usual suspects: How to use board process to make boards better. *Academy of Management Executive,* 17(2): 101–113; Schweiger, D. M., Sandberg, W. R., & Rechner, P. L. 1989. Experiential effects of dialectical inquiry, devil's advocacy, and consensus approaches to strategic decision making. *Academy of Management Journal,* 32(4): 745–772; and Aldag, R. J., & Stearns, T. M. 1987. *Management.* Cincinnati: South-Western Publishing.

10. Finkelstein and Mooney, op. cit.

## APPENDIX TO CHAPTER 14: *Sources of Company and Industry Information**

In order for business executives to make the best decisions when developing corporate strategy, it is critical for them to be knowledgeable about their competitors and about the industries in which they compete. The process used by corporations to learn as much as possible about competitors is often called "competitive intelligence." This appendix provides an overview of important and widely available sources of information that may be useful in conducting basic competitive

*This information was compiled by Ruthie Brock and Carol Byrne, Business Librarians at the University of Texas at Arlington. We greatly appreciate their valuable contribution.

intelligence. Much information of this nature is available in libraries in article databases, business reference books, and on Web sites. This list will recommend a variety of them. Ask a librarian for assistance because library collections and resources vary.

The information sources are organized into 10 categories: Competitive Intelligence; Public or Private, Subsidiary or Division, U.S. or Foreign?; Annual Report Collections—Public Companies; Guides and Tutorials; SEC Filings/EDGAR—Company Disclosure Reports; Company Rankings; Business Metasites and Portals; Strategic and Competitive Analysis—Information Sources; Sources for Industry Research and Analysis; and Search Engines.

# Competitive Intelligence

Students and other researchers who want to learn more about the value and process of competitive intelligence should see five recent books on this subject.

> David L. Blenkhorn and Craig S. Fleisher, eds. *Competitive Intelligence and Global Business*. Westport, CT: Praeger Publishers, 2005.

> Helen N. Rothberg and G. Scott Erickson. *From Knowledge to Intelligence: Creating Competitive Advantage in the Next Economy*. Burlington, MA: Elsevier Butterworth-Heinemann, 2005.

> Murugan Anandarajan, Asokan Anandarajan, and Cadambi A. Srinivasan, eds. *Business Intelligence Techniques: A Perspective from Accounting and Finance*. New York: Springer-Verlag, 2004.

> Benjamin Gilad. *Early Warning: Using Competitive Intelligence to Anticipate Market Shifts, Control Risk, and Create Powerful Strategies*. New York: American Management Association, 2004.

> Conor Vibert, ed. *An Introduction to Online Competitive Intelligence Research: Search Strategies, Research Case Study, Research Problems, and Data Source Evaluations and Reviews*. Mason, OH: Thomson Texere, 2004.

# Public or Private, Subsidiary or Division, U.S. or Foreign?

Companies traded on stock exchanges in the United States are required to file a variety of reports that disclose information about the company. This begins the process that produces a wealth of data on public companies and at the same time distinguishes them from private companies, which often lack available data. Similarly, financial data of subsidiaries and divisions are typically filed in a consolidated financial statement by the parent company, rather than treated independently, thus limiting the kind of data available on them. On the other hand, foreign companies that trade on U.S. stock exchanges are required to file 20F reports, similar to the 10-K for U.S. companies, the most comprehensive of the required reports, although the number of foreign companies doing so is relatively small.

> *Corporate Directory of U.S. Public Companies*. San Mateo, CA: Walker's Research, LLC, 2005.
> The *Corporate Directory* provides company profiles of more than 9,000 publicly traded companies in the United States, including foreign companies trading on the U.S. exchanges (American depository receipts, or ADRs).

> *Corporate Affiliations*. New Providence, NJ: A LexisNexis Group, 2005.
> This directory features brief profiles of major U.S. and foreign corporations, both public and private, as well as their subsidiaries, divisions, and affiliates. The directory also indicates hierarchy of corporate relationships. An online version of the directory allows retrieval of a list of companies that meet specific criteria. Results can be downloaded to a spreadsheet. The online version requires a subscription.

*Ward's Business Directory of U.S. Private and Public Companies.* Detroit, MI: Thomson Gale, 2005. 8 vols.

*Ward's Business Directory* lists brief profiles on more than 110,000 public and private companies and indicates whether they are public or private, a subsidiary or division. Two volumes of the set are arranged using the Standard Industrial Classifications (SIC) and the North American Industry Classification System (NAICS) and feature company rankings within industries.

## Annual Report Collections—Public Companies

A growing number of companies have their Annual Report to Shareholders and other financial reports available on their corporate Web site. A few "aggregators" have cumulated links to many of these Web sites for both U.S. and international corporations.

*AnnualReports.com.* IR Solutions. Weston, FL.
This Web site contains annual reports in HTML or PDF format. Reports can be retrieved by company name, ticker symbol, exchange, industry, or sector.
www.annualreports.com

*Company Annual Reports Online (CAROL).* Carol Ltd. London, UK.
This Web site is based in the United Kingdom; therefore, many reports are European. Links are also provided for companies in Asia and the United States. A pull-down menu allows selection of companies within an industry. Access is free, but registration is required.
www.carol.co.uk/

*Public Register's Online Annual Report Service.* Baytact Corp. Woodstock Valley, CT.
Visitors to this Web site may choose from more than 4,500 company annual reports and 10-K filings to view online or order a paper copy. Access is free, but registration is required.
www.annualreportservice.com/

*Mergent Online.* Mergent, Inc. New York, NY.
*Mergent Online* provides company financial data for public companies headquartered in the United States as well as those headquartered in other countries, including a large collection of corporate annual reports in PDF format. For industry analysis, *Mergent Online* offers an advanced search option. Library subscriptions to *Mergent Online* may vary.

## Guides and Tutorials

*Guide to Corporate Filings and Forms.* U.S. Securities and Exchange Commission. Washington, DC.
This part of the Securities Exchange Commission (SEC) Web site explains and defines a 10-K and other SEC required reports that corporations must file.
www.sec.gov/edaux/forms.htm

*Guide to Financials.* IBM. Armonk, NY.
This guide gives basic information on how to read the financial statements in a company's annual report.
www.ibm.com/investor/financialguide/

*Researching Companies Online.* Debbie Flanagan. Fort Lauderdale, FL.
This Web site provides a step-by-step process for finding free company and industry information on the Web.
www.learnwebskills.com/company/

## SEC Filings/EDGAR—Company Disclosure Reports

SEC Filings are the various reports that publicly traded companies must file with the Securities Exchange Commission to disclose information about themselves. These are often referred to as "EDGAR" filings, an acronym for the Electronic Data Gathering Analysis and Retrieval System.

Some Web sites and commercial databases improve access to these reports by offering additional retrieval features not available on the official (www.sec.gov) Web site.

*EDGAR Database.* U.S. Securities and Exchange Commission. Washington, DC.
The 10-K reports, and other corporate documents, are made available in the EDGAR database within 24 hours after being filed. Annual reports, on the other hand, are typically sent directly to shareholders and are not required by the SEC as part of EDGAR, although some companies voluntarily include them. Both 10-Ks and shareholders' annual reports are considered basic sources of company research.
http://www.sec.gov/edgar/searchedgar/webusers.htm

*EdgarScan—An Interface to the SEC EDGAR Database.* PricewaterhouseCoopers. New York, NY.
Using filings from the SEC's servers, EdgarScan's intelligent interface parses the data automatically to a common format that is comparable across companies. A small Java applet called the "Benchmarking Assistant" performs graphical financial benchmarking interactively. Extracted financial data from the 10-K includes ratios with links to indicate where the data were derived and how it was computed. Tables showing company comparisons can be downloaded as Excel charts.
http://edgarscan.pwcglobal.com/servlets/edgarscan

*LexisNexis Academic—SEC Filings & Reports.* LexisNexis. Bethesda, MD.
EDGAR filings and reports are available through the "Business" option of LexisNexis Academic. These reports and filings can be retrieved by company name, industry code (SIC) or ticker symbol for a particular time period or by a specific report. Proxy, prospectus, and registration filings are also available.

*Mergent Online—EDGAR.* Mergent, Inc. New York, NY.
From the "EDGAR Search" tab within Mergent Online, EDGAR SEC filings and reports can be searched by company name or ticker symbol, filing date range, and file type (10-K, 8-K, ARS). The reports are available in HTML or MS Word format. Using the "Find in Page" option from the browser allows users to jump to specific sections of an SEC report.

# Company Rankings

*Fortune 500.* Time Inc. New York, NY.
The Fortune 500 list and other company rankings are published in the printed edition of *Fortune* magazine, but are available on *Fortune*'s Web site for subscribers only.
www.fortune.com/fortune/fortune500

*Hoover's Handbook of American Business.* Austin, TX: Hoovers, Inc., 2005
This two-volume set gives a company overview, a list of competitors, and basic financial information for large American companies. A special feature is a section called "The List Lovers' Companion," which includes a variety of lists with company rankings, some that include companies listed in *Hoover's Handbooks* and others reprinted from *Fortune, Forbes,* and other publications. In addition to the American edition, *Hoover's Handbooks* are available for private companies, emerging companies, and companies headquartered outside of the United States.

*Ward's Business Directory of U.S. Private and Public Companies.* Detroit, MI: Thomson Gale, 2004. 8 vols.
*Ward's Business Directory* is one of the few directories to rank both public and private companies together by sales within an industry, using both the Standard Industrial Classification system (in Volume 5 only) and the North American Industry Classification System (in Volume 8 only). With this information, it is easy to spot who the big "players" are in a particular product or industry category. Market share within an industry group can be calculated by determining what percentage a company's sales figure is of the total given by Ward's for that industry group.

# Business Metasites and Portals

*@Brint.com, The Biz Tech Network.* Brint Institute. Syracuse, NY.
Brint's business metasite has a concentration of Web links related to e-business, knowledge management, and technology.
www.brint.com/

*CI CorporateInformation.* Winthrop Corporation. Milford, CT.
CorporateInformation's Web site includes information on both U.S. and global public and private companies. It also provides access to company profiles and research reports alphabetically, geographically by specific countries or U.S. states, and by industry sector. Each interactive research report analyzes sales, dividends, earnings, profit ratios, research and development, and inventory and allows up to three companies to be compared to the company selected. Full access requires a paid subscription. Limited access is allowed free with registration.
www.corporateinformation.com/

*Hoover's Online.* Hoover's Inc., Dun & Bradstreet Corporation. Short Hills, NJ.
*Hoover's Online* includes brief company fact sheets, links to corporate Web sites, current company news, and "CEOs on Camera" video clips. The site also provides data on Initial Public Offerings (IPOs) via "IPO Central." Additional information is available to member subscribers only (indicated by the "lock" symbol).
www.hoovers.com/free/

# Strategic and Competitive Analysis— Information Sources

Analyzing a company can take the form of examining its internal and external environment. In the process, it is useful to identify the company's strengths, weaknesses, opportunities, and threats (SWOT). Sources for this kind of analysis are varied, but perhaps the best would be articles from *The Wall Street Journal,* business magazines, and industry trade publications. Publications such as these can be found in the following databases available at many public and academic libraries. When using a database that is structured to allow it, try searching the company name combined with one or more key words, such as "IBM and competition" or "Microsoft and lawsuits" or "AMR and fuel costs" to retrieve articles relating to the external environment.

*ABI/Inform.* Ann Arbor, MI: ProQuest Information & Learning.
*ABI/Inform* provides abstracts and full text articles covering management, law, taxation, human resources, and company and industry information from more than 1,000 business and management journals. *ABI/Inform* includes market condition reports, corporate strategies, case studies, and executive profiles.

*Business & Company Resource Center.* Detroit, MI. Thomson Gale.
*Business & Company Resource Center* provides company and industry intelligence for a selection of public and private companies. Company profiles include parent-subsidiary relationships, industry rankings, products and brands, current investment ratings, and financial ratios. Use the geographic search to locate company contact information. A selection of full-text investment reports from Investext Plus are also available.

*Business Source Premier.* Ispswich, MA. EBSCO Publishing.
*Business Source Premier* is a full text database with over 3,800 scholarly business journals covering management, economics, finance, accounting, international business, and more. The database also includes detailed company profiles for the world's 5,000 largest companies as well as selected country economic reports provided by the Economist Intelligence Unit (EIU). *Business Source Premier* contains over 1,100 peer-reviewed business journals.

*Investext Plus.* Detroit, MI: Thomson Gale.
*Investext Plus* offers full-text analytical reports on more than 11,000 public and private companies and 53 industries. Developed by a global roster of brokerage, investment

banking, and research firms, it is notable that these full-text investment reports include hard-to-find private company data and historical reports useful for evaluating companies over time.

*International Directory of Company Histories.* Detroit, MI: St. James Press, 1988 to present. 68 volumes to date.

This directory covers more than 4,500 multinational companies and the series is still adding volumes. Each company history is approximately three to four pages in length and provides a summary of the company's mission, goals, and ideals, followed by company milestones, principal subsidiaries, and competitors. Strategic decisions made during the company's period of existence are usually noted. This series covers public and private companies and nonprofit entities. Entry information includes a company's legal name, headquarters information, URL, incorporation date, ticker symbol, stock exchange, sales figures, and the primary North American Industry Classification System (NAICS) code. Further reading selections complete the entry information.

*LexisNexis Academic.* Bethesda, MD: LexisNexis.

The "Business" category in *LexisNexis Academic* provides access to a wide range of business information. Timely business articles can be retrieved from newspapers, magazines, journals, wires, and broadcast transcripts. Other information available in this section includes detailed company financials, company comparisons, and industry and market information for over 25 industries.

*LexisNexis Statistical.* Bethesda, MD: LexisNexis.

*LexisNexis Statistical* provides access to a variety of statistical publications indexed in the American Statistics Index (ASI), Statistical Reference Index (SRI), and the Index to International Statistics (IIS). Use the PowerTables search to locate historical trends, future projections, industry or demographic information. *LexisNexis Statistical* provides links to originating government Web sites when available.

*Notable Corporate Chronologies.* Julie A. Mitchell, ed. Detroit, MI: Thomson Gale. 2001.

This two-volume set provides dates of significant changes for over 1,800 corporations that operate in the United States and abroad. Each company entry includes a timeline and a further reading selection. The timeline explains the major events that affected the company's history. Dates of mergers and acquisitions, product introductions, financial milestones, and major stock offerings are also included in the chronologies. The Chronology Highlights in volume 2 provide a historical snapshot of major events for the companies listed.

*CorpTech Database.* Concord, MA: Corporate Technology Information Services, Inc.

The CorpTech CD-ROM database covers over 50,000 technology-related companies, both public and private, headquartered in the United States or affiliated with a foreign parent company. Narrative descriptions of each company, along with sales, number of employees, and other details are provided by the database. CorpTech can be searched by industry, product, geographic location, sales category, employee size, and so forth to create lists of companies that meet certain criteria. Percentage of employment growth compared to prior year is stated. Web site addresses, 800 numbers, or fax numbers are frequently provided. CorpTech is one of the best sources for information on technology-related private companies.

*The Wall Street Journal.* New York: Dow Jones and Reuters Business Interactive.

This respected business newspaper is available in searchable full-text from 1984 to present in the *Factiva* database. The "News Pages" link provides access to current articles and issues of *The Wall Street Journal.* Dow Jones, publisher of the print version of *The Wall Street Journal,* also has an online subscription available at wsj.com.

# Sources for Industry Research and Analysis

*Factiva.* New York: Dow Jones Reuters Business Interactive.

The *Factiva* database has several options for researching an industry. One would be to search the database for articles in the business magazines and industry trade publications.

A second option in *Factiva* would be to search in the Companies/Markets category for company/industry comparison reports.

*Mergent Online.* New York: Mergent Inc.
Mergent's enhanced Basic Search option features searching by primary industry codes (either SIC or NAICS). Once the search is executed, a list of companies in that industry should be shown. A comparison or standard peer group analysis can be created to analyze companies in the same industry on various criteria. The improved Advanced Search allows the user to search a wider range of financial and textual information. Results, including ratios for a company and its competitors, can be downloaded to a spreadsheet.

*Industry Norms and Key Business Ratios.* New York: Dun & Bradstreet, 2004.
*Industry Norms and Key Business Ratios* provides key financial measures and business ratios, based on efficiency, profitability, and solvency, that are used as a benchmark to compare the performance of a company against the industry's average. Industries are presented by the four-digit Standard Industrial Classification (SIC) code and cover agriculture, mining, construction, transportation, communication, utilities, manufacturing, wholesaling, retailing, financial, real estate, and services.

*Standard & Poor's Industry Surveys.* New York: Standard & Poor's, 2005. 3 vols.
*Standard & Poor's Industry Surveys* provide an overview of 52 U.S. industries. Each industry report includes a table of contents, narrative description, history, trends, financial and company information, glossary of terms, and a section on how to perform an analysis of the company. Industry References (associations, periodicals, and Web sites), Composite Industry Data (industry norms and ratios), and Comparative Company Analysis (comparison of 50 major companies, their operating ratios, P/E, revenue, and so forth) complete the industry report section. All charts and graphs cite the information source. NetAdvantage is Standard and Poor's online product that offers online access to industry surveys, stock reports, corporation records, and several other S&P products.

# Search Engines

*Google.* Mountain View, CA: Google, Inc.
Recognized for its advanced technology, quality of results, and simplicity, the Google search engine is highly recommended by librarians and other expert Web "surfers."
www.google.com

*Vivisimo*. Pittsburgh, PA: Vivisimo, Inc.
This search engine not only finds relevant results, but organizes them in logical subcategories.
www.vivisimo.com

*Yahoo Finance.* Sunnyvale, CA: Yahoo! Inc.
This metasite links to information on U.S. markets, world markets, data sources, finance references, investment editorials, financial news, and other helpful Web sites.
http://finance.yahoo.com

# Company Index

## a

A. T. Kearney, 44, 169
ABC, 343
Aberdeen Group, 295
Accenture, 148, 447
Access Health, 148
Ace Hardware, 177
Acer, 417
Activision, 378
Adam's Mark Hotels, 169
Adelphia Communications, 230, 334, 419
Adidas, 22
ADP Corporation, 321
AEP, 447
Aerie Networks, 459
AES, 423
Agillion, Inc., 17
AK Steel Corporation, 63
Alberto-Culver, 184
AllDorm.com, 501
Alliance Semiconductor, 334
Allied Signal, 85
AltiTunes Partners, 497
Amazon.com, 97, 285, 289, 292, 295, 302, 499
AMCI Inc., 76
American Airlines, 10
American Association of Retired Persons, 51
American Builders & Contractors Supply, 221
American Business Information, 61
American Express, 288
American Insurance Group, 420
American Life Project, 294
American Productivity and Quality Center, 150
American Trust, 88
America Online, 296, 332
Ameritech, 199
Ames, 938
Amgen, 12
    altitude management, 12
    collaborations, 380
Amoco, 199–200
Analog Devices, 259
Andersen Consulting, 142, 148
Andersen Windows, 177–178
Andersen Worldwide, 229
Andrew Corporation, 415
Anheuser-Busch Companies, 51
AOL Time Warner, 25, 232, 336
Apple Computer, 187, 190, 278, 399
    bluetooth strategy, 304
    Newton PDA, 458–459
Apple iTunes, 277, 289
Aravind Eye Care, 241
Arco, 199–200
Ariat International, 475
ArrayComm, LLC, 488
ARRIS, 380
Arthur Andersen, 19, 54, 332, 341
Arthur D. Little, 90
Asea Brown Boveri, 26, 261
Aston Martin, 70, 76
AT&T, 86, 87, 217, 218, 459
AT&T Wireless Communications, 220
Autobytel.com, 293, 463
AutoNation, Inc., 34
Avogadro, 142

## b

B. Dalton, 97
Bain & Company, 439, 475
Barnes & Noble, 51, 289
Basset-Walker, 205
BEA Systems, 220
Beecham Group, 221
BellSouth, 220
Beneficial Finance, 220
Berkshire Hathaway, 6, 80, 204, 336
Bertelsmann AG, 276, 447
Bessemer Trust, 175
BestBookBuys.com, 289
Best Buy, 53, 283, 461
Best Practices, LLC, 461
Betacam, 459
BevMark LLC, 6
Big Bowl, 361
BigChampagne LLC, 277
Binney & Smith, 418
Biogen, 227, 380
Biomax, 440
BizRate.com, 289, 292
Bjurman, Barry & Associates, 497
Blockbuster Entertainment, 295
Bluetooth, 303–304
BMG music label, 206, 276
BMW, 56, 68, 169, 170, 238, 299
Body Shop, 446
Boeing Company, 211, 245, 328, 331, 373, 374, 420, 490, 523
Books-a-Million, 285
Booz Allen Hamilton, 335–336
Borders, Inc., 292
Bosch power drills, 250
Boston Consulting Group, 166, 214–215, 270
BP Amoco, 34, 44, 55, 152
Brinker International, 32, 360, 367
    structural change, 361
British Airways, 136, 448
British American Tobacco, 145
British Petroleum, 199–200, 250, 298, 460, 480
    Internet initiatives, 298
    technological innovation, 480
British Sky Broadcasting, 344
Brookstone, 162
BTR, 212
Buckman Laboratories, 145
Bugatti, 238
Buick, 358
Burdines, 82
Burpee Company, 293
Buy.com, 302

## c

Cablevision, 283
Cabot Corporation, 216
Cadbury Schweppes, 327, 523
Cadillac, 238, 358
California Public Employees Retirement System, 337–338
Callaway Golf Clubs, 250
Camelot Communications, 295
Campbell's Soup, 87
    electronic network, 80–81
Cannondale, 170, 212
Canon, 31, 136
    operational effectiveness, 81
CarbWatchers, 488

Cardinal Health, 88, 89, 92
Cargill, 95
Caribbean Shipping & Cold Storage, 491
Carling O'Keefe Breweries, 222
Carnival Corporation, 334
Carrefour Group, 219
Carrier Air Conditioning, 46
CarsDirect, 293
Casas Bahias, 241
Cash-U, 367
Casio, 202–203
Caterpillar, Inc., 31, 170, 184, 362
Cayenne, 70
CBS, 375
Celanese Chemical Corporation, 252
Center for Veterinary Medicine, 227
Cerner Corporation, 145
Cessna Citation, 328
Challenger Electrical Distribution, 375
Champion International, 213
Chaparral Steel, 412, 413
Charles Schwab & Company, 16, 189, 190, 220
    acquisition of U. S. Trust, 198–199
Chase Manhattan Bank, 199
CheckSpace, 142
Chemical Bank, 426
Chevrolet, 358
Chevrolet Corvette, 70
Chevron, 31, 129
Chili's Bar & Grill, 32, 361
Chiquita Bananas, 248
Chiron, 380
Chrysler Corporation, 21, 69, 188, 205
Ciba-Geigy, 202, 243
    portfolio planning, 215–216
Ciba Specialty Chemicals, 87
Cinergy, 132
Cingular Wireless, 219–220
Circuit City, 89
Cirque du Soleil, 445
Cisco Systems, 219, 304, 319, 414, 443, 449
    and technology bubble, 320
Citibank, 25, 133
Citicorp, 258
Citigroup, 20, 133
Citipost, 497
Claria, 288
Claritin, 165
Clayton, Dubilier & Rice, 212
ClearForest, 367
ClickZ.com, 301
CLP, 346
CNBC, 49, 342
CNET, 289, 292
Coca-Cola Company, 15, 136, 184, 246, 249–251, 255, 459
    need for strategy change, 6–8
Coke, 344
Comcast, 283
Commerce One, 54
Compaq Computer, 187, 190
CompUSA, 474
Computer Associates, 144, 288
ConAgra, 63, 95, 361
Cone Communication, 22
Conseco, 220

Consumers Union, 162, 284
Container Store, 400
    as workplace, 401
Context Integration, 149
Continental Airlines, 96
    director selection, 337
Cooley Godward, 143
Cooper Industries, 201, 202, 213
Cooper Software, Inc., 129, 130, 330
Corel, 43
Corporate Interns, Inc., 500
Corporate Library, 334
Corptech, 415
Costco Companies, 219
Country Crisp Catfish Strips, 63
Cox Communications, 283
CP Group, 362
Crate & Barrel, 296
Crescent Real Estate Equities, 334
Crossgain, 142
CSX, 491
CurrentOfferings.com, 302
Custom Research Inc., 171
CVS Pharmacies, 89, 174
Cybercorp Inc., 220
Cypress Semiconductor, 30
Cyveillance, 490

d

Daewoo Motor Company, 266–267
Daimler-Benz, 205
DaimlerChrysler, 56, 199, 250
Datamonitor, 82
deCODE Genetics, 280
Deere & Company, 279
Deja News, 46
Dell Computer Corporation, 107–108, 148, 176, 187,
    243, 246, 278, 288, 292, 296, 300, 376
    customer relations, 374
    direct sales approach, 93–94
    knowledge management, 149
    new production capability, 457–458
    OptiPlex system, 457–458
Deloitte Consulting, 455
Deloitte Touche Tohmatsu, 455
Delta Air Lines, 285
Delta Pride Catfish, 63
Denny's Restaurants, 419
Destiny yachts, 171, 173
Deutsche Bank, 20, 176
Deutsche Telekom, 447
Dickinson theater chain, 417
digiMine, 142
Digital Dimensions, Inc., 492
Digital Directory Assistance, 61
Digital Equipment Corporation, 47, 143, 190
    failure to cope, 191
Ding Dongs, 15
Disneyland, 30
Dodge Neon, 69
Dow Chemical, 367
    talent retention, 138
DreamWorks SKG, 415
Drezler Technology, 9
Driven Image, 176
DuPont Corporation, 24
    environmentalism, 440
    productivity improvement, 24
Duracell, 174, 205
Durkee Famous Foods, 212

e

Earthlink, 296
Eastman Kodak, 146, 246
    and Polaroid, 434–435

EasyJet, 190
eBay, 126, 143, 292, 293, 295, 304, 445, 455
EcoSolution Q, 80
eDonkey, 277
8X8 Company, 283
Electronic Arts, 334, 378
Electronic Data Services, 478
Eli Lilly & Company, 64–65, 205, 211, 226, 308,
    326, 443
    Internet initiatives, 305
    investment in Hybritech, 226
Elixir Springs, 418
E-Loan, 487, 503
eMachineShop.com, 300
E-Mart, 268
EMC, 175, 176, 220
Emerson Electric, 212, 323, 325, 338
    diversification benefits, 217
EMI, 276
Encyclopaedia Britannica, 43, 47, 78
Energizer, 15
Enron Corporation, 19, 20, 54, 229, 230, 334, 341,
    342, 343, 400–402, 418, 419
Enterprise Rent-a-Car, 139
    diversity program, 140
Envirogen, 380
ePinions, 292, 295
eProject.com, 296
Ericsson, 256–257, 266, 384
Ernst & Young, 143
Estée Lauder, 446
E*Trade Financial Corporation, 286, 288
    turnaround, 189
Excel, 93
Exelon, 217
Exel plc, 895
Extremetix, Inc., 286
Exxon, 199
ExxonMobil, 447
    strategy map, 104–105

f

Farm Fresh, 63
Federal Express, 32, 33, 67, 68, 92, 150, 171, 173,
    323, 330, 497
Ferrari, 69, 171, 173
Fidelity Investments, 54, 337, 371
Financial Executives International, 54
Financial News Network, 342
Firestone, 52, 419
Fixx Services, Inc., 495
Fleet Mortgage, 82
Food Lion, 78
Food Network, 663–664
Ford Focus, 70
Ford Motor Company, 15, 25, 52, 70, 126, 136,
    205, 209, 246, 247, 255, 258, 266, 380, 416,
    419, 500
    cultural overhaul, 29
    problems with Jaguar, 76
    transnational strategy, 261
Forest Laboratories, 339
Fortune Brands, 34
Foster-Miller, 480
Fram oil filters, 85
Freemantle Media, 205, 206
FreeMarkets Online, 62
Frost & Sullivan, 283
FTD, 478
Fuld & Company, 45–46

g

Gannett Corporation, 322, 387
Gap, Inc., 22
Garden.com, 293

Gateway Computer, 280, 376, 416
Gatorade, 7, 8
Genentech, 126
General Dynamics, 9, 187
General Electric, 7, 87, 132, 134, 206, 217, 229,
    244, 278, 326, 344, 371, 372, 398, 418, 441
    leadership evaluation, 135
    wind energy, 373
General Electric Aerospace, 187
General Electric Healthcare, 132–133
General Electric Lighting, 371
General Electric Medical Systems, 28, 130
General Electric Power Systems, 373
General Electric Wind Energy, 13, 373
General Mills, 165, 167, 264, 325, 375
General Motors, 25, 56, 176, 209, 229, 246, 339, 358
    partnerships, 266–267
    SmartAuction, 293
Genzyme, 256
George Washington University Aviation
    Institute, 88
Gerber Products Company, 96
Gibbs Aqada, 83
Gibbs Technologies, 83
Gibson guitars, 173
GigaMedia, 266
Gillette Company, 7, 136, 174, 203, 205, 217, 219
    technologies, 93
GlaxoSmithKline PLC, 133, 199, 384
Glaxo Wellcome, 219
Glidden, 212
Glide, 418
Global Brand Management and Advertising, 204
Global Crossing, 229, 342
Glycomex, 380
Goldman Sachs, 88
Goodyear Aerospace, 187
Google, 46, 126, 291, 440, 537
Grameen Bank, 241
Graybar Electric Company, 463
Great Plains Airlines, Inc., 483
    bankruptcy, 470–471
Green Mountain Coffee Roasters, 460
Green Tree Financial, 220
Greyhound, 33
Grokster, 277
Gryphon Technologies, 490
Gucci, 174
Guidant Corporation, 217
Gulfstream, 328
GVO, 402

h

H. H. Cutler, 205
Häagen-Dazs, 268
Hanover Insurance, 411
Hanson PLC, 212, 213–214, 370
Hanson Trust, 362
Harley-Davidson, Inc., 92, 170, 203, 255
Harley-Davidson Café, 92, 203
Harris Interactive, 22
HCI Direct, 82
Headhunter.com, 95
Healthsouth Corporation, 419
Henderson Land Development, 346
Hewlett-Packard, 7, 137, 143, 144, 146, 204, 222,
    243, 246, 267, 323, 374, 376, 447, 448
Hill & Knowlton, 22
Hoffman LaRoche, 243
Home Depot, Inc., 162, 217, 221, 324, 327–329,
    330, 398
    appeal to women, 53
    financial performance, 100
    older employees, 51
Home Pride Carb Action, 42

Honda Goldwing, 170
Honda Motors, 70, 80, 136, 258, 295, 377
Honeywell Corporation, 85, 206
Honeywell ElectroOptics, 187
Hong Kong Securities & Futures Commission, 346
Hotjobs.com, 95
Household International, 220
Hugger Mugger Yoga Products, 495
Hybritech, 226
HyperRoll, 367
Hyundai, 68, 70, 87

IBM, 25, 48, 63, 98, 111, 142, 187, 243, 258, 267, 280, 344, 376, 379–380, 443, 478
  and public education, 23
ICI, 204
Icos Corporation, 64, 226
IDC, 204
Ignition and Greylock, 492
Ignition Corporation, 142
IKEA, 10
ImClone Systems, 19, 420
iNest.com, 295
Infosys, 245
ING Direct, 167, 168
InnoCentive, 205, 308, 443
In-Stat, 304
Intel Corporation, 7, 18, 26, 87, 187, 199, 250, 252, 307, 336, 442
  and bribery problem, 259
  mentoring at, 415
Inter-American Holdings, Inc., 58
IntercomPlus, 87
Interface, Inc., 460
Interland, 281
International Assets Network, 149–150
International Civil Aviation Organization, 415
International Franchise Association, 477
Interstate Bakeries Corporation, 15, 42, 321
Intuit, 136–137, 188, 279, 441
Ionic Breeze Quadra, 162
Iowa Beef Processors, 95
ITT, 257, 362
I-Zone Pocket Camera, 434
Izzo Consulting, 143

J. D. Power & Associates, 171, 224
J. P. Morgan, 20, 199
J. P. Morgan Chase Bank, 426
Jaguar, 15, 70, 76
Jantzen, 205
JCPenney Company, 68, 181
JetBlue Airways Corporation, 85–86
Jobsearch.com, 95
John Hancock Financial Services, Inc., 462–463
Johnson & Johnson, 44, 154, 217, 474, 500
  company credo, 424–425
Johnson Asset Management, 42
Johnson Controls, 453
Juniper Networks, 304
Juno Online Services, 82
Jupitermedia Corporation, 301
Jupiter Media Metrix, 276, 302
Jupiter Research, 302
Justin Boots, 475

Kazaa, 277, 283, 288, 311
KeepSafe, 82
Kellogg Company, 7, 257
Kellogg's Corn Flakes, 318
Kentucky Fried Chicken, 207
Kia, 70
Kidder Peabody, 229

Kinkos, 68
Kiwi Shoe Polish, 250
Kmart, 43, 68, 180, 184, 330
Kmart Holdings Corporation, 217
K'Netix, 145
Kohlberg, Kravis, Roberts & Company, 212
Komatsu, 31
Koos Group, 266
KPMG, 54, 341
Kraft Foods, Inc., 295
Krispy Kreme Doughnuts, 18
  recent problems, 396
Kroger Company, 177
Kyocera Corporation, 498–499

L. A. Gear, 174
Laird Technologies, 480
Lamborghini, 69, 238
Land Rover, 70, 76
Lands' End, 82
Lantech, 17
  incentive plan, 318
LaserCard, 9
Laura Ashley, 398
Lee Jeans, 205
Legend Group, 324
  incentive program, 325
Lego, 48
Lehman Brothers, 185
LendingTree.com, 294, 296
Leonhardt Plating Company, 413
Levi Strauss, 22, 48, 416
Lexmark, 204
Lexus, 76, 170, 171, 172, 173, 238, 323
Liberty Mutual Group, 306
Life Savers, 295
Linens 'n' Things, 495
Li-Ning Company, 250
Litton Industries, 211
Lloyds TSB Bank Plc, 384
LML, 488
Lockheed Martin, 9, 12, 187, 211, 326, 379, 490
Logitech Inc., 365
Loral Corporation, 211
L'Oréal, 446
Lotus Corporation, 98, 149, 267
Louis Vuitton, 250
Lowe's, 53, 398
Lucent Technologies, 443, 448

MACH 3, 93
Macy's, 181, 296
Mail Boxes Etc., 496
Mandalay Entertainment, 30
Manulife Financial Corporation, 463
Marantz, 169
Marriott Corporation, 164, 224
Marshall Industries, 400
Marsh & McLennan, 420
Martha Stewart Living Omnimedia, 420
Martin guitars, 169
Martin Marietta, 12
Massachusetts Bay Transit Authority, 404
Matsushita, 184
Mattel, Inc., 7, 252
Mazda, 380, 416, 552
McAfee, 220
McCaffrey's Markets, 42
McCaw Cellular, 218
McDonald's Corporation, 30, 207, 210, 246, 257, 327, 336, 348, 496
McDonnell-Douglas Corporation, 211, 331
MCI Communications, 199

McKesson, 202
McKinsey & Company, 24, 47, 143, 244, 270, 332
Medtronic, Inc., 30, 135, 169
Meliorra, 488
Menlo Worldwide Freight Forwarding, 33
Mercedes-Benz, 68, 69, 70, 76, 172, 173, 205, 238
Mercer Management Consulting, 200
Merck & Company, 26, 125, 134
  options analysis, 227
Merrill Lynch, 129, 190, 331
M5 networks, 283
MGM, 378
Microsoft Corporation, 83, 125, 130, 146, 171, 199, 224, 244, 245–246, 247, 250, 252, 265, 278, 330, 379–380, 417, 439, 462
  defections from, 142
  innovation challenges, 440
  partnerships in East Asia, 266
Microsoft Encarta, 47, 78
Microsoft Windows, 187
Microsoft Word, 43, 130
MicroUnity, Inc., 480–481
Misiu Systems, 253
  outsourcing, 254
Mobil, 199
Moen, 285
Molson Companies, Ltd., 222
Monsanto, 81, 82, 214
Monster.com, 95
Morgan Keegan Investment, 9
Morgan Stanley, 169, 224
Motel 6, 44, 47
Motorola, Inc., 131, 132, 417, 452, 456, 501
Mountain Dew Code Red, 295
MSA Aircraft Interior Products, Inc., 328–329
MusiKube, LLC, 497
My Docs Online Inc., 287
mySimon, 289

Nabisco Corporation, 480
Napster, 276–277, 278, 289
Nartron Corporation, 501
National Association of Home Builders, 51
National Association of Manufacturers, 51
National Association of Purchasing Managers, 54
National Basketball Association, 334, 408
National Football League, 7
National Health Service (UK), 17, 354
National Retail Federation, 501
Nationjob.vom, 95
Natural Step, 460
NEC, 22, 257
Neiman Marcus, 69
Nestlé Corporation, 207, 254–255
  transnational strategy, 261
NetActive, 447, 451
Netscape, 130
Network Appliance, 175, 176
Newell Rubbermaid, Inc., 323
  marketing innovations, 436
New England Patriots, 7
New York Times Company, 19
New York Yankees, 92
Nextel, 217, 220, 442
NextJet, 33
Nielsen Interactive Entertainment, 295
Nike, Inc., 22, 209, 247, 253, 257, 300, 376, 377, 496
  and child labor issue, 248
Nintendo Entertainment System, 65
Nissan Motors, 87, 238, 380
Nokia Corporation, 169, 222, 299, 384

Nordstrom, 68, 82, 170
Nortel Networks, 222, 331, 446–447, 451
    new ventures, 446–447
North Face, 169
Northrop Grumman, 490
Northstar Group, Inc., 339
Novartis, 87, 202
Novell, 43, 380
NTT DoCoMo, 266
Nucor Steel Company, 140, 323
    incentive compensation, 368–369
    knowledge sharing, 141
Nutmeg Industries, 205

Oakshire Mushroom Farm, Inc., 478–479
OEP Imaging Operating Corporation, 435
Offshore Heavy Transport, 57
Oldsmobile, 358
Onebox.com, 492
1-800 FLOWERS, 478
On the Border, 32
Open Text Livelink, 149
Openwave Systems, 492
Oracle Corporation, 111, 187, 220, 247, 332, 339
Otis Elevator, 46
Outback Steakhouse, 491
Outboard Marine Corporation, 31
Overstock Auctions, 455
Overstock.com, 302, 455
Oxford GlycoSciences, 256
Ozark Air, 470

Pacific Gas & Electric Company, 343
Palm Pilot, 184, 266
Parkdale Mills, 358
Parker Pen, 205
Parmalat, 20
PayPal, 292, 295
Pebbles Big Barney Chase game, 295
PeopleSoft Inc., 220
PepsiCo, 207, 246, 295, 344, 459
    diversification, 8
PestPatrol, 288
Pew Internet, 294
Pfizer, Inc., 64–65, 89, 134, 219, 250, 438
Phaeton, 238
Philadelphia 76ers, 408
Phillips Petroleum, 211
PHPK, 447
Pier 1 Imports, 44, 47
Pilgrim's Pride, 334
Pita Chip Company, 483
Pitney-Bowes, 286, 308
Pizza Hut, 207
PlanetFeedBack, 292
PlayStation, 378, 440, 451, 459
Polaroid, 18, 143
    and Eastman Kodak, 434–435
Pontiac, 176, 267, 358
Porsche, 69, 70, 171, 175, 554
    strategies, 176
Porta-Bote, 85
Post-it Notes, 324
Potash Corporation, 169
PowerBook, 304
PPG, 34
Priceline.com, 94, 229
Price 1 Auto Stores, 453
PriceSCAN, 289
PricewaterhouseCoopers, 54, 139, 371, 378
ProCD, 61, 78
Procter and Gamble, 22, 34, 143, 152, 185–186,
    201, 211, 219, 245, 260, 422, 500

research and development, 101–102
    synergies, 212
    use of ethics, 421
Prufrock Corporation, 111–119
Psion, 266
Public Service Enterprise Group, 217
Publix Super Markets, 19–20
Pure-Ion UV Air, 162
Puritan-Bennett Corporation, 375

Quaker Oats Company,
    7, 8, 183
Quickbook, 188

RadioFrame Networks, 442
Radio Shack, 162, 283
Random House, 497
Raytheon, 211
RealNetworks, 277, 289
Reebok International, 209, 376, 377, 475, 495
REI.com, 293
Remax, 295
Renault, 87
Resource Link, 86
Retail Forward, Inc., 53, 453, 501
Ringling Brothers and Barnum and Bailey, 445
Ritz-Carlton, 223, 224, 327, 491
Ritz-Carlton Leadership Center, 224
Roche, 523
Rolex, 250
Rolls-Royce/Bentley, 238
Rosa Verde Family Health Care Group, 223
Rose International, 492
Rosenbluth International, 129
Rosen Motors, 18
Roxio, 277
Royal Ahold, 331
Royal Air Force Mountain Rescue Service, 85
Royal Dutch/Shell, 456
Rubbermaid, 436
Running Press, 500
RyanAir, 190
Ryder, 179

Sabre, 147
Saflex Windows, 81, 82
Salomon Brothers Smith Barney, 200
SalvageSale, Inc., 302–303
Sam's Club, 268
Sandoz, 243
S&P Compustat, 218
Sanford C. Bernstein & Company, 8, 239
SAP, 111, 244, 304
Sapient Health Network, 511, 512
SAS Institute, 86, 144, 148
Saturn Corporation, 134
SBC Communications, 199, 217, 220, 283
Schering-Plough, 239
Scholastica, 488
Schwab.com, 295
SCM, 212, 214
ScriptLINE, 89
Sears, Roebuck & Company, 21, 43, 51, 68, 104,
    130, 170, 217, 425
Security Mortgage Group, 523
Sensor Excel, 93
Sephora.com, 82
7-Eleven, 300
Seven Networks, 492
SG Cowen Securities, 219
Sharp Corporation, 203, 358, 366–367
    functional structure, 358, 371–372
    related diversification, 369–370

Sharper Image, 16, 193
    and product disparagement, 162
Shaw Industries, 80, 202, 204, 208
    vertical integration, 208
Shell Oil Company, 22, 137
    scenario planning, 48
Siebel Systems, 150, 171, 173, 220, 258
    and technology bubble, 320
Siemens, 447
Siemens Venture Capital, 447
Sikorsky, 46
Silicon Graphics, Inc., 9
Silly Putty, 418
SkyTower Telecommunications, 494–495
Skyworks Technologies, 294, 295
SmartAuction, 293
Smell-O-Vision, 495
Smith-Corona, 212
SmithKline Beecham, 219, 221–222
    vertical boundaries, 371
Smyth Solutions, 283
Sodima, 264
Solar Ventures, 334
Solectron, 131
Sony Computer Entertainment America, 378, 451
Sony Corporation, 24, 223, 276, 277, 440, 449, 459
    outsourcing for talent, 378
    product champion, 451
Sony Entertainment, 378
Sony Pictures, 378
Southwest Airlines, 7, 10, 68, 87, 96, 126, 129,
    130, 136, 295, 298, 323, 324
    performance evaluation, 88
Sports Physical Therapists, 408
Springfield ReManufacturing Corporation, 412–413
Sprint Corporation, 99, 217, 220, 288
Spry Learning Company, 499
Spy Sweeper, 288
Standard & Poor's Corporation, 20
Standard & Poor's 500 Index, 218
Starbucks Corporation, 224, 398, 399, 477–478
    vision for, 399
Stella scooter, 488
STMicroelectronics, 222
Stop & Shop, 331
Strategos Consulting, 456
Subway Sandwiches, 496
Sumerset Houseboats, 279
Sunbeam Corporation, 229, 332, 525
Sun Microsystems, 304, 376
SunTrust Banks Inc., 343
SurModics, Inc., 474
Symantec Corporation, 220

T. Rowe Price, 337
Taco Bell, 207
Taggies, Inc., 488
Tandem Computers, 137
Target Corporation, 42, 180, 181, 184, 189, 292
    late-mover advantage, 185
Taylor Guitars, 418
TCS, 245
Technical Computer Graphics, 381
    boundaryless organization, 382
TechSpace, 486
Tele-Communications Inc., 415
Tellme Networks, 142
Templeton Asset Management, 346
Texaco, 419
Texas Air, 136
Texas Instruments, 87, 501
    and bribery problem, 259
    ethical organization, 422
TGI Friday's, 260

Thermagon, Inc., 480
Thinking Tool's Project Challenge,
     149–150
Third Millennium Communications, 142
Thomson Financial, 367
3M Corporation, 96, 202, 223, 323, 324, 369, 416,
     449, 474
TIAA-CREF, 337, 339–340
     stock-based compensation, 340
Tide, 185
Tiffany's, 296
Timbuk2, 474
Time Inc., 229
Times Mirror Company, 202
     merger, 207
Time Warner, Inc., 130, 222, 232, 331
TollTags, 478
Tony Lama, 475
Toro Company, 411
Tosco, 211
Toshiba, 203, 204
Touareg, 238
Toyota Motor Company, 70, 171, 190, 238, 247, 323
     bluetooth strategy, 304
     fast turnaround, 80
Toyota Production System, 81
Toys "R" Us, 292
Trendsight Group, 53
Treo Palm, 304
Tribune Company, 207
Tricon, Inc., 207
Trimble Navigation Ltd., 9
Tropicana, 8
True Value, 177
Turbotax, 188
Twinkies, 15
Tyco International, 19, 229, 332, 336,
     418, 419

U-Haul, 179, 501
Unilever Bestfoods, 250
Unilever Groups, 186, 250
Union Pacific, 126
Unisys, 490
United Airlines, 96
United Parcel Service, 33, 144, 203, 497
     logistics, 204
United Technologies, 46
Unocal, 211
USAA, 137

*USA Today,* 386–387
     ambidextrous organization, 387
     interactive control system, 322
Usenet, 46
U.S. Trust Corporation, 198–199, 220
UTStarcom, 498

Vaio computers, 459
Value Line, 8
Values Technology, 136
Valvoline Instant Oil Changes, 496
Vanity Fair, 205
Verint Systems, 9
Veritas Software Corporation, 220
Verizon Communications, 283, 683
Vespa, 488
VF Corporation, 205, 817
ViAir, 142
Video Home Source, 184
Viewpoint DataLabs International, 98
Virgin Atlantic, 449
     service quality, 83
Virgin Galactic, 450
Virgin Group, 28, 136, 449, 474
     new ventures, 450
Visteon Corporation, 343
Vivato, Inc., 281
Vivendi Universal, 230
Vivisimo, Inc., 537
Volkswagen, 16, 56, 249, 380
     problems in United States,
     238–239
Volvo, 70, 76, 238
Vonage, 283
Voodoo PC, 172

W. L. Gore & Associates, 418, 456, 457, 474
Walgreen's, 34, 87
Walkabout Travel Gear, 483
Walkman, 459
Wal-Mart Stores, 10, 42, 68, 184, 185, 219, 259,
     277, 296, 298, 324, 398, 446, 453
     competitive advantage, 180–181
     extended value chain, 179
     in South Korea, 268
Walnut Venture Associates, 486
Walt Disney Company, 205, 299, 336,
     362–363
Wang, 43
Warner Brothers, 30, 229

Warner Brothers Publications, 206
Warner-Lambert, 134, 219
Waste Management, 229
Waterman, 205
WD-40 Company, 499
WebMD, 512
Webnoize Research, 276
WeddingChannel.com, 296
Wegman's Food Markets, 81
WellPoint Health Networks, 32, 165, 168
Wells Fargo & Company, 30, 34
Wendy's, 496
Westinghouse Electric Company, 375
Wetherill Associates, 424
WhenU, 288
Whirlpool Corporation, 460
Whole Foods Market, Inc., 413–414
Wildfire, 361
Wildflower Group, 15, 124
Wilshire Associates, 338
WiMax, 488
Winnebago, 208–209
Wipro, 28, 245
Wisk Dual Action Tablets, 185
Wizard, 203
Wonder Bread, 15
WordPerfect, 43
WorldCom, 54, 199, 229, 334, 341,
     343, 419
WPP Group PLC, 145, 404, 449
Wrangler jeans, 205

XBox, 440
Xerox Corporation, 31, 136, 341, 443

Yahoo!, 126, 277, 288, 295, 487, 537
Yale Center for Eating and Weight
     Disorders, 42
Yellow Roadway Corporation, 343
Yesmail.com, 296
Yokogawa, 398
Yoplait, 264
Young & Rubicam, 149, 404
Yugo, 164–165

Zingers, 15
Zurich Financial Services, 258

# Name Index

## a

Aaker, David A., 193, 272
Abell, D. F., 38
Adams, Ed, 140
Adler, P. S., 156
Afuah, A., 297, 312, 391
Ahlstrom, D., 345, 346, 351
Aiman-Smith, L., 466
Albrinck, J., 467
Aldag, R. J., 531
Aldrich, H., 505
Alexander, M., 234
Allard, M. J., 156
Allen, Kent, 295
Allred, B., 382
Amabile, T. M., 156
Amburgey, T. L., 391
Amit, R., 110
Amram, M., 235
Anandarajan, Asokan, 532
Anandarajan, Murugen, 532
Anard, B. N., 234
Anderson, E., 110
Anderson, J. C., 109
Anderson, P., 154
Anderson, Ray, 460
Andrus, Mark, 483
Andrus, Stacy, 483
Angwin, J. S., 235
Anslinger, P. A., 234
Ansoff, H. I., 72
Argawal, A., 350
Argyris, Chris, 319, 349
Arikan, A. M., 38
Arison, Micky M., 334
Armas, G. C., 73
Armstrong, D., 193, 221
Arnadt, M., 88
Arndt, Michael, 54, 193, 218, 234, 351
Arnold, D., 272
Arnold, Jon, 283
Arnott, D. A., 349
Asher, Henry, 339
Ashkenas, R., 371
Asmus, P., 460
Aspelin, D. J., 156
Aston, A., 55, 73
Athitakis, M., 295
Atkins, Ted, 85
Atkinson, A. A., 38
Auger, P., 311
Augustine, Norman R., 12, 38, 194, 326, 373, 379, 391
Aumann, Yonatan, 367

## b

Baatz, E. B., 430
Bader, P., 157
Bahrami, H., 381
Baker, M., 460
Baker, S., 55, 73, 349
Bakke, Dennis, 423, 431
Balfour, F., 250, 346
Ball, D., 350
Ballmer, Steven, 417
Bamford, C. E., 73
Banerjee, S., 311
Bao Degong, 246
Barkema, G. G., 39

Barkema, H. P., 235
Barletta, Martha, 53
Barnes, Christopher, 375, 392
Barnes, L. A., 531
Barnevik, Percy, 39, 156, 450
Barney, J. B., 38, 91, 97, 110, 155, 193
Baron, R. A., 155
Barrett, Amy, 234, 497, 505
Barringer, B. R., 392
Barry, Thomas, 497
Bart, C. K., 39
Bartlett, Christopher A., 155, 194, 271, 272, 360, 391
Bartness, A., 392
Bass, Bill, 82
Baum, A. C., 39
Baum, C. F., 230
Baumgartner, P., 73, 193
Baumol, William J., 278, 311
Bayers, C., 312
Baysinger, B. D., 350
Beamish, Paul W., 77, 271
Bearden, W. O., 194
Becker, Gary S., 155
Beckhard, R., 38, 39, 371, 429
Begley, T. M., 37, 259
Belichick, Bill, 7
Belton, C., 271
Benasou, B. M., 110
Bennet, E., 505
Bennett, N., 350
Bennett, Stephen M., 188
Bennett, Steve, 441
Bennis, Warren, 38
Benson, G. S., 156
Benton, Philip, Jr., 266
Bergen, M. E., 193
Berggren, E., 109
Berkowitz, E. N., 194, 271, 272
Berle, Adolf, 333
Berman, P., 358
Bernardino, Joseph, 229
Bernasek, A., 73
Berner, Robert, 111
Bernstein, A., 28, 73, 344
Berry, Leonard, 401
Berry, M. A., 39
Besley, S., 235
Bezos, Jeff, 499
Bhagat, R. S., 271
Bhatia, Navin, 496
Bhatia, Sue Himanshu, 492, 505
Bhattacharya, C. B., 38
Bhide, A. V., 466
Bick, J., 466
Bierce, Ambrose, 333
Birch, David, 472, 473, 504
Birkinshaw, J., 38, 272, 393, 466
Blake, Dennis, 39
Blake, S., 156
Blanchard, D., 204
Blank, Arthur, 324
Blank, D., 194
Blenkhorn, David L., 532
Block, Z., 467
Bloodgood, J. M., 157
Bloom, Sam, 295
Bloomenkranz, Larry, 204

Blum, Scott, 302
Blyler, M., 110
Bodwell, C., 38
Bogan, C. E., 467
Bogan, Chris, 461
Bolino, M. C., 157
Bolton, L. E., 109
Borden, G., 251
Borrus, A., 426
Bothe, Marie, 424
Bowen, D. E., 430
Bowles, J., 72
Boyd, D. P., 37, 259
Boyle, Brad, 483
Boyle, Gia, 483
Boyztzis, R., 430
Bozzelli, Rick, 42
Brabeck, Peter, 261
Braden, Pam, 490
Brady, D., 37, 399
Brandenburger, A., 65, 66, 73
Brandt, R., 349
Branson, Richard, 28–29, 39, 83, 136, 156, 449, 450
Bratton, William, 404
Breen, B., 467
Breen, S., 313
Brenneman, K., 512
Bresser, R. F., 110
Brezosky, L., 58
Brigham, Bill, 487
Brigham, E. F., 235
Briody, D., 505
Brock, Ruthie, 531
Brockevich, Erin, 243
Brockner, J., 429
Brokaw, L., 408
Brooker, K., 194
Brown, E., 110, 392
Brown, J., 109
Brown, Jeff, 442
Brown, K., 233
Brown, R. H., 271
Brown, R. L., 73
Brown, S. L., 466
Brown, Shona, 441
Browne, John, 44, 72
Brownell, Kelly, 42
Bruch, H., 39
Brush, C., 466, 467
Bruton, G. D., 345, 346, 351
Bryant, James, 61, 78
Brynda, T., 312
Bubbar, S. E., 156
Buchanan, L., 481, 505
Bucher, Mark, 495
Buckingham, M., 430
Buckman, Rebecca C., 141, 157
Buffett, Warren, 6–7, 43, 336, 475
Bunderson, J. S., 391
Burgelman, R. A., 391, 467
Burke, James, 425
Burns, Nanette, 7
Burrows, Peter, 505
Bush, George W., 334
Butz, H. E., 194
Buzzell, R. D., 234
Bygrave, W. D., 473, 482, 485, 505

Byrne, Carol, 531
Byrne, J. A., 350
Byrnes, N., 37, 110

Cadbury, Adrian, 327
Cadbury, S. A., 350
Caegile, D., 63
Camp, B., 467
Campbell, A., 233, 234
Canabou, C., 466
Capelli, P., 156, 157
Caplan, Mitchell, 189
Capozzi, M. M., 312
Carbonara, P., 155
Cardin, R., 130, 155
Carey, D., 234
Carey, J., 38, 373, 504
Carley, W. M., 156
Carlisle, Michael, 124, 154
Carlson, D. S., 430
Carney, Dan, 426
Carr, N. G., 312
Carroll, Chuck, 457
Carroll, Darren J., 305
Carrubba, Frank, 374
Caruso, D., 429
Carvell, T., 467
Case, J., 504
Case, Stephen M., 25
Casey, D., 322
Casico, W. F., 234
Cassar, G., 505
Cassar, Ken, 302
Cassidy, J. C., 194
Castillo, Donna, 137
Cattani, K., 194
Caulfield, B., 466
Cavanaugh, M., 349
Cerny, K., 392
Chakraborty, A., 230
Challenger, J., 73
Chambers, E. Seaworthy, 85
Chambers, John, 414
Chambers, Sara, 495
Chambers, Sil, 419
Champion, David, 173
Champoux, J. E., 429
Champy, James, 383, 393
Chan Kim, W., 404
Chandler, Alfred D., 390, 391
Chang, C., 155
Chapman, Sarah, 499
Charan, R., 135, 397, 429, 466
Charitou, C. D., 72
Charples, S. S., 72
Chatman, J., 155
Chatterjee, S., 39, 350
Cheetham, Stephen, 239
Chen, C. Y., 490
Chen, John, 246
Chen, Winston, 131
Chesbrough, Henry, 443, 466, 480
Cho, H. J., 467
Choi, T. Y., 392
Choo, C. W., 235
Chow, Dan, 250
Chowdhury, N., 266
Chrisman, J. J., 505
Christensen, Clayton M., 38, 191, 195, 311, 466, 480, 481, 531
Chung, M., 157
Ciampa, K., 429
Clark, D., 488
Clayton, V., 235

Clifford, M. L., 271, 346
Clymer, Susan, 512
Cochran, P. L., 350
Cochran, P. S., 431
Coff, R. W., 110, 156, 235, 351
Cogner, J. A., 138
Cohen, D., 157
Colarelli, G., 466
Coleman, D. R., 531
Collett, S., 312
Collins, A., 312
Collins, Art, 136
Collins, D., 157
Collins, D. J., 110, 233, 234, 358, 391
Collins, J., 505
Collins, J. C., 323, 349, 467
Collins, Jim, 493
Colvin, G., 73, 194, 397, 429
Colvin, J. G., 272, 454, 467
Conaty, Bill, 135
Conaway, W., 251
Condit, Philip M., 331
Condon, B., 420
Conley, J. H., 430
Conyon, M. J., 351
Cook, David, 478
Cook, Scott, 136–137
Coolidge, C., 420
Cooney, J., 206
Cooper, Alan, 130
Cooper, S., 505
Copeland, M. V., 83, 367, 475, 488
Copeland, T. E., 234, 235
Corbett, Alistair, 439
Costa, Len A., 110
Courtney, H., 73
Covey, S. R., 429, 430
Cox, T. H., 156
Cox, T. L., 156
Coy, P., 218, 234, 311, 467
Coyle, M., 306
Craig, S., 233
Crawford, Jim, 501
Crick, Francis H. C., 27
Croce, Pat, 408
Crockett, R. O., 467
Cross, Beth, 475
Cross, K., 467
Cross, R., 155
Csere, C., 73
Curley, Tom, 387
Curtis, S., 227
Cusack, M., 234
Cusolito, J., 306

D'Allessandro, David, 462
D'Aquanni, Lissa, 487
D'Aveni, Richard, 397
Dacin, T., 391
Daft, Doug, 6–7
Daft, R., 429
Dahan, E., 194
Dahlvig, Anders, 349
Daily, C. M., 350
Daley, Clayton C., Jr., 212
Daly, Robert, 229
Damanpour, F., 466
Daniels, J. D., 391
Das, T. K., 392
Davenport, Craig, 512
Davenport, T. H., 156, 466
Davidson, Alan, 129
Davies, A., 73
Davis, E., 349, 392

Davis, E. W., 392
Davis, P. S., 194
Davis, S., 193
Dawar, N., 271, 272
Dawn, K., 391
Dawson, J. D., 312
Day, C., Jr., 429
Day, G. S., 110, 194
Day, J. D., 467
Deal, T. E., 349
Dean, B. V., 194
Dean, T. J., 73
Deephouse, D. L., 110
DeKluyver, C. A., 514
Dell, Michael, 374, 392, 467
De Meuse, K. P., 194
Dennis, W. J., Jr., 473, 488, 489, 504, 505
Deogun, N., 234
De Pury, Dave, 26
DeSanctis, G., 392
DeSimone, L. D., 369
DeSio, Tony, 496
Desmond, M., 288
Dess, Gregory G., 38, 78, 110, 151, 154, 155, 193, 194, 233, 234, 235, 273, 349, 390, 392, 400, 429, 430, 454, 467, 504
Detamore-Rodman, C., 505
DeTienne, D. R., 504
Deutschman, A., 457
Devin, L., 420
Dickinson, Wood, 417
Dickson, P., 488, 489
Dickson, P. R., 194
Dienhart, J. W., 54
Doh, J. P., 38
Dolida, Roger J., 375
Domoto, H., 272
Donlon, J. P., 110
Douglas, S. P., 272
Douma, B., 431
Dowling, G. R., 155
Downes, Larry, 286, 312, 313
Doz, Yves L., 272, 392
Dranove, D., 73
Droege, Scott, 194
Drucker, Peter F., 42, 47, 72, 438, 463, 466, 467, 505, 531
Dubini, P., 505
Duncan, Robert E., 390, 393
Dunlap, Al, 332
Dutta, S., 110
Dutton, G., 155
Dwight, Mark, 474
Dwyer, P., 110, 426
Dycjhtwald, K., 138
Dyer, J. H., 109, 155, 157, 273

Eagan, M., 466
Earl, M., 110
Earp, Wyatt, 475
Ebbers, Bernard, 230, 336
Echikson, W., 271, 312
Eckert, Robert A., 7
Eden, L., 271
Edge, A. G., 531
Edmondson, G., 20, 37, 235, 271
Edvisson, Leif, 155
Edwards, C., 378
Ehrenfeld, J. R., 39
Eickhoff, Gerald, 141
Einstein, Albert, 520
Eisenberg, Melvin Aron, 333
Eisenhardt, Kathleen M., 350, 441, 466, 505
Eisner, Michael D., 336, 362–363, 391

Elenkov, D. S., 72
Elkind, P., 420
Ellison, Lawrence J., 332, 339
Ellstrand, A. E., 350
Elson, Charles, 525
Elstrom, P., 234
Emerson, Ralph Waldo, 47
Engardio, P., 28, 271
Engen, Jason, 500
English, M. J., 467
Ensing, I. M., 392
Enz, C., 531
Epstein, J., 48
Erickson, G. Scott, 532
Erickson, T., 138
Eselius, E. D., 234
Esfahani, E., 168
Esrey, William, 99
Estevez, Stella, 133
Ethiraj, S. K., 110
Ettenson, R., 109
Evans, P., 311, 312, 467
Evans, P. B., 73
Evans, Pattie Freeman, 302

Fahey, E., 194
Fahey, J., 233
Fahey, L., 72, 73
Fama, Eugene, 350
Fan Gong, 246
Fanning, Shawn, 276
Farr, David, 217
Fastow, Andrew S., 402
Feeny, D., 109
Ferguson, G., 73
Ferguson, K., 283
Ferrier, W. J., 235
Finegold, D., 38, 156
Finkelstein, S., 154, 531
Fiorina, Carly, 7
Fisher, A., 140, 156
Fisher, George, 417
Fisher, M. L., 109
Fitzgerald, M., 283
Fjeldstad, O. D., 109, 291, 312
Fleisher, Craig S., 532
Flint, J., 194, 271
Folta, T. B., 467
Fontrodona, J., 430
Ford, Henry, 25, 333, 410
Ford, William Clay, Jr., 76
Forest, S. A., 194
Forster, J., 392
Forward, Gordon, 413
Fouladpour, Tony, 238
Foust, D., 37, 497
Fowler, S. W., 110
Fox, Vicente, 58
France, M., 420
Frank, R., 233
Franzke, E., 447
Fraser, J. A., 505
Fraser, Jennifer, 172
Frauenfelder, M., 505
Fredrickson, J. W., 391
Freedman, D. H., 450
Freeman, R. E., 38, 156,
    331n, 350, 390
Friedman, Marc, 415
Friesen, G. B., 280
Friesen, P. H., 391
Fromartz, S., 504, 505
Frost, T., 271, 272
Fry, Art, 324

Fryer, B., 73, 272, 349
Fujii, Akio, 266
Fuld, Leonard, 45–46
Fulmer, R. M., 138
Furchgott, R., 156

Gaal, Stephen, 486
Gadiesh, O., 178, 194
Gaglio, C. M., 504
Gagnie, M., 429
Galbraith, J. R., 356, 390
Gale, B. T., 234
Galvin, Chris, 456, 467
Galvin, Robert, 132
Garman, Ryan, 501
Garrity, B., 311
Garten, J. E., 39, 271
Gartner, W. B., 504
Garvin, D. A., 429
Gates, Bill, 127, 417, 430
Gavetti, G., 466
Gavin, J. H., 401
George, Bill, 135
Georgescu, Peter, 404
Gerstner, Louis V., Jr., 23
Geschke, Jim, 453
Ghemawat, Pankaj, 166
Ghoshal, Sumantra, 39, 72, 155, 271, 272,
    360, 391
Ghosn, Carlos, 7, 37, 87
Gibbert, M., 466
Gibson, C. B., 38, 157, 393
Gikkas, N. S., 271
Gilad, Benjamin, 532
Gilbert, J. L., 178, 194
Gill, Amar, 332
Gilley, K. M., 392
Gilmartin, Ray, 133
Gilmore, J. H., 194
Ginsberg, A., 466
Ginsburg, J., 73
Glass, J. T., 392
Glatz, Hanns, 250
Godwin, J., 467
Goff, John, 334
Goglo, P., 72
Goizueta, Roberto, 6, 7
Goldberg, M., 430
Goldsmith, D., 497
Goldsmith, M., 38, 39, 371
Goldstein, A., 33
Goldstine, J., 194
Goldwasser, Dan, 339
Goleman, Daniel, 405, 406, 408, 429, 430
Goll, I., 73
Gompers, P. A., 467
Goode, Mary, 141
Goodstein, L. D., 194
Goodwin, Joseph D., 7
Goold, M., 233, 234, 349
Gossage, B., 505
Goteman, I., 349
Gottfredson, M., 392
Gourevitch, David, 396
Govindarajan, V., 141, 271, 272
Graen, G. B., 349
Graham, A. B., 391
Grant, K., 475
Grant, P., 73
Grant, R. M., 91, 111
Grassley, Charles, 426
Gray, S., 399
Greatbatch, Wilson, 418
Greco, S., 505

Green, J., 73
Green, S., 271
Greenberg, Jack M., 336
Greenberg, Jeffrey, 420
Greenberg, Maurice, 420
Greene, P., 466, 467
Greenspan, Alan, 281
Greenspan, R., 312
Greenwald, B., 73
Gregg, F. M., 271
Greising, D., 349
Grossman, J., 505
Grossman, L., 440
Grossman, W., 350
Groth, M., 311
Grove, Andrew, 7, 26, 87, 307, 330, 415
Grover, Ronald, 350, 378
Grow, B., 53, 72, 109, 218, 234
Gruber, Peter, 30
Gulati, R., 312
Gull, N., 505
Gupta, A. K., 141, 271, 272
Guth, W. D., 194, 234, 466, 531
Gutierrez, Carlos M., 7

Haas, M. R., 155
Habib, M. M., 391
Haddad, C., 109
Hage, J., 466
Hagel, J., 272
Hagmeier, Katerine, 391
Hall, B. J., 349
Hall, Brian, 136
Hall, D. I., 391
Hall, R. H., 350, 390
Hall, W. K., 194
Halliday, J., 109
Hambrick, D. C., 195, 234, 350
Hamel, Gary, 26, 38, 39, 42, 72, 110, 125, 154,
    156, 193, 233, 392, 450, 467
Hamm, P., 399
Hamm, S., 156
Hammer, Michael, 383, 393, 410–411, 430
Hammonds, K. H., 28, 38, 39, 156, 233
Handy, Charles, 38, 376, 392, 410, 430
Hanrahan, T., 312
Hansen, M. T., 149, 155, 157, 466
Hansen, S., 481
Hanson, James, 370
Harari, O., 430
Hardy, Quentin, 312, 467
Hargreaves, D., 233
Harker, P. T., 311
Harrar, G., 392
Harrigan, K., 233
Harrison, D. A., 431
Harrison, J. S., 38, 156, 350, 390, 392
Hart, M., 466, 467
Hart, Stuart L., 23–24, 39
Hartley, S. W., 194
Hartmann, Joe, 492
Harveston, P. D., 271
Harvey, C. P., 156
Harvey, M. R., 252
Harwick, Julie, 55
Hasan, Fred, 239, 271
Haskins, M. R., 392
Haspelagh, P., 234
Hatch, N. W., 155
Haughton, K., 73
Hawken, P., 460
Hax, A. C., 233, 234
Hayes, R., 466
Healey, J. R., 73, 176

Hegge, Betty-Ann, 169
Heifetz, R., 430
Heinzl, M., 350
Helgesen, Sally, 28, 39, 430
Hellweg, E., 302
Helman, C., 467
Helms, M. M., 38, 194, 271, 272, 390, 430
Helper, S., 73
Hemp, Paul, 12
Henderson, Larry, 252
Hendricks, Ken, 220, 221
Henkoff, R., 110, 155
Henricks, M., 233
Henry, D., 243, 420
Hensler, Bill, 441
Herzog, V. L., 382
Hesselbein, F., 38, 39, 371, 429, 430
Higins, K. T., 72
Hill, A., 233
Hill, C. W. L., 392
Hill, S., 109
Hilmer, F. C., 392
Hirshman, Pamela, 149
Hitt, M. A., 38, 39, 91, 111, 155, 156, 233, 272,
    350, 390, 391
Hodgen, Todd, 254
Hoetker, G., 109
Hof, R. D., 9, 311, 349
Hoffman, Michael, 9
Hofstede, Geert, 272
Hollender, J., 38
Holliday, Chad, 24, 39
Holmes, S., 193, 420
Holt, John W., 417, 430
Hong Liang Lu, 498
Hopkins, M. J., 450
Hornery, J., 467
Horovitz, Bruce, 72
Hoskin, R. E., 235
Hoskisson, R. E., 91, 233, 272, 350, 351, 390,
    391, 392
Hotard, D., 194
House, Andrew, 378
Hout, T., 272
Howell, J. M., 466
Howell, Robert A., 126
Hrebiniak, L. G., 38, 233, 390
Hudspeth, B., 33
Hughes, J., 110
Humer, Franz, 523
Hutt, M. D., 235
Huy, Q. H., 39

Immelt, J., 271
Imperato, G., 45, 109, 430
Ingram, T. N., 194
Inkpen, A. C., 392
Ireland, R. D., 111, 155, 233, 272, 391
Isaacson, W., 430
Isdell, Neville, 7
Iverson, Ken, 369
Ivester, Doug, 6, 37
Izzo, John, 143

Jackson, E. M., 350
Jackson, M., 109
Jacobson, Michael, 143
Jacques, R., 304
Jafari, J., 227
James, David, 354
James, G., 204
Janis, Irving L., 521, 524, 531
Janney, J. J., 235

Jap, S. D., 110
Jenkins, Darryl, 88, 470
Jensen, Michael C., 350, 351
Jespersen, F. F., 351
Jiang, Y., 345, 346, 351
Johannessen, J. A., 466
Johnson, C., 429
Johnson, D., 413
Johnson, G., 224
Johnson, J. L., 350
Johnson, M. W., 195
Johnson, R. A., 350
Jones, J., 33
Jordan, B. D., 111
Joshi, S., 234
Joyce, James, 418
Joyce, W. F., 38, 233, 390
Judge, P. C., 156
Jurgenson, Karen, 387

Kadoorie, Michael, 346
Kahn, J., 73, 420
Kale, P., 110, 273
Kalish, Ira, 453
Kambil, A., 234, 280
Kampur, D., 244
Kanter, Rosabeth Moss, 23, 38, 436, 466
Kao, J., 436, 466
Kaplan, Robert S., 99, 102, 104, 105, 111
Karri, R., 193
Kasten, Tom, 416
Katada, Tetsuya, 31
Katz, J. A., 504
Katz, J. H., 156
Katzenbach, J. R., 392
Kawai, Ryoichi, 31
Kay, Roger, 204
Kaye, Sandy, 85
Kazanjian, R. K., 356, 390
Keats, B., 390
Kedia, B. L., 271
Kee, Lee Shau, 346
Keenan, F., 312, 467
Keenan, P. T., 235
Keighley, G., 295
Kelleher, Herb, 7, 87, 96
Kelly, Bill, 512
Kelly, Gary C., 87
Kennedy, A. A., 349
Kerin, R. A., 194
Kerr, J., 349
Kerstetter, J., 9
Kerwin, Kathleen R., 73, 109
Kets de Vries, M. F. R., 39, 156, 391, 450
Keynes, John Maynard, 34
Khanna, T., 234, 351
Khoury, Ted, 110
Kidd, J. B., 272
Kidwell, R. E., Jr., 350
Kiger, P. J., 430
Kilmann, R. H., 393
Kilts, James, 7
Kim, E., 313
Kim, H., 392
Kim, L., 194
Kim, W. Chan, 444, 445, 466
Kimbrell, Duke, 358
Kini, Mark, 291
Kirby, Michael, 27
Kirchhoff, B., 485
Kirkland, J., 73
Kirkman, B. L., 157
Kirn, S. P., 38, 111
Kitchen, Brent, 470

Kitchen, Garry, 295
Klemp, G., 430
Kletter, D., 467
Kline, D., 39, 110, 272
Kling, K., 349
Knight, Charles, 338
Knight, John, 470
Knox, N., 466
Kocher, Joel, 281
Kogut, B., 272
Kolk, A., 248
Koogle, Timothy, 487
Koppel, B., 391
Koretz, G., 193
Korman, Jonathan, 130
Kosnik, R. D., 351
Kotabe, M., 272
Kotter, John P., 429
Koudsi, S., 157, 234
Koza, M. P., 273
Kozlowski, Dennis, 229, 336
Kripalani, M., 28, 244
Krishnan, H., 234
Krishnan, M. S., 110, 194
Krisnan, R. A., 234
Kroll, M., 194
Kromer, E., 73
Kuczmarski, T. D., 436
Kuedtjam, H., 392
Kuemmerle, W., 391
Kuhlmann, Arkadi, 168
Kulatilaka, N., 235
Kumar N., 73
Kunii, I., 391
Kurlantzick, J., 505
Kurtz, R., 490
Kutaragi, Ken, 451
Kwon, S. W., 156

LaBarre, P., 429
Labianca, G., 157
Labianca, J., 157
Labrada, Lee, 488
Lacity, M., 109
Lacy, S., 302
Lafley, Alan G. "A. G.," 219
Laforge, R. W., 194
LaGuardia, Gina, 501
Lam, Colin, 346
Lambkin, M., 467
Lancaster, Jim, 318
Lancaster, P. R., 349
Lancaster, Pat, 318
Land, Edward, 434
Landes, D. S., 271
Langreth, R., 380
Lanier, Elizabeth, 132
Lashinsky, A., 89
Lassek, P. J., 504
Latham, Carol, 480
Latham, Gary P., 349, 467
Lathan, G., 155
Lavelle, L., 110, 351
Lavelle, Louis, 420
Lavelle, M., 38
Laverty, K. J., 235
Lawler, Edward E., III, 38, 430
Lawrence, Joanne, 221
Lawrence, S., 9
Lawrence, T. B., 110
Lay, Kenneth L., 400–401
Leana, C. R., 157
Lee, J., 349
Lee, L., 193, 233

Lefteroff, T. T., 505
Leggate, John, 298
Lei, D., 157, 194, 272, 391
Leifer, R., 466
Lelii, S. R., 312
LeMay, Ronald T., 99
Lenzer, R., 156
Leonard-Barton, Dorothy, 132, 143, 155, 157, 413, 430
Leonhardt, Daniel, 413
Lerner, J., 467
Leschley, Jan, 133
Letzelter, J., 447
Levering, R., 86, 457
Levin, Gerald M., 336
Levinthal, D., 466
Levitt, Theodore, 254, 272
Lewis, Keami, 129
Lewis, Russell T., 19, 38
Li, J. T., 272
Lichtenthal, John, 252
Licking, E., 27
Lieber, R. B., 156
Lieberman, David, 402
Lieberman, M. B., 467
Lieberthal, K., 271, 272
Light, L., 194
Lii, J., 313
Lim, Y., 194
Limperis, J., 349
Linzmayer, G. W., 311
Lipin, S., 200, 234
Lipparini, A., 110
Lipton, M., 39
Liu Chuanzhi, 325
Livengood, Scott A., 396
Locke, Edwin A., 349
Loeb, M., 38
Lomax, A., 193
London, T., 38
Long, W., 504
Lopez, José Ignacio, 156
Lorange, P., 72, 392, 429
Lorenzoni, G., 110
Lorsch, J. W., 351, 429
Lovins, A., 460
Lovins, H., 460
Low, C. K., 332
Lowery, T., 193, 234
Lowry, T., 233
Lu, J. W., 271
Lubove, S., 156, 430
Luchs, K., 234
Luckey, A., 9
Luehrman, T. A., 111, 235
Lumpkin, G. T., 156, 454, 466, 467, 504
Lundberg, C. C., 531
Lundegaard, K., 293
Luthans, Fred, 429
Lutz, Robert A., 21
Lynton, Michael, 378

m

Ma, H., 193
MacDonald, E., 334
MacDonald-Korth, Holly, 455
MacMillan, I. C., 193, 194, 271, 467
Magretta, J., 149, 392
Maiello, M., 505
Maier, M., 304
Main, J., 430
Majluf, N. S., 233, 234
Makino, S., 271
Malik, Om, 172, 283
Malkin, E., 271

Mallas, S., 467
Malone, John, 415
Malone, Michael S., 155
Mandel, M. J., 311
Mandelker, G., 350
Mandl, Alex, 218
Mang, P. Y., 467
Mannix, E. A., 39
March, J. G., 235, 393, 505
Marcial, G., 73
Marcus, Bernard, 324
Mark, Ken, 77
Markham, S. K., 466
Markides, C. C., 72, 194
Marks, M. S., 194, 271
Marriott, J. W., Jr., 164, 193
Martin, J., 155, 272
Martin, R., 48
Martin, X., 272
Martinez, Angel, 475
Martinez, Arthur, 43
Mass, N. J., 111
Mathur, S., 73
Matias, Yossi, 367
Matin, J., 504
Mauborgne, Renee, 444, 445, 466
Mauboussin, M. H., 227
Maurer, Jeffrey S., 199
May, R. C., 72
Mayer, J. D., 429, 430
Maynard, M., 109
McAfee, A., 110
McAleer, Joseph, 396
McCaleb, Philip, 488
McCarthy, T., 404
McCune, J. C., 272
McDermott, C., 466
McDonald, D., 224, 312
McDonald, Mackey, 205
McDougall, P. P., 356, 391
McDougall, Ronald A., 361
McGahan, Anita M., 66, 67, 73, 194
McGann, R., 281
McGeehan, P., 350
McGowan, W. P., 429
McGrath, R. G., 193, 235, 271, 467
McGuire, D., 311, 312
McKay, N., 312
McKee, A., 430
McKnight, William, 416
McLaughlin, K. J., 392
McLaughlin, T., 466
McLean, Bethany, 243, 351
McMullan, W. E., 504, 505
McNamee, M., 110
McVae, J., 38
McVey, Henry, 169
Means, Gardiner C., 333
Meckling, W. H., 350, 351
Mehta, S. N., 283
Meiland, D., 271
Meindl, J. R., 37
Melcher, R. A., 350
Mellgren, D., 73
Melrose, Ken, 411, 430
Mendelow, A. L., 235
Mendelson, Haim, 320
Menn, J., 311
Merchant, H., 272
Meredith, R., 246
Meremenot, M., 268
Messier, Jean-Marie, 230
Meyer, Peter, 414, 430
Mi-Young, A., 273
Migliorato, P., 81

Milburn, Cindy, 51
Miles, R. E., 381, 382
Miller, A., 38, 193, 349, 390, 429, 430, 467
Miller, D., 349, 391, 454
Miller, D. J., 233
Miller, F. A., 156
Miller, M. J., 304
Miller, W., 392
Minow, Neil, 18, 38, 331, 350
Mintzberg, Henry, 13, 37, 38, 319, 349, 531
Mioniti, M., 473
Mitarai, Fujio, 81
Mitchell, Jordan, 77
Mitchell, Julie A., 536
Mitchell, R., 349
Mittal, Lakshmi, 234
Mochari, I., 467
Moeller, S. B., 200
Mohrman, S. A., 156
Molaro, R., 154
Moldoveanu, M., 38
Monahan, J., 488
Monahan, Tom, 496
Monks, Robert, 18, 38, 331, 350
Monteiro, K. A., 234
Montgomery, C. A., 110, 233, 358, 391
Montgomery, D. B., 467
Moon, I., 378
Mooney, A. C., 531
Moore, Geoffrey A., 458, 467
Moore, J. F., 392
Morison, B., 138
Morita, Akio, 24
Morris, B., 37, 349
Morris, E., 531
Morrison, S., 320
Morrison, T., 251
Morrissey, C. A., 466
Morse, E. A., 110
Moskowitz, M., 457
Moussouris, John, 481
Mowery, D., 392
Mudambi, R., 73
Mui, Chunka, 286, 312, 313
Mullaney, T. J., 195, 467
Muller, J., 193, 234
Mundie, Craig, 440
Munk, N., 110, 156
Muoio, A., 234, 400
Murdoch, James, 344
Murdoch, Rupert, 344
Murphy, D., 429
Murphy, Kevin J., 351
Murray, Roy, 63
Mussberg, W., 392
Myser, M., 288, 501

n

Nacher, T., 109
Nachum, Gal, 367
Nader, Ralph, 243, 344
Nadler, D. A., 337
Nahapiet, J., 155
Nalebuff, B. J., 65, 66, 73
Nally, Dennis, 54
Nam, D., 313
Nambisan, S., 312
Narasimhaiya, Ganesh, 28
Narasimhan, O., 110
Narayanan, V. K., 72, 73
Nardelli, Robert, 329
Nash, John, 7
Nasser, Jacques, 255, 272
Navarez, Raul, 137
Negroponte, N., 311

Neilson, G., 467
Nelson, B., 46
Nelson, M. G., 33
Nerney, C., 280
Neuborne, E., 185
Neufville, R. de, 235
Neumann, Jens, 238
Nguyen, Bill, 491–492, 505
Niblack, J., 466
Nicholls-Nixon, C. L., 504
Nmarus, J. A., 109
Nobel, R., 272
Nohria, N., 149, 157, 312, 466
Nonaka, I., 155
Noot, Walter, 98
Nordstrom, Dan, 82
Norton, David B., 99, 102, 104, 105, 111
Novicki, C., 430
Nulty, P., 349

O'Brien, J. P., 467
O'Brien, William, 411
O'Connor, G. C., 466
O'Dell, Carla, 150
Odlyzko, A., 73
O'Donnell, S. W., 273
Oh, H., 157
Ohannessian, Dikran, 77
Ohmae, Kenichi, 271, 392
Okie, Francis G., 324
O'Leary-Kelly, A. M., 349
Olofson, C., 312
Olsen, B., 466
Olsen, Kenneth H., 47
O'Neill, H. M., 390
Ordonez, L., 431
O'Reilly, B., 429
O'Reilly, Charles A., 385, 386, 387, 393
O'Reilly, J., 155
Osso, Steve, 63
Oster, Sharon M., 166, 233
Otero, Ann, 415
Ouchi, William, 349, 350
Overdorf, M., 191, 195
Overholt, A., 241
Oviatt, B. M., 356, 391
Oxley, J. E., 392
Ozzie, Raymond, 98

Paine, Lynn S., 421, 422, 430, 431
Palmer, A. T., 193
Palmeri, Christopher, 426
Palmisano, Samuel, 63
Pare, T. P., 200, 233
Parise, S., 155
Parloff, R., 193
Pascual, A. M., 193, 234
Patscot, Steven, 130
Patterson, Neal, 145
Pauleen, D. J., 271
Pawlowski, Janina, 487, 505
Peabody, Deborah, 420
Pearce, J. A., II, 38, 194
Pearson, A. E., 429
Pearson, D. R., 328
Peck, S. I., 351
Pedrozza, G. M., 505
Peng, Michael W., 20, 345, 346, 351
Pepper, John E., 421
Perkins, A. B., 155
Perkins, Wendell, 42
Perman, S., 467
Perot, H. Ross, 478
Perrewe, P. L., 430

Petee, S., 273
Peteraf, M., 73, 157
Peters, L. S., 466
Peters, S., 235
Peters, Thomas J., 53, 349
Petry, C., 413
Pfeffer, Jeffrey, 37, 86, 128, 131, 156, 391
Phelan, Dan, 133
Phillips, C., 392
Phillips, Larry, 133
Picken, Joseph C., 78, 110, 151, 154, 155,
    194, 233, 234, 329, 349, 392, 400,
    430
Pickering, C. I., 72
Pidcock, K., 83
Piesch, Ferdinand, 238
Pilgrim, Lonnie, 334
Pinchot, G., 466
Pine, B. J., II, 194
Pinelli, Ron, 176
Pirko, Tom, 6
Pistorio, Pasquale, 222
Pitchford, Mark, 143
Pittman, Brian, 384
Pitts, R. A., 157, 391
Pizana, Lourdes, 222
Pizzo, V. G., 391
Plenge, Robert, 328
Podmolik, M., 204
Poitier, Sidney, 336
Polanyi, M., 155
Polek, D., 235
Pondy, L. R., 393
Porras, J. I., 323, 349, 467
Port, O., 430, 450
Porter, Michael E., 10, 38, 57, 58, 60, 70–71, 73,
    77, 79, 84, 109, 110, 161, 163, 165, 166,
    170, 172, 193, 194, 200, 228, 233, 234,
    235, 237, 240, 243, 244, 245, 269, 270,
    271, 272, 275, 282, 290, 302, 308, 309,
    312, 313, 391
Postrell, Virginia, 293
Pottruck, D. A., 392
Pound, J., 350
Powell, Michael, 283
Powell, T. C., 193
Powell, W. W., 380
Prahalad, C. K., 38, 42, 72, 125, 154, 156, 157,
    193, 194, 233, 241, 271, 272, 279,
    280, 311
Prandelli, E., 311
Pridor, Baradok, 367
Priem, R. L., 72, 392
Prince, C. J., 488
Prince, E. T., 235
Prior, V., 72
Pritchard, David, 330
Prusak, L., 157, 312, 466
Pucik, V., 467
Puryear, R., 392
Putscher, Joyce, 304

Questrom, Allen, 181
Quigley, J. V., 39
Quinn, James Brian, 154, 319, 349, 392,
    467
Quinn, R. C., 430
Quinn, R. T., 38, 111
Quinn, Robert, 411–412

Rabinovitz, J., 447
Rae-Dupree, J., 9
Rahe, Amribeth S., 199

Raisinghani, D., 531
Raisinghani, M., 272
Rajczi, Louis, 447
Rajendra, Eric, 169
Ramamurti, R., 244
Ramaswamy, Venkat, 157, 279, 280, 311
Ramstead, E., 392
Rao, A. R., 193
Rappa, M., 297
Rappaport, A., 234, 349
Rasheed, A., 392
Rasheed, A. M. A., 392
Rasheed, M. A., 73
Raths, D., 512
Rautiola, Norman, 501
Rechner, P. L., 531
Reddy, C. N., 334
Reddy, Damodar, 334
Reed, A., II, 109
Reed, S., 234
Reene, Michael, 141
Reich, Robert B., 125, 155
Reinartz, Werner, 291, 292, 312
Reinemund, Steve, 8
Reinert, U., 271
Reingen, P. H., 235
Reinhardt, A., 235
Reinhardt, F. L., 110
Reuer, J. J., 273
Revell, J., 420
Reynolds, P. D., 485
Rice, John, 373
Rice, M. P., 466
Rich, L., 143
Richter, A., 467
Ridge, Garry, 499
Rigas family, 230
Rigby, D. K., 195, 234
Rivette, K. G., 39, 110
Rivkin, J. W., 110, 351
Robbins, Paul, 491
Roberto, M. A., 429
Roberts, Bari-Ellen, 419
Roberts, D., 271
Roberts, E. B., 466
Roberts, J., 467
Roberts, P. W., 155
Robins, J. A., 110
Robinson, R. B., 194
Robinson, S. L., 349
Rodengen, J. L., 391
Rodenhauser, Tom, 455
Rodin, Rod, 400
Rodriguez, P., 271
Rogers, T. J., 30
Rollag, K., 155
Romanelli, E., 505
Rondinelli, D. A., 38, 39
Ronstadt, R., 531
Root, Alan, 30
Rosen, B., 157
Rosen, S., 39
Rosenblum, J. W., 392, 408
Rosenfeld, J., 194
Rossetti, C., 392
Roth, K., 110
Rothberg, Helen N., 532
Rouse, T., 271
Rowley, I., 378, 399
Rowley, T. J., 38
Rows, S. A., 111
Royer, I., 235, 467
Rubner, J., 373
Rucci, A. J., 38
Rucci, R. S., 111

Rudden, E., 272
Rumelt, R. P., 391
Russo, David, 86
Rutan, Burt, 450
Ryan, L. V., 350

## S

Sacks, D., 418
Sahlman, William A., 514
Saias, M. A., 391
St. Anthony, N., 466
Sakaibara, M., 392
Salancik, G. R., 37
Salman, W. A., 73
Salvoney, P., 429
Sampler, J., 110
Samuel, Phil, 441
Sanborn, Stephanie, 37
Sanchez, Raymond, 523
Sandberg, W. R., 531
Sanders, L., 109
Sanger, Stephen, 165–166
Sant, Roger, 39, 431
Saunders, Anne, 399
Sawhney, M., 311
Schaeffer, Leonard, 165
Schafer, S., 430
Schawlow, Arthur, 136
Schecter, S. M., 195
Schein, Edgar H., 358–359, 390
Schendel, D., 272
Schermerhorn, R. R., Jr., 54
Schindler, Pamela, 524
Schiro, Jim, 139
Schlingemann, F. P., 200
Schmerken, J., 189
Schmidt, Eric, 73
Schmidt, G., 194
Schmitt, W., 436
Schneider, M., 350
Schoemaker, J. H., 110
Schonfeld, E., 373
Schoonhoven, C. B., 505
Schrader, G. E., 504
Schreyogg, G., 72
Schroeder, Gary, 479
Schultz, Howard, 398, 399,
    477–478
Schumpeter, Joseph A., 277, 311
Schwartz, N. D., 272
Schweiger, D. M., 531
Schweitzer, M. E., 431
Schwert, G. William, 200
Scott, B. R., 390
Scott, F. S., 72
Seeger, J., 234
Seglin, J. L., 505
Seiden, Josh, 130
Seijts, G. H., 155, 467
Sellers, P., 234, 349, 420
Sen, S., 38
Senge, Peter M., 11, 25, 28, 38, 39, 410, 430
Server, A., 208
Sexton, D. A., 39
Seybold, P., 312
Shah, B., 73
Shane, S., 467, 504
Shanly, M., 73
Shannon, Robert, 221
Shapira, Z., 235
Shapiro, C., 73, 78
Sharer, Kevin, 12
Shari, M., 271
Sharma, A., 272, 466
Shaw, Peter, 204

Shaw, Robert, 208
Sheng, Andrew, 346
Shepherd, D. A., 504, 505
Sherman, John, 320
Shih, Stan, 417
Shilling, A. G., 233
Shinal, J., 234
Shook, C., 156
Siebel, Tom, 171, 257–258, 272
Siegel, D., 312
Siegel, David, 284
Sigiura, H., 272
Silverberg, Brad, 141, 492
Silverman, B. S., 392
Simmons, Cal, 484
Simon, Anthony, 250
Simon, B., 250
Simons, Mark, 204
Simons, R., 322, 349
Singer, M., 302
Singh, H., 157, 234, 272, 273
Singh, J. V., 110
Sinha, I., 312
Sinkin, Richard N., 58
Sirower, M. L., 234
Slater, R., 133, 156
Slevin, D. P., 393, 467
Slevin, J. P., 454
Sloan, Alfred P., 25, 410
Sloan, P., 206
Sloane, J., 504
Slocum, J. W., Jr., 157, 194, 349, 391
Slowinski, G., 392
Slywotzky, Adrian J., 89, 467
Smith, C., 109
Smith, D., 156, 496
Smith, Douglas K., 382, 392
Smith, Frederick W., 171
Smith, G., 58, 73, 430
Smith, J. A., 73
Smunt, T. L., 306
Snow, C., 382
Snow, C. C., 381
Sole, Kenneth, 523
Solomon, Howard, 339
Song Kye-Hyon, 268
Sood, Rahul, 172
Sood, Ravi, 172
Sorrell, Martin, 145, 449
Soule, E., 430
Spencer, J. W., 157
Spielberg, Steven, 415
Spinelli, S., 482, 505
Spitzer, Eliot, 420
Spraggins, Mike, 328
Spreitzer, Gretchen M., 411–412, 430
Srinivasan, Cadambi A., 532
Srong, Bruce, 150
Stabell, C. B., 109, 291, 312
Stack, Jack, 412–413, 430
Stadter, G., 111
Stafford, E. R., 235
Stanton, Steven A., 411, 430
Staw, B. M., 429
Stearns, T. M., 531
Steenbuch, Frederik, 57
Steensma, H. K., 431
Steere, W. C., Jr., 466
Steere, William, 438
Stein, J., 447
Stein, T., 466
Stephenson, Randall, 220
Stern, David, 408
Sternberg, R., 429
Stevens, J. M., 431

Stewart, C., 358
Stewart, Martha, 420
Stewart, Thomas A., 39, 89, 127, 129, 155,
    156, 505
Stewart, W. H., 72
Stienmann, H., 72
Stiller, Robert, 460
Stimpert, J. L., 313
Stinchcombe, A. L., 505
Stires, D., 429
Stockley, R. L., Jr., 227
Stone, A., 168
Stonecipher, Harry C., 420
Storch, Jerry, 185
Stoughton, S., 185
Stratton, Hal, 250
Straus, S., 157
Strickland, A. J., III, 349
Stringer, R., 467
Strong, Bruce, 149
Stross, R. E., 271
Stuckey, J., 392
Stulz, R. M., 200
Suciu, P., 295
Suhr, J., 176
Sull, D., 466
Summers, Sam, 475
Sundaram, A., 280
Sundarmurthy, C., 230
Sutcliffe, C. L., 306
Sutcliffe, K. M., 72, 391
Swap, W., 155
Swartz, James, 470
Sweeney, Paul, 496
Sweo, R., 72
Symonds, William C., 193, 194

## T

Tabb, L., 233
Takeuchi, I., 155
Tallman, Joseph, 148
Tanner, J., 194, 505
Tanzi, Calisto, 20
Tashiro, H., 346
Taulli, Tom, 302
Taylor, Alex, III, 73, 176, 194
Taylor, Andrew, 140
Taylor, J. T., 430
Taylor, K., 311
Taylor, W. C., 157
Teitelbaum, R., 349
Teng, B. S., 392
Teramoto, Y., 272
Tesler, Larry, 459, 467
Tesluk, P. E., 157
Tetenbaum, T. J., 39
Theirault, John, 250
Theoret, A., 531
Thomas, J. G., 38
Thomas, T., 54
Thompson, A. A., Jr., 349
Thoreau, Henry David, 478
Thorndike, E. L., 429
Thornton, E., 193, 218, 234, 555
Tibbs, K., 227
Tichy, Noel M., 429
Tierney, T. J., 149, 157, 429
Tilin, A., 488, 504
Tillman, Robert, 398
Timmers, P., 297, 312
Timmons, H., 351
Timmons, J. A., 482
Timmons, S., 505
Tindal, Kip, 401
Tischler, L., 73

Toledo, Melissa, 82
Tome, Carol B., 327–329
Torre, Joe, 92
Torres, N. L., 488, 501, 505
Trayford, Richard, 497
Treece, J., 273
Trent, B., 37
Tretter, M. J., 391
Trevino, L. K., 350
Triandis, H. C., 271
Triantis, A., 235
Tsao, A., 53
Tu, H., 194
Tucci, C. L., 297, 312
Tucci, Joseph M., 220
Tulder, R. V., 248
Tully, S., 349, 392
Turk, T. A., 351
Turnley, W. H., 157
Tushman, Michael L., 385, 386, 387, 393
Tyson, D., 109

**U**

Uhl-Bien, M., 349
Uhlenbruck, K., 271
Ulrich, D., 39, 110
Useem, J., 138, 466
Useem, Michael L., 336
Usinier, J. C., 272

**V**

Vagelos, P. Roy, 26, 125
Valeant-Yenichek, Julie, 53
Valikangas, L., 466
Van Aukun, P. M., 39
Van Brugge, Robert, 8
Van Buren, H. J., III, 157
Vance, A., 466, 467
Van Putten, A. B., 271
Varian, H. R., 73, 78
Veen, M., 350
Veitch, M., 467
Venkataraman, S., 504
Vermeulen, F., 235
Verona, C., 311
Veryzer, R. W., 466
Vesper, K. H., 504, 505
Vestring, T., 271
Vibert, Conor, 532
Vicente, J. P., 230
Vickers, M., 311, 467
Victor, B., 391
Viguerie, P., 73
Vogel, C., 505
Volpi, Mike, 234

**W**

Waddock, S., 38
Wagner, M., 467
Wagoner, G. Richard, Jr., 339

Wahlgren, E., 254
Wailgum, T., 312
Waksal, Sam, 420
Walker, B. A., 235
Walker, Jay, 235
Wall, S. J., 430
Wallace, B., 505
Wallace, Jerry, 133
Walsh, J. P., 351
Walters, B. A., 72, 235, 273
Walton, Sam, 324
Wan, W. P., 272
Wang, Charles, 144
Ward, L., 281
Ward, R. D., 350
Ward, S., 194
Warlick, Andy, 358
Warner, F., 415
Warner, M., 51
Warren, Tim, 456
Waterhouse, J. H., 38
Waterhouse, Robert H., 349
Waters, J. A., 13
Watkins, M. D., 73
Watkins, Sherron, 400, 429
Watson, James D., 27
Watson, Thomas, Sr., 25, 410
Weaver, G. R., 350
Weaver, K. M., 488, 489
Webber, A. M., 86, 155
Weber, Alan J., 199
Weber, Joseph, 39, 189, 320, 350, 392
Weber, K., 72
Wedel, Jorgen, 136
Weintraub, A., 193, 312, 467
Weiss, J., 110
Weiss, L. M., 312
Welch, Jack, 7, 87, 128, 229, 235, 278, 326, 371
Welles, E. O., 221
Wellner, A. S., 154
Wells, R. B., 38
Wernerfelt, B., 157
Westcott, Carl, 478
Westerfield, R. W., 111
Weston, J. F., 235
Weston, J. S., 349
Wetlaufer, S., 39, 272, 349, 391, 431
Whalen, C. J., 193, 194, 234
Wheatcroft, P., 390
Wheatley, J., 73
Wheelwright, Steven C., 466
White, D., 392
White, Gordon, 370, 391
White, J., 208
Wiedekig, Wendelin, 176
Wiersema, F., 436, 466
Wiersema, M. F., 110
Wiggett, Jim, 82
Wildstrom, S., 304

Willcocks, L. P., 109
Williams, Devin, 499
Williams, E., 380
Williams, G., 496, 497, 505
Williams, M. A., 156
Williams, Steve, 162
Williamson, Oliver E., 233
Willis, Steve, 460
Wilson, H. J., 466
Wilson, T., 400
Wind, Yoram, 272
Wingfield, N., 235, 293
Winston, S., 157
Wise, R., 73, 89, 193, 467
Wissman, Geoff, 53
Woellert, L., 426
Wolf, Amy Nye, 497
Wolfenson, J., 72
Wolfsried, Sephan, 173
Wood, C., 311
Wood, J., 110
Worrell, D., 447
Wright, P., 194
Wriston, Walter, 25, 229, 410
Wurster, T. S., 73, 311, 312, 467
Wysocki, Bernard, Jr., 142, 157, 504

**X**

Xue, M., 311

**Y**

Yamada, Hiroshi, 81
Yamada, K., 312
Yancey, Ken, 224
Yang, C., 281, 504
Yeoh, P. L., 110
Yi Jiang, 20
Ying Yeh, 246
Yosano, Kaora, 271
Young, Beth, 334
Young, Mike N., 345, 346, 351, 392
Young, Steve, 418

**Z**

Zaccaro, S. J., 157
Zacharakis, A. L., 505
Zaheer, A., 312
Zahra, S. A., 72, 272
Zardkoohi, A., 235
Zelleke, A., 351
Zellner, Wendy, 88, 349
Zeng, Ming, 291, 292, 312
Zesiger, S., 194
Zhang, Victor, 250
Zimmerman, A., 350
Zrike, Stephen, 185
Zwolinski, Steve, 373

# Subject Index

## a

Accounting scandals, 19–20, 54, 327, 400–402
  and corporate governance, 341
Achievable opportunities, 481
Acid-test ratio, 115
Action plans, 326–327
  Aircraft Interior Products, 328–329
Actions, 10
Adaptability, 383–384
Adaptation, 386
Adaptive new entry, 496–498
Administrative costs, 210
Advertising-based business model,
  295, 297
Adware, 288
African Americans, 138–139
Agency theory, 226
  and conflicting goals, 333–334
  and risk sharing, 334
Agents, 333
*Age of Paradox* (Handy), 410
*Age of Unreason* (Handy), 376, 410
Aggregate demand
  in growth stage, 184
  in maturity stage, 185
Aging population, 51
Albany Local Development Corporation, 487
Albany Small Business Development Center, 487
Alignment, 384, 386
Alliances, 380; *see also* Strategic alliances
Ambidextrous organizations, 383–387
  adaptability, 383–384
  alignment, 384
  challenge of achieving, 384
  key design attributes, 385–386
  at *USA Today*, 387
*American Idol,* 205, 206
Americans with Disabilities Act, 52
Analysis, 9
Analysis-decision-action cycle,
  526–531
Angel investors, 484, 486
Annual reports, collections, 533
Antitakeover tactics, 230–231
Asian Americans, 138–139
Asset restructuring, 213
Asset surgery, 188
Asset utilization ratios, 516
  capital intensity ratio, 118
  days' sales in inventory, 117
  days' sales in receivables, 117–118
  inventory turnover, 117
  receivables turnover, 117–118
  total asset turnover, 118
Attractive opportunities, 481
Audio Home Recording Act, 276
Auditors
  and corporate governance, 341
  and Sarbanes-Oxley Act, 342
*Augustine's Law* (Augustine), 373
Automated manufacturing systems,
  177–178
Automobile industry, 7
  globalization, 56
  Internet sales, 293
  profit pool, 178
  strategic groups, 69–70
Autonomy, 454–456
Average collection period, 118
Aviation Consumer Action Project, 344

## b

Baby boomers, 51
Backsolver dilemma, 226
Backward integration, 207, 208
Balanced scorecard, 438
  customer perspective, 103
  financial perspective, 103–104
  functions, 102–103
  innovation perspective, 103
  internal business perspective, 103
Balance sheet, 111–112
Banks
  and corporate governance, 341–342
  new venture financing, 486
Bargaining power
  of buyers, 61–62
  of customers, 284–285
  of employees, 98
  of managers, 99
  of suppliers, 62
Barrier-free organizations
  external constituencies, 374–375
  permeable internal boundaries, 372–374
  risks, challenges, and downsides, 375
Barriers to change
  kinds of, 402
  overcoming, 402–403
Barriers to entry, 59–61, 172–173
  low in digital businesses, 282–283
  for new ventures, 493
Beachhead strategy, 264
Behavioral barriers to change, 402
Behavioral control
  boundaries and constraints, 326–329
  from boundaries to rewards, 329–330
  hiring policy, 330
  levers of, 322–323
  managerial role models, 330
  organizational culture, 323–324
  rewards and incentives, 324–326
  situational factors, 329, 330
  training, 330
Benchmarking, 171
  internal, 414
  types of, 416
Biotechnology, 380
*Blue Marlin,* 57
Blue ocean strategy, 444–446
*Blue Ocean Strategy* (Kim & Mauborgne), 444
Board of directors, 512
  access to employees, 336
  and corporate governance, 18–20, 335–337
  formal evaluation of officers, 337
  independence of, 336
  makeup of, 336
Book publishing industry, 284–285
Book value, 126
Bootstrapping, 483
Boston Consulting Group, 214–216
Bottom-up empowerment, 412
Boundaries, 326–329
  evolving rewards from, 329–330
Boundaryless organizational design, 371–383
  barrier-free organizations, 372–375
  communications, 383
  effectiveness, 381–383
  at General Electric, 373
  horizontal structure, 383
  horizontal systems and processes, 383
  human resource practices, 383

information technology, 383
  modular organization, 375–376
  shared culture and values, 382
  virtual organization, 376–381
Boundary types, 371
Brainstorming, 373
Brand identification dilution, 174
Bribery, 259
British Equestrian Trade Association, 474–476
Broadband, 281
*Built to Last* (Collins & Porras), 323
Bureau of Labor Statistics, 51
*Business 2.0,* 283
*Business Ethics,* 460
Business format franchise, 496
Business groups, 346
Business incubators, 448
Business-level strategy, 160–192
  combination strategy, 177–182
  competitive advantage and sustainability,
    163–182
  differentiation strategy, 169–174
  experience curve, 166
  focus strategy, 175–177
  formulating, 16, 528
  industry life-cycle stages, 182–189
  Internet capabilities, 307
  leveraging human capital for, 150
  overall cost leadership, 164–169
  reward and evaluation systems
    differentiation, 369
    overall cost leadership, 368–369
  at Sharper Image, 162
  turnaround strategies, 188–189
Business metasites and portals, 535
Business models for digital businesses,
  294–298
Business plan framework, 514
Business practices, copying, 461
Business risk taking, 462
Business services, 448
Business Software Alliance, 250
Business-to-business e-commerce, 285
Business-to-consumer e-commerce, 284
*BusinessWeek,* 7, 8, 45, 76, 102, 181, 200, 250,
  342, 390, 396, 415
Buyer channel intermediaries, 284
Buyer power, 173
Buyers, bargaining power, 61–62, 284–285

## c

Capabilities vs. collaborating, 439
Capacity augmentation, 64
Capital intensity ratio, 118
Capitalism, 239–240
Capital requirements, 60
Capital restructuring, 213
Case analysis
  analysis-decision-action cycle, 526–531
  avoiding groupthink, 522–524
  conducting, 511–518
    alternative solutions, 517
    business plan framework, 514
    familiarity with material, 513–514
    identifying problems, 514–515
    making recommendations, 517–518
    participation rate, 512–513
    strategic analysis, 515–517
  getting results from, 518–521
  reasons for, 510–511

Case analysis (*Continued*)
skills for, 510–511
sources of information for, 531–537
teams, 523–524
using conflict-inducing techniques, 521–526
Cash coverage ratio, 116–117
Cash cows, 214
Cash ratio, 115
Causal ambiguity, 96
*Celebrate Your Mistakes* (Holt), 417
Center for Auto Safety, 344
Center for Study of Responsive Law, 344
*Chaebols*, 346
*Chicago Sun-Times,* 436
Child labor, 248
China
emerging middle class, 246
population, 245
product piracy, 250
Co-creation process, 279, 280
Codes of conduct, 424–425
Coercive power, 403
Collective learning, 202–203
College Bound Network, 500
Combination strategies, 163–164, 177–182
automated/flexible manufacturing, 177–178
characteristics, 177
in e-commerce, 305–307
by entrepreneurial firms, 500–502
example, 180
and five-forces model, 179–181
and information technology, 179
pitfalls, 181–182
profit pool concept, 178–179
Commercial Alert, 344
Commission-based business model, 294–295, 297
Commitment, irrational escalation of, 228
Common-size balance sheet, 111–112, 113
Common-size income statement, 112, 113
Communications, 383
Company disclosure reports, 533–534
Company rankings, 534
Compensation plans, 338–339
*Competing for the Future* (Hamel & Prahalad), 42
*Competing on the Edge* (Brown & Eisenhardt), 441
Competition/Competitiveness
in automobile industry, 70
and core competencies, 203
digital business strategies
differentiation, 299–301
focus, 301–304
overall cost leadership, 298–299
and focus strategy, 176
information sources, 535–536
national, 240–243
Competitive advantage
codifying knowledge for, 148
combination strategies, 177–182
from core competencies, 203
creating, 10
differentiation strategies, 169–172
digital businesses
customer feedback, 293–294
entertainment, 294
evaluation activities, 291–292
expertise, 294
problem-solving, 292
search activities, 291
transaction activities, 292
from effective leadership, 397
focus strategy, 175–177
in global markets, 254–263
and innovation, 189–191
in organizational culture, 323
overall cost leadership, 164–169

from pace of innovation, 441
from proactiveness, 458–459
profit pool concept, 178–179
resource-based view, 90–99
sustainability, 163–182, 304–307
from technological innovation, 480–481
types of strategy, 163
value-chain analysis, 77–90
from workforce diversity, 139–140
*Competitive Advantage* (Porter), 77
Competitive aggressiveness, 459–462
Competitive benchmarking, 416
Competitive disruption, 277–282
Competitive environment, 322
five-forces model, 58–66
Competitive intelligence, 45–47, 532
Competitors
alliances with, 488–489
intensity of rivalry, 64–65
Complements, 65–66
Compliance-based ethics, 421–423
Computer-aided design, 300
Computer-aided design/manufacture, 177
Conflict-inducing decision-making techniques, 521–526
Conglomerate, 362
Consolidation, 187
Constraints, 326–329
Consumer price index, 56
Consumer Product Safety Commission, 250
*Consumer Reports,* 174, 284
Consumer spending, 53
Contemporary strategic control, 320–322
Continuous improvement, 456–458
Contracts, 210
Control systems, 85
Core activities, 66
Core assets, 66
Core competencies, 202–203
Corporate Citizenship poll, 23
Corporate credos, 424–425
*Corporate Cultures,* 323
Corporate entrepreneurship, 18, 443–453
blue ocean strategy, 444–446
dispersed approaches, 448–451
entrepreneurial culture, 449
product champions, 449–451
factors influencing, 444
focused approaches
business incubators, 448
new venture groups, 446–447
fostering, 530
measuring success
exit champions, 452–453
real options analysis, 453
strategic vs. financial goals, 451–452
social responsibility, 460
Corporate governance, 17, 330–346
costs of reform, 343
crony capitalism, 334
definition, 318, 331
flawed, 331–332
Hong Kong, 346
and investment decisions, 331
mechanisms
external mechanisms, 340–343
internal control, 335–339
nature of modern corporation, 333–334
research evidence, 332
and stakeholder management, 5, 18–24
and stakeholders, 331n
Corporate lawyers, and Sarbanes-Oxley Act, 342
Corporate-level strategy, 197–232
achieving diversification, 217–224
Charles Schwab & Company, 198–199
corporate parenting, 211–214

economies of scope, 201–205
erosion of value creation, 228–229
financial synergies, 211–217
formulating, 16, 528
internal development, 223–224
Internet capabilities, 308
issues in, 197
joint ventures, 222–223
leveraging core competencies, 202–203
leveraging human capital for, 152
making diversification work, 199–201
market power, 205–211
mergers and acquisitions, 217–222
pooled negotiating power, 217
portfolio management, 214–216
real options analysis, 224–228
related diversification, 201–211
restructuring, 211–214
revenue enhancement, 201–205
reward and evaluation systems, 369–371
risk reduction, 216–217
sharing activities, 203–205
strategic alliances, 222–223
unrelated diversification, 211–217
vertical integration, 207–211
Corporate new venture creation, 444
Corporate parenting, 202, 211–214
Corporate social responsibility, 22–24, 400
costs of, 23–24
and social innovation, 23
Corporate venture capital, 447
Corporations; *see also* Firms; Organizations
agency theory, 333–334
in China, 344
and crony capitalism, 334
definitions, 333
in Japan and South Asia, 346
owner-manager separation, 333–334
patterns of growth, 355–356
risk sharing problem, 334
Cost advantage erosion, 176
Cost argument, 139
Cost disadvantage independent of scale, 60–61
Cost leadership; *see* Overall cost leadership
Cost parity, 171
Cost reduction/saving
from international expansion, 247
reason for international expansion, 254–256
from sharing activities, 204
Cost surgery, 188
Council on Economic Priorities Accreditation Agency, 248
Counterfeit products, 250
Country Risk Rating, 247–248
Creative change, 67, 68
Creative tension, 11
Creativity
enabling, 416–417
fostering, 456
Creativity argument, 139
Credit-card financing, 484
Critical-to-quality model, 133
Crony capitalism, 334
Cross-functional skills, 377
Cross-functional teams, 385
*Crossing the Chasm* (Moore), 458
Cultural differences, 249–252
and packaging, 259
personnel practices, 259
Culture of dissent, 417
Currency risk, 249
Current ratio, 115
Customer feedback, 293–294
Customer perspective, 103

Customers
  bargaining power, 284–285
  choice of substitutes, 287
  end users, 284
Customer service, 82–83
Cyberstorage, 287

DART building blocks, 279, 280
Days' sales in inventory, 117
Days' sales in receivables, 117–118
Debt-equity ratio, 116
Debt financing, 484, 486
Decision, 9
Decision making
  conflict-inducing techniques, 521–526
  devil's advocacy, 525
  dialectical inquiry, 525–526
  guidelines, 524
  operational, 359
  real options analysis, 225–226
  stakeholders in, 11
Decline stage strategies
  consolidation, 187
  exiting the market, 186–187
  harvesting, 186
  maintaining, 186
  remaining profitability pockets, 188–189
Dedication, 491–492
Deliberate strategies, 13
Demand conditions, 240, 242
Demographics, 49–51
Department of Defense, 187, 490
Department of Education, 52
Department of Homeland Security, 9
Development costs, 484–485
Devil's advocacy, 525
Devils' Dictionary (Bierce), 333
Dialectical inquiry, 525–526
Dialogue, access, risk assessment, transparency
  (DART), 279, 280
Diamond of national advantages, 244–245
Differentiation strategy, 163, 169–174
  and cost leadership, 164–165
  and cost parity, 171
  differing perceptions of, 174
  in digital businesses, 299–301
  by entrepreneurial firms, 499
  and five-forces model, 172–173
  forms of, 169–170
  integrated with cost leadership, 177–182
  lack of parity on, 169
  and mass customization, 300
  and multidomestic strategy, 258–260
  parity as basis of, 164–165
  potential pitfalls, 173–174, 301
  reward and evaluation systems, 369
  tactics, 170–172
  too much, 173–175
  value-characteristics, 170
Digital business strategy, 275–308
  adding value
    customer feedback, 293–294
    entertainment, 294
    evaluation activities, 291–292
    expertise, 294
    problem-solving activities, 292
    search activities, 291
    transaction activities, 292
  business models
    advertising-based, 295, 297
    commission-based, 294–295, 297
    fee-for-service-based, 296, 297
    markup-based, 295–296, 297
    production-based, 296–297
    referral-based, 296, 297
    subscription-based, 296, 297

combination strategies, 305–307
competitive advantage
  differentiation, 299–301
  focus, 301–304
  overall cost leadership, 298–299
competitive disruption, 277–282
and five-forces model
  buyer bargaining power, 284–285
  intensity of rivalry, 288–289
  supplier bargaining power, 285–286
  threat of new entrants, 282–283
  threat of substitutes, 286–288
  formulating, 16–17, 529
  leveraging human capital for, 152
  leveraging Internet capabilities, 307–308
  Napster's failure, 276
  strategic management in, 277–282
  sustainable advantages, 304–307
Direction-setting, 398–399
Disintermediation, 286
  to lower costs, 299
Dispersed corporate venturing, 448–451
Disruptive innovations, 190, 191
Distribution channels, 60
  Web-based businesses, 282
Diversification
  criteria for, 326
  excessive, 340
  initiatives, 199–201
  by internal development, 223–224
  by joint venture, 222–223
  and managerial motives, 228–229
  market power from, 205–211
  by merger and acquisition, 217–222
  real options analysis, 224–229
  related, 201–211, 355, 369
  and risk reduction, 216–217
  by strategic alliances, 222–223
  unrelated, 211–217, 362, 370
Divisional structure, 355, 357–362
  disadvantages, 360–361
  holding companies, 362
  strategic business units, 361
DNA experimentation, 27
Dogs, 214
Dot-com boom and bust, 306, 320
Dow Jones Industrial Average, 56
Drive, 491–492
Durable opportunities, 481

Early-stage financing, 483–484
Earnings before interest and taxes, 116–117
Economic indicators, 56
Economic risk, 248–249
Economies of scale, 60, 245
Economies of scope, 201–205
Economist, 296
Economy
  effect of terrorism, 9
  external environment, 56
  role of knowledge in, 124–127
EDGAR database, 533–534
Education of women, 52
Effectiveness-efficiency trade-offs, 11–12
Egotism, 229–230
Electronic Buyers News, 400
Electronic invoice system, 306
Electronic storage, 287
Electronic teams, 145–147
  challenges of, 146–147
  social capital from, 146
Elephants (large firms), 473–474
E-mail, 144–145
Embedded options, 225
Emergent strategies, 13
Emotional intelligence

empathy, 407
motivation, 407
potential drawbacks, 408–410
self-awareness, 405–406
self-regulation, 406–407
social skill, 407–408
Emotional Intelligence (Goleman), 405
Empathy, 407
Employee involvement, 28–29
Employees
  alumni programs, 143
  bargaining power, 98
  in barrier-free organizations, 372–374
  electronic teams, 145–147
  empowering, 411–412
  exit costs, 98–99
  feedback from, 414
  financial and nonfinancial rewards, 137–138
  as free agents, 322
  identifying with mission and values,
    135–136
  older workers, 51
  and Pied Piper effect, 142–143
  replacement cost, 98
  work environment, 136–137
Employee selection, 128–131
  attitudes and skills, 129–130
  by networking, 130–131
  recruiting approaches, 130–131
Employee turnover, 86
Empowerment, 411–412
End users, 284
Enforcement costs, 210
Entering new markets, 222
Entertainment programming, 294
Entrepreneur, 474, 483, 484
Entrepreneurial culture, 449
Entrepreneurial firms; see also New ventures
  compared to small business, 473
  competitive advantage, 480–481
  contribution to economy, 472–473
  strategic alliances, 488–489
  venture capital, 485
Entrepreneurial leadership, 489–493
  commitment to excellence, 492–493
  dedication and drive, 491–492
  vision, 490–491
Entrepreneurial opportunities, 479–481
  characteristics, 481
  feasibility analysis, 479
  formation, 479
  recognizing, 475–481
Entrepreneurial orientation
  autonomy, 454–456
  competitive aggressiveness, 459–462
  definition, 454
  innovativeness, 456–458
  proactiveness, 458–459
  risk taking, 462–463
Entrepreneurial resources
  government resources, 487–489
  human capital, 486
  new venture financing, 482–486
  social capital, 486–487
  strategic alliances, 488
Entrepreneurial strategies
  barriers to entry, 493
  combination strategies, 500–502
  entry
    adaptive entry, 496–498
    imitative entry, 495–496
    pioneering entry, 494–495
  generic
    differentiation, 499
    focus, 499–500
    overall cost leadership, 498–499

Entrepreneurial strategies (*Continued*)
industry analysis, 493–502
threat of retaliation, 494
Entrepreneurial ventures; *see also* New ventures
categories
elephants, 473–474
mice, 474
family business, 477
franchises, 477
gazelles, 471–476
home-based, 477
Entrepreneurship
Great Plains Airlines, 470–471
meaning of, 471
opportunities for, 469
Entry strategies
adaptive, 496–498
imitative, 495–496
pioneering, 494–495
Environmental change, responding to, 318–322
Environmental costs, 23–24
Environmental forecasting, 47–48
Environmentally friendly manufacturing, 80
Environmental monitoring, 44
Environmental Protection Agency, 418
Environmental scanning, 43–44
Equal Employment Opportunity Commission, 418
Equity financing, 484
Equity markets, 56
Equity multiplier, 116
Ethical behavior, 400–402
Ethical crises, 419
Ethical organization, 17
benefits, 419–421
characteristics, 419
codes of conduct, 423–425
corporate credos, 423–425
creating, 530
individual vs. organizational ethics, 417–421
integrity-based vs. compliance-based, 421–423
policies and procedures, 425–426
reward/evaluation system, 425
role models, 423
unethical examples, 420
whistleblowing, 426
Ethics
individual vs. organizational, 417–421
integrity-based vs. compliance-based, 421–423
minimizing improper conduct, 327–328
Ethics management, 422
Ethnic diversity, 138–139
*Euromoney,* 247
European Union, 56
Evaluation activities, 291–292
Evaluation systems
business-level strategies, 368–369
corporate-level strategies, 369–371
and ethics, 425
*Every Business Needs an Angel,* 484
Excellence
commitment to, 492–493
dedication to, 400–402
Excessive product market diversification, 340
Exit barriers, 64
Exit champions, 452–453
Exiting the market, 186–187
Experience vs. initiative, 438–439
Experience curve, 164, 166–167
Experimentation, 456
Expertise, 294
Expert power, 403–404
Exporting, 263–264
by small business, 473
Expropriation, 344–346
Extended value chain, 179, 181
External boundaries, 371

External constituencies, 374–375
External control, 8
External corporate governance mechanisms, 339–343
auditors, 341
bankers and stock analysts, 341–342
market for corporate control, 340–341
media, 342–343
public activists, 342–343
regulatory bodies, 342
External environment, 13
analyzing, 527
competitive, 57–70
general, 49–57
Interstate Bakeries Corporation, 42
scanning, monitoring, and forecasting, 43–49
threats from, 42–43
External information, 414–416
*ExxonValdez* oil spill, 419
Factor conditions, 240, 241–242
Factors of production, and cost leadership, 168–169
Failure, 417, 418
Family business, 477
Family Firm Institute, 477
*Fast Company,* 390, 415
Feasibility analysis, 479
Federal Reserve System, 56
Feedback from employees, 414
Feedback loop, 319
Feedback systems, 133–134
Fee-for-service-based business model, 296, 297
Financial analysis, 516
Financial costs, 23–24
Financial goals, 451–452
Financial/nonfinancial rewards, 137–138
Financial perspective, 103–104
Financial ratio analysis; *see also* Ratio analysis
common-size balance sheet, 111–112, 113
common-size income statement, 112, 113
historical comparisons, 100
industry norms, 101
key competitor comparisons, 101–102
standard financial statements, 111
types of ratios, 99–100
Financial risk taking, 462
Financial statements, 111–113
Financial strategy objectives, 34
Financial synergies, 202, 211–212
Financing, 482–486
bootstrapping, 483
by credit card, 484
debt vs. equity, 484
early-stage, 483–484
later-stage, 484–486
by suppliers, 484
venture capital, 484–486
Firms; *see also* Corporations; Organizations
book value, 126
employee retention mechanisms, 137–139
environmentally aware, 43–44
external control factors, 8
information sources on, 532–537
market value, 125–126
performance evaluation, 99–105
and Pied Piper effect, 142–143
strategy, structure, and rivalry, 240, 243
and war on terrorism, 9
First-mover advantage, 184
First movers, 458
Five-forces model of competition
bargaining power of buyers, 61–62
buying power of suppliers, 62–63
combination strategies, 179–181
and cost leadership, 167–168
criticisms of, 65–66
and differentiation, 172–173

and digital business strategy, 275, 282–290
and focus strategy, 175–176
intensity of rivalry, 64–65
threat of new entrants, 59–61
threat of substitutes, 63–64
use by entrepreneurs, 493
Fixed costs, 64
Flexible manufacturing, 177–178
Focused corporate venturing, 446–448
Focus strategy, 163, 175–177
characteristics, 175
in digital businesses, 301–304
by entrepreneurial firms, 499–500
and five-forces model, 175–176
potential pitfalls, 176–177, 303–304
Food and Drug Administration, 65, 165, 418
*Forbes,* 7, 239, 390, 415
Forecasting, 47–48
Foreign Corrupt Practices Act, 54, 259
*Fortune,* 7, 19, 45, 125, 138, 139, 148, 185, 283, 390, 401, 415
Forward integration, 207, 208
Franchises, 477
U.S. and foreign growth, 63
Franchising, 264–265, 496
*Free-Market Innovation Machine* (Baumol), 278
Functional benchmarking, 416
Functional structure, 355, 357, 385
disadvantages, 358–359
examples, 358
Funding, 448
*Future of Competition* (Prahalad & Ramaswamy), 279
Game theory, 65
Gazelles (rapid-growth firms), 474–476
General administration, 86–87
General Agreement on Tariffs and Trade, 56
General environment
demographic segment, 49–51
economic segment, 56
global segment, 56–57
impact of industries, 59
political/legal segment, 52–53
relationships within, 57
sociocultural segment, 52
technological segment, 53–55
Generic strategies for new ventures, 498–500
Geographical units, 362
Geographic area, 355
Geographic area division, 365
Geographic boundaries, 371
Geographic population shift, 51
German population, 245
Glass-Steagall act, 52
Global capitalism, 239–240
Global economy, 239–240
*Global Entrepreneurship Monitor* survey, 485
Globalization, 25–26, 44, 56–57, 356n
and empathy, 407
and New Economy, 239
Global start-ups, 365–366
Global strategy, 260
for global markets, 257–258
and organizational structure, 365
risks, 258
strengths and limitations, 262
Goals
hierarchy of, 29
organizational, 15
strategic vs. financial, 451–452
Golden parachutes, 231
*Good to Great* (Collins), 323, 493

Government
    and new ventures, 487–489
    online procurement, 285
    requests for proposal, 442
Government contracting, 487
Government work, 490
*Great Game of Business* (Stack), 412
Greenfield venture, 267
Greenmail, 231
Gross Domestic Product
    and family businesses, 477
    knowledge-based, 124–125
Groupthink, 143
    definition, 521
    symptoms and prevention, 522–524
Growth for growth's sake, 228–229
Growth stage strategies, 184

*Harvard Business Review,* 23, 127, 166, 405, 409
Harvesting, 186
Hierarchy of goals, 29
Hiring policy, 128–131, 330
Hispanic Americans, 138–139
Historical comparisons, 100
Holding company structure, 356, 362
Home-based business, 477
H-1B visa program, 53
Hong Kong, 346
Horizontal boundaries, 371
Horizontal organizational structure, 383
Horizontal relationships, 211
Horizontal systems and processes, 383
Hostile takeover, fighting, 230–231
Human capital, 486
    attracting, 128–131
    definition, 126
    developing, 131–135
    emigration of, 142–143
    evaluating, 133–135
    intellectual capital, 127–139
    leveraging, 144–152
    retaining, 135–138
        challenging work environment, 136–137
        identifying with mission and values, 135–136
        rewards and incentives, 137–138
    value creation from, 151
    workforce diversity, 138–140
*Human Equation* (Pfeffer), 373
Human resource management, 85–86
Human resource practices, 383
*Hypercompetition* (D'Aveni), 397

Illegal behavior, 420
Illusion of control, 226–228
Imitation, 299
Imitative new entry, 495–496
Improper conduct, 327–329
Inbound logistics, 79, 80
*Inc.,* 474, 497
Incentive programs
    characteristics, 325
    effective, 325–326
    for managers, 338–339
    potential downside, 324–325
    problems with, 400
Incentives, 137–138
Income statement, 112
Incremental innovation, 437
Incremental launch, 439
Incubators, 448, 485–486
Independent action, 455
Independent business incubators, 485–486
India
    population, 245
    software industry, 244–245

Individual ethics, 417–421
Industry
    fragmented, 500
    mature, 500
Industry analysis
    assumptions, 68
    components, 66–68
    core activities, 66
    core assets of firm, 66
    creative change, 67, 68
    by entrepreneurs, 493
    five-forces model of competition, 58–66
    impact of Internet, 290
    information sources, 536–537
    intermediating change, 67, 68
    progressive change, 67, 68
    and radical change, 66–67, 68
    strategic groups, 68–70
    SWOT analysis, 49
    use of, 65–66
Industry consolidation, 207, 219–220
Industry life cycle stages, 182–191
    and competitive advantage, 109
    decline stage strategies, 186–187
    definition, 182
    growth stage strategies, 184
    importance of, 182
    and innovation, 189–190, 191
    introduction stage strategies, 184
    and late mover advantage, 184, 185
    limitations, 182–183
    maturity stage strategies, 185–186
    personal computer industry, 187–188
    turnaround strategies, 188–189
Industry norms, 101
Inexperience, 30
Infomediary services, 289
Information, external, 414–416
Informational control, 318–322
    contemporary approach, 320–322
    environmental change, 320–321
    feedback loop, 319
    and organizational learning, 321
    traditional approach, 319–320
Information power, 403
Information redistribution, 412–414
Information sharing, 144–145, 414–416
Information systems, 87
Information technology, 54
    in boundaryless organizations, 383
    federal spending, 490
    revolution, 278–279
    and value chain, 179, 181
*InformationWeek,* 189
Inimitability of resources, 95–96
Innovation, 26; *see also* Corporate
        entrepreneurship; New ventures
    challenges of, 438–439
    competitive advantage by, 189–191
    defining scope of, 439–440
    definition, 436
    differentiation by, 171
    dilemmas, 439–440
    disruptive, 190, 191
    in management, 10
    managing, 435–443
    in marketing, 436
    at Microsoft, 440
    open, 443
    pace of, 441
    partners in, 441–442
    Polaroid case, 434–435
    sustaining, 190
    types of, 436–438
*Innovation and Entrepreneurship* (Drucker), 463
Innovation perspective, 103

Innovativeness, 456–458
*Innovator's Dilemma* (Christensen), 480
INPUT, 285
*In Search of Excellence* (Peters & Waterman), 323
*Inside Consulting* (Rodenhauser), 455
Institutional investors, 337–338
Intangible resources, 91, 92
Integrity-based ethics, 421–423
Intellectual assets, 15–16
Intellectual capital, 26–27, 127–139
    analyzing, 528
    components, 125
    global market for, 28
    and value of the firm, 126
Intellectual property, 443
Intended strategy, 13
Interactive control system, 322
Interest rate cuts, 56
Intermediating change, 67, 68
Internal benchmarking, 414
Internal business perspective, 103
Internal corporate governance mechanisms
    board of directors, 335–337
    managerial rewards and incentives, 338–339
    shareholder activism, 337–338
Internal development, 223–224
Internal environment, 13
    analyzing, 527
    Ford Motor Company, 76
    performance evaluation of firm, 99–106
    resource-based view, 90–99
    value-chain analysis, 77–90
Internal information, 412–414
Internal Revenue Service, 476
International divisions, 355, 365
International expansion
    and child labor, 248
    cost reduction goal, 254–256
    entry modes
        exporting, 263–264
        joint ventures, 265–267
        licensing or franchising, 264–265
        strategic alliances, 265–267
        wholly owned subsidiaries, 267–269
    global strategy for, 257–258
    international strategy, 256–257
    local adaptation, 254–256
    motivations, 243–247
    multidomestic strategy for, 258–260
    potential risks, 247–252
        currency risk, 249
        management, 249–252
        political and economic, 248–249
    transnational strategy, 260–263
International Labor Organization, 248
International-level strategy
    formulating, 528–529
    Internet capabilities, 308
International operations, 363–365
International strategy, 237–269
    achieving competitive advantage, 254–263
    entry modes of expansion, 263–269
    formulating, 16
    global dispersion of value chains, 252–254
    global economy, 239–240
    for global markets, 256–257
    leveraging human capital for, 152
    motivation for expansion, 243–247
    national competitiveness, 240–243
    and piracy, 250
    risks of expansion, 247–252
    by Volkswagen, 238–239
Internet, 26, 54; *see also* Digital business strategy
    automobile sales, 293
    and effective strategic management, 279–282
    influence on industry structure, 290

Internet (*Continued*)
  information from, 415
  new business climate, 279, 280
  worldwide users, 281
Internet-based retailers, 82
Internet capabilities
  and business-level strategy, 307
  and corporate-level strategy, 308
  and international-level strategy, 308
Internet sales activity, 284–286
Internet start-ups, 485
Internet strategies, 529
Intrapreneuring, 444
Introduction stage strategies, 184
Inventory turnover, 117
Investment, transaction-specific, 210
*Investors Business Daily,* 342
IQ, 405
Iraq War, 9

Joint ventures, 222–223,
  265–267
Just-in-time systems,
  65, 80

*Keiretsu,* 346
Key competitor comparisons, 101–102
Knowledge
  codifying, 148
  creating and applying, 27
  forms of, 127
  internal, 412–414
  leveraging, 144–152
  minimizing loss of, 148–150
  in today's economy, 124–127
Knowledge economy, 125–126
Knowledge management systems, 149–150
Knowledge transfers, 132–133, 141
Knowledge workers, 127
  Pied Piper effect, 142–143
  and social capital, 140–144

Large firms, 473–474
Late-mover advantage, 184, 185
Later-stage financing, 484–486
Launch, incremental vs. preemptive, 439
Leadership evaluation
  Session C approach, 135
  360-degree assessment, 133–134
Learning organization, 17, 410–417
  accumulating and sharing knowledge, 412–414
  challenging status quo, 416–417
  creating, 530
  critical requirement, 411
  empowering employees, 411–412, 413
  enabling creativity, 416–417
  gathering/integrating external information,
    414–416
  mentoring, 415
  successful, 411
Learning perspective, 103
Legal services, 87
Legislation, 52–53
Legitimate power, 403
Leverage ratios, 116–117
Leveraging core competencies, 202–203
Leveraging human capital
  business-level strategy, 150
  codifying knowledge, 148
  corporate-level strategy, 152
  electronic teams, 145–147
  international-level strategy, 152
  Internet strategies, 152
  by networks, 144–145
  retaining employee knowledge, 148–150

Licensing, 264–265, 488–489
Liquidity measures, 114–115
  cash ratio, 115
  current ratio, 115
  quick (acid-test) ratio, 115
Liquidity ratios, 516
Local adaptation, 254–256, 259–260
Logistics, 204
Long-term perspective, 11
Long-term solvency measures
  cash coverage ratio, 116–117
  times interest earned, 116
  total debt ratio, 116
Low-cost leader, potential pitfalls, 299

Maintaining, 186
*Making the Grass Greener on Your Side*
  (Melrose), 411
Malcolm Baldrige National Quality Award, 223,
  224
Management
  innovation in, 10
  restructuring, 213
Management risk, 249–252
Manager bargaining power, 99
Managerial conceit
  antitakeover tactics, 230–231
  egotism, 229–230
  growth for growth's sake, 228–229
  illusion of control, 226–228
  irrational escalation of commitment, 228
Managerial rewards and incentives, 338–339
Managerial role models, 330
Managers
  credibility and ego, 220–221
  opportunistic behavior, 99
  and Sarbanes-Oxley Act, 342
  in virtual organizations, 380
Managing innovation, 434–435
  at Polaroid, 435–443
Manufacturing
  alliances, 488
  cost reductions, 333
*Maquiladoras,* 57, 247
Market capitalism, 239–240
Market for corporate control, 340–341
Marketing and sales, 79, 81–82
Marketing argument, 139
Marketing to the poor, 241
Market potential, 479–481
Market power, 205–211
  pooled negotiating power, 207
  vertical integration, 207–211
Market pruning, 188
Market research, 287–288
Market share, 185–186
Market-to-book ratio, 120
Market value, 125–126
Market value measures
  market-to-book ratio, 119–120
  price-earnings ratio, 119–120
Market value ratios, 516
Markup-based business model, 295–296, 297
Mass customization, 300
Matrix structure, 362–363
Maturity stage strategies, 185–186
Media, and corporate governance, 342–343
Mentoring, 448
Mergers and acquisitions, 217–222
  leading to consolidation, 219–220
  motives and benefits, 218–220
  to obtain resources, 219
  potential limitations, 220–222
  recent, 217–218
  synergy from, 219

Mice (small firms), 474
Microlending, 241
Mission statement, 32–33, 328
Modular organization, 376–377, 378
Monitoring, 210
Motivation, 407
Multidivisional structure, 359
Multidomestic strategy, 258–260
Multimedia industry, 207
Multinational corporations, 245, 257, 264

Nanotechnology, 54–55
National Association of Home-Based
  Businesses, 477
National Association of Manufacturers, 51
National Association of Purchasing Managers, 54
National competitiveness
  demand conditions, 240, 242
  disparities, 240
  factor conditions, 240, 241–242
  firm strategy, structure, and rivalry, 240, 243
  related and supporting industries, 240, 242–243
National Federation of Independent Business, 488
National Foundation Quarter Horse Association,
  475
National Science Foundation, 490
Negotiating costs, 210
Networking, 130–131, 415, 448
Networks, 144–145
New Economy, 239
New entrants, threat of, 59–61, 282–283
New product introduction, 459
New venture groups, 446–447
New ventures, 18; *see also* Entrepreneur *entries*
  barriers to entry, 493
  categories of, 471–476
  characteristics of opportunities, 481
  creating, 444, 530
  development costs, 484–485
  financing
    bootstrapping, 483
    by credit card, 484
    debt vs. equity, 484
    early stage, 483–484
    later-stage, 484–486
    by suppliers, 484
    venture capital, 484–486
  Great Plains Airlines, 470–471
  leadership qualities, 489–493
  market potential, 479–481
  from new technology, 479
  opportunity analysis framework, 482
  opportunity formation, 479
  opportunity recognition process, 476–481
  and small business, 471–476
  strategic challenges, 469
  strategies for, 493–502
  vulnerability, 482
New York Farm Bureau, 718
*New York Times,* 296, 404, 568
Niche businesses, 301
Niche strategy, 499
No-frills products and services, 166–167
Nonfinancial strategy objectives, 34
Nonprofit sector, boundaries in, 326
North American Free Trade Agreement, 56

Objectives
  in action plans, 328
  criteria for, 34
  short-term, 326–327
  strategic, 33–35
Obsolescence, threat of, 66
Offshoring, 252–254
Older workers, 51

Online music business
    competitive rivalry, 289
    Napster case, 276–277
Online procurement systems, 285
On-the-job consumption, 340
Open innovation, 443
*Open Innovation* (Chesbrough), 480
Operating costs, 246
Operational decision making, 359
Operational effectiveness, 10
Operational efficiency, 327
Operations, 79, 80
Opportunity analysis framework, 482
Opportunity discovery, 478
Opportunity formation, 479
Opportunity recognition process, 475–481
Organizational capabilities, 91, 93–94
Organizational culture
    changing, 28–29
    definition, 323
    nurturing, 400–402
    rewards and incentives, 324–326
    role of, 323
    sustaining, 323–324
Organizational design, 17
    for adaptation and alignment, 386
    ambidextrous organizations, 385–386
    boundaryless, 371–383
    creating, 529–530
    from independent action, 455
    and strategic management, 399–400
*Organizational Dynamics,* 137, 411
Organizational ethics, 417–421
Organizational goals, 10, 13, 527
Organizational learning, 321
Organizational structure
    and business-level strategy, 368–369
    and corporate-level strategy, 369–371
    definition, 355
    global start-ups, 365–366, 367
    influence on strategy formulation, 366
    National Health Service (UK), 354
    traditional forms
        divisional structure, 359–362
        functional structure, 357–359
        growth of large corporations, 355–356
        holding company, 362
        international operations, 363–365
        matrix structure, 362–363
        simple structure, 357
        strategic business units, 361
Organizational vision, 29–32
Organizations; *see also* Corporations; Firms
    ambidextrous, 383–387
    bases of power in, 403–404
    boundaries and constraints, 326–329
    boundary types, 371
    conflict in, 324–325
    global start-ups, 365–366
    mission and values, 135–136
    rule-based controls, 327
    subcultures, 324
Outbound logistics, 79, 80–81
Outside consultants, 512
Outsourcing, 252–254
    advantages, 376
    strategic risks, 377
    for talent, 378
Overall cost leadership, 163, 164–169
    at Buy.com, 302
    and differentiation, 164–165
    in digital businesses, 298–299
    by entrepreneurial firms, 498–499
    examples, 165–168
    experience curve, 153, 166–167
    and five-forces model, 167–168

integrated with differentiation, 177–182
    pitfalls, 168–169
    reward and evaluation systems, 368–369
    tactics, 164
    value-chain activities, 164–165

Packaging, 259
Parenting advantage, 212–213
Parity on basis of differentiation, 164–165
Patents by small business, 473
Path dependency, 96
Pay-for-performance, 339
Peer control, 373
Pension Rights Center, 344
Performance enhancement, 247
Performance evaluation
    balanced scorecard, 102–104
    feedback systems, 133–134
    financial ratio analysis, 111–120, 199–202
    historical comparisons, 100
    industry norms, 101
    key competitor comparisons, 101–102
    strategy maps, 104–105
    360-degree assessment, 133–134
Performance materials, 85
Personal computer, 278
Personal computer industry, 187–188
Personal digital assistants, 303–304, 459
Personal risk taking, 462
Personal time constraints, 403
Physical space, 448
Physical uniqueness, 95
Pied Piper effect, 142–143
Pioneering new entry, 494–495
Piracy, 250
Poison pill, 230, 231
Political barriers to change, 402
Political process, 52–53
Political risk, 248–249
Pooled negotiating power, 205, 207
Population
    diversity in, 138–140
    selected nations, 245
    trends, 49–51, 57
Portfolio management, 214–216
Power, bases of, 403–404
Preemptive launch, 439
Price competition, 64
Price-earnings ratio, 119–120
Price premium, 174
Prices, drastically lower, 461
Primary activities; *see* Value-chain analysis
Principal-agent conflicts, 344–346
Principal-principal conflicts, 343–346
Principals, 333
Proactiveness, 458–459
Problem identification, 514–515
Problem solving, 524
Problem-solving activities, 292
Problem-solving argument, 139
Processes for innovation, 190
Process innovation, 438
Procurement, 86–87
Product champions, 449–451
Product differentiation, 60
Product-function matrix, 362
Product innovation, 437–438
Production-based business model, 296, 297
Productivity improvements, 188
Product life cycle, 246
Product pruning, 188
Professional service firms, 374
Profitability measures
    profit margin, 118–119
    return on assets, 119
    return on equity, 119

Profitability ratios, 516
Profit generation and distribution, 98–99
Profit margin, 118–119
Profit maximization, 33
Profit pool concept, 178–179, 181–182
Progressive change, 67, 68
Project champions, 449–451
Project definition, 450
Project impetus, 450
Public activists, 342–343, 344
Public Citizen, 344

Question marks,
    214
Quick ratio, 115

Radical change, 66–67, 68
Radical innovation, 437, 441
Rapid-growth firms, 474–476
Ratio analysis, 112–120
    asset utilization ratios, 117–118
    liquidity measures, 114–115
    long-term solvency measures, 116–117
    market value measures, 119–120
    profitability measures, 118–119
    summary on, 120, 516
*Reader's Digest,* 478
Realized strategy, 13
Real options analysis, 224–228
    agency theory and, 226
    application to strategic management,
        225–226, 227
    backsolver problem, 226
    corporate entrepreneurship, 453
    pitfalls, 226–228
        illusion of control, 226–228
        irrational escalation of commitment, 228
        managerial conceit, 226–228
Receivables turnover, 117–118
Record Industry Association of America, 276
Recruiting, 130–131
*Reengineering the Corporation* (Hammer &
    Champy), 383
Referent power, 403
Referral-bases business model, 296, 297
Regulatory bodies and corporate governance, 342
*Re-Imagine* (Peters), 53
Reintermediation, 286
Related and supporting industries, 240, 242–243
Related diversification, 355, 369
    economies of scope, 201–205
    market power, 205–211
    revenue enhancement, 201–205
Rents, 98n
Requests for proposal, 442
Research and development, 443
    costs, 246
    investing in, 456–458
    by small business, 490
Resource acquisition argument, 139
Resource-based view, 90–99
    profit generation/distribution, 98–99
    sustainable competitive advantage,
        94–97
    types of resources, 91–94
Resources
    causal ambiguity, 96
    easily imitated, 95
    for innovation, 190
    intangible, 91, 92
    path dependency, 96
    physical uniqueness, 95
    rare, 95
    social complexity, 96
    substitutes for, 97

Resources (*Continued*)
    tangible, 91, 92
    valuable, 95
Restructuring, 202, 213
Retail alliances, 488
Retention mechanisms, 137–138
    and Pied Piper effect, 142–143
Return on assets, 119
Return on book assets, 119
Return on book equity, 119
Return on equity, 119
Return on investment, 451
Return on net worth, 119
Revenue, in growth stage, 184
Revenue enhancement, 201–205
Reward and compensation agreements, 338–339
Reward power, 403
Reward systems
    business-level strategies, 368–369
    characteristics, 325
    corporate-level strategies, 369–371
    effective, 325–326
    and ethics, 425
    evolving from boundaries to, 329–330
    for managers, 338–339
    potential downside, 324–325
Risk factors, 463
Risk reduction, 216–217, 247
Risks
    in global strategy, 258
    in international expansion, 247–252
        currency risk, 249
        management, 249–252
        political and economic risk, 248–249
    in international strategy, 257
    in multidomestic strategy, 259–260
    in transnational strategy, 261–262
Risk taking, 417, 462–463
Rivalry
    in developed nations, 243
    intensity of, 64–65, 288–289
Role models, 423
Rule-based controls, 327

Sales, in growth stage, 184
Sarbanes-Oxley Act, 52–53, 54, 327, 334, 342, 343, 426
SA 8000 standard, 248
Scenario analysis/planning, 47–48
Search activities, 291
Search costs, 210
Search engines, 537
Securities and Exchange Commission, 54, 342
    filings, 533–534
Seeds vs. weeds, 438
Self-awareness, 405–406
Self-regulation, 406–407
Separation of owners and managers, 333–334
Service, 79, 82–83
Service organizations, value-chain analysis for, 88–90
Session C leadership evaluation, 135
Shareholder activism, 337–338
Sharing activities, 203–205
Shifting roles, 44
Shipping industry, 56–57
Shirking, 340
Shopping robots, 289
Short-term objectives, 326–327
Short-term perspective, 11
Short-term solvency measures; *see* Liquidity measures
Silos, 358–359
Simple structure, 355–357

Six Sigma quality control, 441
Skunkworks, 455, 456
Small business, 469
    compared to entrepreneurial firms, 473
    contribution to economy, 472–473
    exporters, 473
    government assistance to, 487–489
    government work, 490
    job creation, 472
    and new ventures, 471–476
    number of employees, 472–473
    patents from, 473
    strategic alliances, 488–489
Small Business Administration, 476, 487, 490
Small Business Development Centers, 487
Small Business Innovation Research, 490
Small firms, 474
Social capital, 140–144
    to attract and retain talent, 142–143
    from electronic teams, 146
    for new ventures, 486–487
    potential downside, 143–144
    value creation from, 151
Social complexity, 96
Social costs, 23–24
Social innovation, 23
Socially complex processes, 127
Social responsibility, 22–24, 460
    and workplace diversity, 139
Social skills, 129, 407–408
Software industry, India, 244–245
SOHO (small office/home office), 47
Southwest Minnesota Initiative Fund, 487
Spyware, 288
Staffing, internal vs. external, 439
Stakeholder management, 5
    and corporate governance, 18–26
    zero-sum or symbiosis, 21
Stakeholders, 99, 398
    and balanced scorecard, 104
    in decision making, 11
    definition, 21
    demand for corporate responsibility, 21
Stakeholder symbiosis, 21
Stakeholder value, 21
Standard financial statements, 111
Standard & Poor's 500 Index, 338
Stars, 214
Start-ups
    categories of, 471–476
    financing for, 482–486
    global, 365–366
    Internet, 485
    in mature industries, 500
    source of opportunities, 476
    from venture capital, 447
Status quo
    challenging, 416–417
    vested interest in, 402
Stock analysts, 341–342
Stock options, 224, 338–339
Storage costs, 64
Storytelling, 324
Stove pipes, 358–359
Strategic alliances, 222–223, 265–267
    drawbacks, 488–489
    kinds of, 488–489
Strategic analysis, 515–517
    information sources, 535–536
Strategic business units, 216, 356
    categories, 214
Strategic control, 17, 317–330
    achieving, 529
    behavioral control, 322–330
        boundaries and constraints, 326–329

        evolving from boundaries to rewards, 329–330
        organizational culture, 323–324
        rewards and incentives, 324–326
        situational factors, 329
    contemporary, 320–322
    informational control, 318–322
    interactive system, 322
    Lantech, 318
    role of corporate governance
        external mechanisms, 339–343
        internal mechanisms, 335–339
        international perspective, 343–346
        modern corporation, 333–334
    rule-based controls, 327
    traditional, 319–320
Strategic decision making, 512
Strategic direction, coherence, 29
Strategic envelope, 439, 441
Strategic goals, 451–452
Strategic implementation, 17–18
Strategic industry groups, 68–70
Strategic leadership; *see also* Entrepreneurial leadership
    bases of power, 403–404
    challenges facing, 6–8
    at Container Store, 401
    creating ethical organizations
        codes of conduct, 423–425
        individual vs. organizational ethics, 417–421
        integrity-based vs. compliance-based ethics, 421–423
        policies and procedures, 425–426
        reward and evaluation systems, 425
        role models, 423
        unethical examples, 420
        whistleblowing, 426
    definition, 397
    developing learning organizations
        accumulating and sharing knowledge, 412–414
        changing status quo, 416–417
        empowering employees, 411–412, 413
        enabling creativity, 416–417
        external information, 416–417
        mentoring, 415
    different altitudes, 12
    effective, 87
    emotional intelligence
        empathy, 407
        motivation, 407
        potential drawbacks, 408–410
        self-awareness, 405–406
        self-regulation, 406–407
        social skill, 407–408
    external control perspective, 8
    from failure to success, 418
    interdependent activities, 397–402
        designing the organization, 399–400
        effective use of power, 402–404
        nurturing culture, 400–402
        overcoming barriers to change, 402–404
        setting direction, 398
    at Krispy Kreme, 396
    at Marshall Industries, 400
    at Starbucks, 399
    successes and failures, 6–7
    three types of, 28
    traits, 405
Strategic management, 8–12
    case analysis for, 510–511
    Coca-Cola Company problems, 6–7
    defining, 9–10
    and digital economy, 277–282
    key attributes, 5, 10–12

ongoing process, 8
real options analysis, 225–226
Strategic management perspective
coherence in direction, 29
driving forces, 25–27
globalization, 25–26
intellectual capital, 26–27
technology, 26
employee involvement, 27–29
mission objectives, 32–33
organizational vision, 29–32
strategic objectives, 32–33
Strategic management process, 12–18
strategic implementation, 17–18
strategy analysis, 13–16
strategy formulation, 16–17
Strategic objectives, 33–35
Strategic partnering, 441–442
Strategic positioning, 500
Strategic priorities, 326
Strategic uncertainties, 321
Strategy analysis, 13–16
Strategy formulation, 16–17
business-level, 150
corporate-level, 152
influence of organizational structure, 366–367
international level, 152
Internet strategies, 152
Strategy maps, 104–105
Strategy/Strategies, 10
deliberate, 13
emergent, 13
entrepreneurial, 493–502
intended, 13
realized, 13
and value of inexperience, 30
*Structure of Corporation Law* (Eisenberg), 333
Subscription-based business model, 296, 297
Substitutes
customer choice, 287
products or services, 63–64
for resources, 97
threat of, 286–288
Supplier power, 173
Suppliers
bargaining power, 62, 285–286
enhancing power of, 63
power from outsourcing, 377
Support activities; *see* Value-chain analysis
Sustainable competitive advantage, 10
in digital businesses, 304–307
and firm's resources, 94–98
Sustainable global economy, 23–24
Sustaining innovations, 190
Switching costs, 60, 64, 284, 289
SWOT analysis, 49, 461
limitations of, 76–77, 78
Synergy, 212
from core competencies, 203
definition, 201
from market power, 205–211
from sharing activities, 203–205
System flexibility argument, 139
Systemic barriers to change, 402

Takeover constraint, 340–341
Takeover premium, 220
Talent
global market for, 28
war for, 131
Tangible resources, 91, 92
Teams, 373
for case analysis, 523–524
cross-functional, 385
unsupported, 385
Technological change, 26

Technological innovation, 278, 282
and competitive advantage, 480–481
new ventures from, 479
Technology, 26
for codifying knowledge, 148
developing and diffusing, 222–223
development of, 84–85
drawbacks, 55
to enhance collaboration, 145–147
in external environment, 53–55
for information sharing, 144–145
new, 456–458
value creation from, 151
Technology alliances, 488
Teleconferencing, 63–64
Terrorist attack of 2001, 8, 9, 22
Test marketing, 287–288, 479
*Theory Z,* 323
360-degree leadership assessment, 133–134
Times interest earned ratio, 116
Time to market, 44
Top-down empowerment, 411–412
Tort reform, 52
Total asset turnover ratio, 118
Total debt ratio, 116
Traditional strategic control, 319–320
Training, 330
Training and development programs, 131–135
evaluation, 133–135
monitoring, 133
Transaction activities, 292–293
Transaction cost perspective, 210
Transaction costs, 298–299, 356n
Transaction-specific investments, 210
Transformational change, 29
Transnational strategy, 152, 260–263
Turnaround strategies, 188–189
Turnover measures, 117–118

Uncertainty, minimizing, 463
UNESCO, 27
Unethical conduct, 327–329, 420
Uniqueness, 173
United States
number of franchise businesses, 477
number of home-based businesses, 477
number of small businesses, 472
population, 245
United Steel Workers, 62–63
*Unleashing the Killer App* (Downes & Mui), 286
Unrelated diversification, 202, 362, 370
Unsupported teams, 385
Upscale market, 171
USS *Cole,* 56–57
Utah Microenterprise Loan Fund, 487

Value added by digital technologies
customer feedback, 293–294
entertainment programming, 294
evaluation technologies, 291–292
expertise, 294
problem-solving, 292
search activities, 291
transaction activities, 292
Value chain
cost savings, 299
extended, 179, 181
global, 252–254
integration, 171
optimizing location of, 246–247
Value-chain analysis, 77–90
applied to services, 88–90
centralizing vs. decentralizing, 261
and cost leadership, 164, 165

cost reductions, 333
focus on one or two activities, 168
harvesting strategy, 186
interrelationships among activities, 87–88
primary activities, 79–83
inbound logistics, 80
marketing and sales, 81–82
operations, 80
outbound logistics, 80–81
service, 82–83
support activities, 83–86
general administration, 86–87
human resource management, 85–86
procurement, 83–84
technological development, 84–85
Value creation
erosion of, 228–231
from human capital, 151
from new opportunities, 481
from social capital, 151
from technology, 151
Value-in-diversity hypothesis, 139
Value net concept, 65
Value of the firm, 126
Values for innovation, 190
Venture capital, 447, 484–486
Vertical boundaries, 371
Vertical integration, 205, 207–211
basic issues in, 209–210
benefits and risk, 208–210
difficulties, 212
example, 208
transaction cost perspective, 211
Videoconferencing, 26
Video games, 378
Virtual organization, 377–381
Virtual research and development, 443
Vision
by entrepreneurs, 490–491
skills for, 491
Vision statement, 30–32, 33
and strategy map, 104
*Vogue Magazine,* 475
Voice over Internet Protocol, 283

*Wall Street Journal,* 45, 142, 342
War for talent, 131
*Web of Inclusion* (Helgesen), 29
Whistleblowing, 426
Wholly owned subsidiaries, 267–269
Wireless communication, 304
Wireless technologies, 281
*Wisdom of Teams* (Katzenbach & Smith), 382
Women
consumer spending decisions, 53
education of, 52
in workforce, 52
Work environment, 136–137
Workforce
and H-1B visas, 53
older employees, 51
women in, 52
Workforce diversity, 138–140
benefits from, 139
*Working with Emotional Intelligence* (Goleman), 405
World Customs Organization, 250
World Health Organization, 250
World population, 245
World Trade Organization, 252, 253
Worldwide functional structure, 355, 365
Worldwide matrix structure, 355, 365
Worldwide product division, 355, 365

Zero-sum thinking, 21

# The Reviewer Hall of Fame

We would like to thank the dedicated instructors who have graciously provided their insights since the inception of *Strategic Management: Creating Competitive Advantages* and *Strategic Management: Text and Cases*.

| | | | |
|---|---|---|---|
| Alessandri, Todd | Syracuse University | Fausnaugh, Carolyn J. | Florida Institute of Technology |
| Alexander, Larry | Virginia Polytechnic Institute | Ferguson, Tamela D. | University of Louisiana at Lafayette |
| Amason, Allen C. | University of Georgia | | |
| Antoniou, Peter H. | California State University, San Marcos | Fox, Isaac | University of Minnesota |
| | | Frankforter, Steven A. | Winthrop University |
| Arnott, Dave | Dallas Baptist University | Fried, Vance | Oklahoma State University |
| Azriel, Jay | Illinois State University | Gilbertson, Diana L. | California State University, Fresno |
| Bailey, Jeffrey J. | University of Idaho | | |
| Barringer, Bruce | University of Central Florida | Gilley, Matt | Oklahoma State University |
| Beal, Brent D. | Louisiana State University | Gilliard, Debora | Metropolitan State College of Denver |
| Bell DeTienne, Kristen | Brigham Young University | | |
| Bernstein, Eldon | Lynn University | Goel, Sanjay | University of Minnesota, Duluth |
| Bodie, Dusty | Boise State University | | |
| Bogner, William | Georgia State University | Harrison, Niran | University of Oregon |
| Calhoun, Mikelle A. | Valparaiso University | Harveston, Paula | Berry College |
| Cappel, Samuel D. | Southeastern Louisiana State University | Hester, Kim | Arkansas State University |
| | | Hironaka, John | California State University, Sacramento |
| Carini, Gary | Baylor University | | |
| Carraher, Shawn M. | Texas A&M University, Commerce | Hoffman, Alan | Bentley College |
| | | Holbein, Gordon | Northern Kentucky University |
| Caruth, Don | Amberton University | Hough, Jill | University of Tulsa |
| Castrogiovanni, Gary J. | University of Tulsa | Humphreys, John | Eastern New Mexico University |
| Chaganti, Radha | Rider University | Ibe, James G. | Morris College |
| Cho, Theresa | Rutgers University | Janney, Jay J. | University of Dayton |
| Coffey, Betty S. | Appalachian State University | Jauch, Lawrence | University of Louisiana - Monroe |
| Coggins, Wade | Webster University, Fort Smith Metro Campus | | |
| | | Johnson, Dana M. | Michigan Technical University |
| Coombs, Joseph | University of Richmond | Katzenstein, James | California State University, Dominguez Hills |
| Cordeiro, James J. | SUNY Brockport | | |
| Covin, Jeffrey | Indiana University | Kellermanns, Franz | Mississippi State University |
| Datta, Deepak | University of Texas at Arlington | Kelley, Donna | Babson College |
| Davis, James | University of Notre Dame | Kelley, Craig | California State University, Sacramento |
| Deresky, Helen | State University of New York, Plattsburgh | | |
| | | Ketchen, Dave | Florida State University |
| DeWitt, Rocki-Lee | University of Vermont | Kilpatrick, John A. | Idaho State University |
| Dobbs, Michael E. | Arkansas State University | Kowalczyk, Stan | San Francisco State University |
| Doh, Jonathan | Villanova University | Kraska, Daniel | North Central State College |
| Douglas, Tom | Clemson University | Kreps, Donald E. | Kutztown University |
| Down, Jon | Oregon State University | Kulkarni, Subdoh P. | Howard University |
| Engle, Clare | Concordia University | Lant, Theresa | New York University |
| Evans, William A. | Troy State University, Dothan | Legatski, Ted | Texas Christian University |
| Fabian, Frances H. | University of North Carolina, Charlotte | Lengnick-Hall, Cynthia | University of Texas at San Antonio |
| Fanelli, Angelo | Warrington College of Business | Lester, Wanda | North Carolina A&T State University |
| Fathi, Michael | Georgia Southwestern University | | |

# IMPORTANT

HERE IS YOUR REGISTRATION CODE TO ACCESS MCGRAW-HILL
PREMIUM CONTENT AND MCGRAW-HILL ONLINE RESOURCES

For key premium online resources you need THIS CODE to
gain access. Once the code is entered, you will be able to
use the web resources for the length of your course.

## Access is provided only if you have purchased a new book.

If the registration code is missing from this book, the registration screen on our
website, and within your WebCT or Blackboard course will tell you how to obtain
your new code. Your registration code can be used only once to establish
access. It is not transferable

### To gain access to these online resources

**1.** USE your web browser to go to: **http://www.mhhe.com/dess3e**

**2.** CLICK on "First Time User"

**3.** ENTER the Registration Code printed on the tear-off bookmark on the right

**4.** After you have entered your registration code, click on "Register"

**5.** FOLLOW the instructions to setup your personal UserID and Password

**6.** WRITE your UserID and Password down for future reference. Keep it in a safe place.

If your course is using WebCT or Blackboard, you'll be able to use this code to
access the McGraw-Hill content within your instructor's online course.

To gain access to the McGraw-Hill content in your instructor's WebCT or
Blackboard course simply log into the course with the user ID and Password
provided by your instructor. Enter the registration code exactly as it appears to
the right when prompted by the system. You will only need to use this code the
first time you click on McGraw-Hill content.

These instructions are specifically for student access. Instructors are not required
to register via the above instructions.

The McGraw-Hill Companies

Thank you, and welcome to your
McGraw-Hill/Irwin Online Resources.

**Dess/Lumpkin/Eisner**
**Strategic Management, 3/e**
**ISBN 10-Digit: 0-07-326694-9**
**ISBN 13-Digit: 978-0-07-326694-7**

PH7P-YTPH-X8YM-MYJ3-UTGM

## REGISTRATION CODE
### REGISTRATION CODE

The McGraw-Hill Companies

McGraw-Hill
Irwin